BOYLE & BIRDS' COMPANY LAW

5th Edition

BOYLE & BIRDS' COMPANY LAW

5th Edition

Editors

John Birds LLM, FRSA
Professor of Commercial Law
University of Sheffield

Iain MacNeil LLB, PhD
Reader in Company Law
University of Glasgow

Gerard McCormack BCL, LLM, PhD
Professor of Law
University of Manchester

Christian Twigg-Flesner LLB, PCHE, PhD
Lecturer in Law
University of Hull

Charlotte Villiers LLM, Solicitor
Reader in Law
University of Bristol

Consultant Editor

A. J. Boyle LLM, SJD, Barrister
Emeritus Professor of Law
Queen Mary
University of London

JORDANS
2004

Published by
Jordan Publishing Limited
21 St Thomas Street
Bristol BS1 6JS

British Library Cataloguing-in-Publication Data
A catalogue record for this book is available from the British Library.

ISBN 0 85308 938 8

Typeset by MFK-Mendip, Frome, Somerset
Printed and bound in England by Antony Rowe Ltd, Chippenham, Wiltshire

Preface to the 5th Edition

The aim of this new edition is the same as that of earlier editions, namely that it seeks to be a comprehensive and reliable textbook providing some detail for company law practitioners and a thorough grounding for students. The opportunity has been taken to rethink the structure a little. We have incorporated a wholly new Chapter 2 on European company law and a final chapter on the future of the subject. The material that relates primarily to public companies, namely that concerning public issues, takeovers, insider dealing and market abuse, has been put in consecutive chapters towards the end of the book. As well as standard updating because of case-law developments, this edition includes in particular the changes implemented under the Financial Services and Markets Act 2000 and the substantial amendments made to corporate insolvency law by the Insolvency Act 2000 and the Enterprise Act 2002.

Deciding whether to update a company law text was not an easy matter given the Review of Company Law, which concluded its business in July 2001, and the Government's response to it in July 2002. However, it has become clear over the past couple of years that producing the next Companies Act will take longer than was originally hoped. The best we can realistically expect is a Bill presented to Parliament after the next general election, say in the autumn of 2005, which may reach the statute book in 2006, but which is unlikely to be brought fully into force for a year or two after that. In the light of this, a new edition at this time will have a reasonable shelf life. The question then becomes one of how to deal with possible reforms arising from the review. Because the Government's response to the Steering Group's recommendations was generally very positive, we have included a reasonable amount of detail in the appropriate chapters, as well as dealing with reform in a general way in the concluding chapter.

Unfortunately Eilís Ferran was unable to be involved in the editing of this edition, but the remaining members of the team were delighted to be joined by Gerry McCormack, Iain MacNeil and Christian Twigg-Flesner. Particular thanks are due to Professor McCormack who stepped in at the last minute to perform the vital task of updating Chapter 21 on insolvency and reconstruction. Apart from that, John Birds was again general editor of this edition and updated chapters 4, 15, 16 and 20. Tony Boyle was responsible for chapters 1, 3 and 17, Iain MacNeil for chapters 7, 8, 9, 18 and 19, Christian Twigg-Flesner for chapters 2, 5, 6 and 10 and Charlotte Villiers for chapters 11, 12, 13, 14 and 22.

John Birds
Tony Boyle
Iain MacNeil
Gerard McCormack
Christian Twigg-Flesner
Charlotte Villiers
July 2004

Contents

Chapter 6   Company Contracts – Capacity, Authority and Form   121

PART 3: THE REGISTRATION OF CHARGES

PART 4: CREDITORS' REMEDIES

Chapter 16   The Duties of Directors

Table of Cases

References are to paragraph numbers.

Table of Statutes

References are to paragraph numbers.

Table of Statutory Instruments

References are to paragraph numbers.

Table of EC Legislation

References are to paragraph numbers.

Table of Overseas Material

References are to paragraph numbers.

Chapter 1

The Development of the Registered Company

1.1   Introduction

This chapter is concerned with issues which have a general bearing on the various specific aspects of company law examined in the chapters that follow, and, in particular, seeks to explain in a concise way how the body of legislation[1] and case-law which today governs the affairs of registered companies[2] first developed and came to take its present form. There are two other issues with an important bearing on company law as a whole. These are the impact of European Union company law on the relatively recent history of company legislation in Britain, which is considered in Chapter 2, and the key concept of corporate personality as developed by the courts, considered in Chapter 3. The chapter concludes with a brief examination of the Department of Trade and Industry's proposals for the fundamental reform of company law, more detail of which is given in Chapter 22. It also looks at the relevance of 'law and economics' theory for company law.

1.2   Historical Background

The first topic is the development of modern company law. The account given is in no sense a history of company law as a whole – too large an undertaking for our purpose. Instead, it is intended to show how the unincorporated joint-stock company of the early nineteenth century was transformed by the legislation of the 1840s and 1850s into a registered company of recognisably modern shape. For an understanding of the earlier history of company law, which had its origins in the sixteenth and seventeenth centuries, the reader is referred elsewhere.[3] There he or she will find an account of how the scandal and financial collapse produced in the early eighteenth century by the 'South Sea Bubble', and the resulting Bubble Act of 1720,[4] not only put down an illicit trade in the charters of incorporated companies but also placed an already flourishing number of unincorporated joint-stock companies under a cloud of official disapproval for over a century. Until the repeal of the Bubble Act in 1825,[5] such companies had a shadowy legal existence. The more favourable legal opinion of them was that, so long as their shares were not freely transferable, they were not liable to prosecution under the Bubble Act. Even after the Act's repeal, the only hope for those forming a corporate business enterprise (however economically important and substantial its operations) was to form a 'statutory company' by means of a private Act of

---

1   Ic the Companies Act 1985 and related legislation.
2   As to other types of business organisation, see **1.5**.
3   For a lively and stimulating summary of this earlier period, see Davies, *Gower's Principles of Modern Company Law* 6th edn (Sweet & Maxwell, 1997), Chapter 2. See further: CA Cooke, *Corporation, Trust and Company* (Manchester, 1950); AB Dubois, *The English Business Company After the Bubble Act, 1720–1800* (New York, 1938); BC Hunt, *The Development of the Business Corporation in England, 1800–1867* (Harvard Economic Studies, 1936).
4   6 Geo I, c 18.
5   6 Geo IV, c 91.

Parliament. This gave the obvious advantage of legal personality with the attendant privilege of limited liability. Only in the case of very major undertakings (such as the canal and railway companies and other early utilities) which needed to raise large amounts of capital from the public, would the delay, trouble and very great expense entailed by the private bill procedure be justified. By this period the modern practice of refusing to grant a Royal Charter of Incorporation to those engaged in trade or commerce was becoming established.[1] It may be noted that, although the common law protected the members of trading corporations from liability, it was common for provisions in their charters to allow the corporation to make 'leviations' on members to pay its debts. The courts of equity permitted creditors direct action against the members.

1.3 The incorporation of joint-stock companies by registration

At common law, despite the repeal of the Bubble Act in 1825, there remained some doubt about the legality of unincorporated joint-stock companies with freely transferable shares. These doubts had been fostered by Lord Eldon, who succeeded in inserting in the repealing Act a provision that their position at common law (with the taint of possible illegality) should be as it was before the Bubble Act was repealed. In the boom of the 1830s there was, nevertheless, a proliferation of unincorporated joint-stock companies, which in turn produced a growing demand for their legal regulation. In particular, there was a need to clarify their right to sue and be sued. There was also a growing demand for limited liability as a protection for shareholders who invested in them. In the case of formal written contracts, this was often obtained by express terms in those contracts, but this was obviously not possible in the case of the everyday informal contracts of a growing number of industrial and commercial companies. It has been seen that incorporation by charter was now deemed unsuitable for industrial and commercial companies, and a private Act of Parliament was prohibitively expensive.

1.3.1 *Legislative control*

The Trading Companies Act 1834 and the Chartered Company Act 1837 made a half-hearted attempt to deal with the problems of joint-stock companies, but the first was very restrictively applied by the Board of Trade and the second had little more success. Without conferring incorporation, these Acts made available some of the incidents of that status (eg the right to sue and be sued) and even (in the 1837 Act) limited liability to those seeking and obtaining the appropriate letters patent.

Especially during the cyclical slumps that followed economic booms in the nineteenth century, fraudulent promotion and other abuses were frequently revealed. This led to the appointment of a Committee of Parliament (eventually chaired by Gladstone when he became President of the Board of Trade). He undoubtedly had a strong influence on the eventual report.[2] This seminal report

---

1   As to types of business organisation other than the registered company, see **1.5**.
2   1844 BPP Vol VII.

resulted in what is still referred to as 'Gladstone's Act' – The Joint Stock Companies Act 1844.[1]

It is this piece of legislation which laid the foundation of the modern registered company; but modern company law still owes very much to those principles of partnership and trust law which the courts had already developed to cope with the unincorporated joint-stock company. However, 'Gladstone's Act' set company law on what is still its modern course by conferring ready access to incorporation by a process of registration.[2] It set up the office of Registrar of Companies who had not only to supervise the original registration, but had to keep up-to-date information about each company's constitution, directors and annual returns and make it available on 'public file'. At this stage the company's constitution was expressed in a 'deed of settlement', essentially the same document used by unincorporated joint-stock companies. It had broadly the same function as the modern articles of association, but in its original form was a trust deed which provided, *inter alia*, for the trustees in whom the assets of the old-style unincorporated joint-stock company might be vested.

The new Act applied henceforth to all joint-stock companies with more than 25 members or which allowed shares to be transferred without the consent of all the members. Thus began the divorce of partnership law from company law and the origin of the legislative practice that limits the size of membership in a 'private partnership'. The limit of 20 partners has now been abolished.[3] Existing unincorporated joint-stock companies could gain the privileges conferred by the Act if they altered their existing deeds of settlement and registered in compliance with the Act's provisions.[4]

1.3.2 Limited liability

Limited liability was not conferred by Gladstone's Act. This was still a hotly debated issue in 1844 both in respect of 'private partnerships' and joint-stock companies. Thus the new type of registered company was like a modern unlimited company. There were some hesitations in the legislature's policy on winding up these new registered companies. The earliest winding-up Acts applied the ordinary bankruptcy law to companies while producing a conflict of jurisdiction between the bankruptcy courts and the Court of Chancery. By 1857, this confusion was resolved by conferring sole jurisdiction on the Chancery.[5] At the same time, certain principles of bankruptcy law were carried over to a new corporate setting.

The question of conferring limited liability on the new registered companies (and also upon certain forms of partnerships) was a strongly debated issue in the mid-nineteenth century in Parliament, in officially appointed committees, and in

---

1 This Act did not apply to Scotland where the more liberal Scots common law applied until the Joint Stock Companies Act of 1856.
2 There was a system of 'provisional registration' prior to the filing of the appropriate deed of settlement. Only after a full registration was the company incorporated.
3 With effect from 20 December 2002; see 24 Co Law 113–114. See further *Gore-Browne on Companies* 44th edn (Jordans, loose-leaf) at 6.1. As to the practical choice to be made between the small private limited company and the limited liability, see **3.3.1**.
4 Those that did not do so still had to file certain information.
5 See the Joint Stock Companies Act 1856 and the Companies Winding Up (Amendment) Act 1857.

the press and the business community.[1] While there was a strong movement for introducing a form of 'limited partnership' (based on the French model of the *société en commandite*), this had to wait in limbo for eventual enactment in the Limited Partnerships Act 1907, by which time it proved to be of little practical utility.[2] Instead, in the mid-nineteenth century, the Government chose to confer limited liability only upon registered companies[3] – or more exactly upon those registered companies which opted to register in compliance with the requirements for a company limited by shares (then, as today, the vast majority).

As at first introduced (in the Limited Liability Act 1855), there were a number of important safeguards attached to the concession of limited liability (some of which have a contemporary ring in that they have been reintroduced in fairly recent legislation). Thus there were requirements of at least 25 members as well as specified amounts in respect of issued and paid-up capital. The word 'limited' had to be added at the end of the company's name everywhere it was displayed as an awful warning of the new risks faced by creditors. There were also safeguards to maintain the capital raised against the hazard of improperly paid dividends or unjustified loans to directors. The company had to have auditors approved by the Board of Trade. However, within a very short time, what had been termed the first 'modern Companies Act' – the Joint Stock Companies Act 1856 – consolidated and reformed earlier legislation. It abolished the old system of registering deeds of settlement and introduced the twin constitutional documents which still govern the modern company – the memorandum of association and the articles of association.[4] Rather less happily, this Act removed most of the safeguards for limited liability in the 1855 Act. In somewhat different form, most of these safeguards have been reintroduced into company law in the legislation of recent years.[5]

Undoubtedly, the grant of the benefit of limited liability helped to make possible the growth of the large modern company which today dominates the private sector of the economy. At an earlier period in the nineteenth century, those enterprises which had need to raise share and loan capital on a grand scale (notably the railway companies) had enjoyed limited liability as statutory companies created by Act of Parliament.[6] The conferment of the same privilege on the registered company made it available to entrepreneurs and investors in industry and commerce generally.

It can be argued that in the case of the old unincorporated joint-stock company, with large numbers of shareholders whose liability was unlimited, this was not (for procedural and practical reasons) of great use in satisfying the claim of the unpaid creditors. Nevertheless the absence of limited liability was undoubtedly a major deterrent to investors in large-scale enterprises under the management of others.

1　　For an account of the 'struggle for limited liability' see Davies, op cit, at pp 40–44.
2　　The more flexible form of the registered company was by then readily available to small private companies. This gave the advantage of limited liability for all members and much else besides.
3　　Banking and insurance companies were at first excluded.
4　　As to the distinctive functions of the memorandum and articles, see Chapter 5.
5　　See eg the provisions of Parts V and VIII of the Companies Act 1985. See Chapters 8 and 14.
6　　The Companies Clauses Consolidation Act 1845 standardised the procedure in respect of statutory companies which were still used for new railways or utilities. This Act allowed the standard provisions normally included in private bills seeking to incorporate companies to be incorporated by reference. A separate Act in 1845 (8 and 9 Vict c 17) dealt with Scottish statutory companies.

This does not of course silence the past and present critics of the unrestricted availability of limited liability for every small private company (or indeed for the subsidiaries of groups of companies). Where such companies are seriously (and deliberately) under-capitalised, the possibilities of abuse are self-evident.[1]

1.4 Developments in the late nineteenth and twentieth centuries

During the remainder of the nineteenth century the legislature made only minor changes in company law, but the courts were responsible for the development of a number of important principles. As regards legislation, a general pattern began in 1862 of reforming legislation followed by a consolidating Act. The Companies Act 1862 was the first Act of that name. This process continued at regular intervals (1908 and 1929) until the Companies Act 1948. The courts were faced with the task of evolving a number of new principles to fill out the statutory structure. In many areas, they could elaborate upon an existing body of partnership, trust and agency law already evolved to meet the needs of the old unincorporated joint-stock companies.[2] Alternatively, they might draw wide inferences from hints dropped by the legislature. Thus, from a somewhat slender statutory foundation, a substantial body of new judge-made principle might be created. Two obvious examples are the *ultra vires* doctrine[3] and the principles governing the raising and maintenance of share capital.[4] In other areas of company law, new concepts owed their origin to commercial practice and the skills of conveyancing counsel. These in due course received the scrutiny and approval of the courts.[5]

In the twentieth century and into the twenty-first century, two issues continued to preoccupy those who write official reports on company law reform and shape the consequent legislation. These issues are the need to increase the disclosure requirements in the Companies Act and the related question of how far to exempt private companies from the accounting and other publicity requirements which apply to public companies. While the expense and administrative burden of disclosure has continued to grow, the question of how to handle the small private company has produced different answers at different times.

As regards publicity in respect of company accounts, this started with an annual balance sheet and then moved to a profit and loss account, to consolidated accounts for groups of companies and certain information as to 'associated companies'.[6] Today it includes further refinements such as information as to turnover and details about methods of valuation of assets, as well as requiring the accounts to be based either on a historical cost basis or, alternatively, on 'alternative accounting rules'. The general effect of these is to allow certain assets to be included in the accounts on the basis of their market value or their current costs. A wide range of other information must also be given about the company's activities, relating to its members and to its share and loan capital. An area of particular growth in respect of disclosure requirements in recent years relates to

---

1   For a valuable review, with references to the earlier literature, see Freedman 'Limited liability: large company theory and small firms' (2000) 63 MLR 317.
2   See eg directors' duties (Chapter 16), minority shareholders' actions (Chapter 17).
3   See Chapter 5.
4   See Chapter 8.
5   Eg preference shares (see Chapter 8), debentures and floating charges (see Chapter 10).
6   See Chapter 14.

directors and their various interests in their company (or group of companies) such as interests in its shares, material contracts with it, loans made to them, etc. All this information is usually disclosed on an annual basis via publicly filed annual returns (or the accounts, or the directors' report). Much of this information (in addition to being made available at the Companies Registry) must be made available on a more immediate basis by means of registers kept at the company's own registered office.[1]

A good deal of the information that must thus be disclosed is (and was) inappropriate in the case of those private companies whose small numbers of shareholders had the remedy in their own hands, and where outside investors (or lenders) could bargain for themselves. Only unsecured trade creditors need the disclosure of such accounting and other information as was appropriate to their needs. Although the private company as a distinct species with certain privileges of its own dates back to the Companies Act 1908, it was not until the Companies Act 1948 that the legislature decided that the burden of the accounting obligations imposed on most companies should not apply to small family or 'closely held' companies. These were termed 'exempt private companies'[2] and were exempt from the necessity to file public accounts (and were given certain other special privileges).[3] The pendulum of policy swung the other way in the Companies Act 1967 which abolished the exempt private company, thus visiting most of the accounting and auditing requirements (increased by that Act) on private limited companies of any size.[4] In the Companies Act 1981 the policy of the 1948 Act was reverted to in some measure. In line with the requirements of the EC Fourth Company Law Directive (on company accounts), new categories of 'medium' and 'small' companies have been created with publicity and accounting requirements appropriately scaled down.[5]

Despite these changes, the general burden of disclosure (both at the Companies Registry and at each company's own registered office) has been the target of considerable criticism both in the business community and in those learned professions concerned with company administration, as well as by some academic writers.[6] The clear lines of segregation between public and private companies first laid down in the Companies Act 1980[7] have already made it possible for the legislature to place a lesser burden on the private company (or at any rate medium or small private companies). However, while limited liability remains overwhelmingly the norm for private companies, and while they are in most instances seriously under-capitalised for the risks involved, there must be a limit on how far the burden of disclosure can be lifted. There is unlikely to be much reduction on the burden placed on public companies either by Parliament or by the UK Listing Authority.[8]

---

1   As to the registered office, see **5.8**.
2   See Schedule 7 to the 1948 Act as to the complex conditions that had to be met to retain exempt status.
3   Loans could be made to directors, and the company's auditors did not need professional qualifications.
4   Unlimited companies provided an escape hatch for those dismayed by the new burden imposed as well as the risk of exposure to competitors.
5   See Chapter 14. There is an audit exemption for 'very small companies'.
6   See L Sealy, 'The Disclosure Philosophy and Company Law Reform', (1981) 2 Co Law 51.
7   See **4.2**, and the Companies Act 1985, Part I, Chapter 1.
8   As to the requirements under the *Listing Rules* as to continuous disclosure, see Chapter 14. The UK Listing Authority is now the Financial Services Authority; see Chapter 18.

Another source of growing complaint among both commentators and the legal profession at large is the complexity and obscure drafting of much recent company legislation. This seems to have had a number of causes. One is undoubtedly the obligation to implement the EU programme for the harmonisation of the company laws of Member States.[1] Particularly in the case of directives which emerged from the Community's complex legislative machinery before the accession of the United Kingdom to the Community in 1973, it is not surprising to find such directives framed in very different terms, and starting from somewhat different basic conceptions, than would be the case with 'home-produced' proposals for law reform. In some instances, a directive may contain a useful reform but may be grudgingly or inadequately implemented by the Department of Trade and Industry (DTI) and its draftsmen.[2] In other cases, the directive provides a 'Continental' solution to a problem of fraud or abuse which is already quite effectively tackled in a different manner by our own company law.

Another source of legislative complexity has been the attempt of the Parliamentary draftsman to curb the ever-present possibility of fraud and self-dealing by the directors of the company. In a perhaps misguided attempt to strive for both comprehensive yet precise prohibitions, while retaining a wide range of 'exemptions' to permit legitimate activities, the result has been legislation far more complex and convoluted than was the case with earlier company legislation.[3] With the prospect of a growing body of harmonisation directives either implemented or yet to be approved by the Council of Ministers, Companies Acts[4] could only grow in bulk and complexity. The programme of company law reform that was conducted by the Company Law Review Steering Group, established by the DTI, is discussed at **1.7** below and in Chapter 22.

1.5 Other types of corporate business organisation

The brief historical account given in this chapter has concerned the development of the registered company, since that is the subject of this book. At the same period of time there also evolved a number of different types of association based not upon the principle of investment for profit by proprietors but on quite distinct principles of co-operation or mutual self-help. In this the archetype was originally the unincorporated friendly society. In the course of the nineteenth century, bodies and associations concerned with specialised activities of this kind came to be regulated by their own special legislation. This usually conferred corporate personality as well as limited liability. One feature common to this type of legislation is that the body for which it was intended might not register under the Companies Acts. This is true of co-operative societies, working men's clubs and other friendly societies. It also applied to trade unions, trustee savings banks and building societies.[5] In the case of trustee savings banks legislation brought their business activities within the sphere of company law. The 'privatisation' of trustee

---

1 This growing body of directives (some in force but many still in the draft stage) is discussed in Chapter 2.
2 See eg the First Directive as originally implemented by section 35 of the Companies Act 1985 before the reform embodied by the Companies Act 1989; see Chapter 6.
3 A notable example is the 'directors' loan provisions' in Part X of the Companies Act 1985 (see Chapter 16).
4 The consolidating legislation of 1985, and subsequent developments, are discussed at **1.6**.
5 As to the legislation applicable, see *Gore-Browne on Companies* 44th edn (Jordans, loose-leaf) at 6.10.3.

savings banks converted them into a public company offering its shares to the public as well as existing investors.[1] The building societies legislation made it possible for them to convert themselves into public limited companies.[2] Many of the larger building societies have converted into public limited companies under this legislation. A new form of business association, which is a hybrid of partnership and company law, suitable for privately owned profit making businesses, was created by the Limited Liability Partnerships Act 2000.[3]

Yet another new form of business enterprise will be the 'community interest company' (CIC), which at the time of writing is the subject of a Bill before Parliament.[4] The CIC will be a new, flexible and easily registered corporate vehicle for businesses whose profits and assets are to be used for the benefit of the community. Bodies wishing to become CICs must pass a community interest test and produce an annual report to show that they have contributed to community interest aims. A new independent regulator will oversee CICs, with wide powers including the power to approve registration, to appoint, suspend or remove directors, to make orders concerning their property, to set a dividend cap and to apply to wind them up.

1.6   The Companies Acts: consolidation and reconsolidation

The unwieldy mass of legislation in the Companies Acts 1948–1983 was consolidated into the Companies Act 1985 and three much smaller related Acts. Two of these latter deal with topics which have a wider application than company law as it is usually conceived. These are the Business Names Act 1985 and the Insider Dealing Act 1985. The Companies Consolidation (Consequential Provisions) Act 1985 relates, as its title implies, to matters (like old public companies) which will not be of long-term significance.

Even at a technical level, it can be argued that neither the timing nor the scope of the 1985 consolidating legislation[5] was entirely happily chosen. While this legislation was going through Parliament, the Bill that became the Insolvency Act 1985 was also being enacted. This process entailed amendment of substantial parts of the Companies Act 1985 in respect of the winding up of insolvent companies. Scarcely were these two Acts of 1985 on the statute book when a change of policy was made. This produced a reconsolidation of the parts of the Companies Act 1985 concerning the winding up of *solvent* companies with the recent legislation on insolvency. This produced the Insolvency Act 1986. At the same time the Department of Trade and Industry decided to reconsolidate the legislation on the disqualification of directors.[6] In this same period, the provisions in the Companies Act 1985 relating to public issues, insider dealing and the compulsory acquisition of shares, were substantially changed by the Financial

---

1   Savings Bank Act 1985.
2   Building Societies Act 1986 as amended by the Building Societies Act 1997.
3   See further **3.3.1**.
4   The Companies (Audit, Investigation and Community Enterprise) Bill, Part 2, introduced into the House of Lords on December 3, 2003.
5   Which came into force on 1 July 1985. A new Table A also came into force for companies registered after that date. See the Companies (Tables A to F) Regulations 1985.
6   The Company Directors Disqualification Act 1986.

Services Act 1986.[1] This Act broke much new ground by introducing a long overdue system of 'securities regulation'. It was itself expanded by the Financial Services and Markets Act 2000.

Since the consolidating legislation of 1985 there has been one major legislative development regarding company law in the strict sense. The Companies Act 1989 contains a mélange of significant legislative innovation and a great number of technical reforms. It implemented the EC Seventh and Eighth Directives on group accounts and the appointment of auditors.[2] It also contains a new regime for private companies.[3] This allows more scope for avoiding the formality of company meetings by means of written resolutions or by the adoption of a more generalised 'elective regime'. In addition to these major changes, the 1989 Act contained a great number of significant reforms of the Companies Act 1985.[4]

There is much to be said in favour of the companies legislation of 1985. In terms of its simplicity and lucidity of style and the ordered clarity of the arrangement of subject matter in the principal Act, it represents a considerable achievement for the draftsman and those who instructed him. Nevertheless, even the most dazzling skills of draftsmanship (in the case of a consolidating Act) cannot cure the substantive defects in the state of existing legislation to be consolidated.

The cogent criticism made of the unconsolidated Companies Acts 1948–1983 by, among others, Professor LS Sealy[5] went beyond matters of legislative style and arrangement. The general thrust of this criticism is that our company legislation (whether carried forward from the past or the subject of recent reform) is over-technical and over-'sanctioned'. It is not directed to enabling businesses large and small to be run honestly and efficiently in the real commercial world. It is law created by civil servants and company lawyers who have had insufficient regard for the real needs of the industrial and commercial world. Our legislation makes very out-of-date assumptions about how private companies are formed, how public companies develop and about the realities of shareholders' meetings and resolutions as a genuine way of expressing shareholders' consent or effectively restraining directors and others who manage companies. While increasingly influenced by the rigid, elaborate and often inappropriate example of the European Union harmonisation programme,[6] our legislation has ignored the more radical and simplifying reforms that have been successfully adopted in the Commonwealth and the United States.

There is much force in Professor Sealy's detailed critique of existing company legislation which is deployed to support this more general thesis. It is inevitable, however, that not everyone will agree that the general policy of those reforming company law (especially in regard to large public companies) should be how best to meet the institutional needs of businessmen. The real political and social world will inevitably demand that company law reflect a more complex, if sometimes competing, range of interests. In that sense, it is entirely understandable that the DTI regard company law (like labour law) as too politically sensitive to be left

---

1   This Act has been substantially amended and extended by the Financial Services and Markets Act 2000.
2   See Chapter 14.
3   See Chapter 13.
4   See in particular Part III 'Investigations and Powers to Obtain Information' and Part VII 'Financial Markets and Insolvency'.
5   See *Company Law and Commercial Reality* (Sweet & Maxwell, 1984), especially Chapter 4.
6   See **1.4**.

without close supervision to the Law Commission or to any other 'neutral' reforming body. The political priorities will inevitably change with the colour of the government in power. Thus, both in Britain and in the European Union, company law remains more than a matter of commercial law. This latter body of law may be well described as 'the totality of the law's response to the needs and practices of the mercantile community. This then is the essence of commercial law – the accommodation of principles, rules, practices and documents fashioned by the world of business: the facilitation, rather than the obstruction, of commercial development'.[1]

Company law, as part of a different body of law – the law of institutions – must inevitably have a different character from that governing the law of commercial transactions. It will retain this character, even when freed from the burden of history and the 'Chancery mentality'.

1.7 Fundamental reform of company law – the Company Law Review

In 1998, the Department of Trade and Industry set in motion a radical and far-reaching programme of company law reform. The outline given here is supplemented by the description in Chapter 22, as well as by specific descriptions in the appropriate chapters. Launched by the then Secretary of State, Margaret Beckett,[2] this was elaborated to form a second stage document which set forth the 'Strategic Framework'[3] for this process. This set up a Steering Group and various working parties whose broad tasks it described. The 'Strategic Framework' of February 1999 embraced all the already recognised shortcomings of the existing body of company law and added some of its own for good measure. Thus the existing company legislation was characterised as 'the current patchwork of largely facilitative core and prescriptive additions accumulated as a result of episodic and reactive reform'.[4] In seeking 'comprehensive coherent reform', the Strategic Framework noted that the present law 'does not measure well up against' the objectives it sets forth for a modern system of company law for 'a competitive economy'.

The subsequent work of the Company Law Review Steering Group evolved through several stages,[5] culminating in its Final Report in July 2001. This programme of reform was then the subject of further reflection by the DTI, resulting in a White Paper, *Modernising Company Law*, which was presented to Parliament in July 2002.[6] This contained a number of definite proposals for reform and was accompanied by a draft Companies Bill embodying some of the proposed reforms.

In many important areas of company law, the White Paper set out proposals for a radical modernisation and simplification of existing company law of real merit.

---

1   RM Goode, *Commercial Law* (Penguin, 1982), p 984 cited by Professor LS Sealy in *Company Law and Commercial Reality*, op cit, at p 81.

2   *Modern Company Law for a Competitive Economy*: DTI, March 1998.

3   *Modern Company Law for a Competitive Economy. The Strategic Framework*, February 1999. See further the 'follow-up' reports: *Company General Meetings and Shareholder Communication (No 2)*; *Company Formation and Capital Maintenance (No 3)* and *Overseas Companies (No 2)* (October 1999).

4   *Strategic Framework* at 2.8.

5   See *Developing the Framework* (March 2000) and *Completing the Structure* (November 2000).

6   Cm 5553-I and II.

These areas include the formation of public and private companies, company constitutions, capital maintenance, financial reports and auditing and general meetings and resolutions. The treatment of directors' duties is rather more tentative, with the proposed reforms left subject to further questions for more consultation.[1] Other areas, where proposals were made by the Steering Group, had not reached the stage where anything could be said in the White Paper. Thus almost nothing was said about minority shareholders' rights, and it is not clear whether, despite much earlier work by the Law Commissions and the Steering Group, any further attempt to reform this complex area will be undertaken.[2] Other important aspects of company law, for example on reconstructions, mergers and takeovers where work was done by the Steering Group,[3] are not mentioned in the White Paper.[4]

Thus, the unfinished task of company law reform has not been carried much further forward in recent years. The cause of this delay would appear to be more than a matter of finding legislative time to present a new Companies Bill to Parliament. The current concerns of the DTI are two issues that primarily affect public listed companies, namely excessive remuneration for company directors[5] and the improvement of accounting and auditing standards.[6] Both are currently the subject of heated debate in the City of London, in Parliament and in the financial press as a result of corporate collapses and other abuses in the USA as well as in Britain.[7]

1.7.1 The comparative law dimension

It is inevitable and entirely appropriate that any process of law reform should have regard to the state of the law (and attempts at reform) in other comparable legal systems. At the outset of the Company Law Review, the Steering Group made it plain[8] that it was very largely in recent reforms of company legislation in leading Commonwealth countries[9] that inspiration must be sought. It is perhaps a pity that, in contrast, a rather negative attitude was taken to the company law of the Member States of the European Union. Likewise, American corporate law was rather dismissively treated. This attitude was reflected in the selection of the membership of the Steering Group.[10] Here the leading 'old' Commonwealth countries were quite properly well represented but there were no representatives

---

1   Ibid, at pp 26–32.

2   See ibid, at 3.18. See further Chapter 17.

3   See the Final Report, Chapter 13.

4   The reform of the law on company charges has been delegated to the Law Commission; see their consultation paper *Registration of Security Interests: Company Charges and Property other than Land*, No 164 (2002).

5   See *Rewards for failure. Directors' remuneration – contracts, performance and severance*, a consultative document, URN 03/652.

6   See *Co-ordinating group on audit and accounting issues, Final Report to the Secretary of State for Trade and Industry and to the Chancellor of the Exchequer*, URN 03/567, and *Review of the regulatory regime for the accounting profession; legislative proposals*, URN 03/717.

7   The Secretary of State has indicated her unwillingness to legislate further on the subject of executive remuneration: Press Statement of February 25, 2004.

8   *The Strategic Framework*, Chapter 4: The Comparative Dimension.

9   Ie Canada, Australia, New Zealand and South Africa.

10 See *Strategic Framework* at Annex A.

(either academics or practitioners) from the Member States of the European Union[1] or indeed the United States.

1.8 The impact of law and economics theory

Some attention may here be given briefly to the work of the law and economics theorists. This theory has been applied to many branches of law, including tort, contract and, above all, commercial law. This intellectual movement has been very influential in the United States[2] but also has a number of adherents in Britain.[3] It will be seen that law and economics theorists have provided a distinct analysis of company law as viewed from the perspective of this type of economic theory. Inevitably, this 'movement' has its critics among other corporate theorists, including economists.[4] Some critics object to the theory as 'anti-regulatory bias', but its adherents reject this charge. They maintain that the aim of their work is to encourage a better quality of legislative intervention based on sound economic theory.[5]

It is not appropriate in a book which does not claim to be influenced by law and economics theory to engage in detailed discussion of the assumptions made and the concepts employed by this theory,[6] except insofar as they have a particular bearing upon company law. One key idea advanced by this type of economic analysis is to stress the contractual basis of company law. In economic terms the company is analysed as a 'network of contracts'. This essentially means that all the relationships within any particular company are best described in terms of a network of explicit or implicit bargains. This way of characterising the company is obviously at odds with the legal conception of the company[7] which centres upon the legal personality of the registered company. Nevertheless, it is argued that, from an economic standpoint, thinking about the company as a nexus of contracts is an illuminating analytical exercise. The key participants – shareholders, directors and employees – can be said to become involved with their company on a voluntary basis, and to continue to interact on the basis of reciprocal expectations and behaviour. A linked theory is that of the 'role of the firm'.[8] Here again, the term 'firm' does not have its usual legal meaning. Theorising about the economic utility of the 'firm' applies to enterprises which may adopt various legal forms (eg a partnership, a private or public limited company, or even a sole proprietorship with a number of employees). In the light of such economic 'realism', it has been observed that 'company legislation has had, in and of itself, only a modest impact on the bargaining dynamics which account for the nature and form of business

---

1   A cautious and wary glance was given to the EU Harmonisation Programme.
2   See RA Posner, *Economic Analysis of Law* (Boston, Little Brown & Co, 1992); FL Easterbrook and DR Fischel, *The Economic Structure of Corporate Law* (Cambridge, MA, Harvard University Press, 1991).
3   Eg AI Ogus, *Regulation, Legal Reforms and Economic Theory* (Oxford University Press, 1994); Brian Cheffins, *Company Law: Theory Structure and Operation* (Oxford, Clarendon Press, 1997).
4   See generally McCahery, Picciotto and Scott (eds), *Changing Structures and Dynamics of Regulation* (Oxford, Clarendon Press, 1993). See further: CAE Goodhart, 'Economics and Law – Too Much One Way Traffic' (1997) 60 MLR 1.
5   See Cheffins, op cit above, at p 7.
6   See generally Cheffins, op cit above, Chapter 1: 'Economics and the Study of Company Law' for an excellent introduction to the subject.
7   See the historical section of this chapter (above) and Chapter 2 as to the concept of legal personality and the consequences of incorporation.
8   See RH Coase, *The Firm, the Market and the Law* (Chicago, University of Chicago Press, 1988).

enterprises. Thus, analytically an incorporated company is, like other types of firms, fundamentally a nexus of contracts'.[1]

Another theory applied by law and economics theory to the company (or any substantial enterprise) is that of 'agency costs'. Here yet again, the term 'agency' (or the correlative 'principal') is not used in a legal sense. The theory of 'agency costs' is designed to deal with inevitable conflicts of interest between the various participants in a business enterprise. From an economic perspective, an agency relationship arises when one participant depends on another for business activity. This obviously applies to the trust that shareholders must place in company directors or officers who manage the assets and undertake the business activity of their company. This delegation by the 'principal' of the power to manage to the 'agent' raises the problem of 'agency costs'. This means the costs of monitoring the performance of the management to prevent an 'agent' putting his own interests above those of his 'principal'. Here again, a bargaining process should establish legal arrangements that will seek to reduce agency 'costs' both in terms of the costs of continuing monitoring and the costs caused by misbehaviour or incompetent management.

In Britain, law and economics theorising about company law has received a mixed reception. Some scholars argue strongly for its application in order to understand the impact of company law upon business enterprises so as to maximise their economic welfare.[2] It has been adopted in a Law Commission Consultative paper concerned with reforming the law of directors' duties.[3]

Other scholars, however, find serious shortcomings in the 'nexus of contracts' analysis of the company and indeed in the whole approach of the law and economics school. They question the neo-liberal economic assumptions on which this theory rests. It can be argued that it is particularly inappropriate when applied to the legal regulation of public listed companies. Its application may compound the weakness and ineffectuality of the present system of company law in restraining corporate abuses in such companies.[4]

The stimulating and continuing debate these arguments have produced may be further pursued in the literature referred to in the footnotes. Any more detailed assessment clearly lies beyond the scope of an introductory chapter to a company law text.

---

1   Cheffins, op cit above, at p 41.
2   Cheffins, op cit above. In a more qualified appraisal, see Simon Deakin and Alan Hughes, 'Economics and Company Law Reform: a fruitful partnership?' (1999) 20 Co Law (Special Issue) 212. See also Riley, 'Contracting out of Company Law: Section 459 of the Companies Act 1989 and the Role of the Court' (1992) 55 MLR 782. See further Maugham and Copp, 'Company law reform and economic methodology revisited' (2000) 21 Co Law 14; Copp, 'Company law and alternative dispute resolution: an economic analysis' (2002) 23 Co Law 361.
3   See *Company Directors: Regulating Conflicts of Interests and formulating a Statement of Duties*. A Joint Consultative Paper of the English and Scottish Law Commission, Law Com No 153 (1998). See Part III by Simon Deakin and Alan Hughes, 'Economic Considerations'. See also the Law Commission's final report: 1B in Law Com No 261 (Cm 4436, 1999).
4   See David Sugarman, 'Is Company Law founded on contract or public regulation? The Law Commission's Paper on Company Directors' (1999) 20 Co Law (Special Issue) at pp 178–183; Janet Dine, 'Fiduciary Duties as default rules, European influences and the need for caution in the use of economic analysis', ibid 190 at pp 193–195.

Other corporate scholars have advanced alternative theoretical approaches to company law which stress many non-economic dimensions in formulating a more comprehensive conceptualisation of company law and corporate reality.[1]

1.9 The market for corporate control

In the case of listed public companies, the role of 'market economics' must be taken seriously at an everyday and severely practical level. Here there is not only a market for the company's goods or services but also an active market for its listed securities. Where all (or at least a controlling majority) of the company's voting shares are issued to the investing public at large,[2] it is clearly possible for control of the company to pass a result of a successful takeover bid.[3] Even where this does not occur, the discipline of market will operate through the rise or fall of the company's share price to reward or punish successful or unsuccessful performance by the management. This may prove much more significant as a sanction against incompetence or carelessness than any legal remedy.

The idea of the market for corporate control has gained increasing attention since the early 1980s. It obviously reflects the neo-liberal ideology which has prevailed in a period when the concept of 'markets' and 'market forces' has been at the centre of most political as well as economic discussion. The undoubted pragmatic basis for this concept is to be found in the regularly occurring battle for control of large public companies by means of contested takeover bids. The conditions that make this possible in Britain (perhaps alone among the Member States of the European Union) require at least a majority of the voting equity shares in the target company to be widely distributed among institutional investors as well as individual shareholders. Institutional investors (such as pension funds, insurance companies and unit trusts) are 'key players' in the takeover market. Their role is an essential one not only in deciding the success or failure of a takeover bid (or rival bids) but in generating such bids in the first place.

There is a significant connection between an active takeover market and the efficient and honest management of large public companies. It has long been argued that in such Stock Exchange listed companies, with very widely distributed shareholding, pressure from institutional investors performs a vital function in disciplining incompetent or corrupt boards of directors. It is the threat or actuality of a takeover bid which brings the main shareholders' voting power to bear.[4]

---

1 See especially JE Parkinson, *Corporate Power and Responsibility, Issues in the Theory of Company Law* (Oxford, Clarendon Press, 1994). This study is especially concerned with directors' duties and the issue of corporate governance. It is further considered in Chapter 11. See also the classical study of the separation of ownership and control in large corporations: AA Berle and GR Means, *The Modern Corporation and Private Property* (New York 1932, rev edn 1967). See a current assessment of this classic work by Paddy Ireland, 'Back to the future', Adolf Berle, the Law Commission and Directors' Duties (1999) 20 Co Law (Special Issue) 203.

2 As to public issues, see Chapter 18.

3 As to the regulation of takeover bids by the City Code on Takeovers and Mergers, see Chapter 19.

4 For a variety of reasons, including board control of the proxy-voting machinery, most general meetings are dominated by the board. This includes the procedure to elect and re-elect directors.

Until relatively recently, the whole question of corporate governance was largely unregulated by company law or indeed by City self-regulation. The corporate governance issue describes the practices and committee structures by which boards of directors conduct their affairs and seek to monitor senior management so as to make them accountable to the board. Such questions were seen as being an internal matter for each listed public company and not one for the law maker or City regulator. As a matter of basic political policy the Government throughout the 1980s regarded the way boards of directors functioned as part of 'the prerogative of management to manage'. It was contended that the market for corporate control would provide the necessary corrective to any corporate abuses that might occur.

In more recent years, the harsh experience of corporate fraud and company failure, extending to well-known public companies, reduced confidence in the market for corporate control to cope on its own with this problem. The system of self-regulation of corporate governance, by what became the 'Combined Code', is examined elsewhere in this book.[1] Currently (2002–04), a new development of 'shareholder activism', mostly by institutional investors, has sought to challenge, sometimes successfully, incompetent senior executives in public listed companies as well as similar executives who have been excessively rewarded despite their obvious lack of success in managing their companies.

---

1   See Chapter 11.

Chapter 2

The European Community and Company Law

2.1 Introduction

Some years ago, an editorial[1] in *The Company Lawyer* criticised the treatment of European company law by academic scholarship in the UK, noting that beyond an 'obligatory introductory section,' few references are made to EC material. It is true that company law is perceived largely as a matter for domestic law and that the influence of the European Community (EC)[2] on domestic company is often treated too superficially. This is despite the fact that several of the central provisions of the Companies Acts 1985 and 1989 are either based on EC directives or have had to be reformed as a result of such measures. Although it is strictly speaking correct that English lawyers apply the provisions of the Companies Acts, they should not ignore the relevance of corresponding EC directives and, crucially, judgments by the European Court of Justice (ECJ).[3] Although this chapter divorces the treatment of EC matters from the corresponding domestic provisions, it does so to raise awareness of the areas which have been affected by EC law. The EC has pursued a wide-ranging programme of harmonisation, and is considering proposals for further harmonising measures. In addition, the provisions of the EC Treaty on the freedom of establishment of companies have given rise to several important judgments by the ECJ, shedding new light on the scope of those provisions. Finally, after many years of negotiation, Member States agreed on a 'European Company Statute' in 2001, which will come into force in October 2004. The EC has therefore made a far-reaching contribution to the development of company law. The purpose of this chapter is to chart these developments, in particular the recent case-law on the freedom of establishment of companies, and the European Company Statute. The harmonisation programme will be presented in outline only, and appropriate reference to the relevant directives will be made when dealing with the corresponding areas of domestic law.[4]

In May 2003, the European Commission outlined its plans to modernise EC Company Law over the next five years or so.[5] This will involve modernisation of existing directives[6] as well as the adoption of several measures that have been in the pipeline for some time. It also intends to take steps to improve corporate

---

1   M Adenas, 'European Company Law Reform and the United Kingdom' (2000) 21 Co Law 36.

2   Although now commonly referred to as the European Union, the law-making powers remain within the Community. This chapter therefore refers to EC law, not EU law.

3   Seminally, see C-106/89 *Marleasing v La Comercial Internacional de Alimentación SA* [1990] ECR I-4135.

4   For a detailed, if now dated, account of the various directives, see V Edwards, *EC Company Law* (Oxford: Oxford University Press, 1999).

5   *Modernising Company Law and Enhancing Corporate Governance in the European Union – A Plan to Move Forward* COM (2003) 284 final, 21 May 2003 and *Reinforcing the Statutory Audit* (2003) OJ C 236/2. *Modernising Company Law* is based on the High Level Group Report *A Modern Regulatory Framework for Company Law in Europe* (November 2002).

6   Noted below where appropriate.

governance in the EC and is expected to put forward proposals for directives which will require greater disclosure, promote communication with shareholders, and require institutional investors to disclose their investment and voting policies. In addition, the Commission intends to legislate to give all listed companies the choice between the one-tier and two-tier board system, as well as to enhance the responsibilities of board members by developing harmonised wrongful trading and disclosure rules. There will also be recommendations on the role of non-executive directors and directors' remuneration.[1] These proposals are still at the planning stage and will therefore not be discussed further in this chapter.

2.2 Fundamental Freedoms: The Free Movement of Companies

2.2.1 A fundamental problem

One of the fundamental objectives of the European Community is to enable the free movement of persons around the Single Market. This includes the right for nationals of a Member State to establish themselves in another Member State. The main provision in this respect is Article 43 EC, which provides as follows:

> Restrictions on freedom of establishment of nationals of a Member State in the territory of another Member State shall be prohibited. Such prohibition shall also apply to restrictions on the setting-up of agencies, branches or subsidiaries by nationals of any Member State established in the territory of any Member State.

This right is extended to companies by Article 48 EC:

> Companies formed in accordance with the law of a Member State and having their registered office, central administration or principal place of business within the Community shall be treated in the same way as natural persons who are nationals of Member States.

Companies which are formed in one of the Member States are therefore, in principle, entitled to move around the internal market in the same way as individuals. This may be done in two ways: either by setting up a *primary* establishment in another Member State by moving the company's registered office there, or merely by opening a *secondary* establishment through the setting up of an agency, branch or a subsidiary formed under the laws of the host Member State. Although this may sound straightforward enough at first sight, it has, in fact, hitherto been very difficult for companies to exercise their right of primary establishment in the Community. A fundamental problem is that a company formed and registered in a particular Member State will only be deemed to have legal capacity and be recognised as a separate legal entity in accordance with the laws of that State. Should a company wish to move its registered office to another Member State, it would have to be wound up in the State of origin and be re-registered as a new company in accordance with the requirements of the host Member State. An attempt was made in 1968 by the then six Member States[2] to enable companies to move freely around the Community by providing for the

---

1   See the consultation documents *Fostering an Appropriate Regime for the Remuneration of Directors* published by the Internal Market Directorate-General on 23 February 2004, and *Recommendation on the Role of (independent) non-executive or supervisory directors*, published on 5 May 2004.

2   Belgium, France, Germany, Italy, Luxembourg and the Netherlands.

mutual recognition of companies with a Convention on the Mutual Recognition of Companies.[1] The Netherlands ultimately chose not to ratify the Convention and it never entered into force. However, in the wake of the adoption of the Statute on a European Company,[2] the European Commission is due to present a proposal for a Fourteenth Directive on the cross-border transfer of a company's registered office some time during 2004, which would be a significant step forward in securing the free movement of companies.[3]

Faced with such difficulties, companies wishing to take advantage of the freedom of establishment have the option of setting up a branch in another Member State, or of incorporating a subsidiary company in another Member State to do business there (secondary establishment). Indeed, an entrepreneur who intends to set up a company might even be tempted to incorporate in a Member State which has a relatively liberal regime, and then, by taking advantage of the right to create a secondary establishment, to conduct most or all of his business in another Member State. A significant difficulty in this context is that the Member States do not follow the same principle of private international law for determining the law applicable to a company (*lex societas*). Broadly speaking, it is possible to divide Member States on the basis of two different, and irreconcilable, theories, the 'incorporation' doctrine (used in Denmark, Finland, Ireland, the Netherlands, Sweden and the UK), and the real seat doctrine (or *siège réel*) (all other Member States).[4] In essence, the real seat doctrine specifies that the law applicable to a company is determined with reference to the location of its head office, its central management or even its centre of activity.[5] A consequence of this is that the company's registered office must be located in the same jurisdiction as the head office. For example, a company which has its head office in Germany (a 'real seat' jurisdiction) would be treated as subject to German law by that legal system. Consequently, if the head office of a company registered in the UK is moved to Germany, the German courts, applying German law, would refuse to recognise its existence unless the company was re-registered as a German company.

In contrast, the 'incorporation' doctrine uses the registered office as the relevant criterion. Consequently, the company will be governed by the law of its country of incorporation. Thus, its legal personality would, for example, depend on the position as it obtains in the jurisdiction where its registered office is based, even if its head office was based in another Member State.

---

1   Article 293 EC provides a legal basis for Member States to negotiate to secure the mutual recognition of companies and the retention of their legal personality in the event of a transfer of their seat from one Member State to another.
2   Discussed below at **2.5**.
3   Press Release IP/04/270, 26 February 2004: 'Company Law: Commission consults on the cross-border transfer of companies' registered offices'.
4   See Wymeersch, 'The Transfer of the Company's Seat in European Company Law' (2003) 40 CML Rev 661–695 for a more detailed exposition of these theories. This does not include the new Member States who joined in May 2004.
5   Sometimes defined as 'the location where the internal management decisions are transformed into day-to-day activities of a company'. See WH Roth, 'From *Centros* to *Überseering*: free movement of companies, private international law and Community law' (2003) 52 ICLQ 177 at 181.

2.2.2 The jurisprudence of the ECJ

The compatibility of the real seat doctrine with the principle of freedom of establishment guaranteed by the EC Treaty has been tested in a number of recent cases. Some of these cases involved companies which were incorporated, but did not trade, in the UK.

In the so-called *Daily Mail* case,[1] a company incorporated under English law wished to transfer its central management to the Netherlands. The primary motive behind this decision was to avoid capital gains tax on the sale of shares.[2] Consent from the Treasury was required before the move could go ahead. Although it was willing to grant such consent, it required that the sale of shares had to be effected *before* the move. The company argued that this was contrary to Article 43. The ECJ held that because of the divergent rules on the transfer of the registered office or head office between the Member States, legislation was required to resolve the problem. There was no right under Article 43 to move the head office of a company to another Member State whilst retaining legal status as a company in the original Member State. Consequently, the home Member State was entitled to impose conditions on a company wishing to exercise its free movement rights.

The position in the host Member State was addressed for the first time in the famous *Centros* decision.[3] A private limited company had been registered in the UK, but it never traded there. It had been formed for the sole purpose of setting up a branch of the company in Denmark to trade there, without having to comply with the Danish minimum capital requirements. These are stricter than in the UK, applying also to private companies.[4] The Danish registrar refused to register the branch because, in his view, rather than being a branch of a company from another Member State, it seemed to be a company with its principal establishment in Denmark. As it had not complied with the minimum capital rules, he refused to register the company, although it was conceded that if Centros had traded in the UK, registration of the branch would not have been refused. The question before the ECJ was therefore whether Centros was entitled to rely on Article 43 EC, or whether the Danish registrar was justified in his refusal to register the branch. The ECJ was unequivocal in its decision, holding that the refusal to register the branch was a breach of EC law and could not be justified in interest of protecting creditors or preventing fraud, especially in light of existing EC rules on accounting. The deliberate choice of a Member State with more lenient requirements for incorporation and subsequent use of the right of secondary establishment was simply an exercise of rights inherent in the notion of freedom of establishment. This in itself would not be an abuse of the right of establishment, even though it had the effect of circumventing requirements in home Member State. Not trading in the Member State where the company was incorporated and only trading

---

1   *R v HM Treasury and Commissioners of Inland Revenue, ex parte Daily Mail and General Trust plc* (Case C-81/87) [1988] ECR 5483.

2   The sum that would have been payable in the UK amounted to some £13 million, whereas following the move to the Netherlands, tax would only have been payable on any increase in the shares' value since the date of the move.

3   *Centros Ltd v Ehrvervs og Selskabsstyrelsen* (Case C-212/97) [1999] ECR I-1459, [2000] 2 WLR 1048, [1999] BCC 983.

4   The 2nd EC Directive requires a minimum capital requirement only for public companies, but many Member States have extended this requirement to private companies, as well. See **2.3.2**, below.

through a branch was not in itself enough to constitute abuse.[1] This decision gave rise to a significant amount of debate among commentators,[2] and many felt that *Centros* marked the beginning of the end of the 'real seat' doctrine.[3] In *Centros*, the company's registered office was located in the UK whereas its activities were carried on in Denmark. In accepting that this was perfectly lawful under EC law, the ECJ appeared to hold that, as a matter of EC law, the registered office, which was not in the same Member State where the company mainly operated, was the law applicable to the company. This, of course, would be in direct conflict with the real seat principle, which, on the facts of *Centros*, would have applied Danish law to the company.

In *Überseering*,[4] the ECJ was given the opportunity to clarify its rulings in *Daily Mail* and *Centros*. In this case, a Dutch company (ÜBV) had acquired land in Germany and contracted with NCC, a German company, for renovation work. This work was not carried out to ÜBV's satisfaction and it tried to sue NCC in the German courts. The shares in ÜBV had been acquired by German shareholders and it seemed to the German court that the company had transferred its real seat to Germany. In German law, a company's legal capacity is determined on the basis of its real seat. As ÜBV had not reincorporated in Germany after the acquisition of its shares by German shareholders, the court refused to recognise the company's legal capacity. The German Federal Supreme Court was concerned about the compatibility of this ruling with Article 43 EC. It referred two questions to the ECJ for a preliminary ruling: (1) If company validly incorporated in A moves its actual centre of administration to B, and rules in B would prevent the company from having legal capacity, can B maintain its rules in light of Article 43 EC? (2) If so, does Article 43 EC require that the legal capacity of a company should be determined according to the law of the State where the company is incorporated? The ECJ first distinguished *Daily Mail* because that case concerned restrictions imposed by the home Member State.[5] In the present case, it held that ÜBV could rely on Article 43 EC, because it was validly incorporated in the Netherlands and had its registered office there. It was of little significance that its shares had been acquired by German shareholders because this had no effect on ÜBV's legal status under Dutch law. On that basis, the refusal of the host Member State (B) to recognise the legal capacity of a company formed in accordance with the law in its home Member State (A) on the ground that the company has moved its centre of administration was in principle incompatible with Article 43. However, it could be justifiable if it was applied without discrimination, required by overriding

---

1   Cf *Segers v Bestuur de de Bedrifsvereniging voor Bank en Verzekeringswezen* (Case C-79/85) [1986] ECR 2375.

2   See eg, E Micheler, 'The Impact of the *Centros* case on Europe's Company laws' (2000) 21 Co Law 179.

3   One aspect of *Centros* (and *Segers*) is open to doubt: the ECJ assumed that Centros Ltd was established in the UK and sought to exercise its right to set up a secondary establishment in Denmark. However, ECJ jurisprudence appears to determine 'establishment' on the basis of both physical presence *and* the exercise of an economic activity. Centros Ltd was not economically active, however, and it may therefore questioned whether it was really established in the UK: see H. Xanthaki, '*Centros*: Is this really the end for the theory of the siège réel' (2001) 22 Co Law 2 at 7.

4   *Überseering BV v Nordic Construction Company Baumanagement GmbH* (Case C-208/00) [2002] ECR I-9919.

5   This has been criticised by WH Roth, 'From *Centros* to *Überseering*: free movement of companies, private international law and Community law' (2003) 52 ICLQ 177.

requirements relating to the general interest, and was proportionate to the objectives pursued. The ECJ accepted that requirements relating to the protection of the interests of creditors, minority shareholders, employees or taxation authorities may justify restrictions on the freedom of establishment, but this did not extend to denying altogether legal capacity to a company and therefore its capacity to bring legal proceedings. Thus, moving the actual centre of management cannot result in loss of legal capacity in the host Member State. In relation to the second question, the ECJ held that where a company has its registered office in Member State A and exercises its right to freedom of establishment in Member State B, Articles 43 and 48 require that B must recognise the legal capacity which the company enjoys under the law of its State of incorporation.[1]

The most recent decision is C-167/01 *Chamber of Commerce Amsterdam v Inspire Art Ltd*,[2] involving a challenge to the legality of a Dutch law on 'formally foreign companies' (FFC law). This law applies to companies incorporated in a Member State other than the Netherlands which predominantly or exclusively operate in the Netherlands. These must be entered in the commercial register as a 'formally foreign company' and comply with detailed disclosure obligations. The law further imposes minimum capital requirements and sanctions for non-compliance. Inspire Art Ltd (IAL) was a company incorporated in England, but it operated exclusively in the Netherlands through a branch in Amsterdam. The Amsterdam Chamber of Commerce demanded that IAL comply with the Dutch law. The Dutch court held that the FFC law applied, but requested a ruling from the ECJ on its compatibility with EC law. The ECJ first held that to the extent that the FFC law reflected the requirements of the relevant company law directives as they applied to IAL, the Dutch law was compatible, provided that the penalties for non-compliance were the same as for Dutch companies. Many of the disclosure provisions implemented the requirements of the Eleventh Directive[3] and were therefore not a problem. However, several disclosure requirements in the FFC law, such as recording in the commercial register that branch is an FFC and providing an auditor's certificate of compliance with minimum capital requirements, went beyond the Eleventh Directive. As the Eleventh Directive was exhaustive, no further requirements could be imposed. The minimum capital requirement fell outside any relevant directive[4] and therefore had to be tested against the relevant Treaty provisions. The ECJ confirmed its holding in *Centros* and *Überseering* that it is immaterial that a company was formed in one Member State solely for the purpose of establishment in a second Member State where its main or entire business is conducted. In the absence of fraud, its reasons for doing so are irrelevant; in fact, incorporating in a particular Member State solely for the purpose of benefiting from more favourable legislation is fully compatible with the Treaty. Imposing the Dutch minimum capital requirement on branches in

---

1   The ruling in this case does not mean that company can move its *registered* office to another
     Member State and demand recognition under Article 43. For this, legislation is required and
     a proposal for a Fourteenth Directive on the transfer of the registered seat is expected during
     2004. A pre-proposal consultation took place between February and April 2004; see Press
     Release IP/04/270, 26 February 2004: 'Company Law: Commission consults on the cross-
     border transfer of companies' registered offices'.

2   *Chamber of Commerce Amsterdam v Inspire Art Ltd* (Case C-167/01) [2003] ECR I-n.y.r (judgment
     of 30 September 2003).

3   See below at **2.3.6.**

4   As noted in the context of *Centros*, EC law only imposes a minimum capital requirement on
     public companies.

such circumstances was contrary to the freedom of establishment, although it might justifiable. On the facts of *Inspire Art*, this was not possible because IAL was clearly held out as English company, and, more significantly, it had not been improper for IAL to have recourse to the freedom of establishment in trying to avoid the stricter incorporation rules of Dutch law.

2.2.3 The impact of the ECJ's case-law

In the wake of these cases, it is perhaps not surprising that commentators have suggested that the 'real seat' doctrine has to all intents and purposes been abolished by the ECJ, although opinions on this diverge. Some clearly think that post-*Überseering*, the incorporation theory is fully accepted.[1] However, that case was concerned with a rather narrow question regarding the legal recognition of a company fully recognised in its home Member State. Although this ruling has a distinct flavour of incorporation theory, it seems difficult to extrapolate a general preference for either the 'real seat' or the 'incorporation' principle from it. It was observed (following *Centros*) that just as the EC Treaty itself does not prefer one of the two principles, referring instead to three alternative criteria in Article 43 EC,[2] so it would be surprising if the ECJ's jurisprudence were to be a departure from these basic alternatives.[3] Indeed, it is likely that the ECJ would have come to a different decision in *Centros*, had the company been incorporated in Austria and tried to establish a branch in Germany.[4] *Überseering* does refer to the country of incorporation for determining the fundamental question of legal capacity, but this does not mean that the incorporation principle should apply to determining all other company law matters.[5] A crucial issue here is the extent to which a host country can impose its rules on a company which is incorporated elsewhere, but active primarily or exclusively in the host Member State. Following *Inspire Art*, it seems that a company would only have to comply with the requirements of its home State (State of registration), unless requirements of the host Member State are justified in public interest. It remains to be seen which rules could be justified on this basis – one possibility might be rules on worker participation imposed by the host Member State on companies which have their registered office in its territory.[6] What does seem clear is that this is a question which will occupy academic commentators for some time to come, and may ultimately only be settled if the EC adopts legislation to allow companies to move freely around the EC.[7]

---

1   See eg, M Ebers, 'Company Law in Member States against the Background of Legal Harmonisation and Competition between legal systems' [2003] ERPL 509 at 511.

2   These are (1) registered office, (2) central administration or (3) principal place of business in the Community. The third factor is relevant for companies incorporated outside the EC.

3   H Xanthaki, '*Centros*: Is this really the end for the theory of the siège réel?' (2001) 22 Co Law 2.

4   Ibid, p 7.

5   I Thoma, 'The *Überseering* ruling: a tale of serendipity' [2003] ERPL 545. Note that UK law applies a 'real seat' criterion in the context of taxation, despite being an 'incorporation' jurisdiction.

6   WH Roth, 'From *Centros* to *Überseering*: free movement of companies, private international law and Community law' (2003) 52 ICLQ 177.

7   M Adenas, 'Free Movement of Companies' (2003) 119 LQR 221 at 226; Roth (2003) 52 ICLQ 177; Wymeersch (2003) 40 CML Rev 661.

The ECJ has, however, given clear support to the existence of a 'market' for incorporation.[1] Because of the variations in the domestic company law systems, Member States could be competing for 'incorporation' business. Indeed, the various recent ECJ cases suggest that there is demand for 'easy incorporation' regimes and that the UK is fairly popular. This raises the suggestion that the UK could even become the EC's Delaware.[2] However, although the Treaty rules grant companies the right to incorporate in any Member State, a significant degree of competition between legal systems could undermine the whole idea of the internal market. To some extent, this is mitigated by the company law harmonisation programme which increasingly deals with those matters which would otherwise make incorporation elsewhere attractive – although does not rule this out altogether. The absence of a minimum capital requirement in the UK has proven to be a significant element – but if plans to modernise the Second Directive include an extension of the minimum capital requirement to private companies, then this may dampen the enthusiasm of those from other Member States to incorporate in the UK and then utilise their rights under the Treaty.

2.3 The Harmonisation Programme: Company Law Directives

The legal basis for the harmonisation programme in the field of company law is Article 44 EC. Harmonisation has proceeded by way of directives, requiring that domestic law is adjusted to comply fully with the requirements of a directive without having to follow the exact wording of each measure.[3] Most of the harmonisation directives have been incorporated into the Companies Act 1985, although some are implemented in free-standing regulations, or in other Acts of Parliament.

It is possible to identify four distinct 'generations' of directives:[4] the first generation (the First and Second Directives) is heavily influenced by the German drafting style and these are therefore very detailed.[5] The second generation (covering the Third, Fourth, Sixth, Seventh and Eighth Directives) is still fairly precisely worded, but there is greater flexibility, thereby allowing for some diversity between the domestic laws and some discretion regarding their implementation. The third generation (Eleventh and Twelfth Directives) follows the so-called 'new approach' to harmonisation, specifying only the essential requirements to be met rather than the detail of how these are to be met. Finally, there may be a fourth generation of 'framework' directives, such as the recently adopted Thirteenth Directive, as well as the proposed Fourteenth Directive on the transfer of the seat.

The purpose of this part is to chart the harmonisation programme in outline, rather than to engage in a detailed discussion of the various directives. Later

---

1   See further Cheffins, *Company Law – Theory, Structure and Operation* (Oxford University Press, 1997), Chapter 9.
2   Although it has been observed that the 'Delaware' effect involves public listed companies, whereas the *Centros* effect is more likely to be relevant to small private companies: E Micheler, 'The Impact of the *Centros* case on Europe's Company laws' (2000) 21 Co Law 179 at 182.
3   For a discussion of harmonisation generally, see J Steiner, L Woods and C Twigg-Flesner, *Textbook on EC Law*, 8th edn, chapter 12 (Oxford University Press, 2003).
4   C Villiers, *European Company Law – Towards Democracy?* (Aldershot: Ashgate, 1998), p 28.
5   Although some of the substantive provisions are based on other jurisdictions, including UK law, eg in respect of some of the capital maintenance rules.

chapters make reference to specific provisions of these directives where appropriate. A general overview helps to illustrate the significance of the EC's harmonisation programme on the development of domestic company law, while also identifying some of the obstacles which are now in the way of reform of domestic company law.[1]

2.3.1 First Company Law Directive

The First Directive[2] is concerned with three basic issues: disclosure, validity of obligations entered into by a company, and nullity of companies. It requires that companies disclose details of their constitutions, including subsequent amendments, company officers, the subscribed capital and their profit and loss accounts. Moreover, all company documents must include basic details, including the company's registration number. All Member States must have a central register of companies. The Directive was recently amended[3] to provide for the creation of an electronic register and disclose of information by electronic means. The national gazette may be kept in electronic form or replaced altogether with an electronic system that will fulfil the same purpose. These amendments must come into force no later than 31 December 2006.

With regard to the validity of obligations entered into by a company, and with an eye on the legal basis for the Directive, there are a number of provisions designed to protect outsiders where particular transactions would not ordinarily bind the company. Thus, in the case of pre-incorporation contracts, it is provided that a person purporting to act for a non-incorporated company may be personally liable to a third party. Moreover, an outsider contracting with a company will be protected in instances where the company has exceeded its capacity (*ultra vires*) or where the relevant organ in the company has exceeded its authority. Finally, the Directive specifies the circumstances when a Member State may declare a company a nullity.[4]

2.3.2 Second Company Law Directive (77/91/EEC)

The Second Directive[5] applies to public companies only and has had a significant impact on domestic rules on capital maintenance.[6] It pursues two broad objectives: first, it imposes further disclosure requirements on public companies in addition to those already contained in the First Directive, and secondly, it lays down numerous rules on capital maintenance.

---

1   See further Chapter 22.
2   Directive 68/151/EEC on co-ordination of safeguards which, for the protection of the interests of members and others, are required by Member States of companies within the meaning of the second paragraph of Article [48] of the Treaty, with a view to making such safeguards equivalent throughout the Community (1968) OJ L 65/8; English Special Edition 1968 (I), p 41.
3   By Directive 2003/58/EC amending Council Directive 68/151/EEC, as regards disclosure requirements in respect of certain types of companies (2003) OJ L 221/13.
4   This provision has no relevance to UK law.
5   Directive 77/91/EEC on co-ordination of safeguards which, for the protection of the interests of members and others, are required by Member States of companies within the meaning of the second paragraph of Article [48] of the Treaty, in respect of the formation of public limited liability companies and the maintenance and alteration of their capital, with a view to making such safeguards equivalent (1977) OJ L 26/1.
6   It was amended once in 1992 by Directive 92/101/EEC (1992) OJ L 347/64, inserting a new Article 24a.

As far as the additional disclosure requirements are concerned, it is required that information is provided about the type and name of company, its objects, and the amount of subscribed and authorised share capital. More detailed disclosure of information on the documents lodged with the registrar of companies is also required.

The Directive requires that all public companies have a minimum subscribed share capital of at least €25,000.[1] There are then several detailed provisions to ensure that the integrity of share capital is preserved. Thus, share capital must be represented in assets capable of economic assessment. Shares may not to be issued at a discount and must be paid up by a minimum of 25%. There is a prohibition against distributions out of capital, and it is further provided that any amount distributed to shareholders must not to exceed the company's net profits. Public companies are permitted to increase or reduce their share capital, but any such changes must be approved by the shareholders. Furthermore, there is a general prohibition against the company providing financial assistance for the acquisition of its own shares, and there are rules on the purchase by a company of its own shares. Finally, there are rules on pre-emption rights of existing shareholders. The provisions of this Directive are very detailed and technical and have been criticised for being overly complex.[2] The Commission recently announced[3] that it would implement legislation to simplify the Directive as a short-term priority. The main changes would enable own-purchase of shares and financial assistance within the limits of distributable profits, the introduction of shares without a par value, and allowing public companies to ignore pre-emption rights where shares are issued at the market price. However, the minimum capital requirement would be retained as a deterrent factor. A proposal for a revised Directive is expected some time during 2004. In the longer term, the Commission will consider whether the capital maintenance system could be replaced with an alternative regime based on a new solvency test before company funds may be used for certain purposes, but this is not expected before 2009.

2.3.3 *Mergers and Divisions of public companies*

The Third Directive[4] deals with mergers of public limited companies. It requires that Member States put procedures into place to facilitate such mergers within their territories.[5] The Directive deals with two types of merger: the first is a merger by acquisition, whereby one of the merging companies will receive all the assets and assume the obligations and liabilities of the other companies. The second is a merger by the formation of a new company, to which all the assets and liabilities of the merging companies will be transferred. In either case, the management bodies of participating companies must draw up terms of proposed merger and provide information on the effect of proposed merger on shareholdings. Furthermore, it must account for any benefits to the management team resulting

---

1   This is about £18,000; note that the minimum capital requirement specified for UK public companies is £50,000.

2   Indeed, the DTI noted that this stood in the way of simplifying the capital maintenance regime for public companies as part of the 'modernising company law' project.

3   See COM (2003) 284 final (EU Action Plan on modernising company law), pp 17–18.

4   Directive 78/855/EEC concerning mergers of public limited liability companies (1978) OJ L 295/36.

5   Note that this Directive does not deal with cross-border mergers. On such mergers, see the proposal for a Tenth Directive (2003) COM final, 18 November 2003.

from the merger. A report by the management and an independent expert report evaluating the proposed merger must be approved by a minimum two-thirds majority of the shareholders in general meeting. Once a merger has been completed details must be publicised in the *Gazette*. The Directive seeks to provide protection for shareholders as well as others affected by the merger (such as employees, creditors or debenture holders). Generally, the management boards must provide detailed information. The Sixth Directive[1] provides for similar rules where a public limited company separates into divisions. Both directives apply to domestic transactions only, but the Commission recently put forward a new proposal for a Tenth Directive on cross-border mergers of public limited companies. Previous proposals for such a directive had not come to fruition because of concerns over worker protection in some Member States. The most recent proposal is discussed below at **2.3.7.**

2.3.4 Accounting and Audit Directives

The Fourth Directive[2] is also known as the Accounts Directive. It sets out the requirements for accounts to be drawn up and submitted to a central registery. The aim of this Directive is to achieve comparability and equivalence of financial information throughout the EC. The Directive provides for a choice of different accounts formats. It also requires that accounts are audited and that the publication of accounts and the auditor's report is duly authorised. The Directive applies to all business forms and not merely to public companies, although it contains a number of exemptions for certain small and medium-sized enterprises. The Seventh Directive[3] extends this to corporate groups. It requires that a parent company, in addition to its annual accounts, also prepares consolidated accounts for the corporate group which it heads.

Both Directives are supplemented by the Eighth Directive[4] which lays down minimum conditions for the approval of auditors. These requirements relate to the competence and independence of auditors and the Directive pursues as its overall objective that accounting of company accounts is carried out with integrity and independence. Auditors must have completed a minimum period of 3 years' training and must have passed an examination of professional competence. The professional bodies for the accounting profession are designated as authorising bodies. The Commission has recently put forward a proposal for the replacement of the Eighth Directive,[5] which marks the culmination of a review process which began in 1996. As well as modernising the existing rules on auditors, it would introduce new rules on auditor independence, quality assurance and, perhaps somewhat controversially, require the establishment of an audit committee for all

---

1   Directive 82/891/EEC concerning the division of public limited liability companies (1982) OJ L 378/47.

2   Directive 78/660/EEC on the annual accounts of certain types of companies (1978) OJ L 222/11. This has been amended several times, most recently by Directive 2003/38/EC on the annual accounts of certain types of companies as regards amounts expressed in euro (2003) OJ L 120/22, and Directive 2003/51/EC on the annual and consolidated accounts of certain types of companies (2003) OJ L 178/16.

3   Directive 83/349/EEC on consolidated accounts (1983) OJ L 193/1.

4   Directive 84/253/EEC on the approval of persons responsible for carrying out the statutory audits of accounting documents (1984) OJ L 126/20.

5   Proposal for a Directive on statutory audit of annual accounts and consolidated accounts and amending Council Directives 78/660/EEC and 84/349/EEC, COM (2004) 177 final, March 2004.

requirements for securities issuers was adopted in 2004.[1] The directive on insider dealing has been replaced by Directive 2003/6/EC on Insider Dealing and Market Manipulation.[2] This was the first to be adopted under the new procedure for the regulation of the European securities markets. Essentially, the directives only specify broad principles. Detailed implementing rules are subsequently drafted by the European Commission, which has to consult the European Securities Regulators Committee.[3] Several implementing measures have subsequently been adopted, including: a regulation providing an exemption for buy-back programmes and stabilisation of financial instruments,[4] a directive on the definition and public disclosure of inside information and the definition of market manipulation,[5] a directive on the fair presentation of investment recommendations and the disclosure of conflicts of interest,[6] and a directive on the definition of inside information.[7] More recently, a new Prospectus Directive[8] was adopted which is intended to require the drafting of one prospectus only, even if securities are offered in more than one Member State. It will require such prospectuses to be vetted by a competent authority even where the securities concerned will not be listed. These are important developments, but it is beyond the scope of the present chapter to discuss these measures in any detail. Appropriate reference will be made in subsequent chapters in this book.

2.5 The European Company Statute[9]

2.5.1 Background

Perhaps one of the most significant contributions in recent years has been the adoption, after a long gestation period, of the European Company Statute.[10] The idea for this particular measure pre-dates establishment of the EC.[11] In 1970, the European Commission presented its first proposal, but negotiations had stalled by 1982. The idea was revived in 1985 when the Commission proposed the two-pronged approach of a Regulation together with a separate Directive on worker participation. The latter issue had been one of the main obstacles in previous negotiations, partly due to the conflicting views of the German and UK Governments. Negotiations progressed slowly, but in 2001, the European

---

1   See, EC Press Release IP/04/398, 30 March 2004 and MEMO/04/110, 12 May 2004.
2   Directive 2003/6/EC on insider dealing and market manipulation (market abuse) (2003) OJ L 96/16.
3   Established by Commission Decision 2001/528/EC (2001) OJ L 191/45.
4   Regulation 2273/2003 (2003) OJ L 336/33.
5   Directive 2003/124/EC, (2003) OJ L 339/70.
6   Directive 2003/125/EC, (2003) OJ L 339/73.
7   Directive 2004/72/EC (2004) OJ L 162/70.
8   Directive 2003/71/EC on the prospectus to be published when securities are offered to the public or admitted to trading (2003) OJ L 345/64. See also Commission Regulation 809/2004 of 29 April 2004 on the content and format of prospectuses.
9   This chapter will not consider the European Economic Interest Grouping (see eg, C Villiers, *European Company Law – Towards Democracy?* (Aldershot: Ashgate, 1998), pp 156–158), nor the Regulation on a European Co-operative Society.
10   Regulation 2157/2001 of 8 October 2001 on the Statute for a European Company (2001) OJ L 294/1. See eg, S Ebert, 'The European Company on the level playing field of the Community' (2003) 24 Co Law 259.
11   See V Edwards; 'The European company – essential tool or eviscerated dream?' (2003) 40 CHL Rev 442. See also C Villiers, *European Company Law – Towards Democracy?* (Aldershot: Ashgate, 1998), pp 58–59 and V Edwards, *EC Company Law* (Oxford University Press, 1999), pp 399–404.

Company Statute and a directive on worker participation were adopted. The Regulation will come into force on October 8, 2004. At this point, it is too early to say if there will be a wide take-up of the Company statute. The earliest date when a European Company may be formed will be October 2004, but it is unlikely that there will be a European Company before 2005. The purpose of this part is to provide an overview of the general framework of the European Company Statute ('ECS').[1]

2.5.2 Scope

Article 1 ECS provides that a is will be possible to set up a new form of public limited-liability company known as a *Societas Europeae*, or SE, which will have legal personality.[2] It must also include the letters 'SE' in its name,[3] and in future, these letters will be reserved for European companies.[4] However, as there is no central registrar of companies for the European Union, an SE will have to be registered in one particular Member State, ie the State where the SE's registered office is to be located.[5] Registration is subject to compliance with the rules on employee involvement.[6] The rules on registration and disclosure in force in the Member States in accordance with the First Directive[7] also apply to SEs.[8] Notice of the registration of an SE will be published in the *Official Journal.*[9]

Each SE will have statutes, which is the term used in the ECS for the instrument of incorporation and, if contained in a separate document, the statutes.[10] For a UK lawyer, therefore, the statutes comprise the SE's memorandum and articles of association, or, in the language of the *Modernising Company Law* White Paper,[11] its 'constitution'.

2.5.3 Interaction between ECS and domestic law

The ECS requires considerable interaction between the ECS and domestic measures. Article 9 ECS specifies the sources for the rules which will govern the formation and operation of an SE. The starting point is the ECS itself,[12] followed by provisions in the SE's statutes,[13] but only to the extent that the ECS authorises this. Where the ECS does not regulate a matter at all, or only partially, the relevant provisions are Member State rules which implement EU measures relating specifically to SEs, followed by the Member State rules applicable to public companies where the SE has its registered office and, finally, the SE's statutes in the same way as the constitution of a public company would apply under the rules

---

1   See further Cavares da Costa and A de Meester Bilreiro, *The European Company Statute* (Kluwer, The Hague, 2003).
2   Article 1(3) ECS.
3   Article 11(1) ECS.
4   Article 11(2) ECS. However, if the abbreviation 'SE' already appears in the names of companies or other business entities, no change in name will be required by the ECS: Article 11(3).
5   Article 12(1) ECS.
6   Articles 12(2)–(4) ECS; see **2.5.10**, below.
7   68/151/EEC. See **2.3.1**.
8   Article 13 ECS.
9   Article 14 ECS.
10 Article 6 ECS.
11 Cm 5543–1, July 2002. See Chapter 22.
12 Article 9(1)(a) ECS
13 Article 9(1)(b) ECS.

of the relevant Member State.[1] If the SE carries on a business activity for which there are specific national provisions, then these apply in full to the SE.[2] In any other respect, an SE should be treated like any other public limited company in the state where it has its registered office.[3] The extent to which domestic law has a role to play in the regulation of SEs is open to the criticism that this approach largely undermines the objective pursued by the ECS, namely the creation of a pan-European business entity which is not restricted by domestic rules. The ECS contains very little of substance as far as the operation of an SE is concerned, and domestic law will be the main determinant in this regard. Although there has been some approximation of the rules applicable to public companies through the harmonisation programme,[4] there will be areas where there is variation.[5] Consequently, rather than creating one SE, there will, in fact, potentially be as many as 25 different types of SEs.[6] The Commission is required to report on the operation of the ECS five years after its entry into force (ie by 8 October 2009),[7] which may provide evidence of the severity of this problem.

2.5.4 Share Capital

The SE will have a share capital and the liability of a shareholder will be limited to the amount he has subscribed.[8] The capital of an SE must be expressed in euros,[9] and there is a minimum share capital requirement of €120,000, [10] except where the domestic law of the country where the SE is registered requires a higher amount for public companies carrying on particular activities.[11] As far as the rules on capital maintenance and variation, and rules on shares, bonds and similar securities are concerned, the provisions applicable to public companies in the Member State where the SE is registered will apply.[12]

2.5.5 Registered and Head Office

The registered office and the head office must be located within the same Member State.[13] This seems to be a nod in the direction of those Member States which adhere to the 'real seat' doctrine.[14] It has been argued[15] that in light of the developing case-law in the context of the freedom of establishment, the compatibility of this provision with the Treaty is in doubt. However, the European

---

1   Article 9(1)(c) ECS.
2   Article 9(3) ECS.
3   Article 10 ECS.
4   This has been outlined above at **2.3**.
5   Now that the draft fifth Directive has been consigned to the scrap heap, the regulation of directors' duties and shareholder remedies will remain a matter for domestic law.
6   M Ebers, 'Company Law in Member States against the Background of Legal Harmonisation and Competition between legal systems' [2003] ERPL 509 at 515 and L Enriques, 'Silence is golden: the European Company as a catalyst for company law arbitrage' (2004) 4 JCLS 77.
7   Article 69 ECS.
8   Article 1(2) ECS.
9   Article 4(1) ECS.
10 Article 4(2) ECS.
11 Article 4(3) ECS.
12 Note that the bulk of the capital maintenance and variation rules is provided by the Second Directive (above at **2.3.2**).
13 Article 7. Member States may require that both offices are based in the same location.
14 See **2.2**, above.
15 M Ebers, 'Company Law in Member States against the Background of Legal Harmonisation and Competition between legal systems' [2003] ERPL 509 at 514.

Court of Justice has not (yet) explicitly declared the real seat doctrine incompatible with the Treaty, and it seems unlikely, therefore, that this provision is problematic. The Commission is required to consider whether the separation of head office and registered office should be enabled when it reports on the ECS in 2009.[1]

If an SE fails to comply with this requirement, the Member State where the SE's registered office is based must take appropriate measures to oblige the SE either to move its head office back to the Member State where its registered office is based, or to transfer its registered office in accordance with the procedure laid down in Article 8.[2] This procedure seeks to ensure that a company may move its registered office to another Member State (effectively change its nationality) without having to wind up the SE in its home Member State or create a new SE in the host State.[3] However, an SE may not move its registered office if it is subject to proceedings for winding up, liquidation, insolvency, or similar proceedings.[4] The management of the SE must draw up a 'transfer proposal' which has to be publicised,[5] as well as a report explaining and justifying the transfer and its implications for shareholders, creditors and employees.[6] There are then a number of steps to be followed to ensure that all the relevant procedures have been followed before the competent authority[7] in the home Member State issues a certificate which confirms that all necessary steps for the transfer have been taken.[8] The transfer of the SE takes effect once it has been registered in the new Member State, of which the registry where it was previously registered must be notified.[9] The SE is then deleted from its old register, but until that has happened, third parties may continue to use the old registered office, unless they are aware of the new registered office.[10]

2.5.6 *Formation*

The bulk of the ECS deals with the procedures for creating an SE. Article 2 ECS specifies the methods by which an SE may be formed, and Title II (Articles 15–37 ECS) lays down the relevant detailed procedures. It must be emphasised that there the ECS does not permit the incorporation of an SE *ab initio*. Furthermore, a general rule is that the companies involved in the creation of an SE must have both

---

1   See Article 69(a).
2   This procedure is expected to form the blueprint for the proposed Fourteenth Directive on the movement of a company's registered office. See **2.3.7**.
3   Article 8(1) ECS.
4   Article 8(15) ECS.
5   In the *Official Journal* in accordance with Article 13, as well as in line with any applicable domestic requirements: Article 8(2) ECS.
6   Article 8(3) ECS.
7   A court, notary or other competent authority, such as, presumably, the registrar at Companies House in the UK.
8   Article 8(8) ECS.
9   Article 8(10)–(12) ECS.
10   Article 8(13) ECS.

their registered and head offices in the Community (but not, it seems, in the same Member State).[1]

The formation procedures are now considered in turn. The starting point is that an SE should be formed in accordance with the rules applicable to the formation of public companies in the relevant Member State, subject to any specific rules laid down in the ECS.[2] As already noted, the SE must be registered in the Member State where its registered office will be based, and it will acquire legal personality from the date of registration.[3] Interestingly, the ECS contains a provision on 'pre-incorporation' contracts based on Article 7 of the First Company Law Directive,[4] according to which the persons (legal or natural) who performed acts in the SE's name before its registration will be jointly and severally liable for these, unless there is an agreement to the contrary.[5] This is subject to the proviso that the SE does not 'assume the obligations arising out of such acts after its registration',[6] a provision which sits rather uneasily with the UK's approach to pre-incorporation contracts.[7]

2.5.6.1   Merger of two public companies

An SE may be formed if two or more public limited companies from at least two different Member States decide to merge.[8] This merger may be carried out in accordance with the procedures for mergers laid down in the Third Company Law Directive[9] and therefore take the form of either a merger by acquisition or a merger by the formation of a new company. However, the ECS imposes several additional requirements. Thus, the management of the merging companies must prepare draft terms of merger which must include numerous details about the SE to be formed, including procedures for employee involvement.[10] Information about the merger must also be published in the national gazette of the relevant Member States.[11] Whereas Article 10 of the Third Directive requires a separate experts' report on each of the merging companies, examining the draft terms of merger and reporting to the shareholders, Article 22 ECS allows for the preparation of a single report covering all of the merging companies.

The legality of the merger, as well as the protection of creditors and debenture holders,[12] is subject to the domestic rules applicable to each of the merging

---

1   Although note Article 2(5) ECS, which permits a Member State to allow a company to participate in the creation of an SE where its head office is based outside the Community, provided that its registered office is in that Member State and the company has a 'real and continuous link' with a (but not 'that'!) Member State's economy. The DTI has indicated that it will not make use of this option. See *Implementation of the ECS – A Consultative Document* (October 2003), paragraph 3.9.
2   Article 15(1) ECS.
3   Article 16(1) ECS.
4   See **2.3.1**.
5   Article 16(2) ECS.
6   Article 16(2) ECS.
7   See eg, C Twigg-Flesner, 'Full Circle: Purported Agent's Right of Enforcement Under s 36C of the Companies Act 1985' (2001) 22 Co Law 274–278.
8   Article 2(1) ECS and Title II, Section 2.
9   Directive 78/855/EEC concerning mergers of public limited companies (1978) OJ L 295/36. The Directive is limited to domestic mergers. See **2.3.3**.
10   Article 20 ECS.
11   Article 21 ECS.
12   Article 24 ECS.

companies.[1] Matters relating specifically to the formation of the SE are subject to the rules applicable in the Member State where the SE will have its registered office.[2] A failure to comply with these rules could lead to the winding up of the SE.[3]

The merger itself takes place and the SE is formed on the date when the SE is registered.[4] If the merger is one by acquisition, all assets and liabilities of the companies being acquired are transferred to the acquiring company,[5] and the shareholders of the companies being acquired become shareholders in the acquiring company.[6] The acquiring company then becomes the SE and the acquired companies cease to exist.[7] However, if the merger is one between a parent company and a subsidiary, some of the rules on disclosure, the expert's report and the exchange of shares in the acquired company for those in the acquiring company do not apply.[8]

If the merger is one by formation of a new company, all assets and liabilities of the merging companies are transferred to the new SE, the shareholders of the merging companies become shareholders in the SE and the merging companies cease to exist.[9] In either case, this is subject to any relevant domestic rules protecting third parties with regard to the transfers of assets, rights and obligations by the merging companies.[10]

This procedure is noteworthy for two reasons: first, it is an instance where the ECS, which is designed to operate in a cross-border context, utilises provisions which are based on existing measures which are applicable only in a domestic context. Secondly, the fact that it has been possible to create a procedure for cross-border mergers in the context of SEs appears to have made it possible to pursue a directive on cross-border mergers of public companies.[11]

2.5.6.2 Formation of Holding Company as SE

The second route for the formation of an SE is available both to public and private limited companies.[12] Two or more companies may come together to form a holding SE, provided that at least two are governed by the law of a different Member State[13] or have had, for at least two years, a subsidiary or branch in another Member State.[14] Once again, the management of the relevant companies must produce draft terms for the formation of the holding SE, providing similar information as in the case of formation by merger[15] as well as the proportion of the shares in each of the companies which the shareholders must contribute to the

---

1   Article 25 ECS.
2   Article 26 ECS.
3   Article 30 ECS.
4   Article 27(1) ECS.
5   Article 29(1)(a) ECS.
6   Article 29(1)(b) ECS.
7   Article 29(1)(c) and (d) ECS.
8   Article 31 ECS.
9   Article 29(2) ECS.
10   Article 29(3) ECS.
11   A new draft Tenth Directive was published by the Commission in November 2003. See **2.3.7**, above.
12   Article 2(2) ECS.
13   Article 2(2)(a) ECS.
14   Article 2(2)(b) ECS.
15   In particular, details required by Article 20(1)(a)–(c) and (f)–(i).

versa.[1] The number of members should be determined by the SE's statutes, although Member States may fix a minimum or a maximum number.[2] The supervisory organ is responsible for supervising the management board and is appointed by the general meeting.[3] It may also elect a chairman. The management organ must report to the supervisory organ at least once every three months about the SE's performance.[4]

Where the SE uses the one-tier system, it has full responsibility for managing the SE.[5] If employee participation is regulated in accordance with the rules of Companion Directive 2001/86/EC,[6] there must be a minimum of three members.[7] The members of the administrative organ are appointed by the general meeting. The organ must elect a chairman, subject to the requirement that if half of the members of the organ are appointed by employees, the chairman must be a shareholder representative.[8] The administrative organ must meet at least once every three months.[9]

The general meeting of the SE will have responsibility for certain matters by virtue of the ECS or companion Directive 2001/86/EC, as well as under the law applicable to public limited companies in the Member State where the SE is registered.[10] Generally, the rules and procedures for convening a general meeting are left for the relevant domestic rules on public companies,[11] although the ECS requires that a meeting be held at least once each calendar year and within six months of the end of the SE's financial year.[12] Furthermore, one or more shareholders holding at least 10% of the SE's subscribed capital may request the SE to convene a meeting, and, if this is not done within two months, a court or competent administrative authority[13] may order that the meeting be convened or allow the shareholders themselves to do so.[14] The general meeting has the power to amend the SE's statutes by a majority of no less than two-thirds[15] of the votes cast.[16] Furthermore, where decisions by the general meeting affect the rights of a particular class of shares, a separate vote of the affected class must be held.[17]

---

1   Article 39(3) ECS.
2   Article 39(4) ECS. The DTI intends to require a minimum of at least one member each for the management and supervisory organ to reflect the requirement in of the Companies Act 1985, section 282, that public companies must have at least two directors. See *Implementation of the ECS – A Consultative Document* (October 2003), paragraph 3.45.
3   Article 40 ECS.
4   Article 41 ECS.
5   Article 43(1) ECS.
6   Discussed below at **2.5.10.**
7   Article 43(2) ECS.
8   Article 45 ECS.
9   Article 44 ECS.
10   Article 52 ECS.
11   Article 53 ECS.
12   Article 54(1) ECS. If the SE carries on a type of business for which domestic law requires more frequent meetings, then the domestic rules apply.
13   In line with the Companies Act 1985, s 367, the DTI proposes to make the Secretary of State the competent authority. See *Implementation of the ECS – A Consultative Document* (October 2003), paragraph 3.38.
14   Article 55 ECS. This procedure differs somewhat from the requisitioning procedure in the Companies Act 1985, s 368. See **13.6.**
15   In the UK, this would be three-quarters (75%), in line with domestic provisions. See *Implementation of the ECS – A Consultative Document* (October 2003), paragraph 3.38.
16   Article 59 ECS.
17   Article 60 ECS.

2.5.8 Accounting

Article 61 ECS provides that an SE is subject to the rules on the preparation of annual and consolidated accounts which apply to public limited companies in the Member State where its registered office is situated.[1] Credit and financial institutions will be subject to the domestic law provisions implementing Directive 2000/12/EC relating to the taking up and pursuit of the business of credit institutions,[2] and insurance companies will be subject to the rules in Directive 91/674/EEC[3] on annual and consolidated accounts of insurance undertakings.[4]

2.5.9 Winding Up, Liquidation, Insolvency and Cessation of Payments

As far as winding up, liquidation, insolvency, cessation of payments and similar matters are concerned, an SE will be governed by the rules applicable to public companies in the Member State where its registered office is based.[5] Where such procedures are initiated, this must be published in the *Official Journal*, as well as in accordance with the relevant domestic rules.[6]

The ECS also provides for the conversion of an SE into a public limited-liability company governed by the law of the Member State where the SE has its registered office, although no such conversion will be permitted within two years from registration as an SE, or before two sets of annual accounts have been approved.[7] Management must prepare draft terms of conversions and a report justifying the proposal to convert the SE into a domestic public company,[8] and an expert's report certifying that the company's assets are at least equivalent to its capital must be drawn up.[9] There then has to be a vote of the general meeting to approve the conversion.[10] Significantly, the conversion will not result in the winding-up of the SE, nor in the creation of a new public company following the conversion.[11]

2.5.10 Employee Involvement

As noted previously, the ECS regulation is supplemented by Directive 2001/86/EC on the involvement of employees in the SE.[12] The Directive needs to be implemented into domestic law and the DTI published draft Regulations in October 2003.[13] Its objective is to govern the involvement of employees in the affairs of an SE.[14]

As soon as the decision is taken to form an SE, by whichever route, a special negotiating body representing the employees of the participating companies

---

1   These will be based on the Fourth and Seventh Directives.
2   (2000) OJ L126/1.
3   (1991) OJ L374/7.
4   Article 62 ECS.
5   Article 63 ECS.
6   Article 65 ECS.
7   Article 66(1) ECS.
8   Article 66(3) ECS.
9   Article 66(5) ECS.
10   Article 66(6) ECS.
11   Article 66(2) ECS.
12   Directive 2001/86/EC supplementing the Statute for a European Company with regard to the involvement of employees (2001) OJ L294/22.
13   See **2.5.11**, below.
14   Article 1(1) of the Directive.

must be set up in accordance with the procedure laid down in Article 3.[1] The purpose of this negotiating body is to come to an agreement on the arrangements for the involvement of employees within the SE.[2] Although parties are free to determine their arrangements, the Directive requires that the agreement covers, among other things, the composition of the body representing employees, its resources, the frequency of meetings, and the implementation of any consultation procedures that may be established. Member States are required to lay down standard rules which regulate the involvement of employees in an SE, and these need to satisfy the provisions specified in the Annex to the Directive.[3] The negotiating body may agree to adopt these rules expressly, or they may come into effect by default if negotiations have not been concluded within the time limit specified in Article 5.[4] Once an agreement has been adopted and a body of employee representatives has been established, the representative body and the competent organ in the SE are required to work together in a spirit of co-operation.[5]

2.5.11 Implementation into domestic law

Although the Regulation is, by definition, directly applicable,[6] there are several provisions which give Member States the option whether to give legal effect to these, and consequently implementing measures need to be adopted by the Member States. In addition, the rules on employee involvement are contained in a Directive which requires separate implementation in any event. Finally, in order to accommodate the new type of company within the existing legal framework of domestic company law, it is necessary to make some adjustments to this. The government set out its position on the options given in the ECS[7] and the proposed implementing measures in a consultation document in October 2003.[8] Final implementing measures had not been published at the time of writing, although the DTI indicated on an informal basis that it expects everything to be in place in good time before the ECS comes into force in October 2004.

2.6 Conclusions

This chapter has revealed the extent to which company law, and the law relating to public companies in particular, is governed by measures based on European directives and regulations. The extensive harmonisation programme of both core company law and the rules on investor protection, adopted to facilitate the completion of the internal market, has left its mark on domestic company law legislation. Furthermore, as the internal market becomes more attractive for companies, the right to move freely and become established in another Member State has become more significant, as evidenced in the string of recent ECJ cases

---

1   For present purposes, it is unnecessary to discuss the exact procedure in detail.
2   Article 4(1) of the Directive.
3   Article 7(1) of the Directive.
4   Article 7(1). The time limits in Article 5 are six months after establishing the negotiating body, subject to an extension by a further six months if the negotiating parties so agree.
5   Article 9 of the Directive.
6   See Article 249 EC.
7   Some of these were noted in the footnotes above accompanying the discussion of the relevant provision in the ECS.
8   *Implementation of the European Company Statute: The European Public Limited-Liability Company Regulations 2004 – A Consultative Document* (DTI, October 2003).

on this matter. Despite its impact, European company law has not displaced domestic initiatives; indeed, the European Company Statute is based on a principle of mutuality, leaving significant aspects of the operation of this new type of business vehicle to the relevant laws of the Member State where the SE is registered. It is hoped that this chapter will assist the reader in placing domestic company law, discussed in the remainder of this book, in the relevant European context.

Chapter 3

Legal Personality: Its Consequences and Limitations

3.1 Introduction

The general issue broached in this chapter is that of the basic principle of corporate personality. The separate[1] personality of the company is an inevitable consequence for a company (or any other body) upon which the privileged status of incorporation has been conferred. This is a judicially created doctrine but the courts have nevertheless shown themselves prepared, when moved by sufficiently strong policy considerations, to depart from this fundamental principle. This process is usually termed 'lifting the veil of incorporation'. The difficulty is to discover by what principle or principles the courts are guided in determining whether to adhere to the safe rule of respecting the separate legal persona of the company or whether to 'lift the veil'. It will be seen that this is an area in which the legislature has intervened on an *ad hoc* basis, especially in the case of 'groups' of holding and subsidiary companies.

Particular attention will also be given to the problem posed, in the case of 'groups', by the separate legal personality of each company in the group. Legislation has created a statutory regime to govern the relationship between member companies in a group for certain statutory purposes. In more general terms, it is necessary to look to case-law for guidance. Here, separate legal personality is usually observed.

Another aspect of legal personality dealt with in this chapter concerns how far the state of mind of directors or senior managers can be attributed to a company for the purpose of making that company criminally or civilly liable.

3.2 The consequences of incorporation

Lord Justice Lindley gave this definition of the old unincorporated joint stock company: 'I understand by a company – an unincorporated company – some association of members, the shares of which are transferable. As distinguished from a partnership, I know of nothing else except the transferability of shares.'[2] But with regard to an *incorporated* company there are other important distinctions: eg that, while in an ordinary partnership each partner is personally responsible for all the debts contracted by the firm, in an incorporated company the members have no individual liability to its creditors for debts owing by the company (and their personal liability is satisfied if they pay the calls properly made upon them by the company or its liquidator. These calls may be limited in amount or unlimited, according as the company is limited or unlimited, but they are enforceable only by the company or its liquidator). The company, moreover, is a distinct legal

---

1 Ie separate from that of the company's directors, shareholders, employees, creditors, etc.
2 *R v Registrar of Joint Stock Companies* [1891] 2 QB 598 at 610.

there will be tax advantages in the corporate form. At a certain level this will become essential.

3.3.1 Limited liability partnerships

A new hybrid form of business organisation was created by the Limited Liability Partnerships Act 2000.[1] In brief, the essential features of an LLP registered under the Act, which are drawn from existing partnership and company law, are as follows. An LLP is a body corporate with a separate legal personality and unlimited capacity, that is it can do anything a natural person can do. The liability of individual members is limited in accordance with their stake in the LLP. It must be registered with the Registrar of Companies, with information including its name, registered office and a list of its members. It must file an annual report and accounts. It will be taxed as a partnership. Certain features of company law in respect of creditor protection and winding up apply to an LLP.[2]

LLPs do offer an alternative to limited companies and in some circumstances have tax advantages. However, their most significant drawback is the lack of the sort of default provisions found in the legislation applying to companies and partnerships.[3] In the case of an LLP this is left to the formation documentation to be drafted prior to its registration.

3.4 The principle of corporate personality

The separate personality of a company and its entity as distinct from its shareholders was established by the House of Lords in *Salomon v Salomon & Co*,[4] where it was held that however large the proportion of the shares and debentures owned by one man, even if the other shares were held in trust for him, the company's acts were not his acts, nor were its liabilities his liabilities; nor is it otherwise if he has sole control of its affairs as governing director.[5] It is important to note that the House of Lords found no evidence whatever of fraud or deliberate abuse of the corporate form. Indeed, Salomon did his best to rescue his company by cancelling the debentures he took and reissuing them to an outside creditor who provided fresh loan capital. The *Salomon* decision gave express recognition to what were even then called 'one man' companies. The modern practice of having undercapitalised private companies (with the founding shareholders as creditors in their own company) stems from this case. This is certainly a use of the corporate form not contemplated when limited liability was made generally available.

---

1   Although originally intended to be restricted to regulated professional partnerships, in its enacted form it is available to any two or more persons carrying on a trade or profession. A proper analysis of the Act's provisions is beyond the scope of a textbook on registered companies. See J Whittacker and J Machell, *Limited Liability Partnerships – the New Law* (Jordan Publishing, 2001).

2   Notably the provisions on fraudulent and wrongful trading and the provisions relating to the disqualification of directors.

3   Eg the Table A model set of articles that can be adopted when registering a limited company.

4   [1897] AC 22.

5   *Inland Revenue Commissioners v Sansom* [1921] 2 KB 492. See also *Re Hydrodam (Corby) (in Liquidation)* [1994] BCC 161. The fact that a body corporate was director of a company did not necessarily mean that that body corporate's directors were therefore directors of the company.

The principle of the *Salomon* case,[1] that a company is a legal entity distinct from its members, is strictly applied by the courts whenever it is sought to attribute the rights or liabilities of a company to its shareholders, or regard the property of a company as belonging in law or equity to the shareholders. Thus the fact that one shareholder controls all or virtually all the shares in a company is not a sufficient reason for ignoring the legal personality of the company.[2] Further, a company cannot be characterised as an agent of its shareholders unless there is clear evidence to show that the company was in fact acting as an agent in a particular transaction or series of transactions.[3] Likewise, the property of a company in no sense belongs to its members.[4] The company is not a trustee of its property for its shareholders even where the directors have been appointed trustees of some or all of the shares in a company.[5] A shareholder does not have an insurable interest in the assets or business of the company.[6]

3.4.1 Corporate personality and directors' liability

As a matter of general principle, corporate personality will prevent directors from being held liable in respect of company obligations. In *Williams v Natural Life Health Foods*,[7] the House of Lords, overruling the Court of Appeal,[8] carefully restricted the circumstances in which a director of a company would be personally liable to plaintiffs for loss which they suffered as a result of negligent advice given them by the company. First, there had to be an assumption of responsibility. This assumption had to be determined objectively. The primary focus had to be on exchanges (including statements and conduct) between the director and the plaintiffs. Secondly, the test of reliance on the assumption was not simply one of reliance in fact but whether the plaintiffs could reasonably rely on the assumption of responsibility.

The action in *Williams* was originally brought primarily against the company on the basis of the 'extended *Hedley Byrne* principle' established by the House of Lords in *Henderson v Merrett Syndicates Ltd.*[9] This decision settled that the assumption of responsibility principle enunciated in *Hedley Byrne* is not confined to statements but may apply to any assumption of responsibility for the provision of services.[10] In *Williams* the company, after judgment for financial loss had been obtained against it, became insolvent and was wound up. The proceedings were continued instead against the defendant director when the judgment against the company remained unsatisfied.

---

1   [1897] AC 22. See *FJ Neale (Glasgow) Ltd v Vickery* 1974 SLT 88 for an application of the *Salomon* principle.
2   See eg *Tunstall v Steigmann* [1962] 2 QB 593 (CA); *Lee v Lee's Air Farming Ltd* [1961] AC 12 (PC).
3   *Ebbw Vale UDC v South Wales Traffic Area Licensing Authority* [1951] 2 KB 366 (CA); *Pegler v Graven* [1952] 2 QB 69 (CA).
4   *Bank voor Handel en Scheepvaart NV v Slatford* [1953] 1 QB 248.
5   *Butt v Kelsen* [1952] Ch 197 (CA).
6   *Macaura v Northern Assurance Co* [1925] AC 619 (HL (Ir)).
7   [1998] 1 WLR 830.
8   [1997] 1 BCLC 131. See the judgment of Hirst LJ at 152, where a more flexible approach to imposing tort liability on a director was taken.
9   [1995] 2 AC 145.
10   See Lord Steyn, [1998] 1 WLR 830 at 834–837. The other members of the court concurred in Lord Steyn's judgment.

In analysing the 'triangular' relationship between the plaintiff, the company and the director, Lord Steyn observed that:

> the *internal* arrangements between a director and his company cannot be the foundation of a director's personal liability in tort. The inquiry must be whether the director, or anybody on his behalf conveyed directly or indirectly to the [plaintiffs] that the director assumed personal responsibility towards [them].[1]

Lord Steyn emphasised the relevance of the basic concept of corporate personality in differentiating between the tort liability of a company and its director. He observed that 'in the context of directors of companies the general principle must not 'set at nought' the protection of limited liability'.[2] The essential issue is that of corporate personality:[3]

> What matters is not that liability of the shareholders of a company is limited but that a company is a separate entity, distinct from its directors, servants or other agents. The trader who incorporates a company to which he transfers his business creates a legal person on whose behalf he may afterwards act as director. For present purposes, his position is the same as if he had sold his business to another individual and agreed to act on his behalf. Thus the issue in this case is not peculiar to companies. Whether the principal is a company or a natural person, someone acting on his behalf may incur personal liability in tort as well as imposing vicarious or attributed liability upon his principal. But in order to establish personal liability under the principle of *Hedley Byrne*, which requires the existence of a special relationship between plaintiff and tortfeasor, it is not sufficient that there should have been a special relationship with the principal. There must have been an assumption of responsibility such as to create a special relationship with the director or employee himself.

The House of Lords concluded that in the circumstances of *Williams* no such duty existed.[4]

In later Court of Appeal cases the reasoning in *Williams* has been carefully followed to determine whether there has been a personal assumption of liability. Liability in respect of negligent misrepresentation may arise where private negotiations between the parties support this inference.[5] A director (and controlling shareholder) can be held liable as a joint tortfeasor with the company in an action for infringement of copyright.[6] Chadwick LJ stressed, however, that a director will not be held liable 'if he does no more than carry out his constitutional role in the governance of the company – that is to say, by voting at board meetings. That, I think, is what policy requires if a proper recognition is to be given to the company as a separate legal person.' He said that for liability to arise, it had to be shown either that the director committed the breach of copyright personally or that he procured or induced such breach by the company or 'that in some other way he and [the company] joined together in concerted action to secure that those acts were done.[7]

The House of Lords has refused to extend the reasoning of its own decision in *Williams* to liability for fraudulent misstatements by a director. Here, while the

---

1   Ibid, at 695.
2   Lord Steyn refers to the judgment of Waite LJ in the Court of Appeal. See [1997] 1 BCLC 131 at p 154 and Cook P in *Trevor Ivory Ltd v Anderson* [1992] NZLR 517 at 524.
3   [1998] 1 WLR 830 at 835.
4   [1998] 1 WLR at 838.
5   *Partco Group Ltd v Wragg* [2002] EWCA Civ 594, [2002] 2 BCLC 323.
6   *MCA Records Inc v Charly Records Ltd* [2001] EWCA Civ 1441, [2003] 1 BCLC 93.
7   [2003] 1 BCLC at 116.

company becomes vicariously liable on ordinary principles, the director committing the tort of deceit remains personally liable.[1]

3.4.2 Controlling shareholders and the corporate veil

A controlling shareholder may also be an employee for the purpose of claiming rights under the Employment Rights Act 1996. Whether or not an employee/employer relationship exists will be determined by having regard to all relevant facts. Having a controlling shareholding will certainly be a significant fact and in some cases may be decisive of the issue. This is a different question from whether there is a controlling shareholder.[2]

3.5 Lifting the veil of incorporation

Notwithstanding the principle of *Salomon's* case[3] there are certain situations where the courts have shown themselves willing to 'lift the veil of incorporation', that is to ignore or set aside the separate legal personality of a company. It is not possible to formulate any single principle as the basis for these decisions, nor are all the decisions, as to when the separate legal entity of the company must be respected or when it may be disregarded, entirely consistent with one another.[4]

It is well established that the courts will not allow the corporate form to be used for the purposes of fraud,[5] or as a device to evade a contractual or other legal obligation. Thus in *Gilford Motor Co v Horne*[6] the respondent had contracted with the appellant company not to solicit its customers when he left its employment. On ceasing employment, Horne formed a company to carry on a competing business and this company started to solicit Gilford Motor Co's customers. The court granted an injunction to enforce the covenant not to solicit against both Horne and the company he had formed as a cloak for his activities. In *Jones v Lipman*[7] the defendant had entered into a contract to sell his house. He sought to escape his obligation to complete by conveying the property to a company in which he and a nominee of his controlled all the shares and were the directors. Russell J, in granting a decree of specific performance, described the company as 'the creature of the first defendant, a device and a sham, a mask which he holds before his face in an attempt to avoid recognition by the eye of equity'.[8]

In some cases, the courts have found on the particular evidence before them that a holding company was in fact carrying on a business through the agency of its subsidiary company. It is important to note that the mere fact that one company is

---

1   *Standard Chartered Bank v Pakistan National Shipping Corp* [2002] UKHL 43, [2003] 1 AC 959. Compare the agency power of directors to bind their company contractually: see **6.19** to **6.33**, below. See further *Gore-Browne on Companies* at 1.8.1 to 1.8.2.

2   *Secretary of State for Trade and Industry v Bottrill* [1999] BCC 177 (CA). See *Ringway Roadmarking v Adbruf Ltd* [1998] 2 BCLC 625 as to a clause in a contract entitling parties to terminate if a 'controlling shareholder in a party' passed to new ownership. The transfer of such control within a group of companies was not 'new ownership'.

3   [1897] AC 22.

4   See eg *Wurzel v Houghton Main Home Service Ltd* [1937] 1 KB 380 and *Trebanog Working Men's Club and Institute Ltd v Macdonald* [1940] 1 KB 576.

5   *Re Darby* [1911] 1 KB 95. See also *Wallersteiner v Moir (No 1)* [1974] 1 WLR 991 (CA) at p 1013.

6   [1933] Ch 935 (CA).

7   [1962] 1 WLR 832. See also *H & H Elliott Ltd v Pierson* [1948] Ch 852.

8   Ibid at 836. See also *Re FG (Films) Ltd* [1953] 1 WLR 483 and *Merchandise Transport Ltd v BTC* [1962] 2 QB 173. See further *International Investment Co v Adhams* [1998] BCC 134.

the subsidiary of another, even a 'wholly owned' subsidiary, is not by itself sufficient to make the subsidiary an agent of its holding company.[1] The activities of the subsidiary must be so closely controlled and directed by the parent company that the latter can be regarded as merely an agent conducting the parent company's business.[2]

For certain purposes, the courts, while respecting the separate legal personality of a company, have treated the conduct or characteristics of its directors, managers or members as attributable to the company itself. This attribution does not in the true sense involve 'lifting the veil of incorporation'. For example, where the courts have had to determine the residence of a company, they look not to the place of registration but to the way the company is actually managed in order to find where the centre or centres of management are in fact located.[3] The cases examined in **3.6** and **3.7,** on the attribution of *mens rea* to a company for the purposes of criminal or civil liability, are another illustration of the same principle. Another example is *Re Greater London Property Ltd's Lease*[4] where a subsidiary company was held a responsible assignee of a lease despite the landlord's contention that it was not financially viable without the support of its holding company. Danckwerts J refused to disregard the real economic link between the holding and subsidiary company. Again, this is not a true case of 'lifting the veil of incorporation'. In *The Abbey, Malvern Wells Ltd v Ministry of Local Government and Planning,*[5] a limited company was formed to run a school for the profit of its shareholders. Later it was converted into a non-profit-making body by vesting its shares in charitable trustees and altering its articles to provide that it would be run by the trustees. Danckwerts J held that the company could claim charitable status so as to exempt it from paying a development charge under the Town and Country Planning Act 1947. This decision is not inconsistent with the generally established rule that a company is not a trustee for its members. In determining whether for a particular statutory purpose it had charitable status, Danckwerts J realistically attributed the characteristics of its shareholders as trustees of a charitable trust to the company itself.

Where fraud or deliberate breach of trust can be shown, the courts show a willingness to set aside the corporate form even where this involves a network of interlocking foreign and English companies. The plaintiff companies in *Re a Company Ltd*[6] were in liquidation and had brought an action against the defendant alleging deceit and breach of trust. The defendant, in the knowledge that the plaintiff companies were insolvent, had disposed of his personal assets so that they were held by a network of interlocking foreign and English companies

---

1   *Kodak Ltd v Clark* [1903] 1 KB 505 (CA); *Gramophone & Typewriters Ltd v Stanley* [1908] 2 KB 89 (CA); *IRC v Sansom* [1921] 2 KB 492 (CA).

2   See the judgment of Atkinson J, in *Smith Stone and Knight Ltd v Birmingham Corporation* [1939] 4 All ER 116 and the cases there cited. See also *Firestone Tyre and Rubber Co v Llewellin* [1957] 1 WLR 464 (HL). As to lifting the veil in the case of groups of companies, see **3.9**.

3   See eg *De Beers Consolidated Mining Ltd v Howe* [1906] AC 455 (HL) and *Unit Construction Co Ltd v Bullock* [1960] AC 351 (HL).

4   [1959] 1 WLR 503. A similarly realistic approach can be found in other cases concerning remedies for minority shareholders (eg *SCWS v Meyer* [1959] AC 324, and *Ebrahimi v Westbourne Galleries Ltd* [1973] 3 AC 360 (HL)) and with the construction of the objects clause of the memorandum (*Charterbridge Corporation Ltd v Lloyds Bank Ltd* [1970] Ch 62).

5   [1951] Ch 728. See also the Court of Appeal's interpretation of the term 'establish a place of business' in section 409 of the Companies Act 1985 in *Re Oriel Ltd* [1985] BCLC 343.

6   [1985] BCLC 333 (CA).

and trusts so that his true beneficial interests were concealed. This was intended to prevent the plaintiffs from recovering those assets in an action against the defendant alleging fraud and breach of trust. The court granted injunctions[1] restraining the defendant from disposing of shares in the foreign companies, or interests under trusts or shares in English or foreign companies entitled to those assets. The injunction also restrained the defendant from procuring the disposition of English assets by the trusts or the companies. The Court of Appeal upheld the grant of these injunctions explicitly on the basis that in the circumstances the court should pierce the corporate veil in order to achieve justice. The only qualification was that the relief granted was restricted to those companies and trusts over which the defendant exercised substantial or effective control.[2] Once again, fraudulent[3] abuse opened doors that would otherwise be kept firmly closed in the absence of that factor. It is clear that the rather loose language in this case, referring to the court using 'its powers to pierce the corporate veil if it is necessary to achieve justice irrespective of the legal efficacy of the company under consideration'[4] must be understood strictly in the context of fraudulent abuse. Later Court of Appeal decisions make it clear that it is not sufficient that the company has been involved in some impropriety *not* linked to the use of the company structure to avoid or conceal that liability.[5]

The question of how far the courts are prepared to lift the veil in groups of companies is separately considered below[6] in its own context. It will be seen that distinctive, if not wholly dissimilar principles have been evolved where groups of companies are concerned.

Parliament is not of course bound by the principle laid down by the House of Lords in *Salomon*.[7] For varying reasons of policy the legislature can, for example, impose personal liability for the company's obligations in shareholders or directors in particular circumstances. This achieves the same result as judicial veil lifting but requires no doctrinal justification by the courts.

Section 24 of the Companies Act 1985 and provisions in the Insolvency Act 1986 create two departures from the principle which respects the separate corporate personality of the company. Section 24 may impose liability where the number of members in a company falls below the minimum required by law. The requirement of a minimum of two members is now confined in practice to public companies, because section 24 ceased to have application to private companies limited by shares or by guarantee when the Companies (Single Member Private Limited Companies) Regulations[8] were brought into effect.[9] Private companies whose members have unlimited liability are not exempt from section 24 as the

---

1   It also granted discovery by interrogatories of an unusually extensive nature.
2   *Re a Company Ltd* [1985] BCLC 333 at 337.
3   The Court of Appeal regarded the decision as a straightforward application of *Wallersteiner v Moir* [1974] 1 WLR 991.
4   [1985] BCLC at 337–338, *per* Cumming-Bruce LJ.
5   See *Adams v Cape Industries plc* [1990] Ch 443 and *Ord v Bellhaven Pubs Ltd* [1998] 2 BCLC 447, as applied in *Trustor AB v Smallbone* [2001] 2 BCLC 437.
6   See **3.9**.
7   [1897] AC 22.
8   SI 1992/1699.
9   On 15 July 1992. Transitional provision is made in respect of section 24 of the Companies Act 1985 by regulation 3. Persons liable under section 24 before the regulation came into effect 'shall not be so liable for the payment of the company's debts contracted on or after the day on which these regulations came into force'.

Where fraud upon the company is alleged in a civil action (or a criminal offence is charged whether under the Theft Act or on the basis of conspiracy) the unanimous consent of shareholders will not bar such criminal proceedings.[1] The purpose of the *alter ego* principle is, in the appropriate circumstances, to impose criminal (or sometimes civil) liability on the company for the acts of those who are regarded in law as its 'deciding mind and will'.[2] Its purpose is not to give such persons a defence for their own wrongdoing at the company's expense.

3.7　Application to civil law

The same principle has been employed by the courts where in civil proceedings it is necessary to attribute a particular mental state to a company. In most civil actions against companies, this question does not arise, since the company may be affixed with liability on some other basis. Thus in tort the ordinary principles of vicarious liability will as a rule determine the matter, and contractual liability will depend on that special adaptation of the principles of agency known to company lawyers as the 'rule in *Turquand's Case*'.[3]

Nevertheless in some cases it is necessary to attribute an intention or actual default to the company. Thus under section 502 of the Merchant Shipping Act 1894 the owner of a vessel has a defence which allows him to exempt himself from liability for injury which is caused without 'his actual default or privity'. But what, as will usually be the case, if the owner is a company? In the leading case of *Lennard's Carrying Company v Asiatic Petroleum Ltd*,[4] the House of Lords held that the default of Lennard, as the managing director and 'directing mind and will' of his company, could be attributed to it so as to deprive it of the defence which section 502 provided. Viscount Haldane's judgments articulated the *alter ego* doctrine peculiar to company law as one quite distinct from the ordinary principles of agency or vicarious liability.

In a justly celebrated passage he observes that:

> ... a corporation is an abstraction. It has no mind of its own any more than a body of its own; its active and directing will must consequently be sought in the person of somebody who for some purposes may be called an agent, but who is really the directing mind and will of the corporation, the very ego and centre of the personality of the corporation.[5]

As in criminal law, the *alter ego* of a company may, depending on the circumstances of the case, be found at a lower level in the managerial hierarchy than that of the board of directors or the managing director. Thus in *The Lady Gwendolen*[6] the marine superintendent, to whom the assistant managing director

---

1　*Belmont Finance Ltd v Williams (No 1)* [1979] Ch 256, *R v McDonnell* [1966] 1 QB 233.
2　On this basis the Court of Appeal distinguished *Tesco Supermarkets v Nattrass* [1972] AC 153.
3　(1856) 5 E & B 248. See **6.25**.
4　[1915] AC 705 (HL).
5　[1915] AC 705 at 713.
6　[1965] P 294 (CA).

and the traffic manager had surrendered 'all the relevant powers of control'[1] over the operation of its ships, was held to be a directing mind for this purpose.

The principle enunciated by Lord Haldane and the significance of the phrase 'directing mind and will' have been scrutinised by the Privy Council in *Meridian Global Funds Management Asia Ltd v Securities Commission*.[2] The judgment of the Board (on an appeal from New Zealand) was delivered by Lord Hoffmann who emphasised that the court must fashion a special rule of attribution for the particular substantive rule.[3]

> This is always a matter of interpretation: given that it was intended to apply to a company, how was it intended to apply? Whose act (or knowledge or state of mind) was *for this purpose* intended to count as the act etc of the company? One finds the answer to this question by applying the usual canons of interpretation, taking into account the language of the rule (if it is a statute) and its context and policy.[4]

Lord Hoffmann, while making it clear that this was the principle applied by Lord Haldane in *Lennard's Case*, warns against the literal application of the phrase 'directing mind and will'. Lord Haldane is not to be taken as 'expounding a general metaphysic of companies'.[5] Lord Hoffmann specifically rejected the 'anthropomorphism' of Denning LJ in *HL Bolton (Engineering) Co Ltd v TJ Graham & Sons Ltd*.[6] It is not possible to make a generalisation about companies 'as such'. Such anthropomorphism 'by the very power of the image distracts attention from the purpose for which Lord Haldane said he was using the notion of directing mind and will, namely to apply the attribution rule derived from section 502 [of the Merchant Shipping Act 1984][7] to the particular defendant in the case'.

In *Meridian Global* the appeal concerned the interpretation of section 20 of the New Zealand Securities Amendment Act 1988. This required every person who became a substantial security holder[8] of a public company listed on the New Zealand Stock Exchange to give notice of his interest in the company to the Stock Exchange. He had to do this as soon as he knew, or ought to have known, that he was a substantial security holder in the company. Where another company became a substantial security holder, the knowledge of two senior investment managers was sufficient to attribute that knowledge to their company for the purposes of section 20 since they acquired the securities with the authority of the

---

1   Ibid, at 355, *per* Winn LJ. The company sought to limit its liability under section 503 of the Merchant Shipping Act 1894 on the basis that a collision occurred without 'actual fault or privity' on the part of the owners. The Court of Appeal held that the company was not entitled to do so. In *Registrar of Restrictive Trading Agreements v WH Smith and Sons Ltd* [1969] 1 WLR 1460 (CA), a branch manager of a company was held not to be a 'manager' or 'officer' for the purposes of section 15(3) of the Restrictive Trade Practices Act 1956 (power to interrogate on oath). See also *Tesco Supermarkets v Nattrass* [1972] AC 153.

2   [1995] 3 WLR 413. See Grantham 'Corporate Knowledge: Identification or Attribution' (1996) 59 MLR 737.

3   Where on other more conventional principles liability can be attributed to a company (eg vicarious liability or agency), there will be no need to seek a 'directing mind and will': see *Deutsche Genossenschaftsbank v Burnhope* [1995] BCC 488 (CA); see further Lord Hoffmann in *Meridian Global Funds* (above) at [1995] 1 WLR 413 at 419.

4   [1995] 1 WLR at 419. See further *Z Bank v DTI* [1994] 1 Lloyd's Rep 656 in respect of contempt by a corporation in respect of a *Mareva* injunction.

5   [1995] 1 WLR at 421.

6   [1957] 1 QB 159 at 172 where Denning LJ likens a company to a human body.

7   [1995] 3 WLR at 421.

8   Defined as holding a relevant interest in 5% or more of the voting shares.

company. It would defeat the policy of the Act to require the board of directors or someone else in senior management to know.[1]

The traditional 'directing mind and will' test has still been retained by the Court of Appeal (Criminal Division) for corporate manslaughter. The court rejected the argument that, on such a charge, a company could be 'personally liable' on the basis of gross negligence. It had to be established that identified individuals who satisfied the directing mind and will requirement (the 'identification principle') had been guilty of such negligence and that this could be attributed to the company.[2]

The same principle, identifying the state of mind of the senior management with that of the company itself, has been employed to determine whether a company intended to occupy premises for its own business under the Landlord and Tenant Act 1954,[3] and to decide whether an inducement to breach of contract operates upon the company itself (as opposed to its servants) to persuade it to break its contract.[4]

The directing mind and will doctrine, which attributes the mind and will of a natural person to the company, was applied by the Court of Appeal in *El Ajou v Dollar Landholdings plc*.[5] Nourse LJ held that, in order to apply the doctrine, it was necessary to identify the person who had actual management and control in relation to the relevant act. The fact that the person so identified in this case was a non-executive nominee director with ostensibly no authority to undertake business decisions is not relevant to the application of the directing mind and will doctrine. The important point is that this director made all the arrangements for receiving and dispersing the moneys and signed all the documents causing the company to become involved in a fraud. In these circumstances this director's state of mind and, in particular, the fact that he knew that the company had received assets representing the proceeds of the fraud, should be attributed to the company as he represented its directing mind and will in relation to these acts.

---

1   Lord Hoffmann contrasted two decisions of the House of Lords interpreting different statutory provisions. In *Tesco Supermarkets Ltd v Nattrass* [1972] AC 153, the failure of a shop manager to comply with section 11(2) of the Trade Descriptions Act 1968 did not prevent the company pleading a defence, under section 24(1) of the Act, that it took 'all reasonable precautions and exercised due diligence'. In contrast, in *Re Supply of Ready Mixed Concrete, Director General of Fair Trading v Pioneer Concrete (UK) Ltd* [1995] 1 AC 456, the House of Lords held that the actions of the company's employees constituted the carrying on of business by the company for the purposes of the Restrictive Trade Practices Act 1976. Thus, when local managers of a company concluded allocation agreements, they were fully competent to make the agreement on behalf of the company and see that it was carried out. The company could not escape liability under the 1976 Act by pleading that a prohibition at senior management level was ignored by certain employees. Here there was no statutory defence based on all reasonable preventative measures being taken. Further, liability for contempt of court for disobedience of a court order did not require any direct intention on the part of the company. The House of Lords in *Ready Mixed Concrete* overruled the Court of Appeal decision in *Director of Fair Trading v Smiths Concrete Ltd* [1992] QB 213.

2   *Re Attorney-General's Reference (No 2 of 1999)* [2000] 2 BCLC 257 at 261–267, *per* Rose LJ. A distinction between common law and statutory offences was drawn. As to a draft Home Office Bill, which would target companies and not individual directors, see (2003) 24 Co Law 245.

3   Landlord and Tenant Act 1954, section 30(1)(g). *Bolton (Engineering) Co Ltd v Graham & Sons* [1957] 1 QB 159. The 1954 Act does not apply in Scotland.

4   *DC Thompson & Co v Deakin* [1952] Ch 646 (CA).

5   [1994] 1 BCLC 464 (CA). Compare *Firststeel Cold Rolled Products Ltd v Anaco Precision Pressings Ltd* (1994) *The Times*, November 21.

Thus, a victim of the fraud was able to enforce a constructive trust against the company on the basis that it had knowingly received the proceeds of the fraud.

3.8 Groups of companies

It is a commonplace of commercial life today that businesses are conducted not only in the form of a single private or public company, but also in the form of a group of companies consisting of a holding company (which may often be a listed public company) and a number of usually wholly owned subsidiaries and possibly sub-subsidiaries. Nowadays the group form may be employed at quite a small level of private business for tax or other reasons. As with larger groups of companies, different branches of the business or different properties will be located in each subsidiary.[1]

3.8.1 *Statutory definition of the group relationship*

The Companies Act 1989 provides two quite distinct statutory concepts to govern holding and subsidiary company relationships. A wholly new definition of 'parent and subsidiary undertaking' was introduced as the basis for consolidated accounts for groups of companies.[2] This is to be distinguished from the general definition of holding and subsidiary company wherever these terms are used elsewhere in the Companies Act (ie other than in Part VII of the Companies Act 1985 as amended by the 1989 Act). The 'new' general purpose definition replaced the 'old' section 736 by inserting new sections 736 and 736A into the Companies Act 1985. The 'parent and subsidiary undertaking' concept is examined in Chapter 14, whereas attention is given here to the more generally applicable provisions of sections 736 and 736A of the Companies Act 1985.[3] It should be noted that the 'parent and subsidiary undertaking' concept has a broader, more flexible and 'judgmental' dimension to it, compared with more traditional legal criteria still employed in sections 736 and 736A.[4]

Before examining the detailed criteria employed in section 736[5] it may be noted that, like the old section 736, it defines a company as a 'wholly owned subsidiary of another company' if it has no members except that other and that other's wholly owned subsidiaries or persons acting on behalf of that other or its wholly owned subsidiaries.[6] As to the wider test of holding and subsidiary (to be examined below) this includes sub-subsidiaries as well.[7] The term 'company' in section 736 (ie both as to holding and subsidiary companies) includes any body

---

1 See further Hadden, *The Control of Corporate Groups* (IALS, 1983).
2 See sections 21 and 22 inserting sections 259 and 260 into the Companies Act 1985. See **14.14**.
3 See Companies Act 1989, section 144.
4 Thus 'parent and subsidiary undertaking' extends to partnerships and unincorporated associations. The provisions of section 258 contain somewhat 'broad brush' terminology, eg 'actually exercising dominant influence' or 'managed on a unified basis', see **14.14.2**.
5 The application of this general definition of the holding and subsidiary company relationship will be found in varying contexts in the later chapters of this book. Among the more important are to be found in Chapter 7 (financial assistance by a company in the acquisition of its shares) and Chapter 16 (statutory fiduciary duties).
6 See section 736(2).
7 'Or if it is a subsidiary of a company which is itself a subsidiary of that company': see section 736(1).

corporate.[1] It does not, therefore, have the wide reach of the term 'undertaking' in the new section 285.

Section 144(2) of the 1989 Act gives the new definition of holding and subsidiary company a wider frame of reference than the Companies Act 1985. It deals with references in other legislation to 'a subsidiary' or 'holding company' within the meaning of section 736 of the 1985 Act. Such references are to be read as referring to the new section 736 subject to 'any express saving or amendment made by or under this Act'.[2]

3.8.2 *Holding or controlling majority voting power*

The most obvious change in the new section 736 is a much more precise statutory definition of control through the exercise of majority voting power. The old section 736(2) required the putative holding company to hold more than half the nominal value of the issued equity share capital in the subsidiary. Since this ignored variations in the right to vote that might be attached to 'equity' shares (as well as to other classes of share), it had the result that a company could be treated in law as a subsidiary of a company which had no voting control over it. Likewise, a company which controlled the majority of votes might not meet the definition of holding and subsidiary company under the old section 736. The essential change in the new section 736(1) is that a company is 'a subsidiary' of another company, its holding company, if that other company 'holds a majority of the voting rights in it'. A further provision[3] is made to cover voting agreements with other shareholders or members.[4] The holding/subsidiary relation will exist under section 736(1)(c) if the holding company is a member of the subsidiary and 'controls alone, pursuant to an agreement with other shareholders or members, a majority of voting rights in it'. This provision would be applicable to a shareholder's agreement between the company as a member (ie shareholder) and other shareholders to put their voting rights at the disposal of the holding company. The voting rights thus controlled would have to confer majority voting powers. Such an agreement might take the form either of an agreement to confer an irrevocable proxy on the holding company,[5] or by means of an agreement which results in the setting up of a voting trust,[6] whereby the shares in the subsidiary are transferred to the trust whose trustees are appointed by the controlling company. In both cases, majority voting power would have to be put at the disposal of the company. If a trustee were a company, the legal ownership of majority voting rights would not make the trustee company a holding company since section 736A(5) provides that rights 'held by a person in a fiduciary capacity shall be treated as not held by him'. The Court of Appeal[7] has held that this term in section 736A(5) includes the situation of a registered shareholder who is a

---

1   Section 736(3).
2   As to which see Schedule 18 to the 1989 Act. As to similar references to 'subsidiaries' or 'holding company' in 'deeds or other instruments or documents' the position is less clear. See section 144(6) of the 1989 Act and *Gore-Browne on Companies* 44th edn (Jordans, looseleaf) at 1.6.4.
3   Section 736(1)(c).
4   This term will apply in the case of companies limited by guarantee.
5   See Murray Pickering (1965) 81 LQR 248 at p 267. As to proxies, see **13.21**.
6   See Murray Pickering, ibid at p 527.
7   *Michaels v Harley House (Marylebone) Ltd* [1999] 1 BCLC 670 at 680 to 683. The Court of Appeal overruled Lloyd J in [1997] 2 BCLC 166 and considered and explained the decision of Russell J in *Musselwhite v CH Musselwhite* [1962] Ch 964 at 969.

vendor of shares under an uncompleted but specifically enforceable contract for the sale of his shares. The voting rights attached to the shares are held in a fiduciary capacity as much as the shares themselves.

It should also be noted that section 736A(6) provides that rights (here voting rights) 'held by a person as a nominee for another shall be treated as held by that other'. Section 736A(6) amplifies this: 'rights shall be regarded as held by a nominee for another if they are exercisable only on his instructions or with his consent or concurrence'. This is clearly of significance in respect of shareholders' agreements which put majority voting power over another company at the disposal of an alleged holding company whether by means of irrevocable proxy, voting trust or in any other way.

It should be noted that the test specified in section 736(1)(c) requires that the alleged holding company must (in addition to controlling a majority of voting rights by agreement) 'be a member of it' (ie of the subsidiary). This requirement would seem to allow an obvious way to evade section 736(1) in this respect. Dominant voting power can be exercised, even if this amounts to control of more than 50% of the voting power, so long as the company which is in a position to exercise this power is not 'a member'[1] of record.

It will be seen that the same lacuna exists in section 736(1)(b) which relates to the right to appoint or remove a majority of the board of directors.

Section 736A(2), which seeks to define various terms used in section 736, thus defines the expression 'voting rights in a company' as used in section 736(1)(a)–(c). These are to be understood as 'rights conferred on shareholders in respect of their shares, or in the case of a company not having share capital, on members to vote at general meetings of the company on all, or substantially all, matters'. This definition would exclude shares that conferred limited voting rights at a class meeting. It would also exclude shares (eg many types of preference shares) that could only be voted in general meetings on matters that directly concerned such shares.[2]

3.8.3 *Power to control a majority of the board*

Section 736(1)(g) provides that a company is a subsidiary of another company if that other company (which thus becomes its holding company) 'is a member of it and has the right to appoint or remove a majority of its board of directors'. As noted above,[3] the requirement of being 'a member of it' (in addition to the power over appointment and removal of a majority of directors) provides a lacuna in this test of the holding and subsidiary company relationship, which might be exploited by appropriate arrangements.

It was seen that section 736A seeks to 'explain expressions used in section 736 and otherwise supplement that section'. Section 736A(3) provides that the reference (in section 736(1)(b)) to 'the right to appoint or remove a majority of the board of directors is to the right to appoint or remove directors holding a majority of the voting rights at meetings of the board on all, or substantially all, matters'. This provision is designed to cope with particular provisions in the

---

1   Ie a registered shareholder in the case of a company with share capital or a member of a company limited by guarantee.

2   See further section 736A(4). See also section 736A(7) as to the treatment of 'rights attached to shares held by way of security'. See further as to the interpretative provision of section 736A in *Gore-Browne on Companies* 44th edn (Jordans, loose-leaf) at 1.6.2.

3   See **3.8.2**.

decisions give scant support to the more optimistic views that the courts were more prepared to lift the veil in the case of groups of companies.[1]

3.9.1 Adams v Cape Industries plc

In its landmark decision in *Adams v Cape Industries plc*,[2] the Court of Appeal took the opportunity to attempt to bring some order to the rather confused body of case-law relating to the question of lifting the veil where groups of companies are concerned. The case was concerned with the enforcement in an English court of judgments obtained in a United States court. One aspect[3] of the question of the exercise of foreign jurisdiction involved the alleged presence of various sub-sidiaries[4] of Cape Industries in the United States. The respondent and its subsidiaries operated an asbestos mining business in South Africa, selling this product in various parts of the world including the United States. The judgments obtained in a Federal Court in Texas were concerned with the liability in tort for asbestos-related injuries. Counsel for the appellant raised three arguments as a basis for asserting that, through its subsidiaries, Cape was present in the United States. The Court of Appeal structured its new and more restrictive approach to lifting the veil around these three possible arguments for the 'presence' of Cape Industries in America.

(1) The single economic unit argument
This concept of the group as a single economic entity found no support as an independent basis on which the corporate veil might be lifted. It could not justify any departure from the normal rule that 'each company in a group of companies . . . is a separate legal entity possessed of separate legal rights and liabilities'.[5] The considerable number of cases where the court has been prepared to ignore the distinction in law between a group of companies on the basis that 'justice so demands' or if 'the business realities' require it were all explained by Slade LJ as being turning 'on the wording of particular statutes or contracts'.[6] While this may be a very satisfactory explanation of some of these cases which explicitly turn on the liberal interpretation of an agreement *in re Mercatoria*,[7] or on the construction of the wording of a particular statutory provision,[8] it cannot satisfactorily explain all of them. It certainly gives a strained interpretation to *DHN Food Distributors Ltd v Tower Hamlets LBC*.[9] Whatever doubts were cast upon the Court of Appeal's decision in this case by the House of Lords in *Woolfson v Strathclyde Regional*

---

1   Some decisions in the field of labour law have been even more hostile to such an approach, and have been prepared to follow the *Salomon* principle to the most artificial extreme. Here policy arguments in favour of the rigorous application of industrial relations legislation may have prevailed. See *Dimbleby v NUJ* [1984] 1 WLR 427 (HL) and *National Dock Labour Board v Pinn Wheeler Ltd* [1989] BCLC 647.

2   [1990] Ch 433.

3   The Court of Appeal also considered whether the defendants had consented to a foreign court exercising jurisdiction over them.

4   In the discussion below of the Court of Appeal's judgment two of these subsidiaries are referred (as in the judgment itself) as AMC and CPC.

5   [1990] Ch 433 at 532 citing Roskill LJ in *The Albazero* [1977] AC 774 at 807.

6   [1990] Ch 433 at 530, *Revlon Inc v Cripps Lee Ltd* [1980] FSR 85 at 105. See [1990] Ch 433 at 534–535.

7   Eg *Harold Holdsworth & Co (Wakerfield) Ltd v Caddies* [1955] 1 WLR 352 at 367. See [1990] Ch 433 at 537.

8   *Scottish Co-operative Wholesale Soc Ltd v Meyer* [1959] AC 324 at 342. See [1990] Ch 433 at 537.

9   [1976] 1 WLR 852 at pp 860 and 861. See [1990] Ch 433 at 533–534.

Council,[1] its authority cannot be wholly dismissed. In particular, the judgment of Lord Denning MR clearly expounds a doctrine about the corporate group as an economic entity which is very different from that of Slade LJ in *Cape Industries.* The Court of Appeal in *Cape Industries* recognised that the rigid doctrine now espoused by the English courts differs markedly from that of the European Court of Justice[2] where a group of companies may be treated as a single economic entity. Clearly, English courts applying EU law to groups of companies must follow the lead of the European Court of Justice.

(2) Piercing the corporate veil

The Court of Appeal in *Cape Industries* accepted that there is 'one well recognised exception to the rule prohibiting the piercing of the "corporate veil"'. This referred to Lord Keith's well-known observations in *Woolfson v Strathclyde Regional Council*[3] that it is appropriate to pierce the corporate veil only where special circumstances exist indicating that it is a mere façade concealing the true facts. Slade LJ in *Cape Industries*[4] cited *Jones v Lipman*[5] as illustrating this principle.[6] As applied to the case itself, the 'façade' principle was applicable to 'AMC' which was not only a wholly owned subsidiary of Cape but had been used by Cape and its subsidiaries as a corporate name on their invoices.[7] This, however, did not help the appellants since the court found that AMC was not in fact carrying on business in the United States. Another company, CPC, was incorporated and carrying on business in the United States but was held not to be a façade. It was an independent corporation which was carrying on its own business in the United States and not that of Cape or its subsidiaries. Significantly, its shares were wholly owned by its chief executive even if it had been set up at the behest of, and with funding from, Cape.[8]

At a more general level, the Court of Appeal stressed that it is legitimate to use a corporate structure 'to ensure that legal liability (if any) in respect of particular future activity of the group ... will fall on another member of the group rather than the defendant company. Whether or not this is desirable, the right to use a corporate structure in this manner is inherent in our corporate law'.[9] The Court of Appeal stressed that the *motive* with which a subsidiary was formed (or an existing subsidiary used) is crucial. Slade LJ stressed that the arrangements involving CPC were not shown to involve actual or potential illegality, nor were they intended to deprive anyone of their existing rights.[10] No doubt future litigation will throw much-needed light upon what is now this crucial if limited basis for lifting the corporate veil.

---

1   1978 SLT 159. See [1990] Ch 433 at 536.
2   See the discussion of *Istitutu Chemioterapico Italiano SPA v The Commission* [1974] ECR 223 in *Cape Industries* at [1990] Ch 433 at 535. See further *SAR Schotte GmbH v Parfums Rothschild SARL* [1992] BCLC 235.
3   1978 SLT 159 at 161.
4   [1990] Ch 433 at 542–543.
5   [1962] 1 WLR 832.
6   Slade LJ found little help in other authorities in terms of reasoned principle. Even the dicta of Lord Denning MR in *Wallersteiner v Moir* [1974] 1 WLR 991 at 1013 and in *Littlewoods Mail Order Stores Ltd v Inland Revenue Commissioners* [1969] 1 WLR 1241 at 1254 were not supported by other members of the Court of Appeal.
7   [1990] Ch 543.
8   Ibid, at 543–544.
9   [1990] Ch at 544.
10   Ibid.

saving in administrative costs for the group. In its Final Report,[1] the Steering Group abandoned the whole idea on the basis the the savings would not justify the loss if information in respect of substantial groups. The injustice caused in particular to involuntary tort creditors remains to be addressed.

---

1   Volume 1 at 8.23–8.28; see Boyle, 'The Company Law Review and "group reform"' (2002) 23 Co Law 35.

Chapter 4

Registration, Formation and Promotion of Companies

4.1 Introduction

This chapter describes the different types of company that can exist and the mechanisms which are provided for their registration and, occasionally, re-registration. Although the vast bulk of registered companies are companies limited by shares, the legislation makes provision also for unlimited and guarantee companies. The nature of these is briefly explained later in this chapter.[1] It is appropriate also to consider the law which applies to those people, known as promoters, who are actually engaged in the business of forming a company, and, briefly, the law which applies to foreign companies doing business in Britain.

Historically, the registered company form was made available for enterprises wishing to involve a large or at least reasonable number of investors. However, as has been seen in Chapter 1, it was also adopted by small concerns, even where there was only one person really involved, a move that was sanctioned by the House of Lords in *Salomon v Salomon & Co*.[2] At the time of this decision, the law made no distinctions between different types of registered company; that happened in 1909 when the concept of the private company, as something distinct from the basic form, the public company, was introduced. Under the law then, the private company was a special category meeting particular requirements (eg as to the number of members). All companies not registered as private fell into the residual category of public company. In order to implement the provisions of the EC's Second Directive on Company Law,[3] a new way of classifying public and private limited companies was introduced by the Companies Act 1980. Many of the more onerous requirements first imposed by this Act (which stem from the Directive)[4] apply only to public companies. To prevent evasion of these requirements it was necessary to introduce a more rigid and watertight dividing line between public and private companies.[5] Under this modern system of classification, which better reflects the reality of company registration, all proposed companies must be registered as private unless they are specifically registered as public companies and meet the special requirements of such. The most important of these are a minimum capitalisation for public companies and an addition to their name (public limited company) indicating a public company's special status.

---

1   A further registered business association is the European Economic Interest Grouping.
2   [1987] AC 22; see **3.4**.
3   77/91/EEC, OJ 1977 L 26/1.
4   As to these, see Chapter 7.
5   This applies to the original registration of public and private companies and also to the re-registration of a private company as a public company or vice versa.

The Review of Company Law[1] looked closely at many aspects of the law described in this chapter and a very brief indication of what might eventually emerge in new companies legislation is given in **4.17**.

4.2   The classification of public and private companies

Section 1(3) of the Companies Act 1985 defines 'public company' as a company limited by shares (or limited by guarantee and having a share capital)[2] whose memorandum of association states that it is a public company and in relation to which the provisions of the 1985 Act or the former Companies Acts as to the registration or re-registration of a company as a public company have been complied with. The Registrar of Companies must register intended companies as public or private, and in the case of a company registered as public the amount of share capital stated in the memorandum must not 'be less than the authorised minimum',[3] which is defined by section 118(1) to mean £50,000.[4]

A public company must have a minimum of two members, while a private limited company can have just one member.[5] Section 25(1) requires that the name of a public company must end with the words 'public limited company',[6] which can be abbreviated to 'plc'.[7] Section 1(3) defines 'private company', as 'a company that is not a public company'. This obviously includes all companies limited by shares which, when they are registered under section 13, are not specifically registered as public companies. It also includes all companies already registered as private companies under earlier Companies Acts 1948–1976 and all unlimited companies or companies limited by guarantee, whatever their previous status.

Sections 43 to 47 provide for the various types of company to be re-registered as another type of company. These provisions are described below.

It is an offence for a public company (other than an old public company) 'to use a name which may reasonably be expected to give the impression that it is a public company in circumstances in which the fact that it is a public company is likely to be material to any person'.[8]

4.3   The memorandum of association

The fundamental document which must be prepared for the registration of a company is the memorandum of association. The purpose and drafting of the memorandum are examined in detail in Chapter 5, but we must note the contents

---

1   See generally **1.7** and Chapter 22.
2   Guarantee companies with a share capital cannot be formed as such now (section 1(4)), but those existing prior to 1980 could re-register as public.
3   Sections 11 and 14.
4   Or 'such other sum as the Secretary of State may by order made by statutory instrument specify instead'.
5   The Companies (Single Member Private Limited Companies) Regulations 1992, SI 1992/1699, implementing Directive 89/667 and amending section 1 of the 1985 Act.
6   It is an offence for a 'person' (eg a private company) which is not registered as a public company to carry on any trade, profession or business under a name which includes as its last part the words 'public limited company' or their Welsh equivalent: section 33(1).
7   Section 27. In the case of companies whose registered office is stated by the memorandum to be in Wales, this may be rendered in Welsh as 'cwmni cyfyngedig cyhoeddus', which may be abbreviated as 'ccc'.
8   Section 33(2).

here. Section 2 of the Companies Act 1985 requires the memorandum of a company limited by shares to contain the following clauses:[1]

(1) the Name Clause;
(2) the Registered Office Clause;
(3) the Objects Clause;
(4) the Limited Liability Clause;
(5) the Share Capital Clause.

In the case of a public company, an additional clause stating that it is a public company must be inserted between (1) and (2), above.

The memorandum may contain optional provisions (which might otherwise be inserted in the articles).[2] It should then conclude with a formal declaration of association by the subscribers.[3] Section 2(6) requires that the memorandum 'must be signed by each subscriber in the presence of at least one witness who must attest the signature'. In practice, subscribers usually sign for only one share each; but there is no reason why they should not sign for as many shares as they intend to take up and pay for. The fact that they have subscribed makes them members of the company from the date of registration.[4]

The name, address and occupation of each subscriber must be stated fully, giving the number, street, city or town, and county. The memorandum may be subscribed by or on behalf of a firm or corporation. Any signature for a firm should be followed by the signature of all the partners. Minors (ie persons under age) should not subscribe, although the Registrar's certificate is conclusive evidence that the company is duly registered.[5] An agent may sign the memorandum on behalf of his principal, and the authority to sign may be given orally. The execution will be good, whether the agent simply writes his principal's name or adds words showing that it is signed by an attorney.[6] The signatures must be attested by one or more witnesses. A witness should be a disinterested person, and not a subscriber. He should give his address and occupation in the same manner as the subscribers.[7] The document may be signed at different times and different places, and be witnessed by different persons.

The memorandum should be in correct form when presented for registration, and any alterations and interlineations in it should be initialled by each subscriber, or the witness should certify that the alterations were made before the document was executed. For the purpose of registration, the memorandum may be either entirely typed upon a sheet or sheets of foolscap; or it may be typed upon the forms provided for that purpose, in which case it will be partly written and partly printed; or it may be entirely printed. As, however, every member is entitled to be supplied with a copy on payment of 5p (or any less sum the company may

---

1   See the model forms in the Companies (Tables A to F) Regulations 1985 at Table B (private company limited by shares) and Table F (public company limited by shares).

2   Eg as to the rights attached to shares. See Chapter 8.

3   Note that there is no bar on all the subscribers to a British company being foreigners: *Re General Company for Promotion of Land Credit* (1870) 5 Ch App 464.

4   See further **12.2.1**.

5   Section 14 of the Companies Act 1985. In Scotland, however, a minor (in the Scots law sense) may subscribe.

6   *Re Whitely Partners* (1886) 42 Ch D 447 (CA). In the latter case, the Registrar will require production of a written authority, stamped as a power of attorney.

7   It is not necessary for a witness to state his occupation in the case of a company registered in Scotland: see the Requirements of Writing (Scotland) Act 1995.

prescribe), printing is almost indispensable. Printing the document has the further advantage that every copy is an exact reproduction of the registered original.

4.4   The articles of association

The other document which must be prepared for registration is the articles of association. Articles must be printed and divided into numbered paragraphs.[1] The original articles must be signed by each subscriber to the memorandum and attested by a witness.[2] The purpose, contents and drafting of the articles of association are considered further in Chapter 5.

Companies limited by guarantee and unlimited companies must register articles, but a company limited by shares need not register articles, in which case the articles of the company will be the regulations contained in Table A.[3] If a company limited by shares is to be registered without articles, the fact must be stated on the back of the memorandum. It is important in the case of a private company that the articles should be so drafted to meet the requirements of the particular 'corporate partners' as to the distribution of voting power attached to shares, the power to issue further shares, pre-emptive rights, etc. The provisions of Table A (especially the 1985 Table A) may be far from suitable for preventing or resolving problems of deadlock, oppression, etc and for controlling the transfer of shares.[4] Where an existing registered company is to be used, the articles should be appropriately amended.

4.5   Registration of memorandum, articles, etc

Section 10 of the Companies Act 1985 requires that the memorandum and articles of association (if any) be delivered to the Registrar for registration.[5] Under section 12, the Registrar may not register the memorandum unless he is satisfied that all the requirements of the Act in respect of registration and of matters precedent and incidental to it have been complied with. Section 11 further requires that, where a memorandum delivered to the Registrar concerns a public company, the amount of share capital stated in the memorandum to be that with which the company proposes to be registered must not be less than the 'authorised minimum'.[6]

Section 12(3) also requires a statutory declaration of compliance with the requirements of section 10 in respect of registration. This must be made by a solicitor engaged in the formation of the company or by a person named in the articles as a director or secretary of the company in the statement delivered under section 10(2) of the 1985 Act.

---

1   Companies Act 1985, section 7(3).
2   Ibid.
3   See section 8(1) and, for companies registered since 1 July 1985, the Companies (Tables A to F) Regulations 1985. Unless it has resolved to alter its articles appropriately since then, a company registered prior to 1 July 1985 is governed by the then applicable version of Table A, which was always in a Schedule to the Companies Act, to the extent that it was adopted by that company.
4   A variety of models is provided in the standard works on precedents. See eg Jordan's Model Forms, reproduced in *Secretarial Administration* (Jordans, loose-leaf), FP2.4.
5   This will be the English Registrar (in Cardiff) if the company is to be registered in England and Wales or the Scottish Registrar (in Edinburgh) if the company is to be Scottish.
6   See **4.2**.

With every memorandum delivered for registration under section 10 of the Act there must be delivered a statement containing particulars of the first director or directors and first secretary or joint secretaries of the company. In the case of an individual director, the particulars required by Schedule 1 to the Companies Act 1985 are his present name and any former name,[1] his usual residential address, his nationality, his business occupation (if any), particulars of any other directorships held by him or which have been held by him,[2] and his date of birth. The corporate name and registered or principal office of a corporate director must be given. As far as the secretary is concerned, the particulars required are his present name, any former name and his usual residential address,[3] and the same is required of joint secretaries unless all the partners in a firm are joint secretaries, in which case disclosure of the name and principal office of the firm will suffice.

The statement delivered under section 10 must be signed by or on behalf of the subscribers to the memorandum,[4] and must contain a consent signed by each of the persons named as director or secretary. Those named are deemed, on the incorporation of the company, to have been appointed to the office in question,[5] and any appointment by any articles delivered with the memorandum is void if it does not accord with the statement.[6]

The section 10 statement must also contain a statement of the intended situation of the company's registered office. The matter of the registered office is considered below in **4.8**.

The other requirement for registration of a company is payment of the appropriate fee. The amount of this is governed by regulations.[7]

4.6 The certificate of incorporation

Section 13(1) of the Companies Act 1985 requires that on registration of the memorandum of a company, the Registrar shall certify that the company is incorporated and, in the case of a limited company, that the company is limited.[8] Where the memorandum of the company registered states that it is a public company, the certificate must state that it is a public company.[9] From the date mentioned in the certificate, the subscribers of the memorandum together with such other persons as may from time to time become members of the company shall be:

(1) a body corporate by the name contained in the memorandum,

---

1   'Name' is defined in paragraph 4 of Schedule 1 to mean Christian name or forename and surname, with qualifications for peers. 'Former name' is further defined.

2   Directorships last held more than five years before the statement and in dormant companies and companies 'grouped with' the company delivering the document do not have to be disclosed here.

3   In the case of a corporation or Scottish firm, its corporate or firm name and registered or principal office.

4   Where the memorandum is delivered by a person as agent of the subscribers of the memorandum the statement required by this section shall specify that fact and the name and address of that person: section 10(4).

5   Section 13(5).

6   Section 10(5).

7   See the Companies (Fees) Regulations 1991, SI 1991/1206, as amended.

8   As to the rights to inspect and require a copy of the certificate, see sections 709 and 710.

9   Section 13(6). The certificate may be signed by the Registrar or authenticated by his official seal. Note that it is possible to obtain registration on the same day as the documents are handed in.

(2) capable forthwith of exercising all the functions of an incorporated company,
(3) but with such liability on the part of the members to contribute to the assets of the company in the event of its being wound up as is provided by the Act and the Insolvency Act.

Section 711 of the 1985 Act requires the Registrar to publish in the *London Gazette* notice of the issue by him of any certificate of incorporation of a company. He must state in the notice the name of the company, a description indicating that it is a certificate of incorporation and the date of its issue.

Section 13(7) deals with the problem of irregularities in the process of registration. It provides that a certificate shall be conclusive evidence that the reqirements of the Act in respect of registration and matters precedent and incidental to it have been complied with, and that the association is a company authorised to be registered and is duly registered under the 1985 Act, and, if the certificate contains a statement that the company is a public company, that the company is such a company.

It has been held that the certificate of incorporation is conclusive evidence that there is a company, and that it is duly incorporated.[1] The certificate is also conclusive evidence that the registration and incorporation of the company were fully effected on the day mentioned in the certificate. The date mentioned in the certificate is the first day of the company's existence, and the company is deemed to have been incorporated on the first moment of that day.[2] However, section 13(7) deals only with ministerial acts, and a certificate does not establish the fact that the company is not a trade union and therefore capable of registration.[3] The House of Lords has held that the certificate of the Registrar is conclusive that the terms of the memorandum are within the law, and that accordingly the court's only function is to construe the memorandum as it stands.[4] The Registrar will refuse registration if he is of the opinion that any object of the company is illegal, and an appeal from his decision can be brought to the High Court by way of judicial review seeking an order that he be required to register.[5] Where the Registrar permits registration, the Attorney-General may be given leave for judicial review where the objects of the company involve entering into contracts which are sexually immoral.[6]

4.7 Certificate for public companies

As a way of guaranteeing that a newly incorporated public company satisfies the requirement as to its authorised minimum capital, section 117 of the Companies Act 1985 provides an administrative safeguard. A company registered as 'a public

---

1   *Hammond v Prentice Brothers* [1920] 1 Ch 201.
2   *Jubilee Cotton Mills v Lewis* [1924] AC 958 (HL).
3   *Edinburgh and District Aerated Water Manufacturers' Defence Association v Jenkinson* (1904) 5 F 1159 (Ct of Sess): *British Association of Glass Bottle Manufacturers v Nettlefold* (1911) 27 TLR 527. Whether a certificate of incorporation is conclusive when a friendly society purports to register as a company but adopts an extended memorandum or otherwise offends against the law was left open in *Blythe v Birtley* [1910] 1 Ch 229.
4   *Cotman v Brougham* [1918] AC 514 (HL).
5   *R v Registrar of Companies, ex parte More* [1941] 2 KB 197 (CA). If the conditions laid down in the Act have been complied with (and the object is not illegal) the court will compel the Registrar to issue a certificate of incorporation: *R v Registrar of Companies, ex parte Bowen* [1914] 4 KB 1161.
6   *R v Registrar of Companies, ex parte Attorney-General* [1991] BCLC 476.

company on its original incorporation' may not do business or exercise any borrowing powers unless the Registrar issues a certificate as to its authorised minimum capital. If he does not do so, the company must re-register as a private company.

In order for the Registrar to issue this certificate an application must be made to him by the company in prescribed form, signed by a director or secretary, which satisfies him that the nominal value of the company's allotted share capital is not less than the authorised minimum; further, there must be delivered to him a statutory declaration complying with the matters set out below.[1] Shares allotted in pursuance of an employees' share scheme may not be taken into account in determining the nominal value of the company's allotted share capital unless they are paid up at least as to one-quarter of their nominal value and the whole of any premium.[2]

The statutory declaration must state:

(1) that the nominal value of the company's allotted share capital is not less than the authorised minimum;
(2) the amount paid up, at the time of application, on the allotted share capital of the company;
(3) the amount, or estimated amount, of the preliminary expenses of the company and the persons by whom any of those expenses have been paid or are payable;
(4) the details of any amount or benefit paid or given or intended to be paid or given to any promoter of the company, and the consideration for the payment or benefit.

The Registrar 'may accept a statutory declaration as sufficient evidence of the matters stated therein',[3] which presumably still leaves him the discretion in an appropriate case to enquire further.

A certificate issued under section 117(1) is 'conclusive evidence that the company is entitled to do business and exercise any borrowing powers'.[4] Where a company does business or exercises borrowing powers in contravention of the section, criminal penalties are imposed on the company and any officer in default. There are, however, two further sanctions. First, the Secretary of State may present a petition to wind up a company on the ground that it is a public company which was registered as such on its original incorporation but that it has not been issued with a certificate under section 117 and more than a year has expired since it was registered.[5] It may be noted that, unlike the criminal penalties, this sanction may be invoked against a company incorporated as public even though it has not otherwise infringed section 117 by doing business, etc. The fact that it has lain dormant for a year would be sufficient. However, section 117(1) permits such a company (eg where it is unable to raise the authorised minimum capital) to re-register as a private company. An undertaking to do so might persuade the court not to grant a winding-up order.

---

1   See section 117(3).
2   Section 117(4).
3   Section 117(5).
4   Section 117(6). In view of the protection given to third parties even where no certificate is issued (see below), this must be intended to protect the company and its officers.
5   Insolvency Act 1986, sections 122(1)(b) and 124(4). This would not seem to exclude others entitled to present a petition under section 124(1) doing so on this ground.

The second additional sanction imposed by section 117 concerns transactions entered into by a company in contravention of its provisions.[1] It is important to note that such transactions are expressly declared to be valid. If, however, a company fails to comply with its obligations under such a transaction within 21 days of being called upon to do so (ie by the other party), the directors become jointly and severally liable to indemnify the other party to the transaction in respect of any loss or damage suffered by him by reason of the failure of the company to comply with those obligations.

4.8 Unlimited companies

So far in this chapter it has been assumed that a company is formed with the liability of its members limited, but it has long been possible to register a company with unlimited liability. However, before the Companies Act 1967 very few companies, other than estate companies, were registered with unlimited liability, and many banking and other companies originally constituted as unlimited companies were re-registered with limited liability. When the 1967 Act relieved unlimited companies from the disclosure requirements in respect of accounts that apply to limited companies (private or public),[2] some encouragement was provided for the registration or re-registration of unlimited companies. The members of an unlimited company are liable in a liquidation to contribute until the whole of the company's debts or obligations (however heavy they may be) are paid, but their primary liability is at an end once they have ceased to be members.[3] An unlimited company must always now be classified as a private company.

Unlimited companies may be registered either with or without a capital divided into shares. The memorandum of association must state the name of the proposed company, whether the registered office of the company is to be situated in England and Wales or Scotland, and the objects for which the company is to be established.[4] It must be accompanied by articles of association,[5] for which Table E may be used as a model.[6] The articles must be printed[7] and must state the amount of its share capital (if any).[8] The capital (if the company has a capital), being stated in the articles of association, may be varied at any time by special resolution without the sanction of the court, and, if the articles allow it, capital may be returned to members, and they may cease to be members on such terms as may be agreed upon.[9]

So far as regards the powers of an unlimited company and of its directors, the conduct of its business and proceedings, the alteration of its memorandum or

---

1   Section 117(8).
2   Although many private limited companies are now relieved from many of the disclosure requirements; see **1.4** and Chapter 14.
3   Past members may in certain circumstances escape liability, eg if they have ceased to be members of the company a year or more before the commencement of the winding-up; see section 74 of the Insolvency Act 1986.
4   Section 2(1).
5   Section 7(1).
6   See section 8(4). Though the general form of the tables in the Companies (Tables A to F) Regulations 1985 must be followed, their contents may be changed: *Gaiman v National Association for Mental Health* [1971] 1 Ch 417.
7   Section 7(4).
8   Section 7(2).
9   *Re Borough Commercial and Building Society* [1894] 2 Ch 242.

articles of association, and its winding up, the same considerations apply as in the case of a limited company. The returns required to be made by unlimited companies are the same as those by other companies, except that an unlimited company with a share capital is under no obligation to lodge a return of allotments.

4.9 Companies limited by guarantee

Companies limited by guarantee are usually formed for the purpose of carrying on business as mutual insurance and trade protection societies, social, athletic and other clubs, and concerns in which it is not intended to make a profit. There are two kinds of guarantee company still provided for under the Companies Act 1985:[1] companies limited by guarantee and not having a share capital; and companies limited by guarantee and having a share capital. It is only the first kind that is considered here, since the hybrid variety was in practice rarely used. Furthermore, since the Companies Act 1980, it has not been possible to register any more such companies. It should be noted that there is no provision for a company limited by shares to re-register as a company limited by guarantee or vice versa.

The principle on which these companies are constituted is that each person who becomes a member 'undertakes to contribute to the assets of the company in the event of its being wound up while he is a member, or within one year after he ceases to be a member, for payment of the debts and liabilities of the company contracted before he ceases to be a member, and of the costs, charges, and expenses of winding up, and for adjustment of the rights of the contributories among themselves, such amount as may be required, not exceeding a specified amount'.[2] This amount has to be stated in the memorandum of association, and may be any sum the subscribers to that document think fit – £1 or £1,000, or any other sum, large or small. The amount is not part of the capital of the company, and cannot be mortgaged or charged by debentures.[3]

In the form which is usually adopted the amount of the guarantee of each member remains the same, whatever his pecuniary interest in the company may be, and (beyond that interest) is the utmost extent to which he can be a loser in the event of the company going into liquidation. The guarantee, moreover, is only so much per member, and accordingly, if the number of members is reduced, the aggregate amount guaranteed is also reduced. Thus the security of the creditor is lessened to that extent unless the memorandum provides for membership continuing until some other person takes the place of the member then on the register.

In all companies limited by guarantee, articles of association must be registered with the memorandum of association, and must be printed. Section 8(4) requires that the memorandum and articles of a company limited by guarantee (and not having a share capital) shall be in accordance with the form set out in Table C of the Companies (Tables A to F) Regulations 1985. In *Gaiman v National Association for Mental Health*,[4] Megarry J held that the draftsman of the articles, provided that he followed the general form of the relevant Table was free to add to, subtract

---

1   See sections 3 and 8.
2   Section 2(2) and (3).
3   *Re Pyle Works* (1890) 44 Ch D 544 at 574 and 584; *Re Irish Club Co* [1906] WN 127.
4   [1971] 1 Ch 317.

from or vary the model set out in the Table 'as the needs of the case suggest'.[1] Section 15(1) provides that 'every provision in the memorandum or articles or in any resolution of the company purporting to give any person a right to participate in the divisible profits of the company otherwise than as as member shall be void'.

4.9.1 Exemption from using 'limited' as part of the name

A private guarantee company may take advantage of the procedure in sections 30 and 31 of the Companies Act 1985 to omit the word 'limited' from its name (while of course retaining limited liability).[2] The objects of the company must be the promotion of commerce, science, education, religion, charity or any profession and anything incidental or conducive to those objects. In addition the following restrictions on profits, dividends and capital must be contained in the company's memorandum or articles. The memorandum or articles must require that its profits, if any, or other income be applied in promoting its objects, and prohibit the payment of dividends to members. The memorandum or articles must also require all the assets (which would otherwise be available, on a winding-up, to its members generally) to be transferred on its winding up either to another body with objects similar to its own, or to another body whose objects are the promotion of charity and anything incidental or conducive to it.

A statutory declaration must be made that the company complies with the requirements of section 30(3). In the case of a company about to be formed, this may be made by a solicitor engaged in the formation of the company or by a person named as a director or secretary of the company in the 'statement of first directors and secretary' delivered under section 10(2).[3] In the case of a company which is proposing to drop the word 'limited' from its name, the statutory declaration must be made by a director or secretary of the company. On the delivery of such a declaration to the Registrar, he may accept it as sufficient evidence of the matter stated in it. Companies to which section 30 applies are exempt not only from the use of the word 'limited' as part of their name, but also from the requirements of the 1985 Act as to the publishing of its name[4] and the sending of lists of members to the Registrar of Companies.[5] These practical advantages may be even more beneficial to companies qualifying for exemption under section 30.

A company so exempt may not alter its memorandum or articles 'so that it ceases to be a company to which this section applies'.[6] If it appears to the Secretary of State that a company exempt under section 30 is in fact ignoring the requirements, he may, in writing, direct the company to change its name (by resolution of the directors) so that the name ends with 'limited'. The directors must do so within such period as may be specified in the Secretary of State's direction. Such a resolution by the directors must be treated as one to be registered under section 380 of the 1985 Act.[7] A company which has received a

---

1   Ibid, at 328.
2   Before the original introduction of these provisions, in 1981, Department of Trade and Industry approval was required.
3   See **4.5**.
4   See **4.5**.
5   See **12.7**.
6   Section 31(1).
7   See **14.18**.

direction under section 31 may not thereafter be registered with a name which does *not* include the word 'limited' without the approval of the Secretary of State.[1]

Section 351(1) requires a company exempt under section 30 to display in legible characters on all its business letters and order forms the fact that it is limited.[2]

4.10 The re-registration of companies

The Companies Act provides for a number of ways in which a company may be re-registered, for example from private to public. The principal requirements are examined in the following paragraphs.[3]

4.11 The re-registration of private companies as public

Sections 43 to 47 of the Companies Act 1985 provide for the re-registration of private companies as public companies. Section 43 requires the company to pass a special resolution making the necessary changes in its memorandum and articles and then to make an application accompanied by certain required documents. It must also meet certain conditions specified in section 45 as to the nominal value of its share capital, as described in **4.11.1**.

The special resolution that the company should be re-registered as a public company must alter the memorandum so that it states that the company is a public company. The resolution must also make such other alterations in the memorandum necessary to make it conform with the memorandum of a public company. The special resolution must also 'make such alterations in the articles as are requisite in the circumstances'. For example, articles restricting the transfer or transmission of shares, or entrenching the position of the existing directors on the board, might have to be changed. This would certainly be necessary where admission of the shares to trading on a recognised investment exchange listing was contemplated.

Section 43(3) requires that, having passed the special resolution to re-register as a public company, an application in prescribed form, signed by a director or secretary of the company, be delivered to the Registrar. The application must be accompanied by the following documents.

(1) A printed copy of the memorandum and articles as amended by the special resolution required by section 43.

(2) A copy of a written statement by the company's auditors that, in their opinion, the 'relevant balance sheet' shows that at the balance sheet date the amount of the company's net assets was not less than the aggregate of its called-up share capital and 'undistributable reserves'. 'Relevant balance sheet' means a balance sheet prepared as at a date not more than seven months before the

---

1   Section 41(4).

2   See **5.5**.

3   In addition to those described, there is provision for 'old public companies', ie those incorporating before the Companies Act 1980 came into force and which have not hitherto re-registered as public companies, to re-register as private companies. These are described in *Gore-Browne on Companies* 44th edn (Jordans, loose-leaf) at 7.10–7.10.4.

company's application for re-registration under section 43.[1] 'Undistributable reserves' has the same meaning as in section 264(3).[2]

(3) A copy of the relevant balance sheet, together with a copy of an 'unqualified report by the company's auditors in relation to that balance sheet'.[3]

(4) A copy of the experts' report required where shares have been issued for non-cash consideration. This is further explained in **4.11.1**, below.

(5) Finally, there must be a statutory declaration in the prescribed form by a director or secretary of the company as to the following. First, that the requirements of section 43(1) as to the special resolution altering the company's memorandum and articles have been complied with; secondly, that the conditions specified in section 44[4] where this applies and in section 45 (as to authorised share capital, etc)[5] have been complied with; thirdly, that between balance sheet date and the application of the company for re-registration, there has been no change in the financial position of the company that has resulted in the amount of the company's net assets becoming less than the aggregate of its called-up share capital and undistributable reserves. The Registrar may accept the statutory declaration called for by section 43(3)(e) as sufficient evidence that the special resolution has been passed and that the other conditions have been satisfied.[6]

4.11.1 Requirements as to share capital

Section 45(1) provides that a private company shall not be re-registered as a public company unless, at the time the special resolution required by section 43 is passed, the following requirements as to the company's share capital are satisfied.

(1) The nominal value of the company's allotted share capital is not less than the authorised minimum.

(2) Each of the allotted shares is paid up at least as to one-quarter of the nominal value of that share and the whole of any premium on it.

(3) Where any share in the company or any premium payable on it has been fully or partly paid up by an undertaking given by any person that he or another should do work or perform services for the company or another, the undertaking has been performed or otherwise discharged.

(4) Where any shares in the company have been allotted as fully or partly paid up as to their nominal value or any premium payable on them otherwise than in cash and the consideration for the allotment consists of or includes an undertaking (other than one to which paragraph (3) above applies) to the company, then either
     (a) that undertaking must have been performed or otherwise discharged, or

---

1   Section 43(4).
2   See **7.21.3**.
3   See section 46.
4   See **4.11.1**.
5   Ibid.
6   Section 47(2).

(b) there must be a contract between the company and any person pursuant to which that undertaking must be performed within five years from that time.

A further condition that must be met by a private company seeking to re-register as a public one[1] applies only where shares are allotted by the company between the balance sheet date[2] and the passing of the special resolution as fully or partly paid up as to their nominal value or any premium on them otherwise than in cash. In this event, section 44(2) adapts the provisions of section 108 of the 1985 Act.[3] A private company may not make an application for re-registration unless before doing so consideration for the allotment has been valued in accordance with the provision of section 108. Further, a report with respect to its value must have been made in accordance with section 108 during the six months immediately preceding the allotment of the shares.

4.11.2 The effect of re-registration under section 43

If the Registrar is satisfied that a company may be re-registered as a public company, he must retain the application and accompanying documents. He must then issue the company with a certificate of incorporation stating that the company is a public company.[4] Upon the issue of this certificate, the company becomes a public company and the alteration in the memorandum (and any alteration in the articles) set out in the special resolution required by section 43(1) takes effect accordingly.[5]

4.12 Re-registration of unlimited companies as public companies

In principle, where an unlimited company wishes to re-register as a *public* limited company, the procedure and requirements of section 43 of the Companies Act 1985 must be followed. However, this is subject to certain modifications appropriate to the change from unlimited to limited status.[6] It should be remembered that, under the modern system of classification, an unlimited company is a private company and may not, while it remains such, register as a public one.[7] However, section 48 allows it to change its status by re-registering as a public limited company. Where an unlimited company wishes to become a private limited company, then it should re-register under section 51.[8]

---

1 See section 43(1) and (3)(e).
2 Ie the date when the balance sheet (required as part of the documents contained with the application under that section) was prepared.
3 See **7.14.3**.
4 Section 47(1). The Registrar may not issue such a certificate where it appears to him that the court has made an order confirming a reduction of capital and where this brings the nominal value of the issued capital below the authorised minimum: section 47(3).
5 Section 47(5).
6 See sections 43(1) and 49(1).
7 See **4.2**, above.
8 See **4.15**, below.

4.13 Public companies re-registering as private

Section 53 of the Companies Act 1985 allows companies registered under the Act as public companies to re-register as private companies. This can apply to companies registered on incorporation as public and also to private companies which have re-registered as public.

The procedure for re-registration follows the usual pattern in requiring a special resolution that the company be re-registered. This must alter the company's memorandum so that it no longer states that the company is a public company. It must also make such 'other alterations in the company's memorandum and articles as are requisite in the circumstances'.[1] The name of the company (ending 'public limited company') will of course be changed to simply 'limited'. The articles may take the form of specially drafted articles suitable to a private company.

This special resolution may be challenged by dissenting shareholders applying to the court to have the resolution cancelled under section 54. An application may be made to the court within 28 days after the passing of the resolution 'on behalf of persons entitled to make the application by such one or more of their number as they may appoint in writing for the purpose'. The persons entitled to make the application are shareholders (or members) who meet any of the following criteria:

(1) holders of not less in aggregate than 5% in nominal value of the company's issued share capital or any class thereof;
(2) if the company is not limited by shares, by not less than 5% of the company's members; or
(3) by not less than 50 of the company's members.

Where an application is made by those entitled, the company must 'forthwith' give notice in the prescribed form to the Registrar. The company must also, where on the hearing of that application the court cancels or confirms the resolution, deliver an office copy of the court order to the Registrar within 15 days from the making of the order or within such longer time as the court may at any time by order direct.

The court which hears an application to cancel or confirm a resolution is given wide powers. It may make that order (either cancelling or confirming the resolution) 'on such terms or conditions as it thinks fit'. Further, the court may, if it thinks fit, adjourn the proceedings in order that an arrangement may be made to the satisfaction of the court for the purchase of the interest of dissentient members. It may give such directions and make such orders as it thinks expedient for facilitating or carrying into effect any such arrangement. The court is given the further power to provide for the company itself to purchase the shares of any member of the company. Where that is ordered, the company's capital will be reduced accordingly. Such an order may make the necessary alterations in the memorandum and articles that are required in consequence. Quite apart from the power to order the company to purchase dissenters' shares, there is a further power to require the company to make any, or any specified, alteration in the memorandum or articles of the company. The company will then require the leave of the court before it may further alter the memorandum or the articles in breach of what has been required. However, any alterations in, or additions to, the

---

1 Section 54(2).

memorandum or articles, ordered by the court under section 54, have the same effect as if made by the resolution of the company. The provisions of the Companies Act are to apply accordingly.

The wide powers which section 54 confers on the court are similar to those conferred on a court hearing a petition by unfairly prejudiced minority shareholders under sections 459–461 of the Companies Act 1985.[1] It remains to be seen how the courts will exercise these new powers in this context, since the ground for giving relief is quite distinct from that of unfair prejudice under section 459. Since the complainants under section 54 will, if the resolution is confirmed, be deprived of a market for their shares (eg the company will cease to be a listed company, where that had been the case), it is to be hoped the court will as a rule be prepared to grant some form of relief where it decides not to cancel the resolution. The most obvious solution is that indicated by section 54 – the purchase of the dissenter's shares by or on behalf of the majority shareholders or by the company itself.

4.14 Re-registration of private limited companies as unlimited companies

Section 49 allows the conversion of a limited company into an unlimited one on application to the Registrar for re-registration.[2] The conditions that must be met are:

(1) that the unanimous consent of the members has been obtained;[3]
(2) that the memorandum is altered to bring it, both in substance and form, into conformity with the requirements of the Companies Act 1985 as to the memorandum of an unlimited company with a share capital.[4]

If it is not to have a share capital, the memorandum must set out such alterations as are 'requisite in the circumstances'. If the company had previously registered articles and it is to have a share capital, then the application must set out such alterations to the articles as 'are requisite to bring them, both in substance and form, into conformity with the requirements' of the 1985 Act as to the substance and form of the articles required for an unlimited company with share capital.

A public company cannot re-register directly as an unlimited company, because section 53(3) provides that a company cannot under this section be re-registered 'otherwise than as a company limited by shares or by guarantee'. Thus a public limited company seeking to become a private unlimited company will have first to re-register as a private limited company under section 53. There is nothing to prevent it then applying for re-registration as an unlimited company under section 49. However, the unanimous consent of the members will be required. At

---

1   See **17.12**.
2   This procedure was first introduced by the Companies Act 1967 to enable private companies to escape the disclosure obligations imposed on them by that Act. Section 49(4) provides that a public company cannot re-register as an unlimited company. It also provides that a company that has previously been registered as unlimited may not re-register under this section.
3   Section 49(8).
4   Section 49(5)(a).

the stage of re-registration under section 53, dissenting shareholders might apply to the court under section 54. As already noted, the court may make an order for the purchase of the shares of the dissentient members.

4.15 Re-registration of unlimited companies as private limited companies

The converse procedure for re-registering an unlimited company as a private limited company follows broadly the same pattern. However, instead of the unanimous consent of all the members, section 51 requires the passing of a special resolution. This resolution must state whether the liability of members is to be limited by guarantee or by share capital and, if the latter, what the capital is to be. The resolution must also make appropriate alteration in the memorandum and articles to fit the requirements of the Companies Act 1985 as to the substance and form of the memorandum and articles suitable to the type of limited liability chosen.

Section 77 of the Insolvency Act 1986 provides that those who were members at the time of re-registration shall remain liable to contribute if the company is wound up within three years of the re-registration, even though they have become past members by the time the winding-up commences. Such past members remain liable to contribute to the company's debts and liabilities incurred before the re-registration as if the company had not been re-registered as limited. Further, where none of the members at the time of the re-registration remain members at the commencement of the liquidation, those who were existing or past members at the time of re-registration are liable to contribute without limit to the debts and liabilities incurred before re-registration. This is notwithstanding the fact that the existing members at the time of winding up have 'satisfied the contribution required to be made by them' under the Companies Act 1985 and the Insolvency Act 1986.

4.16 Prohibited forms of re-registration

Neither section 49 nor section 51 permits a limited company to change to a different form of limited liability (ie a company limited by share capital to one limited by guarantee or vice versa). However, section 51 permits an unlimited company to re-register as a company limited by shares or by guarantee. The prohibition on the use of these sections by a company which is or wishes to become a public company has already been noted. Furthermore, section 51 does not permit an unlimited company to re-register as a limited one if it has previously changed from a limited to an unlimited company under section 49. Likewise, section 49 prohibits the converse process when a limited company seeking to re-register as an unlimited one has previously changed from unlimited to limited.

4.17 Reform of the law on registration and formation

The Company Law Review[1] identified[2] the formation of companies as one area of the law where modernisation and simplification was necessary. Among the ideas

---

1   See **1.7**.
2   See especially *Modern Company Law for a Competitive Economy, The Strategic Framework*, February 1999, Chapter 5.4, and *Modern Company Law for a Competitive Economy, Company Formation and Capital Maintenance*, Chapter 2.

that might be taken up are: (1) allowing all companies to be formed with a single member; and (2) simplifying registration by replacing the memorandum and articles of association by a single constitutional document, to be delivered with a standard Registration Form. The Constitution would be similar to the articles of association as presently required. The Registration Form would contain most of the matters currently required to be in the memorandum together with one or two additions, such as the intended address of the registered office, although private companies would no longer have to state their objects.[1] The 'subscribers' would become the 'founder members', and the directors would be required to confirm that they had informed themselves about their duties.[2]

4.18 Promoting companies

It is now appropriate to consider the legal position regarding those who are involved in the formation of a company, conventionally called promoters. The courts have always refused, rightly, to define what constitutes a 'promoter'. If a rigid definition were given, those who want to avoid the liabilities of the position would be careful to come very close to the line without crossing it. The best description is that of Bowen LJ: 'The term "promoter" is a term not of law but of business, usefully summing up in a single word a number of business operations, familiar to the commercial world, by which a company is generally brought into existence.'[3] To this there should probably be added 'and by which its original capital is provided'. The promotion does not necessarily cease with the registration of the company, for 'a person not a director may be a promoter of a company which is already incorporated but the capital of which has not been taken up'.[4]

In seeking to ascertain who are the promoters of a company, it is useful to ask the following questions.

(1) Who started the idea of forming a company for the purpose in question?
(2) Who decided what was to be included in the memorandum and articles of association and in the prospectus, or gave the lawyers instructions to prepare them and information upon which they might be prepared?
(3) Who undertook the liability for the costs of preparing those documents, registering the company and making the preliminary agreements?
(4) Who sought out the persons who ultimately became the first directors, and induced them to undertake the office?
(5) Who procured the subscription of the capital?
(6) Who benefited by the formation of the company?

---

1 Unless and until aspects of the 2nd EC Directive are renegotiated, public companies will continue to have to state their objects, although these would no longer have any effect on the capacity of the company; see **6.40**.
2 See the similar recommendation made by the Law Commissions (*Company Directors: Regulating Conflicts of Interest and Formulating a Statement of Duties*, Law Com No 261, Scot Law Com No 174, September 1999), discussed at **16.25**.
3 *Whaley Bridge Calico Printing Co v Green* (1880) 5 QBD 109.
4 *Emma Silver Mining Co v Lewis* (1879) 4 CPD 396 at 407.

However, none of these questions is decisive. A person may have done one or more of these things, and yet not be a promoter; or a person may have kept in the background and have appeared to do none of these things, and yet be a promoter. Usually, however, persons who have busied themselves in procuring subscriptions or underwriting will find it very hard to escape from being held to be promoters. Further, a person may be a promoter who is acting only as agent for others, or as a director of a promoting syndicate, if he has personally taken an active part in the promotion.[1]

Frequently, the vendors of property to a company are the promoters,[2] but if they have done no more than agree to sell, they will not be promoters; nor will the solicitors who, as part of their professional duty, prepared the contracts.[3] However, the courts will look at the substance of a transaction, and vendors or others who are in reality the promoters will not escape liability by the interposition of a nominal vendor or a nominal promoter, who professes to purchase and resell the property or to undertake the financial operations incidental to forming and floating a company.[4]

4.19 Duties of promoters

The relation of a promoter to the company he is about to form, although not strictly that of a trustee to his beneficiary, or of an agent to his principal, is of the same nature. It follows that he may not secretly make a profit for himself, nor otherwise benefit at the expense of the company. Thus Lindley LJ described the relationship between a promoter and his company as follows:

> Although not an agent of the company nor a trustee for it before its formation, the old familiar principles of the law of agency and of trusteeship have been extended, and very properly extended, to meet such cases. It is perfectly well settled that a promoter of a company is accountable to it for all moneys secretly obtained by him from it, just as if the relationship of principal and agent, or of trustee and *cestui que trust*, had really existed between him and the company when the money was so obtained.[5]

The fiduciary relationship extends, moreover, not only to the company as constituted at the time, but also to future allottees of shares. Thus disclosure of profits made by the promoters must be made not only to the subscribers to the memorandum.

The fiduciary position commences as soon as the promoter begins to act for or promote the company, but not earlier. The fact of acquiring a property with the intention of ultimately forming a company which shall acquire and develop it does not render the purchaser accountable for the profit he makes on the resale, so long as the company, on coming into existence, is informed that the person selling

---

1   *Lydney and Wigpool Iron Ore Co v Bird* (1886) 44 Ch D 85 at 94.

2   *Twycross v Grant* (1877) 2 CPD 469; *Gluckstein v Barnes* [1990] AC 240 at 249 (HL).

3   *Re Great Wheal Polgooth Co Ltd* (1884) 54 LJ Ch 42.

4   See *Twycross v Grant* (1877) 2 CPD 469; *Bagnall v Carlton* (1877) 6 Ch D 471; *Emma Silver Mining Co v Lewis* (1879) 4 CPD 496; *Erlanger v New Sombrero Phosphate Co* (1878) 3 App Cas 1218 (HL); *Emma Silver Mining Co v Grant* (1879) 11 Ch D 918; *Nant-y-Glo and Blaina Ironworks Co v Grave* (1878) 12 Ch D 748; *Lydney and Wigpool Iron Ore Co v Bird* (1886) 33 Ch D 85.

5   *Lydney and Wigpool Iron Ore Co v Bird* (1886) 33 Ch D 85 at 94.

to the company and the promoter are identical.[1] The same rule applies even though the acquisition is only in the form of an option or uncompleted contract,[2] or where the promoter contracted to sell 'the benefit of a lease agreed to be granted', and in fact there was no agreement for the lease, but only negotiations which ultimately resulted in a lease which was assigned to the company.[3] But any profit which the promoter makes after he has begun to promote the company, and the benefit of any contracts into which he enters during the period, *prima facie* belong to the company.[4] It is, however, too much to say that what a promoter acquires after he has commenced the promotion *ipso facto* belongs to the company. The question whether the promoter is in fact acquiring as agent for the intended company or for himself is one of fact; but where the scheme thoughout is that he shall resell at a profit, the natural inference is that he is not acting as agent for the company, and if there is no concealment of the fact that he is the vendor when he resells the company, the company cannot claim the profit.[5]

If the promoter was not at the time he bought in a fiduciary position, though subsequently and at the time of his resale of the company he is in a fiduciary position and does not disclose his interest, the company is entitled to rescind. If in such a case rescission has become impossible, the company cannot recover from the promoter, as money had and received, the profit he has made, or damages.[6]

However, if an additional secret profit has been made under a separate transaction which it is still open to the company to rescind, or under an ancillary transaction to which it was not a party, such a profit may be recovered.[7] Furthermore, a promoter will be liable in deceit if it can be shown that he has caused loss to the company by making fraudulent statements.[8]

---

1   *Cavendish Bentinck v Fenn* (1887) 12 App Cas 652 (HL); *Gover's Case* (1875) 1 Ch D 182; *Erlanger v New Sombrero Phosphate Co* (1878) 3 App Cas 1218; *Ladywell Mining Co v Brookes* (1887) 35 Ch D 400. Compare *Burland v Earle* [1902] AC 83 (PC): the case of a director purchasing privately and selling to his company.

2   *Gover's Case* (1875) 1 Ch D 182, followed in *Ladywell Mining Co v Brookes* (1887) 35 Ch D 400.

3   *Omnium Electric Palaces v Baines* [1914] 1 Ch 332 (CA).

4   *Ladywell Mining Co v Brookes* (1887) 35 Ch D 400; *Re Cape Breton Co* (1885) 29 Ch D 795, affirmed *sub nom Cavendish Bentinck v Fenn* (1887) 12 App Cas 652 (HL).

5   *Omnium Electric Palaces v Baines* [1914] 1 Ch 332 (CA).

6   *Gover's Case* [1875] 1 Ch D 182; *Re Cape Breton Co* (1885) 29 Ch D 795; *Ladywell Mining Co v Brookes* (1887) 35 Ch D 400; *Re Lady Forrest (Murchison) Gold Mine* [1901] 1 Ch 582; *Burland v Earle* [1902] AC 83; *Re Jacobus Marler Estates v Marler* (1913) 114 LT 640 note; *Cook v Deeks* [1916] AC 554 (PC). But in *Cavendish Bentinck v Fenn* (1887) 12 App Cas 652 (HL) Lord Hershell, at 664, suggested there might be a remedy in damages.

7   *Gluckstein v Barnes* [1900] AC 240 (HL); *Jubilee Cotton Mills v Lewis* [1924] AC 958 (HL).

8   *Re Leeds & Hanley Theatre of Varieties* [1902] 2 Ch 809 (CA). Where misstatements are made negligently which induce the company to enter into a contract in reliance on them, there may now be liability under section 2(1) of the Misrepresentation Act 1967 (this Act does not apply in Scotland, but the Law Reform (Miscellaneous Provisions) (Scotland) Act 1985, section 10, allows for the award of damages for a negligent misrepresentation). Where the promoter can establish a reasonable ground for belief, he will have a defence to an action under section 2(1). However, the court under section 2(2) may now award damages in lieu of rescission when this latter remedy would otherwise be available for innocent misrepresentation. Finally, the company may have an action for negligent misstatement at common law within the principle laid down in *Hedley Byrne & Co Ltd v Heller & Partners Ltd* [1964] AC 465 (HL).

4.19.1   To whom disclosure must be made

Promoters will not be protected by disclosures made before the public have joined the company unless there is an independent board or body of shareholders to receive and act upon the information, and the directors who participate in the profits must not be counted as independent.[1] Thus mere communication to the subscribers to the memorandum of association who are clerks in the vendor's office is obviously a farce, even though they hold a meeting and are the only members of the company. Equally, disclosure to directors who are mere nominees of the vendors or promoters will not be sufficient.[2] In such a case the information should be given in the prospectus;[3] and even if all the facts are known to all the members of the company at the time the contract is made, but a misleading prospectus is subsequently issued by the promoters to the public inviting them to join the company, the promoters will be liable.[4] If, however, there is no intention of making a public issue of shares, and no such issue is in fact made, the knowledge by all the directors and members of the company of the facts will exonerate the promoters, even where the purchase price has been greatly inflated.[5]

Where a promoter has to account to the company for secret profits, the measure of recovery is the amount of profit made by the promoter,[6] but he is allowed to deduct from the amount all reasonable expenses he has been put to, and is liable only for the net profits made.[7]

4.20   The remuneration of promoters

The traditional way for promoters to obtain their reward was in the form of the profit made on property sold to the company or in some other ancillary transaction connected with its formation. It has been seen that if proper disclosure is made, such transactions are binding on the company.[8]

Promoters have no right to any remuneration simply because the articles state that the promoters are entitled to a certain sum for their services. This does not of itself create a contract between the promoter and the company.[9] The promoter must prove the existence of a binding contract with the company,[10] and, as will be explained below, a contract purporting to be made with a company before it is

---

1   *Re Leeds and Hanley Theatre of Varieties* [1902] 2 Ch 809 (CA); *Erlanger v New Sombrero Phosphate Co* (1878) 4 App Cas 1218 (HL); *Re Olympia* [1898] 2 Ch 153, affirmed *sub nom Gluckstein v Barnes* [1900] AC 240 (HL).

2   *Re Olympia* [1898] Ch 153 affirmed *sub nom Gluckstein v Barnes* [1990] AC 240. Cf *Kaye v Croydon Tramways* [1898] 1 Ch 358 (CA) and *Lagunas Nitrate Co v Lagunas Syndicate* [1899] 2 Ch 392 at 431 (CA).

3   *Re Leeds and Hanley Theatre of Varieties* [1902] 2 Ch 809 (CA).

4   *Lagunas Nitrate Co v Lagunas Syndicate* [1899] 2 Ch 392 at 428 (CA).

5   *Re Ambrose Lake Tin and Copper Mining Co* (1880) 14 Ch D 390; *Re British Seamless Paper Box Co* (1881) 17 Ch D 467; *Re Innes & Co* [1904] 2 Ch 254; *Attorney-General for Canada v Standard Trust Co* [1911] AC 498 (PC).

6   *Re Leeds and Hanley Theatre of Varieties* [1902] 2 Ch 809 (CA).

7   *Emma Silver Mining Co v Grant* (1879) 11 Ch D 918; *Lydney and Wigpool Iron Ore Co v Bird* (1886) 33 Ch D 85.

8   Payments, etc, made to promoters must also be disclosed where shares are to be traded on a recognised investment exchange; see *Listing Rules*, paragraph 6.C.21.

9   *Re Rotherham Alum and Chemical Co* (1883) 25 Ch D 103 (CA). Moreover the directors may not rely on such a clause authorising payment unless they have made proper enquiry: *Re Englefield Colliery Co* (1878) 8 Ch D 388.

10   *Re English & Colonial Produce Co* [1906] 2 Ch 435 (CA).

formed is not binding upon it. This applies even to a claim for the preliminary expenses connected with the formation, such as registration fees.[1]

4.21 Underwriting commission

The function at one time performed by the traditional promoter is now carried out in the case of public companies by a city issuing house. The remuneration of such a body will take the form of an underwriting commission[2] and there are a number of statutory provisions governing such commission. Section 97 of the Companies Act 1985 allows an underwriting commission of up to 10% of the price at which the shares were issued to be paid if this is authorised by the company's articles and the commission paid or agreed to be paid does not exceed 10% of the price at which the shares are issued or the amount or rate authorised by the articles,[3] whichever is the less. Section 98(4) allows vendors or promoters the power to apply part of the money or shares received from the company in the payment of an underwriting commission which would have been lawful under section 97 if paid directly by the company.

Section 98 prohibits a company, save as authorised by section 97(1), from applying any of its shares or capital money either directly or indirectly in payment of commission; this applies to private as well as public companies.[4] However, there is no prohibition against paying commission unconditionally *out of profits* and this would seem to be lawful unless contrary to any stipulation in the articles.[5] Section 98 is very wide in its language, subsection (2) extending the prohibition in the following way: 'whether the shares or money be so applied by being added to the purchase money of any property acquired by the company or to the contract price of any work to be executed for the company, or the money be paid out of the nominal purchase money or contract price, or otherwise'. Further, the court will look at the substance of the transaction, and will prohibit a pretended purchase and resale which is in fact only a device to cover payment of a commission.[6] However, an agreement giving underwriters an option to subscribe for further shares as consideration for underwriting is not an application of shares in payment of commission within the section and is lawful.[7] The Company Law Review proposes to retain the substance of sections 97 and 98 for public companies, but abolish them as far as private companies are concerned.[8]

Commission paid in respect of shares[9] must be disclosed in the annual return filed with the Registrar,[10] and companies whose shares are traded on a recognised investment exchange must disclose details in their listing particulars.[11]

---

1   *Re National Motor Mail Coach Co* [1908] 2 Ch 515 (CA).
2   As to the standard terms of underwriting contracts, see *Gore-Browne on Companies* 44th edn (Jordans, loose-leaf) at 8.4.2.
3   If the articles allow a commission at a specified rate. This is not satisfied by a commission consisting of a lump sum: *Booth v New Afrikander Gold Mining Co* [1903] 1 Ch 295 (CA).
4   *Dominion of Canada General Trading & Investment Syndicate v Brigstocke* [1911] 2 KB 648.
5   In addition, the share premium account (see **7.15**) can be applied to paying commission.
6   *Booth v New Afrikander Gold Mining Co* [1903] 1 Ch 295 (CA).
7   *Hilder v Dexter* [1902] AC 474 (HL).
8   *Modern Company Law for a Competitive Economy, Company Formation and Capital Maintenance,* October 1999.
9   And debentures.
10   See Chapter 12.
11   *Listing Rules*, paragraph 6.B.15.

What is now section 36C of the Companies Act 1985[1] made a change in the law as regards the liability of those who purport to act on behalf of the company before it is incorporated. It provides as follows:

> A contract which purports to be made by or on behalf of a company at a time when the company has not been formed has effect, subject to any agreement to the contrary, as one made with the person purporting to act for the company or as agent for it, and he is personally liable on the contract accordingly.[2]

This provision does not change the position of the company once it is formed. It is not bound by such contracts and cannot ratify them.

The purpose of section 36C would appear to be to remove the subtle distinction between _Kelner v Baxter_ and _Newborne v Sensolid (GB) Ltd_. Its effect is that even if the defendant did not contract as agent _or_ assume personal liability but (as in _Newborne_) his signature is appended to that of the company's name to authenticate it, he will nevertheless be personally liable. Here there will be a contract which 'purports to be made by the company' which 'has effect as a contract entered into by the person purporting to act for the company'. This interpretation was adopted by the Court of Appeal in _Phonogram Ltd v Lane_,[3] where it was held that 'purports' does not require that there should be a representation that the company is already in existence. The court also held that the section is not confined to the case where the company is already in the course of formation. In this case, no steps had been taken to do so.[4]

It should be noted that where liability is imposed by section 36C, it is not based on breach of warranty of authority but on the personal liability 'on the contract'. This will be so even where the contract has been made 'by a person as agent for a company'. Although this is not made explicit, the Court of Appeal[5] has clarified the issue and held that the agent is made 'personally liable on the contract' and consequently has a right to enforce it. This construction was based not on the Directive (whose text would not require this) but on the application of common law principles to give meaning to what Parliament has decreed by employing the words 'personally liable on the contract'.[6] This means that in some situations the 'agent' would not succeed (eg if there had been a misrepresentation, or if the identity of the unformed company as, say, an employer, were significant to the

---

1   Section 36C was derived initially, as section 36(4), from section 9(2) of the European Communities Act 1972 implementing a provision of the EC First Directive on Company Law. The current version was inserted by the Companies Act 1989, with some improved wording, to extend its coverage to deeds. See further, Green, 'Security of transactions after Phonogram v Lane' (1984) 47 MLR 671. The Court of Appeal has held that in section 9(1) and (2) of the 1972 Act, 'company' meant registered company and not a foreign corporation created by its own special statute: _Janred Properties v Ente Nazionale Italiane per il Turismo_ (1983) 14 July (unreported). See also _Rover International Ltd v Cannon Film Sales Ltd_ [1987] BCLC 540 in respect of section 36(4).

2   By section 36C(2), the section applies to the making of a deed (obligation in Scotland) as it applies to the making of a contract.

3   [1981] 3 WLR 746.

4   The Court of Appeal rejected an argument which rested on the French text of the First EEC Directive on Company law. The court observed that under Article 189 (now Art 249) of the EC Treaty a directive is binding insofar as its spirit and intent are concerned. Section 36C satisfied this requirement, and its plain meaning should be applied even if it went further than the scope of the directive.

5   _Braymist Ltd v Wise Financing Co Ltd_ [2002] EWCA Civ 127, [2002] 1 BCLC 415.

6   See Arden LJ [2002] 1 BCLC at 425–429.

third party). Thus the general right to enforce the contract under s 36C(1) cannot be allowed to prejudice the third party.[1] Where he is a promoter, he might in some circumstances have to account to the company for the fruits of the contract.[2]

The qualifying proviso to section 36C – 'subject to any agreement to the contrary' – appears to require, for the application of the section to be excluded, that there should be an express term to that effect in the contract, whether oral or written.[3]

The courts have imposed sensible limits on the protection afforded by section 36C. So, it has been held that it did not apply to save a contract in the name of a company which had not existed for five years by the registration of a new company, because there was no intention to form the new company when the contract was made.[4] It does not apply to a company awaiting a new certificate of incorporation on a change of name,[5] since that is not a company that 'has not been formed'.[6] Similarly, there is no basis for applying the section to a contract made by a company which has been formed but which is not accurately named.[7]

4.24   Oversea companies

It is appropriate to conclude this chapter with a brief examination of the law concerning companies which are not registered in Great Britain.[8] The law has long recognised the existence of companies incorporated abroad and as regards those which set up business in some way in Britain, imposes a number of formal requirements.

Part XXIII of the Companies Act 1985 applies to such oversea companies. Following amendments introduced pursuant to the Eleventh EC Directive,[9] the provisions now distinguish between companies which have established a place of business in Great Britain,[10] and those which have a 'branch' in Great Britain.[11] Curiously, neither the directive nor the regulations define the term 'branch', and it is probably proper to refer to relevant decisions of the European Court of

---

1   See Arden LJ ibid at 428–431, and Judge LJ at 434–435.
2   See **4.19**.
3   See *Phonogram Ltd v Lane*, above. See Green (1984) 47 MLR 671 at pp 677–82 as to the effect of the parol evidence rule where an oral 'agreement to the contrary' relates to a written contract.
4   *Cotronic (UK) Ltd v Dezonie, t/a Wendaland Builders Ltd* [1991] BCC 200 (CA).
5   See **4.6**.
6   *Oshkosh B'Gosh v Dan Marbel Inc* [1989] BCLC 507 (CA).
7   *Badgerhill Properties Ltd v Cottrell* [1991] BCLC 805 (CA).
8   For detail on this and on how the Companies Act applies to unregistered companies and certain other associations, see *Gore-Browne on Companies* 44th edn (Jordans, loose-leaf) Chapter 47. Of course, a British-registered subsidiary of a foreign company is not an oversea company. The Company Law Review proposes to simplify considerably the law governing oversea companies: see *Modern Company Law for a Competitive Economy, Reforming the Law Concerning Oversea Companies,* October 1999.
9   89/666/EC, introduced by the Oversea Companies and Credit and Financial Institutions (Branch Disclosure) Regulations 1992, SI 1992/3179.
10   'Place of business' includes a share transfer or share registration office (section 744); otherwise it requires some degree of permanence or recognisability in addition to the setting up of a place of business at a specific location: see especially *Re Oriel Ltd* [1989] BCLC 444 (CA).
11   Companies registered in Northern Ireland or Gibraltar can register only under the old place of business regime.

Justice.[1] From these it seems that the concept of a branch implies the actual transaction of business to a greater extent than that of a place of business. So if the oversea company can enter into contracts, etc through its office in Great Britain, it will be subject to the branch registration regime.[2]

The traditional place of business regime requires the delivery to the Registrar, within one month of establishment, of: a certified copy of the charter, statutes or memorandum and articles or other instrument constituting or defining the constitution of the company; and a return including details of the company's directors and secretary, the names and addresses of one or more persons resident in Great Britain authorised to accept, on the company's behalf, service of process and any notices required to be served on it and a statutory declaration stating the date on which the place of business was established.[3] Alterations to the appropriate details must also be filed. The Secretary of State can control the name used by an oversea company[4] in a similar way to the controls over the names of British registered companies,[5] and the name, country of incorporation and whether the liability of the members is limited must be disclosed at the place of business and on all billheads and letters.[6] Audited accounts must be filed,[7] and charges over British property registered. Companies registered in the Channel Islands or the Isle of Man must in addition file an annual return.[8]

The branch registration regime differs only relatively slightly.[9] There is a similar registration requirement within one month with the same basic details required, and the provisions regarding names, etc apply to all oversea companies. One change relates to the registration of reports and accounts, so that, *inter alia*, accounts which are prepared, audited and disclosed according to the law of the country of incorporation can be filed in Great Britain, but if accounts are not required in that country, accounts meeting the requirements of the 1985 Act must be filed. In addition, letters, etc of branches must disclose the place of registration and registered number of the branch, and branches of companies from outside the EC have to disclose further detail.[10]

---

1   Mentioned in *Gore-Browne on Companies* 44th edn (Jordans, loose-leaf) at 42.8.4, especially
      Etablissements Somafar SA v Saar-Ferngas AG [1979] 1 CMLR 490.
2   In general, it may be that only Northern Irish and Gibraltarian companies (see footnote 11 at
      p 91) will in practice still be subject to the old regime.
3   Section 691.
4   Section 694.
5   See **4.2**.
6   Section 693.
7   Section 700.
8   Section 699.
9   Although the Registrar has had to establish a new register of branches. The detail regarding
      the branch regime is contained in sections 690A, 690B and 92A and Schedule 21A.
10   Section 693(3) and (4).

Chapter 5

The Memorandum and Articles of Association

5.1 The memorandum of association

The constitution of every registered company is embodied in its memorandum of association and articles of association. The memorandum of association is the more fundamental of the two documents.[1] In it the basic characteristics of the company's particular corporate personality are identified. Section 2 of the Companies Act 1985 requires the memorandum of every company to state its name, the situation of the registered office (ie whether in England and Wales or in Scotland) and its objects. A company limited either by share capital or by guarantee must have further clauses stating: (a) that the liability of its members is limited; and (b) the amount of the share capital or guarantee. Where a company is registered as a public limited company (plc), this must be stated in the memorandum, and the words 'public limited company' (or the abbreviation 'plc') must come at the end of its name.[2] The first part of this chapter examines the law concerning each one of these essential 'clauses' in the memorandum with the exception of the 'objects clause'. This clause is so important in defining the limits of the authority of the directors, officers and other agents to act on the company's behalf that it is treated separately in the next chapter. Other matters may also be included in the memorandum, at the option of those forming the company. The legal effect of such provisions is also considered in this chapter. In the case of each type of clause the extent to which, if at all, it may be altered after the company is formed will be examined. The question of the subscription of the memorandum has been considered at **4.3**.

The statutory requirements relating to the formation of companies, including the form and content of the constitutional documents, were considered by the Company Law Review and largely accepted by the Government. The reform proposals are considered at **5.31**.

5.2 Initial registration of a company name

Those forming a company can choose any name for the company provided it does not infringe certain prohibitions which are set out in section 26 of the Companies Act 1985. The principal prohibition is that the chosen name must not be the same as a name which already appears on the Registrar's index of company and corporate names.[3] The founders of a new company should search the index of names to ensure that the name they have chosen has not already been registered.[4] It is possible to search against the names of companies on the website of

---

1   The articles of association, and the contract of association formed by both the memorandum and the articles, are discussed at **5.16** to **5.23**.
2   Companies Act 1985, sections 1(3) and 25(1).
3   Section 26(1)(c). The index is maintained in accordance with section 714.
4   Section 709 authorises inspection of any records kept by the Registrar for the purposes of the Companies Acts.

Companies House. There is nothing to stop a new company being registered with a name that is very similar to one that is already registered but, under section 28, a company can be required within 12 months of registration of a name[1] to change its name if, in the opinion of the Secretary of State, it is too like a name which appeared in the Registrar's index of company names at the time of registration of the new company, or which should have appeared in the index at that time.[2] It could prove to be an expensive and time-consuming exercise to change all of the accounts, stationery and other materials in the event of the company being required to change its name and, ordinarily, this would deter the founders of a company from choosing a name that is very like a name that is already registered.[3]

There are also prohibitions on the registration of a company with a name whose use would constitute a criminal offence or which is offensive.[4] Except with the approval of the Secretary of State, a company cannot be registered with a name which would be likely to give the impression that it is connected in any way with HM Government or with any local authority.[5]

Section 32 gives the Secretary of State a power to direct a change of name by which a company is registered if he is of the opinion that the name gives so misleading an indication of the nature of the company's activities as to be likely to cause harm to the public. The company has the right to apply to the court to set the Secretary of State's direction aside.[6] The court must consider the matter afresh on the matter brought before it and its role is to consider the evidence from both sides and then to form a view on whether the name offends under section 32 or not.[7]

5.3 'Limited'

Section 25(2) of the Companies Act 1985 also requires that, in the case of a private company limited by shares or by guarantee, 'limited' must form the last word of its name as stated in the memorandum. Such companies may also use the abbreviation 'Ltd' or the Welsh equivalent. The name of a public company must

---

1   If misleading information has been given for the purposes of registration with a particular name or undertakings or assurances have not been fulfilled, the Secretary of State can require a name change within five years of initial registration: section 28(3).

2   Under section 26(3) certain matters are disregarded in determining whether names are too similar: section 28(2). Note also the prohibition in sections 216 and 217 of the Insolvency Act 1986 regarding names which are so similar to that of a company which has gone into liquidation as to suggest an association with that company discussed at **5.7**, below.

3   Those trading under a name that is like the name of another company would also risk incurring liability in tort for passing off.

4   Section 26(1)(d) and (e). In both cases, it is for the Secretary of State to decide whether the use of the particular name would be a criminal offence or would be offensive. The words or expressions 'Limited', 'Unlimited' or 'Public Limited Company', or abbreviations thereof, or Welsh equivalents, must not be included otherwise than at the end of a name: section 26(1) (a) and (b).

5   Section 26(2). The Secretary of State has the same power in respect of any words or expressions specified in regulations made under section 29 (see Company and Business Names Regulations 1981, as amended, SI 1981/1685 (these regulations remain in force despite consolidation of the Companies Acts)). Section 29 also makes provision for a procedure for obtaining the consent of government departments and other bodies for the use of a name which suggests that there is some connection: section 29(2).

6   As to the procedure, see section 32(2) and (3).

7   *Association of Certified Public Accountants of Britain v Secretary of State for Trade and Industry* [1997] BCC 736.

end with 'public limited company' (or plc) or the Welsh equivalent of either of these terms. In certain circumstances, companies limited by guarantee (and some other private companies) may be dispensed from the requirement to place 'limited' after their name.[1] Section 33 makes it an offence for a person who is not a public company to carry on any trade, profession or business under a name which includes, as its last part, the word 'public company'. Likewise, a public company is guilty of an offence, if in circumstances in which the fact that it is a public company is likely to be material to any person, it uses a name which may reasonably be expected to give the impression that it is a private company.[2]

5.4 'Business names'

In addition to the restrictions imposed by the Companies Act 1985, the Business Names Act 1985 regulates the use, control and disclosure of business names. This Act is relevant where a company has a place of business in Great Britain and carries on business in Great Britain under a name which is not its corporate name.[3] It contains provisions, which mirror those of the Companies Act, regarding the use of certain names such as those which are likely to give the impression of a connection with HM Government or with a local authority. The Act also requires disclosure of the corporate name in business letters and other documents, and at business premises.[4]

5.5 The display and use of the company's name

There are various requirements concerning the use and display of the corporate name. Every company must have its name printed or affixed, and kept painted or affixed, 'in letters easily legible' in a conspicuous position on the outside of every office or place in which it transacts business.[5] The company's name must also be mentioned 'in legible characters' on its seal if it has one[6] and must appear 'in all business letters of the company and in all notices and other official publications of the company, and in all bills of exchange, promissory notes, endorsements, cheques, and orders for money or goods[7] purporting to be signed by or on behalf of the company, and in all bills of parcels, invoices, receipts, and letters of credit of the company'.[8]

If an officer of the company, or a person on its behalf, signs or authorises to be signed on behalf of the company any bill of exchange, promissory note, endorsement, cheque or order for money or goods in which the company's name is not correctly stated in legible characters, by virtue of section 349(4), he is personally liable to the holder of any such bill of exchange, promissory note, cheque or order for money of goods for the amount in question unless this is duly

---

1 See **4.9.1**.
2 As to the sanctions imposed, see section 33(3). If the 'person' guilty of an offence is a company, any officer of the company who is in default is also liable.
3 The Act also applies to partnerships and sole traders.
4 See further *Gore-Browne on Companies* 44th edn (Jordans, loose-leaf) at 2.2.4–2.2.5.
5 Section 348. Penalties for default are specified in section 348(2) and Schedule 24.
6 Section 350.
7 This does not include services: *East Midlands Electricity Board v Grantham* (1980) 6 Current Law paragraph 35.
8 Section 349. In the event of default, the company and the responsible individuals are liable to a fine: section 349(2) and (3).

paid by the company.[1] In the case of an order for goods, the 'holder' to whom the person signing is made liable by this section is the person to whom the order is given.[2]

Personal liability under section 349(4) comes into existence on the date when a cheque (signed in breach of that section) is not duly paid. This liability cannot be affected thereafter in the way in which liability of a surety under a contract of guarantee might be affected under the law of principal and surety.[3] The fact that the company in question has been sued to judgment under dishonoured cheques is no bar to recovery under section 349(4) since the remedies are concurrent and not alternative.[4]

In the case of *Atkin v Wardle*,[5] it was decided that the directors of a company were personally liable for the amount of a bill of exchange accepted by them as directors of the company, because, although the word 'limited' appeared in the bill in one place, the name of the company was not correctly given in either the draft or the acceptance. Where a cheque was signed which omitted the ampersand in the company's name, it was held that the directors who had signed the cheque had not complied with what is now section 349 and were personally liable.[6] This decision was distinguished in a later case where one letter had been omitted from the spelling of the company's name: the omission of a letter in the middle of a word was not to be equated with the omission of a whole word and, therefore, the directors were not held personally liable.[7] The later decision is based on a less semantic approach than that which characterises some of the earlier authorities.

In another case, where a bill contained more than the correct name, the directors were held personally liable[8] but they escaped where the name of the company had been impressed with a rubber stamp and the word 'limited' had overlapped, and did not appear on the bill.[9] The use of the abbreviation 'Ltd' has been held not to render the statement of the name incorrect.[10]

It should be noted that the directors can be liable under section 349 even though the 'holder' was not misled by the misdescription.[11] However, the 'holder'

---

1   Section 349(4). In *Penrose v Martyr* (1858) EB&E 499, which was decided upon a similar worded clause in the Act of 1856, the secretary, who had accepted on behalf of the company a bill directed to the company in which the word 'limited' as part of its name was omitted, was held personally liable on the bill, the same not having been paid by the company.

2   *Civil Service Co-operative Society v Chapman* [1914] WN 369.

3   *British Airways Board v Parish* [1979] 2 Lloyd's Rep 361 (CA).

4   *Maxform SpA v Mariani and Goodville* [1979] 2 Lloyd's Rep 385, affirmed [1981] 2 Lloyd's Rep 54.

5   (1899) 58 LJ QB 377 and, on appeal 5 TLR 734. An example of misspelling is provided by *Durham Fancy Goods Ltd v Michael Jackson (Fancy Goods) Ltd* [1968] 2 QB 839 at p 846 where this case is mistakenly referred to as *Atkins v Wardle*.

6   *Hendon v Adelman* (1973) *The Times*, 16 June.

7   *Jenice Ltd v Dan* [1993] BCLC 1349, [1994] BCC 43.

8   *Nassau Steam Press v Tyler* (1894) 70 LT 376.

9   *Dermatine Co v Ashworth* (1905) 21 TLR 510.

10   *F Stacey & Co v Wallis* (1912) 106 LT 544. See also *Banque de L'Indochine v Euroseas Group Finance Co* [1981] 3 All ER 198.

11   *Scottish and Newcastle Breweries Ltd v Blair* 1967 SLT 72 at 74; *Lindholst & Co A/S v Fowler* [1988] BCLC 166. Cf *Jenice Ltd v Dan*, above.

may be estopped from suing under section 349 where he is responsible for the misdescription.[1]

5.6 Change of name of a company

A company can change its name by passing a special resolution to that effect.[2] As on initial incorporation, the new name must not be the same as a name which appears on the Registrar's index of names at the time of registration of the new name;[3] if, in the opinion of the Secretary of State, the new name is too like a name which was, or was entitled to be, registered earlier the company can be required to change its name again.[4] The other restrictions on the choice of name, discussed above, also apply.

When a company has resolved to change its name it must inform the Registrar of Companies. The Registrar will enter the new name in the register in place of the former name and issue 'a certificate of incorporation altered to meet the circumstances of the case': section 28(6). The change of names will take effect from this date: section 28(6).

A change of name does not affect the legal identity of the company. Thus section 28(7) provides that it will not affect any rights or obligations of the company or render defective any legal proceedings by or against the company. Any legal proceedings that might have been continued or commenced against the company by its former name may be continued or commenced against it by its new name.[5]

A company which is in the process of changing its name and which is awaiting a certificate of incorporation with its new name is *not* a company that has not been formed. Accordingly, there can be no question of the contracts which it enters into at that time being 'pre-incorporation' contracts for which those who act on its behalf could incur personal liability under section 36C of the Companies Act 1985.[6]

5.7 'Phoenix companies'

The Insolvency Act 1986 attempts to stamp out the notorious practice of incorporating 'phoenix companies'. A phoenix company is one which is formed with a name which is the same as, or very similar to, the name of a company which has recently gone into liquidation. The reason for choosing the same, or a very similar, name is usually to try to hide the fact that the earlier company has gone into liquidation from its creditors and thus ensure that the new company can

1   *Durham Fancy Goods Ltd v Michael Jackson (Fancy Goods) Ltd* 1968] 2 QB 839; cf *Blum v OCP Repartition SA* [1988] BCLC 170, (1988) 4 BCC 771 and *Rafsanjan Pistachio Producers Cooperative v Reiss* [1990] BCLC 352, [1990] BCC 730.
2   Section 28(1).
3   Or which ought to have appeared in that index at the time of the registration under the new name: section 28(2)(b).
4   Section 28(2).
5   Cf *Lin Pac Containers (Scotland) Ltd v Kelly* 1983 SLT 422.
6   *Oshkosh B'Gosh Incorporated v Dan Marbel Incorporated Ltd* [1989] BCLC 507, (1988) 4 BCC 795, [1989] 1 CMLR 94. The directors could incur personal liability under section 349(4) if they use the new name before the process of changing the name is complete because the company would have been misdescribed: *Allied Irish Bank plc v GFT Sales and Service Ltd* 1993 GWD 28 1789.

continue to enjoy the goodwill of the old business.[1] Under section 216 of the Insolvency Act 1986, the directors[2] of a company which has gone into insolvent liquidation are prohibited[3] for a period of five years from being involved in another company which has the same name as one by which the old company was known[4] at any time in the period of 12 months preceding its liquidation or a name which is so similar as to suggest some association with the old company. Contravention of this prohibition attracts civil and criminal penalties.[5]

Under section 216(3), the court may authorise the continued use of a prohibited name. In considering applications under this provision, the court should have regard only to the purposes for which section 216 was enacted, namely, the danger that the business of the old company has been acquired at an undervalue to the detriment of its creditors and that those creditors may be misled into the belief that there has been no change in the corporate vehicle.[6]

5.8 The registered office

Section 2(1)(b) of the Companies Act 1985 requires the memorandum of every company to state 'whether the registered office of the company is to be situated in England and Wales, or in Scotland'.[7] The registered office of a company is the office to which all communications and notices may be addressed,[8] and any writ, notice, summons or order is well served if left at, or sent by post[9] to the registered office.[10] Service at other places where the company carries on business is not sufficient.[11]

The precise location of the registered office is not stated in the memorandum but this address must be notified to the Registrar of Companies as part of the process of incorporation.[12] The clause of the memorandum stating the jurisdic-

---

1   But section 216 is not limited in its application to this particular form of abuse: *Thorne v Silverleaf* [1994] BCC 109 and *Ricketts v Ad Valorem Factors Ltd* [2003] EWCA Civ 1706, [2004] 1 BCLC 1.
2   That is the persons who were directors at the time of liquidation or at any time in the preceding 12 months. Shadow directors are also caught: section 216(1).
3   Except with the leave of the court or as permitted by the Insolvency Rules 1986 (rules 4.228–4.230): section 216(3).
4   This includes business names as well as corporate names: section 216(6).
5   Section 216(4) and section 217. See *Thorne v Silverleaf*, above. The offence under section 216 is a strict liability offence: *R v Cole, Lees & Birch* [1998] BCC 87.
6   *Penrose v Official Receiver* [1996] 1 BCLC 389.
7   Special provision is made for companies whose registered office is in Wales to state this fact in their memorandum: section 2(2). On companies with a registered office in Wales see *Gore-Browne on Companies* 44th edn (Jordans, loose-leaf) at 2.3.2.
8   Section 287(1).
9   Section 725(1).
10   *Pearks, Gunston & Tee v Richardson* [1902] 1 KB 91. See further as to the service of writs at the registered office *Gore-Browne* 44th edn (Jordans, loose-leaf) at 2.3.1.
11   *Re British and Foreign Gas Generating Apparatus Co* (1865) 12 LT 368; *Re Fortune Copper Mining Co* (1871) 10 Eq 390. This is subject to section 42 (official notification) and section 287(4) (service at previous registered office).
12   Section 10(6).

tion in which the registered office is situated cannot ordinarily[1] be changed but, subject to that limit, a company can change the precise location of its registered office by giving notice to the Registrar of Companies.[2] As a measure to ensure that any change in the precise location of a company's registered office is brought to the attention of the wider public, the Registrar must give official notification of the change in the *London Gazette*.[3]

Section 351 of the Companies Act 1985 requires the place of registration (ie England or Scotland), the registration number and the address of its registered office to be mentioned in legible characters in all business letters and order forms of the company.

5.9 The objects of the company

This clause in the memorandum is dealt with separately in Chapter 6.

5.10 The liability of the members

In the cases of companies limited by shares or by guarantee, with or without share capital, the fourth clause of the memorandum must simply state that 'The liability of the members is limited'. Those are the words contained in the forms given in the regulations made under the Companies Act 1985[4] and they should not be departed from. It is wrong to insert 'The liability of the *company* is limited' because the company itself will be liable without limit for its debts and obligations.

The most usual course is to frame the memorandum of association so as to limit the liability of each member or shareholder to the amount of the shares held by him. This means that at no time can he be called upon to pay, either for the purpose of carrying on the company's business or of satisfying the claims of its creditors, a larger sum than remains unpaid on the shares which at the time of the call, or within a year before the commencement of the winding up of the company, were registered in his name. For example, if a member holds 50 shares of £1 each, his utmost liability is £50 plus, if the shares were issued at a premium, the amount of that premium. When he has paid a part, the balance only can be recovered from him. No alteration of the memorandum or articles of association after he becomes a member can bind him either to take up more shares than he held at the date when the alteration was made, or in any way increase his liability as at that date to contribute to the share capital of, or otherwise to pay money to, the company, unless he agrees in writing, either before or after the alteration is made, to be bound thereby.[5] Should he transfer his shares before the full amount is called up, his unsatisfied liability passes to the person who acquires them; but a

---

1   Except that a company with a registered office in Wales can alter its memorandum to state
     that its registered office is situated in Wales rather than 'England and Wales': section 2(2).
     Otherwise the Companies Act 1985 does not authorise amendments to this clause of the
     memorandum. A company could seek to obtain a private Act of Parliament for this purpose
     but the more practical alternative may be to form a subsidiary in the desired jurisdiction and
     to transfer the business of the company to it.
2   Section 287(3). The change takes effect when registered by the Registrar but for a period of
     14 days thereafter a person may validly serve a document on a company at its previous
     registered office: section 287(4).
3   Section 711. The consequences of official notification are discussed further at **4.14**.
4   See the Companies (Tables A to F) Regulations 1985, SI 1985/805, Tables B to D.
5   Section 16.

contingent liability still attaches to a former holder to the limited extent that, if the company should go into liquidation within one year from the time of his parting with his shares, he may be called upon to contribute towards the payment of any debts contracted before he ceased to be a member, in the event of the company being unable to meet its liabilities in full, and the person who has acquired his shares failing to pay the balance owing on them.

Under the provisions of sections 306 and 307 of the 1985 Act, the directors or managers may take upon themselves an unlimited liability, although the liability of the other members is limited, this being similar to the distinction between general and limited partners under the Limited Partnerships Act 1907. Since the protection of limited liability is the main reason for registering a limited company, it is almost unknown for resort to be had to these provisions.

The second way of limiting the liability of members is by so framing the memorandum of association as to make each member guarantee a certain sum, which he can only be called upon to pay in the event of the company being wound up, and which will remain the same whatever his pecuniary interest in the company may be.[1]

5.11 The nominal capital

In the case of companies limited by shares the capital must[2] be divided into shares of a certain fixed amount, and a statement to that effect included in the memorandum: eg 'The share capital of the company is ten thousand pounds, divided into ten thousand shares of one pound each'.[3]

In the case of a company registered as a public limited company, the share capital clause must state a minimum share capital complying with that required for a public limited company (ie £50,000).[4]

A company limited by shares or by guarantee and having a share capital, if so authorised by its articles, may increase its nominal share capital by new shares of such amount as it thinks fit or may diminish the nominal share capital by cancelling shares which have not been taken up.[5]

5.12 Optional conditions in the memorandum

A matter which might be provided for in the articles of association can instead be inserted in the memorandum. This is not wholly unusual in regard to the special class rights attaching to preferred shares. It is possible in this way to entrench such rights more strongly than if they were contained in the articles. The general question of class rights and their variation is examined later in Chapter 8. Here the restricted power to alter such provisions in the memorandum is considered.

---

1 See **4.9**. As to unlimited companies, see **4.8**.
2 Section 2(5)(a).
3 The share capital can comprise shares of fixed amounts expressed in varying currencies (but each individual share must be expressed in one currency only): *Re Scandinavian Bank Group Plc* [1988] Ch 87.
4 Section 118; see **4.2**.
5 Section 121(2)(a) and (c). Cancellation of shares which have not been taken up is not a reduction of capital within the meaning of section 135.

5.13 Alteration of optional conditions in the memorandum

Section 2(7) of the Companies Act 1985 prohibits the alteration, except in accordance with the Act, of the conditions contained in a company's memorandum. This prohibition is partly relaxed by section 17 which provides that any such condition which could lawfully have been contained in the articles instead of in the memorandum may be altered by special resolution. This is not to apply where the memorandum itself provides for or prohibits the alteration of such conditions. Nor does it authorise any variation or abrogation of class rights, which accordingly, if contained in the memorandum and not thereby made alterable,[1] will require either the unanimous consent of all the members of the company[2] or a scheme of arrangement under section 425 to effect a variation.[3]

The power given by section 17 is, moreover, subject to any restriction on the alteration of the memorandum existing by virtue of an order of the court under Part XVII of the 1985 Act;[4] nor will an alteration made under section 17 imposing a monetary liability on existing members bind them without their consent.[5]

Apart from provisions declaring the rights attached to different classes of shares, the memorandum rarely provides for matters which can be dealt with in the articles. Accordingly, it would seem that section 17 will have only a limited application as, for example, in such cases as *Re Society for Promoting Employment of Women*,[6] where the memorandum contained a clause restricting the application of income of the society, and it was held that the court had no jurisdiction to sanction an alteration of the provision, not being a provision with respect to the objects of the society.

When an alteration is made under the section, the shareholders (but not debenture holders) have the same rights to apply to the court to cancel the variation as they have under section 5 in the case of an alteration of objects.[7]

5.14 Requirements as to the alteration of memorandum or articles

Section 711 of the Companies Act 1985 requires various documents there described to be published by the Registrar in the *Gazette*. Section 711(1)(b) includes among this category a 'document making or evidencing an alteration in the memorandum or articles of association of a company'. The Registrar is required to state in the *Gazette* notice the name of the company, the description of the document and the date of receipt.

---

1   Where the memorandum does contain a provision for the alteration of class rights, the
     procedure stated must be followed. In certain cases, the requirements of section 125 must be
     met. See **8.7.3**.
2   Section 125(5).
3   Cf *Re RAC Motoring Services Ltd* [2000] 1 BCLC 307. See also Chapter 18.
4   This gives the court power to give relief to minority shareholders. See **17.13**.
5   See section 16.
6   [1927] WN 145.
7   The section 5 procedure for objecting to an alteration to the objects is examined at **6.15**.
     Section 17(3) states that section 5 (except subsections (2)(b) and (8)) and section 6(1) and
     (3) apply in relation to any alteration and to any application under section 17 as they apply to
     applications made under sections 4 to 6 of the 1985 Act.

A company which does not furnish the Registrar with such information is put under a disability. Section 42(1) provides that a company shall not be entitled to rely against other persons on the happening of certain 'events' – which include the alteration of the memorandum or articles of association – if the 'event' had not been officially notified (ie in the *Gazette*) at the material time.

Section 42(1) then goes on to provide, as a qualification to the requirement of official notification, 'and is not shown by the company to have been known at the time to the person concerned'. Since the section is there not for the protection of the company but of outsiders dealing with the company, an outsider who is shown to have actual knowledge of the relevant event cannot insist that the company may not rely on the event because it failed to '*Gazette*' it.[1] Furthermore, it has been held by the Court of Appeal[2] that official notification of an event in the *Gazette* (as required by section 42(1)) does not give constructive notice of the event in question to third parties. Its effect is merely to prevent the company relying on such an event which has not been duly '*Gazetted*'.

The term 'other person' in section 42(1) would appear to bear the same meaning as 'a person dealing with the company' in section 35A.[3]

Section 42(1) further provides that a company will not be entitled to rely on an event 'if the material time fell on or before the fifteenth day after the date of official notification (or where the fifteenth day was a non-business day,[4] on or before the next day that was not) and it was shown that the person concerned was unavoidably prevented from knowing of the event at that time'.

5.15 Filing of amendments to the memorandum and articles

Section 18 makes provision for the forwarding to the Registrar of a printed copy of any Act or instrument which varies a company's memorandum or articles together with a printed copy of the memorandum or articles as altered. Members of a company have a right to request copies of the memorandum and articles (if any) on payment of a fee.[5]

5.16 The contents of the articles of association

The articles of association govern the internal affairs of the company, and may from time to time be altered by the members to an almost unlimited extent.

The articles of association regulate a great range of matters affecting almost every aspect of company law as it applies to each individual company. Such internal regulations are of course subject to the requirements of the Companies Acts and the general principles of company law laid down by the courts. The

---

1   See Article 3(5) of the First Company Law Directive (see **2.3.1**) and *Official Custodian for Charities v Parway Estates Developments* [1985] Ch 151.
2   *Official Custodian for Charities v Parway Estates*, above.
3   See the discussion of the latter term at **6.21**. In appropriate circumstances, this might include the shareholders: *EIC Services Ltd v Phipps* [2003] EWHC 1507 [2003] 3 All ER 804.
4   Defined by section 42(2)(b).
5   Section 19. This right extends to any Act of Parliament amending the memorandum.

following[1] are some of the important matters which are commonly governed by the articles: voting rights and proxies,[2] the status and the powers of management of the board of directors,[3] shareholders'[4] and directors' meetings,[5] the payment of dividends,[6] the capitalisation of profits,[7] the transfer and transmission of shares,[8] the alteration of capital.[9] Detailed provisions in the articles are discussed in their proper context in later chapters, in terms of the relevant articles of Table A. The purpose of this chapter is to examine certain more general questions about the articles of association. These are:

(1) the status of the articles as a contract of membership as defined by section 14;
(2) the drafting of articles of association and the adoption of Table A; and
(3) the power to alter the articles under section 9 and the equitable doctrine whereby the court may restrain the exercise of this power.

5.17   The articles as a contract: section 14

Section 14(1) of the Companies Act 1985 provides that the memorandum and articles of association when registered bind the company and its members to the same extent as if each member had signed and sealed them and they contained a covenant by him to observe all the provisions contained in them. The effect of this[10] is to create an obligation binding alike on the members in their dealings with the company,[11] on the company in its dealings with the members as members,[12] and on the members in their dealings with one another as members.[13] Thus where the articles impose a duty on shareholders to purchase the shares of a member who wishes to dispose of them, such as individual right of membership can be directly enforced against the other shareholders without making the company a party.[14] It is not clear how far the rule in *Foss v Harbottle*[15] permits a minority shareholder to enforce any provision in the articles, as part of his contract of membership, where no individual right of membership is concerned.[16] A member may seek to challenge a failure to comply with the articles under Part XVII of the 1985 Act on the grounds that this failure amounts to unfairly prejudicial conduct.

---

1   As to companies registered before 1 July 1985, see Table A in Schedule 1 to the 1948 Act (as amended). As to companies registered thereafter (under the 1985 Act), see the Companies (Tables A to F) Regulations 1985. References in this chapter to articles are to articles contained in the Companies (Tables A to F) Regulations 1985 unless otherwise indicated.
2   Articles 54–63.
3   Articles 64–87.
4   Articles 36–53.
5   Articles 88–98.
6   Articles 102–108.
7   Article 110.
8   Articles 23–31.
9   Articles 32–34.
10   For a full discussion of the earlier authorities, see *Hickman v Kent or Romney Marsh Sheep-Breeders' Association* [1915] 1 Ch 881.
11   *Bradford Banking Co v Henry Briggs & Co* (1886) 12 App Cas 29 (HL); *Wood v Odessa Waterworks Co* (1889) 42 Ch D 636; *Quin & Axtens v Salmon* [1909] AC 442 (HL); *Hickman v Kent or Romney Marsh Sheep-Breeders' Association*, above.
12   *Oakbank Oil Co v Crum* (1882) 8 App Cas 65 (HL).
13   *Eley v Positive Government Security Life Assurance* (1876) 1 Ex D 88 (CA).
14   *Rayfield v Hands* [1960] Ch 1.
15   (1843) 2 Hare 461.
16   This question is further considered at **17.3**.

However, trivial or technical infringements of the articles are not intended to give rise to petitions under this Part.[1]

Although section 14 uses the language of contract, the section 14 contract is of a special kind, as was noted by Steyn LJ in *Bratton Seymour Service Co Ltd v Oxborough*.[2] Distinctive features of the section 14 contract include the following:[3]

(1) it derives its binding force not from a bargain struck between the parties but from the terms of the statute;

(2) it is binding only insofar as it affects rights and obligations between the company and its members acting in their capacity as members;[4]

(3) it can be altered by special resolution without the consent of all of the contracting parties;[5]

(4) it is not defeasible on the grounds of misrepresentation, common law mistake, mistake in equity, undue influence or duress;

(5) it cannot be rectified on the grounds of mistake.[6]

In addition, the principles regarding the implication of terms are different, the courts taking a very restrictive attitude. In *Bratton Seymour*, the Court of Appeal refused to imply a term into articles on the grounds of business efficacy which would have had the effect of imposing on members an obligation to make a financial contribution to certain expenses incurred by the company. The Court of Appeal indicated that terms would not easily be implied into articles from extrinsic circumstances because of the special nature of the contract. Steyn LJ and Sir Christopher Slade emphasised the importance of third parties (in particular potential shareholders) being able to rely on the articles as registered.[7] In *Re Benfield Greig Group plc*,[8] in the context of a share transfer restriction in the articles requiring an independent valuation of the shares concerned, Arden J refused to imply a term giving both parties to the transaction the right to be treated equally because this was not a matter of necessity, irrespective of whether it was a matter of fairness or reasonableness.[9] However, in *Folkes Group plc v Alexander*,[10] Rimer J did add five words to a specific provision in the articles of a listed public company. The articles contained a definition of 'qualifying shares' for the purposes of calculating the shareholding of the Folkes family, which originally included a reference to 'any voting share which is for the time being beneficially owned by or held in trust for a member of the Folkes family. . .'. This was amended in 1999 to

1   *Re Saul D Harrison & Sons plc* [1994] BCC 475.
2   [1992] BCC 471, [1992] BCLC 693. See also *Shareholder Remedies* (Law Commission Consultation Paper No 142, 1996) paragraphs 2.6–2.14.
3   [1992] BCC at 475, [1992] BCLC at 698.
4   This feature is discussed further at **4.18**.
5   Discussed at **4.24**.
6   *Evans v Chapman* [1902] WN 78; *Scott v Frank F Scott (London) Ltd* [1940] 1 Ch 794.
7   See also *Mutual Life Insurance Co v The Rank Organisation* [1985] BCLC 11 where Goulding J refused to imply pre-emption rights into articles. Limited pre-emption rights are now provided by statute: see **7.5**. *Bratton Seymour* was followed in *Towcester Racecourse Co Ltd v The Racecourse Association Ltd* [2002] EWHC 214 (Ch), [2003] 1 BCLC 260.
8   [2000] 2 BCLC 488; decision reversed by the Court of Appeal on different grounds [2001] EWCA Civ 397, [2002] 1 BCLC 65.
9   It had been argued that the valuation requirement should be subject to Lord Hoffmann's observations in *O'Neil v Phillips* on the valuation of shares in the context of a section 459 petition (see [1999] 2 BCLC 1 at 17; [1999] 1 WLR 1092 at 1107) and that a term to that effect should be implied.
10   [2002] EWHC 51 (Ch), [2002] 2 BCLC 254.

read 'any voting share which is for the time being beneficially owned by a member of the Folkes Family Company or held in trust for a member of the Folkes family. . .'. This seemed to remove shares beneficially owned by the family from the definition, although it created a new category of qualifying shares based on membership of the Folkes Family Company, although there was no such company. The consequence of this was a reduction of the family's voting shares from 40% to 24%. Having concluded that 'an interpretation of [the article] according to the face value of the words is so absurd that something must have gone seriously wrong with its drafting',[1] Rimer J construed the article by supplying the words 'or by a Folkes Family', inserted before 'Company'. Although he regarded this still as an exercise of construction, Rimer J acknowledged that it was 'close to the limits of what is permissible'.[2] This is an unusual case where the court added words to a term primarily to correct what the evidence showed to be a drafting error.[3]

5.18　Outsiders' rights and the articles as a contract

In accordance with normal contractual principles, those who are not members cannot enforce the provisions of the articles either against the company or its members.[4] A special feature of the section 14 contract is that even a member cannot enforce provisions for his benefit in some other capacity than that of member: eg he cannot assert a right to be appointed solicitor, secretary, or director[5] by reason of provisions contained only in the articles.[6] So an article providing for the reference of disputes to arbitration may be enforceable by or against a member in his capacity as such, but not in some other capacity, eg that of director.[7] On the other hand, the shareholder is not bound in his personal capacity. 'The purpose of the memorandum and articles is to define the position of the shareholder as shareholder, not to bind him in his capacity as an individual.'[8]

The somewhat unclear wording of section 14 (and its predecessor, eg section 16 of the 1862 Act and section 20 of the 1948 Act) long gave rise to conflicting judicial interpretation. This stemmed in part from the fact that though the memorandum

---

1　Ibid, para [20].

2　Ibid, para [22].

3　See also *Stanham v NTA* (1989) 15 ACLR 87 at 90–91 to support the possibility of implying a term purely from the language of the document itself.

4　*Re Rotherham Alum and Chemical Co* (1883) 25 Ch D 103; *Melhado v Porto-Allegre Co* (1874) LR 9 CP 503; *Re Empress Engineering Co* (1881) 16 Ch D 125 (CA); *Re English and Colonial Produce Co* [1906] 2 Ch 435. These cases establish that a clause in the articles requiring the company to pay preliminary charges cannot be enforced unless some other contract has been made. Equally, a contract made with a trustee before the company is formed does not become enforceable merely because the articles purport to adopt the contract: *Re Northumberland Avenue Hotel Co* (1886) 33 Ch D 16 (CA).

5　*Eley v Positive Government Security Life Assurance Co*, above; *Browne v La Trinidad* (1888) 37 Ch D 1.

6　The Contracts (Rights of Third Parties) Act 1999, which allows a third party to enforce a term in a contract to which he is not party but which seeks to confer a benefit on him, expressly excludes the section 14 contract from its application: section 6(2) of the 1999 Act.

7　*Hickman v Kent or Romney Marsh Sheep-Breeders' Association* [1915] 1 Ch 881; *Beattie v E and F Beattie* [1938] Ch 708; *London Sack and Bag Co v Dixon* [1943] 2 All ER 763 (CA).

8　*Per* Buckley LJ, *Bisgood v Henderson's Transvaal Estates* [1908] 1 Ch 743 at 759 (CA). See also *Baring-Gould v Sharpington Combined Pick and Shovel Syndicate* [1899] 2 Ch 80 (CA).

and articles 'shall, when registered, bind the company and the members' this is based on a putative statutory signing and sealing by the members and not by the company. Likewise, the memorandum and articles are deemed to contain 'covenants on the part of each member' (but not the company) to observe their provisions.[1] Until the end of the nineteenth century the courts were divided as to the parties to this statutory contract of association (ie parties in the sense of having rights of action and liabilities thereunder). There were authorities both for and against there being a contract between the members *inter se*,[2] as well as both for and against section 14 creating a contract between the company and its members.[3]

As indicated above, the modern law was eventually settled that the section 14 contract confers rights between the company and its members and between the members *inter se*. However, the still conflicting reasoning in the cases (considered by Astbury J in *Hickman v Kent or Romney Marsh Sheep-Breeders' Association*[4]) induced his attempt to provide a perhaps novel reconciling principle with regard to the scope of the contractual effect of the articles.[5] This has received substantial criticism from some academic commentators.[6] It is argued that Astbury J's decision in *Hickman* conflicts with earlier decisions which do not recognise the principle which he attempted to elicit from them. Moreover, it is said that the *Hickman* principle appears to ignore the wording of (what is now) section 14(1) of the 1985 Companies Act, which creates a contractual obligation in respect of 'all the provisions of the memorandum and of the articles'. The view contended for by these commentators is that an 'outsider', so long as he sues in his capacity as shareholder, can compel the company not to depart from the contract with him under the articles. This is so even if that results indirectly in the enforcement of 'outsider' rights vested in third parties or in the plaintiff shareholder. The case-law, which remains in a state of some confusion, reveals that in some situations the courts have allowed a member, suing as such, to enforce a non-shareholder right conferred by the articles. This has been done to protect shareholder-directors whose rights to hold office, or to participate in management, or to exercise a veto over board decisions or to commence litigation, have

---

1   The explanation of this omission lies in the conveyancing background to this section. See 44 MLR 526 at pp 528–529. Under the Companies Act 1844, each shareholder executed an indenture with a trustee for the company. This incorporated or referred to the company's constitution. This requirement was dropped in the Companies Act 1856. The covenant was simply deemed to exist by the statute but no covenant with the company was expressed.

2   Cf *Eley v Positive Government Security Life Association Co* (1870) LR 1 Ex 88 at 89, with *Welton-Saffery* [1897] AC 299 at 315 *per* Lord Herschell.

3   Cf *Johnson v Lyttle's Iron Agency* (1877) 5 Ch D 687 at 693, with *Browne v La Trinidad* (1888) 37 Ch D 1 at 12 and 15.

4   Above.

5   The earlier cases were influenced by other grounds than the *Hickman* principle: eg the old view that members were not parties to the contract (*Baring-Gould v Sharpington Combined Pick and Shovel Syndicate* [1899] 2 Ch 80) or that the article in question was directory rather than mandatory (*Pritchard's Case* (1873) 8 Ch App 956 at 960), or that the plaintiff, as a matter of procedural form, sued not as a member but in some external capacity (eg as a solicitor or promoter): *Eley v Positive Government Security Life Association Co*, above. See (1981) 44 MLR 531–539.

6   See Gregory, 'The Section 20 Contract' (1981) 44 MLR 526. This amplifies views earlier expressed by Lord Wedderburn: [1957] CLJ 194 at pp 212–13.

been brushed aside in breach of a provision in the articles.[1] However, it is a long step from this to conclude that every shareholder has a right to have all and every one of the articles enforced by declaration or injunction.[2] To do so is to ignore not only the authorities on the *Hickman* principle (which, whatever its questionable provenance, has never been overruled and has been applied by the Court of Appeal).[3] It also overlooks the rule in *Foss v Harbottle*[4] and the related question of the majority shareholders' right to ratify some, but not all, breaches of the articles.[5] The Court of Appeal has, on more than one occasion, indicated that the members' contract of association cannot be used to 'short-circuit' the rule in *Foss v Harbottle*, especially in the case of shareholders' actions to remedy directors' breaches of fiduciary duty to the company.[6] This is clearly of more significance than the confusion of the courts in the late nineteenth century as to the parties to the statutory contract of association.[7] The point is reinforced by Steyn LJ's comments in *Bratton Seymour* which indicate that it is incorrect to attach too much importance to the 'contractual' nature of the relationship formed by section 14 between a company and its members (and between the members *inter se*) since the normal incidents of a contract do not necessarily apply.

The restrictions on a shareholder's ability to bring a personal action to enforce the provisions of the articles of association were considered by the Law Commission in the context of its wide-ranging review of shareholder remedies.[8] The Law Commission concluded that no hardship was being caused by potential difficulties in identifying enforceable personal rights conferred by the articles and accordingly, it declined to recommend reform of section 14. The question of reform of section 14 has also been raised by the Company Law Review Steering Group in its general review of company law. In consultation documents,[9] the Review questioned whether the articles should continue to be treated as a

---

1   *Imperial Hydropathic Hotel v Hamson* (1882) 23 Ch D 1, *Pulbrook v Richmond Consolidated Mining Co* (1878) 9 Ch D 610, *Quin and Axtens v Salmon* [1909] AC 442, *Hayes v Bristol Plant Hire* [1957] 1 All ER 685, *Breckland Group Holdings Ltd v London and Suffolk Properties Ltd* [1989] BCLC 100, noted Wedderburn (1989) 52 MLR 401. Attempts have been made by commentators to explain, on 'organic' or constitutional grounds, when the courts will allow 'non-shareholder rights' in the articles to be enforced. See Goldberg (1972) 35 MLR 362, Bastin [1977] JBL 17, Prentice (1980) 1 Co Law 179.

2   It is clear that (claims for arrears of dividend and the like aside) damages will not be awarded for breach of this very special contract. This alone may indicate its special character: a case perhaps of *ibi remedium, ubi jus*.

3   *Beattie v E and F Beattie Ltd* [1938] Ch 708 at 713–14. See also *London Sack and Bag Co Ltd v Dixon* [1943] 2 All ER 763.

4   (1843) 2 Hare 461.

5   See *Grant v UK Switchback Railways* (1889) 40 Ch D 135 (CA).

6   See *Bamford v Bamford* [1970] Ch 212. *Prudential Assurance v Newman Industries (No 2)* [1982] Ch 204. See a further discussion of these issues at **17.5** and **17.6**.

7   See further R R Drury, 'The Relative Nature of a Shareholder's Right to Enforce the Company Contract' [1986] CLJ 219. This is an interesting attempt to reconcile the cases on the basis that the courts weigh various factors in the balance in deciding whether to enforce the shareholder's 'relative right'. This is more satisfying than some earlier theories in coming to grips with the institutional reality produced by the shareholder's contract. It still remains open to the criticism levied at earlier theories that it is essentially an *ex post facto* rationalisation.

8   *Shareholder Remedies* (Law Commission Consulation Paper No 142, 1996) paragraphs 2.13–2.28 and *Shareholder Remedies* (Law Commission Report No 246, 1997) paragraph 7.4–7.11.

9   *Modern Company Law for a Competitive Economy: Company Formation and Capital Maintenance* (1999) and *Developing the Framework* (March 2000) paragraphs 4.72–4.99.

contract, although it decided not to recommend a specific change.[1] Nevertheless, the Review did recommend that in future, all duties imposed on the members by the constitution should be enforceable by individual shareholders, subject to specific disapplication of this right in relation to particular provisions.[2] The draft clauses in the White Paper, *Modernising Company Law*, do not contain a new version of section 14 nor any indication that an equivalent provision would apply to the proposed constitution (see **5.31**).

5.19　Contracts incorporating provisions in the articles

If individuals have been engaged in some capacity without an agreement setting out the terms of employment,[3] the articles may be looked at to see what these terms are. On this footing the directors may be sued for payment of their qualification shares or sue for the remuneration specified in the articles,[4] although it seems that a director cannot derive a prospective entitlement to remuneration from a contract inferred on this basis.[5] In any other case where a contract is established, but the terms are not specified, the articles may be referred to for the purpose of supplying the terms.[6]

5.20　The character of obligations in the memorandum or articles

All money payable in pursuance of the memorandum or articles becomes in England a 'specialty debt' from the members to the company,[7] so that the debt remains enforceable for 12 years before the Limitation Act 1980 affords a good defence to proceedings. It has been held that money payable from the company to the members in pursuance of the articles is not a specialty debt so that the relevant limitation period is that which applies to actions based on simple contract, namely six years.[8] It is doubtful, however, whether the practical benefit of the longer limitation period applying to specialty debts outweighs the burden of complexity that retention of this concept in section 14 entails.[9]

5.21　Drafting articles: examples of invalid provisions

The articles cannot vary rights given by the Companies Act, and must be rejected if inconsistent with the Act or the general law.

1　*Completing the Structure* (November 2000) paragraphs 5.68–5.69, where it was proposed that the desired result about the status of the constitution should be explained to the draftsman, leaving him to find the best way of expressing the result in the drafting.

2　*Completing the Structure* (November 2000) paragraph 5.73; *Final Report* (July 2001), paragraphs 7.34–7.40.

3　*Boston Deep Sea Fishing and Ice Co v Ansell* (1888) 39 Ch D 339 (CA).

4　*Re New British Iron Co, ex parte Beckwith* [1898] 1 Ch 324. On the relevance of the articles to directors' service contracts, see **15.4**.

5　*Re New British Iron Co, ex parte Beckwith* [1898] 1 Ch 324.

6　*Pritchard's Case* (1873) 8 Ch App 956; *Swabey v Port Darwin Co* (1889) 1 Meg 385 (CA); *Boston Deep Sea Fishing and Ice Co v Ansell* (1888) 39 Ch D 339 at 366 (CA).

7　Section 14(2).

8　*Re Compania de Electricidad de la Provincia de Buenos Aires Ltd* [1980] 1 Ch 146.

9　See *Modern Company Law for a Competitive Economy. Company Formation and Capital Maintenance* (Company Law Review Steering Group Consultation Document, 1999) paragraph 2.9, which proposes that debts owing to the company should cease to be specialty debts.

Articles cannot deprive a company of the powers which are conferred on it by statute: thus a provision in the articles which purports to make them unalterable is invalid because a company is empowered by section 9 of the Companies Act 1985 to alter its articles by special resolution.[1]

Articles cannot free a member from paying in full for his shares, or deprive members of their right to petition for the winding up of the company or to dissent in a reconstruction under what is now section 110 of the Insolvency Act 1986,[2] nor can they validly provide for the transfer of shares without a written instrument of transfer where one would otherwise be required by virtue of section 183.[3]

5.22 Drafting articles: adoption of Table A

Companies limited by guarantee, and unlimited companies,[4] must register articles of association with the memorandum; but a company limited by shares may either be registered with special articles of association, or may, without registering articles, rely upon the regulations in Table A. When special articles are not adopted, the memorandum must be endorsed 'registered without articles of association', and every member of the company will be bound by the regulations contained in Table A.[5]

A new Table A (prescribed by regulations of the Secretary of State[6]) came into operation with the Companies Act 1985 and, unless excluded, this applies to all companies (public and private) which register under that Act. The 1985 Act Table A will obviously apply to more and more companies as time goes by, but very many companies now in existence were registered under the Companies Act 1948 and 1980, and for those companies the applicable Table A (so far as it is not excluded) is the Table A contained in Schedule 1 to the Companies Act 1948 or, depending on the date of incorporation, the 1948 Act Table A as amended by subsequent companies legislation.[7] There are still of course a number of companies registered under the Companies Acts of 1862, 1908 and 1929 and in each case the relevant Table A is applicable.

---

1   *Walker v London Tramways Co* (1879) 12 Ch D 705; *Allen v Gold Reefs of West Africa* [1900] 1 Ch 656 at 671; *Southern Foundries (1926) Ltd v Shirlaw* [1940] AC 701 at 739; *Russell v Northern Bank Development Corporation* [1992] 3 All ER 294, [1992] 1 WLR 588, [1992] BCLC 1016, [1992] BCC 578. The power to alter articles and the extent to which (if it all) it can be fettered are discussed further at **5.24–5.25**.

2   *Welton v Saffery* [1897] AC 299 (HL): *Re Peveril Gold Mines* [1898] 1 Ch 122 (CA); *Payne v Cork Co* [1900] 1 Ch 308.

3   *Re Greene* [1949] Ch 333. Listed shares may now be transferred without the use of a written instrument; see **9.3.3**.

4   Unlimited companies registering under the Companies Act 1985 may adopt the form of articles contained in Table E of the Companies (Tables A to F) Regulations 1985, SI 1985/805. See section 8(4) of the Companies Act 1985. Likewise, a private company limited by guarantee and not having a share capital may adopt Table C and a company limited by guarantee and having a share capital may adopt Table D of those Regulations.

5   Section 8(2).

6   Section 8(1) and the Companies (Tables A to F) Regulations 1985, SI 1985/805. Having Table A in regulations rather than as a Schedule to primary legislation (as was previously the position) provides greater flexibility because it means that amendments can be made without the need for primary legislation.

7   Section 8(3) makes it clear that companies registered before the Companies Act 1985 came into operation continue to be governed by the articles which were in force at the time of registration.

Large companies almost always adopt their own special regulations in which case the articles begin with a provision to the effect that the relevant Table A is excluded. Where a company is adopting new articles and excluding Table A, the Table A to be excluded is that in force at the date of the company's registration. Other companies, instead of wholly excluding Table A, may adopt the suitable parts of that Table, with a few special articles containing the desired modifications. In such cases, the articles will commence with a provision to the effect that the regulations contained in the relevant Table A are to apply to the company, save in so far as they are excluded or varied. Table A, or such portions of it as are adopted, need not be registered.

The articles must be printed and divided into paragraphs numbered consecutively.[1] The original articles must be signed by each subscriber to the memorandum and attested by a witness.[2]

Every company is bound to supply any of its members, on request, with a copy of its memorandum and articles (if any), upon payment of a sum not exceeding 5p. Where alteration has been made in the memorandum every copy issued after the alteration must be in accordance with the alteration. There must also be supplied on request, at a charge not exceeding the published price thereof, a copy of any Act of Parliament which alters the memorandum.[3]

When Table A was contained in a Schedule to the Companies Act of the day, it clearly had statutory force and, accordingly, companies could safely adopt any operative regulations it contained without fear of such regulations proving invalid.[4] It may still be argued that the Table A to the Companies Act 1985 (though contained in a statutory instrument and no longer a Schedule to the Act itself) has statutory force by virtue of the wording of section 8.

5.23 Table G

The Companies Act 1989 inserted a provision into the Companies Act 1985 which empowers the Secretary of State to prescribe by regulations a Table G containing articles of association for a partnership company. A 'partnership company' is defined for this purpose as a company limited by shares whose shares are intended to be held to a substantial extent by or on behalf of its employees.[5] This provision has not been brought into effect, and as the White Paper (see **5.31**) does not mention it at all,[6] it now seems certain that it never will be.

5.24 Alteration of articles: section 9

Section 9 of the Companies Act 1985 provides that the articles of a company may, subject to the provisions of the Act and to the conditions in the memorandum, be altered by special resolution. The company can amend both its own tailor-made articles and the provisions of Table A which it has adopted. The fact that articles may be altered with the consent of three-quarters of those voting on the resolution

---

1   Section 7(3).
2   For the procedure on registration of memorandum and articles see **4.5**.
3   Sections 19 and 20.
4   *Lock v Queensland Investment and Mortgage Co* [1896] AC 461 (HL).
5   Section 8A of the Companies Act 1985, inserted by section 128 of the Companies Act 1989.
6   Draft clause 11 on the power to prescribe model constitutions makes no reference to partnership companies.

(ie the majority required for a special resolution[1]) and unanimity is not required is a further illustration of different nature of the statutory contract formed by the articles of association compared to a normal contract.[2] Where all of the members who would have been entitled to attend and vote at a meeting to consider a resolution to change the articles consent informally to an alteration, that is also effective[3] but altering the articles by unanimous consent is likely to be feasible only in the very smallest of companies. Exceptionally, a long period of acquiescence under particular articles may be held to be effective even though they have not been adopted as the articles of the company.[4] Articles may also be altered by statute.[5]

The company has power to adopt any new article which could lawfully have been included in the original articles.[6] However, it is clearly established that no majority of shareholders can by altering the articles retrospectively affect, to the prejudice of non-consenting owners of shares, rights already existing under a contract,[7] nor take away rights already accrued: for example, after a transfer of shares is lodged the company cannot create a right of lien so as to defeat the transfer.[8]

Requirements as to the procedure for effecting an alteration of the articles were introduced by the European Communities Act 1972 and are now contained in sections 18, 42 and 711 of the Companies Act 1985. These are the same as for alterations of provisions in the memorandum. They are discussed under this heading at **5.14–5.15**. The power to alter articles is subject to any class rights which may be attached to particular shares. Class rights are discussed in Chapter 8.

5.25 Agreements not to alter the articles and voting agreements

It is clear that a company cannot deprive itself of the power to alter its articles by a statement to that effect in its articles of association,[9] but can it agree not to alter (some of) the articles through a separate contract? In principle, there are three possible answers to the question whether, or to what extent, an extrinsic contract by a company not to alter its articles is valid, namely:

(1) such a contract is entirely ineffective;
(2) such a contract cannot prevent a company from exercising its statutory power to alter the articles but in that event the company will be in breach of contract and may be liable to pay damages to the other contracting party;

---

1   Section 378(2).
2   *Bratton Seymour v Oxborough*, above.
3   *Cane v Jones* [1981] 1 All ER 533, [1980] 1 WLR 1451.
4   *Ho Tung v Man On Incee Co* [1902] AC 232.
5   Section 18 of the Companies Act 1985.
6   *Sidebottom v Kershaw Leese & Co* [1920] 1 Ch 154.
7   *Per* Rigby LJ in *James v Buena Ventura Syndicate* [1896] 1 Ch 456 at 466; *per* Lord Watson in *Welton v Saffery*, above at 309; *per* Vaughan Williams LJ in *Allen v Gold Reefs of West Africa*, above at 676.
8   *McArthur v Gulf Line* 1909 SC 732.
9   *Walker v London Tramways Co*, above; *Allen v Gold Reefs of West Africa*, above; *Southern Foundries (1926) Ltd v Shirlaw*, above; *Russell v Northern Bank Development Corporation*, above.

(3) such a contract is effective and in a suitable case the company can be prevented by injunction from seeking to exercise the statutory power to alter its articles.

Which of these propositions is correct depends essentially on the extent to which the powers conferred by the Companies Act 1985 must be viewed as a mandatory code which cannot be modified, as opposed to a series of standard provisions which a company might ordinarily want to adopt but which it can depart from as it thinks fit. The issue was clarified by the House of Lords in *Russell v Northern Bank Development Corporation.*[1] This case concerned a contract by a company not to alter the nominal capital clause in its memorandum but the principles discussed are equally applicable to contracts not to alter the articles. The House of Lords ruling means that an extrinsic contract by a company not to alter its articles was as obnoxious as a provision to that effect contained in the articles themselves. It is entirely invalid and cannot be enforced even by way of damages.

Despite this unequivocal rejection of the freedom of the company to contract out of its statutory powers, the House of Lords upheld the right of individual shareholders to enter into contracts regarding the exercise of their votes.[2] This right is consistent with the well-established principle that a vote attached to a share is a property right to be exercised as its owner thinks fit.[3] Thus, the position now is that a company may not contract not to alter its articles,[4] but its shareholders may agree amongst themselves that they will not vote in favour of a proposal to alter the articles and in a suitable case this shareholders' agreement can be enforced by injunction.[5] This means that it may be possible to achieve the aim of ensuring that articles are entrenched by drafting the agreement in the form of a shareholders' agreement rather than a covenant by the company itself. However, it may not be practicable to enter into a shareholders' agreement which is effective for this purpose where the company has a large number of shareholders: a shareholders' agreement will ensure only that the articles cannot be changed where the parties to it have sufficient voting strength to block the passing of a special resolution, since, as a normal contract, a shareholders' agreement will of course not be binding on non-contracting shareholders. Even where a company has only a few

---

1   [1992] 1 BCLC 1016, HL. See further Ferran, 'The Decision of the House of Lords in *Russell v Northern Bank Development Corporation Limited*' [1994] CLJ 343. A narrower interpretation of the ratio in *Russell* is suggested by Davenport. 'What Did *Russell v Northern Bank Development Corporation Ltd* Decide?' (1993) 109 LQR 553. Other comments on the decision in *Russell* include Riley, 'Vetoes and Voting Agreements: Some Problems of Consent and Knowledge', (1993) 44 NILQ 34: Sealy, 'Shareholders' Agreements – An Endorsement and a Warning from the House of Lords' [1992] CLJ 437: Shapira, 'Voting Agreements and Corporate Statutory Powers' (1993) 109 LQR 210.

2   Lord Jauncey of Tullichettle, who delivered the Opinion of the House, found support for this conclusion in *Welton v Saffery* [1897] AC 299 at 331.

3   Leading authorities are *Pender v Lushington* (1877) 6 Ch D 70: *Northern Counties Securities Ltd v Jackson & Steeple Ltd* [1974] 1 WLR 1133: *North-West Transportation Co Ltd v Beatty* (1887) 12 App Cas 589.

4   In *Cumbrian Newspapers Group Ltd v Cumberland & Westmorland Herald Newspaper & Printing Co Ltd* [1987] Ch 1, Scott J suggested that the power to alter articles belonged to the members rather than to the company, an interpretation which seems rather at odds with the wording of section 9: '. . . a *company* may by special resolution alter its articles' (emphasis added). Scott J thought that a promise by a company not to alter the articles amounted to no more than a promise not to *initiate* the process of alteration.

5   The possibility of a shareholders' agreement being enforced by injunction was accepted in *Russell*, although the only remedy sought and granted in that case was a declaration.

shareholders, the entrenching effect of a shareholders' agreement not to vote in favour of an alteration to the articles may not survive when a new shareholder, who is not party to the agreement, joins the company.[1]

Shareholders' agreements are often encountered in the type of company which is commonly referred to as a 'quasi-partnership' company where, despite the corporate form, the individuals forming the company intend to run their operations on partnership lines. By entering into a shareholders' agreement each individual seeks to protect himself against the principle of majority rule, which is the normal hallmark of corporate decision making, and to ensure that the bargain which he reached with his 'partners' when they established the business cannot be changed without his consent.

5.26 Acting on altered articles

Although a company cannot contract not to alter its articles, acting on altered articles may amount to a breach of an earlier contractual promise which the company has given. The distinction between the situations is illustrated by *Southern Foundries (1926) Ltd v Shirlaw*,[2] where the company altered its articles to remove directors from office and then used this power to remove Shirlaw, the managing director, from his office. The House of Lords held that this action breached Shirlaw's service contract and ordered the company to pay damages. Lord Porter summarised the approach of the House in the following terms:

> The general principle therefore may, I think, be thus stated. A company cannot be precluded from altering its articles thereby giving itself power to act upon the provisions of the altered articles – but so to act may nevertheless be a breach of contract if it is contrary to a stipulation in a contract validly made before the alteration.[3]

In a suitable case, an injunction might be granted to prevent a company acting on its altered articles in breach of an earlier contract.[4] Although the distinction may be quite fine, this does not infringe the principle that a company cannot fetter its power to alter the articles, because the company is not actually prevented from altering the articles and can rely on the altered articles against everyone apart from parties to the earlier contract in whose favour the court is persuaded to grant the discretionary remedy of an injunction.

The same principle seems to apply where there is a contract between the shareholders not to alter the articles but an alteration is subsequently made. That this may give rise to a claim for damages in the event of breach was supported by *Punt v Symons*.[5] This was subsequently considered in *British Murac Syndicate Ltd v*

---

1   To bind the new shareholder, the agreement regarding voting rights would have to be in the articles but such a provision in the articles would be regarded as an invalid fetter on the statutory power: *Russell* [1992] 3 All ER at 167. But this would not preclude the formation of a new shareholders' agreement to which the new shareholder is a party.

2   [1940] AC 701. *Baily v British Equitable Life Assurance Co*, above, is also more concerned with the consequences of acting on altered articles than with a contract not to alter articles.

3   Ibid, at 740–741.

4   *Allen v Gold Reefs of West Africa* at 672 *per* Lindley LJ, quoted by Lord Wright in *Shirlaw* at 725. On this point see further Trebilcock, 'The Effect of Alterations to Articles of Association' (1967) 31 Con (NS) 95 at 113–116.

5   [1903] 2 Ch 505 following an unreported case in the Court of Appeal. *Malleson v National Insurance Corp* [1894] 1 Ch 200, in spite of the headnote, is not an authority for this proposition.

Alperton Rubber Co Ltd[1] where it was held that a contract not to alter articles was capable of being enforced by way of injunction, *Punt v Symons* being treated as having been implicitly overruled by a later Court of Appeal decision. On closer examination the analysis in *British Murac* is questionable. In the Court of Appeal decision relied upon, *Baily v British Equitable Assurance Co*,[2] the court actually granted a declaration rather than an injunction. Also, this decision was not precisely in point, because the Court of Appeal was mainly concerned with the wider principle (well established by other authorities) that a company cannot by altering its articles justify a breach of an extrinsic contract.

5.27 'Bona fide for the benefit of the company as a whole'

The power conferred by section 9 of the Companies Act 1985 to alter the articles by resolution may not be abused by a majority of shareholders so as to oppress the minority.[3] Even though a special resolution, valid in all respects as to form, has been passed as required by section 9, the minority may have it set aside for 'fraud on a minority'.[4] The courts will intervene where it is established that the majority have *not* acted '*bona fide* in the interests of the company as a whole'. This equitable principle was first clearly stated by Lord Lindley in *Allen v Gold Reefs of West Africa*.[5]

Later cases have sought to elucidate the precise meaning of the phrase '*bona fide* for the benefit of the company as a whole'.[6] It is clear that a heavy burden of proof rests on those seeking to prevent alteration of the articles. It must be shown that the object of the majority in altering the articles is not capable of being for the benefit of the company as a whole.[7]

Some first instance decisions suggest that '*bona fide*' and 'the interests of the company as a whole' are separate requirements so that, regardless of the view of the majority, an alteration can be held to be invalid where, on an objective assessment, the court concludes that it is not in the interests of the company.[8] These cases have not been overruled but the Court of Appeal has strongly

---

1 [1915] 2 Ch 186.

2 [1904] 1 Ch 373 (reversed by House of Lords [1906] AC 35 but not on grounds relevant to this point).

3 The same principle would apply to a resolution altering shareholders' rights where these are set forth in the memorandum, though the decided cases have concerned the alteration of the articles.

4 The principle considered here is only one form of the wider concept of 'fraud on a minority'. See further **17.4**.

5 [1900] 1 Ch 656 at p 671 (CA). A provision in the original articles of association, which might be open to attack if introduced as an alteration, will not be set aside on this basis. *Borland's Trustee v Steel Bros Co Ltd* [1901] 1 Ch 279: *Phillips v Manufacturers' Securities Ltd* (1917) 86 LJ Ch 305 (a power of compulsory acquisition of shares).

6 These cases are examined thoroughly by Rixon, 'Competing Interests and Conflicting Principles: An Examination of the Power of Alteration of Articles of Association', (1986) 49 MLR 446.

7 *Dafen Tinplate Co v Llanelly Steel Co* [1920] 2 Ch 124 at 137; *Sidebottom v Kershaw, Leese & Co* [1920] 1 Ch 154 at 163(4) and 169 (CA); *Shuttleworth v Cox Bros & Co* [1927] 2 KB 9 at 18, 23 and 27 (CA).

8 *Brown v British Abrasive Wheel Co* [1919] 1 Ch 290; *Dafen Tinplate Co v Llanelly Steel Co* [1920] 2 Ch 124.

criticised the reasoning in the earlier first instance judgments[1] and has repeatedly affirmed that corporate benefit is not an independent ground for intervention: '*bona fides* in the interests of the company' is a single composite standard by which the majority decision is to be judged.[2] The better view is that it is primarily for the majority to decide what is in the interests of the company, since in principle the majority is best qualified to decide this question. It is thus a subjective rather than an objective test.

5.28 A malicious alteration

If it can be shown that the majority acted maliciously or fraudulently, the alteration will not be allowed to stand because it cannot be said that the majority has acted *bona fide* in the interests of the company.[3] Malice for this purpose is used in the sense of a desire to harm or injure the minority.[4] Even if, on objective grounds, the alteration would be justifiable as being for the benefit of the company, it will be tainted by the bad motive of the majority. In *Sidebottom v Kershaw & Leese*, the articles were altered to allow the company compulsorily to acquire the shares of any member who was in competition with the company's business. The Court of Appeal considered that this alteration in fact benefited the company, but indicated that it would not have stood if the evidence had shown that the alteration was directed at an individual for any malicious motive or with any dishonest intention.[5] In *Shuttleworth v Cox*, the articles were altered to add an additional event which disqualified a director from office. In the circumstances, the Court of Appeal concluded that there was no 'trace of any vindictiveness or bad motive'[6] or of the decision having been taken 'maliciously', or with any desire to spite the plaintiff, or from any motive but that of doing what they thought best 'in the interest of the company';[7] it can be inferred that the alteration would not have stood if there had been such evidence.

Those seeking to prevent an alteration to articles becoming effective may find it difficult to establish positive evidence of malice, especially since, in all but the very smallest of companies, what will be in issue will be the motives of the group of persons who comprise the majority of the shareholders, rather than that of one majority shareholder. An inference may be drawn where an alteration is so oppressive of the minority as to cast suspicions on the honesty of the majority[8] but it is important to note that the mere fact that an alteration is directed at a particular individual and may involve expropriation of that person's shares does not, in itself, constitute sufficient evidence of oppression for such an inference to

---

1   *Sidebottom v Kershaw, Leese & Co Ltd*, above at 172 where Astbury J in *Brown* is said by
     Warrington LJ to have 'confused himself' by treating *bona fides* and corporate benefit as
     separate things: see also Lord Sterndale MR at 167. The reasoning in *Dafen* was criticised by
     the Court of Appeal in *Shuttleworth*, especially at 19, 22 and 27.
2   See *Sidebottom* at 163 and 172; *Shuttleworth* at 18 and 22; and *Greenhalgh v Arderne Cinemas Ltd*
     [1951] Ch 286 at 291.
3   *Sidebottom*, above at 163.
4   *Sidebottom*, above at 161 *per* Lord Sterndale MR.
5   At 166 *per* Lord Sterndale MR and at p 172 *per* Warrington LJ.
6   At 17 *per* Bankes LJ.
7   At 21 *per* Scrutton LJ.
8   *Shuttleworth* at 18 *per* Bankes LJ, and at 27 *per* Atkin LJ; *Rights & Issues Investment Trust Ltd v
     Stylo Shoes Ltd* [1965] 1 Ch 250.

be drawn.[1] In both *Sidebottom* and *Shuttleworth*, the articles were altered to enable the company to rid itself of a particular individual but in both cases the Court of Appeal considered that in the circumstances the action of the majority was not suspicious: in *Sidebottom* the circumstances surrounding the alteration were that the individual against whom it was directed could exploit the information which came to him as a shareholder for the benefit of his own business and to the detriment of the company, whilst in *Shuttleworth* the individual had already been validly dismissed from his employment as managing director because of his laxity in running the company's affairs. Again, in *Allen v Gold Reefs of West Africa*, the company altered its articles to impose a lien on fully paid shares. The background to the alteration was that one shareholder owed a particularly large debt to the company and the imposition of the lien was one way of giving the company some security for the debt. Although the alteration was thus directed at one particular individual, it was upheld.

The reluctance of the English courts to strike down alterations to articles even where they are directed at particular individuals is to be contrasted with the more interventionist approach of the High Court of Australia in *Gambotto v WCP Ltd*.[2] In *Gambotto*, the company altered its articles so as to include a provision which would give the holder of 90% or more of its shares the right to buy out the minority. The High Court held that a test of proper purchase and fairness, rather than that of acting *bona fide* for the benefit of the company as a whole, governed the question of the validity of the new expropriation article and that the onus lay on those supporting expropriation to prove the validity of the article.

5.29   An alteration outside the bounds of reasonableness

It is not for the court to impose its own view of what is reasonable on the company but if the alteration is such that no reasonable body of persons could consider it for the benefit of the company, it will not be allowed to stand.[3] In *Shuttleworth*, Bankes LJ indicated that an apt analogy is that of the grounds on which an appellate court will quash the verdict of a jury.[4] Bankes LJ also stated an alternative test which could be suitable in some cases: whether the action of the majority is capable of being considered for the benefit of the company.[5]

The absence of any reasonable grounds for deciding that an alteration is for the benefit of the company does not necessarily indicate malice but the alteration can still be set aside because the majority has not considered the matters which it ought to have considered.[6] In this respect, the 'jury' test is slightly wider than the malice test. Nevertheless, as the decisions of the Court of Appeal in *Sidebottom* and *Shuttleworth* indicate, it is still extremely difficult to persuade a court to set aside an alteration on this ground. An example of a claim that might succeed is where the

---

1   *Sidebottom* at 173 *per* Eve J.
2   (1995) 16 ACSR 1, noted Prentice, 'Alteration of Articles of Association – Expropriation of Shares' (1996) 112 LQR 194.
3   *Shuttleworth* at 18 *per* Bankes LJ.
4   Ibid, at 18.
5   Ibid, at 18–19.
6   *Shuttleworth* at 23 *per* Scrutton LJ. *Estmanco (Kilner House) Ltd v GLC* [1982] 1 All ER 437 at 444 *per* Megarry V-C: 'Where the majority shareholders genuinely believe that it is in the best interests of the company as a whole ... that is decisive, unless no reasonable shareholder in their position could hold this belief'.

articles are altered to allow the majority an unlimited power to expropriate or acquire compulsorily the shares of the minority and there are no valid commercial reasons, as there were in *Sidebottom* and *Shuttleworth*, to explain that alteration.[1] Another is if the majority alter the articles so as to restrict the dividend that would otherwise be due to the minority.[2]

5.30 The discrimination test and the 'interests of the company as a whole'

In *Greenhalgh v Arderne Cinemas Ltd*,[3] Lord Evershed MR formulated another way of testing whether an alteration is *bona fide* in the interests of the company as a whole: an alteration would be liable to be impeached 'if the effect of it were to discriminate between the majority shareholders and the minority shareholders, so as to give the former an advantage of which the latter were deprived'. Taken out of context, this comment may suggest that the circumstances in which the court can invalidate an alteration are judged on objective grounds but passages elsewhere in the judgment of the Master of the Rolls confirm that what is for 'the benefit of the company' is primarily for the majority of the shareholders to decide.[4] Also, the actual decision in *Greenhalgh* indicates that the discrimination test is not satisfied simply because, objectively, the alteration favours the majority over the minority: the articles were altered to allow existing members to sell their shares to outsiders provided they had the sanction of an ordinary resolution of the shareholders in general meeting; if the majority wanted to sell its shares to an outsider it would be assured of obtaining the necessary resolution but the minority would not; this objective discrimination against the minority did not invalidate the alteration. Unfortunately, the decision leaves open what type of discrimination is required for the court to intervene on this ground.[5]

Lord Evershed MR also formulated his test in this way:[6] 'the case may be taken of an individual hypothetical member and it may be asked whether what is proposed is, in the honest opinion of those who voted in favour, for that person's benefit'. The concept of 'an individual hypothetical member' is difficult to grasp and this test has not proved to be easy to apply. In *Clemens v Clemens*,[7] the company had two shareholders and, in purported reliance on the *Greenhalgh* hypothetical member test, Foster J considered whether in voting on a particular resolution the majority shareholder had honestly believed that it would benefit the plaintiff who was the minority shareholder. The representative member chosen by Foster J

---

1   *Dafen Tinplate & Llanelly Steel*, on its facts, could support the proposition in the text because the alteration went further than what was required in the company's interest.
2   *Dafen* at 143.
3   Above at 291.
4   At 291.
5   Discrimination as a basis for impeaching an alteration of articles is mentioned by Pennycuick J in *Rights & Issues Investment Trust Ltd v Stylo Shoes Ltd* [1965] 1 Ch 250 but the meaning of 'discrimination' for this purpose is not explained.
6   At 291.
7   [1976] 2 All ER 268.

could hardly be described as hypothetical;[1] but how such a member could have been constructed from the circumstances of the dispute defies description since it is difficult to see what common benefit could have transcended the interests of the warring factions. A further criticism of the hypothetical member test is that it seems to require the majority to act altruistically; this does not sit easily with the principle that a vote attached to a share is a property right which can be used as the owner of the share thinks fit. Lord Evershed MR himself acknowledged that persons in the majority did not have to dissociate themselves from their own interests when voting on the resolution to alter the articles.[2]

An important aspect of the decision in *Greenhalgh* is what Lord Evershed MR had to say about the meaning of the phrase 'the company as a whole'. The company is of course an entity distinct and separate from its shareholders and in cases such as *Allen v Gold Reefs*, *Sidebottom* and *Shuttleworth* it may be sufficient to consider whether the alteration is capable of being in the interests of the company as a commercial entity. However, cases such as *Greenhalgh* involve alterations which affect groups of shareholders differently but which have little or no effect on the company as a commercial entity; accordingly, 'the phrase, "the company as a whole", does not (at any rate in such a case as the present) mean the company as a commercial entity, distinct from the corporators: it means the corporators as a general body'.[3]

In *Peter's American Delicacy Co Ltd v Heath*,[4] the High Court of Australia accepted the need to distinguish alterations to articles which affected the rights *inter se* of shareholders from those which affected the interests of the company as a separate entity.[5] In cases of alterations involving competing shareholders' interests, 'the interests of the company as a whole' was thought to be an inappropriate, if not meaningless, test.[6] Inhuman altruism was not expected of the shareholders in the majority. According to Dixon CJ, provided the resolution to alter the articles involved no oppression, no appropriation of an unjust or reprehensible nature and did not imply any purpose outside the scope of the power, it would be allowed to stand.[7] Latham CJ expressed the test in slightly different language, but to the

---

1   The decision in *Clemens* can also be criticised on other grounds: see Joffe (1977) 40 MLR 71. The resolution in question did not relate to an alteration of the articles and the court's assertion of a general power to review shareholder decisions is questionable. The subjecting of majority power to equitable constraint on the basis of the decision in *Ebrahimi v Westbourne Galleries Ltd* [1973] AC 360 is doubtful because that case concerned a specific discretion conferred by statute in particular circumstances, see **17.17** (but note also *Pennell v Venida Investments* (1974) which is unreported but is discussed extensively by Burridge (1981) 44 MLR 40). *Clemens* hints at a fiduciary relationship between majority and minority shareholders but, although this has been accepted in certain American and Commonwealth jurisdictions, it is not yet part of English company law: Sealy, 'Equitable and Other Fetters on the Shareholder's Freedom to Vote' in Eastham and Krivy (eds), *The Cambridge Lectures* (1981) p 80. See also Rider [1978] CLJ 148: Prentice (1976) 92 LQR 502.

2   At 291.

3   *Greenhalgh* at 291 *per* Lord Evershed MR.

4   (1939) 61 CLR 457.

5   At 481 *per* Latham CJ: at 512–13 *per* Dixon J.

6   *Per* Dixon CJ at 513. Similarly, Latham CJ at p 481: 'The benefit of the company cannot be adopted as a criterion which is capable of solving all the problems in this branch of the law. . . . In cases where the question which arises is simply a question as to the relative rights of different classes of shareholders the problem cannot be solved by regarding merely the benefit of the corporation'. Also Rich J at 495.

7   At 513.

same effect: a resolution altering articles would be held to be invalid if there was 'fraud or trickery' or 'evidence of oppression' or if the alteration could be 'described as extravagant, so that reasonable men could not regard it as a fair alteration'.[1] In *Gambotto v WCP Ltd*,[2] Mason CJ said that where a change to articles gave rise to a conflict of interests and advantages the general test for judging its validity was whether it was '*ultra vires*, beyond any purpose contemplated by the articles or oppressive as that term is understood in the law relating to corporations'. If, however, the article involved expropriation or shares or other valuable proprietary rights, it would be subject to the stricter test of proper purpose and objective fairness.

The judgments of the High Court of Australia in *Peter's American Delicacy* and *Gambotto* explicitly address the considerations which underlie the court's assertion of a power to review decisions to alter articles of association and the factors which restrict the scope of this power of review. It is a well-established principle of company law that voting rights attached to shares are property rights which shareholders can in general use as they think fit. It would be impossible to investigate the thoughts and motives with which each shareholder casts his votes. However, the court must set some limit on the power of the majority because of, in the words of Dixon J, 'the fear or knowledge that an apparently regular exercise of power may in truth be but a means of securing some personal or particular gain, whether pecuniary or otherwise, which does not fairly arise out of the subjects dealt with by the power and is outside and even inconsistent with the contemplated objects of the power'.[3]

Emphasising misuse of power by the majority[4] as a trigger which allows the court to intervene seems in many ways a much more realistic and workable test than those outlined in *Greenhalgh*. It is becoming increasingly unlikely, though, that the courts will have much opportunity in the future to refine further the meaning of the 'bona fide in the interests of the company' test enunciated in *Allen v Gold Reefs* because a minority which objects to an alteration to the articles can now voice the complaint by petitioning the court under Part XVII of the Companies Act 1985 for relief from unfairly prejudicial conduct. This form of statutory relief is very flexible, both in terms of the conduct which can be regarded as 'unfairly prejudicial' and with regard to the remedies which the court can grant where a claim is made out. The section is discussed further at **17.13** *et seq.*

5.31 Reform proposals

Following the review of company law carried out by the Company Law Review Steering Group, the Government's White Paper *Modernising Company Law*[5] contained a number of significant reform proposals. This section will outline the main changes regarding the company's constitution. The requirement for the two separate documents, the memorandum and articles of association, would be replaced with the requirement to have a constitution contained in a single

---

1   At 491, and see also 482.
2   (1995) 16 ACSR 1 at 8–9.
3   *Peter's American Delicacy* at 511–512.
4   Or as it may be described in equity: 'fraud on a power' *Estmanco (Kilner House) Ltd v GLC*, above at 445.
5   Cm 5553, July 2002.

document.[1] As noted above, it is not clear whether the new constitution would retain the contractual character of the present articles and memorandum. In its *Final Report*, the Steering Group adopted a neutral position, preferring instead to explain to the draftsman of the new Companies Bill how the constitution is intended to operate and how this could best be reflected in the drafting. The White Paper itself is silent on this issue altogether, and it remains to be seen what the juridical character of the new constitution would be.

A company will be able to change its constitution by special resolution,[2] although an alteration requiring an existing member to subscribe for more shares or to increase his liability will not bind him.[3] It will also be possible to include an 'entrenching provision', either on incorporation or by subsequent agreement of all the members. This provision would, in turn, specify those articles in the constitution which could only be altered with a majority greater than that required for a special resolution, or not at all. The entrenching provision could only be removed if all the members agreed.[4]

The standard Table A would be replaced with separate model constitutions for private and public companies, thus acknowledging that the one-size-fits-all approach in the current Table A is out of step with modern practice.[5] A company which intends to adopt a constitution which differs in some way from the model constitution would have to register the text of its constitution as before. If the relevant model constitution contains a provision for which there is no equivalent in the constitution thus registered, and that provision has not been excluded expressly or by implication, then it will be deemed to be included in the company's constitution.[6]

The White Paper also makes it clear that the 'objects clause' in the memorandum (discussed in detail in the next chapter) no longer serves a useful purpose and should be abolished, although companies would be permitted to include an objects clause in their constitution, but this would only have internal effect between the directors and members.[7] However, the total removal of the objects clause must be limited to private companies for the time being due to the requirement in the Second Company Law Directive[8] for public companies to state their objects, although this is purely an information requirement and the Directive does not deal with acts which fall outside the objects clause.

---

1   *Modernising Company Law* (July 2002), paragraphs 2.2–2.5.
2   Draft clause 20.
3   Draft clause 22.
4   Draft clause 21.
5   See draft clause 11. The *Final Report* contains a draft model constitution for private companies.
6   Draft clause 11(3).
7   *Modernising Company Law*, paragraph 2.2.
8   Directive 77/91/EEC, (1977) OJ L26/1. See **2.3.2**.

Chapter 6

Company Contracts – Capacity, Authority and Form

6.1 Introduction

This chapter is concerned with the ability of a company to make legally binding contracts and to enter into other transactions with valid effect. In the past this would have involved detailed examination of two quite distinct areas of law, namely the *ultra vires* doctrine and agency principles. The *ultra vires* doctrine is related to the capacity of the company: in its original and strictest form, the *ultra vires* doctrine meant that no transaction which was beyond the capacity of a company could ever be binding on it.[1] The strictness of the *ultra vires* doctrine was first ameliorated as a consequence of the United Kingdom's accession to the European Community because it was incompatible with Community law. The European Communities Act 1972 contained a provision[2] which allowed transactions which were beyond a company's capacity to be enforced against it in certain circumstances; this provision was consolidated as section 35 of the Companies Act 1985. The wording of section 35 proved to be unsatisfactory and with effect from February 1991 it was replaced by sections 35, 35A, 35B and 322A of the Companies Act 1985, as amended by the Companies Act 1989. If the proposals contained in the White Paper, *Modernising Company Law*,[3] are implemented, the requirement for an objects clause and consequently the *ultra vires* doctrine would be completely abolished.[4]

Broadly, the effect of the provisions which are now in force is to reduce very significantly the importance of the *ultra vires* doctrine. The underlying purpose of the provisions is to allow outsiders dealing with a company to assume that the company has unlimited capacity and, although there are some uncertainties because of the way the legislation is drafted, this purpose is almost certainly achieved. The *ultra vires* doctrine remains relevant as an internal control mechanism: the directors will be in breach of duty if they fail to observe limits on the company's capacity and shareholders may be able to obtain injunctions to restrain acts which would be beyond those limits. Lord Strathclyde, the Government spokesman who introduced the relevant clauses of the Companies Bill to the House of Lords, explained their purpose in the following terms:[5]

1　It is now generally accepted that the courts will not apply the ultra vires doctrine to limit a company's liability in tort or crime: Welch, 'The Criminal Liability of Corporations' (1946) 62 LQR 345.

2　Section 9.

3　Cm 5553, July 2002.

4　See **5.31**.

5　*Hansard*, HL Debs, 21 February 1989, cols 508–512, esp at 512. As a result of the decision of the House of Lords in *Pepper v Hart* [1993] AC 593, [1993] 1 All ER 42, [1992] 3 WLR 1032, it may be possible to look to this statement to clarify any ambiguities in the drafting of the sections.

The clause[s] will in practice abolish the effect of the *ultra vires* rule on relations between a company and other parties . . . The *ultra vires* rule will still operate internally; that is for the purpose of defining the directors' duties to their shareholders.

In 1986, the DTI published a report by Professor Prentice entitled *Reform of the Ultra Rule*. The proposals outlined in the Prentice Report went further than the provisions which were eventually enacted because that report advocated the entire abolition of the *ultra vires* doctrine. The retention of the doctrine for internal purposes means that all of the old learning on *ultra vires* cannot be jettisoned completely, and this is reflected in this chapter. It also means that the statutory provisions which now govern the position are rather more complex than might have been the case if the proposal to give companies unlimited capacity had been adopted instead. Proposals to rid English law of the last vestiges of the *ultra vires* rule have been accepted by the Government and would form part of a new Companies Bill. These proposals are considered at the end of this chapter.

Agency principles remain extremely important in determining when a company is bound by a transaction. As a legal, as opposed to a natural, person a company must act though others,[1] but simply because someone purports to act on a company's behalf does not mean that it is bound: the authority of those who act on behalf of the company to bind it is governed by agency principles together with a special principle of company law known as the *Turquand* rule. Agency principles are derived mainly from case-law but the statutory reforms to the *ultra vires* doctrine have affected these principles to a certain extent.

It is important to understand the distinction between 'capacity' and 'authority' at the outset. References to 'capacity' normally relate to the ability of the *company* to enter into a particular transaction. If it does not have this ability, the act is *prima facie* '*ultra vires*' (see **6.2**). In contrast, the term 'authority' refers to acts by *individuals* who purport to take a decision on behalf of the company, such as its directors or managers. Their power to take decisions in the company's name is not restricted, and if they exceed this, they are acting 'without authority'. This chapter will examine the law relevant to both matters of capacity and authority.

6.2   The term '*ultra vires*'

The term '*ultra vires*' used in a strict sense in relation to a registered company means acts which are outside the scope of the objects of the company set forth in the objects clause of its memorandum.[2] Prior to the statutory reforms, the distinguishing feature of a transaction which was *ultra vires* in the strict sense was that it was beyond the company's capacity and could not be ratified even by a

---

1   *Meridian Global Funds Management Asia Ltd v Securities Commission* [1995] 2 AC 500 (PC).

2   In the case of statutory companies created by private Acts of Parliament, the Act itself will define the company's objects. This will usually be done in much narrower terms than the objects clause of a modern registered company. The *ultra vires* doctrine does not apply to companies incorporated by Royal Charter. A chartered company which fails to observe restrictions in its charter may find itself subject to proceedings in the nature of *scire facias* for the revocation of its charter: *British South Africa Co v de Beers Mines* [1910] 1 Ch 354. A member may obtain an injunction to restrain the company from acting in a manner inconsistent with its charter: *Rendall v Crystal Palace Co* (1858) 4 K & J 326; *Bray v Royal British Nurses Association* [1897] 2 Ch 272; *Jenkins v Pharmaceutical Society of Great Britain* [1921] 1 Ch 392.

unanimous vote of the shareholders.[1] The consequences of an act which is *ultra vires* in the strict sense (which is the sense in which the term is used in this chapter unless otherwise indicated) are now governed by statute.

In company law, the term '*ultra vires*' is sometimes used to describe acts which are not beyond the *capacity* of the company, but simply beyond the authority of either the board of directors or a simple majority of the shareholders. Such acts may be in breach of the articles of association, but they are not, strictly speaking, beyond the powers of the company. Acts of this type can be ratified and, once properly ratified, they become binding on the company. Another use of the term *ultra vires* in a wider sense is to describe transactions which, although within the scope of the powers of the company, are entered into for an unauthorised purpose. These transactions are not void and can confer rights on a third party who is unaware of the improper purpose.[2] In *Rolled Steel Products (Holdings) Ltd v British Steel Corp*,[3] Slade and Browne-Wilkinson LJJ rightly commented on the potential for confusion caused by the use of the term '*ultra vires*' in these wider senses and suggested that its use should be confined to its strict sense.

An act may also be void on the ground of illegality as being contrary to the provisions of the Companies Acts. A company cannot take power to do something which is contrary to the Companies Acts so that an act which is illegal can also properly be described as being *ultra vires*.[4]

6.3 Drafting of objects clauses

To counteract the effect of the *ultra vires* rule, it has long been the established practice for companies to adopt very long objects clauses which authorise a wide range of activities. Also, a well-drafted objects clause usually confers numerous powers on the company and authorises the company to exercise these powers regardless of whether the exercise is incidental or conducive to the specified activities.[5] It is also usual for the objects clause to include a subjective incidental powers provision whereby the company is empowered to do anything which, in the opinion of its directors, is incidental or conducive to the activities or powers stated in the other paragraphs of the objects clause. The Companies Act 1989 introduced a provision into the 1985 Act that was intended to make it unnecessary for companies to continue to follow this practice. Companies were given the option of incorporating with a short-form objects clause or of amending their memoranda to adopt it. The short-form objects clause was to the effect that the object of the company was to carry on business as a general commercial company. By virtue of section 3A of the Companies Act 1985, an objects clause in this form

---

1   *Ashbury Railway Carriage & Iron Co v Riche* (1875) LR 7 HL 653; *Rolled Steel Products (Holdings) Ltd v British Steel Corp* [1986] Ch 246, [1985] 3 All ER 52, [1985] 2 WLR 908, [1984] BCLC 466, (1983–1985) 1 BCC 99 at 158.

2   *Rolled Steel Products (Holdings) Ltd v British Steel Corpn* [1982] Ch 478, [1982] 3 All ER 1057, [1982] 3 WLR 715 (Vinelott J). See Birds (1982) 3 Co Law 123.

3   [1986] Ch 246.

4   In *Aveling Barford Ltd v Perion Ltd* [1989] BCLC 626, (1989) 5 BCC 677 the term '*ultra vires*' is used in respect of an illegal act. Because such acts are illegal as well as void, third parties will not be entitled to the same consequential relief that is open to a party to a contract that is *ultra vires* but not contrary to the Companies Acts. The rules as to illegal contracts are applied: *South Western Mineral Water Co v Ashmore* [1967] 1 WLR 1110.

5   Whether, or to what extent, a provision which purports to confer an independent 'power' is effective is discussed at **6.6–6.8**.

objects clause as being ancillary to that main object.[1] Thus, for example, if the company's objects clause commenced with a paragraph authorising it to acquire rubber and tobacco estates but a subsequent paragraph gave it the power to underwrite shares,[2] under the main object rule of construction, the underwriting power would be viewed as ancillary to, and to be exercisable only for the purposes incidental or accessory to, the acquisition of rubber or tobacco estates. With a view to avoiding the operation of the main object rule of construction altogether, companies then started to include wording in their objects clause to the effect that each paragraph of the clause was to be read separately and without limitation by reference to the other clauses.

The effect of this wording was considered by the House of Lords in *Cotman v Brougham*.[3] The House held that once a company was registered, its memorandum of association had to be viewed as a valid instrument and the provisions which it contained had to be given effect to accordingly.[4] Therefore, effect had to be given to an independent objects paragraph by treating every object and power specified in the objects clause as independent objects, and not as ancillary to the main object. On that basis, the underwriting of shares by a rubber company, as permitted by its objects clause, could not be held to be *ultra vires* even though the underwritten shares were in a company with a business which had no apparent connection with rubber.

Their Lordships expressed unhappiness with this result and suggested that the Registrar of Companies should refuse to register companies which had objects clauses containing multifarious objects, powers expressed as objects and independent objects provisions, on the ground that this practice did not satisfy the statutory requirement to state the objects of the company.[5] This course was not taken by the Registrar and it is now standard practice for registered companies to include an extensive range of businesses in their objects clause, as well as every conceivable power that they could ever wish to use, and to provide that each paragraph of the objects clause is to be interpreted independently.

Anglo-Overseas Agencies v Green[6] provides an illustration of an independent objects clause and its effect.[7] The plaintiff company's objects clause had the usual series of paragraphs setting forth various objects of the company and then concluded with the following provision:

> The intention is that the object is specified in any paragraph of this clause shall, except where otherwise expressed in this clause, be in no wise limited or restricted by reference to or reference from the terms of any other paragraph or the name of the company.

---

1   As explained in *Anglo-Overseas Agencies v Green* [1961] 1 QB 1 at 8. For cases considering whether to wind up a company on the grounds that its principal object had failed, see *Re Haven Gold Mining Co* (1882) 20 Ch D 151; *Re German Date Coffee Co* (1882) 20 Ch D 169 (CA); *Re Kitson & Co* [1946] 1 All ER 435; *Re Eastern Telegraph* [1947] 2 All ER 104.

2   The factual situation is taken from *Cotman v Brougham* [1918] AC 514 (HL).

3   Above. This must be taken to overrule *Stephens v Mysore Reefs (Kangundy) Mining Co* [1902] 1 Ch 745.

4   But the Crown can bring proceedings to quash the registration of a company which is registered with illegal objects: **6.3**.

5   Now contained in section 2(1)(c) of the Companies Act 1985.

6   [1961] 1 QB 1.

7   See [1961] 1 QB 1 at 8, for a discussion of the effect of the 'main object' rule where no such provision is made.

Salmon J upheld the contention that these concluding words had the effect of making each paragraph an independent main object. This allowed a company, whose apparent main objects set out in paragraphs (A) and (B) were the export and import of merchandise, to obtain a building lease of a site from a local authority by virtue of a widely drafted paragraph (E), even though there was no paragraph expressly permitting property development.[1]

6.5 'Subjective' provisions in the objects clause

This liberal policy of allowing the draftsman of the objects clause to defeat the apparent purpose of the *ultra vires* doctrine was carried a stage further by the Court of Appeal in *Bell Houses Ltd v City Wall Properties Ltd.*[2] In that case, clause 3(c) of the memorandum of association allowed the company to 'carry on any other trade or business whatever which can, *in the opinion of the board of directors,*[3] be advantageously carried on by, in connection with, or ancillary to, any of the above businesses or general businesses of the company'. The appellant company maintained that clause 3(c) allowed them to charge a procuration fee for introducing a source of finance (which they did not wish to use themselves at the time) to another property company, even though there was no express power to do so. The Court of Appeal held that, provided the directors of the plaintiff company honestly formed the view that that particular business could be carried on advantageously in connection with, or as an ancillary to, the company's main business,[4] then the agreement to charge a procuration fee was within the company's powers by virtue of clause 3(c).

The decision in *Bell Houses Ltd* also rested on the alternative ground that, apart from the subjective discretion conferred on the directors, the obtaining of the procuration fee was, as a matter of objective construction, reasonably incidental to certain specific objects of the company.[5] However, Salmon LJ made it quite clear that the discretion conferred on the directors may allow them in good faith to extend the company's activities in ways which, strictly as a matter of objective construction, are *not* reasonably incidental to the activities specified in the objects clause:

---

1   Paragraph (E) read: 'To obtain the grant of, purchase, or otherwise acquire any concessions, contracts, rights, patents, privileges, monopolies, undertakings or businesses, or any right or option in relation thereto and to perform and fulfil the terms and conditions thereof, and to carry the same into effect, operate thereunder, develop, turn to account, maintain and sell, and dispose of and deal with the same.'

2   [1966] 2 QB 656. For an application of this case in New Zealand, see *American Home Assurance Co v Tjmonis Properties* [1984] NZLR 452 (CA). See also *H & H Logging Co Ltd v Random Services Corp Ltd* (1967) 63 DLR (20) 6 and *HA Stephenson & Sons Ltd v Gillanders, Arbuthnot & Co Ltd* (1931) 45 CLR 476 (Aust HC).

3   Italics supplied.

4   This is an important qualification to the discretion conferred on directors to determine what is within the objects clause of the company. It is clear that the courts would not accept an unqualified discretion which allowed the company to do anything the directors thought fit to decide: *Re Crown Bank* (1890) 44 Ch D 634; *Introductions Ltd v National Provincial Bank* [1970] Ch 199 at p 209 *per* Harman LJ. This should be contrasted with a more expansive approach (to a less qualified discretion conferred upon the directors) taken by the Australian High Court in *HA Stephenson Ltd v Gillanders, Arbuthnot & Co* (1931) 45 CLR 476. See the judgment of Dixon J at 490–491.

5   See [1966] 2 QB 656 at 680 (Danckwerts LJ) and 692–693 (Salmon LJ).

As a matter of pure construction the meaning of these words seems to me to be obvious. An object of the company is to carry on any business which the directors genuinely believe can be carried on advantageously in connection with or as an ancillary to the general business of the company. It may be that the directors take the wrong view and in fact the business in question cannot be carried on as the directors believe. But it matters not how mistaken the directors may be. Providing they form their view honestly, the business is within the plaintiff company's objects and powers . . .[1]

6.6 Objects and powers

The *Bell Houses* decision appeared to indicate a marked shift in the judicial attitude towards the value of the *ultra vires* doctrine. It permitted the draftsman by a simple and flexible drafting device to give the company's management reasonable freedom of manoeuvre in developing and diversifying the company's activities. However, in a later Court of Appeal decision a more rigorous approach was taken.

In *Introductions Ltd v National Provincial Bank Ltd*,[2] a company originally formed for the purpose of offering services and information to overseas visitors to the Festival of Britain was taken over and, under new management, it began pig-breeding as its only business. A bank which had advanced money to finance this business was held unable to recover on the company's liquidation. The bank was fully aware of the purpose of the loan and that the objects for which the company was formed were those set out in its memorandum, of which the bank had a copy. It was contended for the bank that, even if pig-breeding were *ultra vires*,[3] it might rely on a sub-clause (N) of the objects clause that enabled this company 'to borrow or raise money in such manner as it thought fit'. This was linked with a provision (similar to that in *Anglo-Overseas Agencies v Green*) that each sub-clause 'should be construed independently of, and should be in no way linked by, reference to any other sub-clause, and that the objects set out in each sub-clause were independent objects of the company'.

The Court of Appeal made a sharp distinction between *powers* as opposed to *objects* in the memorandum. On the true construction of the sub-clause conferring a general power to borrow, this was a power not an object. Thus the power to borrow had to be used for the legitimate *intra vires* objects of the company. Since the explicit purpose of the loan (pig-breeding) was *ultra vires*, the borrowing itself was *ultra vires*. Despite the final provision declaring all the objects set forth to be independent, the power to borrow on sub-clause (N) was not on its wording capable of being a wholly independent object. As a power it was necessarily ancillary to the objects of the company.

It should be noted that the Court of Appeal's decision in the *Introductions* case did not, so far as *objects* were concerned, in any way repudiate attempts to exclude the main objects principle of construction. It did, however, have a limiting effect in respect of *powers*. In the case of an ordinary trading company, whilst it could specify a number of different objects (in the sense of trades and businesses) in its objects clause, ranging, say, from acquiring rubber plantations through to promoting festivals or pig-breeding, and each of those objects would be construed

---

1   [1966] 2 QB 656 at 690.
2   [1970] Ch 199 (CA).
3   Buckley J had held that pig-breeding was *ultra vires* the company and this point was not contested on appeal: [1968] 2 All ER 1221.

independently provided there was an appropriate independent objects clause, the paragraphs of the objects clause containing true powers, such as the power to borrow or to give guarantees, would always be construed as ancillary to the objects, notwithstanding any independent objects clause.[1]

Attempts have been made to exclude the distinction drawn in *Introductions* between objects and powers by explicitly providing that no such distinction is to be made, but the effect of this wording has not been tested in the courts. In any event, in restrospect it can be seen that *Introductions* was a high point of judicial antipathy to the practice of drafting very broad objects clauses. Since then, two important cases decided by the Court of Appeal have greatly reduced the significance of the distinction between objects and powers.[2]

6.7   Objects and powers: *Re Horsley & Weight* and *Rolled Steel*[3]

In *Re Horsley & Weight Ltd*,[4] the objects clause of a company which carried on the business of shopfitters authorised it: 'to grant pensions to employees and ex-employees and directors and ex-directors'. There was also an independent objects clause. The Court of Appeal held that the granting of pensions was capable of subsisting as a substantive object rather than as an ancillary power and that, having regard to the independent objects clause, it was to be so construed in this case. The Court of Appeal thus confirmed the existence of a distinction between objects and powers but, by classifying a provision as an object when it might easily have been regarded as a power, sidestepped the need to consider whether a power had been exercised otherwise than in pursuit of the objects, and the consequences in that event.

Rolled Steel Products (Holdings) Ltd v British Steel Corporation[5] provided an opportunity for a more detailed examination of the distinction between objects and powers and its consequences because, despite an independent objects clause, the relevant provision authorising the giving of guarantees and debentures was classified by the first instance judge, Vinelott J, and by the Court of Appeal as a mere power. This led to the question: given that the power to give guarantees and debentures had been exercised otherwise than in pursuit of the substantive objects of the company, were the guarantee and debenture binding on the company? The Court of Appeal held that they were not, not because they were beyond the company's capacity but because the directors had exceeded the authority and the contracting party was aware of this. The judgments of Slade and Browne-Wilkinson LJJ contain a valuable restatement of the law relating to the use

---

1   For a Scottish case following the restrictive approach in *Introductions* see *Thompson v J Barke & Co (Caterers) Ltd* 1975 SLT 67.

2   Note also *Re New Finance and Mortgage Co* [1975] Ch 420 and *Newstead v Frost* [1980] 1 All ER 363, [1980] 1 WLR 135 (HL) where the courts did not adopt a restrictive approach in determining the scope of objects clauses.

3   Notes on the decision of Vinelott J at first instance and of the Court of Appeal include Wedderburn (1983) 46 MLR 204; McMullen [1983] CLJ 58; Sealy [1985] CLJ 39; (1986) 102 LQR 169.

4   [1982] Ch 442, [1982] 3 All ER 1045, [1982] 3 WLR 431.

5   Above.

of a power in the objects clause otherwise than in pursuit of the objects.[1] The learned Lord Justices sought to explain earlier decisions such as *Introductions* so as to reconcile them with their own analysis of the position. When the judgments in some earlier cases are compared closely with those of Slade and Browne-Wilkinson LJJ in *Rolled Steel* it is questionable whether the reconciliation is entirely persuasive[2] but, consistent with legislative developments in this area of the law, the approach in *Rolled Steel* embodies the policy of not penalising innocent outsiders dealing with a company when those who act on the company's behalf fail to observe limits which are imposed by the company's constitution.

It is far from clear how far this line of argument can be pushed. It is debatable whether *Rolled Steel* supports the use of any and every power in the memorandum to justify a wholly new area of activity which is to be conducted on a permanent basis (eg pig-breeding as the sole activity of a company whose express objects give no hint of this type of animal husbandry). But if *Rolled Steel* comes to be further considered by the courts, the impact of sections 35 and 35A (and such statutory protections for third parties as may be enacted in future) in protecting third parties may make that aspect of the reasoning in the case redundant.

6.8 The use of powers in the memorandum for improper purposes

The essence of the restatement of the law in *Rolled Steel* is that if an act performed pursuant to an ancillary power stated in the memorandum is of a category which, on a true construction of the company's memorandum, is capable of being performed as reasonably incidental to the attainment or pursuit of its substantive objects, it will not be rendered *ultra vires* the company merely because in a particular instance its directors, in performing the act in its name, are doing so for purposes other than those set out in its memorandum.[3] Thus, if the directors exercise a power in the memorandum to borrow money, provided borrowing money is *capable* of being reasonably incidental to the pursuit or attainment of the company's objects (a test that would ordinarily be satisfied) a particular borrowing by a company is not *ultra vires* even though the purpose for which the directors borrowed the money falls outside the scope of the company's substantive objects.

The only limitation put upon the protective shield thus thrown around the use of powers in the memorandum, is that 'due regard must be paid to any express condition attached to, or limitation on, powers contained in a company's

---

1   Lawton LJ gave a brief judgment in which he considered the misfeasance aspects of the case (and certain matters arising from the handling of the case by the trial judge) but otherwise he agreed with Slade LJ. Browne-Wilkinson LJ also expressed agreement with Slade LJ.

2   It is particularly difficult to reconcile *Rolled Steel* with the decision of the House of Lords in *Sinclair v Brougham* [1914] AC 398. Their Lordships were mainly concerned with the consequences of *ultra vires* but accepted that the power to borrow money must be limited to borrowing for the purposes of the company, borrowing for any other purpose being *ultra vires*. This aspect of the decision in *Sinclair v Brougham* is unaffected by the House of Lords' departure from it in *Westdeutsche Landesbank Girozentrale v Islington Borough Council* [1996] AC 669.

3   [1986] 1 Ch 246 at 295 *per* Slade LJ and at 306–307 *per* Browne-Wilkinson LJ. For an application of *Rolled Steel* to a housing association registered under the Industrial and Provident Societies Act 1965, see *Halifax Building Society v Meridian Housing Association Ltd* [1994] 2 BCLC 540.

memorandum' (eg a power to borrow only up to a specified amount).[1] However, the court will not ordinarily construe a statement in the memorandum that a particular power is 'exercisable for the purpose of the company' (or similar phraseology) as a condition limiting the company's corporate capacity to exercise the power (as opposed to limit on the authority of the directors).[2] In the view of Browne-Wilkinson LJ such a limitation 'does not put the third party on enquiry as to whether the power is being so exercised, ie does not give constructive notice of excess or abuse of such power'.[3]

Some[4] earlier cases had suggested that the consequences of an exercise of a mere power specified in the objects for an improper purpose could depend on the state of mind of the person who dealt with the company: taking the borrowing power as an example, if the lender knew that the directors were borrowing the money for a purpose which was not authorised by the company's memorandum, the loan would be *ultra vires*, but the loan would be binding if the lender did not have the requisite knowledge.[5] In *Introductions*, Harman LJ said: 'if the defendant bank did not know what the purpose of the loan was it need not enquire, but it did know, and I can find nothing . . . to protect it notwithstanding that knowledge'; in that case, the loan and related debenture were held to be not binding on the company.[6]

In *Rolled Steel*, it was held that the knowledge of the person dealing with the company was generally irrelevant to the question of *corporate capacity* but that it was significant with regard to matters of *authority*. Slade LJ explained this on the basis that the directors of a company are held out as having ostensible authority to bind the company in any transaction falling within the express or implied powers in its memorandum.[7] Unless put on notice to the contrary, a person dealing in good faith with a company which is carrying on an *intra vires* business is entitled to assume that the directors are properly exercising these powers for the purposes of the company set out in the memorandum and can therefore hold the company to any transaction of this nature. However, if a person dealing with a company is on notice that the directors are exercising the relevant power for purposes other than the purposes of the company, he cannot rely on the directors' ostensible authority to hold the company to the transaction.

To explain the decision in *Introductions*, the Court of Appeal considered the various senses in which the term '*ultra vires*' can be used in company law and reinterpreted certain passages in the relevant judgments in the earlier case as being concerned with '*ultra vires*' in the wider sense of being beyond the authority of the directors rather than in its narrow strict sense of being outside the

---

1   Slade LJ at 295 summarising his conclusions.
2   Ibid.
3   Slade LJ at 307.
4   But not all: Pennyquick J's reasoning in *Charterbridge Corporation Ltd v Lloyds Bank Ltd* [1970] Ch 62 is similar to that of the Court of Appeal in *Rolled Steel*. See also *Re Halt Garage (1964) Ltd* [1982] 3 All ER 1016. Both of these cases are considered further at **6.13**.
5   *Re David Payne & Co Ltd* [1904] 2 Ch 608; *Re Jon Beauforte* [1953] Ch 131; *Introductions*, above.
6   Buckley J at first instance, [1968] 2 All ER 1221 at 1225 described the loan and debenture as '*ultra vires*'. This categorisation is not expressly stated in any of the judgments in the Court of Appeal but Harman and Russell LJJ both expressed agreement with Buckley J (the third Lord Justice, Karminski LJ, agreed with the dismissal of the appeal without giving reasons).
7   At 295.

company's capacity.[1] This interpretation made sense of the references in those judgments to the knowledge of the bank of the intended unauthorised purpose for which the loan was sought, because, in accordance with agency principles, such knowledge may displace the ostensible authority that the directors would otherwise have had to bind the company.

The vigorous restatement of the nature and proper scope of the *ultra vires* doctrine in *Rolled Steel* is to be welcomed both for its logical character and the evident judicial policy aimed at reducing the scope of possible harm it may cause to innocent third parties. The proposition that the capacity of the company could in some circumstances depend on the knowledge of persons dealing with it was always logically dubious.[2] However, certain queries and doubts about the Court of Appeal's decision arise when what is unquestionably a 'restatement' of a difficult and confused body of case-law, is related to well-established principles and authorities.

The distinction between substantive objects and ancillary powers will, sometimes at least, be difficult to draw, although it must be accepted that not only *Re Introductions*[3] but *Re Horsley & Weight Ltd*[4] and *Rolled Steel v British Steel Corporation*,[5] too, are adamant that this distinction must be made.[6] Moreover, the doctrine enunciated by the Court of Appeal in *Rolled Steel* is not easy to square with the treatment of subordinate powers by Buckley LJ in *Horsley v Weight* or with that of Harman LJ in *Re Introductions*. The contention in *Rolled Steel* that in the latter case Harman LJ was not concerned with *ultra vires* acts beyond the company's corporate capacity (as regards the bank's reliance on the power to borrow) seems open to serious question.

6.9　*Ultra vires* at common law and ratification

At common law, a transaction which was *ultra vires* in the strict sense was void and could not be ratified even with the unanimous consent of all of the shareholders.[7] Thus, an act which was not authorised by the substantive objects or express powers stated in the memorandum, and which could not be regarded as falling within the scope of the company's implied powers, was entirely[8] void at common law. In contrast, a transaction which went beyond the authority of the directors under the articles could normally be ratified by an ordinary resolution of the shareholders in general meeting. What of a transaction in which the directors used an ancillary power expressly or impliedly conferred by the memorandum for a purpose which was beyond the company's substantive objects? Such transactions were not *ultra*

1　At 293 and 294 *per* Slade LJ and at 306 *per* Browne-Wilkinson LJ. The judgment of Russell LJ in *Introductions* was not susceptible to this interpretaton; Slade LJ held that the judgment was confined to its own facts, at 293. *Re David Payne*, above was subjected to similar reinterpretation. *Re Jon Beauforte*, above was not separately considered by Slade LJ or Browne-Wilkinson LJ but the reasoning in that case is undermined by *Rolled Steel.*

2　A perceptive article by Baxter, 'Ultra Vires and Agency Untwined' [1970] CLJ 280, made this point and interpreted the authorities in a way very similar to that subsequently adopted by the Court of Appeal in *Rolled Steel.*

3　[1970] Ch 199 (CA).

4　[1982] Ch 442 (CA).

5　[1986] Ch 246.

6　However, it is not beyond argument that it may still be possible to draft a way out of this distinction.

7　*Ashbury Railway Carriage v Riche* (1875) LR 7 HL 653.

8　On the question of who can plead *ultra vires*, see **6.10**.

vires and, according to the decision of the Court of Appeal in *Rolled Steel*, were capable of being ratified; but a further complication raised by that case was the suggestion (although the point was not fully explored) that ratification of such transactions required the unanimous consent of all of the shareholders rather than the normal principle of ratification by a majority.[1] It is possible that the Court of Appeal had in mind situations where ratification is given informally as opposed to ratification by resolution: informal corporate decision-making is only effective where it is unanimous but majority consent normally suffices where decisions are taken at properly convened company meetings.[2] As a result of statutory reforms, even an act which is *ultra vires* in the strict sense can now be ratified by a majority[3] and it would be illogical if the ratification of an act which is not *ultra vires* in that sense but which is tainted by an improper purpose is subject to a more rigorous procedure.

6.10   Other consequences of *ultra vires* at common law

This needs only a brief review by way of background to the present position which is governed by statute.

As against the company 'an *ultra vires* agreement could not become intra vires by reason of estoppel, lapse of time, ratification, acquiescence or delay'.[4] At common law, a company could always plead in its defence that any contract or other transaction was *ultra vires*. A minority shareholder could prevent the company carrying out an *ultra vires* transaction by obtaining an injunction to restrain the company.[5] An ordinary creditor of the company had no such *locus standi* in seeking to prevent an *ultra vires* transaction.[6] This was somewhat at odds with the idea that one of the purposes of the *ultra vires* doctrine was to protect creditors.[7]

There was no unequivocal ruling on whether the other party to an *ultra vires* contract could raise the issue of the company's capacity when sued by the company. The Court of Appeal in *Bell Houses* left open the question whether it was proper to allow *ultra vires* to be raised as defence against a company, but Salmon LJ

---

1   At 295 *per* Slade LJ.
2   Sealy [1985] CLJ 39 at pp 40–41. This suggestion gathers weight from the fact that the cases cited by Slade LJ in support of the need for unanimity were concerned with shareholders' informal decision-making rather than with decisions taken at shareholders' meetings.
3   Section 35(3) which is discussed further at **6.11**. A special resolution, ie three-quarters majority (of those voting), is required.
4   *Per* Russell J in *York Corporation v Henry Leetham & Sons Ltd* [1924] 1 Ch 557 at 583.
5   *Parke v Daily News Ltd* [1962] Ch 927. An executed *ultra vires* transacton is one of the exceptions to the rule in *Foss v Harbottle* in respect of which a minority shareholder may bring a derivative action: *Russell v Wakefield Waterworks* (1875) LR 20 Eq 374 at 481. It has been held that, to have standing to proceed with a derivative action, a minority shareholder must establish that the wrongdoers are in control of the company and that his action has the support of those who are not implicated in the wrongdoing: *Smith v Croft (No 2)* [1988] Ch 144; see **17.5**.
6   *Mills v Northern Rly of Buenos Ayres* (1870) 5 Ch App 621; *Lawrence v West Somerset Rly* [1918] 2 Ch 520. A debenture-holder holding security over the company's property was allowed to sue in *Cross v Imperial Continental Gas Assoc* [1923] 2 Ch 553.
7   See **6.12**.

cast some doubt on the propriety of this.[1] The objection in principle to allowing *ultra vires* to be pleaded as a defence against a company was that this would subvert a doctrine which was intended to protect companies, and their shareholders and creditors.

It was a breach of fiduciary duty for directors to engage in *ultra vires* acts and the directors were liable to make good any loss suffered by the company as a result of an *ultra vires* transaction.[2] The court could relieve the directors under section 727 of the Companies Act 1985 of liability arising from *ultra vires* acts if it was satisfied that they had acted honestly and reasonably and ought fairly to be excused.[3]

6.11 Consequences of *ultra vires*: section 35 of the Companies Act 1985

Section 35(1) of the Companies Act 1985 provides that 'the validity of an act done by a company shall not be called into question on the ground of lack of capacity by reason of anything in the company's memorandum'.[4] This clearly reverses the common-law rule that *ultra vires* could be raised as a defence to any contractual claim brought against a company. Subject to a query arising from the drafting of a later sub-section,[5] the effect of section 35(1) is also to ensure that lack of capacity cannot be pleaded against a company by the other party. In other words, section 35(1) is two-way in its effect, operating to protect both the company and those who deal with it from the consequences of *ultra vires*.

When is an act done by a company for the purposes of section 35(1)? In contractual matters, English company law has not adopted an organic theory whereby the acts of the board and of the general meeting are treated automatically as acts of the company.[6] Whether a company is bound by a transaction or other act which purports to be done on its behalf is normally determined by reference to agency principles, as modified by the *Turquand* rule and by section 35A of the Companies Act 1985 which is discussed later in this chapter.[7] Nothing in section 35(1) appears to displace or override these principles and, although this is not spelt out, it would therefore seem that they should determine what is an 'act of the

---

1   [1966] 2 QB 656 at 694. At first instance in the same case [1965] 3 All ER 427, Mocatta J suggested that, if the company had performed its side of an *ultra vires* contract, it could claim in quasi-contract. See also Lawson J in *International Sales and Agencies Ltd v Marcus* [1982] 3 All ER 551 at 561.

2   *Re Sharpe* [1892] 1 Ch 154; *Cullerne v London & Suburban Building Society* (1890) 25 QBD 485 at 490.

3   *Re Claridge's Patent Asphalte Co* [1921] 1 Ch 543. See further on section 727, **16.24.4**.

4   There are special rules in relation to charitable companies: section 35(4) and section 65(1) of the Charities Act 1993, and section 112(3) of the Companies Act 1989 amending the Charities Act 1960. Also note section 322A which applies where the person dealing with the company is a director or an associate of a director: **6.23**.

5   Section 35(3).

6   See eg *Rolled Steel* at 295 *per* Slade LJ and at 304 *per* Browne-Wilkinson LJ. Article 9 of the First Company Law Directive (68/151/EEC), the underlying Community provision implemented into English law by section 35 and the immediately following sections, is based rather more on the organic theory: 'acts done by the organs of the company shall be binding on it even though those acts are not within the objects of the company'. A purposive construction is to be adopted in respect of domestic legislation implementing a directive so as to ensure, so far as practicable, compliance with Community obligations: *Pickstone v Freemans plc* [1989] AC 66; *Litster v Forth Dry Dock Engineering Co Ltd* [1990] 1 AC 546.

7   See **6.20–6.22**.

company' for this purpose: so interpreted, section 35(1) ensures that an act done on behalf of a company which would otherwise be enforceable against it does not cease to be so simply because it is not authorised by the company's memorandum.[1]

The reference in section 35(1) to the company's *memorandum* is significant because if the provision had simply referred to the company's objects clause[2] that would have provided scope for companies to reintroduce the *ultra vires* doctrine via restrictive additional clauses in the memorandum. In *Re Cleveland Trust*,[3] where an additional clause in the memorandum restricted the funds available for the payment of dividends, dividend payments in breach of the restriction were held to be *ultra vires*. Although this restriction was not contained in the objects clause, it would now presumably be subject to section 35(1) and such payments could therefore no longer be challenged on the grounds of lack of capacity. However, dividend payments made in breach of the restrictions on distributions imposed by the Companies Acts would still be illegal and might be described as *ultra vires* for that reason.[4]

The memorandum of a company may seek to limit its capacity either by express restrictions or by failing to make provision for matters that would not otherwise be implied as incidental to the stated objects. Since the capacity problems in respect of acts which are not expressly or implicitly authorised by the company's memorandum have their roots in what is expressly provided for in the memorandum, it is suggested that section 35(1) applies in cases where the memorandum is silent and that the reference in that provision to anything *in* the company's memorandum does not limit its application to situations where an express limitation in the memorandum is breached.[5]

Section 35(2) and (3) preserve some of the common-law consequences of *ultra vires*. Section 35(2) gives statutory force to the right of a minority shareholder to bring proceedings to restrain the doing of an *ultra vires* act. No such proceedings may be brought in respect of any act which is to be done in fulfilment of a legal obligation arising from a previous act of the company. Where, as is typical in larger companies, the shareholders are mainly passive investors and are not involved in the management of the company's affairs, they are unlikely to be able to take advantage of the right to seek an injunction because they will not know of what is proposed until such time as it is too late and the company has already incurred legal obligations.[6] The right is likely to be most useful in companies where all of the shareholders are also involved in management but, if relations in that type of

---

1   This interpretation of the phrase 'act of the company' is explored further in Ferran, 'The Reform of the Law on Corporate Capacity and Directors' and Officers' Authority' (1992) 13 Co Law 124. See also Poole, 'Abolition of the Ultra Vires Doctrine and Agency Problems' (1991) 12 Co Law 43.

2   An early version of the bill was couched in these terms but the wording was changed during its passage through Parliament.

3   [1991] BCLC 424, [1991] BCC 33.

4   See *Precision Dippings Ltd v Precision Dippings Marketing Ltd* [1986] Ch 447, [1985] 3 WLR 812, [1985] BCLC 385, (1983–1985) 1 BCC 99, 539 (CA).

5   See also a publication of the Legal Risk Review Committee (a precursor of the Financial Law Panel, a City body which provides guidance to practitioners on areas of legal uncertainty) entitled *Reducing Uncertainty, The Way Forward*, (1992), Annex to Appendix 1, paragraph 10.

6   This point was discussed in the House of Lords during the passage of the Companies Bill through Parliament. See *Hansard* HL Debs col 512, 7 November 1989, col 681 and Poole (1991) 12 Co Law 43.

company have broken down, proceedings to restrain the doing of an act which is not authorised by the company's memorandum may be only one aspect of a larger dispute.

Section 35(3) preserves the common-law position in respect of directors' duties and corporate capacity: 'it remains the duty of the directors to observe any limitations on their powers flowing from the company's memorandum'. Section 35(3) provides that the shareholders may by special resolution relieve directors from liability for failing to observe limits flowing from the company's memorandum. Section 35(3) also refers to ratification by separate special resolution of action by directors which, but for subsection (1), would be beyond the company's capacity. At a basic level, it confirms the change to the common-law position that an *ultra vires* act is not ratifiable. Ratification may be desirable to prevent a shareholder from exercising his right under section 35(2), for example.[1] Moreover, to the extent that it prevents shareholders from being misled by a composite special resolution which simultaneously ratifies the transaction and relieves the directors from liability, it is sensible and uncontroversial. In circumstances where the company chooses to ratify a transaction which is beyond the limits of its memorandum,[2] the clause makes clear that the ratification must be effected by a separate special resolution. However, it is arguable that the clause has a wider effect.

The wider interpretation of section 35(3) is that to enforce any act of the directors which is beyond the limits of its memorandum, a company must ratify the action by special resolution. The argument on which this interpretation is based is that, until ratification, the company cannot claim the act as one of its own because the directors had no authority to do the act on its behalf. Although, by virtue of section 35A which is discussed later in this chapter, the person dealing with the company may be able to enforce it against the company despite the directors' lack of authority, that provision does not allow a company to enforce the act against the outsider. [3] This interpretation, which has been described as 'strained',[4] undermines the unqualified two-way wording of section 35(1) that an act 'shall not be called into question'. It is also objectionable in principle because in effect it subverts what was the underlying principle of the *ultra vires* doctrine, namely, protection of the company and its creditors and shareholders. Even when the *ultra vires* doctrine was most vigorously enforced at common law, it was doubtful whether *ultra vires* could be pleaded against the company; it would run

---

1   Davies, *Gower and Davies' Principles of Modern Company Law*, 7th edition (London: Sweet & Maxwell, 2003).

2   Eg where the transaction is voidable under section 322A because the other party is a director or a person connected with a director.

3   See Poole (1991) 12 Co Law 43 at p 45 and Ferran (1992) 13 Co Law 124 at p 128 where this argument is further considered.

4   *Gore-Browne on Companies* 44th edn (Jordans, loose-leaf) at 3.1.1. Commencing on the relevant clause of the Companies Bill during its passage through Parliament, Lord Strathclyde, the Government spokesperson, stated that ratification 'would, among other things, enable the company to enforce the contract if that is what the shareholders believe to be in the interests of the company', *Hansard*, HL Debs, 21 February 1989, col 516. In similar vein is his Lordship's later statement that 'ratification by the company of an *ultra vires* act that would not otherwise bind the company on the grounds of the lack of authority of the directors does not affect any liability incurred by the directors', *Hansard*, HL Debs, 7 November 1918, col 675. These comments tend to support the wider view.

entirely counter to the purpose of the statutory reforms if, by arguing lack of authority, a plea which is to substantially the same effect could now succeed.

Reading section 35 as a whole, it is questionable whether the wide interpretation of the offending clause in section 35(3) is correct but, unless it is considered by a court, the matter cannot be regarded as entirely free from doubt. In theory, it would be prudent for a company to ratify by special resolution any acts which fall outside what is authorised by its memorandum but this advice might well be outweighed by practical considerations. Obtaining a special resolution can be a time-consuming and expensive task since, unless the company is so small that it is possible for all of the shareholders to reach agreement by informal means, this will involve convening a general meeting for the purpose. The safest course remains to have an objects clause which is drafted in the widest possible terms, because this minimises the circumstances in which recourse will have to be had to the statutory provisions. This is reinforced by the fact that failure to observe the limitations imposed by the company's memorandum remains a breach of duty by the directors and, if discovered far enough in advance, can be restrained by an injunction obtained by a shareholder. The consequences of an act falling outside the scope of a company's memorandum are now much less severe than they were previously, but companies, or more particularly their directors, are still likely to appreciate the advantages of avoiding those consequences altogether by appropriate drafting of the company's memorandum.[1] Ultimately, once the proposal to abolish the *ultra vires* doctrine altogether has been adopted, this will no longer be an issue.

6.12   The decline of the *ultra vires* doctrine

When the *ultra vires* doctrine was first developed by the courts in the nineteenth century, it was perceived to be a valuable protection to shareholders and creditors from risky and wasteful ventures by the directors: shareholders and creditors could be assured that their money would not be put to uses beyond those authorised by the company's memorandum. As companies began to draft their way around the restrictions of the doctrine by devising ever more extensive objects, the usefulness of the objects clause as a source of information to shareholders and creditors about the uses to which their money could be put declined. Judicial antipathy to devices such as the independent objects clauses ultimately failed to prevent companies from ensuring, by suitable drafting, that they had capacity to do virtually anything.

At the same time, company law was developing alternative rules to protect shareholders and creditors against dissipation by the directors of the funds made available to the company. Throughout the twentieth century, the rules regarding the funds which could be used to pay dividends or make other distributions to shareholders were progressively tightened.[2] Provisions of the insolvency legislation attacking preferences or transactions at an undervalue also sought to prevent unwarranted disposals of corporate funds.[3] Accounting and reporting obligations imposed on directors by the companies legislation became more

---

1   For persons dealing with the company, an advantage of a widely drafted memorandum is that it minimises the possibility of becoming implicated in a breach of duty by the directors flowing from their failure to observe the limits of the memorandum.

2   See **7.21**.

3   See **21.55.2** and **21.55.3**.

onerous thus giving those dealing, or considering dealing, with a company the opportunity to monitor the stewardship of its affairs by consulting its published financial information.[1] Fiduciary duties, as well as specific personal liabilities under the insolvency legislation for wrongful trading,[2] also served as deterrents against abuse of position by directors.

When Professor Prentice reviewed the *ultra vires* doctrine in 1986, he concluded that 'the doctrine of *ultra vires* no longer serves any useful purpose' because 'the doctrine is for all intents and purposes defeasible at the discretion of the draftsman'.[3] Virtually all of those consulted by Professor Prentice were of the view that the doctrine of *ultra vires* failed to provide any significant protection to the interests of shareholders[4] and were critical of its operation in relation to creditors.[5] Professor Prentice concluded that the published accounts and reports of a company were a more helpful source of information than its objects clause.[6] He thought[7] that the provisions of the insolvency legislation relating to wrongful trading, preferences and transactions at an undervalue provided adequate protection to creditors against dissipation of assets without the need in addition for the *ultra vires* doctrine[8] and that shareholders were also protected against gratuitous dispositions by fiduciary duties, rules about maintenance of capital and unlawful distributions, reporting requirements and the provisions of the companies and insolvency legislation entitling them to seek relief from unfair prejudice[9] or to have the company wound up on just and equitable grounds.[10]

The DTI chose not to accept Professor Prentice's recommendation that a company should have the capacity to do any act whatsoever and opted instead for the rather more complex position reviewed in this chapter. However, because companies have tended to continue to adopt prolix objects clauses[11] and the short-form 'general commercial company' object has proved not to be an attractive alternative, the Government has now accepted that the *ultra vires* principle should be abolished altogether.[12]

6.13 Corporate gifts

The topic of corporate gifts provides a good illustration of the way in which, historically, the courts used the *ultra vires* doctrine to control the application of corporate funds but how, with the decline of that doctrine, other rules have developed to serve that purpose. Glosses were added to the *ultra vires* doctrine to accommodate control of corporate gifts, but in recent years the courts have stripped away those glosses as being incompatible with *ultra vires* in its strict sense

---

1   See Chapter 14.
2   See **15.17.2**.
3   DTI, *Reform of the Ultra Vires Rule*, Part II, Chapter 2, paragraph 6.
4   Ibid, Chapter 3, paragraph 3.
5   DTI, *Reform of the Ultra Vires Rule*, Part II, Chapter 3, paragraph 9.
6   Ibid, Chapter 5, paragraphs 7 and 11. He recommended that this should be bolstered, in respect of both private and public companies, by a specific obligation to file an annual activities and business statement: Chapter 5, paragraphs 11, 19 and 26.
7   Ibid, Chapter 6, paragraphs 28–30.
8   Ibid, Chapter 6, paragraph 25.
9   Section 459; see **17.13**.
10   Section 122(1)(g) of the Insolvency Act 1986. See **17.16**.
11   Or have retained existing long-form objects which were in place before the short-form 'general commercial company' object was introduced.
12   *Modernising Company Law* (July 2002).

of outside corporate capacity. The need to have those glosses diminished as other forms of control were put in place.

In *Re Lee, Behrens & Co*,[1] Eve J laid down three tests by which improper gifts, charitable or otherwise, might be distinguished from those which formed a legitimate *intra vires* expenditure by the company. To be valid, any payment had to be:

(1) for the benefit of the company;
(2) reasonably incidental to its business; and
(3) made *bona fide* in the interest of the company.

Charterbridge Corporation v Lloyds Bank[2] repudiated the principles set forth in *Re Lee, Behrens & Co*, above, so far as they applied to the interpretation of express powers. Pennycuick J rejected the test of the 'benefit of the company' as placing a limit upon the use that may be made of an express provision in the objects clause. He indicated that the question of good faith[3] on the part of the directors related to their fiduciary duty to the company and not to the question of *ultra vires*.

In *Re Horsley & Weight Ltd*,[4] the Court of Appeal endorsed the approach taken in *Charterbridge*. Where on its true construction a clause in the memorandum allowed for the payment of pensions as a separate object, and not merely as an ancillary power or object to the main object of the company, the purchase of a pension policy could not be challenged by the liquidator as *ultra vires* the objects of the company. Buckley LJ discarded Eve J's criteria as they applied to express powers as 'no more than *obiter dictum*'. The clause in this case also allowed the making of grants for charitable, benevolent or public purposes or objects. Buckley LJ observed that 'the objects of a company need not be commercial; they can be charitable or philanthropic; indeed, they can be whatever the original incorporators wish, provided that they are legal. Nor is there any reason why a company should not part with its funds gratuitously or for non-commercial reasons if to do so is within its declared objects'.

However, whilst a gift or gratuitous payment may not be challenged as *ultra vires* for the reasons stated, it may still be impugned as an unlawful return of capital (eg where a payment is made under the guise of directors' remuneration where the real intention is to make a gift of capital to shareholders)[5] or as a transaction at an undervalue under section 238 of the Insolvency Act 1986.[6] Directors who authorise the making of corporate gifts at a time when, to their knowledge, the company's solvency is in doubt may also be liable for misfeasance under section

---

1   [1932] 2 Ch 46.
2   [1970] Ch 62. Pennycuick J's reasoning in *Charterbridge* was followed in *Thomson v J Barke & Co (Caterers) Ltd* 1975 SLT 67 at 70–71.
3   As to the directors' duty of good faith, see **16.4**. For an illustraton of such lack of good faith, see *Re W & M Roith Ltd* [1967] 1 WLR 432.
4   [1982] 3 All ER 108. See also *Re Halt Garage (1964) Ltd* [1982] 3 All ER 1016, where Oliver J adopted a similar approach. He regarded the test of 'good faith' and 'the benefit of the company' as irrelevant to express powers.
5   *Re Halt Garage*, above; *Aveling Barford Ltd v Perion Ltd* [1989] BCLC 626; *Barclays Bank plc v British and Commonwealth Holdings plc* [1995] BCC 19, affirmed [1996] 1 All ER 381 (indirect return of capital). See **7.11**.
6   The company must have gone into liquidation or an administrator must have been appointed. The conditions which must be satisfied for section 238 to apply are discussed in Chapter 19. Note also section 423 of the Insolvency Act 1986 (transactions defrauding creditors).

212 of the Insolvency Act 1986.[1] An argument based on misfeasance will not succeed where gifts are made with the knowledge and consent of all of the shareholders at their instigation and the company is fully solvent.[2] It has been held that in addition to rules prohibiting the return of capital to members, a company which has no distributable profits cannot make gifts to outsiders except for the advancement of the company's business.[3] The best explanation for this rule would appear to be that the making of such gifts amounts to a fraud on the company's creditors, which is something that the shareholders are powerless to authorise.[4]

Where no express power has been conferred by the memorandum, the extent of the company's implied powers to make gifts must be determined. In the early case of *Attorney-General v Great Eastern Rly*,[5] it was said that whatever could fairly be regarded as incidental to, or consequential upon, the stated objects would be implied. Eve J's second test – reasonably incidental to its business – is no more than a restatement of this conventional test for implying powers into an objects clause and, to that extent, the reasoning in *Re Lee, Behrens* may still be regarded as authoritative.[6]

With regard to the element of benefit to the company, in *Charterbridge* Pennycuick J commented that this was appropriate in part to the scope of implied powers and in part, and perhaps principally, to the duty of directors.[7] Oliver J was more explicit in *Re Halt Garage* stating that the test of benefit to the company was, in his view, really only appropriate to the question of the propriety of an exercise of a power.[8] Pennycuick J in *Charterbridge* and Oliver J in *Re Halt Garage* had the same view of the *bona fides* test: that it was relevant to the fiduciary duties of the directors and did not affect the construction of the company's implied powers.[9]

Neither *Charterbridge* nor *Re Halt Garage* required the court to rule on the scope of a company's implied powers and the comments on implied powers were therefore strictly *obiter*. This was also the position in *Rolled Steel* where the actual decision of the Court of Appeal related to the company's express power in its memorandum to give guarantees. Nevertheless, the Court of Appeal took the opportunity to consider the *Re Lee, Behrens* tests generally and, although not formally overruled, the force of the criticisms voiced by Slade and Browne-Wilkinson LJJ means that little of Eve J's reasoning in the earlier case can be regarded as still relevant to the question of construction of implied power to make corporate gifts.

Without distinguishing between express and implied powers, Slade LJ stated simply that the three tests of *ultra vires* suggested by Eve J:[10]

> ... should, in my opinion, now be recognised as being of no assistance, and indeed positively misleading, when the relevant question is whether a particular gratuitous transaction is within a company's corporate capacity. To this extent, the tests should, I

---

1   *Re Horsley & Weight*, above.
2   *Brady v Brady* [1989] AC 755 at 776.
3   *Barclays Bank plc v British and Commonwealth Holdings plc*, above.
4   *ANZ Executors & Trustee Co Ltd v Qintex Australia Ltd* (1990) 8 ACLC 980; *Plain Ltd v Kilney & Royal Trust Co* (1931) 1 DLR 468; *Re George Newman & Co* [1985] 1 Ch 674.
5   (1875) LR 7 HL 653. Note also *Hutton v West Cork Railway co* (1883) 23 Ch D 654 at 671 *per* Bowen LJ.
6   *Charterbridge* at 71; *Re Halt Garage (1964) Ltd* [1982] 3 All ER 1016 at 1034.
7   At 71.
8   At 1034.
9   *Charterbridge* at 71; *Re Halt Garage* at 1034.
10   At 288.

think, be finally laid to rest, though they may well be helpful in considering whether or not in any given case directors have abused the powers vested in them by the company.

Browne-Wilkinson LJ endorsed Pennycuick J's analysis in *Charterbridge* and regarded the reasoning in *Re Lee, Behrens* as 'wrong'.[1]

Three types of corporate gifts require special mention. These are pensions to former employees and their dependants, redundancy payments, and charitable or political donations.

6.13.1 Pensions

Where the paying of pensions is an independent object of the company, pensions paid under that power in the company's memorandum cannot be *ultra vires*.[2] Where the memorandum authorises the paying of pensions but, as a matter of construction, that provision is only a power and is not a substantive object, provided that power is capable of being used in a manner which is reasonably incidental to the attainment or pursuit of its substantive objects, its use in particular cases will not be *ultra vires* although the directors may be liable for breach of their fiduciary duties if they have abused the power.[3] The power to pay pensions could be viewed as being capable of being exercised reasonably incidentally to the company's business on the grounds that it is conducive to business to seek to retain the workforce by being seen to be a generous employer.[4]

If there is no express power in the memorandum to pay pensions, the test is whether this can be implied as being reasonably incidental to the company's business.[5] In an ordinary trading company that test would normally be satisfied; thus Plowman J in *Re W & M Roith Ltd*[6] was 'disposed to agree' with counsel 'that a widow's pension is reasonably incidental to carrying on a company's business'. In *Roith*, a pension granted under an express power in the memorandum was held to be *ultra vires* by application of the *Re Lee, Behrens* tests; in view of *Re Horsley & Weight* and *Rolled Steel*, *Roith* may now be better regarded as an instance where the directors abused the corporate powers in breach of their fiduciary duties.

6.13.2 Charitable or political donations

Parliament requires that charitable and political donations which exceed £200 in any financial year must be disclosed in the directors' report.[7] This provision does not of itself validate gifts, being concerned simply with disclosure. Where a political or charitable gift is covered by an express provision in the memorandum, *Re Horsley & Weight Ltd*[8] makes it clear that like any other gift it is not open to challenge on grounds of lack of capacity. If there is no express power, the question of the company's capacity to make charitable donations would depend on whether this is reasonably incidental to the company's business.

---

1 At 304–305.
2 *Re Horsley & Weight*, above.
3 *Rolled Steel*, above.
4 Similar arguments could be used to justify the provision of sporting and social welfare facilities.
5 *Henderson v Bank of Australasia* (1888) 49 Ch D 170; *Normandy v Ind Coope & Co Ltd* [1908] 1 Ch 84, 104; *Cyclists' Touring Club v Hopkinson* [1910] 1 Ch 179.
6 [1967] 1 WLR 432 at 437.
7 See the Companies Act 1985, Schedule 7, paragraph 3.
8 [1982] 3 All ER 1045.

In *Simmonds v Heffer*,[1] Mervyn Davies J was dealing with a charitable company whose main object was to prevent and oppose cruelty to animals. The plaintiff first challenged a gift of £50,000 to the general election fund of the Labour Party. This gift had been made on the ground that the party was committed to introducing legislation to ban hare-coursing and stag-hunting. This gift was held to be *ultra vires* as it could be used for purposes unconnected with the League Against Cruel Sports' purposes. This was despite an ancillary power 'to affiliate, to combine or co-operate with, subscribe to, aid or support any institution having objects similar to the main objects of the League or any of them'. This was because the Labour Party, by its constitution, had vastly wider aims than the League and therefore did not have aims similar to the League's main objects. However, another gift of £30,000, made on the understanding that it would be used specifically for activities advertising the Labour Party's commitment to animal walfare, was upheld as being within the League's main objects as supported by ancillary powers in its objects clause.

This case was decided before *Rolled Steel v British Steel Corporation*,[2] and its reasoning is not entirely consistent with the Court of Appeal's restatement of the principles applicable to powers (as opposed to objects) in the memorandum. The voluntary recipients of political or charitable donations could now claim the protection of sections 35 and 35A if there is any doubt about the capacity of the donor company, since those provisions are not limited in their application to commercial transactions, but apply also to other acts.

For most practical purposes, the *ultra vires* rule has thus faded away as a mechanism for controlling the funding of political parties or the making of charitable gifts by companies. Directors remain subject to fiduciary duties and they must make decisions about the use of company money in accordance with the duty to act in the interests of the company.[3] In recent years, there has been concern from some institutional investors and from government about the accountability of directors to shareholders with regard to these matters and the perception has grown that fiduciary duties and disclosure requirements may not be sufficient to prevent directors from choosing to use company money to support causes that reflect their own personal interests rather than those of the company. A recommendation from the Committee on Standards in Public Life, chaired by Lord Neill, that any company wishing to make a donation to a political party should have the prior authority of its shareholders[4] has been accepted by the Government. The Political Parties, Elections and Referendums Act 2000 inserted a new Part XA (sections 347A to 347K) into the Companies Act 1985 to give effect to this proposal.[5] In essence, political donations and other political expenditure require the approval by the sharehoders of a company before donations are made.[6] Such approval is not, however, required for a particular transaction, but

---

1   [1984] BCLC 298.

2   Above. But see a similar decision by Mervyn Davies J in *Rosemary Simmons Memorial Housing Association v United Dominions Trust* [1985] 1 WLR 1440. Though *Rolled Steel* was taken into account, *ultra vires* was strictly applied to a charitable company.

3   See Chapter 16.

4   Cm 4057–I *The Funding of Political Parties in the United Kingdom* (October 1998), recommendation 34. The Government's views are set out in *Political Donations by Companies* (URN 99/757), (Consultative Document, March 1999).

5   These new provisions are only summarised briefly here.

6   Section 347C.

rather sanctions political donations and expenditure up to a specified amount for a period of up to four years ('approval resolutions'). Directors are liable to repay to the company any donations made in breach of these provisions,[1] and may also have to pay compensation for any loss or damage suffered by the company as a result.

6.13.3 Redundancy payments

In *Parke v Daily News*,[2] it was held that gratuitous redundancy payments paid to former employees were in breach of the *Lee, Behrens* principles since they were motivated by a desire to treat the employees generously, and were not made to benefit the company (which was to cease to be an employer in the newspaper industry). The categorisation of these payments as '*ultra vires*' the powers of the company might now be reassessed because of the reliance placed by Plowman J on the discredited *Lee, Behrens* tests. In any event, two statutory innovations originally made by the Companies Act 1980 would mean that a different decision would now be made where employees are affected. Where the company is a going concern, section 309 of the Companies Act 1985 provides that the 'matters to which the directors of a company are to have regard in the performance of their function include the interests of the company's employees in general as well as the interests of its members'.[3] Further, section 719 states that the powers of the company shall be deemed to include a power to make provision 'for the benefit of persons employed or formerly employed by the company or any of its subsidiaries in connection with cessation or transfer to any person of the whole or part of the undertaking of that company or that subsidiary'.

The power conferred by section 719 may be exercised notwithstanding that its exercise is not in the best interests of the company.[4] Section 719(3) makes it clear the section is concerned with extending the capacity of the company and freeing it from a restriction that the *ultra vires* doctrine might otherwise impose on such voluntary (ie non-statutory) redundancy or retirement payments. It does not dispense with the proper authorisation within the company itself. Section 719(3) provides that the power it confers may be exercised, if so authorised by the company's memorandum or articles, by a resolution of the directors. If, however, the memorandum or articles require the exercise of the power to be 'sanctioned by a resolution of the company of some other description for which more than a simple majority of members voting is necessary', it must be exercised with the sanction of a resolution of that description: section 719(3)(b) and (c). Where no provision for the exercise of the power conferred by section 719 is made in the memorandum or articles, it may be exercised by ordinary resolutions of the company: section 719(3)(a). On the winding up of a solvent company (whether by the court or a voluntary winding up), the liquidator may make any payments which the company decided to make before commencement of the winding up. Provision is also made for the liquidator to exercise this power himself if the company's liabilities have been fully satisfied and provision made for the costs of winding up. He must also obtain the authorisation of the shareholders by a

---

1   Section 347F.
2   [1962] Ch 927.
3   See **16.6**.
4   Section 719(2). See also section 187 of the Insolvency Act 1986.

resolution.[1] In the case of payments made before commencement of winding up, these must be made out of the profits of the company available for dividend. In the case of payments made after the commencement of winding up, these must be made out of the assets of the company which are available to its members on its winding up.[2]

6.14 Alteration of objects

The companies legislation which was in force between 1856 and 1890 did not permit the objects of a company to be altered. Once it became possible to alter objects with the consent of only a majority of the shareholders and without the consent of the creditors (although dissident shareholders and creditors might, in limited circumstances, be able to raise objections), the idea that the objects clause was a safeguard against shareholders' and creditors' money being put to purposes which they had not authorised was undermined.

A company may by special resolution, under the power conferred by section 4, alter the provisions of its memorandum of association. This section does not authorise an alteration of the memorandum which does not relate to the objects of the company.[3] But the whole objects of a company are not necessarily contained in the objects clause of the memorandum;[4] and provisions not relating to the objects may, if they could lawfully have been contained in the articles, be alterable under section 17.[5] Under section 4, a company now has unrestricted power to limit or narrow the scope of its objects and to increase them.

6.15 The procedure for objecting to an alteration to the objects

Dissenting shareholders or, to a more limited extent, creditors are permitted by section 5 to apply to the court to have the alteration cancelled. An application by shareholders must be made by the holders of not less in the aggregate than 15% of the company's issued share capital or of any class of shares. If the company is not limited by shares, not less than 15% of the members must make the application. The creditors entitled to make the application are limited to the holders of debentures secured by a floating charge which were issued or first issued before 1 December 1947, or which form part of the same series as any debentures so issued; and an application by debenture holders must be made by the holders of not less than 15% of such debentures.

A person – whether a shareholder or debenture holder – who has consented to or voted in favour of the alteration cannot make an application under the section.

---

1   See section 187 of the Insolvency Act 1986. This may be an ordinary resolution or one by more than a simple majority if the memorandum or articles so require. A resolution of the directors will not suffice.
2   Section 719(4) and 187(3) of the Insolvency Act 1986.
3   *Re Society for Promoting Employment of Women* [1927] WN 145; cf *Re Scientific Poultry Breeders' Association* [1933] 1 Ch 227; *Re Scottish Special Housing Association* 1947 SC 17.
4   *Incorporated Glasgow Dental Hospital v Lord Advocate* 1927 SC 400.
5   See **5.13**.

The application must be made within 21 days after the date of the passing of the resolution, and the persons entitled to make it may in writing appoint one or more of their number for the purpose.[1]

6.16 The court's discretion

On the hearing of an application under section 5(4), the court may confirm the alteration either wholly or in part and on such terms and conditions as it thinks fit, or, it may adjourn the proceedings in order that an arrangement may be made to the satisfaction of the court for the purchase of the interests of dissentient members, and may give directions and make orders for facilitating or carrying into effect any such arrangement.

Section 5(5) provides that, if the court thinks fit, an order under section 5 may provide for the purchase by the company of the shares of any members of the company and for the reduction accordingly of the company's capital. The court may make such alterations in the memorandum and articles as are required in consequence of such provision. Quite apart from this, the court may require the company to make any, or any specified, alteration in the memorandum or articles of the company. The company will not then have power without leave of the court to make any further alteration in breach of what the court has required.[2] Alterations of the memorandum or articles required by the court have the same effect as if duly altered by resolution of the company.[3]

Applications under section 5 are very rare.[4] Shareholders who are aggrieved by an alteration to the objects have the option of seeking alternative relief under Part XVII of the Companies Act 1985 (the unfair prejudice remedy) or may even seek to have the company wound up under section 122(1)(g) of the Insolvency Act 1986.[5] These alternative remedies are not subject to the strict time-limit imposed on section 5 applications and there is no minimum shareholding requirement which must be met.

6.17 Publicity for alterations of the memorandum

The requirements imposed by sections 42 and 711 of the Companies Act 1985 in regard to alteration of the memorandum have been examined at **5.14–5.15**. As regards the alteration of the objects clause, certain additional points should be noted. Section 18 (regarding forwarding printed copies of the altered memorandum and the instrument of alteration to the Registrar) does not apply to a special resolution under section 4 of the Companies Act 1985. However, section 6(1) of the Companies Act 1985 itself requires, *inter alia*, the delivery of a printed copy of the memorandum as altered.

---

1   As to the necessity for obtaining within the 21 days the authority of the holders of the requisite number of shares or debentures cf *Re Suburban & Provincial Stores* [1943] Ch 106; *Re Sound City (Films)* [1947] Ch 169.
2   Section 5(6).
3   Section 5(7). For similar powers conferred on the court under sections 459 to 461 (relief where members are unfairly prejudiced) and section 54 of the 1985 Act (cancellation of special resolutions by the court where a public company becomes a private company), see respectively **17.16** and **4.13**.
4   Since the Companies Act 1948 there has been only reported application under the relevant section: *Re Hampstead Garden Suburban Trust Ltd* [1962] Ch 806.
5   See **6.18**.

Section 17, which is concerned with the alteration of optional conditions in the memorandum, gives dissenting shareholders the same right to apply to the court as is given by section 5 to those who dissent from an alteration of the objects clause (see **5.13**). However, even though section 17 invokes the procedure laid down by certain subsections of section 5, the resolution altering optional provisions in the memorandum is a resolution under section 17. Consequently, it is not exempt from the requirements of section 18.

6.18 Just and equitable winding-up

Shareholders who object to a company undertaking a new type of activity when its original business is abandoned may have a form of relief open to them other than invoking the *ultra vires* doctrine. They may petition the court under section 122(1)(g) of the Insolvency Act 1986 for a compulsory winding-up order on the ground that it is just and equitable to do so. One basis on which the court will make a just and equitable winding-up order is that the substratum of the company, the main object for which it was incorporated, has ceased to exist.[1] A winding-up order may be made even though the new activity is technically within the scope of an express power. Even if the memorandum provides that each of the powers conferred by the objects clause shall be a main object, the court may still find that the company has abandoned the real purposes for which it was founded.[2]

6.19 Authority to bind the company

Where the company possesses undoubted contractual capacity in respect of a particular contract, there still remains the question whether those who purported to make a contract on the company's behalf had the authority to do so. The authority to bind the company must be conferred either directly by the articles of association or by delegation under a power contained in them. Almost invariably, the general power to manage the company will be conferred upon the board of directors[3] and the board itself will usually have a power to delegate their power to manage the company's affairs (eg to one or more managing directors[4]). On some important matters, the approval of the general meeting may be required.[5]

Any want of authority can be cured by ratification by a resolution of the shareholders in general meeting.[6] An ordinary resolution normally suffices but where the lack of authority results from the provisions of the company's memorandum, a special resolution is required.[7] Where a contract is neither originally binding upon the company nor subsequently ratified, the third party may be entitled to recover on a restitutionary basis if the company has received money or goods have been supplied or services have been rendered.

---

1   For detailed treatment of the grounds on which a court will make a just and equitable order, see **17.17**, where the cases on the disappearance of the substratum of a company are examined.
2   *Cotman v Brougham* [1918] AC 514 at 520 *per* Lord Parker.
3   Article 70 of the Companies (Tables A to F) Regulations 1985. References in this chapter to articles are to articles of the Table A contained in these regulations.
4   Eg Table A, articles 84 and 72.
5   Eg Table A, article 70, in respect of the directors' powers relative to the company's powers.
6   *Grant v United Kingdom Switchback Railway Co* (1889) 40 Ch D 135 (CA); *Phosphate of Lime Co v Green* (1871) LR 7 CP 43; *Campbell's Case* (1873) 9 Ch App 1.
7   Section 35(3).

A director or other lesser agent who lacks the authority to bind the company that he claims, may be liable for breach of warranty of authority. Where a wilful or reckless misrepresentation on the part of the directors can be established, an action for deceit might be brought.[1]

A contract for which there is no actual authority (express or implied) may nevertheless become binding on the company under a number of principles. The directors or other officers of a company have no actual authority to bind the company in matters falling outside the constitutional limits imposed by its memorandum and articles. However, by virtue of section 35A of the Companies Act 1985, transactions authorised by the board which are outside the constitutional limits can usually be enforced against the company.[2] Under the doctrine of ostensible (or apparent) authority, a person who has no actual authority to act on the company's behalf may be able to bind the company if he has been held out by someone with appropriate authority as a duly authorised agent of the company. The doctrine of ostensible authority is part of the general law of agency and it applies irrespective of whether the principal is a company or a natural person. A special modification of the doctrine known as the 'rule in *Turquand's* case' applies only in relation to corporate principals.

6.20 The protection of persons dealing with the company in good faith: section 35A

It is through section 35A (and the surrounding sections) that the United Kingdom seeks to comply with its obligation to implement article 9 of the First Company Law Directive.[3] Article 9 seeks to protect third parties in transactions with a company from 'limitations upon the powers of the competent organs imposed by the Charter or by a decision of the competent organs'. Such limitations 'may never be invoked against third parties even if they have been published'. The First Directive was adopted before the United Kingdom joined the European Community and its language is unfamiliar because, in contractual matters, English law traditionally has not regarded the board and the general meeting as 'organs' of a company. Possibly because of differences in established terminology, article 9 was badly implemented by section 9 of the European Communities Act 1972 (which, on consolidation of the companies legislation, became section 35 of the Companies Act 1985).[4] The current section 35A (and surrounding sections) is therefore the United Kingdom's second attempt to implement the Directive. Section 35A meets many of the criticisms which were levelled at its predecessor but some points of uncertainty or difficulty remain.

Section 35A(1) provides that:

> In favour of a person dealing with a company in good faith, the power of the board of directors to bind the company, or to authorise others to do so, shall be deemed to be free of any limitation under the company's constitution.

---

1   Or an action for negligent misstatement under *Hedley Byrne & Co v Heller Partners* [1964] AC 465.

2   See **6.20**.

3   Directive 68/151/EEC, (1968) OJ L65/8. See **2.3.1**. As to the European Community's programme of company law directives generally, see **2.3**.

4   Commentaries on the implementation of Article 9 by the European Communities Act 1972 include: Prentice (1973) 89 LQR 518; Farrar & Powles (1973) 36 MLR 270; Sealy & Collier [1973] CLJ 1; Wyatt (1978) 94 LQR 182.

Thus, if a person negotiates a contract with the board of directors of the company and it subsequently emerges that the board's authority to conclude that contract was in fact limited by the company's constitution, that person can nevertheless hold the company to the contract provided he is in 'good faith'. The limitation on the board's authority may stem from the company's memorandum where it is beyond the company's express (or implied) objects and powers to enter into contracts of that type. A limitation imposed by the company's articles is also a limitation under the company's constitution: thus section 35A applies where the board exceeds a limit imposed by the articles on its power to manage the company's affairs. By virtue of section 35A(3), limitations under the company's constitution also include limitations deriving from a resolution of the company in general meeting or a meeting of any class of shareholders, or from any agreement between the members of the company or any class of shareholders.

It is usually not practicable for the board of a company to play a significant role in the day-to-day contracts which are entered into in the ordinary course of the company's business. These contracts are normally the responsibility of individual directors and other corporate officers. Typically, the board of directors is only involved in major contracts such as acquisitions of new businesses, disposals of existing divisions of the company, or loans and other financing agreements. A criticism of section 9 of the European Communities Act 1972 was that it applied only in respect of 'transactions decided upon by directors'; although the courts did attempt to interpret this provision robustly,[1] it appears that, in all but exceptional cases,[2] transactions which were authorised within the company at a level below that of the board fell outside the scope of the statutory protection.

In this respect, section 35A is more helpfully drafted because, as well as protecting outsiders who deal with the board directly, it also deems the power of the board to authorise others to bind the company to be free of any limitations under the company's constitution. But for section 35A, if the board purports to delegate, say to a managing director, in breach of limitations on its powers to delegate in the company's constitution, the managing director cannot be said to have authority to bind the company. Although, in a factual sense, the managing director may have been held out by the board as having authority, the principle of ostensible authority does not apply because the board itself has no authority under the company's constitution to make the representation.[3] In favour of an outsider, section 35A deems the board to have that authority.

An apparent lacuna in section 35A is that it does not expressly protect an outsider against specific constitutional limitations on persons other than the board. If the articles limit the authority of the managing director to contracts of a particular type or impose a ceiling on the amounts involved, that is obviously not a limit on the board's power to bind the company and, read literally, it is not a limit on the board's power to delegate authority. Accordingly, this is not covered by section 35A unless it is possible to argue that section 35A, by deeming the board to have unlimited power to authorise others to bind the company, overrides any

---

1   *TCB v Gray* [1986] Ch 621 (informal consent of all directors to the granting of a debenture), *affirmed* [1987] Ch 458n; *International Sales and Agencies Ltd v Marcus* [1982] 3 All ER 551.

2   In *International Sales and Agencies Ltd v Marcus* above at p 560 Lawson J observed that the statutory protection could apply where there was a 'sole effective director to whom all actual authority to act for the board had been delegated'.

3   See further **6.31**.

specific limitation whether expressed to apply to the board or to an individual.[1] In practice, it would be uncommon for the authority of individual directors or officers to be limited by the company's constitution; such limitations are more usually imposed in the contracts of employment of the relevant individuals. These contractual limitations fall outside the scope of section 35A and their effect on outsiders is governed by agency principles and the rule in *Turquand's* case.

Section 35A applies to limitations on the powers of the board. One difficult question in this context has been whether the requirements regarding the constitution of the board, such as quorum requirements, fall within the section. This was debated during the passage of the Companies Act 1989 through Parliament. The view of the government spokesperson was that articles specifying the quorum for board meetings, voting rights at board meetings and the like were to be regarded as provisions which defined the board rather than limitations on the powers of the board.[2] If so,[3] a transaction which is entered into by an inquorate board is not protected by section 35A. This issue was considered in the recent case of *Smith v Henniker-Major & Co.*[4] In that case, a director had attempted to assign to himself the company's right of action against a firm of solicitors by passing a resolution at an inquorate board meeting. He subsequently sought to rely on section 35A to defeat a challenge to the validity of the assignment. At first instance,[5] Rimer J held that section 35A did not apply to an inquorate board, because that section refers to the 'powers of the board of directors', which can only be exercised if directors act as a board. An inquorate board is not a board at all and therefore has no powers, and consequently cannot exceed these.[6] If the quorum requirement were a limitation within section 35A, which would then effectively override this requirement, no useful effect would be served by having a quorum requirement in the articles. The Court of Appeal differed on this issue, undoubtedly influenced by the unusual facts of the case. Robert Walker LJ disagreed with Rimer J and thought that section 35A could apply to an inquorate board, provided that the 'irreducible minimum' of a 'genuine decision taken by a person or persons who can on substantial grounds claim to be to board of directors acting as such'[7] had been attained. On the facts, therefore, the director could benefit from section 35A, although the company could have recourse to section 322A to avoid the transaction (see **6.23**). Carnwath LJ, whilst accepting that a purposive interpretation of section 35A might admit its application to a decision by an inquorate board, took the view that this case, the facts of which he regarded as 'exceptional' was inappropriate for laying down a general rule. Instead, he held that because the director was also the company's chairman and therefore under a duty to ensure that the constitution was properly applied, he could not rely on section 35A 'to turn his own decision, which had no validity of

---

1   Note the robust interpretation of 'limitations' in *TCB v Gray*, above. Even if section 35A can be interpreted in this way, it would still be necessary to refer to agency principles to determine whether the company is actually bound by the acts of an individual.

2   *Hansard*, HL Debs, 7 November 1989, cols 685–687.

3   It was challenged by Lord Wedderburn in the House of Lords in the debate on the relevant clauses of the Companies bill: *Hansard*, HL Debs, 7 November 1989, cols 685–687.

4   [2002] EWCA Civ 762, [2002] 2 BCLC 655.

5   [2002] BCC 544.

6   The views are reproduced at paragraph [32] in Robert Walker LJ's judgment in the Court of Appeal. See also Howell (2002) 23 Co Law 96.

7   [2002] 2 BCLC 655, paragraph [41].

any kind under the company's constitution, into a decision of 'the board'.[1] Schiemann LJ expressed no view on the quorum point at all, preferring instead to hold that a director who is responsible for exceeding any limitations in the company's constitution cannot benefit from the section.[2] The reasoning of Carnwath and Schiemann LJJ is rather unsatisfactory for not giving clear guidance on the question whether section 35A does apply to a decision by an inquorate board.[3] For the time being, it seems that the better view is that section 35A does *not* apply to an inquorate board, although a clear decision on this matter is still required.[4] In any event, it is well established in English company law that the rule in *Turquand's* case protects outsiders against internal irregularities of which they are unaware. The fact of a board being improperly constituted is an internal irregularity and an outsider would not usually be aware of it in his dealings with the company. Accordingly, even if section 35A does not apply in this situation, the outsider could still be protected under the older *Turquand* rule.[5] Rimer J adopted this reasoning at first instance, and also held that the director in question could not benefit from *Turquand* because he was, or ought to have been, aware of the quorum requirement. The final outcome, ie, that the director could not overcome the consequences of the inquorate board, are the same whether one adopts Rimer J's reasoning or the rather more strained reasoning favoured by Carnwath and Schiemann LJJ, although Rimer J's approach is preferable for its clarity and avoidance of putting an unnecessary gloss on section 35A.[6]

6.21 A person dealing with a company in good faith

A person deals with a company if he is a party to any transaction or other act to which the company is a party.[7] The reference to 'any other act' makes clear that the protection of the section extends beyond purely commercial matters and includes charitable gifts and other gratuitous distributions of assets. Under the predecessor section, this point was doubtful.[8] Shareholders are not excluded from the protection of section 35A, and it seems that that section can be invoked even in connection with a claim based on a transaction in breach of the company's articles, such as the procedure to be followed when issuing bonus shares,[9] although not where there was a failure to honour pre-emption rights in a transfer

---

1   [2002] 2 BCLC 655, paragraph [110].
2   Ibid, paragraph [128].
3   See also Howell (2003) 24 Co Law 264.
4   Although the head-note to the report of the case at [2002] 2 BCLC 655 suggests that Robert Walker LJ's 'irreducible minimum' forms part of the *ratio* (with Carnwath LJ dissenting), this does not correspond with what Carnwath and Schiemann LJJ actually say in their judgments. See also *Gower and Davies' Principles of Modern Company Law*, p 151.
5   Note that the protection afforded by the *Turquand* rule is more limited than that given by section 35A. Section 35A protects persons who are in good faith, and good faith is not incompatible with knowledge that a limitation under the constitution has been breached: **6.21**. However, an outsider who knows of an internal irregularity or who is put on enquiry cannot rely on the rule in *Turquand's* case: **6.25**.
6   See Walters (2002) 23 Co Law 325.
7   Secton 35A(2)(a).
8   In *Re Halt Garage* [1982] 3 All ER 1016 above at 1039–1040, Oliver J took the view, without deciding the point, that section 9 of the European Communities Act only protected those who were in a contractual relationship with the company. See also *International Sales v Marcus*, above at 560.
9   *EIC Services Ltd and another v Phipps and others* [2003] EWHC 1507, [2003] 3 All ER 804.

between shareholders.[1] Special provision is made for directors who deal with their company, although there is no reason, in principle, to exclude directors from the benefit of section 35A altogether.[2] This is discussed in **6.23**.

Good faith[3] is presumed so that the burden of proof lies with the person who asserts that the outsider did not deal in good faith.[4] The burden of proof would thus normally fall on the company. Section 35A(2)(b) expressly provides that a person is not to be regarded as acting in bad faith by reason only of his knowing that an act is beyond the powers of the directors under the company's constitution. This provision clarifies some doubts that were created by the wording of the predecessor section but it also gives rise to some new uncertainties. Section 9 of the European Communities Act 1972 protected those who dealt with a company 'in good faith' but gave no guidance as to the meaning of that phrase. In *International Sales v Marcus*,[5] Lawson J judged lack of good faith to be found either in actual knowledge or where 'it can be shown that such a person could not in view of all the circumstances have been unaware'.[6] In *Barclays Bank Ltd v TOSG Trust Fund Ltd*,[7] Nourse J rejected objective standards, stating that in his judgment a person acted in good faith if he acted 'honestly and genuinely in the circumstances of the case'. It is now clear from section 35A(2)(b) that even actual knowledge of the constitutional limits does not amount to bad faith. An example of the type of situation where an outsider might be held to be in good faith, notwithstanding its knowledge, is where the outsider is itself a large organisation which is deemed[8] to have technical knowledge of the company's constitutional limitations, because they are known to some of its departments, but the particular individuals within the organisation who are dealing with the company lack the relevant knowledge.[9] Another example is where the outsider reads but fails to understand, or to interpret properly, the company's memorandum and articles.

However, what would now constitute bad faith cannot be stated with any certainty. If, for example, the outsider knows that the directors are acting contrary to constitutional limitations and also that the transaction is part of a scheme by the directors to defraud the company, there could surely be no question of his sheltering behind a protection given only to those who are in good faith. It is not

---

1   It seems that such a transaction is one between the shareholders only and does not involve 'dealing with the company', even though the company has a role to play in the mechanics of the transfer: *Cottrell v (1) King (2) T A King (Services) Ltd.* [2004] EWHC 397 (Ch).

2   *Smith v Henniker-Major* [2002] EWCA Civ 762, [2002] 2 BCLC 655 (Robert Walker LJ at paragraphs [50]–[52] accepting the full application; Carnwath LJ leaving open the question at paragraph [110], and Schiemann LJ excluding the directors who have overstepped the relevant limitation in the constitution at paragraph [129]). Neuberger J in *EIC Services* has interpreted *Smith v Henniker-Major* as meaning that directors could benefit in principle except in facts such as those in that case (paragraphs [198]–[202]).

3   See also Griffiths, 'An Assessment of Sections 35–35B and 322A of the Companies Act 1985 and the protection of third parties dealing with companies' in De Lacy (ed) *The Reform of United Kingdom Company Law* (London: Cavendish Publishing, 2002).

4   Section 35A(2)(c).

5   Above.

6   At 559.

7   [1984] BCLC 121. Nourse J's judgment was reversed on appeal but not on grounds relevant to this point: [1984] AC 626.

8   Law Commission, *Fiduciary Duties and Regulatory Rules: A Consultation Paper* (No 124) (HMSO, 1992), section 2.3 considers the ways in which a firm can acquire knowledge.

9   This example was given by Lord Fraser of Carmyllie during the passage of the Companies Act 1989 through Parliament: *Hansard* HL Debs, 7 November 1989, col 683.

The qualification contained in section 35A(4) preserves the binding nature of transactions with outsiders who are protected by section 35A but it means that shareholders can seek only to restrain contemplated transactions or those which are not binding on the company because the other party is not protected by section 35A, such as where he is a director or connected person. The practical effect of section 35A(4) is likely to be limited because shareholders will rarely discover the directors' plans at a time before a legal obligation has been incurred.

Section 35A(5) preserves any liability incurred by the directors, or any other person,[1] by reason of the directors exceeding their powers. Entering into an unauthorised transaction may amount to a breach of the directors' fiduciary duties.[2]

6.25   The *Turquand* rule: the indoor management principle

The purpose of the rule first clearly set forth in *Royal British Bank v Turquand*[3] is to provide some measure of protection for those who enter into contracts with the company from the consequences of the complex internal organisation of companies. The essence of the *Turquand* rule is that those dealing with a company are not affected by what is called the 'indoor management' of companies. They are entitled to assume that the internal procedures of a company, both at directors' and shareholders' meetings, have been regularly conducted in the absence of actual notice to the contrary. Section 382(4) of the Companies Act 1985 gives indirect support to this principle. It provides that where the minutes of shareholders' or directors' meetings are kept as the section requires, there is a presumption, until the contrary is proved, that all meetings have been regularly convened and conducted.[4] However, where it applies, the *Turquand* rule is conclusive and does not simply raise a rebuttable presumption.

It has been held by the Court of Appeal that the rule in *Turquand's* case is not a mere plea of law (which therefore does not have to be pleaded). It is a plea of mixed law and fact. It must therefore be pleaded and may not be raised if it has not been pleaded unless the court permits the pleadings to be amended.[5]

The rule in *Turquand's* case ameliorated the severity of the constructive notice rule whereby outsiders were deemed to know the contents of documents registered at the Companies Registry. With the enactment of the wide-ranging protection afforded to those dealing with a company by sections 35 and 35A of the Companies Act 1985, the importance of the *Turquand* rule has decreased. In many circumstances it overlaps with section 35A: for example, if the articles cap the directors' borrowing power by requiring them to seek the approval of the

---

1   A person dealing with a company may become implicated in the directors' breach of duty and thus incur liability to the company as a constructive trustee. It seems that a person who is in good faith for the purposes of section 35A could nevertheless be held to be a constructive trustee. In *International Sales v Marcus*, Lawson J held that section 9 of the European Communities Act 1972 did not affect constructive trust liability. See also *Coöperatieve Rabobank 'Vecht en Plassengebied' BA v Minderhoud* [1998] 2 BCLC 507 (enforceability as against third parties of acts done by directors in circumstances where there is a conflict of interest with the company fall outside the normative framework of the First Directive).

2   See Chapter 16, below.

3   (1856), 6 E & B 327 (Exch Ch).

4   This presumption extends to all appointments of directors, managers and liquidators.

5   *Rolled Steel Products v British Steel Corporation*, above.

shareholders in general meeting by ordinary resolution for borrowings over a certain amount, the lender can either assume that the ordinary resolution has been obtained, because, under the *Turquand* rule, this is a matter of internal management, or can disregard the need for the resolution because this is a limitation on the directors' power which is overridden by section 35A.[1]

The rule in *Turquand's* case cannot be relied upon by an outsider who knows the true position or who is put on enquiry.[2] The very nature of a proposed transaction can be sufficient to put an outsider on enquiry.[3] In circumstances where there is an overlap between section 35A and the rule in *Turquand's* case, section 35A may thus offer greater protection because even actual knowledge of the irregularity does not amount to 'bad faith' putting the person dealing with the company outside the scope of that section.

As noted above,[4] one situation to which the *Turquand* rule applies but to which section 35A seems to have no application is in respect of decisions made by a body which purports to be the board of the company but which is improperly constituted. Although the issue remains unclear, the judgment in *Smith v Henniker-Major*[5] appears to suppport the interpretation of section 35A that it applies only to acts of a properly constituted board and has no relevance to the question of what constitutes the 'board'.[6]

6.26 'Outsiders'

The *Turquand* rule is designed to protect 'outsiders' dealing with the seemingly authorised agents of the company. If they are unaware of any irregularity, the rule will protect not only complete outsiders, such as creditors, but also the members of the company (at any rate *vis-à-vis* the conduct of board meetings). Even a director in some circumstances may be treated as an outsider. If a director has not acted on behalf of the company in connection with the transaction he seeks to enforce, he may invoke the *Turquand* rule in order to bind the company.[7] Where he has acted on behalf of the company and it is his duty to have knowledge of the true state of affairs, he will not be able to rely on the rule.[8]

Section 322A does not draw a distinction between insider and outsider directors. A contract between a director and his company which infringes

---

1   In practice, lenders may insist on seeing a copy of the resolution as a pre-condition of the loan especially if the amounts involved are significant.

2   *B Liggett (Liverpool) Ltd v Barclays Bank Ltd* [1928] 1 KB 48; *Morris v Kanssen* [1946] AC 459; *Rolled Steel*, above.

3   *AL Underwood Ltd v Bank of Liverpool and Martins* [1924] 1 KB 775; *Northside Developments Pty Ltd v Registrar-General* (1989–1990) 2 ACSR 161, (1990) 64 ALJR 427, noted [1991] CLJ 47.

4   See **6.20**.

5   [2002] EWCA Civ 762, [2002] 2 BCLC 655.

6   See **6.20**.

7   *Hely-Hutchinson v Brayhead Ltd* [1968] 1 QB 549, *per* Roskill J. (The decision was confirmed on other grounds in the Court of Appeal.)

8   *Morris v Kanssen* [1946] AC 459 (HL); *Howard v Patent Ivory Co* (1888) 38 Ch D 156. Where the third party is a company, notice will not be binding unless given to an officer in the course of the company's business, or in such circumstances that it was his duty to communicate it to the company. Thus, one of two companies having directors, or a secretary, in common will not by reason of that fact be taken to have notice of the manner in which the acts of the other are carried out: *Re Hampshire Ltd Co* [1896] 2 Ch 743; *Re Marseilles Extension Rly Co* (1871) 7 Ch App 161; *Re Fenwick, Stobart & Co* [1902] 1 Ch 507; *Re David Payne & Co* [1904] 2 Ch 608 (CA).

constitutional limits is voidable irrespective of the director's involvement on behalf of the company. A director cannot rely on the *Turquand* rule in relation to a transaction which is voidable under section 322A.[1]

6.27 General agency principles and the *Turquand* rule

Although the *Turquand* rule will protect an outsider in regard to internal procedures at general meetings and board meetings, when it comes to the powers of individual officers and agents of the company the outsider cannot rely solely on the internal management rule. Whether a company is bound by acts which are done on its behalf depends on whether the director, or other individual, who acted for the company had authority to do so.

There are two main types of authority, namely actual authority and ostensible (or apparent) authority. Actual authority is authority which the principal confers, either expressly or impliedly, on the agent. The board of directors of a company has express actual authority to exercise such powers of the company as are vested in it by the company's memorandum and articles; an executive director appointed under a written service contract has express actual authority to bind the company to the extent that this is authorised by his contract. Where the terms on which someone is appointed to an executive position within a company are not spelt out in an express service contract, actual authority to bind the company may nevertheless be implied from the circumstances. Such authority may also be implied where a person is allowed *de facto* to assume a position but is never expressly appointed. In *Hely-Hutchinson v Brayhead Ltd*,[2] the Court of Appeal held that the *de facto* managing director (or chief executive officer (CEO) as persons holding this office are now commonly described in practice) of the company had implied actual authority to bind the company to contracts of guarantee and indemnity.

The crucial distinction between actual authority and ostensible authority is that actual authority is a relationship between the principal and agent[3] and ostensible authority is the authority of an agent as it *appears* to others.[4] Ostensible authority is created 'by a representation, made by the principal to the contractor, intended to be and in fact acted upon by the contractor, that the agent has authority'.[5] The agent is not a party to the relationship created by the principal's representation and the representation, when acted upon, acts as an estoppel preventing the principal from claiming that it is not bound.[6] Actual authority and ostensible authority can coincide[7] but an important feature of ostensible authority is that it can exist in circumstances where the agent has no actual authority. Thus, if the company restricts the powers of its managing director in some respect, the managing director has no actual authority, whether express or implied, to bind the company in matters covered by the restriction; but an outsider dealing with

---

1   Nor can he rely on the rule where he knows that a board meeting is improperly constituted and unable to act: *Smith v Henniker-Major*, above.

2   [1968] 1 QB 549.

3   The scope of which is to be ascertained by applying ordinary principles of construction: *Freeman & Lockyer v Buckhurst Park Properties (Mangal) Ltd* [1964] 2 QB 480.

4   *Freeman & Lockyer* [1964] 2 QB at 503 *per* Diplock LJ; *Hely-Hutchinson v Brayhead* [1968] 1 QB at 583 *per* Lord Denning MR.

5   *Freeman & Lockyer* [1964] 2 QB at 503 *per* Diplock LJ.

6   Ibid. Also at 498 *per* Pearson LJ.

7   *Freeman & Lockyer* at 502 *per* Diplock LJ; *Hely-Hutchinson* at 583 *per* Lord Denning MR.

the managing director who is unaware of the restriction may be able to hold the company to the transaction on the basis of ostensible authority.

Ostensible authority can take one of two forms: either the directors and officers have a 'usual' authority attached to their office, giving a certain scope of authority implied by law; or the company may be estopped from denying that it held out its agent as having authority to act in a particular transaction. If this representation by words or conduct is relied upon by an outsider, who acts to his detriment in entering into the contract, the company will be bound.

The *ultra vires* doctrine and the constructive notice rule (as ameliorated by the *Turquand* rule) have, in their time, complicated the application of the principles of ostensible authority in relation to companies. The complications have largely disappeared either through statutory developments or through judicial reassessment of the scope of the constructive notice rule, but it is important to have their earlier significance in mind when considering some of the relevant authorities.

6.28   Usual authority

Depending on the context in which it is used, the term 'usual authority' can denote a species of implied actual authority or, alternatively, a form of ostensible authority.[1] A person who is appointed to a particular office may be said to have usual authority by which it is meant that he has implied actual authority to do whatever falls within the usual scope of that office.[2] Implied actual authority to do whatever acts are necessarily incidental to the performance of the agency is a form of usual authority.[3]

When a person is appointed to an office, he may also be said to have usual authority, meaning that he has ostensible authority to do whatever falls within the usual scope of the office.[4] In this case, the company will be bound where the agent acts within the scope of his usual authority even though he may exceed specific restrictions which the company has imposed on his actual authority. Appointing someone to an office can be regarded as one form of 'holding out'[5] but it is helpful to distinguish ostensible authority in the form of usual authority from ostensible authority in the form of holding out. This is because where someone has been appointed to a position, there is no doubt that the factual element of holding out has been satisfied and the relevant issue of potential dispute is as to the scope of the usual authority attached to that position.[6]

6.29   Directors, executive directors and chairmen

The exact scope of the usual authority of individual directors, chairmen of boards, managing directors and other executive directors and officers of the company

---

1   *First Energy UK (Ltd) v Hungarian International Bank Ltd* [1993] BCLC 1409, [1993] BCC 533. In *Armagas Ltd v Mundogas SA* [1986] AC 717 (ostensible) usual authority is described as 'general ostensible authority'.

2   *Hely-Hutchinson*, above.

3   *First Energy* [1993] BCLC at 1418 *per* Steyn LJ.

4   Ibid.

5   *Egyptian International Foreign Trade Co v Soplex Wholesale Supplies Ltd, The Raffaela* [1985] BCLC 404 at 411.

6   The courts often distinguish between ostensible authority in the form of usual authority and in the form of holding out: see, eg *Freeman & Lockyer, The Raffaella, Armagas v Mundogas, First Energy*, above.

differs considerably. In the case of managing directors, most modern articles empower the board to delegate to them wide powers of management (under the general supervision of the board).[1] In consequence, the courts have held that a managing director's usual authority has a wide scope. It extends to the management of the ordinary business of the company.[2] It will be seen that, where no managing director has been appointed despite a power to do so, the courts will readily infer, on the basis of estoppel, that either a chairman of the board or another director, acting *de facto* as chief executive, has been held out by the company as managing director.[3] However, the better view is that a chairman, *qua* chairman, has no wider usual authority than a director.[4] Individual directors, as such, have almost no usual authority[5] beyond a power to execute documents to clothe a transaction with formal validity which has already been authorised by the board or the managing director.[6] It has been held that a single director has usual authority to sign cheques or other negotiable instruments on behalf of the company.[7] Where a director has a service agreement which requires him to perform a particular task (eg sales manager[8]) then, like any other management executive, he will possess the usual authority that his function requires.[9] This is a matter of ordinary agency law but, in terms of general powers of management, directors must act collectively as a board, unless the articles give a power to delegate to individual directors.[10] This is subject to section 35A because, where that section applies, the board is deemed to have power to authorise others to act on behalf of the company free of any limitations under the company's constitution. For this purpose, a 'limitation' should include a matter on which the constitution is silent as well as express restrictions.[11]

---

1   Article 72 of Table A.
2   *Freeman & Lockyer v Buckhurst Park Properties (Mangal) Ltd* [1964] 2 QB 480 (CA).
3   *Freeman & Lockyer v Buckhurst Park Properties Ltd*, above; *Hely-Hutchinson v Brayhead* [1968] 1 QB 549, *per* Roskill J, affirmed by the Court of Appeal on other grounds.
4   Some of the earlier cases appear to invest the chairman with a usual authority equivalent to a managing director: *British Thomson-Houston Co v Federated European Bank Ltd* [1932] 2 KB 176 (CA) and *Clay Hill Brick Co v Rawlings* [1938] 4 All ER 100, but the sounder view is that the company is liable because the chairman has been held out as managing director. See *Biggerstaff v Rowatts Wharf Ltd* [1986] 2 Ch 93 (CA); *Hely-Hutchinson v Brayhead Ltd* [1968] 1 QB 549 at 560 (Roskill J) and 586 (Lord Wilberforce in CA).
5   *Rama Corporation Ltd v Proved Tin & General Investments Ltd* [1952] 2 QB 147; *Houghton & Co v Nothard, Lowe & Wills* [1927] 1 KB 247 (CA) – affirmed on other grounds [1928] AC 1.
6   The power to execute documents is discussed below.
7   *Re Land Credit Co of Ireland* (1869) LR 4 Ch 460. See also section 37 of the Companies Act 1985 and *Dey v Pullinger Engineering Co* [1921] 1 KB 77.
8   Cf. *SMC Electronics Ltd v Akhter Computers Ltd and others* [2001] 1 BCLC 433, CA.
9   But if an executive goes beyond the confines of his routine duties, he will lack authority: *Kreditbank Cassel GmbH v Schenkers* [1927] 1 KB 826 (CA); *British Bank of the Middle East v Sun Life Assurance Co of Canada* [1983] 2 Lloyd's Rep 9 (HL). See *Harmond Properties Ltd v Gajdzis* [1968] 1 WLR 1858 (a director acting as general agent of his company in giving notice to quit).
10   Article 72 of Table A. However, even though it is not uncommon for the articles to provide for this, delegation cannot be assumed, ie such an article does not add to a director's 'usual' authority.
11   See **6.11**.

The position of company secretary has grown in importance over the years. In the nineteenth century, the company secretary was described as a mere servant[1] but, by the 1970s, it was accepted by the Court of Appeal that the company secretary was the chief administrative officer of the company and that, as such, he had ostensible authority to bind the company in contracts of an administrative nature such as employing staff and hiring cars.[2]

Where three companies were controlled by one individual, who was the major shareholder in and chairman, managing director and the organiser of, each of the three companies, it was held that the affairs of these companies were so 'mixed up' that the individual controlling them must be regarded as having actual or ostensible authority to act for any of the companies.[3]

6.30   When an outsider cannot rely on usual authority

There are a number of general rules which limit the right of an outsider to rely on the usual authority of any agent of the company. As in agency law in general, if the third party has knowledge of a relevant restriction on a particular agent's authority, the company will not be liable.[4] The result will be the same if the circumstances surrounding the transaction are sufficiently suspicious to put the third party on enquiry as to the agent's authority.

Restrictions on an agent's usual authority which are contained in the company's articles give rise to special considerations. The constructive notice rule means that outsiders dealing with a company are deemed to know of such restrictions and therefore cannot rely on an agent's usual authority in respect of any matter within the scope of the restrictions. Where the restrictions are not absolute but require a particular use of power to be authorised by the shareholders in general meeting or by the board, sometimes the internal management may be invoked to mitigate the constructive notice rule and to enable the outsider to hold the company to the transaction. This is possible where the required authorisation takes the form of an ordinary resolution of the shareholders or of a board resolution because these are matters of internal management.[5] It is not possible where the required authorisation takes the form of a special resolution, because an outsider can discover from the Registrar of Companies whether a special resolution has been passed and is therefore fixed with constructive notice of the existence or otherwise of such a resolution.[6]

It should be stressed, however, that, so far as the usual authority of directors and officers is concerned, an outsider need not have read the articles. The articles can have a negative effect in limiting authority but they need not have been read as a positive basis for the usual authority of a particular agent. Here it is the

1   *Barnett, Hoares & Co v South London Tramways Co* (1887) 18 QBD 815 at 817, approved by Lord Macnaghten in *George Whitchurch Ltd v Cavanagh* [1902] AC 117 at 124 and supported by the decision in *Ruben v Great Fingall Consolidated* [1906] AC 439.

2   *Panorama Developments (Guildford) Ltd v Fidelis Furnishing Fabrics Ltd* [1971] 3 All ER 16. See also *First Energy*, above at 1422.

3   *Ford Motor Credit Co v Harmack* (1972) *The Times*, 7 July (CA).

4   *AL Underwood Ltd v Bank of Liverpool*, above; *Rolled Steel*, above.

5   *Mahoney v East Holyford Mining Co* (1875) LR 7 HL 869. This was provided that the outsider did not know that the required internal authorisation had not been obtained and there was no ground for suspicion.

6   *Irvine v Union Bank of Australia* (1877) 2 App Cas 366 at 379. Copies of special resolutions must be filed with the Registrar of Companies: section 380.

appearance of authority with which a particular agent is commonly vested that determines the scope of his usual authority.[1]

6.31 The 'holding out' principle

The classic statement of the principles of ostensible authority in the form of holding out as applied to companies is to be found in Diplock LJ's judgment in *Freeman & Lockyer*, where he summarised the conditions which had to be fulfilled for a contractor to be entitled to enforce a contract against a company in the following terms:[2]

(1) a representation that the agent had authority to enter on behalf of the company into a contract of the kind sought to be enforced must be made to the contractor;

(2) such representation must be made by a person or persons who had actual authority to manage the business of the company either generally or in respect of those matters to which the contract relates;

(3) the contractor must be induced by the representation to enter into the contract (ie in fact he must rely on it); and

(4) under the memorandum or articles of association of the company, the company must not be deprived of the capacity to enter into a contract of the kind sought to be enforced or to delegate authority to enter into a contract of that kind to the agent.

Section 35A modifies conditions (2) and (4). The board may make a representation of authority to a contractor which exceeds its actual authority under the company's memorandum and articles but, by virtue of section 35A, the contractor, provided he is in good faith, is entitled to assume that the board's authority is unlimited. The reference to lack of capacity in (4) must now be read in the light of section 35. It is now not a bar to a contract being binding on a company that it is outside the limits of the company's memorandum.

The elements of holding out and reliance embodied in conditions (1) and (3), as stated by Diplock LJ in *Freeman & Lockyer*, are essentially matters that will be determined by reference to the factual circumstances of each case. It is not essential for the body with actual authority to state expressly that the agent has authority, as the holding out may be inferred from the circumstances.[3] The representation by which the company may be said to have held out the individual as having authority will usually take the form of knowingly permitting a director or officer to assume an authority he does not in fact possess. In a one-off transaction, however, an express holding out may be necessary for an estoppel to arise.[4]

---

1   *Freeman & Lockyer v Buckhurst Park Properties (Mangal) Ltd* [1964] 2 QB 480 at 496 (Willmer LJ). There was formerly some uncertainty on this point, which this case has dispelled. See the reporter's note appended to *British Thomson-Houston Co v Federated European Bank* [1932] 2 KB 176, and the subsequent history of this note in *Clay Hill Brick Co v Rawlings* [1938] 4 All ER 100 and in *Rama Corporation v Proved Tin & General Investments Ltd* [1952] 2 QB 147.

2   At 506, Diplock LJ's analysis in *Freeman & Lockyer* has been applied in numerous subsequent cases including *IRC v Ufitec Group Ltd* [1977] 3 All ER 924; *British Bank of the Middle East v Sun Life Assurance of Canada*, above; *Rhodian River Shipping v Halia Maritime* [1984] 1 Lloyd's Rep 373; *The Raffaella*, above.

3   See the remarks of Pearson LJ in *Freeman & Lockyer* at 498 as qualified by his later remarks in *Hely-Hutchinson* at 593.

4   *Armagas v Mundogas*, above at 777.

Most of the cases illustrating this form of ostensible authority have concerned directors who were held out as managing directors, even though they had never been appointed to that office.[1] The estoppel principle overcomes the lack of valid appointment and confers on the director the same scope of usual authority as if he were a regularly appointed managing director. In accordance with the second of Diplock LJ's conditions, the representation must have been made by an individual or organ of the company with actual authority to make the appointment. In the case of the appointment of the managing director, most articles (eg article 72 of Table A) confer this power on the board of directors. The board will be estopped by their conduct in knowingly allowing a director either expressly to represent himself as managing director, or by his conduct impliedly to represent that he has the powers of such. In *Freeman & Lockyer v Buckhurst Park Properties*,[2] for example, no managing director had been appointed, despite a power in the articles to do so, in a company formed to purchase and develop certain properties. Two directors allowed the third director, Kapoor, the whole management of the company's business. The Court of Appeal held that the company was estopped from denying that Mr Kapoor was managing director and that it was within the usual authority of such to engage a firm of architects to obtain planning permission for the development of certain properties.

6.32   Knowledge of the articles

As in cases involving usual authority, where liability is founded on the holding out principle, it is *not* essential that the third party should have read the articles. The conduct of the board in acquiescing in the pretensions of a self-styled managing director will bind the company, even though the articles conferring the power to appoint a managing director have not been read. Conversely, the existence of a power to delegate, eg to a managing director, will not of itself raise an estoppel where no managing director has been appointed. The *Turquand* rule cannot be invoked by a person who knows of the contents of the articles to raise an estoppel against the company in circumstances where the articles permitted delegation but there is no evidence of an individual having being held out. The significance of a power to delegate in the articles, if known, is simply that this may help to establish[3] that the company is estopped, but it can scarcely do so alone without more positive evidence that a particular individual was held out as holding an executive position by an organ which had the authority to appoint him.

In *Freeman & Lockyer*, the Court of Appeal was divided on whether the holding out principle could bind the company even where the articles did not specifically provide a power to appoint a managing director.[4] The point may now be covered by section 35A which, irrespective of the actual contents of the articles, allows a

---

1   The holding out principle may also extend the scope of the actual authority of an agent of the company: *Mercantile Bank of India v Chartered Bank of India* [1937] 1 All ER 231. (Agents authorised to borrow by power of attorney. A limitation on the amount imposed by the directors did not appear in the power of attorney. A charge granted to secure an amount in excess of the limitation was held to estop the company, since it had held out the agents by the power of attorney as having unlimited power to borrow.)

2   Above.

3   See *Houghton & Co v Nothard, Lowe & Willis Ltd* [1927] 1 KB 246 at 266 *per* Sargant LJ.

4   Diplock LJ at 505–506 thought that this was possible but Willmer LJ at 492 and Pearson LJ at 480 thought otherwise.

person dealing with the company in good faith to assume that the directors have unlimited powers to authorise others to act on the company's behalf.

6.33 'Self-authorising' agents

The second of the conditions of ostensible authority outlined by Diplock LJ in *Freeman & Lockyer* is that the agent must be held out by someone who has actual authority in the matter to which the representation relates. It follows from this that an agent should not be able to increase his own power to bind the company by holding himself out as having more authority than he actually has. Likewise, an agent who lacks authority should not be able to bind the company by over-representing someone else's authority. These propositions are supported by the decision of the House of Lords in *British Bank of the Middle East v Sun Life Assurance Co of Canada (UK) Ltd,*[1] where it was held that the general manager of a branch office of an insurance company had no authority to give an undertaking on the company's behalf and had no authority to represent that a more junior employee, a unit manager, had the requisite authority.[2]

A gloss on this is, however, indicated by *The Raffaella*[3] where Browne-Wilkinson LJ said:

> It is obviously correct that an agent who has no actual or apparent authority either (a) to enter into a transaction or (b) to make representations as to the transaction cannot hold himself out as having authority to enter into the transacton so as to affect the principal's position. But, suppose a company confers actual or apparent authority on X to make representations and X crroneously represents to a third party that Y has authority to enter into a transaction; why should not such a representation be relied on as part of the holding out of Y by the company? By parity of reasoning, if a company confers actual or apparent authority on A to make representations on the company's behalf but no actual authority on A to enter into the specific transaction, why should a representation made by A as to his authority not be capable of being relied on as one of the acts of holding out?

This was applied by the Court of Appeal in *First Energy (UK) v Hungarian International Bank,*[4] where it was held that a bank manager who had no authority to make an offer on the bank's behalf had ostensible authority by virtue of his position (ie what has been described in this chapter as a form of usual authority) to communicate that head office approval had been given to the transaction in question. Whether it was possible to draw a distinction between authority to enter into a transaction and authority to represent that it had been approved at a higher level, had been put in some doubt by the decision of the House of Lords in *Armagas v Mundogas.* However, the Court of Appeal distinguished the earlier House of Lords decision on two grounds: first, *Armagas* was not concerned with the ostensible authority of an agent arising from his position but with ostensible authority arising from holding out on specific occasions, and the evidence in that case did not establish that such authority existed; secondly, the House of Lords had not ruled out altogether the possibility of an agent who had no authority to

1   Above.
2   See also *Armagas v Mundogas*, above.
3   Above.
4   Above.

conclude the transaction having authority to communicate decisions, but had merely decided that it would be somewhat rare for that situation to arise.[1]

The pragmatic commercial considerations that underlie agency principles, and also the rule in *Turquand's* case, were emphasised by the Court of Appeal in *First Energy*. On the one hand, a contractor who is dealing with an agent acting on behalf of a company cannot know, nor be expected to enquire into, all of the internal approval procedures within the company; on the other hand, merely because someone (who may have no other connection with the company) purports to act for a company should not necessarily mean that the company is bound, since this could facilitate fraud and operate to the detriment of the company's innocent creditors and shareholders. A balance has to be struck which allows a contractor to hold the company to a transaction, without having to go to the (usually impossible) lengths of ensuring that the transaction is approved at board level, in circumstances where the contractor acts reasonably in assuming that appropriate corporate approvals have been obtained. Normally, the contractor will rely on the authority of the agent to conclude the transaction, but the decision of the Court of Appeal in *First Energy* recognises that an agent who lacks the authority to conclude the transaction may, in limited circumstances, bind the company by communicating, within the scope of his authority, that it has been approved at a higher level.[2]

6.34 Forgery, the *Turquand* rule and agency principles

There is authority from the House of Lords for the proposition that a forgery as such is a *nullity* and cannot bind the company.[3] On the other hand, if an organ or official of the company with the authority to bind the company held out the person who committed the forgery as having authority to execute the document in question, the company may be estopped from denying the validity of the forgery. In *Ruben v Great Fingall Consolidated*,[4] a company secretary, without authority to do so, issued a share certificate with the company's seal attached and under his own signature and the forged signatures of two directors. The execution of the share certificate was therefore a nullity, and there was no ground for holding the company estopped from denying this. In other cases, a director or other official has been held to have 'forged' his own signature to a parol agreement.[5] This would seem to be a misuse of the word 'forgery' and such cases should have been decided instead on the basis of lack of authority (whether actual or ostensible).[6] Indeed, it is difficult to see why even forgery, as in *Ruben's* case, must be treated as being governed by a special rule. So far as actual authority is concerned a forgery is clearly a nullity. However, whether or not it binds the company should depend on the general principles. It is clear that under general agency law[7] forgeries are not

---

1   *British Thomson-Houston Co Ltd v Federated European Bank Ltd* [1932] 2 KB 176 can be explained as a case where the agent's authority to conclude transactions was not commensurate with his authority to communicate decisions.

2   For a criticism of the decision, see Reynolds (1994) 110 LQR 21.

3   *Ruben v Great Fingall Consolidated* [1906] AC 439 (HL) *per* Lord Loreburn at 443.

4   [1906] AC 439 (HL); see further *Slingsby v District Bank* [1931] 2 KB 588 at 605 *per* Wright J (*affirmed* by [1932] 1 KB 544 (CA)).

5   *Kreditbank Cassel GmbH v Schenkers Ltd* [1927] 1 KB 826; *South London Greyhound Racecourses v Wake* [1931] 1 Ch 496.

6   See *Northside Developments Pty Ltd v Registrar-General*, above, where this distinction is drawn.

7   *Uxbridge Building Society v Pickard* [1939] 2 KB 248 (CA).

treated differently from other fraudulent acts which may be binding on the principal if the agent acts within his usual or apparent authority.[1]

6.35 Statutory provisions affecting appointments

Section 285 of the Companies Act 1985 appears to give additional protection to an outsider dealing with a director or manager who has been invalidly appointed. This section provides that 'the acts of a director or manager are valid notwithstanding any defect that may afterwards be discovered in his appointment or qualification'.[2] However, the House of Lords in *Morris v Kanssen* gave a very restricted interpretation to this section. Lord Simonds distinguished 'between (a) an appointment in which there is a defect or, in other words, a defective appointment and (b) no appointment at all'.[3] Thus it will validate a mere slip or procedural defect in the appointment of a director, but it will not cover even an originally valid appointment which has been vacated by reason of a statutory provision[4] requiring qualification shares to be taken up within two months.[5] Thus the *Turquand* rule and agency principles will normally give an outsider better protection in dealing with invalidly appointed officers than does section 285.[6]

The publicity that the Companies Act 1985 requires about the identity of directors may, in some circumstances, prevent the company from denying the validity of an appointment of a director or officer. Thus the company is required to keep a register of directors and file a copy of this with the Registrar of Companies.[7] Further, the names of the directors may have to be shown on the company's notepaper and other business documents.[8] Where names of invalidly appointed directors are publicised in this way, third parties who have read and relied on this information might hold the company liable if the company could be shown to have acquiesced in the registration or display of erroneous information as to the identity of any of the directors. It might then be argued that there was implied actual authority for their appointment even though there had been no formal election to the board. Such an argument is more likely to succeed in the case of a private company with a small number of members.

6.36 Publication in the *Gazette* of returns relating to the register of directors

Section 711 of the Companies Act 1985 requires the Registrar to publish in the *Gazette* 'any return relating to a company's register of directors, or notification of a change among its directors'. Under section 42 of the 1985 Act, 'any change among the company's directors' is an 'event' on which 'the company shall not be entitled

---

1   *Lloyd v Grace, Smith & Co* [1912] AC 716 (HL).
2   A similar provision is found in the articles of most companies (eg Article 92 of Table A). See also section 382(4), discussed in **6.25** as to presumption of regularity at meetings where proper minutes are kept.
3   [1946] AC 459 at 471.
4   Now section 291.
5   *Morris v Kanssen*, above.
6   Although section 285 includes members as well as outsiders, it will not protect anyone who knew or ought to have known of the defect: *Re Staffordshire Gas and Coke Co* (1892) 66 LT 413; *Tyne Mutual Steamship Insurance Association v Brown* (1896) 74 LT 283. See also *John v Rees* [1969] 1 WLR 1294 at 1320.
7   Section 288.
8   Section 305. See **15.20**.

to rely against other persons' if the event has not been officially notified at the material time. See further **5.14**.

6.37 The form of contracts by companies

A company may make a contract in writing under its common seal and a contract may be made on its behalf by its duly authorised agent.[1] Any formalities required by law in the case of a contract made by an individual also apply, unless a contrary intention appears, to a contract made by or on behalf of a company.[2]

6.38 The execution of company documents[3]

Certain special rules apply to the execution of documents. Here a distinction has to be drawn between *formal* authority to execute a document and *substantive* authority to enter into the transaction (which is then clothed with formal validity by the execution of the document). Although the substantive validity of a transaction may require a decision by the board of directors or a managing director, the execution of documents will usually be left to lesser officers of the company. So long as the requirements of the articles have been complied with, the outsider will not have to prove that there was actual authority to execute the document. Where a document has to be sealed, most articles provide that this may be done by a director and the secretary, or by two directors.[4] The cases establish that where a document is executed with the signature or signatures that the articles require, its formal validity cannot be contested by the company,[5] but where this is not the case the document is not binding on the company[6] unless section 35A of the Companies Act 1985 applies.[7]

Section 36A of the Companies Act 1985 provides that a document is executed by a company by the affixing of its common seal. It is not now obligatory for a company to have a common seal.[8] Whether or not a company has a common seal, a document signed by a director and the secretary of the company or by two directors of the company, and expressed (in whatever form of words) to be executed by the company has the same effect as if executed under the common seal of the company.[9] A document executed by a company which makes it clear on its face that it is intended by the person or persons making it to be a deed has effect, upon delivery, as a deed; and it is presumed, unless a contrary intention is proved, to have been delivered upon it being so executed.[10]

---

1 Section 36 (as substituted by the Companies Act 1989).
2 Ibid.
3 See generally on this topic: *The Execution of Deeds and Documents by or on Behalf of Bodies Corporate* (Law Com CP No 143, 1996); *The Execution of Deeds and Documents by or on Behalf of Bodies Corporate* (Law Com Rep No 253, 1998).
4 Eg article 101 of Table A.
5 *County of Gloucester Bank v Rudry Merthyr, etc, Colliery Co* [1895] 1 Ch 629 (CA); *Duck v Tower Galvanizing Co* [1901] 2 KB 314.
6 *TCB Ltd v Gray*, above.
7 Ibid, at 125.
8 Section 36A(3). Where a company has a common seal, the name of the company must be engraved on it in legible characters: section 350(1).
9 Section 36A(4).
10 Section 36A(5).

It is common practice for the comon seal to be affixed to important documents which are not deeds such as share and stock certificates.[1]

6.39 Protection for purchasers

Section 36A(6) provides that in favour of a purchaser[2] a document is deemed to have been duly executed by a company if it purports to be signed by a director and the secretary of the company and, where it makes it clear on its face that it is intended by the person or persons making it to be a deed, to have been delivered upon its being executed. The meaning of 'purports to be signed' is not certain. It would presumably cover any lack of authority on the part of the signing officers but it is open to argument whether it would also encompass forged signatures. If this were the case, section 36A(6) would, in effect, repeal *Ruben v Great Fingall*[3] in respect of documents within its scope. The Law Commission has noted the uncertainty on this point but its view is that the presumption[4] does not and should not give protection where the signature of the company's officers has been forged.[5] According to the Law Commission, the presumption in section 36A(6) should apply where the signatures are genuine but the officers in question lack authority to sign the document, and where the document is attested by persons who are no longer office-holders but notice of their resignation has not yet been filed with the Registrar of Companies or where there was some defect in their appointment.

Section 36A(6) is in similar terms to a more limited protection for purchasers provided by section 74 of the Law of Property Act 1925.

6.40 Reform proposals

The White Paper, *Modernising Company Law*, accepted the proposal that in future a company should have unlimited capacity and that a provision to this effect should replace section 35 of the Companies Act 1985. This would achieve the effect advocated by Professor Prentice when the law on corporate capacity was last reviewed in 1986, but which was rejected at that time.[6] As discussed in Chapter 5, the requirement to state objects would disappear for private companies but would have to remain for public companies to comply with the requirement of the Second Company Law Directive (unless this is also reformed). However, it would be an insignificant requirement since all companies would have unlimited capacity in any event. Companies could continue to include restrictions in their registration documents but these would have no external effect and would be

---

1   A share certificate is not a deed: *South London Greyhound Racecourses v Wake* [1931] 1 Ch 496 at 503 *per* Clausen J. See section 186 as to the effect of sealing a share certificate. A company which has an official seal may have a securities seal which is a facsimile of its common seal (with the addition of the word 'securities') specifically for use in sealing documents creating and evidencing securities: section 40.
2   For this purpose, a purchaser means a purchaser in good faith for valuable consideration and includes a lessee, mortgagee or other person who, for valuable consideration, acquires an interest in the property.
3   See **6.34**.
4   In section 74(1) of the Law of Property Act 1925 as well as in section 36A(6).
5   *The Execution of Deeds and Documents by or on Behalf of Bodies Corporate* (Law Com Rep No 253, 1998) paragraphs 5.34–5.37.
6   See **6.12**.

relevant only to issues of directors' duties and the ability of shareholders to take proceedings. All actions contrary to such provisions would be capable of ratification by ordinary resolution.

The abolition of the doctrine of deemed notice is also proposed, but in a form that would seek to avoid the problems created by the poorly drafted, and never implemented, section of the Companies Act 1989 that represented the last attempt to address this issue. Sections 35A, 35B and 322A would be replaced with a single provision, currently contained in draft clause 17.[1] This would deem the board of directors to have autority to exercise all the powers of the company and authorise others do so irrespective of any limitations in the company's constitution (including resolutions by the company). However, as far as transactions with directors and connected persons are concerned, this rule would not apply. This changes the current position which grants provisional validity to such transactions but makes them voidable, by removing these from the scope of the statutory rule altogether. Furthermore, it would be provided that no reference may be made to the company's constitution when determining questions of ostensible authority, thus aiding the application of the *Turquand* principle insofar as the ostensible authority of the relevant person would not be affected merely by the existence of a provision to the contrary in the constitution.

1　See CM 5553–II.

Chapter 7

Share Capital – Allotment and Maintenance

7.1 Introduction

This chapter is concerned with the capital which is raised by companies by means of issuing shares. All companies, of course, need capital and, although in practice share capital is often less important than other sorts of capital, company law has traditionally paid particular attention to share capital in two particular respects. The first concerns allotment of shares,[1] where rules exist primarily to protect shareholders. The second is the rules that seek to ensure that share capital is properly raised and maintained for the benefit of the company's creditors. The Company Law Review[2] has recommended a number of changes to the law described in this chapter. The likely shape of those changes is considered in **7.25**.

7.2 Methods of capitalising companies[3]

The overwhelming majority of private companies are small businesses which have chosen for tax or other reasons to incorporate. They are 'small' both in their capitalisation and in the number of their participators. They frequently take the form of 'one-man companies' or small 'corporate partnerships'. Almost without exception, they will register as a private company limited by shares. The capital of such a company will typically comprise a mixture of loan capital (eg debentures) and share capital. The participators will fix the initial capital at a level appropriate to the activities of the company, but this has no direct relationship with the economic value of the enterprise. The function of share capital in such a company is largely to allocate control rights in the manner agreed by the participators. The function of loan capital is generally to enable the company to acquire (possibly from the participators) the assets required by the company to run its business. Issuing loan capital to the participators allows them to become creditors (possibly secured) in their own business.

This common form of initial capitalisation in the case of small companies has tax advantages for the company. Interest payments are deductible from operating profits for taxation purposes,[4] whereas dividend payments are not. When all the shareholders/debenture-holders are likely also to be directors, and to be closely involved in working for and running the company, there may be tax advantages in

---

1   Note that, as confirmed by the House of Lords (*National Westminster Bank plc v IRC* [1995] 1 AC 119), the terms 'issue' and 'allotment' in relation to shares have different technical meanings. Shares are allotted when there is a contract to take them in accordance with the procedures described later in this chapter; they are issued only when the allottee has been entered in the register of members (as to which, see Chapter 12) to complete the title of the allottee.

2   See generally, **1.7**.

3   For a detailed account of corporate financing, see Ferran, *Company Law and Corporate Finance* (Oxford University Press, 1999), especially Chapter 2.

4   However, a shareholder/creditor who receives dividend/interest payments remains liable to tax on them.

participating in profits in the form of salaries (or other remuneration) rather than in the form of dividends. When it comes to 'ongoing' finance for such companies, this is most likely to take the form of bank borrowings[1] and retaining (instead of distributing) profits earned by the company.[2] Other factors may come into play as further finance is needed. Thus the company may seek 'venture' capital from institutions or individuals prepared to take an 'equity stake' in the company. As the business matures the original 'participators' may need to dispose of their interest in the company. These and other factors may lead to the company issuing a substantial share capital as it continues to grow in size. The ultimate stage of such development may be a public issue of some or all of the company's share capital.[3]

In the case of large public listed companies, share capital obviously has a much more significant role. Nevertheless, in terms of continuing sources of fresh finance, share capital[4] is nowadays less important than loan capital[5] and self-financing through retained profits. However, the concept of 'gearing' in the prudent financing of public companies will discourage companies from relying too heavily on loan capital. 'High gearing' means that the ratio of loan capital (as well as preference shares on which there is a fixed return) to equity capital (ordinary shares) is too high[6] in regard to the proportion of the former to the latter. High gearing makes profits more volatile and puts the owners of equity shares at risk in that it may increase the chances of insolvency. The owners of such shares will also suffer in a period of low profits or actual losses in the company's (or group's) trading operations. Thus, especially in a time of high interest rates, capital and income repayments in respect of loan capital may absorb much too high a proportion of the company's earnings from its business activities. This may necessitate a fresh issue of equity shares to the existing ordinary shareholders in the form of a rights issue[7] in order to restore an appropriate balance between equity and loan capital.

7.3 Allotment of shares

The next part of this chapter looks at the two forms of statutory protection for shareholders against the traditional power of control of the board of directors over the issue of a company's share capital and is followed by a brief examination of the common-law control. The statutory protection was first introduced in 1980 to implement what was required by the Second EC Directive on Company Law.[8]

---

1   And other forms of commercial credit such as industrial hire-purchase and 'factoring' of debts owed to the company.
2   This is limited by the tax regime established for 'close' companies. See *Gore-Browne on Companies* 44th edn (Jordans, loose-leaf) at 24.35.
3   See Chapter 6.
4   This is true of both ordinary and preference shares. See the Committee to Review the Functioning of Financial Institutions (the Wilson Committee) (Cmnd 7937, 1980, Table 34 at p 133).
5   See Chapter 10. Today this takes the form of bank borrowings over a relatively short term rather than a public issue of debentures over a medium-to long-term period.
6   What this ratio should be will depend on a number of factors, primarily the cost of (equity or loan) capital and the profitability of the company's business.
7   See **6.9**.
8   See **2.3.2**.

The first form requires the authority of the shareholders for the allotment[1] of shares. Secondly, in the case of equity shares, the Companies Act 1985 confers what are known as 'pre-emptive' rights on holders of existing equity shares in proportion to their holdings of such shares.

There is an evident need to circumscribe the power of the directors of public companies and of larger private companies to issue share capital. They may be tempted to do this to resist external takeover bids, or to entrench themselves when threatened by internal struggles for control of majority voting power at shareholders' meetings. There is also the problem of what is known as dilution following a new issue of shares. 'Vote dilution' means that the existing shareholders will lose their existing voting strength and this process, if carried far enough, may tip the balance of control. 'Earnings dilution' is of most concern to existing equity shareholders.[2] Following a new issue, the existing and future earnings of the company will be divided among a larger number of shareholders. If the return on new capital does not match that on existing capital a new issue of shares will cause earnings per share to fall. This will have obvious implications for the value of those shares on the stock market or their value in a private company.[3]

The statutory provisions provide a somewhat less than satisfactory bulwark against both vote and earnings dilution. Section 80, described below, has only limited criminal sanctions for breach, and the pre-emption provisions can be fairly easily disapplied.

7.4 Authority required to allot shares

Section 80 of the Companies Act 1985 restricts the power of directors of a company to allot 'relevant securities' unless, in accordance with that section, they are authorised to do so either by the company in general meeting or by the articles of the company.[4] 'Relevant securities' means shares in the company other than shares shown in the memorandum to have been taken by the subscribers to the memorandum, or shares allotted in pursuance of an employees' share scheme. It also includes any right to subscribe for, or to convert, any security into the kind of shares of the company defined above.[5]

Any authority (given in general meeting or by the articles) may be given for a particular exercise of that power or for its exercise generally.[6] It may be unconditional or subject to conditions. An authority must state the maximum amount[7] of shares that may be allotted under it and the date on which it will

---

1 Their prior authority for the creation of the company's 'authorised' but unissued share capital was always required. This, however, allowed the directors to have a 'bank' of unissued shares at their disposal.

2 It will usually also have the effect of vote dilution but this need not be the case (eg where the fresh issue consists of non-voting equity shares).

3 If a share is valued on a price/earnings basis, any increase in the number of shares that is not matched by a similar increase in earnings per share will lead to a fall in the share price and a loss to shareholders.

4 Section 80(1). As to the relationship between section 80 and section 125 protecting class rights, see **8.7.3**.

5 Section 80(2).

6 Section 80(3).

7 Where the 'securities' are not shares but rights to subscribe for shares or to convert any security into shares, then the 'maximum amount' of relevant securities means the maximum which may be allocated pursuant to the rights: section 80(6).

expire, which must not be more than the five years from the relevant date applicable. This date, in the case of an authority contained at the time of the original incorporation of the company in the articles, is the date of incorporation. In any other case, it is the date on which the resolution is passed by which the authority required by section 80 is given.[1] Any authority may be renewed by the company in general meeting for further successive periods not exceeding five years. The resolution renewing such authority must state (or restate) the amount of shares which may be allotted or, as the case may be, remains to be allotted under its authority, and the date on which the renewed authority will expire.[2] Even though any authority required by section 80 has expired, the directors may allot shares if they are allotted in pursuance of an offer or agreement made by the company before the authority expired. However, the authority must have allowed the company to make an offer or agreement which would or might require shares to be allotted after the authority expired.[3]

A company may give, vary, revoke or renew an authority by ordinary resolution even though it alters the articles of the company. However, the requirements of section 380 of the 1985 Act (registration of copies of certain resolutions) apply to such a resolution.[4] While criminal penalties are provided for any director who knowingly and wilfully contravenes, or permits or authorises the contravention of, section 80,[5] this will not affect the validity of any allotment of shares.[6]

A private company which has opted for the elective regime described in **13.4.6** may, instead of following the requirements of section 80, give the directors authority to allot shares for an indefinite period or for a fixed period longer than the five years permitted by section 80.[7] A fixed period authority may be renewed or further renewed by the company in general meeting.[8]

7.5 Pre-emption rights

As already noted, statute has, since 1980, conferred pre-emptive rights on existing equity shareholders when further shares are allotted.[9] This right applies to both public and private companies, but private companies may exclude it by a provision in their memorandum or articles.

The right conferred by section 89(1) of the Companies Act 1985 may, subject to various qualifications and exemptions to be considered later, be stated as follows. A company proposing to allot any 'equity securities' shall not allot any of those equity securities on any terms to any person, unless it has first made an offer to each person who holds 'relevant shares' or 'relevant employee shares' to allot to

---

1 Section 80(4).
2 Section 80(5).
3 Section 80(7).
4 Section 80(8). The provisions of section 711 (documents to be published by the Registrar in the *Gazette*) apply to such a resolution. See section 711(1)(d).
5 Section 80(9) and Schedule 24.
6 Section 80(10).
7 Section 80A.
8 This requires only an ordinary resolution or the statutory written resolution procedure (see **13.4.1**) can be used; the original elective resolution must be unanimous.
9 It has been common for the articles of private companies to make such provision. The *Listing Rules* confer what amounts to a right of pre-emption upon existing holders of equity shares in listed companies. Such rights do not exist at common law: *Mutual Life Insurance Co v The Rank Organisation* [1985] BCLC 11. The common law in the United States recognised such rights at an early stage. See generally I MacNeil 'Shareholders' Pre-Emptive Rights' [2002] JBL 78.

him, on the same or more favourable terms, a proportion of those securities which is as nearly as practical equal to the proportion in nominal value held by him of the aggregate of 'relevant shares' and 'relevant employee shares'.[1] 'Relevant shares', in relation to a company, means shares of the company *other than* (a) shares which as respects dividends and capital carry a right to participate up to only a specified amount in a distribution, and (b) shares held or to be held by a person who acquired them in pursuance of an employees' share scheme.[2] Conversely, 'relevant employee share' means shares of the company which would be relevant shares (as above) but for the fact that they are held under an employees' share scheme. Thus 'relevant shares' excludes preference shares which do not have rights to participate in both profits and capital.[3] 'Equity security', in relation to a company, means a relevant share in a company or a right to subscribe for, or convert any securities into, relevant shares of a company. 'Equity security' does not include, however, a bonus share or a share shown in the memorandum to have been taken by a subscriber thereto.[4]

There is a 21-day period during which the pre-emptive rights may be taken up or refused. The offer may not be withdrawn before the end of that period.[5] During this period, the company may not allot any securities subject to the pre-emptive rights conferred by section 89 to any other person, unless the period during which any such offer may be accepted has expired, or the company has received notice of the acceptance or refusal of every offer so made.[6] Shares offered by virtue of section 89(1) may be allotted either to the holders of relevant shares (or relevant employee shares) *or* to anyone in whose favour such a person has renounced his right to allotment.[7]

Special provision is made to meet the situation where a company's memorandum or articles confer pre-emptive rights which require a company proposing to allot equity shares of a particular class to offer those shares to the holders of relevant shares or relevant employee shares of that class. Section 89(3) provides that where that is the case, an offer to allot in compliance with such a provision will prevent the application of section 89(1) in the event that the recipient, or anyone in whose favour the recipient has renounced his right to allotment, accepts the offer. The 21-day period during which an offer must be made and the manner in which it must be served, is governed by section 90 and not by what the memorandum or articles may prescribe.[8]

Section 89(1) does not apply to an allotment of equity securities if they are to be paid up (or are in fact paid up) wholly or partly otherwise than in cash.[9] Further, it does not apply in relation to the allotment of any securities which would, apart from a renunciation or assignment of the right to their allotment, be held under

---

1   Section 89(1)(a).
2   See section 94(5). As to the meaning of 'employees' share scheme', see section 743.
3   See **8.4**. So, for example, preference shares with a preferential right to dividend, but the same capital rights as ordinary shares, are within the definition and caught by section 89.
4   Section 94(2).
5   Section 90(6). Section 90(2)–(5) makes provision for the communication of pre-emption offers to shareholders (eg delivery personally or by registered post).
6   Section 89(1)(b).
7   Section 89(4). This facilitates the existence of a market in 'nil paid rights' in which a shareholder can sell the right to allotment to a third party.
8   Section 90(7). In other respects the provisions of the memorandum or articles to which section 89(3) applies will remain valid.
9   Section 89(4).

an employees' share scheme.[1] Subject to these exemptions and the provision described in **7.5.1**, pre-emptive rights are mandatory in the case of public companies. However, the rights conferred by section 89 may be excluded by a provision contained in the memorandum or articles of a private company. Furthermore, a requirement or authority contained in the memorandum or articles of a private company, if it is inconsistent with the requirements of sections 89(1), 90(1) to (5) (mode of service) and 90(6) (period of offer), shall have effect as a provision excluding the pre-emptive rights conferred by section 89(1).[2]

Section 92(1) provides a civil, but not a criminal, sanction for a contravention of sections 89 and 90. The company, and every officer of the company who knowingly authorised or permitted the contravention, are jointly and severally liable to compensate any person to whom an offer should have been made[3] for any loss, damage, costs or expenses which that person has sustained or incurred by reason of that contravention.[4] However, no such proceedings may be commenced after the expiration of two years from the delivery to the Registrar of Companies of the return of allotments in question.[5] Section 92(1) does not appear to invalidate any allotment not complying with shareholders' pre-emptive rights.[6] They are simply left to the civil remedy provided by the subsection. It has been left to the courts to determine the measure and scope of loss or damage that may be recovered. It is not clear whether the loss of 'control' of a company would be compensable over and above the market price for shares of that class.

7.5.1 *When authority under section 80 overrides pre-emptive rights*

Section 95 attempts to reconcile the requirements of section 80 with those of section 89. It does this by providing for the disapplication of section 89 in certain circumstances. Section 95(1) provides that where directors of a company are *generally* authorised for the purposes of section 80,[7] they may be given power by the articles or by special resolution to allot equity securities pursuant to their section 80 authority as if section 89(1) did not apply to the allotment. Alternatively, section 89(1) may apply to the allotment with such modifications as the directors may determine. Where the directors are not generally authorised for the purposes of section 80, section 89(1) can be disapplied or modified in respect of an allotment by special resolution.[8]

The power conferred by section 95 will cease to have effect when the authority to which it relates is revoked or would, if not renewed, expire. However, if the authority required by section 80 is renewed, the power conferred by section 95 (in the articles or by special resolution) may also be renewed (for a period not longer

---

1   Section 89(5). As to the definition of 'employees' shares scheme', see section 743.
2   Section 91(1) and (2). The 'implied' exclusion referred to in the text does not of course extend to provisions in the memorandum or articles conferring pre-emptive rights of the kind contemplated by section 89(2) and (3).
3   Ie an offer under section 89(1) or (3).
4   Section 92(1).
5   Where equity securities other than shares are granted it is two years from the date of the grant: section 92(2).
6   This is probably so in the case of an allotment to a large number of shareholders, but an allotment in a small company where the 21-day period was not allowed was declared invalid in *Re Thundercrest Ltd* [1994] BCC 857.
7   See section 80(3).
8   Section 95(2).

than that for which the authority is renewed) by a special resolution of the company.[1]

As in the case of an authority for the purposes of section 80, the directors may allot equity securities in pursuance of an offer or agreement previously made by the company even though the power or resolution required by section 95 has expired at the time of the allotment. However, the power or resolution must have enabled the company to make an offer or agreement which would or might require equity securities to be allotted after it expired.[2]

A special resolution conferring the power given by section 95(2) (which applies where the directors are authorised for the purposes of section 80 generally and *otherwise*) may not be proposed unless it is recommended by the directors.[3] In addition, there must be circulated with the notice of the meeting at which the resolution is proposed, to the members entitled to have that notice, a written statement by the directors. This must set out:

(1) their reasons for making the recommendation;
(2) the amount to be paid to the company in respect of the equity securities to be allotted; and
(3) the directors' justification of that amount.[4]

7.6 Common-law controls on allotments

The statutory controls on allotments have their limitation. The remedies for breach are limited and do not appear to include avoidance of an allotment even for a breach of the pre-emption provisions. Where the directors of a company are in control of the voting power at general meetings, there will still be the possibility of abuse notwithstanding section 80 of the Companies Act 1985. The observance of statutory pre-emption rights in a private company may amount to an indirect method of squeezing out minority shareholders who lack the means to take up their proportionate share of a new issue.[5] Further, as has been seen, pre-emption rights do not apply to certain types of issue, in particular issues of equity shares not paid for wholly in cash; this leaves a very wide gap in the statutory protection, as it seems that a minor amount of non-cash consideration will suffice. In all of these cases, the only possible remedies for abuse will be for breach of directors' duties in respect of an allotment and/or for breach of controlling shareholders' duties, perhaps by way of a petition under section 459. The latter is considered elsewhere,[6] but it is appropriate to look briefly here at the law regarding directors' duties in this area.[7]

In deciding upon the making of allotments, the directors 'must dispose of their company's shares on the best terms obtainable, and must not allot them to themselves or their friends at a lower price in order to obtain a personal benefit.

---

1   Section 95(3).
2   Section 95(4).
3   Special resolutions required by section 95 must be also gazetted under section 711.
4   Section 95(5). A criminal sanction is imposed in respect of misleading, false, or deceptive matters in the statement: section 95(6).
5   See the unreported decision in *Pennell v Venida Invesements*, 25 July 1974, discussed in *Burridge* (1981) 44 MLR 40.
6   See **17.4** for the common-law controls on majority shareholders' voting, and **17.13** *et seq* for section 459.
7   For directors' duties in general, see Chapter 16.

They must act *bona fide* for the interests of the company'.[1] But this does not mean that when the market price is at a premium, shares cannot be issued at par. In *Hilder v Dexter*, Lord Davey observed that he was not aware 'of any law which obliges a company to issue its shares above par because they are saleable at a premium in the market. It depends on the circumstances of each case whether it will be prudent or even possible to do so, and it is a question for the directors to decide'.[2] When the shares command a premium, the directors must not allot them at par to members of their own body or their friends, for they should either offer them equally to all the shareholders or obtain the benefit of the premium for the company.[3] However, an allotment to the directors sanctioned by a general meeting of the company has been held to be unimpeachable notwithstanding that the directors held the majority of the shares and voted in favour of the allotments of the shares to themselves.[4] Directors, moreover, must not allot shares to themselves or their friends for the purpose of obtaining the control of the voting power in the company. If they do so, the court will declare the allotment invalid and rectify the register, and in the meantime will restrain the allottees from voting in respect of the shares thus allotted.[5] Directors may, however, purchase shares from existing members to increase their voting power.[6] But they must not, when allotting shares to themselves or their friends, make the terms or time of payment more favourable to themselves than to the general body of members or to the public unless the latter are expressly informed of the arrangement.[7] Any profit the directors make out of shares improperly allotted to themselves will belong to the company, or if they have retained the shares they will be liable for the difference between the nominal value and the market value at the time of allotment.[8]

7.7   The contract of allotment

The contract to take shares is generally made by application and allotment, and for this purpose in public issues, a form of application for shares is usually issued with the prospectus, to be filled up by the applicant and left at the office of the company or with its bankers, accompanied by a deposit of a specified amount for each share applied for.[9]

7.8   Letters of allotment

Public companies do not, in making an allotment in response to an application, immediately issue a share certificate to the allottee. Instead, the allottee receives a letter of allotment which will be replaced by the share certificate (or its

---

1   *Per Swinfen Eady J, Percival v Wright* [1902] 2 Ch 421 at 425.
2   [1902] AC 474 at 480 (HL).
3   *York and North Midland Railway Co v Hudson* (1853) 16 Beav 485; *Parker v McKenna* (1874) 10 Ch App 96; *Shaw v Holland* [1900] 2 Ch 305 (CA).
4   *Ving v Robertson and Woodcock* (1912) 56 SJ 412.
5   *Fraser v Whalley* (1864) 2 H & M 10; *Punt v Symons & Co* [1903] 2 Ch 506; *Piercy v Mills Co* [1920] 1 Ch 77; *Hogg v Cramphorn* [1967] Ch 254; *Bamford v Bamford* [1969] 2 WLR 1107 (CA). See further, **16.7**.
6   *North-West Transportation Co v Beatty* (1887) 12 App Cas 589 (PC).
7   *Alexander v Automatic Telephone Co* [1900] 2 Ch 56 (CA).
8   *Shaw v Holland* [1900] 2 Ch 305 (CA).
9   However, a letter or even a verbal application for shares is perfectly valid: *Cookney's Case* (1859) 3 De G & J 170; *Bloxam's Case* (1864) 4 De GJ & S 447.

equivalent[1]) only when the full issue price has been paid.[2] The position of the allottee,[3] before his name is entered on the register of members and a share certificate is issued to him, is that he is a shareholder and enjoys the rights and is subject to the liabilities of such. However, he is not yet a member of the company and, unless the articles otherwise provide, he cannot exercise a membership right such as the right to vote or attend meetings.[4] However, as a shareholder, he is entitled to any dividends declared and must pay any calls that are made.[5] If the company is wound up he may be made a contributory if the contract of subscription is still enforceable against him.[6]

The Companies Act 1985 gives an allottee of shares the right to apply to the court to have his name entered on to the register[7] and to have a share certificate issued to him if the company fails to do so within two months of allotment.[8] The company also has the right to register a subscriber if he (or his renouncee) does not apply for registration.[9] It should be noted that none of the above references to share certificates will apply if, as is normally the case for listed companies, the shares in question are 'dematerialised'.[10]

Nowadays a letter of allotment issued by a public company will always have attached to it a blank letter of renunciation and a registration application form. The former allows the original allottee to renounce his right to allotment in favour of whoever completes the appropriate registration application form.[11] However, the allottee may not wish to renounce and will then himself complete his registration application form and submit the letter of allotment to the company. Alternatively, the allottee may wish to renounce some shares in his allotment and retain others. He will do this by executing the letters of renunciation in respect of those shares he wishes to renounce and submitting the letter of allotment to the company. The company will then issue 'split letters of allotment' to the allottee and the renouncee.[12]

---

1   When shares have been dematerialised certificates are replaced by electronic records of ownership. See **9.3.3**.
2   As to share certificates, see **9.10**.
3   Subscribers to the memorandum are members from the time of subscription: see **12.2**.
4   Section 370(6), which confers the right on 'every member . . . of one vote in respect of each share' in the case of companies 'originally having a share capital' insofar as the articles 'make no other provision'.
5   See *McEuen v West London Wharves & Warehouses Co* (1871) 6 Ch App 655 at 661–662.
6   See *Re Direct Birmingham, Oxford, etc, Rly Co, ex parte Capper* (1851) 20 LJ Ch 148, 151; *Re Pennant and Craigwen Mining Co, Fenn's Case* (1852) 1 Sm & G 26 and the definition of contributories in section 79 of the Insolvency Act 1986.
7   Section 359(1).
8   Section 185(1).
9   *McEuen v West London Wharves and Warehouses Co* (1871) 6 Ch App 655.
10 See generally **9.3.3**. Regulation 38 of the Uncertificated Securities Regulations 2001, SI 2001/3755 prohibits the issue of a share certificate in respect of dematerialised (uncertificated) shares.
11 The directors cannot refuse to accept a renouncee by relying on the article entitling them to refuse transfer because this does not amount to a transfer: *Re Pool Shipping Co* [1920] 1 Ch 251. An article might be so drawn as to allow the directors to refuse to register the renouncee, but this is not usually done.
12 For specimen forms of allotment letter and split allotment letter, see *Secretarial Administration* (Jordans, 1984, loose-leaf), Part 6. The allotment letter will always state the last date on which it may be split or renounced.

It should be noted that where a public issue is made by way of 'offer for sale'[1] by an issuing house, the allotment is made by the issuing house and not the company. The applicant is sent in response to his application a 'letter of acceptance' (instead of an allotment letter). Until the allottee (or his renouncee) has his name entered on the register of members, his contract of subscription is with the issuing house which may sue him if he is in default.

The usual practice in the case of allotments of shares by private companies is to dispense with the letter of allotment and, on allotment, to proceed at once to the issue of a share certificate and entry of the allottee's name on the register of members.[2] Sometimes public companies issue 'renounceable share certificates'. Within the period provided the renouncee may send it to the company to be entered on the register of members. An ordinary share certificate will then be sent to him. If the original allottee decides not to renounce, he may retain the original share certificate as permanent evidence of title by cancelling or destroying the attached letters of renunciation.[3]

7.9 Restrictions on allotment of shares by public companies

There are two restrictions on the power of public companies to make a valid allotment of shares. First, section 84 of the Companies Act 1985 imposes a restriction on the allotment of any share capital of a public company. Such an allotment may not be made unless either that capital is subscribed in full, or the offer states that, even if the capital is not subscribed for in full, the amount of that capital subscribed for may be allotted in any event or in the event of the conditions specified in the offer being satisfied. Where such conditions are imposed, no allotment must be made unless those conditions are satisfied. The 'offer' document will, in the normal case of a public company offering shares to the public, be listing particulars or a prospectus subject to the requirements described in Chapter 6.

Section 84(2) and (3) provides for the consequences of allotting shares in breach of section 84(1). Thus all money must be repaid to applicants within 40 days from the first issue of the prospectus. Personal liability is imposed on directors if this money is not repaid within 48 days of the issue of the prospectus. The director has the defence open to him of proving that this was not due to any misconduct or negligence on his part. Such an allotment will also be voidable at the instance of the applicant under section 85. Section 84 applies in the case of shares offered as wholly or partly payable otherwise than in cash as well as to shares offered for subscription in cash.[4]

The second restriction is that a public company may not allot a share except as paid up at least as to one-quarter of the nominal value of the share and any premium on it.[5] Where a public company allots a share in contravention of this

---

1 See **6.8**.
2 Since shares in private companies are not as a rule freely transferable, there is no reason to issue renounceable allotment letters.
3 The reason for this practice is to save unnecessary expense, but it will only be used where the shares are to be paid in full at the time of allotment or in the case of a capitalisation issue.
4 Section 84(4).
5 Companies Act 1985, section 101(1). This section does not apply to shares allotted in pursuance of an employees' share scheme: section 101(2).

provision, the share will be treated as if one-quarter of its nominal value together with the whole of any premium had been received. However, the allottee shall be liable to pay the company the minimum amount which should have been received in respect of the share less the value of any consideration actually supplied in payment (up to any extent) of the share and any premium on it, and the interest at the appropriate rate on the amount so payable.[1] This liability will not apply in relation to an allotment of a bonus share unless the allottee knew or ought to have known that the share was allotted in contravention of section 101.[2]

7.10 Return of allotments

Whenever a company limited by shares or limited by guarantee and having a share capital makes any allotment of its shares, either upon public subscription or otherwise, it must within one month thereafter lodge with the Registrar for registration the following documents:

(1) a return of the allotments in the prescribed form stating the number and nominal amount of the shares comprised in the allotment, the names and addresses of the allottees, and the amount (if any) paid or due and payable on each share whether on account of the nominal value of the shares or by way of premium;

(2) when shares are allotted as fully or partly paid up otherwise than in cash, a contract in writing constituting the title of the allottee to the allotment, together with any contract of sale or for services or other consideration in respect of which the allotment was made, and a return stating the number and nominal amount of the shares so allotted, the extent to which they are to be treated as paid up, and the consideration for which they have been allotted.[3]

In the absence of a contract in writing, a document containing the prescribed particulars must be stamped with the same stamp as if it were a contract for the purpose, and must be lodged with the Registrar for registration.[4] The court may grant relief and extend the time for delivery of the document if the omission was accidental or due to inadvertence or if it is just and equitable to grant relief.[5]

7.11 Maintenance of capital

As we have seen earlier in this chapter, although the raising of finance by the issue of shares is often the least important method, company law has always paid special attention to share capital and has developed sophisticated rules relating to what is called 'the raising and maintenance of capital'. It should be noted that the term 'capital' here means only capital in the narrow sense of money raised by the issue of shares and the assets (eg land, plant and machinery) acquired with that money. It bears no necessary relationship to the more normal use of that word in

---

1   Section 101(4). As to the liability of subsequent holders, see section 112; see **7.14**.
2   Section 101(5).
3   Section 88(2). Fines may be imposed for default on an officer of the company 'knowingly a party to the default'. This means knowing of the default at the time, not subsequently: *Beck v Solicitor to Board of Trade* (1932) *The Times*, 23 April; see *Gore-Browne on Companies* 44th edn (Jordans, loose-leaf) at 9.9.
4   Section 88(3). As to payment for shares other than in cash generally, see **7.13** *et seq.*
5   Section 88(5).

economic jargon, which is simply the net worth of a business, the amount by which the value of its assets exceeds its liabilities. The purpose of the legal rules is primarily to protect the creditors of a company limited by shares, whose existence is of course quite independent of any individual members of it, so that the creditors can be sure that there is something they can look to for payment of their debts. The fact that share capital may play a very small role in a company's financing means that these rules often have less significance than their volume and complexity would otherwise suggest.

The artificiality of these rules is compounded by the fact that there is no minimum share capital for private companies. Of course, public companies must have such a minimum,[1] but the figure of £50,000 is paltry indeed compared to the actual worth of the vast majority of public companies. Despite these points, detailed attention must be paid to the law relating to the raising and maintenance of capital. This was initially developed by the courts and the general principle established by the cases may be stated as requiring that a company with a share capital is bound to obtain a proper consideration for the shares which it issues and to refrain from handing back any or all of the fund so acquired to its members except by a lawful distribution of profits or a lawful reduction of capital. Although much of the detail is now consolidated and modified by statute, as will be seen in ensuing paragraphs, the common-law principle is by no means redundant. Recent case-law has illustrated its vitality: denying the validity of 'unearned' remuneration awarded to a director who was also a shareholder;[2] striking down a sale of company A's assets to B, a company controlled by A's sole substantial shareholder, at a gross undervalue;[3] and holding unlawful an agreement which sought to impose a liability to make a gratuitous payment at a future date when it was likely that the company would have no distributable profits.[4]

The statutory provisions are contained in Part V of the Companies Act 1985. This Part is the consolidation of part of the Companies Act 1980 which implemented the Second EC Directive,[5] the measure which necessitated the statutory enactment of the rules. It must be said that some of the Directive's provisions – and hence those of the statute – appear to be rather pointless in practice; this is considered, where appropriate, in the following description of the legal rules and it is likely that some simplification of the rules will emanate from the Department of Trade and Industry's review.[6] The issues surrounding the nature and rights of shares themselves and the ways in which a company may reorganise its capital structure are considered in the next chapter.

7.12 Price of allotted shares

The principle of maintenance of capital requires that as a general rule the total consideration received by a company in return for each share allotted by it must not be less than the nominal amount, or 'par value', of the share; that is, shares

---

1   See **3.2**.
2   *Re Halt Garage* (1964) Ltd [1982] 3 All ER 1045; see also *Re George Newman & Co* [1895] 1 Ch 974 at 686 and the discussion of corporate gifts at **5.13**.
3   *Aveling Barford Ltd v Perion Ltd* (1989) 5 BCC 677.
4   *Barclays Bank plc v British & Commonwealth Holdings plc* [1996] 1 BCLC 1 (CA).
5   (1977) OJ L26/1.
6   See **7.25**. See also Ferran, 'Creditors' Interests and "Core" Company Law' (1999) 20 Co Law 314; Armour, 'Share Capital and Credit Protection: Efficient Rules for a Modern Company Law' (2000) 63 MLR 355.

must not be allotted at a discount.[1] The basis of the rule is that a company should not overstate the size of its share capital, which is the money paid to it in return for shares. This rule applies whether the shares are issued fully paid or partly paid in the first instance.[2] It is, however, relaxed by the Companies Act 1985 in one specific instance, namely where commission or brokerage is paid under section 97.[3] Except in this case, where shares are allotted at a discount, the allottee is liable to pay the company the amount of the discount and interest thereon at the appropriate rate.[4] A subsequent holder of the shares is jointly and severally liable with the allottee unless he is a purchaser for value without actual notice of the issue at a discount at the time of the purchase or he derived title, directly or indirectly, from such a purchaser.[5] Sections 100 and 112 impose this liability upon an actual allottee and the subsequent holders described. It seems, therefore, that a mere contract to issue or allot shares at a discount is void and unenforceable under previous authority.[6]

Any liability to pay the amount of a discount may be enforced in a winding-up for the benefit of creditors or other shareholders,[7] as the case may be, but the mere fact that some members received their shares at a discount does not entitle other members holding shares properly issued to bring a winding-up petition.[8] As an alternative to these remedies, the company may make the directors who were responsible for the shares issue liable to pay the amount of the discount as damages for breach of duty.[9]

The rule that a proper consideration must be obtained for issued shares is applicable in a wide range of situations which clearly survive the statutory confirmation of the principle. For example, the issue of £1 debentures at a discount with a provision that they may be exchanged for fully paid £1 shares immediately or at any time before a fixed date, is unlawful, as the shares would be issued at a discount.[10] A company cannot issue 200 £1 shares in satisfaction of a debt of £100,[11] nor can it allot 200 £1 shares for 50p each in consideration of the allottee making a loan of £100 to the company.[12]

The rule does not go so far as to require that shares must be paid for in cash. That payment in money's worth is sufficient is confirmed in respect of both nominal value and premium by section 99(1).[13] Furthermore, section 738 provides that payment in cash includes the following: cash in foreign currency; cheques received by the company which the directors have no reason for suspecting will not be paid; the release of a liability of the company for a liquidated

---

1 Section 100, confirming *Ooregum Gold Mining Co of India v Roper* [1892] AC 125 (HL).
2 As to the minimum price payable on allotment of a public company's shares under section 101, see **7.9**. As to the minimum capital requirements for public companies, see **3.2**.
3 See **4.21**.
4 Section 100(2), the appropriate rate for interest is 5% per annum or such other sum as is specified by statutory instrument: section 107.
5 Section 112(1).
6 *Re Almada & Tirito Co* (1888) 38 Ch D 415 (CA).
7 *Welton v Saffery* [1897] AC 299 (HL).
8 *Re Pioneers of Mashonaland Syndicate* [1893] 1 Ch 731.
9 *Hirsche v Sims* [1894] AC 654.
10 *Mosley v Koffyfontein Mines Ltd* (No 1) [1904] 2 Ch 108 (CA).
11 *Re Wragg Ltd* [1897] 1 Ch 796, 831 (CA).
12 *Re James Pitkin & Co Ltd* [1916] WN 112.
13 'Money's worth' is expressly stated to include goodwill and know-how.

sum;[1] and an undertaking to pay cash to the company at a future date. However, apart from these cases, the Companies Act 1985 provides important qualifications in respect of the payment for shares in public companies by non-cash consideration. Thus, this question must be considered separately in respect of private and public companies respectively.

7.13   Allotments of shares for non-cash consideration by private companies

As far as private companies are concerned, any valuable consideration *prima facie* suffices – for example an agreement to render services, as by becoming manager for five years.[2]

However, a company cannot by a contract make that which is not a good consideration in law a valid payment for shares – for example past services for which the company was not liable to pay.[3] But if the consideration is in kind, the court will not inquire whether it was really of a value equal to the nominal amount of shares issued, unless the consideration was illusory or had an obvious money value showing that a discount had been allowed.[4] Thus, a private company can agree to purchase property and pay for services at any price it thinks proper, and may make the payment in shares, provided that it does so honestly and not colourably, and has not been so imposed as to be entitled to repudiate the bargain.[5] The bargain must, however, represent a real valuation of the property transferred as an equivalent for the shares issued. Thus, if the directors have not considered at all whether the property and the shares are of equivalent value, the issue is bad.[6]

7.14   Allotments of shares for non-cash consideration by public companies

In accordance with the requirements of the Second EC Directive on Company Law, the Companies Act 1985 contains detailed provisions governing the payment for shares allotted by public companies otherwise than in cash.[7]

In one case, payment other than in cash is totally prohibited. This is where shares are taken by a subscriber to the memorandum by virtue of an undertaking by him in the memorandum; the nominal value and any premium on the shares must be paid up in cash.[8]

In the other cases described below, the Act imposes various sanctions for breach.[9] Criminal liability to pay a fine may be imposed on the company and on

---

1   This does not cover the case where a price for property is stated to be satisfied by an allotment of shares: *Re Bradford Investments plc (No 2)* [1991] BCLC 688.

2   *Re Theatrical Trust Ltd, Chapman's Case* [1895] 1 Ch 771.

3   *Re Eddystone Marine Insurance Co* [1893] 3 Ch 9 (CA). In Scotland, past consideration may be good: *Park Business Interiors Ltd v Park* [1990] BCC 914.

4   *Re Wragg Ltd* [1897] 1 Ch 796.

5   Ibid.

6   *Tintin Exploration Syndicate Ltd v Sandys* (1947) 177 LT 412.

7   As to what is payment in cash, see section 738, discussed in **7.12**. The payment of, or an undertaking to pay, cash to any person other than the company is non-cash consideration.

8   Section 106.

9   Note that where the consideration is an undertaking caught by the provisions described in **7.14.1** and **7.14.2**, the company can still enforce the undertaking: section 115(1).

every officer in default.[1] The recipient of the shares is immediately liable to pay in cash[2] the difference between any cash actually paid and the nominal value of, plus any premium payable on, the shares. A subsequent holder of the shares is jointly and severally liable with an original recipient, unless he is a purchaser for value from him without actual notice[3] of the contravention at the time of purchase, or unless he derived title, directly or indirectly, from such a purchaser.[4] The court can grant relief from civil liability subject to the conditions of section 113. Among other things,[5] these conditions impose a requirement to have regard to the principle of capital maintenance and to whether or not the company has benefited from the transaction which was in breach of the statute. It has been held that very good reasons will be required before the court can accept that it is just and equitable to exempt an applicant from liability, notwithstanding that the company has not received sufficient value,[6] but relief is more than likely to be given if the company has in fact received good value for shares, notwithstanding a failure to observe the valuation requirements described in **7.14.3**.[7]

7.14.1 Prohibited non-cash consideration

One form of non-cash consideration is prohibited by section 99(2). This is consideration which consists of an undertaking to do work or perform services for the company or any other person, whether in respect of payment of the nominal value of shares or any premium payable on them.

7.14.2 Future non-cash consideration

By section 102, it is prohibited for a public company to allot shares as fully or partly paid up, whether as to their nominal value or in respect of any premium payable on them, other than for cash, if the consideration for the allotment is or includes an undertaking which is to be or may be performed more than five years after the allotment.[8]

---

1   Section 114.
2   See *Re Bradford Investments plc* [1990] BCC 740, where it was held that, as a result, until cash is paid or the recipient of the shares is relieved from liability, under standard articles the recipient will be disenfranchised in respect of the shares (see Table A, article 57).
3   This means actual notice of the facts constituting the breach; ignorance of the statutory requirements is no defence: *System Control plc v Munro Corporate plc* [1990] BCLC 659.
4   Section 112(1) and (3).
5   For details, see *Gore-Browne on Companies* 44th edn (Jordans, loose-leaf) at 13.4.6. The list of matters in section 113 to which the court should have regard is not exhaustive: *Re Bradford Investments plc (No 2)* [1991] BCLC 688.
6   *Re Bradford Investments plc (No 2)*, above.
7   *Re Ossory Estates plc* [1988] BCLC 213.
8   Section 102(1). Any variation of a contract to allot shares, or an ancillary contract relating to payment in respect of those shares, which originally complies with subsection (1), which purports to vary its terms so that the subsection would have been broken had the variation been in the original contract, is void (section 102(3)); and this applies to the variation by a public company of the terms of such a contract entered into before it was re-registered as a public company (section 102(4)).

7.14.3 *Valuation of non-cash consideration*

In those cases where it is permissible for a public company to allot shares for a non-cash consideration, ie in cases other than those just described, section 103 imposes a general requirement of valuation of the consideration. [1]

For the allotment to be valid, a report on the value of the consideration must have been made to the company within the six months preceding the allotment, and a copy of the report sent to the proposed allottee. The requirement does not apply, however, to the following:

(1) a bonus or capitalisation issue of shares (section 103(2));
(2) allotments in connection with take-overs and mergers falling within the terms of section 103(3) and (4);
(3) allotments in connection with a proposed merger within the terms of section 103(5).

The 'curious and arcane'[2] provisions of section 108 lay down the requirements for the valuation of and report on the non-cash consideration, which must be made by an independent person qualified at the time of the report to be appointed or to continue to be auditor of the company, whom the Act refers to as the valuer.[3] However, he may arrange for or accept a valuation of the consideration or part of it made by another person, eg a surveyor, where it appears to him to be reasonable for it to be made by that person and where that person appears to him to have the requisite knowledge and experience and is not an officer or servant[4] of the company or its subsidiary or holding company or of another subsidiary of the company's holding company or a partner or employee of such an officer or servant. If the valuation is thus delegated, the delegate must also make a report that will enable the independent person to make his own report and to provide a note in accordance with subsection 6, described below.[5]

The valuer's report must state:

(1) the nominal value of the shares to be wholly or partly paid for by the consideration in question;
(2) the amount of any premium payable on the shares;
(3) the description of the consideration and of that part of it which he himself has valued, the method used to value it and the date of the valuation; and
(4) the extent to which the nominal value of the shares and any premium are to be treated as paid up on allotment by the consideration and in cash.[6]

Where the valuation was made by a delegate, the report must also state this fact and the name of the delegate and the knowledge and experience he had to carry

---

1   This applies whether the shares are fully or partly paid up and the requirement also applies when an allotment of shares is mixed with other consideration given by the company in exchange for non-cash consideration.Here the valuer must also value the other consideration to determine what proportion of the consideration provided by the allottee is attributable to the shares.
2   *Per* Harman J in *Re Ossory Estates plc* [1988] BCLC 213 at 215.
3   Section 108(1). This can clearly be the company's own auditor. As to who is qualified to be an auditor, see **14.20.3**.
4   Other than an auditor; see section 108(3).
5   Section 108(2).
6   Section 108(4).

out the valuation, and must describe so much of the consideration as was valued by the delegate, the method used to value it and the date of valuation.[1]

In addition, the report must contain, or be accompanied by a note containing, statements to the following effect:

(1) in the case of a valuation made by a delegate, that it appeared to the valuer reasonable to arrange for it to be so made or to accept a valuation so made;
(2) that the method of valuation was reasonable in all circumstances;
(3) that it appears to the valuer that there has been no material change in the value of the consideration in question since the valuation; and
(4) that on the basis of the valuation, the value of the consideration, together with any cash by which the nominal value of the shares or any premium payable on them is to be paid up, is not less than so much of the aggregate of the nominal value and the premium as is treated as paid up by the consideration and any such cash.[2]

Any person making a valuation or report under section 103 is by section 110 given the right to require from the officers of the company such information and explanation as he thinks necessary.[3]

A copy of any report must be delivered to the Registrar of Companies for registration at the same time as the return of the allotment of the shares concerned is made under section 88.[4]

By way of comment, it may be thought that the provisions described in this section were a complex overreaction to a not very real problem, given that the shares of many public companies are or will be traded on The Stock Exchange or dealt in under the auspices of some other body recognised under the Financial Services and Markets Act 2000, the rules of which should ensure the full disclosure of all relevant information. Like some other measures emanating from the Second Directive, they have complicated company law without any apparent benefit thereto and it is a pity that these considerations were not in the minds of those negotiating or implementing the Directive.[5]

7.14.4 *Non-cash assets acquired from subscribers and others*

Sections 104 and 105 deal with certain agreements which may be entered into by public companies which, although they are not necessarily confined to allotments of shares, will often be so concerned and which it is convenient to describe here.[6] The sections impose valuation, report and public filing requirements similar to those just described,[7] where a public company enters into an agreement with an appropriate person for the transfer by him to the company or another person of one or more non-cash assets[8] equal to one-tenth or more of the company's issued share capital within what is described as the 'initial period'.

---

1   Section 108(5).
2   Section 108(6).
3   It is an offence for an officer to mislead the valuer, section 110(2) and (3).
4   Section 111; see **7.10**.
5   See, also, Sealy, *Company Law and Commercial Reality*, pp 68 and 82.
6   This is a very brief account of the provisions; for more detail, see *Gore-Browne on Companies* 44th edn (Jordans, loose-leaf) at 13.4.5.
7   Note that both valuations will be required when a company is allotting shares as all or part of the consideration for the transfer of a non-cash asset to it.
8   Property or interests in property: section 739.

Where a company is formed as a public company, the appropriate person is any subscriber to its memorandum and the initial period is two years from the issue of the company's trading certificate.[1] Where a joint-stock company is registered as a public company, or a private company is re-registered as a public company, the appropriate person is any member of the company at the time of registration or re-registration and the initial period is two years from the date of registration or re-registration.

These sections are open to even more criticism than the related ones on valuation discussed above. Their purpose is presumably the prevention of fraud by promoters of public companies, but they can be easily evaded. Public companies are never in practice formed as such and hence the provision as to their subscribers to the memorandum is in effect redundant. When public companies are converted from private companies, the sections apply, as described above, only to members at the time of registration or re-registration; an intending fraudster need only ensure that he does not become a member of a company at the appropriate time.

7.15   Issue of shares at a premium

It is very common for shares in a company to be issued in return for a consideration greater than the par or nominal value of the shares, whether the company is a public company making a public issue or a private company formed with a £100 share capital which is issued in return for the transfer of property worth much more than £100. The fact that such a premium is obtainable does not of itself impose a duty on the company to demand it.[2] However, if shares are issued at a premium, whether for a cash or non-cash consideration,[3] *prima facie* section 130 of the Companies Act 1985 requires the company to transfer a sum equal to the aggregate amount or value of the premiums on those shares to a share premium account which, like issued share capital, must appear on the liabilities side of the balance sheet.[4] In certain cases where shares are issued in return for shares or in other consideration from another company, section 130 does not apply by reason of sections 131 to 134, which are described below.

Where section 130 does apply, the share premium account is to some extent treated as if it were share capital so that the provisions regarding reduction of capital apply to it and it cannot be used to finance a payment of dividends.[5] However, it may be applied:

(1) to finance an issue of fully paid bonus shares (though not a partly paid issue nor to finance an issue of debentures);

(2) in writing off preliminary expenses or the expenses of, or commission paid or discount allowed on any issue of shares or debentures; and

---

1   Under section 117; see **4.7**.

2   *Hilder v Dexter* [1902] AC 474 (HL). But it may be a breach of duty by the directors who fail to obtain such a premium; see **7.6**.

3   *Henry Head & Co Ltd v Ropner Holdings Ltd* [1952] Ch 124; *Shearer v Bercain* [1980] 3 All ER 295.

4   Schedule 4, Part I; see Chapter 14, below.

5   Although, using the reduction of capital procedure (see Chapter 8), a company may be able to cancel the share premium account and in effect convert it into distributable profits: *Quayle Munro Ltd, Petitioners* [1994] 1 BCLC 410.

(3) in providing for the premium payable on redemption of any debentures.[1]

The Company Law Review Steering Group (CLRSG) has proposed that it should no longer be possible to use the share premium account for the second and third purposes.[2]

7.15.1 Relief from section 130

In *Shearer v Bercain Ltd*,[3] it was clearly established that the obligation to create a share premium account applied wherever a company in fact acquired assets worth more than the par value of the shares issued, and particularly in the case of a merger of companies by exchange of shares where the shares acquired by the new holding company were worth more than the par value of the shares issued by it.[4] This decision, though logically unimpeachable on the construction of what is now section 130, was felt to cause unnecessary difficulties in certain contexts, and mergers by exchange of shares were frequently effected since the introduction of what is now section 130 (as section 56 of the 1948 Act) on the basis of a different interpretation.[5] As a result, the Companies Act 1985 provides for exemptions from the need to establish a share premium account in limited circumstances. These are principally mergers by exchanges of equity shares which satisfy the provisions of section 131 and capital reconstructions within a group which satisfy the requirements of section 132.[6]

7.16 Acquisition by a company of rights in respect of its own shares

One of the most fundamental common-law principles relating to the maintenance of capital was that which made it illegal for a limited company to purchase its own shares.[7] To have allowed otherwise would in many cases have permitted a company unilaterally to reduce the capital fund available for creditors. The prohibition is now in statutory form (Companies Act 1985, section 143(1)) and applies to the acquisition by a company of its own shares by purchase, subscription or otherwise except, *inter alia*, when fully paid shares are acquired other than for valuable consideration. This exception permits, for example, a company acting as trustee to hold its own shares in that capacity, provided that someone else paid for them. An acquisition in breach of section 143 is void and the company and every defaulting officer is liable to a criminal penalty.[8] Section 143 does not apply where

---

1   Section 130(2). It may also be used by private companies making a lawful purchase of shares out of capital under the provisions of the 1985 Act; see **7.17**.

2   See *Completing the Structure* para 7.8 and *Modernising Company Law* (Cmnd 5553) paragraphs 76 and 77.

3   [1980] 3 All ER 295.

4   It was also decided that the pre-acquisition profits of the acquired company were to be treated as capital, not profit. As to pre-acquisition profits, see **14.15**.

5   For an account of the debate that *Shearer v Bercain* stimulated, see (1980) 1 Co Law 293.

6   For detail, see *Gore-Browne on Companies* 44th edn (Jordans, loose-leaf) at 13.5.1–13.5.7.

7   *Trevor v Whitworth* (1887) 12 App Cas 409 (HL).

8   See section 143(2). In *Vision Express (UK) Ltd v Wilson* [1995] 2 BCLC 419, part of a *Tomlin* order under which a company was to purchase all the rights in shares in itself held by the other party was void for infringing section 143.

a company acquires the whole of the issued share capital of another company where the sole asset of the latter is a shareholding in the first company.[1]

However, shortly after the introduction of what is now section 143, the 1981 Act made substantial inroads into the prohibition and, as will be seen in the following sections, statute does permit the purchase by a company of its own shares under stringent conditions. There are other exceptions to section 143[2] covering reductions of capital,[3] purchases pursuant to court orders under various sections of the Companies Act 1985, and forfeitures and surrenders of shares for failure to pay calls.[4]

The basic prohibition in section 143 cannot be evaded by the issue of shares to someone acting as nominee for the company or by such a nominee acquiring partly paid shares in the company. In most cases, by section 144, the nominee is deemed to hold the shares on his own account and is liable to pay for them.[5] However, this does not apply where the company does not have any beneficial interest in such shares, for example because it did not provide or agree to provide any consideration. In addition, if the nominee of a public company acquires shares in the company with financial assistance given to him directly by the company, the shares must be disposed of or cancelled under section 146.[6]

A nominee for a company has always been able to acquire from a member, and hold, already issued fully paid shares in the company – provided that the company provides no consideration.[7] If, however, the company is a public company, the regime of section 146[8] applies and the nominee cannot exercise any voting rights attached to the shares.[9]

## 7.17	The redemption or purchase of a company's own shares

The Companies Act 1985 contains a number of important provisions (first introduced in the 1981 Act) which allow companies to purchase their own shares and, in respect of private companies, permit this to be financed out of capital. Although in part these represent a considerable departure from traditional principles of maintenance of capital, they were to some extent only an extension of a longstanding provision which allowed companies to issue preference shares which would be redeemable by the company.[10]

There seems little doubt that the idea underlying these provisions was worthwhile, since there is no reason why a purchase of its own shares by a company should necessarily infringe the capital maintenance principle and this is certainly

---

1   *Acatos & Hutcheson plc v Watson* [1995] BCC 446. In this case, the provisions of section 23 (see **7.19**) apply.
2   See section 143(3).
3   See **8.14**.
4   See **8.16**.
5   See section 144(2) which also provides that if the nominee fails to pay a call, then the subscribers to the memorandum or the directors, as the case may be, are liable to pay it.
6   See **8.16**.
7   *Kirby v Wilkins* [1929] 2 Ch 444; *Re Castiglione's Will Trusts* [1958] Ch 549. This course is unnecessary now that section 143, as described above, permits the company itself to hold such shares.
8   See **8.16**.
9   Section 146(4).
10   Section 58 of the Companies Act 1948.

not the case if the consideration is not provided out of capital, and it may be economically advantageous for unwanted capital to be freed in this way. However, it may be wondered whether the legislature was not far too cautious. As will be seen, the provisions are complex and the exercise of the power to redeem or purchase is surrounded by restrictive requirements. Some relaxation seems likely, however, as a result of the proposals made by the CLRSG.[1]

7.17.1 Redeemable shares

By section 159, a company limited by shares or limited by guarantee and having a share capital may, if authorised to do so by its articles and subject to the conditions laid down, issue shares of any class which are to be redeemed or are liable to be redeemed at the option of the company or the shareholder. No redeemable shares may, however, be issued by a company unless it has at the time issued shares which are not redeemable. Subject to the relevant provisions of the Act, the redemption of shares may be effected on such terms and in such manner as may be provided by the articles of the company.[2]

The conditions of redemption are as follows.

(1) Redeemable shares may be redeemed only if they are fully paid.
(2) The terms of redemption must provide for payment on redemption.
(3) The redeemable shares of public companies may be redeemed only out of distributable profits[3] or out of the proceeds of a fresh issue of shares made for the purposes of the redemption, and except as described below, any premium payable on redemption must be paid out of distributable profits.

Private companies may additionally redeem shares out of capital.[4]

Where redeemable shares were issued at a premium, any premium payable on their redemption may be paid out of the proceeds of a fresh issue of shares made for the purposes of the redemption up to an amount equal to the lesser of: (a) the aggregate of the premiums received by the company on the issue of the shares redeemed; and (b) the current amount of the company's share premium account (including any sum transferred to that account in respect of premiums on the new shares). In such a case, the amount of the company's share premium account must be reduced by a sum corresponding (or by sums in the aggregate corresponding) to the amount of any payment made under this provision out of the proceeds of the issue of the new shares.

Shares redeemed under section 160 must be treated as cancelled on redemption and the amount of the company's issued capital[5] is diminished by the nominal value of the shares. However, capital is maintained either because the proceeds of a fresh issue are used or by the requirement to create a capital redemption

---

1   See further **7.25**.
2   Section 160. This last provision (section 160(3)) was due to be replaced by a more
     prescriptive regime in section 159A (inserted by Companies Act 1989, section 133(2)), but
     section 159A will not be implemented. A redemption (or purchase) of shares made when a
     company does not have distributable profits is invalid: *BDG Roof-Bond Ltd v Douglas and Others*
     [2000] 1 BCLC 401.
3   That is (section 181) profits distributable under section 263(2), as to which, see **7.21** *et seq*. A
     redemption (or purchase) of shares made when a company does not have distributable
     profits is invalid: *BDG Roof-Bond Ltd v Douglas and Others* [2000] 1 BCLC 401.
4   As to private companies, see **7.17.10–7.17.13**.
5   But not its authorised capital.

reserve.[1] Where in pursuance of the section a company is about to redeem any shares, it has power to issue shares up to the nominal amount of the shares to be redeemed as if those shares had never been issued.

Notice of every redemption (and purchase, including treasury shares) within section 159 must be given to the Registrar within one month, failing which, the company and every officer in default is liable to a default fine.[2]

7.17.2 Purchase by a company of its own shares

Section 162 gives companies limited by shares or limited by guarantee and having a share capital the power to purchase their own shares, including any redeemable shares, if authorised to do so by their articles, provided that a purchase must not result in there being no member holding other than redeemable shares in the company. Section 162(2) incorporates all except one of the provisions of sections 159 and 160. Thus purchases of companies' own shares may take place on the same conditions and with the same consequences as the redemption of redeemable shares, as described above. The one distinction is that the terms and manner of purchase need not be determined by the articles.

However, the exercise of a purchase of a company's own shares is governed by strict additional requirements, in terms of the authority which must be obtained for particular purchases, the publicity which must be given and certain other matters. These are described in the following sections. They are not purely procedural and for the benefit of current members, but also exist to protect creditors; there is thus no basis for waiving them.[3]

A purchase by a company of shares that are to be held by the company as treasury shares is subject to additional provisions.[4] Treasury shares are qualifying shares[5] purchased by a company out of distributable profits that are held by the company pending future sale, transfer or cancellation of the shares.[6] The requirement that shares redeemed or purchased by a company be cancelled does not apply to treasury shares.[7] The company must be entered on the register as the owner of treasury shares and therefore cannot hold them through nominees. The maximum holding of treasury shares is 10% of the nominal value of any class. If that limit is exceeded the company must dispose of or cancel the excess shares within 12 months. Dividend and voting rights associated with treasury shares are suspended.[8] Proceeds of the sale of treasury shares are treated as a realised profit to the extent that they are less than or equal to the purchase price, while proceeds above that level must be transferred to the share premium account.[9]

---

1   As to the capital redemption reserve, see **7.17.9**.
2   Section 122(1)(e).
3   See *Re RW Peak (Kings Lynn) Ltd* [1998] 1 BCLC 193, especially at 204–205, where the informal consent of all shareholders was not sufficient to validate an off-market purchase under section 164 (see below).
4   See generally The Companies (Acquisition of Own Shares) (Treasury Shares) Regulations 2003, SI 2003/1116, which authorise a company (with effect from 1 December 2003) to hold its shares as treasury shares. Holding shares in treasury provides an additional tool to companies for managing their financing requirements.
5   See section 162 CA 1985 (as amended).
6   See section 162 CA 1985 (as amended) and (new) sections 162A and 162D.
7   Section 162(2B) CA 1985 (as amended).
8   (new) Section 162C CA 1985.
9   (new) Section 162F CA 1985. Treatment of proceeds as distributable profits recognises the origin of the purchase funds as distributable profits.

7.17.3 *Authority required for off-market purchases*

The Act draws a distinction between what are described as 'off-market purchases' and 'market purchases' of a company's own shares. Off-market purchases are defined as purchases otherwise than on a recognised investment exchange and purchases on a recognised investment exchange but not subject to a marketing arrangement on that exchange.[1] Shares are subject to such a marketing arrangement if either: (a) they are listed under Part VI of the Financial Services and Markets Act 2000;[2] or (b) the company has been accorded facilities for dealings in those shares to take place on that investment exchange without prior permission for individual transactions from the authority governing that investment exchange and without limit as to the time during which these facilities are to be available. Principally, therefore, purchases by private and non-listed public companies and over-the-counter purchases by listed companies are 'off-market' purchases .

An off-market purchase may be made only if the terms of the contract of purchase are authorised before the company enters into the contract by a special resolution of the company[3] or if the company has previously authorised a contingent purchase contract under section 165 (as described in **7.17.4**). The authority can be varied, revoked or from time to time renewed by special resolution. In the case of a public company, the special resolution conferring or renewing authority must specify a date for its expiry which must be within 18 months of the date of the resolution.

If a member (or his proxy) whose shares are the subject of a proposal to purchase them votes on the special resolution, on a poll or otherwise, his votes must not be counted. Notwithstanding anything in a company's articles, any member of the company (or his proxy) may demand a poll on the question whether any such resolution shall be passed.

In addition to the notice which will be required for a special resolution under section 164,[4] no such resolution is effective unless a copy of the proposed contract of purchase, if it is in writing, or a written memorandum of its terms, if it is not in writing, is available for inspection by members of the company both at the registered office of the company for at least 15 days before the date of the meeting at which the resolution is passed, and at the meeting itself.[5] Any memorandum must include the names of any members holding shares to which the contract relates, and any copy of the contract must have annexed to it a written memorandum specifying any such names which do not appear in the contract itself.

A variation of an existing approved contract may be made by the company but only if authorised by special resolution. The same requirements as described above apply to such a special resolution and a copy or memorandum of the original contract (and any previous variations) must be available for inspection as well as a copy or memorandum of the proposed varied contract.

No specific or civil penalties are prescribed if the requirements of section 164 are not complied with, but a contract purportedly entered into in pursuance of a

---

1   Section 163(1).
2   See Chapter 6.
3   Section 164. The provisions are modified if authority is conferred by a statutory written resolution (see **13.4**), rather than by special resolution.
4   Under section 380; see **13.18**.
5   The requirement here is modified where the statutory written resolution procedure is used.

resolution which is not effective according to the section is void as a contract to perform an unlawful act, namely an unauthorised purchase by a company of its own shares, and the criminal penalties specified in section 143 will apply.[1] An agreement between the company and a shareholder for the purchase of his shares is not enforceable until it has been sanctioned under section 164,[2] but specific performance of such a contract may be granted subject to such sanction.[3]

7.17.4 Contingent purchase contracts

An alternative procedure in respect of off-market purchases is provided for by section 165. This allows the company to enter into what is described as a contingent purchase contract for its own shares. This is a contract not amounting to an actual contract to purchase but under which the company may, subject to any conditions, become entitled or obliged to purchase its own shares, in other words, an option.

The purchase of shares pursuant to a contingent purchase contract may be made only if the terms of the proposed contract are authorised by special resolution before the company enters into the contract, and the relevant provisions of section 164 (described in **7.17.3**) apply to such a resolution and to variations of existing contingent purchase contracts.

7.17.5 Authority required for market purchase

A market purchase is defined by section 163(3) as a purchase made on a recognised investment exchange other than a purchase on an investment exchange of shares not subject to a marketing arrangement. Most purchases by companies whose shares are listed on a stock market will be market purchases.

Section 166 requires such a purchase to have the prior authority of the company in general meeting, that is by ordinary resolution only.[4] The resolution may confer general authority to purchase the company's own shares of any particular class or description, and the authority may be unconditional or conditional. By section 166(3), the authorising resolution must do three things.

(1) It must specify the maximum number of shares authorised to be acquired.
(2) It must determine both the maximum and minimum prices which may be paid for those shares either by specifying a particular sum or by providing a basis or formula for calculating the amount of the price in question without reference to any person's discretion or opinion.
(3) It must specify a date within 18 months on which the authority is to expire. Note though that a purchase can be made outside the time-limit, where the contract was concluded before it and the terms of the authority permitted the company to make a contract which could or might be executed wholly or partly after the authority expires.

Subject to these requirements, any authority may be varied, revoked or renewed from time to time by the company in general meeting.

---

1   *Re RW Peak (Kings Lynn) Ltd* [1998] 1 BCLC 193.
2   *Western v Rigblast Holdings Ltd* 1989 GWD 23–950.
3   *Vision Express (UK) Ltd v Wilson* [1998] BCC 173.
4   Listed companies are required by ABI guidelines to adopt a special resolution in these circumstances. See Ferran, footnote 3 at p 167.

A printed copy of any resolution conferring, varying, revoking or renewing authority within section 166 must be forwarded to the Registrar within 15 days.

7.17.6 Assignments and releases of a company's right to purchase its own shares

The rights acquired by a company under any contract to purchase its own shares, whether a contract for an off-market purchase approved under section 164 or section 165 or a contract for a market purchase authorised under section 166, cannot be assigned.[1]

If a company proposes to release its rights under a contract for an off-market purchase approved under section 164 or 165, the terms of the proposed release agreement must be authorised by special resolution before the company enters into the agreement. In the absence of such a resolution, any such agreement to release rights is void.

7.17.7 Payments other than of the purchase price

Certain payments which may be made by companies in connection with a purchase of their own shares, other than payments of the purchase price for the shares, must be made out of distributable profits.[2] The payments in question are any payments made by a company in consideration of:

(1) acquiring any right to purchase its own shares under a contingent purchase contract;

(2) the variation of any contract or contingent purchase contract for an off-market purchase of its own shares;

(3) the release of any of the company's obligations to purchase any of its own shares under any contract for an off-market or market purchase of its own shares.

If any such payment is not made out of distributable profits, a purchase of shares within (1) above and a purchase of shares following a variation within (2) above is unlawful, and a release within (3) above is void.

7.17.8 Publicity for purchases

The requirements that companies disclose purchases of their own shares are contained in section 169. It should be noted that private companies taking advantage of the power to purchase out of capital are subject to the additional requirements described in **7.17.10**. Within 28 days of the date of delivery of the shares to the company, it must deliver to the Registrar a return in the prescribed form stating with respect to shares of each class purchased the number and nominal value of those shares and the date they were delivered to the company. A single return may cover shares delivered on different dates and under different contracts of purchase. The return sent by a public company must also state the aggregate amount paid by the company for all the shares covered by the return and the maximum and minimum prices paid in respect of shares of each class purchased.

---

1   Section 167(1).
2   Section 168. As to distributable profits, see **7.21.2**.

In addition, the company must keep a copy of any contract to purchase its own shares (and any variation of it), or a memorandum of its terms if it was not in writing, at its registered office for the period from the conclusion of the contract to the date ten years after the date on which the purchase of the shares was completed. Every copy or memorandum must be open to the inspection of any member of the company without charge and, if the company is a public company, to the inspection of any other person without charge. Inspection must be permitted during business hours, subject to such reasonable restrictions as the company in general meeting may impose, but for at least two hours in each day.[1]

Failure to deliver the return, to keep copies or memoranda, or to permit an inspection may be punished by fines on the company and every officer in default, and the court may order immediate inspection of a copy or memorandum where an inspection has been refused.

7.17.9 The capital redemption reserve

Often when a company redeems redeemable shares or purchases its own shares, it will be obliged to transfer a sum to its capital redemption reserve under the provisions of section 170. This reserve, like share capital, appears on the liabilities side of the balance sheet[2] and is treated as capital. It can be reduced only by a proper reduction of capital.[3] However, it can be used to finance an issue to existing members of fully paid bonus shares.[4]

The requirement to transfer to this reserve applies only to the extent that the shares redeemed or purchased are not represented by new shares, that is when their redemption or purchase is financed wholly or partly by the use of distributable profits. So, when profits alone are used, the amount to be transferred is the nominal value of the shares redeemed or purchased. When a combination of profits and the proceeds of a new issue of shares is used, it is the amount, if any, by which the nominal value of the shares redeemed or purchased exceeds the amount of the proceeds of the new issue. Note, however, that by section 170(3), this latter requirement does not apply when a private company makes an authorised payment out of capital to finance a redemption or purchase, as described in the next section; this is because when a company is permitted to use capital, there is obviously no point in having the same capital maintenance requirement.

7.17.10 Private companies redeeming or purchasing shares out of capital

As has been mentioned earlier, section 171 permits private companies limited by shares or limited by guarantee and having a share capital, if authorised by their articles and subject to the stringent conditions laid down in the Act, to redeem redeemable shares and purchase their own shares out of capital. In effect, the relevant provisions lay down an easier procedure whereby private companies may

---

1 The right of inspection is governed by section 723A and the Companies (Inspection and Copying of Registers, Indices and Documents) Regulations 1991, SI 1991/1998.
2 Details of any redeemable shares must be given in the notes to the accounts: Schedule 4, paragraph 38(2).
3 See **8.14**.
4 See **7.23**. So far as the company at least is concerned, this really amounts to no more than a juggling around of the items on its balance sheet.

reduce their share capital,[1] as well as making it easier for them, for example, to satisfy the claims of a retiring member or the estate of a deceased member.[2]

The payment which may be made out of capital, described as 'the permissible capital payment for the shares', is such an amount as, taken together with any available profits and the proceeds of a fresh issue of shares made for the purpose of the redemption or purchase, is equal to the price of redemption or purchase. It seems that a company must use its 'available profits', the meaning of which is described below, before it can touch capital. This somewhat restricts the advantages of the section.

Where the permissible capital payment for any shares redeemed or purchased is not combined with the proceeds of a fresh issue, and it is less than the nominal amount of the shares redeemed or purchased, the amount of the difference must be transferred to the capital redemption reserve. If it is greater than the nominal amount of the shares redeemed or purchased, the amount of the difference may be used to reduce the amount of any capital redemption reserve, share premium account or fully paid share capital of the company and any amount representing unrealised profits of the company for the time being standing to the credit of any reserve maintained by the company in accordance with Schedule 4, paragraph 34 (the revaluation reserve).[3] In any case where the proceeds of a fresh issue of shares are applied in the redemption or purchase of a company's own shares, in addition to a payment out of capital, if the aggregate of the proceeds and payment is less than the nominal amount of the shares, the amount of the difference must be transferred to the capital redemption reserve.[4] If the aggregate is greater, the difference may be used to reduce any capital redemption reserve, share premium account or fully paid share capital of the company, together with any amount in the revaluation reserve, as described above.

For the purpose of section 171, available profits are profits available for distribution within the meaning of Part VIII[5] but determined in the way laid down in section 172 rather than in accordance with the accounts normally required[6] to determine a company's distributable profits. They must be determined within the period of three months before the date of the statutory declaration of the directors required by section 173[7] by reference to such accounts prepared within that period as are necessary to enable a reasonable judgment to be made of any of the company's profits, losses, assets, liabilities, provisions, share capital and reserves. For the purpose of determining the amount of the permissible capital payment for any shares, the amount of the company's available profits thus determined is to be treated as reduced by the amount of any distributions lawfully made by the company after the date of the relevant accounts and before the date of the statutory declaration.

Payments out of capital under section 171 must comply with the procedural requirements of sections 173 and 174 and the publicity requirements of section 175. In addition, there is provision for objecting members or creditors to apply to

---

1   As to reduction of capital otherwise, see **8.14** *et seq.*
2   For a full description of the circumstances where the power may be taken advantage of, see the 'Green Paper', *The Purchase by a Company of its own Shares* Cmnd 7944 (1980).
3   As to the revaluation reserve, see **14.7.1**.
4   Section 171(6).
5   As described in **7.21.2–7.21.4**.
6   See **7.21.1**.
7   See **7.17.11**.

the court (sections 176 and 177), and liabilities may arise under the terms of section 76 of the Insolvency Act 1986 where a winding-up ensues within one year of payment out of capital. These matters are examined in the following sections.

7.17.11 Procedure and publicity

Sections 173 to 175 specify the following requirements to secure an effective payment out of capital.

(1) The directors must make a statutory declaration which states the permissible capital payment and is otherwise essentially a declaration of existing solvency and that, in the view of the directors, the company will continue to trade and be solvent for one year.

(2) The auditors of the company must make a report to the directors which confirms the permissible capital payment and that they are not aware of anything to indicate that the statutory declaration is unreasonable.

(3) A special resolution must be passed approving the payment out of capital on, or within one week of, the date of the statutory declaration, at a general meeting at which the statutory declaration and auditors' report are available for inspection and in respect of which resolution the votes of any member holding shares to which it relates cannot be counted.[1]

(4) The payment out of capital can be made only between five and seven weeks after the date of the resolution.

(5) The company must publish notice in the *Gazette* and either notice in a national newspaper or notice in writing to each of its creditors within one week of the special resolution. The notice must give the details specified in section 175, namely the fact and date of the resolution, the amount of the permissible capital payment, that the statutory declaration and auditors' report can be inspected at the company's registered office, and that any creditor can seek to restrain the payment out of capital by applying to the court under section 176. From the date of this notice the declaration and report must be kept at the registered office and be open to inspection by any member or creditor without charge until the end of the fifth week following the special resolution.

(6) Copies of the statutory declaration and auditors' report must be delivered to the Registrar by the date of the public notice.

Criminal penalties are specified for directors making a knowingly false declaration and for refusals to allow inspections of the declaration and report. The latter can also be remedied by court order.

7.17.12 Applications to the court

Within five weeks of a special resolution under section 173, any member of the company other than one who consented to or voted in favour of the resolution and any creditor may apply to the court for the cancellation of the resolution.[2]

---

1   This requirement is appropriately modified when a company uses the statutory written resolution procedure (see **13.4**).
2   Section 176.

The court has wide powers.[1] It may adjourn proceedings so that arrangements can be made to purchase the interest of dissentient members or protect creditors. Failing this, it must confirm or cancel the resolution on such terms and conditions as it thinks fit. It has the specific power to provide for the company to purchase the shares of any member, reducing capital in consequence, and to make any necessary alterations in the memorandum and articles.

The Act does not spell out when the court might accede to such an application. It would obviously do so for a serious default in procedure or if available profits had not been fully utilised. However, it is not clear whether, for example, a minority shareholder would succeed if he could show that he was discriminated against because the chance to have his shares bought by the company was denied to him whereas the majority had caused the company to purchase some or all of theirs. Compare, for example, section 127 which gives the court power to disallow a variation of class rights[2] and expressly directs the court to consider fairness. It is thought that section 176 should not be used for such complaints, given the absence of any reference to fairness in section 177 and given the fact that the minority which has been unfairly treated can use the statutory remedy under sections 459 to 461.[3]

7.17.13   Liability of past shareholders and directors

Where, in redeeming or purchasing any of its own shares, a company has made a payment out of capital, and it is subsequently wound up, and is insolvent, on winding-up commencing within one year of the payment, liability to contribute to the assets of the company may be imposed under section 76 of the Insolvency Act 1986 upon the person from whom the shares were redeemed or purchased to the extent of the amount of capital he received and the directors of the company who signed the relevant statutory declaration who are jointly and severally liable with that person, except a director who shows that he had reasonable grounds for forming the opinion set out in the declaration.

7.17.14   Failure of a company to redeem or purchase its own shares

Section 178 contains provisions dealing with cases where a company has issued redeemable shares or agreed to purchase any of its own shares, under the provisions described in the preceding sections, and has failed to perform its obligations.

A company cannot be liable in damages for any failure to perform its obligations, but other remedies for a breach of contract are available to the shareholder, provided that the court must not grant an order for specific performance if the company shows that it is unable to meet the cost of redeeming or purchasing the shares in question out of distributable profits. The exclusion of liability for damages refers to claims in respect of a company's breach of duty to redeem or purchase shares; it does not prevent other damages claims, eg for breach of a covenant contained in a financing agreement entered into to facilitate redemption.[4]

---

1   Section 177.
2   See **8.7.5**.
3   See **17.13.1**.
4   *Barclays Bank plc v British & Commonwealth Holdings plc* [1996] 1 BCLC 1 (CA).

Where a company is being wound up and, at the commencement of the winding-up, has failed to meet an obligation to redeem or purchase its own shares which has already accrued, the terms of redemption or purchase may be enforced by the shareholder, provided that, during the period between the due date for redemption or purchase and the date of the commencement of the winding-up, the company could have lawfully made a distribution equal in value to the price at which the shares were to have been redeemed or purchased.

Any money so owed is deferred to the claims of all creditors and preference shareholders having capital rights ranking in preference to those of the shares redeemed or purchased; but it ranks before the claims of other shareholders.

7.18 Financial assistance by a company for the acquisition of its own shares

Sections 151 to 154, which consolidate the replacement of section 54 of the Companies Act 1948, act as a reinforcement of the rule that a company may not, except subject to the strict conditions described in the preceding sections, purchase its own shares. Uncertainty surrounding the exact scope of the repealed section 54[1] led to the introduction in 1981 of what are now sections 151 to 154. The prohibitions in these sections are relaxed in respect of private companies which comply with the requirements of sections 155 to 158 as described in **7.18.3**. Notwithstanding this relatively recent revision of the statutory provisions, there are still many uncertainties surrounding the operation of them which continue to cause difficulties in practice. A further revision of the provisions, with greater scope for private companies to disapply them, is likely to result from the Department of Trade and Industry's Review of Company Law.[2]

7.18.1 Prohibited under section 151

The basic prohibition, which is subject to the exceptions discussed below, is twofold. First, where a person is acquiring or is proposing to acquire any shares in a company, it is unlawful for the company or any of its subsidiaries to give financial assistance directly or indirectly for the purpose of that acquisition[3] before or at the same time as the acquisition of the shares takes place.[4] Secondly, where a person has acquired any shares in a company and any liability has been incurred by him or any other person for the purposes of that acquisition, it is unlawful for the company or any of its subsidiaries to give any financial assistance directly or indirectly for the purpose of reducing or discharging the liability incurred.[5]

The reference above to a person incurring any liability includes the case of a person changing his financial position by making any agreement or arrangement

---

1   See in particular the cases of *Belmont Finance Corp Ltd v Williams Furniture Ltd (No 2)* [1980] 1 All ER 393 (CA) and *Armour Hich Northern Ltd v Whitehouse* [1980] 1 WLR 1520, discussed in (1980) 1 Co Law 99 and 145. Section 54 was notorious for often hitting the innocent and failing to deter the guilty; see the Jenkins Report (Cmnd 1749, paragraphs 170–176) for a general review.

2   See **7.25**.

3   The equivalent words in section 54 were 'purchase or subscription'. 'Acquisition' is wider since it covers cases where the payment for shares is not in cash.

4   Section 151(1).

5   Section 151(2).

(whether enforceable or unenforceable and whether made on his own account or with any other person) or by any other means.[1]

The reference to a company giving financial assistance to reduce or discharge a liability incurred by a person for the purpose of acquiring shares in the company includes the case where the company gives financial assistance for the purpose of wholly or partly restoring his financial position to what it was before the acquisition took place.[2]

Financial assistance is defined in section 152(1)(a) as meaning any of the following:

(1) financial assistance given by way of gift;
(2) financial assistance given by way of guarantee, security or indemnity, other than an indemnity in respect of the indemnifier's own neglect or default, or by way of release or waiver;[3]
(3) financial assistance given by way of a loan or any other agreement under which any of the obligations of the person giving the assistance are to be fulfilled at a time when, in accordance with the agreement, any obligation of any other party to the agreement remains unfulfilled or by way of the novation or assignment of any rights arising under the loan or such other agreement;[4] or
(4) any other financial assistance given by a company the net assets[5] of which are thereby reduced to a material extent[6] or which has no net assets.

It is thought that 'assistance' necessarily involves the existence of at least two persons, one giving and one receiving the assistance. So where, for example, a company borrows money and gives security in order to finance a purchase of its own shares, this can hardly be regarded as the giving of financial assistance within section 151. A surrender of tax losses by a subsidiary company to another company within the same group, as part of a wider agreement for the sale of its shares to one of its directors, was held not to amount to the giving of financial assistance where there was no evidence that the surrender reduced the price which the director would otherwise have paid.[7] *Barclays Bank plc v British & Commonwealth Holdings plc*[8] concerned the issue of liability to pay damages for breach of a covenant given under a court-sanctioned scheme of arrangement. The company in question had given the covenant to the plaintiff banks as part of a scheme under which the banks became liable to finance the purchase by another party of shares in the company. This was held not to amount to financial assistance given by the

---

1　Section 152(3)(a).

2　Section 152(3)(b).

3　The words 'guarantee' and 'indemnity' bear their ordinary legal meaning: *Barclays Bank plc v British & Commonwealth Holdings plc* [1996] 1 BCLC 1 at 37–40.

4　See eg the facts in *Coulthard v Neville Russell* [1998] BCC 359.

5　In this context 'net assets' means the actual net assets, not necessarily those as stated in the company's accounting records, at the time of the giving of assistance, so that any value received by the company in return for the assistance should be taken into account: *Parlett v Guppys (Bridport) Ltd* [1996] BCC 299.

6　'Material extent' is not defined. In *Parlett v Guppys (Bridport) Ltd* [1996] BCC 299, where counsel were disposed to agree that a reduction of 5% or more would have been material, Nourse LJ commented that there can be no rule of thumb and the question is one of degree to be answered on the facts of the particular case.

7　*Charterhouse Investment Trust Ltd v Tempest Diesels Ltd* [1986] BCLC 1.

8　[1996] 1 BCLC 1 (CA).

company; while the giving of the covenants may have induced the banks to enter into the commitments that they did, they did not financially assist anybody to acquire shares. In *Parlett v Guppys (Bridport) Ltd,*[1] an agreement to transfer shares in one member of a group of companies was entered into where the consideration was the payment of a salary and pension by all the members of the group. As the agreement could be performed lawfully without breaching section 151, by the payment being made by members of the group other than the company whose shares were the subject of the agreement, it did not infringe the prohibition against the giving of financial assistance. On the other hand, in the leading case of *Brady v Brady,*[2] in order to effect the reorganisation and division of a company, Brady Ltd, between the two principal shareholders (brothers who had fallen out), two new companies (A and B) were created which would ultimately each be owned by one brother and run one side of the previously merged businesses. Company A acquired the share capital of Brady in return for loan stock issued to company B. Subsequently, A was to redeem the loan stock by arranging for Brady to transfer to B one half of Brady's assets. It was accepted that Brady would give financial assistance by this transfer when A redeemed stock to discharge the liability it had incurred in acquiring the shares in Brady. Payment by a target company of expenses incurred by a bidder prior to making a takeover offer has been held to constitute financial assistance.[3]

Further examples of the sorts of transactions prohibited by section 151 can be found in some of the cases decided on its predecessor: a loan made by a company to finance the borrower's purchase of shares in the company;[4] the case of a purchaser of shares undertaking a liability as part of the consideration which he never discharges or causes the company to discharge;[5] or the purchase by a company of assets at an inflated price to enable the vendor of the assets to buy shares in the company.[6]

The company which is prohibited by section 151 from giving financial assistance must be a company registered in Britain.[7] In addition, the phrase 'any of its subsidiaries' must be construed as limited to British companies.[8] So the section does not prohibit a foreign subsidiary of an English parent company from giving financial assistance for an acquisition of shares in its parent, nor, it seems, does it prohibit the giving of financial assistance by an English subsidiary to acquire shares in its foreign parent.[9]

A contravention of section 151 attracts severe criminal sanctions,[10] and the transaction itself is void and unenforceable.[11] However, the directors responsible

---

1 [1996] BCC 299. See also *Grant v Lapid Developments Ltd* [1996] BCC 410.
2 [1989] AC 755 (HL). The significance of the decision lies in the construction of the purpose exceptions, discussed below. See also *Plant v Steiner* (1989) 5 BCC 352.
3 *Chaston v SWP Group plc* [2002] EWCA Civ 1999, [2003] 1 BCLC 675.
4 See eg *Selangor United Rubber Estates Ltd v Cradock (No 3)* [1968] 1 WLR 1555.
5 See the 'circular cheque' transaction in *Wallersteiner v Moir (No 1)* [1974] 1 WLR 991.
6 See *Belmont Finance Corp Ltd v Williams Furniture Ltd*, above.
7 Section 735.
8 *Arab Bank plc v Mercantile Holdings Ltd* [1994] 1 BCLC 330.
9 Ibid.
10 See section 151(3) and Schedule 24.
11 See *Brady v Brady*, above; *Selangor United Rubber Estates Ltd v Cradock*, above.

and, possibly, any third parties involved, can be sued for breach of trust[1] to compensate the company for any loss suffered.

7.18.2 Exceptions provided for by section 153

It is important that, for financial assistance to be given unlawfully, it is given *for the purpose of* an acquisition or discharge of liability.[2] This requirement is reinforced by section 153(1) and (2). Section 153(1) provides that section 151(1) does not prohibit a company from giving any financial assistance if:

(1) the company's principal purpose in giving it is not to give it for the purpose of an acquisition or the giving of it for that purpose is but an incidental part of some larger purpose of the company; and

(2) the assistance is given in good faith in the interests of the company.

Section 153(2) contains similar provisions to cover the prohibition in section 151(2). Thus, for example, a transaction under which a company buys from another a chattel or commodity it genuinely wants but with the intention also of putting the vendor in a position to acquire shares in the company is not prohibited provided that the latter purpose is not the principal purpose and the transaction is entered into in good faith in the interests of the company.[3] Whether the purpose exceptions have much more scope is doubtful following the House of Lords' decision in *Brady v Brady*.[4] Here they were said to contemplate two alternative situations. The first envisages a principal and a secondary purpose and was enacted to cover the sort of situation just described. The second situation is where it is not suggested that the financial assistance was intended to achieve any object other than the giving of assistance or the reduction or discharge of indebtedness, but where the result is merely incidental to some larger purpose of the company. Lord Oliver stated that in construing the word 'purpose' in the context of the sections regulating the provision of finance by a company in connection with the purchase of its own shares, there had always to be borne in mind the mischief against which section 151 was aimed. If this section was not to be deprived of any useful application, it was important to distinguish between a purpose and the reason why a purpose was formed. The reason for a scheme which involved the provision of financial assistance might be a needed reorganisation or takeover which was regarded as commercially desirable or even necessary, but that could not be regarded as a larger purpose:

> The purpose and the only purpose of the financial assistance is and remains that of enabling the shares to be acquired and the financial or commercial advantages flowing from the acquisition, whilst they may form the reason for forming the purpose

---

1   *Steen v Law* [1964] AC 287 (PC); *Selangor United Rubber Estates Ltd v Cradock*, above; *Wallersteiner v Moir (No 1)*, above; *Belmont Finance Corp Ltd v Williams Furniture Ltd (No 2)*, above. On appropriate facts, an alternative cause of action is in the tort of conspiracy: see the *Belmont Finance* case.

2   In section 54 of the 1948 Act, it was sufficient in the alternative that assistance was given 'in connection with' an acquisition, and this caught some otherwise legitimate transactions; see *Armour Hick Northern Ltd v Whitehouse*, above.

3   This phrase is traditionally used to describe the fundamental duties of company directors (see **16.4**) and in this context requires consideration of the interests of creditors: see *Brady v Brady* above.

4   See above. It was correctly pointed out that the section is complex and not altogether easy to construe.

of providing financial assistance, are a by-product of it rather than an independent purpose of which the assistance can properly be said to be an incident.[1]

So, in the case itself,[2] the purpose of the financial assistance was to enable the acquisition of shares and the commercial desirability of the reorganisation was not a larger corporate purpose. The scheme was not saved by section 153(2).[3] It has to be said that this construction leaves very little room for the operation of the second situation.[4]

Quite apart from the 'purpose' exception, section 153(3) lists a number of things which are totally outside the prohibition in section 151. These are:

(1) a distribution of a company's assets by way of a dividend lawfully made or a distribution made in the course of the company's winding up;
(2) the allotment of bonus shares;
(3) any reduction of capital confirmed by order of the court under section 137;[5]
(4) a redemption or purchase of any shares made in accordance with the provisions described above;[6]
(5) anything done in pursuance of an order of the court made under section 425, that is a court-approved reconstruction,[7]
(6) anything done under an arrangement made in pursuance of section 110 of the Insolvency Act 1986, that is a reconstruction linked to a voluntary winding up;[8] and
(7) anything done under an arrangement made between a company and its creditors which is binding on the creditors by virtue of Part I of the Insolvency Act 1986.[9]

Section 153(4) provides for more exceptions, but so far as a public company is concerned, advantage can be taken of these only if they do not reduce the company's current worth according to the value of its assets and liabilities in its accounting records or, to the extent that they do reduce it, if the financial assistance is provided out of distributable profits.[10] The first section 153(4) exception exempts the lending of money in the ordinary course of its business by a company whose ordinary business includes moneylending.[11]

The other three exceptions are all essentially concerned with the acquisition of or dealing in a company's shares by employees and are thus designed to encourage employee shareholding. First, a company can provide financial

---

1   [1989] AC at 780.
2   The facts are given briefly above.
3   Although it was open to be saved by sections 155–158 (see **7.18.3**).
4   Which partly explains why a further legislative attempt to recast the provisions is likely; see **7.25**.
5   See **8.14**.
6   See **7.17** *et seq.*
7   See **19.18**.
8   See **19.13**.
9   See Chapter 19.
10   See section 154(1) and (2)(a).
11   A loan made by a moneylending company for the specific purpose of financing a purchase of its shares is not made 'in the ordinary course of business'; *Steen v Law* [1964] AC 287 (PC); *Fowlie v Slater* (1979) 129 NLJ 465.

assistance for the purposes of an employees' share scheme[1] for the acquisition of fully paid shares in the company or its holding company. Secondly, it, or a subsidiary of it, can provide assistance for the purposes of or in connection with anything done by it, or by a company in the same group, to enable or facilitate transactions in its shares between or for the benefit of employees and others.[2] Thirdly, it can make loans to *bona fide* employees, other than directors, with a view to enabling them to acquire fully paid shares in it or its holding company to be held by way of beneficial ownership.[3]

7.18.3 *Exemption from section 151 for private companies*

Private companies are permitted to provide financial assistance for the acquisition of their shares and are thus wholly exempted from the prohibition in section 151, provided that they comply with the conditions prescribed in sections 155 to 158. This 'whitewash procedure', as it is commonly known, broadly speaking, requires a special resolution following a statutory declaration of solvency by the directors and a report by the auditors. The exemption covers in addition financial assistance given by a private company which is a subsidiary of another private company in connection with the acquisition of shares in that holding company, unless the company is also a subsidiary of a public company which is itself a subsidiary of that holding company.[4]

The statutory declaration and the auditors' report have to comply with broadly the same technical requirements, *mutatis mutandis,* as those required for a redemption or purchase of shares out of capital.[5] The failure of the directors properly to inform themselves about the financial situation of the company will invalidate the declaration and hence the whole procedure.[6]

However, by section 155(2) a company may give financial assistance to any person within the exemption only if according to its accounting records the company has net assets which are not thereby reduced or, to the extent that these assets are thereby reduced, if the financial assistance is provided out of distributable profits. For this purpose,[7] net assets are defined as the amount by which the aggregate amount of the company's assets exceeds the aggregate amount of its liabilities, taking the amount of both assets and liabilities to be as stated in the company's accounting records immediately before the financial assistance is given, that is 'book' value, and 'liabilities' includes any amount retained as reasonably necessary for the purpose of providing for any liability or loss which is either likely to be incurred, or certain to be incurred but uncertain as to amount or as to the date on which it will arise, that is 'provisions'. The proper treatment of assets and liabilities for the purpose of determining whether net

---

1   Section 153(4)(b). An employees' share scheme is defined in section 743 as a scheme for encouraging or facilitating the holding of shares or debentures in a company by or for the benefit of the *bona fide* employees or former employees of the company, its subsidiary or holding company or a fellow subsidiary, or the wives, husbands, widows, widowers or children or stepchildren under the age of 18 of such employees or former employees.

2   Section 153(4)(bb). The 'others' are the same people as are mentioned in section 743; see footnote 1, above.

3   Section 153(4)(c).

4   The exemption was partly designed to facilitate 'management buy-outs'.

5   See **7.17.11**. For more details, see section 156.

6   Re *In a Flap Envelope Co Ltd* [2003] EWHC 3037 (Ch), [2004] 1 BCLC 64.

7   Section 155(2) applying the definition in section 154(2).

assets are reduced, for example as to the amount of a provision, or whether provision is necessary in the circumstances, is essentially a question for accountants.[1]

A special resolution is required unless the company proposing to give the financial assistance is a wholly owned subsidiary.[2] In addition, where the financial assistance is to be given by a company in any case where the acquisition of shares in question is or was an acquisition of shares in its holding company, a special resolution is also required of the holding company and any other company which is both the company's holding company and a subsidiary of that other holding company, except in the case of any company which is a wholly owned subsidiary.[3] Any such special resolution must be passed on the date of or within the week immediately following the date of the statutory declaration made by the directors, and the statutory declaration and the auditors' report must be available for inspection at the meeting.

There is a strict time-scale dictating when the financial assistance can be given. It must not be given until four weeks after the date of the special resolution (or the last of the resolutions, where appropriate). This allows for the expiry of the time within which a dissentient shareholder can apply to the court to cancel the resolution,[4] and naturally it does not apply if the resolution(s) was (were) passed by all members entitled to vote. In addition, the assistance must not be given after the expiry of eight weeks from the date of the statutory declaration (or the earliest of the statutory declarations, where appropriate).[5]

7.19 The holding by a subsidiary of shares in its holding company

A further statutory reinforcement of the rule that a company may not purchase its own shares is contained in section 23. This section forbids a body corporate[6] from being a member (or having its nominee as a member) of its holding company, and any allotment or transfer of shares in a company to its subsidiary (or nominee) is void.[7] This would be tantamount to the holding company owning its own shares. The provision is of long standing, although it was revised in 1989, and these days appears somewhat inadequate because it is limited to situations where there is a holding company/subsidiary company relationship. Control of another company

---

1 *Hill v Mullis & Peake* [1999] BCC 325.
2 The requirements are modified when the company uses the statutory written resolution procedure (see **13.4**).
3 In this case, more than one statutory declaration will also be required.
4 The relevant provisions governing the application to the court are similar to those concerning applications to cancel a payment for shares out of capital (see **7.17.12**), save that dissentient shareholders must hold 10% of the company's issued shares or of a class of issued shares and there is no provision for creditors to apply.
5 Unless the court resolves otherwise following an unsuccessful application by a dissenting shareholder (in which case the eight-week limit is likely to have expired long before the issue is resolved).
6 This term is defined in section 740 and comprehends all companies, including foreign companies, except for corporations sole and Scottish firms.
7 For the definitions of 'holding company' and 'subsidiary company', see sections 736 and 736A of the Companies Act 1985.

may be obtained by a holding of less than 50% of voting shares, for example by the use of cross and circular holdings,[1] but section 23 will not apply in those cases.[2]

In any event, the section has no application where a subsidiary holds shares in its holding company as personal representative or as trustee, unless the holding company or a subsidiary thereof is beneficially interested[3] under the trust and is not so interested only by way of security for the purpose of a transaction entered into by it in the ordinary course of a business which includes the lending of money.[4]

7.20 Serious loss of capital by public companies

Section 142 consolidates a provision first introduced in the 1980 Act as a result of the Second EC Directive. It provides that where the net assets of a public company are half or less of the amount of the company's called-up share capital, the directors of the company must duly convene an extraordinary meeting of the company to consider whether any, and if so, what, measures should be taken to deal with the situation. The meeting must be convened not less than 28 days after the earliest day on which a director learns of the fact, to take place at a date not later than 56 days after that day.[5]

Failure to comply with the section renders the director responsible liable to criminal sanctions,[6] but there are no civil consequences, nor does the section provide any specific guidance as to the position, if, following the meeting, the company resolves to do nothing. It is really a rather curious provision which looks like another example of an ill-thought-out implementation of the Second Directive. In fact it may be wondered whether it really does implement Article 17 of the Directive, which requires the meeting 'to consider whether the company should be wound up or any other measures taken' and which thus at least has a more specific point in mind than section 142.

7.21 Dividends

The next sections of this chapter are concerned with profits and dividends, namely how profit is assessed and how it is distributed or otherwise dealt with. The differing entitlement of different classes of shares to such profits, where appropriate, is considered in the next chapter.

---

1 See the example cited in Gower, *Principles of Modern Company Law* 4th edn (Sweet & Maxwell) p 226, footnote 63: company A holds 45 per cent of the voting shares of company B and company B holds 45% of the voting shares of company A. In effect, the directors of both are irremovable and the companies are grouped together, but sections 736 and 736A will not apply. See also Pickering at (1965) 81 LQR 248.

2 The Jenkins Committee thought that it should, but that enacting the appropriate provision would be too difficult: Cmnd 1749, paragraph 153.

3 The meaning of 'beneficial interest' is qualified by the provisions of Schedule 2, as to which see *Gore-Browne on Companies* 44th edn (Jordans, loose-leaf) at 13.10.1–13.10.4.

4 In addition, it does not apply where shares in the holding company are held by the subsidiary in the ordinary course of its business as an intermediary involved in dealing in securities and satisfying certain other conditions: see section 23(3) as inserted by the Companies (Membership of Holding Company) (Dealers in Securities) Regulations 1997, SI 1997/2306.

5 The section does not dispense with the need for proper notices, etc, of any resolution which might be proposed: subsection (3).

6 Section 142(2).

The common-law rule, in accordance with the general principle of maintenance of capital, was that dividends could not be paid out of capital,[1] but this rule
has now been largely overtaken by statute.[2] The basic rule now is that a
distribution, a generic term including a dividend,[3] can only be made out of profits
available according to the rules laid down in Part VIII of the Companies Act 1985
and only by reference to properly prepared accounts. The latter point will be
examined first.

7.21.1 The relevant accounts

Section 270 requires that companies determine the question of whether a
distribution can be made, and its amount, by reference to a list of items in the
'relevant accounts'. The items amount to the basic contents of accounts, that is
profits, losses, assets, liabilities, provisions, share capital and reserves.[4] There are
three descriptions of relevant accounts; in all cases they must have been properly
prepared so as to give a true and fair view,[5] but only the first two descriptions must
have been audited.[6] They are:

(1) the last annual accounts, that is the standard accounts prepared annually
     under Part VII of the Act;[7]
(2) initial accounts, that is accounts prepared to allow for a distribution to be
     made by a recently formed company, during the company's first accounting
     reference period or before accounts are laid in respect of that period;[8]
(3) interim accounts, that is accounts prepared by a public company which
     wishes to declare an interim dividend, as such companies frequently do in the
     course of the financial year.[9]

---

1   *Re Exchange Banking Co, Flitcroft's Case* (1882) 21 Ch D 519.
2   The common-law rule was notoriously out of touch with good commercial and accounting
     practice; see Yamey (1941) 4 MLR 273.
3   The full definition in section 263(2) is every description of distribution of a company's assets
     to members of the company, whether in cash or otherwise, except distribution made by way
     of: (1) a fully or partly paid issue of bonus shares (see **7.23**); (2) the redemption or purchase
     of any of the company's own shares under Chapter VII of Part V (see **7.17** *et seq*); (3) the
     reduction of share capital by extinguishing or reducing the liability of any partly paid shares
     or by paying off paid-up share capital (see **8.14** *et seq*); and (4) a distribution of assets to
     members of the company on its winding-up. It might be argued that the width of this
     definition means that it covers such distributions as the payment of remuneration to directors
     of a small company, especially where they are its only members and this is the usual way in
     which profits are shared. However, in *Macpherson v European Strategic Bureau Ltd* [1999] 2
     BCLC 203, it was held that provision made in a severance agreement for the retrospective
     remuneration of shareholders for the work they had done as executives was not a distribution
     within section 263(2).
4   Section 270(2).
5   As to this classic formula, see **14.4**.
6   If the audit is qualified and the qualification does not state whether it is material to
     determining the legality of a distribution, a distribution thus in breach of the statute (as a
     result of section 271(4)) is unlawful: *Precision Dippings Ltd v Precision Dippings Marketing Ltd*
     [1985] 3 WLR 812 (CA). The same consequence must apply to any breach of the relevant
     accounts provisions. Certain small companies can dispense with the audit requirement, for
     this as well as general, purposes, see **14.26**.
7   See section 271 and, further, **14.2.3**.
8   Section 272.
9   Section 273.

Where a company has made a distribution by reference to particular accounts and wishes to make a further distribution by reference to the same accounts, it must take account of the earlier distribution and of certain other payments made, if any, as listed in section 274.[1]

7.21.2 Determination of profits

The Act, consequent upon the need to comply with the Second EC Directive, lays down what can be termed the 'balance sheet surplus method' of determining profits available for distribution.[2] Under this, a company can distribute what is the net profit on both capital and revenue at the particular time, that is according to the relevant accounts.

Section 263(3) lays down the basic rule, but it does not apply to investment companies[3] and is qualified in respect of public companies by section 264.[4] It states that a company's profits available for distribution are its accumulated, realised profits (on both revenue and capital)[5] not previously distributed or capitalised,[6] less its accumulated realised losses (on both revenue and capital) not written off in a proper reduction or reorganisation of capital.[7]

Under section 275(1), realised losses to be taken account of in the calculation include amounts written off or retained for depreciation.[8] Development costs must also *prima facie* be treated as a realised loss.[9]

The inclusion of 'accumulated' is important, making it clear that the current year's position cannot be taken in isolation. As indicated, realised profits include both trading profits and profits on the sale of capital assets,[10] but obviously not unrealised profit arising as a result of a revaluation of assets. An unrealised profit cannot be used to pay up debentures or amounts outstanding on partly paid shares.[11] However, such a profit can sometimes be capitalised,[12] and in certain circumstances can be treated as realised if made on a revaluation of fixed assets and a sum is set aside for depreciation of the assets.[13]

---

1   These relate to various categories of financial assistance given for the purpose of an acquisition of a company's shares (see **7.18** *et seq*) and various payments in respect of a company's purchase of its own shares (see **7.17** *et seq*).

2   For a very clear general account, see Renshall, 1 Co Law 194 (1980).

3   See *Gore-Browne on Companies* 44th edn (Jordans, loose-leaf) at 13.14.9.

4   See **7.21.3**.

5   Section 280(3).

6   This means used to finance a bonus issue or the purchase or redemption of the company's own shares with a resulting transfer to the capital redemption reserve: section 280(2).

7   The ability to write off losses by a reduction of capital has led to an increased use of the reduction procedure under section 135 since these provisions were first introduced in 1980: see *Re Jupiter House Investments* [1985] 1 WLR 975 and *Re Grosvenor Press plc* [1985] 1 WLR 980, discussed in **8.14.2**.

8   These are 'provisions', as to which see **14.5**.

9   But there are exceptions; see section 269.

10   'Realised' is not defined and its application could cause difficulties in certain cases; see Renshall, op cit, p 195.

11   Section 263(4).

12   Section 278; see **7.23**.

13   See section 275(2).

7.21.3 Public companies

It is not sufficient that a public company has made a distributable profit under section 263. Section 264 imposes an additional capital maintenance requirement, to ensure that the net worth of the company is at least equal to the amount of its capital. A public company can only distribute profit if at the time the amount of its net assets, that is the total excess of assets over liabilities, is not less than the total of its called-up share capital and its undistributable reserves, and only if and to the extent that the distribution does not reduce the amount of the net assets to less than that total. Undistributable reserves are:

(1) the share premium account;
(2) the capital redemption reserve;
(3) the amount by which unrealised uncapitalised profits exceed unrealised losses not written off; and
(4) any other reserve which the company is prohibited from distributing by statute or its memorandum or articles.

7.21.4 Improperly paid dividends

The Act provides[1] that a member who knows or has reasonable grounds to believe that a distribution or part of it is unlawful is liable to repay it or that part of it,[2] but it does not specify any further consequences of an improper dividend.

It is clear, though, that the additional remedies provided by the common law in respect of a dividend out of capital will apply to a payment illegal under the Act. Thus directors are liable to compensate the company if they know or should know that a distribution is illegal.[3] Any member can restrain a proposed illegal distribution by injunction,[4] but a member who has knowingly received such a distribution cannot bring a derivative action against the directors,[5] and will be liable to account to the company as a constructive trustee.[6] It is not possible for the members to ratify an illegal distribution or absolve directors from their liability in making such a distribution.[7]

Rather curiously, perhaps, a creditor has no *locus standi* to restrain an illegal distribution, unless he has an enforceable security which is thereby put in jeopardy.[8] His only remedy is to seek a winding-up.

---

1   Section 277.
2   This remedy does not apply to any unlawful financial assistance given to members in contravention of section 151 (see **7.18.1**) or to payments in respect of the redemption or purchase of a company's own shares (see **7.17** *et seq*).
3   See eg *Flitcroft's* Case (1882) 21 Ch D 519 and *Bairstow and Others v Queens Moat Houses plc* [2000] 1 BCLC 549. Where directors do not know, eg because they rely upon others, the question becomes one as to their liability for negligence, as to which see **16.23**.
4   See eg *Hoole v Great Western Railway Co* (1867) 3 Ch App 262.
5   *Towers v African Tug Co* [1904] 1 Ch 558. As to derivative actions, see **17.8–17.10**.
6   *Precision Dippings Ltd v Precision Dippings Marketing Ltd* [1985] 3 WLR 812 (CA).
7   *Aveling Barford Ltd. v Perion* [1989] BCLC 626.
8   *Mills v Northern Railway of Buenos Aires* (1870) 5 Ch App 621.

7.22 Reserves

Directors have power to set aside a proportion of profits, before a dividend is declared, to form a reserve.[1] Whether or not a company chooses to set aside profits in this way depends on its particular circumstances. A reserve generally remains undivided profit and can be used, for example, to pay dividends in bad years. However, it can be capitalised, and thus cease to be profit, as described in the next section.

Reserves in the sense described above must be distinguished from provisions, that is amounts written off or retained to provide, for example, for depreciation or bad debts.[2] It should also be noted that, despite its name and despite the fact that it is often funded from distributable profits, the capital redemption reserve required under section 170[3] is, for most purposes, a capital account.

7.23 Capitalisation of profits

In times of prosperity it is common practice for companies which have large undistributed profits to convert them into capital and distribute fully paid bonus shares representing the increased capital amongst the members in proportion to their right. This requires express sanction in the memorandum or articles.

Under the common-form article, article 110 of Table A, the directors may, with the authority of an ordinary resolution, capitalise any undivided profits not required for paying any preferential dividend, whether or not they are available for distribution,[4] or any sum standing to the credit of the share premium account[5] or capital redemption reserve.[6] They may then appropriate the capitalised sum to the members who would have been entitled to it by way of dividend, by issuing fully paid-up bonus shares to them.[7] A bonus issue may be declared void for mistake if it was made on the false premise that there were profits available for capitalisation.[8]

7.24 Mode of distribution of profits

Unless the memorandum or articles provide or imply otherwise, a dividend is not payable until it has been declared,[9] and any proceedings to recover it from the company before it has been declared are premature. However, it has been stated that members are entitled to have profits distributed so far as is commercially possible, and that directors who fail to make an appropriate recommendation are

---

1   This may be expressed in the articles, but is not on the modern Table A. If not, it is implied from the fact that, usually, no dividend can exceed the amount recommended by the directors (see **7.24**).
2   See further **14.5**.
3   See **7.17.9** and **7.23**.
4   Thus including unrealised profits.
5   See **7.15**.
6   See **7.17.9**.
7   If the capitalisation is of distributable profits, it can also be used to fund the issue of fully paid-up debentures and to pay up, wholly or partly, any amount owing on hitherto partly paid-up shares.
8   *Re Cleveland Trust plc* [1991] BCC 33.
9   *Bond v Barrow Haematite Steel Co* [1902] 1 Ch 353.

exercising their powers for an improper purpose.[1] Once a dividend is properly declared, it is a debt payable to the members. The articles generally state which organ of the company has the power to declare a dividend. Under Table A, article 102, this power is vested in the general meeting,[2] subject to the proviso that it may not declare a dividend exceeding the amount recommended by the directors. Under article 103 the directors also have power to pay 'interim dividends', ie dividends on account of the 'final dividend' declared by the general meeting.[3] The general meeting cannot interfere with the directors' exercise of this power.[4] But the power to resolve that a distribution of profits should take some other form than that of a cash dividend is vested by article 105 in the general meeting.

Dividends can only be paid in cash, unless there are words authorising payment by the issue of shares or debentures in the company fully or partly paid up (ie capitalisation), or the distribution among the members of assets (as, for instance, shares in other companies) *in specie*.[5]

If the articles are silent as to the distribution of profit, or declare that it shall be divided among the shareholders 'in proportion to their shares', the division must be made in accordance with, not the amount paid up on the shares, but the nominal amount of the shares, so that a shareholder whose shares are fully paid up gets no more per share than one whose shares are only partly paid up.[6] However, section 119(c) of the Companies Act 1985 authorises companies, if they so wish, to pay dividends in proportion to the amount paid up on the shares, where a larger amount is paid up on some shares than others and article 104 of Table A so provides.

Unless the articles otherwise provide, dividends and bonuses are payable to those who are registered holders at the time of the declaration.[7]

7.25 The Company Law Review

The previous edition of this book set out a number of options that were considered by the Company Law Review Steering Group in respect of the law described in this chapter. Since then, the CLRSG has published its final report and the Government has published its White Paper on the reform of company law. While there must inevitably remain some doubt over which reforms will be introduced and the manner in which they will be formulated, the following proposals seem likely to be implemented.

The concept of authorised share capital is likely to be abolished. This follows from the recommendation that companies formed under the new legislation should not have a separate memorandum and articles of association.[8] The details of share capital given by companies with shares at the time of formation would, if

---

1   *Re a Company, ex parte Glossop* [1988] BCLC 570 at p 577. Habitual abuse may justify a winding-up on the just and equitable ground (see **17.16**) or a petition under section 459: *Re Sam Weller & Sons Ltd* [1989] 3 WLR 923.

2   It is usually exercised at the company's annual general meeting.

3   There must be a legitimate profit available according to the rules already set out.

4   *Scott v Scott* [1943] 1 All ER 582. The directors can, however, rescind their decision before the date for payment: *Lagunas Nitrate Co. v Schneder* (1901) 85 L.T. 22.

5   *Wood v Odessa Waterworks Co Ltd* (1889) 42 Ch D 645: see Table A, article 105.

6   *Oakbank Oil Co v Crum* (1882) 8 App Cas 65 (HL).

7   The question of entitlement to dividends upon shares which have been transferred or transmitted is dealt with at **9.5** and **9.15**.

8   See para 9.4 of *Final Report*.

this change were made, relate to the share capital allotted to members on formation.

It is proposed that the provisions of section 80 of the Companies Act (authority for allotment of shares) be relaxed in the case of private companies so as to allow directors to allot shares under their general management powers. The requirement for authorisation will continue to apply to public companies as required by the second EC company law directive.[1] The objective is to give private companies greater freedom to issue shares. Section 80 will, however, continue to apply where a company has, or will have after the issue, more than one class of share, so as to prevent any unauthorised change in the relative power of the different classes of shares.[2]

Changes to the present legal provisions regarding par (or nominal) value shares and pre-emption rights were canvassed during the course of the review but were ultimately rejected. The CLRSG favoured in principle the introduction of no par value shares, noting that such a system was already operating satisfactorily in other countries such as Australia. However, as the Second Directive requires shares in public companies to have a par value, the CLRSG was limited to proposing options that would affect only private companies. It was ultimately concluded that it would be inappropriate to abolish par value shares for private companies so long as the Second Directive requirement relating to public companies remains in force. However, the CLRSG took the view that the abolition of par value shares for all companies should be the long-term objective and has recommended that the Secretary of State be given powers to enable him to achieve this without the need for primary legislation if and when the EU constraint is removed.

The subject of pre-emption rights attracted relatively little discussion in the review, which was surprising given the attention given to other (arguably less significant) aspects of the law relating to capital and the willingness to look to the experience of other jurisdictions which operate successfully under different rules. Retention of the existing law and self-regulatory rules on pre-emption rights was justified on the basis that they command widespread support both from investors and companies.[3]

An alternative to the present court procedure for capital reduction is likely to be introduced. At present, the law requires a company to seek court approval for any reduction in its share capital. It is proposed to replace this for private companies by a requirement that a capital reduction should be decided by a special resolution of the company, and that to protect creditors the directors should be required to make a formal declaration of solvency. For public companies, the same procedure would apply, except that in order to comply with the Second Directive, creditors would be given the opportunity, at their initiative, to challenge the reduction in court.[4]

The provisions relating to the giving of financial assistance by a company for the acquisition of its shares (presently contained in sections 151 to 158 of the Companies Act 1985) are likely to be made applicable only to public companies (where article 23 of the Second Directive requires a prohibition to be main-

---

1   Directive 77/91, [1991] OJ L26/1.
2   See *Developing the Framework* paras 7.28–7.32, *Completing the Structure* para 2.16, *Final Report* para 4.5.
3   See paragraphs 5.49–5.52 of *Completing the Structure*.
4   See paragrapg 3.27 of *Company Formation and Capital Maintenance* and draft clauses 50–67 of a new Companies Bill in the White Paper *Modernising Company Law* (Cm 5553-II).

tained).[1] The CLRSG considered that the effect of the present law on private companies was arbitrary and that financial assistance can only threaten the interests of creditors in a situation of potential insolvency, when directors' duties and the provisions on fraudulent and wrongful trading are likely to be relevant. If this change were made, the present 'whitewash' procedure applicable to private companies would become redundant. As far as public companies are concerned there are likely to be some revisions to the existing exemptions from the prohibition on giving financial assistance and the introduction of new exemptions. Of most significance is the proposal to reformulate the exemption presently contained in section 153(1) so that it would refer to a company's 'predominant reason' for giving financial assistance rather than its 'principal purpose'. This follows an earlier recommendation made by the DTI in 1996, which was intended to avoid the narrow interpretation placed on the present wording by the House of Lords in the *Brady* case.[2]

It is also proposed to change the definition of financial assistance given 'after the event' presently contained in section 151(2), which is not conditional on there having been a prior understanding as to the finance being made available for that purpose.[3] The proposal is to define financial assistance to include reimbursing by the company of expenditure, or the reducing or discharging by the company of a liability, incurred by any person in pursuance of an agreement or understanding to acquire the company's shares, whether or not the company itself is party to the agreement or understanding.

The CLRSG has proposed clarification of the scope of Part VIII of the Companies Act 1985 relating to distribution of profits and assets by providing that it applies (only) to transfers of assets to members, or to others at the direction or substantially at the direction, of members.[4] This would remove the need to consider the potential impact of the current law on distributions to transactions with outsiders who have no connection with a company.[5] The legislation would displace any common law rules prohibiting distributions as such. But this would be without prejudice to the general fiduciary duties and duties of care and skill of the directors, and to any provisions in an enactment or the company's constitution.

---

1   See paragraph 10.6 of *Final Report*, paragraphs 7.12–7.15 of *Completing the Structure* and
    paragraphs 3.41–3.48 of *Company Formation and Capital Maintenance*.
2   *Brady v Brady* [1989] AC 755; see **7.18.2**.
3   See para 7.13 of *Completing the Structure*.
4   See paras 7.20–7.23 of *Completing the Structure*.
5   See **7.21**.

Chapter 8

Rights and Liabilities Attached to Shares: Reorganisations of Capital

8.1 Shares

The ways in which a company may raise capital were described in a general way at the beginning of the previous chapter. It now falls to consider the nature of shares, the rights and liabilities attached to them and different classes thereof, and the ways in which share capital may be recognised.

Looking first at the nature of a share, we find that the Companies Act 1985 describes it as an item of personal property transferable in the manner provided by the company's articles.[1] A share is in fact a chose-in-action (in Scotland, incorporeal moveable property), one of those property interests which do not give the owner the right to possess anything physical. This bare description does not in fact seem to help very much. A more vivid description is provided by the oft-cited *dictum* of Farwell J:

> A share is the interest of a shareholder in the company, measured by a sum of money for the purpose of liability in the first place and of interest in the second, but also consisting of a series of mutual covenants entered into by all the shareholders *inter se* in accordance with section [14] of the Companies Act [1985] ... A share is not a sum of money ... but is an interest measured by a sum of money, and made up of various rights contained in the contract.[2]

This points to a share having a dual nature as both contract and property. It also distinguishes the share from the debenture, the other standard form of security issued by companies, the holder of which, a lender of money to the company,[3] simply has rights against the company and not in it.

In practice, however, as regards the securities of at least a public listed company, this distinction is to some extent illusory.[4] What is really important is to distinguish a security which gives real ownership rights in terms of votes at company meetings from one that does not. In practice, only ordinary shares confer such rights. The nature of the preference share is described below, as it is still conventional to compare and contrast it with the ordinary share, but it must not be forgotten that in practice it is lumped together with the debenture and the two are collectively referred to as preferred stock or securities. This is because, as well as having no or limited voting rights, the preference share usually shares the characteristic of the debenture of having the right to a prior, but fixed, rate of return.

---

1   Section 182(1); as to transfer, see Chapter 9. A share must also have a fixed nominal value (see **4.11**).
2   *Borland's Trustee v Steel Bros & Co Ltd* [1901] 1 Ch 279 at 288. As to section 14, see **5.17**.
3   See Chapter 10.
4   It will normally hold for private companies, since the issue by them of more than one class of share is unusual.

8.2 Classes of shares

As the above introductory remarks have indicated, a company may divide its share capital into different classes, although this would be relatively unusual for a private company. The power to create shares with varying rights is normally contained in the articles,[1] but occasionally it is found in the memorandum.[2]

Whatever preferences or postponements or other special rights are intended to be created for a class of shares should be clearly expressed in the memorandum or articles or in the resolution authorising the issue, and also in the prospectus inviting subscriptions for the shares. The mere use of a name such as 'preference shares' or 'preferred ordinary shares' is not enough of itself to indicate what special rights are to be attached to the shares. It is particularly important to express clearly what are the rights of the various holders in the case of a winding-up.

If there is any conflict between the memorandum and the articles as to what rights are conferred on a particular class of shareholders, the memorandum prevails.[3] Where, however, there is an ambiguity in the memorandum, resort may be had to the articles to resolve the ambiguity.[4] *Prima facie*, the memorandum, the articles, the resolution authorising the issue and, it is submitted, the share certificates express all the rights of the holders, and the prospectus cannot be looked at for the purpose of interpreting them.[5] This rule as to interpretation does not, however, exclude proof that the prospectus did, in fact, contain part of the contract, or constitute a binding collateral contract.[6]

8.3 Ordinary shares

Except in so far as the memorandum, articles or terms of issue provide otherwise, an ordinary shareholder is entitled to receive dividends when declared (subject to any priority as to dividend enjoyed by preference shareholders), to have his appropriate proportion of the company's assets after payment of creditors paid or transferred to him on a winding-up (subject again to any priority enjoyed by preference shareholders) and to exercise one vote for each share that he holds at the general meetings of the company.[7] It should be noted that these rights as to dividend and return of capital include a right to participate in any surplus; thus in a winding-up, the holder of a £1 ordinary share is not confined to receiving back his £1 if the value of the assets available for distribution among the ordinary shareholders exceeds the nominal amount of the issued ordinary shares.

These rights of an ordinary shareholder may be, and often are, varied in specific respects by express provision in the memorandum, articles or terms of issue. A company may, for instance, have two or more classes of ordinary shares, with each

---

1 See article 2 of Table A for the standard form.
2 If necessary, a company can generally adopt the power by altering the memorandum or articles.
3 *Re Duncan Gilmour and Co Ltd* [1952] 2 All ER 871; *Guinness v Land Corp of Ireland* (1883) 22 Ch D 349 (CA).
4 *Angostura Bitters Ltd v Kerr* [1933] AC 550 (PC).
5 *British Equitable Assurance Co Ltd v Baily* [1906] AC 35 at 38–41 (HL).
6 *Jacos v Batavia and General Plantations Trust Ltd* [1924] 2 Ch 329 (CA) (which related to an issue of short-term notes).
7 See Companies Act 1985, section 370(6).

class carrying different voting rights, or indeed, with one such class having no voting rights at all.[1]

8.4   Preference shares

Preference shares may give a preferential right as to dividend only, or as to return of capital only, or both as to dividend and to return of capital. In either case the preferential dividend may be cumulative, or it may be payable only out of the profits of each year.

In addition to their fixed preferential rights, preference shares sometimes give further rights to participate in profits or assets. In this case, they may be known as 'participating preference shares'.

In the last resort, the rights of a preference shareholder as to dividend and capital turn upon the construction of the relevant parts of the memorandum or articles, or of the terms of issue. The courts have developed certain rules to govern this task of construction, as it is not always an easy one. It is proposed now to examine these rights, first as regards dividend and secondly as regards capital.

8.4.1   Preferential rights

The dividend on a preference share is generally a fixed one: that is, it is expressed in terms of a fixed percentage of the par value of the share.

A fixed preferential dividend is *prima facie* cumulative.[2] That is, arrears in one year must be made up from profits in subsequent years before any ordinary dividends are declared.[3] But this presumption may be rebutted, eg where the dividend is declared to be payable from 'yearly profits'[4] or 'out of the net profits of each year'.[5]

Payment of a preference dividend is dependent on 'distributable profits'[6] being available for that purpose. The holders of preference shares cannot prevent the company setting aside profits earned in any year to make good the losses sustained in previous years or to build up reserves if good faith is observed, even where they are entitled to a cumulative preferential dividend at a fixed rate. Their right to dividend is, in the absence of express bargain to the contrary, subject to the director's right to carry sums to reserve, and as with ordinary dividends, it only accrues when the dividend is declared.[7]

When a winding-up supervenes, the question arises whether the holders of cumulative preference shares have a right to receive the whole or any part of undeclared dividends from surplus assets.[8] There is no rule applicable to all circumstances as the issue turns on the construction of the relevant memorandum and articles of association.[9] If there are no constitutional provisions regarding distribution of assests on winding up, the assets are shared equally between all

---

1   See **8.6**.
2   *Webb v Earle* (1875) LR 20 Eq 556.
3   However, the payment of such arrears is a dividend for the year in which it was declared, not in respect of the year when no payment was made: *Re Wakley* [1920] 2 Ch 205.
4   *Adair v Old Bushmills Distillery Co* [1908] WN 24.
5   *Staples v Eastman Photographic Materials Co* [1896] 2 Ch 303 (CA).
6   See **7.21.2**.
7   See **7.24**.
8   This is sometimes referred to as arrears of dividend. See further *Palmer's Company Law* paragraph 6.110.
9   See eg *Re Walter Symons Ltd* [1934] Ch 308.

members, including preference shareholders. This conclusion follows from the presumption that *prima facie* all shareholders rank equally.[1]

If the memorandum or articles declare that the preference shares do confer priority in a winding-up, or that the surplus assets shall be applied first in repaying the preference shares, but do not further deal with the capital, it is in every case a question of construction whether the preferential rights are given by way of priority only or by way of delimitation. Generally speaking, however, such a provision will constitute an exhaustive declaration of the preference share-holders' rights in a winding-up,[2] so as to exclude them from participation in any surplus remaining after repayment of the ordinary capital.[3] Any preference shareholder who wishes to displace the presumption must shoulder the onus of so doing.[4] The fact that his shares carry a right of participation in any surplus profits available for dividend does not displace the presumption; indeed it strengthens it if anything.[5]

Where the preference shareholders do have a right to participate, it extends to all the available assets, including those representing profits which before the winding-up the company could have been distributed as an ordinary dividend,[6] unless a provision in the memorandum or articles makes it clear that such profits 'belong to' the ordinary shareholders[7] or in some other way reserves them for such holders.

8.5   Other classes of shares

There is no limit to the classes of shares which can be created, even within a single company. Founders' shares, often issued to promoters, in respect of which the receipt of a dividend was deferred until after the preference and ordinary shares had been paid a dividend at a specified rate, used to be common but are now rare.[8]

Alternatively, a company may issue shares which, like preference shares, carry the right to a fixed preferential dividend, but, like ordinary shares, carry the right to participate in surplus profits after their own fixed dividend and a fixed dividend attached to the ordinary shares have been paid. Such 'hybrid' shares are sometimes labelled 'participating preference shares' or 'preferred ordinary shares'. Also commonly found in practice are employees' shares, the issue of which has been encouraged by recent British governments.[9] Shares of any class may be issued as redeemable under the terms of section 159 of the Companies Act 1985.[10]

---

1   *Birch v Cropper* (1889) 14 App Cas 525 at 543 and 546, *per* Lord Macnaghten.
2   This question is also especially relevant in a reduction of capital: see **8.14.3**.
3   *Scottish Insurance Corporation Ltd v Wilsons & Clyde Coal Co Ltd* [1949] AC 462 (HL (Sc)); *Re Isle of Thanet Electricity Supply Co Ltd* [1950] Ch 161 (CA); *Re Saltdean Estate Co Ltd* [1968] 1 WLR 1844.
4   *Re Isle of Thanet Electricity Supply Co Ltd*, above.
5   Ibid.
6   *Dimbula Valley (Ceylon) Tea Co Ltd v Laurie* [1961] Ch 353; *Re Saltdean Estate Co Ltd*, above; cf *Scottish Insurance Corp Ltd v Wilsons & Clyde Coal Co Ltd*, above.
7   *Re Bridgewater Navigation Co Ltd* [1891] 2 Ch 317 (CA).
8   As to these and the requirements of the Companies Act in respect of them, see *Gore-Browne on Companies* 44th edn (Jordans, loose-leaf) at 14.5.
9   See further *Gore-Browne on Companies* 44th edn (Jordans, loose-leaf) at 14.12.
10 See **7.17.1**.

8.6 Voting rights

The holders of all classes of shares have equal rights of voting[1] unless restrictions are specifically imposed. But a provision in the articles that holders of any class of shares shall not have votes or shall have only limited rights of voting in respect of those shares is good; and resolutions passed by those having votes may be binding even when they affect the interests of all classes.[2] It has been suggested from time to time that voteless shares should be made illegal,[3] but this suggestion has never been implemented, and even listed shares may be voteless provided that they are clearly designated as such.[4]

Often, by the provisions of the articles, the holders of preference shares are not entitled to receive notice of or to attend or vote at general meetings in respect of their preference shares; but it is desirable that they should have the right to vote on any resolution involving a variation of their rights or a reduction of capital or a winding-up, and usually cumulative preference shareholders are given voting rights during any period when their dividend is in arrears for longer than a specified period.[5]

Sometimes even the holders of debentures are given votes in pursuance of a provision to that effect in the articles of association, and accordingly have a voice in the management of the company; but such votes could not be counted upon a special or extraordinary resolution, for the Companies Act 1985 provides that such a resolution must be passed by the specified majority of *members* entitled to vote.[6]

An article which vests the primary right to vote at meetings in persons other than the registered shareholders or members is not lawful.[7] The articles generally determine how joint holders of shares are to vote. Of course, only one of such holders can vote, and the right is usually (as in Table A, article 55) given to the senior who tenders a vote, seniority for this purpose being determined by the order in which the names stand in the register of members. Under articles in the usual form, a joint holder can give a proxy without the concurrence of the other joint holders.

Every shareholder is entitled to vote in accordance with his own interests, although they may appear to be different from those of the company at large, unless the vote is given to him as a member of a class, in which case he must conform to the interest of the class itself when seeking to exercise the power conferred on him in his capacity of a member of that class,[8] or unless in so doing he infringes the broad principle, discussed elsewhere,[9] that members must exercise their voting power in what they *bona fide* believe to be the interests of the

---

1 See also **13.19**.
2 *Re Barrow Haematite Steel Co* (No 1) (1888) 39 Ch D 582; *Re Mackenzie & Co Ltd* [1916] 2 Ch 450. This proposition is, however, subject to the specific rules governing variation of class rights, discussed at **8.7** *et seq*.
3 See eg the Note of Dissent in the Report of the Jenkins Committee (Cmnd 1749), p 207.
4 *Listing Rules*, Chapter 6.B5(a).
5 See eg *Re Bradford Investments plc* [1990] BCC 740, where it was held that the preference shareholders' right to vote if their dividend had not been paid for six months after the due date was exercisable, whether or not there were profits available to pay the dividend.
6 See section 378(1), (2), discussed at **14.15**.
7 *Shears v Phosphate Co-operative Co of Australia Ltd* (1988) 14 ACLR 747.
8 *Re Holders Investment Trust Ltd* [1971] 1 WLR 583.
9 See **17.4**.

company. Subject to this principle, a shareholder may, for example, vote in favour of property being purchased from himself even though he is also a director, and the resolution will be binding even though passed by the votes of such shareholders.[1] An agreement by a vendor of shares with the purchaser that until they are transferred he will vote in a particular way will be enforced by the court by a prohibiting injunction[2] (although it seems the company could not take notice of the fact that a vote was given in breach of such an agreement) and an agreement in a mortgage that the mortgagor should retain the right of voting has in fact been enforced by a mandatory injunction.[3] An agreement made for a money consideration to vote for the advantage of another person in the course of a winding-up is, however, void.[4]

If by transferring his shares into other names or altering the order of the names a member can increase his voting power, he is entitled to do so.[5]

8.7 Variation and abrogation of the class rights of shareholders

Special provisions exist in the Companies Act 1985, principally sections 125 to 127, to protect the 'class rights' of shareholders, so that they cannot simply be varied or altered or, indeed, removed by alteration of the documents in which they are contained, ie the memorandum or articles or a resolution passed under the authority of the articles. Where a company has only one class of shares, then variation of their rights would in general be effected by such alteration, although even in these circumstances, it seems that rights may be class rights.[6]

A number of questions arise, including:

(1) What is a 'class right'?
(2) What constitutes a 'variation' or 'abrogation' of such a right?
(3) What is the appropriate procedure for varying or abrogating class rights?

Further questions will arise once these have been considered.

8.7.1 The concept of a 'class right'

When Parliament enacted the statutory provisions protecting class rights,[7] it chose not to define what it meant by 'class rights' or, to use the statutory phase, 'rights attached to any class of shares', nor even what it meant by 'class'. This was probably because it was thought that there was no difficulty in determining what class rights were – if the shares in a company are divided into different classes according to the criteria set out earlier in this chapter, so that they have differing

---

1   *North-West Transportation Co v Beatty* (1887) 12 App Cas 589 (PC); *Pender v Lushington* (1877) 6 Ch D 70; *Burland v Earle* [1902] AC 82 at 94 (PC); *Dominion Cotton Mills Co Ltd v Amyot* [1912] AC 546 (PC). See **17.4**, for a more detailed discussion of the fiduciary aspects of voting at general meetings by directors.

2   *Greenwell v Porter* [1902] 1 Ch 530. As to the duration of a voting agreement, see *Greenhalgh v Mallard* [1943] 2 All ER 234 (CA).

3   *Puddephatt v Leith* [1916] 1 Ch 200.

4   *Elliot v Richardson* (1870) LR 5 CP 744.

5   *Pender v Lushington*, above; *Moffat v Farquhar* (1878) 7 Ch D 591; *Burns v Siemens Brothers Dynamo Works Ltd* [1919] 1 Ch 225.

6   See **8.7.1**.

7   Section 125 was introduced only in 1980, implementing part of the Second EC Directive. Section 127 was first introduced in 1929.

rights in respect of dividend, capital and voting or any of these, then the rights specifically conferred in contrast to one or more of the other classes are class rights.[1] The rights might be conferred by the memorandum, the articles, the terms of issue or the resolution authorising the issue (as originally framed or subsequently varied).[2] That such rights are class rights was confirmed in the only reported case properly to consider the meaning of the term, namely *Cumbrian Newspapers Group Ltd v Cumberland & Westmoreland Herald Newspaper & Printing Co Ltd,*[3] although, as will be seen below, the actual decision in that case went somewhat further. It was also, clearly correctly, decided in that case that a right unrelated to any shareholding cannot by any stretch of imagination be a class right.[4]

In addition to rights conferred specifically on a class, it is thought that the basic rights of all the classes as to dividends, capital and voting should be treated as class rights even when on a particular aspect there happens to be no difference between the various classes. Thus, for example, where preference and ordinary shares are clearly demarcated as regards dividend, but both classes participate *pari passu* in the assets on a winding-up, a resolution giving the preference shareholders the normal position of priority without further participation on a winding-up should be treated as varying a class right of the preference shares. Furthermore, the right to insist upon a variation of rights clause[5] is a class right, not least since section 125(7) provides that any alteration of a variation of rights clause in the articles or the insertion of such a clause into the articles shall be treated as a variation of class rights.

As well as rights of the sort already described which are clearly class rights, articles of association in particular often confer other sorts of rights on shareholders not attached to a conventional 'class' of shares, for example weighted voting rights in certain circumstances[6] or rights of pre-emption over shares. These will normally be found only in the articles of private companies. In the *Cumbrian Newspapers* case, the question arose as to whether such rights, even when not conferred on a shareholder as a member of a conventional class, could be class rights. Here, the plaintiff was given rights under the defendant's articles, including a pre-emptive right regarding the transfer of any shares in the defendant and the right to nominate a director to the board of the defendant so long as it held 10% of the issued ordinary shares of the defendant. It was held that rights of this sort were class rights, provided that they were conferred on a shareholder as such,[7] and thus subject to the protection of section 125. The learned judge, Scott J, found no basis for this result in the wording of the statute

---

1   *Re John Smith's Tadcaster Brewery Co Ltd* [1953] Ch 308 at 319–320 (CA), *per* Jenkins LJ.

2   As in *Re Old Silkstone Collieries Ltd* [1954] Ch 159 (CA).

3   [1986] 3 WLR 26.

4   See also *Re Blue Arrow plc* [1987] BCLC 587 at 590 rejecting, in line with the reasoning of Scott J in *Cumbrian Newspapers*, the idea that a right in the articles to be 'president' of the company, unrelated to any shareholding, could be a class right.

5   This is not contained in the modern Table A because of the existence of section 125, but will still be relevant to companies which have the former Table A, article 4 (see footnote 3 at p 221).

6   Cf *Bushell v Faith* [1970] AC 1099 (HL), discussed in **15.7**. The right which was the subject of this decision – weighted voting on a resolution to remove a director – was used as an example of a class right in the *Cumbrian Newspapers* case; scc [1986] 3 WLR at 37.

7   This limitation was not framed as narrowly as that which is often said to surround the statutory contract created out of the memorandum and articles by section 14; see **4.18**.

and justified it by what he perceived to be the legislative purpose behind section 125, namely the protection of such rights lest they be subject to removal by simple alteration of the articles.

It is submitted, with respect, that this conclusion is open to question.[1] There are other bases for protecting minority shareholders, both at common law[2] and under statute.[3] The purpose of section 125 was to implement part of the Second EC Directive, whose purpose was the harmonisation of provisions relating to shares and share capital in *public* companies. Section 125(1) provides that the section is concerned with the variation of the rights attached to any class of shares in a company *whose capital is divided into shares of different classes*.[4] This seems to require conventionally different classes. If the decision is correct and followed, it has wide-ranging implications for rights often conferred by the articles of private companies, as already indicated. In effect, these rights are unalterable save with the consent of the individual shareholder concerned, since that person alone would constitute the class for the purposes of section 125 which, as will be seen below, requires the consent of a proportion of the class by itself to a variation of class rights. It is submitted that, if it is thought proper that such rights should be unalterable, this should be provided for in the context of a properly thought-out code for private companies, not by a 'surprisingly wide'[5] construction of a provision which had its origins in a code for public companies.

8.7.2 The meaning of 'varying' or 'abrogating' class rights

It is easy to discern that a class right is being 'varied' or 'abrogated'[6] when the proposed alteration directly conflicts with, and purports to override, the particular provision under which the right arises. Thus a resolution reducing a preferential dividend from 10% to 5% clearly involves the 'variation' of a class right, and a resolution depriving a class of preference shares of a right, guaranteed by a previous special resolution, to participate in compensation accruing to the shareholders under impending nationalisation legislation, has been held to involve the 'modification or abrogation' of a class right attached to the preference shares.[7]

This is not to say that variation or abrogation of a class right belonging to a particular class cannot arise in some other way, eg through a variation of the literal terms of the class rights of another class, or through some measure not on its face involving class rights at all. It would seem, for example, that a resolution raising the voting power of one class of shares from one vote to ten votes per share alters the class rights, not only of that particular class, but of all other classes carrying

---

1   See also (1986) 7 Co Law 202; [1986] CLJ 399. Sealy, *Cases and Materials in Company Law* 5th edn (Butterworths, 1992) at p 424 refers to the decision as 'surprisingly wide'. Davies, *Gower's Principles of Modern Company Law* 6th edn (Sweet & Maxwell, 1997) at p 720 welcomes it.
2   See **4.27**.
3   Especially under section 459; see **17.12**.
4   Italics supplied.
5   See footnote 1, above.
6   These are the vital words in sections 125 and 127. Further by virtue of section 125(8), in any provision for the variation of class rights, except where the context requires otherwise, references to variation include references to abrogation.
7   *Re Old Silkstone Collieries Ltd* [1954] Ch 169 (CA).

voting rights.[1] Equally, it has in general been assumed[2] that a reduction of capital under which the various classes are not treated in accordance with their capital rights on a winding-up involves a variation of class rights. Probably the removal of a modification of rights clause constitutes such a variation also. The articles can extend the meaning of a variation of class rights, for example by providing that any reduction of capital is deemed to be such.[3]

The general tendency of the courts has, however, been to rule that the class rights attached to (say) 'class X' of shares have not been 'varied' or 'abrogated', or even 'affected' or 'dealt with',[4] by a resolution which alters the literal terms of the class rights of another, 'class Y', or on its face does not bear upon class rights at all. The following measures have been held not to vary or abrogate the class rights attached in each case to 'class X' and therefore not to fall within the scope of a modification of rights clause:

(1) an issue of new shares ranking *pari passu* with class X;[5]
(2) an issue ranking in priority to class X,[6] there being no extrinsic contractual promise to the holders of class X that this would not be done;[7]
(3) an issue of bonus shares (whether ordinary or preference) to the holders in class Y (ordinary shares), when it had the effect of greatly increasing their voting power as against that of the holders in class X (preference shares),[8] or of reducing the amount which would come in a liquidation, on a distribution of surplus assets, to the holders in class X (preference shares);[9]
(4) a subdivision of shares in class Y so that the holders in that class acquired a greatly increased voting power in comparison to class X;[10]
(5) the cancellation of paid-up capital to an equal extent on both class X (preference shares) and class Y (ordinary shares), with the result that the fixed preferential dividend payable to class X, though unaltered in percentage, was substantially reduced in amount, whereas the dividend for class Y remained at large;[11] and

---

1   *Greenhalgh v Arderne Cinemas Ltd* [1946] 1 All ER 512 at 516 (CA); *Lord St David's v Union Castle Mail Steamship Co Ltd* (1934) *The Times*, November 24. But cf the actual decision in the *Greenhalgh* case, referred to in the next paragraph, and cf the approach of the Court of Appeal in *White v Bristol Aeroplane Co Ltd* [1953] Ch 65 (CA) and *Re John Smith's Tadcaster Brewery Co Ltd* [1953] Ch 308 (CA).

2   See eg *Scottish Insurance Corp Ltd v Wilsons & Clyde Coal Co Ltd* [1949] AC 462 (HL (Sc)); *Re Old Silkstone Collieries Ltd*, above. The adjustment of rights as between different classes of shareholders on a reduction of capital is discussed more fully at **8.14.3**.

3   See *Re Northern Engineering Industries plc* [1993] BCC 267. As to reductions of capital and class rights generally, see **8.14.3**.

4   These extra terms are sometimes inserted in modification of rights clauses in an attempt to widen their scope, but no decision to date has shown them to have any substantial effect. In *Re Mackenzie & Co Ltd* [1916] 2 Ch 450, they seem to have been ignored, but in *White v Bristol Aeroplane Co Ltd*, above, and *Re John Smith's Tadcaster Brewery Co Ltd*, above, they did come under discussion by the Court of Appeal.

5   *Re Schweppes Ltd* [1914] 1 Ch 322 (CA) (a decision under the Companies (Consolidation) Act 1908).

6   *Pulbrook v New Civil Service Co-operation* (1878) 26 WR 11; *Underwood v London Music Hall Ltd* [1901] 2 Ch 309; *Hodge v James Howell & Co Ltd* [1958] CLY 446 (CA).

7   See *Allen v Gold Reefs of West Africa Ltd* [1900] 1 Ch 656 at 673–674 and 679 (CA).

8   *White v Bristol Aeroplane Co Ltd*, above; *Re John Smith's Tadcaster Brewery Co Ltd*, above.

9   *Dimbula Valley (Ceylon) Tea Co Ltd v Laurie* [1961] Ch 353.

10   *Greenhalgh v Arderne Cinemas Ltd* [1946] 1 All ER 512 (CA).

11   *Re Mackenzie & Co Ltd*, above.

(6) the alteration of the place of payment (and thus the currency) of dividends from England to Australia, causing the fixed preferential dividend payable to class X to be of lesser value because the Australian pound was worth less than the English pound sterling.[1]

Lord Evershed MR[2] suggested an explanation for such decisions, namely that it was not the class rights of the complaining class that were varied or abrogated or affected, but merely the 'enjoyment' of those rights.[3] No doubt this is a valid theoretical distinction. It is submitted, however, that more than once minority classes have lost the benefit of their rights, without any class meeting being held, in circumstances where the relevant modification of rights clause seems clearly to have been intended to supply protection to them.[4] A narrow and literal approach to the concept of 'variation of rights' has in general been the cause.

8.7.3 *Procedure for variation*

Once it is clear that a 'class right' is being sought to be 'varied' or 'abrogated', the procedure to be adopted depends upon two factors in particular: whether the memorandum, articles or terms of issue contain an express provision for variation (ie a 'variation of rights clause') and whether the right in question has been set out in the memorandum, the articles, the resolution authorising the issue, or any other contractual document containing the terms of issue. The procedure is largely governed by section 125.

Where class rights are set out in the memorandum and no variation of rights clause exists, either in the memorandum or the articles, then they may be varied if all the members of the company agree,[5] or by a virtue of a scheme of arrangement under section 425.[6] Where the rights are set out in the memorandum which also provides for their variation, then clearly the procedure there laid down must be followed. However, more than this may be required if the variation proposed is concerned with the giving, variation, revocation or renewal of an authority to issue securities for the purposes of section 80,[7] or is concerned with a reduction of capital under section 135.[8] In these cases, rights can be varied only by either the consent in writing of the holders of 75% in nominal value of the issued shares of the class, or by an extraordinary resolution passed at a separate general meeting of the class,[9] together with any other requirement laid down in the memorandum in so far as it is not comprised in the statutory requirements.[10]

Where class rights are set out in the memorandum and a variation of rights clause exists in the articles, then, provided that the variation of rights clause was

---

1   *Adelaide Electric Supply Co Ltd v Prudential Assurance Co* [1934] AC 122 (HL).
2   In *White v Bristol Aeroplane Co Ltd* [1953] Ch 65 at 74 (CA).
3   A distinction was drawn in this case between the rights attached to a share within a particular class and the relative influence (in terms of voting) of that class within the company following a variation. The latter was categorised as 'enjoyment' of rights, as it could be varied without any variation in the former (eg as a result of the issue of new voting shares of a different class).
4   Notably in *Greenhalgh v Arderne Cinemas Ltd*, above, and *Re Mackenzie & Co Ltd*, above.
5   Section 125(5).
6   *Ashbury v Watson* (1885) 30 Ch D 376 (CA); *City Property Investment Trust Corp Ltd* 1951 SC 571. As to schemes of arrangement, see **18.18**.
7   See **7.4**.
8   See **8.14** *et seq*.
9   See below for the statutory requirements relating to such meetings.
10   Section 125(3).

included in the articles at the time of the company's original incorporation, and subject to the qualification to be mentioned shortly, the rights may be varied only in accordance with the variation of rights clause.[1] The qualification is that, if the proposed variation concerns either an authority under section 80 or a reduction of capital under section 135, as described above, then the rights can be varied only by either the consent in writing of the holders of 75% in nominal value of the issued shares of the class or by an extraordinary resolution passed at a separate general meeting of the class, together with any other requirement laid down in the memorandum in so far as it is not comprised in the statutory requirements.

Where class rights are set out in the articles or in some independent document, for example the resolution under which the shares were issued, and there is no variation of rights clause in the articles, then those rights may be varied, but only if the holders of 75% in nominal value of the issued shares of the class consent in writing to the variation, or the variation is sanctioned by an extraordinary resolution passed at a separate general meeting of the holders of the class.[2]

If the articles do contain a variation of rights clause,[3] then this must be complied with.[4] Further, if the proposed modification concerns either an authority under section 80 or a reduction of capital under section 135, as described above, then the requirements as to 75% class consent in writing or an extraordinary resolution at a class meeting as described earlier must be complied with if not imposed by the articles.[5]

8.7.4 Notice for class meetings and statement to the Registrar

If, under any of the circumstances described, a class meeting is held, whether required by the statute or by a variation of rights clause, then the requirements of section 369 as to the length of notice for calling meetings, section 370 concerning general provisions regarding meetings and votes,[6] and sections 376 and 377 regarding the circulation of members' resolutions,[7] and any relevant provisions in the articles must be complied with. In addition, the quorum at any such meeting must be two persons at least holding or representing by proxy one-third of the issued shares of the class concerned, except at an adjourned meeting where one person holding shares of the class is sufficient; any holder of shares of the class concerned present in person or by proxy may demand a poll.[8]

---

1   Section 125(4). Presumably, if the variation of rights clause was not included in the articles at the time of incorporation, the previous law applies and the memorandum should expressly or impliedly refer to or contemplate variation of the rights according to the clause in the articles. If there is no such indication, variation of the rights in the memorandum must be carried out as if the clause in the articles did not exist, ie under section 125(5) or by a scheme of arrangement under section 425, as described earlier.
2   Section 125(2). Any other requirement, however imposed, is automatically complied with.
3   The common form clause was exemplified by Table A, Part I, article 4 in the Companies Act 1948, which provided that where the share capital was divided into different classes of shares, the rights attached to any class might be varied with the consent in writing of the holders of three-fourths of the issued shares of that class, or with the sanction of an extraordinary resolution passed at a separate general meeting of the holders of the shares of the class. There is no standard form clause in the modern Table A, because of the statutory protection afforded by section 125, first introduced in 1980.
4   Section 125(4).
5   Section 125(3).
6   See **13.10.1**.
7   See **13.15**.
8   Section 125(6).

Where a company allots shares with rights which are not stated in its memorandum or articles or in any resolution or agreement to which section 380 applies,[1] the company must (unless the shares are in all respects uniform with shares previously allotted) deliver to the Registrar of Companies within one month from allotting the shares a statement in the prescribed form containing particulars of those rights.[2] Where the rights attached to any shares of a company are varied otherwise than by an amendment of the company's memorandum or articles (or a resolution or agreement to which section 380 applies), the company must within one month from the date of the variation deliver to the Registrar a statement in prescribed form containing particulars of the variation.[3] A similar statement must be delivered to the Registrar where (without otherwise varying them) the company assigns a name or other designation (or a new name or other designation) to any class of its shares.[4] A criminal sanction is imposed upon the company and every officer who is in default if the company fails to comply with section 128.[5]

8.7.5 Protection for minority in class

Where a variation of rights clause in the memorandum or articles has been invoked to vary or abrogate class rights, or where there is no such clause but class rights have been varied or abrogated under section 125(2), section 127 provides that the holders of not less than 15% of the issued shares of the class affected, if they did not consent to or vote in favour of the variation, may apply to the court to have the variation cancelled. The court may, if satisfied that the variation would unfairly prejudice the shareholders of the class represented by the applicant, disallow the variation; if not so satisfied, it must confirm it. Application may be made by such one or more of the shareholders affected as may be appointed by them in writing and must be made within 21 days after the appropriate consent was given or resolution passed.[6]

Section 127 does give a measure of protection to minorities within a class of shareholders who consider that their rights have been unjustly overridden by the majority. But its narrow scope must be noted. It applies only where there is: (a) a variation of rights clause in the memorandum or articles or a variation under section 125(2); and (b) a genuine 'variation' or 'abrogation' of a 'class right'. The narrow meaning of these terms has already been described. Further, there is no

---

1   Section 380 concerns registration of certain resolutions and agreements. See **13.18**. Any statement or notice delivered under section 128 to the Registrar will be gazetted under section 711.

2   Shares are not treated as being different by reason only of the fact that they do not carry the same rights to dividends for the first 12 months after allotment; section 128(2).

3   Section 128(3).

4   Section 128(4).

5   Section 128(5). See section 129 for a similar obligation imposed on companies without a share capital, but with different classes of members, in respect of the creation or variation of class rights.

6   Section 127(3). The court's decision is final (section 127(4)) and a copy of any order made must be lodged with the Registrar within 15 days of the date thereof (section 127(5)).

reported use of the section. On the other hand, there are House of Lords *dicta*[1] to the effect that a minority shareholder within the relevant class has a right at general law to challenge a class resolution on the ground of lack of good faith and that section 127 is not intended to deprive him of such right. To enforce this general law right, a holding of 15% of shares of the class in question is not necessary.[2]

8.8   Liabilities on shares

The fact of becoming a member of a company renders the person liable to contribute to its assets to the extent and in the manner prescribed by the Companies Act 1985, taken along with the general law and the memorandum and articles of association, as outlined below.

In an unlimited company the members are liable while the company is a going concern to pay to it the nominal amount of the shares (if any) held by them as and when called up, together with any premium payable on issue, and upon winding up to pay whatever amount is necessary to satisfy the debts of the company and the expenses of liquidation,[3] but as far as possible all the members contribute rateably.

In a company limited by guarantee, the members are liable while the company is a going concern to pay to it the amount payable on the shares (if any) held by them as and when called up, and on a winding-up they are liable for any balance of the amount of their shares unpaid and, in addition, the amount guaranteed by them in the memorandum of association, if required for the purpose of paying the debts of the company and the costs of liquidation, but no more.[4]

In the case of a company limited by shares each member is liable to pay only the nominal amount of the shares held by him (together with any premium which he may have agreed to pay);[5] and notwithstanding any provision of the memorandum or articles, no member is bound by any alteration thereof, to which he has not previously or at the time thereof given his assent in writing, which requires him to subscribe for more shares than he then holds or in any way increases his liability to pay money to the company.[6]

In each of the above cases, until a liquidation takes place, the amounts are payable at the times and in the manner prescribed by the articles of association, which almost invariably declare that so much as is not paid on application and/or allotment may be called up by the directors as and when they think fit.[7]

---

1   *Carruth v Imperial Chemical Industries Ltd* [1937] AC 707 at 756 and 765; see too *British American Nickel Corp v O'Brien* [1927] AC 369 (PC) and *Re Holders Investment Trust Ltd* [1971] 1 WLR 583. The latter case, which is described in **8.14.4** and where the issue arose on a petition to confirm a reduction of capital, is perhaps the best reported example of what might be regarded as 'unfair prejudice' under section 127.

2   The matter could also be litigated on a petition to confirm a reduction of capital (see footnote 1 at p 232) or by a petition under section 459, the general remedy for unfairly prejudiced minority shareholders (see **17.13**).

3   Insolvency Act 1986, section 74(1); and see section 1(2)(c) of the Companies Act 1985.

4   Ibid, section 74(3); and see section 1(2)(b) of the Companies Act 1985.

5   Ibid, section 74(2)(d); and see section 1(2)(a) of the Companies Act 1985. In exceptional circumstances the liability of a member or a director may become unlimited: see **5.10**.

6   Section 16 of the Companies Act 1985.

7   See eg Table A, article 12. As to calls by a liquidator when a company is being wound up, see **21.52**.

8.9   Initial payments on shares

Payments on applications for shares and/or allotment are dealt with in connection with the general topics of public issues and allotment of shares.[1] For present purposes it is sufficient to note that, subject to certain specific statutory provisions relating to public companies only,[2] and to any provisions in the articles or any agreement between the company and the member, the mere fact of becoming a member, whether as a subscriber to the memorandum or otherwise, does not of itself impose any obligation on the member to make an immediate payment to the company in respect of his shares.[3] In practice, of course, at least part of the price of the shares will in any event be made payable on application where the process of application is resorted to. Similarly, all, or the balance outstanding, or a part, will be payable on allotment.

8.10   Calls

A call is the way in which amounts due on shares not fully paid up on application are raised.[4] These amounts can in general be called up by a proper authority at any time, subject to the articles.[5] In the early days of company law, when the holding of partly paid shares for a considerable time was common, calls would be made at regular intervals. This is infrequent, and perhaps unknown, these days, but the articles, as in Table A, article 16, usually deem any amount payable in respect of a share on allotment or at any fixed date in the future to be a call. The result is that, for example, a failure to pay the balance or an instalment due on allotment of shares, a sum having been paid on application, or to pay the balance due at a later specified date, will attract the prospect of the shares being forfeited.[6]

Article 12 of Table A provides that, subject to the terms of allotment, the directors may from time to time make calls upon the members in respect of any moneys unpaid on their shares (whether in respect of nominal value or premium),[7] and requires at least 14 days' notice to be given to the members, who are then liable to pay at the time(s) and place(s) appointed by the directors.

If calls remain unpaid, the members liable should be sued for the amount. In England, a call is specialty debt,[8] and accordingly can be recovered by action at

---

1   See Chapters 7 and 18, above.

2   Especially section 101, by which shares in a public company must not be allotted to any person unless not less than one-quarter of the nominal value of the shares together with the whole of any premium has been received by the company (see **7.9**).

3   *Alexander v Automatic Telephone Co* [1900] 2 Ch 56 (CA).

4   For more detail, see *Gore-Browne on Companies* 44th edn (Jordans, loose-leaf), 14.10 *et seq.*

5   A member cannot escape liability unless he shows that he has been wrongly made a member and has used all diligence to have his name removed from the register: see **12.5**.

6   As to forfeiture, see **8.15**. Note that in the absence of a provision like article 16, payments on application or allotment are not calls (*Croskey v Bank of Wales* (1863) 4 Giff 314) and that in the absence of a provision to the contrary in the articles or in some other agreement, there is no obligation to make any payment on shares subsequent to allotment until a call is made; *Re Russian Spratt's Patent Ltd* [1898] 2 Ch 149 (CA).

7   They must act in good faith and not for a collateral purpose. For example, it is prima facie improper to make calls on only some of a class of members: *Galloway v Hallé Concerts Society* [1915] 2 Ch 233. See further, as to directors' duties, Chapter 16.

8   Companies Act 1985, section 14(2) and Insolvency Act 1986, section 80.

any time within 12 years of the date of the call.[1] In Scotland, five years is the equivalent period.[2]

Table A provides that calls in arrear shall bear interest.[3] Any dividends becoming payable upon the shares of defaulting members should be retained by the company, and in addition any rights of lien[4] or refusal to register a transfer of the shares[5] exercised. As a last resort (if the articles give the power) the shares should be forfeited.[6]

8.11 Liens on shares

Articles[7] generally give a company a lien on the shares of a member for the calls or any debts as are due to the company from such member. Such a lien is valid so far as private companies are concerned.[8] It can generally be enforced by sale[9] or forfeiture[10] of the shares concerned.[11]

As far as public companies are concerned, section 150 of the Companies Act 1985 restricts their right to take liens or other charges on their shares. Section 150(1) provides that a lien or other charge of a public company is void unless permitted by the section.[12] This permits only the following categories of lien or charge:

(1) in respect of any public company, a charge on partly paid shares for any amount payable in respect of the shares;
(2) in respect of a public company whose ordinary business includes the lending of money or consists of the provision of credit or the bailment or (in Scotland) hiring of goods under a hire-purchase agreement, or both, a charge on any of its shares, fully or partly paid, which arises in connection with a transaction entered into by the company in the ordinary course of its business;
(3) in respect of a company which is re-registered as a public company or registered under section 680[13] as a public company, a charge on its own shares in existence immediately before its application for re-registration or registration.

---

1   Limitation Act 1980, section 8.
2   Prescription and Limitation (Scotland) Act 1973.
3   Article 15.
4   See **8.11**.
5   See **9.3**.
6   See **8.15**.
7   See eg Table A, article 8, in which a lien for calls or other moneys payable on the shares is given in respect of partly paid shares. Under the *Listing Rules*, the articles of a company seeking quotation must not provide for any lien on fully paid shares.
8   *Bradford Banking Co Ltd v Henry Briggs & Co Ltd* (1886) 12 App Cas 29 (HL); *Bank of Africa Ltd v Salisbury Gold Mining Co* [1892] AC 281 (PC).
9   See eg in Table A, articles 9–11.
10   See **8.15**.
11   For more detail on liens, see *Gore-Browne on Companies* 44th edn (Jordans, loose-leaf) at 14.11 *et seq*.
12   Or by section 6 of the Companies Consolidation (Consequential Provisions) Act 1985, which concerns 'old public companies', that is pre-1980 public companies which have not re-registered. See generally, *Gore-Browne on Companies* 44th edn (Jordans, loose-leaf) at 7.10–7.10.3. *Quaere* whether there are any left.
13   These are old (pre-1862) joint-stock companies.

8.12 The reorganisation of capital

A company may reorganise its capital structure in various ways.

(1) It may increase its capital.
(2) It may reduce its capital.
(3) It may enforce forfeitures of shares and, under certain conditions, accept surrenders.
(4) It may consolidate its shares into shares of larger amount, and convert its paid-up shares into stock, and subsequently reconvert the stock into shares.
(5) It may subdivide its shares.

The Company Law Review[1] recommended changes to the law governing reorganisations of capital. These are considered further at **8.17**.

8.13 Increase of capital

The 'capital' referred to here is the nominal capital authorised by the memorandum of association, and must not be confused with the issued capital or the paid-up capital. It follows that to make an issue of shares already authorised, or to make a call upon the shares already issued, would increase the issued share capital or the paid-up capital respectively, but neither proceeding would be such an increase of capital as to fall within the provisions of the Companies Act described below.

By virtue of section 121 of the Companies Act 1985, a company limited by shares, or a company limited by guarantee and having a share capital, may, if authorised by its articles,[2] increase its share capital by new shares of such amount as it thinks expedient.[3] The increase must be effected by the company in general meeting.[4] The nature of the resolution – whether special, extraordinary, or ordinary – may be prescribed by the articles. If it is not, an ordinary resolution suffices. Notice of the increase must be given in the prescribed form to the Registrar of Companies within 15 days after the passing of the resolution authorising the increase.[5]

8.14 Reduction of capital

The provisions as to reduction of capital are set out in sections 135 to 141 of the Companies Act 1985.

Under section 135, a company limited by shares or a company limited by guarantee and having a share capital,[6] may, if authorised by its articles, by passing

---

1   See generally, **1.7** and Chapter 22.
2   See eg Table A, article 32.
3   Section 121(1) and (2)(a).
4   Section 121(4).
5   Section 123.
6   An unlimited company may reduce capital at will, without the confirmation of the court being required, as long as there is power in the articles: *Re Borough Commercial and Building Society* [1893] 2 Ch 242.

a special resolution[1] and obtaining the sanction of the court,[2] reduce its share capital 'in any way'. The words 'in any way' indicate that the power to reduce capital is unlimited, but section 135(2) gives also special instances, providing expressly that such a company may:

(1) extinguish or reduce the liability on any of its shares in respect of share capital not paid up; or

(2) either with or without extinguishing or reducing liability on any of its shares, cancel any paid-up share capital which is lost or unrepresented by available assets; or

(3) either with or without extinguishing or reducing liability on any of its shares, pay off any paid-up share capital which is in excess of the wants of the company.

A further common use of the power to reduce capital is to reduce the share premium account. In addition, a company may take power under section 121(2)(e) to cancel shares which at the date of the passing of the relevant resolution have not been taken or agreed to be taken by any person and to diminish the amount of share capital to that extent; it may take power to issue redeemable shares and to purchase its own shares subject to the conditions of Chapter VII of Part V of the Act.[3] The fact that a private company can in certain circumstances purchase its own shares out of capital provides in effect for a much easier procedure for reducing capital. However, none of these measures is deemed to be a reduction of share capital within the meaning of the Act.[4] The court has power to make an order for reduction of capital under section 461.[5]

Section 135 deals with the reduction of *share capital,* so that, in cases under (3) above, a reduction may be confirmed, although the money to make the payment off is to be borrowed,[6] and even if it is to be borrowed (eg on the security of debentures) from the very persons whose shares are to be reduced.[7] The amounts by which the share capital is to be reduced may be satisfied by the distribution of assets in specie even though the value of those assets may exceed the nominal amount by which the share capital is reduced.[8]

8.14.1 *Matters incidental to a reduction*

In the course of reducing its capital with the court's confirmation, a company may do things which would otherwise be illegal, such as repurchasing its own shares.[9] A reduction may also be confirmed even though its purpose is one not apparently

1   The requirement for a special resolution is not usually displaced by the unanimous agreement of all the shareholders: *Re Barry Artist Ltd* [1985] BCLC 283, but a private company can use the statutory written resolution procedure; see **13.4**. The court can correct a trivial error in the resolution: *Re Willaire Systems plc* [1986] BCLC 67.

2   The court can confirm a reduction of capital which does not actually exist, provided that the resolution is conditional on other resolutions which will increase the capital to the necessary amount: *Re TIP-Europe Ltd* (1987) 3 BCC 647.

3   See **7.17** *et seq.*

4   See sections 121(5) and 160(4).

5   See **17.14**.

6   *Re Nixon's Navigation Co* [1897] 1 Ch 872.

7   *Re Thomas de la Rue & Co Ltd* [1911] 2 Ch 361.

8   *Ex parte Westburn Sugar Refineries Ltd* [1951] AC 625 (HL (Sc)).

9   *British and American Trustee Corp v Couper* [1894] AC 399 (HL); of course it is not now always illegal to do so: see **7.17.2**.

contemplated by the section provided that it has a discernible purpose; for example, where the company has ceased to carry on business and the only aim of the reduction is to distribute the assets,[1] where a holding company wishes to reduce its share premium account in order to eliminate goodwill arising on consolidation of the group's accounts,[2] where a subsidiary company wishes to cancel its share premium account to increase its distributable reserves and produce a tax advantage for its holding company,[3] or where the company wishes to convert ordinary shares into redeemable deferred shares.[4]

8.14.2 Matters relevant to confirmation

Once provision has, where relevant, been made for creditors,[5] the court's attitude to confirming a reduction of capital depends on three factors:

(1) that the reduction is fair and equitable between the different classes of shareholders in the company, where there is more than one class;

(2) that the proposal affects all shareholders of the same class in a similar manner, unless those treated differently have consented to it; and

(3) that the causes of the reduction were properly put to shareholders so that they could exercise an informed choice and that the cause is proved by evidence before the court.[6]

8.14.3 Shareholders' class rights

The first two of these factors have traditionally posed the most problems and merit examination here. There is no general rule that a reduction of capital must bear equally upon all the shares of the company, or even upon all the shares in a particular class, and reductions have been confirmed as fair and equitable where only some of the shares in a particular class have been wholly or partly paid off[7] or

---

1   See *Scottish Insurance Co Ltd v Wilsons & Clyde Coal Co Ltd* [1949] AC 462 (HL (Sc)).

2   *Re Ratners Group plc* (1988) 4 BCC 293; *Re Thorn EMI plc* (1988) 4 BCC 698.

3   *Re Ransomes plc* [1999] 1 BCLC 775. On appeal ([1999] 2 BCLC 591), the decision was confirmed even though, subsequently to the decision at first instance, the company no longer wished to distribute the reserve so created. The case had become 'very unusual' (at 603).

4   *Forth Wines Ltd, Petitioner* [1991] BCC 638.

5   As to creditors, see **8.14.5.**

6   See the *dictum* of Harman J in *Re Jupiter House Investments (Cambridge) Ltd* [1985] BCLC 222, 224. This *dictum* actually omits the first factor, but its importance is well established by the cases cited in the next section. See also *Re Ratners Group plc* (1988) 4 BCC 293 and *Re Thorn EMI plc* (1988) 4 BCC 698, requiring that all shareholders be treated 'equitably'. Note that Harman J expressed disapproval of *dicta* to the effect that the public interest, in terms of people who might become shareholders in the future, was a relevant factor (*per* Lord Macnaghten in *Poole v National Bank of China Ltd* [1907] AC 229 at 239 (HL)); see also *Re Grosvenor Press plc* [1985] BCLC 286 at 290–291. It was clear, previously, that the public interest, if relevant, did not extend to the interests of the community at large: *Ex parte Westburn Sugar Refineries Ltd* [1951] AC 625 (HL). As regards the third factor, although the court has recently forgiven a less than full explanation where the matter was urgent and it was satisfied as to the substantive fairness of the scheme, it was stated that 'no company would be well advised to follow [this] course ... if it has any minority shareholders on whose agreement it cannot count': *Re Ransomes plc* [1999] 1 BCLC 775 at 786. See also [1999] 2 BCLC 591 at 599–600 (CA).

7   Eg *British and American Trustee Corporation v Couper*, above; *Re Robert Stephen Holdings Ltd* [1968] 1 WLR 522 (but note that in this case the court suggested that a scheme of arrangement under section 425 would have been a more appropriate procedure, because minority interests would have been better protected thereby).

cancelled.[1] Where, however, different shareholders or classes of shareholders have different rights as to return of capital on a winding-up, there is a *prima facie* rule that a reduction of capital should be framed so as to conform with these rights, unless consent is obtained from the particular shareholders or classes of shareholders whose rights are prejudiced.[2]

The most important instance of this rule is that where there are preference shares having priority as to return of capital (but no rights of further participation in surplus assets) and there are ordinary shares as well, then in a reduction involving a return of capital in excess of the company's wants, the preference shares should be paid off first,[3] whereas in a reduction involving partial or total cancellation of shares on account of losses, it is the ordinary shares that should first be cancelled.[4] Sometimes the preference shareholders in a prosperous company may feel aggrieved at losing a favourable investment through being thus paid off at par in advance of the ordinary shareholders, but this of itself gives them no legal grounds of objection,[5] not even if under the articles they had a right of participation in distribution of surplus profits by way of dividend.[6] It is only when they have clearly defined[7] rights of participation in surplus assets on a winding-up (whether under the memorandum or articles or terms of issue, or under some special statutory provision),[8] or (perhaps) where there is an independent agreement between them and the company that capital will not be reduced without their consent,[9] that they can raise the objection that their rights are not being strictly observed. This vulnerability of preference shareholders who have no such rights of participation is sometimes overcome in quoted companies by the use of the so-called 'Spens formula', namely a provision in the memorandum or articles or terms of issue that where preference shares are paid off, the price should be tied to the quoted market value at the time and the preference shareholders should have voting rights on the resolution for reduction. An alternative method of protection is to provide that any reduction of capital is deemed to be a variation of class rights, so that the special procedure described in **8.7.3** must be complied with.[10]

---

1   Eg *Re Gatling Gun Ltd* (1890) 43 Ch D 628; *Re Pinkney & Sons Steamship Co* [1892] 3 Ch 125.

2   *Bannatyne v Direct Spanish Telegraph Co* (1887) 34 Ch D 287 at 300 (CA).

3   *Re Chatterley-Whitfield Collieries Ltd* [1948] 2 All ER 593 at 596 (CA) affirmed sub nom *Prudential Assurance Co Ltd v Chatterley-Whitfield Collieries Ltd* [1949] AC 512 (HL); *Re Saltdean Estate Co Ltd* [1969] 1 WLR 1844; *House of Fraser plc v ACGE Investments* [1987] AC 387 (HL) and see *Scottish Insurance Corporation Ltd v Wilsons & Clyde Coal Co Ltd* [1949] AC 462 (HL (Sc)).

4   *Re Floating Dock Co of St Thomas Ltd* [1895] 1 Ch 691; *Re London and New York Investment Corporation* [1895] 2 Ch 860; *Poole v National Bank of China Ltd* [1907] AC 229 (HL).

5   *Scottish Insurance Corporation Ltd v Wilsons & Clyde Coal Co Ltd*, above.

6   *Re Saltdean Estate Co Ltd*, above; *House of Fraser plc v ACGE Investments*, above.

7   Inchoate rights (eg an expectation of compensation under the Coal Industry Nationalisation Act 1946, section 25) will not suffice: *Scottish Insurance Corp Ltd v Wilson & Clyde Coal Co Ltd*, above; *Prudential Assurance Co Ltd v Chatterley-Whitfield Collieries Ltd* [1949] AC 512 (HL).

8   Eg where their expectation of compensation under the Coal Industry Nationalisation Act 1946, section 25, has been confirmed by resolution, as in *Re Old Silkstone Collieries Ltd* [1954] Ch 169 (CA).

9   See ibid.

10   *Re Northern Engineering Industries plc* [1993] BCC 267.

8.14.4 Reduction not in accordance with class rights

In certain cases, the courts were prepared to confirm reductions that did not accord with class rights on a winding-up, even though the consent of the shareholders or classes affected had not been obtained. In such a case, however, the onus lay on the company to prove that the reduction was fair and equitable, and the court would examine its terms and effect with particular care.[1] It appears that this is no longer permissible owing to the provisions of section 125, providing that any variation of class rights in connection with a reduction of capital must be sanctioned by a three-quarters majority of the class.[2]

Even if the variation procedure has *prima facie* been complied with, the court can still disallow the variation and hence the reduction if the variation was improper. In one case,[3] the court refused to confirm a reduction whereby redeemable preference shares were cancelled and the holders received an equivalent amount of unsecured loan stock, it being conceded by the company that this entailed a modification of the class rights of the preference shareholders. The court found: (a) that the resolution for class consent was ineffectual because the majority had not voted with a view to the interests of the class; and (b) that, having regard to the terms of issue of the loan stock, the reduction had not been shown by the company to be fair and equitable.

Where class consent is obtained (which may be done under section 125, a 'modification of rights clause' or under an accompanying scheme of arrangement under section 425),[4] class rights may on a reduction be changed or overridden to a substantial degree: for example, the preference shareholders may agree to surrender their priority as to capital[5] or to forgo arrears of cumulative preferential dividend,[6] or the voting powers of the respective classes may be altered,[7] or the reduction may be accompanied by other arrangements reconstituting for the future the class rights of the different classes.[8]

8.14.5 Rights of creditors

Under section 136, if a reduction involves any diminution of liability or any repayment of capital, and in any other case if the court so directs, creditors are entitled to object. The court can, however, under section 136(6), dispense with creditors' rights and will generally do so if there is obtained a guarantee of their debts from a bank or if satisfied that the company has cash and liquid assets exceeding the claims of the creditors and the amount of the capital to be returned.

A typical 'other case' where the rights of creditors are relevant is where a company is reducing capital in order to write off a loss, but the loss is not expected

---

1   *British and American Trustee Corp v Couper* [1894] AC 399 at p 406 (HL); *Carruth v Imperial Chemical Industries Ltd* [1937] AC 707 at 744 and 749 (HL); *Re Holders Investment Trust Ltd* [1971] 1 WLR 583.
2   As to section 125 in more detail, see **8.7.3**.
3   Re *Holders Investment Trust Ltd*, above.
4   As to section 425 see **19.18**.
5   *Re Hyderabad (Deccan) Co Ltd* (1897) 75 LT 23; *Re National Dwellings Society Ltd* (1898) 78 LT 144; *Balmenach Glenlivet Distillery Ltd v Croall* (1907) 8 F 1135.
6   *Oban and Aultmore Glenlivet Distillery Ltd* (1904) 5 F 1141.
7   *Re James Colmer Ltd* [1898] 1 Ch 524.
8   *Re Allsopp & Sons Ltd* (1903) 51 WR 644 (CA); *Re Welsbach Incandescent Gas Light Co Ltd* [1904] 1 Ch 87 (CA).

to be permanent, for example because the company has acquired a loss-making business which it is hoped will prove profitable in the future.[1] Here the reduction will be confirmed if the company undertakes to put into a capital fund not available for distribution any money received in respect of the business up to the amount of the reduction.[2]

If the rights of creditors are not dispensed with, section 137 requires the court to be satisfied on the hearing of the petition to confirm the reduction with respect to every creditor that either: (a) his consent to the reduction has been obtained; or (b) his debt or claim has been discharged or determined, or has been secured by setting apart and appropriating, in such manner as the court may direct, a sufficient sum.[3]

8.14.6 *Procedure on a reduction of capital*

Detailed consideration of the procedure involved in the presentation of a petition to confirm a reduction of capital is unnecessary here.[4] If the court sanctions the reduction, the order and a minute, approved by the court, showing the particulars of the capital as reduced must be registered with the Registrar,[5] and notice of this registration must be published in such manner as the court directs. The reduction does not take effect until the registration has been carried out.[6] The Registrar then certifies the registration and his certificate is conclusive evidence that all the requirements of the Act have been complied with, and that the capital is as stated in the minute.[7] All future copies of the memorandum must contain the minute, which on registration is deemed to form part thereof,[8] in substitution for the original statement of the capital of the company.[9]

The court can require the company to publish the reasons for the reduction,[10] but rarely does so.

8.15 Forfeiture and surrender of shares

A forfeiture or surrender of shares is a reduction of capital and in consequence cannot usually be carried out without the confirmation of the court under section 135. It is, however, established that without such confirmation shares may be forfeited, but only for non-payment of calls and provided it is done under an

---

1   See *Re Jupiter House Investments (Cambridge) Ltd* [1985] BCLC 222 and *Re Grosvenor Press plc* [1985] BCLC 286, which illustrate that using the reduction procedure in this way can increase the amount of profits available for distribution under section 239 (as to which, see **7.21** *et seq.*).

2   Ibid. These authorities also make it clear that the interests of future creditors are irrelevant.

3   For more detail as to procedure in respect of creditors, see *Gore-Browne on Companies* 44th edn (Jordans, loose-leaf) at 15.3.8. Note also the provisions of section 140 whereby a creditor ignorant of the reduction and who did not therefore object to it, may be entitled if the company is wound up insolvent, to receive payment from the shareholders whose shares were reduced up to the amount of the reduction.

4   See *Gore-Browne on Companies* at 15.3.7–15.3.11.

5   Section 138(1) and (3).

6   Section 138(2).

7   Section 138(4).

8   Section 138(5).

9   Section 138(6). This constitutes an alteration of the memorandum within the meaning of section 20.

10   Section 137(2).

express power in the articles.[1] In cases where such a forfeiture would be permissible, the shares may be validly surrendered.[2] A company's articles may be altered so as to introduce a power of forfeiture,[3] subject to the general limitations upon alteration of articles.[4]

Where shares are forfeited in the absence of any such authorisation in the articles, or in a manner falling outside the relevant clause thereof, the forfeiture is invalid and cannot be ratified, even by a majority of shareholders.[5]

By the same token, a surrender of partly paid shares in circumstances not justifying a forfeiture is invalid, because the shareholder is purportedly released from his liability for uncalled capital.[6] A voluntary surrender of fully paid shares in such circumstances may perhaps be valid if it is authorised by the articles and new shares are issued in exchange so as to prevent diminution of the company's capital.[7] A surrender in return for any other form of valuable consideration is clearly invalid as being in substance a purchase by the company of its own shares.[8] On the other hand, a voluntary transfer of fully paid shares to a nominee to hold them as trustee for the benefit of the company is valid. In such a case, the company pays nothing for the shares, and its capital is not reduced.[9]

The procedure specified by the articles for forfeiture must be strictly complied with,[10] and directors must exercise the power for a proper purpose, not, for example, simply to get rid of an obnoxious shareholder.[11]

If a forfeiture is invalid, the invalidity is not cured by lapse of time and the holder remains a member of the company as regards both liabilities and rights.[12]

8.15.1 Reissue of forfeited shares

The company usually has power to reissue forfeited shares (eg under Table A, article 20)[13] and on such reissue may treat them as paid up to any extent not exceeding the amount paid by the former holders. If in exercise of this power it reissues shares irregularly forfeited, it may be liable in damages to the original holder.[14] When forfeited shares have been reissued, the company may make a

---

1   *Lane's Case* (1862) 1 De GJ & Sm 504; *Kipong v Todd* (1878) 3 CPD 350 (CA). See Table A, articles 18–22 permitting forfeiture and note the extended meaning of 'call' under Table A; see **8.10**.

2   *Trevor v Whitworth* (1887) 12 App Cas 409 at 417, 429, 438 (HL).

3   *Dawkins v Antrobus* (1881) 17 Ch D 615 (CA).

4   See **5.24**.

5   *Spackman v Evans* (1868) LR 3 HL 171; *Houldsworth v Evans* (1868) LR 3 HL 263.

6   *Bellerby v Rowland and Marwood's Steamship Co Ltd* [1902] 2 Ch 14 (CA).

7   *Re County Palatine Loan & Discount Co Teasdale's case* (1873) 9 Ch App 54.

8   *Trevor v Whitworth* (1887) 12 App Cas 409 at 438 (HL).

9   *Kirby v Wilkins* [1929] 2 Ch 444. See further **7.16**. However, as far as public companies are concerned, the consequences of a lawful acquisition by a nominee are the same as those of a forfeiture, by virtue of sections 146 to 149. See **8.15.2**.

10 See eg *Johnson v Lyttle's Iron Agency* (1877) 5 Ch D 687.

11 As to directors' duty to act for the proper purpose, see **16.5**.

12 *Garden Gully United Quartz Mining Co v McLister* (1875) 1 App Cas 39. However, a shareholder may be precluded from setting aside a forfeiture after acquiescing in it over a long period: *Jones v North Vancouver Land and Improvement Co* [1910] AC 317.

13 A public company is in effect obliged to reissue them by virtue of section 146, described in **8.15.2**.

14 *Re New Chile Gold Mining Co* (1890) 45 Ch D 598.

fresh call upon the new holder in respect of the amount remaining unpaid by the former holder upon which the forfeiture was made.[1]

8.15.2 Treatment of forfeited and surrendered shares in public companies

By section 146, shares in public companies[2] which are forfeited or surrendered for failure to pay calls and shares which are subject to the other circumstances described below are subject to a special regime. The other circumstances are:

(1) where shares in the company are acquired by the company other than as a result of a redemption or purchase under Chapter VII of Part V,[3] or a reduction of capital,[4] or of a court order under the various provisions whereby the court can order a company to purchase its own shares[5] and it has a beneficial interest[6] in them;

(2) where the nominee of the company acquires shares in the company from a third person without financial assistance being given directly or indirectly by the company and the company has a beneficial interest[7] in those shares;[8]

(3) where any person acquires shares in the company with financial assistance given to him directly or indirectly by the company for the purpose of or in connection with the acquisition[9] and the company has a beneficial interest in those shares.[10]

If such shares are not disposed of within the relevant period of the date of forfeiture, surrender or acquisition, the company must cancel them and diminish the amount of its share capital by the nominal value of the shares concerned and, where the effect of the cancellation will be to bring the level of the company's allotted share capital below the authorised minimum,[11] apply for re-registration as a private company, stating the effect of the cancellation.[12] The relevant period in all cases except that described in paragraph (3) above is three years. In the cases of shares acquired in the circumstances described in paragraph (3), it is one year.[13] In addition, shares forfeited, surrendered or acquired in these circumstances cannot carry voting rights.[14] Failure to comply with either of the requirements

---

1   *New Balkis Eersteling Ltd v Randt Gold Mining Co* [1904] AC 165 (HL) but any payment by the former holder goes to reduce this amount (*Re Randt Gold Mining Co* [1904] 2 Ch 468) and, conversely, any payment by the new holder reduces the debt of the former holder (*Re Bolton* [1930] 2 Ch 48).

2   Where a private company is re-registered as a public company (see **3.11**), and shares in it have been forfeited, surrendered or otherwise acquired in circumstances to which section 146 applies, the provisions of the section apply, the relevant period for disposal or cancellation of the shares (see below) commencing with the date of re-registration; section 148.

3   See **7.17** *et seq.*

4   See **8.14** *et seq.*

5   That is, section 5 (see **6.16**); section 54 (see **4.13**); and section 461 (see **17.12.1**).

6   'Beneficial interest' is subject to the qualifications in Schedule 2; see *Gore-Browne on Companies* 44th edn (Jordans, loose-leaf) at 15.4.6.

7   See footnote 6, above.

8   On the acquisition of shares by a nominee, see **7.16**.

9   See **7.18**.

10   Section 146(1).

11   See **4.2**.

12   Section 146(3).

13   Section 146(3).

14   Section 146(4).

mentioned renders the company and every officer in default liable to a fine.[1] Failure to comply with the requirement to apply to be re-registered as a private company within the relevant period means that the company is treated as a private company for the purpose of section 81;[2] ie it is unable to offer its securities to the public, but otherwise it continues to be treated as a public company until it is re-registered.[3]

The cancellation procedure required may be effected by a resolution of the directors of the company without complying with the statutory procedures for a reduction of capital under sections 135 and 136[4] and a resolution of the directors can alter the memorandum of the company so that it no longer states that it is to be a public company and so as to make such other alterations as are required.[5]

Where a public company or its nominee acquires shares or an interest in shares in the company, and those shares or that interest are shown in a balance sheet of the company as an asset, an amount equal to the value of the shares or the interest must be transferred out of profits available for dividend[6] to a reserve fund and is not available for distribution.[7]

8.16   Other capital alterations

'If so authorised by its articles', a company limited by shares or a company limited by guarantee and having a share capital can under section 121(2) of the Companies Act 1985 consolidate and divide all or any of its share capital into shares of larger amount than its existing shares, convert all or any of its paid-up shares into stock and reconvert that stock into paid-up shares of any denomination or subdivide its shares into shares of a smaller amount. The power must be exercised by the company in general meeting.[8] Every copy of the memorandum issued thereafter must be in accordance with the alteration.[9] Notice of any such consolidation or conversion or of any reconversion must be given to the Registrar of Companies[10] on the proper form.

Stock is 'simply a set of shares put together in a bundle'.[11] It is in fact the holding of the stockholder expressed in pounds instead of in so many shares of so much each. Unless forbidden by the articles any fraction may be transferred, but it is usual to provide that the directors may fix the minimum amount of stock transferable, which minimum, however, is not to exceed the nominal amount of the shares from which the stock arose.

It should be noted that a company cannot make an original issue of stock. If it desires to have a capital held as stock it must first issue shares, and only when they

---

1   Section 149(2).
2   See **18.3**.
3   Section 149(1).
4   Section 147(1). As to these, see **8.14** *et seq.*
5   Section 147(2). If the requirement to apply for re-registration applies, the conditions of section 147(3) and (4) must be complied with.
6   See **7.21.2**.
7   Section 148(4).
8   The form of resolution required depends on the articles, but a private company can use the statutory written resolution procedure.
9   Section 20.
10   Section 122.
11   *Morrice v Aylmer* (1875) LR 7 HL 717 at 725, *per* Lord Hatherley.

are fully paid convert them into stock. Conversion of shares into stock is a very rare phenomenon these days.

8.17   Reform of the law on reorganisations of capital

The Company Law Review Steering Group recommended a number of changes to the law described in the latter part of this chapter, which were accepted by the Government.[1] The provisions described in **8.16** will be retained, except where they become unnecessary as a consequence of other changes. So, for example, the proposed abolition of the concept of authorised capital will remove the need for power to alter it and to cancel unissued capital. It is also thought that the power to convert shares into stock and vice versa will be obsolete.

A radical change to the provisions on reduction of capital is envisaged. The requirement to seek court approval would disappear. Private companies would be able to reduce capital by special resolution, provided that the directors made a formal declaration of solvency.[2] Public companies would *prima facie* observe the same procedure but, in order to satisfy the Second EC Directive on Company Law, any creditor would have the right to object to the court in respect of any reduction.[3] The grounds for objection would be that the proposed reduction did not offer security or other safeguards for the debt and that the level of the company's assets made this necessary.[4] A public company would have to give public notice of the passing of the resolution to reduce capital.[5] If provisions along these lines are enacted, the result will be a significant simplification of an area of company law that in practical terms is quite complex and time-consuming. It would seem that creditors' rights would be sufficiently protected, and shareholders would retain the right to object to a reduction which was not in accordance with their class rights by virtue of the general protection of such rights discussed earlier in this chapter.[6]

---

1   *Modernising Company Law*, Cm 5553, July 2002. As to other possible changes to the law on share capital, see **7.25**.
2   Clause 51 of the draft Companies Bill.
3   Clause 54 of the draft Companies Bill.
4   Clause 56 of the draft Companies Bill.
5   Clause 52(3) of the draft Companies Bill.
6   See **8.7–8.7.5**.

Chapter 9

Transfer and Transmission of Shares

9.1 The transfer of shares

The original allottee of the shares of a company remains personally entitled to the benefits and subject to the obligations of the shares until he has disposed of them either:

(1) by transfer;
(2) by death or bankruptcy;
(3) by forfeiture or surrender; or
(4) on a reduction of capital or other form of capital reorganisation.

The last two processes have been considered in the previous chapter. The first two, which are commonly referred to as 'the transfer and transmission of shares', will be dealt with in this chapter. In cases of transfer the transferee takes the place of the transferor, and in cases of transmission the estate of the former holder takes his place as regards benefits and liabilities.

It should be noted that, unless the contrary is provided, the term 'transfer' in a company's articles refers only to a transfer of the legal title to shares, that is the registered membership,[1] and not to transfer of an equitable interest.[2] This can have important consequences as regards restrictions on the transfer of shares, as will be discussed in the following sections.

The legal technique by which shares are transferred is novation.[3] Strictly speaking, it is inaccurate to refer to shares being 'transferred' by novation, as the process of novation establishes a new contract (the 'statutory contract' created by section 14 of the Companies Act 1985) as between a company and a (new) member and as between the new member and existing members. But the economic effect of novation is similar to transfer as the old and new contract are on the same terms.[4] A purchaser of shares becomes a member by being entered in the company register of members[5] and thereby becomes a party to the statutory contract. This process differs from assignment (the legal technique by which unregistered securities are transferred) in that novation extinguishes the old and creates a new contract, whereas an assignee takes legal title from an assignor subject to equities.[6]

---

1   As to the register of members, see Chapter 12 below.
2   *Theakston v London plc* [1984] BCLC 390. As to the consequences of this, see **9.2.2**; neither an allotment nor the renunciation of an allotment of shares is a transfer of them: *System Control plc v Munro Corporate plc* [1990] BCLC 659 at 662–663.
3   Novation is a general principle of contract law: see *Chitty on Contracts* (28th edn. London: Sweet & Maxwell 1999) paragraph 20–086, 1067.
4   See generally J Benjamin, *Interests in Securities* (OUP 2000) paragraph 2.04.
5   Section 22. See in respect of dematerialised securities **9.3.3**.
6   Although equitable interests in property are not recognised in Scotland, a similar distinction can be drawn between novation and assignation as an assignee takes legal rights subject to the principle *assignatus utitur jure auctoris*.

9.2 Transferability of shares

Subject to certain limited restrictions imposed by law,[1] a shareholder has *prima facie* the right to transfer his shares when and to whom he pleases.[2] This freedom to transfer may, however, be significantly curtailed by provisions in the articles. Restricting provisions are legal;[3] on the other hand, the transfer of fully paid listed shares must not be restricted by the articles in any way.[4] In determining the extent of any restriction on transfer contained in the articles, a strict construction is adopted; that is to say, the restriction must be set out expressly, or must arise by necessary implication, and any ambiguous provision is construed in favour of the shareholder wishing to transfer.[5]

Two common forms of restriction found in articles of association are: (a) provisions that the board of directors should have a power, general or limited in scope, to refuse to register transfers as they should deem fit; and (b) pre-emption clauses, ie provisions that a member wishing to transfer should first offer his shares to other specified persons, such as the directors or the other members. These two forms of restriction will now be discussed in turn, although it must be borne in mind that many other forms of restriction exist as well.

9.2.1 Power to refuse registration

Any discretionary power vested in the directors to refuse to register transfers of shares is a fiduciary power, which must be exercised *bona fide* in what the directors conceive to be the interests of the company.[6] If the transferor can show that the directors have acted wantonly or capriciously or from an improper motive or with a collateral purpose in refusing to register the transfer, the court will order the transfer to be registered.[7] Evidence that the directors were acting upon undertakings given to outsiders would be evidence that their discretion was being improperly exercised,[8] as too would evidence that they had an explicit policy of refusing to allow a particular shareholder to transfer his shares to anyone.[9]

If the directors, having a general and absolute power of refusal, decide to reject a transfer, the court will not interfere provided the requirements as to *bona fides* are satisfied.[10] Furthermore, it will not compel the directors to state their reasons for the rejection.[11] But the power will be construed strictly, in the sense that in the absence of clear words it will not be held to authorise the directors to refuse to

---

1   These are briefly discussed at **9.2.4**.
2   *Re Smith Knight & Co, Weston's Case* (1868) 4 Ch App 20: *Re Bede Steam Shipping Co* [1917] 1 Ch 123 at 132–133 (CA).
3   Since 1980 there has not been any obligation on private companies (as existed previously) to restrict the right of transfer, although restrictions of the sort discussed below are still usual. Article 24 of Table A restricts certain transfers, including transfers of partly paid shares.
4   *Listing Rules*, Chapter 3, paragraph 3.15. This rule does not prohibit the imposition of purely formal requirements as to transfer.
5   *Re Smith & Fawcett Ltd* [1942] Ch 304 at 306 (CA); *Moodie v W & J Shepherd (Bookbinders) Ltd* [1949] 2 All ER 1044 (HL (Sc)).
6   *Re Smith & Fawcett Ltd* [1942] Ch 304 (CA); and see **16.4**.
7   *Ex parte Penney* (1873) 8 Ch App 446; *Re Coalport China Co* [1895] 2 Ch 404 (CA).
8   *Clark v Workman* [1920] 1 Ir R 107.
9   *Robinson v Chartered Bank* (1865) LR 1 Eq 32.
10 *Re Smith & Fawcett Ltd* [1942] Ch 304 (CA); *Charles Forte Investments Ltd v Amanda* [1964] Ch 240 (CA); *Village Cay Marina Ltd v Acland* [1998] 2 BCLC 327 (PC).
11 *Ex parte Penney* (1873) 8 Ch App 446; *Berry v Tottenham Hotspur Football and Athletic Co Ltd* [1935] Ch 718.

register the executor of a deceased member on a transmission[1] or, in the case of shares being issued to members with a right to renounce, a person to whom a member has duly renounced his right to subscribe.[2] Neither of these transactions involves a 'transfer' strictly so-called.

Where the board's power of refusal is limited to grounds specified in the articles, the board's reasons for a particular refusal are again not examinable.[3] The court is, however, concerned to see that the refusal really is based on at least one of the specified grounds; accordingly, unless the articles stipulate otherwise,[4] the directors may be compelled to identify the particular ground on which their decision to refuse is based.[5] In general, the rule of strict construction applies again. Thus, if the directors' power is expressed to be a right to refuse to register a transfer to a person of whom they do not approve, or whose membership would, in their opinion, be contrary to the interests of the company, their objection must be to something personal to the transferee (for instance, that he cannot pay calls or is a quarrelsome person, or is acting in the interests of a rival business), and if their refusal is on the ground of something which relates only to the transferor (such as that the transfer is made only to increase his voting power), or is on the ground that the directors desire that only members of a particular family should be shareholders, or that there should not be a number of small holdings, this is in excess of the power, and the court will order registration of the transfer.[6]

Unless the articles expressly make the directors' approval of transfers a condition precedent to their registration, a transfer fails only if there is a positive decision by the directors to reject it; thus if the directors are equally divided on the matter, or there is no board at all, the transfer is entitled to registration.[7] The same applies if a decision is not reached within a reasonable time after lodgment of transfer[8] and since section 183(5) of the Companies Act 1985 requires that any company refusing to register a transfer must notify the transferee accordingly within two months of lodgment, it will normally be safe to say that once the two-month period has elapsed, the transfer can no longer be rejected.[9] However, if a proper decision to refuse to register a transfer is taken, a failure to communicate that decision within the two-month period does not render the transfer void.[10] Subject to these rules, mere silence on the part of the directors does not amount to acquiescence in the transfer.[11]

---

1   See *Re Bentham Mills Spinning Co* (1879) 11 Ch D 90 (CA).
2   *Re Pool Shipping Co Ltd* [1920] 1 Ch 251.
3   *Re Coalport China Co* [1895] 2 Ch 404 (CA).
4   *Berry v Tottenham Hotspur Football and Athletic Co Ltd* [1935] Ch 718.
5   *Sutherland v British Dominions Land Settlement Corp* [1926] Ch 746.
6   These instances are taken from *Moffat v Farquhar* (1878) 7 Ch D 591; *Re Bell Brothers Ltd* (1891) 65 LT 245; *Re Bede Steam Shipping Co* [1917] 1 Ch 123 (CA).
7   See three cases on transmission: *Re Hackney Pavilion Ltd* [1924] 1 Ch 276; *Moodie v W & J Shepherd (Bookbinders) Ltd* [1949] 2 All ER 1044 (Sc); *Re New Cedos Engineering Co Ltd* [1994] 1 BCLC 797.
8   *Re Joint Discount Co, Shepherd's Case* (1866) 2 Ch App 16.
9   *Re Swaledale Cleaners Ltd* [1968] 1 WLR 1710 (CA); *Tett v Phoenix Property and Investment Co Ltd* [1984] BCLC 599; *Re Inverdeck Ltd* [1998] BCC 256. During the two-month period, the transferee has no rights, even if the company has no directors to exercise the right of refusal: *Re Zinotty Properties Ltd* [1984] 1 WLR 1249.
10   *Popely v Planarrive Ltd* [1997] 1 BCLC 8.
11   *Re European Central Rly Co, Gustard's Case* (1868) LR 8 Eq 468.

9.2.2 Pre-emption clauses

Pre-emption clauses constitute valid restrictions upon the transfer of shares.[1] They are enforceable against individual members by the company[2] and by the persons upon whom the rights of pre-emption are bestowed, at least if they are members of the company.[3] A pre-emption clause will be strictly construed; in particular, the court will be reluctant to hold that such a clause fetters the right of a member to transfer his shares to another member at any price that may be agreed upon between them.[4] On the other hand, the court will be prepared to construe a pre-emption clause with sufficient liberality to prevent its obvious purpose being thwarted.[5] Thus, in *Lyle & Scott Ltd v Scott's Trustees*[6] when a company's articles provided that any member 'desirous of transferring his shares' should serve a 'transfer notice' upon the company, thereby setting in train certain procedures whereby other members could exercise rights of pre-emption, the House of Lords held that a member who in return for a sale price executed a transfer of his shares to a non-member and gave him an irrevocable proxy in respect of the votes thereon was 'desirous of transferring' within the meaning of the article, even though both parties to the sale had sought to evade the article by refraining from requesting registration of the transfer. The member was accordingly directed to serve a 'transfer notice'.

This decision was distinguished in *Safeguard Industrial Investments Ltd v National Westminster Bank Ltd.*[7] Here, subject to certain exceptions, the articles required a 'proposing transferor' to give notice to the company to set in motion a pre-emption procedure. The bank, executor of a deceased member who had bequeathed his shares to two members of the company, was registered as holder of the shares which it would hold for the latter on completion of the administration of the estate. However, at their request, it did not propose to transfer the shares to the two members. It was held that the bank did not fall within the articles. It had no intention of transferring the shares and the word 'transfer' was apt to cover only the transfer of the legal title to the shares, not the transfer of beneficial interests.

The court left open the question of the effect of an uncompleted agreement to sell shares on the operation of the articles. It may be that, unless the articles are drafted to cover dispositions of equitable interests, nothing short of a declaration of trust or the execution of a transfer and the handing over of an irrevocable

---

1   Altering the articles to remove such a clause may be unfairly prejudicial conduct within section 459: *Re Kenyon Swansea Ltd* [1987] BCLC 514; see **17.12** *et seq.*

2   *Borland's Trustee v Steel Brothers & Co Ltd* [1901] 1 Ch 279; *Lyle & Scott Ltd v Scott's Trustees* [1959] AC 763 (HL (Sc)); *Jarvis Motors (Harrow) Ltd v Carabott* [1964] 1 WLR 1101.

3   Cf *Rayfield v Hands* [1960] Ch 1, where a clause entitling members who wished to sell their shares to require the directors (who were subject to a share qualification) to buy them out at a fair price was held to be enforceable against the directors without the company having to be joined as a party to the proceedings. See further **4.17** and **4.18**.

4   *Delavenne v Broadhurst* [1931] 1 Ch 234; *Greenhalgh v Mallard* [1943] 2 All ER 234 (CA).

5   *Lyle & Scott Ltd v Scott's Trustees* [1959] AC 763 (HL(Sc)); and see *Jarvis Motors (Harrow) Ltd v Carabott* [1964] 1 WLR 1101.

6   Above.

7   [1982] 1 All ER 449 (CA).

proxy, as in the *Lyle & Scott* case, would suffice to bring a member within the terms of standard-form pre-emption provisions such as these.[1]

Where a company's articles provided in essence that shares could not be transferred to any person not already a member of the company if any member was willing to purchase the same, it was held that a term would be implied requiring a member wishing to transfer to take reasonable steps to give notice of his wishes to existing members.[2]

Pre-emption clauses often provide that for the purpose of any sale carried out in accordance therewith the value of the shares should be determined by an accountant, who in performing this task is to act as an expert and not as an arbitrator. An accountant acting under such a clause cannot be compelled to state the basis on which he makes his valuation. If he does not, the valuation is referred to as 'non-speaking' and can be challenged only if not made honestly by the correct person. If the valuer does give reasons (a 'speaking' valuation), his valuation can also be challenged if its basis is significantly erroneous.[3] If the auditor or accountant reaches an incorrect valuation through negligence, he can be sued in damages by the aggrieved party; his function is not sufficiently akin to the judicial to render him immune from such proceedings.[4]

If shares are sold in contravention of a pre-emption clause and the purchase price is paid, the purchaser acquires an equitable title to them, so that, for instance, a subsequent charging order purporting to bind them in the hands of the vendor is ineffective.[5] There is, of course, no transfer of the legal title while the vendor remains on the register. However, a person who is entitled under the

---

1 See the comments of Vinelott J at first instance, [1980] 3 All ER 849 at 859. The *Safeguard* decision was followed in *Theakston v London Trust plc* [1984] BCLC 390, where a member had taken a transfer of shares (not restricted by the articles) with the aid of a loan, charging the shares to the lender as security. At the chargee's request, he was obliged to set in motion the pre-emption procedure in the company's articles. The loan was interest-free and only repayable if and when the member disposed of the shares. It was held that he was not a 'person proposing to transfer' as there was 'no unequivocal obligation to execute any instrument at all at present' (*per* Harman J at 401). See also *Re Ringtower Holdings plc* (1989) 5 BCC 82 at 99 and *Re Macro (Ipswich) Ltd* [1994] 2 BCLC 354. In the latter case, there had been declarations of trust and transfer documents completed and Arden J had no difficulty in holding (at 401–403) that the members in questions were 'desiring to sell'.

2 *Tett v Phoenix Property Co* [1986] BCLC 149 (CA). It was held on the facts that the transferor had failed to give such notice and thus the alleged transfer of his shares was void. However, the 'transferee' who had paid the price held the equitable interest in the shares. See also footnote 5, below.

3 See, in particular, *Dean v Prince* [1953] Ch 590, [1954] Ch 409 (CA); *Burgess v Purchase & Sons Ltd* [1983] 2 All ER 4; for more detail, see *Gore-Browne on Companies* 44th edn (Jordans, loose-leaf) at 16.2.2.

4 *Arenson v Casson, Beckman Rutley & Co* [1977] AC 405 (HL).

5 *Hawks v McArthur* [1951] 1 All ER 22. Despite dicta to the contrary in *Hunter v Hunter* [1936] AC 222 at 261 (HL), *Hawks v McArthur* was followed in *Tett v Phoenix Property Co* [1984] BCLC 599 by Vinelott J. The point was not argued and was left open by the Court of Appeal ([1986] BCLC 149), where the decision of Vinelott J was overruled on other grounds (see footnote 2, above), but it seems implicit in the Court of Appeal judgment that the purchaser obtains *an* equitable title and this is consistent with the notion that the question of title to property of any sort is relative: cf Battersby and Preston (1972) 35 MLR 268 arguing in favour of the notion of relative title to goods, but whose argument is applicable, *mutatis mutandis*, to intangible personal property such as shares. See also Borrowdale [1988] JBL 307 and Luxton [1990] JBL 14. Scots law does not recognise equitable ownership and therefore a transferee has no proprietary right until his name appears on the register.

pre-emption clause to have the shares first offered to him can sue to have the register rectified by insertion of his name as legal holder.[1]

9.2.3 Compulsory transfer

A clause to the effect that in the event of bankruptcy a member should sell his shares to particular persons at a particular price cannot be impeached by the member's trustee in bankruptcy, unless the price stipulated is shown to be less than the fair price which could otherwise be obtained. It is likewise not open to attack on the ground that such a restriction upon ownership is repugnant to the nature of personal property.[2]

A company's articles may furthermore contain a clause to the effect that a member infringing any specified regulation or regulations may be compelled by resolution to sell his shares to other members at a specified price. Any resolution passed in pursuance thereof will be valid and effective provided that it is passed *bona fide* in what the members conceive to be the interests of the company as a whole.[3]

9.2.4 Restrictions not arising out of the articles

Where the articles impose no restrictions upon the transfer of shares, the right to transfer fully paid shares is unlimited,[4] except as follows:

(1) the transferee must have capacity to hold the shares;[5]
(2) the principle of maintenance of capital must be observed;[6] and
(3) certain important restrictions come into operation once a winding-up has commenced.

There is thus nothing objectionable, for instance, in a member transferring some of his shares in order to increase his voting power,[7] and a misdescription of the transferee, even if intentional, gives no ground for setting a transfer aside.[8]

With regard to partly paid shares, the restrictions just mentioned apply, and in addition there are certain grounds upon which a liquidator may in a winding-up set aside transfers made before the commencement thereof.[9]

9.3   The mode of transfer of shares

The formalities of a transfer of shares in an unlisted company are in general regulated by the articles and, when applicable, the Stock Transfer Act 1963. If the

1   *Hunter v Hunter*, above. As to rectification of the register, see **12.5.3**.
2   *Borland's Trustee v Steel Brothers & Co Ltd* [1901] 1 Ch 279. A provision for compulsory transfer without consideration or compensation may be valid in exceptional circumstances: *Money Markets International Stockbrokers Ltd v London Stock Exchange Ltd* [2002] 1 WLR 1150.
3   See *Phillips v Manufacturers' Securities Co* (1917) 116 LT 290 (CA); *Sidebottom v Kershaw, Leese & Co* [1920] 1 CH 154 (CA); *Gaiman v National Association for Mental Health* [1971] Ch 317. As to the application of the same test in determining whether the introduction or deletion of such a clause by an alteration of the articles is valid, see **5.27**.
4   Assuming of course that the transferor is the beneficial owner free from any encumbrance.
5   See **12.5**.
6   See **7.11**.
7   *Re Stranton Iron and Steel Co* (1873) LR 16 Eq 559.
8   *Re Smith, Knight & Co, Battie's Case* (1870) 39 LJ Ch 391; *Re Financial Insurance Co, Bishop's Case* (1872) 7 Ch App 296n.
9   As partly paid shares are rare nowadays, no detail is given here; see *Gore-Browne on Companies* 44th edn (Jordans, loose-leaf) at 16.2.4.

articles provide for the issue of share warrants to bearer, the transfer of shares comprised in any warrants that are issued is effected by delivery of the warrant.[1] In all other cases, however, section 183(1) of the Companies Act 1985 provides that, notwithstanding anything in the articles, a 'proper instrument of transfer' must be delivered to the company. Otherwise the company is prohibited from registering the transfer.[2] This phrase means a written instrument 'such as will attract stamp duty under the relevant fiscal legislation'; it does not carry any further implication as to the form of the transfer.[3] As a result of section 183(1), an oral transfer is ineffective even if the articles purport to make it effective. Furthermore, a clause in the articles purporting to effect an automatic transfer of shares in stipulated circumstances without any written instrument (eg from a deceased member to his widow as a beneficial holder) is invalid.[4]

Except where partly paid shares are involved, the actual form of the instrument of transfer may be one of those provided by the Stock Transfer Act 1963; as these are relatively short and simple, they are used for the vast majority of transfers of unlisted shares[5].

The transfer of listed securities is increasingly effected under the CREST system described in **9.3.3**.

9.3.1   *The Stock Transfer Act*

Under section 1 of the Stock Transfer Act 1963, simplified forms are provided for the transfer of fully paid shares or stock[6] in any company within the meaning of the Companies Act 1985 except an unlimited company or a company limited by guarantee. The section provides for transfer by an instrument in the form set out in Schedule 1, called a 'stock transfer', or any form substantially corresponding thereto.[7] This instrument must be executed by the transferor, execution under hand being sufficient, but need not be executed by the transferee. It must contain particulars of the transferor and of the description and number or amount of the shares or stock and, save where the transfer takes place in pursuance of a 'stock exchange transaction',[8] the nature and amount of the consideration and the full name and address of the transferee must be included. Attestation is unnecessary, and, where the transfer is in pursuance of a stock exchange transaction, these particulars of the consideration and of the transferee may be inserted either in the stock transfer or supplied by means of separate instruments in the form set out in Schedule 2, called 'broker's transfers', or in any form substantially corresponding thereto. Each of these instruments identifies the stock transfer and the particular shares to which it relates, and specifies the consideration paid for such shares.

---

1   As to share warrants, see **9.12**.
2   Note, however, that the section expressly disclaims any effect on the power of the company to register as shareholder any person to whom the right to any shares in the company has been transmitted by operation of law: see **9.15**.
3   *Re Paradise Motor Co Ltd* [1968] 1 WLR 1125 at p 1141 (CA); *Nisbet v Shepherd* [1994] 1 BCLC 300 (CA).
4   *Re Greene* [1949] Ch 333.
5   When they are not used, the transfer must accord with the articles, of which article 23 in Table A is the standard example. As to this, see *Gore-Browne on Companies* 44th edn (Jordans, loose-leaf) at 16.3.1.
6   The section also covers debentures and other specified forms of security: see section 4 (4).
7   The relaxation in favour of 'forms substantially corresponding' is contained in section 3(1).
8   'Stock exchange transaction' is defined by section 4(1), coupled with the Stock Transfer (Recognition of Stock Exchanges) Order 1973, SI 1973/536.

Section 1 of the Stock Transfer Act 1963 provides forms which are permissible alternatives to, and not in substitution for, those provided for by the articles. Furthermore, any instrument purporting to be in any form which was common or usual for the transfer of shares before the commencement of the Act, or in any other form authorised or required for that purpose save under section 1 itself, is sufficient to transfer shares falling within section 1, whether or not it is completed in accordance with such form, provided that it complies with the requirements as to execution and contents which apply to a stock transfer.[1]

Section 1 of the Act does not affect any right of the company to refuse to register a transfer on any ground other than the form of the transfer, nor does it affect the existing position as regards execution of documents by companies or other bodies corporate. It does, however, apply notwithstanding anything to the contrary in any enactment or instrument relating to the transfer of shares; thus its provisions cannot be excluded by a company's memorandum or articles.[2] Any enactment or instrument relating to the transfer of fully paid shares such as falls within section 1 applies, *mutatis mutandis*, in relation to stock transfers and broker's transfers authorised by that section.[3]

9.3.2 *Procedure on transfer of unlisted shares*

Provided that the share certificate currently issued in respect of unlisted shares does not also contain shares which are not being transferred as part of the same transaction, the transferor normally delivers the certificate to the transferee along with the executed transfer, receiving in exchange any consideration that is payable. Where, however, the certificate contains more shares than those being transferred, an alternative procedure is adopted. The transferor lodges the certificate at the company's office and the fact of lodgment is certified by the company's secretary on the margin of the form of transfer.[4] The certified transfer is returned by the company to the transferor, who in due course delivers it to the transferee, receiving the consideration, if any, payable. After lodgment and registration, two new certificates are made out by the company: one in the name of the transferee, for the shares transferred, and the other in the name of the transferor, for the shares retained by him.

After execution and delivery of the form of transfer to the transferee, it must be stamped, and duty paid[5] within thirty days of execution.[6] Registration of an improperly stamped transfer cannot operate to bring about a legal transfer of the shares into the name of the transferee.

After stamping, the instrument of transfer is delivered to the company, with a request that a new certificate may be prepared and issued to the transferee. Either

---

1   Section 1(3).
2   Section 2(1).
3   Section 2(2). Where both a stock transfer and a broker's transfer are used, any reference in any enactment or instrument to the delivery or lodging of an instrument (or proper instrument) of transfer is to be taken as referring to the delivery or lodging of the stock transfer and the broker's transfer; any such reference to the date of lodgment is to be taken as referring to the date on which the later of the two forms of transfer to be lodged was lodged; and it is the broker's transfer that operates as the conveyance and transfer for stamp duty purposes.
4   As to this, see **9.11**.
5   Generally, a transfer on sale attracts *ad valorem* duty of 0.5%. See further, *Gore-Browne on Companies* 44th edn (Jordans, loose-leaf) at 16.3.3.
6   Stamp Act 1892, section 15.

the transferor[1] or the transferee may be the party who delivers it. Except where the transfer has been certified, the old certificate should accompany the instrument of transfer for the purpose of being cancelled or destroyed, and a new certificate issued in its place. Indeed, the articles usually provide that unless the certificate is produced the transfer will not be passed,[2] and a company receiving the purchase money for shares, the certificate for which was, to the knowledge of the directors, in the hands of a stranger, has been held liable to pay over the amount to the holder of the certificate, who was, in fact, a mortgagee of the shares.[3]

Upon receiving a transfer,[4] it is the secretary's duty to satisfy himself that the instrument is properly executed and bears the requisite stamp, and is correct in other particulars, such as the distinctive numbers (if any) of the shares, and that the transferor is the registered holder of the shares expressed to be transferred. If he is a responsible person, the directors are not personally liable to the transferee if they accept his investigations as sufficient.[5]

Before issuing the new certificate to the transferee the secretary may, for the company's protection, send notice of impending registration of the transferee to the transferor.[6]

If the transfer is in order, and no objection is received from the reputed transferor, the secretary should bring the document before the directors at the next board meeting.

On a transfer being brought before the board, the directors should consider whether or not it should be passed for registration.[7] In addition, if they know that a transfer is made in breach of trust or in fraud of a person having equitable rights, they should not pass the transfer without notifying the person interested,[8] and if they do pass the transfer they may come under a personal liability, although the company is protected by section 360 of the Companies Act 1985[9] which forbids notices of trusts being entered in the register.

If the transfer is passed, a certificate in favour of the transferee must be prepared and ready for delivery to him within two months, unless the terms of issue of the shares otherwise provide.[10]

---

1   See Companies Act 1985, section 183(4).
2   See eg Table A, article 24.
3   *Rainford v James Keith and Blackman Co* [1905] 2 Ch 147 (CA).
4   The secretary giving a receipt for the transfer is no warranty that the transfer will be accepted for registration: *Longman v Bath Electric Tramways Ltd* [1905] 1 Ch 646 (CA).
5   *Dixon v Kennaway & Co* [1900] 1 Ch 833, but note that the position of a director who actually signs the certificate in the transferee's favour was left open.
6   But the sending of such a notice does not protect the company where the transfer is forged, even if the true owner makes no reply: *Barton v London & North-Western Rly Co* (1890) 24 QBD 77 (CA); *Welch v Bank of England* [1955] Ch 508.
7   In accordance with the principles discussed in **9.2.1**.
8   Notification is mandatory when a 'stop notice' has been served on the company: see **9.8.1**.
9   *Société Générale de Paris v Walker* (1885) 14 QBD 424 (CA); (1886) 11 App Cas 20 (HL). As to section 360, see **12.6**.
10   Section 185; see further **9.10**.

9.3.3 *Procedure on transfer of listed shares*

Increasingly, listed shares and other securities are transferred under the paperless and computerised system known as CREST.[1] Section 207 of the Companies Act 1989 provides the foundation for the legal regime. The detailed rules are contained in the Uncertificated Securities Regulations 2001.[2] The section and the regulations provide for title to securities[3] to be evidenced and transferred[4] without a written instrument, a process described as 'dematerialisation'.[5] Provision is made for securities to become dematerialised[6] but there is no requirement for this to occur. Securities can be admitted to the system if the articles of the company permit,[7] or if the directors resolve to join.[8] It remains possible for the ownership and transfer of listed securities to be managed in the traditional manner using certificates.[9] The CREST system is run by what the Regulations call an Operator who requires Treasury approval and is subject to on-going Treasury supervision.[10]

An Operator is required to maintain an 'Operator register of members' in respect of every company which is a participating issuer.[11] This register is required to show, in respect of each class of participating security, the names and addresses of members who hold uncertificated shares and the number of shares held.[12] A participating issuer is required to maintain an 'issuer register of members' showing the date on which each person was registered as a member, a statement of the certificated shares held by each member and the amount paid or agreed to be paid on those shares. A participating issuer is also required to maintain a 'record

---

1   CREST is a recognised clearing house under the Financial Services and Markets Act 2000 and an approved system under the Uncertificated Securities Regulations 2001. It is part of Euroclear, the leading securities settlement organisation in Europe. CREST calculates and collects stamp duty on behalf of the Inland Revenue.

2   SI 2001/3755.

3   Including any legal or equitable interest in securities: section 207(1)(b). The very wide definition of 'securities' is shares, stock, debentures, debenture stock, loan stock, bonds, units of a collective investment scheme, rights under a depositary receipt and other securities of any description; and interests in a security.

4   References within the section to a transfer of title include a transfer by way of security: section 207(1)(c).

5   See generally R. Goode, 'The Nature and Transfer of Rights in Dematerialised and Immobilised Securities' in F Oditah (ed) *The Future for the Global Securities Market: Legal and Regulatory Aspects* (Oxford, Clarendon Press 1996).

6   The form of transfer under which 'certificated' securities become 'dematerialised' (ie held in electronic form by a system member) is prescribed in the Stock Transfer (Addition and Substitution of Forms) Order 1996, SI 1996/1571.

7   Uncertified Securities Regulations 2001, regulation 15; the articles must be consistent with Regulations.

8   Ibid, regulation 16; this is subject to the right of the general meeting to veto the directors' resolution.

9   There are, however, economic incentives favouring the dematerialisation of listed securities as transaction costs are higher for certificated transfers. Over 80 per cent of the UK equity market by value is now dematerialised.

10   See Part II and Schedule 1 of the Uncertificated Securities Regulations 2001. In principle, it is possible for another operator to compete with CREST by seeking approval as a 'relevant system'.

11   Regulation 20(3) of and Schedule 4, paragraph 4 to the USR 2001.

12   Only system members can be shown in this register as holders of uncertificated shares. Non-members (such as private investors) must arrange for a system member to hold uncertificated shares as trustee.

of uncertificated shares'[1], which replicates the entries made in the 'Operator register of members'. A participating issuer is not required to comply with section 352 (obligation to keep and enter up a conventional register of members), the rationale presumably being that all the information required to be entered in a conventional register is shown in the registers (above) required by the Uncertificated Securities Regulations 2001.

References in any enactment or instrument to a company's register of members shall, unless the context otherwise requires, be construed in relation to a company which is a participating issuer as referring to the company's issuer register of members and Operator register of members.[2] An entry on both the Operator and issuer register of members has the same legal effect in respect of title to dematerialised shares as does a certificate in respect of certificated shares. In each instance the entry or certificate is *prima facie* evidence (in Scotland sufficient evidence unless the contrary is shown) of legal title to shares.[3]

Transfer of title to uncertificated shares is effected by the Operator, which gives an Operator-instruction,[4] pursuant to which the company must register the transfer on its register of securities; the company must then notify the Operator it has done so by what is called an issuer-instruction. Except in a case where title has been transmitted by operation of law, a company cannot register a transfer of title to uncertificated units of a security unless instructed by an Operator or by court order or in certain other limited situations, and any other purported transfer of title is of no effect.[5] From the time that an Operator-instruction is generated which will require a company to register a transfer of title, until that transfer is registered, the transferee acquires an equitable interest in the requisite number of uncertificated units of the security in question, notwithstanding that the units in question or in which an interest arises may be unascertained.[6] It does not matter that the transferor acquires his equitable interest at the same time as the transferee in a situation, for example, where there is a series of transactions all entered in the system at more or less the same time.[7]

The Regulations contain a number of miscellaneous provisions to ensure, among other things, that holders of uncertificated shares are not prejudiced by not having paper evidence of their holdings. By regulation 37, references in any enactment or rule of law to a proper instrument of transfer of securities, or any expression having like meaning, is to be taken to refer to a reference to an Operator-instruction to a participating issuer to register a transfer of title on the relevant register of securities in accordance with the Operator-instruction. Regulation 40 exonerates trustees and personal representatives from any liability for breach of trust or default in dealing with uncertificated securities, unless they

---

1   Regulation 20(6) of and Schedule 4, paragraph 5 to the USR 2001.
2   See eg section 356, providing for the right to inspect the register of members.
3   Section 186 and regulation 24 of the USR 2001.
4   Regulation 27(7) USR 2001. See Part IV of the Regulations regarding authentication etc of dematerialised instructions.
5   Ibid, regulation 28(6).
6   Ibid, regulation 31.
7   The CREST system implements the principle of 'delivery versus payment', meaning that transfer of legal title and payment occur simultaneously. In principle this limits the need to refer to equitable interests as a party to a transaction will have either legal title or payment at any point in time during which a transfer is taking place (unlike the position prior to the introduction of CREST).

are expressly prohibited from so dealing, but also mirrors the general principle of company law[1] in providing that the Operator is not bound or compelled to recognise any express, implied or constructive trust or other interest in respect of uncertificated units of a security, even if he has actual or constructive notice of the said trust or interest.[2] By regulation 38, any requirements in an enactment or rule of law which apply in respect of the transfer of securities otherwise than by means of a relevant system shall not prevent an Operator-instruction from requiring a participating issuer to register a transfer of title to uncertificated units of a security. Notwithstanding any enactment, instrument or rule of law, a participating issuer may not issue a certificate in relation to any uncertificated units of a participating security, and a document issued by or on behalf of a participating issuer purportedly evidencing title to an uncertificated unit of a participating security shall not be evidence of title to the unit; in particular section 186 of the Companies Act 1985[3] shall not apply to any document issued with respect to uncertified shares.[4] Transfers of uncertificated shares are made subject to stamp duty reserve tax, at the rate of 0.5% of the consideration, payable by the purchaser.[5]

9.4 The position as between transferor and transferee

Quite apart from the effect of a proper transfer of shares as between the transferor or transferee and the company, questions may arise as to the legal relationship between the transferor and the transferee, particularly when the transfer is, quite properly, refused registration[6] or the parties choose not to seek registration of the transfer. The answers may vary depending on the nature of the transfer, namely whether it was a sale, a gift or a mortgage. These points are explored in the following sections.

9.5 Sales of shares

A contract for the sale of shares may be oral. If the shares are sold through a stock exchange, the usages of the exchange are incorporated into and form part of the contract;[7] an important effect of this principle is that once a vendor and a purchaser are brought together by the negotiations of their brokers on the exchange, the brokers 'drop out' and in general are not parties to the contract of sale ultimately formed.[8]

---

1   Companies Act 1985, section 360; see **12.5.1**.
2   Uncertified Securities Regulations 1995, regulation 40(3) Note that section 360 does not apply to Scottish companies and Regulation 40(3) does not prevent an Operator giving notice of a trust to such a company.
3   See **9.10**.
4   As to the special provisions regarding notice of and attending and voting at meetings, see Uncertified Securities Regulations 1995, regulation 41. Regulation 42 makes special provision to enable the exercise of the powers of compulsory purchase in Part XIIIA of the Companies Act 1985; as to these, see **19.23**.
5   See Part IV of the Finance Act 1986. Stamp duty is a tax on documents and therefore a special regime had to be established for dematerialised securities. The Treasury is authorised to abolish both stamp duty reserve tax and stamp duty on certificated share transfers (see Finance Act 1990 section 110) but has not yet exercised this power.
6   In accordance with a restriction on transfer of the sort discussed earlier in this chapter.
7   *Coles v Bristowe* (1868) 4 Ch App 3; *Bowring v Shepherd* (1871) LR 6 QB 309.
8   *Bowring v Shepherd*, above.

If the shares to be sold are not specified by the contract, they may be specified at a later stage by appropriation; in some cases this may not occur until the transfer form is filled in. Once the shares have been specified (whether by the contract, or subsequently) the contract becomes enforceable in most cases[1] by specific performance.[2]

A further effect of the shares being specified is that whilst the vendor remains the holder of the legal title to the shares, and is treated by the company as the owner thereof,[3] beneficial ownership passes to the purchaser,[4] even though the sale is in breach of a pre-emption clause in the articles.[5]

Once the beneficial ownership thus passes, a number of consequences ensue. In the absence of express provision in the contract, the purchaser becomes entitled as against the vendor to any dividends subsequently declared in respect of the shares, even if such dividend relates back wholly or partly to a period prior to the passing of beneficial ownership.[6] Dividends declared before the beneficial ownership passes but paid thereafter may, however, be retained by the vendor.[7] In practice, where shares are sold on The Stock Exchange near the time of declaration of a dividend the contract normally provides whether the sale is to be *ex div* or *cum div*. If after the beneficial ownership has passed a call is made or a contribution sought in a winding-up in respect of the shares, the vendor is the person liable to the company,[8] but he is entitled to an indemnity from the purchaser[9] (unless the contract of sale provides otherwise), or indeed against any sub-purchaser who has become beneficially entitled to the shares.[10] As to calls made before the beneficial ownership passes, the vendor has no indemnity, but if he fails to pay, the company may make a fresh call against the purchaser after registration of the transfer.[11]

Voting rights are subject to slightly different principles. The vendor, while he remains the registered holder, is from the company's point of view the person entitled to exercise the voting rights attached to the shares. The purchaser acquires the right to direct how the votes should be cast, not when the beneficial ownership passes to him, but when he has paid the full purchase price for the shares.[12] When the purchaser is in default in paying for the shares, a clause in the contract of sale providing that all rights pass to the purchaser on a specified date

---

1   An exception is where a winding-up supervenes, because a transfer would prima facie be void under what is now section 127 of the Insolvency Act 1986; *Sullivan v Henderson* [1973] 1 WLR 333.

2   *Duncuft v Albrecht* (1841) 12 Sim 189; *Grant v Cignan* [1996] 2 BCLC 24.

3   See section 360, discussed at **12.5.1**.

4   *Re National Bank of Wales, Taylor, Phillips and Rickard's case* [1897] 1 Ch 298 at pp 305–6 (CA); *Wood Preservation Ltd v Prior* [1969] 1 WLR 1077 (CA). As to the passing of beneficial ownership where an option is granted, see *Hare v Nicoll* [1966] 2 QB 131 (CA).

5   *Hawks v McArthur* [1951] 1 All ER 22; and see **9.2.2**.

6   *Black v Homersham* (1879) 4 Ex D 24; *Re Wimbush* [1940] Ch 92. The vendor is, moreover, bound to take steps to collect the dividend so as to be able to pay it over to the purchaser; *Stevenson v Wilson* 1907 SC 445.

7   *Re Kidner* [1929] 2 Ch 121.

8   *Ex parte Hennessy* (1849) 2 Mac & C 201.

9   *Bowring v Shepherd* (1871) LR 6 QB 309; *Re National Bank of Wales Taylor, Phillips and Rickard's Case* [1897] 1 Ch 298 at 305–306 (CA).

10 *Spencer v Ashworth, Partington & Co* [1925] 1 KB 589 (CA).

11 *New Balkis Eersteling v Randt Gold Mining Co* [1904] AC 165 (HL).

12 *Musselwhite v C H Musselwhite & Son Ltd* [1962] Ch 964; see also *Re Piccadilly Radio plc* [1989] BCLC 683 at 696.

before completion will be construed, in the absence of compelling language to the contrary effect, as not depriving the unpaid vendor of his right to vote.[1]

Upon a sale of shares the seller is bound only to execute a proper transfer and deliver it with the share certificate to the purchaser. He does not warrant that the company will accept the transferee,[2] and even if the company wrongfully refuses to register the purchaser he can, it seems, keep the purchase money.[3] He must not, however, do anything to hinder registration; if he does, he may be made liable in damages.[4]

Subject to the terms of the contract, the obligations of the purchaser are to prepare the form of transfer[5] (though often in practice the vendor takes over the task), to execute it (if this is necessary to obtain registration), to pay the purchase price and stamp duty and to lodge the transfer for registration.[6]

Where an unpaid vendor of shares executes a transfer and delivers it to the purchaser along with the share certificate, he has, unless the contract of sale otherwise provides, a lien upon the shares for payment of the purchase price. The company cannot, however, be required to accept notice of the lien, which may therefore be overridden if the shares are transferred to a *bona fide* purchaser for value without notice.[7]

9.6   Gifts of shares

Where shares are transferred by way of gift, the beneficial ownership does not pass to the donee until the donor has done all within his power to implement registration of the donee as transferee.[8] In the ordinary course, this means executing a transfer in the proper form and delivering it to the donee or to the company along with the relevant certificate, but if further requirements are imposed upon the donor by the articles or by statute these must also be complied with.[9] Until the donor has done all within his power to implement registration, the intended gift is revocable, the donee having no equity to compel the donor to perfect it and no right to ask the court to construe it as a declaration of trust.[10] On the other hand, if the donor has done everything that is required of him, but registration does not occur through some act or omission of one or more third parties (eg a refusal by the board to register the transfer, in exercise of a power in the articles), the donor is, it seems, treated as a trustee of the shares for the donee.[11] Further, if there is a clear declaration of trust of shares, whether oral or written, and even if expressed as simply a percentage of the donor's holding of

---

1   *JRRT (Investments) Ltd v Haycraft* [1993] BCLC 401, applying the principle in *Alghussein Establishment v Eton College* [1988] 1 WLR 587 (HL), that it is to be presumed that the parties did not intend that either should enjoy benefits between the contract date and completion arising from their own default.
2   *Skinner v City of London Marine Corp* (1885) 14 QBD 882 (CA).
3   *London Founders Association v Clarke* (1888) 20 QBD 576 (CA).
4   *Hooper v Herts* [1906] 1 Ch 549 (CA).
5   *Birkett v Cowper-Coles* (1919) 35 TLR 298.
6   *Re Stranton Iron and Steel Co* (1873) LR 16 Eq 559. The vendor may do this if the contract so permits; section 183(4).
7   *Langen & Wind Ltd v Bell* [1972] Ch 85; and see the discussion of priorities at **9.8**.
8   *Re Rose* [1949] Ch 78; *Re Rose* [1952] Ch 499 (CA); *Re Paradise Motor Co Ltd* [1968] 1 WLR 1125 (CA); *Vandervell v CIR* [1967] 2 AC 291 at 330 (HL).
9   *Re Fry* [1946] Ch 312.
10   *Milroy v Lord* (1862) 4 De G F & J 264.
11   *Re Rose* [1952] Ch 499 at 510 (CA) *per* Evershed MR.

shares in a particular company, this is effective to pass the equitable interest in the shares.[1] In addition, the modern view appears to proceed on the rather more liberal basis that 'although equity will not aid a volunteer, it will not strive officiously to defeat a gift'.[2] Thus the execution of a transfer form, in circumstances where there was a plain intention to make an immediate gift of shares, but without delivery of the share certificate has been held to constitute a valid equitable assignment of the shares.[3]

9.7 Mortgages of shares

A legal mortgage of shares can be implemented only by registration of a transfer to the mortgagee, though the parties will, of course, agree between themselves that it is a transfer by way of security only. From the point of view of the company the transfer will operate as an out-and-out transfer, so that, if the shares are partly paid, the mortgagee will be personally liable for calls.[4] Equally, anyone inspecting the share register or the share certificate issued to the mortgagee will be induced, if he does not know the true position, to treat the mortgagee as the absolute owner of the shares at law and in equity. The mortgagor may accordingly protect his equity of redemption by serving a 'stop notice' on the company.[5]

An equitable mortgage or charge upon shares can be created simply by deposit of the share certificate as security for the relevant advance.[6] Alternatively, or in addition, the parties may execute and deliver to the mortgagee a transfer in blank. If the mortgagee receives both the share certificate and a transfer in blank, he may exercise his power of sale in the event of default by the mortgagor without having to apply to the court for an order for sale just as a legal mortgagee may do.[7] Furthermore, subject to certain difficulties which arise when the transfer is required by the articles to be by deed,[8] he may at any time convert the mortgage into a legal mortgage by filling in his own name as transferee and procuring registration of the transfer.[9] While the mortgage remains equitable only, it is the mortgagee who should consider protecting his interest; this he may do by serving a stop notice.[10]

---

1   *Hunter v Moss* [1994] 1 WLR 452 (CA); and see *Re Harvard Securities Ltd* [1997] 2 BCLC 369.
2   *T Choithram International SA v Pagarini* [2001] 1 WLR 1 at 11 (PC), per Lord Browne-Wilkinson.
3   *Pennington v Waine* [2002] EWCA Civ 227, [2002] 1 WLR 2075 (CA). However, this may be in breach of a pre-emption clause in the company's articles of association and thus the company will be able to resist registration of the donee as legal owner: *Hurst v Crampton Bros (Coopers) Ltd* [2002] EWHC 1375 (Civ).
4   *Re Land Credit Co of Ireland, Weikersheim's Case* (1873) 8 Ch App 831.
5   See **9.8.1**. This is not possible in a Scottish company.
6   *Harrold v Plenty* [1907] 2 Ch 314. In a Scottish company, only registration of the mortgagee by the company will constitute a valid mortgage.
7   *Stubbs v Slater* [1910] 1 Ch 632 (CA). This is not possible in a Scottish company.
8   See *Gore-Browne on Companies* 44th edn (Jordans, loose-leaf) at 16.5.1.
9   *Re Tahiti Cotton Co* (1874) LR 17 Eq 273.
10   See **9.8.1**.

9.8 Priorities in England

Competing claims to the beneficial entitlement to shares sometimes arise in the context of share transfers in England.[1] Contests may arise between the registered holder of the shares and a claimant asserting a prior or a subsequent equity, or between two equitable claimants.[2]

Generally speaking, the registered holder, as legal owner, will prevail over a prior equitable claimant if he gave valuable consideration for the transfer through which he acquired his legal title[3] unless before the time of giving such consideration he had notice of the prior equity.[4] As against a subsequent equitable claim not created by his own act or with his authority, he will generally prevail, but not if his conduct has been such as to disentitle or estop him from asserting his rights against the person asserting the claim.[5]

As between two equitable claimants, the earlier in point of time prevails,[6] unless his conduct has been such to disentitle or estop him,[7] or, it has been said, the later claimant has acquired 'a present, absolute unconditional right to registration'.[8] It is not clear what this last phrase means, as in a later case a transferee for value who had lodged a transfer for registration was held not to have acquired such a right even though the directors had no power to refuse to register the transfer.[9]

Some authority is available as to the type of conduct that will disentitle or estop a legal or equitable claimant as against a subsequent equitable claimant. The mere fact that the beneficiaries under a trust of shares leave the share certificate in the hands of the trustees does not constitute such conduct,[10] but, according to an Irish case, a first mortgagee who fails to obtain the certificate relating to the mortgaged shares will be 'disentitled' as against a subsequent claimant who has acquired an equitable interest for value from the mortgagor, *bona fide* believing him to have an unencumbered title because he held the certificate.[11]

9.8.1 Notice to the company

In cases involving questions of priority, the mere fact that the company has notice of an equitable claim is not enough of itself to give that claimant priority over other claims of which the company has no notice; in other words, the rule in *Dearle*

---

1   The problems discussed here do not arise in Scots law, which does not recognise purely equitable interests in property.
2   It should be noted that particular problems can arise when transfers of shares are executed in blank. These are considered in *Gore-Browne on Companies* 44th edn (Jordans, loose-leaf) at 16.5.1.
3   *Shropshire Union Railways and Canal Co v R* (1875) LR 7 HL 496; *Guy v Waterlow Brothers and Layton Ltd* (1909) 25 TLR 515; *Langen & Wind Ltd v Bell* [1972] Ch 685. Where the articles give a company a 'first and paramount' lien over the shares of any shareholder indebted to it, this will prevail over an equitable charge over those shares given to a third party: *Champagne Perrier-Jouet SA v HH Finch Ltd* [1982] 3 All ER 713.
4   See *Dodds v Hills* (1865) 2 H & M 424. *Sheffield v London Joint Stock Bank* (1888) 13 App Cas 333 (HL). For a recent example of a transfer without valuable consideration where the legal title was therefore held subject to a prior equity, see *Cottrell v King* [2004] EWHC 397 (Ch).
5   *Fry v Smellie* [1912] 3 KB 282 (CA).
6   *Roots v Williamson* (1888) 38 Ch D 485; *Peat v Clayton* [1906] 1 Ch 659.
7   See *Shropshire Union Railways and Canal Co v R*, above, in which disentitling conduct was said to comprise 'misconduct or fraud or negligence' (at 514).
8   *Société Générale de Paris v Walker* (1886) 11 App Cas 20 at 29 (HL).
9   *Ireland v Hart* [1902] 1 Ch 522.
10 *Shropshire Union Railways and Canal Co v R*, above.
11 *Kelly v Munster and Leinster Bank* (1891) 29 LR Ir (Eq) 19.

v Hall has no application.[1] The company is bound by statute not to enter on the register notice of any trust, express, implied or constructive,[2] and this rule is often widened in the articles[3] to take in any equitable interest whatsoever. On receiving notice of an equitable claim, the company may, however, decide against registering a competing transferee,[4] or may even remove such a transferee from the register,[5] in which event this transferee's position may be weaker through being based on equitable rights only.

With the same purpose in mind – that of preventing a competing claimant from strengthening his position by obtaining registration of a transfer – any person claiming a beneficial interest in shares may apply *ex parte*, by summons or motion in the Chancery Division, for an order prohibiting the registration of any transfer of the shares.[6] This will serve to 'freeze' the position while the rights of the competing claimants are worked out.

A final form of protection for equitable claimants is the serving of a 'stop notice', a procedure which is regulated by the Rules of the Supreme Court, Order 50, rules 11–14. By the terms of these rules, any person who has such an interest may, upon making and filing an affidavit of his interest, and serving an office copy of the affidavit and a notice on the company, require it to stop the transfer of or the payment of dividends upon the shares in question. This notice is not enough to give the server priority over a claimant to whom, under the rules just discussed, he ranks subject.[7] However, it prevents the company from registering a transfer of the shares or paying the dividends without giving the server an opportunity of applying to the court to prevent the transfer or payment. But if the person in whose name the shares stand requests the company to transfer or pay, the company must notify the server of the notice, and if he does not within 14 days obtain an order from the court, the company may proceed, despite the notice, to deal with the shares or pay the dividends as requested. This course is, in practice, very little resorted to; but it will be obvious that a very valuable method is provided for checking any anticipated or possible misappropriation of shares by a trustee or person whose title to them is not absolute. If such a notice is served on the company, it must be careful not to register any transfer or pay any dividend without referring to the server of the notice. If it does register a transfer, so as to cause the interest asserted by the server of the notice to be overridden, the directors,[8] and possibly also the company itself, will be liable to him in damages for the loss which he has suffered.

A judgment-creditor who has taken out a charging order in respect of shares does not thereby obtain the right to receive notice of and oppose the impending registration of any transfer presented by the registered holder. He does, however,

---

1   *Société Générale de Paris v Walker* (1886) 11 App Cas 20 (HL).

2   Companies Act 1985, section 360. For an instance of the application of a similar provision in Commonwealth legislation, see *Simpson v Molson's Bank* [1895] AC 270 (PC). This rule apparently extends to notice of an unpaid vendor's lien: see *Langen & Wind Ltd v Bell* [1972] Ch 85. In this case, Brightman J may, however, have been thinking of common-form provisions in company articles such as the provision referred to in the next footnote.

3   See eg Table A, article 5.

4   See eg *Roots v Williamson* (1888) 38 Ch D 485; and see **9.3.2**.

5   This was done in *Peat v Clayton* [1906] 1 Ch 659.

6   RSC Order 50, rule 15.

7   *Wilkins v Sibley* (1863) 4 Giff 442 at p 446.

8   *Société Générale de Paris v Walker* (1884) 14 QBD 424 at p 453 (CA) (affirmed (1885) 11 App Cas 20 (HL)).

have a sufficient interest in the shares to provide the basis for a stop notice, and if he proceeds to serve such a notice, he will be protected to the extent described.[1]

9.9 Forged transfers

A forged transfer is in law no transfer, and gives the alleged transferee no rights, not even if the company issues to him a certificate stating that he is the holder of the shares which the transfer purports to assign.[2] If the company, acting upon a forged transfer, removes the true owner from the register and substitutes the supposed transferee, it can be compelled to reinstate the true owner and replace or restore his shares.[3] In England, the Limitation Act 1980 only runs against the true owner as from the time when his demand for reinstatement to the register is refused.[4] He can claim any intervening dividends from the company, which can in turn claim them from the transferee.[5]

By reason of a general law principle of estoppel discussed in the next section, persons who suffer damage through relying on the share certificate issued pursuant to a forged transfer can in general recover compensation for their loss from the company.[6] But estoppel cannot be invoked by a person who has presented for registration a forged transfer in his favour. Indeed, such a person may instead be required by the company to reimburse it for any damages that it has been compelled to pay out to a third party under the estoppel principle.[7] Thus a transferee taking a forged transfer can claim damages only under the estoppel principle when two conditions are satisfied: (a) that someone other than him presented the transfer for registration; and (b) that he relied on the certificate to his detriment, eg in being 'put to rest' thereby so that he delayed in taking action against the forger until the forger, through becoming bankrupt or for some other reason, ceased to be able to satisfy the transferee's claim against him in respect of the forgery.[8]

The proposition, just stated, that a company can claim reimbursement for any damages it has had to pay out on a forged transfer, from the person who presented the transfer for registration, stems from the wider principle that a person presenting a transfer impliedly warrants that it is genuine and given with due authority. Thus a broker who deposits a forged transfer in good faith is liable to the company for loss it may suffer thereby,[9] and, if a broker represents, whether in good faith or not, that he has authority to act for the supposed transferor when in

---

1   *Adams v Bank of England* (1908) 52 SJ 682.
2   *Simm v Anglo-American Telegraph Co* (1879) 5 QBD 188 (CA).
3   *Barton v North Staffordshire Rly Co* (1888) 38 Ch D 458. This applies even if the true owner has been notified of the transfer before its registration but has failed to make any objection to it: see **9.3**.
4   *Barton v North Staffordshire Rly Co*, above: *Welch v Bank of England* [1955] Ch 508.
5   *Foster v Tyne Pontoon and Dry Dock Co* (1893) 63 LJQB 50.
6   *Re Bahia and San Francisco Rly Co* (1868) LR 3 QB 584; *Dixon v Kennaway & Co* [1900] 1 Ch 833.
7   *Sheffield Corp v Barclay* [1905] AC 392 (HL); *Welch v Bank of England*, above; *Yeung v Hong Kong and Shanghai Bank* [1981] AC 787 (PC); *Royal Bank of Scotland plc v Sandstone Properties Ltd* [1998] 2 BCLC 429.
8   *Dixon v Kennaway & Co*, above.
9   *Sheffield Corp v Barclay*, above; *Yeung v Hong Kong and Shanghai Bank*, above. It may be, though, that this principle should be reviewed in the light of the Civil Liability (Contribution) Act 1978; ibid, at 799–800, but only the House of Lords can do this: *Royal Bank of Scotland plc v Sandstone Properties Ltd*, above.

fact he has not, he is liable to the company upon an implied warranty that he has authority.[1]

9.10 Share certificates

The articles almost invariably give to each member a right, free of charge, to a certificate or certificates indicating the share or shares to which he is entitled;[2] indeed, by virtue of section 185(1) of the Companies Act 1985, a member is entitled to a certificate unless this right is expressly excluded by the conditions of issue.[3] The usual practice is to include in one certificate all the shares of the same class held by a member. The articles also generally state how such a certificate is to be signed. Table Λ, articles 6 and 101, require it to be under the seal of the company, and to be signed by a director and by the secretary or by a second director, unless the directors determine that some other or others shall sign it. The certificate is not a deed,[4] however, and it does not attract stamp duty.

Section 185(1) requires every company, unless the conditions of issue otherwise provide, to complete and have ready for delivery the certificates of shares within two months after allotment or lodgment of any transfer of shares.[5] If notice has been served requiring the company to make good any default with respect to the issue of certificates and the default is not made good within ten days after service of the notice, the court may, on the application of the person entitled to have the certificate delivered to him, order the company and any officer of the company to make good the default within a specified time, and the order may provide that all costs of and incidental to the application shall be borne by the company or by any officer responsible for the default.[6]

A share certificate (as opposed to the share itself which is a chose in action, in Scotland incorporeal moveable property) is a personal chattel (in Scotland corporeal moveable property) and can be the subject of a claim in conversion at the suit of someone who has either possession or an immediate legal right to possession at the time of conversion. However, someone with merely an equitable title, such as the beneficiary of a trust, has no standing to bring such an action.[7]

9.10.1 Evidence of title

A certificate under the seal of the company is *prima facie* evidence of the title of the person named to the shares;[8] but it does not give the person an indefeasible right to the shares. If it can be shown that the holder obtained the shares from some person who could not give him a title to them, the name of the true owner will be

---

1 *Starkey v Bank of England* [1903] AC 114 (HL). This is not affected by the fact that the company or its registrar has issued a duplicate share certificate to the fraudster: *Royal Bank of Scotland plc v Sandstone Properties Ltd* [1998] 2 BCLC 429.

2 See eg Table A, article 6.

3 In the case of 'dematerialised' securities, in respect of which legal title is evidenced by an electronic record, there is no right to a certificate. See **9.3.3** above.

4 *South London Greyhound Racecourses v Wake* [1931] 1 Ch 496; *R v Williams* [1942] AC 541 (PC).

5 'Transfer' here means a transfer duly stamped and otherwise valid, and does not include any transfer which the company is for any reason entitled to refuse to register and does not register.

6 Section 185(6) and (7).

7 *MCC Proceeds Inc v Lehman Brothers International (Europe)* [1998] 2 BCLC 659 (CA).

8 Section 186.

retained upon or restored to the register, and the holder will lose the shares.[1] But if the holder acquired the shares in good faith and for value, relying upon an untrue certificate issued to his predecessor by the company, the company will be estopped from denying his title to the shares which he has been induced to buy or pay for by being shown the certificate.[2] Similarly, if after acquiring the shares in good faith and for value, he makes a contract to resell them in reliance on an untrue certificate issued to him and is then compelled to pay damages to his purchaser or buy other shares in order to fulfil the contract, he may recover his loss from the company.[3] If, however, the certificate is a forgery, the company comes under no liability, even when the forgery was the act of its secretary.[4] Furthermore, if the certificate is in fact correct, stating that a certain person is the registered holder of the shares, the company will not be liable to a purchaser from him by reason of having certified a previous transfer of the shares to another person, even though the company has parted with the certificate to the registered holder after certifying the transfer, thus enabling the registered holder to deal with the shares again. The proximate cause of the loss by the purchaser is taken to be the fraud of the registered holder and not the negligence (if any) of the company, and in any event any duty of the company to ensure that the certificate in such circumstances is sent to the registered holder is owed to the registered holder only, not to third paries such as purchasers.[5]

Another form of estoppel may arise against the company if it issues a certificate which states that the shares comprised in it are fully paid when in fact they are only partly paid or have nothing paid up on them. If the shares come into the hands of a *bona fide* transferee for value who relied upon such a statement in the certificate held by his predecessor and had no knowledge of the true position, the company will be estopped as against him from denying that they are fully paid and thus will be prevented from claiming from him the amount unpaid on the shares or any part thereof.[6]

9.11 Certification of transfers

The act of certification of a transfer of shares is often a step in the process of transfer; its general nature and purpose have already been described.[7] The position of persons, such as transferees, who act on the faith of a certification by the company is dealt with in section 184:

> The certification by a company of any instrument of transfer[8] of shares in or debentures of the company is to be taken as a representation by the company to any

---

1   See **9.9**.
2   *Re Bahia and San Francisco Rly Co* (1868) LR 3 QB 584; *Re Ottos Kopje Diamond Mines Ltd* [1893] 1 Ch 618 (CA). This estoppel arises when the holder, having been refused registration or having been removed from the register to make way for the true owner, sues the company for damages for wrongful refusal or wrongful removal.
3   *Balkis Consolidated Co Ltd v Tomkinson* [1893] AC 396 (HL).
4   *Ruben v Great Fingall Consolidated* [1906] AC 439 (HL); *South London Greyhound Racecourses Ltd v Wake* [1931] 1 Ch 496; but these cases may not be followed today – see **5.34**.
5   *Longman v Bath Electric Tramways Ltd* [1905] 1 Ch 646 (CA).
6   *Burkinshaw v Nicholls* (1878) 3 App Cas 1004 (HL); *Re British Farmers' Pure Linseed Cake Co* (1878) 7 Ch D 533 (CA).
7   See **9.3.2**.
8   'Instrument of transfer' includes a broker's transfer under the Stock Tranfer Act 1963; see section 2(2) of that Act.

person acting on the faith of the certification that there have been produced to the company such documents as on their face show a prima facie title to the shares or debentures in the transferor named in the instrument of transfer. However, the certification is not to be taken as a representation that the transferor has any title to the shares or debentures.

For the purposes of the section, a transfer is to be deemed to be certified if it bears the words 'certified lodged', or words to this effect.[1]

The section further provides that when any person acts on the faith of a false certification made negligently, the company is to be under the same liability to him as if the certification had been made fraudulently.[2]

Decisions[3] prior to 1948 established that where an agent of a company had authority to certify transfers but fraudulently did so without the share certificates having been lodged, he was not acting within the scope of his authority and accordingly his act was not the act of the company. These decisions were substantially overruled by what is now section 184(3)(b), which provides that certification is to be deemed to be made by the company if: (a) the person issuing the instrument is a person authorised to issue certificated transfers on the company's behalf; and (b) the certification is signed by a person authorised to certificate transfers on the company's behalf or by any officer or servant of the company or of another company which is so authorised. It would seem, however, that the old law still applies where the secretary or other officer fraudulently certifying the transfer had no authority to certify transfers at all.

A certification is to be deemed to be signed by a person if it purports to be authenticated by his signature or initials (whether handwritten or not), unless it is shown that the signature or initials were placed there neither by himself nor by a person authorised to use the signature or initials for the purpose of certificating transfers on the company's behalf.[4]

9.12   Share warrants

By virtue of the Companies Act 1985, section 188(1), the articles of any company limited by shares may contain a power to issue 'share warrants' to bearer in respect of fully paid shares.[5] The effect of the issue of a share warrant is to make the bearer of it absolutely entitled to the shares named in it, and the ownership can accordingly be passed by mere delivery.[6] No person purchasing a share warrant need make any enquiry as to the title of the person who sells it, any more than if he were receiving a banknote, but if the holder has in fact stolen or fraudulently obtained a share warrant, he can, of course, be compelled to surrender it in the same way as a thief would have to give up a banknote.

The company may provide for the payment of dividends by coupons or otherwise.[7] It is usual to do this by coupons attached to the warrant, each stating

---

1   Section 184(3)(a).
2   Section 184(2).
3   *George Whitechurch Ltd v Cavanagh* [1902] AC 117 (HL); *Kleinwort v Associated Automatic Machine Corp* (1934) 50 TLR 244 (HL).
4   Section 184(3)(c).
5   Table A contains no relevant article. Share warrants have not been popular, partly because of former exchange control legislation, but there is evidence of their increasing use: see *Gore-Browne on Companies*, 44th edn (Jordans, loose-leaf) at 16.9.
6   Section 188(2).
7   Section 188(3).

that the bearer is entitled to the dividend for a certain year or half-year, or to the first, second, or third dividend declared, and in such case the bearer of the coupon, and not of the warrant, is entitled to the dividend.

Subject to the regulations of the company, the bearer of a share warrant can return it to the company, and be re-entered upon the register as a shareholder, the warrant being thereupon cancelled.[1] The company will be responsible for any loss incurred by any person if the name of a bearer of a share warrant is entered in the register without the warrant being surrendered and cancelled.[2]

Without exception, the bearer of a share warrant may, if the articles of the company so provide, be deemed to be a member of the company, either to the full extent or for any purposes defined in the articles.[3] For the purpose, however, of any provision in the articles requiring a director or manager to hold a specified share qualification the bearer of a share warrant is not to be deemed to be the holder of the shares specified in the warrant.[4]

On the issue of a share warrant a company must strike out of its register the name of the holder of the shares represented, and enter particulars as to the date of issue of the warrant, and a statement of the shares represented by it, distinguishing each share by its number (if any). If the warrant is surrendered the date of the surrender must be entered in the register.[5]

9.13   The transmission of shares

A transmission of shares occurs upon the holder dying, becoming a patient under the Mental Health Act 1983, or becoming bankrupt. The persons or person with whom the company must deal in such a case are the executors or administrators of a deceased shareholder, the committee or receiver of a Mental Health Act patient, or the trustee of a bankrupt, all of whom may be described by the words 'the representatives of the former holder'.

9.14   Trustees in bankruptcy

The title of the trustee in bankruptcy to the shares of the bankrupt is conferred by the Insolvency Act 1986, which vests the property in the shares in him,[6] empowers him to exercise the right of transfer to the same extent as the bankrupt could have done,[7] and authorises him to disclaim the shares.[8] Thus, unless the articles otherwise provide, the trustee can take the shares into his own name, leave them in the name of the bankrupt, transfer them without first taking them into his own name, or disclaim them, but in each case the rights of third parties are left unaffected.[9]

---

1   Section 355(2).
2   Section 355(3).
3   Section 355(5), to which cf section 22(2).
4   Section 291(2).
5   Section 355(1) and (4).
6   Section 306. The equivalent in Scotland is section 31(1) of the Bankruptcy (Sc) Act 1985.
7   Section 314 and Schedule 5. For Scotland, see section 39 of the Bankruptcy (Sc) Act 1985.
8   Section 315. As to the trustee's power to disclaim, see *Gore-Browne on Companies* 44th edn (Jordans, loose-leaf) at 15.5.
9   See *Re Cannock and Rugeley Colliery Co* (1885) 28 Ch D 363 (CA); *Wise v Lansdell* [1912] 1 Ch 420.

When the trustee takes the shares into his own name he can insist upon a 'clean' certificate; ie he can object to an entry in the register or upon the certificate to the effect that he holds them as trustee or subject to a lien.[1] By taking partly paid shares into his own name, he becomes personally liable for calls on them.

If the trustee elects to leave the shares in the bankrupt's name, the bankrupt can vote upon the shares and give proxies, but he must exercise these powers in accordance with the trustee's directions.[2] He cannot sue the company to enforce his personal rights, but in appropriate cases he probably has the *locus standi* to bring a derivative action to redress a wrong done to the company.[3] The trustee for his part does not have the *locus standi* to present a petition to wind up the company.[4] The bankrupt estate, and not the trustee, is liable for calls on any partly paid shares, and the company can prove for the estimated value of any future calls.[5]

9.15   Executors and administrators

On the death of a shareholder other than a joint holder, even if he bequeaths his shares to a specific legatee, the executor or administrator is the person entitled to the shares so far as the company is concerned, because he has the legal title to them.[6] The title of the executor or administrator is shown by the probate or letters of administration, which must be produced to the company for registration.[7] Thereafter, the executor or administrator is the person with whom the company must deal in all matters relating to the shares. His title cannot be bypassed by an article purporting on the death of the holder to vest the shares in someone else.[8] Equally, the directors cannot reject an executor's claim to be registered as the holder of shares held by the testator, relying upon an article which enables them to refuse transfers, because such an article does not apply to a transmission by operation of law.[9] There must instead be an express power of veto conferred by the articles to justify a refusal to enter the name of an executor on the register of members.[10] The articles may give the directors in such a case the same right to decline registrations they would have had in the case of a transfer of the share by the deceased.[11] A provision in the articles that on the death of a member his shares must be offered to the other members at par can be enforced against the executors of a deceased member, and has been construed so as to operate even when there is only one member surviving.[12] Where the articles of a company

---

1   *Re W Key & Sons Ltd* [1902] 1 Ch 467.
2   *Morgan v Gray* [1953] Ch 83.
3   *Birch v Sullivan* [1957] 1 WLR 1247; and see **17.8**.
4   *Re H L Bolton Engineering Co Ltd* [1956] Ch 677. There is nothing to prevent the bankrupt presenting a petition on the trustee's behalf: see *Re K/9 Meat Supplies (Guildford) Ltd* [1966] 1 WLR 1112.
5   *Re McMahon* [1900] 1 Ch 173.
6   See *Roberts v Letter 'T' Estates Ltd* [1961] AC 795 (PC). This is normally confirmed in the articles: see eg Table A, article 29.
7   See the Companies Act 1985, section 187. In a Scottish estate, confirmation as executor is the equivalent.
8   *Re Greene* [1949] Ch 333.
9   *Re Bentham Mills Spinning Co* (1879) 11 Ch D 900 (CA).
10   *Scott v Frank F Scott (London) Ltd* [1940] Ch 794 (CA).
11   This is the effect of article 30 in Table A; and see, eg, the particular articles in issue in *Village Cay Marina Ltd v Acland* [1998] 2 BCLC 327 (PC).
12   *Jarvis Motors (Harrow) Ltd v Carabott* [1964] 1 WLR 1101.

permitted the transfer of shares to, among others, 'privileged relatives', while allowing the directors to refuse to register other transfers, and incorporated the provisions of Table A[1] providing for the same position to apply in the case of transmission by death or bankruptcy, it was held that the personal representatives of a deceased member could not be prevented from transferring the shares to his beneficiary who was within the class of privileged relative.[2]

Articles sometimes compel representative holders either to take the shares in their own names, assuming all the responsibilities of a member of the company, or to nominate some other person to take the shares. If such provisions are not in the articles, there is nothing to prevent representative holders from continuing to allow the shares to remain in the name of the deceased shareholder.[3] But in the absence of express provisions in the articles,[4] the representatives are not entitled to have any notice sent to them or to the registered address of the deceased unless such representative holders become members by formal registration.[5] If the company has not been notified of the death of a member, it is entitled to assume that a notice sent to his registered address has been duly received.[6]

While the shares remain in the name of the deceased holder, his estate is *prima facie* entitled to any subsequent benefits deriving from the shares and is liable to pay any subsequent calls.[7] It follows that, if the articles require that new shares must be offered to the members, the estate of a deceased member must not be ignored when a new issue is made.[8] Similarly, in the event of reconstruction under section 110 of the Insolvency Act 1986, an executor or administrator can exercise the statutory right of dissent.[9] He has also the necessary *locus standi* to present a petition to wind up the company,[10] or to challenge a resolution for voluntary winding up,[11] or to institute proceedings under section 459[12] or section 653,[13] but he is not to be counted in determining whether there is a sufficient quorum at a general meeting unless the articles otherwise provide,[14] nor in determining whether the company's membership has fallen below the statutory minimum prescribed by sections 1 and 24.[15]

Whether the personal representatives have taken the shares into their own names or not, they can transfer them.[16]

---

1   The relevant Table A articles were articles 30 and 31 of the 1948 Table A, but in this respect the 1985 Table A has the same effect.
2   *Re William Steward (Holdings) Ltd* [1994] BCC 284 (CA).
3   *City of Glasgow Bank in Liquidation, Buchan's Case* (1879) 4 App Cas 549 at 588–9 (HL (Sc)).
4   See eg Table A, article 38.
5   See *Allen v Gold Reefs of West Africa Ltd* [1900] 1 Ch 656 (CA), where, however, the point was expressly covered by an article.
6   *New Zealand Gold Extraction Co (Newbery-Vautin Process) v Peacock* [1894] 1 QB 622 (CA).
7   *James v Buena Ventura Syndicate Ltd* [1896] 1 Ch 446 at 464–465 (CA); and see Table A, articles 29 and 31.
8   *James v Buena Ventura Syndicate Ltd*, above.
9   *Llewellyn v Kasintoe Rubber Estates Ltd* [1914] 2 Ch 670.
10 See *Re Cuthbert Cooper & Sons Ltd* [1937] Ch 392; *Re Chesterfield Catering Co* [1976] 3 WLR 879.
11 *Howling's Trustee v Smith* (1905) 7 F 390.
12 Section 459(2); see **17.13.**
13 *Re Bayswater Trading Co Ltd* [1970] 1 WLR 343.
14 *Re J Franklin & Son Ltd* [1937] 4 All ER 43.
15 *Re Bowling and Welby's Contract* [1895] 1 Ch 663 (CA); and see **12.6.**
16 Section 183(3). See further as to the procedure to be adopted on a transmission of shares, *Gore-Browne on Companies* 44th edn (Jordans, loose-leaf) at 16.13.

Chapter 10

Debentures, Charges and Creditors' Remedies

10.1 Introduction

The immediately preceding chapters have been concerned with various aspects of share capital.[1] This chapter is concerned with loan capital raised by companies. Loan capital is a form of corporate finance that is mainly governed by the law of contract, and lenders and borrowers are free to bargain for such contractual terms as are appropriate to their particular circumstances and their assessment of risk. It is inappropriate in a general company law text such as this to delve too far into the detail of the corporate debt financing structures and loan terms that are used in practice (not least because of the dynamic and evolving nature of the debt capital markets),[2] but some general considerations that are relevant to corporate borrowing are briefly outlined. The types of charge that can be issued by companies, and the distinction between fixed and floating charges, are then considered. This in turn leads to an examination of the relative priority of fixed and floating charges *inter se* and in respect of various other interests. This necessarily involves consideration of the system for the registration of charges created by companies.

In Part 4 of the chapter some of the remedies available to lenders are explored. Principal attention is given to the enforcement of secured loans. Until September 2003, the appointment of an administrative receiver (in the case of a floating charge) was the normal remedy. However, section 72A of the Insolvency Act 1986, inserted by the Enterprise Act 2002, now prohibits the appointment of an administrative receiver by the holder of a 'qualifying floating charge' and the administration procedure, also replaced by a new system, will now form the main remedy for a floating charge holder.[3]

There are many defects in the existing system for the creation and registration of company charges. One is the complexity of the rules governing the relative priority of the floating charge in relation to fixed charges. Recent case-law has also made the task of distinguishing between fixed and floating charges more difficult. Another problem with the existing system is that some transactions commonly used by companies to obtain credit, such as industrial hire-purchase and leasing agreements, are not considered to involve the creation of a charge and therefore will not appear on the register of charges. Even certain types of undoubted charge (eg over shares in other companies) are not registrable.

---

1   As to the relationship between equity and loan capital, known as 'gearing', see **7.2**.

2   For more detailed treatment, see standard banking law texts such as Cranston, *Principles of Banking Law* (Oxford University Press, 1997). Specifically with regard to corporate debt finance, see also *Gore-Browne on Companies* 44th edn (Jordans, loose-leaf), Chapter 17; Ferran, *Company Law and Corporate Finance* (Oxford University Press, 1999) Chapters 14–16; Pennington, *Bank Finance for Companies* (Sweet & Maxwell, 1987).

3   See further, **10.39**. As to the administration procedure under the new Part II of the Insolvency Act 1986 (now contained in a new Schedule B1 to that Act), see **21.13**. As to the effect of a voluntary arrangement (whether consequent upon an administration order or not) under Part I of the 1986 Act, see **21.7**.

Radical proposals for the reform of the law relating to security interests have been made periodically, albeit with no success, although the Law Commission has now been asked to report on this.[1] At the end of the chapter, there is a brief account of the main proposals which have been made previously and an attempt is made to assess why the proposals have not made it onto the statute books. One exception to this general failure to advance reform much beyond the discussion stage was in relation to the registration of charges where new requirements were enacted in the Companies Act 1989. However, those requirements, which were interim measures designed to correct some of the more obvious defects in the systems rather than radical reforms, have not been brought into force and although they remain on the statute books, it is now clear that they will never be implemented.[2]

PART 1: GENERAL CONSIDERATIONS

10.2 Borrowing powers

Besides raising capital by means of shares, companies frequently, either at the time of their incorporation or subsequently, raise money by borrowing.[3] This may be done in various ways – by an ordinary unsecured loan, by making bills of exchange or promissory notes, by a mortgage on the property of the company, or by the issue of debentures. In all these cases, it is necessary to see, first, whether the company has power to borrow; secondly, whether the directors have authority to exercise the company's borrowing powers without a resolution of the company or, as is sometimes required, the consent of a class of shareholders; thirdly, whether there is any limit on the amount which may be borrowed, and, if so, whether that limit is reached; and, fourthly, whether the company or the directors have power to secure the repayment of the money borrowed by a mortgage or charge on all or any part of the assets of the company.

These general questions as to the capacity of a company and as to the authority of the directors and officers to bind the company have been examined in an earlier chapter.[4]

If a company has power (express or implied) to borrow, it can create mortgages or charges to secure the repayment of the loan;[5] but if the power is express, its directors must observe any limitations in the power. Thus, if the memorandum contains the necessary authority, the company can charge or mortgage all its property, of whatever nature, including future property, such as book debts not

---

1   Law Commission, *Registration of Security Interests: Company Charges and Property other than land*, Consultation Paper 164 (2002).
2   See *Company Law Review: Proposals for Reform of Part XII of the Companies Act 1985* (DTI Consultative Document, November 1994).
3   For the exemption of borrowing by companies under the Consumer Credit Act 1974, see sections 8, 16 and 189.
4   See Chapter 5.
5   *Re Patent File Co* (1870) LR 6 Ch App 83: *Australian Auxiliary Steam Clipper Co v Mounsey* (1858) 4 K & J 733; *Byron v Metropolitan Saloon Omnibus Co* (1858) 3 De G & J 123.

yet due.[1] It may also charge its uncalled capital,[2] although this is, 'strictly speaking, more in the nature of power than of property'.[3] Uncalled capital capable of being charged does not include capital which can only be called up in the event of a winding-up as provided by section 120,[4] nor the amount payable under the guarantee in the case of a company limited by guarantee, this not being part of the capital of the company nor at any time under the control of the directors.[5]

10.3 Borrowing on debentures

One form of borrowing by a company is on debentures. When the term 'debenture' is used in its familiar commercial sense, it means a series of bonds which evidence the fact that the company is liable to pay the amount specified, with interest, and generally charge the payment of it upon the property of the company. They may be offered to the public by means of a prospectus in the same manner as shares. The procedure governing the application for and allotment of debentures is similar to that in the case of shares; but, as a debenture-holder is a creditor, and not a member of the company, widely different results follow.[6]

Although debentures are well-known instruments in the business world and are the subject of various provisions in the Companies Act 1985, there is no complete legal definition of them. It was said by Chitty J that 'a debenture means a document which either creates a debt or acknowledges it, and any document which fulfils either of these conditions is a debenture'.[7] But this is possibly too wide a definition[8]: for example, a bank statement may be an acknowledgment of a debt, but it would not ordinarily be regarded as a debenture. At any rate, an acknowledgment of indebtedness fulfils the primary qualification of a debenture. It does not matter by what name the company calls the document. Thus an 'income stock certificate' containing such an acknowledgment but no charge has been held to be a debenture, having regard to the terms and conditions under which it was issued.[9] A document, with coupons attached, promising to 'pay the amount of this debenture to A. B. or order', has been held to be liable to duty as a

1   *Illingworth v Houldsworth* [1904] AC 353 (HL); *Bloomer v Union Coal Co* (1873) 16 Eq 383: cf
      Tailby v Official Receiver (1888) 13 App Cas 523 (HL).
2   *Newton v Anglo-Australian Investment Co* [1895] AC 244 (PC); *Re Pyle Works (No 1)* (1890) 44 Ch
      D 534 (CA).
3   *Bank of South Australia v Abrahams* (1875) LR 6 PC 265 at 271.
4   *Bartlett v Mayfair Property Co* [1898] 2 Ch 28 (CA).
5   *Re Pyle Works (No 1)* (1890) 44 Ch D 534 at 574: but capital which can be called up only with
      the sanction of a special resolution may be charged, and the charge enforced in a winding-up
      even though no such resolution has been passed: *Newton v Anglo-Australian Investment Co*
      [1895] AC 244 (PC).
6   Companies, like individuals and partnerships, may resort to other means of obtaining credit
      (eg overdrafts on bank accounts, and the issue of negotiable instruments). Companies also
      obtain finance by means of hire-purchase agreements and commercial leasing arrangements.
      Such arrangements, however, have no special provision (eg as to registration) made for them
      in the Companies Act 1985.
7   *Levy v Abercorris Slate and Slab Co* (1887) 37 Ch D 260. See also *Edmonds v Blaina Furnaces Co*
      (1887) 36 Ch D 215; *Knightsbridge Estates Trust v Byrne* [1938] Ch 741 at 769 *et seq*, and *R v*
      Findlater [1939] 1 KB 594 (CCA).
8   See (*per* North J) *Topham v Greenside Co* (1888) 37 Ch D 281 at 291.
9   *Lemon v Austin Friars Investment Trust* [1926] 1 Ch 1 (CA).

debenture and not as a promissory note.[1] A document may be a debenture even though the debt to which it relates it not quantified at the date of its creation.[2]

Section 744 of the Companies Act 1985 states that for the purpose of the Act[3] 'debenture' includes debenture stock, bonds, and any other securities of a company, whether constituting a charge on the assets of the company or not. An ordinary mortgage of freehold land is a debenture within this section.[4]

In *Re SH & Co (Realisations) 1990 Ltd*,[5] Mummery J acknowledged the absence of a precise definition of the term 'debenture' but commented that this rarely seemed to cause problems in practice.

Debentures may be either: (a) a mere promise to pay; or (b) a promise to pay secured by a mortgage or charge. The mortgage or charge may be created by words in the debenture itself, or by a deed to the benefit of which the debenture holders are declared to be entitled or by a combination of these two methods.[6]

Debentures may be payable to the registered holder and those persons to whom he assigns or to bearer, in which latter case they pass by delivery.

10.4 Significance of the term 'debenture'

Various provisions of the Companies Act 1985, the Insolvency Act 1986, the Financial Services and Markets Act 2000 and the Public Offers of Securities Regulations 1995 relate to debentures. These include the following.

(1) Section 185(1) of the Companies Act 1985 requires debenture certificates to be complete and ready for delivery within two months after allotment, unless the conditions of issue provide otherwise.

(2) Section 194 of the Companies Act 1985 allows a company that has redeemed debentures to re-issue them or to issue other debentures in their place.[7] The re-issued or replacement debentures enjoy the same priority as if the debentures had never been redeemed.[8] Thus, if the company has created a security that ranks behind the original debentures, the security does not take priority over the re-issued debentures, even though it would rank before an entirely new issue of debentures.[9]

(3) Section 195 of the Companies Act 1985 makes a contract with a company to take up and pay for debentures of the company enforceable by an order for specific performance.

---

1   *British India Steam Navigation Co v Commissioners of Inland Revenue* (1881) 7 QBD 165.
2   *NV Slavenburg's Bank v Intercontinental Natural Resources* [1980] 1 All ER 955 at 976.
3   And unless the contrary intention appears.
4   *Knightsbridge Estates Trust v Byrne* [1940] AC 613 (HL).
5   [1993] BCC 60.
6   The extent of the company's indebtedness covered by the security given will depend in the proper construction of the debenture itself. It was held in *Re Quest Cae Ltd* [1985] BCLC 266, that even a widely drafted 'all moneys' debenture did not cover unsecured loan stock issued to a third party and subsequently acquired by the debenture holder.
7   This power can be excluded in the articles or by contract, or by a manifestation by the company of its intention to cancel the debentures: section 194(1)(a)–(b).
8   Section 194(2).
9   *Fitzgerald v Persse* [1908] 1 Ir R 279.

(4) If a register of debenture-holders is kept, sections 190 and 191 of the Companies Act 1985 impose certain obligations regarding the maintenance, inspection and provisions of copies thereof.

(5) Under section 29(2) of the Insolvency Act 1986, a receiver or manager appointed by or on behalf of the holders of debentures (other than a qualifying floating charge)[1] may be an administrative receiver. The position and powers of an administrative receiver are considered further later in this chapter.[2]

(6) The admission of debentures to listing must comply with Part VI of the Financial Services and Markets Act 2000. A public offer of unlisted debentures must be done in accordance with the Public Offers of Securities Regulations 1995. The regulation of public offers and listing of securities is considered in Chapter 18.

10.5 Main terms of loans

The main terms of loans relate to the payment of interest and the repayment of principal.

10.5.1 Principal

The loan agreement fixes the date when, or the circumstances in which, the principal is repayable. A loan may be for a fixed term, or may be repayable on demand or on notice. The equitable rule which invalidates restrictions on a mortgagor's[3] right to redeem does not apply to debentures, with the consequence that a debenture may be 'perpetual' or 'irredeemable'.[4] It may be slightly misleading to describe a debenture as 'irredeemable'[5] or 'perpetual' because closer examination of the terms will usually indicate that, although the holder has no right to redeem, the company has an option to redeem in given circumstances.[6]

As well as specifying a final redemption date or period, the terms of the loan agreement may also give the company the power to make early repayment or may provide for the establishment of a sinking fund which the company is obliged to apply in repaying principal from time to time.

10.5.2 Interest

At common law, interest is not payable on a debt except by agreement.[7] The loan agreement must therefore contain a covenant to pay interest, and should provide

---

1 Section 72A of the Insolvency Act 1986.

2 See **10.42–10.54**.

3 For this purpose, this includes a company which has given a floating charge: *Kreglinger v New Patagonia Meat Co* [1914] AC 25 (HL) dispelling doubts expressed in *De Beers Consolidated Mines v British South Africa Co* [1912] AC 52.

4 Section 193 of the Companies Act 1985; *Knightsbridge Estate Trust v Byrne*, above.

5 'Irredeemable' may mean, if the context so requires, 'not liable to be called in': *Willey v Joseph Stocks & Co* [1912] 2 Ch 134n.

6 Stock which is expressed to be 'redeemable at the option of the company' is not repayable on the demand of the holder: *Edinburgh Corporation v British Linen Bank* [1913] AC 133 (HL (Sc)).

7 *Higgins v Sargent* (1823) 2 B & C 348; *Page v Newman* (1829) 9 B & C 378.

that if the capital is not paid at the due date, interest shall continue to be payable at the agreed rate. If there is no such provision, although interest may be recovered as damages for non-payment of the principal, it will be allowed only at the 'merchantable rate', or at the rate previously paid, whichever is less.[1] The interest on a loan is a debt, and, although usually expressed to be payable half-yearly, accrues from day to day.[2] It is payable whether or not there are profits. Sometimes, however, interest is declared to be payable only out of profits, in which case the company must apply all available profits for this purpose, and not set aside any part as reserve until the interest is paid in full.[3] Debentures in this form are sometimes called 'income bonds'.

10.6   Debentures issued at a discount

Debentures may be issued at a discount: eg a debenture for £100 may be issued in consideration of £95 advanced to the company, the effect of the discount being an addition to the interest paid,[4] and commission may be paid to underwriters or others for placing or guaranteeing the taking up of debentures. However, convertible debentures must not be issued at a discount so as to evade the rule against issuing shares at a discount. In *Moseley v Koffyfontein Mines*,[5] debentures issued at a discount entitled the holder to call for the allotment of fully paid up shares in satisfaction of the same nominal amount as the debentures. Since the debentures here were immediately convertible it was obviously a device for issuing shares at a discount. Cozens-Hardy LJ left open the question of whether an option to convert is valid if it is not exercisable until some time after the debentures are issued.[6] Although convertible debentures are frequently issued, there will usually be a premium element in the conversion terms so that a discount will not arise.

PART 2: CHARGES

10.7   Fixed and floating charges

The charge created by a debenture may be either 'fixed' or 'floating'. When the charge is fixed it is like an ordinary mortgage and affects the title to the property, so that the company can only deal with the property affected, subject to the charge. But where the charge is a 'floating' one the company may in the ordinary

---

1   *Price v Great Western Rly* (1847) 16 M & W 244; *Re Roberts* (1880) 14 Ch D 49 (CA); *Mellersh v Brown* (1890) 45 Ch D 225.
2   Apportionment Act 1870, sections 2 and 5; *Re Rogers' Trusts* (1863) 1 Dr & Sm 338.
3   *Heslop v Paraguay Central Rly* (1910) 54 SJ 234.
4   *Re Anglo-Danubian Steam Co* (1875) 20 Eq 339; *Campbell's Case* (1876) 4 Ch D 470; *Webb v Shropshire Rly Co* [1893] 3 Ch 307 (CA).
5   [1904] 2 Ch 108 (CA).
6   Ibid, at 120.

course of its business[1] deal with the property covered by the charge, mortgaging it so that the mortgage takes priority over the floating charge, or selling or disposing of it, free from the floating charge, or using it up as the business requires at any time before the charge attaches.[2]

It is common to create the security in such manner that the lands and immovable property of the company are covered by a fixed charge, while the stock-in-trade, chattels, and book debts of the company and its future property are included in a floating charge. In recent years, however, attempts to create fixed charges on present and future book debts have become more common.[3] The debentures usually specify in what events (such as liquidation, default in payment of principal or interest for a stated period, etc) the charge is to be enforceable, and in interpreting these the court will always lean against treating the charge on goods required for the business as being fixed while the business is going on.[4] Where an intention appears that the company should receive and deal with the property charged, it is assumed that only a floating security is intended.[5] A charge, though expressed in words which would otherwise suffice to create a fixed mortgage, will be treated as a floating charge if it appears that it was intended that the company should continue to use the articles charged and turn them over in its business.[6]

The test for classifying a charge as 'fixed' or 'floating' requires the court first to construe the relevant document to ascertain the parties' intentions,[7] and then to

---

1   *Re Old Bush Mills Distillery Co* [1897] Ir R 488. What is within the 'ordinary course of business' will depend on the circumstances of each case. A specific mortgage to raise money for the purpose of carrying on the business of the company is within the words: *Cox Moore v Peruvian Corp* [1908] 1 Ch 604. Some cases have equated the 'ordinary course of business' to what is permitted by the company's objects clause: *Re HH Vivian & Co Ltd* [1900] 2 Ch 654; *Re Borax Co* [1901] 1 Ch 326 at 342; *Re Automatic Bottle Makers Ltd* [1926] Ch 412 at 421; *Hamilton v Hunter* (1982) 7 ACLR 295. But *intra vires* transactions which would cause a cessation of the company's business may fall outside the ordinary course: *Hubbuck v Helms* (1887) 56 LJ Ch 536. The consequences of acting outside the ordinary course have been discussed more in Australia than in England: *Hamilton v Hunter*, above; *Torzillu Pty Ltd v Brynac Pty* (1983) 8 ACLR 52; see generally Worthington, 'Floating Charges – An Alternative Theory' [1994] CLJ 81 at pp 99–102. The absence of relevant English authority suggests that this point rarely causes difficulty in practice. In England, because 'ordinary course' has been linked to issues of vires, there is a question concerning the effect (if any) of section 35 of the Companies Act 1985.

2   *Re Florence Land Co* (1878) 10 Ch D 530 (CA): *Wheatley v Silkstone etc Coal Co* (1885) 29 Ch D 715; *Re Hamilton's Windsor Ironworks* (1879) 12 Ch D 707; *Re Colonial Trusts Corporation* (1879) 15 Ch D 465 at p 472; *In re HH Vivian & Co* [1900] 2 Ch 654.

3   See **10.9**.

4   *Government Stock Investment Co v Manila Rly* [1897] AC 81 (HL): *Evans v Rival Granite Quarries* [1910] 2 KB 979 (CA).

5   *Illingworth v Houldsworth* [1904] AC 355 (HL); *Re GE Tunbridge Ltd* [1995] 1 BCLC 34; *Agnew v Commissioner of Inland Revenue* [2001] 2 BCLC 188 (PC).

6   *National Provincial Bank v United Electric Theatres* [1916] 1 Ch 132; *United Builders Pty Ltd v Mutual Acceptance Ltd* (1980) 33 ALR 1; *Boambee Bay Resort Ltd (in Liquidation) v Equus Financial Services Ltd* (1991) 6 ACSR 532.

7   As does the determination of the extent of the property covered by the charge: *Northern Bank Ltd v Ross* [1991] BCLC 504, [1990] BCC 883 (charge on book debts did not extend to bank account); *Re HiFi Equipment (Cabinets) Ltd* [1998] BCLC 65, (1987) 3 BCC 478 (machines were not 'fixed plant and machinery' and were therefore not caught by a fixed charge (not following *Tudor Heights Ltd v United Dominion Corporation Finance Ltd* [1977] 1 NZLR 532).

categorise this on the basis of relevant legal principles, as stated by Lord Millet in *Agnew v Commissioner of Inland Revenue*:[1]

> In deciding whether a charge is a fixed charge or a floating charge, the court is engaged in a two-stage process. At the first stage it must construe the instrument of charge and seek to gather the intentions of the parties from the language they have used. But the object at this stage of the process is not to discover whether the parties intended to create a fixed or floating charge. It is to ascertain the nature of the rights and obligations which the parties intended to grant each other in respect of the charged assets. Once these have been ascertained, the court can then embark on the second stage of the process, which is one of categorisation. This is a matter of law. It does not depend on the intention of the parties.[2]

The principal indicia of a floating charge have been stated by the Court of Appeal as follows: first, if it is a charge upon all of a certain class of assets, present and future; secondly, if the assets charged would in the ordinary course of business be changing from time to time; and, thirdly, if expressly or by necessary implication the company has the power, until some step is taken by the debenture-holders or trustees, of carrying on its business in the ordinary way so far as regards the assets charged.[3]

It is important to bear in mind that these tests are descriptive and that they do not amount to a precise definition of a floating charge.[4] Thus, although there is a *prima facie* rule that the property secured by a floating charge on the company's undertaking includes future property as well as such property as is owned by the company when the charge is created,[5] it has been held that a charge on present property only can be a floating charge.[6] Equally, a charge can be a fixed charge where the property secured includes future, as well as present, property.[7]

Land owned by a company which is not in the business of property trading would not be regarded as a class of asset changing from time to time in the course of the company's business. Nevertheless, in *Welch v Bowmaker (Ireland) Ltd*,[8] the majority of the Irish Supreme Court[9] held that a charge secured on land could be a floating charge.

The essence of a floating charge is embodied in the third of the characteristics outlined in *Re Yorkshire Woolcombers* and relates to control. Millett LJ (as he then

---

1   [2001] 2 BCLC 188. This case is also known as *Re Brumark Investment* (the name in the New Zealand Courts: see [2000] 1 BCLC 353), but will here be referred to as *Agnew*.

2   Ibid, at paragraph [32]. For an example of how this test is applied, see *Re Txu Europe Group plc* [2004] 1 BCLC 519.

3   *Re Yorkshire Woolcombers' Association* [1903] 2 Ch 284 (CA), affirmed in the House of Lords *sub nom Illingworth v Houldsworth* [1904] AC 355, where it was held that a general charge on book debts, present and future, was a floating charge, although not expressed to be so, and required registration under the Companies Act 1900.

4   *Re Yorkshire Woolcombers* at 295 *per* Romer LJ and 298 *per* Cozens Hardy LJ; *Re Croftbell Ltd* [1990] BCLC 844, [1990] BCC 781.

5   *Re Panama, New Zealand and Australia Royal Mail Co* (1870) LR 5 Ch App 318; *Illingworth v Houldsworth* [1904] AC 355; *Re Croftbell Ltd*, above. This rule can assist where there is some doubt about the extent of the security: *Re Alfred Priestman & Co Ltd* [1936] 2 All ER 1340.

6   *Re Bond Worth Ltd* [1980] 1 Ch 228 at 267; *Re Atlantic Medical Ltd* [1992] BCC 653 at 658 ('it is very unusual indeed that a floating charge would be limited to existing assets of a company'); *Re Cimex Tissues Ltd* [1994] BCC 626 at 637–639.

7   *Tailby v Official Receiver* (1883) 13 App Cas 543. See further, **10.9**.

8   [1980] IR 251.

9   Kenny J dissented precisely because the second characteristic of a floating charge, as outlined in *Yorkshire Woolcombers*, was not present.

was) once said that whether a charge is fixed or floating depends on the freedom of the chargor to deal with the proceeds of the charged assets in the ordinary course of business free from the security,[1] but in a later case he reformulated the correct question as being whether the chargee is in control of the charged assets.[2] In *Agnew*, Lord Millett noted that:

> ... [I]n construing a debenture to see whether it creates a fixed or a floating charge, the only intention which is relevant is ... whether the charged assets were intended to be under the control of the company or of the charge holder.[3]

The 'control test' recognises that some restrictions on the chargor's powers to deal with the charged assets, for instance limitations on the power to create further charges ranking in priority, may be compatible with a floating charge. The degree of control (or freedom) required to create a fixed (or floating) charge has been discussed extensively in cases concerned with the nature of charge on book debts (discussed at **10.9**).

Precisely because it confers greater control, lenders might be expected to prefer fixed security and to take floating security only on assets where the frequency of turnover makes fixed security impracticable. An inherent risk in a floating charge is that the company will dissipate the subject-matter of the security through imprudent trading, leaving the lender with a security that is virtually worthless. Also, a lender who has taken only floating security, risks finding himself postponed to other creditors of the company who have themselves obtained fixed security or who are afforded a preferential status by the insolvency legislation.[4]

The Insolvency Act 1986 provides a reason[5] why it can be important for a lender to take a floating charge, either on its own or in addition to fixed security.[6] Under the Act, an administrator can be appointed by the court, and, following changes made by the Enterprise Act 2002, the holder of a 'qualifying floating charge',[7] to administer the affairs of a company in financial difficulties. Administration is a collective insolvency procedure and no one creditor, or group of creditors, is entitled to control the administrator in the exercise of his powers. The administrator's statutory powers are extensive and include the ability to sell property which is subject to a charge without the consent of the holder of that security.[8] The significant restriction on the administration procedure is that an

---

1   *Royal Trust Bank v National Westminster Bank plc* [1996] BCC 613 at 616. In *Re ASRS Establishment Ltd* [2000] 1 BCLC 631, Otton LJ advised that this should be approached 'with some caution' (at 643).

2   *Re Cosslett (Contractors) Ltd* [1997] BCC 724 at 734. See also *Re Cimex Tissues Ltd* [1994] BCC 626 and cases such as *Re Brightlife Ltd* [1987] 1 Ch 200 and *Re Westmaze Ltd* [1999] BCC 441 (charge on book debts was a floating charge despite restrictions on the chargor's power to assign or factor the debts). For a fixed charge, the chargee must enjoy his power to control the charged assets as chargee and not in some other capacity, such as director of the chargor company: *Re Double S Printers Ltd* [1999] BCC 303.

3   [2001] 2 BCLC 188 at paragraph [32].

4   Although the number of preferential creditors has been greatly reduced by the Enterprise Act 2002.

5   Another reason, also provided by the Insolvency Act 1986, is that an administrative receiver, but not an ordinary receiver, enjoys a wide range of implied statutory powers. See **10.51**.

6   On this function of the floating charge, see Mokal, 'The Floating Charge – An Elegy' in Worthington (ed), *Commercial Law and Commercial Practice* (Oxford: Hart, 2003).

7   See **10.39**.

8   The administrator requires the consent of the court to sell property which is subject to a fixed charge; the court's consent is not required where the security is a floating charge: section 15(1) and (2).

administrator may not be appointed where an administrative receiver[1] has been appointed to the company unless the appointor of the administrative receiver consents.[2]

An administrative receiver is defined by section 29(2) of the Insolvency Act 1986 as a receiver or manager of the whole (or substantially the whole) of a company's property, appointed by or on behalf of the holders of any debentures of the company secured by a charge which, as created, was a floating charge, or by such a charge and one or more other securities.[3] However, following the changes made to the Insolvency Act by the Enterprise Act 2002, the holder of a 'qualifying floating charge'[4] created after 15 September 2003[5] may no longer appoint an administrative receiver.

Since the coming into force of the administration procedure contained in the Insolvency Act 1986, there has emerged the concept of the 'lightweight' floating charge.[6] Where a company's assets consist wholly or mainly of property which is not expected to be the subject of rapid turnover, an example being a holding company with assets consisting almost entirely of shares in subsidiaries, the lender can take a fixed charge on the assets without unduly impeding the company's business affairs. This fixed charge will largely satisfy the lender's desire for control, save for the fact that it will not enable the lender to prevent the appointment of an administrator. Prior to 15 September 2003, this need could be met by also taking a floating charge over the company's undertaking. This floating charge may be almost identical in scope to the fixed charge and the detailed covenants which would usually be required from the company if the floating charge stood alone can be dispensed with, thus making the charge 'lightweight'.

10.8 The nature of a floating charge

A floating charge is a present charge, not a future one, but it does not specifically affect any item until some event happens which causes it to become fixed.[7] Thus the debenture holder has under his floating charge an immediate equity or charge on the property, but the company can continue to deal with the property charged in the course of its business until the charge attaches as a fixed charge, or, as it is often described, 'crystallises'.

Some of the earlier cases,[8] reasoning by analogy to the fixed charge, explained what was then a novel form of security as being like a specific mortgage plus a licence to the mortgagor to dispose of the company's assets in the ordinary course

---

1   See Part 4, below. An administative receiver may now not be appointed by a creditor who holds a 'qualifying floating charge': section 72A of the Insolvency Act 1986, as amended.

2   Section 39(1) of Schedule B1 to the Insolvency Act 1986 (inserted by the Enterprise Act 2002).

3   Or a person who would be such a receiver or manager but for the appointment of some other person as the receiver of part of the company's property: section 29(2)(b).

4   Defined in section 14 of Schedule B1 to the Insolvency Act 1986.

5   Section 72A and the Insolvency Act 1986, section 72A (Appointed Date) Order 2003 (S.I. 2003/2095), regulation 2.

6   Oditah, 'Lightweight Floating Charges' [1991] JBL 49; Marks and Emmet, 'Administrative Receivers: Question of Identity and Double Identity' [1994] JBL 1.

7   See (*per* Buckley LJ) *Evans v Rival Granite Quarries* [1910] 2 KB at 999; *Mercantile Bank of India v Chartered Bank of India & Co* [1937] 1 All ER 231.

8   Eg *Re Florence Land Co* (1878) 10 ChD 543; *Davey & Co v Williamson* [1898] 2 QB 194 at 200.

of business. Buckley LJ[1] repudiated this explanation of the floating charge in favour of the concept of 'a floating mortgage applying to every item comprised in the security, but not specifically affecting any item until some event occurs, or some act on the part of the mortgagee is done, which causes it to crystallize into a fixed security'. This notion of a floating charge, characterising it as a 'present security on a shifting fund of assets',[2] better accords with the detailed rules governing the functioning of the floating charge between the time of its creation and its crystallisation.

The nature of the lender's interest in the company's property created by a floating charge and the related question of the basis of the company's power to continue to deal with the assets are issues which have intrigued commentators and on which there is an extensive amount of literature.[3] Gough argues that a floating charge gives the lender no proprietary interest in the company's property until such time as the charge crystallises into a fixed charge[4] but this view has been disputed by many other writers.[5] The cases are not consistent and whilst the argument that a floating charge confers a proprietary interest has support,[6] so too does the alternative view.[7] Although its true nature has proved to be somewhat elusive, this has not prevented the floating charge from becoming an important element of corporate financing. Bearing this in mind, it may be that it is unnecessary to attempt to pinpoint in an absolute sense the proprietary interest created by a floating charge and that a more fruitful line of enquiry is to consider whether in specific contexts, the floating charge gives the lender an interest which, for the purpose in question, is to be regarded as 'proprietary'.[8] In *Re Margart Pty*, the Supreme Court of New South Wales[9] held that a statutory provision[10] which invalidated dispositions of a company's property after the

---

1   *Evans v Rival Granite Quarries* [1910] 2 KB 979 at 999. See also *Biggerstaff v Rowatts Wharf Ltd* [1896] 2 Ch 93 at 105 *per* Kay LJ.
2   *Re Cimex Tissues*, above, at 635.
3   Gough, *Company Charges* 2nd edn (Butterworths, 1996).
4   A view also asserted by the same author in Chapter 9 of Finn (ed), *Equity and Commercial Relationships* (Law Book Company, 1978).
5   For example: Goode, 'It can now be taken as settled that the floating charge creates an immediate interest *in rem*' in *Legal Problems of Credit and Security* 2nd edn (Sweet & Maxwell, 1988), p 46: Farrar, 'World Economic Stagnation Puts the Floating Charge on Trial' (1980) 1 Co Law 83; Ferran, 'Floating Charges – the Nature of the Security' [1988] CLJ 213; Worthington, 'Floating Charges – An Alternative Theory' [1994] CLJ 81; and Worthington, *Proprietary Interests in Commercial Transactions* (Oxford University Press, 1996), Chapter 4. See also Pennington, 'The Genesis of the Floating Charge' (1960) 23 MLR 630.
6   *Driver v Broad* [1893] 1 QB 744; *Wallace v Evershed* [1899] 1 Ch 891; *Landall Holdings Ltd v Caratti* [1979] WAR 97 at 102–103; *Hamilton v Hunter* (1982) 7 ACLR 295 at 306; *Re Margart Pty Ltd, Hamilton v Westpac Banking Corp* (1984) 9 ACLR 269 at 271–272; *Canadian Imperial Bank of Commerce v Coopers & Lybrand* (1989) 57 DLR (4th) 633; *Wily v St George Partnership Banking Ltd* (1997) 30 ACSR 204.
7   *Tricontinental Corp v FCT* (1987) 12 ACLR 421, citing, *inter alia, Evans v Rival Granite Quarries Ltd* [1910] 2 KB 979.
8   See *Wily v St George Partnership Banking Ltd* (1997) 30 ACSR 204 at 204 *per* Sackville J: 'That different views continue to be expressed on such an apparently fundamental question [the juridical nature of the floating charge] reflects the fact that particular cases (like the present) usually turn on more prosaic issues, such as the construction of a statute or the terms of the particular charge.'
9   Although an Australian decision, this was followed by Vinelott J in *Re French's Wine Bar Ltd* [1987] BCLC 499 and would seem to represent English law.
10 The equivalent provision in the Insolvency Act 1986 is section 127.

commencement of its liquidation did not apply to dispositions made to a debenture holder who held an uncrystallised floating charge, because, for that purpose, the debenture-holder had a beneficial interest in the property trans-ferred. In *Re Goldcorp Exchange Ltd*[1] Lord Mustill, delivering the judgment of the Judicial Board of the Privy Council, stated that the chargor's freedom to deal with the secured assets prior to crystallisation did not mean that the chargee's right to the assets was circumscribed by an indebtedness of a purely personal nature and held that the floating charge gave its holder a sufficient proprietary interest to defeat a claim by a third party to an estoppel arising from statements made by the company.

10.9   Charges on book debts

The characteristics of fixed and floating charges have received close judicial scrutiny in a line of cases concerned with charges on book debts or other debts or receivables such as rental payments.[2] 'Book debts' are simply debts which, as a matter of accounting practice, would ordinarily be entered in the books of the company.[3] The case law was recently clarified by the decision in *Agnew v Commissioners of Inland Revenue*,[4] but to put that decision in context, it is necessary to review several previous decisions eventually leading to the ruling in *Agnew*.

In the landmark decision of *Siebe Gorman & Co Ltd v Barclays Bank Ltd*,[5] the court held that a debenture effectively created a fixed charge on present and future book debts. The significant terms of the debenture obliged the company not to assign or charge its book debts without the lender's consent and required the company to pay the proceeds of book debts into an account held with the lender. Slade J held that the bank effectively had a lien on the proceeds paid into the bank account and could prevent the company from making withdrawals in the course of its business. It was held that the restrictions on the book debts and on their proceeds together gave the lender a degree of control which was inconsistent with the freedom to the company that was the vital characteristic of a floating charge. Despite condemnation from the Review Committee on Insolvency Law and Practice,[6] the decision in *Siebe Gorman* was not reversed by the 1980s'

---

1   [1994] 3 WLR 199 at 212–213.
2   For an explanation of the tendency of banks in recent years to move from a floating charge
     to a series of fixed charges giving a greater degree of protection, see Robbie and Gill, 'Fixed
     and Floating Charges. A New Look at the Banks' Position' [1981] JBL 95. For further analysis
     of the cases, see Pennington, 'Fixed Charges over Future Assets of a Company' (1985) 6 Co
     Law 9; McCormack, 'Fixed Charges over Future Book Debts' (1987) 8 Co Law 3; Pearce,
     'Fixed Charges Over Book Debts' [1987] JBL 18.
3   *Tailby v Official Receiver; Independent Automatic Sales Ltd v Knowles and Foster* [1962] 1 WLR 974;
     Paul & Frank Ltd v Discount Bank (Overseas) Ltd [1967] Ch 348.
4   [2001] 2 BCLC 188 (PC). This has subsequently been followed by the House of Lords in
     Smith (Administrators of Cosslett (Contractors) Ltd) v Bridgend County Borough Council [2001]
     UKHL 58, [2002] 1 BCLC 77.
5   [1979] 2 Lloyd's Rep 142.
6   Cmnd 8558 (1982), paragraphs 1584–1586.

insolvency legislation and it has since been followed,[1] and distinguished,[2] although post-*Agnew*, its days seem to be numbered.[3]

In *Re New Bullas Ltd*, the Court of Appeal[4] established that control of the debts *and* of their proceeds is not the prerequisite of a fixed charge on book debts: the charging document can treat the debts and their proceeds as divisible and create a fixed charge on the debts, but only a floating charge on the proceeds of those debts.[5] The debenture in question was expressed to create a fixed charge over debts and provided for their proceeds to be paid into a current account or another designated account. In the absence of directions from the debenture-holder, on payment into the account the proceeds were released from the fixed charge and became subject to a floating charge. Even though the proceeds of the debts could thus cease to fall within the debenture-holder's control as soon as they were paid into the account, the charge on the debts themselves was held to be a fixed charge. This decision attracted much comment[6] and doubts were soon cast over the *New Bullas* concept of the divisibility of debts and their proceeds in the courts.[7] *New Bullas* and subsequent cases[8] left the law on the identifying characteristics of fixed and floating charges on book debts or other receivable in a state of disarray. However, much-needed clarity was restored by the Privy Council decision in *Agnew*.[9] In that case, Brumark Investment Ltd had granted a *New Bullas* style charge in favour of its bank, and, having gone into liquidation, the question arose who would be entitled to the proceeds of the outstanding book debts. The Privy Council had to consider whether a charge over uncollected book debts which the company was free to collect and which allowed it to use the proceeds in the

---

1   *Re Keenan Bros Ltd* [1986] BCLC 242 (Supreme Court (Ireland)); *William Gaskell Group Ltd v Highley* [1993] BCC 200.

2   *Re Brightlife Ltd* [1987] Ch 200, [1986] 3 All ER 673, [1987] 2 WLR 197, [1986] BCLC 418, (1986) 2 BCC 99 at 359. *Siebe Gorman* was not followed on indistinguishable facts in *Supercool Refrigeration & Air Conditioning Ltd v Hoverd Industries Ltd* [1994] 3 NZLR 300. See further Ferran, *Company Law and Corporate Finance* (Oxford University Press, 1999) pp 517–529.

3   *Re Spectrum Plus Ltd* [2004] EWHC 9, [2004] 1 All ER 981, Ch.D.

4   [1994] BCLC 485, [1994] BCC 36 noted, (1994) 110 LQR 340, [1994] CLJ 225. See also Goode, 'Charges over Book Debts: a Missed Opportunity' (1994) 110 LQR 592.

5   Cf *Waters v Widdows* [1984] VR 503, Victoria, Australia and *Re Holidair Ltd* [1994] ILRM 481 (Ireland, Supreme Court).

6   See Berg 'Charges Over Book Debts – a Reply' [1995] JBL 433; Worthington, 'Fixed Charges over Book Debts and Other Receivables' (1997) 113 LQR 562; Gregory, 'Fixed Charges on Book Debts – The Conceptual Light Still Hid From Our Eyes' (1996/97) 3 RALQ 65; Gregory and Walton, 'Book Debt Charges – The Saga Goes On' (1999) 115 LQR 14.

7   *Royal Trust Bank v National Westminster Bank plc* [1996] BCC 613 at 619 *per* Millett LJ. See also *Oakdale (Richmond) Ltd v National Westminster Bank plc* [1997] 1 BCLC 63 at 75 *per* Chadwick J.

8   Such as the *Atlantic* decisions (*Re Atlantic Computer Systems plc* [1992] Ch 505 and *Re Atlantic Medical Ltd* [1992] BCC 653). The Court of Appeal's conclusion in *Computer* that the charge in question was a fixed charge seems to have been strongly influenced by the fact that the subject-matter of the security was a set of present assets and did not extend to future assets. However, it is well established (as was acknowledged by Vinelott J in *Medical*) that that specifity of the charging clause is not determinative of the nature of the charge as fixed or floating. The authorities to this effect were not, however, considered by the Court of Appeal. See further, Bridge (1994) 107 LQR 394; Goode (1994) 110 LQR 340; Berg [1995] JBL 433; Worthington (1997) 113 LQR 562 and Ferran, *Company Law and Corporate Finance* (Oxford University Press, 1999) pp 517–529.

9   Known at first instance in New Zealand as *Re Brumark Investments Ltd* (16 February 1999, unreported), NZHC, noted (1999) 115 LQR 365, which followed *New Bullas*, but the NZ Court of Appeal reversed that decision [2000] 1 NZLR 223. *Agnew* was an appeal from the NZ CA decision.

ordinary course of its business was a fixed or a floating charge. The opinion was given by Lord Millett, who undertook an extensive review of the relevant case-law that eventually resulted in the decision in *New Bullas*. His conclusion was that *New Bullas* was 'wrongly decided'[1] for a number of reasons: first, the Court of Appeal in *New Bullas* had taken an approach to construction which was 'fundamentally mistaken'[2] because it focused exclusively on the parties' intentions.[3] Secondly, Nourse LJ's argument that the book debts ceased to be subject to the fixed charge because of what the parties had agreed rather than because the company was free to collect the debts would be 'entirely destructive of the floating charge'.[4] The third, and most crucial, point related to the question whether debts can be separated from their proceeds, a matter crucial to the *New Bullas*-style charge. Lord Millett accepted that property and its proceeds are two different assets, and a book debt could be assigned, as well as realised by collection (when the debt is wholly extinguished).[5] However, the value of a debt, which is a right to receive payment, can only be exploited by exercising that right; separating ownership of debts from that of their proceeds 'makes no commercial sense'.[6] Consequently, in determining whether the charge was fixed or floating, the crucial question was not merely whether the company was free to collect the debts, but whether it could do so for its own benefit. It is not necessary that the company is prevented from realising the debt, as long as the proceeds are not at the company's disposal. A *New Bullas* style charge left the company free to realise the debt and to replace it with assets not subject to a fixed charge and therefore at the free disposal of the company, and that is why it could not be a fixed charge.

This decision restores much-needed clarity,[7] although it does not resolve all difficulties.[8] In particular, it raises fresh doubts over the decision in *Siebe Gorman*, which assumed that where the proceeds of the book debts are paid into a bank account with the lender (a clearing bank), the charge would be a fixed charge. The difficulty with this has always been that the company was free to draw on the account,[9] and several comments by Lord Millett in *Agnew* are thought to be critical of *Siebe Gorman*.[10] The matter was addressed by Sir Andrew Morritt V-C in *Re Spectrum Plus Ltd*,[11] a case involving a charge almost identical to that in *Siebe Gorman*. This followed an announcement by the government that it intended to challenge the *Siebe Gorman* decision, although only with regard to insolvency

---

1   Paragraph [50].
2   Paragraph [32].
3   See **10.7**, above, for the correct approach.
4   Paragraph [34].
5   Paragraph [43].
6   Paragraph [46].
7   A similar approach had been adopted by Hart J in *Chalk v Khan* [2000] 2 BCLC 361. In that case, the company did not have a current account with the charge holder, and had therefore been directed to pay any proceeds into an account held at another bank, which it was free to access. See also *Re ASRS Establishment Ltd* [2000] 1 BCLC 631 (CA).
8   See eg, McCormack (2002) 23 Co Law 84; Capper (2003) 24 Co Law 325.
9   Contrast *Re Keenan Brothers* [1986] BCLC 242, Irish Supreme Court.
10 At paragraph [38], he used the words '. . . was thought to obtain in *Siebe Gorman* . . .', and at paragraph [48], it was noted that 'their Lordships would wish to make it clear that it is not enough to provide in the debenture that the account is a blocked account if it is not operated as one in fact'. See also Capper (2003) 24 Co Law 325.
11 [2004] EWHC 9 (Ch) [2004] 1 BCLC 335.

proceedings arising after the date of the decision in *Agnew*,[1] and *Spectrum* was that challenge. Morritt V-C reviewed the opinion given in *Agnew* and concluded that because the account into which the proceeds were paid was an ordinary current account on which no restrictions had been imposed and which had been set up to provide working capital for the company, the charge was a floating, and not a fixed, charge. Although this outcome was inevitable, it was unusual because it required the court to depart from a previous judgment of the same court, and it is likely that the matter will have to be resolved conclusively by the Court of Appeal.

10.10 Floating charges and the Bills of Sale Acts

A debenture of a company formed under the Companies Act 1985 is not within the Bills of Sale Acts 1878 and 1882, and may therefore create a charge on chattels, without being in the form prescribed by or registered under the last-named Act.[2]

As a consequence of the requirements of the Bills of Sale Acts, it is generally thought that it is not practicable for partners (or sole traders) to create an effective floating charge. This inability was made the greater by the 'reputed ownership' provision of the Bankruptcy Act 1914[3] (now repealed), which used to apply in the bankruptcy of partnerships and individuals but not in the liquidation of insolvent companies.[4] The report of the Review Committee on Insolvency Law and Practice[5] proposed the abolition of 'reputed ownership' together with 'appropriate amendments' of the Bills of Sale Acts so as to permit individuals (and partners) to create effective floating charges over their business undertaking.[6] This would not extend to assets not used in the debtor's business, trade or profession. Professor Diamond in his review of security interests in property other than land also proposed that the floating charge form of security should be made available to businesses generally, irrespective of the form in which the business was carried on.[7] There is no indication that repeal or reform of the Bills of Sale Acts is likely to be forthcoming in the immediate future. However, under the Limited Liability Partnerships Act 2000, limited liability partnerships are bodies corporate[8] and have the capacity to grant a floating charge.

10.11 Crystallisation of the floating charge

The charge crystallises or becomes fixed when the chargee takes possession or appoints a receiver on the occurrence of one of the events which under the provision of the charge renders the security enforceable. Moreover, if the company goes into liquidation the charge will crystallise, even though the liquidation is for reconstruction purposes and the provisions of the charge

---

1   Capper (2003) 24 Co Law 325 at 332 notes that as the decision technically 'declares' the law, previous decisions in conflict with it could be unscrambled. In the case of *Siebe Gorman*-style charges, this would be an impossible undertaking.
2   See section 17 of the Bills of Sales Act 1882. *Re Standard Manufacturing Co* [1891] 1 Ch 627 (CA); *Richards v Overseers of Kidderminster* [1896] 2 Ch 212. Registration is, however, necessary under the Companies Act 1985, section 395; see **10.23**.
3   Section 38(c).
4   See *Gorringe v Invell Rubber Co* (1886) 34 ChD 128.
5   Cmnd 8558, June 1982.
6   Ibid, paragraphs 1093 and 1569.
7   *A Review of Security Interests in Property* (HMSO, 1989), paragraph 16.15.
8   Section 1(2) of the Limited Liability Partnerships Act 2000.

stipulate only that the principal shall become payable on the company going into liquidation otherwise than for the purpose of reconstruction.[1] But while the company continues in business,[2] the charge does not crystallise merely by the happening of the events which entitle the chargee to intervene,[3] for 'unless something has occurred entitling the debenture holders to make such an application' (ie an application to the court for a receiver), 'and the application has in fact been made, or an action brought by them or on their behalf to realise their security, or unless something has happened which entitles the debenture holders to determine their licence to the company to carry on their business, and they have actually done so, the company is entitled to do all the things which the licence entitles them to do'.[4] If, therefore, the company assigns a book debt which is covered by the floating charge, it becomes the property of the assignee, and the receiver subsequently appointed cannot obtain priority by giving the debtor notice to pay him after the assignment.[5] Equally, a contractual lien will take priority over a floating charge where it arises from a contract made in the ordinary course of business before crystallisation.

It is established that a floating charge will crystallise in the event of the cessation of business of the chargor company.[6] It is uncertain whether the commencement of administration proceedings or the appointment of an administrator would cause a floating charge to crystallise in the absence of express provision to that effect in the charge.[7] Since 1986, when the administration procedure was first introduced, it has become common for debenture terms to provide expressly for crystallisation in the event of administration.

The crystallisation of a floating charge over the undertaking of the company effects an equitable assignment to the debenture-holders of the company's present assets which are comprised in the security[8] and also, unless excluded by the terms of the charge, of future assets accruing to the company as they arise. In

---

1   *Player v Crompton & Co* [1914] 1 Ch 954.
2   The 'cessation of the company's business' is preferable to 'ceasing to be a going concern' as a description of this crystallising event. *Re Woodroffes (Musical Instruments) Ltd* [1986] Ch 366, [1985] 2 All ER 908, [1985] 3 WLR 543, [1985] BCLC 227.
3   *Edward Nelson & Co v Faber* [1903] 2 KB 367. The text assumes that the charge does not contain an automatic crystallisation clause. Such clauses are discussed in **10.12**.
4   *Evans v Rival Granite Quarries* [1910] 2 KB 979 *per* Vaughan Williams LJ at 986. At 993, Fletcher Moulton LJ says, 'Mere default on the part of the company does not change the character of the security; the debenture holder must actually intervene.' At 1002, Buckley LJ says, 'No equity arises in a debenture holder whose security is a floating charge from his merely giving notice to seize a particular asset of the company. He must do something to turn his security from a floating into a fixed charge.'
5   *In re Ind, Coope & Co* [1991] 2 Ch 223.
6   *Re Woodroffes (Musical Instruments) Ltd* [1986] Ch 366; *Re Brightlife Ltd* [1987] Ch 200; *Bank of Credit and Commerce International SA v BRS Kumar Brothers Ltd* [1994] 1 BCLC 211; *Re The Real Meat Co Ltd* [1996] BCC 254.
7   In *Re GE Tunbridge Ltd* [1994] BCC 563, the parties conceded that the appointment of an administrator would not cause crystallisation.
8   *George Barker (Transport) Ltd v Eynon* [1974] 1 All ER 900, [1974] 1 WLR 462, [1974] 1 Lloyd's Rep 65; *Leyland DAF Ltd v Automotive Products Ltd* [1993] BCC 389 at 392; *Re ELS Ltd, Ramsbottom v Luton Borough Council* [1994] 3 WLR 616, [1994] BCLC 743, [1994] BCC 449 (local authority precluded from levying distress on goods for non-payment of rates after charge had crystallised).

NW Robbie & Co Ltd v Witney Warehouse Co Ltd,[1] the majority of the Court of Appeal held that after the appointment of a receiver each future debt to the company became, as it arose, a chose in action belonging to the company subject to an equitable charge in favour of the debenture-holder.

10.11.1 Notices of crystallisation

It has become increasingly common for floating charges to include a provision whereby the holder is entitled to cause the charge to crystallise by serving a notice to that effect on the company. In *Re Woodroffes*, above, the effectiveness of a notice of crystallisation was assumed and in *Re Brightlife*, above, Hoffmann J decided the point. Hoffmann J held that crystallising events were not prescribed by law[2] and were to be determined by the parties to a charge as a matter of contract; crystallisation on winding up, receivership or cessation of business would be implied into a charge unless expressly excluded but it was open to the parties to agree upon additional crystallising events. A notice of crystallisation served in accordance with the terms of the charge would therefore be effective to cause the crystallisation of a floating charge.

10.12 Automatic crystallisation

Crystallisation on the service of a notice requires positive action by or on behalf of the chargee. Is it possible to dispense altogether with the need for positive action and to provide for crystallisation to occur automatically upon the occurrence of specified events? It is established that an event which is of such magnitude as to lead to the cessation of the company's business is an implied automatic crystallising event: in that situation the *raison d'être* of the floating charge, namely continued freedom for the chargor company to use the charged assets in the course of its business, disappears. Greater controversy has in the past surrounded the possibility of providing for automatic crystallisation upon the happening of some lesser event which is not necessary incompatible with continued trading by the company, such as the creation of a second mortgage or charge without the debenture-holder's consent; but it is now clear that freedom of contract prevails in this area of the law.

The validity of an automatic crystallisation clause was upheld in New Zealand in *Re Manurewa Transport Ltd.*[3] The concept of automatic or 'self-generating' crystallisation has also been accepted in Australia,[4] although it has been rejected

1   [1963] 1 WLR 1324 (CA). The reasoning in *Witney Warehouse* was applied in *Rendell v Doors & Doors Ltd* [1975] 2 NZLR 199. See also *Security Trust v Royal Bank of Canada* [1976] 2 WLR 437 (PC) at 491 in respect of land acquired after a floating charge has crystallised by the appointment of a receiver.

2   As suggested by *Edward Nelson & Co Ltd v Faber & Co* [1903] 2 KB 367 at 376. Hoffmann J explained the statements in the earlier case by saying that the judge (Joyce J) was simply stating the crystallising events that would be implied unless expressly excluded by the parties.

3   [1971] NZLR 909. See McLauchlan [1972] New Zealand Law Journal at p 330.

4   *Stein v Saywell* (1969) 121 CLR 529; *DCT (Vic) v Horsburgh* [1984] VR 773; *Fire Nymph Products Ltd v The Heating Centre Pty Ltd (in Liquidation)* (1991–1992) 7 ACSR 365. Cf *Re Bismark Australia Ltd* [1981] VC 527. See also Burns, 'Automatic Crystallisation of Company Charges: Contractual Creativity or Confusion' (1992) 290 ABLR 125.

in Canada.[1] In England, *dicta* of Buckley LJ in *Evans v Rival Granite Quarries Ltd*[2] supported automatic crystallisation, but both Vaughan Williams and Fletcher Moulton LJJ stated in the same case (also *obiter*) that the debenture-holder was required to intervene. The matter finally arose for decision in England in *Re Permanent House (Holdings) Ltd*[3] where, confirming views which he had expressed *obiter* in *Re Brightlife*, above, Hoffmann J held that an automatic crystallisation clause was valid and effective. In *Brightlife*, Hoffmann J preferred the New Zealand authority to the approach taken in Canada and did not feel constrained by earlier English decisions to reach the opposite conclusion. In his view, automatic crystallisation was essentially a matter of explicit contractual provision. The rights and duties which the law might or might not categorise as a floating charge were derived from the agreement of the parties, as supplemented by implied terms, and merely because some terms deviated from what might be regarded as the 'standard' terms of a floating charge did not preclude the charge from being a floating charge. Hoffmann J considered that any policy objections to automatic crystallisation were matters to be settled by an appellate court or by Parliament.

Policy objections to automatic crystallisation clauses include the potential prejudice that they may cause to innocent third parties, who may be unaware (and have no means of knowing) that the charge has crystallised.[4] There is also the uncertainty that could result from a situation where a debenture-holder tacitly waives a crystallisation which has occurred in accordance with an automatic crystallisation clause and allows the company to continue its business.[5]

A particular objection, considered in *Re Brightlife* and *Re Permanent Houses*, above, but now, because of legislative developments, of no more than historical interest, was the effect of automatic crystallisation clauses on the position of preferential creditors. In a receivership or liquidation, preferential debts rank before debts secured by a floating charge,[6] but before reforms enacted by the 1980s insolvency legislation, it was held[7] that the preferential status could only be

---

1   *The Queen in Right of British Columbia v Consolidated Churchill Copper Corporation Ltd* (1978) 5
     WWR 652.
2   [1910] 2 KB 979.
3   (1989) 5 BCC 151.
4   The policy objections have been considered by various commentators and review bodies. The
     literature includes Farrar, 'The Crystallisation of a Floating Charge' (1976) 40 Conv 397;
     Gough, *Company Charges* 2nd edn (Butterworths, 1996), Chapters 11 and 16 and 'The
     Floating Charge' in Finn (ed), *Equity and Commercial Relationships* (Law Book Company, 1987)
     p 239; Boyle, 'The Validity of Automatic Crystallisation Clauses' [1979] JBL 231; Dean,
     'Crystallisation of a Floating Charge' (1982–4) 1–2 *Company and Securities Law Journal* 185;
     Review Committee on Insolvency Law and Practice, (Cmnd 8558, 1982) paras 1577–80;
     Goode, *Legal Problems of Credit and Security* 2nd edn (Sweet & Maxwell, 1988) pp 69–75;
     Pennington, 'Loans to Companies' in Pettet (ed), *Company Law in Change* (Stevens, 1987) pp
     99–107.
5   McLauchlan [1972] New Zealand Law Journal at 330. On 'decrystallisation' see Goode, op cit
     pp 73–6 and Lightman and Moss. *The Law of Receivers of Companies* 2nd edn (Sweet & Maxwell,
     1994), at paragraphs 3.41 to 3.45. See also Grantham, 'Refloating a Floating Charge' [1997]
     CfiLR 53; Tan, 'Automatic Crystallisation, De-Crystallisation and Convertibility of Charges'
     [1998] CfiLR 41.
6   Sections 40 and 175 of the Insolvency Act 1986. The categories of preferential debts are set
     out in Schedule 6 to the Act, although after the Enterprise Act 2002, there are only a few
     categories left. Preferential debts are therefore much less significant now than they once
     were.
7   *Re Griffin Hotel Co* [1941] Ch 129; *Re Christonette International* [1982] 3 All ER 227; *Re Brightlife*,
     above; *Re Permanent Houses*, above; *William Gaskell v Highley*, above.

claimed over debts secured by a floating charge which *was floating at the time of the receivership or liquidation*. If a floating charge had crystallised prior to the receivership or liquidation, the preferential debts ranked behind the debt secured by the charge. An automatic crystallisation clause could thus enable the holder of a floating charge to be repaid before the preferential debts. It may be noted that this objection could be levelled not just at automatic crystallisation clauses but also at clauses permitting crystallisation on the service of a notice and at crystallisation upon cessation of business prior to receivership or liquidation. However, automatic crystallisation clauses attracted particular criticism because they were thought to increase significantly the power of creditors lending money on the security of a floating charge to structure the lending to their advantage at the expense of the holders of preferential debts. This objection to automatic crystallisation has disappeared because, for the purposes of the relevant provisions of the Insolvency Act 1986, a floating charge is now defined as a charge which as created was a floating charge.[1] The status of the charge when it is created is all important and it now makes no difference that the charge may have crystallised before receivership or liquidation.

The possible ill effects of such clauses on innocent third parties remain.[2] A potential solution was offered by a provision of the Companies Act 1989,[3] whereby the Secretary of State was to be empowered to make regulations requiring notice of the occurrence of crystallising events to be filed at the companies registry. It was envisaged that the regulations could provide for the crystallisation to be ineffective until notified. This provision of the Companies Act 1989 is part of the extensive amendments to the requirements for the registration of company charges which are not now to be brought into force.

10.13 Crystallisation and rights of set-off

A right of set-off which accrues to a debtor of the company before crystallisation can be raised against a claim by the receiver against the debtor: in *Rother Iron Works Ltd v Canterbury Precision Engineers Ltd*[4] Russell LJ distinguished *Robbie v Witney Warehouse Co Ltd*,[5] where the cross-claim was assigned to the debtor after the crystallisation of the charge. Moreover, there the claim made by the receiver arose out of a contract made by the receiver subsequent to his appointment. In *Rother Iron Works* the contract to sell goods, which the receiver was seeking to enforce, had been made before his appointment.[6]

---

1   Sections 40 and 251 contain the definition.
2   Goode, op cit, argues that potential unfairness to third parties disappears if the position is analysed on agency principles. He suggests that automatic crystallisation may terminate the company's actual authority to use the charged assets in the course of its business, but that, until the fact is brought to their attention, outsiders can continue to rely on the company's apparent authority.
3   Section 100.
4   [1973] 2 WLR 281 (CA).
5   [1963] 1 WLR 1324 (CA).
6   See further, as to the legal position of an 'administrative receiver' appointed under a general floating charge, Part 4 of this chapter. The right to appoint an administrative receiver has been removed for floating charges created after 15 September 2003.

10.14   Priorities and the floating charge

The rules as to priority between charges created by a company are basically the same as those governing legal and equitable charges generally. These rules are derived from the cases and they have not been codified in statutory form. The registration requirements of the Companies Act 1985 may affect the operation of the priority rules but it is important to note that they do not supplant those rules. The absence of clear statutory rules governing priority is open to criticism because it leads to uncertainty. The position is different in Scotland where clear statutory rules are laid down as to priority.[1]

As between equitable charges, priority is governed by the order of creation, the charge created first ranking first in order of priority. A legal mortgage will rank before a previous equitable security where the legal interest is acquired by a *bona fide* purchase for value without notice of the earlier interest. The special qualities of the floating charge mean that these general rules are modified in relation to a security of that type. In principle, a floating charge will be postponed to any subsequently created fixed security (legal or equitable) regardless of notice, because the company is permitted to continue to deal with the assets which are the subject-matter of the floating charge and this dealing power includes the power to charge or mortgage them.[2]

As between two floating charges, the first created will prevail since there is no implied authority to create subsequent floating security ranking first. A second floating charge will only have priority if either: (a) the instrument creating the first floating charge gave an express power to create later floating charges ranking first;[3] or (b) the second floating charge is over part only of the company's assets and the court construes the express reservation in the general floating charge of the right to create prior charges as embracing particular types of floating charge.[4] Crystallisation of a second floating charge before a first floating charge should not enable the second charge to move ahead of the first charge, because that result would be inconsistent with the bargain between the company and the holder of the first charge.[5]

To avoid the risk of being postponed to future charges by the creation of fixed mortgages or charges on all or part of the property of the company, it has become common in the case of floating charges to insert a declaration that the company shall not have the power to mortgage the property in priority to or equally with the floating charge created by the debentures. This restriction is not incompatible with the nature of the floating charge.[6] The effect of inserting this restriction,

---

1   Sections 463 to 464 of the Companies Act 1985. For an example of the application of the statutory ranking provisions see *AIB Finance Ltd v Bank of Scotland* [1994] BCC 184.

2   *Wheatley v Silkstone and Haigh Moor Coal Co* (1885) 29 ChD 715.

3   *Re Benjamin Cope & Sons Ltd* [1914] 1 Ch 800.

4   *Re Automatic Bottlemakers Ltd* [1926] Ch 412. The second floating charge must not affect substantially the whole of the company's property: ibid, 423.

5   *Re Benjamin Cope & Sons Ltd,* above; *Re Household Products Co Ltd* (1981) 124 DLR (3d) 325. But note *Griffiths v Yorkshire Bank* [1994] 1 WLR 1427, where a contrary view is taken. The statutory order of priority governing Scottish floating charges does not depend on, nor is it affected by, order of crystallisation.

6   *Re Brightlife* [1987] 1 Ch 200 at 209; *Re Cimex Tissues* at 635.

which is sometimes referred to as a negative pledge, into a floating charge is that, if the equities are otherwise equal, it will bind a subsequent equitable fixed chargee even without notice.[1] Equities will not be equal where the debenture-holder allows the company to retain the title deeds to the property which is the subject of the subsequent security.[2] In that event, the holder of the subsequent security will not be bound in the absence of notice of the restriction in the earlier floating charge.[3] The owner of a subsequent legal mortgage will be bound only where he has notice of the restriction.[4] Merely because a lender is aware of the existence of an earlier floating charge does not put the lender on enquiry or fix him with notice of a restriction that may be contained in that charge.[5]

10.15   The effect of registration on priorities

The requirement of registration under section 395 of the Companies Act 1985 affects the rules as to priorities in two ways. First of all, a charge which is not duly registered[6] within the 21-day period is void and will lose all priority it would otherwise possess.[7] Secondly, registration, besides giving actual notice to those who search the register, has been held to give constructive notice to subsequent mortgagees or chargees.[8] Thus a registered fixed equitable charge will be protected as against a legal mortgage created after the time of registration of the equitable charge.

It should be noted that, subject to the effect of constructive notice, priority is based on the date of creation, not that of registration, though subsequent registration is necessary if the charge is to be effective.

It was held in *Wilson v Kelland*[9] that registration of a charge gave constructive notice of the charge, but not of the terms contained in the deed creating it. Thus registration of a floating charge will not by itself give constructive notice of the prohibition contained in that charge so as to postpone a subsequent mortgage.[10]

In order to give greater protection to floating charges, the practice has developed, which the Registrar has accepted, of including the prohibition in the charging document among the registered particulars of the charge. It is sometimes thought that this will give constructive notice of the prohibition but

---

1   *Re Castell & Brown Ltd* [1898] 1 Ch 315.
2   As in *Castell & Brown*, above.
3   Ibid.
4   *English & Scottish Mercantile Investment Co v Brunton* [1892] 2 QB 700 at 707.
5   *English & Scottish Mercantile Investment Co v Brunton*, above (where enquiries were in fact made); *Re Valletort Sanitary Steam Laundry Co Ltd* [1903] 2 Ch 654.
6   See **10.32** as to the possibility of rectifying the register. But this will not be allowed so as to regain priority.
7   *Re Monolithic Building Co* [1915] 1 Ch 643.
8   *Wilson v Kelland* [1910] 2 Ch 306; *Re Standard Rotary Machine Co* (1906) 95 LT 829.
9   [1910] 2 Ch 306.
10   *Re Valletort Laundry* [1903] 2 Ch 654; *Re Standard Rotary Machine Co* (1906) 95 LT 829.

this is doubtful. The practice has not yet been tested in the courts in England,[1] and it has been rejected in New Zealand and Ireland.[2]

A provision enacted in the Companies Act 1989 was designed to clarify the position with regard to registration and notice. This provision is not now to be brought into force, but it is nevertheless useful to consider it briefly. Under this provision,[3] a person taking a charge over a company's property was deemed to have notice of any matter requiring registration and disclosed on the registration at the time the charge was created. Otherwise, a person was not to be taken to have notice of any matter by reason of its being disclosed on the register or by reason of his having failed to search the register in the course of making such enquiries as ought reasonably to have been made. Thus, under this provision, a chargee (which would include a mortgagee) was conclusively presumed to have notice of the matters which required registration and which were disclosed on the register but a purchaser was conclusively presumed not to have such notice.

The Companies Act 1989 also provided for the matters requiring registration to be prescribed by the Secretary of State in regulations. When that legislation was enacted, it was envisaged that the Secretary would follow existing provisions governing registration of charges under Scottish law[4] and make the existence, or otherwise, of restrictions in floating charges a matter requiring registration, and hence bring such restrictions within the ambit of the notice provision.[5]

10.16 Further advances and subsequent charges

A particular case should be noted. Mortgages and debentures are often created in favour of banks and others to secure a current account. In such a case, if a subsequent mortgage is created on the same property and the bank entitled to the prior security has notice of such subsequent mortgage, it cannot make further advances upon its own security to the prejudice of the later mortgagee. Further, if it continues the current account, payments made by the debtor company will go in reduction of the debt existing at the time of the later mortgage,[6] so that in course of time the bank or lender on current account will become postponed to the later lender, for all subsequent advances will rank after the amount advanced by the

---

1   See also the effect of a clause providing for 'automatic crystallisation', discussed at **10.12**. For an argument that constructive notice is not given by including the prohibition among the registered particulars, see Farrar, 38 *Conveyancer* 315 at p 325 *et seq*. The author argues in favour of the different concept of 'inferred notice'. This inference would rest on the common practice but would be open to rebuttal; ibid p 319. This distinction was made in *Siebe Gorman v Barclays Bank* [1979] 2 Lloyd's Rep 142.

2   *Dempsey v The Traders Finance Corporation Ltd* [1933] NZLR 1258 (New Zealand); *Welch v Bowmaker (Ireland) Ltd* [1980] IR 251 (Ireland). The problem does not arise in Scotland, because the existence of a clause in a floating charge which prohibits, restricts or regulates the power of the company to grant further securities ranking in priority to or *pari passu* with the floating charge is a registrable particular: section 417(3)(e) and section 413(2)(e).

3   Section 103 of the Companies Act 1989.

4   Sections 417(3)(e) and 413(2)(e) of the Companies Act 1985.

5   Section 103 of the Companies Act 1989 expressly mentioned restrictions in floating charges as one of the matters which the Secretary of State could prescribe as a particular requiring registration.

6   Under what is known as the rule in *Clayton's Case* (1816) 1 Mer 572: see also next footnote.

later lender.[1] To meet this danger banks usually rule off and close the current account as soon as they learn of the subsequent mortgage, thus retaining their charge for the balance then due on current account.

10.17 Purchase money, security interests and floating charges

If property is acquired subject to an existing charge or upon the terms of the purchase price being advanced on the security of the property, these charges will take priority over a floating charge on the company's undertaking or a fixed charge on the company's present and future assets of a description which covers the property so acquired. The implications of acquiring property on a mortgage and the priority position of the mortgagee as against others with competing interests in the same property were considered by the House of Lords in *Abbey National Building Society v Cann*.[2] This case concerned an individual acquiring residential property with the help of a mortgage, but the reasoning of their Lordships is equally applicable to corporate finance.

The House of Lords held that where a conveyance and a mortgage or charge take place at approximately the same time, in reality the purchaser never acquires more than an equity of redemption.[3] According to Lord Jauncey of Tullichettle:

> a purchaser who can only complete a transaction by borrowing money ... cannot in reality even be said to have acquired even for a scintilla temporis the unencumbered freehold or leasehold interest in the land whereby he could grant interests having priority over the mortgage ...

Thus a pre-existing charge must rank behind a later purchase-money security.

10.18 Postponement and avoidance of floating charges by statute

Certain special provisions affect the priority or validity of floating charges. The position of preferential debts has already been noted: preferential debts[4] which cannot otherwise be met have priority over debts secured by a charge which as created was a floating charge.[5] In *Re GL Saunders Ltd*,[6] it was settled that where the

---

1   *Deeley v Lloyds Bank* [1912] AC 756 (HL); *Hopkinson v Rolt* (1861) 9 HLC 514; *London and County Bank v Ratcliffe* (1881) 6 App Cas 722 (HL); *Bradford Banking Co v Henry Briggs & Co* (1886) 12 App Cas 29 (HL). *Siebe Gorman v Barclays Bank* [1979] 2 Lloyd's Rep 142.

2   [1991] 1 AC 56, [1990] 1 All ER 1085, [1990] 2 WLR 832. Gregory, 'Romalpa Clauses as Unregistered Charges – a Fundamental Shift' (1990) 106 LQR 550; McCormack, 'Charges and Priorities – The Death of the Scintilla Temporis Doctrine' (1991) 12 Co Law 11; de Lacy, [1991] LMCLQ 531; Bennett and Davis, 'Fixtures, Purchase Money Security Interests and Dispositions of Interests in Land' (1994) 110 LQR 448. Commentators note some uncertainty regarding the application of the Companies Act registration requirements to purchase money securities: eg [1991] LMCLQ 531 at 535–537, (1994) 110 LQR 448 at 479–483.

3   Following *Re Connolly Brothers Ltd (No 2)* [1912] 2 Ch 25 and *Security Trust Co v Royal Bank of Canada* [1976] AC 503, [1976] 1 All ER 381, [1976] 2 WLR 437, and overruling the *scintilla temporis* approach favoured in *Church of England Building Society v Piskor* [1954] Ch 553.

4   These are now limited to contributions to occupational pension schemes, remuneration of employees, and, where relevant, levies on steel and coal production, following amendments by section 251(1) of the Enterprise Act 2002.

5   Sections 40 and 175 of, and Schedule 6 to, the Insolvency Act 1986, as amended by the Enterprise Act 2002.

6   [1986] BCLC 40.

realisation of a fixed charge produced a surplus (after satisfying the claims of the chargee) the surplus was not part of the assets subject to the floating charge. The company was in receivership and the significance of the decision was that it meant that the receiver had no obligation to pay preferential debts from the surplus because that obligation was limited to payment out of floating-charge assets.[1] Moreover, section 176A of the Insolvency Act 1986[2] now requires a liquidator, administrator or receiver to set aside a prescribed part[3] of the company's net property for the benefit of the company's unsecured creditors. This part may not be given to the holder of a floating charge. However, this provision does not apply if the company's net value is less than £10,000[4] and the liquidator, administrator or receiver thinks that making a distribution to the unsecured creditors would be disproportionate to the benefits.[5]

In a winding-up, section 245[6] of the Insolvency Act 1986 renders invalid certain floating charges created within twelve months of the winding-up in favour of persons not connected with the company. In the case of 'connected persons' this period is two years. The charge may be valid where value has been given to the company. All charges, fixed as well as floating, may be open to attack under section 239 of the Insolvency Act 1986 on the basis that the transaction has given one of the company's creditors (or a surety or guarantor of its debts) a preference.[7] All these matters are examined at length in the context of the winding up of companies.[8]

10.19 Priority agreements

If a fixed charge is expressed to be subject to an earlier floating charge it will rank behind the earlier floating charge even though it would otherwise have taken priority.[9] Also, where there are two (or more) existing securities affecting the same property, the holders of the securities can agree amongst themselves to alter their priority and this does not require the company's consent.[10]

A priority agreement between the holders of fixed and floating charges can produce circularity problems concerning preferential debts: this problem arises where, under the insolvency legislation, the preferential debts rank behind debts secured by a fixed charge but before debts secured by a floating charge, whilst under the priority agreement, the debts secured by the floating charge rank before those secured by the fixed charge. How is this conundrum to be resolved?

---

1   See further **10.49** on the obligation of a receiver to pay preferential debts.
2   Inserted by section 252 of the Enterprise Act 2002.
3   This is calculated in accordance with regulation 3 of the Insolvency Act 1986 (Prescribed Part) Order 2003 (SI 2003/2097). If the company's net property is below £10,000, the prescribed part is 50% of the property. Where the company's net property exceeds £10,000, the prescribed part is 50% of the first £10,000 and 20% for the part of the company's property exceeding £10,000 in value. However, the total value of the prescribed part is fixed at £600,000.
4   Section 176A(3)(a) of the Insolvency Act 1986 and regulation 2 of the Insolvency Act 1986 (Prescribed Part) Order 2003 (SI 2003/2097).
5   Section 176A(3)(b).
6   See further **21.55.6**
7   Sections 239 to 241. See **21.55.3**.
8   See Chapter 21.
9   *Re Robert Stephenson & Co* [1913] 2 Ch 201 (CA); *Re Camden Brewery Ltd* (1912) 106 LT 598.
10   *Cheah Theam Swee v Equiticorp Finance Group Ltd* [1992] 1 AC 472, [1991] 4 All ER 989, [1992] BCLC 371, [1992] BCC 98.

The question was considered by Chadwick J in *Re Portbase (Clothing) Ltd, Mond v Taylor.*[1] Chadwick J held that the effect of the priority agreement was to postpone the fixed charge to the floating charge. Preferring the approach taken in the Australian case of *Waters v Widdows,*[2] to the *obiter* views of Nourse J in *Re Woodroffes,*[3] he concluded that this postponement meant that the preferential debts ranked before the debt secured by the floating charge and also the debt secured by the fixed charge. If Chadwick J had followed the solution suggested in *Re Woodroffes* (where construction of a priority agreement did not arise for decision),[4] the debt secured by the floating charge would have ranked before the preferential debts to the extent of the fixed-charge security. Chadwick J noted that this solution might apply where the parties, by their agreement, exchanged their rights under their respective securities but that, as a matter of construction, it was not the effect of the agreement in question.

10.20   Retention of title clauses and floating charges

A receiver appointed on behalf of a debenture-holder has no better title to goods in the company's possession whose ownership lies elsewhere than the company itself. Consequently, the owner of goods which are hired to the company or are the subject of a hire-purchase agreement may recover them from the receiver. The same principle will apply to a 'title retention' clause in a sale of goods contract. Such clauses are known as *Romalpa* clauses from the leading case[5] in which their validity was upheld. They provide that the goods purchased shall remain the property of the seller until the purchase price is paid (as well, sometimes, as money outstanding in other contracts between the buyer and seller). In consequence the unpaid purchaser will be able to recover goods still in the company's possession against the claims of a receiver subsequently appointed under a floating charge. In *Romalpa,*[6] there was a further provision that if the purchasing company resold any of the contract material it should do so as agent of the seller. It was held on that basis the buyer was accountable to the seller for the proceeds of the sub-sales. As agent a fiduciary duty was owed in respect of these proceeds which could be traced in equity.

Subsequent cases have tended to limit the protection which is afforded by a title retention clause to an unpaid seller who is in competition with the claims of a receiver appointed by a debenture-holder.[7] The simplest type of clause where the

---

1   [1993] Ch 388, [1993] 3 All ER 829, [1993] 3 WLR 14, [1993] BCLC 796, [1993] BCC 96.
2   [1984] VR 503.
3   [1986] Ch 366. Nourse J adopted the analysis in Goode, *Legal Problems of Credit and Security* 1st edn (Sweet & Maxwell, 1982), pp 54–55 (see also 2nd edn 1988, pp 97–98).
4   The solution adopted by Nourse J was conceded by counsel.
5   *Aluminium Industrie Vaassen BV v Romalpa Aluminium Ltd* [1976] 1 WLR 676 (CA). The Scottish courts have also recognised title retention clauses: *Armour v Thyssen Edelstahlwerke AG* [1991] 2 AC 339, [1990] 3 All ER 481, [1990] 3 WLR 810, [1991] 1 Lloyd's Rep 395, [1991] BCLC 28, [1990] BC 925.
6   Above.
7   There is a large amount of literature on retention of title clauses, including the following: Goodhart and Jones, 'The Infiltration of Equitable Doctrine into English Commercial Law' (1980) 43 MLR 489; McCormack, 'Reservation of Title – Past, Present and Future' [1994] Conv 129, and for a recent comprehensive review of this area, see Bradgate, '25 years of *Romalpa*' in Davies (ed), *Security Interests in Mobile Equipment* (Aldershot: Ashgate, 2002).

seller retains title[1] to the very goods sold (as provided for in the Sale of Goods Act 1979, section 19(1)) until specified debts are paid[2] is effective and it does not create a charge which must be registered so long as the goods supplied are identifiable and in the possession of the buyer.[3] If the goods supplied are subjected to a manufacturing process[4] with other materials, ordinarily a title retention clause does not vest title to the new product in the supplier[5] and, furthermore, does not give a right to trace into the resulting new product.[6] Any rights[7] given by the contract in the newly created product would normally be a charge granted by the buyer to the seller and requiring registration under the Companies Act 1985.[8]

Despite the fact that such a claim was successful in *Romalpa* itself, suppliers' claims to the proceeds of resale of goods supplied on title retention terms (irrespective of whether those goods are processed before resale) have usually failed.[9] The obstacles are that the supplier must establish that there is a fiduciary relationship between himself and the buyer in respect of the proceeds of sale and that he has a beneficial interest in the proceeds of sale otherwise than by way of charge. The courts are reluctant to characterise the relationship between buyer

---

1   That is, legal title. 'Retention' of equitable ownership has been held to amount to a charge granted by the buyer in favour of the supplier; *Re Bond Worth Ltd* [1980] Ch 228, [1979] 3 All ER 919, [1979] 3 WLR 629; *Stroud Architectural Systems Ltd v John Laing Construction Ltd* [1994] BCC 18.

2   The title retention clause in *Armour v Thyssen*, above, was an 'all monies' clause; title was retained pending payment of all debts between the parties. On 'all monies' retention of title clauses see further McCormack [1991] LMCLQ 154; Mance [1992] LMCLQ 35; McCormack [1994] Conv 129.

3   *Clough Mill v Martin* [1984] 3 All ER 982, [1985] 1 WLR 111, [1985] BCLC 64 (CA), noted Goodhart, (1986) 49 MLR 96; *Armour v Thyssen*, above; *Hendy Lennox (Industrial Engines) Ltd v Grahame Puttick Ltd* [1984] 2 All ER 152, [1984] 1 WLR 485; *Re Andrabell Ltd* [1987] 3 All ER 407 at 414.

4   The extent of the processing to which the goods are subjected may be significant. In *Armour v Thyssen*, some of the goods supplied (steel strips) had been cut but this did not prejudice the claim of the original supplier.

5   In *Clough Mill v Martin* [1984] 3 All ER 982 at 989–990, 993, Goff and Oliver LJJ thought that in principle it would be possible for parties to agree that title to manufactured goods would vest in the supplier of part of the goods used in the manufacturing process but that, in practice, it was unlikely that they would so agree. Goff LJ at 989 noted problems that would result from the conclusion that an agreement conferred absolute ownership of (or a right to trace in respect of manufactured goods) in a supplier: (1) buyer may have paid for some of the goods supplied; (2) buyer may have supplied part of the materials used in the manufacturing process and will have borne the cost of the manufacturing process; and (3) part of the materials used in the manufacturing process may have been supplied, subject to a title retention clause, by another supplier.

6   *Borden (UK) Ltd v Scottish Timber Products* [1981] Ch 25, [1979] 3 All ER 961, [1979] 3 WLR 672 (CA); *Re Peachdart Ltd* [1984] Ch 131, [1989] 3 All ER 204, [1983] 3 WLR 878, [1983] BCLC 225, (1983) 1 BCC 98 at 920; *Specialist Plant Services Ltd v Braithwaite* (1987) 3 BCC 119 and *Ian Chisholm Textiles Ltd v Griffiths* [1994] BCC 96.

7   In *Borden*, the court found that the seller had no interest whatsoever in the manufactured product.

8   *Re Peachdart Ltd; Clough Mill: Modelboard Ltd v Outer Box Ltd* [1993] BCLC 623. Note *Hendy Lennox (Industrial Engines) Ltd v Grahame Puttick Ltd* (diesel engines supplied subject to title retention clause incorporated into generators but remained readily identifiable and easily disconnected; title retention effective despite incorporation).

9   In *Tatung (UK) Ltd v Galex Telesure Ltd* (1989) 5 BCC 325 (noted McCormack [1989] LMCLQ 198; Wheeler (1989) 10 Co Law 188), Phillips J questioned whether *Romalpa* had been correctly decided on the point.

and supplier as fiduciary. Instead, any interest of the supplier in the proceeds which is defeasible upon the payment of specified debts owing from the buyer to the supplier is usually characterised as a charge granted by the buyer to the supplier and, as such, it requires registration under the Companies Act 1985.[1]

10.21 Execution creditors and floating charges

If the chargee takes steps promptly to enforce its security then its rights under a floating charge to the property comprised in their security take precedence over those obtained by an execution creditor where execution is incomplete. Execution is incomplete for this purpose where even though a sale by the sheriff has been avoided by the payment of money by the chargee, provided the money still remains in his hands;[2] but where money has been paid by the debtor company to the sheriff on the terms that he shall not sell the property seized, the title of the execution creditor to the money prevails as against the receiver.[3] If an execution is put in, or garnishee order obtained, the chargee ought at once to give the sheriff notice to withdraw, or to the debtor not to pay the garnishor, and proceed to the appointment of a receiver, for if the security becomes a fixed one before the goods are sold or the debt paid the charge will prevail.[4]

The equities of the holder of the charge entitle him to oust the sheriff after he has seized if the security has crystallised before he has sold,[5] or to deprive the garnishor of his advantage if the crystallisation of the security has taken place before he has collected the money.[6] But if the security is allowed to continue to float, the execution creditor's or garnishor's right will prevail, and a garnishee order *nisi* will be made absolute notwithstanding the opposition of the holder of the charge or a claim made by him on the debtor to pay the money direct to him,[7] for a debenture-holder cannot single out and take a particular debt or piece of property while allowing the company to trade with the rest of its assets.[8]

PART 3: THE REGISTRATION OF CHARGES

10.22 Legislative framework

Part XII of the Companies Act 1985 governs the registration of company charges. Details of most, but not all, charges created by companies must be delivered to the

1   *Re Peachdart Ltd; Re Andrabell Ltd; E Pfeiffer Weinkellerei-Weineinkauf GmbH & Co v Arbuthnot Factors Ltd* [1988] 1 WLR 150, [1998] BCC 608; *Tatung v Galex Leisure Ltd Re Weldtech Equipment Ltd* [1991] BCC 16, [1991] BCLC 393, noted de Lacy (1991) 65 MLR 736; *Compaq Computers Ltd v Abercorn Group Ltd* [1991] BCC 484, noted Hicks (1992) 13 Co Law 217; de Lacy (1992) 13 Co Law 164; *Modelboard v Outer Box*, above.
2   *Re Opera* [1891] 3 Ch 260 (CA); *Taunton v Sheriff of Warwickshire* [1895] 2 Ch 319 (CA).
3   *Robinson v Burnell's Vienna Bakery* [1904] 2 KB 624.
4   *Davey & Co v Williamson & Sons Ltd* [1898] 2 QB 194, as explained in *Evans v Rival Granite Quarries* [1910] 2 KB 979 at 1000 (CA); *Norton v Yates* [1906] 1 KB 112.
5   *Re Opera* [1891] 3 Ch 260; *Davey & Co v Williamson & Sons Ltd* [1898] 2 QB 194; *Duck v Tower Galvanising Co* [1901] 2 KB 314.
6   *Norton v Yates* [1906] 1 KB 112.
7   *Evans v Rival Granite Quarries* [1910] 2 KB 979 (CA).
8   *Robson v Smith* [1895] 2 Ch 118; approved by CA [1910] 2 KB at 989 and 998.

companies registry within 21 days of creation. The Registrar of Companies is required to maintain a register of charges and this is available for public inspection. Failure to deliver the requisite particulars to the companies registry results in the charge becoming void against certain categories of person. There is provision for late filing but this requires an order of the court. Where particulars are duly filed in accordance with the statutory requirements, the priority of the charge depends on the rules already discussed.[1] Priority of company charges is not governed by order of filing at the companies registry.

The system for the registration of company charges is open to criticism. The 21-day period allowed for delivery of particulars means that the register may not give a searcher an accurate picture of the existing registrable charges on a company's property. The fact that not all charges which can be created by companies require registration further detracts from the register as a comprehensive source of information. The company also has to keep its own register of charges at its registered office and this register, which extends to all charges, can be searched to obtain a more complete picture; but a charge is not rendered void if it is not entered on this register, which means that there is less incentive to ensure its accuracy. The existence of financing arrangements, such as conditional sales and hire purchase agreements, which are not in law regarded as charges will not be disclosed by either register. A further criticism of the existing system is that it preserves old, complex priority rules. A system of priority is based on date of filing would be far more straightforward than a series of rules which depend on order of creation of competing securities, equality of equities and notice.

Professor Diamond in his *Review of Security Interests in Property* (HMSO, 1989) made various criticisms of the statutory regime for the registration of charges. The main thrust of Professor Diamond's report was directed at recommending a fundamental overhaul of the law relating to security interests generally, but he also made specific recommendations regarding company charges which were intended as interim measures pending the larger reform.[2] The proposed interim measures included amending the list of registrable charges, streamlining the registration procedure and, in particular, reducing the burden of the Registrar of Companies, making 'negative pledge' restrictions in floating charges registrable, introducing a system of priorities related to the date of registration, eliminating the need to apply to court for an order authorising late registration, and removing anomalies in the law relating to the registration of charges by oversea companies.

Some of Professor Diamond's interim measures were included in the Companies Act 1989.[3] Part IV of that Act contained a set of provisions which were designed to replace in their entirety the existing sections of Part XII of the Companies Act 1985. Part IV of the Companies Act 1989 has not been brought into force. One difficulty with the new provisions that became apparent was their relationship with other applicable registration requirements, in particular those relating to registered land. At the time of writing, it is uncertain when the existing regime for the registration of charges will be reformed and whether the new provisions will bear much resemblance to those enacted in the Companies Act

---

1   See **10.14**.
2   *Review of Security Interests in Property*, Part III.
3   In September 1987 the DTI had heralded the amendments by publishing its own proposals for amendment of the company charges requirements: 'Outline Proposals for Amendment of Sections 395 to 424 Companies Act 1985', noted (1988) 9 Co Law 101 and (1988) 9 Co Law 220.

1989. What is clear is that the DTI does not intend to bring Part IV of the Companies Act 1989 into force in its entirety. This is apparent from the outcome of a consultation exercise launched by the DTI in November 1994 with the publication of a consultative document, *Proposals for Reform of Part XII of the Companies Act 1985*. This paper outlined three options for reform, namely: (a) retention of the present legislation; (b) retention of the core provisions of the present legislation and incorporating improvements introduced by Part IV of the 1989 Act (but omitting some of the more controversial aspects of that Part); and (c) replacement of the present system with an entirely new one based on notice filing. The DTI later reported that the majority of the responses to this document favoured the second option and indicated that it was also the Department's preferred option.

The following account focuses mainly on the provisions which are currently in force. Brief mention is made of some of the ways in which the position might be better under the regime contained in the Companies Act 1989.[1] The more wide-ranging and fundamental reforms proposed by Professor Diamond, and also by previous review bodies, are considered at the end of this section, as is the most recent push for reform in the Law Commission's consultation document of 2002.

Charges created by oversea companies may require registration at the English companies registry. Part IV of the Companies Act 1989 also included new provisions which were designed to apply to charges created by oversea companies.[2]

10.23   Charges requiring registration

Every limited company must keep a register of charges, and enter therein particulars of all charges specifically affecting property of the company and of all floating charges.[3]

In addition to keeping such a register, sections 395 to 399 require particulars of certain mortgages and charges[4] created by companies registered in England to be delivered to the Registrar within 21 days after the date of their creation if they come within any of the descriptions mentioned below:

(1) a charge for the purpose of securing any issue of debentures;
(2) a charge on uncalled share capital of the company;
(3) a charge created or evidenced by an instrument, which if executed by an individual, would require registration as a bill of sale;
(4) a charge on any land, wherever situate, or any interest therein, but not including a charge for any rent or other periodical sum issuing out of land;
(5) a charge on book debts of the company;
(6) a floating charge on the undertaking or property of the company;

---

1   For more detailed examination of the 1989 Act see McCormack, 'Registration of Company Charges: The New Law' [1990] LMCLQ 520; Ferran and Mayo, 'Registration of Company Charges – The New Regime' [1991] JBL 152. The application of the requirements of the 1989 Act to various types of retention of title clauses is considered by McCormack, 'Reservation of Title and the Company Charges Registration System' in Palmer and McKendrick (eds), *Interests in Goods* (Sweet & Maxwell, 1993).
2   This was recommended in the Diamond report: Chapter 27.
3   Section 407, see **10.37**.
4   For the purposes of Chapter 1 of Part XII, 'the expression "charge" includes mortgage'; section 396(4).

(7) a charge on calls made but not paid;

(8) a charge on a ship or aircraft or any share in a ship;

(9) a charge on goodwill or on any intellectual property.[1]

Anything which creates a charge in equity or law (being of any of the classes above described) therefore requires registration: that is to say, anything which would create a charge as between individuals will suffice. 'When there is a contract for value between the owner of a chose in action and another person which shows that such person is to have the benefit of the chose in action, that constitutes good charge on the chose in action. The form of words is immaterial so long as they show an intention that he is to have such benefit.'[2]

However, an absolute assignment (eg of book debts) is not a charge and will not require registration. Thus in *Lloyds and Scottish Finance Ltd v Cyril Lord Carpets Ltd*,[3] the House of Lords held that assignments to a finance house of credit sale agreements, under a block discounting agreement, were absolute assignments and therefore did not require registration under section 93 of the Northern Ireland Companies Act 1960 (the equivalent of section 395 of the 1985 Act). Factoring arrangements are equally effective and do not require registration.[4] A company may enter into a complex financing arrangement, involving the sale of assets rather than a loan secured on those assets, specifically in order to avoid the need for registration (such arrangement may also fall outside the ambit of covenants in the company's existing loans whereby it has promised not to create any new security). This sale may be accompanied by an option in favour of the company allowing it to recover the assets at a later date so that, in economic terms, the arrangement may be indistinguishable from a secured loan. In *Welsh Development Agency v Export Finance Co Ltd*,[5] a complex sale of this type was challenged by a debenture-holder as amounting in substance to no more than a secured loan on the assets supposedly sold. The Court of Appeal rejected the claim on its facts but emphasised that the label attached to a financing arrangement is not conclusive and, if it is a sham or the substance of the arrangement does not accord with the label the parties have given it, the arrangement will not be allowed to stand.

---

1   'Intellectual property' for this purpose is defined by section 396(3A) which was inserted by the Copyright, Designs and Patents Act 1988.

2   *Gorringe v Irwell India Rubber Works* (1886) 34 ChD 128 at 134 *per* Cotton LJ (CA). In *National Provincial and Union Bank of England v Charnley* [1924] 1 KB 431 (CA) at 449, 450, Atkin LJ expressed his views as follows: 'I think there can be no doubt that where in a transaction for value both parties evince an intention that property, existing or future, shall be made available as security for the payment of debt, and that the creditor shall have a present right to have it made available, there is a charge, even though the present legal right which is contemplated can only be enforced at some future date, and though the creditor gets no legal rights of property, either absolute or special, or any legal right to possession, but only gets a right to have the security made available by an Order of the Court.... If, on the other hand, the parties do not intend that there should be a present right to have the security made available, but only that there should be a right in the future by agreement, such as a licence to seize the goods, there will be no charge.'

3   [1992] BCLC 609.

4   *Re George Inglefield Ltd* [1933] Ch 1.

5   [1992] BCLC 148, [1992] BCC 270, noted Oditah [1992] JBL 541. See also *Orion Finance Ltd v Crown Financial Management Ltd* [1996] 2 BCLC 78 (assignment of rentals was by way of security rather than sale and repurchase).

Space does not permit even a cursory consideration of the special characteristics of various types of charge listed in section 396.[1] However, it should be noted that fixed charges over certain types of property are not included in the list in section 396.[2] The most important of these omissions is that of any fixed charge over shares held by the company in any other company.[3] The Review Committee on Insolvency Law and Practice proposed[4] that charges over stocks and shares (and other marketable securities) be registrable under section 395. Professor Diamond reached the opposite conclusion and no provision for the registration of such charges was included in the Companies Act 1989. It is probable that a 'floating charge' (in section 396(1)(f)) includes such a charge over a class of the company's assets. A charge 'for securing any issue of debentures' (in section 396(1)(a)) would not seem to require a public issue of debentures (or debenture stock), but it would seem to require a series of debentures.

10.24 Effect of failing to register a charge

Any registrable mortgage or charge not registered within 21 days after the date of its creation is, 'so far as any security on the company's property or undertaking is conferred by the charge', void against the liquidator, the administrator and any creditor of the company,[5] and this is so even though the creditor is a second mortgagee who had notice of the prior unregistered mortgage.[6] Although the section refers only to the 'liquidator or administrator', it also applies to the company in liquidation or administration itself.[7] It is to be noted that the charge is not avoided as against the company *before* liquidation or administration, and a chargee of goods who has seized the goods before liquidation, in pursuance of a licence to seize contained in the charge, is entitled to the benefit of the security as against the liquidator, despite non-registration of the charge.[8] An unregistered registrable charge is not avoided against purchasers, a point that would have been reversed in the registration regime of the Companies Act 1989. Section 395 does not invalidate the contract or obligation for repayment of the money thereby secured, which will accordingly, even if not registered, rank in a liquidation as an unsecured debt; and before liquidation the charge will be enforceable against the company by all the remedies of a mortgagee, although void against an execution creditor of a secured creditor.[9] Section 395(2), moreover, makes the money secured become immediately payable when the mortgage or charge becomes void. It has been held that an unregistered charge is void in a solvent liquidation as

---

1   See further, *Gore-Browne on Companies* 44th edn (Jordans, loose-leaf) at 18.8–18.9.9, where the question of 'dual registration' under other legislation is also considered.

2   Apart from charges upon shares referred to in the text, other examples are charges upon *non-book* debts and charges upon registered designs.

3   *Arthur D Little Ltd (in administration) v Ableco Finance LLC* [2002] EWHC 701 (Ch), [2002] 2 BCLC 799.

4   Cmnd 8558 (1982), paragraph 1520.

5   Section 395(1). As to the similar provision made for Scotland, see section 410(2).

6   *Re Monolithic Building Co* [1915] 1 Ch 643 (CA).

7   *Smith (Administrator of Cosslett (Contractors) Ltd) v Bridgend County Borough Council* [2001] UKHL 58, [2002] 1 BCLC 77.

8   *Mercantile Bank of India v Chartered Bank of India* [1937] 1 All ER 231. See also *Re Toomer, ex parte Blaiberg* (1883) 23 ChD 254 (CA).

9   Note that there was some concern about the compatibility of section 395 with the Human Rights Act 1998, a matter which is now unlikely to give rise to further worry in light of the House of Lords ruling in *Wilson v First Country Trust Ltd* [2003] UKHL 40, [2003] 3 WLR 568.

well as where the company is wound up insolvent. That interpretation of what is now section 395(1) must be correct as a literal interpretation of the words 'void against any liquidation or creditor of the company'. It may, however, be doubted that that was the real intention of the draftsman. Where in the course of liquidation it is still unclear (as was here the case) whether the company is or is not insolvent, the validity of a charge will still be of great concern to the secured creditor.[1]

Failure to effect registration of a charge renders the company, and every officer in default, liable to a fine.[2]

10.25   The particulars of a charge to be registered

Under section 401(1), the Registrar is to keep a register of all charges required to be registered, and to enter the following particulars:

(1) in the case of a charge to the benefit of which the holders of a series of debentures are entitled, the particulars as are specified in section 397(1), namely:
   (a) the total amount secured by the whole series;
   (b) the dates of the resolutions authorising the issue of the series and the date of the covering deed, if any, by which the security is created or defined;
   (c) a general description of the property charged; and
   (d) the names of the trustees (if any) for the debenture-holders;
(2) in the case of any other charge:
   (a) if the charge was created by the company, the date of its creation, and if the charge was a charge existing on property acquired by the company, the date of the acquisition of the property;
   (b) the amount secured;
   (c) short particulars of the property charged; and
   (d) the names of the persons entitled to the charge.

Any person may inspect such register.[3]

The registration of a series of debentures under this subsection protects all debentures properly issued in the series, and also agreements to issue such debentures, without separate registration, even when such agreements are to be found only in documents which were intended to be debentures, but from a technical defect can only be treated as agreements for debentures.[4]

Section 397(2) requires the amount or rate of any underwriting commission paid, or any allowance or discount made on the placing or issue of debentures, to be included in the particulars filed; but omission to do this will not affect the validity of the debentures issued, and the deposit of debentures to secure a debt of the company is not, for the purposes of this subsection, an issue of the debentures at a discount.

1   *Re Oriel Ltd* [1984] BCLC 241.
2   Sections 399(3) and 400(4). See Section 410 for the equivalent provision in Scotland.
3   Section 401(3).
4   *Re Fireproof Doors* [1916] 2 Ch 142.

10.26 The 'date of creation' for purposes of registration

Registration of a mortgage or charge under section 395(1) is required to be effected within 21 days after the date of its creation. The 'date of creation' of a charge may differ from the 'date of issue' of the debenture it secures. The date of creation is the date when the trust deed or agreement creating the charge is executed or entered into.[1] This will be so even though no money is owing when the deed is executed.[2] Where a series of debentures is issued, the charge must be registered within 21 days after the date of issue of the first debenture.

Where, under a power in the debenture trust deed, other property of the company is substituted for the property originally charged, no new registration is required. No new charge requiring registration is thereby created.[3]

The charge created in equity by an agreement to issue debentures, if duly registered, will give an equal protection to the debenture-holder as a complete debenture,[4] and so will a debenture informally issued if the holder had no notice of the informality.[5]

10.27 The registration obligation

Prescribed particulars of the charge,[6] together with any instrument creating or evidencing the charge, must be delivered to the Registrar of Companies within 21 days after the date of creation of the charge.[7] The duty to fulfil this registration requirement falls on the company but registration may instead be effected by any person who is interested in the charge.[8] It is in the lender's interest to take responsibility for registration, because the security will become void if it is overlooked. Section 399(2) allows the lender to recover from the company any fee which has to be paid to the Registrar.

The Registrar of Companies is required to check the details of the prescribed particulars which are submitted against the charging document. When the checking process is complete, the Registrar registers the charge and issues a certificate of registration. Professor Diamond, echoing comments made previously by the Jenkins Committee,[9] thought that the obligation to check delivered

---

1   *Watson & Co v Spiral Globe Co* [1902] 2 Ch 209; *Re New London & Suburban Bus Co* [1908] 1 Ch 621. Cf *Re Harrogate Estates Ltd* [1903] 1 Ch 495. The Companies Act 1989 contained a specific provision dealing with the date of creation of a charge: section 103.

2   *Esberger & Sons v Capital & Counties Bank* [1913] 2 Ch 366 and see *Transport & General Credit Corporation v Morgan* [1939] Ch 531.

3   *Cunard SS Co Ltd v Hopwood* [1908] 2 Ch 564.

4   *Simultaneous Colour Printing Syndicate v Foweraker* [1901] 1 KB 771.

5   *Duck v Tower Galvanising Co* [1916] 2 Ch 142.

6   Note that a company's registered number, although necessary to complete the application for registration, is not a particular of the charge. Consequently, providing an incorrect number does not amount to a failure to comply with section 395: *Grove v Advantage Healthcare (T10) Ltd* [2000] 1 BCLC 661, ChD (A (T10) had granted charge but the application contained the number for A (T9). The companies had swapped names shortly before the relevant transactions took place).

7   Companies Act 1985, section 395. Note also section 397 which specifies the documents which must accompany particulars relating to a series of debentures.

8   Section 399. If a charge is not registered, the company and its responsible officers are liable to a fine: section 399(3).

9   *Report of the Company Law Committee*, 1965 Cmnd 1749, paragraph 302.

prescribed particulars against charging documents was an unreasonable burden to impose on the Registrar. The registration regime contained in the Companies Act 1989 relieved the Registrar of Companies of this obligation but, as discussed in **9.38**, this proposed change was related to one of the most controversial provisions of the 1989 Act, namely the abolition of the conclusive certificate of registration.

10.28   The Registrar's certificate as conclusive evidence

The Registrar must give a certificate of the registration of any mortgage or charge, stating the amount thereby secured, and the certificate will be conclusive evidence that the requirements of the Act as to registration have been complied with.[1] The company must cause a copy of the certificate so given to be endorsed on every debenture or certificate of debenture stock issued, the payment of which is secured by the charge so registered.[2] Where, however, the company has issued debentures or certificates of debenture stock, and further charges are created, to the benefit of which the holders are entitled, it will not be necessary for the company to endorse on the debentures or debenture stock certificates already issued a certificate of the registration of the charge.[3] Any person who knowingly and wilfully authorises or permits the issue of any debenture or certificate of debenture stock requiring registration without a copy of the Registrar's certificate being endorsed thereon incurs liability to a fine.[4]

The certificate of the Registrar is conclusive evidence that the requirements of the Act as to registration have been complied with, even if there is an omission in supplying the necessary particulars, eg the date of the resolution authorising the issue of the series,[5] or of some class of property which is to be subject to the charge.[6] The court will refuse to go behind this certificate, and will not enquire whether there has been any irregularity.[7] Thus, where a creditor sent in defective particulars, omitting to state that the instrument conferred a charge over chattels, and the Registrar, by mistake or oversight, omitted to mention that charge in the register, his certificate was held to be conclusive that the document creating the charge was properly registered.[8] In the same case, it was also decided that the requirement as to stating in the certificate 'the amount thereby secured' is sufficiently complied with by the words 'all sums now due or to become due'.

If the particulars submitted at the time the charge is registered do not give the true date of creation, and as a result the charge is registered and a certificate is issued by the Registrar, the charge will be valid even though more than 21 days have elapsed between the creation and registration of the charge.[9] The decision

---

1   Section 401(2). This certificate will either be signed by the Registrar or authenticated by his official seal: section 401(2)(b).
2   Section 402(1).
3   Section 402(2).
4   Section 402(3). As to the fine that may be imposed, see Schedule 24.
5   *Cunard SS Co v Hopwood* [1908] 2 Ch 564.
6   *National Provincial and Union Bank of England v Charnley* [1924] 1 KB 431 (CA); *Re Mechanisations (Eaglescliffe) Ltd* [1966] Ch 20.
7   *Re Yolland, Husson and Birkett* [1908] 1 Ch 152 (CA); *National Provincial and Union Bank of England v Charnley*, above.
8   *National Provincial and Union Bank of England v Charnley*, above; *Re Mechanisations (Eaglescliffe) Ltd*, above.
9   *Re Eric Holmes (Property) Ltd* [1965] Ch 1052.

of the Court of Appeal in *Re CL Nye Ltd*[1] illustrates the degree of protection afforded by section 401(2). A company was granted loan and overdraft facilities by a bank against the security, *inter alia*, of its business premises. All the necessary documents for registration (including an undated charge) were delivered to the bank's solicitor on 28 February 1964. The charge was stamped on 19 March, but thereafter was mislaid in the office of the bank's solicitor, and was not discovered until 19 June 1964. The solicitor thereupon inserted that date as being the date when the charge was created, and lodged for registration on 3 July the prescribed particulars of the charge in accordance with section 395(1). The Court of Appeal held that, notwithstanding that the date of the charge was incorrectly stated in the particulars delivered to the Registrar, once the certificate was granted section 401(2) applied. The certificate was conclusive evidence that all the requirements of the Act as to registration had been complied with. The requirement for delivery of the particulars within 21 days in section 395(1) was not a condition precedent to the Registrar's jurisdiction to register a charge or grant a certificate.[2]

In *R v Registrar of Companies, ex parte Central Bank of India*,[3] it was held that judicial review should not be allowed so as to challenge the Registrar's decision to register a charge where there were defects in the original registration of a charge in respect of the time allowed. What is now section 401(2) did not exclude the jurisdiction of the court. It merely excluded the admission of evidence to challenge the decision of the Registrar in the exercise of his statutory duty. Only the Attorney-General could obtain judicial review of the Registrar's decision to register a charge because the Crown was not bound by section 401(2).[4]

If inaccurate or incomplete particulars are delivered to the Registrar, he is not obliged to register the charge[5] and can return the particulars for correction.[6] Where defective particulars are returned, the obligation to file within 21 days remains unfulfilled and the lender may have to move quickly to ensure that correct particulars are filed within the 21-day period.

The registration regime contained in the Companies Act 1989 abolished the conclusive certificate of registration. Instead, the Registrar was merely required to send to the company, the chargee and, if the particulars were delivered by another person, to that person a copy of the filed particulars and of the note made by him of the date of delivery.[7] The Registrar's note of the date of delivery did not constitute conclusive evidence of the date of delivery, but the Registrar could be required by any person to provide a certificate stating the date on which particulars were delivered to him and this certificate was conclusive evidence that they were delivered no later than that date.[8]

---

1   [1971] 1 Ch 442.
2   [1971] 1 Ch 442 (applying *National Provincial Bank v Charnley* [1924] 1 KB 431) *per* Harman LJ (470), Russell LJ (472 and 474) and Megaw LJ (476).
3   [1986] QB 1114, [1986] 2 WLR 177, [1986] 1 All ER 105 (CA), overruling Mervyn Davies J, in *R v Registrar of Companies, ex parte Esal Commodities* [1985] 2 WLR 447.
4   Except that the Court of Appeal left open the possibility of a challenge by someone other than the Attorney-General where the certificate disclosed an error on its face, or the challenge was based on fraud or duress.
5   *Sun Tai Cheung Credits Ltd v AG of Hong Kong* (1987) 3 BCC 357.
6   The Registrar's practice of not accepting defective particulars in satisfaction of the filing obligations was endorsed by Lawton and Slade LJJ in *Central Bank of India*.
7   Section 95 of the Companies Act 1989.
8   Section 94. There was also a presumption that the particulars were delivered on the stated date, but that could be rebutted by evidence to the contrary.

The abolition of the conclusive certificate of registration, although part of the streamlining measures advocated by Professor Diamond,[1] was one of the obstacles to implementation of the registration regime contained in the Companies Act 1989. Under the existing regime, the production of a certificate of registration gives a purchaser from a debenture-holder (or a receiver acting on the debenture-holder's behalf) the assurance that the charge under which the sale is made has not become void for want of registration. A purchaser would not have that assurance had the provisions in the Companies Act 1989 been implemented.[2]

10.29 The transfer of charges

Where the benefit of a mortgage or charge on land owned by a company is transferred, and the company is a party to the transfer, the practice is to register the transfer as a new charge, but the question of registration does not arise if the company is not a party to the transfer.

The proper means of obtaining a decision of the court as to whether registration is necessary is by proceedings instituted for the purpose.[3]

10.30 Property acquired subject to a charge

Section 400 requires companies registered in England which acquire property already subject to a charge to register the charge within 21 days of the completion of the acquisition.[4] Although a penalty is provided for failure to register such charges on the register of charges kept by the Registrar, this failure does not render the charge void, as is the case with charges created by the company and not registered under section 395.[5] Where property was conveyed to a company, which created a legal mortgage in favour of the vendor for the unpaid balance of the purchase price, it was held that registration had to be effected under what is now section 395 and not under section 400.[6] Some doubt has been cast on this by the decision of the House of Lords in *Abbey National Building Society v Cann*[7] because it is now the case that there is never a moment when the purchaser of a property on a mortgage holds the property free of the security so that it is arguable that the

---

1   The Registrar would no longer be required to check filed particulars against original charging documents and would therefore no longer be in a position to determine whether the requirements as to registration had been complied with.

2   The Land Registry is understood to have opposed implementation for this reason (*Company Law Review: Proposals for Reform of Part XII of the Companies Act 1985*, DTI consultative document, November 1994). Note section 99 which attempted to deal with the issue by providing that a chargee or receiver could give a good title to a purchaser (defined as a person who acted in good faith and who gave valuable consideration) even though the charge had become void but that the chargee must then hold the proceeds of sale on a statutory trust.

3   *Re Cunard SS Co* [1908] WN 160.

4   If the property charged is situated outside Great Britain the material date becomes 21 days after the copy of the instrument could in due course of post, if dispatched with due diligence, have been received in the United Kingdom: section 400(3).

5   *Capital Finance Co Ltd v Stokes* [1969] 1 Ch 261 (CA).

6   Ibid. Equivalent provision is made for Scotland by section 416.

7   [1991] 1 AC 56.

purchaser does not create a charge over its own property for the purposes of section 395.[1]

10.31 Registration and priorities

Registration of a registrable charge 'perfects' the security against others who have competing interests in the same property and prevents the security becoming void. Registration, however, does not determine priority. Thus, the priority of two fixed charges on the same property, both of which are duly registered, is determined by order of creation, not by order of registration. Registration of a charge does give notice of the existence of that charge to subsequent charges, so that where priority depends on notice (eg where a fixed charge is followed by a legal mortgage of the same property), compliance with the registration require-ment can be a significant factor in establishing priority.[2]

10.32 Rectification of the register of charges[3]

Section 404 of the Companies Act 1985 provides that the register of charges may be rectified by supplying any omission or correcting any misstatement,[4] or the time for registration may be extended. Any such rectification or extension must be authorised by the court on the application of the company or any person interested.[5] But this will be allowed only if the court is satisfied that the omission to register a charge within the time required by the 1985 Act, or that the omission or misstatement of any particular with respect to any such charge, or in a memorandum of satisfaction, was accidental, or due to inadvertence or to some other sufficient cause, or is not of a nature to prejudice the position of creditors or shareholders of the company, or that on other grounds it is just and equitable to grant relief: section 404(1).[6] The court may impose terms as the condition of the grant of relief. Where a solicitor had advised that it was not necessary to register, that was held to be 'sufficient cause'.[7]

It is now[8] usual to make the order in the following form: 'That the time for registering the debentures [*or* mortgage] be extended until the day of ; and this order is to be without prejudice to the rights of parties acquired during the period

---

1   The arguments against this view which are put forward in de Lacy [1991] LMCLQ 531 at pp 536–537 are, however, persuasive.

2   For a general discussion of the rules governing the priority of competing securities, see **10.24**.

3   McCormack, 'Extension of Time for Registration of Company Charges' [1986] JBL 282.

4   Eg cancelling a notice of satisfaction of a mortgage entered by mistake. *Re C Light & Co* [1917] WN 77. When once a certificate of registration has been given by the Registrar, it is, apparently, unnecessary for the secured creditor to take any seps to rectify the register, however defective or even misleading it may be: *National Provincial and Union Bank of England v Charnley* [1924] 1 KB 431 (CA).

5   Swinfen-Eady J has held that it is not proper to apply for an extension of time as a means of determining whether or not registration is necessary: *Re Cunard SS Co* [1908] WN 160.

6   *Re Chantry House Developments plc* [1990] BCC 646, [1990] BCLC 813 (relief granted by means of an interlocutory notice of motion).

7   *Re S Abrahams & Sons Ltd* [1902] 1 Ch 695.

8   This contains the new form of proviso introduced as a result of *Watson v Duff Morgan & Vermont (Holdings) Ltd* [1974] 1 WLR 450.

between the date of creation of the said (charge) and the date of its actual registration).'[1]

Where a charge was created but not registered within the specified time, and leave to register was subsequently given, the charge was held to be postponed to a duly registered mortgage given before such registration to a director who had full knowledge of the earlier charge at the time he advanced his money.[2] Where, however, the only directors of a company learnt that the company had failed to fulfil its obligation to register a charge and then registered a charge in their own favour, the order extending time for registration of the earlier charge did not include the normal proviso which would have protected the rights of the directors.[3] The reasoning behind this is that the court will modify the order to exclude the proviso where its inclusion would facilitate an equitable fraud.[4] A chargee who discovers that, by mistake, he is unregistered, should act without delay. He should not deliberately defer action to see which course suits him best.[5]

10.33   Effect of a winding-up

Except in very exceptional circumstances, an order extending the time for registration will not be made once a winding-up has commenced,[6] because a winding-up, whether compulsory or voluntary, is a proceeding for the benefit of the unsecured creditors, so as to establish their right not to be postponed to the holders of debentures subsequently registered.[7] It has been held that where a winding-up is imminent, the court may exercise its discretion to refuse registration out of time.[8] Alternatively, where liquidation appears to be imminent, the court may insert a proviso permitting the company to make an application to discharge the extension order within a specified period after a winding-up becoming effective on or before a specified date.[9]

Where there is no winding-up before the actual registration of the debentures, an order in the usual form does not prevent the debentures, when registered, from taking priority over existing unsecured creditors who have not levied execution or taken some effective step to enforce their debts before the registration of the debentures.[10] Thus it is clearly established that the order only

---

1   *Re The Mendip Press* (1901) 18 TLR 38; *Re Joplin Brewery Co* [1902] 1 Ch 79 as to the original form of the proviso. A more elaborate form is given for the case where there are duly registered debentures in *Re IC Johnson & Co* [1902] 2 Ch 101 (CA).

2   *Re Monolithic Building Co* [1915] 1 Ch 643 (CA).

3   *Re Fablehill Ltd* [1991] BCLC 830, [1991] BCC 590.

4   *Re Telomatic Ltd, Barclays Bank plc v Cyprus Popular Bank Ltd* [1993] BCC 404.

5   *Victoria Housing v Ashpurton Estates* [1982] 3 All ER 655; *Re Telomatic*, above.

6   *Re S Abrahams & Sons* [1902] 1 Ch 695 (the order was refused on the ground that it would be of no value); *Re Anglo-Oriental Carpet Co* [1903] 1 Ch 914; *Re Mechanisations (Eaglescliffe) Ltd* [1966] Ch 20 at 36–37. *Re Spiral Globe Company* [1902] 1 Ch 396 and *Re RM Arnold & Co Ltd* [1984] BCLC 535 are examples of exceptional cases where an order was granted after the commencement of winding up. In *Re Resinold and Mica Products Ltd* [1982] 3 All ER 677, the Court of Appeal did not accept any qualification to the general rule, but earlier authorities were not cited to the court.

7   *Re Anglo-Oriental Carpet Co* [1903] 1 Ch 914.

8   *Re Ashpurton Estates* [1983] Ch 110.

9   *Re LH Charles & Co Ltd* [1935] WN 15; *Re Braemar Investments Ltd* [1989] Ch 54, (1988) 4 BCC 366, [1988] BCLC 556; *Exeter Trust Ltd v Screenways Ltd* [1991] BCLC 888, [1991] BCC 477, *Barclays Bank plc v Stuart Landon Ltd* [2001] EWCA Civ 140, [2001] 2 BCLC 316.

10 *Re Ehrmann Bros* [1906] 2 Ch 697 (CA); *Re IC Johnson & Co* [1902] 2 Ch 101; cf *Re Cardiff Workmen's Cottage Co* [1906] 2 Ch 627.

protects creditors who have acquired a security or levied execution on the property which is the subject matter of the charge, and that the court will not insert any terms for the protection of the unsecured creditors of the company.[1]

The registration provisions of the Companies Act 1989 dispensed with the need to apply to court for an extension order where a charge was not duly registered within 21 days. Under that regime, late filing[2] could be made at any time but, for a period of up to two years from the time of the late filing, the charge was vulnerable and liable to be avoided as against a liquidator or an administrator.[3] The priority of charges created before the late registration of an earlier charge was also preserved.

10.34   Memorandum of satisfaction

When a registered charge is paid or satisfied in whole or in part, a memorandum of satisfaction in the prescribed form, verified by a statutory declaration by a director and the secretary, should be lodged with the Registrar. Registration of the satisfaction or partial satisfaction of the debt is optional and may be effected at any time[4] but it is obviously desirable to record the fact that the company's indebtedness has been discharged or reduced. A similar memorandum may be lodged with the Registrar where part of the property or undertaking charged has been released from the charge or has ceased to form part of the company's property or undertaking. Section 403 requires that the memorandum be recorded by the Registrar on his register.

Omissions or misstatements in a memorandum of satisfaction may be rectified by the court under section 404, discussed above.

10.35   Charges over foreign property

Section 398(3) of the Companies Act 1985 provides that if the mortgage or charge is created within the United Kingdom[5] but comprises property outside the United Kingdom, the instrument purporting to charge such property must be lodged for registration. Registration must be effected even if further proceedings (eg registration in a foreign country) are necessary to make the charge valid in accordance with the law of the country in which such property is situate. Section 398(1) provides that 'in the case of a mortgage or charge created out of the United Kingdom comprising property situate outside the United Kingdom', a copy verified in the prescribed manner, delivered to or received by the Registrar, with the proper particulars, within 21 days after the date on which the instrument or copy could in due course of post, if dispatched with due diligence, have been received, will be sufficient to comply with the requirements of the Act. Companies

---

1   *Re MIG Trust* [1933] 1 Ch 542; *Re Kris Cruisers* [1949] Ch 138.
2   Or filing to correct incomplete or inaccurate particulars (section 96), a situation which, because of the conclusive nature of the certificate of registration and the Registrar's practice (post-*Esal*) of refusing to accept defective particulars, cannot occur under the existing registration requirements.
3   Section 95.
4   *Scottish & Newcastle plc Petitioners* [1993] BCC 634 (on the equivalent Scottish provision).
5   Ie Great Britain and Northern Ireland. Equivalent provision for Scotland is made by section 411.

instructing their agents abroad to create a mortgage must therefore be careful also to instruct them to forward a verified copy of the mortgage by the earliest possible post.

When a charge comprises property situate in Scotland or Northern Ireland and registration in the country where the property is situate is necessary to make the charge valid or effectual according to the law of that country, the delivery to and the receipt by the Registrar of a copy, verified in the prescribed manner, of the instrument by which the charge is created or evidence, together with a certificate in the prescribed form stating that the charge was presented for registration in Scotland or Northern Ireland, as the case may be, on the date on which it was so presented is, for the purposes of section 395, to have the same effect as the delivery and receipt of the instrument itself.[1]

10.36   Charges on property in Britain created by an oversea company

By section 409, the provisions of Part XII, Chapter I of the Companies Act 1985 are extended to charges on property in England and Wales which are created, and to charges on property in England and Wales which is acquired, by a company (whether a company within the meaning of the Act or not) incorporated outside Great Britain which has an established place of business in England and Wales. The Court of Appeal has had to determine the meaning of 'established place of business' for the purposes of section 409 in the case of an Isle of Man company which had acquired seven petrol stations in Lancashire, and then created charges over these properties in favour of an oil company.[2] The charges had not been registered under what is now section 409. Oliver LJ (giving the judgment of the court) held that evidence that a company has 'carried on business' may not be substantial enough to show that the company has 'an established place of business'. 'The concept, as it seems to me, is of some more or less permanent location not necessarily owned or even leased by the company, but at least associated with the company and from which habitually or with some degree of regularity business has been conducted.'[3] On this basis, only three of the seven charges were registrable under section 409 since, by the time they were created, the evidence showed that the company had established a business in the sense defined by Oliver LJ.

When an oversea company establishes a place of business or a branch in Great Britain, it is supposed to register under Part XXIII of the Companies Act 1985. Whether or not such registration has been effected, an oversea company which has an established place of business in Great Britain is subject to section 409 and must therefore register any charges on its property in England and Wales.[4] This creates an anomaly because it is the practice of the Registrar not to accept particulars of charges for registration under section 395 unless an oversea company is already registered under what is now Chapter I of Part XXIII of the

---

1   Section 398(4).
2   *Re Oriel* [1985] BCLC 343 at 347.
3   Oliver LJ applied *Lord Advocate v Huron and Eric Loan and Savings Association* 1911 SC 612. See also *Deverall v Grant Advertising Inc* [1955] Ch 111; *Act Dampskip Hercule v Grand Trunk Pacific Railway* [1912] 1 KB 222; *South India Shipping Corp v Export Import Bank of Korea* [1985] 1 WLR 585.
4   *NV Slavenburg's Bank v Intercontinental Natural Resources* [1980] 1 WLR 1076.

1985 Act.[1] In order to preserve the validity of the charge the owner of the charge must deliver particulars of the charge, together with the instrument (if any) by which it is created or evidenced. This will save the charge despite the lack of actual registration.[2] This divergence of the obligation imposed by section 409 from the Registrar's practice in administering section 395 would seem unsatisfactory both from the point of view of the owner of the charge and others who continue to deal with the company. Doubtless the policy of the Registrar is to provide further encouragement for oversea companies which establish a place of business in England to register under Chapter I of Part XXIII of the 1985 Act.

The Companies Act 1989 contained a new set of provisions governing the registration of charges by oversea companies. Under these provisions (which are not in force), the anomaly highlighted by the *Slavenburg* decision would disappear.

It has also been held[3] that the term 'liquidator' in section 395 (as extended by section 409 to companies incorporated outside England) includes a liquidator appointed in a foreign winding-up where the foreign winding-up was similar in character to an English winding-up. In any event, representative creditors may be joined, under RSC Order 15, rule 6(i), to plead the liquidator's case under section 395. Section 395 applies to floating charges as well as to fixed charges and when applied to oversea companies by virtue of section 409 includes a charge on future property in England. It is not confined to property existing in England when the charge was created. Further, if the charge initially came within section 395 by virtue of section 409, it remains within section 395 even if the company ceased to have a place of business in England before the commencement of the liquidation.[4]

10.37   The company's register of charges: section 407

In addition to registering with the Registrar those charges specified in section 396, section 407 of the Companies Act 1985[5] requires that every limited company must keep at its registered office a register of all charges specifically affecting property of the company and of all floating charges on the undertaking or any property of the company. In this register must be entered a short description of the property charged, the amount of the charge, and except in the case of securities to bearer, the names of the persons entitled to such charge. If any property of the company is charged[6] without such entry being made, every officer of the company who knowingly and wilfully authorises or permits the omission is liable to fine.[7]

---

1   See **4.24**.
2   [1980] 1 WLR 1076 *per* Lloyd J following a *dictum* of Scrutton LJ in *National Provincial Bank v Charnley* [1924] 1 KB 431 at 447.
3   [1980] 1 WLR 1076.
4   Ibid.
5   Equivalent provision is made for Scotland by section 422. Section 422 is, however, not confined to limited companies. A floating charge is in principle assignable by the holder, and on due intimation of the assignation the particulars of the assignee must be entered in the company's own register of charges. Intimation of the assignation must be in writing, in such terms (on a reasonable interpretation) as to convey to the debtor company that the debt has been transferred to the assignee: *Libertas Kommerz GmbH* 1978 SLT 222.
6   The expression 'charge' includes mortgage: section 396(4).
7   See now the Companies Act 1985, Schedule 24.

A person entitled to the benefit of a charge, however, even though a director of the company, does not lose his security by an omission to see that it is entered in the company's Register of Charges.[1] (It has been seen that he does so if the charge is one that requires registration under section 395 and is not registered with the Registrar.) The priority of charges is not affected by any imperfection of the register kept by the company.[2] Debentures containing a specific charge on the property of the company must be included in this register, and also those only containing a floating charge.

The company must also keep at its registered office a copy of every instrument creating a charge requiring registration.[3] In the case of a series of uniform debentures, it will suffice to keep a copy of one of such debentures.[4]

Under section 408, the register of charges, and copies of all instruments creating charges which are required to be registered with the Registrar, must be open at all reasonable times to the inspection of any creditor or member of the company without fee. The register of charges, but not copies of charging documentation, must be open to inspection by any other person on payment of a fee not exceeding 5p; but on a winding-up, the register cannot be inspected without an Order of Court.[5] The right to inspect the register of charges involves a right to take copies of it.[6] Any officer refusing to allow such inspection is liable to a penalty. In the case of such refusal in relation to a company registered in England, the court may by order compel an immediate inspection.[7]

An advantage for a creditor, or prospective creditor, in searching the company's register of charges in addition to the register maintained by the Registrar of Companies is that this may disclose the existence of charges which do not require registration with the Registrar. Some idea of the amount of a company's existing secured debt can also be gleaned from its last annual return, but this is necessarily a historical record of the amount as at the date of the annual return, which may since have become out of date.

10.38   The reform of the law of security over personal property

Prior to the Law Commission review, the law of security over personal property had been the subject of two major reviews since the 1970s. The first review was conducted by the Committee on Consumer Credit, chaired by Lord Crowther (the 'Crowther Committee').[8] The Crowther Committee put forward a proposed new framework for the law relating to security over personal property. This framework was largely based on article 9 of the United States Uniform Commercial Code which governs all secured transactions over personal property.[9]

---

1   *Wright v Horton* (1987) 12 App Cas 371 (HL).
2   *Re General South American Co* (1876) 2 ChD 337 (CA).
3   Section 406(1). Equivalent provision is made for Scotland by section 423.
4   Section 406(2).
5   *Somerset v Land Securities Co* [1897] WN 29.
6   *Nelson v Anglo-American Land, etc Co* [1897] 1 Ch 130. Note that, as these sections do not give the persons inspecting a right to have a copy supplied on payment, the case is different from that of the register of members. See **12.5.2**.
7   Section 408(4).
8   1971, Cmnd 4596.
9   Article 9 also formed the foundation of the Canadian Personal Property Security Act.

In a White Paper published in 1973,[1] the Government accepted that aspects of the law caused difficulty and announced its intention to institute consultations to determine whether there was a need for a major recasting of the law on new principles and whether the proposed Crowther scheme commanded general support. Apart from a report relating to Scottish law[2] and limited reference to the Crowther scheme in the *Report of the Review Committee on Insolvency Law and Practice*,[3] thereafter there were few significant developments with regard to possible reform of personal security law until, in March 1986, the Department of Trade and Industry appointed Professor AL Diamond to undertake a 'review of security over property other than land'. One of his criticisms was that the law was too fragmented and treated transactions which were similar in different ways. An illustration of the fragmentation of the law is the fact that a genuine[4] sale of assets coupled with an option to repurchase which is entered into to enable the company to raise finance, although it may be economically indistinguishable from a loan secured on those assets, does not require registration at the companies registry because it is not, in legal terms, a 'charge'. The non-registrable status of retention of title clauses and hire-purchase agreements also illustrates the point. Professor Diamond's final report was published in 1989.[5]

He advocated[6] the introduction of a new simplified law which was similar to the Crowther scheme and which was based on the United States and Canadian models. Under the new law, substance would have precedence over form, and any arrangement, having as its true purpose the transfer or creation of rights over or interests in property other than land, as security for the provision of finance or the performance of any other obligation, would be treated as giving rise to a 'security interest'. Hire-purchase agreements and retention of title clauses, which are not presently registrable, would become security interests under this scheme, as could sales of assets entered into for financing purposes.

The creation of security interests enforceable against third parties would require a degree of formality in the form of a written financing agreement,[7] and as a general rule non-possessory securities interests would be required to be made public by some form of registration or filing.[8] Priority of competing securities would be governed by date of filing, not, as is presently the case, by date of creation and questions of notice.[9] One particular question raised by Professor Diamond at the consultative stage was the treatment of floating charges under a new scheme. In his final report, he recommended[10] the preservation of the essence of the floating charge, namely the freedom for the debtor to dispose of the property secured in the ordinary course of business, and the attachment of the charge to after-acquired property falling within the description of the security. Professor

1   *Reform of the Law on Consumer Credit* (Cmnd 5427).
2   Halliday Working Party Report, published by the Scottish Law Commission in March 1986.
3   1982, Cmnd 8558.
4   *Welsh Development Agency v Export Finance Co Ltd* (CA), above. Cf *Re Curtain Dream plc* [1990] BCLC 925 where a transaction which the parties designated a sale was held to be a registrable charge.
5   *Review of Security Interests in Property*. See also Diamond, 'The Reform of the Law of Security Interests' [1989] CLP 231.
6   Chapter 9 of the report sets out the main recommendations.
7   Chapter 10 of the report.
8   Chapter 11 of the report.
9   Ibid.
10   Chapter 16 of the report.

Diamond specifically recommended that the floating-charge form of security should be made available to all businesses, whether incorporated or not.

Reaction to Professor Diamond's final proposals was muted[1] and in 1991 the Secretary of State for Trade and Industry indicated that they would not be adopted.[2] The Minister stated that consultations had established that the majority of interested parties were opposed to major reform and that it could not be commercially justified. One argument against reform is that, although it is widely accepted that the current law is complex and lacking in any functional basis, it is a system with which lenders, and their advisers, are familiar and which does allow lenders to achieve the object of obtaining adequate security for their loans. Another is that radical reform initiatives should not be pursued in domestic law in advance of European Union harmonisation measures.[3]

As part of the Review of Company Law which was launched in 1998 and culminated in the *Modernising Company Law* White Paper in 2002, the Law Commission was asked to investigate and review the registration of security interest. A consultation paper setting out the Law Commission's preliminary recommendations was published in 2002,[4] and it is anticipated that its final report will appear some time in 2004. Any recommendations should become part of the Companies Bill announced by the Government in *Modernising Company Law*.[5] The Law Commission does not believe that the shortcomings of the existing system could be remedied and it therefore argues that an entirely new system for registration should be adopted.[6] The system favoured by the Law Commission is a 'notice filing system'. This would be an electronic system: the relevant information would be entered into an on-line form and processed automatically, thereby ensuring that the relevant information appears on the register much more quickly than is the case at present. The form would be known as a 'financing statement', and require as a minimum details of the debtor and secured party, debtor's registration number at Companies House and a brief description of the secured property.[7] A significant advantage of the proposed system would be that it would not be transaction-specific, and a single filing could cover multiple security transactions between the same parties. Priorities would be determined on the basis of their date of creation, although it is also proposed to remove the possibility that a floating charge can give the company the authority to create a later fixed charge that ranks ahead of the floating charge.[8] A further crucial proposal is that the new system would encompass not only those securities

---

1   The Company Law Committee of the Law Society and the Joint Working Party of the Bar and the Law Society on Banking Law were against implementation of the radical reforms: 'Comments on "A Review of Security Interests in Property"' (November 1989, Memorandum No 211).

2   *Hansard*, HC vol 189, col 482, 24 April 1991.

3   The memorandum published by the Company Law Committee of the Law Society and the other bodies mentioned in footnote 1, above, cites possible European developments as a reason for not adopting the Diamond reforms at this stage: 'it would be unfortunate if a major change in the law were to be implemented and then followed by another major change to accommodate any EEC requirements', paragraph 8.2.10.

4   Law Commission, *Registration of Security Interests: Company Charges and Property other than Land*, Consultation Paper 164.

5   See CM 5553–I, paragraph 6.20.

6   Consultation Paper 164, Part III, and paragraphs 4.2–4.5.

7   Ibid, paragraph 4.108.

8   Ibid, paragraph 4.142.

recognised as registrable at present, but also any arrangements which are functionally equivalent ('quasi-securities'),[1] such as hire-purchase and conditional sale agreements and retention of title clauses. It is beyond the scope of this book to review the details of this proposal, in particular because of their preliminary nature. There is a reasonable chance that the proposals eventually put forward by the Law Commission will be accepted by the Government and form part of a new Companies Act.

PART 4: CREDITORS' REMEDIES

10.39 Scope

This part is mainly concerned with the remedy which used to be employed when a debenture is secured by a floating charge, namely the appointment of a receiver under an express power in the debenture trust deed. This is likely to fall out of use over the coming years as a result of major changes made by the Enterprise Act 2002.[2] A key change is that the holder of a 'qualifying floating charge' created after 15 September 2003[3] is prohibited from appointing an administrative receiver.[4] A 'qualifying floating charge' is defined in section 14(2) of a new Schedule B1 of the Insolvency Act 1986 as follows:

(a) it is stated that the floating charge falls within section 14(1) of Schedule B1.

(b) it purports to empower the holder of the charge to appoint an administrator of the company.

(c) it purports to empower the holder of the charge to make an appointment which would be the appointment of an administrative receiver; or

(d) it purports to empower the holder of a floating charge in Scotland to appoint a receiver who on appointment would be an administrative receiver.

A person is a holder of a qualifying floating charge where his security arrangements include one or more qualifying floating charges which together cover the whole or substantially the whole of the company's property.[5] This means that a lender holding several forms of security will be caught by the prohibition in section 72A if one of these is a qualifying floating charge. It seems that such a lender could not exercise a right to appoint an administrative receiver based on a floating charge which is not a qualifying charge.

The overall objective pursued by these change is to promote a 'rescue culture', and the main procedure that should now be invoked where a company is in financial difficulties is the administration procedure.[6] This has also been significantly reformed by the Enterprise Act 2002, which replaced the old Part II of

---

1   Ibid, paragraph 7.20.
2   For a summary, see Walters (2004) 25 Co Law 1.
3   The date is confirmed in the Insolvency Act 1986, section 72A (Appointed Date) Order 2003 (SI 2003/2095), regulation 2.
4   Section 72A of the Insolvency Act 1986.
5   Section 14(3) of Schedule B1.
6   It has been argued that the new scheme effectively heralds the demise of the floating charge: see Mokal, 'The Floating Charge – An Elegy' in Worthington (ed), *Commercial Law and Commercial Practice* (Oxford: Hart, 2003).

the Insolvency Act 1986 with Schedule B1 which now contains the administration procedure. An important change here is that it the holder of a qualifying floating charge now has the right to appoint an administrator.[1] The administration procedure is examined in detail in Chapter 21.

Administrative receivership is therefore likely to disappear very quickly. It will still be available in respect of non-qualifying floating charges, but only if the holder of such a charge is not also the holder of a qualifying floating charge. Moreover, there are some exceptions to the prohibition in section 72A in sections 72B–72G. The discussion of receivership and administrative receivership has therefore been retained in this edition. However, the recourse open to the holder of a qualifying floating charge is to appoint an administrator under the new administration procedure.[2]

10.40 The categories of receiver

In English company law there have traditionally been two types of receiver (or receiver and manager): the receiver appointed by the court and the receiver appointed by debenture holders under a power in the debenture trust deed. The Insolvency Act 1986 introduced a new category of receiver – the 'administrative receiver'.[3] Such a receiver is now subject to a distinct statutory regime over and above the rules which apply to receivers and managers generally.[4] An administrative receiver[5] is defined as a receiver or manager of the whole (or substantially the whole) of a company's property. He must be appointed by or on behalf of the holders of any debentures of the company secured by a floating charge, or by a floating charge and one or more fixed charges.[6]

As noted above, there is another institution, the 'administrator'. Such an individual is appointed in accordance with Part II of, and Schedule B1 to the Insolvency Act 1986 to help a company in financial difficulties. Since administration is not exclusively a remedy for secured creditors, it is discussed elsewhere in this book in the context of the law[7] of insolvent companies.

---

1   Subsections 14–21 of Schedule B1 to the Insolvency Act 1986.

2   See **21.3**.

3   See sections 42 to 49.

4   References in the Companies Act 1985 or in the Insolvency Act 1986 to a receiver or manager of the property of a company include a receiver or manager of part of that property or of income arising from the property or part of it. This also includes references to a receiver who is not a manager. Likewise, references to appointment of a receiver or manager under powers contained in an instrument includes appointment under powers which, by virtue of any enactment, are implied in and have effect as if contained in an instrument: section 29(1).

5   See section 29(2)(a).

6   This extends to a person who would be such a receiver or manager but for the appointment of some other person as the receiver of part of the company's property. On whether there can be more than one administrative receiver in office at the same time (apart from joint appointments), see Oditah, 'Lightweight Floating Charges' [1991] JBL 49; Marks and Emmet, 'Administrative Receivers: Questions of Identity and Double Identity' [1994] JBL 1. A receiver appointed to a foreign company can be an administrative receiver: *Re International Bulk Commodities Ltd* [1993] Ch 77; [1993] 1 All ER 361, [1992] BCLC 1074, [1992] BCC 463. Cf *Re Devon and Somerset Farmers Ltd* [1993] BCC 410.

7   See Part 3 of Chapter 21.

10.41　Unsecured lending

A company's creditors may bring an action in debt if their principal or interest is in arrears. A creditor may, when his principal or interest is in arrears, petition for the winding-up of the company[1] and may also seek an administration order. In the case of unsecured creditors these are the only remedies ordinarily available.[2]

10.42　Secured lending

If default is made in the payment of the principal or interest on secured loans,[3] the holders have all the remedies which mortgagees would have in like circumstances, ie: they may sue on the covenant to pay; they may obtain a receiver of the rents and profits, or apply for a sale of the mortgaged property;[4] they may, if all of the debenture-holders are parties to the action,[5] proceed by way of foreclosure;[6] or, if they have legal estate or a power to enter, they may take possession.[7] In each case, the debenture and trust deed (if any) must be consulted to see, first, whether there has really been a default, and, secondly, what remedies are available without the assistance of the court, and what remedies require an action to be commenced. The strict performance of all conditions is of the utmost importance, for without this the powers cannot be exercised nor will any order be made by the court for the appointment of a receiver or execution of the trust. For instance, if payment is stipulated to be made at a certain time and place, the condition is not broken unless demand is made by the debenture holder at that place;[8] but if the condition is only that the principal shall be paid at a named place, demand of the interest need not be made at such place.[9] So if the consent of a majority of the debenture holders is required by the deed before an action is brought, a debenture holder who has not obtained such consent cannot obtain the appointment of a receiver.[10]

The usual remedy today, where the debentures or debenture stock are secured by a charge, is to seek to enforce the powers given by the terms of the debentures in the trust deed to appoint a receiver out of court. The power to appoint a receiver may be either express or implied by reference to the Law of Property Act 1925;[11] but, as the power under that Act is very meagre, being primarily intended

---

1　*Re Borough of Portsmouth etc Tramways Co* [1892] 2 Ch 362.

2　The court will not normally appoint a receiver unless the debentures are secured by a charge: *Harris v Beauchamp Bros* [1896] 1 QB 801 (CA): *Re Swallow Footwear Ltd* (1956) *The Times*, 23 October. Moreover, in Scotland only the holder of a floating charge can appoint a receiver. The possibility of the court appointing a receiver on behalf of an unsecured lender has been considered in Australia: *Bond Brewing Holdings v National Australia Bank* (1990) 1 ACSR 445, noted (1991) 107 LQR 551, [1990] 8 JIBL 330, [1991] 10 JIBL 405.

3　The company cannot by making default compel debenture holders to accept immediate repayment: *Re General Motor Cab Co (No 2)* (1912) 56 SJ 573.

4　An action by one debenture holder for a receiver in the Chancery Division is no impediment to an action by another debenture holder in the Queen's Bench Division for the payment of arrears of interest: *Cleary v Brazil Rly Co* [1915] WN 178.

5　*Elias v Continental Oxygen Co* [1897] 1 Ch 511.

6　*Oldrey v Union Works* [1895] WN 77.

7　The examples relate to English law, but the principle is true in Scotland also.

8　*Thorn v City Rice Mills* (1889) 40 ChD 357; *Re Escalera Silver Co* (1908) 25 TLR 87.

9　*Re Harris Calculating Machine Co* [1914] 1 Ch 920.

10　*Pethybridge v Unibifocal Co* [1918] WN 278.

11　Sections 101 and 109.

only to deal with real estate, there is usually an express power in elaborate terms to appoint a receiver without the need to resort to a debenture holder's action.[1] Where a debenture provides for the repayment of all moneys thereby secured on demand and for the debenture-holder to become entitled to appoint a receiver in default of compliance with such demand, the debenture-holder is required to give the debtor a reasonable opportunity of implementing the mechanics of payment before appointing a receiver.[2] The 'mechanics of payment' test means that the debenture-holder must allow the debtor time to effect the transfer from its account but it does not extend to giving the debtor time to raise new money to meet the demand.[3] There is some concern that precipitate action by banks in appointing receivers has the effect of denying companies' management the opportunity to mount rescues and reconstructions. A response to this concern has been the development of a self-regulatory statement of principles agreed by the majority of UK banks, which sets out the framework for the relationship between banks and their business customers.[4]

A receiver appointed out of court will usually be given wide powers, including a power of sale. The powers conferred on an administrative receiver are also deemed to include a wide range of statutory powers, except in so far as these are inconsistent with the terms of the debenture under which he was appointed.[5]

If the power to appoint a receiver is conferred on one or some of the debenture-holders, it must be exercised as a trust for the benefit of all of the holders of the debentures: otherwise the court will intervene and itself appoint a receiver.[6]

Appointing a receiver under an express power in the charging documentation avoids the trouble, delay and expense of applying to court. Nowadays, it should rarely be necessary to resort to seeking an appointment of a receiver by the court unless there is some defect in the express power. One circumstance where the court may be asked to appoint a receiver is where the debenture holder's security is 'in jeopardy' and the debenture trust deed does not provide for the appointment of a receiver in that situation.[7]

On grounds of jeopardy, a receiver may be appointed, even before the principal or interest is in arrear if the assets are in danger[8] or a sale will be necessary in the

---

1   *Gore-Browne on Companies* 44th edn (Jordans, loose-leaf) at 19.3–19.6, contains a full account of the procedure governing debenture holders' actions.

2   *Cripps (Pharmaceuticals) Ltd v Wickenden* [1973] 2 All ER 606, [1973] 1 WLR 944; *Bank of Baroda v Panessar* [1987] Ch 335, [1986] 3 All ER 751: *NRG Vision Ltd v Churchfield Leasing Ltd* [1988] BCLC 624, (1988) 4 BCC 56; *Sheppard & Cooper Ltd v TSB Bank plc* [1996] 2 All ER 654; *Lloyds Bank plc v Lampert* [1999] BCC 507.

3   *Cripps (Pharmaceuticals) Ltd v Wickenden*, above.

4   See *A Review of Company Rescue and Business Reconstruction Mechanisms* (Insolvency Service, 1999), p 9.

5   Section 42 of the Insolvency Act 1986, see **10.51**.

6   *Stuart v Maskelyne Typewriter etc Co* [1898] 1 Ch 133 (CA).

7   The court will not imply a term into a debenture trust deed entitling the debenture-holder to appoint a receiver in the event of jeopardy: *Cryne v Barclays Bank plc* [1987] BCLC 548.

8   *McMahon v North Kent Iron Works Co* [1891] 2 Ch 148; *Edwards v Standard Rolling Stock Syndicate* [1893] 1 Ch 574; *Thorn v Nine Reefs* (1892) 67 LT 93 (CA); *Wissner v Levison & Steiner* [1900] WN 152; *Re London Pressed Hinge Co* [1905] 1 Ch 576; *Re Braunstein and Marjolaine* [1914] WN 335.

near future.[1] Many appointments have been made under this power,[2] but if any opposition is offered, the court scans closely the circumstances, and will not allow a debenture-holder to obtain a receiver merely because the security he has accepted is a risky one or the assets of the company are not sufficient to pay the debenture in full.[3] A receiver will, however, be appointed if the company's business is practically at an end, and the only asset remaining is a reserve fund created out of profits earned at an earlier date,[4] or if the business is about to be shut down and the premises let.[5] Indeed, it now seems that the jeopardy must be from some act which would be wrongful as against the debenture-holders or amounts or may amount to a destruction of his security.

If there is a specific charge on part of the assets and a floating charge on the rest, jeopardy, by reason of threatened executions on the specifically charged assets, will be a ground for the appointment of a receiver of them, without a receiver and manager of others assets not in jeopardy, the security being ample.[6]

Since debenture-holders rarely seek the assistance of the courts to enforce their security, the remainder of this part is concerned only with receivers who are appointed out of court under powers contained in debentures or debenture trust deeds.[7] Once again, it must be emphasised that this is no longer possible in the case of qualifying floating charges (see **10.39**).

10.43 Receivers and managers: capacity to act as a receiver

In England,[8] a body corporate is not qualified for appointment as receiver of the property of a company; any body corporate acting as receiver is liable to a fine.[9]

If an undischarged bankrupt acts as receiver or manager of the property of a company on behalf of debenture-holders, he is liable to imprisonment and/or a fine. This does not apply if the appointment was made by the court[10] but it is difficult to envisage circumstances where the court would be inclined to appoint a bankrupt as a receiver.

A receiver or manager may now be disqualified from 'managing' other companies by a court order under the Company Directors (Disqualification) Act 1986. Such an order may disqualify a person from acting as a receiver or manager where he has committed certain serious offences.[11]

---

1   *Smith v Wilkinson* [1897] 1 Ch 158.
2   The jeopardy is usually the danger of the assets charged being taken in execution by unsecured creditors under judgments. The right of the debenture-holders thus to make their security attach was discussed by Buckley J in *Re London Pressed Hinge Co* [1905] 1 Ch 576.
3   *Re New York Taxicab Co* [1913] 1 Ch 1.
4   *Re Tilt Cove Copper Co* [1913] 2 Ch 588.
5   *Re Braunstein and Marjolaine* [1914] WN 335.
6   *Grigson v George Taplin & Co* (1915) 112 LT 985.
7   *Gore Browne on Companies* 44th edn (Jordans, loose-leaf) at 19.9–19.13, considers court-appointed receivers.
8   For receivers in Scotland, see ibid, 19.16–19.33.
9   Section 30 of the Insolvency Act 1986.
10   Section 31 of the Insolvency Act 1986.
11   See **15.16** *et seq*.

An administrative receiver acts an 'insolvency practitioner'.[1] Insolvency practitioners, as a category, are regulated by the Insolvency Act 1986.[2] Persons must be qualified to act as insolvency practitioners, usually through membership of an appropriate authority such as the regulatory bodies of the accounting profession, and they must provide security for the performance of their functions.[3] It is an offence to act as an insolvency practitioner when not qualified to do so.[4]

An administrative receiver must vacate office if he ceases to be qualified to act as an insolvency practitioner in relation to the company. He may also resign office[5] but can be removed from office only by order of the court.[6] The fact that the debenture holder who appointed an administrative receiver cannot remove him from office without a court order gives an administrative receiver security against removal without cause (but note that the administrative receiver's freedom to act independently is curtailed by his duty to act in the interests of his appointor[7]). Where an administrative receiver vacates office (otherwise than by death) he must send notice to the Registrar of Companies within fourteen days.[8]

10.44   Notification of the appointment of a receiver

Within seven days after the appointment of a receiver or manager, the person making the appointment under the powers contained in any instrument must give notice of the fact to the Registrar, who must enter it in the register of charges.[9] If default is made, a fine may be imposed.[10] There is no statutory obligation on a receiver who is not an administrative receiver or on his appointor to notify the company of the appointment, but this would be done at an early stage in the ordinary course of events. On his appointment an administrative receiver must at once send notice of his appointment to the company. He must also publish this notice in the 'prescribed manner', that is in the *London Gazette* and in an appropriate newspaper. He must send notice of his appointment within twenty-eight days to all the creditors of the company (so far as he is aware of their addresses).[11]

---

1   Section 388 of the Insolvency Act 1986.
2   Part XIII.
3   The details of the qualification requirements are fleshed out in the Insolvency Practitioners Regulations 1990, SI 1990 No 439.
4   Insolvency Act 1986, section 389(1). This does not apply to the Official Receiver: section 389(2).
5   Ibid, section 45. There is no statutory provision which entitles a receiver who is not an administrative receiver to resign and the matter is governed by the debenture under which the receiver is appointed.
6   Ibid, section 45.
7   See **10.49**.
8   Ibid, section 45(4). See also the Insolvency Rules 1986, SI 1986 No 1925 which impose further notification requirements. When an administrative receiver vacates office the remuneration and expenses to which he is entitled are charged on the property of the company under his custody or his control at the time he leaves. This secures the payment of these claims. The same principle also applies to any indemnity to which he is entitled out of the assets of the company. See section 45(3).
9   Section 405(2) of the Companies Act 1985. The corresponding obligation to notify the Registrar of ceasing to act as a receiver or manager falls on the receiver or manager himself: section 405(3).
10   Section 405(4) of the Companies Act 1985.
11   Section 46 of the Insolvency Act 1986 and Insolvency Rules 1986, rule 3.2.

Where any receiver or manager has been appointed, every invoice, order for goods or business letter issued on behalf of the company or the receiver or manager or the liquidator, being a document on which the name of the company appears, must state that a receiver or manager has been appointed.[1]

10.45   Defective appointments

Section 34 of the Insolvency Act 1986 deals with the consequences of invalid appointments of receivers or managers.[2] Whether this is caused by the invalidity of the instrument under which the appointment is made or otherwise, the court may order the person making the appointment, or the person on whose behalf the appointment was made, to indemnify the appointee against liability arising solely by reason of the invalidity of the appointment.[3] In practice, receivers may prefer to ensure that their appointors give them a contractual indemnity to avoid the need to obtain a court order.

Also of note in this context is section 232 of the Insolvency Act 1986, which provides that the acts of an individual as administrative receiver are valid notwithstanding any defect in his appointment, nomination or qualifications.[4]

10.46   Application to the court to fix a receiver's remuneration

The court may, on application by the liquidator, fix the remuneration of a receiver or manager appointed under the powers contained in any instrument, and may from time to time, on the application of the liquidator, receiver or manager, vary or amend any order so made.[5] The power to fix the remuneration extends to fixing the remuneration for any period before the making of the order or the application, and is exercisable notwithstanding that the receiver or manager has died or has ceased to act before the making of the order or the application. Further, where the receiver or manager has been paid, or has retained for his remuneration for any period prior to the order any amount in excess of that fixed for that period, it extends to requiring him or his personal representatives to account for the excess or such part thereof as may be specified in the order. Such a requirement is not to be made in respect of any period before the making of the application unless there are special circumstances.[6]

A receiver is entitled to charge the property in his custody in respect of his right to remuneration.[7] Accordingly, the amount of remuneration paid to a receiver

---

1   Section 39(1) of the Insolvency Act 1986. See section 39(2) as to the fine that may be imposed on those who have knowingly and wilfully authorised a default.

2   *Shamji v Johnson Bankers Ltd* [1991] BCLC 36 is an example of an (unsuccessful) challenge to the appointment of a receiver.

3   An invalidly appointed receiver may be liable as a trespasser on the company's property: *Re Goldburg (No 2)* [1912] 1 KB 606.

4   This is similar to section 285 of the Companies Act 1985, which deals with defectively appointed directors. On the limits of the protection afforded by that section, see *Morris v Kanssen* [1946] AC 459, which is discussed in **6.35**.

5   Insolvency Act 1986, section 36.

6   Section 36(2). Where a debenture incorporates section 109 of the Law of Property Act 1925, then the receiver is entitled to the 5% commission allowed by section 109(6) even though the debenture did not otherwise specify the remuneration. The receiver may fix this rate without applying to court unless he wants a higher rate: *Marshall v Cottingham* [1981] 3 All ER 8.

7   Sections 37(4) and 45(3) of the Insolvency Act 1986.

diminishes the amount remaining for the unsecured creditors. The power to apply to court is a safeguard against abuse and it is intended to protect unsecured creditors.[1] However, the courts will not interfere lightly: in *Re Potters Oils Ltd (No 2)*,[2] it was said that the power of the court to fix a receiver's remuneration should be confined to cases in which the remuneration could clearly be seen to be excessive.

10.47 Receiver's right to indemnity

If a receiver and manager properly incurs expenses in carrying on business, he is entitled to be repaid out of the property in priority to the rights of the persons for whose benefit he acted, and where he is not declared to be the agent of the company he may sue the debenture-holders who appointed him for his remuneration.[3] Receivers are now also given statutory indemnities.[4] The usual practice is for receivers to be appointed as agents of the company.[5]

10.48 Application to the court for directions

A receiver or manager appointed under the powers contained in any instrument may apply to the court for directions in relation to any particular meeting arising in connection with the performance of his functions: and the court may give such directions or make such order declaring the rights of persons before the court or otherwise as it thinks just.[6] This power to apply is also given to those by whom or on whose behalf a receiver or manager has been appointed.

A receiver may apply for directions from the court in order to resolve disputes about entitlements to the secured property.[7] In *Tudor Grange Holdings Ltd v Citibank NA*,[8] Browne-Wilkinson V-C suggested that a receiver could use the power to apply to court for directions to cure any embarrassment involved in making a decision whether to commence proceedings on the company's behalf against the debenture-holder who had appointed him.

10.49 Duties of a receiver

A receiver is subject to a statutory duty imposed by section 40 of the Insolvency Act 1986 to pay preferential debts in priority to any claims for principal or interest in respect of debentures secured by a floating charge. Preferential debts are specified in section 386 of and Schedule 6 to the Act, although following changes made by the Enterprise Act 2002, these are now restricted mainly to contributions to occupational pension schemes and remuneration.[9]

If a receiver disposes of the assets, or allows them to be taken by others, without providing for claims having a right to preferential payment, with knowledge of the

---

1   *Re Greycaine Ltd* [1946] Ch 269.
2   [1986] 1 All ER 890, [1986] 1 WLR 201, [1986] BCLC 98, (1985) 1 BCC 99 at 593.
3   *Deyes v Wood* [1911] 1 KB 806 (CA).
4   As to the statutory right of indemnity conferred by sections 37 and 44 of the Insolvency Act 1986, see **10.52** and **10.55**.
5   See **10.52** and **10.55**.
6   Insolvency Act 1986, section 35.
7   As in *Re Ellis, Son & Vidler Ltd* [1994] BCC 532.
8   [1992] Ch 53, [1991] 4 All ER 1, [1991] 3 WLR 750, [1991] BCLC 1009. Cf *Lascomme Ltd v UDT (Ireland) Ltd* [1994] 1 ILRM 227. See further **10.51**.
9   See **21.51.1**.

claims, he will be personally liable to those entitled to the extent to which they are prejudiced.[1] Once a receiver has collected assets he is liable to the extent of those assets to pay preferential creditors of whose claims he has notice. This is equally the case where payment is made to the company by the direction and on the indemnity of the debenture-holder. A receiver is neither bound nor entitled, when he is removed from his appointment as a receiver, to account to the company for the moneys he has collected. Although those assets belong to the company, they are (in the case of a receiver appointed to enforce a floating charge) subject to a charge which has crystallised in favour of the debenture-holder. The receiver cannot therefore pay the company and ignore the statutory rights of preferential creditors. A receiver so doing is liable to the preferential creditors for breach of statutory duty: *CIR v Goldblatt.*[2]

Payments made to preferential creditors out of floating-charge assets can be recouped out of assets of the company available for payment of the general creditors.[3] This ensures that the burden of paying the preferential debts falls ultimately on the company's unsecured creditors, to the extent that the company's assets exceed what is owing to the debenture-holder under the floating charge. Any other result would fail to give effect to the debenture-holder's priority over unsecured creditors.

A floating charge is defined by section 40 as a charge which, as created, was a floating charge. Crystallisation of the floating charge prior to the appointment of the receiver does not take the situation outside the scope of that section. Also, the reference to debentures in section 40(2) is not limited to those debentures under which the administrative receiver is actually appointed.[4]

Aside from the statutory duty to pay preferential debts, the primary duty of a receiver is to realise the security on behalf of his appointor.[5] The receiver is under no obligation to the company or to its other creditors to carry on the company's business at the expense of his appointor, nor need he delay realising the security even though he might have obtained a higher price at a later date.[6]

A receiver is subject to equitable duties in his dealings with the company's property. He must not himself buy the property which he is appointed to realise, since such a purchase would infringe the self-dealing rule.[7] A sale of the property by a receiver to a company in which he has an interest infringes the fair-dealing rule and is liable to be set aside, unless he can show that the sale was made in good

---

1   *Woods v Winskill* [1913] 2 Ch 303; *Westminster City Council v Haste* [1950] Ch 442.

2   [1972] Ch 498 (applying *Woods v Winskill,* above; *Westminster City Council v Haste,* above).

3   Section 40(3).

4   *Re H & K (Medway) Ltd v IRC* [1997] 1 BCLC 545, not following *Griffiths v Yorkshire Bank plc* [1994] 1 WLR 1427.

5   *Re B Johnson & Co (Builders) Ltd* [1955] Ch 634 at 661–662 *per* Jenkins LJ, approved by Lord Templeman in *Downsview Nominees Ltd v First City Corporation* [1993] AC 295, [1993] 3 All ER 626, [1993] 2 WLR 286, [1993] BCC 46.

6   Ibid. Also *Cuckmere Brick Co Ltd v Mutual Finance Ltd* [1971] Ch 949; *Bank of Cyprus (London) Ltd v Gill* [1980] 2 Lloyd's Rep 51. Note also *AIB Finance Ltd v Debtors* [1998] 1 BCLC 665 (mortgagee had no duty to preserve business pending realisation of the security). Cf *Standard Chartered Bank Ltd v Walker* [1982] 1 WLR 1410 at 1415 *per* Lord Denning: 'It is at least arguable that, in choosing the time, he must exercise a reasonable degree of care'. If a receiver sells at the worst possible time, this may be seen as evidence of bad faith.

7   *Watts v Midland Bank plc* (1986) 2 BCC 98 at 961; *Nugent v Nugent* [1907] WN 169; *Re Magadi Soda Co* (1925) 94 LJ Ch 217.

faith and that he took reasonable precautions to obtain the best price reasonably obtainable at the time.[1]

In *Downsview Nominees Ltd v First City Corporation*,[2] the Privy Council held that a receiver acting on behalf of a debenture-holder[3] owes duties to second and subsequent debenture-holders and to the company to use his powers for the sole purpose of securing repayment of the moneys owing under the debenture under which he was appointed, and to act in good faith. He also owes specific duties in equity to these persons, such as the duty to keep premises in repair and to avoid waste.[4] The Privy Council accepted that the receiver owes a specific equitable duty to take reasonable care to obtain a proper price for any assets he decided to sell.[5] However, the Privy Council denied the existence of a general duty of care in tort owed by a receiver to subsequent encumbrancers or to the company in respect of dealings with the security. Some earlier first-instance and appellate decisions of the English courts had assumed the existence of a duty of care in tort owed by debenture-holders and their receivers to the company and subsequent encumbrancers, and also to guarantors of the company's debts.[6] Yet, although there is no duty of care in tort, in particular circumstances equity may impose a similar duty. In *Medforth v Blake*,[7] the Court of Appeal considered the scope of the receiver's equitable duties and held that where, as in this case, the receiver chose to manage the mortgaged property he owed a duty to the mortgagor and anyone else interested in the equity of redemption[8] to do so with reasonable diligence. In such circumstances, the receiver's duties were not confined to a duty of good faith.

A debenture-holder who is contractually entitled to appoint a receiver is under no duty to refrain from doing so on the grounds that it might cause loss to the company or its creditors. The debenture-holder is free to exercise his rights even if it is alleged that the appointment of a receiver is unnecessary because it would simply duplicate the efforts of the liquidator.[9]

---

1   *Tse Kwong Lam v Wong Chit Sen* [1983] 1 WLR 1349; *Watts v Midland Bank* at 98, 968.

2   Above. The Court of Appeal has held that a mortgagee's duty arises in equity rather than tort: *Parker-Tweedle v Dunbar Bank* [1991] Ch 12; *AIB Finance Ltd v Debtors* [1998] 1 BCLC 665. See further Berg, 'Duties of a Mortgagee and a Receiver' [1993] JBL 213; Nolan (1994) Co Law 28; Grantham (1993) Conv 401; Fealy, 'Receivers' Duties: A Return to Orthodoxy' [1994] NILQ 61.

3   Or the debenture-holder itself.

4   These equitable duties would also include those mentioned in the previous paragraph.

5   This is consistent with *Cuckmere Brick Co Ltd v Mutual Finance Ltd*, above.

6   The existence of such a duty of care (extending to guarantors of the company's debts) was supported by *Standard Chartered Bank v Walker* [1982] 3 All ER 938, [1982] 1 WLR 1410 (CA), *American Express International Banking v Hurley* [1986] BCLC 52 (duty owed to guarantor of the secured debt) and *Knight v Lawrence* [1991] BCC 411, [1993] BCLC 215 (duty of care owed by a receiver to joint borrowers, which was breached when the receiver failed to put in motion rent review procedures contained in leases of properties owned by one of the joint borrowers); *Downsview* is consistent with other decisions of the House of Lords which have sought to restrict the ambit of the tort of negligence: *Caparo Industries plc v Dickman* [1990] 2 AC 605; *Murphy v Brentwood DC* [1991] AC 398. See also *China & South Sea Bank Ltd v Tan* [1990] 1 AC 536 (no duty in tort to surety (PC)).

7   [1999] 3 WLR 922.

8   The duty owed to those interested in the equity of redemption does not extend to shareholders or directors of the debtor company nor to a guarantor who has not been called to pay under the guarantee: *Burgess v Auger* [1998] 2 BCLC 478.

9   *Re Potters Oil Ltd (No 2)*, above; *Shamji v Johnson Matthey Bankers Ltd* [1986] BCLC 278.

10.50 Powers of receivers and administrative receivers

It is in relation to their respective powers that the distinction between administrative and other receivers is most significant. An administrative receiver derives his powers from the Insolvency Act 1986 as well as from the instrument under which he is appointed, whereas other receivers must look to the terms on which they were appointed to determine the scope of their powers.[1]

Generally speaking, an administrative receiver is in a far more powerful position than a receiver who is not an administrative receiver. By definition, an administrative receiver takes charge of the whole (or substantially the whole) of the property of the company to which he is appointed, whereas an ordinary receiver or manager is concerned merely with a limited part of the company's assets. Where an administrative receiver is appointed, effective control of the company's business affairs passes from the board to the administrative receiver. Under the Insolvency Act 1986, an administrative receiver has power to deal with assets which are subject to other securities in ways which a debenture holder would never be competent to grant by contract to a receiver who is not an administrative receiver.

10.51 The administrative receiver's powers

Section 42 of the Insolvency Act 1986 provides that the powers conferred on an administrative receiver 'by the debentures by virtue of which he was appointed' shall be deemed to include a list of powers set out in Schedule 1 to the 1986 Act. These deemed powers are to operate 'except in so far as they are inconsistent with any of the provisions of those debentures'. The powers specified in Schedule 1 are as follows.

(1) Power to take possession of, collect and get in the property of the company and, for that purpose, to take such proceedings as may seem to him expedient.

(2) Power to sell or otherwise dispose of the property of the company by public auction or private contract.[2]

(3) Power to raise or borrow money and grant security therefor over the property of the company.

(4) Power to appoint a solicitor or an accountant or other professionally qualified person to assist him in the performance of his functions.

(5) Power to bring or defend any action or other legal proceedings in the name and on behalf of the company.

(6) Power to refer to arbitration any question affecting the company.

(7) Power to effect and maintain insurances in respect of the business and property of the company.

(8) Power to use the company's seal.

(9) Power to do all acts and to execute in the name or on behalf of the company any deed, receipt or other document.

---

1 Subject to the specific statutory right already considered to apply to court for directions, and the limited powers which may be implied by the Law of Property Act 1925.

2 'or in Scotland, to sell, feu, hire out or otherwise dispose of property of the company by public coup or private bargain'. An English floating charge can affect property situated in Scotland.

(10) Power to draw, accept, make and endorse any bill of exchange or promissory note in the name and on behalf of the company.

(11) Power to appoint any agent to do any business which he is unable to do himself or which can more conveniently be done by an agent, and power to employ and dismiss employees.

(12) Power to do all such things (including the carrying out of works) as may be necessary for the realisation of the property of the company.

(13) Power to make any payment which is necessary or incidental to the performance of his functions.

(14) Power to carry on the business of the company.

(15) Power to establish subsidiaries of the company.

(16) Power to transfer to subsidiaries of the company the whole or any part of the business and property of the company.

(17) Power to grant or accept a surrender of a lease or tenancy of any of the property of the company, and to take a lease or tenancy of any property required or convenient for the business of the company.

(18) Power to make any arrangement or compromise on behalf of the company.

(19) Power to call up any uncalled capital of the company.

(20) Power to rank and claim in the bankruptcy, insolvency, sequestration or liquidation of any person indebted to the company and to receive dividends, and to accede to trust deeds for the creditors of any such person.

(21) Power to present or defend a petition for the winding-up of the company.

(22) Power to change the situation of the company's registered office.

(23) Power to do all other things incidental to the exercise of the foregoing powers.

The powers to establish subsidiaries and to transfer to those subsidiaries the whole or any part of the business and property of the company enable an administrative receiver to effect what is commonly known as a 'hive-down'.[1] A hive-down involves the transfer of the viable parts of a company's business to a new subsidiary with a view to selling the subsidiary to a purchaser. A 'clean' subsidiary which is not saddled with bad debts and unprofitable contracts is likely to be far more attractive to potential purchasers than the old business would have been. A hive-down can thus lead to the continuation of at least part of the business, where the only other alternative would have been to break up and sell separately the assets of the company. A sale of a going concern tends to be more profitable than a sale of assets on a 'break up' basis so that, as well as facilitating repayment of the debenture holder's debt, a hive-down may produce a surplus from which unsecured creditors can be paid. Employees can also benefit from a hive-down where their employment is transferred to the new subsidiary.

The Committee on Insolvency Law and Practice had this to say about the role of a receiver appointed under a floating charge over the whole of a company's undertaking:[2]

> There is, however, one aspect of the floating charge which we believe to have been of outstanding benefit to the general public and to society as a whole; we refer to the power to appoint a receiver and manager of the whole property and undertaking of a company. This power is enjoyed by the holder of any well-drawn floating charge, but

---

1　A hive-down may cause the company to cease to carry on business and a floating charge to crystallise; *William Gaskell Group Ltd v Highley* [1993] BCC 200.

2　1982 Cmnd 8558, at paragraph 495.

by no other creditor. Such receivers and managers are normally given extensive powers to manage and carry on the business of the company. In some cases, they have been able to restore an ailing enterprise to profitability, and return it to its former owners. In others, they have been able to dispose of the whole or part of the business as a going concern. In either case, the preservation of the profitable parts of the enterprise has been of advantage to the employees, the commercial community and the general community.

The Committee suggested the codification of the extensive powers normally given to receivers appointed under floating charges; this was done.[1] The Committee also recommended that the advantages of floating-charge receivership should be made more widely available. The administration procedure now contained in the Insolvency Act 1986 was the legislative response to this suggestion. This procedure is based on the model of floating-charge receivership.[2]

The directors must not interfere with the administrative receiver in the discharge of his functions.[3] In view of the wide range of powers conferred on an administrative receiver, this means that the directors can play little active role in the company's affairs whilst it is in receivership, although they do remain in office despite the appointment of an administrative receiver. The directors retain certain residual powers, one of which, it was held by the Court of Appeal in *Newhart Developments Ltd v Co-operative Commercial Bank Ltd,* is that of bringing proceedings in the company's name against the person who appointed the administrative receiver.[4] Browne-Wilkinson V-C (as he then was) has since doubted whether *Newhart* was correctly decided, and has held that its scope is limited to the comparatively unusual situation where the company has been indemnified from outside sources not only for its own costs but also for costs that it might be ordered to pay to the other party. Only in these circumstances, can it be said that the costs of the directors' action would not in any way prejudice the property for which the receiver was responsible.[5]

It has been held that the directors are entitled to reasonable information about the assets remaining in the company's hands, in addition to a redemption statement showing how much is still owing, provided that they show a *bona fide* intention and ability to redeem the security.[6]

Section 42(3) provides that a person dealing with an administrative receiver 'in good faith and for value' is not concerned to enquire whether the administrative receiver is acting within his powers. This provision is clearly intended to increase the protection which would in any event be given by conferring the powers set out in Schedule 1. For example, in the event of a conflict between the powers in the debenture and the Schedule 1 powers (which would be caught by the phrase in

---

1   Section 42 and Schedule 1.

2   See Part 3 of Chapter 17.

3   *Newhart Developments Ltd v Co-operative Commercial Bank Ltd* [1978] QB 814, [1978] 2 All ER 896, [1978] 1 WLR 636.

4   *Newhart Developments v Co-operative Commercial Bank,* above. See also *Watts v Midland Bank plc* (1986) 2 BCC 98, 961, where Peter Gibson J canvasses the possibility of the company (acting through its directors or shareholders) bringing an action against the administrative receiver himself where he is alleged to be acting improperly.

5   *Tudor Grange Holdings Ltd v Citibank NA* [1992] Ch 53, [1991] 4 All ER 1, [1991] 3 WLR 750, [1991] BCLC 1009. Compare the Irish decision, *Lascomme Ltd v UDT (Ireland) Ltd* [1994] 1 ILRM 227.

6   *Gomba Holdings UK Ltd v Homan & Bird* [1986] 3 All ER 94, [1986] 1 WLR 1301, [1986] BCLC 331, (1986) 2 BCC 99, 102; *Rottenberg v Monjak* [1992] BCC 688, [1993] BCLC 374.

section 42(1) 'except insofar as they are inconsistent with any provisions in those debentures'), a third party acting in good faith, etc, would not be required to investigate the powers in the debenture (or in the Schedule) unless such a problem were brought expressly to his attention.

Section 43 of the Insolvency Act 1986 confers a power on an administrative receiver, with the consent of the court, to sell company property free of the fixed charge or security to which it is subject. On the application of the administrative receiver, the court may so authorise him if it is satisfied that the disposal (with or without other assets) of any property of the company, subject to a fixed charge or security, would be likely to promote a more advantageous realisation of the company's assets than would otherwise be effected. The court may then authorise the receiver to dispose of the asset as if it were not subject to the security. It must be a condition of the court's authorisation under section 43 that the net proceeds of sale shall be applied towards discharging the sums secured by the fixed charge or security.[1] Where these proceeds are less than the amount, as may be determined by the court, which would have been realised on a sale of the property in an open market by a willing vendor, the deficiency must be made up.[2] The power conferred by section 43 does not apply to securities held by those who have appointed the administrative receiver. This is also true of any security to which such security (ie held by the person appointing) has priority.[3]

The power conferred by section 43 is analogous to that given to administrators by Schedule B1, paragraph 7 of the Insolvency Act 1986.[4]

10.52   The administrative receiver's agency and liability for contracts

Section 44 of the Insolvency Act 1986 provides that an administrative receiver of a company is deemed to be the company's agent unless and until the company goes into liquidation. The consequence of this is that he is personally liable on any contract entered into by him in the carrying out of his functions except in so far as the contract otherwise provides. In the case of employment contracts, he is liable for those contracts adopted by him in the carrying out of those functions. However, he is not to be taken to have adopted a contract of employment by reason of anything done or omitted to be done within a fortnight of his appointment.[5] This provision allows the receiver to use the essential services of the company's employees in this initial period before he commits himself to their continued employment.

What amounts to 'adoption' was considered by the House of Lords in *Powdrill v Watson, Re Paramount Airways Ltd (No 3)*.[6] An administrative receiver cannot avoid adoption by merely informing employees that he does not intend to adopt their contracts, because adoption is a matter of fact rather than words. Continuing, after the 14-day grace period, to employ staff and to pay them in accordance with the terms of their previous contracts, amounts to implicit adoption. The effect of

---

1   See section 43(4) as to when there are two or more fixed charges and a sale is ordered. The proceeds of sale must be applied so as to respect priorities.
2   Section 43(3).
3   Section 43(2).
4   See **21.22**.
5   See section 44(1) and (2).
6   [1995] 2 AC 314.

adopting employment contracts is that the administrative receiver assumes personal liability for all liabilities incurred under the adopted contracts while he is in office.[1]

The Insolvency Act 1994 amended section 44 of the Insolvency Act 1986 with effect from 15 March 1994. The effect of the amendments is to limit the administrative receiver's personal liability in respect of contracts of employment adopted on or after that date, to sums payable by way of wages or salary[2] for services rendered after adoption of the contracts.

Section 44 gives the administrative receiver a right to an indemnity out of the assets of the company to recoup the liability to which the section exposes him. The section does not limit any other right of indemnity he may have. It also preserves the receiver's liability on contracts entered into (or adopted) without authority. Here he has no right of indemnity.[3]

An administrative receiver does not incur any personal liability in respect of contracts of the company (apart from employment contracts) which are already in existence when he is appointed. This principle is consistent with the administrative receiver's position as the company's agent and it has been explained in the following terms: an administrative receiver:

> is not personally liable for the rent payable under an existing lease, or for the purchase charges under an existing hire-purchase agreement. This is not a surprising conclusion. It does not offend against basic conceptions of justice or fairness. The rent and hire charges were a liability undertaken by the company at the inception of the lease or hire-purchase agreement. The land or goods are being used by the company even when an administrative receiver is in office. It is to the company that, along with other creditors, the lessor and the owner of the goods must look for payment.[4]

The appointment of an administrative receiver does not terminate existing contracts of the company,[5] but the administrative receiver may decide not to continue or complete contractual performance, thereby placing the company in breach of its obligations.[6] A third party who interferes with contractual relationships would ordinarily risk liability in tort, but this does not apply where, as is the case with an administrative receiver, the interferer is acting as an agent of

---

1   *Re Leyland Daf* [1994] 4 All ER 300, [1995] 2 WLR 316 varied to this extent by the House of Lords in *Powdrill.*

2   Or by way of contribution to an occupational pension scheme: section 44(2A). The position regarding wages and salary payable during sickness or holidays is clarified by section 44(2C) and (2D).

3   See section 44(3).

4   *Re Atlantic Computer Systems plc* [1992] Ch 505 at p 524, [1992] 1 All ER 476 at 486, [1990] BCC 859 at 866 *per* Nicholls LJ.

5   This includes employment contracts: *Re Mack Trucks (Britain) Ltd* [1967] 1 WLR 780; *Re Foster Clark's Indenture Trusts* [1966] 1 WLR 125 at 132 *per* Plowman J. But there can be special circumstances where receivership does operate to terminate contracts of employment, such as where the continuation of a particular employee's employment is inconsistent with the role and function of the receiver and manager: *Griffiths v Secretary of State for Social Services* [1974] QB 468 (continued employment of managing director held not to be inconsistent with receivership).

6   Although note that in unusual circumstances, an order for specific performance might be made notwithstanding the appointment of an administrative receiver: *Land Rover Group Ltd v UPF (UK) Ltd* [2003] 2 BCLC 222.

one of the contracting parties.[1] The proposition that a receiver can repudiate an existing contract of the company is justifiable in principle, because obliging the administrative receiver to perform the company's existing contracts would mean that contractors would be paid before the debenture-holder who made the appointment, which would be inconsistent with the debenture-holder's priority.[2]

One aspect of the administrative receiver's position as an agent of the company is that transactions authorised by him are 'company contracts'. As such, they are subject to the rules on substantial property transactions in section 320 of the Companies Act 1985 and must therefore be approved by the shareholders in general meeting if the consideration is above the thresholds mentioned in that section and the other parties are directors or connected persons.[3] Although this result would seem to be a correct interpretation of section 320 it is, none the less, somewhat odd that shareholders, whose investment in the company has probably been wiped out by company's losses, should retain a power of veto over certain transactions that a receiver may wish to enter into.[4]

10.53 The effect of liquidation on administrative receivership

A company which is in administrative receivership can go into liquidation. On liquidation, an administrative receiver ceases to be an agent of the company. It has been held, in relation to receivers, that a receiver does not automatically become his appointor's agent upon termination of the agency relationship with the company,[5] but that he may become so if his appointor treats him as such.[6]

10.54 Statements of affairs, investigations and reports

Section 47 of the Insolvency Act 1986 requires the company's officers to submit a report to the administrative receiver showing particulars of its assets, debts and liabilities. It must also include the names and addresses of the company's creditors and information about the securities over the company's property held by them.

---

1   *Said v Butt* [1920] 3 KB 497; *Re Walter J Jacob & Co Ltd* (1987) 3 BCC 532; *Lathia v Dronsfield Bros Ltd* [1987] BCLC 321; *Welsh Development Agency v Export Finance Co Ltd*, above. See also *Airlines Airspares v Handley Page Ltd* [1970] Ch 193, [1970] 1 All ER 29, [1970] 2 WLR 163 at 199 and *Telemetrix v Modern Engines of Bristol (Holdings) plc* [1985] BCLC 213, (1985) 1 BCC 99, 417.

2   *Airlines Airspares Ltd v Handley Page Ltd*, above. The administrative receiver cannot, however, interfere with any equitable right which ranks before the debenture-holder's security: *Freevale v Metrostore (Holdings) Ltd* [1984] Ch 199; *Astor Chemical Ltd v Synthetic Technology Ltd* [1990] BCLC at 11, [1990] BCC at 105; *Ash & Newman v Creative Devices Research Ltd* [1991] BCLC 403 at 404.

3   *Demite Ltd v Protec Health Ltd* [1998] BCC 638, noted Frisby, 'Receivers and the Companies Act 1985, s 320: A Very Real Agency' [1999] CfiLR 143. Section 320 is considered further at **16.16**.

4   For this reason, the Law Commissions have recommended the alternative of allowing the administrative receiver to seek court approval: *Company Directors: Regulating Conflicts of Interests and Formulating a Statement of Duties*, Law Com No 261, Scot Law Com No 173, paragraphs 10.14 to 10.19.

5   *Gosling v Gaskell* [1897] AC 575; *Thomas v Todd* [1926] 2 KB 511.

6   *American Express International Banking Corp v Hurley* [1985] 3 All ER 564 at 568, citing *Re Wood* [1941] Ch 112. See further **10.55**.

This statement will assist the administrative receiver in forming a picture of the state of the company to which he has been appointed. An administrative receiver is an 'office holder' for the purposes of the Insolvency Act 1986 and, as such, has powers to take control of the company's books, to compel co-operation from those who were involved in its formation or management, and to invoke the assistance of the court in conducting inquiries into the company's dealings.[1] The powers of office-holders are considered further in the context of liquidations.[2]

Within three months[3] of his appointment, an administrative receiver must send to the Registrar of Companies, to the debenture-holder by whom, or on whose behalf, he was appointed, and to any trustee for those debenture-holders, a report as to the following matters:

(1) the events leading up to his appointment;
(2) the disposal or proposed disposal by him of any property of the company and the carrying on, or proposed carrying on, by him of any business of the company;
(3) the amounts of principal and interest payable to the debenture-holders by whom or on whose behalf he was appointed, and the amounts payable to preferential creditors;
(4) the amounts (if any) likely to be available for the payment of other creditors.[4]

Within the same three-month period the administrative receiver must make available this report to all creditors.[5] He must also lay a copy of the report before a meeting of the company's creditors summoned for that purpose on not less than 14 days' notice. Where a meeting of creditors is summoned under section 48, the meeting may, if it thinks fit, establish a creditors' committee to supervise the administrative receiver in carrying out his functions. If such a committee is established, it may require the administrative receiver to appear before it and furnish such information (as it may reasonably require) which relates to his functions.[6]

The court is given a power to release the administrative receiver from laying his report before a creditors' meeting. The court may *not* give a direction releasing the administrative receiver from an obligation to lay his report before a meeting of the company's creditors, unless the report states that it is his intention to apply for such a direction and the report has been made available[7] to creditors not less than 14 days before the application.[8]

---

1   Sections 234 to 237 of the Insolvency Act 1986.
2   See Chapter 21.
3   Insolvency Act 1986, section 49. The court may allow a longer period.
4   The report must also include a summary of the statement of affairs submitted to the administrative receiver under section 47. See section 48(5).
5   Section 48(4). He may do this *either* by sending copies to all the creditors (so far as he is aware of their addresses) *or* publishing a notice stating an address where creditors may write for a copy.
6   Section 49.
7   By either of the methods allowed by section 48(2).
8   Section 48(3). For the administrative receiver's obligation where the company goes into liquidation, see section 48(4).

10.55   The status of a receiver appointed by the debenture-holders who is not an administrative receiver

For the purpose of ascertaining the status of a receiver who is not an administrative receiver, the debentures and trust deed must be consulted to find out whether there are words declaring him to be the agent of the company or incorporating the provisions of the Law of Property Act 1925 to that effect.[1] If these words are found, then, the receiver being appointed under the power declaring him to be agent for the company, his dealings will (subject to the provisions of what is now section 37 of the Insolvency Act 1986, referred to below) be governed by the ordinary principles relating to the acts of an agent, the company being his principal[2] until liquidation, whether compulsory or voluntary, when it ceases to hold that position.[3] But the receiver does not then become the agent of the debenture-holders (or their trustees) who appointed him, nor are they liable for the debts incurred by him upon the company going into liquidation, unless they perform some act authorising him to pledge their credit or otherwise treat him as their agent.[4] In the unlikely event that there are no words declaring the receiver to be the agent of the company, the debenture-holders who appoint him are his principals and are liable for his faults or omissions, as well as upon the contracts he makes on their behalf, and to indemnify him against any liabilities he incurs as their agent, and to pay him his remuneration.[5] If appointed under powers in the debentures authorising him to carry on the business, but not declaring him to be agent of the company, he may even pledge the personal credit of the debenture-holders.[6]

The agency relationship between a receiver and the company to which he is appointed is an unusual form of agency.[7] Essentially, it is a device to protect the debenture-holder from liability in respect of the receiver's actions and instead, to make the company, whose agent he is, liable. Section 44 of the Insolvency Act 1986, in making an administrative receiver the agent of the company until liquidation, codifies what was in any event the usual practice for all receivers prior to that Act and what remains the practice with regard to receivers who are not administrative receivers. One aspect of the unusual nature of a receiver's agency relationship with the company is that the duties normally owed by an agent to his

---

1   *Central London Electricity Ltd v Berners* [1945] 1 All ER 160.
2   *Owen & Co v Cronk* [1895] 1 QB 265 (CA); *Bissel v Ariel Motors* (1910) 27 TLR 73; *Gosling v Gaskell* [1897] AC 575 (HL); *Central London Electricity Ltd v Berners*, above.
3   *Thomas v Todd* [1926] 2 KB 511; *Re S Brown & Son (General Warehousemen)* [1940] Ch 961; but see *Re Northern Garage* [1946] Ch 188.
4   *Gosling v Gaskell* [1897] AC 575 (HL); *Jeffereys v Dixon* (1866) 1 Ch App 183 at 190; *Cox v Hickman* (1860) 8 HLC 268. As to when receivership will be regarded as being 'rateable occupation', see *Ratford v Northavon DC* [1986] BCLC 391.
5   *Deyes v Wood* [1911] 1 KB 806 (CA); *Re Vimbos* [1900] 1 Ch 470. Since the decision in *Deyes v Wood*, a common form of debenture previously in use has been altered by the addition of the following words: 'and the holder of this debenture shall not in making or consenting to such appointment (ie of a receiver) incur any liability to the receiver for his remuneration or otherwise.' These additional words protect the debenture-holder not only from liability to the receiver, but also from liability for debts incurred in the course of the carrying on by the receiver of the company's business: *Cully v Parsons* [1923] 2 Ch 512.
6   *American Express International Banking Corp v Hurley* above.
7   *Lawson v Hosemaster Machine Co Ltd* [1965] 1 WLR 1399; *Gomba Holdings UK Ltd v Minories Finance Ltd* [1989] BCLC 115.

principal do not apply. A receiver owes his duties primarily to his appointor and not to the company.[1]

The position of a receiver in respect of the company's existing contracts (other than employment contracts) is the same as that of an administrative receiver. With regard to new contracts entered into by him, section 37 of the Insolvency Act 1986 provides that a receiver or manager of the property of a company appointed under the powers contained in any instrument is, to the same extent as if he had been appointed by the court, personally liable on any contract entered into by him in the performance of his functions, except in so far as the contract otherwise provides. He is also personally liable on any contract of employment adopted by him in the performance of those functions, but he is entitled in respect of that liability to any indemnity out of the assets. This is not to limit any right of indemnity that he would otherwise have, or to limit his liability on contracts entered into without authority, or to confer any right to indemnity in respect of that liability.

Where a receiver is appointed in such circumstances as to be agent of the company, and the company subsequently goes into liquidation, the receiver ceases to be the agent of the company.[2] Although a winding-up deprives a receiver, appointed under a debenture, of power to bind the company personally, because he ceases to be its agent, this does not affect the exercise of his powers given by the debenture to hold and dispose of the property charged.[3]

10.56 Powers of a receiver

A receiver who is not an administrative receiver derives his powers from the instrument under which he is appointed. Under a debenture in common form which declares the receiver to be agent of the company, and confers on him power 'to take possession of and get in the property hereby charged', he is not limited to the right to take proceedings to get in the income of the property charged given by section 109(3) of the Law of Property Act 1925. He can bring, without the consent of the company, an action in its name to recover any of the property charged.[4] Even when the words declaring the receiver to be the agent of the company are omitted, he is agent of the company 'to such an extent as may be necessary to enable him to exercise the powers conferred on him by the debenture'.[5]

A receiver duly appointed under a debenture, which has the usual clause to take possession of all assets charged and to perform such acts as are incidental or conducive thereto, may present a winding-up petition on which an order will be made at the court's discretion.[6] The protection and preservation of assets is incidental to their possession, and where a winding-up order in respect of an insolvent company would achieve this aim, the receiver had power to petition.[7]

---

1 See **10.49**.
2 *Gosling v Gaskell* [1897] AC 575; *Thomas v Todd* [1926] 2 KB 511; cf *Re Northern Garage* [1946] Ch 188.
3 *Sowman v David Samuel Trust* [1978] 1 WLR 22.
4 *M Wheeler & Co v Warren* [1928] 1 Ch 840 (CA). *Gough's Garages v Pugsley* [1930] 1 KB 615.
5 *Per* Warrington J *Robinson Printing Co v Chic Ltd* [1905] 2 Ch 123, approved by Vaughan Williams LJ in *Deyes v Wood* [1911] 1 KB 806 at 821.
6 See **21.35.2**.
7 *In Re Emmadart Ltd* [1979] 2 WLR 868 at 875.

10.57   Receivership accounts

Section 38 of the Insolvency Act 1986 imposes an obligation on a receiver or manager appointed out of court (other than an administrative receiver, for whom separate provision is made) to deliver accounts to the Registrar on a periodic basis.

It should be noted that these statutory obligations are not exhaustive of a receiver's duty to provide accounts or other information to a debtor company. The extent of this obligation can be deduced from the nature of the receivership and the express or implied terms of the debenture. A company's right to such information depends upon it being shown that the information is needed to enable the board of directors to exercise its residual powers or perform their duties. However, this right is qualified by the receiver's primary responsibility to the debenture-holder who appointed him. Thus the receiver may withhold information where he forms the opinion that this would be contrary to the interests of the debenture-holder.[1]

---

1   *Gomba Holdings UK Ltd v Homan* [1986] BCLC 331. Here the receiver was on the facts held not obliged to furnish additional information. See also *Smiths Ltd v Middleton* [1979] 3 All ER 842.

Chapter 11

Corporate Governance

11.1 Introduction

This chapter focuses upon the control mechanisms available for ensuring that managers and directors do not abuse their corporate powers and seeks to set the background to the descriptions of the law in the following chapters. Corporate governance is traditionally concerned with how the company is directed and the relationship between the board of directors, management and shareholders.[1] The structure of the company as recognised by company law is central to corporate governance. Corporate governance contributes both to business prosperity and to accountability and requires an appropriate balance to be established for these two important goals. In the United Kingdom, concern about standards of financial reporting and accountability, heightened by a series of major corporate collapses and controversy over directors' pay have brought corporate governance to the centre of attention. As discussed later, the question also arises whether or not it should be the proper concern of company law to ensure that interests other than those of the traditional constituents are protected.

11.2 Corporate structure

Traditionally, company directors have been regarded effectively as agents who act on behalf of the company in general meeting.[2] In practice, they have been required to act on behalf of the shareholders collectively. This approach has shaped the legal duties of directors.[3] Yet, as companies grew in size, the position of directors and managers altered. This corporate demographic change led to a delegation of wide powers to the board of directors with the general meeting unable to interfere in the exercise of those powers. This situation is generally

---

1   There is a vast literature on corporate governance. For a comprehensive discussion and extensive bibliography, see Sheikh and Rees (eds), *Corporate Governance and Corporate Control* 2nd edn (Cavendish, 2000); see also Parkinson, Gamble and Kelly (eds) *The Political Economy of the Company* (OUP, 2000), Charkham, *Keeping Good Company: a study of corporate governance in five countries* (OUP, 1994), Hopt (ed) *Comparative Corporate Governance* (Clarendon Press, 1998), Proctor and Miles, *Corporate Governance* (Cavendish, 2002), Smerdon, *A Practical Guide to Corporate Governance* (Sweet & Maxwell, 1998), Kay and Silberston 'Corporate Governance' (1995) 153 National Institute Economic Review 84, Dine and Villiers, 'Listed Company Structures and Corporate Governance in the United Kingdom', in Artigas et al (eds) *The Listed Corporation: Corporate Governance Structure and Markets* (Revista de Derecho de Sociedades, Aranzadi, Spain, English Version, forthcoming) and the other writings referred to later in this chapter.

2   See Chapter 15. For discussions of the relationship between directors and shareholders historically and today, see, eg Stokes 'Company Law and Legal Theory' in Twining (ed), *Legal Theory and Common Law* (Blackwell, 1986) p 155, Ireland, 'Property and Contract in Contemporary Corporate Theory' (2003) 23 Legal Studies 453. See further, Ferran, *Company Law and Corporate Finance* (Oxford University Press, 1999) chapter 4.

3   See Chapter 16.

known as the 'separation of ownership and control' following the seminal work of Berle and Means,[1] who described the new position of the shareholder in the 1930s:

> The shift of powers from the individual to the controlling management combined with the shift from the interests of the individual to those of the group have so changed the position of the stockholder that the current conception with regard to him must be radically revised. Conceived originally as a quasi-partner, manager and entrepreneur, with definite rights in and to property used in the enterprise and to the profits of that enterprise as they accrued, he has now reached an entirely different status. He has, it is true, a series of legal rights, but these are weakened in varying degree (depending upon the completeness with which the corporation has embodied in its structure the modern devices) by the text of the contract to which the stockholder is bound. His power to participate in management has, in large measure, been lost to him, and has become vested in the 'control'. He becomes simply a supplier of capital on terms less definite than those customarily given or demanded by bondholders; and the thinking about his position must be qualified by the realization that he is, in a highly modified sense, not dissimilar in kind from the bondholder or lender of money.[2]

Berle and Means were describing the corporate environment of the United States of America in the early twentieth century. A similar pattern occurred in the UK. However, there are two objections that can be raised today against the description of the corporate structure as one that encompasses a separation of ownership and control. First, in small private companies it is often the same people who are the owners and the controllers so that those same individuals have management and shareholder roles. Secondly, in public companies there has been a dramatic growth in the level of institutional investment. This growing dominance of institutional shareholders on both sides of the Atlantic during the 1980s and 1990s and into the twenty-first century[3] means that the shareholders' position might not be as weak as the analysis of Berle and Means would suggest. However, arguably, the divide continues because shareholders are not cohesively organised to enable them to use their potential collective weight to bring the managers to account. The key decisions are still for the board to take. Moreover, if the roles of the shareholders and directors are not wholly clear then directors may be in a position to pursue their own interests rather than act in the interests of the company or even of the shareholders.

11.3   Defining corporate governance

The most authoritative definition of corporate governance in the United Kingdom was provided by the Cadbury Committee, which reported on the Financial Aspects of Corporate Governance in 1992. The Cadbury Committee's Report defined corporate governance as 'the system by which companies are

---

1   Berle and Means, *The Modern Corporation and Private Property* (New Brunswick, Transaction Publishers, 1991, originally published in 1932).
2   Ibid, at p 245.
3   The Hampel Report notes that approximately 80% of shares in listed United Kingdom companies are held by institutions: *The Hampel Report on Corporate Governance* (Gee, 1998) paragraph 5.1. Davies estimates around 60%: Davies *Gower and Davies' Principles of Modern Company Law*, 7th edn (London, Sweet & Maxwell, 2003), at p 338. The Myners Report suggests that in 1999 the institutional investors held 51.9%: Paul Myners, *Institutional Investment in the UK: A Review*, HM Treasury, April 2001, at p 27.

directed and controlled'.[1] The Cadbury Committee explained this definition further in the following manner:

> Boards of directors are responsible for the governance of their companies. The shareholders' role in governance is to appoint the directors and the auditors and to satisfy themselves that an appropriate governance structure is in place. The responsibilities of the board include setting the company's strategic aims, providing the leadership to put them into effect, supervising the management of the business and reporting to shareholders on their stewardship. The board's actions are subject to laws, regulations and the shareholders in general meeting.

This definition was adopted by the DTI in 1998 in the paper that established the company law review.[2] In this relationship, responsibility rests with directors to establish the company's policies and to supervise how the company is managed. The directors are, in turn, accountable to the shareholders. Auditors have a role of acting as a representative for the shareholders collectively by guarding against financial irregularities and aiming for the directors to provide a 'true and fair view' of the company's performance.[3] As the shareholders supply equity capital to the company, they seek maximisation of their financial return from the company so that the general aim of the system of corporate governance may be to maximise the company's profits. Indeed, the Hampel Report on corporate governance, published in 1998, stated that the single overriding objective shared by all listed companies, whatever their size or type of business, is the preservation and the greatest practicable enhancement over time of their shareholders' investment.[4]

11.4 How is this system to be achieved?

This relationship in which the directors monitor the activities of management and then report to the shareholders rests on the assumption that the shareholders have the ability to exercise their powers in general meeting. This they do by voting on resolutions. In particular, the shareholders have power to appoint or remove the directors from office.[5] Managers are forced to recognise the risk that shareholders will use their voting powers to limit their discretion or indeed to remove them from office. Yet, in reality, in large public companies at least, the voting powers of shareholders comprise a limited form of control of management activities. In reality, shareholders are more likely to sell their shares if they are dissatisfied with the manner in which the company is being run. This is generally regarded as shareholders using powers of 'exit' rather than 'voice' to influence the company's management.[6] This response of 'rational apathy' by shareholders occurs because in reality there is little incentive for them to attend and vote at

---

1 Cadbury Committee *Report on the Financial Aspects of Corporate Governance* (Gee, 1992), paragraph 2.5. The Department of Trade and Industry adopted this definition in its consultation paper *Modern Company Law for a Competitive Economy* (HMSO, March 1998), paragraph 3.5 at p 9. See also Hampel Report op cit, paragraph 1.16.

2 *Modern Company Law for a Competitive Economy*, 1998, paragraph 3.5, at p 9. As to the review, see **1.7** and Chapter 22.

3 As to auditors, see Chapter 14.

4 Hampel Report on Corporate Governance, (Gee, 1998), paragraph 1.16.

5 For powers of appointment, see Table A, articles 73–80. Section 303 of the Companies Act 1985 provides shareholders with the right to remove directors. As to these, see **15.2** and **15.7**.

6 These terms were introduced by Hirschman in *Exit, Voice and Loyalty: Responses to Decline in Firms, Organizations and States* (Cambridge, MA, Harvard University Press, 1970).

general meetings.[1] Each individual shareholder's vote is unlikely to carry sufficient weight and collective action is difficult when shareholders are dispersed. In addition, existing corporate governance provisions seem to place obstacles in the way of shareholders who question decisions of directors rather than assist them. Indeed, shareholders who seek to challenge directors' actions in the courts[2] face procedural barriers and judicial reluctance to intervene in commercial decisions.[3] This fact brings about a requirement for more effective controls upon management activity. The increased proportion of shares held by institutional investors has given to them a greater significance in corporate governance. However, empirical evidence suggests that rather than exercise their votes, institutional investors prefer to influence the managers through dialogue.[4] They are generally prepared to intervene only to a limited extent, regarding their role primarily as investors rather than as managers.[5] In practice this approach has resulted in a poor level of shareholder activism. Thus, the 2002 White Paper *Modernising Company Law* noted failure of some institutional investors and fund managers to intervene actively to protect and enhance the value of the investment in cases where companies are being ineffectively, or even dishonestly, managed by their boards.[6]

An additional control mechanism arising from the analysis of Berle and Means is that of the so-called market for corporate control,[7] which imposes on managers the threat of displacement. According to this theory, 'inefficient managers, if not responsible to, and subject to displacement by, owners directly, can be removed by stockholders' acceptance of take-over bids induced by poor performance and a consequent reduction in stock value'.[8] This control mechanism operates to the effect that if a company is not managed efficiently this will reduce its share prices. This will present a control opportunity for a 'predator' to acquire the company and replace the managers with a new board. The new board will manage the company more efficiently and maximise the share price. This precedent will encourage managers in other companies to act efficiently in order to avoid being displaced. This ability of the market for corporate control to curtail inefficient or

---

1   The problems and limitations of shareholders' meetings are described at **13.1**.

2   All UK company lawyers are familiar with the difficulties caused by *Foss v Harbottle* (1843) 2 Hare 461; see Chapter 17.

3   See eg Lord Greene MR stating in *Re Smith & Fawcett Ltd* [1942] Ch 304 at 306 (CA) that directors are bound to exercise the powers conferred upon them 'bona fide in what they consider – not what a court may consider – is in the interests of the company'.

4   Holland, *Corporate Communications with Institutional Shareholders: Private Disclosures and Financial Reporting* (Edinburgh, Institute of Chartered Accountants of Scotland, 1998). For example, in the United States, the California Public Employees Retirement Scheme (CalPERS) adopts 'intensive dialogue' and 'heightened monitoring' to assert its influence.

5   Thus for example the Institutional Shareholders' Committee *Statement of Principles on the Responsibilities of Institutional Shareholders and Agents* (2002) states in its introduction: 'The policies of activism set out below do not constitute an obligation to micro-manage the affairs of investee companies, but rather relate to procedures designed to ensure that shareholders derive value from their investments by dealing effectively with concerns over under-performance. Nor do they preclude a decision to sell a holding, where this is the most effective response to such concerns.'

6   Cm 5553–I, paragraph 2.43 at p 24.

7   See also **1.9** and for a detailed discussion of the theory of the market for corporate control see Bradley, 'Corporate Control: Markets and Rules' (1990) 53 MLR 170.

8   See Herman, *Corporate Control, Corporate Power* (Cambridge University Press, 1981) at p 10, quoted by Bradley, op cit.

irresponsible managerial behaviour is subject to a number of qualifications. First, the ability of the market to respond speedily to inefficient management is limited. Secondly, a company's managers may be able to defend themselves against takeover threats, eg, by using devices such as 'poison pills'.[1] Thirdly, the market for corporate control could cause managers to be too preoccupied with the company's short-term results. In turn this could lead to various social costs, such as job losses or reduced training opportunities.

A number of legal controls exist which seek to ensure that directors and managers act within their powers and run the company effectively. There is a broad range of common law and statutory directors' duties.[2] For example, there are fiduciary duties aimed at promoting honesty and disclosure, and at combating conflicts of interest. Thus directors have a duty to act *bona fide* in the interests of the company and not to exercise their powers for any collateral purpose; a duty not to make a secret profit by use of their position; and a duty to avoid a conflict between their duty to the company and their personal interests. These fiduciary duties are backed by statutory provisions that guard against self-dealing by directors. In particular, Part X of the Companies Act 1985 contains obligations such as disclosure of interest in relevant transactions. Criminal and civil sanctions apply against breach of many of the provisions in Part X. There are also detailed financial disclosure provisions and obligations with regard to disclosure of remuneration.[3] Many of these disclosure obligations are supplemented by requirements and standards set by City institutions such as the London Stock Exchange and relevant professional bodies such as the Institute of Chartered Accountants, and now by the Financial Services Authority as UK Listing Authority.[4]

Despite the existence of these internal, market and legal controls the concerns about corporate governance have not disappeared. The response in the United Kingdom to the inadequacies of these control mechanisms has not been to introduce new statutory provisions. Instead, self-regulation has been encouraged as a supplement to existing legislative provisions and it has been noted by the Law Commissions of both Scotland and England and Wales that a 'significant interdependency now exists between voluntary codes and formal law'.[5] A number of Committees have been central to the development of corporate governance, their efforts culminating in a Combined Code implemented by the Financial Services Authority as an Appendix to the *Listing Rules*.[6] The Company Law Review[7] has expressed the view that there is no intention to replace the use of best

---

1   Poison pills are tactics used by companies threatened with unwelcome takeover bids to make
     themselves unattractive to the bidder, eg the target company issues large amounts of shares to
     the shareholders in order to dilute the shareholding that the hostile acquirer might establish.
2   For further detail on directors' duties, see Chapter 16.
3   See Chapter 14.
4   See **18.4**.
5   Law Commissions, *Regulating Conflicts of Interests and Formulating a Statement of Duties: A Joint
     Consultation Paper*, No 153 and Discussion Paper No 105, paragraph 1.21 at p 8.
6   Combined Code on Corporate Governance, revised by the Financial Reporting Council,
     2003, available at www.frc.org.
7   See generally, **1.7**.

practice, for which the Combined Code is said to be more suitable, provided best practice is seen to be working.[1]

11.5　The corporate governance committees

Since the beginning of the 1990s the corporate governance debate has been shaped to a large degree by the work of the Cadbury Committee, the Greenbury Committee, the Hampel Committee and the Turnbull Committee. An understanding of the approach towards corporate governance adopted in the United Kingdom requires a brief description of the work of these Committees. The collapse of ENRON and other companies in the United States and Western Europe also led to further moves to strengthen the protections afforded by the corporate governance regime.

11.5.1　*The Cadbury Committee*

The Cadbury Committee was set up as a private initiative in response to a number of corporate collapses, notably the demise of the Bank of Credit and Commerce International, Polly Peck, a FT-SE 100 company and the Maxwell empire. The Cadbury Committee regarded the public attention on its work as an opportunity to raise standards of financial reporting and accountability. It sought to ensure that boards would be free to drive their companies forward in a competitive environment but that they would exercise that freedom within an effective framework of accountability. The Committee focused on the control and reporting functions of boards and on the role of auditors. Thus while its remit was limited to the aspects of corporate governance specifically related to financial reporting and accountability, it was hoped that the proposals would contribute positively to the promotion of good corporate governance as a whole.

In its *Report on the Financial Aspects of Corporate Governance*, the Committee concentrated on the tripartite relationship between the board, auditing and the shareholders. The Committee created a Code of Best Practice to be complied with by public listed companies. This Code was based on the principles of openness, integrity and accountability. Briefly, the Code included, *inter alia*, the following provisions: the board should meet regularly, retain full and effective control over the company and monitor the executive management; there should be a clearly accepted division of responsibilities at the head of the company to ensure a balance of power and authority; the board should include non-executive directors of sufficient calibre and number for their views to carry significant weight in the boards' decisions; non-executive directors should bring an independent judgment to bear on issues of strategy, performance, resources, and standards of conduct and their fees should reflect the time which they commit to the company; there should be full and clear disclosure of directors' total emoluments and those of the chairman and highest-paid UK director and executive directors' pay should be subject to the recommendations of a remuneration committee; the board should establish an audit committee of at least three non-executive directors; the directors should report that the business is a going concern, with supporting assumptions or qualifications as necessary.

1　Department of Trade and Industry, *Modern Company Law for a Competitive Economy* (HMSO, March 1998) paragraph 3.7 at p 9. The 2002 White Paper did not suggest any change to this approach.

The Committee also recommended that companies should expand their interim reports to include balance sheet information and that interim reports should be reviewed by the auditors; that fees paid to audit firms for non-audit work should be fully disclosed; that the accountancy profession should draw up guidelines on the rotation of audit partners; and that institutional investors should disclose their policies on the use of their voting rights.

11.5.2 The Greenbury Committee

The Greenbury Committee was established on the initiative of the CBI in January 1995 in response to public and shareholder concerns about directors' remuneration. The terms of reference were to identify good practice in determining directors' remuneration and prepare a code of such practice for use by public companies. The Committee focused on similar themes to the Cadbury Committee: accountability, responsibility, full disclosure, alignment of director and shareholder interests, and improved company performance. The Committee published its Report in July 1995.[1]

In brief, the Greenbury Committee recommended:

(1) that directors' remuneration be determined by an independent remuneration committee directly accountable to shareholders and consisting exclusively of non-executive directors;

(2) full disclosure to shareholders of the salaries of named directors, with information covering all aspects of pay, including share options and pension entitlements;

(3) that directors' service contracts with notice periods for longer than one year should be disclosed and the reasons for the longer notice period explained;

(4) that shares should not vest and options should not be exercisable in under three years and that directors should be encouraged to hold onto them; and

(5) that gains from executive share options should be taxed as income at the time of the exercise rather than capital gains on disposal.

The Committee urged performance-based pay and compensation so that poor performance should not be rewarded, and that compensation payments should be paid in instalments so that they can be mitigated if the director obtains new employment or earns money elsewhere.

11.5.3 The Hampel Committee

The Hampel Committee published its final *Report on Corporate Governance* in January 1998, just over two years after the Committee was established on the initiation of the Financial Reporting Council. The Hampel Committee built on the recommendations of the Cadbury and Greenbury Committees and had a broader remit, covering the more general aspects of corporate governance. The Report covered corporate governance, principles of corporate governance, the role of directors, directors' remuneration, the role of shareholders and accountability and audit.

In summary, the Committee recommended, *inter alia*:

(1) that executive and non-executive directors should continue to have the same duties under the law;

---

1   Greenbury Committee, *Report on Directors' Remuneration* (Gee, 1995).

(2)   that new directors should receive appropriate training;

(3)   that the majority of non-executive directors should be independent and that to be effective, non-executive directors should make up at least one-third of the membership of the board comprising of people from a wide range of backgrounds;

(4)   that a senior non-executive director should be identified in the annual report to whom concerns could be conveyed;

(5)   that all directors should submit themselves for re-election at least every three years;

(6)   that a remuneration committee should be established and made up of independent non-executive directors to develop a policy on remuneration and devise remuneration packages for individual executive directors;

(7)   simplification of disclosure requirements for remuneration;

(8)   that institutional investors should vote the shares under their control but that voting should not necessarily be compulsory;

(9)   that shareholders should be able to vote separately on each substantially separate issue;

(10)   that the chairman should provide questioners with written answers to significant questions which cannot be answered on the spot;

(11)   that each company should establish an audit committee of at least three non-executive directors;

(12)   and that the audit committee should keep under review the overall financial relationship between the company and its auditors.

11.5.4   The Combined Code

The Combined Code, embracing the work of the Cadbury, Greenbury and Hampel Committees, was initially produced in June 1998. In the wake of the collapse of ENRON in the United States it was revised by the Financial Reporting Council in 2003, incorporating recommendations in the Higgs Review on non-executive directors and the Smith Review on the role of audit committees. In addition, the Turnbull Working Party was established by the Institute of Chartered Accountants in England and Wales to provide guidance to assist listed companies to implement the new requirements in the Combined Code relating to internal control. The purpose of this guidance is to help manage and control risk appropriately rather than to eliminate it. This Working Party published its final report in September 1999.[1]

The Combined Code comprises principles of corporate governance and a code of best practice. It focuses on structural issues, including membership of the board of directors, directors' remuneration[2] and relations between the board and shareholders, as well as accountability issues, including financial reporting, internal control and the relationship between the board and the company's auditors. The specific role of institutional investors is also covered. The aim of the Combined Code is to allow companies to create and establish their own governance policies in the light of the main and supporting principles set out in

---

1   *Internal Control: Guidance for Directors on the Combined Code* (ICAEW, 1999). See also *The Combined Code: A Practical Guide* (KPMG and Gee Publishing, October 1999).

2   Though now the reporting aspects of directors' remuneration are regulated by the Directors' Remuneration Report Regulations 2002, SI 2002/1986, inserting section 234B into the Companies Act 1985; see Chapter 15.

the Code. This seeks to offer flexibility for companies in order to take account of their diversity but within a broad framework of requirements. Listed companies must make a disclosure statement in two parts. In the first part of the statement the company must report on how it applies the Code's principles. It is for the companies to define and explain their own governance policies and for their shareholders and others to evaluate this part of the company's statement. In the second part of the statement the company must confirm that it complies with the Code's provisions or explain why it does not. Again the shareholders and others must evaluate such explanations. In the same way as its predecessor the Code reflects the Hampel Committee's objective 'to restrict the regulatory burden on companies e.g. by substituting principles for detail wherever possible'.[1] Alongside the Combined Code and associated requirements many companies have also created their own codes of conduct. Bodies such as the Organisation for Economic Co-operation and Development[2] and the International Labour Office have also published codes and guidelines.

The various Committees had in common their preference for a self-regulatory approach to the issue of corporate governance. The adoption of a Combined Code avoids resort to statute and the courts. The obvious point to note is that codes of practice are not legally binding. In *Re Astec (BSR) plc*,[3] it was held that the exercise of a majority shareholder of its legal rights contrary to the Cadbury Code was not capable of giving rise to a claim for unfair prejudice even though investors might expect compliance with voluntary codes on corporate governance.[4] Furthermore, as was noted by the Law Commissions,[5] the civil and criminal remedies are far less than those available for a breach of a rule of the general law or of some legislative provision.

The principles established in the Combined Code apply to listed companies but unlisted and private companies are also encouraged to adopt the principles recommended. The flexibility offered by self-regulation and the opportunity it provides for speedy action compared with legislative regulation makes it an attractive form of regulation for corporate governance, as was recognised both by the DTI and the Law Commissions. However, the principles for best practice adopted in the self-regulatory codes have also been subjected to considerable criticism.[6] As is stated by Dignam,[7] the codes are 'at the very loose end of any regulatory control system'. The flexibility that they offer may allow directors to

---

1   Hampel Report, op cit Annex B, at p 66.
2   On 22 June 1999; the text was recently revised in 2002 and can be downloaded from www.oecd.org.
3   [1999] BCC 59.
4   Cf *Re BSB Holdings Ltd (No 2)* [1996] 1 BCLC 155 and *Re Macro (Ipswich) Ltd* [1994] 2 BCLC 354.
5   Law Commissions of Scotland and of England and Wales, op cit, September 1998, paragraph 1.44, at p 15.
6   For discussion of the Cadbury Report, see Belcher, 'Regulation by the Market: The Case of the Cadbury Code and Compliance Statement' (1995) JBL 321; 'Compliance with the Cadbury Code and the Reporting of Corporate Governance' (1996) 17 Co Law 11; for discussion of the Greenbury Report, see Villiers, 'Directors' Pay: An Ill Not yet Cured' (1995) Utilities Law Review 100; for discussion of the Hampel Report, see Dignam 'A Principled Approach to Self-Regulation? The Report of the Hampel Committee on Corporate Governance' (1998) 19 Co Law 140; Villiers 'Self-Regulatory Corporate Governance: Final Attempt or Last Rites?' (1998) 3 Scottish Law and Practice Quarterly 208.
7   Op cit.

abuse the system. Heavy reliance is placed upon the disclosure of information and the monitoring of management activity by non-executive directors.

11.5.5 *Disclosure*

Disclosure of information is required for many activities, the most obvious being in the accounts and the annual report and directors' remuneration.[1] Sealy has noted that this has been an underlying principle of company law in the UK 'ever since companies were accorded the twin privileges of incorporation and limited liability by the legislation of 1844 and 1855'.[2]

The claim that the disclosure philosophy stems from the privilege of limited liability might imply that it is third parties rather than shareholders who should benefit from such disclosure. Indeed, shareholders ought to be responsible for ensuring that information is provided and to bear the costs of that publicity. However, the disclosure obligations, in particular financial disclosure obligations, require directors to furnish the shareholders with this information. Additionally, the corporate governance reports of the 1990s emphasise the role of shareholders as recipients of information by the directors. The Hampel Report, for example, states that the directors are accountable to shareholders. These facts suggest that shareholders are entitled to information that might affect their investment and that, for corporate governance purposes, shareholders are expected to monitor the directors.

In the UK, disclosure activity falls into three categories: legal disclosure obligations, self-regulatory disclosure requirements and voluntary disclosure. Each of these categories of disclosure may cover the same or distinct areas of corporate activity. For example, financial disclosure is covered by legal obligations as well as requirements imposed by the accounting professional bodies, in particular the Accounting Standards Board. Although the 'accounting standards' do not have the force of law they do have a measure of underpinning in the Companies Act which provides for such standards to be issued by those bodies prescribed by the regulations.[3] Additionally, for listed companies there are detailed financial disclosure requirements under the *Listing Rules*. It may also be possible that companies provide financial details above the legal and self-regulatory demands. On the other hand, there may be areas which are not covered by legal or self-regulatory rules, but which are offered by the company, such as certain aspects of social reporting.[4]

Disclosure is a key aspect of corporate governance but it has a number of limitations. An example of the limitations of disclosure may be provided by a brief examination of directors' remuneration. The Greenbury Report and Code of Best Practice laid down detailed provisions relating to disclosure of directors' remuneration as a step towards ensuring a closer relationship between pay and performance. The Greenbury Report suggested that one of the benefits of disclosure would be that it might encourage remuneration committees to be sensitive to the wider scene. Yet the Hampel Report noted that full disclosure had

---

1   For the detail, see Chapter 14.
2   Sealy, 'The Disclosure Philosophy and Company Law Reform' (1981) 2 Co Law 51. See also Villiers 'Disclosure Obligations in Company Law: Bringing Communication Theory into the Fold' (2001) 1 JCLS 181.
3   Companies Act 1985, section 256.
4   See Parkinson, 'Disclosure and Corporate Social and Environmental performance: Competitiveness and Enterprise in a Broader Social Frame' (2003) 3 JCLS 3.

led to an upward pressure on remuneration in a competitive field. In addition, it has been observed by Ernst and Young that the Greenbury Code has led to an increase in the length of annual reports, with the result that such reports are less likely to be read by the shareholders.[1] Importantly, the Secretary of State for Trade and Industry in a speech[2] noted that disclosure by itself is not a sufficient guarantee of aligning executive pay with company or individual executive performance. Disclosure also requires vigilance by the shareholders. The Secretary of State stressed that accountability can work properly only if there is a framework in place that allows shareholders to exercise their influence effectively over remuneration policy. The eventual outcome is that increasingly stringent and detailed disclosure requirements have developed over time to remedy the problems arising from previous less demanding disclosure rules.[3] These steps indicate clearly that disclosure is only a part of corporate governance and that to be effective it requires a response by those to whom it is aimed. Vigilance is required by non-executive directors and by shareholders, in particular the institutional shareholders.

11.5.6 *Non-executive directors*

The various corporate governance reports and codes have stressed the importance of non-executive directors for corporate governance.[4] They have both strategic and monitoring functions. They may also contribute expertise or act as mentors to relatively inexperienced executives. A survey report published by BDO Binder Hamlyn in 1995 reveals that their monitoring role is perceived generally to be the most important role for non-executives.[5] Recognising the importance of their monitoring role, the Cadbury and Hampel Reports express the need for a majority of non-executive directors to be independent. Both adopt the same definition of independence: that non-executive directors are 'independent of management and free from any business or other relationship which could materially interfere with the exercise of their independent judgement'. Despite these statements, empirical data indicates that the presence of significant

---

1   Ernst and Young, *Corporate Governance: Greenbury Implementation* (1996).
2   Speech of Stephen Byers, Secretary of State for Trade and Industry, 19 July 1999.
3   See now the Directors' Remuneration Report Regulations 2002, SI 2002/1986.
4   For an overview of the role of non-executive directors, see Ferran, *Company Law and Corporate Finance* (Oxford University Press, 1999) pp 217–223.
5   BDO Binder Hamlyn, *Non-executive Directors – Watchdogs or Advisers?* (City Research Associates, 1994): 85% of those who responded to the survey considered the role of non-executive directors in protecting shareholder interests as either very or fairly important, 80% considered they should be custodians of good corporate governance, and only 13% considered as very or fairly important the role of providing detailed advice and assistance to executive management in the running of the company. Most respondents felt that it was realistic for non-executive directors to shoulder responsibility for ensuring the maintenance of high standards of corporate practice: see especially p 5 and p 14.

numbers of 'insider' non-executives does not seem consistent with independent outsider judgments.[1]

One problem is that companies (especially small companies) may have difficulty in appointing independent non-executive directors. The Hampel Report suggests that non-executive directors could be chosen from a variety of backgrounds beyond political and technical expertise, and overseas knowledge. However, the report does not state which other backgrounds it envisages for these non-executive directors. In any event, research by BDO Binder Hamlyn promises little optimism in this regard. That survey reveals that 78% of the respondents considered a top level management role in another company to be the most relevant career background compared with 21% supporting a merchant banker, 15% supporting a practising accountant, 10% supporting a practising solicitor and 9% supporting a career non-executive director.[2] One problem may be that the skills and qualifications relevant to other careers may not necessarily contribute to successful corporate or commercial performance.

This issue received attention in the Company Law Review as well as in the post-ENRON scrutiny of corporate governance. The Company Law Review acknowledged concerns by respondents about 'the genuineness of the independence of non-executive directors, their real ability to hold management to account, the absence of clear legal support for the Code, the effectiveness of the current disclosure approach and the weight which this approach gives to institutional enforcement'.[3]

The 2002 White Paper *Modernising Company Law* identified the role of non executive directors as key in corporate governance in respect of accountability and business prosperity. This gave support to the work of Derek Higgs. The Higgs *Review of the role and effectiveness of non-executive directors* was subsequently published in January 2003. The Trade and Industry Select Committee in its Sixth Report welcomed the Higgs Report, stating that its proposals were modest but could contribute to good corporate governance standards without being overly prescriptive.[4] Following endorsement by the Committee and the Government the proposals set out in the Higgs Report have been incorporated into the revised Combined Code. Primarily these include: challenging and helping to develop proposals on strategy; scrutiny of management's performance in meeting agreed goals and objectives and monitoring the reporting of performance; checking the integrity of financial information and ensuring robust and defensible financial controls and systems of risk management; monitoring remuneration levels and appointing and removing executive directors.[5] Additionally, a senior independent non-executive director should be available to shareholders and in particular

---

1   Cosh and Hughes, 'The Changing Anatomy of Corporate Control and the Market for Executives in the United Kingdom' (1997) 24 Journal of Law and Society 104–123 at p 111 and p 121. See also Brudney, 'The Independent Director – Heavenly City or Potemkin Village?' (1982) 95 Harv LR 597; Prodham, *Corporate Governance and Long-Term Performance*, Management Research Paper, Templeton College, Oxford, 93/13 (1993); Lowry, 'Directorial Self-Dealing: Constructing a Regime of Accountability' (1997) 48 NILQ 211–242, at pp 234–235.

2   See footnote 5 at p 337.

3   *Completing the Structure*, (2000) paragraph 4.47. These concerns were highlighted by Brenda Hannigan in *Company Law* (London, Butterworths, 2003).

4   Trade and Industry Select Committee Sixth Report, *White Paper, Modernising Company Law*, HC 439, paragraph 49.

5   See Higgs Review, chapter 6 and Combined Code, Section 1A.

to act as an alternative contact with the chairman, chief executive or finance director when the normal channels have failed or are inappropriate.[1] What is not clear is how the non-executive directors will communicate with the shareholders, or more fundamentally, how they will increase accountability to the shareholders.[2] Ultimately, as Davies suggests, 'executive management is unlikely easily to accept supervision by the non-executives, so that the non-executives may well have a battle on their hands to impose their will where there is a divergence of view'.[3]

11.5.7 *The auditors and institutional investors*

The role of the auditors and their independence are key issues, as was stated in the various Committee Reports, yet arguably these remain insufficiently clarified. Auditors have a statutory role of providing shareholders with independent and objective assurance on the reliability of the financial statements and of certain other information provided by the company but their role is limited insofar as they do not have an executive role in corporate governance. They may identify only the deficiencies of directors in this regard but they cannot make good those deficiencies. The independence of auditors is an important principle and the Hampel Committee acknowledged that audit firms have strong commercial reasons for maintaining independence but could be tempted to compromise on independence where they depend for a significant proportion of income on a single audit client. [4] The issue of non-audit work that has a strong potential to compromise the independence of auditors has further come under the spotlight in the wake of scandals like the collapse of ENRON in the United States.[5]

The Government stated its intention to put in place a package of measures on auditor independence set out in detail in the CGAA Report[6] and the Auditing Practices Board is also to develop necessary standards on auditor independence. In summary the CGAA Report proposed that some non-audit services should not be provided if they would involve the audit firm performing management functions for their client or if it would mean auditing its own work. Auditors should also avoid providing valuations services that would involve a degree of subjectivity. The CGAA Report also recommended stronger disclosure provisions relating to non-audit services as well as regular rotation of auditor partners. Many of these recommendations have been put into effect by professional bodies such

---

1   See Higgs Review, Chapter 7 and Combined Code Provision A.3.3. It is notable that the role of the senior independent director is essentially a passive one. See Trade and Industry Select Committee Sixth Report, White Paper, *Modernising Company Law*, HC 439, paragraph 44.
2   Davies, Gower and Davies, *Principles of Modern Company Law* 7th edn, (Sweet & Maxwell, London) at p 326.
3   Ibid at p 326.
4   For further details on auditors, see Chapter 14 and on independence, see eg Macgregor and Villiers, 'Independence of Auditors: A Comparison between Spain and the UK' (1998) 3 European Business Law Review 318.
5   See the discussion in the *Report of the Co-ordinating Group on Audit and Accounting Issues* DTI and Treasury, URN 03/567 (January 2003).
6   Ibid.

as the ICAEW.[1] Legislative support will be provided when the Companies (Audit, Investigations and Community Enterprise) Bill is enacted.

The importance of institutional investors lies in the proportion of their shareholdings, in particular in listed companies where they own approximately 80% of the shares. The Combined Code emphasises the responsibility of institutional shareholders to make considered use of their votes and to be ready, where practicable, to enter into a dialogue with the company based on mutual understanding of objectives. The Code provisions also require institutional investors to endeavour to eliminate unnecessary variations in the criteria which they apply to the corporate governance arrangements and performance of the companies in which they invest. They should, on request, make available to their clients information on the proportion of resolutions on which votes were cast and non-discretionary proxies lodged. Additionally, they should take steps to ensure that their voting intentions are being translated into practice. The Committees also expressed consistently the need for institutional investors to exercise their votes, even if they do not attend the annual general meeting.

The evidence on institutional shareholder vigilance[2] has been mixed with earlier reports demonstrating a significant level of indifference.[3] However, other reports provide evidence of such investors acting to influence the behaviour of company boards.[4] In practice the low-key approach adopted has resulted in a poor level of shareholder activism. Thus, the 2002 White Paper noted failure of some institutional investors and fund managers to intervene actively to protect and enhance the value of the investment in cases where companies are being ineffectively, or even dishonestly, managed by their boards.[5] The Company Law Review also noted a number of problems connected with the role of institutional investors. Thus, for example, it highlighted concerns about failures in the vote execution process and lack of transparency in the voting system as well as possible conflicts of interest that might inhibit institutional investors in the performance of their governance role.[6]

The Treasury took up the issue of shareholder activism as part of its response to the Myners Report on Institutional Investment in the UK. The Government endorsed the proposals of the Company Law Review for improving the effectiveness of the voting process in quoted companies, in particular by a requirement to disclose the results of polls at general meetings on their websites and in annual reports as well as a new right for members to require a scrutiny of any poll.[7] The Government appeared, in the White Paper, to be more reluctant to tackle the conflicts of interests issue through company law and said that it would set out its

---

1   See for example, *Additional Guidance on the Independence of Auditors* which supplements their *Guide to Professional Ethics*. See also the Guidance in the Combined Code on the Role of the Audit Committee, following recommendations made by the Smith Report: Report to the FRC (January 2003) *Audit Committee Combined Code Guidance*.

2   See generally, Ferran, *Company Law and Corporate Finance* (Oxford University Press, 1999) at pp 248–249 and 271–275.

3   See eg Cosh and Hughes 'The Changing Anatomy of Corporate Control and the Market for Executives in the United Kingdom' (1997) 24 Journal of Law and Society 104.

4   See cg Holland, *The Corporate Governance Role of Financial Institutions in their Investee Companies*, Research Report 46 (London, ACCA, 1995).

5   White Paper *Modernising Company Law* Cm 5553–I, paragraph 2.43 at p 24.

6   Company Law Review, *Modern Company Law for a Competitive Economy: Completing the Structure* paragraphs 4.49–4.62 and *Final Report* Chapter 6, paragraphs 6.19–6.40.

7   White Paper, paragraph 2.45.

position fully at a later date.[1] The Government's view is that best practice guidelines are the most efficient way of achieving higher levels of corporate behaviour. The Government has stated that it will monitor the situation and take action if necessary.[2] Thus the current position is that the ISC Statement of Principles will continue to guide the actions of institutional investors and will be reviewed during 2004.[3]

11.6 The narrow framework of corporate governance in the United Kingdom

One limitation on corporate governance in the United Kingdom is the narrow perspective that has arguably been adopted. The Hampel Committee, accepting the Cadbury definition of corporate governance, also conceded that it is a restrictive definition that 'excludes many activities involved in managing a company which may nevertheless be vital to the success of the business'.[4] Indeed, it is limited by the fact that it concentrates only on the internal structure of the company. This approach limits the goal of corporate governance to profit maximisation since it prioritises the interests of the shareholders. Thus the Hampel Committee, in its Report, states that a board's first responsibility is to enhance the prosperity of the business over time.[5]

The market place requires companies to attract investment, not only in terms of purchase of shares but also in obtaining credit for the supply of goods and services as well as in terms of purchase of goods and services offered by companies. However, the participants in these aspects, creditors and suppliers, are normally viewed as outside the company and are not therefore in a position to bargain so effectively with regard to positional conflicts with the company or its managers. The United Kingdom's corporate governance system, framed by Cadbury's definition that concentrates on the internal processes, does not adequately address these needs.[6] Despite the Hampel Committee's claims that good governance ensures that constituencies (stakeholders) with a relevant interest in the company's business are fully taken into account,[7] the system adopted makes this objective difficult to achieve in practice. Section 309 of the Companies Act 1985 is a classic example of the problem. Directors are required to take the interests of the employees into account when performing their functions for the company, but since their duties are owed only to the company, the employees are not able to pursue their interests under this provision.[8]

---

1   White Paper, paragraphs 2.46–2.47.
2   Trade and Industry Select Committee, Thirteenth Report, Government Response, paragraph 23.
3   HM Treasury Budget Report 2003, Chapter 3, paragraph 3.108. Hannigan, *Company Law*, suggests that if there is still dissatisfaction with the level of institutional shareholder activism by then, the government might consider taking additional legislative measures: at p 172.
4   Hampel Report, at paragraph 1.15.
5   Ibid, at paragraph 1.1.
6   For a more detailed argument against this narrow approach see Dine and Villiers, noted above.
7   Ibid, at paragraph 1.3.
8   See further as to section 309, **16.6**. See also Villiers, 'Section 309 of the Companies Act 1985: Is it Time for a Reappraisal?' in Collins, Davies and Rideout, *Legal Regulation of the Employment Relation*, (Kluwer, 2000), p 593.

Sheridan and Kendall[1] provide a broader definition of corporate governance that recognises the relationship between the company and the community and goes beyond the notion that profit maximisation is the only relevant objective of the enterprise. They argue that good corporate governance consists of a 'system of structuring, operating and controlling a company' such as to achieve the following:

> (i) Fulfil the long-term strategic goal of the owners, which, after survival may consist of building shareholder value or establishing a dominant market share or maintaining a technical lead in a chosen sphere, or something else, but will certainly not be the same for all organisations.
>
> (ii) Consider and care for the interests of employees, past, present and future, which we take to comprise the whole life-cycle including planning future needs, recruitment, training, working environment, severance and retirement procedures, through to looking after pensioners.
>
> (iii) Take account of the needs of the environment and the local community, both in terms of the physical effects of the company's operations on the surroundings and the economic and cultural interaction with the local population.
>
> (iv) Work to maintain excellent relations with both customers and suppliers, in terms of such matters as quality of service provided, considerate ordering and account settlement procedures, etc.
>
> (v) Maintain proper compliance with all the applicable legal and regulatory requirements under which the company is carrying out its activities.[2]

This approach is much broader than that of the Cadbury Committee and its successors since it addresses the 'external' as well as the 'internal' aspects of corporate activity. It suggests that the shareholders' profit-oriented interest is not the only relevant goal of the company but that other constituent interests are also relevant to the company.[3] Such other constituent interests must influence how that company is run as well as the control structure that seeks to ensure that the company's activities are managed properly. In order for these other groups to have an effective influence, mandatory rules will be required because they have less bargaining power, and market forces alone are unlikely to protect them adequately. Others have argued for a similarly broad approach to the question of corporate governance. John Parkinson's *Corporate Power and Responsibility*[4] is a most important contribution to the debate, informed as it is by detailed knowledge and discussion of current company law rules. The Royal Society of Arts' work on *Tomorrow's Company* is a further important development.[5] Obviously,

---

1   *Corporate Governance* (Financial Times and Pitman, 1992).
2   Op cit, pp 27–28.
3   For interesting arguments challenging the whole basis for the primacy of shareholders, see Ireland, 'Corporate Governance, Shareholding and the Company: Towards a Less Degenerate Capitalism' (1996) 23 Journal of Law and Society 287; Grantham, 'The Doctrinal Basis of the Right of Company Shareholders' [1998] CLJ 554; Ireland, 'Company Law and the Myth of Shareholder Ownership' (1999) 62 MLR 32. A major focus of these writers is to dispel the notion that shareholders own the company which, they argue, is the basis for the law as traditionally understood. Perhaps, though, the law is based more on the concept of membership. It does not seem surprising that the traditional view of the law is that prima facie any association must be run primarily in the interests of its members. This is not to say that this is necessarily an appropriate view for today's company law.
4   Oxford University Press, 1993. See also Parkinson, Gamble and Kelly (eds), *The Political Economy of the Company* (Hart, 2001).
5   *Tomorrow's Company: The Role of Business in a Changing World* (1995). See also www.tomorrowscompany.com.

fundamental changes to the current system and corporate law framework would be necessary to achieve the goals argued for by these contributions to the debate.

A key aspect of these contributions is the stakeholder concept.[1] This represents a view that company law should recognise interests beyond those of the shareholders. Its most critical, although not the only, application is in terms of the fundamental duty of company directors to act *bona fide* 'in the interests of the company'.[2] Among these 'stakeholder' interests might be included employees, creditors and consumers as well as the wider community. The work of the Royal Society of Arts' Centre for *Tomorrow's Company* seems to show that encouraging worker and community links and involvement produces not only a better and more productive operational environment, but in the long term more secure and 'successful' financial performance.

Whether or not British company law moves in this sort of direction depends on what emanates from the Review of Company Law.[3] The Consultation Document issued in February 1999[4] discussed the interests which company law should serve, focusing on the actual changes to the law which different approaches would imply. A case was recognised for ensuring that company managers have regard, where appropriate, to the need to ensure productive relationships with a range of interested parties and have regard to the longer term. A distinction was drawn between the 'enlightened shareholder value' approach, which asserts that this can be achieved within present principles, but ensuring that directors pursue shareholders' interests in an enlightened and inclusive way, and the 'pluralist' approach, which asserts that co-operative and productive relationships will be optimised only where directors are permitted (or required) to balance share-holders' interests with those of others committed to the company. The pluralist approach would require changes to company law, especially to the fundamental duties of directors.

The subsequent Consultation Document from the Company Law Review Steering Group gave primary consideration to issues of corporate governance.[5] Following responses to the earlier consultation, the Steering Group provisionally concluded that 'the overall objective should be pluralist in the sense that companies should be run in a way which maximises overall competitiveness and wealth and welfare for all'. However, it continued by stating that 'the means which company law deploys for achieving this objective must take account of the realities and dynamics which operate in practice in the running of commercial enterprise. It should not be done at the expense of turning company directors from business decision makers into moral, political or economic arbiters, but by harnessing focused, comprehensive, competitive business decision making with robust, objective professional standards and flexible, but pertinent, accountability'.[6] To this end, the final proposal, supported in the White Paper, was for an 'inclusive'

---

1   See Kelly and Parkinson, 'The conceptual foundations of the law: a pluralist approach' [1998] CfiLR 174. Cf Goldenberg, 'Shareholders v Stakeholders: The Bogus Argument' (1998) 19 Co Law 34.
2   Discussed in **16.5**.
3   See generally, **1.7** and Chapter 22.
4   *Modern Company Law for a Competitive Economy: The Strategic Framework*, Chapter 5.1, 'The scope of company law'.
5   *Modern Company Law for a Competitive Economy: Developing the Framework*, March 2000, chapters 2 to 5.
6   Ibid, paragraph 2.21.

statement of directors' duties, which would continue to give primacy ultimately to the interests of shareholders as a whole, together with an 'inclusive' Operating and Financial Review for public and large private companies.

The Company Law Review and the White Paper, *Modernising Company Law*, have effectively endorsed a shareholder-centred approach but with an additional dimension which requires the directors to take account in good faith of all the material factors that might be relevant to the company's success.[1] This 'enlightened shareholder value' approach is intended to take into account the interests of other participants in the company whose interests materially affect the success of the company – 'the basic goal for directors should be the success of the company in the collective best interests of shareholders, but that directors should also recognise, as the circumstances require, the company's need to foster relationships with its employees, customers and suppliers, its need to maintain its business reputation, and its need to consider the company's impact on the community and the working environment'.[2] The draft put forward[3] by the Government in the White Paper states that a director must:

(a) act in the way he decides, in good faith, would be most likely to promote the success of the company for the benefit of its members as a whole, and
(b) in deciding what would be most likely to promote that success, take account in good faith of all the material factors that it is practicable in the circumstances for him to identify.

The material factors to be taken into account include: the short and long term consequences of the director's actions and matters such as the company's need to foster its business relationships, including those with its employees and suppliers and the customers for its products or services; the need to have regard to the impact of its operations on the communities affected and on the environment; its need to maintain a reputation for high standards of business conduct; and the need to achieve outcomes that are fair as between its members. Additionally the draft requires a director to exercise the care, skill and diligence of a reasonably diligent person with both the knowledge, skill and experience which may reasonably be expected of a director in his or her position; and any additional knowledge, skill and experience which the particular director has.[4]

It could be argued that the draft statement offers little to the non-shareholder interest groups. First, the directors would still be required to act from a shareholder-centred perspective. Other participant interests remain secondary to the interests of the shareholders. Their interests are recognised but only where they are considered *by the directors* to be relevant to the company's overall success *for the benefits of the shareholders as a whole*. Regard to other interests is purely at the discretion of the directors acting in good faith and they have only to take such interests into account. The directors are not compelled to give priority to such other interests. Nor do other interest groups gain from this proposed draft a right to challenge the decisions of directors. Such action will still depend on the shareholders.

---

1   See Company Law Review, *Developing the Framework* (2000) paragraphs 3.40; 3.45–3.48; *Completing the Structure* (2000) paragraphs 3.13–3.14; *Final Report*, Vol I (2001) Annex C and also *Modernising Company Law* (2002) Cm 5553–I.
2   White Paper, paragraph 3.3.
3   White Paper, Volume II, clause 19 and Schedule 2, principle 2.
4   White Paper, Volume II, Schedule 2, principle 4.

The proposed Operating and Financial Review (OFR) continues this 'enlightened shareholder' stance.[1] The main objective of the proposed OFR is to provide more qualitative and forward looking reporting, in addition to information that is quantitative, historical or concerns internal company affairs. The detailed rules for the compilation of the OFR will be devolved to the Standards Board. However, the Government gives an indication of the basic contents of the OFR in the White Paper.

Draft Clause 73 sets out the objective of the Operating and Financial Review: 'providing such information as will permit the members of the company, as of the approval date, to make an informed assessment of the company's operations; its financial position; and its future business strategies and prospects'. The Government proposes a compulsory content with core elements as well as a duty on directors to consider other matters that would be relevant to achieving the review objective. The compulsory matters, or core elements, include: a statement of the company's business in the financial year to which the operating and financial review relates; a fair review of performance during the financial year and of the position of the company at the end of that year; and a fair projection of the prospects for the company's business and of events which will, or are likely to, substantially affect that business. Those non-mandatory matters which must be considered for inclusion if the directors feel they are materially relevant include:

(a) the management structure of the company;
(b) receipts from, and returns to, members of the company in the financial year to which the operating and financial review relates in relation to shares held by them;
(c) the company's policies in relation to employment by the company;
(d) the company's policies on environmental issues relevant to the company's business;
(e) the company's policies on social and community issues relevant to the company's business;
(f) the company's performance, in the financial year to which the operating and financial review relates, in carrying out the policies mentioned in paragraphs (c) to (e);
(g) matters not falling within the preceding paragraphs which affect, or may affect, the company's reputation.

Despite a favourable opinion from the Trade and Industry Select Committee, a number of concerns can be raised against the proposed operating and financial review. As with the proposals concerning directors' duties, much depends on the discretion of the directors. This increases the difficulties of challenging decisions by the directors. So long as their decision is made in good faith the courts are likely to refuse to provide an opinion about their reports. In any event, whilst the White Paper suggests that directors are open to challenge and may need to defend their actions in the courts it is not likely that such challenge will be possible for non-shareholders. The issue of materiality is the subject of a consultation exercise by a working group on the OFR. The consultation paper suggests that a procedural approach to the issue of materiality is probably more effective than a substantive approach. Thus a challenge might be based on the failure of a director

---

1   See DTA, *Draft Regulations on the Operating and Financial Review and Directors' Report, A Consultative Document*, May 2004.

to acquire sufficient information to make a reporting decision or a failure to give due regard to the various matters listed but the substance is left to the directors to decide.

11.7 Corporate governance outside the UK

In contrast to the position in the United Kingdom, the 'stakeholder' approach has for a long time influenced corporate governance developments more strongly in other countries, especially in some fellow European Union Member States. The Peters Report in the Netherlands[1] opens by stating that 'companies and the enterprise connected therewith play an important role in society' and 'they must seek a good balance between the interests of the providers of risk capital (investors) and the other stakeholders'. In France, the Viénot Report[2] emphasised that the 'interests of the company may be understood as an overriding claim of the company as a separate economic agent, pursuing its own objectives which are distinct from those of shareholders, employees, creditors including the internal revenue authorities, suppliers and customers. It none the less represents the common interest of all these persons which is for the company to remain in business and prosper'. In Japan, the 'kairetsu' system[3] pursues the general welfare of the company based on continued growth, guaranteed employment, favourable business relationships with creditors, suppliers and distributors, and share-holders' interests have traditionally not been such a primary concern. Under German law, a management board is required to run the company in the interests of the company as a whole. Shareholders are regarded as only a part of the differing groups of 'stakeholders'.[4]

The European Commission is currently in the process of developing plans for the harmonisation of roles relating to corporate governance.[5] The plans at European level include improvements in transparency with a requirement for listed companies to provide an annual corporate governance statement as well as introduction of minimum standards relating to the role and responsibilities of directors. Longer term plans include improved shareholder democracy as well as more options for different board structures. The introduction of the European Company Statute,[6] whilst greatly compromised from its earlier versions, at least introduces the possibility of a variety of board structures across the European Union.

---

1   *Corporate Governance in the Netherlands: Forty Recommendations* (25 June 1997).
2   *The Boards of Directors of Listed Companies in France*, Report of the 'Viénot Committee' (July 1995).
3   For a description of the Japanese 'kairetsu' see Gilson and Roe 'Understanding the Japanese Kairetsu: Overlaps between Corporate Governance and Industrial Organization' (1993) 102 Yale Law Journal 871.
4   German law heavily influenced the draft Fifth EC Directive, with its proposals for compulsory employee representation, but this Directive has now been abandoned; see **2.3.8**.
5   See eg European Commission Communication, *Modernising Company Law and Enhancing Corporate Governance in the European Union – A Plan to Move Forward*, Com (2003) 284 final, 21.5.2003.
6   See **2.5**.

Chapter 12

Membership of a Company

12.1 Introduction

A number of varied issues arise under the heading of membership of a company, including some which have already been considered in earlier chapters, particularly the effect of the contract of membership under section 14 of the Companies Act 1985[1] and the transfer of shares by members.[2] This chapter is concerned with the general characteristics of membership of a company, with the register of members which every company must maintain, with the obligation to file an annual return and with the disclosure of interests by substantial shareholders holding voting shares in public companies. It is, however, appropriate to introduce the chapter with a brief discussion of who in effect owns and/or controls companies; that is, who are the real members. This relates closely to some issues discussed below, not least the disclosure provisions described in **12.8** *et seq.*

It has long been recognised that the control of a company with a widely held shareholding[3] may in fact be obtained by the holding of considerably less than a majority of the company's issued voting shares.[4] As long ago as 1932, Berle and Means[5] found that the ownership of shares in typical large American corporations was so widely dispersed that no individual or group was in a position to control the corporation; instead management was in control. This was probably not quite so true of British public companies, where at least a substantial proportion were controlled by their owners.[6] In recent years, the crucial factor in the United Kingdom has been the level of institutional shareholding, which has risen considerably while the level of individual shareholding has fallen dramatically.[7] This complicates the question of control even more. While institutions are likely, at least together, to be in a position to have actual control of a majority of voting power in many large public companies, the fact is that they very rarely

---

1   See **4.17**.
2   See Chapter 9.
3   That is, the typical public company. Much of this discussion is irrelevant to the numerically much more common private company.
4   For a much more detailed discussion of this question, see Farrar, *Company Law* 4th edn (Butterworths, 1998) Chapter 34.
5   *The Modern Corporation and Private Property*; see **11.2**.
6   See Florence, *Ownership, Control and Success of Large Companies* (1961) and *The Logic of British and American Industry* 3rd edn (1972).
7   The figures are not consistent but what can be said with confidence is that institutional investors are in the majority. The Hampel Report indicated figures as high as 80%: Hampel Committee, (1998) *Combined Code on Corporate Governance and Report*, London, Gee, paragraph 5.1, at p 40. Davies estimates around 60%: Davies (2003) *Gower and Davies' Principles of Modern Company Law*, 7th edn (London, Sweet & Maxwell), at p 338. The Myners Report suggests that in 1999 the institutional investors held 51.9%: Paul Myners, *Institutional Investment in the UK: A Review* (HM Treasury, April 2001), at p 27. See also Farrar and Russell (1984) 5 Co Law 107. Note the attempts by the Conservative governments to reverse this trend, particularly in respect of nationalised industries which have been 'privatised'.

appear to use this control openly.[1] Of course their decision will be crucial in a takeover battle and there is no doubt a considerable amount of behind-the-scenes lobbying and discussion, but it is probably safe to say that on the whole the management of large public companies is in *de facto* control.[2]

The law's response to these factors has generally been piecemeal.[3] It could well be argued that the problem of supervising management remains a critical and important one and that present practices leave much to be desired.[4] Following the Myners Review published in April 2001, the Government's White Paper, responding to the Company Law Review, included observations about the role of institutional investors. The Government's stance was significantly cautious. The White Paper identifies three specific concerns: shareholder activism, lack of transparency in the voting system and conflicts of interest.[5] The Treasury took up the issue of shareholder activism as part of its response to the Myners Report on Institutional Investment in the UK. The Government endorsed the proposals of the Company Law Review for improving the effectiveness of the voting process in quoted companies, in particular by a requirement to disclose the results of polls at general meetings on their websites and in annual reports as well as a new right for members to require a scrutiny of any poll.[6] The Government appeared, in the White Paper, to be more reluctant to tackle the conflicts of interests issue through company law and said that it would set out its position fully at a later date.[7]

The response to the Government's comments by the Trade and Industry Select Committee in the Sixth Report was still less enthusiastic about the role of institutional investors as corporate governance actors: 'Ultimately, the primary concern of institutional investors is to maximise the returns on their investments.

---

1   Institutions often prefer to 'vote with their feet', ie sell out rather than interfere. Perhaps this is inevitable given that the principal institutions are pension funds and insurance companies which have duties to their beneficiaries and policyholders. See for information on the role of Institutional Shareholders: *The Responsibilities of Institutional Shareholders in the UK* (Institutional Shareholders' Committee, 1991). See also Finch (1992) 55 MLR 179; Prodham, Management Research Paper, Templeton College, Oxford No 92.13 (1993); Stapledon *Institutional Shareholders and Corporate Governance* (Clarendon, 1996); Myners, *Developing a Winning Partnership – How Companies and Institutional Investors are Working Together* (DTI, URN, 95/551).

2   See also **13.1**. The law generally recognises this; see **15.11**. For a discussion of behind the scenes lobbying see Holland, *Corporate Communications with Institutional Shareholders. Private Disclosures and Financial Reporting* (Edinburgh, Institute of Chartered Accountants of Scotland, 1997).

3   Attempts can be made, as in Farrar, *Company Law*, chapter 34, to bring together various themes in the case-law regarding control and the duties of institutional investors, but it seems clear that in this country there are still no coherent principles, and it is not certain that there is much likelihood of these being developed, however desirable that might be. There is no doubt, though, that the concept of control can be relevant at common law, especially regarding the 'fraud on a minority' exception to the rule in *Foss v Harbottle*; see **17.2**. As far as statute is concerned, there are isolated provisions in the Companies Act 1985 which recognise that control of a company can be obtained by a holding of less than 50% of voting shares, eg section 314(1)(c) (see **16.20**) and section 346(4) (see **16.14**), and there are the disclosure provisions in Part VI described in detail in **12.8** *et seq*. The question of control of a company may also arise in other areas of law, especially in relation to taxation and employment law. Regarding the latter, see especially the discussion by McMullen [1986] Law Society's Gazette 2923.

4   See Chapter 11 above; Boyle (1978) 24 ICLQ 487.

5   White Paper, *Modernising Company Law*, (2002) Cm 5553–I, paragraphs 2.43–2.44

6   Ibid, paragraph 2.45.

7   Ibid, paragraphs 2.46–2.47.

Whilst this may bring with it some pressure on companies hoping to attract funds from institutional investors to ensure that they have adequate corporate governance systems in place, there is a limit to the extent to which the institutional investors are willing or able to police the probity of the UK's companies'.[1] The Government, in contrast, said that it believes institutional investors have a key role to play in ensuring the good governance of the companies in which they invest and considers best practice guidelines to be the most efficient way of achieving higher levels of corporate behaviour. The Government added that it would monitor the situation and take action if necessary.[2] Thus the current position is that the ISC Statement of Principles will continue to guide the actions of institutional investors and will be reviewed during 2004.[3]

12.2   The members of a company

The law defines the members of a company in section 22 of the Companies Act 1985 as comprising, first, the subscribers to a company's memorandum, who are deemed to have agreed to become members and on registration must be entered on the register of members, and, secondly, every other person who agrees to become a member of a company and whose name is entered in its register of members. These two categories must be examined in more detail.

12.2.1   Subscribers to the memorandum

As section 22 provides, a subscriber to the memorandum is a member whether he has otherwise agreed to become so or not, and whether or not his name is entered in the register, and he is bound to take and pay for the number of shares written opposite his name,[4] although if he subsequently applies for and receives an allotment of an equal or greater number of shares this may be treated as a satisfaction of his obligation under the memorandum.[5] The directors have no power to release a subscriber from his obligation to take shares,[6] and he can therefore escape only by taking up and transferring the shares. He will, however, be relieved from liability if the whole of the shares are allotted to other persons, so that no shares are left in respect of which he can be registered.[7] When the liability is thus extinguished, it does not revive on a forfeiture of shares putting shares at the disposal of the directors.[8]

12.2.2   Entry in the register of members

As stated above, the other persons who are members are those who have agreed to take shares *and* whose names are entered in the register. Even if they are not so entered, if there is complete agreement between them and the company, subject

---

1   Trade and Industry Select Committee Sixth Report, HC 439, paragraph 120, at p 38.

2   Trade and Industry Select Committee, Thirteenth Report, Government Response, paragraph 23.

3   HM Treasury Budget Report 2003, Ch 3, paragraph 3.108.

4   *Re Tyddyn Sheffrey Slate Co* (1869) 20 LT 105; *Drummond's Case* (1869) 4 Ch App 772; *Pell's Case* (1869) 5 Ch App 11. See further, Smith, 'Subscribers: their status on incorporation', (1982) 3 Co Law 99 which, after an exhaustive examination of the cases, comes to the same conclusion as that expressed in the text.

5   *Gilman's Case* (1886) 31 Ch D 420.

6   *Re London and Provincial Consolidated Coal Co* (1877) 5 Ch D 525.

7   *Tuffnell and Ponsonby's Case* (1885) 29 Ch D 421 (CA).

8   *Mackley's Case* (1875) 1 Ch D 247.

to the possibility of that agreement being rescinded by mutual consent,[1] they will not escape liability, for the register can be amended under section 359 while the company is a going concern,[2] or under section 148 of the Insolvency Act 1986 when the company is in liquidation.[3] However, the entry in the register of the name of a person does not make him a member if he never agreed to become one, and his name can be removed in the same way. It is possible for the court to make an order for removing his name retrospectively in order to free him from liability as a contributory, if that name has remained on the register when it should have been removed.[4]

A corporation may be a member if authorised by its constitution to hold shares,[5] but an English partnership should not be entered in the firm name, as the firm is not a 'person', and the names of the individual holders of the shares must be entered in the register.[6] If, however, the firm name is in fact entered with the consent of the partners, they become liable as members.[7] A Scottish firm is a 'person' and may be entered in its firm name.[8]

The simplest and most usual form of agreement to become a member is an application for and an allotment of shares.[9] But an agreement may be made in other ways.[10] For instance, it may be part of the preliminary contract with the vendor that he shall take shares; persons may by underwriting letters bind themselves to take any shares not subscribed for by the public; or there may be contracts to take shares which are not in writing, for a person may agree with the company by word of mouth, or even by conduct, to become a member. An agreement for value to take up shares in a company if called upon is enforceable notwithstanding the death of the person making the contract.[11] 'A formal agreement is not necessary ... If the substance of an agreement is made out the form is not material'.[12] Thus, if a person who has not previously agreed to take shares knows that they have been allotted to him, and afterwards acts as a member of the company (for instance, by attending meetings, giving proxies, or selling or attempting to sell some of the shares), he will be held to have accepted the allotment and to be a member in respect of the shares. Or a person accepting the office of director when the articles make it a condition of his office that he shall take shares from the company may be held to have agreed to become a member.

1   *Nicol's Case* (1885) 29 Ch D 421 at 444, *per* Bowen LJ (CA).
2   See **12.5.3**.
3   *Winstone's Case* (1879) 12 Ch D 239; cf *Portal v Emmens* (1877) 1 CPD 664 (CA).
4   *Nation's Case* (1866) 3 Eq 77; cf *Re Sussex Brick Co* [1904] 1 Ch 598 (CA).
5   *Bath's Case* (1878) 8 Ch D 334; *Re Barned's Banking Co, ex parte Contract Corporation* (1867) 3 Ch App 105.
6   A purported transfer to a firm in its firm name may be rejected: *Re Vagliano Anthracite Collieries* [1910] WN 187.
7   *Weikersheim's Case* (1873) 8 Ch App 831.
8   The same may be said for the Limited Liability Partnership.
9   This is dealt with at **7.7**.
10   See section 22(2) and *Re Nuneaton Borough Association Football Club* [1989] BCLC 454, where the Court of Appeal held that the phrase 'agrees to become a member' in section 22(2) is satisfied where someone assents to become a member. It does not require that there be a binding contract between the person and the company. Thus, where a person is entered on the register of members with his consent, he is a member of the company.
11   *William Beardmore v Park's Executrix* 1927 SLT 143. See also *Warner Engineering Co v Brennan* (1913) 30 TLR 191 at 196.
12   *Per* James LJ in *Risto's Case* (1877) Ch D 782.

Where the articles specify a procedure for admission to membership this must be complied with. Where, for example, admission to membership of a company required a decision of the company's council, but where in practice the procedure followed was a virtual automatic admission on an administrative basis of any person who applied for membership, this does not comply with the company's articles.[1]

A statement in the prospectus that directors or others have agreed to take shares will not alone be sufficient to render them liable.[2]

An agreement to take shares may be made through an agent.[3] The authority of the agent must be considered under the ordinary doctrines of principal and agent.

If an agreement to take shares (not arising merely by subscribing the memorandum) is brought about by misrepresentation, made either by the company or its agents, the member can, before a winding-up, obtain rescission of the contract, repayment of what he has paid, and removal of his name from the register. However, a contract procured by misrepresentation being only voidable and not void, if the company has gone into liquidation and other interests have come into existence, it is too late to set the contract aside, and the person remains a member.[4] If, however, there was in fact no contract to take shares, the supposed member can at any time have his name removed from the register, for he was never really a member.[5]

12.3 The termination of membership

A person ceases to be a member of a company upon a transfer of his shares being made and the name of the transferee being entered in the register of members,[6] but he remains liable to a limited extent in the event of a liquidation occurring within one year after the transfer. On the death of a shareholder his membership, of course, ceases, but his estate remains entitled to the benefits and subject to the burdens arising from his membership until some other person is entered in the register in respect of his shares. An executor or administrator, however, does not become a member unless he consents to be treated as such and to be entered in the register:[7] subject to the provisions of the articles, he is entitled, if he desires, to have his name entered in the register.[8] A person may also cease to be a member by a surrender or forfeiture of his shares properly made; and in the case of unlimited companies the articles may provide for a person ceasing to be a member in any manner which may be agreed, for in such cases the company has power to reduce its capital without reference to the court.[9] Thus in the case of mutual ship

---

1   *POW Services Ltd v Clare* [1995] 2 BCLC 435.

2   *Re Moore Bros & Co* [1899] 1 Ch 627; *Todd v Miller* 1910 SC 869.

3   *Levita's Case* (1870) 5 Ch App, 489; *Fraser's Case* (1871) 24 LT 746; *Barnett's Case* (1864) 4 De GJ & S 416. See further, *Gore-Browne on Companies* 44th edn (Jordans, loose-leaf) at 20.3.

4   On the effect of misrepresentation on a contract to subscribe for shares see **6.33** *et seq.*

5   *Oakes v Turquand* (1867) LR 2 HL 325; *Alabaster's Case* (1869) 7 Eq 273.

6   The rights and liabilities of the transferor and transferee of shares, both *inter se* and in relation to the company, are discussed in Chapter 9.

7   *Bowling and Welby's Contract* [1895] 1 Ch 663 at p 670 (CA).

8   *Scott v Frank F Scott (London)* [1940] Ch 794. The executor can (subject to the provisions of the articles of association) insist on being entered as a member in his own right: *Re T H Saunders & Co* [1908] 1 Ch 415.

9   See *Re Borough Commercial and Building Society* [1893] 2 Ch 242.

insurance companies, it is often provided that a person is a member only so long as he has ships insured in the company. It would seem, however, that in a company limited by shares a person cannot cease to be a member in any manner which would reduce the capital of the company other than in the ways referred to above. Therefore, as a company cannot purchase its own shares, except in the ways provided by Chapter VII of Part V of the Companies Act 1985,[1] a transfer purporting to be made to the company will not relieve the transferor from liability.[2]

The fully paid shares of a company can be bequeathed or transferred to a nominee of the company.[3] The shares of a company can also be held on trust for it.[4]

The representatives of a deceased or bankrupt member are entitled to receive on behalf of the estate any dividends, bonuses, or benefits attaching to the shares, and are liable to contribute in respect of the estate in their hands and to be put on the list as representative contributories (see section 81 of the Insolvency Act 1986), but are not themselves members unless they take the shares into their own names.[5] Until they do this, however, they are not entitled to receive notices from the company,[6] unless the articles expressly so direct.

A shareholder who is bankrupt may continue to use his right to vote at shareholders' meetings while his name remains on the register, but he is obliged to do so in accordance with the instructions of his trustee in bankruptcy.[7] Such a shareholder may also bring a minority shareholders' action.[8]

The company cannot refuse to enter executors in the register or insist on inserting a notice that they hold in a representative capacity unless the articles contain some authority to do so,[9] and must enter the names in the order desired by the executors – a matter which often affects the right to vote and receive notices. Moreover, where articles allowed only the person first named upon the register to vote, as such person might be unable to attend meetings, the court, with a view to protecting the voting rights of the joint holders, ordered the company to enter the names in its register so that one name came first in respect of some of the shares and another name came first in respect of other of the shares.[10]

12.4   Minors as members

The following refers to persons domiciled in England who are 'minors' in English law in reference to their membership of a company. The Scots law in relation to capacity is now contained in the Age of Legal Capacity (Scotland) Act 1991.

---

1   See **7.16** *et seq.* As to reduction of capital, see **8.14**.
2   *Trevor v Whitworth* (1877) 12 App Cas 409 (HL).
3   See **7.16**.
4   *Re Castiglione's Will Trusts* [1958] Ch 549; *Kirby v Wilkins* [1929] 2 Ch 444.
5   *James v Buena Ventura Syndicate* [1896] 1 Ch 456 (CA); *New Zealand Gold Extraction Co v Peacock* [1894] 1 QB 622 (CA); cf *Bowling and Welby's Contract* [1895] 1 Ch 633.
6   *Allen v Gold Reefs of West Africa* [1900] 1 Ch 656 (CA).
7   *Morgan v Gray* [1953] Ch 83.
8   *Birch v Sullivan* [1957] 1 WLR 1247.
9   *Re TH Saunders & Co* [1908] 1 Ch 415; *Scott v Frank F Scott (London)* [1940] Ch 794.
10   *Burns v Siemens Brothers Dynamo Works* [1919] 1 Ch 225; see also *Re Hobson, Houghton & Co* [1929] 1 Ch 300.

A minor[1] may become a member of a company and hold shares either by subscribing to the memorandum of association[2] or by taking a transfer of shares,[3] but the company has power to refuse to accept a minor as a shareholder or transferee of shares,[4] and should always do so in any case where a liability is attached to the shares, for the minor can, on or before attaining his majority, repudiate the shares if they are then burdensome.[5]

12.5 The register of members

Every company is required to keep a register of its members and section 352 of the Companies Act 1985 prescribes that the following particulars shall be entered therein:

(1) the names and addresses of the members, and in the case of a company having a share capital a statement of the shares held by each member distinguishing each share by its number so long as the share has a number,[6] and, where the company has more than one class of issued shares, by its class, and of the amount paid or agreed to be considered as paid on the shares of each member;[7]
(2) the date at which each person was entered in the register as a member; and
(3) the date at which any person ceased to be a member.

In the case of a private company limited by shares or by guarantee, if the number of members falls to one, on that event occurring a statement that the company has only one member (and the date on which this happened) must be entered into the register of members.[8]

By section 353, the register is to be kept at the registered office of the company, except that it may instead be kept at any office of the company where the work of making it up is done or, where it is made up by some other person on behalf of the company, at the office of that person at which the work is done.[9] It is not, however, to be kept, in the case of a company registered in England and Wales, at a place

---

1 At common law the age of majority was 21. By the Family Law Reform Act 1969, section 1, the age of majority was reduced to 18 as from 1 January 1970. Section 12 of that Act authorises the use of the term 'minor' to describe those not of full age in place of the term 'infant' previously used.
2 *Re Laxon & Co (No 2)* [1892] 3 Ch 555; *Re Nassau Phosphate Co* (1876) 2 Ch D 610.
3 *Lumsden's Case* (1868) 3 Ch App 31.
4 *Symon's Case* (1970) 5 Ch App 298; *Castello's Case* (1869) 8 Eq 504.
5 *Dublin and Wicklowe Rly Co v Black* (1852) 8 Ex 181; *Ebbett's Case* (1870) 5 Ch App 302; *Re Laxon & Co (No 2)* [1892] 3 Ch 555. See further as to the legal position of minors who become members by allotment or transfer, *Gore-Browne on Companies* 44th edn (Jordans, loose-leaf) at 20.5.
6 As to when shares have to be numbered, see section 182(2).
7 As to the entries to be made on the register in relation to share warrants, see **9.12**. As to when shares have been converted into stock, see section 352(3)(b).
8 Section 352A, inserted by the Companies (Single Member Private Limited Companies) Regulations 1992, SI 1992/1699, Schedule, paragraph 4.
9 See the Companies (Registers and Other Records) Regulations, SI 1985/724 as to the keeping of the register of members in computerised form.

outside England and Wales, or in the case of a company registered in Scotland, at a place outside Scotland.[1]

Notice is to be sent to the Registrar of the place where the register of members is kept and of any change in that place. Such notice need not, however, be given where the register has, at all times during its existence or since 1 July 1948, been kept at the company's registered office.[2]

In the case of joint holders, it is their right to determine in what order their names shall be entered, a matter which will under most articles affect the right of attending meetings and voting.[3] An article declaring that only the first named shall be entitled to attend and vote will not be so construed as to prevent shareholders from fairly and reasonably exercising their powers as members of the company. Accordingly, where shares were registered in the joint names of two trustees, and the first-named holder might not be able to attend meetings and the second-named holder could neither vote nor be appointed a proxy for a poll, the court rectified the register and directed the company to have the names of the holders entered as to some of such shares in one order and as to other of such shares in the reverse order.[4]

There are special provisions in section 362 and Schedule 14 relating to 'overseas branch registers'. These allow the keeping in a particular country or territory of a register of members resident in that country or territory by a company with a share capital transacting business there in accordance with its objects.[5]

12.5.1   *The register, equitable interests and notice*

The register of members is *prima facie* (but not conclusive) evidence of any matters directed or authorised to be inserted therein.[6] By section 360, it is provided that no notice of any trust shall be entered on the register or be receivable by the Registrar in the case of English companies,[7] and the company may not enter particulars of a lien it may claim to have on the shares.[8] 'It seems to me extremely important', said Lord Coleridge in the Court of Appeal, 'not to throw any doubt

---

1   Section 353(1). See *International Credit and Investment Co (Overseas) Ltd v Adham* [1994] 1 BCLC 66 at 72. Harman J applied the principle that shares in a company are choses in action which (for the purposes of serving a writ out of jurisdiction) are situate at the place where the existence of the choses in action are recorded. The situs of the shares in a company is at the registered office of the company at which the register of shares is kept in accordance with section 353(1).

2   As to when an index to the register must be kept, see section 354.

3   *Re TH Saunders & Co* [1908] 1 Ch 415; see also Table A, article 55.

4   *Burns v Siemens Brothers Dynamo Works* [1919] 1 Ch 225; see also *Re Hobson, Houghton Co* [1929] 1 Ch 300.

5   For more detail, see *Gore-Browne on Companies* 44th edn (Jordans, loose-leaf) at 20.11. The countries and territories in question are Northern Ireland, any part of Her Majesty's Dominions outside the United Kingdom, the Channel Islands and the Isle of Man and any in the list in Part I of Schedule 14.

6   Section 361.

7   *Société Générale v Tramways Union Co* (1884) 14 QBD 424 (CA), affirmed sub nom *Société Générale de Paris v Walker* (1885) 11 App Cas 20 (HL), where it was held that the company is not liable, though the directors may be, for ignoring notices of trust. See also *Simpson v Molson's Bank* [1895] AC 270 (PC). Scottish companies may recognise trusts (although this is excluded for most purposes by the articles if article 5 of Table A applies), and this discussion of equitable rights relates only to English law.

8   *Re W Key & Son* [1902] 1 Ch 467. A person who has only a beneficial interest in shares cannot exercise the rights of a member, eg to have proposals included in a circular sent to members prior to a meeting: *Verdun v Toronto-Dominion Bank* (1996) 139 DLR (4th) 415, SC (Can).

on the principle that companies have nothing whatever to do with the relation between trustees and their *cestuis que trust* in respect of the shares of the company'.[1] But the court will intervene to protect equitable rights by injunction if application is made before a transfer is complete.[2]

The rule does not mean that the company, with knowledge of the rights of other people, can make advances to the registered holder on the security of the shares, ignoring the rights of which it has knowledge, for the company is not relieved from the obligation of giving effect to equitable rights of which it in fact has notice: eg its own lien will not take precedence of charges prior in date of which it has notice at the time of making the advance which gives rise to the lien.[3] Nor can it enforce its own lien against the holder upon shares held by trustees if at the time of making the advance it knew that the shares were held in trust.[4] Where a company had notice of a transfer to trustees for creditors or others, it was held that it was justified in refusing to give effect to a subsequent transfer by the debtor to a purchaser for value.[5] When a company upon receiving a transfer has notice of an adverse claim, it usually gives notice to the claimant that it will register the transfer unless he takes proceedings within a specified time. But a company is not concerned to enquire whether trustees who are registered as shareholders are acting within their powers in dealing with the shares,[6] and can enforce its own rights against the actual holders of shares irrespective of the rights of the persons for whom they are trustees.[7] Nor does priority in giving notice to the company affect the priority of two charges one against another.[8] If a person having equitable rights in shares desires protection he should serve a notice under RSC Order 50, rules 11–15.[9]

If an official of the company, under a mistake, strikes out the name of a member properly registered, this is a nullity and must be disregarded, and if disputes arise as to the propriety of the act the court will, on being satisfied that a mistake was made, order rectification of the register so as to 'restore and retain' the name of the person entitled to the shares.[10]

The register of members gives particulars of the shares as they were originally issued, with the changes from time to time made. A register of transfers which is

1   *Re Perkins* (1890) 24 QBD 613 (CA). In a case, however, where it was alleged that an irregular disposition of the company's property by the directors had been authorised or approved by all the shareholders, the Privy Council seem to have thought it material to consider whether the shareholders were the beneficial owners of the shares; see *EBM v Dominion Bank* [1937] 3 All ER 555 (PC).

2   *Binney v Ince Hall Coal Co* (1866) 35 LJ Ch 363.

3   *Bradford Banking Co v Henry Briggs & Co* (1886) 12 AC 29 (HL); *Rearden v Provincial Bank of Ireland* [1896] 1 Ir R 532 (CA); *Binney v Ince Hall Coal Co* (1866) 35 LJ Ch 363.

4   *Mackereth v Wigan Coal and Iron Co* [1916] 2 Ch 293.

5   *Peat v Clayton* [1906] 1 Ch 659; *Roots v Williamson* (1888) 38 Ch D 485; *Moore v North-Western Bank* [1891] 2 Ch 599.

6   *Simpson v Molson's Bank* [1895] AC 270 (PC).

7   *London and Brazilian Bank v Brocklebank* (1892) 21 Ch D 302 (CA). But it would seem that if the company had notice of the trust before the debt to itself was incurred, the doctrine of *Bradford Banking Co v Henry Briggs & Co* (1886) 12 AC 29 would apply, and the company would be postponed.

8   *Société Générale de Paris v Walker* (1886) 11 AC 20 (HL).

9   See **9.8.1**.

10 *Re Indo-China Steam Navigation Co* [1917] 2 Ch 100. If the company loses its register, it should apply to the court before compiling a new one: *Re Data Express Ltd* (1987) *The Times*, 27 April.

usually kept, though not specifically required by the Companies Act 1985, gives particulars of the changes which take place in the ownership of shares.

A company not entering in the register the name of a person entitled to be put therein is liable to pay him damages for any loss he may have sustained by its neglect or refusal to do its duty.[1] By section 352(7), any liability incurred by a company from the making or deletion of any entry in its register of members or from a failure to make or delete any such entry, is not enforceable more than 20 years after the date on which the entry was made or deleted or, in the case of any such failure, the failure first occurred. This provision is 'without prejudice to any lesser period of limitation'.

Section 352(6) allows any entry relating to a *former* member of the company to be removed from the register of members after the expiration of 20 years from the date on which he ceased to be a member.

12.5.2   Inspection and copies of the register

The register of members, and the index (where required to be kept) must, except when the register is duly closed, be open for a period of at least two hours a day to the inspection of any member *gratis*, and to the inspection of any other person on payment of a fee not exceeding £2.50 per hour or part thereof during which the right of inspection is exercised.[2] Further, the company must permit a person inspecting the register and index to copy any information therein by means of the taking of notes, the transcription of the information, or photographic reproduction (by means provided by that person). The obligation to permit copying does not oblige the company to provide any facilities additional to those provided for the purpose of facilitating inspection. The person inspecting may require a copy or extract on payment of the prescribed fee.[3] The company is not obliged to present the register or index for inspection in a manner which groups together entries by reference to whether a member has given an address in a particular geographical location, is of a particular nationality, has a holding of a certain size, is a natural person or not, or is of a particular gender.[4]

The court is given powers where inspection is refused or copies of the register are not supplied to order an immediate inspection or direct copies required to be sent to the persons requiring them.[5]

A person desiring to inspect cannot be required to give the reason for his desire,[6] and even if it be known that the object of inspecting the register or of requiring a copy thereof is antagonistic to the company, it is illegal to refuse such

---

1   Section 359(2). See *Re Ottos Kopje Diamond Mimes* [1893] 1 CH 618 (CA); *Tomkinson v Balkis Consolidated Co* [1893] AC 397 (HL).
2   Sections 356 and 723A and the Companies (Inspection and Copying of Registers, Indices and Documents) Regulations 1991, SI 1991/1998. The penalties for failing to comply with section 356 are imposed upon the company and 'every officer in default', which includes any person at whose office the register is kept as permitted by section 353(1)(b) (section 357).
3   Not more than £2.50 for the first 100 entries (or part thereof), £20 for the next 1,000 entries (or part thereof) and £15 for every subsequent 1,000 entries (or part thereof).
4   The Companies (Inspection and Copying of Registers, Indices and Documents) Regulations 1991, SI 1991/1998, regulation 4. Nor is it obliged to extract entries from the register by reference to any of these criteria.
5   Section 356(6).
6   *Holland v Dickson* (1888) 37 Ch D 669.

inspection or copy.[1] But the right to inspect ceases upon the commencement of a winding-up,[2] and if inspection is required after liquidation an order of the court must be obtained under section 155 of the Insolvency Act 1986.[3] Such an order entitles the party to inspect and take copies himself. He need not pay the liquidator a fee for having them made.[4]

A company may close its register for a period not exceeding thirty days in each year, upon giving notice thereof by advertisement in some newspaper circulating in the district in which the registered office is situate.[5] The main objects of closing the register are that entries of transfer may be deferred until after dividends have been declared and paid, and that lists of members may be made out in the event of polls being demanded, and the like. But closing the register is sometimes resorted to with the object of preventing hostile action, in which case the courts will usually grant relief, as this is not a proper use of the power.

12.5.3 *Rectification of the register*

It is of the greatest importance that the register of members should be promptly and accurately entered up, as delay or inaccuracy may lead to an expensive lawsuit. Section 359 of the Companies Act 1985 prescribes that if the name of any person is without sufficient cause entered in or omitted from the register of members of any company, or if default is made or unnecessary delay takes place in entering in the register the fact of any person having ceased to be a member, the person aggrieved, or any member of the company, or the company itself, may apply for the order of the court[6] that the register be rectified, and the court may 'either refuse the application or may order rectification of the register, and payment by the company of any damages sustained by any party aggrieved'.[7] Such an order must be notified to the Registrar of Companies.[8] Where the issue is not rectification but damages, the court cannot give damages upon a motion made under section 359, the proper course being for the person aggrieved to bring an action.[9] The court has power to determine any question relating to the title of any party to the application.[10] If no dispute arises as to the rights of the person who seeks to have his name entered in or removed from the register, this section presents no difficulty. But as the inclusion or exclusion of a person's name in or from the register determines his right to the benefit of the shares or his liability to pay calls upon them, a number of cases have arisen under the similar section in the earlier Acts.

The court will interfere and rectify the register, upon a motion made under section 359, where the error is due to the neglect or default of the company, and

---

1   *R v Wilts and Berks Canal Navigation Co* (1874) 29 LT 922 (CA): *Mutter v Eastern and Midlands Railway* (1888) 38 Ch D 92 (CA); *Davies v Gas Light and Coke Co* [1909] 1 Ch 708 (CA).

2   *Re Kent Coalfields Syndicate* [1898] 1 QB 754 (CA).

3   This section in terms applies only to a winding-up by the court, but in the case of a voluntary winding-up, section 112 allows an order to be made under section 155 (*per* Chitty LJ in *Re Kent Coalfields Syndicate,* above).

4   *Re Arauco Co* [1899] WN 134.

5   Section 358.

6   'The court' means the court having jurisdiction to wind up the company (section 744).

7   As to the measure of damages see *Re Ottos Kopje Diamond Mines* [1893] 1 Ch 618.

8   Section 359(4).

9   See *Re Ottos Kopje Diamond Mines* [1893] 1 Ch 618 (CA).

10   Section 359(3).

generally when the question arises between the company and a member or alleged member whether his name is properly included or excluded.[1] The power of the court is discretionary, and regard must be had to the 'justice of the case'.[2] In a dispute between two individuals as to which ought to be registered as a member of the company, if the matter is a simple one the court will decide it upon a motion under this section, and will make the necessary order for rectifying the register. But if the question is complicated, or if the rights of third parties intervene, the court will not make an order upon a motion, but will allow the party aggrieved to seek his remedy by an action.[3] In a case where the issue is whether there was an enforceable contract for the allotment of shares, the discretion under section 359 is the same as the discretion whether or not to order specific performance of the contract and can therefore be affected by delay on the part of the applicant and prejudice to a third party.[4]

There is authority for the proposition that where a person on the register has a right to rectification and the company recognises that right, the register may be rectified without an application to the court.[5] It has been said, however, that 'the protection of the court's order is in the ordinary case essential to any rectification of the register by the removal of the name of a registered holder of shares'.[6] The company cannot, however, unilaterally alter the register by removing the name of a person who continues to assert his right to be a member.[7]

12.6 Carrying on business with less than the minimum number of members

If a public company carries on business without having at least two members and does so for more than six months, a person who, for the whole or any part of the period that it so carries on business after those six months (a) is a member of the company, and (b) knows that it is carrying on business with only one member, is liable (jointly and severally with the company) for the payment of the company's debts contracted during the period (or, as the case may be, that part of it).[8] The

---

1   *Ward and Henry's Case* (1867) 2 Ch App 431; *Reese River Silver Mining Co v Smith* (1869) LR 4 HL 64 at 75.

2   *Sichell's Case* (1868) LR 3 Ch App at 122; *Re Dronfield Silkstone Co* (1880) 17 Ch D 76 at 97 (CA); *Trevor v Whitworth* (1888) 12 App Cas 409 (HL), *per* Lord Macnaghten at 440.

3   *Ward and Henry's Case* (1867) 2 Ch App 431; *ex parte Shaw* (1877) 2 QBD 463; *ex parte Sargent* (1874) 17 Eq 273; *Re Greater Britain Products Development Corp* (1924) 40 TLR 488.

4   *Re Isis Factors plc* [2003] EWHC 1653 (Ch), [2003] 2 BCLC 411.

5   *Reese River Silver Mining Co* (1869) LR 4 HL 64 at 74; *Re Poole Firebrick Co* (1875) 10 Ch App 157; *First National Reinsurance Co v Greenfield* [1921] 2 KB 260 at 278–280.

6   *Re Derham and Allen* [1946] Ch 31 at 36. For a further discussion of the procedure under section 359 and the cases decided on application under this section (and its predecessors), see *Gore-Browne on Companies* 44th edn (Jordans, loose-leaf) at 20.10.

7   *Majujaya Holdings Sdn Bhd v Pens-Transteel Sdn Bhd* [1998] MLJ 399, CA (Malaysia).

8   Section 24. This provision ceased to apply to private companies when the Companies (Single Member Private Limited Companies) Regulations 1992, SI 1992/1669 came into force on 15 July 1992.

company may also be wound up by the court.[1] It is not, however, illegal for a company to have less than the minimum number of members.[2]

12.7 The annual return

Companies are required to file annual returns with the Registrar of Companies at least once each year. The rules relating to this requirement were changed substantially by section 139 of the Companies Act 1989, which inserted new sections 363 to 365 in place of the existing sections in Part XI of the Companies Act 1985.[3]

Section 363(1) requires every company to deliver to the Registrar successive annual returns, each of which is made up to the company's return date. The return date is defined as the anniversary of the company's incorporation or the anniversary of the date to which the company's last annual return was made if that date is different. Section 363(2) requires the return to be in the prescribed form[4] containing the information required by section 364 (and 364A where applicable) and that it must be signed by a director or the company secretary. In practice, the Registrar now sends out a partially completed 'shuttle document' which the company is required to complete and return.

The return must be delivered within 28 days from the date on which it is made up.[5] The company and its officers face penalties for failure to comply and a daily default fine is imposed for continuous contravention.

12.7.1 The contents of the annual return

Section 364 sets out the required contents of annual returns in respect of every type of registered company.[6] Companies which have a share capital where further particulars of share capital and shareholders are required are dealt with by section 364A. Section 364 requires the following:

(1) Information about the company[7]
   (a) the address of the company's registered office;
   (b) the type of company it is and its principal business activities.
(2) Information about officers
   (a) the name and address of the company secretary;
   (b) the name and address of every director of the company;
   (c) the nationality, date of birth and business occupation of each individual director.
(3) Information as to registers

---

1   Section 122(1)(e) of the Insolvency Act 1986. For the purposes of these sections, it seems that past members and persons who are merely representatives of deceased members, without having put themselves on the register, must not be counted: *Re Bowling and Welby's Contract* [1895] 1 Ch 663 (CA).

2   See *Jarvis Motors (Harrow) Ltd v Carabott* [1964] 1 WLR 1101 and *Nisbet v Shepherd* [1994] 1 BCLC 300 (CA) concerning private companies before the 1992 Regulations came into effect.

3   The Companies (Contents of Annual Return) Regulations 1999, SI 1999/2322 amended the requirements of section 364.

4   See the Companies (Forms) (No 2) Regulations 1991, SI 1991/1259.

5   Section 363(2), (3).

6   Section 365 allows the Secretary of State by regulation to amend the contents of the annual return.

7   Including the date to which the annual return is made up.

(a) if the register of members is not kept at the company's registered office, the address of the place where it is kept;

(b) if any register of debenture-holders (or a duplicate of any such register or a part of it) is not kept at the company's registered office, the address of the place where it is kept.

(4) Particulars of share capital and shareholders (section 364A) – a company having a share capital is required to supply the following information in its annual returns

(a) the total number of issued shares of the company at the date to which the return is made up and the aggregate nominal value of those shares;

(b) with respect to each class of shares in the company
(i) the nature of the class, and
(ii) the total number and aggregate nominal value of issued shares of that class at the date to which the return is made up;

(c) the names and addresses of every person[1] who
(i) is a member of the company on the date to which the return is made up, or
(ii) has ceased to be a member of the company since the date to which the last annual return was made up (or since the incorporation of the company if the first return);

(d) the number of shares of each class held by each member of the company at the date to which the return is made up; and

(e) the number of shares of each class transferred since the date to which the last return was made up (or in the case of the first return, the date of incorporation of the company) by each member, or person who has ceased to be a member, and the dates of registration of the transfers.

Regarding (c), (d) and (e), if either of the two immediately preceding annual returns still provides accurate information at that date, the current return need only give changes in membership[2] since the date of the last annual return and shares transferred since that date.[3]

12.8 Disclosure of interests in the voting shares of public companies

While, as we have seen in **12.5.1**, a company with a share capital is prima facie concerned only with the registered ownership of its shares, there have long been felt to be good reasons why the true beneficial ownership of the shares in public companies should be discoverable.[4] Otherwise, for example, the real identity of persons building up an interest, perhaps with a view to obtaining control by a cheaper means than the making of a takeover bid, may be concealed. The Secretary of State has wide powers to investigate the beneficial ownership of companies.[5] Our present concern is with the provisions which require the disclosure of interests in the voting shares of public companies. These provisions are contained in Part VI of the Companies Act 1985 which consolidated

---

1   If the names are not arranged in alphabetical order, the return shall be annexed with an index sufficient to enable the name of any person in the list to be easily found.

2   Ie 'persons ceasing to be or becoming members': section 364A(6).

3   Section 364A(6).

4   See also the discussion in **12.1**.

5   See **17.27**.

provisions, first introduced in 1967, which were beefed up considerably by the 1981 Act. The latter for the first time required the notification of group interests of persons acting together and gave a minority of members the right to require their company to exercise its powers to compel the disclosure of information about interests in its voting shares.

12.9   The obligation of disclosure

Any person who has certain interests in the shares with voting rights in a public company may, on the occurrence of certain events, come under an obligation to notify the company. If such a person to his knowledge acquires an interest in shares 'comprised in a public company's relevant share capital' or ceases to be interested in such shares, or becomes aware that he has acquired such an interest or that he has ceased to have such an interest, he is under the 'obligation of disclosure' of his interests.[1]

Section 198(3) extends the obligation to notify beyond the knowledge of acquisition or loss of interests specified in section 198(1). Where a person is aware at the time when it occurs of any change of circumstances affecting facts relevant[2] to the application of the notification requirement to an existing interest of his in shares comprised in a company's share capital of any description, then he comes under the obligation of disclosure. This will also apply if such a person 'otherwise becomes aware of any such fact (whether or not arising from any such change of circumstances)'.

'Relevant share capital' means issued share capital of a public company of a class[3] carrying rights to vote in all circumstances at general meetings of the company.[4]

The obligation of disclosure arises in the following events:[5]

(1) under section 198(1) or (3), if a person has a notifiable interest[6] immediately after the 'relevant time', but did not have such an interest immediately before that time;
(2) under section 198(1),
    (a) if he had a notifiable interest immediately before the 'relevant time' but does not have such an interest immediately after it, or
    (b) if he had a notifiable interest immediately before that time and has such an interest immediately after it, but the percentage levels have changed.

The 'relevant time' for these purposes is the time of the event or change of circumstances or the time at which the person becomes aware of the facts in question, as appropriate.[7]

---

1   Section 198(1).
2   Eg full voting rights becoming exercisable in respect of shares on the satisfaction of a condition.
3   Where the relevant share capital is divided into different classes, a percentage (the relevance of which is discussed below) means a percentage of the nominal value of the issued shares in each class taken separately.
4   Section 198(2); any temporary suspension of voting rights does not affect the application of Part VI.
5   Section 199(4) and (5).
6   As to the meaning of this, see **12.9.3**.
7   Section 198(4).

12.9.1   The percentage level

The obligation of disclosure arises when a person is interested in a prescribed percentage of relevant share capital. Section 199(2) states that a person has a 'notifiable interest' at any time when he is interested in shares, comprised in relevant share capital of a company, of an aggregate nominal value equal to, or more than, the percentage of the nominal value of the share capital[1] which is 'for the time being the notifiable percentage'.[2] This percentage is 3% or such other percentage as may from time to time be prescribed by regulations under section 201.[3] The percentage level is found by expressing the aggregate nominal value of the shares, comprised in the share capital concerned, in which a person is interested, immediately before or (as the case may be) after the relevant time, as a percentage of the nominal value of that share capital. The figures must be rounded down if it is not a whole number, to the next whole number.[4] Where the nominal value of the share capital is greater immediately after the relevant time than it was immediately before, the percentage level of the person's interests immediately before (as well as immediately after) that time is determined by reference to the larger amount.[5]

12.9.2   The form of notification required

A notification required by section 202(1) must be in writing and must specify the share capital to which it relates.[6] Such notification must also state the number of shares in that share capital in which the person making it knows he was interested immediately after the time when the obligation to make the notification arose. In the event that a person making notification no longer has a notifiable interest, the notification must state that he no longer has such an interest. Notification must be given within two days after the obligation to notify arises.[7]

A notification must give[8] particulars of the identity of each registered holder of any shares to which the notification relates and the number of those shares held by each registered holder.[9] Any person who has a notifiable interest must notify the company in writing within two days of any particulars in relation to those shares (or any change in those particulars) of which he becomes aware after the 'interest notification date' and before the first occasion following that date on which he

---

1 When the 'relevant share capital' is divided into different classes of shares, the 'percentage level' means the percentage level of the nominal value of the issued shares in each of these classes taken separately (section 198(2)).

2 'All the facts relevant to determining for the purposes of this section whether a person has such an interest at any time (or the percentage level of his interest) shall be taken to be what he knows them to be at the time.'

3 Section 210A, inserted by the Companies Act 1989, section 134.

4 Section 200(1).

5 Section 200(3).

6 Section 202(2).

7 Excluding Saturdays, Sundays or bank holidays; sections 202(1) and 220(1). See the amendment of section 202(1) by section 134(3) of the Companies Act 1989.

8 So far as this is known to the person making the notification at the date of the notification. Section 202(3) does not apply to a notice stating that there is no longer a notifiable interest.

9 Section 202(3).

becomes subject to any further obligation to make notification.[1] The term 'interest notification date' is defined as being either: (a) the date of any notification made by him with respect to his interest under Part VI; or (b) where he has failed to make any such notification, the date on which the period allowed for making it came to an end. A person who at any time has an interest in shares is regarded for the purposes of section 202(4) as continuing to have an interest in those shares subject to that requirement, unless and until he becomes subject to an obligation to make notification that he no longer has such an interest: section 202(6).

12.9.3 'Notifiable interest in shares'

The meaning of 'notifiable interest in shares' for the purposes of sections 198 to 202 is defined in sections 203, 208 and 209. Under section 203(1), a person is 'taken to be interested in any shares' in which his spouse or any infant child or stepchild of his is interested. A person is also so taken if a body corporate is interested in shares and: (a) that body or its directors are accustomed to act in accordance with his directions or instructions; or (b) he is entitled to exercise, or control the exercise of, one-third or more of the voting power at general meetings of that body corporate.[2] It should be noted that a corporation (controlled in either of these ways) need not be the registered holder; it need only have an interest in accordance with the rules discussed below. Furthermore, where a person is entitled to exercise, or control the exercise of, one-third or more of the voting power at general meetings of a body corporate, and that body corporate is entitled to exercise, or control the exercise of, any of the voting power at general meetings of another body corporate (the 'effective voting power'), then for the purposes of section 203(2)(b), the effective voting power is taken as exercisable by that person.[3] Here the degree of control of the first body corporate over the second would be insufficient to make it a holding and subsidiary relationship within section 736.[4]

Section 208 lays down certain general rules for determining, for the purposes of sections 198 to 202, whether a person has a notifiable interest in shares. These rules are subject to section 209 (discussed below) which provides for certain interests to be disregarded.

Section 208(2) casts a wide net by providing that 'a reference to an interest in shares is to be read as including an interest of any kind whatsoever in the shares, and accordingly there are to be disregarded any restraints or restrictions to which the exercise of any right attached to the interest is or may be subject'. Section 208(3) then provides that where any property is held on trust, any beneficiary of

---

1 Ie 'with respect to his interest in shares comprised in that share capital': section 202(4). A person who at any time has a notifiable interest in shares is regarded under section 202(4) as continuing to have an interest in those shares subject to that requirement unless and until he becomes subject to an obligation to make notification that he no longer has such an interest: section 202(6).

2 Section 203(2).

3 Section 203(3). For the purposes of section 203(2) and (3), a person is entitled to exercise or control the exercise of any voting power if he has a right (whether subject to conditions or not) the exercise of which would make him so entitled, or is under an obligation (whether so subject or not) the fulfilment of which would make him so entitled: section 203(4).

4 See **3.8.3**.

that trust who apart from the subsection does not have an interest in the shares is
to be taken as having such an interest.

A person is also taken to have an interest in shares if he enters into a contract for
their purchase by him (whether for cash or other consideration).[1] Section
208(4)(b) also casts a wide net by providing that a person is taken to have an
interest in shares if (not being the registered holder) he is entitled to exercise any
right conferred by the holding of those shares, or is entitled to control the exercise
of any such right. A person is entitled to exercise, or control the exercise of, any
right conferred by the holding of shares if he has a right (whether subject to
conditions or not) the exercise of which would make him so entitled, or if he is
under an obligation (whether so subject or not) the fulfilment of which would
make him so entitled.[2] However, section 208(4)(b) does not apply to someone
appointed a proxy to vote at a specified meeting of a company,[3] nor to corporate
representatives at *any* meeting of a company or any class of its members.[4] The
reference to 'specific meeting' (in respect of the appointment of proxies) clearly
indicates that not only irrevocable proxies but the grant of a proxy for more than
one meeting would be caught by section 208(4)(b). Section 208(6) would also
catch 'voting trust' or 'voting pool' agreements (see also the wide terms of section
208(2), as already discussed).

A person is taken to have an interest in shares if (otherwise than by virtue of
having an interest under a trust) he has a right to call for delivery of the shares to
himself or his order (a call option).[5] This will also be the case where he has a right
to acquire an interest in shares or is under an obligation to take an interest in
shares.[6] Persons having a joint interest are taken each of them to have that
interest.[7] It is immaterial that the shares, ie the precise shares, in which a person
has an interest are unidentifiable.[8]

Regulations[9] made under section 201A[10] qualify the above provisions by
distinguishing between material and non-material interests. Material interests
must be disclosed if they represent at least 3% of the company's nominal share
capital, whereas non-material interests must be disclosed if they represent at least
10% or if the various interests of the shareholders (whether or not material) when
aggregated are at least 10%.

12.9.4 *Sanctions to enforce notification of interests*

If a person authorises an agent to acquire or dispose of interests in shares
comprised in the relevant share capital of a public company, he must secure that
the agent notifies him immediately of acquisitions and disposals which may give

---

1   Section 208(4)(a).
2   Section 208(6).
3   Including class meetings or adjourned meetings: section 209(2).
4   Section 209(2).
5   Section 208(5)(a).
6   Section 208(5)(b). Here 'interest' will have the meaning indicated by the other provisions of
     section 208.
7   Section 208(7).
8   Section 208(8).
9   SI 1993/1819 and SI 1993/2089.
10   Inserted by section 134(5) of the 1989 Act. This section gives wide powers to amend the
     provisions for certain stated purposes.

rise to an obligation of disclosure under Part VI.[1] A notification of disclosure is not adequate unless it identifies the person obliged to give it and his address, and if the person notifying is a director of the company, states that the notice is given in fulfilment of the obligation.[2] An offence is committed by a person who:[3]

(1) fails to fulfil an obligation of disclosure under Part VI;
(2) gives a notification containing a false statement made knowingly or recklessly;
(3) fails to give a notification to other parties to an 'acquisition agreement' within the time allowed under section 206; or
(4) fails to comply, without reasonable excuse, with section 210(1).

However, it is a defence to a charge under (3) that it has not been possible to give the notification, or that the notification was given as soon as it became possible to do so.[4] If a person is convicted of any of the above offences (other than failing to give notification of ceasing to be interested in shares), the Secretary of State may impose restrictions under Part XV[5] (restrictions on transfer, voting, payment of dividends and issue of further shares) on the shares in respect of which the offence was committed.[6]

12.9.5 The register of interests in shares

A public company must keep a register in which it must record contents of notifications received by it under sections 198 to 202 in chronological order within three days after receipt of notifications, and where notification is that any person has ceased to be a party to an acquisition agreement within section 204, the company must record that fact against the name of the person concerned in every place in the register where his name appears as a party to the agreement.[7] The company is not affected by notice of any matter or put on inquiry as to rights of any person by reason of anything done for purposes of keeping the register.[8] Unless the register is in the form of an index, an index of names entered in the register must be kept by the company.[9] If a public company is converted into a private company, it must keep the register kept by it under section 211 for a further six years.[10] The register and index must be kept at the same place as its register of directors' interests in shares and debentures is kept and must be available for

---

1   Section 210(1). As to the liability of the directors and officers where bodies corporate commit offences under section 210, see section 733. Members who manage a body corporate's affairs may also be liable under section 733.

2   Section 210(2).

3   Section 210(3) and (4). As to the power to prosecute, see section 732.

4   Section 210(4). The accused must show that it was not possible for him to give the notice required by section 206 within the proper time period, and either: (a) that it has not since become possible for him to give the notice so required; or (b) that he gave the notice as soon after the end of that period as it became possible for him to do so.

5   Section 210(5).

6   These provisions apply notwithstanding any provisions in the articles or memorandum imposing a similar restriction. Increasing concern about nominee shareholdings may lead to more drastic sanctions, particularly automatic disenfranchisement, if interests are not notified.

7   Section 211(1)–(3).

8   Section 211(4).

9   Section 211(6).

10   Section 211(7).

inspection by members and others.[1] The register and index shall not be open to inspection in respect of information about a company's interests in shares of a public company which need not be disclosed in the shareholding companies' annual accounts.[2]

12.9.6 'Acquistion agreements'

Sections 204 to 206 make provision for the notification of 'group interests of persons acting together'. For brevity such agreements are hereafter referred to as 'acquisition agreements'. Section 204 is the statutory equivalent of the City Code rules[3] in respect of 'concert parties' in the context of a takeover bid. These provisions are intended to provide some sanction against the practice of 'warehousing' and the more recent development of 'dawn raids' as a method of takeover, or a preliminary to a takeover bid.

Section 204 applies to an agreement between two or more persons which includes provisions for the acquisition, by any one of more of them, of interests in shares in a particular company (the target company)[4] where the following conditions are met. To be caught, the acquisition agreement must include provisions imposing obligations or restrictions on any one or more parties to it with respect to their use, retention or disposal of interests in that company's shares acquired in pursuance of the agreement,[5] and any interests in that company's shares must *in fact* be acquired by any of the parties in pursuance of the acquisition agreement. The reference to 'the use of interests in shares in the target company' is to the exercise of any rights or of any control or influence arising from those interests. This includes the right to enter into any agreement[6] for the exercise, or for control of the exercise, of any of those rights by any other persons.[7] Once any interest in shares in the target company has been acquired in pursuance of an acquisition agreement, section 204 will still apply despite certain changes in the parties to, or term of, the agreement. Likewise, the section will continue to apply 'whether or not any further acquisitions of interests in that company's shares take place in pursuance of the agreement'.[8] Furthermore, references to 'the agreement' include any agreement having effect (whether directly or indirectly) in substitution for the original agreement.

This is the first of a number of subsections to section 204 containing 'catch-all' provisions designed to defeat the common legal techniques of statutory evasion.

---

1   See section 211(8) and section 219 as to the inspection of the register 'during business hours' by members and other persons and their right to obtain copies. See **12.9.10**.
2   Section 211(9). The exemption referred to is conferred by paras 3 and 10 of Schedule 5 (exemption of a company from requirement to disclose in its accounts particulars of substantial shareholdings in subsidiaries or other bodies corporate incorporated or carrying on business outside the United Kingdom in circumstances where disclosure would be harmful to business), ibid.
3   See **19.6**.
4   In relation to acquisition agreements, references to 'target company' elsewhere in sections 205 or 206 arc to the company which is the target company for that agreement in accordance with section 204(1) and (2).
5   Whether or not together with any other interests of theirs in that company's shares to which the agreement relates.
6   Eg an option agreement giving the right referred to in section 204(2). But such an 'agreement' need not necessarily be a legally binding contract. See section 204(5) and (6).
7   Section 204(3).
8   Section 204(4). 'So long as the agreement continues to include provisions of any description mentioned in section 204(2)(a).'

Their far-reaching character may in practice place difficult evidential burdens upon the prosecution. Thus, by section 204(5), references in section 204 (and elsewhere in Part VI) to the term 'agreement' include any agreement or arrangement. The reference in section 204 to the 'provisions' of an agreement accordingly includes 'undertakings, expectations or understandings operative under any arrangement'. The term 'provision' extends to 'any provisions whether express or implied and whether absolute or not'. However, section 204 'does not apply to an agreement which is not legally binding unless it involves mutuality in the undertakings, expectations or understanding of the parties to it'.[1]

One consequence of section 204 applying to an acquisition agreement is that each party to such an agreement shall be taken to be interested in all the shares in the target company in which any other party to the agreement is interested *apart* from the agreement. This is so whether or not the interest of the other party in question was acquired, or includes, any interest which was acquired, in pursuance of the agreement.[2]

Thus a reporting shareholder must notify the company not only as to his own interests (under the agreement or otherwise), but also as to all the interests of other parties to the agreement. This may include interests (in shares in the same target company) arising under separate agreements to which other parties to the agreement are party.[3]

Section 205(4) defines the contents of the notification of interests required by Part VI as this applies to acquisition agreements. Any notification must state that the person making the notification[4] is a party to an agreement to which this section applies. It must indicate the name and (so far as known) the addresses of the other parties to the agreement, 'identifying them as such'. It must also state whether or not any of the shares to which the notification relates are shares in which he is interested by virtue of section 204 and, if so, the number of those shares.[5]

It should be noted that section 204 does not apply to any agreement to underwrite or sub-underwrite any offer of shares (not just public issues) so long as the agreement is confined to that purpose and matters incidental to it.[6]

12.9.7 'Persons acting together' to keep each other informed

Section 206 imposes an obligation 'on persons acting together' (ie parties to an acquisition agreement within section 204) to keep each other informed of relevant particulars of their interests (if any) apart from the agreement, in shares comprised in the 'relevant share capital'[7] of the 'target company'. This obligation arises only when the target company is a public company, and the

---

1   Section 204(6).
2   Section 205(1).
3   See section 205(2) as to the meaning of 'an interest apart from that agreement'.
4   The Department of Trade and Industry seems to envisage that a single notification could be made by the member of a section 204 'acquisition agreement' as agent for all its members: Department of Trade consultative document, May 1981, *The Disclosure of Interests in Shares*, Annex B, Clause E.
5   If a person ceases to be interested in shares because he or another person ceases to be a party to the agreement, the notifications must where appropriate give particulars of that person and the fact that he has ceased to be a party: section 205(5).
6   Section 204(6).
7   See **12.9**.

shares in that company to which the agreement relates consist of, or include, shares comprised in relevant share capital of that company. The person liable to the obligation[1] imposed by section 206 must know the facts which make the agreement one to which section 204 applies, the status of the target company and the type of share capital affected.

The 'relevant particulars' that must be notified in writing[2] are: (a) the number of shares (if any) comprised in the relevant share capital in which he would be required to state his interest if he were under an obligation of disclosure with respect to his interest in those shares, apart from the agreement immediately after the time when the obligation to give notice under section 206(2) arose; and (b) the relevant particulars with respect to the registered ownership of those shares,[3] so far as it is known to him at the date of the notice.

A person for the time being subject to section 206 is also under an obligation to notify in writing each party to the agreement of relevant particular,[4] and of changes therein, of which he becomes aware at any time after any 'interest notification date',[5] and before the first occasion following that date on which he becomes subject to any further obligations to give notice under section 206(2) with respect to his interest in shares comprised in that share capital.[6]

Anyone who is a party to a section 204 acquisition agreement is under an obligation to notify each other party to the agreement, in writing, of his current address. He must do this on first becoming subject to the requirements of section 206, and on any change of address while he is still subject to those requirements.[7]

12.9.8 The investigation by a company of interests in its shares

Section 212 gives a public company the power to require information with respect to interests in its voting shares. Such a company may by notice in writing require any person whom the company knows, or has reasonable cause to believe, to be interested in shares comprised in 'relevant share capital'[8] of that company to confirm the fact or (as the case may be) to indicate whether or not it is the case. The company has the like power where it knows, or has reasonable cause to believe, that a person has been interested in shares at any time during the three years immediately preceding the date on which the notice was issued. The notice may also require, where the person holds (or has held during the three-year

---

1   An obligation to give notice imposed by section 206 must be performed within two days 'next following the day on which the obligation arises': section 206(8) (as amended by section 134(3) of the Companies Act 1989).

2   This must be done '(a) on his first becoming subject to the requirements [of section 206], and (b) on each occurrence after that time, while he is still subject to those requirements, of any event or circumstances within section 198(1) as it applies to his case otherwise than by reference to interests treated as his under section 205 as it applies to that agreement': section 206(2).

3   This has the same meaning as in section 203(3)(a) and (b): section 206(7).

4   Ie with respect to the registered ownership of any shares comprised in relevant share capital of the target company in which he is interested apart from the agreement, and changes in these particulars: section 208(4).

5   See section 206(5) as to the meaning of 'interest notification date' for the purpose of section 206(4).

6   Section 206(4).

7   Section 206(6).

8   See **12.9** as to the meaning of 'relevant share capital' for Part VI; see sections 198(2) and 220(1).

period) any interest in shares (in relevant share capital), the further information specified in section 212(2).

(1) He must give particulars of his own past or present interest in shares, comprised in relevant share capital of the company, held by him at any time during the three-year period referred to above.

(2) Where his interest is a present interest, and any other interest in the shares subsists, or, in any case, where another interest in the shares subsisted during that three-year period at any time when his own interest subsisted, he must give (so far as lies within his knowledge) such particulars with respect to that other interest as may be required by the notice.

(3) Where his interest is a past interest, he must give (so far as lies within his knowledge) particulars of the identity of the person who held the interest immediately upon his ceasing to hold it.

The particulars required by section 212(2) include particulars of the identity of persons interested in the shares in question. They also include whether persons interested in the same shares are, or were, parties to a section 205 'acquistion agreement', or to any agreement or arrangement relating to the exercise of any rights conferred by the holding of shares.[1]

A recipient of a notice under section 212 must provide the information requested in writing, and within such reasonable time as may be specified in the notice.[2] The question of what is meant by 'reasonable time' in a notice served under section 212(4) was explored by Vinelott J in *Re Lonrho plc*[3] in which he came to the conclusion that where such a notice is served on a person outside the United Kingdom, two clear working days should be allowed. The same concept of 'interest in shares' and 'persons interested in shares' applies to section 212 as it does to sections 198 to 201.[4] Thus section 203 (family and corporate interests)[5] and section 205[6] (group interests of persons acting together) apply, as do the general rules about 'interests to be notified' laid down in section 208.[7] However, the effect of section 209 (interests to be disregarded) is excluded for the purpose of section 212.

Section 212 also applies to a person 'who has or previously had, or was entitled to acquire, a right to subscribe for shares in a public company which would on issue be comprised in relevant share capital of that company'. References to 'interests in shares' in section 212 are to be construed accordingly.[8]

Section 214 allows a certain fraction of the members of a public company a right of requisition so as to enforce the powers conferred on the company under section 212. A company may be required to exercise its powers under section 212 on the requisition of members of the company holding, at the date of the deposit of the

---

1   Section 212(3).
2   Section 212(4).
3   [1989] BCLC 315.
4   But not the 3% requirement.
5   See **12.9.3**.
6   See **12.9.6**.
7   See **12.9.3**.
8   Section 212(6).

requisition, not less than one-tenth of such of the paid-up capital of the company as carries at that date the right of voting at general meetings of the company.[1]

The requisition must state that the requisitionists are requiring the company to exercise its powers under section 212, and must specify the manner in which they require those powers to be exercised. They must also give 'reasonable grounds' for requiring the company to exercise those powers in the manner specified.[2] Who is to determine (short of litigation) whether the grounds are 'reasonable' (in the event of dispute between the company and the requisitionists) is not made clear. A requisition must be signed by the requisitionists and deposited at the registered office of the company. However, it may consist of several documents 'in the form each signed by one or more of the requisitionists'.[3]

On the deposit of a requisition complying with these requirements, it then becomes the duty of the company to exercise its powers under section 212 in the manner specified in the requistion.[4] Seemingly the company can argue that the grounds given are not reasonable and this affects the validity of the requisition (see above). On the conclusion of an investigation by the company, in consequence of a requisition under section 214, it is 'the duty of the company to cause a report of the information received in pursuance of that investigation to be prepared'. This report must be available at the company's registered office within a reasonable period after the conclusion of the investigation.[5]

By section 213, a public company (to which section 212 applies) must include information obtained as a result of an enquiry under section 212 in a separate part of the register of interests in shares it must keep under section 211.[6] The company may not enter on the register information acquired about the ownership of its shares other than under section 212.[7]

Section 216 provides sanctions for the failure to provide information under section 212. If a person who is or was interested in shares of a public company fails to give the information required in response to a notice served on him by the company (under section 212), then the company may apply to the court for an order imposing restrictions on the shares (to which the notice relates) under Part XV.[8] The company is entitled to its costs on an application for a 'freezing' order

---

1   Section 214(1).
2   Section 214(2).
3   Section 214(3).
4   Section 212(4).
5   Section 215(1). Section 215 makes further provision for interim reports where the investigation takes more than three months (section 215(2)); for the period of making the report available (section 215(3)); for exempting substantial holdings in bodies incorporated, etc, outside the United Kingdom (section 215(4)); and for informing the requisitionists of the availability of the report (section 215(5)). Further provision is made as to when an investigation is to be regarded as concluded (section 215(6)); as to where reports prepared under section 215 are to be kept (section 215(7)), and for sanctions in the event of default in complying with section 215; section 215(8).
6   Section 211(3) to (10) applies correspondingly to information so recorded: section 213(3). See also the definition of 'register of interests in shares' in section 220(1).
7   *Re TR Technology Investment Trust plc* [1988] BCLC 256.
8   Section 216(1). See also *House of Fraser, Petitioners* [1983] SLT 500. As to the provisions of section 454 (giving a power to impose restrictions on transfer, voting rights, payment of dividends and issue of further shares) see **17.29**. See also *Gore-Browne on Companies* 44th edn (Jordans, loose-leaf), note 7 to 20.24.

under section 216. The costs will be paid by those who have failed to do their best to provide the information.[1]

Such an order may be made notwithstanding any power in the articles or memorandum to make similar restrictions.[2] A person who fails to comply with a notice under section 212, or who knowingly or recklessly makes statements false in a material particular in response to such a notice, is guilty of an offence. However, it is a defence to a charge of failure to comply with a notice under section 212 that the requirement was frivolous or vexatious.[3] The Secretary of State may (after consultation with the Governor of the Bank of England) exempt a person from complying with notices under section 212. However, he must be satisfied that, having regard to the undertaking given by that person with respect to the shares held or to be held by him, there are special reasons why that person should not be subject to section 212. A person fails to give information under section 216 if he fails to give a full and truthful answer to a section 212 enquiry.[4]

12.9.9   *Removal of entries from the register*

Section 217 makes provisions for the removal of certain entries from the register of interests in shares.[5] The company may remove an entry in the register after more than six years have elapsed since the entry was made if the entry in question either: (a) related to a person ceasing to be interested in shares; or (b) has been superseded by a later entry against the same person's name.

Where anyone, 'in pursuance of an obligation imposed upon him by any provision' of Part VI, notifies the company that another person is interested in shares, the company must, within 15 days of the date on which it was given the information, notify that person and give him particulars of the entry made in the register in consequence of the information given to the company. He must also be informed of his right to apply to have the entry removed (ie if it is incorrect) in accordance with the provisions of section 217 (discussed immediately below).[6] A person thus notified may apply to the company for the removal of the entry relating to him. The company must then remove such an entry it satisfied that it is incorrect.[7] Where a person, shown in the register of interests in shares as being a party to a section 204 acquisition agreement,[8] ceases to be such a party, he may apply to the company in writing for the inclusion of that information in the register.[9] The company, if satisfied that he has ceased to be a party to the agreement, must record that information, if it has not already done so, 'at every place where his name appears as a party to that agreement in the register'. If a company refuses an application, made under section 217(3) or (4), the applicant

---

1   *Re The Bestwood plc* (1989) 5 BCC 620.
2   Section 216(2).
3   Section 216(4). Where a body corporate is guilty of an offence under section 216(3), directors, managers and other officers involved may incur liability (as may members where they manage the company's affairs): section 733(2) and (3).
4   *Re TR Technology Investment Trust plc* [1988] BCLC 256. See further, *Gore-Browne on Companies* 44th edn (Jordans, loose-leaf) at 20.24.
5   As to the register of interests in shares kept in accordance with section 211, see **12.9.5**.
6   Section 217(2).
7   Section 217(3).
8   See **12.9.6**.
9   Section 217(4).

may apply to the court for the appropriate order.[1] The court may if it thinks fit make such an order.[2]

Entries in the register of interests in shares, kept under section 211, may not be deleted except in accordance with the provision of section 217 (set out above).[3] An entry deleted in contravention of this provision must be restored as soon as reasonably practicable. Sanctions are provided for default in compliance with sections 217 and 218.[4]

12.9.10 *Inspection of the register and of reports*

Section 219 regulates the right of inspection afforded both in respect of the register of interests in shares kept by virtue of section 211 and of any reports by the company under section 215. Both the register and reports (if any) must be available for inspection without charge by members of the company and other persons.[5] Any person may require the company to provide a copy of the register and any reports (or a part of them) on payment of the prescribed fee.[6] If either an inspection or the provision of copy required is refused, a court order may be obtained requiring the company to comply.[7]

---

1   Ie for an order directing the company to remove the entry in question from the register or (as the case may be) to include the information in question in the register.
2   Where names are removed from the register by the company or under court order, the company must alter the 'associated index' within 14 days: section 217(6).
3   Section 218.
4   See sections 217(7) and 218(3).
5   Section 219(1). As to the detailed rights of inspection, see the Companies (Inspection and Copying of Registers, Indices and Documents) Regulations 1991, SI 1991/1998.
6   Section 219(2). The fee is prescribed in the 1991 Regulations.
7   For the criminal sanction for refusal of inspection or the right to obtain copies, see section 219(3).

Chapter 13

Shareholders' Meetings

13.1 Introduction

This chapter is concerned with what is sometimes called the 'machinery of corporate democracy' – ie the legislation and case-law which regulates the summoning and conduct of meetings (including voting, proxies and quorums). There is a certain artificiality about the way this machinery works in respect of the modern company, even if it worked well enough in the world of Victorian shareholders and their companies.

In the case of small private companies (by far the most numerous type of company) the formal rules about holding shareholders' meetings (and directors' meetings) wear an awkward air of unreality. A handful of 'corporate partners' (ie shareholders/directors) will tend to meet perhaps every day just to run the company's business. In practice, they may often forget the formalities of shareholders' and directors' meetings and may be unsure which corporate 'hat' they are wearing on any particular occasion. To some extent modern company law (in the Companies Act 1985, in Table A and in the case-law) recognises this problem. The provisions allowing waiver of notice, and permitting resolutions to be passed by circulating for signature a document so as to avoid the need for a meeting, go some way in this direction, as does the case-law on 'informal agreements'.[1] More important in this respect are the provisions of the Companies Act 1989 which provided for the de-regulation of private companies (see **13.4**).[2] However, company law nowhere approaches the ease and informality of partnership law in respect of the conduct of internal affairs by partners.

In the case of large public companies, the law of meetings, voting, etc, operates in a somewhat unreal context of a different order from that affecting small private companies. Of course, shareholders' meetings will be summoned and conducted, and votes counted, with scrupulous regard for what the law requires. The problem is that such public company meetings are extremely poorly attended (even where every effort is made to encourage good attendance). Although there may be thousands (or hundreds of thousands) of shareholders, research has shown that about one in a thousand bothers to attend.[3] This stems in part from the obvious trouble and time involved in travelling to company meetings, where individual shareholders have a small interest at stake.

---

1   See **13.2** and **13.3**.
2   These changes followed debate concerning the requirements and their effect on small firms. See eg Gower, *A New Form of Incorporation for Small Firms*, (1981) Cmnd 8171: a consultative document, *A Code for Incorporated Firms*, Annexe A (Department of Trade and Industry); and an Institute of Directors' paper, 'The Deregulation of Small Companies', December 1986.
3   See Midgley, 114 Lloyds Bank Review 24 (1974). Even where a company has well-advertised problems and stormy shareholders' meetings, the average attendance only rises to 1%. See further Midgley, *Companies and Their Shareholders: The Uneasy Relationship* (The Institute of Chartered Secretaries and Administrators, 1975); Butcher, 'Reform of the General Meetings' in Sheikh and Rees, *Corporate Governance and Corporate Control* 2nd edn (Cavendish, 2000).

The use of what is called the 'proxy voting machinery' by the board of directors ensures that where an issue is contested at a company meeting (and the vote goes beyond a show of hands to a poll),[1] the board is extremely likely to win. This stems from the power of the board to 'solicit proxies'[2] at the company's expense. The evidence of experience is that the vast number of individual shareholders, who do not attend company meetings, either return a proxy vote in favour of the board's proposal (or counter proposal) or remain passive. It is true that the growth of 'institutional shareholders' (pension funds, unit trusts, etc) has in recent decades tended to redress the balance somewhat.[3] However, as was pointed out in **12.1**, it is not the usual practice of institutional shareholders to contest issues at company meetings. It is much more common for a prestigious institution to raise a matter 'behind the scenes' by approaching the chairman of the board (or other senior executive) directly. This may be done either by a number of institutional investors individually, or through various shareholder protection committees to which they belong.[4] This can sometimes be quite successful in rectifying the abuses or inadequacies of management, or in preventing what are thought to be undesirable initiatives by the board.

It must be conceded that the unstated threat behind such pressure by the institutions obviously comes from the proportion of voting shares held by them. This can be used to override the de facto control exercised by the boards of most large public companies. Thus, at the end of the day, the 'machinery of corporate democracy' has a vital role to play but rather through the implied threat it presents than in its actual use.[5]

13.2 Informal agreement

It is well established that if all the shareholders are present at a meeting and unanimously give their assent to a proposal, it does not matter that no formal resolution was put to the vote.[6] Likewise, any requirements as to the length of notice for a meeting (or for a resolution thereat), whether imposed by the

---

1 See **13.19**.

2 See **13.20.1**.

3 About two-thirds of the shares in listed companies are now owned by institutional investors. The Hampel *Report on Corporate Governance* states that about 60% of the shares in listed companies are owned by United Kingdom institutional investors, and about 20% are owned by overseas institutions: Hampel *Report on Corporate Governance* (Gee, 1998) paragraph 5.1. The figures are not consistent but what can be said with confidence is that institutional investors are in the majority. The Hampel Report indicated figures as high as 80%: Hampel Committee, (1998) *Combined Code on Corporate Governance and Report*, London, Gee, paragraph 5.1, at p 40. Davies estimates around 60%: Davies (2003) *Gower and Davies' Principles of Modern Company Law*, 7th edn, (London, Sweet & Maxwell), at p 338. The Myners Report suggests that in 1999 the institutional investors held 51.9%: Paul Myners, *Institutional Investment in the UK: A Review* (HM Treasury, April 2001), at p 27.

4 See the Wilson Committee, Cmnd 7937, Chapter 19 at paragraphs 909–913. The institutions each have their own Investment Protection Committee as well as the collective body for all types of institution – the Institutional Shareholders' Committee.

5 See also the discussion in **12.1**.

6 *Re Express Engineering Works* [1920] 1 Ch 466 (CA). Here the meeting consisted of directors who were also all the shareholders. See also *Baroness Wenlock v River Dee Company* (1883) 36 ChD 675n at 681. This has been applied to unanimous agreement to vary a provision in the articles: *Cane v Jones* [1980] 1 WLR 1451, and to a reduction of capital: *Re Barry Artist plc* [1985] BCLC 283 (although only here 'with great reluctance' and with a warning that this procedure would not be accepted in future reductions).

Companies Act 1985 or by the articles, may be waived by the consent of all the members of a company.[1] It would also appear that, if all the shareholders have given their consent to a proposal, it is not necessary that they should have held a meeting. Although in *Re George Newman Ltd*[2] the Court of Appeal held that 'for the purpose of binding a company in its corporate capacity individual assents given separately are not equivalent to the assent of a meeting',[3] more recent decisions have come to a different conclusion. In two cases the members of a company were held to have informally ratified acts by directors beyond their powers even though no shareholders' meeting had been held. In *Parker and Cooper v Reading*,[4] it was held that all the members had informally ratified a debenture granted by the directors even though no meeting had been held. In *Re Duomatic Ltd*,[5] directors' salaries had been paid without the authority of a shareholders' resolution. It was held by Buckley J that the agreement of the two directors who held all the voting shares, even though they had not constituted themselves as a shareholders' meeting, amounted to an informal ratification of the payment of unauthorised salaries. This decision also establishes that all that is required is the unanimous assent of the shareholders with the right to vote.[6] It is of course only in small private companies that the informal agreement of all the shareholders is likely to occur.[7] In *Cane v Jones*,[8] it was held that by unanimous agreement the members might without passing a special resolution alter the articles so that the chairman should no longer have the casting vote. Such an agreement will be registrable under section 380 of the Companies Act 1985.[9] In *Atlas Europe Ltd v Wright*,[10] the Court of Appeal applied the principle in recognising the approval of a director's service contract under section 318. The principle will also apply to a requirement of consent of a class of shareholders[11] and in respect of provisions in a shareholders' agreement and will therefore allow unanimous agreement to abrogate procedural requirements therein.[12] However, it cannot be effective to

---

1   *Re Oxted Motor Co* [1921] 3 KB 32. There is also provision in section 369(4) permitting notice to be waived by 95 per cent in value of the shares carrying a right to vote at the meeting (or if the company has no share capital 95 per cent of the total voting rights): section 369(3) requires unanimous consent in the case of twenty-one days' notice for an annual general meeting. See **13.10.1**.

2   [1895] 1 Ch 674 (CA). A possible explanation of this decision is that it concerned acts beyond the powers of the company.

3   Ibid, at 686, *per* Lord Lindley, who noted, however, that such assents would preclude those who had given them from complaining of what had been sanctioned.

4   [1926] Ch 975.

5   [1969] 2 Ch 365.

6   In *Re Duomatic Ltd* [1969] 2 Ch 365, the company had a share capital of 100 £1 ordinary shares and 80,000 £1 non-voting preference shares. The shareholder who held all the preference shares had not been consulted. But a different conclusion was reached as to disclosure to 'members' for the purposes of section 312. See also *Souter of Stirling (Sports Turf) v The Monument Golf Club Ltd* 1996 GWD 736.

7   See *Attorney-General for Canada v Standard Trust Co* [1911] AC 498 (PC); *Re Innes & Co* [1903] 2 Ch 254 (CA). These cases suggest that as a matter of legal principle the rule as to the effect of unanimous consent is confined to such companies. *Sed quaere.*

8   [1980] 1 WLR 1451.

9   See **13.19**.

10   [1999] BCC 163. See **16.15**. Cf *Demite Ltd v Protec Health Ltd* [1998] BCC 638, where it was doubted whether the principle applied to approval under section 320, although a different view was taken in *Re Conegrade Ltd*, [2002] EWHC 2411, [2003] BPIR 358, ChD (see **16.16**).

11   *Re Torvale Group Ltd* [1999] 2 BCLC 605.

12   *Euro Brokers Holdings Ltd v Monecor (London) Ltd* [2003] EWCA Civ 105, [2003] 1 BCLC 506.

validate something that a general meeting itself cannot do, such as a purported ratification of a director's breach of duty that is not ratifiable even with the consent of all shareholders.[1]

A single person cannot normally constitute a general[2] meeting[3] – a rule may have considerable importance now that a company may consist of only two persons, of whom one may be absent or ill – except that, where the court makes an order under section 371 for a meeting to be held,[4] or the Department of Trade and Industry calls or directs the calling of a general meeting under section 367,[5] it may direct that one member present in person or by proxy shall be deemed to constitute a meeting.[6] This problem has, however, been effectively solved by the Companies (Single Member Private Limited Companies) Regulations 1992.[7]

13.3 Resolutions in writing signed by all members

The articles of association usually provide for written resolutions signed by all members to be as valid and effective as if they had been passed at a general meeting. The standard model, applicable to all companies limited by shares, is article 53 of Table A to the Companies Act 1985.[8]

> A resolution in writing executed by or on behalf of each member who would have been entitled to vote upon it if it had been proposed at a general meeting at which he was present shall be as effectual as if it had been passed at a general meeting duly convened and held and may consist of several instruments in the like form each executed by or on behalf of one or more members.

13.4 De-regulation of private companies

Sections 113–117 of the Companies Act 1989[9] provide for the de-regulation of private companies, and were intended to simplify company procedures in respect of small private companies where unanimous consent can be obtained for a particular proposal without the necessity for a general meeting (the written resolution procedure) or where such consent can be obtained to disapply a Companies Act requirement for a particular type of resolution (the elective resolution procedure).

---

1 *Bowthorpe Holdings Ltd v Hills* [2002] EWHC 2331 (Ch), [2003] 1 BCLC 226; as to ratification in this context, see further **16.24.2**.
2 *Secus* as regards class meetings: see *East v Bennett Brothers* [1911] 1 Ch 163.
3 *Sharp v Dawes* (1876) 2 QBD 26 (CA); *Re Sanitary Carbon Co* [1877] WN 233; *Prain & Sons* 1947 SC 325; *Re London Flats* [1969] 1 WLR 711.
4 See **13.5**.
5 Ibid.
6 See *Re El Sombrero Ltd* [1958] Ch 900. A private company with one member is catered for by statute; see **13.22**.
7 SI 1992/1699.
8 A similar provision appeared (though with the addition of words making it subject to the Companies Acts) in the 1948 Act Table A. Originally it was article 5 in Part II of Table A (and thus applicable automatically only to private companies). Following the Companies Act 1980, which abolished Part II, it became article 73A and applicable to all companies adopting it.
9 Inspired by a report by the Institute of Directors: *De-regulation for small private companies*, November 1986.

13.4.1 *Written resolutions of private companies*

The purpose of Section 113 of the Companies Act 1989 (which inserted new sections 381A, 381B and 382A into the Companies Act 1985) is to allow more effective and widespread use by small private companies of written resolutions so as to avoid company meetings. The statutory power has a more extensive scope than the provisions in article 53 of Table A. Section 381A allows the replacement not only of ordinary resolutions in general meetings, and resolutions in class meetings, but also special and extraordinary resolutions.[1] It also extends to an 'elective resolution'[2] by a private company to apply the 'elective' regime described in **13.4.6**.

The written resolution procedure will apply even in those cases where the existing provisions in the Companies Act 1985 insist on a special resolution passed at a shareholders' meeting.[3] However, provisions such as article 53 of Table A remain an alternative to the statutory procedure,[4] and the common-law rule as to informal unanimous consent is also preserved.[5]

13.4.2 *The procedure*

This requires 'without a meeting and without any previous notice', a 'resolution in writing by or on behalf of all the members of the company who at the date of the resolution would be entitled to attend and vote at such meeting'.[6] The signatures need not be in a single document so long as each signature is on a document which accurately states the terms of the resolution.[7] The date of the resolution is deemed to be the date when the resolution is signed by or on behalf of the last member.[8] This date will in general be regarded as 'the date of the passing of the resolution', but this is subject to the provisions of section 381B which defines the rights of auditors in relation to written resolutions.[9]

13.4.3 *Rights of auditors*

Section 381B[10] imposes a duty on the directors and secretary of a company to send to the company's auditors a copy, or otherwise inform them of the contents, of any written resolution proposed under section 381A at or before the time that resolution is supplied to a member for signature. Breach of this statutory duty is a criminal offence but does not affect the validity of any resolution passed under section 381A. In any criminal proceedings under section 381B(3), the accused will

---

1   See section 381A(4) and (6).
2   See section 379A.
3   Eg section 4 (alteration of the memorandum) or section 135 (reduction of capital). As to the
     necessity of a special resolution under the old law, see *Re Barry Artists Ltd* [1985] BCLC 283.
4   Section 381C(1), as inserted by the Deregulation (Resolutions of Private Companies) Order
     1996, SI 1996/1471. The earlier version of section 381C(1) was ambiguous in this respect.
     Proceeding under such an article removes the need to inform the auditors (see **13.4.3**).
5   Section 381C(2).
6   Section 381A(1).
7   Section 381A(2).
8   Section 381A(3).
9   See section 381A(5) and section 381B.
10   As inserted by the Deregulation (Resolutions of Private Companies) Order 1996,
     SI 1996/1471. The previous version of section 381B was ambiguous with regard to whether or
     not, taken together with the original section 381C(1), it applied to written resolutions
     effected under a provision in the articles rather than under the statutory provisions. It is now
     clear that section 381B applies only to the statutory procedure.

have available the following defences: (a) that the circumstances were such that it was not practicable for him to comply with section 381B; or (b) that he believed on reasonable grounds that a copy of the resolution had been sent to the auditors or that they had otherwise been informed of its contents.

13.4.4 Minuting written resolutions

Section 382A makes provision for recording written resolutions. The company must cause a record of the resolution (and of the signatures) to be entered into a book in the same way as minutes of a general meeting of the company. Such a record, if purporting to be signed by a director or secretary, is 'evidence of the proceedings in agreeing the resolution'. Where a record is made in accordance with section 382A then, until the contrary is proved, the requirements of the Act with respect to the proceedings are deemed to be complied with.[1]

Section 382B applies to private companies limited by shares or by guarantee which have only one member.[2] Where such a member takes a decision 'which may be taken by the company in general meeting[3] and which has effect as if agreed by the company in general meeting' he must[3] provide the company with a written record of that decision. A criminal sanction[4] is provided for failure to comply, but this does not affect the validity of the decision taken by the single member.[5]

13.4.5 Additional requirements for particular types of written resolution

The procedure set out in section 381A for written resolutions is specifically subject to Schedule 15A.[6] Part I of the Schedule bars the use of a written resolution altogether in two cases. These are a resolution under section 303 (removing a director before the expiration of his office) and a resolution under section 391 (removing an auditor before the expiration of his terms of office). In these cases, the person to be removed has a right to speak in his own defence at the meeting to consider the resolution, making the written resolution procedure inappropriate. Part II of the Schedule deals with resolutions (mostly concerning share capital) that are for a particular statutory purpose which has a specific statutory requirement not applicable to company resolutions generally.

Part II adapts certain procedural requirements to the written resolution procedure. This may relate to specific statements or documents to be circulated with the notice of meeting, which by virtue of Part II are to be supplied to each member 'by whom or on whose behalf the resolution is required to be signed in accordance with that section'.[7] This applies to resolutions concerned with disapplication of pre-emption rights under section 95,[8] with financial assistance

---

1   The penalties for failing to comply with section 382A are carried over from those applicable to section 382. The same applies to the right of inspection of minute books given by section 383: see section 382A(3).

2   See the Companies (Single Member Private Limited Companies) Regulations 1992, SI 1992/1699, Schedule, paragraph 6.

3   'Unless that decision was taken by written resolution': section 382B(1).

4   Section 382B(2), Schedule 24, as amended.

5   Section 382B(3).

6   See section 381A(7).

7   Schedule 15A, paragraph 2.

8   Schedule 15A, paragraph 3: see **7.5.1**, above.

for the purchase of a company's own shares,[1] with authority for off-market purchases, or contingent purchase contracts of a company's own shares.[2] It also applies to resolutions under section 319 (approval of a director's service contract),[3] and section 337 (funding of a director's expenditure in performing his duties).[4] In some cases, members holding shares to which the resolution relates are disqualified from voting. This has likewise been adapted to the written resolution procedure.[5]

13.4.6 The elective resolution procedure

The elective resolution procedure under section 379A of the Companies Act 1985 allows certain requirements to pass resolutions to be disapplied. The elective resolution may take the form of the written resolution procedure. The matters subject to elective resolution[6] are authority to issue shares,[7] laying accounts before a general meeting,[8] consent to short notice of meetings,[9] and the appointment of auditors.[10] The same procedure can be used by a private company to dispense with the need to hold an annual general meeting, unless a member requires one to be held. The Secretary of State has power to extend this by statutory instrument.[11] Generally speaking, the elective regime will be confined to matters of internal administration and will not impinge upon the protection of creditors or other outsiders.

13.4.7 Procedure for elective resolutions

The procedure for an elective resolution is set out in section 379A(2).[12] Such a resolution usually requires 21 days' notice in writing given of the meeting, stating that an elective resolution is to be proposed and the terms of the resolution. As a result of a recent amendment of s 379A, less than 21 days' notice may be given on a meeting at which an elective resolution is proposed, provided that all the members entitled to attend and vote at that meeting agree to short notice.[13] It must then be agreed to at the meeting, in person or by proxy, by all the members entitled to attend and vote.[14] The elective resolution may be revoked by ordinary resolution.[15] The passing or revoking of elective resolutions under section 379A

---

1   Ie under section 155 (see **7.17.3**). See Schedule 15A, paragraph 4.
2   Ie under sections 164, 165 and 167 (see **7.17.4**). See Schedule 15A, paragraph 5.
3   Schedule 15A, paragraph 7. See **16.15**.
4   Ibid, paragraph 8. See **16.17.3**.
5   Ie in respect of sections 164 and 174. See Schedule 15A, paragraphs 5 and 6.
6   Section 379A(1).
7   See **7.4**.
8   See **14.2.4**.
9   See **13.10.1**.
10 See **14.20.1**.
11 See section 117 of the Companies Act 1989. Such regulations may make different provisions for different cases. They may also amend or repeal provisions of the Companies Act 1985 and 'may provide for such provisions to have effect, where an election is made, subject to such adaptions and modifications as appropriate': section 117(2), (3).
12 Such a resolution can of course be passed as a written resolution.
13 See the Deregulation (Resolutions of Private Companies) Order 1996 SI 1996/1471.
14 Section 379A(3).
15 Section 379A(5). If a private company re-registers as a public one, an elective resolution ceases to have effect: section 389A(4).

have effect notwithstanding any contrary provision in the articles.[1] An elective resolution must be registered under section 380 within 15 days.[2]

13.5 Annual general meetings

Every company, except a private company which elects otherwise,[3] must in each year hold a general meeting as its annual general meeting in addition to any other meetings in that year, and must specify the meeting as such in the notices calling it. Not more than 15 months must elapse between the date of one annual general meeting and the next. But so long as a company holds its first annual general meeting within 18 months of its incorporation, it need not hold it in the year of its incorporation or the following year.[4]

If default is made in holding such a meeting, the Secretary of State may, on the application of any member, call or direct the calling of a general meeting, and give such ancillary or consequential directions as he thinks expedient. These may include directions modifying or supplementing[5] the operation of the company's articles, including a direction that one member present in person or by proxy shall be deemed to constitute a meeting.[6] Failure to hold a meeting in accordance with section 366 or in complying with any directions of the Department of Trade and Industry under section 367, renders the company and every officer in default liable to a fine.[7] Repeated failure to hold annual general meetings and to lay annual accounts before the members may establish unfair prejudice in a petition under section 459.[8]

A general meeting held under section 367 is (subject to any directions of the Secretary of State) deemed to be an annual general meeting, but, where a meeting so held is not held in the year in which the default in holding the company's annual general meeting occurred, such meeting is not to be treated as the annual general meeting for the year in which it is held unless at that meeting the company resolves that it shall be so treated.[9] Where a company does so resolve, a copy of the resolution must, within 15 days after its passing, be forwarded to the Registrar of Companies and recorded by him.[10]

It is customary to provide in the articles[11] that all business except such as is therein mentioned (eg declaring a dividend, considering the accounts, balance sheets, and the reports of the directors and auditors, and electing directors and

---

1   Section 379A(5).
2   Section 380(4)(bb).
3   See **13.4.6**.
4   Section 366. As to the sanctions, see section 366(4), Schedule 24.
5   '... in relation to the calling, holding and conducting of the meeting'. Where a meeting is held after the prescribed time, voting rights are determined as of the actual time of the meeting, not as they would have been if the meeting had been held at the proper time: *Musselwhite v CH Musselwhite Ltd* [1962] Ch 964.
6   Section 367(1) and (2).
7   Sections 366(4) and 367(3). As to the fines that may be exacted, see Schedule 24 to the 1985 Act.
8   *Re a Company, ex parte Shooter* [1990] BCLC 384.
9   Section 367(4).
10   For the sanctions for failure to send a copy to the Registrar, see section 367(5).
11   The 1948 Table A, Part I, article 52 so provided, but, rather curiously, there is no equivalent provision in the 1985 Table A.

appointing auditors and fixing their remuneration)[1] shall be deemed special, and that notice must be given of the general nature of all special business. Without such a provision in the articles, it seems that no business could be transacted of which previous notice had not been given,[2] and where such provisions are included, any business not specially mentioned as an exception can only be transacted if notice has been given.

13.6 Requisitioning extraordinary general meetings

In addition to annual general meetings, a company may also from time to time hold other general meetings, which are usually called extraordinary general meetings. Under all usual forms of articles only the special business of which notice has been given can be transacted. Extraordinary meetings can be convened by the directors whenever they think proper[3] and in certain circumstances may be convened by the members themselves, subject to the conditions contained in section 368 of the Companies Act 1985 which overrides any regulations of the company. By this section, the directors are bound forthwith to convene an extraordinary general meeting on the requisition of:

> ... (a) members of the company holding at the date of the deposit of the requisition not less than one-tenth of such of the paid-up capital of the company as at that date carries the right of voting at general meetings of the company, or (b) in the case of a company not having a share capital, members of the company representing not less than one-tenth of the total voting rights of all the members having at the date of deposit of the requisition a right to vote at general meetings of the company.[4]

The requisition (which may consist of several documents in like form each signed by one or more requisitionists) must state the objects of the meeting and must be signed by the requisitionists and deposited at the registered office of the company. If joint holders of shares join in the requisition all must sign, unless the articles specifically authorise one to sign for all: the signature of one on behalf of all is of no avail.[5] If the directors do not within 21 days from the date of the requisition being deposited proceed duly to convene a meeting,[6] to consider the matters

---

1   As to the special requirements when an auditor other than the retiring auditor is proposed, see **14.21.2**.

2   *Per* LittledaleJ in *R v Hill* (1825) 4 B & C 444.

3   As to the directors' duty of good faith in respect of their power to call meetings, see *Pergamon Press Ltd v Maxwell* [1970] 1 WLR 1167; *Smith v Sadler* (1997) 25 ACSR 672, SC(NSW) (annual general meeting called for a time and a place where the directors knew a particular member would be unable to attend). An extraordinary general meeting has been held not to be validly constituted where the procedure by which the applicants were admitted to membership did not comply with the articles of association: *POW Services Ltd v Clare* [1995] 2 BCLC 435.

4   If the articles allow a small number to requisition a meeting, this, being an additional power not inconsistent with the Act, will be effective.

5   *Patent Wood Keg Syndicate v Pearse* [1906] WN 164.

6   The 21-day period refers to the time by which the directors must have decided to *convene* the extraordinary general meeting. The meeting so convened need not be held within this period so long as it has been convened and this will prevent the requisitionists themselves convening a meeting: *Re Windward Islands Enterprises* [1983] BCLC 293. This decision of Nourse J allows extensive delay by the directors. It indicates a need to tighten the wording of section 368: see (1983) 4 Co Law 219. See also *McGuinness v Bremner plc* [1988] BCLC 673, Ct of Sess.

specified in the requisition,[1] the requisitionists, or any of them representing more than one-half of the voting rights of all of them, may themselves convene the meeting; but it must be held within three months from the date of the deposit of the requisition.[2] Any meeting convened by requisitionists is to be convened as nearly as possible in the same manner as that in which meetings are to be convened by directors.[3] Unreasonable and unjustifiable delay may, however, amount to 'unfair prejudice' for the purposes of section 459.[4]

A meeting requisitioned by members under section 368 cannot deal with a resolution not included in the objects for which the meeting was requisitioned. Unless the articles otherwise provide, the requisitionists will not be able to insist on any matter not in the requisition being included in the notice of meeting sent out by the company.[5]

Any reasonable expenses incurred by the requisitionists by reason of the failure of the directors duly to convene a meeting shall be repaid by the company, and the company must deduct any sum so repaid from any sums due or to become due from the company by way of fees or other remuneration in respect of their services to such of the directors as were in default.[6] For the purposes of the section directors are, in the case of a meeting at which a resolution is to be proposed as a special resolution, deemed not to have duly convened the meeting if they do not give such notice thereof as is required by section 378(2).[7]

There is no provision in the Companies Act 1985 similar to that usually inserted in articles, that at a meeting convened by requisitionists no business is to be done other than that mentioned in the requisition. However, this is perhaps implied in the provision that the requisition must state the objects of the meeting. In any case, due notice must be given of any business to be transacted.

The directors have a duty, as well as a right, to circularise the members for the purpose of advising them as to the prudence or propriety of any proposed resolution, and may use the company's money for this purpose or for procuring proxies in their own favour.[8]

If there are no directors,[9] or no special provisions in the articles to meet the case, any two or more members holding not less than one-tenth of the issued share capital or, if the company has not a share capital, not less than 5% in number of

---

1   If the directors convene a meeting to consider part only of the specified matters, the requisitionists may ignore it, and call their own meeting: *Isle of Wight Rly Co v Tahourdin* (1883) 25 ChD 320 (CA). If the requisition contains matters which, though apparently irregular, may be carried out in a lawful manner, the court will not restrain the holding of the meeting (same case).

2   The secretary cannot without the sanction of the board summon the meeting on receipt of the requisition. Whether the requisitionists can employ him to give the notice after the twenty-one days have elapsed is still an open question: *Re State of Wyoming Syndicate* [1901] 2 Ch 431.

3   Section 368(5).

4   *McGuinness v Bremmer plc* [1988] BCLC 673.

5   *Ball v Metal Industries* 1957 SC 315.

6   Section 368(6).

7   Section 368(7).

8   *Peel v London and North-Western Rly* [1907] Ch 5 (CA); *Campbell v Australian Mutual Provident Society* (1909) 77 LJPC 117; *Wilson v LMS Rly Co* [1940] Ch 393 (CA); but if invitations to appoint proxies are issued at the company's expense, they should be sent to all the members entitled to be sent a notice of the meeting and to vote thereat by proxy: section 372(6); see **13.21.1**.

9   See *Re Brick & Stone Co* [1878] WN 140, a decision under the Companies Act 1862.

the members of the company, may call a meeting.[1] The court may also order a meeting to be held if it is impracticable otherwise to call or conduct it.[2]

A minority shareholder seeking an order that an extraordinary general meeting of the company be convened under section 371 must fail if the claim cannot be brought within an exception to the rule in *Foss v Harbottle*.[3] Such a claim should be brought not by way of originating summons but in a contentious action with pleadings.[4]

Where the hearing of an unfair claim under section 459 is pending, and quorum requirements and refusal to attend meetings by a minority shareholder prevent the holding of shareholders' meetings, the court will order a meeting under section 371 so as to allow directors to be appointed and accounts to be approved.[5] However, to protect the minority shareholder until the section 459 petition is heard, restrictive provisions will be placed upon what could be done or in consequence of the meeting ordered by the court. For example, directors could not effect any alteration in the constitution or capital of the company.[6] The existence of a section 459 petition at the date of hearing of the section 371 application is a matter which bears upon the discretion of the court but does not prevent it exercising its discretionary powers under section 371.[7]

13.7 Representatives of corporate members

Only members of the company (and the auditors)[8] are, in the absence of express provisions in the articles, entitled to be present. A member cannot insist on his solicitor or other agent being allowed to accompany him, although a solicitor or other agent may be appointed proxy, as a proxy need not be a member of the company.[9] Section 375 empowers any corporation (whether a company within the meaning of the Companies Act 1985[10] or not), if it is a member of another corporation which is a company within the meaning of the Act, to authorise, by resolution of its directors or other governing body, such person as it thinks fit to act as its representative. A representative of a corporate member may attend any meeting of the company or of any class of members of the company, and, if a creditor, any meeting of any creditors of the company held in pursuance of the Act or of any rules made thereunder, or in pursuance of the provisions contained in any debenture or trust deed, as the case may be. Such person need not be a member. A person so authorised is entitled to exercise the same powers on behalf of the corporation which he represents as that corporation could exercise if it were an individual shareholder, creditor, or holder of debentures, of the other company. Such representative must be counted in estimating the quorum

---

1   Section 370(3).
2   Section 371.
3   (1843) 2 Hare 461. See Chapter 17.
4   *Re Downs Wine Bar* [1990] BCLC 839 at 842.
5   *Re Sticky Fingers Restaurant Ltd* [1992] BCLC 84.
6   Ibid at 89–90.
7   *Re Whitchurch Insurance Consultants* [1994] BCC 51 at 56. *Re Sticky Fingers* was distinguished on the ground that there the hearing of the section 459 petition was imminent: *Re Opera Photographic* [1989] 5 BCC 601 followed.
8   Section 387.
9   Section 372(1). As to the appointment and powers of proxies at general meetings, see **13.21**.
10   The word 'company', when used in the Act, is defined in section 735: 'company' means a company formed and registered under this Act or an existing company.

present.[1] If the chairman allows the vote of a person claiming to represent a company, it is no objection that no proxy has been produced if it subsequently appears that such person was duly appointed by resolution;[2] but there is no English authority[3] as to whether the chairman can insist upon evidence of the appointment before receiving the vote. Unless the articles deal with the matter, a chairman should allow a person claiming to represent a company to attend, but specially note how he votes, and require evidence subsequently of his appointment by resolution of the directors.[4]

13.8   Class meetings

Meetings of a class of shareholders will often be held in order to vary the rights of the class by extraordinary resolution. Provision for this may be made by the articles,[5] but in practice it is usually regulated by the provisions of section 125 of the Companies Act 1985.[6] If a class of shareholders consists of only one person (eg holding all the preference shares), clauses in the memorandum or articles requiring the consent of a meeting of such class may be satisfied by a resolution in writing signed by that one person.[7] Class meetings may also be summoned by order of the court under section 425.[8]

Prima facie a separate meeting of a class should be attended only by members of that class, but if, the presence of strangers being known, no objection is taken at the meeting to their presence, the members present must be taken to have assented to the meeting being so conducted.[9]

13.9   Adjourned meetings

In the absence of express directions in the articles the chairman of a general meeting can, on proper grounds, adjourn the meeting,[10] but usually the articles only give him power to do so with the consent of the meeting, in which case he cannot, by leaving the chair before the business is completed, bring the meeting to a close; if he purports to do so, the meeting may appoint another chairman and proceed with the business.[11] If the articles provide that 'the chairman, with the consent of the meeting, may adjourn', the majority cannot compel the chairman to adjourn the meeting if he thinks it ought to proceed.[12] But Table A (article 45) requires the chairman to adjourn the meeting if so directed by the meeting,

---

1   *Re Kelantan Coco Nut Estates* [1920] WN 274.
2   *Colonial Gold Reef v Free State Rand* [1914] 1 Ch 382.
3   In New Zealand, it has been held that the right to vote depends on whether a valid resolution has been passed by the appointing body, and not upon production of evidence at the meeting that this has been done: *Maori Development Corp Ltd v Power Beat International Ltd* [1995] 2 NZLR 568, HC (NZ).
4   As to the appointment of a corporate representative by a company in liquidation, the power conferred by section 375 may be exercised by the liquidator: *Hillman v Crystal Bowl Amusements* [1973] 1 WLR 162 (CA).
5   See eg article 4 in the 1948 Table A. There is no equivalent provision in the 1985 Table A because of the statutory provisions, first introduced in 1980, referred to below.
6   See **8.7** *et seq.*
7   *East v Bennett Bros* [1911] 1 Ch 163.
8   See **18.19**.
9   *Carruth v Imperial Chemical Industries* [1937] AC 707 (HL).
10   *R v D'Oyly* (1840) 12 A & E 139; *R v Wimbledon Local Board* (1882) 8 QBD 459 (CA).
11   *National Dwellings Society v Sykes* [1894] 3 Ch 159; *John v Rees* [1969] 2 WLR 1294.
12   *Salisbury Gold Mining Co v Hathorn* [1897] AC 268 (PC).

further providing (by article 51) that a poll demanded on the question of adjournment shall be taken forthwith.[1]

The Court of Appeal reviewed and clarified the legal principles governing the chairman's power to adjourn a meeting in *Byng v London Life Association Ltd*[2] in which the relevant article expressly conferred on the chairman power to adjourn but only with the consent of a quorate meeting. In any circumstances where there is a meeting at which the views of the majority cannot be validly ascertained, the chairman has a residual common-law power to adjourn.

The Court of Appeal also held that for a meeting to be validly constructed it was not necessary for all the members to be physically present in the same room. 'Overflow' rooms may be used if adequate audio-visual aids are used to allow all members to see and hear what is going on in other rooms and to communicate properly. Where, as in *Byng*, such arrangements break down, the meeting becomes incapable of transacting any business but it is not a nullity.[3] The chairman still retains his power under the articles to adjourn so long as this is properly exercised.

An adjourned meeting is merely a continuation of the original meeting,[4] and all the requirements as to the original meeting must have been complied with to make the adjourned meeting valid. In the absence of special regulations no further notice is necessary, and if any notices have to be given before 'the meeting' this will be read as being before the commencement of the original meeting.[5] The same quorum will be required as for the original meeting unless the articles otherwise provide.[6] Proxies given for the original meeting are available for an adjourned meeting; but where articles require proxies to be lodged so many hours before a meeting, they have to be lodged that number of hours before the commencement of the original meeting.[7] To avoid this, it is often provided that proxies must be lodged not less than so many hours[8] before 'the meeting or adjourned meeting', as in Table A, article 62.[9]

Section 381 provides that where a resolution is passed at an adjourned meeting of a company, or the holders of any class of shares in a company, or the directors of a company, the resolution shall for all purposes be treated as having been passed on the date on which it was in fact passed, and shall not be deemed to have been passed on any earlier date. It must be remembered, however, that the taking of a poll is not an adjournment of a meeting.[10]

---

1   As to the chairman's power to adjourn a meeting, see *Byng v London Life Association Ltd* [1989] BCLC 400, which stated that where there is a meeting at which the views of the majority cannot be validly ascertained, the chairman has a residual common-law power to adjourn.

2   [1989] BCLC 400.

3   See the judgment of Browne-Wilkinson V-C at 406 to 409.

4   *Wills v Murray* (1850), 4 Ex 843; *Scadding v Lorant* (1851) 3 HLC 418; *McLaren v Thomson* [1917] 2 Ch 261. As to the date of a resolution passed at an adjourned meeting, see section 381 described below.

5   See further, as to notice in respect of adjourned meetings, at **13.11**.

6   Table A, article 41 requires the same quorum for an adjourned meeting.

7   *McLaren v Thompson* [1917] 2 Ch 261.

8   *Spiller v Mayo (Rhodesia) Co* [1926] WN 78, and **13.21**. For some purposes the date of the original meeting may be the governing date: see *Cousins v International Brick Co* [1931] 2 Ch 90. See further, **13.21**.

9   This must not exceed 48: section 372(5).

10 As to the court's power to adjourn a meeting which it has previously ordered to be held, see *Northern Counties Securities v Jackson* [1974] 1 WLR 1133.

13.10   Notices of general meetings

Notice of all general meetings must be given to the members entitled thereto[1] in manner prescribed by the company's articles or by Table A, and also to the auditors.[2] If all the members do not attend, a company is not 'corporately assembled', so as to be able to do business, unless the meeting is held upon notice given to every member entitled thereto, and complies with the provisions of the articles as to stating the objects for which the meeting is held.[3] If the registered address of a member entitled to notice under the articles is situate in enemy territory or enemy occupied territory, or the right to receive notices is otherwise suspended by operation of law, the company can conduct its business without serving notices upon such members.[4]

A provision in the articles that the accidental omission to give notice to or the non-receipt of notice by any person entitled to receive notice shall not invalidate the proceedings (see Table A, article 39) will prevent any such omission being relied upon as a ground for questioning any resolutions or proceedings of a meeting of which a member did not receive notice. It has been held that such a provision in the articles will validate a meeting where some members did not receive notice of a meeting because their addressograph plates had been separated from the rest. This had been done because their dividend warrants had previously been returned undelivered and uncashed.[5] Presumably, this would also cover a situation where the whereabouts of a shareholder was unknown to the company (eg communications had been returned from an old address and where no later address was known). However, it has been held that an article such as article 39 of Table A will not cover a deliberate omission even if based on a mistaken belief that a member is not entitled to notice.[6] Where all the shareholders attend a meeting of which no notice or insufficient notice has been given, they can waive the informality, and pass valid resolutions.[7] A member who is in fact present and has allowed the business determined upon to be carried out for a long period cannot subsequently set up an irregularity in summoning the meeting.[8]

13.10.1   Length of notice

By section 369(1), any provision of a company's articles is void in so far as it provides for the calling of a meeting of the company (other than an adjourned meeting) by a shorter notice than:

(1) in the case of the annual general meeting, 21 days' notice in writing; and

---

1   Where restricted voting rights are conferred on a class (see **8.6**), the entitlement to receive notice of or to attend at the meeting is usually expressly made to depend on the same circumstances as the right to vote. Even if it is not, the same result may follow: *Re Mackenzie & Co* [1916] 2 Ch 450.
2   Section 387.
3   *Baillie v Oriental Telephone Co* [1915] 1 Ch 503 (CA); cf *Young v Ladies' Imperial Club* [1920] 2 KB 523.
4   *Re Anglo-International Bank* [1943] Ch 233.
5   *Re West Canadian Collieries Ltd* [1962] Ch 370. See also *Royal Mutual Benefit Society v Sharman* [1963] 1 WLR 581.
6   *Musselwhite v CH Musselwhite & Sons Ltd* [1962] Ch 964.
7   See the cases discussed at **13.2**.
8   *Re British Sugar Refining Co* (1857) 3 K & J 408.

(2) in the case of a meeting other than an annual general meeting or a meeting for the passing of a special resolution, 14 days' notice in writing in the case of a company other than an unlimited company and seven days' notice in writing in the case of an unlimited company.

By section 369(2), a meeting of the company (other than an adjourned meeting) may (unless the company's articles make some other provision not being a provision invalidated by section 369(1)) be called:

(1) in the case of the annual general meeting, by 21 days' notice in writing; and
(2) in the case of a meeting other than an annual general meeting or a meeting for the passing of a special resolution, by 14 days' notice in writing in the case of a company other than an unlimited company and by seven days' notice in writing in the case of an unlimited company.

These provisions are confirmed in article 38 of Table A, which also adds to the 21 days' notice requirement notice of a meeting to pass a resolution appointing a director, and refers to the periods being 'clear days', ie exclusive of the day of giving the notice and the day of the meeting. Article 111 requires that the notice is in writing and article 115 provides that proof that an envelope containing a notice was properly addressed, prepaid and posted is conclusive evidence that the notice was given, and that a notice is deemed to be given at the expiration of 48 hours after the envelope containing it was posted.

It has been seen that the articles may provide for giving longer notice than specified, but not shorter notice. Section 369(3) and (4) do, however, go on to provide some latitude, by saying that a meeting shall, although called by shorter notice than that specified in subsection (2) or in the company's articles, be deemed to have been duly called if it is so agreed:

(1) in the case of a meeting called as the annual general meeting, by all the members entitled to attend and vote;
(2) in the case of any other meeting, by a majority in number of the members having a right to attend and vote at the meeting, being a majority together holding not less than 95% in nominal value of the shares giving a right to attend and vote at the meeting, or, in the case of a company not having a share capital, together representing not less than 95% of the total voting rights at that meeting of all the members.[1]

A private company may elect to reduce the percentage to anywhere between 90 and 95%.[2] In general, no notice is required to be given of adjourned meetings, if held within the limits prescribed by the articles of association, as they are merely continuations of the previous meetings, at which, if notice was properly given, all the members have had the opportunity of being present, and those who were present have agreed to the time and place of adjournment. But under Table A, article 45 if the adjournment is for 14 days or more, fresh notice is required.

---

1   Provision to the same effect is contained in article 38 of Table A. Section 378(3) allows a special resolution to be validly passed without the usual 21-day period of notice where a majority in number of the members having the right to attend and vote at the meeting, and holding 95% in nominal value of the shares giving that right, agree to accept a lesser period of notice. But the members must, in giving their consent, have knowledge of the special resolution which it is proposed to pass on a shorter period of notice: *Re Pearce Duff & Co Ltd* [1960] 1 WLR 1014. See **13.16–13.17** as to special and extraordinary resolutions.
2   As to elective resolutions generally, see **13.4.6**.

Although the adjourned meeting is only a continuation of the original meeting,[1] if notice to propose a director is required to be given so many days before 'the day of election', and the election takes place at an adjourned meeting, the notice is sufficient if given the specified time before the day of holding the adjourned meeting.[2] It would be otherwise if the article required notice before the meeting at which the election is to take place.[3]

When notice has been duly given of a meeting, the meeting cannot be postponed by a subsequent notice;[4] the proper course is for the meeting to be held and adjourned.

In the absence of some special provision in the articles, it is not necessary to give notice to the representatives of deceased shareholders unless such representatives have become members by formal registration.[5] Under article 38 of Table A such notice is required to be given to representatives of deceased shareholders: the use to which they can put this notice is not clear, since article 31 prevents them attending the meeting, and, of course, voting thereat. Even if the articles allowed them to attend and vote, their votes could not be counted on an extraordinary or special resolution, because under section 378 the votes to be counted are those of members.

A notice of meeting, to be good, must be given by persons authorised to summon the meeting. Resolutions passed at a meeting convened by the secretary without the authority of the board are invalid; nor will the consent of directors separately given suffice.[6] But if the notice purports to be issued by the authority of the directors and is subsequently ratified by them at a board meeting, it will be valid.[7] A statement in the report of the directors sent with the notice of meeting that certain business will be proposed is a sufficient notice.[8]

13.10.2 Misleading notices

The articles usually provide that notice must be given of the general nature of any special business to be transacted,[9] and by section 378(1) notice must be given of the intention to propose an extraordinary or special resolution. In the absence of provisions in the articles of association, and if Table A be excluded, no business can be brought on without notice. The notice must 'give at any rate a fair, candid, and reasonable explanation' of the business proposed, and if something is wrapped up or kept back it will invalidate the proceedings.[10] Thus Kekewich J held that a notice of a meeting to adopt new articles which might be seen at the

---

1   *Wills v Murray* (1850) 4 Ex 843; *Scadding v Lorant* (1851) 3 HLC 418.
2   *Catesby v Burnett* [1916] 2 Ch 325.
3   See *McLaren v Thomson* [1917] 2 Ch 261.
4   *Smith v Paringa Mines* [1906] 2 Ch 193.
5   *Allen v Gold Reefs of West Africa* [1900] 1 Ch 656 (CA).
6   *Re Haycraft Gold Reduction Co* [1900] 2 Ch 230; *Re State of Wyoming Syndicate* [1901] 2 Ch 431.
7   *Hooper v Kerr Stuart & Co* (1900) 83 LT 729.
8   *Boschoek Proprietary Co v Fuke* [1906] 1 Ch 148.
9   Table A has this provision (Table A of 1862, article 35; Table A of 1908, article 49; Table A of 1929, article 42; Table A of 1948, article 50; Table A of 1985, article 38).
10 *Kaye v Croydon Tramways* [1898] 1 Ch 358 (CA); cf *Young v Ladies' Imperial Club* [1920] 2 KB 523 (CA), where in a club case the rules required that the expulsion of a member should only be effected at a meeting of the committee specially convened for that purpose. A notice 'to elect directors' constitutes a sufficient notice to elect directors up to the maximum number authorised by the articles: *Choppington Collieries v Johnson* [1944] 1 All ER 762 (CA).

company's office was not sufficient where the new articles increased the directors' remuneration and borrowing power, and made other important changes.[1]

Directors who are to derive some benefit under resolutions have sometimes attempted to cover it up in the notice of meeting in such a way that it shall not be fully understood by the shareholders. Such a notice is insufficient, and a resolution passed in pursuance of it will be invalid.[2] Thus, where in a reconstruction directors did not state that they were participating in the purchase consideration to be received by the selling company,[3] or where in seeking the sanction of the company to the retention by the directors of remuneration they had received irregularly no proper statement was made as to the amount,[4] the resolutions passed were held to be invalid. The holding of extraordinary general meetings without sufficient notice, where this results in the ineffective creation of new shares, may amount to unfairly prejudicial conduct of the company's affairs within section 459 of the Companies Act 1985.[5]

13.11   Minutes of business done at meetings

Every company must, pursuant to section 382 of the Companies Act 1985, cause minutes of all proceedings of general meetings, and of meetings of its directors or managers, to be entered in books kept for the purpose. Such minutes if purporting to be signed by the chairman of the meeting or of the next succeeding meeting are evidence of the proceedings. Until the contrary is proved every meeting of the company, or of the directors or managers, of which minutes have been so made, is deemed duly held and convened, and all proceedings thereat duly had, and all appointments of directors, managers, or liquidators are deemed to be valid.[6]

The absence of any reference to a matter in the minutes is treated as evidence that it was not brought before the company or the board, but express evidence may be given to prove what was in fact done and what resolutions have been passed.[7] Where the articles provide that the minutes of meetings when signed shall be conclusive evidence of the facts therein stated, as between members of the company, the minutes are in the absence of fraud conclusive, and unless bad faith or fraud is alleged, evidence tendered for the purpose of contradicting the facts set forth in the minutes is inadmissible.[8]

Directors present when the minutes of a previous meeting are read and signed are not thereby made responsible for the resolutions passed at the previous meeting, although they thus are fixed with notice of what has been done.[9] If any

---

1   *Normandy v Ind Coope & Co* [1908] 1 Ch 84.
2   *Pacific Coast Coal Mines v Arbuthnot* [1917] AC 607 (PC).
3   *Kaye v Croydon Tramways* [1898] 1 Ch 358 (CA); *Tiessen v Henderson* [1899] 1 Ch 861. See also *Clarkson v Davies* [1923] AC 100 (PC).
4   *Baillie v Oriental Telephone Co* [1915] 1 Ch 503 (CA).
5   *Re a Company, ex parte Shooter* [1990] BCLC 385 at 394.
6   Section 382, and see Table A, article 100. This must of course mean in regard to matters properly entered in the minutes, and the evidence will only be that such and such proceedings were had, and not that the statements of fact contained therein are true.
7   *Knight's Case* (1867) 2 Ch App 321; *Re Great Northern Salt Co* (1890) 44 ChD 472; *Re Pyle Works (No2)* [1891] 1 Ch 172; *In re Fireproof Doors* [1916] 2 Ch 142.
8   *Kerr v John Mottram* [1940] Ch 657, and see *Re Hadleigh Castle Gold Mines* [1900] 2 Ch 419, and *Arnot v United African Lands* [1901] 1 Ch 518 (CA).
9   See **15.12**.

matter is debated afresh, this should be the subject of a separate minute. It is improper to remove a page from the minute book. If it requires rewriting, a line should be drawn through it, leaving the page in its place. The mutilation of any book gives rise to suspicion of bad faith.[1] The minutes should be full and accurate because they are constantly referred to in legal proceedings.

It is advisable to have separate minute books for general and board meetings. Under section 383(1), the books containing minutes of proceedings of general meetings are required to be kept at the registered office of the company and to be open to the inspection of members for not less than two hours during the period between 9 am and 5 pm on each business day free of charge;[2] but the directors' minute book, containing as it does a record of the private affairs of the company, should not be accessible to any but the directors, secretary, and auditors, who will be entitled to see it for purposes of the audit. The covers of the directors' minute book are frequently secured by a lock. While carrying out an inspection of the minutes under section 383(1), a member is entitled to be accompanied by an adviser of his own choice.[3]

13.12   The conduct of general meetings

It is only at general meetings that the shareholders can exercise any control over the affairs of the company. The Companies Act 1985 requires the directors to lay before the company in general meeting profit and loss or income and expenditure accounts, balance sheets and directors' and auditors' reports.[4] Subject to the articles, the chairman of directors, or, if there be no such chairman, the person elected by the meeting, takes the chair. It is his duty to preserve order, conduct proceedings regularly, and take care that the sense of the meeting is properly ascertained with regard to any question before it.[5] The conduct of a meeting is largely in the hands of the chairman with the assent of the persons properly present.[6] Under the general law of meetings, if the person appointed does not attend, those present may appoint someone else to chair the meeting.[7] The articles may sometimes provide that, where there is no chairman of the board of directors and no directors present, the members may choose a chairman of the

---

1   In *Hearts of Oak Assurance Co v Flower & Sons* [1936] Ch 76, BennettJ held that loose leaves fastened between two covers in such a way that leaves could be taken out by any person and fresh ones substituted was not a book within the meaning of section 120 of the 1929 Act: but what is now section 722(1) of the 1985 Act reverses this.

2   Members also have the rights to copies and to take notes, conferred by section 383(3) and the Companies (Inspection and Copying of Registers, Indices and Documents) Regulations 1991, SI 1991/1998.

3   *McCusker v McRae* 1966 SC 253. A director has a common-law right to inspect the minutes of directors' meetings, even though the Companies Act 1985 makes no provision for this. The director is entitled to be accompanied by an adviser of his choice: ibid. Although a Scottish decision, this is true of English law. As to the director's right to inspect his company's books of account, see the English cases discussed at **15.13**.

4   The Companies Act 1985 no longer requires that the auditors' report be read before the general meeting: see section 241(1), as amended by the Companies Act 1989, section 11.

5   *Per* Chitty J in *National Dwellings Society v Sykes* [1894] 3 Ch 159.

6   *Carruth v Imperial Chemical Industries* [1937] AC 707 (PC) at 767 *per* Lord Maugham: see also the observations of Lord Russell of Killowen in the same case at 761. See *John v Rees* [1969] 2 WLR 1294 in respect of the chairman's power to adjourn the meeting in the event of disorder. He must act in good faith and should exercise this power only in the last resort. He should not adjourn the meeting for longer than is necessary.

7   *Re Salcombe Hotel Development Corporation Ltd* (1989) 5 BCC 807.

general meeting from one of their number.[1] *Prima facie* every member has a right to be heard and to advocate or oppose any resolution before the meeting;[2] but if a matter has been fairly debated, the chairman, with the sanction of the majority, can stop the discussion, or, in modern phrase, 'the closure may be adopted' after resolutions have been reasonably debated.[3]

13.13 Publication of reports of meetings

As has been seen, minutes must be taken; but there is no obligation upon the company to print and publish a report of the proceedings at general meetings, although such a report is sometimes circulated among the shareholders by large companies. On the ground that members have a common interest in the affairs of the company, speeches at a meeting and circulars sent by directors or share-holders to the members are privileged, and in the absence of malice will not support an action for slander or libel.[4] The Defamation Act 1952, section 7, extends the defence of privilege to reports in the press of the meetings of public companies. These must be fair and accurate reports of the proceedings at general meetings of companies registered or certified under any Act of Parliament or incorporated by Royal Charter not being a private company[5] within the meaning of the Companies Act 1985.[6]

13.14 Notices of resolutions and amendments

Only such motions can be submitted to a meeting as fall within the notice given of business to be transacted;[7] but if all the members of the company are present they can waive any irregularity.[8] By section 378(3) of the Companies Act 1985, a resolution may be passed as a special resolution at a meeting of which less than the 21 days' notice prescribed by the section has been given, if it is so agreed by a majority in number of the members having the right to attend and vote, being a majority together holding not less than 95% in nominal value of the shares giving that right, or in the case of a company not having a share capital, together representing not less than 95% of the total voting rights at that meeting. It would seem that this proviso would be ineffective in a case where a special resolution was sought to be passed at an annual general meeting, because section 369(3) requries, as a prerequisite to the meeting being deemed to have been duly called,

---

1   See *Re Bradford Investments Ltd* [1991] BCLC 224 for an illustration of this rule and the authority of the chairman's ruling at such a meeting.

2   *Const v Harris* (1824) Turn & R 496 at 525. A proxy appointed to attend and vote instead of a member of a private company has the same right as the member to speak at the meeting: section 372(1).

3   *Wall v London and Northern Assets Corp* [1898] 2 Ch 469 (CA): *Carruth v Imperial Chemical Industries* [1937] AC 707 *per* Lord Maugham at 767 (HL).

4   *Lawless v Anglo-Egyptian Co* (1869) LR 4 QB 262; *Quartz Hill Co v Beall* (1882) 20 ChD 501 (CA).

5   See the definition of a private company at **3.2**.

6   The Faulk's Committee on Defamation (Cmnd 5909, 1975) proposed extending the defence of qualified privilege to reports on documents issued by the board of directors (or auditors) to shareholders and to documents circulated to shareholders concerning the appointment, resignation, retirement or dismissal of directors.

7   See **13.10.2**.

8   *Re Express Engineering Works* [1920] 1 Ch 466 (CA); *Re Oxted Motor Company* [1921] 3 KB 32. See further at **13.2**.

agreement of all the members entitled to attend and vote. Where all the members agree, and the transaction is honest and intra vires, and entered into for the benefit of the company, they can waive the formality of a meeting.[1] The chairman usually proposes the resolutions necessary for the business brought forward by the board, and if notice has been given of other resolutions calls upon the giver of the notice to bring forward his motion. If a member during the meeting proposes a motion, then in cases where notice is required, and has not been given, or where insufficient notice has been given, the chairman should refuse to put the motion to the meeting. But an amendment of which notice has not been given may be proposed to a motion properly moved, so long as it is within the scope of the notice originally given.[2] If the notice of meeting is accompanied by the directors' report, stating that certain business will be proposed, this is a sufficient notice.[3] It has been held that where the notice was of a resolution to appoint as directors three persons named in the notice, it was competent for the company to add three others by way of amendment.[4] If the chairman improperly refuses to submit an amendment to the meeting, the resolution actually carried will be invalidated.[5]

13.14.1 Special notice

The Companies Act 1985 requires special notice of certain resolutions. These are:

(1) a resolution at the annual general meeting appointing as auditor a person other than a retiring auditor or providing expressly that a retiring auditor shall not be reappointed (section 388);

(2) a resolution to remove a director under section 303 or to appoint somebody instead of a director so removed at the meeting at which he is removed; and

(3) a resolution appointing or approving the appointment of a director over the age limit of seventy for the purposes of section 293(5).[6]

Section 379 deals with special notice. It provides that where special notice is required of a resolution, the resolution is not to be effective unless notice of the intention to move it has been given to the company not less than 28 days before the meeting at which it is moved. Then the company must give its members notice of any such resolution at the same time and in the same manner as it gives notice of the meeting or, if that is not practicable, must give them notice thereof, either by advertisement in a newspaper having an appropriate circulation or in any other mode allowed by the articles, not less than 21 days before the meeting. But if, after notice of the intention to move such a resolution has been given to the company, a meeting is called for a date 28 days or less after the notice has been given, the notice though not given within the time required by the section is to be deemed to have been properly given for the purposes thereof.

Section 379 does not give to any individual shareholder a right (which he does not otherwise possess) to compel the inclusion of a resolution the agenda for a

---

1   *Parker and Cooper v Reading* [1926] 1 Ch 975.

2   *Torbock v Lord Westbury* [1902] 2 Ch 871; *Henderson v Bank of Australasia* (1890) 45 ChD 330 (CA). The latter case also decided that an amendment need not be submitted in writing, but is good if its effect be made reasonably clear to the meeting orally.

3   *Irvine v Union Bank of Australia* (1877) 2 App Cas 366 at 376 (PC); *Boschoek Proprietary Co v Fuke* [1906] 1 Ch 148.

4   *Betts & Co v Macnaghten* [1910] 1 Ch 430.

5   *Henderson v Bank of Australasia* (1890) 45 ChD 330 (CA).

6   See **15.2.1**.

company meeting.[1] To do so, a member must either be given such a right by the articles or enjoy sufficient support to make a requisition under section 376. This section is discussed immediately below.

13.14.2 Electronic communications

Companies can now communicate with their members and with Companies House electronically, including giving notices of general meetings and resolutions.[2] Notice sent in this way, eg to an email address notified to the company by the member is deemed to have been served 48 hours after the time it was sent, unless the articles provide otherwise. An alternative, if it has been agreed, is for the company to notify members by posting details on its website. The company must comply with the provisions of section 369[3] and specify the place, date and time of the meeting and whether it is to be an annual or extraordinary general meeting.

13.15 Members' resolutions and circulars

Section 376 of the Companies Act 1985 confers certain rights on members in regard to resolutions to be moved at annual general meetings and to the circulation of statements in relation to any general meeting.[4] Section 376(1) requires the company on written requisition of the specified number of members and (unless the company otherwise resolves) at the expense of the requisitionists:

(1) to give to members of the company entitled to receive notice of the next annual general meeting notice of any resolution which may properly be moved and is intended to be moved at that meeting; and
(2) to circulate to members entitled to have notice of any general meeting sent to them any statement of not more than 1000 words with respect to the matter referred to in any proposed resolutions or the business to be dealt with at that meeting.

These, it will be observed, are quite separate and distinct matters: (a) resolutions to be moved at an annual general meeting; and (b) circulars relating to *any* general meeting. With regard to (a), section 376(6) provides that, notwithstanding anything in the articles, the business which may be dealt with at an annual general meeting is to include any resolution of which notice is given in accordance with the section.[5] There is no restriction on the nature of the resolution (except that it must not seek to achieve anything beyond the powers of the company), but if it seeks to do something which by law or under the articles is required to be done, for example, by special resolution, it would be prudent that the requisition should indicate what type of resolution it is to be.

The specified number of members necessary for an effective requisition is either any member representing not less than one-twentieth of the total voting rights of all the members who have at the date of the requisition a right to vote at the meeting to which the requisition relates, or not less than 100 members

---

1   *Pedley v Inland Waterways Association* [1977] 1 All ER 209.
2   The Companies Act 1985 (Electronic Communications) Order 2000, SI 2000/3373, made under section 8 of the Electronic Communications Act 2000.
3   See **13.10.1**.
4   As to the sanctions imposed for default, see Schedule 24.
5   Notice is to be deemed to have been so given 'notwithstanding the accidental omission, in giving it, of one or more members' (*sic*): section 376(6).

holding shares on which there has been paid up an average sum per member of not less than £100.

Notice of any such resolution is to be given, and any such statement is to be circulated, to members of the company entitled to have notice of the meeting sent to them, by serving a copy of the resolution or statement on each such member in any manner permitted for service of notice of the meeting, and notice of any such resolution shall be given to any other member of the company, by giving notice of the general effect of the resolution in any manner permitted for giving him notice of meetings of the company. The copy must be served, or notice of the effect of the resolution given, in the same manner and, so far as practicable, at the same time as notice of the meeting. Where this is not practicable, it must be served or given as soon as practicable thereafter.[1]

But the company is not bound to give notice of a resolution or to circulate a statement unless:[2]

(1) a copy of the requisition signed by the requisitionists (or two or more copies which between them contain the signatures of all the requisitionists) is deposited at the registered office of the company

    (a) in the case of a requisition requiring notice of a resolution, not less than six weeks before the meeting but if, after a copy of such a requisition has been so deposited an annual general meeting is called for a date six weeks or less after the copy has been deposited, the copy though not deposited within this time is deemed to have been properly deposited; and

    (b) in the case of any other requisition, not less than one week before the meeting; and

(2) there is deposited or tended with the requisition a sum reasonably sufficient to meet the company's expenses in giving effect thereto.

The company is also not bound to circulate any statement if, on the application either of the company or of any other person who claims to be aggrieved, the court is satisfied that the rights conferred by the section are being abused to secure needless publicity for defamatory matter.[3] The court may order the company's costs on an application under this section to be paid in whole or in part by the requisitionists, notwithstanding that they are not parties to the application.

13.16 Extraordinary resolutions

For certain acts of the company an ordinary resolution does not suffice, and either an 'extraordinary resolution' or a 'special resolution' must be passed. The requirements of section 378 of the Companies Act 1985 which govern such resolutions must be carefully followed, for any departure from the procedure there laid down will render the resolution void.

By section 378(1), a resolution is an extraordinary resolution 'when it has been passed by a majority of not less than three-fourths of such members, as being entitled so to do, vote in person or, where proxies are allowed, by proxy, at a general meeting, of which notice specifying the intention to propose the

---

1   Section 376(3)–(5).
2   See section 377(1) and (2).
3   Section 377(3).

resolution as an extraordinary resolution has been duly given'.[1] Notice of a meeting is to be deemed to be duly given and the meeting to be duly held when the notice is given, or the meeting is held in the manner provided by the Act or the articles.[2] A notice will therefore be 'duly given' if given and served in accordance with the articles so long as the provisions in the articles are not avoided by section 369(1).[3] If the articles make no valid provision as to the giving of notices, the length of notice will be that prescribed by section 369(2), namely 14 days for companies other than unlimited companies and seven days in the case of unlimited companies.[4] The method of giving it will be that prescribed by the articles, or if they do not prescribe a method, the method prescribed by section 370(2). This provides that where no provision in that behalf is made in the articles, the notice shall be served on every member in the manner required by Table A for the time being in force, ie at present as set out in articles 111, 112, 115 and 116 of Table A. The number of days required by the Act is that number of *clear* days.[5] If the meeting is convened by the court under section 371, the court will give directions as to notice and service.

The company's articles may require an extraordinary resolution for any purpose other than one for which a special resolution is made necessary by the Companies Act 1985 but for certain purposes an extraordinary resolution is required by the Act. The precise terms of the resolution, and the fact that it is to be proposed as an extraordinary resolution, must be stated in the notice.[6]

As a rule an extraordinary resolution is resorted to in cases where a company is insolvent and wishes to go into voluntary liquidation.[7] In such cases the resolution must declare that the company cannot, by reason of its liabilities, continue its business, and that it is advisable to wind up. Extraordinary resolutions may also be used in a voluntary winding up for sanctioning arrangements with creditors, and in the case of a members' voluntary winding up is required for empowering the liquidator to pay any classes of creditors in full or to make any compromise with creditors, or persons alleging any claims against the company whereby the company might be rendered liable, or with debtors, or contributories, or for determining how the books and papers of the company and of the liquidator are to be disposed of.

13.17 Special resolutions

A resolution is a special resolution 'when it has been passed by such a majority as is required for the passing of an extraordinary resolution and at a general meeting of which not less than twenty-one days' notice, specifying the intention to propose the resolution as a special resolution, has been duly given'.[8]

---

1   As to the substantial identity required between the notice and the resolution, see *Re Moorgate Mercantile Holdings Ltd* [1980] 1 WLR 227 discussed at **13.17**.
2   Section 378(6).
3   A resolution may be a good special resolution if the terms of the section are complied with, even though the articles contain further requirements which have not been complied with: *Etheridge v Central Uruguayan Northern Extension Rly* [1913] 1 Ch 425.
4   As to the shorter period of notice allowed by section 369(3) and article 38 of Table A, see **13.11**.
5   *Re Hector Whaling Co* [1936] Ch 208. *Secus Neil McLeod & Sons Ltd, Petitioners* 1967 SC 16.
6   *McConnell v E Prill & Co* [1916] 1 Ch 794, CA.
7   Insolvency Act 1986, s. 84(1)(c)
8   Section 378(2).

A notice of intention to propose a special resolution for the purpose of section 378(2) of the Companies Act 1985 is valid only if it identifies the intended resolution by specifying either the text or the entire substance of the resolution it was intended to propose. Thus a special resolution is validly passed in accordance with the subsection only if it is the same resolution as that identified in the preceding notice.

In *Re Moorgate Mercantile Holdings Ltd*,[1] Slade J reaffirmed the need for substantial concordance between the notice of a special resolution and the terms of the resolution passed. There is no room for the application of the *de minimis* principle in deciding whether there is complete identity between the substance of the resolution as passed and the substance of the intended resolution as notified. However:

> ... a resolution as passed can properly be regarded as 'the resolution' identified in the preceding notice even though (i) it departs in some respects from the text of a resolution set out in such notice (for example by correcting those grammatical or clerical errors which can be corrected as a matter of construction, or by reducing the words to more formal language) or (ii) it is reduced into the form of a new text which was not included in the notice, provided only that in either case there is no departure whatever from the substance.[2]

A departure from the rigour of this rule can be made only with the unanimous consent of the shareholders concerned.[3] Slade J observed that propositions (expounded above) in respect of notices of special resolutions were intended to include circulars accompanying notices. In those cases where notices are so accompanied, the notices and circulars can and should ordinarily be treated as one document.[4] What is said about special resolutions will also apply to extraordinary resolutions.

At any meeting at which an extraordinary or a special resolution is submitted to be passed, a declaration of the chairman that the resolution is carried is, unless a poll is demanded, conclusive evidence of the fact without proof of the number or proportion of the votes recorded in favour of or against the resolution.[5]

Failure either to set out the resolution or to specify that it is to be an extraordinary or a special resolution will invalidate the resolution if passed,[6] and the result of the requirement as to giving notice of 'the resolution' is that no amendment can be made to any proposed extraordinary or special resolution.

As to the requisite majority on a show of hands, it will be observed that there must be in favour of the resolution not less than three-quarters of such members as, being entitled so to do, vote in person, or, where proxies are allowed, by proxy, and, accordingly, any member present but not voting should be ignored.[7] On a poll, the requisite majority is three-quarters of the total number of votes cast.[8]

An irregularity in an ordinary resolution may be cured by a subsequent ratification by the company, but for a resolution to be good as a special resolution

---

1   [1980] 1 WLR 227 at 242.
2   Ibid. However, so long as there is identity, no court can, under its inherent jurisdiction, correct insignificant errors in the resolution: *Re Willaire Systems plc* [1987] BCLC 67.
3   Ibid. See further, **13.2**.
4   Ibid.
5   Section 378(4). As to demanding a poll, see **13.20.1**.
6   *MacConnell v E Prill & Co* [1916] 2 Ch 57.
7   Section 378(1).
8   Section 378(5).

it must be carried *modo et forma* as required by the Act: that is to say, on proper notice, and by the requisite majority. Accordingly, the company cannot by an ordinary resolution or by conduct make good an invalid special resolution, nor is it an objection to an action by a single shareholder to say that the company ought to be plaintiff on the ground that it can ratify the resolution, for this is not the case.[1]

Unless the Companies Act 1985 provides that an ordinary resolution or an extraordinary resolution is sufficient,[2] any kind of business may be declared by the articles of association to require a special resolution; but for the following[3] a special resolution is required by law:

(1) Changing the name of the company: section 28.
(2) Altering the objects as stated in the memorandum: section 4.
(3) Altering the conditions contained in the memorandum which could have been contained in the articles: section 17.
(4) Altering, or adding to the articles or any existing special resolutions: section 9.[4]
(5) Reducing capital: section 135.
(6) Declaring any portion of the unpaid capital shall only be capable of being called up in the case of a winding up: section 120.
(7) Rendering the liability of directors, managers, or managing director unlimited: section 307.
(8) Approving assignment of office by director: section 308.
(9) Procuring the company to be wound up by the court: Insolvency Act 1986, section 122(1)(a).
(10) Winding up voluntarily in certain cases: Insolvency Act 1986, section 84(1)(c).
(11) Where a company is proposed to be or is in the course of being wound up voluntarily, sanctioning a sale by the liquidator to another company in consideration of shares, policies, or other like interests: Insolvency Act 1986, sections 110 and 111.
(12) Substitution of memorandum and articles for deed of settlement by company registered under part XII of the Act: section 690.

13.18   Registration of resolutions

Within fifteen days after the passing of a special or extraordinary resolution, section 380(1) of the Companies Act 1985 requires that a copy[5] must be lodged with the Registrar of Companies.[6] This obligation of forwarding copies of resolutions to the Registrar applies, in addition to special and extraordinary resolutions, to the following:

---

1   *Baillie v Oriental Telephone Co* [1915] 1 Ch 503 (CA). But the articles may be varied by unanimous agreement of the members: *Cane v Jones* [1980] 1 WLR 1451: see **13.2**.
2   See section 303(1) (removal of directors); section 598(1)(a) (liquidator's powers in a voluntary winding up), section 606(1) (arrangements with creditors on voluntary winding up); section 640 (disposal of books and papers in a voluntary winding up).
3   Though this is not an exhaustive list.
4   The court has no jurisdiction to rectify articles adopted by mistake: *Evans v Chapman* [1902] WN 78 and *Scott v Frank F Scott (London)* [1940] 1 Ch 794 (CA).
5   Either printed or in a form approved by the Registrar.
6   A fine may be imposed on the company and every officer of the company in default.

(1) resolutions or agreements[1] which have been agreed to by all the members of a company, but which, if not so agreed to, would not have been effective for their purpose unless passed as special resolutions or extraordinary resolutions;

(2) resolutions or agreements which have been agreed to by all the members of some class of shareholders but which, if not so agreed to, would not have been effective for their purpose unless passed by some particular majority or otherwise in some particular manner, and all resolutions or agreements which effectively bind the members of any class of shareholders though not agreed to by all those members;

(3) a resolution passed by the directors of the company in compliance with a direction under section 31(2) (change of name on the Secretary of State's direction);

(4) a resolution giving, varying, revoking or renewing an authority to the directors under section 80 (allotment of securities);

(5) a resolution of the directors under section 147(2) (alteration of the memorandum following a company ceasing to be a public company following an acquisition of its own shares);

(6) a resolution conferring, varying, revoking or renewing authority under section 166 (market purchase of a company's own shares);

(7) resolutions requiring a company to be wound up voluntarily passed under section 84(1)(a) of the Insolvency Act 1986 (ie ordinary resolutions which are effective to wind up a company, as where the period fixed for the duration of the company, or the event in which it is to be wound up, is specified in the articles);

(8) a resolution of the directors of an old public company (under section 2(1) of the Companies Consolidation (Consequential Provisions) Act 1985) that it should be re-registered as a public company.

The Registrar requires the copy to contain particulars of the date and place of passing the resolution, and to be authenticated by the signature of the chairman, a director, or the secretary of the company. A copy of every resolution or agreement, a copy of which is required to be forwarded to the Registrar and which is for the time being in force must, where articles have been registered, be annexed to or embodied in every copy of the articles issued after the passing of the resolution or the making of the agreement. Where articles have not been registered every member of the company is entitled to a printed copy of every such resolution or agreement upon request and payment of 5p or such lesser sum as the company may direct.[2] Any company not complying with these provisions of the Act is liable to a penalty, and every officer in default is alike liable.[3]

---

1   The inclusion of 'agreements' brings within the ambit of section 380 such things as an agreement of all members effecting an alteration in the articles (as in *Cane v Jones* [1980] 1 WLR 1451, **13.2.1**). Note, however, that a failure to register under section 380 does not affect the validity of any resolution or agreement.

2   Section 380(2) and (3).

3   A liquidator is deemed to be an officer for the purpose of liability under section 380. See section 380(7).

13.19 Votes at general meetings

A right to vote is property, and the courts will intervene to protect a member from being deprived of this right.[1] Where shares are mortgaged, but the mortgagor's name remains on the register of members, he alone can vote, but he must do so in accordance with the dictation of those entitled to the beneficial interest in the shares unless[2] it is otherwise agreed. However, an unpaid or partly paid vendor of shares remaining on the register after a contract of sale retains, *vis-à-vis* the purchaser, the right to decide how to exercise the voting rights.[3] The company, however, is not concerned to inquire as to the beneficial interest and must accept the vote of the registered holder of the shares, and where shares are mortgaged and placed in the names of trustees for the mortgagee, these trustees may vote contrary to the wishes of the mortgagor even though no interest is in arrear and the principal is not payable.[4]

The articles of association usually provide how many votes each shareholder shall have. If the articles are silent and the 1985 Table A does not apply, every member has, in the case of a company originally having a share capital, one vote in respect of each share or each £10 of stock held by him, and in any other case every member has one vote.[5] Special articles of association frequently provide for a different apportionment of votes,[6] but a vote for every share on a poll is usual and is adopted in Table A, article 54. The register of members should be in readiness at the meeting to refer to for the number of shares held by each member, and the consequent number of votes to which he is entitled on a poll. Under Table A, article 50, and most special articles, the chairman has a second or casting vote in the case of an equality of votes, but he has no such right at common law.[7]

Where there is a mode of voting known to the community, that mode should be followed unless a binding rule is found in the articles to the contrary, and likewise any common-law rule as to voting will prevail unless inconsistent with the articles.[8] Thus, votes in the first instance are taken by a show of hands, each shareholder having a single vote for himself, but none for any persons whose proxies he

---

1   *Pender v Lushington* (1877) 6 ChD 70; *Osborne v Amalgamated Society of Railway Servants* [1911] 1 Ch 540 at 567 *per* Buckley LJ (CA).

2   *Wise v Lansdell* [1921] 1 Ch 420; *Puddephatt v Leith* [1916] 1 Ch 200.

3   *Musselwhite v CH Musselwhite & Son* [1962] 1 Ch 965. See also **9.5.**

4   *Siemens Brothers Dynamo Works v Burns* [1918] 2 Ch 324 (CA).

5   Section 370(6).

6   See **8.6** as to the voting rights attached to shares. An article which gives a director three votes for every share held by him only in respect of a resolution to remove him from office is perfectly valid. It is not an infringement of section 303, which provides that 'a company may by ordinary resolution remove a director before the expiration of his period of office notwithstanding anything in its articles or in any agreement between it and him': *Bushell v Faith* [1970] AC 1099 (HL). For comment on this decision, see **15.7.** Where the Act confers a power to do a particular thing by special resolution, an article which purports to require a larger majority than that prescribed by the Act for a special resolution is ineffective: see *Ayre v Skelsey's Adamant Cement Company Ltd* (1904) 20 TLR 587 (affirmed on other grounds at (1905) 21 TLR 464). The above rule is not affected by the decision in *Bushell v Faith* (above).

7   If the chairman has not voted in the first instance he can, upon an equality appearing, give an original vote and so determine the question in issue, but if he has voted, and as a result an equality arises, the common law has provided no way out of the difficulty: *Nell v Longbottom* [1894] 1 QB 767.

8   *Per* Jessel MR, *Re Horbury Bridge Coal Co* (1879) 11 ChD 109 at 113, 115 (CA).

holds.[1] But if a sufficient number of shareholders are dissatisfied with the result of the count of hands, they can demand a poll.

In the absence of specific provision in the company's articles, a specified majority of votes may be calculated by reference to the number of members present and voting at the meeting.[2]

13.20 Polls at general meetings

13.20.1 *The right to demand a poll*

The right to demand a poll depends on the company's articles, but section 373 of the Companies Act 1985 contains provisions which in effect fix the maximum which can be imposed by the articles. This section invalidates any provision in articles of association in so far as it would have the effect of either:

(1) excluding the right to demand a poll at a general meeting on any question other than the election of the chairman of the meeting or the adjournment of the meeting; or

(2) making ineffective a demand (including a demand by a person as proxy) for a poll on any such question which is made
    (a) by not less than five members having the right to vote at the meeting; or
    (b) by a member or members representing not less than one-tenth of the total voting rights of all the members having the right to vote at the meeting; or
    (c) by a member or members holding shares in the company conferring a right to vote at the meeting, being shares on which an aggregate sum has been paid up equal to not less than one-tenth of the total sum paid up on all the shares conferring that right.

Article 46 of Table A follows the requirements of section 373 in defining who may demand a poll. However, it allows a minimum of two persons present in person or by proxy to demand a poll.

The section also provides that the instrument appointing a proxy is to be deemed also to confer authority to demand or join in demanding a poll. It would seem that section 373(1)(b)(ii) and (iii) refer to the potential voting rights irrespective of whether or not those rights are in fact represented at the meeting.

Where the articles gave the right to demand a poll to 'members holding' a specified number of shares, it was held that two trustees holding that number could demand the poll without the support of any other member. But in this case there was also an article that words importing the plural include the singular.[3]

---

1   *Ernest v Loma Gold Mines* [1897] 1 Ch 1 (CA); but if a person not a member is allowed to be a proxy, it seems he can vote on a show of hands (see [1897] 1 Ch at 8). But most articles in modern form expressly confer a vote on a show of hands only on a member present in person. If the articles require a vote by show of hands on any resolution, this must be taken even though there is no opposition: *Citizens Theatre* 1946 SC 14; *Fraserburgh Commercial Co* 1946 SC 444.

2   *Cullen v Galloway Cattle Society of Australia Inc* (1998) 27 ACSR 648, SC (NSW). However, where there is a select and definite group, such as a board of directors or councillors, a specified majority should, prima facie, be calculated by reference to all of those in the group (ibid).

3   *Siemens Brothers & Co v Burns* [1918] 2 Ch 324 (CA): see Law of Property Act 1925, section 61.

13.20.2   The conduct of a poll

The chairman must decide whether a poll is properly demanded, having regard to the articles (which usually require a poll to be demanded before or on the declaration of the result of the show of hands), and the Act. The chairman has generally also to determine how the poll is to be taken (see eg article 49 of Table A). At common law, there is no requirement of confidentiality for poll votes. Those who organise a poll vote are entitled to know how people voted so that the validity of the votes can be scrutinised.[1]

If there is a question of much importance to be decided, the chairman may well fix a future day, and notice should be given to all the shareholders of the appointed place and time. If the matter is not of great importance, or if there is a representative gathering of shareholders present, the poll may be taken at once.[2] In any case, the votes should be taken in writing and an entry made of how many votes each shareholder is entitled to give and actually does give. Each shareholder should sign his name as a guarantee that there is no personation. A shareholder who has not voted at the meeting may vote on the poll. A member entitled to more than one vote need not, if he votes, use all his votes or cast all the votes he uses in the same way.[3] This provision, which at first sight may be thought to be of a somewhat eccentric character, is designed principally for the benefit of trust corporations and the like, which may (and often do) hold precisely similar shares under totally different trusts. The chairman should fix the hours during which the poll is to be held. If he does not do so he cannot close the poll as long as votes are coming in;[4] but after waiting a reasonable time, if no more voters present themselves, he may declare the poll closed.[5] If he improperly excludes a voter it will invalidate the poll. The chairman must declare the result of the poll, but it is most desirable that there should be scrutineers present on each side at the counting. If there are several resolutions, the poll must be taken on each separately, though all may be included on one sheet of paper, to be marked by the voters.[6] If the vote is taken on a number of resolutions together, they cannot be validly passed.[7]

Where a poll takes place at a later date than the meeting, the resolution will not be deemed to have been passed until the result of the poll is declared, and the meeting will be regarded as continuing until then. Thus in *Holmes v Keyes*,[8] where the articles required the directors to acquire qualification shares within two months of election, their election dated from the declaration of the poll. It is a question of construction as to whether, under the relevant articles, a poll can be demanded before there has been a vote on a show of hands. In *Holmes v Keyes*,[9] the articles stated (as does Table A, article 47) 'a resolution put to the vote of the meeting shall be decided on a show of hands unless a poll is (before or on the declaration of the show of hands) demanded' etc. The Court of Appeal held that

---

1   *Haarhus & Co GmbH v Law Debenture Trust Corporation plc* [1988] BCLC 640.
2   *Re Chillington Iron Co* (1885) 29 ChD 159.
3   Section 374.
4   *R v St Pancras* (1839) 11 A & E 15.
5   *R v Lambeth* (1938) 8 A & E 356.
6   *In re RE Jones Ltd* (1933) 50 TLR 31.
7   *Patent Wood Keg Syndicate v Pearse* [1906] WN 164.
8   [1959] Ch 199 (CA).
9   Ibid. See also *Carruth v ICI* [1937] AC 707 (HL).

under such an article a poll could be demanded without going through a vote by show of hands.

Under the common form of articles or under Table A, a poll cannot be taken by sending voting papers to the members to be returned by post. They or their proxies must attend and give the votes personally.[1]

Unless a poll is demanded by the proper number of persons, the chairman's declaration of the result of the voting on a special or extraordinary resolution will be conclusive.[2]

Table A, article 47 extends this effect of the chairman's declaration, if accompanied by an entry in the minute book, to other resolutions. This will prevent the question being reopened in legal proceedings, even if evidence is tendered that the declaration by the chairman was wrong,[3] unless an error appears in the face of the declaration, for example where it states the number of votes given and they are insufficient,[4] or an error is plain on the face of the proceedings,[5] or bad faith or fraud in writing up the minutes is proved.[6]

The right of bearers of share warrants to vote depends on the regulations of the company.[7] When the articles give this privilege they usually contain special terms under which the power of voting is to be exercised, for example on depositing the warrants with the company.

13.21 Proxies at general meetings

When a company is governed by the regulations of Table A 'on a poll votes may be given either personally or by proxy'[8] (Table A, article 59), and special articles of association generally have a similar provision. In the absence of this provision there was at one time no legal right of a member to have his vote by proxy accepted.[9] Now, however, the Companies Act 1985 confers upon any member of a company having a share capital who is entitled to attend and vote at a meeting of the company or of a class of members of the company the right to appoint a proxy to attend and vote instead of him.[10] The proxy need not be a member. In the case of a private company, the proxy has the same right as the member to speak at the meeting.[11] These provisions do not apply to a company not having a share capital

---

1 *McMillan v Le Roi Mining Co* [1906] 1 Ch 331.
2 Section 378(4).
3 *Arnot v United African Lands* [1901] 1 Ch 518 (CA); *Re Hadleigh Castle Gold Mines* [1900] 2 Ch 419, not agreeing with Kekewich J in *Young v South African Development Syndicate* [1896] 2 Ch 268.
4 *Re Caratal (New) Mines* [1902] 2 Ch 498.
5 *Clark & Co* 1911 SC 243.
6 *Kerr v John Mottram* [1940] Ch 657.
7 Section 355(5): 'The bearer of a share warrant may, if the articles of the company so provide, be deemed to be a member of the company ... either to the full extent or for any purposes defined in the articles.' Thus, if the articles provide that bearers of warrants shall be members, and do not exclude the right to vote, they will have votes; but if the articles state that they shall have the rights of members in respect of defined objects, and do not include the right to vote, they will have no votes.
8 The appointment of a proxy is to be distinguished from a corporation which is a member of another company appointing a corporate representative under section 375. See **13.7**.
9 *Harben v Phillips* (1883) 23 ChD 14 (CA). No such right exists at common law (*per* Bowen LJ at 35).
10 Section 372(1).
11 Ibid.

unless the articles otherwise provide. In the absence of a provision in the articles, a member of a private company is not entitled to appoint more than one proxy to attend on the same occasion and a proxy is not entitled to vote except on a poll.

Some explanation is required of the reference to appointing more than one proxy to attend on the same occasion. It has been suggested that a form of proxy appointing X, or failing him, Y, appoints more than one proxy to attend on the same occasion, but it is arguable that an alternative appointment such as that is not what the section is referring to. One inference to be drawn is that a member of a company not being a private company is entitled to appoint more than one proxy as of right.

Notices convening the meetings have to indicate these statutory rights in respect of proxies.[1] Table A, article 62 requires the instrument of proxy and the power of attorney or other authority, if any, under which it is signed, or a notarially certified copy, to be deposited at the registered office not less than 48 hours before the meeting or adjourned meeting at which it is to be used. But special articles sometimes reduce the time to twenty-four hours. The Act prevents the time being more than 48 hours.[2]

It has been held that a 'resumed meeting' is not an adjourned meeting for the purpose of an article such as article 62 of Table A. In *Jackson v Hamlyn*,[3] a motion to adjourn was lost, but shortly afterwards the hall where the meeting was being held had to be vacated. It was held that new proxies could not be lodged before the resumption of the meeting, because a resumed meeting after such an unavoidable interruption was not an adjourned meeting.[4]

A proxy may in the first instance be given with a blank left for the name of the person entitled to vote if there is an authority to some person to fill in the blank,[5] and if stamped at the time of execution it is no objection that the blanks are subsequently filled up.[6] Where a member had notice that a requisition had been lodged to summon a meeting, and gave authority to another member to fill up a proxy for him, but the requisition was withdrawn and another lodged, the authority was held to extend to the meeting called on the later requisition.[7] The proxy need not be actually named if he is sufficiently described to be identified.[8] Sometimes the form of proxy authorises 'the chairman of the meeting' to vote for the absent shareholder; but this is very inadvisable.

It is the duty of the secretary to examine the instruments of proxy that may be sent in, and to report any irregularity to the directors.

Where articles required that proxies should be lodged two days before the day for holding the meeting, and the meeting was adjourned, proxies lodged after the original day and before the adjourned meeting were invalid.[9] It would be different if the article said 'not less than 48 hours before the time for holding the meeting of adjourned meeting', as is now usually the case (see eg Table A, article 62).

---

1   Section 372(3).
2   Section 372(5).
3   [1953] Ch 577.
4   As to stamp duty in respect of proxies, see *Gore-Browne on Companies* 44th edn (Jordans,
5   *Re Lancaster* (1877) 5 ChD 911 (CA). The authority may be oral only.
6   *Sadgrove v Bryden* [1907] 1 Ch 318.
7   *Bombay Burmah Trading Co v Shroff* [1905] AC 213 (PC).
8   Ibid.
9   *McLaren v Thomson* [1917] 2 Ch 261.

As a poll is a continuance of the meeting, which is not at an end until the poll is taken, a proxy vote at the meeting includes authority to vote on the poll.[1] But if the articles require the proxies to be lodged so many hours 'before the meeting or adjourned meeting', it is not sufficient that they should be lodged this length of time before the taking of the poll, for the occasion of taking the poll is not an adjournment of the meeting.[2] The taking of a poll is not a meeting of the company in the strict sense, but a mere continuation of the meeting at which the poll was directed to be taken. So that if the articles provide that a proxy is to be valid notwithstanding the death of the principal or revocation of the proxy or transfer of the share, unless intimation of the death, revocation, or transfer is received at the office before the meeting, a revocation of the proxy between the date of the meeting and the taking of the poll is inoperative. It is given 'during' and not 'before' the meeting.[3] It seems also that, where a meeting is adjourned, the adjourned meeting is not a separate meeting, but a continuation of the original one.[4] It follows that, under articles to the above effect, a revocation between the dates of the original and adjourned meetings is equally inoperative. But a shareholder who has given a proxy can, unless the articles otherwise expressly provide, attend the meeting and vote personally. He has an option to vote either personally or by proxy, which he can exercise at any time up to the moment when the vote must be given. By thus attending and voting he supersedes the proxy, and it does not matter whether he has revoked it or not.[5] Where the revocation is out of time and the shareholder who has given the proxy does not attend the meeting, the person to whom the proxy has been given may commit a breach of duty if he uses the vote after notice of the withdrawal of his authority.[6]

'The right of a shareholder to vote by proxy depends on the contract between himself and his co-shareholders, ... and all the requisitions of the contract as to the exercise of the right must be followed.'[7] Accordingly, proxies which are not in accordance with the regulations of the company must be rejected as invalid: for example if the articles of association require an instrument of proxy to be witnessed, it is invalid if not so witnessed.[8] It is for the chairman of the meeting to receive or reject proxies, and his decision is binding, unless it is proved to the court to be wrong.[9] A proxy holder may assume the position of temporary

---

1   Section 372(1).
2   *Shaw v Tati Concessions* [1913] 1 Ch 292.
3   *Spiller v Mayo (Rhodesia) Co* [1926] WN 78.
4   So held by Luxmoore J in *Cousins v International Brick Co* [1931] 2 Ch 90. His view was not dissented from in the Court of Appeal, although the Master of the Rolls (at 99) indicated the possibility that an adjourned meeting might be treated as a separate meeting. Inasmuch as the articles in common use (see eg article 45 in Table A) provide that no business may be transacted at an adjourned meeting other than the business left unfinished at the meeting from which the adjournment took place, the circumstances under which an adjourned meeting can be treated as a separate meeting must be very special.
5   *Cousins v International Brick Co* (above).
6   Ibid, at 104, *per* Romer LJ.
7   *Per* Cotton LJ, *Harben v Phillips* (1883) 23 ChD 14 at 32. While the first phrase of this quotation no longer represents the law, having regard to section 372 it is submitted that, subject to the provisions of the Act, the second phrase remains apposite.
8   *Harben v Phillips* (1883) 23 ChD 14 (CA).
9   *Re Indian Zoedone Co* (1884) 26 ChD 70. But the chairman is not entitled to reject properly executed proxy forms because he believes them to have been obtained by misrepresentations: *Holmes v Jackson* (1957) *The Times*, 3 April. Nor can the chairman reject proxies because of some minor misstatement in them: *Oliver v Dalgleish* [1963] 1 WLR 1274.

chairman to supervise the election of a proper chairman. This applies where the articles provide that, where there is no chairman of the board of directors and no directors present, the members should choose a chairman of a general meeting from one of their own number.[1]

Unless the articles of association or other document governing the meeting so require, it is not essential that the proxies should be produced at the meeting, and if duly lodged at the place required by the regulations the result of the proxies may be communicated by telegram or letter.[2]

13.21.1 Solicitation of proxies

The directors may employ the company's funds in printing or sending out to shareholders proxy forms filled up with the names of the directors or their nominees as the proxies, and in stamping the forms (when required) or the envelopes in which to return them. Indeed, it is their duty thus to advocate the policy which they believe to be in the interests of the company.[3] But if at the company's expense they invite appointments of proxies they must send the invitations to all members entitled to be sent notice of the meeting and to vote thereat by proxy.[4]

Two alternative forms of proxy are contained in Table A, articles 60 and 61, the latter being what is known as a 'two-way' proxy, to enable members to instruct their proxies whether to vote for or against a resolution.

It has been held that if one proxy represents a number of members, some of whom have given proxy forms for and some against a particular resolution, and he votes for the resolution without indicating how many votes he is casting, his vote is valid to the extent of the shares in respect of which he has been given affirmative proxy forms.[5] It would seem that a proxy is not, in the absence of a contractual obligation or a special fiduciary relationship, obliged to use the proxy he has been given. It should be noted that those who solicit proxies (whether it is the board of directors or others) are *not* obliged by law to use 'two-way' proxy forms (which enable members to vote for or against a resolution). It became common practice for the board of directors to use proxy forms in their own favour. However, The Stock Exchange requires that the directors must undertake to send out 'two-way' proxy forms with notices calling meetings of shareholders or debenture-holders.[6]

13.22 Quorum at general meetings

No business can be done at a meeting unless a quorum is present.[7] By section 370(4) of the Companies Act 1985, two members personally present are a quorum, unless the articles otherwise provide.[8] Since the Companies (Single

---

1   *Re Bradford Investments Ltd* [1991] BCLC 224 at 229–230. This is so even if the temporary chairman then has to rule on the admissibility of the votes of all the shareholders present.

2   *Re English, Scottish and Australian Chartered Bank* [1893] 3 Ch 385 (CA).

3   *Peel v London and North-Western Rly* [1907] 2 Ch 5 (CA). *Campbell v Australian Mutual Society* (1908) 77 LJPC 117. *Wilson v LMS Rly Co* [1940] Ch 393 (CA), where it was held to be in order for directors to send stamped proxies at the expense of the company to the larger shareholders only, is now overruled on this point by section 372(6).

4   Section 372(6).

5   *Oliver v Dalgleish* [1963] 1 WLR 1274.

6   See *The Listing Rules*, paragraph 13.28.

7   *Howbeach Coal Co v Teague* (1860) 5 H & N 151; *Re Romford Canal Co* (1883) 24 ChD 85.

8   Table A, article 40, is to the same effect.

Member Private Limited Companies) Regulations 1992[1] came into force (on 15 July 1992), in the case of private companies limited by shares or by guarantee having only one member, one member present in person or by proxy is a quorum. This is so 'notwithstanding any provision to the contrary in the articles'.

Apart from requirements as to quorum under the articles, it is well established that there must be at least two members present who remain throughout the meeting.[2] However, under Table A to the 1948 Act (article 53), it is sufficient if a quorum exists at the beginning of the meeting.[3] The 1985 Table A, article 41, requires a continuing quorum.[4]

Unless the articles provide otherwise, 'presence' at a meeting for the purpose of a quorum means presence in person and not by proxy.[5] However, it has also been held that a member present in two capacities (eg as an individual member and as a trustee) counts as two members personally present.[6]

Where a company is represented under section 375, its representative must be counted in estimating the quorum.[7] An executor or administrator is not a member until he has taken the shares of the deceased into his own name;[8] he cannot therefore be counted in estimating a quorum, unless the articles expressly allow it.[9]

13.23 Reforming the law of company meetings

The Company Law Review,[10] acknowledging the widespread dissatisfaction with the current law and practice regarding shareholders' meetings,[11] led to recommendations for substantial changes to the law, particularly as it applies to the annual general meetings of larger and particularly listed companies. A wide range of issues was addressed in its consultation paper – *Modern Company Law for a Competitive Economy: Company General Meetings and Shareholder Communication* – published in October 1999. These were followed up in the *Developing the Framework* paper in March 2000, addressing responses to the October 1999 document. The starting point was that the annual general meeting is ineffective in fulfilling its role in the governance of public companies. The possibility of public companies being able to dispense with the AGM was canvassed, although it was recognised that

---

1   Section 370A, inserted into the Companies Act 1985 by the Companies (Single Member Private Limited Companies) Regulations 1992, SI 1992/1699, Schedule, paragraph 5.
2   *Sharp v Dawes* (1876) 2 QBD 76 (CA); *Re Sanitary Carbon Co* [1877] WN 223; *Prain and Sons* [1947] SC 325; *Re London Flats* [1969] 1 WLR 711.
3   *Re Hartley Baird Ltd* [1955] Ch 143.
4   This could be awkward for small private companies, which would be well advised not to adopt this aspect of the 1985 Table A.
5   *M Harris Ltd* 1956 SC 207.
6   *Neil McLeod & Sons Ltd, Petitioners* 1967 SC 16. This was decided in respect of what is now section 370(4), which makes provision for a quorum in the absence of provision by the articles.
7   *Re Kelantan Coco Nut Estates* [1920] WN 274.
8   *Re Bowling & Welby's Contract* [1895] 1 Ch 663 at 670 (CA).
9   The court has powers to order a meeting under section 371, which will prevent a minority abusing the quorum requirement to frustrate the desire of a majority shareholder to hold a meeting: *In re HR Paul & Son Ltd* (1973) *The Times*, 17 November. See also *Re Opera Photographic Ltd* [1989] BCLC 763, *Harman v BML Group Ltd* [1994] 1 BCLC 674 (CA), *Ross v Telford* [1998] 1 BCLC 82 (CA), *Re Woven Rugs Ltd* [2002] 1 BCLC 324, *Union Music Ltd v Watson* [2003] EWCA Civ 180, [2003] 1 BCLC 453 and *Gore-Browne on Companies*, 21.21.1.
10   See generally **1.8**.
11   See **13.1**.

detailed requirements would be necessary to find another satisfactory method for communication with, and decision-making by, shareholders. On balance, the Review Steering Group favoured retaining a requirement for public companies to hold an AGM but allowing wholly owned public company subsidiaries to dispense with them and any public company to opt out by unanimous decision of all shareholders. The Steering Group suggested provisions to facilitate the holding of meetings using information technology, including audio-visual techniques and the Internet.

In its White paper[1] the Government put forward a number of proposals with regard to the AGM. Thus, whilst public companies will be required to hold AGMs they will also have the option of deciding unanimously to dispense with the AGM.[2] The proposed Companies Bill is also likely to contain provisions to enable companies to take advantage of communications technology as an alternative means of fulfilling the functions of a meeting.[3]

The notice periods for company meetings are likely to be aligned to a minimum of 14 days and shorter notice if a sufficient number of majority of shareholders agree.[4] Additionally the voting powers of proxies are likely to be enhanced so that proxies will be able to speak and to vote on a show of hands as well as on a poll and join with others in demanding a poll.[5] The Government also proposes a new right for a sufficient body of members to require a scrutiny of any poll that would be conducted by a registered auditor.[6] In order to link the AGM more closely to the annual reporting cycle the draft Bill requires the AGM of public companies the AGM to take place within six months of the financial year-end.[7]

With regard to resolutions, the White Paper states that the Bill will effectively abolish the extraordinary resolution as a separate category of resolution and any current extraordinary resolutions will be replaced by a requirement for a special resolution, with the latter requiring 14 days' notice in line with the intended revised minimum notice period for general meetings.[8] Members' resolutions and statements received in time to be circulated with the notice of the meeting should be circulated to all members at the company's expense.[9] At least as far as the AGM is concerned, the proposals do indicate attempts to address the procedural difficulties that shareholders have in their efforts to hold dialogue with the directors.

As far as smaller companies are concerned, the Steering Group and the Government have supported the policy of a 'think small first' regime, which would mean that extended deregulatory provisions (see **13.4**) would apply by default to most private companies.[10]

---

1   *Modernising Company Law* Cm 5553–I and II, 2002.
2   Ibid, paragraph 2.13.
3   Ibid, paragraph 2.15.
4   Ibid, paragraph 2.17.
5   Ibid, paragraph 2.18.
6   Ibid, paragraph 2.19.
7   Ibid, paragraph 2.16.
8   Ibid, paragraph 2.22.
9   Ibid, paragraph 2.24.
10 See *Developing the Framework*, Chapter 7.

Chapter 14

Accounts and Reports

PART 1: COMPANY ACCOUNTS

14.1 Introduction

Limited companies have for many years been required to produce annual accounts for circulation to members.[1] The basic purpose of such accounts is to provide an account of the stewardship of the directors to the shareholders and creditors, rather than to provide information to the investing public generally. It was at one time acceptable practice deliberately to understate the value of a company's assets. Investors required assurance that their investment was safe and creditors that the company could pay its debts. Now, however, greater accuracy is expected in accounts, and the deliberate understatement of assets or overstatement of liabilities is considered to be incompatible with the fundamental requirement of the Companies Act that accounts should give a true and fair view.[2]

Accounting standards are governed by an independent Accounting Standards Board[3] with the assistance of an Urgent Issues Task Force,[4] which endeavours to reach a consensus where unsatisfactory or conflicting interpretations have developed in respect of accounting treatment. The Accounting Standards Board issues Statements of Standard Accounting Practice (SSAP)[5] and Financial Reporting Standards, the latter being based on the Statement of Principles for Financial Reporting, which provides a framework for the consistent and logical formulation of accounting standards. Accounting Standards do not have direct legal effect but they may have indirect effect on the interpretations that the courts would give to true and fair concepts.[6] The court is likely to infer that, in general, compliance with accounting standards is necessary to meet the true and fair requirement, and that departures will result in a breach of that requirement unless it is clearly justified and explained. An accounting standard which the court upholds must be complied with to meet the true and fair requirement becomes, in cases where it is applicable, a source of law in the widest sense of that term.

The adoption of the European Community's Fourth Company Law Directive in July 1978 foreshadowed new legislation in the United Kingdom governing the format and content of limited companies' accounts. The provisions of this directive, which were initially implemented by the Companies Act 1981 and were

---

1   Companies were first compelled to publish a balance sheet by the Companies Act 1908. The Companies Act 1929 required them additionally to circulate to their members a copy of the profit and loss account.

2   See **14.4**.

3   This replaced the Accounting Standards Committee in August 1990. For a brief history of the developments in this context, see *Gore-Browne on Companies* 44th edn (Jordans, loose-leaf) at 23.1.

4   Created in March 1991.

5   These were adopted from the SSAPS that were developed by the Accounting Standards Committee, the predecessor of the Accounting Standards Board.

6   See *Gore-Browne on Companies* at 23.1.

then consolidated in the Companies Act 1985, represented a major departure from previous United Kingdom practice in that, for the first time, the basic rules for the presentation and accounting measurement of income, expenditure, assets and liabilities were laid down by law. Before that, UK company law had been more concerned with the disclosure of accounting information than with precise methods of presentation or with measurement. The Companies Act 1989 extended the influence of the EC legislation by implementing the European Community's Seventh Company Law Directive, which includes detailed rules for preparing consolidated financial statements. This largely reflected existing accounting standards, but also changed the emphasis in defining a subsidiary undertaking from legal ownership to effective control. The 1989 Act[1] also implemented the Eighth Company Law Directive on the qualification and supervision of auditors. All references in this chapter to the Companies Act 1985 are, where appropriate, references to that Act as amended by the 1989 Act.

The Review of Company Law has led to proposals for fundamental changes to the reporting and accounting regime, emphasising the need for a more inclusive approach to reporting for public and large private companies, while simplifying the requirements for small companies.[2]

In addition, the European Regulation on the application of international accounting standards has led the Government to take steps towards extending the use of international accounting standards by all public companies as an alternative to the accounting standards.[3]

14.2   The directors' obligation to keep accounting records

14.2.1   The definition of accounting records

The directors of a company are required to ensure that accounting records sufficient to show and explain the company's transactions are kept. The accounting records must be such as to disclose with reasonable accuracy, at any time, the financial position of the company at that time and enable the directors to ensure that any balance sheet or profit and loss account of the company, prepared in accordance with the Companies Act, gives a true and fair view of its state of affairs or of its profit or loss. In particular, the accounting records must contain entries from day to day of all sums of money received and expended by the company and the matters in respect of which the receipt and expenditure takes place, a record of the assets and liabilities of the company and (where the company's business involves dealing in goods) information relating to stock and to purchases and sales. This information comprises statements of stock held by the company at the end of each financial year, all statements of stocktaking from which these statements have been or are to be prepared and (except in the case of goods sold by way of ordinary retail trade) statements of all goods sold and

---

1   Especially Part II.

2   Ibid, chapter 8.

3   For an overview of the European level initiatives see Villiers, 'European Integration and Globalisation: The Experience of Financial Reporting' in *The Cambridge Yearbook of European Legal Studies*, Volume 5 (Hart, 2003–2004), p 105. See for more detail on the European measures and the UK's position, DTI, *Modernisation of Accounting Directives/IAS Infrastructure: A consultation document on the implementation of the accounting modernisation directive and arrangement for the use of IAS for companies and building societies*, March 2004.

purchased, showing the goods and the buyers and sellers in sufficient detail to enable those goods and those buyers and sellers to be identified.[1]

Accounting records may be kept in non-legible (eg computerised) form so long as the recording is capable of being reproduced in a legible form.[2]

14.2.2 The custody of accounting records

The accounting records must be kept either at the company's registered office or at such other place as the directors think fit and must be open to inspection by the company's officers at all times. Shareholders have no statutory right to inspect accounting records. If the accounting records are kept outside Great Britain, accounts and returns must be sent to and retained in Great Britain, where they must be open to inspection by the company's officers.

Subject to any direction under the insolvency rules, the accounting records which companies, as a minimum, are required to keep by law must be preserved for at least six years (or, in the case of a private company, three years) from the date on which they are made.[3]

14.2.3 The preparation of accounts

The directors of every company are responsible for the regular preparation of accounts for presentation to the shareholders. The period covered by these accounts (the 'financial year') must coincide with the company's accounting reference period or, for the benefit of companies which prefer to make up their accounts for a 52 or 53-week period, may end at a date within seven days of the accounting reference date.[4] For this purpose, the accounting reference period means the period between two successive accounting reference dates and the accounting reference date means the date registered as such with the Registrar of Companies. The basic accounting reference date for a company incorporated on or after 1 April 1996 is the last day of the month in which the anniversary of its incorporation falls.[5] Companies incorporated before that date had a period of nine months from the date of incorporation to select another date than that set out in the statute, which was 31 March for a company incorporated before 1 April 1990, and the last day of the month in which the anniversary of its incorporation fell for companies incorporated on or after 1 April 1990 but before April 1996.[6] In all cases, the accounting reference of a newly incorporated company must be such as to give the company a first accounting reference period of more than six but not more than 18 months.[7]

A company may alter its accounting reference date (and thereby its accounting reference period) by giving notice to the Registrar of Companies in prescribed form. Notice must normally be given before the end of the accounting reference

---

1   Section 221.
2   For VAT purposes, the Customs and Excise must approve the form of any accounting records kept in non-legible form. See also FRAG 5/92, a statement issued in March 1992 by the Council of the Institute of Chartered Accountants in England and Wales, which gives guidance on the contents of such accounts.
3   Companies Act 1985, section 222.
4   Ibid, section 223(3).
5   Section 224(3A), as inserted by the Companies Act 1985 (Miscellaneous Accounting Amendments) Regulations 1996, SI 1996/189.
6   Section 224(2) and (3).
7   Section 224(4).

period affected, but retrospective notice may be given if the company is the holding company or a subsidiary of another company and the new accounting reference date coincides with the accounting reference date of that other company – provided that the period for laying and delivering accounts[1] has not expired. If the change in accounting reference date will have the effect of increasing the length of an accounting reference period, the period so increased may not exceed 18 months. An application to increase the length of an accounting reference period must also meet one of the further conditions that the period is being extended for the first time, or that it was last extended more than five years previously, or that the change is being made to make the date coincide with the accounting reference date of an European Economic Area (EEA) parent or subsidiary undertaking, or that the Department of Trade and Industry has given its consent.[2]

The accounts required consist of a balance sheet, a profit and loss account and notes, all complying with the requirements of the Companies Act 1985, Schedule 4.[3]

As from 21 July 1993, limited companies which form partnerships with other companies are responsible for preparing accounts for the partnership and for causing them to be audited.[4]

14.2.4 *Laying and delivering accounts*

It is the duty of the directors to lay before the company in general meeting a copy of every document required to be comprised in the accounts for each financial year[5] and to deliver a copy of them to the Registrar of Companies[6] within a specified period after the accounting reference date. The documents required to be comprised in the accounts are those specified in **14.2.6**, and, where appropriate, group accounts.[7] A private company may elect to dispense with the laying of accounts before the company in general meeting,[8] but must send copies of the accounts to members and others entitled to receive them whilst an election is in force. A shareholder has the right to require the laying of accounts.[9]

Although the accounts laid before the shareholders must comply with the requirements of the Companies Act 1985, Schedule 4, small and medium-sized companies (see **14.17.1**) are permitted to deliver to the Registrar (or otherwise publish) abbreviated accounts.[10] The accounts that a company is permitted to deliver to the Registrar (whether they are in the normal format specified by the Companies Act, or whether they are in one of the abbreviated formats appropriate

1   Companies Act 1985, section 225(3).
2   Companies Act 1985, section 225 as amended by the Companies Act 1985 (Miscellaneous Accounting Amendments) Regulations 1996, SI 1996/189.
3   Companies Act 1985, section 226. Besides this statutory requirement FRS1 'Cash Flow Statements (Revised 1996)' requires most medium-sized and large companies to provide a cash flow statement in their annual accounts. See **14.4**.
4   The Partnerships and Unlimited Companies (Accounts) Regulations 1993, SI 1993/1820.
5   Companies Act 1985, section 241(1).
6   Ibid, section 242(1).
7   Ibid, section 227(1).
8   Ibid, section 252(1).
9   Ibid, section 253(2).
10   Ibid, section 246(1).

to small or medium-sized companies) are referred to in the Act (together with the report of the directors) as the 'statutory accounts'.[1]

The period allowed for laying and delivering accounts is, in the case of private companies, ten months and, in the case of other companies, seven months after the end of the relevant accounting period. A company which carries on business or has interests abroad and gives notice in prescribed form to the Registrar of Companies within the periods mentioned above may obtain an extension of these periods by three months to 13 months and ten months respectively. The Secretary of State may further extend them in special circumstances.[2]

If the company fails to deliver its accounts to the Registrar within the period of time allowed, the company and every person who was a director of the company immediately before the end of that period may be liable to a fine. The Registrar also has the right under section 242A to obtain fixed penalty fines from companies that are late in filing accounts.

Certain unlimited companies are not required to deliver accounts to the Registrar.[3]

14.2.5 Signing of accounts

Every balance sheet of a company and every copy of such a balance sheet which is laid before the company in general meeting or delivered to the Registrar of Companies must be signed on behalf of the board by two of the directors or by one if there is only one director.[4] There is no legal requirement that the directors should also sign a consolidated balance sheet, although this is usually done. Section 238(4), however, requires the board to approve the group accounts.

14.2.6 Documents to be annexed or attached to the balance sheet

The profit and loss account and any group accounts must be annexed to the balance sheet, these documents together, with any notes thereto, comprising the accounts. The board must approve the profit and loss account and group accounts before the balance sheet is signed on their behalf. The auditors' report and the directors' report must be attached to a company's full individual (or group) accounts.[5]

14.2.7 Persons entitled to receive copies of the accounts

A copy of every balance sheet which is laid before the company in general meeting, together with the documents required to be annexed thereto and a copy of the auditors' and directors' reports, is to be sent to every member and

---

1   Ibid, section 240. See also SI 1992/2452, SI 1996/189 and SI 1997/220. As to accounts in a foreign language, see section 242(1) and for the possibility of delivering accounts with the amounts translated into Euros, see section 242B. The latter section still refers to ECUs, but as the ECU was abolished on 31 December 1998, it should presumably be read as a reference to Euros.

2   Companies Act 1985, section 244(5).

3   Companies Act 1985, section 254(1).

4   Ibid, section 233.

5   As to the penalties for failing to attach the auditors' report to the full individual accounts and the position with regard to the publication of abridged accounts, see **14.3**.

debenture-holder, except as stated in a footnote below,[1] and every other person entitled to receive notices of general meetings of the company not less than 21 days before the meeting. If they are sent less than 21 days before the meeting, they shall nevertheless be deemed to have been duly sent if it is so agreed by all the members entitled to attend and vote at the meeting. Any member of a company and any debenture-holder is entitled to be furnished on demand and free of charge with a copy of the most recent balance sheet of the company including every document required to be annexed thereto and a copy of the auditors' report and directors' report.[2]

14.3 The publication of accounts

Except in the case of small companies exempt from audit, the statutory accounts of any company (see **14.2.4**) may not be published otherwise than with the relevant auditors' report. In addition, where a company is required to produce group accounts, any full individual accounts that the company publishes must be accompanied by full group accounts. Similarly, full group accounts of any company may not be published otherwise than with either the company's full individual accounts for the period or the relevant auditors' report.[3]

Accounts that are neither statutory individual accounts nor statutory group accounts are called 'non-statutory accounts'. Where a company chooses to publish non-statutory accounts, they must be accompanied by an explanatory statement that indicates that they are not the statutory accounts, and states whether the statutory accounts have been delivered to the Registrar of Companies, whether the auditors have made a report under section 235 in respect of the statutory accounts to which the non-statutory accounts relate, and whether that report was qualified. However, that report may not be published with the non-statutory accounts.

If the accounts or directors' report do not comply with the provisions of the Companies Act 1985, the directors may prepare revised accounts or reports.[4]

14.4 The contents of accounts

Every balance sheet of a company must give a true and fair view of the state of affairs of the company as at the end of its financial year, and every profit and loss account a true and fair view of the profit or loss of the company for the financial

---

1   Except that it need not be sent to: a member or debenture-holder who is not entitled to receive notices of general meetings and of whose address the company is unaware; to more than one of the joint holders of any shares or debentures none of whom are entitled to receive such notices; or in the case of joint holders of shares or debentures some of whom are and some of whom are not entitled to receive such notices, to those who are not so entitled. In the case of a company not having a share capital, it need not be sent to a member or debenture-holder who is not entitled to receive notices of general meetings.

2   Companies Act 1985, sections 238 and 239. See **14.18** for the penalties for the failure to comply with these provisions. Where the accounts of a company fail to comply with what is now Schedule 9, a shareholder may not sue the directors of a company on the basis that the accounts distributed to the members did not conform with Schedule 9: *Devlin v Slough Estates Ltd* [1983] BCLC 497. See (1982) 2 Co Law 261.

3   Companies Act 1985, section 254.

4   Ibid, sections 245, 245A and 245B.

year. A financial year is the period for which the accounts are made up and need not be a calendar year, or a period of 12 months.[1]

The balance sheet and profit and loss account must comply with the Companies Act 1985, Schedule 4. There are, however, some exceptions to this general rule.[2] The requirement that the accounts must comply with Schedule 4 is, with certain exceptions,[3] without prejudice to the requirement that a true and fair view be shown and to any other requirements of the Companies Act. The Secretary of State may add to or alter the requirements of the Companies Act in respect of balance sheet, profit and loss account and group accounts.[4] Any reference to a balance sheet or profit and loss account includes any notes to the accounts in question which give any information required by the Act.

Most of the detailed requirements of information to be disclosed in a company's accounts are set out in the Companies Act 1985, Schedule 4, which provides a company with a choice of two fixed formats for the balance sheet and four fixed formats for the profit and loss account. These formats specify the information that must be given on the face of the accounts and the information that may be given in a note to the accounts.[5] From 1 March 1997 eligible small companies may instead prepare their accounts in accordance with the new Schedule 8.[6] When a company has adopted a particular format, that format may not generally be changed in subsequent years. Regardless of where in the accounts an item is disclosed, assets and income may not be set off against liabilities and expenditure, or vice versa (immaterial items need not be disclosed).[7] Unless otherwise stated, the corresponding amounts for the preceding financial year for all items required to be disclosed in the balance sheet or profit and loss account should be shown on the face of those accounts. Where an amount for the previous year is not comparable with the amount shown for the current year, the prior year amount must be adjusted.

Schedule 4 contains a number of fundamental accounting principles which must be observed in drawing up the accounts. The company must be presumed to be carrying on business as a going concern (but this presumption is, of course, rebuttable if the facts do not support it). There must be consistency in accounting policies from one year to the next. The amounts included in the accounts must be arrived at on a prudent basis; in particular, only profits realised at the balance sheet date may be included in the profit and loss account[8] and provision must be

---

1   As to the method of determining the financial year, see **14.2.3**.

2   See *Gore-Browne on Companies* 44th edn (Jordans, loose-leaf) at 23.6.

3   For holding companies see **14.14.6**. For exemptions provided by Part III of Schedule 9, see **14.17**.

4   Companies Act 1985, section 256 – for purposes of adapting them to the circumstances of the company.

5   Banking companies must comply with the requirements of Schedule 9 (sections 255 and 255A, as amended by the Companies Act 1989, section 18, and further amended by the Companies Act 1985 (Bank Accounts) Regulations 1991, SI 1991/2705). Insurance companies may choose to comply with the requirements of Schedule 9A, as amended by SI 1991/2705. No detail is given in this book of these particular rules.

6   See SI 1997/220.

7   Companies Act 1985, Schedule 4, paragraphs (2) and (5).

8   The United Kingdom accounting bodies have issued their interpretation of realised profits in guidance statement TR81 (September 1982), which interprets 'principles generally accepted' for a definition of 'principles', for which see *Associated Portland Cement Manufacturers Ltd v Price Commission* [1975] ICR 27.

made for all liabilities and losses relating to the financial year, or to a previous
financial year, even if they do not become apparent until a date between the end
of the financial year and the date when the directors sign the balance sheet. All
income and expenditure relating to the financial year must be taken into account,
regardless of when it is received or paid. In arriving at the amounts to be included
in the accounts, each individual asset and liability must be considered separately.[1]

Where, in special circumstances, the directors consider that it is appropriate to
depart from any of the above principles, they may do so, but particulars of the
departure, the reasons for it, and its effect on the accounts must be explained in a
note.[2]

It is a requirement of the Act that the accounting policies adopted in
determining the company's profit or loss should be stated in the notes to the
accounts.[3] These policies may vary from one company to another. It must also be
stated whether applicable accounting standards have been complied with and
particulars of and reasons for any material departures from them must be given.[4]

14.5 The balance sheet: share capital, reserves and provisions

A company that is required to prepare its accounts in accordance with Schedule 4
to the Companies Act 1985 must use one of two fixed formats for the balance
sheet.[5] Every balance sheet must show the capital and reserves of the company,
categorised as specified in these standard formats. The amount of the allotted
share capital and the amount of the called-up share capital that has been paid up
must be shown separately on the face of the balance sheet under the heading
'Called-up share capital' (Schedule 4, Part I, note 12 to the balance sheet formats).
In addition, a company must show, either on the face of the balance sheet or in the
notes, the amount of the company's authorised share capital and where shares of
more than one class have been allotted, the number and aggregate nominal value
of the shares of each class so allotted (Schedule 4, paragraph 38(1)). If a company
has allotted shares during the financial year, information must be given about the
classes of shares allotted and (for each class) the number allotted, their aggregate
nominal value and the consideration received for each class respectively
(Schedule 4, paragraph 39). Where any part of the allotted share capital consists
of redeemable shares, there must be shown the earliest and latest dates on which
the company has power to redeem such shares, whether they must be redeemed in
any event or are redeemable at the option of the company and any premium
payable on redemption or the fact that no premium is payable (Schedule 4,
paragraph 38(2)).

---

1   Schedule 4, paragraphs 10–14. These principles follow closely those set out in FRS 18
    'Accounting Policies' (effective for accounting periods ending on or after 22 June 2001) and
    previously SSAP No 2 – Disclosure of accounting policies. See also FRS 3 'Reporting financial
    performance' and Urgent Issues Task Force Abstract (see *Gore-Browne on Companies* 44th edn
    (Jordans, loose-leaf) at 23.1). 'Disclosure of changes in accounting policy' 21 November 1995.
2   Schedule 4, paragraph 15.
3   Schedule 4, paragraph 36. This is also a requirement of FRS 18 'Accounting Policies'
    (effective for accounting periods ending on or after 22 June 2001) and previously SSAP No 2
    – Disclosure of accounting policies.
4   Schedule 4, paragraph 36A.
5   Section 226(3): see *Gore-Browne on Companies* 44th edn (Jordans, loose-leaf) at 23.7.

The number, description and amount of any shares in the company for which any person has an option to subscribe are required by paragraph 40 of Schedule 4 to be shown, as are the periods during which the option is exercisable and the price to be paid for the shares when the option is exercised.

If a company holds any of its own shares among its investments the nominal value of the shares must be shown separately (Schedule 4, Part I, note 4 to the balance sheet formats).[1]

Provisions may not be shown under the heading of capital and reserves and, except for provisions for depreciation or diminution in the value of assets, should be shown under the heading of provisions for liabilities and charges. A provision is any amount written off or retained by way of providing for depreciation, renewals or diminution in value of assets or retained by way of providing for any known liability of which the amount or the date cannot be determined with substantial accuracy (Schedule 4, paragraphs 88 and 89). Reserves are not defined in Schedule 1, but it is generally accepted that they do not include any amounts which fall within the definition of a provision, or any sum set aside to prevent undue fluctuations in taxation charges.

In respect of each category of reserves and provisions for liabilities and charges, particulars must be given of the opening and closing balances and the source and amount of any increase or decrease during the financial year. Particulars must also be given of any transfer from provisions for liabilities and charges made otherwise than for the purpose for which the provision was established, and of any material provision included under the balance sheet heading of 'other provisions': Schedule 4, paragraph 46.

The amount of any provisions for taxation, other than deferred taxation, shall be stated separately in the notes to the balance sheet (Schedule 4, paragraph 47).[2]

All movements on reserves should be accounted for through the profit and loss account, except for prior year adjustments and unrealised surpluses on valuation of fixed assets, which should be taken directly to reserves, and capital gains and losses of investment trust companies (whether realised or unrealised) which may be, and in practice are, dealt with in the same way. Prior year adjustments are defined for this purpose as material adjustments applicable to prior years arising from changes in accounting policies and from the correction of fundamental errors.

While there is no legal requirement to do so, it is good practice to state in the accounts the respective amounts of distributable and non-distributable reserves. In effect, this practice is encouraged by Financial Reporting Standard No 2 – Accounting for subsidiary undertakings.[3]

As regards the need to create a revaluation reserve and the use to be made of it, see **14.7.1**.

14.6 Liabilities

There are various kinds of liabilities that must appear separately in the accounts under the headings 'Creditors' and 'Accruals and deferred income'. For each item under the heading 'Creditors', amounts falling due within one year and

---

1   Further information of a similar nature must be given in the directors' report. See **14.26.1**.
2   However, disclosure of any provision for deferred taxation is required by FRS No 15 (revised) – Deferred taxation.
3   See **7.21.2** regarding what are distributable and non-distributable profits.

amounts falling due after more than one year must be stated separately, as also must convertible debenture loans and creditors for taxation and social security (Schedule 4, Part I, notes 7, 9 and 13 to the balance sheet formats).[1]

Where a company has issued debentures during the financial year, the following information must be given either on the face of the accounts or in the notes: the classes of debentures issued and, as respects each class of debenture, the amount issued and the consideration received for the issue (Schedule 4, paragraph 41(1)).

Particulars of any redeemed debentures which the company has power to reissue must also be given (Schedule 4, paragraph 41(2)). When a debenture is given, for example, to a bank to secure an overdraft, the debenture is not deemed to have been redeemed only because the account has ceased to be in debit while the debenture remains so deposited. If any of the company's debentures are held by a nominee or trustee for the company, the nominal amount of the debentures and the amount at which they stand in the company's books must be stated (Schedule 4, paragraph 41(3)). The number, description and amount of its debentures held by subsidiaries or their nominees must also be shown (Schedule 5, paragraph 6).

In respect of each item shown under the heading 'Creditors', there should be stated the aggregate amount of any debts included under that item which are payable or repayable otherwise than by instalments and fall due for payment or repayment more than five years after the balance sheet date or are repayable by instalments any of which fall due after that date.[2] For each such item the payment or repayment terms and rates of interest must be given, except that if the number of loans is such that, in the opinion of the directors, compliance would result in a statement of excessive length, a general indication of such payment or repayment terms and interest rates may be given (Schedule 4, paragraph 48(1) to (3)).

In respect of each item shown under the heading 'Creditors' there must be stated the amounts of any liabilities included under that item in respect of which any security has been given and an indication of that security (Schedule 4, paragraph 48(4)).[3] Particulars must be given of any charges on the assets of the company to secure the liabilities of another person and the amount secured must be stated. Particulars must also be given of the amount or estimated amount and legal nature of any other material contingent liability not provided for, and of any valuable security that the company may have provided in connection with such a contingent liability (Schedule 4, paragraph 50(1) and (2)).

The amount recommended for distribution as a dividend and the amount of any arrears of fixed cumulative dividends must be stated separately for each class, as must the periods to which such arrears relate (Schedule 4, paragraph 49).

Where practicable, the amount of any contracts for capital expenditure which have not been provided in the accounts should be stated (Schedule 4, paragraph 50(3)).

---

1   For these purposes, a loan is treated as falling due for repayment on the earliest date on which the lender could require repayment: Schedule 4, paragraph 85. See also SI 1996/189.

2   For a more detailed analysis of maturity dates of borrowings required under the continuing obligations of companies whose securities are admitted to listing, see *Gore-Browne on Companies* 44th edn (Jordans, loose-leaf) at 23.21.5.

3   See Chapter 10, above, as to the creation and registration of charges under the Companies Act 1985. All charges required to be entered in a company's own register of charges here apply.

The amount of any pension commitments included in the balance sheet, and any such commitments that have not been provided for, must be stated. Where those commitments relate wholly or partly to pensions payable to past directors of the company, separate particulars must be given (Schedule 4, paragraph 50(4)). Particulars must also be given of any other material financial commitments not provided for in the accounts (Schedule 4, paragraph 50(5)).

14.7 Fixed assets

The fixed formats of balance sheet contained in Schedule 4 to the Companies Act 1985 require assets to be classified as fixed or current (with the exception that, at the company's option, called-up share capital not paid and prepayments and accrued income may be treated as separate categories). A fixed asset is defined as one that is intended for continuing use in the company's activities.[1]

14.7.1 Types of fixed asset and general rules for their treatment in accounts

Three main categories of fixed asset are recognised in the standard balance sheet formats in Schedule 4: intangible assets; tangible assets; and investments held for the long term.

Fixed assets with a limited useful economic life must be wholly written off, or written down to their estimated residual value (if any), by systematic charges for depreciation spread over the asset's useful economic life (Schedule 4, paragraph 18). In addition, if a fixed asset has diminished in value and diminution in value is expected to be permanent, the value of the asset concerned must be written down accordingly. If a fixed asset investment has diminished in value (but the diminution is not expected to be permanent) the value of the asset concerned may (but need not) be similarly written down. Any such provision for diminution in the value of a fixed asset must be disclosed separately or in aggregate, either in the profit and loss account or the notes. If it subsequently transpires that a provision for diminution in value of a fixed asset is no longer required, any surplus provision must be written back and the amount written back must be disclosed either in the profit and loss account or in the notes (Schedule 4, paragraph 19). However, investment companies may account for profits and losses arising on the valuations of investments through reserves (Schedule 4, paragraph 71(2)). The accounting policies adopted which relate to the depreciation and diminution in value of assets must be disclosed in a note to the accounts (Schedule 4, paragraph 36).

As an alternative to the historical cost accounting rules discussed above, companies may include certain fixed assets in their accounts on the basis of alternative accounting rules. These alternative accounting rules in general allow certain assets to be included in the accounts on the basis of their market value, or their current cost, instead of on the basis of their purchase price or production cost.

Where any of the alternative accounting rules are adopted, the assets affected and the basis of valuation used for determining the amounts at which those assets are stated in the accounts must be disclosed in a note. There must also be shown (except in the case of stocks), either separately on the face of the balance sheet or

---

1   Section 262(1).

the notes, the comparable amounts determined according to the historical cost accounting rules, or the differences between the two amounts (Schedule 4, paragraph 33).

If fixed assets (other than listed investments) are included in the accounts on the basis of one of the alternative accounting rules, there must be shown the years (to the extent known) in which the assets were valued, their respective values and, in respect of any valuation taking place during the financial year, the names or qualifications of the persons who undertook the valuation (Schedule 4, paragraph 43).

Where, as a result of adopting the alternative accounting rules, a profit or loss arises, it must be either credited or debited to a separate reserve called the 'revaluation reserve'. This reserve may be subsequently reduced to the extent that amounts standing to its credit are, in the opinion of the directors, no longer necessary. Transfers from the reserve to the profit and loss account may, however, be made only if either the amount transferred was previously charged to that account, or if the transfer represents a realised profit. The amount of the revaluation reserve must be shown on the face of the balance sheet. The taxation effect of any movements on the reserve must be disclosed in a note unless the company is an investment company (Schedule 4, paragraph 34).

Regardless of the method used for determining the value of a fixed asset for inclusion in the accounts, there must be shown for each category of fixed assets, either on the face of the balance sheet or in the notes, the cost at valuation of that item at the beginning and the end of the financial year, together with any revaluation adjustment and the amounts of any acquisitions, disposals or transfers that have taken place during the year. There must also be shown the cumulative amount of all provisions for depreciation or diminution in value of each such category of fixed assets, the amount of such provisions made in the financial year, the amount of any adjustments to such provisions arising from the disposal of any fixed assets and the amount of any other adjustments made to such provisions during the year (Schedule 4, paragraph 42).

14.7.2 *Intangible assets*

The categories of intangible asset that must be disclosed in the accounts are set out in Schedule 4.

Development costs may be included in the balance sheet only in special circumstances and, if they are so included, the notes to the accounts must state the period over which they are being written off and the reason why they were not written off in the year in which the expenditure took place.

Goodwill may be included in a company's balance sheet only if it has been purchased for valuable consideration. Its treatment is also covered by FSR 10.[1]

As an alternative to the historical cost accounting rules, intangible assets (other than goodwill) may be included in the accounts at their current cost (Schedule 4, paragraph 31(1)).

The following items may not be treated as assets in a company's balance sheet: preliminary expenses; expenses of and commission on any issue of shares or debentures; and costs of research (Schedule 4, paragraph 3(2)).

---

1   Schedule 4, Part I, Note (3) to Balance Sheet format. For details on FSR 10, see *Gore-Browne on Companies* 44th edn (Jordans, loose-leaf) at 23.7.5.

14.7.3 *Tangible assets*

The categories of tangible fixed asset that must be disclosed in the accounts are set out in Schedule 4.

In contrast to the general rule for accounting for fixed assets, tangible assets whose overall value is not material and whose quantity, value and composition are not subject to material variation, may be included in the accounts at a fixed quantity and value (Schedule 4, paragraph 25(1)(a) and (2)).

As an alternative to historical cost accounting rules, tangible fixed assets may be included in the accounts at a market value, determined as at the date of their last valuation, or at their current cost (Schedule 4, paragraph 31(2)).

Regardless of the accounting rules adopted, there must be shown, in respect of the land and buildings, either on the face of the balance sheet or in the notes, the amounts ascribable to freehold property and leasehold property respectively. This latter amount must be further subdivided between the amounts ascribable to long leases (50 years' unexpired term or more) and those held on short leases.

Where the market value of the land differs substantially from the value at which it is stated in the balance sheet and the difference is, in the opinion of the directors, of such significance as to require that the attention of members or debenture-holders should be drawn to it, it should be shown in the directors' report (Schedule 7, paragraph 1(2)).[1] Alternatively, it may be stated in the notes to the accounts.

14.7.4 *Investments (other than in group companies)*

The categories of investments that must be disclosed in the accounts, either as fixed or current assets, are set out in Schedule 4.

The accounts must shown how much of the value of the investments is ascribable to listed investments (ie investments that have been granted listing on a recognised stock exchange or any stock exchange of repute outside Great Britain (Schedule 4, paragraph 84).

The aggregate market value of any listed investment must be given where it differs from the amount stated, and, if the market value of any investments is taken as being higher than The Stock Exchange value, both The Stock Exchange value and the market value must be shown (Schedule 4, paragraph 45).

If, at the balance sheet date, a company holds more than 20% of the allotted shares of a class of equity capital in an undertaking other than a subsidiary, it must show the name of the undertaking in which it holds shares, the country of incorporation or registration,[2] the identity of the class of shares held, the proportion of the shares held to the total of the allotted shares of that class, and similar details of shares of other classes which it holds in the same undertaking (Schedule 5, paragraph 7). There is, however, no requirement to refer separately to different classes of shares held in the same undertaking. These particulars need not be given if the undertaking in which shares are held is either incorporated outside the United Kingdom or incorporate in the United Kingdom but carries on business abroad, if, in the opinion of the directors, to give them would be harmful to the business of the shareholding company or the other company, and the

---

1   See **14.26**.
2   The country of incorporation must be shown if it is incorporated outside Great Britain. The place of registration must be shown if the company holding shares is registered in England and the other in Scotland (or vice versa).

Department of Trade and Industry agrees that the information need not be disclosed.[1]

Further particulars of that other company must be given in a note to the accounts. These further particulars are the aggregate amount of that other company's capital and reserves as at the end of its financial year ending with, or last before, the financial year of the investing company and its profit or loss for that year.[2] These further particulars need not be given, however, where the investment in that other company is accounted for by the equity method of accounting.[3]

A further exemption from disclosure of the information referred to above in respect of holdings in excess of 20% is available if the directors are of the opinion that so many undertakings are involved that particulars of excessive length would have to be given; in that event, the information need be given only in respect of those investments that principally affect the company's assets and profit or loss. However, if any particulars are omitted from the accounts for that reason, that fact must be stated, and the full particulars must be given in the annual return.[4]

14.8 Current assets

A current asset is defined as one that is not intended for use on a continuing basis in the company's activities.[5]

Four main categories of current assets are recognised in the standard balance sheet formats in Schedule 4: stocks; debtors; investments;[6] and bank balances and cash in hand.

Loans made under the authority of section 153(4)(b) or (c) or section 155 of the Companies Act 1985 are to be disclosed either on the face of the balance sheet or in the notes (Schedule 4, paragraph 51(2)). These provisions enable companies in limited circumstances to provide financial assistance for the purpose of purchasing their own shares.[7]

The requirements of the Act as regards disclosure in the accounts of information relating to loans to directors and officers are set out in **14.12–14.13**.

14.9 The profit and loss account

A company that is required to prepare its accounts in accordance with Schedule 4 of the Companies Act 1985 must use one of four fixed formats for the profit and loss account.[8] Any of the information contained in these formats may be combined where either their individual amounts are not material, or their combination permits a readier appreciation of the company's profit or loss, but where any of these items are combined on the face of the profit and loss account

---

1   Companies Act 1985, section 231(3).
2   Schedule 5, paragraph 9.
3   Schedule 5, paragraph 9. Companies falling within this definition will normally be associated companies or joint ventures within the meaning of FRS 9 'Associates and joint ventures' see *Gore-Browne on Companies* 44th edn (Jordans, loose-leaf) at 23.7.7, note 2.
4   Schedule 5, paragraphs 11 and 12. Section 231 provides that the company and every officer in default should be liable to a fine for failure to give the particulars in the annual return.
5   Section 262.
6   See **14.7.4**.
7   See **7.18**.
8   Section 226.

for the latter of these reasons, they must be disclosed separately in a note (Schedule 4, paragraph 3(4)).[1]

14.10 Directors' emoluments

The requirements governing disclosure of directors' emoluments and related benefits for accounting periods ending on or after 31 March 1997 are set out in Schedule 6 to the Companies Act 1985.[2] These provisions were introduced in response to the Cadbury Committee Report on the *Financial Aspects of Corporate Governance* published in December 1992 and the Greenbury Report on *Directors' Remuneration* published in July 1995.[3] The information to be disclosed consists of:

(a) aggregates relating to directors' emoluments (paragraph 1);
(b) details of the emoluments of the highest paid director, where applicable (paragraph 2);
(c) excess retirement benefits of directors and past directors, if any (paragraph 7);
(d) compensation to directors for loss of office (paragraph 8); and
(e) sums paid to third parties in respect of directors' services (paragraph 9).[4]

Compensation for loss of office includes compensation for the loss of the office of director or of any other office connected with the management of the company or of any subsidiary.[5] Compensation for the loss of the office of director must be distinguished from that for the loss of any other office. Any sum for which a director must account by reason of section 315[6] need not be included (Schedule 6, paragraph 10).

The amounts to be shown include sums paid by or receivable from the company, its subsidiaries and any other person. In the case of compensation for loss of office the aggregate amounts received from sources in each of these categories must be shown separately. The relevant amounts are any amounts receivable in respect of the year, whenever paid, and sums that are not receivable in respect of any particular period but are paid in the year. If any sums are omitted from one year's figures because they are sums for which directors must account by virtue of section 315 and the liability is subsequently released or is not enforced within two years, or if any expense allowances are not charged to income tax until after the end of the relevant year, these must be shown in the first accounts in which it is practicable to do so, and must be shown separately. The directors may make such an apportionment as they consider necessary.

---

1   For further detail, see *Gore Brown on Companies* 44th edn (Jordans, loose-leaf) at 23.9.1–23.9.6.
2   Companies Act 1985, section 232, and Schedule 6, Part I, as amended by the Companies Act 1989, section 6 and Schedule 4, paragraph 3, and as further amended by the Company Accounts (Disclosure of Directors' Emoluments) Regulations 1997, SI 1997/570.
3   See Chapter 11.
4   For further detail, see *Gore Browne on Companies* 44th edn (Jordans, loose-leaf) at 23.10.
5   Companies Act 1985, Schedule 6, para 8(4) as amended by the Company Accounts (Disclosure of Directors' Emoluments) Regulations 1997, SI 1997/570.
6   See **16.20**.

14.10.1 Directors' Remuneration Report

Section 243B of the Companies Act 1985[1] requires quoted companies to prepare a directors' remuneration report. This report should be approved by the board of the company and signed by either a director or the company secretary on the company's behalf. A quoted company for the purpose of this section means a company whose equity share capital is listed on the UK Official List, is officially listed in an EEA State or is admitted to dealing on either the New York Stock Exchange or NASDAQ.

The contents of the directors' remuneration report are specified in Schedule 7A. The information to be disclosed is set out in two parts, Part 2 and Part 3. Part 2 sets out information that is not subject to audit while the information required by Part 3 is subject to audit.

The information required in Part 2 which is not subject to audit includes details of the membership of the remuneration committee and its advisers, a statement of the company's policy on directors' remuneration, duration of service contracts and the notice periods and termination payments under such contracts. In addition the company should provide a detailed summary of the performance conditions relating to each director's entitlement to share options or under a long-term incentive scheme together with a performance graph for the last five financial years.

The information required in Part 3 which is subject to audit is similar to the information required for other companies in Schedule 6 of the Companies Act except that the information is required to be shown for each director rather than in aggregate.[2]

14.11 Staff costs

Staff costs must be disclosed either in the accounts under the separate heading of 'Wages and salaries', 'Social security costs' and 'Other pension costs', or under such separate headings in the notes to the accounts depending on the format of accounts chosen.[3] In addition, all companies must show in the notes to their accounts the average number of employees during the financial year and the average number of persons employed in each category of employees.[4] Self-employed persons should not be included in calculating staff costs.

14.12 Transactions with directors

Particulars must be given in the notes to the accounts of any of the following transactions: a loan, quasi-loan or credit transaction or a guarantee, security assignment or arrangement relating thereto, which is of the type described in section 330 of the Companies Act 1985 (see **16.17**), and which the company has entered into for anyone who was a director of the company or its holding company or who was connected with such a director at any time during the financial year; an

---

1 Inserted for accounting periods on or after 31 December 2002 by the Directors' Remuneration report Regulations 2002, SI 2002/1986.
2 For further details see *Gore-Browne on Companies*, 44th edn, 23.10.5–23.10.7.
3 FRS 17 Retirement benefits – requires further details to be disclosed.
4 The Companies Act 1985 does not define what is meant by a 'category of person' but states that the directors may determine these categories by reference to the manner in which the company's activities are organised: Schedule 4, paragraph 56(5).

agreement by the company to enter into such a transaction or arrangement; and any other transaction or arrangement with the company in which a person who at any time during the financial year was a director of the company or its holding company had a material interest. If a director of the company or its holding company, or a person connected with him, is a party to a transaction or an arrangement, he is presumed to have an interest in it and his interest is presumed to be material unless a majority of the other directors who are preparing the accounts considers it not to be material. Where a director or his connected person is not a party to the agreement with the company, there is no presumption of interest. If the company is itself a holding company, the particulars given must relate to any transaction, arrangement or agreement made by a subsidiary, as well as any such arrangements made by the company itself.[1]

The particulars which must be given are the principal terms of the transaction or arrangement concerned, including, without limitation, the following: a statement that the arrangement was made, or existed, during the financial year; the name of the person with whom it was made and (if applicable) the name of the director with whom that person was connected or of the director who had a material interest; in respect of a loan or an arrangement relating thereto, the liability for principal and interest at the beginning and end of the financial year, the maximum amount of the liability during that period, the amount of any unpaid interest and the amount of any provision made in the accounts for failure or anticipated failure to repay; in respect of any guarantee or security or arrangement relating thereto, the amount for which the company was liable at the beginning and end of the financial year, the maximum amount for which it could become liable, and any amount paid or liability incurred in connection therewith; and (in respect of any other transaction, arrangement or agreement) the value of the transaction or arrangement concerned.[2] Corresponding amounts need not be given in the notes to the accounts. If the particulars required to be given are omitted from the accounts, the auditors must give them in their report, so far as they are reasonably able to do so.[3]

14.13 Transactions with officers (other than directors)

Summarised particulars must be given in the notes to the accounts (except in the accounts of banking companies) of loans, quasi-loans and credit transactions and guarantees, securities and agreements relating thereto, which are of the type described in section 330 of the Companies Act 1985 (see **16.17**) and which the company has entered into for any persons who were officers of the company (other than directors) at any time during the financial year. If the particulars required to be given are omitted from the accounts, the auditors must give them in their report, so far as they are reasonably able to do so.[4]

---

1   Companies Act 1985, sections 232 and 233, and Schedule 6, Parts I and II. Schedule 9, Part IV, paragraph 2 exempts recognised banks from a part of these provisions, as to which see *Gore-Browne on Companies* 44th edn (Jordans, loose-leaf) at 23.12. Schedule 4, paragraph 63(b) exempts companies from sections 232 and 234 where they are producing consolidated accounts that are not group accounts.
2   Schedule 6, Part II.
3   Section 237(4).
4   Section 237(4).

14.14 Parent and subsidiary companies

14.14.1 Group accounts

A company which, at the end of its financial year, is a parent company is, with certain exceptions, required to produce group accounts, which must be consolidated accounts dealing with the state of affairs and profit or loss of the parent company and its subsidiary undertakings.[1] Group accounts are to be approved by the board of directors before the balance sheet is signed on their behalf and must be included in the documents which the company lays before its members and delivers to the Registrar. The exceptions are that:

(1) Where a parent company is itself a subsidiary undertaking and its immediate parent undertaking is established in the EC it need not produce group accounts if the company is a wholly owned subsidiary of that parent or the parent holds more than 50% of the shares, provided that no notice has been received from minority shareholders requesting group accounts. Certain other conditions must be complied with including the requirements that the company is included in consolidated accounts of an EC group drawn up in accordance with the Seventh Directive and that a copy of these accounts is delivered to the Registrar of Companies. This exemption is not available to companies listed on any EC stock exchange.

(2) All the subsidiary undertakings are required to be excluded from consolidation by the effect of section 229.[2]

(3) In certain circumstances, the parent companies of small and medium-sized groups may be exempt from preparing group accounts.

14.14.2 The definition of a subsidiary

The Companies Act 1989 changed the definition of a subsidiary, for accounting purposes,[3] to include all undertakings which are controlled by a parent company rather than considering only legal ownership.

A subsidiary undertaking is defined as one where there is a parent undertaking that:

(1) holds a majority of the voting rights; or
(2) is a member and has a right to appoint or remove directors holding a majority of the voting rights at meetings of the board;
(3) has the right to exercise a dominant influence by virtue either of provisions in its memorandum or articles or a control contract; or
(4) is a member and controls a majority of the voting rights; or
(5) has a participating interest and actually exercises a dominant influence over the undertaking or is managed on a unified basis with it.[4]

---

1   Section 227, implementing the Seventh EC Directive. The Accounting Standards Board issued Financial Reporting Standard No 2 – Accounting for subsidiary undertakings – in July 1992, which requires that group accounts should in all circumstances take the form of a single set of consolidated accounts, covering the holding company and all its subsidiaries except those which are required to be excluded, see **14.14.4**.
2   See further *Gore-Browne on Companies* 44th edn (Jordans, loose-leaf) at 23.15.1A.
3   As to the general definition of a parent–subsidiary relationship, see **2.8.3**.
4   Companies Act 1985, section 258.

An undertaking need not be a company and may be a partnership or unincorporated body. A participating interest is an interest in shares held by an undertaking on a long-term basis to secure a contribution to its activities by the exercise of control or influence arising from that interest. A holding of 20% or more is presumed to be a participating interest unless the contrary is shown.

14.14.3 The financial year of a subsidiary

Unless there are special reasons to the contrary, the financial year of a company should coincide with that of its parent undertaking.[1] If the financial year of a subsidiary does not coincide with that of the parent undertaking, the group accounts must deal with the state of affairs of the subsidiary, as at the end of its latest financial year ending before that of the parent company and the profit or loss of the subsidiary for that year.[2]

14.14.4 Form of group accounts

Group accounts should normally take the form of a consolidated balance sheet and profit and loss account dealing with the accounts of the parent undertaking and those of all the undertakings to be included in the group accounts. The Companies Act 1985, Schedule 4A, permits that if, in the directors' opinion, it is better for the purpose of presenting the same or equivalent information in such a way that it may be readily appreciated by the members of the company, the group accounts may be prepared in some other way.

14.14.5 The profit and loss account of a parent company

Certain modifications to the normal disclosure requirements apply to the accounts of parent and subsidiary undertakings. If a parent undertaking's profit and loss account is framed as a consolidated profit and loss account dealing with the company and all or any of its subsidiaries, it need not comply with the requirements of the Companies Act relating to profit and loss accounts, so far as concerns the company itself, provided that the consolidated profit and loss account complies with the relevant requirements of the Companies Act and shows how much of the consolidated profit or loss for the year is dealt with in the accounts of the company.[3] Where a separate profit and loss account is not prepared, that fact must be disclosed in a note to the group accounts.[4] In practice, a separate profit and loss account in respect of the parent company itself is seldom published. However, the company must prepare a profit and loss account, although it need not contain the supplementary information required by Schedule 4, paragraphs 52–7. The profit and loss account must be approved by the board of directors but need not be filed with the Registrar of Companies.

---

1 Ibid, section 223(5). Contrary to the general rule, companies are permitted to change their accounting reference date after the accounting reference period has ended, if the object is to make the date coincide with that of a holding company or subsidiary. See **14.2.3**.
2 See Schedule 4A paragraph 2(2) and Schedule 5, paragraphs 4 and 19.
3 Section 228(7).
4 Companies Act 1985, section 230(4).

14.14.6 A parent company's balance sheet

A parent company is required to show in a note to the balance sheet thereto the number, description and amount of the shares in the company held by its subsidiaries or their nominees.[1]

There must be stated in a note to the company's accounts, the name and country of incorporation or registration[2] of every subsidiary and the identity of each class of shares held and the proportion of the nominal value of the shares of each class of the shares in the subsidiary held.

14.14.7 A subsidiary company's balance sheet

A subsidiary company is required to show guarantees and financial commitments in fellow or other group undertakings separately from other commitments.[3]

The subsidiary is required to state in its accounts or in a note thereto the name and, if known, the country of incorporation of the company regarded by the directors as being the company's ultimate parent company. This information need not be given by a company which carries on business outside the United Kingdom if the directors are of the opinion, and the DTI agrees, that to give it would be harmful to the holding company, the subsidiary in question or any other of the holding company's subsidiaries.[4]

14.14.8 Group accounts to give a true and fair view

Group accounts must give a true and fair view of the state of affairs and profit or loss of the company and the subsidiaries dealt with in the group accounts, so far as concerns the members of the parent company. Group accounts that are required to be prepared in accordance with Schedule 4 to the Companies Act 1985 must, so far as is practicable, give the same information as that required by the balance sheet and profit and loss formats for individual companies.

14.14.9 Consolidated accounts

With certain exceptions, consolidated accounts, which are the most usual form of group accounts, are required to combine the information which has to be shown in the individual balance sheets and profit and loss accounts of the parent company and subsidiaries, with such adjustments as the directors deem necessary, and consolidated accounts are to comply, as far as possible, with the requirements of Schedule 4 to the Act, together with the other requirements of the Act as if they were the accounts of a single company.[5]

Consolidated accounts are required to show, in respect of subsidiaries not consolidated, the same information, relating to amounts attributable to dealings with, or interests in, any subsidiary and the number, description and amount of shares and debentures of the company held by the subsidiary, as a parent company is required to show in respect of its subsidiaries in its own accounts. There must

---

1　Schedule 5, paragraph 6.
2　The country of incorporation must be shown if the subsidiary is incorporated outside Great Britain. The place of registration must be shown if the holding company is registered in England and the subsidiary in Scotland (or vice versa). See Companies Act 1985, Schedule 5, paragraph 1.
3　Schedule 4, paragraphs 59 and 59A. See also SI 1996/189.
4　Companies Act 1985, section 231, Schedule 5, Part IV.
5　Schedule 4A.

also be shown in a note to the accounts, in respect of subsidiaries not consolidated, the same information, relating to the profits and losses of subsidiaries, qualifications contained in audit reports, and notes to the accounts, as a parent company must give when group accounts are not submitted. The same information as is required when there are no consolidated accounts, in respect of subsidiaries with financial years ending on a different date from that of the parent company, must also be given in respect of subsidiaries not consolidated when group accounts are produced.[1]

14.15   Pre-acquisition profits

Any balance on a company's profit and loss account or other revenue reserves at the time the company becomes a subsidiary of another represents undistributed profits earned or losses incurred before the date of the acquisition of shares in the company by the holding company. Such profits or losses, adjusted as appropriate, are referred to as pre-acquisition profits or losses.[2]

14.16   Summary financial statements of listed public companies

A listed public company may send to its members what is called a 'summary financial statement', in place of a copy of the full accounts and reports.[3] This concession was introduced as a cost-saving measure following a great increase in the number of shareholders to whom otherwise full copies of all the documents would have to be sent, particularly in privatised companies. Shareholders, debenture-holders and entitled persons must be alerted on the summary financial statement of their right to receive the full accounts and reports and must be issued with a pre-paid card or form on which they can notify the company of their wish to receive the full set of accounts and reports for the current and/or future years.[4]

Summary financial statements must be derived from the full accounts and reports and contain a statement that they are only a summary. They must be approved by the board of directors and signed on their behalf by one director. The detail of what they must contain is prescribed in the Companies (Summary Financial Statements) Regulations 1992.[5]

14.17   Exemptions

14.17.1   Small and medium-sized companies

The requirements of Schedule 4 to the Companies Act 1985 may be modified by companies that are defined in section 247 of the Act as either 'small' or

---

1   Companies Act 1985, Schedule 5, Part I. See also FRS 2, Accounting for subsidiary undertakings.

2   See *Gore-Browne on Companies* 44th edn (Jordans, loose-leaf) at 23.16 as to the treatment of dividends paid by a subsidiary out of pre-acquisition profits and their availability for distribution by the parent company.

3   Section 251, as amended by the Companies Act 1985 (Amendment of Sections 250 and 251) Regulations 1992, SI 1992/3003. As well as summarising the accounts, the statement summarises the directors' and auditors' reports, described below.

4   Companies Act 1985, section 251(1) as amended by the Companies Act 1985 (Amendment of Sections 250 and 251) Regulations 1992, SI 1992/3003 and as further amended by the Companies Act 1985 (Summary Financial Statement) Regulations 1995, SI 1995/2092.

5   SI 1992/3075. See further, *Gore-Browne on Companies* 44th edn (Jordans, loose-leaf) at 23.16B.

'medium-sized'. The concessions are not available, however, to any company that is, or was at any time during the financial year in question, a public company, a banking or insurance company or an authorised person under the Financial Services and Markets Act 2000, or a member of an ineligible group (that is, a group which includes such a company within it or which includes within it a body corporate, other than a company, that has powers to offer its shares and debentures to the public or is a recognised bank or authorised person, or an insurance company).[1] A company qualifies to be treated under the amended rules as a small or medium-sized company if it satisfies, both for the financial year in question and the preceding year, two of the three following criteria. For a small company: the turnover (or its annual equivalent) must not exceed £2.8 million; the balance sheet total must not exceed £1.4 million; the average number of employees during the financial year must not exceed 50. For a medium-sized company: the turnover (or its annual equivalent) must not exceed £11.2 million; the balance sheet total must not exceed £5.6 million; the average number of employees during the financial year must not exceed 250.[2] In determining whether a company satisfies the qualifying conditions for a preceding financial year for which the accounts are not drawn up in accordance with Schedule 4, amounts corresponding with those set out above should be aggregated.

Once a company's category has been established, it remains in that category until it has failed to meet the criteria, or has met a new set of criteria, for two consecutive years.

Where a company qualifies as a small company, the exemptions apply both to the accounts it must prepare and, unless it has elected otherwise, lay before the shareholders in general meeting and to those delivered to the Registrar.[3] The requirements for the contents of small company accounts are now set out in Schedule 8.[4] Further, those delivered to the Registrar may omit the profit and loss account and the directors' report entirely.

The modifications permitted to the accounts delivered to the Registrar of Companies by a medium-sized company relate mainly to the format of the profit and loss account. The accounts of medium-sized companies that are laid before the shareholders in general meeting must be in the normal, unmodified form.

The directors of a company delivering abbreviated accounts must state prominently on the balance sheet and/or on the directors' report, as appropriate, immediately above the signature required, that the accounts are prepared in accordance with the provisions relating to small companies or medium-sized companies, as the case may be.[5] All abbreviated accounts delivered to the Registrar must be accompanied by a special auditors' report stating that, in their opinion, the company is entitled to deliver abbreviated accounts and that they are

---

1   Section 247A.
2   The method used for determining the average number of employees must be that prescribed by Schedule 4, paragraph 56(2) and (3). The turnover threshold must be proportionately adjusted where a company does not prepare its accounts for a full year: section 247(4).
3   Companies Act 1985, section 246, as substituted by SI 1997/936. See also the exemption from audit for certain small companies – **14.24**.
4   Small companies may prepare their individual accounts using the Financial Reporting Standard for Small Entities, introduced by the Accounting Standards Board and regularly updated. See further *Gore-Browne on Companies* 44th edn (Jordans, loose-leaf) at 23.17A.
5   Sections 246(8), 246A(4).

properly prepared.[1] In this case, the full auditors' report does not have to be delivered, unless that report was qualified.[2]

A parent company that is required to produce group accounts may take advantage of the exemptions available to small or medium-sized companies if the group as a whole meets the criteria.[3]

14.17.2 Dormant companies

A company which meets the size criteria for treatment as a small company but which would otherwise be unable to claim the relevant exemptions because it is a member of an ineligible group may nevertheless have the benefit of the relevant exemptions if it is a dormant company within the meaning of the 1985 Act, if it has been so since its formation or since the beginning of the financial year, and if it has taken advantage of the provisions available to dormant companies under section 250 not to appoint auditors (see **14.20.1**). A dormant public company may also claim the exemptions. For these purposes, a company is regarded as dormant when no transaction of any accounting significance takes place during the period under review. Where the directors of a company take advantage of this exemption they must include in the balance sheet a statement that the company was dormant throughout the financial year ending with the date of that balance sheet.[4]

14.18 Penalties in respect of accounting requirements

The Companies Act imposes penalties for failure to comply with certain requirements. If a company fails to keep the required accounting records, every officer who is in default is liable to imprisonment or a fine or both. Likewise, a person who dishonestly falsifies accounting information is liable to imprisonment. The penalty for other offences is confined to a default fine.[5]

14.19 Requirements for listed companies

Listed companies must comply with the rules in the *Listing Rules*.[6] The continuing obligations of companies after admission to listing impose a general requirement to notify information necessary to enable holders of the company's listed securities and the public to appraise the position of the company and to avoid the establishment of a false market in its listed securities.[7]

The main requirements as to information to be disclosed under the continuing obligations are summarised below.

(1) *Particulars of any company (not being a subsidiary) in which the group has an interest in the equity of 20%.*

The requirement is additional to that required by Schedule 5, Part II to the

---

1   Section 247B.
2   Or the circumstances specified in section 247B(3)(b) apply.
3   Sections 248–249.
4   Section 250. A transaction is a significant accounting transaction if it would fall to be entered in the company's accounting records under section 221 and does not arise from the taking of shares in the company by a subscriber to the memorandum in accordance with an undertaking therein.
5   See further, *Gore-Browne on Companies* 44th edn (Jordans, loose-leaf) at 23.20.
6   See Chapter 18. These are now the responsibility of the Financial Services Authority.
7   See further, *Gore-Browne on Companies* 44th edn (Jordans, loose-leaf) at 23.21.

Companies Act 1985. In addition to particulars of share and loan capital, the principal country of operation must be shown.

(2) *Borrowing and interest.*
Interest capitalised must be stated and bank and other borrowings must be separately analysed over repayment periods.

(3) *The tax status of the company.*
An investment trust must disclose any change in its status for taxation purposes and must include a statement confirming that the Inland Revenue has approved the company as an investment trust.

(4) *Standard accounting practices.*
The directors must state their reasons for any significant departure from standard accounting practice.

(5) *Interests of directors and substantial shareholders in share capital.*
A listed company must give a statement in the annual report showing any changes in the interests of each director appearing in its register of directors' interests that have occurred between the end of the financial year and a date not more than one month prior to the date of the notice of the meeting[1] and a similar statement concerning the interests of substantial shareholders.[2]

(6) *Waiver of emoluments or dividends.*
Particulars must be given of any arrangement under which a director has waived or agreed to waive any emoluments from a company or any of its subsidiaries, and of any arrangement under which a shareholder has waived or agreed to waive any dividends.

(7) *Interests of directors and substantial shareholders in contracts.*
Particulars must be given of any contract of significance between the company (or any of its subsidiaries) and a controlling shareholder,[3] or such a contract in which a director is or was materially interested. A contract of significance is, broadly, one worth 1% or more of the company's share capital and reserves. In addition, particulars are required of contracts for the provision of services to the company by a controlling shareholder.

(8) *Purchase by the company of its own shares.*
More details are required than under the Companies Act 1985 of these purchases.[4]

(9) *Earnings per share.*
A company which issues summary financial statements[5] must include in them the earnings per share.

---

1   Ie under section 325: see **15.22.5**.
2   Ie under section 211: see **12.9.5**.
3   A controlling shareholder is one who is entitled to exercise or control the exercise of 30% or more of the voting power at general meetings, or who is able to control the appointment of directors who are able to exercise a majority of votes at board meetings.
4   See *Gore-Browne on Companies* 44th edn (Jordans, loose-leaf) at 23.21.8.
5   See **14.16**.

(10) *Corporate governance.*

A company incorporated in the United Kingdom with an accounting year ending on or after 31 December 1998 must include a statement in its annual report and accounts as to how it applied the principles set out in section 1 of the Combined Code and whether or not the company has complied throughout the accounting period with the relevant sections of the Combined Code.[1]

(11) *Going concern.*

Companies' accounts should include a statement by the directors that the business is a going concern, with supporting assumptions or qualifications as necessary.

(12) *Long term incentive schemes.*

Details must be given in the first annual report published after the relevant event, of any long term incentive scheme established where the only participant is a director of the company (or whose appointment as such is being contemplated) and the arrangement is established specifically to facilitate, in unusual circumstances, that person's recruitment or retention.[2]

(13) *Half yearly report.*

In addition to their annual accounts, the UK Listing Authority requires listed companies to issue reports on their activities for the first six months of the financial year.[3]

PART 2: AUDITORS

14.20 The appointment, qualifications and remuneration of auditors

14.20.1 *Appointment*

With the exceptions noted below, every company is required to appoint at each general meeting before which accounts are laid an auditor or auditors to hold office from the conclusion of that meeting until the conclusion of the next such general meeting.[4] Reappointment of a retiring auditor is not automatic and a resolution concerning the appointment or reappointment of auditors should therefore be put before each meeting held to consider the accounts.

Special notice[5] is required of a resolution concerning the appointment of the auditors, unless the resolution is for the continuation of the appointment of auditors whose appointment was approved at the previous general meeting held to consider the accounts.[6]

---

1   This includes requirements of disclosure of details about directors' remuneration. See further *Gore-Browne on Companies* 44th edn (Jordans, loose-leaf) at 23.21.12A–C.
2   See *Gore-Browne on Companies* 44th edn (Jordans, loose-leaf) at 23.21.13.
3   Ibid at 23.21.14.
4   Section 384(1).
5   See **13.14.1**. Section 379 provides that at least 28 days' notice of the intention to move such a resolution must be given to the company and that the company must give at least 21 days' notice to its members.
6   Sections 388(1) and 391A.

The first auditors of a company may be appointed by the directors at any time before the first general meeting held for consideration of the accounts, to hold office until the conclusion of that meeting. If the directors fail to do so, the company in general meeting may appoint them.[1]

A private company which has elected to dispense with the laying of accounts before the company in general meeting must appoint auditors at a general meeting held at least 28 days before copies of the company's annual accounts are sent to members. It may, however, elect to dispense with the annual appointment of auditors, in which case the auditors are deemed to be reappointed in each succeeding year unless a resolution is passed ending their appointment.[2]

The directors or the company in general meeting may fill any casual vacancy.[3] If no auditors are appointed or reappointed at a general meeting held to consider the accounts, the Secretary of State may appoint a person to fill the vacancy. Within a week of the power becoming exercisable the company must give notice to him of that fact. The company and every officer in default are liable to a fine for failure to give the required notice.[4]

The first exception mentioned above to the general rule is that a dormant company (see **14.17.2**) that is not required to prepare group accounts, may by special resolution exclude the obligation to appoint auditors. Such a resolution may be passed, either at any general meeting of the company at which copies of the accounts are laid before the company under section 241 in the normal way, or at any time before the first general meeting of the company, provided that the company has been dormant from the time of its formation. Where the resolution is passed at a general meeting that is not the first such meeting, the company must, in addition, be entitled to the benefit of the accounting exemptions available to small companies, or must be ineligible for those exemptions by reason only of the fact that it is a member of an ineligible group (see **14.17.1**); it must also have been dormant since the end of that financial year.[5]

The second exception is that a private company exempt from the audit requirement as described in **14.24**, is also exempt from the obligation to appoint an auditor.[6]

14.20.2   *Removal or resignation*

A company may remove an auditor by ordinary resolution before the expiration of his term of office, notwithstanding any previous agreement to the contrary. The Registrar of Companies must be informed within 14 days of any such resolution having been passed.[7]

If a company receives special notice of a resolution proposing the removal of an auditor before the expiration of his term of office, or proposing a change of

---

1   Section 385(3)(4).
2   Sections 385A and 386.
3   Section 388(1).
4   Section 287. As to the fines that may be imposed, see Schedule 24.
5   Section 250, as amended by the Companies Act 1985 (Amendment of Sections 250 and 251) Regulations 1992, SI 1992/3003, regulation 2. The requirement for an eligible dormant company to pass the resolution required by section 250 is abolished for accounting periods ended on or after 26 July 2000. Section 249AA provides that such companies are exempt from the requirement for audit.
6   Section 388A.
7   Section 391(1)(2).

auditor when the present auditor's term of office expires, it must forward a copy of that notice to the retiring auditor, or to the auditor who is to be removed. The auditor may make representations in writing to the company and, if he so requests and the representations are not received too late, the company must, in any notice of the resolution given to members of the company, state that representations have been received and send a copy to every member to whom notice of the meeting is sent.

If an auditor wishes to resign his office before its term expires, he may do so by depositing a notice in writing to that effect at the company's registered office, containing either a statement that there are no circumstances connected with his resignation which he considers should be brought to the notice of the members or creditors of the company, or a statement of any such circumstances as may exist. The company must, within 14 days of receipt, send copies of the notice to the Registrar of Companies and, if the notice contains a statement of circumstances connected with the resignation as described above, to the members of the company and to any other persons who are entitled to receive a copy of the company's accounts.[1] If the notice of resignation states that there are circumstances which the auditor considers should be brought to the notice of members or creditors, he may call on the directors to convene an extraordinary general meeting of the company to consider his explanation. He may also require the company to circulate to the members a written statement of the circumstances connected with his resignation (of reasonable length) and to state in the notice of the meeting that such a statement has been issued.[2]

If the company does not, within 14 days,[3] circulate an auditor's notice of resignation, or does not, within 21 days, convene an extraordinary general meeting which has been requisitioned by the auditor then, unless the company has obtained a court order excusing it from so doing, the company and every officer who is in default will be liable to a fine.[4]

An auditor who has been removed or who has resigned is entitled to attend the general meeting of the company at which his appointment would otherwise have expired and any general meeting at which it is proposed to fill the vacancy caused by the removal or resignation, to receive notices relating to those meetings and to be heard on any business which concerns him as former auditor.[5]

14.20.3 *Qualifications*

The Companies Act 1989 implemented the Eighth EC Company Law Directive[6] on the qualifications and training of auditors. The stated purposes of the Act are 'to secure that only persons who are properly supervised and appropriately qualified are appointed as company auditors, and that audits by persons so appointed are carried out properly and with integrity and with a proper degree of independence'.[7]

---

1 Section 392.
2 Section 392A.
3 See *P & P Designs plc v PriceWaterhouseCoopers* [2002] 2 BCC 645.
4 Sections 392(3) and 392A(5).
5 Sections 391(4) and 392A(8).
6 Directive 84/253/EEC.
7 Companies Act 1989, section 24.

To qualify for appointment as a company auditor, a person, either an individual or a firm, must be[1] a member of a recognised supervisory body; and eligible for appointment under the rules of that body.

To be eligible, the auditor must hold an appropriate qualification, which may be:

(1) by virtue of membership immediately before 1 January 1990 of a body recognised for the purposes of section 389(1)(a) of the Companies Act 1985;[2] or

(2) a recognised professional qualification obtained in the United Kingdom from a qualifying body; or

(3) an overseas qualification approved by the Secretary of State, provided that the person also satisfies any additional educational qualifications that the Secretary of State may require.[3]

Certain classes of person are disqualified from appointment as auditors. They are officers or servants of the company, persons who are partners or employees of an officer or servant of the company and bodies corporate. Nor may a person be appointed auditor of a company if he is disqualified from appointment as auditor of its parent or subsidiary company. Any person who acts as auditor of a company when he knows he is disqualified, or who fails to vacate his office and to give notice of that fact to the company when to his knowledge he becomes disqualified, is liable to a fine.[4] Section 28(5) of the Companies Act 1989 now provides that it is a defence for a person to show that he did not know and had no reason to believe that he was, or had become, ineligible for appointment.

14.20.4 Remuneration

The remuneration of the auditors of a company is normally fixed by the company in general meeting or in such a way as the company in general meeting may decide.

A company's profit and loss account must show the remuneration of the auditors, including expenses.[5] A consolidated profit and loss account must show the remuneration of the auditors of all the companies included in the consolidated accounts. Disclosure of remuneration including expenses paid to the auditors or their associates in respect of services other than audit must also be made.[6]

---

1   Ibid, section 31.
2   The Institute of Chartered Accountants in England and Wales, The Institute of Chartered Accountants of Scotland, the Chartered Association of Certified Accountants, the Institute of Chartered Accountants in Ireland and the Association of Authorised Public Accountants. See *R v Institute of Chartered Accountants in England and Wales ex parte Brindle* [1994] BCC 297.
3   Companies Act 1989, section 33.
4   Section 28.
5   Schedule 4, paragraph 53(7).
6   Section 390B and the Companies Act 1985 (Disclosure of Renumeration for Non-Audit Work) Regulations 1991, SI 1999/2128.

14.21 The rights and duties of an auditor

14.21.1 *Right of information*

An auditor[1] has a right of access at all times to the books and accounts and vouchers of the company and a right to require from the officers of the company such information and explanations as he thinks necessary for the performance of his duty.[2]

An officer of a company who makes to an auditor (orally or in writing) a misleading statement which conveys, or purports to convey, any information or explanation which the auditor requires, or is entitled to require in his capacity as auditor, may be liable to imprisonment or to a fine or both.

A company's articles may not limit the auditor's statutory right to information. 'Any regulations which preclude the auditors from availing themselves of all the information to which under the Act they are entitled as material for the report which under the Act they are to make as to the true and correct state of the company's affairs are, I think, inconsistent with the Act.'[3]

The auditor of a parent company also has the right of access to information about the subsidiaries.[4]

14.21.2 *Attendance at meetings*

The auditors of a company are entitled to attend any general meeting of the company and to receive notice of, and other communications relating to, any general meeting which any member of the company is entitled to receive. They also have a right to be heard at a general meeting on any part of the business of the meeting which concerns them as auditors.[5]

---

1   In March 1976 the major professional accounting bodies set up an Auditing Practices Committee to develop standards to which all audits should be carried out. In 1980, the Committee published a series of auditing standards and guidelines which, although they do not have legal backing, are intended to be followed by all members of the professional accounting bodies concerned. They apply to the audits of the accounts of all enterprises and not only to the audits of accounts of limited companies. The standards, which simply codify current good practice, consist of an operational standard and two standards relating to the audit report and are effective for the audit of accounts relating to periods starting on or after 1 April 1980. The operational standard requires an auditor adequately to plan, control and record his work; to ascertain the enterprise's system of recording and processing transactions and assess its adequacy as a basis for the preparation of accounts; to obtain relevant and reliable audit evidence sufficient to enable him to draw reasonable conclusions therefrom; to ascertain, evaluate and test the operation of any internal controls on which he wishes to place reliance in his work; and to carry out such a review on the accounts as is sufficient, in conjunction with the conclusions drawn from the other audit evidence obtained, to give him a reasonable basis for his opinion on the accounts. In April 1991 the APC was replaced by a new body called the Auditing Practices Board (APB), which is committed to leading the development of auditing practice in the United Kingdom and the Republic of Ireland so as to: establish the highest standards of auditing; meet the developing needs of users of financial statements; and ensure public confidence in the auditing process. See Statement of Objectives, Scope and Authority, May 1993, and SAS 600 – Auditors' reports on financial statements, May 1993. The APB has subsequently published a number of SASs which amend and update standards and guidelines previously issued by the APC. See *Gore-Browne on Companies* 44th edn (Jordans, loose-leaf) at 23.23.1.

2   Section 389A.

3   *Newton v BSA* [1906] 2 Ch 378 at 389 *per* Buckley J.

4   Section 389A.

5   Section 390.

14.21.3   *The auditors' report*

The auditors of a company are required to make a report to the members on the accounts examined by them and on every balance sheet and profit and loss account and all group accounts, a copy of which is laid before the company in general meeting during their tenure of office. A copy is to be attached to the accounts and sent with them to every shareholder and debenture-holder who is entitled to receive a copy of the accounts.[1]

14.21.4   *The contents of the auditors' report*

Section 235 of the Companies Act 1985 sets out the statutory requirements for the auditors' report.

When preparing a report under section 235 the auditors must consider whether the information given in the directors' report is consistent with the accounts. Where the information so given is inconsistent, that fact must be noted in their report.[2]

The auditors must carry out such work as to enable them to form an opinion as to: (a) whether proper books of account have been kept by the company and adequate returns received from branches not visited by them; and (b) whether the company's balance sheet and profit and loss account (unless it is framed as a consolidated profit and loss account) are in agreement with the books of account and the returns from branches.

If the requirements imposed by section 232 and Schedule 6 for the disclosure in the accounts of certain information about the emoluments of directors and certain employees and transactions with directors and officers are not observed, the auditors are required to give in their report the information which has been omitted.[3]

Where the audit report is qualified, the auditors must state whether in their opinion the qualification is material for the purpose of determining whether a proposed distribution would contravene the relevant section in Part VIII of the Act.[4]

Auditors who are not satisfied that the accounts comply with the Companies Act or show a true and fair view of the state of affairs or of the profit or loss of a company must refer to those matters explicitly in their report.[5] They may not just hint at them.

In addition to their obligation to report on the accounts, the auditors have a duty to examine the register of directors' loans and similar transactions maintained by a recognised bank in accordance with section 343 before it is made available to the members of the company and to report to the members on that statement, stating whether in their opinion it contains the particulars required; if, in their opinion, it does not, they must include the missing particulars in their report, so far as they are reasonably able to do so.[6]

The form and content of the auditors' report has been changed and expanded with effect for accounting periods ending on or after 30 September 1993 by

---

1   Section 238(1).
2   Section 235(3). As to the special report where abbreviated accounts are concerned, see
     12.17.1.
3   Section 237(4).
4   Section 273(4).
5   *Newton v BSA* [1906] 2 Ch 378.
6   Section 343(6).

Statement of Auditing Standards – Auditors' report on financial statements (SAS 600).[1]

Effective reporting depends in part on the ability of auditors to check and report on the annual accounts. Yet, a number of questions about the role of and quality of auditors arose after the collapse of ENRON. The issue of auditor independence was a particular concern. The Government stated that it would put in place a package of measures on auditor independence set out in detail in the CGAA Report[2] and the Auditing Practices Board is also to develop necessary standards on auditor independence. In summary the CGAA Report proposed that some non-audit services should not be provided if they would involve the audit firm performing management functions for their client or if it would mean auditing its own work. Auditors should also avoid providing valuations services that would involve a degree of subjectivity. The CGAA Report also recommended stronger disclosure provisions relating to non-audit services as well as regular rotation of auditor partners. Many of these recommendations have been put into effect by professional bodies such as the ICAEW.[3] The Government, in its White Paper[4], also gave support to the Review's recommendations to extend the statutory role of auditors in relation to the OFR and the cash flow statement, as well as an extension of auditors' rights to information from the company. The legislative changes required to implement these proposals are contained in Part I of the Companies (Audit, Investigations and Community Enterprise) Bill, which at the time of writing is before Parliament.

14.22 The auditor as an officer of the company

The Companies Acts do not make it clear whether or not an auditor is an officer of the company. Section 385(2) of the 1985 Act refers to an auditor holding office. The Companies Act 1989, section 27(1), by excluding an auditor from its provisions, implies that, but for the exclusion, he might be considered an officer: 'For this purpose an auditor of the company is not to be regarded as an officer or employee of the company'. Further doubt arises from sections 434(4) and 310 of the 1985 Act, which indicate that they apply to auditors whether or not they are officers of the company.

The court has held that an auditor is an officer for the purposes of section 212 of the Insolvency Act 1986 (a misfeasance summons in a liquidation).[5] He is also an officer for the purposes of the other sections dealing with offences antecedent to or in the course of winding up and may, therefore, be liable under, for example, section 206 of the 1986 Act for making, or being party to the making of, a false entry in the books or section 207 for fraud.[6]

---

1   See further APB Bulletin 2001/02. See also *Gore-Browne on Companies* 44th edn (Jordans, loose-leaf) at 23.24.1.
2   DTI/Treasury, URN 03/567, January 2003.
3   See for example, *Additional Guidance on the Independence of Auditors* which supplements their *Guide to Professional Ethics*. See also the Guidance in the Combined Code on the Role of the Audit Committee, following recommendations made by the Smith Report: Report to the FRC (January 2003) *Audit Committee Combined Code Guidance*.
4   HMSO, White Paper, *Modernising Company Law*, Cm 5553–I.
5   See eg *Re London and General Bank Ltd* [1895] 2 Ch 166, and *Kingston Cotton Mill Co (No 1)* [1895] 1 Ch 6. See **15.17.4**.
6   *R v Shacter* [1960] 2 QB 252.

It seems that an auditor appointed under the provisions of section 384 of the 1985 Act will be considered by the court to be an officer of the company. If, however, he is appointed for a more limited purpose, he may not be so considered.[1]

14.23 Liability for negligence

The auditor's potential civil liability[2] for negligence, which may arise in contract or tort, merits brief examination here.

14.23.1 Liability in contract

An auditor performs his duties under a contractual relationship with his company. If he is negligent in the performance of his contractual duties he may be liable to the company for loss arising from his negligence. If the company is in liquidation, proceedings may be brought by way of misfeasance summons under section 212 of the Insolvency Act 1986.[3] The duties of an auditor were discussed extensively in *Re London and General Bank Ltd (No 2)*,[4] *The Kingston Cotton Mill Co*[5] case and *Re City Equitable Fire Insurance Co.*[6]

Lopes LJ defined an auditor's duties as follows:[7]

> It is the duty of an auditor to bring to bear on the work he has to perform that skill, care and caution which a reasonably competent, careful and cautious auditor would use. What is reasonable skill, care and caution must depend on the circumstances of each case. An auditor is not bound to be a detective, or, as was said, to approach his work with suspicion. He is a watchdog, but not a bloodhound. He is justified in believing tried servants of the company in whom confidence is placed by the company. He is entitled to assume that they are honest, and to rely upon their representations, provided he takes reasonable care. If there is anything calculated to excite suspicion, he should probe it to the bottom, but in the absence of anything of that kind he is only bound to be reasonably cautious and careful.[8]

14.23.2 Liability in tort for negligent misstatement

The possibility of an auditor being held liable in negligence to persons relying on his report and with whom he does not stand in a contractual or fiduciary relationship has been raised by the decision of the House of Lords in *Hedley Byrne and Co Ltd v Heller and Partners Ltd.*[9] The Court of Appeal in the earlier case of

---

1 See *Re Western Counties Steam Bakery & Milling Co Ltd* [1897] 1 Ch 617 and *R v Shacter*, above.
2 As to potential criminal liability, see *Gore-Browne on Companies* 44th edn (Jordans, loose-leaf) at 23.27.
3 See **15.17.4**.
4 [1895] 2 Ch 673.
5 [1896] 2 Ch 279.
6 [1925] Ch 407.
7 *Kingston Cotton Mill Co (No 2)* [1896] 2 Ch 279 at 288, 289.
8 See also *Henry Squire (Cash Chemist) Ltd v Ball, Baker & Co* [1911] 106 LT 197. Cf *Fomento (Sterling Area) Ltd v Selsdon Fountain Pen Co* [1958] 1 WLR 45 at 61 *per* Lord Denning. See also *Re Thomas Gerrard & Son Ltd* [1968] Ch 455.
9 [1964] AC 465 (HL). See also *WB Anderson Ltd v Rhodes* [1967] 2 All ER 850, *Mutual Life & Citizens' Assurance Co Ltd v Evatt* [1971] 1 All ER 150 (PC). There is no ground for excluding liability for negligence in relation to statements made in the course of negotiations which culminate in the making of a contract (though such statements may also create liability under the contract or the Misrepresentation Act 1967; *Esso Petroleum Company v Mardon* [1976] 2 WLR 587 (CA)).

Candler v Crane Christmas[1] had held that a firm of accountants was not liable in negligence to someone who had relied on a report negligently prepared by them and which they had known would be acted on by him, and suffered loss as a result, because there was no contractual relationship between the parties. The House of Lords in *Hedley Byrne v Heller*[2] held that a duty of care could arise when there was no contractual relationship.

A landmark decision in the context of the law on negligent statements by professional people which cause economic loss was given by the House of Lords in *Caparo Industries plc v Dickman*.[3] The directors of a public limited company announced results for the financial year end which fell short of the predicted figure, and the share price dropped dramatically. The accounts had been audited by the auditors and approved by the directors before the results were announced. Caparo was an investor which had relied on the auditor's report on the company accounts and consequently suffered considerable financial loss. The Court of Appeal ruled that there was no sufficiently proximate relationship between an auditor and a potential investor to give rise to a duty of care at common law, but that an auditor had a duty of care to individual shareholders, entitling an individual shareholder to recover in tort where he suffered loss by acting in reliance on negligently prepared accounts. On appeal, the House of Lords ruled that the auditors did not owe a duty of care to individual shareholders and agreed with the Court of Appeal that the auditors did not owe a duty of care to potential investors. Foreseeability alone was not sufficient to impose such a duty and the requisite relationship of proximity should also be present to limit what would otherwise be an unlimited duty of care owed by the auditors for the accuracy of their accounts to all who may foreseeably rely on them. The conclusion was that auditors owe no duty of care to members of the public at large who rely on the accounts to buy shares as, if it did, the duty would then extend to all who rely on the accounts such as investors deciding to buy shares, lenders or merchants extending credit. It was necessary to prove that the defendant knew that his statement would be relied upon by the plaintiff in deciding whether or not to enter upon a particular transaction. Thus even if reliance was probable, it was also necessary to have regard to the transaction for the purpose of which the statement was made. In the view of their Lordships the purpose of the statutory requirement for an annual audit was to enable shareholders to review the past management of the company and to exercise their rights to influence future management. They saw nothing in the statutory duties of an auditor to suggest that they were intended to protect the interests of the public at large or investors in the market. The statutory duty was owed to shareholders as a body and not as individuals, and this meant also that they did not owe duties to potential investors. It is still not clear whether there is a duty to protect individuals from losses in the value of the shares they hold.[4]

In recent decisions, it has been held that where auditors make statements concerning the reliability of the accounts to purchasers of the company, they may be liable for their negligence within the principles laid down in *Caparo*. This is so

---

1   [1951] 2 KB 164 (CA).
2   [1964] AC 465, [1963] 2 All ER 575.
3   [1990] 2 AC 605. For a review of the earlier case-law see *Gore-Browne on Companies* 44th edn (Jordans, loose-leaf) at 23.26.3.
4   See *Morgan Crucible Co plc v Hill Samuel & Co Ltd & Ors* [1990] BCC 686, [1991] BCC 82, and *James McNaughton Paper Group Ltd v Hicks Anderson & Co* [1990] BCC 891.

even if the main purpose of the statement was to enable the purchaser to extract a warranty from the vendors.[1] The duty of care will not be displaced by the purchasers having their own accountants conduct a review, where the review was a limited one and the accountants had to rely on information provided by the auditors.[2] Where a statement is made at a meeting with the purchasers, the auditor may be held to have assumed responsibility to the purchaser. It is not necessary that they assume a role of persuasion.[3] The Court of Appeal has held that the auditors of the accounts of a subsidiary company may owe a duty of care to its parent company. This is so even though the information was supplied to enable the parent company to prepare group accounts as required by statute.[4] The parent company was not prevented from suing because damages, for which the auditor might be liable to the parent company, might include liability to the subsidiary.[5]

14.23.3 Duty of auditor valuing shares

Where an auditor of a private company is called upon to value shares in the company in the knowledge that his valuation would determine the price to be paid on the sale of such shares, the auditor owes a duty of care to those affected by his valuation. The House of Lords has held that an auditor valuing shares has no general immunity from an action for negligence. In order to establish such an immunity, the auditor acting as valuer must show that a formulated dispute between at least two parties has been remitted to him to resolve in such a manner that he was called upon to exercise a judicial (ie arbitral) function, and that the parties had agreed to accept his decision.[6]

A valuer must also be seen to be truly independent of the company whose shares he has to value. If the valuer is independent then the valuing of the shares might reasonably be left to him.[7] It is also only possible to challenge a certificate of valuation of shares for mistake when the mistake is of such a nature that the expert has not performed what he was appointed to do.[8] Where a company's articles

---

1   *Peach Publishing Ltd v Slater & Co* [1996] BCC 751; see also *Bank of Credit and Commerce International (Overseas) Ltd v Price Waterhouse* [1997] BCC 584. See further *Electra Private Equity Partners v KPMG Peat Marwick* [2001] 1 BCLC 589 (CA).

2   Ibid. See *Sayers v Clarke-Walker (a firm)* [2002] 2 BCLC 16 as to the scope of the duty in respect of a retainer to give advice as regards the purchase of a company as a facilitator. The claimant must have relied on the auditor's report when embarking on the transaction which resulted in the loss: *Barings plc (in liq) v Coopers & Lybrand (a firm) (No 1)* [2002] 2 BCLC 364. See also *Barings v Coopers & Lybrands* [2002] 2 BCLC 410 as to auditors certifying accounts on the basis of representation letters by a finance director of a subsidiary. Such letters did not provide the auditors with a defence since they were written in honest belief and without recklessness.

3   *ADT Ltd v BDO Binder Hamlyn* [1996] BCC 608.

4   *Barings plc v Coopers & Lybrand* [1997] 1 BCLC 427.

5   Ibid. A risk of recovery could be avoided by bringing both actions together. The principle of *Prudential Assurance Co Ltd v Newman Industries (No 2)* [1982] Ch 204 was held not applicable.

6   *Arenson v Casson, Beckman, Rutley & Co* [1977] AC 405; *Suttcliffe v Thackrah* [1974] All ER 859 applied. However, even if an action against the auditors in negligence would lie, the purchaser is still entitled to buy the shares at the price certified by the auditors. In the absence of fraud, collusion or error on the face of the certificate, it cannot be challenged: *Baber v Kenwood Manufacturing Co* [1978] 1 Lloyd's Rep 175 (CA).

7   *Re Boswell & Co (Steels) Ltd* (1989) 5 BCC 145.

8   *Jones v Sherwood Computer Services Plc* [1992] 2 All ER 170.

provide for shares to be valued by an auditor, the standard of care is that of a reasonable auditor, not that of a specialist valuer.[1]

14.23.4 The limitation or exclusion of liability

The Limitation Act 1980, as amended by the Latent Damage Act 1986, serves to limit the auditor's civil liability in England and Wales[2] for negligence to losses arising within six years before the commencement of an action. Any provision contained either in a company's articles or in a contract to exempt an auditor from or to indemnify him against any liability which would otherwise attach to him in respect of any negligence, default or breach of duty or trust in relation to the company is void. The company may, however, indemnify him in respect of costs incurred in a successful defence of a civil or criminal action or in connection with an application for relief under section 727.[3]

14.24 Small company exemption from audit

As a part of the Government's policy of deregulation and 'lifting the burdens' on small businesses, the Companies Act 1985 (Audit Exemption) Regulations 1994[4] removed the requirement for audit from private companies which qualify as 'small companies',[5] are not part of a group, have a balance sheet total of not more than £1.4 million, and comply with the further requirements specified.[6] An appropriate company with a turnover of not more than £350,000 in respect of the year in question is in effect totally exempt from the audit requirement.[7]

The exemption cannot be taken advantage of if a member or members of the company, holding not less in the aggregate than 10% in nominal value of the company's issued share capital or any class thereof, or, in the case of a company without a share capital, being not less than 10% in number of the members of the company, require the company to obtain an audit of its accounts for a particular financial year. The only formality is that a written requisition is deposited at the registered office during the year in question and at least one month before the end of the year.[8]

---

1   *Whiteoak v Walker* (1988) 4 BCC 122.
2   In Scotland, the prescriptive period is five years: Prescription and Limitation (Scotland) Act 1973.
3   Section 310. As to relief under section 727, see **16.23.4**.
4   SI 1994/1935, inserting new sections 249A to 249E into the Companies Act 1985. See also SI 1997/936 which amended sections 249A and 249B with effect from 15 June 1997.
5   See **14.17.1**.
6   Section 249A. The further requirements include the need for an appropriate statement by the directors on the balance sheet. Companies regulated under the Financial Services and Markets Act 2000 cannot claim exemption.
7   Different rules may apply to charitable companies. No copy of an auditors' report need be delivered to the Registrar or laid before the company in general meeting, and members' rights to receive or demand copies of accounts and reports do not extend to the right to a copy of the auditors' report. In addition, distributions of profits may be made without reference to an auditors' report: section 249E(1). See *Gore-Browne on Companies* 44th edn (Jordans, loose-leaf) at 23.17.B1 for further details. The Government is consulting on raising the threshold to a turnover of around £4.2 million; see the DTI's Consultative Document, *The Statutory Audit Requirement for Small Companies* (URN 99/1115, October 1999), and it will be raised to £1 million for financial periods ending after 31 July 2000.
8   Section 249B(2) and (3).

PART 3: THE DIRECTORS' REPORT

14.25 Introduction

Section 234 of the Companies Act 1985 requires the directors to produce a report for each financial year.[1] Small companies which take advantage in relation to their accounts of the exemptions described in **14.17** are not required to deliver to the Registrar a copy of the directors' report.[2]

Following the Company Law Review, the Government in its White Paper has recommended the abolition of the directors' report, with appropriate disclosure requirements imposed by other means, especially the Operating and Financial Review.[3]

14.26 The information required in the directors' report

The report must contain a fair review of the development of the business of the company and its subsidiary undertakings during the financial year and of their position at the end of it and state the amount, if any, which they recommend should be paid as dividend and the amount, if any, which they propose to carry to reserves. The additional matters of a general nature required to be stated are listed below.

(1) The report must state the names of those persons who at any time during the financial year were directors of the company, the principal activities of the company and its subsidiary undertakings in the course of the year and any significant changes in those activities in the year: section 234(2).

(2) In respect of the fixed assets which consist of interests in land, if their market value at the end of the year differs substantially from the amount at which they are included in the balance sheet and the difference is, in the directors' opinion, of such significance as to require that the attention of members of the company or holders of its debentures should be drawn to it, the report must indicate the difference with such degree of precision as is practicable: Schedule 7, para 1(2).

(3) As respects each person who was a director at the end of the financial year, the report must state whether or not he was interested in shares in or debentures of the company or its subsidiary or holding company or fellow subsidiary, and, if he was, the number and amount of shares in and debentures of each company (specifying it) according to the company's register of directors' interests.[4] The same information must be given in relation to the beginning

---

1   A director who fails to comply is guilty of an offence and liable to a fine, subject to the defence that he took all reasonable steps to secure compliance; section 234(5) and (6).
2   Section 246(5). Further they are exempted from some of the contents of the directors' report: section 246(4).
3   *Modern Company Law for a Competitive Economy: Developing the Framework*, March 2000, paragraph 5.102. See Chapters 11 and 22 for details of the proposed OFR.
4   As to this register, see **15.22.5**.

of the year or, if he was not then a director, when he became a director: Schedule 7, paragraphs 2, 2A and 2B.[1]

(4) The report must contain:
  (a) particulars of any important events affecting the company or any of its subsidiaries which have occurred since the end of the financial year;
  (b) an indication of likely future developments in the business of the company and of its subsidiaries;
  (c) an indication of the activities (if any) of the company and its subsidiaries in the field of research and development; and
  (d) an indication of the existence of branches[2] outside the United Kingdom: Schedule 7, paragraph 6.

(5) If a company employs an average number of persons exceeding 250,[3] the report must state such policy as the company has applied during the financial year for:
  (a) giving fair consideration to applications for employment by disabled persons;
  (b) continuing the employment of, and arranging appropriate training for, disabled persons;
  (c) training, career development and promotion of disabled persons employed by the company (Schedule 7, paragraph 9).

(6) If the company during the financial year has had an average weekly number of at least 250 employees,[4] the report must contain a statement describing the action that has been taken during the financial year to introduce, maintain or develop arrangements aimed at:
  (a) providing employees systematically with information on matters of concern to them as employees;
  (b) consulting employees or their representatives on a regular basis so that the views of employees can be taken into account in making decisions which are likely to affect their interests;
  (c) encouraging the involvement of employees in the company's perform-ance through an employees' share scheme or by some other means; and
  (d) achieving a common awareness on the part of all employees of the financial and economic factors affecting the performance of the company: Schedule 7, paragraph 11.

14.26.1 *Particulars of acquisition of a company's own shares*

Section 234(4) requires the directors' report to include the information specified in Schedule 7, Part II, where shares in the company are:

---

1 'Interest in shares or debentures' is defined in Schedule 13, Part I and has the same meaning as in sections 324 to 328, as to which see **15.22.2**; references to a person 'becoming a director', in the case of a person who became a director on more than one occasion, are to be construed as a reference to when he first became a director: Schedule 7, paragraph 2(2). The information required by this paragraph can be given by way of notes to the accounts instead of in the directors' report: Schedule 7, paragraph 2(1).

2 See **3.24**.

3 Excluding those employed to work wholly or mainly outside the United Kingdom: Schedule 7, paragraph 9(4).

4 Ibid.

(1) purchased by the company by forfeiture or surrender, or in pursuance of section 143(3) of the Act;[1]
(2) acquired by another person in circumstances where para (c) or (d) of section 146(1) applies;[2] or
(3) made subject to a lien or other charge taken (whether expressly or otherwise) by the company and permitted by section 150(2) or (4) of the Act and section 6(3) of the Consequential Provisions Act 1985.[3]

The information required is:

(1) the number and nominal value of shares so purchased, the aggregate amount of the consideration paid by the company for such shares and the reasons for their purchase;
(2) the number and nominal value of the shares so acquired by the company, acquired by another person in such circumstances and so charged respectively during the financial year;
(3) the maximum number and nominal value of such shares which are held at any time by the company or the other person during the year;
(4) the number and nominal value of such shares which are disposed of by the company or that other person or cancelled by the company during the year;
(5) where the number and nominal value of the shares of any particular description are stated in pursuance of any of the above paragraphs, the percentage of the called-up share capital which shares of that description represent;
(6) where any of the shares have been so charged, the amount of the charge in each case;
(7) where any of the shares have been disposed of by the company or the person who acquired them in such circumstances for money or money's worth, the amount or value of the consideration in each case.

14.26.2 *Charitable and political gifts*

Schedule 7, paragraphs 3–5 of the Companies Act 1985 provide that if a company, other than a wholly owned subsidiary[4] of a company incorporated in Great Britain, has given more than £200 during the financial year for either political or charitable purposes, the directors' report must state the amount given under each category and, in the case of political gifts: (a) the name of each person to whom more than £200 was given and the amount of the gift; and (b) if more than £200 is given by way of donation or subscription to a political party, the identity of the party and the amount of the gift.

By para 5(2), a company is to be treated as giving money for political purposes if, directly or indirectly: (a) it gives a donation or subscription to a political party of the United Kingdom or of any part thereof; or (b) it gives a donation or subscription to a person who, to its knowledge, is carrying on, or proposing to carry on, any activities which can, at the time of the donation or subscription, reasonably be regarded as likely to affect public support for such a political party.

---

1   As to forfeiture and surrender, see **8.15**; as to section 143(3), see **7.16**.
2   As to this, see **8.15.2**.
3   As to this, see **8.11**.
4   Defined in section 736, as to which see **2.8.1**.

Money given for charitable purposes means purposes which are exclusively charitable,[1] the latter presumably having the technical meaning as it does in the general law of charities. Money given for charitable purposes to a person ordinarily resident outside the United Kingdom is to be ignored.[2]

In the case of companies which at the end of the financial year have subsidiaries, Schedule 7, para 4(2) provides for the disclosure on a group basis of political and charitable gifts if the amount given by the company and its subsidiaries exceeds £200 in total. Certain types of EU political expenditure incurred by companies are exempt from the requirement of approval by the company.[3]

14.26.3 Policy and practice on payment of creditors

Part VI of Schedule 7 concerns the company's policy and practice in paying creditors. It applies to public companies and to private companies which did not qualify as a small or medium-sized company and which were at any time within the year a member of a group of which the parent company was a public company.

For such companies the report must contain a statement of the company's policy and practice on the payment of suppliers. The report must state the figure, expressed in days, which bears the same proportion to the number of days in the year as the amount owed to trade creditors at the year end bears to the amount invoiced by suppliers during the year.[4]

The report must state whether in respect of some or all of its suppliers it is the company's policy to follow any code or standard on payment practice, and, if so, the name of the code or standard and the place where information about, and copies of, the code or standard can be obtained. It must also state whether in respect of some or all of its suppliers it is the company's policy: (a) to settle the terms of payment with those suppliers when agreeing the terms of each transaction; (b) to ensure that those suppliers are made aware of the terms of payment; and (c) to abide by the terms of payment.[5] If the company's policy is different for different suppliers or classes of suppliers, the report must identify the suppliers to which the different policies apply.

14.27 Duty of the auditors

Section 235(3) of the Companies Act 1985 provides that in preparing their report on the accounts[6] the auditors are under a duty to consider whether the information given in the directors' report relating to the financial year in question is consistent with those accounts. If they consider that it is not, they must state that fact in their report.

---

1   Schedule 7, paragraph 5(4).
2   Schedule 7, paragraph 5(3).
3   Companies (EU Political Expenditure) Exemption Order 2001, SI 2001/245.
4   For the detailed criteria for making this calculation, see Companies Act 1985, Schedule 7, Part VI, paragraph 12(3) to (5).
5   Where the company's policy is not as described in the text in respect of some or all of its suppliers, the report must state what the policy is with respect to payment of those suppliers.
6   As to the auditors' report under section 235, see **14.21.3**.

14.28 Distribution of the directors' report

Section 238 of the Companies Act 1985 provides that the directors' report is among the documents to be included in the company's accounts and thus confers the same right to receive on demand the directors' report as is given by section 239 in respect of copies of the accounts and the auditors' report.[1]

---

1   As to these, see **14.2.7**.

Chapter 15

Management of a Company

15.1 Introduction

The important question of the management of a company is obviously a part of what is nowadays called corporate governance; this was discussed in a general way in Chapter 11. There it was seen that the United Kingdom now has a system of 'self-regulation' which requires listed companies to observe the Combined Code. The subject matter of this chapter is the current legal position in the strict sense of what is required by the Companies Act 1985 and associated legislation regarding the management of a company. Although the 1985 Act requires that every company must have a director or directors,[1] and although it attributes many functions to and casts many obligations on directors, it does not of itself prescribe how the business of the company is to be managed.[2] This and some other aspects of the law relating to directors and other officers are left to the articles which in practice will adopt or follow, with modifications, the relevant parts of Table A. Thus the articles will, among other things, determine the number of directors, the powers of the board as against those of the members in general meeting and the ability of directors to delegate their powers. In this permissive respect, British company law is very different from the law in most other Member States of the European Union and at one time the Draft Fifth Directive proposed the imposition of a formal legal structure regarding the management of public companies.[3] However, further consideration of this issue at the European level is off the agenda for the foreseeable future.[4]

The present law applying to directors and other officers includes the questions of their appointment, removal, functions and procedures, remuneration and service contracts, and the complex rules laid down to ensure that members (and often the public) are aware of the interests directors have in their companies. This chapter is also an appropriate place to examine the law regarding the disqualification of directors and their potential responsibility for fraudulent or wrongful trading. Although some of these issues touch on the duties of directors, consideration of these duties in general is deferred to the next chapter. The other important question not considered here is the extent of directors' agency powers,

---

1   Section 282; see **15.2.1**.
2   Nor, perhaps surprisingly, does it define the term 'director'; see **16.2**.
3   This included the representation of a company's employees on its board of directors or in some other formal way. Other proposals for employee directors include those of the Bullock Committee on Industrial Democracy, Cmnd 6706 (1977). The whole question of 'industrial democracy' has given birth to many different proposals and reactions over the last 25 years or so, and there have been a number of changes in company law which reflect increasing recognition of employees' interests: see in particular section 309 of the 1985 Act, discussed in **16.2** and Part V of Schedule 7, discussed in **14.26**. See also the fiscal and other measures introduced to encourage employee share ownership. See also the discussion of the 'stakeholder' question in **11.6**.
4   Except as regards the European Company; see **2.3.8.** and **2.5**.

namely when liability for their dealings will be attributed to their companies; this question has already been considered in Chapter 6.

15.2 Appointment of directors

The articles usually provide how the directors are to be appointed (see Table A of the Companies Act 1985, articles 73 to 80), and in practice the first directors are normally either named in the articles or directed to be appointed by the subscribers to the memorandum. If appointment lies with the subscribers, then, until they have made the appointment, a general meeting of the company must be held to perform any acts. A majority of the subscribers must act at a meeting in making the appointment of directors[1] but the appointment may be made in writing by all the subscribers without a meeting.[2]

The provisions for the appointment of future directors usually declare that vacancies[3] may be filled, or additional directors appointed, by the board of directors and that a certain proportion of the directors (usually one-third) must retire at each annual general meeting and the places be filled by the company at the meeting;[4] further, a director retiring by rotation is deemed to be reappointed if his place is not filled, unless it is expressly resolved not to reappoint him or not to fill the vacated office.[5]

A company has an inherent power to fill vacancies,[6] unless restricted by its articles, and even where this is restricted, the general meeting has a residual power if the directors cannot or will not act, for example because of deadlock or the failure of the directors to meet or if the directors are equally divided.[7]

If the articles authorise it, but not otherwise,[8] the directors may delegate the power to appoint directors to a third party.[9] If the appointment of directors requires the confirmation of the company at the next general meeting, the directors cannot by appointing a managing director for a fixed period dispense with this confirmation nor give him a right to damages for breach of contract.[10]

15.2.1 Statutory requirements

There are a number of statutory requirements relating to the appointment of directors. Section 282 requires that every private company and every public company registered before 1 November 1926 should have at least one director, and that every other public company should have at least two directors. Subject to this, the number of directors may be varied from time to time within the limits (if any) specified in the articles. In practice, the articles often specify the minimum

1   *John Morley Building Co v Barras* [1891] 2 Ch 386.
2   *Re Great Northern Salt and Chemical Works Co* (1890) 44 Ch D 472.
3   That is, all vacancies occurring other than through retirement by rotation, such as by death, resignation, disqualification or failure to accept office. The power to fill vacancies continues even if a general meeting has been held, if the vacancy has not been filled: *Munster v Cammell Co* (1882) 21 Ch D 187.
4   See **15.5**.
5   Table A, article 75.
6   *Worcester Corsetry v Witting* [1936] Ch 640.
7   *Barron v Potter* [1914] 1 Ch 895; *Foster v Foster* [1916] 1 Ch 532; see **15.11**.
8   *James v Eve* (1873) LR 6 HL 335.
9   *British Murac Syndicate v Alperton Rubber Co* [1915] 2 Ch 186.
10   *Bluett v Stutchbury's Ltd* (1908) 24 TLR 469 (CA).

and maximum number of directors.[1] Section 10 requires the directors of all companies to sign a statement giving their consent to act at the time the company is registered.[2]

As far as public companies are concerned, section 292 prohibits the appointment of two or more persons as directors by a single resolution unless this procedure has been approved by the meeting without dissent.[3] A resolution contravening section 292 is void, but section 285[4] will apply to validate the acts of the improperly appointed 'directors' and such a resolution will prevent the operation of a provision in the articles (eg article 75 in Table A) for the automatic reappointment of retiring directors in default of another appointment. Section 293 provides that a person who has attained the age of seventy cannot be appointed director of a public company or a private company which is a subsidiary of a public company, and a director reaching that age must vacate office at the conclusion of the next annual general meeting, unless the articles provide otherwise or the director is appointed or approved by a resolution of which special notice[5] stating his age has been given.[6]

15.2.2 Directors' qualification shares

The Companies Act 1985 does not require that a director be a shareholder, but articles may require it.[7]

Where the articles prescribe a share qualification, section 291 requires directors to acquire it within two months after appointment, or such shorter time as may be fixed by the articles,[8] and declares that the office of any director not acquiring his qualification within such time, or ceasing to hold it after such time, shall be vacated, and that the disqualified person shall not be capable of reappointment as director until he has obtained his qualification.[9]

Articles sometimes provide that the holding of the necessary shares is a condition precedent to election,[10] but it is more usual to require the obtaining of the qualification after appointment. The articles may also require that a director cannot act before acquiring his qualification. In this case, he must qualify before

---

1   The articles of many private companies appoint a person, eg the vendor of a business to the company, as a director. He may be styled a 'governing director' with extensive powers, eg the right to appoint a successor and to appoint and remove other directors. As to whether the exercise of such powers may amount to an assignment of office and thus be subject to the requirement of a special resolution under section 308, see *Gore-Browne on Companies* 44th edn (Jordans, loose-leaf) at 25.1.2.

2   See further, **4.5**.

3   'Appointment' includes approving a person's appointment or nominating a person for appointment.

4   See further, **6.35**.

5   See **13.14.1**.

6   Under section 294, a person appointed or proposed to be appointed a director of such a company at a time when he has reached 70 (or the retiring age under the articles) must give notice of his age to the company, unless he is a retiring director reappointed, when the register of directors will give his date of birth.

7   There is no reference at all to share qualifications in the modern Table A.

8   Where directors are elected on a poll, the time runs from the date of the declaration of the poll: *Holmes v Keyes* [1959] Ch 199 (CA).

9   A criminal penalty is imposed by subsection (5). Bearing a share warrant is not compliance: subsection (2).

10   See, eg, *Barber's Case* (1877) 5 Ch D 963 (CA); *Jenner's Case* (1877) 7 Ch D 132 (CA).

he acts and within a reasonable time (not more than two months) after his appointment, even though he has not acted in the meantime.[1]

If the articles do not prescribe that a director must take his qualification shares from the company, he may purchase them or obtain them from any person possessed of shares.[2] Shares held jointly with another person are a sufficient qualification unless the articles require a sole holding.[3]

A director may pay for his qualification shares out of the purchase money owing to him from the sale of property to the company, or in any acceptable form of money's worth.[4] It is a breach of duty to accept the shares as a gift from a promoter or any person having contracts with the company,[5] in respect of which the director will be liable to account to the company for the value of the shares, but shares so acquired will suffice to form his qualification.[6]

Section 285[7] and (usually) the articles provide that the acts of an unqualified director are valid until the defect is discovered, but an appointment vacated by reason of section 291 is not validated by section 285.[8]

15.3   Remuneration of directors

Directors *qua* directors are not entitled as of right to any remuneration, whether upon a *quantum meruit* or otherwise.[9] A 'director is not a servant; he is a person doing business for the company, but not upon ordinary terms. It is not implied from the mere fact that he is a director that he is to be paid for it'.[10] However, this proposition may be, and of course, normally is, qualified.[11] First, the articles may provide for director's fees.[12] Secondly, there may be a service contract between a director and his company which entitles him to a salary or other remuneration, in other words, a director is often an employee as well as holding the office of director. Further, if a director performs services which are not comprehended by the terms of any service contract (or where there is no service contract), he may claim in *quantum meruit*. This applies to a director who continues to perform services for the benefit of his company after he ceases to be qualified as a director.[13] However, where a managing director is appointed under article 84 (of Table A, or a similar article) which confers on the board of directors the power to determine the managing director's remuneration, and the board have not determined his remuneration, the managing director will have no claim in

---

1   *Molineaux v London, Birmingham and Manchester Insurance Co* [1902] 2 KB 589 (CA).
2   *Brown's Case* (1873) 9 Ch App 102; *Miller's Case* (1876) 3 Ch D 661.
3   *Dunster's Case, Re Glory Paper Mills* [1894] 3 Ch 473 (CA).
4   *Dent's Case* (1873) 8 Ch App 768 at 776. As to payment for shares in money's worth, see **7.12** *et seq.*
5   *Eden v Ridsdale's Railway Lamp and Lighting Co* (1889) 23 QBD 368 (CA).
6   *Re Hercynia Copper Co* [1894] 2 Ch 403 (CA).
7   See further, **6.35**.
8   *Morris v Kanssen* [1946] AC 459 (HL).
9   *Re Geo Newman and Co* [1895] 1 Ch 674 (CA).
10   *Per* Bowen LJ in *Hutton v West Cork Rly* (1883) 23 Ch D 654 at 671 (CA).
11   'Excessive' remuneration for executive directors of public companies has been the subject of public concern in recent years; see Ramsay [1993] JBL 351; Villiers, 'Executive Pay: Beyond Control' (1995) 14 LS 260, and was one of the factors behind the moves to improve corporate governance; see Chapter 11. As to the specific disclosure requirements introduced for the directors of quoted companies, see **14.10.1**.
12   See article 82 of Table A, described below.
13   *Craven-Ellis v Canons* [1936] 2 KB 403 (CA).

quantum meruit; since he has agreed to serve the company on the basis of this provision in the articles, this excludes a quasi-contractual claim in *quantum meruit*.[1]

In practice, the articles usually declare that directors shall receive remuneration and fix the amount, in which case when earned it becomes a debt for which the directors can sue.[2] Their own right in such cases arises from the contract to employ them as directors, and the articles must be looked at to see what are the terms agreed upon for their remuneration.[3] If the articles provide that a director is to be paid such remuneration as the board of directors determines, and the company is wound up before the board has passed any such resolution as to remuneration, then a director will *not* be entitled to recover for any services he has performed on a contractual basis (since the contractual amount has not been determined in the way the article required). Further, as described above, a claim on a *quantum meruit* is also excluded by the terms of the articles.[4] If the articles are silent, the company in general meeting may vote remuneration; but in such case the remuneration is a gratuity, and not a matter of right.[5] So in an operative company a general meeting may vote a gratuity beyond the amount prescribed by the articles, but upon liquidation this cannot be done.[6] Standard articles[7] provide that the directors are entitled to such remuneration as the company may by ordinary resolution determine.[8] Where the remuneration of the directors is governed by such an article, it is incompetent for the board to fix it.[9]

Liquidation puts an end to a director's service,[10] but the appointment of a receiver and manager does not determine the director's right to remuneration.[11] If remuneration is payable 'at such time as the directors may determine', one of the directors cannot sue for fees until the board have fixed the time for payment.[12]

If a director's appointment is not validly made he cannot recover remuneration as a director, either under the articles or under a *quantum meruit*, although he may have served for a long period,[13] and if it be discovered that fees have been paid for a period after the director has vacated office under the terms of the articles, the company, in a case where the facts negate the probability of an intention to grant remuneration, can recover the amount paid by mistake.[14] It should, however, be

---

1   *Re Richmond Gate Property Co* [1965] 1 WLR 335. The contract of service in this case was not constituted by the articles but was a contract of service created by the conduct of the parties based on, or incorporating, the articles – 'those were the terms on which he accepted office'.

2   *Nell v Atlanta Gold and Silver Consol Mines* (1895) 11 TLR 407 (CA); *New British Iron Co, ex parte Beckwith* [1898] 1 Ch 324; *Re Dover Coalfields Extension Co* [1908] 1 Ch 65 (CA).

3   *Molineaux v London, Birmingham, and Manchester Insurance Co* [1902] 2 KB 596 (CA).

4   *Re Richmond Gate Property Co* [1965] 1 WLR 335.

5   *Re Geo Newman & Co* [1895] 1 Ch 674 (CA); see generally the discussion of 'corporate gifts' in **6.13**.

6   *Hutton v West Cork Rly Co* (1883) 23 Ch D 654.

7   See article 82 of Table A.

8   As to variations on this method of calculation which may be found in articles of association, see *Gore-Browne on Companies* 44th edn (Jordans, loose-leaf) at 25.3.2.

9   *Kerr v Marine Products* (1928) 44 TLR 292. But a formal resolution in general meeting may be dispensed with if *all* the shareholders entitled to attend and vote at a general meeting have approved the remuneration: *Re Duomatic* [1969] 2 Ch 365. See further, **12.2**.

10   *In Re Central de Kaap Gold Mines* [1899] WN 216; *Re T N Farrer* [1937] Ch 352.

11   *Re South Western of Venezuela Rly* [1902] 1 Ch 701.

12   *Caridad Copper Mining Co v Swallow* [1902] 2 KB 44 (CA).

13   *Woolf v East Nigel Gold Mining Co* (1905) 21 TLR 660.

14   *Re Bodega Co* [1904] 1 Ch 276.

noted that a person purported to be appointed *managing director* by the supposed board may recover remuneration as such on the basis of a *quantum meruit*, notwithstanding that such appointment was altogether void, neither he nor any person constituting such board being a director, through failure to qualify.[1]

The remuneration of a director as such covers travelling expenses, and unless specially authorised by the articles (see Table A, article 83) or by resolution of a general meeting, expenses of travelling to or from board meetings must not be paid in addition.[2]

Section 311 contains provisions prohibiting the payment to a director of tax-free remuneration, whether paid to him as a director or otherwise. The prohibition extends to the payment of remuneration calculated by reference to or varying with the amount of his tax, or the rate of income tax. Provisions in any other contract or in the articles or any resolution for payment of remuneration tax-free or calculated by reference to tax are to have effect as if they provided for payment, as a gross sum subject to tax, of the net sum actually provided for.[3]

15.4 Directors' service contracts and the articles

Where a managing director or other director has a service contract with the company and he is dismissed in breach of his service contract, a provision in the articles which enables the general meeting or the board to dismiss him from the office of director or managing director will not prevent him from suing for damages for breach of contract.[4] Thus, where, as in *Southern Foundries v Shirlaw*,[5] a director is appointed managing director for a term of years, and the articles provide that a managing director shall be subject to the same provisions for removal as any other director 'subject to the provisions of any contract between him and the company', it is an implied term of the contract that the company will not remove the managing director from his office as director. In *Nelson v James Nelson & Sons*,[6] it was held that even without such a phrase the directors could not revoke an appointment otherwise than in accordance with the terms of the service agreement.

Although section 303 of the Companies Act 1985 allows the company in general meeting to dismiss a director by ordinary resolution,[7] section 303(5) specifically provides that nothing in the section deprives a director removed under it 'of compensation or damages payable to him in respect of the termination of his appointment or of any appointment terminating with that as a director' (eg as managing director). In *Shindler v Northern Raincoat Co*,[8] the plaintiff was appointed a managing director of the defendant company for ten years. The company's articles included article 68 of Table A of the 1929 Act, which gave the company in general   meeting   a   power   to   determine   the   appointment   of   a

---

1   *Craven-Ellis v Canons* [1936] 2 KB 403 (CA). See also *Re Richmond Gate Property Co* [1965] 1
     WLR 335 (see footnote 1 at p 451).
2   *Young v Naval and Military Co-operative Society* [1905] 1 KB 687.
3   The Law Commissions have recommended the repeal of section 311 on the ground that it no
     longer serves any useful purpose: Law Com No 261, Scot Law Com No 173; see further, **16.25**.
4   It is most unlikely that he will have any prospect of obtaining an injunction: see, eg, *Walker v
     Standard Chartered Bank plc* [1992] BCLC 535 (CA).
5   [1940] AC 707 (HL). See further as to the powers and status of managing directors, **15.14.1**.
6   [1913] 2 KB 471 (CA).
7   See further as to section 303, **15.7**.
8   [1960] 1 WLR 1038.

managing director.[1] As a result of a change in the control of the defendant's holding company, resolutions were passed at a general meeting removing the plaintiff from office as director and terminating his service agreement as managing director. It was held that the plaintiff could sue for damages for wrongful dismissal since it was an implied term in his service agreement that the defendant company would do nothing of its own motion to put an end to the circumstances which enabled the plaintiff to continue as managing director. In another case,[2] where a managing director was appointed under an identical article, his service contract was held to incorporate article 68 (which allowed the company to dismiss him without notice by a resolution in general meeting). Here the plaintiff was not appointed for any specific period. It was held that in the absence of a contract independent of the articles there was no ground for implying a term as to reasonable notice. Where the plaintiff's conduct involves a breach of fiduciary duty to his company a claim for wrongful dismissal will be rejected. It is the director's own wrongful repudiation of his contract of service which produces its termination.[3]

Where a director has a claim for damages for wrongful dismissal, he is of course subject to the general contractual rule that he must seek to mitigate his loss. It has been held, however, that where a managing director is dismissed and is offered the position of assistant managing director at the same salary, he is entitled to refuse the offer because of the loss of status involved.[4] In estimating the amount of damages, the court must apply the principle of *British Transport Commission v Gourlay*[5] and take into account what would have been his liability for income tax.

In addition to, and as apart from, any common-law claim for wrongful dismissal, a director who has a service contract and is therefore an employee of his company may bring a claim for unfair dismissal before an industrial tribunal.[6]

15.5 Vacating the office of director

Table A, article 73 provides that at the first annual general meeting all the directors shall retire from office, and that at the annual general meeting in every subsequent year one-third of the directors for the time being, or, if their number is not three or a multiple of three, then the number nearest to one-third, shall retire. Most articles of public companies have similar provisions for the retirement of a certain proportion of the directors by rotation, although most private companies will not provide for this.

Articles usually also provide[7] that the office of director is to be vacated if he does or suffers certain things, such as becoming bankrupt or insolvent, and on grounds such as failure to acquire or hold the necessary share qualification,

---

1   The equivalent article in respect of the appointment of managing directors in the 1985 Act (article 84) does not give this power. The general meeting can, however, act under section 303.

2   *Read v Astoria Garage* [1952] Ch 637 (CA). Cf *James v T Kent & Co Ltd* [1951] 1 KB 551 (CA) where a term as to reasonable notice was implied.

3   *Neptune (Vehicle Washing Equipment) Ltd v Fitzgerald (No 2)* [1995] BCC 1000.

4   *Yetton v Eastwoods Froy Ltd* [1967] 1 WLR 104. As to the measure of damages in respect of various 'heads' (loss of salary and commission, reduction in pension, loss of life insurance cover, etc), see *Bold v Brough, Nicholson and Hall Ltd* [1964] 1 WLR 201.

5   [1956] AC 185 (HL).

6   Ie under the Employment Rights Act 1996.

7   See article 81 of Table A.

absence from meetings for a long period or disqualification under the statutory provisions. The vacation of office is automatic,[1] but unless the cause of disqualification is a continuing one, or is bankruptcy, the director may be re-elected.

As far as bankruptcy is concerned, section 11 of the Company Directors Disqualification Act 1986 (consolidating a long-established provision in the companies legislation) provides that it is a criminal offence[2] for an undischarged bankrupt to act as a director of, or directly or indirectly take part in or be concerned in the promotion, formation or management of, a company, without the leave of the court by which he was adjudged bankrupt. In England, the court may not give leave unless notice of the application is served on the Official Receiver, who may attend and oppose it.

The provisions under which directors (and others) may be disqualified from management are considered later in this chapter at **15.16** *et seq.*

15.6   Resignation

Articles usually permit a director to resign. Even in the absence of such a power, unless the articles contain conditions, he may resign, and his resignation is complete when notice is given to the secretary, and cannot subsequently be withdrawn,[3] even though no acceptance has taken place. Notwithstanding that the articles contemplate a written resignation, a verbal notice of resignation given and accepted at a general meeting of the company is binding.[4]

15.7   Removal by ordinary resolution

Section 303 of the Companies Act 1985 provides that a company may, by ordinary resolution, remove a director before the expiration of office, notwithstanding anything in its articles or in any agreement between the company and the director.[5] Even assuming that a director may be entitled, having been removed under section 303, to petition for a just and equitable winding-up on the principles laid down by the House of Lords in *Ebrahimi v Westbourne Galleries Ltd*,[6] this does not affect the validity of the removal under the section and the court will not grant an injunction.[7] The director's only remedy is to petition for a winding-up or, perhaps more likely now, for an order under sections 459 to 461.[8]

An important limitation on the effectiveness of section 303 may arise, however, as the result of the decision in *Bushell v Faith*.[9] Here the articles of a private company provided that 'in the event of a resolution being proposed at any general

---

1   *Re Bodega Co* [1904] 1 Ch 276.
2   It is an offence of strict liability: *R v Brockley* [1994] 1 BCLC 606 (CA).
3   *Maitland's Case* (1853) 4 De GM & G 769. See also *POW Services Ltd v Clare* [1995] 2 BCLC 435.
4   *Latchford Premier Cinema Ltd v Ennion* [1931] 2 Ch 409.
5   The only exception, which is unlikely to be relevant today, is in the case of a director of a private company holding office for life on 18 July 1945: section 14, Companies Consolidation (Consequential Provisions) Act 1985.
6   [1973] AC 360; see **17.17**.
7   *Bentley-Stevens v Jones* [1974] 1 WLR 638. *Quaere*, though, whether on exceptional facts if the removal was a breach of a contract with the company, eg between it and a debenture-holder, an injunction might be awarded: see the discussion in **5.25**.
8   The remedy for 'unfair prejudice', fully discussed in **17.13** *et seq.*
9   [1970] AC 1099; see Prentice (1969) 32 MLR 693.

meeting for the removal from office of any director any shares held by that director shall on a poll in respect of such resolution carry the right of three votes per share'. The House of Lords, affirming the Court of Appeal, upheld this provision for weighted voting in resolutions under section 303. The House held that this was not an infringement of the requirement imposed by section 303 to the effect that, despite any contrary provision in the articles, any director may be removed by ordinary resolution. The following passage[1] from Lord Upjohn's judgment stresses the distinction between voting rights attached to shares and the scope of section 303.

> Parliament has never sought to fetter the right of the company to issue a share with such rights or restrictions as it may think fit. There is no fetter which compels the company to make the voting rights or restrictions of general application and it seems to me clear that such rights or restrictions can be attached to special circumstances and to particular types of resolution. This makes no mockery of section [303]; all that Parliament was seeking to do thereby was to make an ordinary resolution sufficient to remove a director. Had Parliament desired to go further and enact that every share entitled to vote should be deprived of its special rights under the articles it should have said so in plain terms by making the vote on a poll one vote one share.

There was a strong dissent by Lord Morris[2] to the effect that this construction made a mockery of what Parliament really intended and it is possible that, in future legislation,[3] section 303 will be strengthened to prevent evasion in this manner. On the other hand, an article of the kind considered by the House of Lords arguably is legitimate in the context of small private companies where majority rule may work to the prejudice of a minority shareholder-director.[4]

A resolution to remove a director under this section, or to appoint a director in his place at the meeting at which he is removed, requires special notice;[5] and on receipt of notice of an intended resolution to remove a director under section 303 the company must send a copy to the director, who has then the right to make representations and have them notified to the members: if this is not done, the representations must be read out at the meeting. The obligation of the company to circularise the representations or have them read at the meeting may, if the representations contain defamatory matter, be avoided by an application to the court.[6]

A director removed under the section does not lose any right to compensation or damages he may have for the termination of his appointment as director or of any other appointment (eg that of managing director) which terminates with his directorship.[7]

If the vacancy created by the removal of a director is not filled at the meeting at which he is removed, it may be subsequently filled as a casual vacancy. A person appointed to the vacancy is to be treated, for purposes of retirement by rotation or otherwise, as if appointed on the day on which his predecessor was last appointed.[8]

---

1   [1970] AC 1099, at 1109.
2   Ibid, at 1106.
3   See the lapsed Companies Bill 1973, clause 44(1).
4   See the speech of Lord Donovan in [1970] AC 1099 at 1110–11.
5   As to which see **13.14.1**, above.
6   Section 304.
7   See **15.4**.
8   Section 303(3) and (4).

It should be noted that the provisions of the section do not affect or apply to any other power (eg under the articles) to remove a director. Prior to the Companies Act 1948, which first introduced what is now section 303, articles commonly contained a power to remove a director by extraordinary resolution, and such a power may still be taken with advantage, since proceeding under the articles will not involve the complication of special notice or the statutory rights in regard to making representations. It should also be noted that the administrator of a company appointed under Part II of the Insolvency Act 1986[1] has, under section 14(2) of that Act, power to remove any director of the company.

15.8 Alternate directors

It is a fairly common practice for the articles to provide for the representation of a director who will be absent from board meetings for a lengthy period by enabling him to appoint an 'alternate' or 'substitute' director. Such an appointment is not an 'assignment' of the office under section 308 of the Companies Act 1985, because the appointing director continues in office. Under the model form in Table A (articles 65 to 69), an alternate director is regarded as a director 'for all purposes'.

15.9 Directors' meetings

Directors must obviously meet as a board to transact the business vested in them by the Companies Act or the articles of association. The common law has developed a number of rules, in many cases drawing on common-form articles, relating to the conduct of and jurisdiction of directors' meetings. These are examined in the following sections.

15.9.1 Quorum

The presence of all the directors at a board meeting is not required if, as is usually the case (eg article 89 of Table A), the articles provide that a specified number of directors shall form a quorum. If a quorum is not so prescribed, a majority of the board is required to attend,[2] unless a quorum can be established by the practice of the board.[3] If the articles so provide, questions may be decided by a majority of the directors present; but where such provision is made and controlling powers are vested in joint governing directors, those powers must be exercised by all of them.[4] If there is a clause in the articles stating that the continuing directors may act notwithstanding vacancies, a number less than the minimum number of directors prescribed by the articles is capable of binding the company.[5] Article 90 in Table A so provides, but with the qualification that if the number of directors is below that fixed as the quorum, the continuing directors may act only for the purpose of filling vacancies or of summoning a general meeting. In reckoning a

---

1   See Chapter 19.
2   *York Tramways Co v Willows* (1882) 8 QBD 685.
3   *Re Regent's Canal Ironworks* [1867] WN 79; *Lyster's Case* (1867) LR 4 EQ 233.
4   *Perrott & Perrott Ltd v Stephenson* [1934] Ch 171. But see *Bersel Manufacturing Co v Berry Ltd* [1968] 2 All ER 552 (HL) where a husband and wife were the two permanent life directors who had the power under the articles to terminate the directorship of the ordinary directors. It was held, on the construction of the article in question, that the power was exercisable by the husband after the wife's death.
5   *Re Scottish Petroleum Co* (1883) 23 Ch D 413 (CA).

quorum, directors not entitled to vote (eg as being interested in the contract under discussion) must not be counted.[1]

15.9.2 *Notice*

Notice of the meeting must be given to all the directors, for business done at a meeting of which some directors had no notice is invalid even though the latter are in a minority, and a director has no power to waive his right to notice,[2] but if a director is abroad and out of reach of notices, a meeting held without notice to him is valid.[3] There is a conflict of judicial opinion as to whether it is necessary to give notice of a board meeting to a director who, under the articles, has no vote thereat: for example an ordinary director, when all the powers of the directors are vested in permanent directors.[4] The notice may be a very short one; even a few minutes' notice will suffice if the director can attend, and where he objects to the shortness of the notice he should make his objection at once, or will not prevail.[5] A verbal notice is also sufficient.[6] It is not necessary that the notice should state what business is to be transacted, unless the articles require that certain business shall only be transacted at a meeting specially convened for that purpose, in which case the notice must sufficiently indicate the business to be considered.[7] A casual meeting of the two directors, even at the company's office, cannot be converted into a board meeting if one of them denies that it is a board meeting and has not received notice calling such a meeting.[8]

Articles (eg article 88 of Table A) usually declare that the chairman shall have a casting vote in case of the directors being equally divided upon any question.[9]

15.10 The validity of directors' acts

If the articles authorise it, but not otherwise,[10] the board may delegate any of its powers to a committee, which may consist even of a single director,[11] but the board does not by making such delegation lose its power to act in the matter,[12] and the board cannot deprive itself of power to control the company's business.[13] Each director has not alone power to bind the company unless he has had this power specially delegated to him. By section 284 of the Companies Act 1985, a provision requiring or authorising a thing to be done by or to a director and the secretary is

---

1   *Yuill v Greymouth-Point Elizabeth Rly* [1904] 1 Ch 32; *Victors v Lingard* [1927] 1 Ch 323; *Re Cleadon Trust* [1939] Ch 286 (CA). See further, **16.8** as to this and the provisions of Table A, articles 94 and 95.

2   *Re Portuguese Copper Mines* (1889) 42 Ch D 160 (CA); *Young v Ladies Imperial Club* [1920] 2 KB 523 (CA).

3   *Halifax Sugar Refining Co Ltd v Franklyn* (1890) 59 LJ Ch 591. However, there must still be a quorum: *Davidson and Begg Antiques Ltd v Davidson* [1997] BCC 77.

4   *John Shaw & Sons (Salford) v Shaw* [1935] 2 KB 113; *per* Greer LJ at 133 and *per* Slesser LJ at 138–41 (CA).

5   *Browne v La Trinidad* (1888) 37 Ch D 1 at 9 (CA).

6   *La Compagnie de Mayville v Whitley* [1896] 1 Ch 788 (CA).

7   *Young v Ladies' Imperial Club* [1920] 2 KB 523 (CA).

8   *Barron v Potter* [1914] 1 Ch 895.

9   But this does not validate the casting vote of an improperly appointed chairman: *Clark v Workman* [1920] IR R 107.

10 *Howard's Case* (1886) 1 Ch App 561.

11 *Re Taurine Co* (1884) 25 Ch D 118 (CA). See Table A, article 72.

12 *Huth v Clarke* (1890) 25 QBD 391.

13 *Horn v Faulder & Co* (1908) 99 LT 524.

not satisfied by its being done by or to the same person acting both as director and as, or in place of, the secretary.

Articles (eg Table A, article 93) normally provide that a resolution in writing signed by all or a majority of the directors shall have the same effect as a resolution passed at a meeting of the board. There is authority for the proposition that, in the absence of such a provision, directors can act unanimously but informally,[1] but where only a majority of the directors give their oral assent informally (and an article like article 93 does not apply), such assent does not amount to a valid resolution.[2] However, this defect can be cured by a subsequent resolution at a board meeting which may take the form of authorising the chairman to sign minutes which record that a particular resolution has been passed.[3] Articles like article 93 are intended to be used on occasions when a directors' meeting is not necessary. It is not intended to allow directors to avoid the requirements of a quorum by passing resolutions when other directors have left the country and are therefore not entitled to notice of meetings.[4]

The directors must not exclude any of their body from their meetings, and unless the company has by resolution declared that it does not desire a director to act,[5] an excluded director can obtain an injunction restraining his continued exclusion.[6] However, it is possible for the articles to confer a power to remove a director on the board.

The directors are the proper persons to perform any act in the name of the company, and in particular to commence actions in the name of the company, to make contracts, and to affix the seal of the company to deeds.

15.11 The relationship between board and general meeting

The question whether the company in general meeting has any power to direct the directors in their management of the company's business is one that has been much discussed over the years. The answer depends upon the construction of the appropriate article of association vesting powers of management in the directors.[7] It has long been established that, in principle, it is perfectly acceptable for the board to have powers quite free from interference by the shareholders. Thus the court has refused to allow the general meeting to take the conduct of the business out of the directors' hands, or to compel them to adopt a particular line of action, such as sealing a draft deed or effecting a sale of the company's

---

1 See *Collie's Claim* (1871) LR 12 Eq 246 at 258; *Bolton Engineering Ltd v T J Graham & Sons Ltd* [1957] 1 QB 159. Cf other decisions which hold the contrary (*D'Arcy v Tamar Hill Railway Co* (1867) LR 2 Ex 158; *Re Haycraft Gold Reduction Co* [1900] 2 Ch 230; *Re Homer District Gold Mines* (1888) 39 Ch D 546 (CA)), but in these cases there was no unanimous agreement, only the informal consensus of a quorum.

2 *Municipal Mutual Insurance Ltd v Harrop* [1998] 2 BCLC 540 at 551.

3 Ibid at 551–3, applying *Re Portuguese Consolidated Copper Mines Ltd* (1890) 45 Ch D 16.

4 *Hood Sailmakers Ltd v Adford and Bainbridge* [1996] 4 All ER 830; *Davidson & Begg Antiques Ltd v Davidson* 1997 SLT 301, [1997] BCC 77.

5 *Bainbridge v Smith* (1889) 41 Ch D 462 at 474 (CA); *Harben v Phillips* (1883) 23 Ch D 14 at 40 (CA).

6 *Pullbrook v Richmond Consolidated Mining Co* (1878) 9 Ch D 610. *Hayes v Bristol Plant Hire Ltd* [1957] 1 WLR 499.

7 There is no doubt in law that this 'contract-based' view is the correct one. Whether it should be or not is another matter.

property,[1] or discontinuing legal proceedings commenced in the name of the company on the instructions of the board,[2] or to interfere in the exercise of the directors' power to appoint a managing director.[3] In most of these cases, the article in question was based on the standard article in Table A, which in the 1948 Act was article 80, and this was generally thought to permit interference only by special resolution. However, the wording of articles based on article 80 was not free from difficulty,[4] one particularly contentious area concerning the question of the use of the company's name in litigation.[5]

While companies registered prior to 1 July 1985 adopting this part of Table A will continue to have article 80 as their regulation in this respect, unless and until they amend their articles appropriately, the matter has been clarified in respect of companies adopting Table A to the 1985 Act.[6] Article 70 of this Table A makes it clear that, subject to the provisions of the Act and to any special provisions in a company's memorandum or articles, the general meeting can interfere only by 'any directions given by special resolution' and further that no such direction (or alteration of the memorandum or articles) can operate retrospectively to validate any prior act of the directors.[7]

However, if the directors are unable or unwilling to exercise the powers conferred upon them, whether by reason of there being no independent quorum or by reason of disputes among the directors, the company in general meeting can perform the duties which the directors fail to carry out.[8] In addition, the general meeting has wide powers to ratify an excess of power by directors, ie an act beyond the authority vested in the directors under the articles,[9] or to ratify or cure an

---

1   *Automatic Self-Cleansing Filter Co v Cunninghame* [1906] 2 Ch 34 (CA); *Gramophone and Typewriter v Stanley* [1908] 2 KB 89 at 105 (CA); *Salmon v Quin & Axtens Ltd* [1906] AC 442 (HL).

2   *John Shaw & Sons (Salford) Ltd v Shaw* [1935] 2 KB 113 (CA); *Scott v Scott* [1943] 1 All ER 582 (CA); cf *Marshall's Valve Gear Co v Manning, Wardle & Co* [1909] 1 Ch 267, which may be explained as authorising the shareholders to commence proceedings when the board refuses to do so.

3   *Thomas Logan v Davis* (1911) 104 LT 914, 105 LT 419.

4   It conferred on the directors 'all such powers of the company as are not by [the legislation] or by these regulations, required to be exercised by the company in general meeting, subject, nevertheless, to any of these regulations, to the provisions of the [legislation] and to *such regulations, being not inconsistent with the aforesaid regulations or provisions, as may be prescribed by the company in general meeting*' (emphasis added). The judicial construction put on the word 'regulations' was that throughout article 80 it meant 'articles' or 'new or amended articles', but this made the passage in italics somewhat tautologous and led certain writers to take a different view as to its meaning: see, especially, Goldberg, (1970) 33 MLR 177, and Sullivan 93 LQR 569 (1977). In *Beckland Group Holdings Ltd v London & Suffolk Properties Ltd* (1988) 4 BCC 542, Harman J ignored these difficulties.

5   In *Marshall's Valve Gear Co v Manning, Wardle & Co* [1909] 1 Ch 267, it was held that the majority shareholder had the right to commence proceedings in the company's name, even where general management powers were vested in the directors. While this right has been confirmed in situations of deadlock or where there are no directors (see *Alexander Ward v Samyang, Navigation Co*, below, and *Re Argentum Reductions (UK) Ltd* [1975] 1 WLR 191), it was totally swept aside in the *Breckland Group Holdings* case, above. See further Wedderburn (1976) 39 MLR 327 and (1989) 52 MLR 401.

6   Ie in the Companies (Table A to F) Regulations 1985.

7   See the discussion in Davies, *Gower's Principles of Modern Company Law* 6th edn (Sweet & Maxwell, 1977) pp 185–187.

8   *Barron v Potter* [1914] 1 Ch 895; *Foster v Foster* [1916] 1 Ch 532.

9   *Irvine v Union Bank of Australia* (1877) 2 App Cas 366.

abuse of power by directors, ie an act in breach of duty though not necessarily beyond the directors' powers.[1]

Further, the House of Lords has held that the absence of validly appointed directors does not prevent a company taking proceedings to recover its debts.[2] Lord Kilbrandon had this to say about an article similar to article 70 (and article 80 in the 1948 Table A) in respect of the management of the company's business:

> I think the article probably means no more than this, that the directors, and no one else, are responsible for the management of the company, except in the matters specifically allotted to the company in general meeting. This is a term of the contract between the shareholders and the company. But it does not mean that no act of management, such as instructing the company's solicitor, can validly be performed without the personal and explicit authority of the directors themselves.[3]

Article 70 of Table A is concerned with the board's powers of *management*. Thus it does not, for example, confer authority on a board to present a winding-up petition[4] or to apply to set aside an order restoring the company's name to the register.[5]

The court can appoint a receiver and manager where the company is in a condition in which there is no properly constituted governing body, or there is such dissension in the governing body that it is impossible to carry on the business with advantage to the parties interested. Such an appointment would be made for only a limited time, ie until a meeting of the company could be held and a governing body appointed.[6]

15.12   Minutes of directors' meetings

Minutes must be kept of all proceedings at every meeting of directors. Such minutes, when kept in a proper book[7] and signed by the chairman of that or the next succeeding meeting, are evidence of the proceedings. Where minutes have been made in accordance with the provisions of the section, then, until the contrary is proved, every such meeting is deemed to have been duly held and convened, and all proceedings to have been duly had, and all appointments of directors, managers, or liquidators shall be deemed to be valid.[8]

The adoption of minutes at a subsequent meeting of directors does not make those taking part in such adoption responsible for the acts of the earlier meeting if such acts were complete before the minutes came up for consideration.[9]

---

1   See **16.23.1** as to which breaches of duty are ratifiable.
2   *Alexander Ward v Samyang Navigation Co* [1975] 1 WLR 673.
3   Ibid, at 683.
4   *Re Emmadart Ltd* [1979] Ch 540. But this power is now conferred by section 124(1) of the Insolvency Act 1986.
5   *Re Regent Insulation Co Ltd* (1981) *The Times*, 5 November.
6   *Featherstone v Cooke* (1873) LR 16 Eq 298.
7   By section 722, a minute book may be kept either by making entries in bound books or by recording the matters in question in any other manner.
8   Section 382.
9   *Re Lands Allotment Co* [1894] 1 Ch 616 at 634 (CA).

15.13   A director's right to inspect company books

A director has the right to inspect the company's books either at a board meeting or elsewhere. This right extends both to the minutes of directors' meetings,[1] and to the company's accounting records,[2] but the court has a discretion as to whether or not to order an inspection which is conferred on a director not for his own advantage but to enable him to carry out his duties as a director.[3]

15.14   The officers of a company

For the purposes of the Companies Act 1985, 'officer' includes a director, manager or secretary.[4] The position of directors in general has already been discussed; the position of the other usual officers of a company will now be dealt with.[5] The terms of their employment depend upon their contract, whether written or verbal, with the company, although the position of a managing director may in some respects be governed by the articles.[6]

15.14.1   The manager or managing director

Most companies, even small private companies, are actually managed on a day-to-day basis by one or more people who will be described as 'managing director' or 'chief executive'. Perhaps surprisingly, the general law is that the directors cannot appoint one of themselves to an office of profit or delegate power to a managing director unless expressly empowered by the articles or by a resolution of the company.[7] It is therefore usual to insert in the articles power for the directors to appoint one or more of their body to be managing director or directors, and to pay him or them special remuneration, delegating to him or them such powers as are necessary.[8] Modern practice, at least in the case of larger companies, is to call such a person the 'chief executive', but this terminology is not reflected in the Companies Act 1985 or Table A.

Modern articles, as exemplified by article 84 of Table A, allow the directors to appoint a managing director (and other executive directors) on such terms as they determine, and, by article 72, to delegate to such persons such of their powers and on such conditions as they consider desirable; such delegation may be altered or revoked. These articles do not, however, permit revocation of the appointment.[9] It has been held that a managing director has no power, under the standard provisions of Table A, to commence proceedings on behalf of the

---

1   See *McCusker v McRae* 1966 SC 253. Note that the Scottish court held that the director was entitled to be accompanied by an adviser of his choice. English authorities (see below), which established the directors' right to inspect accounting records, do not discuss that point.

2   *Burn v London and South Wales Coal Co* [1890] WN 209.

3   *Conway v Petronius Clothing Co* [1978] 1 WLR 72. Here an immediate order was refused because misconduct was alleged against the two plaintiff directors and a meeting to consider their removal was held.

4   Section 744.

5   The auditor may or may not be an 'officer'. As to him, see **14.22**.

6   A mere statement in the articles that someone shall be secretary, manager or other officer is not a contract with that person: *Eley v Positive Government Assurance Co* (1876) 1 Ex D 88 (CA); *Browne v La Trinidad* (1888) 37 Ch D 1 (CA); see **5.18**.

7   *Boschoek Proprietary Co v Fuke* [1906] 1 Ch 148 at 159; *Nelson v James Nelson & Sons* [1914] 2 KB 770 at 779 (CA).

8   Such a power is conferred by Table A, articles 72 and 84.

9   Cf article 107 of Table A to the Companies Act 1948.

company. Delegation to him of such a power by the board is not presumed by the mere fact of his appointment as a managing director.[1] A managing or other executive director is not usually subject to retirement by rotation.[2] If a managing director is removed from his office of managing director, where the articles permit the directors to do this,[3] or from his directorship by the company in general meeting,[4] before the expiry of the term of his contract of service, the removal is valid, but he will have a claim to damages for breach of contract if he complied with his part of the bargain.[5]

There is very little case-law as to the nature of the relationship between the board and a managing or other executive director. In *Harold Holdsworth & Co (Wakefield) Ltd v Caddies*,[6] the House of Lords held that the board of Holdsworth were entitled to direct Caddies to confine his attention to a subsidiary company. Under his contract of employment, Caddies had been appointed a managing director of Holdsworth itself. The contract provided that he should perform the duties and exercise the powers in relation to the business of the company and the business of its existing subsidiaries 'which may from time to time be assigned to or vested in him by the board of directors of the company'. Up until the time when a dispute arose between Caddies and his fellow directors, he had managed Holdsworth itself and a subsidiary of it. The decision of the House of Lords (that Caddies could be so demoted without a breach of his contract of employment) turned on the particular wording of his contract. This conferred a discretion on the board as to the mode or extent of his employment in managing the company and any of its subsidiaries. Thus under the more usual terms of employment of a managing director this option would not be available to the board without committing a breach of contract.[7]

Thus the exact status and powers of a managing director depend both upon the articles which confer a power on the board to appoint a managing director and upon the terms of the contract by which he is employed. Although he must be a director, his status as managing director derives from his appointment by the

---

1   *Mitchell & Hobbs (UK) Ltd v Mills* [1996] 2 BCLC 102 at 107–108.
2   See article 84 of the modern Table A. If the articles do not so provide, a managing director not reappointed by the general meeting will lose his office even though expressed to be appointed for a term of years: *Bluett v Stutchbury's* (1908) 24 TLR 469 (CA).
3   As under article 107 of the 1948 Table A.
4   Under section 303; see **15.7**.
5   *Nelson v James Nelson & Sons* [1914] 2 KB 770 (CA); see **15.4**. An appointment for an indeterminate period may be determined, however, at any time, without the company being liable for breach of contract: *Foster v Foster* [1916] 1 Ch 532.
6   [1955] 1 WLR 352 (HL).
7   See also *Yetton v Eastwoods Froy* [1967] 1 WLR 104, where a managing director was dismissed and then offered the position of assistant managing director at the same salary; he was held entitled to refuse the offer because of the loss of status involved.

board to this office. He is thus both a director and, as managing director, an employee of the company.[1]

15.14.2 The secretary

The secretary is the other important officer of a company. Every company must have a secretary, and a sole director of a company, or a corporation the sole director of which is a sole director of a company, may not be the secretary of the company.[2] A provision requiring or authorising anything to be done by or to a director and the secretary is not satisfied by being done by or to the same person acting both as director and as, or in the place of, the secretary.[3] However, if at any time the office of secretary is vacant, or there is no secretary capable of acting, his functions may be carried out by any assistant or deputy secretary or, if there is no such, by an officer duly authorised by the directors.

The importance of the office of secretary is recognised by the fact that secretaries of public companies must since 1980 have been qualified. Under section 286, it is the duty of the directors of a public company, when appointing the secretary, to take all reasonable steps to secure that he is a person who appears to them to have the requisite knowledge and experience to discharge the functions of secretary, and such a person must have one of several possible types of experience or professional qualification. The professional qualifications include chartered secretaryship, accountancy and the legal profession. Sufficient experience is provided by the person having been secretary (or assistant or deputy secretary) of the company on 22 December 1980, by his having been secretary of a public company for at least three of the previous five years or, by virtue of his holding or having held any other position, or his being a member of any other body, by his appearing to the directors capable of discharging the function of secretary.[4]

---

1   See *Anderson v James Sutherland (Peterhead) Ltd* 1941 SC 203, where Lord Carmont relied upon *Southern Foundries Ltd v Shirlaw* [1940] AC 701 (HL) and *Fowler v Commercial Timber Co* [1903] 3 KB 1. See also *Trussed Steel Concrete v Green* [1946] Ch 115; *Lee v Lees Air Farming Ltd* [1961] AC 12 (PC); *Boulting v ACTAT* [1963] QB 600 (CA). Although a managing director was held (*Re Newspaper Proprietary Syndicate Ltd* [1900] 2 Ch 349) not to be a 'clerk' or 'servant' when these were the relevant persons described as preferential creditors on a winding-up in the former legislation (consolidated in Schedule 19 to the Companies Act 1985), the appropriate legislation now (Schedule 6, paragraph 9 to the Insolvency Act 1986) refers simply to 'employee' and there seems no reason why this should not include a managing director. As to preferential debts, see **21.51.1**.

2   Section 283. Particulars of the secretary must be notified to the Registrar: see **15.19**. The Company Law Review may recommend abolition of the requirement for a secretary for at least small private companies (see *Modern Company Law for a Competitive Economy: Developing the Framework*, March 2000, paragraphs 7.34–7.36).

3   Section 284. 'Provision' is not expressed to be limited to 'statutory provision', and the enactment presumably applies to provisions in the articles, eg an article requiring the presence and signature of a director and the secretary for the affixing of the seal.

4   The date is the date when the previous section (in the 1980 Act) came into force. The last qualification by experience is rather odd, since it seems to negate the general purpose of section 286.

Case-law has also recognised the important position that the secretary holds in respect of a company's administrative affairs.[1] He is wholly or partly responsible for the accuracy of documents lodged with the Registrar, and if the company defaults in this respect, the liability to a fine is almost invariably incurred by the secretary. He is the agent through whom the clerical work of the company is done. He must obey the orders of the directors and give effect to their resolutions by issuing notices, sending circulars, writing letters, etc. He will also prepare the agenda for directors' meetings and general meetings, and usually write up the minutes, either from his own notes or from those of the chairman.[2]

15.15   Disqualification and other sanctions against miscreant directors and others involved in company management

Legislation contains various provisions under which directors and others may be disqualified from office or subjected to personal liability for the debts of their companies or under which other forms of sanction may be imposed.[3] These are essentially aimed at situations where the privileges of corporate personality and limited liability have been abused. The provisions are a mixture of ones which have existed for some years and ones which were introduced relatively recently.[4] Others were first introduced by the Insolvency Act 1985.[5] They are now all consolidated in the Company Directors Disqualification Act 1986 and the Insolvency Act 1986, as amended.

The legislation has spawned a vast amount of case-law and continuing government attempts to enforce the provisions, but an important survey[6] which looked particularly at disqualifications for unfitness[7] concluded that the disqualification of directors of small companies, which is where the provisions have been most used, is a very costly and not particularly effective way of dealing with abuses of limited liability. This aim would be better achieved by providing an alternative business form for the small business. It is suggested that the most effective policy would be to pursue unfit directors of larger companies.[8]

---

1   *Panorama Developments (Guildford) Ltd v Fidelis Furnishing Fabrics Ltd* [1971] 2 QB 711 (CA); the
    company was held liable to pay care hire charges incurred by the secretary in the company's
    name, but where the cars were fraudulently used by the secretary for his own pleasure, on the
    ground that the hiring fell within the apparent authority of a company secretary; see **5.29**.
2   For more detail as to the secretary's functions, see *Gore-Browne on Companies* 44th edn
    (Jordans, loose-leaf) at 26.10.
3   In addition to those reviewed here, see also **5.7**.
4   In the Companies Acts 1976 and 1981.
5   There was a considerable amount of controversy surrounding these. Originally, the
    Government introduced provisions providing for the automatic disqualification of directors
    of insolvent companies, with the onus on such directors to prove to the court the reason why
    they should not be disqualified. These were based on, but not identical to, proposals
    recommended by the Review Committee on Insolvency Law and Practice (the Cork
    Committee), Cmnd 8558 (1982), Chapter 45. Opposition from such influential bodies as the
    CBI and the Institute of Directors, as well as in Parliament, led to the dropping of these
    provisions and their replacement by the provision relating to 'unfitness' described in **15.16.3**.
6   Andrew Hicks, *Disqualification of Directors: No Hiding Place for the Unfit?*, ACCA Research Report
    59, 1998.
7   See **15.16.4**.
8   For a review of the DTI's exercise of their powers, see the report of the National Audit Office,
    Company Director Disqualification – a Follow-up Report, HC424, May 1999.

15.16 Disqualification of directors and others

The powers of the court to make disqualification orders[1] are contained in the Company Directors Disqualification Act 1986 and the statutory references in this and the following sections are to that Act.[2]

15.16.1 The meaning of disqualification

'Disqualification order' is defined as follows.[3] It is an order that a person shall not, without leave of the court,[4] be a director of a company, or a liquidator or administrator of a company, or a receiver or manager of a company's property, in any way, whether directly or indirectly, be concerned or take part in the promotion, formation or management of a company, or act as an insolvency practitioner, for a specified period beginning with the date of the order. Being concerned or taking part in management has been widely construed to cover the position of management consultant or the giving of advice on the financial management and reconstruction of a company.[5]

The various sections provide for maximum penalties of five years' disqualification in respect of persistent default (see below) and in all disqualifications by courts of summary jurisdiction, and of fifteen years in any other case. 'Tariffs' have been established, particularly for disqualification on the ground of unfitness, so that there are three 'brackets': ten or more years for serious cases, six to ten years for middling cases, and two to five years for minor cases.[6] The period of any subsequent disqualification imposed against a person already subject to an order runs concurrently with the existing period.[7] An order may be made on grounds which are or include matters other than criminal convictions, notwithstanding that the person in question may be criminally liable in respect of those matters.[8] There are heavy penalties for breach of a disqualification order.[9]

---

1   As to the nature of disqualification proceedings regarding admissible evidence, the applicability of natural justice, and other procedural matters, see *Re Churchill Hotel (Plymouth) Ltd* [1988] BCLC 341; *Re Rex Williams Leisure plc* [1993] BCLC 568; *Re Polly Peck International plc* [1993] BCLC 886; *Re Moonbeam Cards Ltd* [1993] BCLC 1099; *Re Polly Peck International plc* [1994] BCC 15. See *Gore-Browne on Companies* 44th edn (Jordans, loose-leaf) at 25.7.3 for detailed consideration of these and other cases. As to the impact of the European Human Rights Convention on disqualification proceedings, see *EDC v United Kingdom* [1998] BCC 370, *R v Secretary of State for Trade and Industry, ex parte McCormick* [1998] BCC 379 (CA), *Re Westminster Property Management Ltd, Official Receiver v Stern* [2000] 2 BCLC 396 (CA) and the discussion in *Gore-Browne* at 25.7.4G.
2   See generally, Dine (1991) 12 Co Law 6, [1994] JBL 325.
3   Section 1, as amended by section 5 of the Insolvency Act 2000.
4   Applications for leave are governed by section 17; the case law relevant thereto is examined in *Gore-Browne on Companies*, 25.7.4F.
5   *R v Campbell* [1984] BCLC 83. An order cannot be restricted to the holding of a directorship in a public company: *R v Ward; R v Howarth* [2001] EWCA Crim 1648, [2002] BCC 953.
6   See eg *Re Sevenoaks Stationers (Retail) Ltd* [1991] BCLC 325 and the other cases referred to in *Gore-Browne on Companies* 44th edn (Jordans, loose-leaf) at 25.7.4. See also *Re Westmid Packing Services Ltd* [1998] 2 BCLC 646 (CA).
7   Section 1(3).
8   Section 1(4).
9   Section 13.

15.16.2 Application for disqualification

An application to a court with jurisdiction to wind up companies to obtain a disqualification order under sections 2 to 5 may be made by the Secretary of State or the Official Receiver, or the liquidator or any past or present member or creditor of any company in relation to which the person in question has committed or is alleged to have committed an offence or default.[1] In respect of disqualification on the ground of unfitness, only the Secretary of State, or the Official Receiver acting under the direction of the Secretary of State, has *locus standi* to apply.[2]

An alternative cost-saving procedure to making an application to the court was introduced by the Insolvency Act 2000, inserting a new section 1A into the 1986 Act.[3] This allows the Secretary of State to accept a 'disqualification undertaking' from a person, which will have the same effect as a court order, if it appears to him to be expedient in the public interest to do so instead of applying, or proceeding with an application, for a disqualification order.[4]

15.16.3 Grounds for disqualification

The grounds for disqualifying a person from acting as a director, etc, are as follows.

(1) *Conviction of an offence.* The court can disqualify a person convicted of an indictable offence (whether on indictment or summarily) in connection with the promotion, formation, management or liquidation of a company or with the receivership or management of a company's property.[5] This ground is very wide as there is no requirement that the offence be committed in the course of the internal management of a company's affairs. So, for example, convictions for theft or other offences of dishonesty against outsiders or for insider dealing[6] are sufficient.[7]

(2) *Persistent default.* Disqualification can be imposed if it appears to the court that a person has been 'persistently in default' in relation to provisions of the companies legislation requiring any return, account or other document to be filed with, delivered or sent, or notice of any matter to be given, to the Registrar.[8] There is a presumption of persistent default where the person has

---

1   Section 16; the other procedural aspects are also prescribed in this section and section 17, and are described in detail in *Gore-Browne on Companies*, 44th edn (Jordans, loose-leaf) at 25.7.3. The courts are prepared to be flexible regarding these aspects where feasible; see eg the treatment of the 'requirement' for ten days' notice of an application for a disqualification order by the Court of Appeal in *Secretary of State for Trade and Industry v Langridge* [1991] BCLC 543. As to guidance regarding the conduct of applications under section 17 for leave for someone to act notwithstanding a disqualification order, see *Re Westmid Packing Services Ltd* [1998] 2 BCLC 646 (CA).

2   Section 7(1).

3   For detail, see *Gore-Browne on Companies*, 44th edn (Jordans; loose-leaf) at 25.7.3A.

4   See the review of this power by the Court of Appeal in *Re Blackspur Group plc (No 3), Secretary of State for Trade and Industry v Davies (No 2)* [2001] EWCA Civ 1595, [2002] 2 BCLC 263.

5   Section 2.

6   See **20.2**.

7   *R v Corbin* (1984) 6 Cr App R (S) 17, see 6 Co Law 183 (1985); *R v Austen* (1985) BCC 99, 528, see 7 Co Law 68 (1986). See also *R v Georgiou* (1988) 4 BCC 322 (CA); *R v Goodman* [1994] 1 BCLC 349 (CA).

8   Section 3.

been convicted of relevant offences or default orders have been made against him on three or more occasions. Otherwise, there is no need to show culpable disregard, merely a need to show some degree of continuance or repetition.[1] Under section 5, disqualification on this ground can be imposed by a magistrates' court (in England and Wales) at the same time as a person is convicted of an offence relevant to the filing of returns etc.

(3) *Fraud.* The court can disqualify if, in the course of winding up a company, it appears that a person:
   (a) has been guilty of an offence for which he is liable (whether or not he has been convicted) under section 458 of the Companies Act 1985, that is the offence of fraudulent trading;[2] or
   (b) has otherwise been guilty, while an officer or liquidator of the company, of any fraud in relation to the company or of any breach of his duty as such officer, liquidator, receiver or manager.[3]
   The reference to any breach of duty in (b) above obviously makes this potentially a very wide ground for disqualification.

(4) *Unfitness.* This ground for disqualification, and the next, are the most recent and this is potentially the broadest of all. It arises under sections 6 to 9 and its introduction (in the Insolvency Act 1985) gave rise to considerable controversy.[4] Because of its importance, it is dealt with separately in the next section.

(5) *Wrongful and fraudulent trading.* The concepts of wrongful and fraudulent trading are examined below, but it is appropriate to note at this stage that any person found liable under the relevant provision to contribute to a company's assets may also be disqualified under section 10.

(6) *Competition infringements.* Section 9A, inserted by the Enterprise Act 2002, section 204, allows for disqualification if a company of which the person is a director commits a breach of competition law and the court considers that his conduct as a director makes him unfit to be concerned in the management of a company.

15.16.4 Disqualification for unfitness

As has already been pointed out, only the Secretary of State (or the Official Receiver in most cases)[5] can apply for disqualification on the ground of unfitness, and he can do so if he thinks that 'it is expedient in the public interest,'[6] but liquidators and others[7] are under a duty to report what can be described as suspected cases of unfitness to the Secretary of State, and the latter (and the Official Receiver) can require those persons to produce information and

---

1   *Re Arctic Engineering Ltd* [1986] BCLC 253; see (1986) 7 Co Law 27.
2   See **15.17.1**.
3   Section 4.
4   See footnote 5 at p 464.
5   Only the Secretary of State can act in respect of a director of a company in voluntary liquidation; section 7(1); see *Re Probe Data Systems Ltd* [1989] BCLC 561.
6   Section 7(1).
7   The Official Receiver in respect of a company being wound up by the court, the liquidator (company being otherwise wound up), the administrator (company in administration) and the receiver (company in receivership).

documents which he 'may reasonably require for the purpose of determining whether to exercise, or of exercising, any function of his' under the section.[1] Except with the leave of the court,[2] an application under section 6 may not be made more than two years after the company in question becomes insolvent.[3]

Section 6 allows the court to disqualify only a director or shadow director[4] for unfitness, and is thus narrower in this respect than the other disqualification provisions, but director for this purpose includes a *de facto* director, that is someone who acted as a director although not formally appointed.[5] The court must be satisfied of two things: (a) that the person in question is or has been a director of a company which has at any time become insolvent[6] (whether while he was a director or subsequently); and (b) that his conduct as a director of that company (either taken alone or taken together with his conduct as a director of any other company or companies)[7] makes him unfit to be concerned in the management of a company.[8] Under section 8, an application for disqualification for unfitness may be made by the Secretary of State from a different route, namely where he thinks it expedient to apply following an inspection under the provisions of the Companies Act 1985.[9]

Obviously, the concept of 'unfitness' is central to applications under both sections 6 and 8. Section 9 directs the court to determine the question by reference to the matters listed in Schedule 1. These matters are divided into those applicable in all cases, and those applicable where the company has become insolvent. The first head comprises misfeasance or breach of duty as a director, the responsibility of the director for a transaction liable to be set aside as a fraud on creditors,[10] and the extent of his responsibility for any breaches of many of the filing requirements of the Companies Act 1985. The second includes the extent of the directors' responsibility 'for the causes of the company becoming insolvent' and for failing to supply paid-for goods or services, the extent of his responsibility for any voidable preference[11] or failure to summon a creditors' meeting in a

---

1   Section 7(4).
2   As to the principles on which the court should grant leave, see especially *Secretary of State for Trade and Industry v Davies* [1997] 2 BCLC 317 (CA).
3   Section 7(2). Insolvency is widely defined for these purposes as when either: (a) a company goes into liquidation at a time when its liabilities and the expenses of winding up exceed its assets; (b) an administration order (not an interim administration order: *Secretary of State for Trade and Industry v Palmer* [1993] BCC 650) is made in relation to the company; or (c) an administrative receiver of the company is appointed: section 6(2). The period runs from when the first one of these events occurs: *Re Tasbian Ltd (No 1)* [1991] BCLC 54 (CA).
4   As to the meaning of this, see **15.2**.
5   *Re Moorgate Metals Ltd* [1995] 1 BCLC 503.
6   As to the meaning of insolvency, see footnote 00 on p 000 above.
7   There is no territorial limit on the conduct that may be considered: *Re Seagull Manufacturing Co Ltd (No 2)* [1994] Ch 91. See also *Secretary of State for Trade and Industry v Ivers* [1997] 2 BCLC 339.
8   Section 6(1). References to conduct include, where a company has become insolvent, references to a person's conduct in relation to any matter connected with or arising out of the insolvency of that company: section 6(2). As to the relationship between different sets of disqualification proceedings or between disqualification proceedings and other disciplinary proceedings, see the cases discussed in *Gore-Browne on Companies*, 44th edn (Jordans, loose-leaf) at 25.7.4D.
9   Sections 437 and 447 or 448; see Part 3 of Chapter 17.
10 Under Part XVI of the Insolvency Act 1986; see **21.55** *et seq*.
11 Under the Insolvency Act 1986, sections 127, 238 or 241.

creditors' voluntary winding-up[1] and any failure to comply with any obligations to deliver statements of affairs to the liquidator, administrator or receiver.[2]

The extent to which these provisions are successful in curbing the abuses at which they are directed depends upon a number of factors. These include the willingness of insolvency practitioners to report suspected cases, made more likely by their obligation to make appropriate returns to the Department of Trade and Industry and the willingness of the DTI to pursue individual cases. Also of crucial importance is the attitude of the court when faced with applications for disqualification. We now have a large volume of case-law on the unfitness provisions, which is summarised in the following paragraph.

Basically, what must be shown to justify disqualification is conduct that is dishonest, is in breach of standards of commercial morality or is grossly incompetent, such as to convince the court that it would be a danger to the public to allow the person in question to continue to be involved in the management of companies.[3] On the other hand, commercial misjudgment by itself does not constitute unfitness. What constitutes dishonesty does not need to be considered further here. It is clear that commercial morality and competence are separate matters, so that a director can be shown to have been grossly incompetent even if his conduct was 'commercially moral'. Even if, for example, it is regarded as moral to use money owed to the Crown in respect of taxes (especially PAYE, VAT and national insurance) to finance the company's trading activities,[4] and the director in question knows or ought to know what is happening, this can still be sufficiently incompetent.[5] So also, incompetence is evidenced by failure to file accounts and returns as required by the Companies Act 1985, pressure of work being no excuse.[6] The Court of Appeal has confirmed that in general the test for acting incompetently is whether the director caused the company to trade while insolvent and had no reasonable prospect of meeting creditors' claims; it is not enough for the company to have been insolvent to the knowledge of the director.[7] A clear illustration of conduct contrary to commercial morality is provided by *Re Ipcon Fashions Ltd*.[8] The director had carried on business in the

---

1   Ibid, section 98.

2   Ibid, sections 22, 47, 66, 99, 131, 234, or 235.

3   This was first clearly set out by Hoffman J in *Re Dawson Print Group Ltd* [1987] BCLC 601. Other leading cases include *Re Stanford Services Ltd* [1987] BCLC 607; *Re Lo-Line Electric Motors Ltd* [1988] Ch 477; *Re Bath Glass Ltd* [1988] BCLC 329; *Re Churchill Hotel (Plymouth) Ltd* [1988] BCLC 341; *Re Majestic Recording Studios* [1989] BCLC 1; *Re McNulty's Interchange Ltd* [1989] BCLC 709; *Re C U Fittings* [1989] BCLC 556; *Re Ipcon Fashions Ltd* (1989) 5 BCC 773; *Re Cladrose Ltd* [1990] BCLC 204, *Re ECM Europe Electronics* [1991] BCLC 268, *Re Wimbledon Village Restaurant Ltd* [1994] BCC 753, *Secretary of State for Trade and Industry v Gray* [1995] 2 BCLC 276 (CA) and *Re Kaytech International plc* [1999] 2 BCLC 351. The last case and *Re Pamstock Ltd* [1996] BCC 341 (CA) also give guidance as to when an appeal court can interfere with the trial judge's findings as to unfitness.

4   It will not always be such.

5   The use of Crown money to continue trading has on the balance of the cases been viewed as a much more serious matter than the failure to pay ordinary creditors.

6   See, in particular, *Re Churchill Hotel (Plymouth) Ltd*, above, and *Re Cladrose Ltd*, above, referring to Schedule 1 which, as indicated above, directs the court to have regard to the extent of a director's responsibility for a failure to comply with a duty. See also *Secretary of State for Trade and Industry v Van Hegel* [1995] 1 BCLC 545.

7   *Secretary of State for Trade and Industry v Creegan* [2001] EWCA Civ 1742, [2002] 1 BCLC 99.

8   Above. See also on the 'Phoenix syndrome', *Re Travel Mondial (UK) Ltd* [1991] BCC 224; *Re Swift 736 Ltd* [1992] BCC 93; *Re Linvale Ltd* [1993] BCLC 654.

clothing trade for 15 years through a succession of companies which had become insolvent. In the four months before Ipcon Fashions was wound up, knowing it was insolvent, he abandoned it to its fate and transferred the business to a new company, while still incurring liabilities to suppliers and paying himself and his wife salaries without accounting for tax.

The court's refusal to regard mere incompetence as revealing unfitness has been criticised, on the ground that the courts seem to view the policy behind section 6 as punitive rather than as protecting the public against incompetent directors.[1] Judicial reluctance to disqualify without blameworthiness may be influenced by the mandatory nature of the duty under section 6,[2] and it has been observed on a number of occasions that the court must use its jurisdiction to protect the public against those who abuse limited liability, but must be careful not to stultify all enterprise. It may not be easy to resolve what exactly is or should be the dominant purpose of disqualification, and consideration of this cannot be divorced from looking at the impact of other measures such as the wrongful trading provision.[3] What cannot be denied is that the law seems much more effective than it used to be at penalising rogue directors and thus protecting the public from them, even if it may not yet be working perfectly.[4]

15.16.5 Register of disqualification orders

Under section 18 and regulations made thereunder,[5] the Secretary of State maintains a register of disqualification orders on the basis of information which it is the duty of the officers of the courts making the orders to supply. Entries must be deleted on the expiry of any order. The register is open to public inspection on the payment of a fee of 5 pence.

15.17 Liability of directors (and others) to contribute to the assets or for the debts of their companies

There are now three provisions under which directors and, in certain cases, others may be made liable by the court in effect for the debts of their companies. A person may be made liable for fraudulent trading, for wrongful trading or for acting while disqualified. All these situations provide for statutory exceptions to the principle of the separate legal personality of a company from its members.[6] For many years, companies legislation has made 'fraudulent trading' a criminal offence, and also the basis on which personal liability could be imposed on directors and others responsible. Criminal liability was, and continues to be, imposed by section 458 of the Companies Act 1985, which applies whether or not there is a winding up. In a winding up, civil liability for fraudulent trading is imposed on the same grounds as attract criminal liability. For this reasons it was suggested[7] that, the object of civil liability being compensation rather than

---

1   Finch (1990) 53 MLR 385.
2   In contrast to its predecessor, section 300 of the Companies Act 1985, which afforded a discretion.
3   See **15.17.2**.
4   See the Report by Hicks, footnote 6 at p 464.
5   The Companies (Disqualification Orders) Regulations 1985, SI 1985/829.
6   See Chapter 3.
7   Report of the Review Committee on Insolvency Law and Practice, Cmnd 8558 (1982), paragraph 1776 *et seq.*

punishment, civil liability for fraudulent trading should be replaced by a wider liability imposed without proof of fraud or dishonesty. Liability for 'wrongful trading' was introduced by what is now section 214 of the Insolvency Act 1986, but civil liability for fraudulent trading remains in force under section 213. It is more likely than not that in a case where there is any reasonable prospect of establishing fraud or dishonesty there will also be liability for wrongful trading and, therefore, an application in respect of fraudulent trading against a director is likely to be pointless.[1] Section 213 does, however, apply to a wider category of persons than does section 214 and recent section 213 litigation has focussed on attempts to obtain contributions from those who would not be subject to section 214.

15.17.1 Fraudulent trading

Section 213 of the Insolvency Act 1986 provides that if in the course of winding up a company it appears that any business of the company has been carried on with intent to defraud creditors of the company or creditors of any other person, or for any fraudulent purpose, the court, on the application of the liquidator, may declare that any persons who were knowingly parties to the carrying on of the business in that manner are to be liable to make such contributions (if any) to the company's assets as the court thinks proper.

Despite the propounding of a somewhat looser test in an early case on the predecessor to section 213,[2] it is clear that the words 'defraud' and 'fraudulent purpose' connote 'real dishonesty involving, according to current notions of fair trading among commercial men at the present day, real moral blame'.[3] It is sufficient if directors allow the company to incur credit at a time when it is clear that the company will never be able to pay its creditors. It may be sufficient if they so allow it at a time when they know the company is unable to meet all its liabilities as they fall due.[4]

It does not matter for the purpose of the section that only one creditor is defrauded and by a single transaction, if it is shown that the transaction can properly be described as a fraud on the creditor perpetrated in the course of carrying on business.[5] The phrase 'carrying on business' is not necessarily synonymous with actively carrying on trade. The collection in and distribution of assets in payment of debts can constitute a carrying on of business. However, where the only allegation is that a company or its officers preferred one or more creditors over others, that cannot constitute fraud within the meaning of the

---

1   See, eg, *Official Receiver v Doshi* [2001] 2 BCLC 235 as a case which before 1986 might well have been argued on the basis of fraudulent trading but was brought successfully under section 214. It is possible that the level of compensation might be higher under section 213 since the level of contribution may include a punitive element: *Morphites v Bernasconi* [2001] 2 BCLC 1.

2   *Re William C Leitch Bros* [1932] 2 Ch 71.

3   *Per* Maugham J in *Re Patrick and Lyon* [1933] Ch 786. The need to show dishonesty was more recently stressed in *R v Cox and Hedges* (1982) 75 Crim App R 291 and *Re Augustus Barnett & Son Ltd* [1986] BCLC 170. See also *Re L Todd Swanscombe Ltd* [1990] BCLC 454 and *Re Sobam BV* [1996] 1 BCLC 446. The dishonesty involved in fraudulent trading may justify an order which includes a punitive element: *Re a Company* [1990] BCC 526.

4   *R v Grantham* [1984] 3 All ER 166 (CA), disapproving the decision to the contrary in *Re White and Osmond (Parkstone) Ltd*, unreported, 30 June 1960. See also *R v Lockwood* (1986) 2 BCC 99, 333 (CA).

5   *Re Gerald Cooper Chemicals Ltd* [1978] 1 Ch 262. It does not matter that the creditor is not owed a present debt at the time of the fraud: *R v Kemp* [1988] BCLC 217 (CA).

section.[1] A false representation that the company would make a payment that the defendants did not intend to make could amount to fraudulent trading; it is not necessary for the liquidator to show that credit had in fact been given or that the creditor had relied on the fraud.[2]

In order to be subject to liability under section 213, it is necessary to have knowingly[3] been a party to the carrying on of the business in the fraudulent fashion. Any person who actively and dishonestly assists in or benefits from the fraudulent conduct can be liable; it is not necessary to have exercised a controlling or managerial function within the company in liquidation.[4] The expression 'party to' in the section indicates no more than 'participates in', 'takes part in', or 'concurs in', but involves more than mere passivity. A person, such as an employee, who was merely carrying out orders, or another company carrying on bona fide business with the company, would not be caught by section 213. Mere omission by a company secretary to give certain advice to the directors was held not to render the secretary liable under the section,[5] though this is not to say that a secretary who does more than the duties appropriate to his office might not be liable, and it is clear that given the necessary evidence, a creditor[6] or a parent company could fall within the expression.[7] In this respect, section 213 contrasts with the wrongful trading provision, discussed next, under which only directors and shadow directors can be found liable.

Under section 215(2), the court, on making a declaration, may also provide that the liability of a person is to be a charge on any debt or obligation due from the company to him, or on any mortgage or charge on any assets of the company held by or vested in him, or any company or person on his behalf. It can from time to time make such further orders as may be necessary to enforce any such charge. By section 215(5), the section applies notwithstanding that the person concerned may be criminally liable in respect of the matters on the ground of which a declaration is made.

15.17.2 *Wrongful trading*

As we have seen, section 214 of the Insolvency Act 1986 is an alternative to alleging fraudulent trading under section 213.[8] It should be noted though, that the section imposes liability for omissions and goes beyond the examples given by the Review Committee regarding continuing to trade while insolvent. It imposes a

---

1   *Re Sarflax Ltd* [1979] 1 Ch 529.
2   *Morphites v Bernasconi* [2001] 2 BCLC 1.
3   *Morris v Bank of America National Trust* [2001] 1 BCLC 771 (CA) involved an application by the defendant to strike out proceedings under section 213 on the basis that the allegation that it was 'knowingly' a party to fraudulent trading was bound to fail. It was common ground for the purposes of the appeal that 'knowingly' includes wilful blindness or reckless indifference and that the defendant must be shown to have acted dishonestly. The liquidators' case was that individual senior executives either had the requisite knowledge or recklessly ignored it or, in the alternative, that the knowledge of all its senior executives should be aggregated and attributed to the defendant. The Court of Appeal held that the defendants had failed to discharge the burden of establishing that the liquidators had no prospect of establishing any aspect of their case.
4   *Re BCCI, Banque Arabe Internationale d'Investissement SA v Morris* [2001] 1 BCLC 263.
5   *Re Maidstone Building Provisions Ltd* [1971] 1 WLR 1085.
6   *Re Sarflax*, above.
7   Note that by section 215(4), if a creditor is found liable, his debt can be deferred to rank for payment after all the other debts owed by the company.
8   See section 214(8).

new liability to contribute and is not concerned with enforcing some past or existing liability.[1]

Application under section 214 may only be made by the liquidator of a company, and only in respect of a person who is or has been a director or shadow director[2] of the company. The court may declare that person liable to make such contribution (if any) to the company's assets as it thinks fit if:

(1) the company has gone into insolvent liquidation;[3]
(2) at some time before the commencement of the winding-up, that person knew or ought to have concluded that there was no reasonable prospect that the company would avoid going into insolvent liquidation; and
(3) that person was a director (or shadow director) of the company at that time.

However, the court must not make a declaration in relation to any person if satisfied that, after he first realised the likelihood of insolvent liquidation, ie the time in (2) above, he took every step with a view to minimising the potential loss to the company's creditors as (assuming him to have known that there was no reasonable prospect that the company would avoid going into insolvent liquidation) he ought to have taken.[4] In respect of this point and (2) above, the facts which a director of a company ought to know or ascertain, the conclusions which he ought to reach and the steps which he ought to take are those which would be known or ascertained, or reached or taken, by a reasonably diligent person having both (a) the general knowledge, skill and experience that may reasonably be expected of a person carrying out the same functions as are carried out by that director in relation to the company, and (b) the general knowledge, skill and experience which that director has.[5]

The subjective criterion will work against, rather than in favour of, the director; the function of (b) is to catch a director who fails to live up to his own standards when those are higher than would usually be expected, having regard to his functions within the company. Conversely, (a) will catch those who simply fail to match the standards of performance 'reasonably expected' of directors having similar functions. In particular cases, the scope of a director's 'functions in relation to the company' will be of decisive importance. A director may be an executive or non-executive director, full-time or part-time; he may be elected for his financial acumen or business experience, for his knowledge of particular products or services, or to provide, for example, technical expertise.[6] All these are

---

1 *Re Howard Holdings Inc* [1998] BCC 549. Thus, in the case of a foreign company being wound up in England, it was irrelevant whether the liability existed or could exist under any system of foreign law.

2 As to shadow directors, see **16.2**. In *Re Hydrodam (Corby) Ltd* [1994] 2 BCLC 180, it was held that a parent company, but not its directors, could be a shadow director of its subsidiary for the purposes of section 214. The judgment of Millett J contains important and helpful guidance as to the meaning of the term. Where a director has died, the claim may be maintained against his estate: *Re Sherborne Associates Ltd* [1995] BCC 40. A director may be entitled to enforce an indemnity given by the person who appointed him if the true construction of the indemnity so permits: *Burgoine v London Borough of Waltham Forest* [1997] BCC 347.

3 Ie its assets are insufficient to pay its liabilities and the expenses of winding up: section 214(6).

4 Section 214(3). For an argument that the burden of proof in this aspect continues to lie on the liquidator, see *Gore-Browne on Companies* 44th edn (Jordans, loose-leaf) at 35.4.2.

5 Section 214(4).

6 Eg in a 'high-tech' company.

matters which may be relevant in determining what a particular director's 'functions' are, although it will also be necessary to examine the 'functions' which are actually conferred upon him. This is made clear by section 214(5), which provides (as might well have been implied) that a director's functions include those 'which he does not carry out but which have been entrusted to him'.[1]

The courts have recognised that the degree of competence found among directors will vary from company to company,[2] and the criterion of 'functions ... in relation to the company' may reflect this to some extent. The nature of the company must be relevant, since the standards reasonably to be expected of directors of a large public company cannot be the same as those of directors of an incorporated family business. The courts will no doubt recognise this, but cannot be expected to allow the argument to be pressed too far; the function of section 214 is to protect the company's creditors against neglect and incompetence, and even a small family concern will have creditors whose position, relatively speaking, may be as vulnerable to such neglect and incompetence on the board as that of the creditors of a much larger company. Even within a small company, therefore, there will inevitably be one or more directors whose functions include monitoring the company's solvency.[3] In any event, and in any company, there must come a point when a director ought to realise from information which he has received[4] that the company faces solvency problems, and it seems that the effect of section 214 must be that, at that point, his duties include the function of ascertaining the true position and, if necessary, taking action. There will, therefore, be a duty to supervise under section 214, and that duty may be broken either by individual directors, or by the whole body of directors in failing to institute or to operate an adequate monitoring process. In *Re Produce Marketing Consortium Ltd (No 2)*,[5] the company's accounts were prepared some considerable time after the statutory periods had expired. The court imputed to the directors the knowledge that timely delivery of the accounts would have given them. It is clear that directors will usually, if not invariably, be taken for the purposes of section 214 to have knowledge of the accounts, at the latest by the time when they should have been delivered. The director's position will be even weaker if the failure to prepare accounts is accompanied by obvious warning signs, such as a supplier's refusal to make further deliveries, or pressure for payment from the company's creditors. In

---

1   The word 'entrusted' may raise questions. The court may feel itself free to disregard formal requirements as to delegation of functions and pay attention instead to the company's actual working arrangements. It may also feel that it may look at what actually occurred by way of 'entrusting' functions even if it was in complete disregard of the articles. This would mean, in all probability, that there might be liability both in a director to whom a function was in fact entrusted and in a director who should, strictly speaking, have been exercising that function. Further, it seems likely that it will be a 'function' of all directors to some extent to oversee the activities of the company, including those of other directors.

2   *DHSS v Evans* [1985] 2 All ER 472.

3   *Re DKG Contractors Ltd* [1990] BCC 903; *Re Sherborne Associates Ltd* [1995] BCC 40. In the latter case, it was accepted that two non-executive directors, recruited for reasons quite different from financial expertise, were entitled to rely on an active chairman, who had far greater involvement with the company and its figures. The case concerned a company whose only prospects of survival depended on increased sales, and – given a consistent pattern of losses and optimistic forecasts – it is submitted that the decision that the directors in question were not liable under section 214 can be justified only on the basis that it survived for only two years, during which it may still have been reasonable to believe there would be a turnaround.

4   Or ascertained or, indeed, ought to have ascertained: section 214(4).

5   [1989] BCLC 520.

Re DKG Contractors Ltd,[1] the company was a small works contractor managed by the two directors, a husband and wife team. The wife kept a 'black book' recording payments and invoices received, which was a basis on which proper accounts might have been prepared, but this was never done. It was held that, given the warning signs referred to above, the directors should have instituted some form of financial control. That would have revealed that there was no reasonable prospect of avoiding liquidation. The two directors had thus failed to satisfy the standards set by subsection (4)(a). The 'hopeless inadequacy' of their knowledge, skill and experience could not protect them. It is the duty even of the directors of an incorporated family business to acquire some basic knowledge of their legal obligations and financial responsibilities. Nor, in this case, was it sufficient answer to say that the directors had relied on assurances that money would come into the company; although these came from a quantity surveyor, his task had been merely to supervise contract income, and he had no information about the company's finances. *Re Brian D Pierson (Contractors) Ltd*[2] concerned, among other things, a claim for wrongful trading against the directors of a company that constructed and maintained golf courses. The company had two directors who were also husband and wife. The wife had taken almost no part in management, she had no separate areas of responsibility, and she had left all management decisions to her husband. The court was satisfied that the case was made out by the liquidator even having regard to the seasonal nature of the business and to the fact that the company had not suffered losses continuously over a number of years. It had suffered increasing losses and certain investments had become worthless. The loss of the investments was not so important by itself, but to regard them as current assets as the active director had done amounted to a refusal to face facts. There was no evidence that the directors had sought advice from the bank or the company's auditors, and in any event it was their responsibility to review critically the position of the company and it was they who had or should have had fullest knowledge of the position of the company. The wife's lack of involvement did not exclude her from liability. Although she had little practical involvement in the company she was still a director, drawing a salary and other fees, and certain minimum responsibilities were expected of her. The courts have distinguished between those cases where the directors, being clearly aware of the possibility and consequences of insolvent trading, had considered the position carefully before deciding to trade on and those cases where the directors had made no real attempt to address the issue. The courts have stressed the need to avoid hindsight; the fact that a decision to trade on, taken after careful consideration, turned out to be wrong should not in itself give rise to liability. In *Re Continental Assurance of London plc*, Park J commented that if he had had to find the directors liable for wrongful trading in the circumstances of the case, it would be 'hard to imagine any well-advised person ever agreeing to accept appointment as a non-executive director of any company'. The liquidators' initial argument was that the accounting information available was inadequate to enable the directors to form a view as to the solvency of the company; by the end of the trial this argument had fallen away and the liquidators were left to argue that appropriate accounting

---

1   [1990] BCC 903; see also *Re Purpoint Ltd* [1991] BCC 121 at 127–128, where Vinelott J clearly contemplates that there may be companies which no prudent director would allow to begin trading.

2   [1999] BCC 26.

policies had not been applied to the raw data in the accounts and that, if they had been, the company would have been seen to be insolvent and the directors ought to have realised that. After detailed consideration of the adjustments which the liquidators argued should have been made to the accounts, the judge concluded that even if he had accepted all the adjustments so that the accounts should have shown the company to be in a state of insolvency, he would not have held that the directors should have been aware of the position. This would have required an understanding of accounting concepts of a particularly specialised and sophisticated nature which should not be expected even of the directors of such a specialised business.[1]

It has already been mentioned that section 214 of the 1986 Act goes far beyond the active trading to which the Review Committee on Insolvency Law and Practice addressed its recommendations. In covering the whole area of a company's financial affairs, and in attaching liability to omission as well as commission, the section imposes a potentially limitless duty on the director to pay constant attention to all aspects of his company's affairs, for fear that with hindsight a court may find that a reasonably diligent person in his position would have been able to evaluate the company's performance and prospects.[2] This will no doubt be mitigated in practice by allowing a measure of 'business judgment' to the board, but it seems unlikely that this can excuse complete omission. Further, a duty to inquire is clearly placed upon a director by judging him in the light of facts which he ought to know or *ascertain*: section 214(4). At the least, this means that when a director feels, or, it seems, ought to feel, that the information available to him is inadequate he must press for more. This may place an individual director in some difficulties since (apart from provoking hostility, which section 214 presumably expects him to suffer rather than avoid) a failure to obtain satisfactory answers seems itself to be a ground upon which a liquidator might later rely. In order to assess his own and the company's position, a director may have to seek advice and assistance from outside the company.[3] Section 214 may also produce a certain amount of 'defensive management', since an alert director will wish to keep very clear records of his own activities.

Section 214(3) is equally and deliberately imprecise in requiring the director, on actual or imputed foresight of insolvent liquidation, to take 'every step ... with a view to minimising the potential loss to the company's creditors[4] as ... he ought' to take, the only limitation being that he is liable only for failure to take steps

---

1 It would not have been acceptable for them to be totally ignorant of the accounting concepts to be applied to an insurance company but the 'proceedings are in substance an accountant's negligence action brought against the laymen who employed the accountants'. All the directors (except the company's finance director, against whom the case had been settled) were to be regarded as laymen in this regard despite the fact that they included two non-practising chartered accountants, one of whom had previously been a finance director himself albeit in a different type of insurance business.

2 In *Re Produce Marketing Consortium Ltd (No 2)* [1989] BCLC 520, the judge stressed in making the order under section 214 that the case was not one of deliberate wrongdoing but of 'failure to appreciate what should have been clear'. It is the nature of this liability which prevents a director from claiming relief under section 727 of the Companies Act 1985; *Re Produce Marketing Consortium Ltd* [1989] 1 WLR 745; *Re DKG Contractors Ltd* [1990] BCC 902 (see **16.23.4**).

3 It is a moot point whether his duties under section 214 will in all cases override obligations of confidentiality.

4 Presumably, those who are likely to be creditors in an insolvent liquidation, and not merely those who happen at present to be creditors.

which a reasonably diligent person in his position would have taken. The director is, subject to that qualification, expected to follow the course of conduct which will not merely reduce but reduce as far as possible the potential loss, and it appears to follow that, given a range of possible actions, he must take that course which satisfies that criterion; he may use his business judgment in evaluating the consequences of each course which is open, but once that is done he has no choice but to follow the course which minimises the loss. Resignation from the board is manifestly not such a course,[1] and it is difficult to avoid the conclusion that the section will, whatever its true intentions, make insolvency proceedings the likeliest outcome. The director is still, however, required to decide what form of proceedings (ie receivership, administration or liquidation) will in fact minimise the creditors' losses, and for this purpose the preliminary step of seeking advice[2] may not be only permissible but necessary. There is a real risk that section 214 will actually precipitate insolvency proceedings which in some cases may have been avoidable, particularly as directors face possible disqualification if held liable under the section.[3] Even if some form of insolvency proceedings is the step which the section itself contemplates, however, there may be cases where a decision to trade on, albeit for a limited period, may be justified insofar as it appears reasonably likely to increase the assets available to creditors, although it may be wondered whether directors or their advisers will in practice be prepared to support such a decision. Conversely, if the directors have properly considered the possible courses of action open to them, concluded reasonably that some form of insolvency proceedings are inevitable, and honestly and reasonably begun the process of realising assets by sale, they are probably not to be judged by the standards of an insolvency practitioner; provided that they obtain a reasonable price, they are not required to conduct a full-scale investigation of other offers which might produce a better price.[4]

What is absolutely clear from section 214(2) to (4) of the 1986 Act is the vital importance of the time element. It must be established at what moment the conditions set out in section 214(2) first applied to a particular director before the question of complying with section 214(3) can arise. In a wider sense, the impact of the section may be determined by the willingness or unwillingness of the court, with hindsight, to trace a company's affairs backwards in time from an insolvent liquidation to the first warning signs.

15.17.3 Liability for acting while disqualified

Section 15 of the Company Directors Disqualification Act 1986 contains a further provision under which a person can be liable for the debts of a company, and in this case liability is for those debts as such,[5] rather than, as in the cases of fraudulent and wrongful trading just described, liability to contribute to a company's assets.

A person is 'personally responsible' for all the relevant debts of a company if at any time either: (a) he is involved in the management of a company in

---

1   Still less, of course, abandoning the company while seeking fresh starts elsewhere: *Re Purpoint Ltd* [1991] BCC 121 at 125.
2   As expeditiously as possible.
3   See **15.16.3**, above.
4   Cf *Welfab Engineers Ltd* [1990] BCC 600 (directors' duties at common law).
5   Jointly and severally with the company and any other person who, whether under the section or otherwise, is liable: section 15(2).

contravention of a disqualification order[1] or section 11 of the Act (ie acting as a director while an undischarged bankrupt);[2] or (b) as a person involved in management he acts or is willing to act on instructions given without the leave of the court by a person whom he knows at that time to be disqualified or to be an undischarged bankrupt.

'Relevant debts' are those debts and liabilities incurred at a time when the person was involved in management or those incurred when he acted or was willing to act on the instructions of a person disqualified, etc.[3] Involvement in management is given a wide meaning, namely being a director or being concerned, directly or indirectly, or taking part in the management of a company.[4] For the purposes of situation (b), a person who has acted at any time on instructions as described above is presumed, unless the contrary is shown, to have been willing at any time thereafter to act on instructions.[5]

The attraction of section 15 to creditors of a company is that it can be used by them directly without the need for action by a liquidator or even for the company in question to be in liquidation. It should also therefore prove a strong deterrent to those disqualified.

15.17.4 Summary remedy

Finally, it is convenient to note the summary remedy available against directors and others in a liquidation, provided for by section 212 of the Insolvency Act 1986, and available not just to the liquidator or the official receiver, but also to any creditor and, subject to the leave of the court, contributory. This provision replaced and extended what was section 631 of the Companies Act 1985.

15.18 Publicity about directors and their interests

The Companies Act 1985 and associated legislation contains many provisions designed to ensure that the members of companies, and in some instances creditors and others dealing with companies, are protected from abuse by directors of their position. Some of these provisions have already been considered earlier in this chapter.[6] Some require disclosure in the accounts of certain transactions entered into by directors and have been considered in Chapter 14. Others relate directly to the duties of directors and are considered in the next chapter. The remainder of this chapter is devoted to those provisions which require publicity to be given to directors and others and to the interests which they may hold in their companies.

15.19 The register of directors and secretaries

Under sections 288 to 290 of the Companies Act 1985, every company is required to keep a register of its directors[7] and secretaries, and to file copies thereof or of

---

1 Made under any of the provisions described above.
2 See **15.5**.
3 Section 15(3).
4 Cf the wide construction of the similar words in section 1; see **15.16.1**.
5 Section 15(5).
6 Eg section 303 and the disqualification provisions.
7 Including shadow directors (see **16.2**).

any changes therein with the Registrar of Companies within 14 days of the appointment of the first directors or any change, as the case may be.[1]

Under section 289, the register must contain the following particulars with respect to each director:

(1) in the case of an individual, his present name,[2] any former name,[3] his usual residential address, his nationality, his business occupation (if any), particulars of any other directorships held by him or which have been held by him[4] and the date of his birth; and

(2) in the case of a corporation, its corporate name and registered or principal office.

The register must contain the following particulars with respect to the secretary or where there are joint secretaries, with respect to each of them: (a) in the case of an individual, his present name, any former name and his usual residential address; and (b) in the case of a corporation or a Scottish firm, its corporate or firm name and registered or principal office. Where all the partners in a firm are joint secretaries, the name and principal office of the firm may be stated.[5]

The register must be open to the inspection of any members of the company without charge, and of any other person on payment of the prescribed fee.[6] If inspection of the register is refused, the court may by order compel an immediate inspection of it.[7]

The annual return required by sections 363 to 365[8] must also state most of the same particulars as to the persons who are the directors and secretary of the company at the date of the return as are required to be inserted in the register.

15.20 Business letters

Section 305 of the Companies Act 1985 contains provisions as to the names of directors on business letters which apply to every company registered under the Companies Acts on or after 23 November 1916, and to every company incorporated outside Great Britain with an established place of business in Great Britain if such place of business was established on or after the said date.

Section 305(1) provides that a company to which the section applies shall not state in any form the name of a director[9] otherwise than in the text or as a signatory on any business letters on which the company's name appears, unless it

---

1   Any notification of a change must contain a signed consent to act by the new director or secretary. Any change must also be notified in the *Gazette* under section 711. The register may be computerised: the Companies (Registers and Records) Regulations 1985, SI 1985/724.

2   'Name' throughout the section means Christian or other forename and surname, with qualifications regarding titles: see section 289(2).

3   See section 289(2)(c).

4   Subject, in the case of past directorships, to the exceptions in section 289(3) which, broadly speaking, refer to directorships not held for five years or more and directorships in dormant companies (as to which see **14.17.2**) or companies which are part of the same group of companies where all the subsidiaries and sub-subsidiaries are wholly owned.

5   Section 290.

6   Section 288(3). As to the fee and the detailed rights of inspection and copying, see the Companies (Inspection and Copying of Registers, Indices and Documents) Regulations 1991, SI 1991/1998.

7   Section 288(5). As to the penalties for breach of section 288, see section 288(4).

8   See **12.7** above.

9   'Director' includes shadow director, as to which see **16.2**.

states on the letter in legible characters the Christian name or the initials thereof and surname of every director of the company who is an individual, and the corporate name of every corporate director. Prior to the Companies Act 1981, the obligation to state the names of directors applied without qualification to those companies subject to the equivalent section. It is surprising that Parliament should choose to amend the requirement, given that it was some, albeit small, protection against small company fraud.[1]

15.21 Directors' service contracts

Section 318(1) of the Companies Act 1985 requires every company to keep copies of each director's service contract, or where such contract is not in writing, a written memorandum setting out the terms of the director's contract of service.[2] In the case of each director who is employed under a contract of service with a subsidiary of the company, a similar obligation is imposed. Section 318(2) requires copies and memoranda of service contracts to be kept in one place. Section 318(3) states that the following are 'appropriate places' for this purpose:

(1) its registered office;
(2) the place where its register of members is kept (if other than its registered office);
(3) its principal place of business, provided that it is situated in that part of Great Britain in which the company is registered.

The company must give notice to the Registrar as to the place where these copies and memoranda are kept and any change of place, except where this has always been the registered office. These documents are to be open to inspection by any member of the company. Section 318 provides for heavy penalties for the company and every officer in default, and empowers the court by order to compel an immediate inspection where this has been refused.

Section 318 does not apply in relation to a director's service contract with the company, or with a subsidiary of the company, if that contract requires him to work wholly or mainly outside the United Kingdom. However, even in such a case the company must keep, in the case of a contract of service with the company, a memorandum setting out the names of the director and the provisions of the contract relating to its duration. In the case of a contract of service with a subsidiary of the company, the company must keep a memorandum, setting out the names of the directors, the name and place of incorporation of the subsidiary and the provisions of the contract relating to its duration.

The Law Commissions[3] have recommended a number of changes to section 318, including that it should be extended to directors' contracts for services and non-executive directors' letters of appointment and that the exemption in relation to contracts to work abroad should be abolished.

---

1   See (1981) 2 Co Law 125–126.
2   This obligation applies also to a variation of a director's service contract: section 318(10). As to the statutory controls on the length of directors' service contracts, see **16.15**.
3   *Company Directors: Regulating Conflicts of Interest and Formulating a Statement of Duties*, Law Com No 261, Scot Law Com No 173, paragraphs 9.5 to 9.23. See generally, **16.25**.

15.22   Directors' interests in shares or debentures

Section 324 of and Schedule 13 to the Companies Act 1985 place anyone who becomes a director[1] under an obligation to notify the company in writing of his interest in shares in or debentures of the company, or its subsidiary, holding company or co-subsidiary within five days of his becoming a director or, if he is ignorant of his interest, within five days after it comes to his knowledge. He is required to give notice of his interests in terms of the number of shares of each class and the amount of debentures of each class in the company or its subsidiary, etc. The meaning of being 'interested in shares in or debentures of the company' is defined in Schedule 13, Part I, which will be considered below.[2]

While he remains a director of a company, a director is under an obligation to notify the company of the occurrence of any of the following events:[3]

(1)   any event in consequence of whose occurrence he becomes, or ceases to be, interested in shares in, or debentures of, the company or any other body corporate, being the company's subsidiary or holding company or a subsidiary of the company's holding company;[4]

(2)   the entering into by him of a contract to sell any such shares or debentures;[5]

(3)   the assignment by him of a right granted to him by the company to subscribe for shares in, or debentures of, the company;[6] and

(4)   the grant to him by another body corporate, being the company's subsidiary or holding company or a subsidiary of the company's holding company, of a right to subscribe for shares in, or debentures of, that other body corporate, the exercise of such a right granted to him as aforesaid and the assignment by him of such a right so granted.[7]

In each case he must state the number or amount, and class, of shares or debentures involved.

15.22.1   *Duty to notify an investment exchange*

Section 329(1) imposes upon a company a duty, in certain cases, to notify an investment exchange of information obtained from directors in compliance with section 324. The obligation arises where the company has shares or debentures listed on a recognised investment exchange and it is notified by a director, in

---

1   This includes a shadow director: section 324(8).

2   A few technical changes to these provisions are recommended by the Law Commissions, footnote 3 at p 480, at paragraphs 11.18 to 11.46.

3   The same five-day period as above applies.

4   He must state the price to be paid under the contract: Schedule 13, paragraph 17(1). 'Price' includes 'any consideration other than money'.

5   He must state the price received under the contract: Schedule 13, paragraph 17(2). 'Price' includes 'any consideration other than money'.

6   He must state the consideration for the assignment or that there is none: Schedule 13, paragraph 18(1).

7   Where he assigns such a right he must state the consideration: Schedule 13, paragraph 18(2). Where he is granted a right to subscribe for shares or debentures he must state: (a) the date on which the right was granted; (b) the period during which or time at which the right is exercisable; (c) the consideration for the grant (or the absence of it); and (d) the price to be paid for the shares or debentures. Where he *exercises* such a right to subscribe for shares, etc, he must state the number of shares or amount of debentures in respect of which the right was exercised, and the names of those in whose name the shares are registered: Schedule 13, paragraph 19.

compliance with section 324, in respect of the acquisition, etc, of an interest in the securities of a company and those securities are listed on the investment exchange. This obligation must be fulfilled before the end of the next day following that on which it arises (ie the day on which the company was notified by the directors). The period allowed to the company excludes Saturdays, Sundays or Bank Holidays.[1] The investment exchange 'may publish, in such manner as it may determine, any information received' under section 329(1).

15.22.2 The meaning of 'interest' in shares and debentures

Part I of Schedule 13 contains elaborate provisions as to what is meant by 'interest' in shares or debentures for the purposes of a director's disclosure obligations under section 324.

Paragraph 1 starts with the wide proposition that interest includes a reference to any interest of any kind whatsoever in shares or debentures. Accordingly, there must be disregarded any restraints or restrictions to which the exercise of any right attached to the interest is or may be subject. Where trust property includes any interest in shares or debentures, any beneficiary of the trust who, apart from this provision, does not have any interest in the shares or debentures, is taken to have such an interest (without prejudice to the later provisions of Part I).[2]

The entering into a contract to purchase shares, for cash or other consideration, gives a person an interest for these purposes,[3] as does the right, when a person is not the registered holder, to exercise or to control the exercise of any rights conferred by the holding of shares or debentures.[4]

Paragraph 4 deals with interest in shares or debentures held through 'controlled' companies. A person is taken to be interested in shares or debentures if a body corporate is interested in them and either of the following two criteria is met: (a) that body corporate or its directors are accustomed to act in accordance with his directions or instructions; or (b) the person in question is entitled to exercise or control the exercise of one-third or more of the voting power at a general meeting of the body corporate. When condition (b) is met and the body corporate in question is entitled to exercise or control the exercise of *any* of the voting power at general meetings of another body corporate (the 'effective voting power'), then for the purposes of condition (b) the effective voting power is taken to be exercisable by the person in question.

A person is taken to have an interest in shares or debentures if, otherwise than by virtue of having an interest under a trust, he has a right to call for delivery of the shares or debentures to himself or his order (a call option), or if he has a right to acquire an interest or is under an obligation to acquire an interest.[5] However, rights or obligations to *subscribe* for shares or debentures do not for these purposes

---

1   Section 329(2).
2   Schedule 13, paragraph 2.
3   Ibid, paragraph 3(1)(a).
4   Schedule 13, paragraph 3(1)(b). This includes the cases when a person has an option, conditional or not, to exercise or control the exercise of such rights and when he is under an obligation, conditional or not, the fulfilment of which would make him so entitled. However, appointment as a proxy at a *specified* company meeting or class meeting or the appointment of someone as the representative of a corporation at *any* company meeting or class meeting does not amount to an interest.
5   Ibid, paragraph 6(1).

amount to rights or obligations to acquire (but this is without prejudice to the general concept of interest in shares or debentures in paragraph 1).[1]

Those who have a joint interest are each deemed to have that interest,[2] and it is immaterial that shares or debentures in which a person has an interest are unidentifiable.[3]

15.22.3   Types of interest disregarded

Certain types of interest in shares or debentures are disregarded, including an interest in reversion or remainder[4] so long as someone is entitled to receive, during the lifetime of himself or another, income from trust property comprising shares or debentures.[5] A person who holds shares or debentures as a bare trustee or custodian trustee[6] is treated as uninterested in them.[7]

Those who invest in an authorised unit trust scheme are not regarded as having an interest in the underlying investments.[8] Certain statutory investment schemes are also exempted.[9] The Secretary of State has power by regulation to except other categories of interest in shares or debentures.[10]

15.22.4   Spouses and children of directors

Sections 327 and 328 extend section 324 by treating the interests of the spouses or children of directors as being those of the director. 'Spouse' means a husband or wife of a director, not being herself or himself a director of that company. Likewise, 'children' means the infant son or daughter of a director, not being himself or herself a director of that company. 'Son' includes stepson and adopted son, and 'daughter' includes stepdaughter and adopted daughter. A contract, assignment or right of subscription entered into, exercised or made by, or grant made to, such a spouse or child (in respect of shares or debentures) is treated, for the purpose of section 324, as having been entered into, etc by the director.

Consequently, a director of a company is under an obligation to notify the company in writing of the occurrence (while he or she is a director) of either: (a) the grant to his wife or her husband or to his or her infant son or infant daughter, by the company, of a right to subscribe for shares in, or debentures of, the company; or (b) the exercise by his wife or her husband or by his or her infant son or infant daughter of such a right.

In either case, he must report the same information as section 324 requires where a director is granted a right to subscribe or exercises it. The five-day period

---

1   Ibid, paragraph 6(2).
2   Ibid, paragraph 7.
3   Ibid, paragraph 8.
4   Or as regards Scotland, in fee.
5   Schedule 13, paragraph 9.
6   Ie under English law. The same applies to a simple trustee in Scots law.
7   Schedule 13, paragraph 10.
8   Schedule 13, paragraph 11.
9   See ibid, paragraphs 11 and 12.
10   Section 324(3). See the Companies (Disclosure of Directors' Interests) (Exceptions) Regulations 1985, SI 1985/802. These except, *inter alia*, disclosure to a company which is the wholly owned subsidiary of a body corporate incorporated outside Great Britain of interests in that body corporate or any other body corporate so incorporated, and disclosure by a director of a wholly owned subsidiary of his interests in the subsidiary when he is also a director of its holding company and the latter is obliged to keep a register of directors' interests.

during which written notice must be given runs from 'the day next following that on which the occurrence of the event that gives rise to it comes to his knowledge'.

15.22.5 The register of directors' interests

Section 325 requires every company to keep a register to record the information about those interests in shares and debentures which section 324 requires directors to notify to the company. Under the Companies (Registers and other Records) Regulations,[1] this register may be kept in non-legible (eg computerised) form. Every company is also under an obligation, without such notification, to record on this register the grant of a right to subscribe in shares in or debentures of the company to a director. It must inscribe:

(1) the period during which or the time at which the right is exercisable;
(2) the consideration for the grant (or the fact that there is no consideration);
(3) the description and the number and amount of shares or debentures involved;
(4) the price or other non-monetary consideration to be paid for them.

Whenever such a right to subscribe is exercised, the company must inscribe this fact on the register as well as the following information:

(1) the number or amount of shares or debentures in respect of which a right is exercised;
(2) if they are registered in his name, that fact;
(3) if they are not registered in his name, the name or names of those in whose name they are registered.[2]

Part IV of Schedule 13 makes detailed provision as to the way in which this register must be maintained.[3] This register must be kept at the company's registered office if the company's register of members is kept there. If the company's register of members is not so kept, it may be kept at the company's registered office or at the place where its register of members is kept.

This register must be open to inspection by members free of charge, and by members of the public on payment of the prescribed fee.[4] The company is required to send notice to the Registrar of Companies as to the whereabouts of the register and of any change of place (unless it has at all times been kept in the company's registered office). Any member of the company or other person may require a copy of the register or part of it. The company is required to send such a copy within ten days. The register must be produced at the company's annual general meeting and remain open and accessible throughout it to any person attending.

Section 326 provides penalties for failing to maintain the register properly or for refusing a request for inspection or copying. Further, a court order compelling

---

1   SI 1985/724.
2   Together with (if they are registered in the name of two or more persons) the number or amount registered in the name of each of them.
3   See paragraph 21 (entries for each director in chronological order); paragraph 28 (index of names); paragraph 22 (obligation to inscribe to be fulfilled within three working days). The index of names may, like the register itself, be kept in non-legible form. See the Companies (Registers and Other Records) Regulations 1985, SI 1985/724.
4   As to the fee and the detailed rights of inspection and copying, see the Companies (Inspection and Copying of Registers, Indices and Documents) Regulations 1991, SI 1991/1988.

compliance can be obtained where an inspection is refused or there is a failure to send a copy.

15.22.6 *Powers of inspection by Secretary of State*

By section 446(1), where it appears to the Secretary of State that a contravention of section 324 may have occurred in relation to shares in, or debentures of, a company, he may appoint one or more competent inspectors. The latter will carry out such investigations as are necessary to establish whether or not contraventions have occurred. The procedure and purpose of this and other powers to appoint inspectors will be considered in Chapter 17 below.

Chapter 16

The Duties of Directors

16.1 Introduction

This chapter is concerned with the scope and content of various duties which the law imposes upon a director of a company by virtue of his holding office as such.[1] Since, as we have seen in the previous chapter, the management of a company is vested in its directors and, as described in Chapter 11, the issue of corporate governance is generally regarded as perhaps the most important issue in company law today, the question of the duties that directors owe is a critical one. Broadly speaking, the duties discussed fall into two categories, fiduciary duties (ie duties of good faith and honesty) and duties of skill and care. Although it seems clear as a matter of principle that a breach of fiduciary duty and a breach of the duty to exercise care and skill could arise on the same facts, it is clear that negligence is not per se a breach of fiduciary duty.[2] The general purpose of these duties is the protection of present and future shareholders and (to a lesser extent) creditors, though, as will be seen,[3] they are generally expressed as being owed to 'the company'. Much of the content of the duties to be discussed has been developed by way of analogy with rules governing legal relationships comparable to that between a director and his company, a point which is briefly discussed in the next section. In part these have been supplemented by often complex statutory provisions. The result is a large number of heads of duty, many of which overlap with one or more others.

The Law Commissions examined some aspects of directors' duties and made important recommendations for legislative change.[4] These were then considered as part of the Review of Company Law,[5] which also examined the central question of what should be the proper meaning of 'the company' for the purpose of the director's primary fiduciary duty.[6] Further general consideration of these questions of reform, including the Steering Group's recommendation for an exhaustive statutory code, is left to the end of this chapter, but the Law Commissions' detailed recommendations to amend the statutory duties are noted at the appropriate places in the text that follows.

---

1   As to when a director may be liable in tort to third parties in respect of his actions as director, see *Williams v Natural Life Health Foods Ltd* [1998] 1 WLR 830 (HL), discussed at **3.4.1**. See also *Standard Chartered Bank v Pakistan National Shipping Corp* [2002] UKHL 43, [2003] AC 959.

2   *Extrasure Travel Insurances Ltd v Scattergood* [2003] 1 BCLC 598.

3   See **16.3**.

4   *Company Directors: Regulating Conflicts of Interests and Formulating a Statement of Duties*, Law Com No 261, Scot Law Com No 173, September 1999.

5   See generally, **1.7** and Chapter 22. See especially *Modern Company Law for a Competitive Economy: Developing the Framework*, March 2000, paragraphs 3.9–3.89.

6   See the detailed examination of the Steering Group's eventual proposal, as accepted by the Government in *Modernising Company Law*, Cm 5553–I and II, July 2002, at **11.6**.

16.2   The legal nature of the office of director

The Companies Act 1985 does not define directors. There is, however, a general provision that, for the purposes of the Act, the expression 'director' includes 'any person occupying the position of director by whatever name called'.[1] The meaning of 'director' is to be derived from the words of the Act as a whole and varies according to the context in which it is found. In respect of certain provisions, someone who acts as a director but is not actually appointed as such, ie a *de facto* as opposed to a *de jure* director, will be treated as a director.[2] Furthermore, in respect of certain provisions, obligations are cast on any 'shadow director', who is 'a person in accordance with whose directions or instructions the directors of a company are accustomed to act'.[3] It should be noted that the concept of *de facto* director is quite different from that of shadow director.[4] As far as the latter is concerned, the Court of Appeal has established[5] that:

(1) the term should not be strictly construed;
(2) a shadow director must have a real influence in the corporate affairs of the company, but not necessarily over the whole field of its activities;
(3) the directions or instructions do not necessarily have to be proved to have been understood or expected;
(4) non-professional advice may be within the meaning of 'directions or instructions'; and
(5) it is not necessary in all cases to show that the actual directors or some of them act in a subservient manner or surrender their discretion to the shadow director.

The absence of a definition of 'director' renders it somewhat difficult to ascertain the exact nature of the director's office. He is certainly an agent of the company but is rather more than that as in practice he is not subject to much control by his principal, the company acting through the shareholders in general meeting.[6] In certain respects, the director is a trustee[7] and there is no doubt that many of his duties developed from the law of trusts, but he is certainly not a full trustee, not least because his very function is an entrepreneurial one and he may properly take risks with the company's funds which a trustee in the strict sense cannot. If a director performs more than the tasks of a director pure and simple, such as attending board meetings and the like, he may well also be an employee of

---

1   Companies Act 1985, section 74(1). This means persons described as governors or managers rather than as directors, but performing the same function.
2   *Re Lo-Line Electric Motors Ltd* [1988] BCLC 698, *Re Kaytech International plc* [1999] 2 BCLC 353. This will be particularly so in respect of the disqualification provisions (see **15.16**).
3   Section 741(2). These provisions are noted in the appropriate parts of the text. A person is not deemed a shadow director by reason only of the fact that the directors act on advice given by him in a professional capacity, and the definition does not catch a holding company, which could clearly fall within it in some situations, in respect of the sections listed in section 741(3).
4   *Re Hydrodan (Corby) Ltd* [1994] BCC 161.
5   *Secretary of State for Trade and Industry v Deverell* [2000] 2 WLR 907 (CA) at 919 to 920, applied in *Secretary of State for Trade and Industry v Becker* [2002] EWHC 2200 (Ch), [2003] 1 BCLC 555.
6   The 'separation of ownership and control', recognised by Berle and Means in *The Modern Corporation and Private Property* (Harcourt, Brace & World Inc, revised edn, 1967). See especially, **11.2**.
7   See **16.8**.

the company and as such subject to a stricter duty of care and skill[1] and the beneficiary of important statutory rights if he is declared redundant or unfairly dismissed.[2]

In short, the director's office is *sui generis*, although for certain purposes the analogies of agency, trusteeship and employment may be useful.

It should be noted that a director need not be an individual person and another company may even, if it has the requisite power, be appointed the sole director.

16.3   The scope of directors' fiduciary duties

It is an established general rule that, insofar as a director of a company is bound by fiduciary duties at general law, these duties are owed to the company only. Thus they are not owed to other companies or bodies corporate with which the company is associated, eg its holding company[3] or subsidiary,[4] nor do they operate in favour of any person simply because he is a person to whom the company itself stands in a fiduciary relationship.[5] This proposition stems from *Percival v Wright*,[6] in which a group of shareholders in a company approached the directors with a request that the directors purchase their shares; some of the directors did so without disclosing that a purchase of the company's undertaking was imminent, this being a piece of information which was known to them and to the other members of the board, though not to any of the shareholders who were not directors. It was held that the directors in question were not under any duty to the shareholders to disclose this information, even though the price being offered for the undertaking represented a substantial amount more per share than they paid to the shareholders on the purchase, and that accordingly the shareholders could not have the purchase set aside. The judgment does, however, stress that there was no 'unfair dealing' by the directors and seems to suggest that it was significant that the initial approach in the matter was made by the shareholders.[7] The possibility that fiduciary duties would have arisen between the directors and the shareholders if the directors had instigated the purchase is thus not entirely ruled out.

Furthermore, directors, in supplying information to their shareholders regarding a takeover offer and expressing a view as to whether the offer should be accepted, have 'a duty towards their own shareholders which ... clearly includes a duty to be honest and a duty not to mislead'.[8] It has also been laid down that if in a particular transaction a director expressly or by his conduct constitutes himself as

---

1   See **16.23**.

2   See further, **15.4**. In acting as an employee, a director can bargain as he wishes over the terms of his service contract, provided that there is compliance with the articles; in practice, these remove any possibility of conflict of duty and interest. See further, **16.15** and **16.16** and *Jackson v Invicta Plastics Ltd* [1987] BCLC 329.

3   *Bell v Lever Bros Ltd* [1932] AC 161 at p 228 (HL).

4   *Lindgren v L & P Estates Ltd* [1968] Ch 572 (CA); but note the effects of *Scottish Co-operative Wholesale Society Ltd v Meyer* [1959] AC 324 (HL (Sc)).

5   *Wilson v Bury (Lord)* (1880) 5 QBD (CA).

6   [1902] 2 Ch 421. See also *Dawson International plc v Coats Paton plc* (1988) 4 BCC 305, *Towcester Racecourse Co Ltd v The Racecourse Association Ltd* [2002] EWHC 2141 (Ch), [2003] 1 BCLC 260.

7   Ibid, at 426–427.

8   *Gerthing v Kilner* [1972] 1 WLR 337 at 341, *per* Brightman J. See also *Dawson International plc v Coats Paton plc*, above, at 310, 312.

agent for one or more of the shareholders, he thereby becomes subject to fiduciary duties to the shareholder or shareholders concerned.[1] Such duties arise, however, by virtue of his agency, not his directorship. In the decision of the New Zealand Court of Appeal in *Coleman v Myers*,[2] a fiduciary relationship between directors and shareholders was held to have arisen where, in a private company with the shareholding spread over a few associated family groups, the directors had a high degree of inside knowledge which they failed to disclose to the other shareholders when the shares in the company were the subject of a takeover offer from a company owned by one of the directors. The court stressed, however, that the existence of such a relationship depended entirely on the facts of any particular case and dissented from the view expressed by the trial judge[3] that the decision in *Percival v Wright* was wrong and should be ignored.[4] English case-law has referred to and followed the decision in *Coleman v Myers*, holding that a fiduciary relationship between directors and shareholders can arise in special circumstances like those subsisting in that case.[5] A further example of a duty which may be owed directly to shareholders is the duty to allot shares for a proper purpose.[6]

The time at which a director's fiduciary duties to the company arise is the time when he becomes a director. He is not bound by them when he is merely a 'director-elect'.[7]

The form in which a director's fiduciary duties are expressed is that of a number of general law and statutory rules, varying greatly in their range of application and at many points overlapping with each other. The lack of any precise and logical pattern makes orderly exposition of these rules difficult, and no doubt makes it especially difficult for company directors themselves fully to comprehend the duties they are subject to, which is why the Law Commissions[8] recommended the introduction of a partial codification of directors' duties and the Company Law Review Steering Group went further and recommended a complete codification.[9] What follows is an attempt to summarise and explain them with as much coherence as the subject-matter permits. Except where the text expressly indicates otherwise, it is assumed that the conduct of the directors being dealt with is within the literal terms of the powers conferred on them by the memorandum and articles. It is arguable, of course, that merely to act in excess of those powers is *ipso facto* a breach of fiduciary duty; such conduct is certainly invalid unless and

---

1   *Allen v Hyatt* (1914) 30 TLR 444 (PC); and see *Briess v Woolley* [1954] AC 333 (HL); and see *Platt v Platt* [1999] 2 BCLC 745.

2   [1977] 2 NZLR 297; see Rider (1978) 41 MLR 585. This decision was followed by the British Columbia Court of Appeal in *Dusik v Newton* (1985) 62 BCLR 1 and by the New South Wales Court of Appeal in *Glandon Pty Ltd v Strata Consolidated Ltd*(1993) 11 ACLC 895; see *Gore-Browne on Companies* 44th edn (Jordans, loose-leaf) at 12.17.

3   [1977] 2 NZLR 22.

4   These cases involved what is generally known as 'insider dealing'. The statutory prohibitions against such dealing are described below at **16.21**.

5   *Re Chez Nico (Restaurants) Ltd* [1992] BCLC 192 at 208; *Stein v Blake (No 2)* [1998] 1 BCLC 573 at 576, 579 (CA); *Platt v Platt* [1999] 2 BCLC 745 (affirmed [2001] 1 BCLC 698, CA); *Peskin v Anderson* [2000] 1 BCLC 1 at 11 to 14 (affirmed [2001] 1 BCLC 372 at 378–380).

6   See *Re a Company* [1987] BCLC 82; *John Crowther Group plc v Carpets International plc* [1990] BCLC 460 at p 464. This relates in particular to the question of minority shareholders' remedies; see **17.6**.

7   *Lingren v L & P Estates Ltd* [1968] Ch 575 (CA).

8   See **16.1**.

9   See **16.25**.

until effectively ratified.[1] But for the purposes of the present discussion, it is treated as a breach of fiduciary duty only when, through causing loss to the company, it involves the relevant director or directors in liability to the company.

16.4 Duty to act *bona fide* in the interest of the company

As Lord Greene MR said in the case of *Re Smith & Fawcett Ltd*,[2] directors are bound to exercise the powers conferred upon them 'bona fide in what they consider – not what a court may consider – is in the interests of the company ...'. This duty of honesty and good faith in the exercise of his powers is in fact the primary duty of a director. As Lord Greene's formulation indicates, the duty is subjective, in that the court will not consider it broken merely because, in the court's own opinion, the particular exercise of power was not in the company's interests;[3] *a fortiori* the court will not take it upon itself to order that a particular power vested in directors should be exercised in a particular way.[4] On the other hand, the court will insist that, save in so far as the articles expressly permit, it should be the directors, and not some other person or body to whom they have purported to delegate their powers, who determine how the powers vested in the directors are best used to serve 'the interests of the company'.[5]

16.5 The interests of the company

This last phrase merits some special consideration. Modern management often takes the view that the interests to be taken into account by directors in running a company should include the interests of not only the present and future shareholders, but also the company's employees, its customers and its creditors and, in the case of large public companies at least, the State and the general public. No doubt this represents an adequate practical guide for most decisions that a director has to take. It is, however, thought that from the point of view of strict law at present,[6] while the 'interests of the company' may now include the interests of the company's employees,[7] and in certain situations the interests of its creditors,[8] it otherwise means the interests of the company as a commercial entity, to be judged in most cases by reference to the interests of present and future shareholders alone. Thus the only circumstances in which the directors may

---

1   Although third parties dealing with the directors are protected: see Chapter 6.
2   [1942] Ch 304 (CA) at p 306; see also *Alexander v Automatic Telephone Co* [1900] 2 Ch 56 at 72 (CA); *Charterbridge Corporation Ltd v Lloyd's Bank Ltd* [1970] Ch 62 at 74; *Gething v Kilner* [1972] 1 WLR 337 at 341 to 342; *Clemens v Clemens Bros Ltd* [1976] 2 All ER 268 to 280; *Hindle v John Cotton Ltd* (1919) 56 Sc LR 625 at 631, (HL Sc); *Regentcrest plc v Cohen* [2001] 2 BCLC 80.
3   No doubt it will hold, however, that a breach has occurred if the relevant exercise of power could not possibly be considered by a reasonable man to be in the interests of the company; cf *Shuttleworth v Cox Bros & Co (Maidenhead) Ltd* [1927] 2 KB 9 (CA), and other authorities on the fiduciary duties of the shareholders in general meeting, cited at **5.27**.
4   *Pergamon Press Ltd v Maxwell* [1979] 1 WLR 1167.
5   *Re County Palatine Loan and Discount Co, Cartnell's Case* (1874) 9 Ch App 691.
6   This would be modified under the Company Law Review Steering Group's proposal; see **11.6**.
7   Under section 309 which is discussed in **16.6**.
8   See below.

legitimately promote the interest of any other groups or entities are those where to do so ultimately advances the interests of the shareholders.[1]

Where a particular decision to be taken by the directors bears differently upon different classes of shareholders, their duty is to act fairly having regard to the interests of all classes,[2] although ultimately they must act in the interests of the company.[3] Similarly, they should, in appropriate circumstances, seek to balance short-term considerations, affecting the present shareholders only, against long-term considerations which involve future shareholders as well.[4] This is because, as explained above, the interests of the company are equated to the interests of the shareholders as a whole, not simply to present shareholders nor, *a fortiori*, simply to one class of shareholders. In contrast, where a company is to be taken over and the only issue is as to which of competing bids is to succeed, the interests of the company are the interests of its current shareholders only,[5] but this does not necessarily mean that the directors are under a positive duty to recommend the higher bid nor that they cannot agree to recommend a particular bid or agree not to encourage or co-operate with another would-be bidder.[6] The mere fact that, in a particular transaction, the directors of a company having a holding company and/or subsidiaries and/or co-subsidiaries looked to the interests of the group as a whole does not of itself mean that they are in breach of duty, provided that an 'intelligent and honest man' in the position of the directors could have reasonably believed the transaction to be in the interests of the company.[7]

When a company is insolvent or on the verge of insolvency, but not otherwise, it is the creditors' interests that become paramount.[8] This recognition of creditors' interest by the common law is a relatively recent development, and has probably been heavily influenced by the same factors as led to the introduction of statutory provisions designed to give more effective protection to creditors.[9] Although it has been said that a duty is owed by the directors to the company and to the creditors of the company to ensure that the affairs of the company are properly

---

1　*Hutton v West Cork Rly Co* (1883) 23 Ch D 654 (CA); *Parke v Daily News Ltd* [1962] Ch 927. Although these decisions were concerned with gratuitous payments, where the matter may concern the validity of a resolution of shareholders as well as or rather than a decision of the directors, it is submitted that the same meaning of the 'interests of the company' applies when an issue is solely one of the duties of directors: see further, Birds (1980) 1 Co Law 67; *contra* Instone [1979] JBL 221. As to the statutory reversal by what is now section 719 of the Companies Act 1985 of the actual decision in *Parke v Daily News Ltd*, see **6.13.3** where the topic of gratuitous payments is also discussed more fully.

2　*Henry v Great Northern Rly* (1857) 1 De G & J 606 at 638.

3　*Mutual Life Insurance Co of New York v Rank Organisation Ltd* [1985] BCLC 11; *Re BSB Holdings Ltd* [1996] 1 BCLC 155 at 246–249.

4　See the report of the Inspector, Mr E Milner-Holland QC, in the Savoy Hotel Investigation (HMSO, 1954); see Gower (1955) 68 Harv LR 1176.

5　*Heron International Ltd v Grade* [1984] BCLC 244, esp at 264–265 (CA).

6　See *Re a Company* [1986] BCLC 382 at 389–390 and *Dawson International plc v Coats Paton plc* (1989) 5 BCC 405.

7　*Charterbridge Corporation Ltd v Lloyds Bank Ltd* [1970] Ch 72 at 74.

8　See especially, *Lonrho Ltd v Shell Petroleum Ltd* [1980] 1 WLR 627 at 634 (HL) *per* Lord Diplock; *West Mercia Safetyware Ltd v Dodd* [1988] BCLC 250 at 252–253 (CA) *per* Dillon LJ. See also *Brady v Brady* [1989] AC 755 (HL), *Facia Footwear Ltd v Hinchcliffe* [1998] 1 BCLC 218; *Colin Gwyer & Associates Ltd v London Wharf (Limehouse) Ltd* [2002] EWHC 2748 (Ch), [2003] 2 BCLC 153.

9　Especially the wrongful trading provision (section 214 of the Insolvency Act 1986); see **15.17.2**.

administered and that its property is not dissipated or exploited for the benefit of the directors themselves to the prejudice of the creditors,[1] it is submitted that this is not a duty owed directly to creditors, but rather a duty to the company, which in the event of liquidation can be enforced by the liquidator for the benefit of the creditors.[2] Further, it is a duty owed to the creditors as a whole, not to an individual creditor or section of creditors with special rights in a winding up.[3]

If a power is found not to have been exercised by the directors *bona fide* in the interests of the company, the exercise may be declared void. Any agreement made with a third party is voidable against the third party if he was aware of the lack of *bona fides*,[4] and if the exercise of the power causes loss to the company, the directors responsible may be liable to make good the loss.

16.6 The interests of the employees

By section 309,[5] the matters to which the directors of a company are to have regard in the performance of their functions include the interests of the company's employees in general as well as the interests of its members. This welcome acknowledgement of the fact that modern management does often take into account the interests of employees[6] is based upon a recommendation of the Committee of Inquiry on Industrial Democracy (the Bullock Report).[7] However, this duty is, by subsection (2), owed only to the company, and not to employees individually, and is enforceable in the same way as any other fiduciary duty.[8]

It is submitted that the full import of this section is not entirely clear.[9] Before the enactment of its predecessor in 1980, directors were entitled to take account of the interests of employees provided that in so doing they ultimately advanced the interests of the shareholders. Section 309 goes further and requires them to have regard to those interests.[10] So if it could be shown that in taking a decision

---

1   *Winkworth v Edward Baron Development Co Ltd* [1987] BCLC 193 at 197 (HL) *per* Lord Templeman.
2   *Re Horsley & Weight Ltd* [1982] 3 All ER 1045 at 1055 (CA) *per* Buckley LJ; *Kuwait Asia Bank EC v National Mutual Life Nominees Ltd* [1990] BCLC 868 at 888 (PC) *per* Lord Lowry. See also *Yukong Line Ltd of Korea v Rendsberg Investment Corp of Liberia* [1998] 4 All ER 82 at 99. It is not a breach of duty for a director to cause the company to prefer one creditor to another: *Knight v Frost* [1999] 1 BCLC 364 at 381–382; see also *Re Brian D Pierson (Contractors) Ltd* [1999] BCC 26 at 46. In practice, it seems more likely that the matter will be litigated and decided under the statutory wrongful trading provision rather than as a common-law duty.
3   *Re Pantone 485 Ltd* [2002] 1 BCLC 266 at 285–287.
4   *Charterbridge Corporation Ltd v Lloyd's Bank Ltd* [1970] Ch 72 at 69, 75; *Lindgren v L & P Estates Ltd* [1968] Ch 572 (CA); *Rolled Steel Products Ltd v British Steel Corporation* [1984] BCLC 466 (CA); *Criterion Properties plc v Stratford UK Properties LLC* [2002] EWCA Civ 1883, [2003] 2 BCLC 129. See also *John Crowther Group plc v Carpets International plc* [1990] BCLC 460, holding invalid an agreement by directors to recommend a course of action or to propose a resolution which was entered into in breach of duty. See also *Rackham v Peck Foods Ltd* [1990] BCLC 895.
5   See also section 719, which is discussed at **6.13.3**.
6   See also **16.5**.
7   Cmnd 6706 (1977), Chapter 7, paragraph 12, and Chapter 8, paragraph 38. It seems unlikely though that it will survive the proposed codification of the core aspect of directors' duties, where employees' interests are 'relegated' to rank alongside a whole range of other 'stakeholders'; see **11.6**.
8   See **16.25**. *Quaere* where a minority shareholder's derivative action would lie, particularly if the shareholder is also an employee; see **17.7**.
9   See also (1980) 1 Co Law at pp 72–73.
10 See *Fulham Football Club Ltd v Cabra Estates plc* [1992] BCC 863 at 876 (CA).

directors failed to consider the interests of employees, they would be in breach of duty. Whether, however, directors are entitled to subordinate the interests of shareholders to those of employees must be open to doubt, because section 309 does not alter the legal meaning of 'interests of the company'[1] which must ultimately be paramount. For example, a board might be faced with a decision whether or not to close down a factory that is unprofitable but employs a considerable number of people who would lose their jobs if the decision to close were taken. Provided that the directors considered this latter point, it is submitted that they would not be in breach of section 309 if they decided to close the factory. Indeed, if they did not so decide they might be liable for not acting *bona fide* in the interests of the company, if it could clearly be shown that they had acted against the interests of the shareholders.

16.7 Duty to act for proper purposes

In the judgment of Lord Greene MR in *Re Smith & Fawcett Ltd*, the principle already cited is supplemented by the statement that directors' powers must not be exercised for any 'collateral purpose'.[2] Thus, if the directors exercise a power conferred by the articles for a purpose other than that for which, upon its proper interpretation, it was so conferred, their conduct is open to challenge, and in such a case it is no answer for them to maintain that they *bona fide* believed their conduct to be in the interests of the company. The court will not substitute its own view for that of the board as to the correctness of the board's exercise of its management powers, but where, on an objective review of the situation, it finds that a requirement allegedly underlying the board's action was not urgent or critical, it may have reason (particularly where the action was taken was unusual or extreme) to doubt or discount the assertions of the directors that they acted solely to deal with this requirement.[3] To this limited extent, their assessment of the company's interests in the exercise of their powers is open to review, on an objective basis, by the court.[4]

This principle was brought into prominence in the cases, described in the next paragraph, dealing with a power vested in the directors of a company to allot the company's shares. Since the introduction of what are now sections 80 and 89 to 96 of the Companies Act 1985, which restrict directors' powers of allotment,[5] the principle is of less importance thereto. However, those provisions may in certain cases be excluded and thus the common-law principle can be relevant. Further, as the cases discussed below reveal, the principle has often been used in modern times to question the validity of defensive tactics used by directors fighting a takeover bid for their company or of another means or maintaining directors' control. Thus it can be used in respect of any power exercised with these aims in mind whose purpose can clearly be discerned from the articles, as for example in the Savoy Hotel case, where it was the directors' power to lease the company's

---

1   See **16.5**.
2   [1942] Ch 304 at 306 (CA). See generally, Nolan, 'The Proper Purposes Doctrine and Company Directors' in Rider (ed), *The Realm of Company Law* (1998) p 1.
3   *Howard Smith Ltd v Ampol Petroleum Ltd* [1974] AC 821 at 823 (PC).
4   For an argument that this test is not objective enough, see Birds (1974) 37 MLR 580. The proper purposes duty has been held to be one owed to shareholders directly rather than to the company (see **16.3**) and as such may be relevant in an unfair prejudice petition (see **17.12**).
5   See **7.3–7.5**.

property as a means of forestalling an anticipated takeover bid which was in issue.[1] Further examples concerned the directors entering into a management agreement which had the effect of depriving the shareholders of their constitutional right to appoint new directors with full managerial powers,[2] and directors entering into a supplementary partnership agreement that exposed the company to a serious contingent liability.[3]

In *Hogg v Cramphorn Ltd*,[4] the directors of the defendant company, fearing a takeover bid and their own dismissal from the board, allotted shares to persons who would support them in office. They honestly believed that, in acting to preserve their position on the board, they were serving the company's best interests, but it was held that they had used the power of allotment for a purpose for which it was not intended to be used and that the allotment was accordingly voidable. However, the court ruled that if a meeting of the shareholders existing prior to the allotment approved the allotment by a majority it would thereby be rendered valid, and ordered that such a meeting be held. In *Howard Smith Ltd v Ampol Petroleum Ltd*,[5] two shareholders holding between them 55% of the shares in a company announced that they would jointly reject any offer from a particular intending takeover bidder, or from any other source. The board of directors then allotted new shares to the intending bidder. Although the company did not need new capital at the time, the primary purpose of the directors in making this allotment was to reduce the proportionate shareholding of the two majority shareholders to below 50% and thus enable the bidder to make an effective bid. In proceedings brought by one of the two majority shareholders against, *inter alia*, the directors and the bidder, it was held by the Privy Council that the board had acted with an improper purpose, albeit honestly and within their powers, and that the issue of shares to the bidder (which was on notice of the impropriety) should accordingly be set aside. Giving the Privy Council's judgment, Lord Wilberforce said that a decision of directors to issue shares could be set aside on the ground of improper purpose even though there was no element of self-interest involved, and that while it might in some circumstances be proper to issue shares for purposes

---

1   This *cause célèbre*, which was never litigated, was the subject of a Board of Trade Inspector's Report in 1954; see footnote 4 at p 494. For reported examples of the use of a proper purposes principle outside the context of a struggle for control and unrelated to an allotment of shares, see *Stanhope's Case* (1866) 1 Ch App 161 (power to forfeit shares), *Bennett's Case* (1867) 5 De GM & G 284 (power to approve transfers of shares), *Galloway v Hallé Concerts Society* [1915] 2 Ch 233 (power to make calls) and *Gaiman v NAMH* [1971] Ch 317 (power to expel members).

2   *Lee Panavision Ltd v Lee Lighting Ltd* [1992] BCLC 22 (CA).

3   *Criterion Properties plc v Stratford UK Properties LLC* [2002] EWCA Civ 1883, [2003] 2 BCLC 129.

4   [1967] Ch 254. The principles adopted in this case, which was actually decided in 1963, were approved of and applied in *Bamford v Bamford* [1970] Ch 212 (CA). Earlier authorities are *Punt v Symons & Co Ltd* [1903] 2 Ch 506 and *Piercy v S Mills & Co Ltd* [1920] 3 Ch 77. It is clear that some Commonwealth authorities reject the breadth of the principle confirmed in *Hogg v Cramphorn Ltd* and in effect deny the existence of this objective restraint on directors' powers, despite Lord Wilberforce's valiant attempt in *Howard Smith Ltd v Ampol Petroleum Ltd* [1974] AC 821 (see below) to explain them as consistent with *Hogg v Cramphorn Ltd*; see in particular *Harlowe's Nominees Ltd v Woodside (Lake Entrance) Oil Co* (1968) 121 CLR 483 (Australian HC) and *Teck Corporation Ltd v Millar* (1972) 33 DLR (3d) 288 (Sup Ct BC). See also the unreported English decision in *Pennell v Venida Investments Ltd*, discussed in Burridge, (1981) 44 MLR 40. Cf, however, for example, *Whitehouse v Carlton Hotel Pty* (1987) 162 CLR 285 (HCA). The many other Commonwealth authorities are referred to in *Gore-Browne on Companies*, 27.5.

5   [1974] AC 821 (PC).

other than raising capital for the company, 'it must be unconstitutional for directors to use their fiduciary powers over the shares in the company purely for the purpose of destroying an existing majority, or creating a new majority which did not previously exist'. Further, he said that the case was all the stronger against the directors where there was 'an ulterior purpose to enable an offer for shares to proceed which the existing majority was in a position to block'.[1]

It is submitted that, except as regards the possibility of ratification by the general meeting,[2] the consequences of infringement of this principle are the same as apply in relation to the principle of *bona fides* just discussed. Thus, where a power of forfeiture was exercised for improper purposes, the members concerned, who knew of the impropriety, could not rely on the forfeiture as a defence to an action for payment of the balance due on the shares.[3] In order to set aside an agreement entered into for an improper purpose, it is necessary to consider the actions and knowledge of the other party in the context of the continuing commercial relationship between the parties. Knowledge of the relevant facts is not enough to establish that the other party had sufficient knowledge about the motivation of the directors to disable it from relying on the directors' apparent authority to commit the company to the contract.[4]

16.8 Trusteeship of the company's assets

Directors are regarded as trustees of company property which is in their hands or under their control. The primary consequence of this principle of trusteeship is that a director is answerable as a trustee for any misapplication of the company's property in which he participated and which he knew or ought to have known to be a misapplication.[5] A misapplication in this context means any disposition of the company's property which by virtue of any provision of the company's constitution or any statutory provision or any rule of general law the company or the board is forbidden or incompetent or unauthorised to make, or which is carried out by the directors otherwise than in accordance with their duty to act *bona fide* in the interests of the company and for the proper purposes. This second limb covers not only misappropriations of the company's property, but also dispositions in favour of third parties which do not satisfy the test of *bona fides*.

---

1   Ibid at p 837. This is analogous to '*Wednesbury* unreasonableness' in public law cases; see *Re a Company, ex parte Glossop* [1988] BCLC 570.
2   See **16.23.1**.
3   *Re London and Provincial Starch Co, Gower's Case* (1868) LR 6 Eq 77.
4   *Criterion Properties plc v Stratford Properties LLC* [2002] EWCA Civ 1883, [2003] 2 BCLC 129, applying the principles established by the earlier Court of Appeal decision in *BCCI (Overseas) Ltd v Akindele* [2001] Ch 437, in the context of claims based on liability for constructive trusteeship
5   For a full statement of the nature of the director's liability, see *Selangor United Rubber Estates Ltd v Cradock (No 3)* [1968] 1 WLR 1555 at 1575–1576. Alternatively the director may be liable to pay equitable compensation: *Gwembe Valley Development Co Ltd v Koshy* [2003] EWCA Civ 1048, [2004] 1 BCLC 131 at paragraph 142. Third parties who participate in such a breach of trust may themselves be liable to the company as constructive trustees: see *Gore-Browne on Companies* 44th edn (Jordans, loose-leaf) at 27.6.3.

16.8.1 The scope of the trusteeship

Provided that the directors have possession or control of the property beneficially owned by the company, their trusteeship will arise whether the property is legally vested in the company, in one or more of the directors, or in a third party.

A director's trusteeship has been held to cover funds standing to the company's credit in a bank account.[1] Its scope is, moreover, widened by the fact that property which can be misapplied can include property which is not yet vested in the company or in any person on its behalf, but which comes to the directors in circumstances where they are in duty bound, for example through some express or implied mandate, to acquire and hold it for the company's benefit.[2] Furthermore, the term 'property' in this context may cover confidential information of a special and valuable nature (such as secret manufacturing processes and patents, but not mere 'know-how')[3] and also business advantages such as the opportunity to enter into a favourable contract within the company's existing line of business.[4] Thus, a director who makes an invention or other valuable technical discovery in the course of performing active duties as an employee of the company holds the benefit of his discovery (including any patent rights that he has acquired in respect thereof) on trust for the company; it would not matter that he was not specifically commissioned by the company to make the relevant discovery, provided that it fell within the company's line of business.[5] It is equally a breach of trust for a director to make use of 'trade secrets' to the company's detriment, and in appropriate cases he can be prevented by injunction from so doing.[6]

In *Cook v Deeks*,[7] three directors of a private company, holding a majority of the shares, appropriated to themselves an opportunity to enter into a highly favourable business contract, it being evident that the opportunity was only presented to them because they were directors of the company and that the company's business would have greatly benefited from having the contract. They purported to ratify this breach of duty by using the votes attached to their shares to pass an ordinary resolution, but were none the less held liable to account to the

---

1   *Selangor United Rubber Estates Ltd v Cradock (No 3)*, above.
2   *Benson v Heathorn* (1842) 1 Y & CCC 326; *Burland v Earle* [1902] AC 83 at 98–99 (PC); *Cook v Deeks* [1916] 1 AC 554 (PC). For a detailed discussion of when such a duty arises, see the South African case of *Robinson v Randfontein Estates Gold Mining Co Ltd* [1921] AD 168 (South African SC).
3   See eg *Saltman Engineering Co Ltd v Campbell Engineering Co Ltd* [1963] 3 All ER 413n (CA); *Heyting v Dupont* [1964] 1 WLR 843 (CA); *Cranleigh Precision Engineering Ltd v Bryant* [1965] 1 WLR 1293; *Phipps v Boardman* [1967] 2 AC 46 (HL). In relation to such 'property', the positions of directors, ordinary employees and other fiduciary agents are virtually the same, though the duty not to misuse confidential information 'applies with particular force as between a director and his company': *Baker v Gibbons* [1972] 1 WLR 693 at 700. See also *Thomas Marshall (Exports) Ltd v Guinle* [1979] Ch 227, especially at 248, for a discussion of what constitutes confidential information; cf *Island Export Finance Ltd v Umunna* [1986] BCLC 460.
4   *Burland v Earle*, above, at 93; *Cook v Deeks*, above.
5   *Cranleigh Precision Engineering Ltd v Bryant*, above; and see *British Syphon Co Ltd v Homewood* [1956] 1 WLR 1190.
6   *Measures Bros Ltd v Measures* [1910] 1 Ch 336 (affirmed in [1910] 2 Ch 248 (CA)); *Cranleigh Precision Engineering Ltd v Bryant*, above; and see *Printers & Finishers Ltd v Holloway* [1965] 1 WLR 1.
7   [1916] 1 AC 554 (PC). See also *Canadian Aero Service Ltd v O'Malley* [1973] 40 DLR (3d) 371 (Canadian SC).

company for the profits derived from the contract, on the basis that the contract 'belonged in equity to the company'.[1] An alternative remedy for the company in such a situation may be damages for breach of the director's contract of service (assuming that he has one); in the assessment of these damages the court will take into account the extent to which the company was likely to obtain the business contract for itself.[2] If misapplied assets have already been returned to the company, the director will be under no further liability,[3] but the director who is accountable cannot claim to set off against this anything owed to him under a contract of employment.[4]

16.8.2 Further examples of misapplications

Many further instances of directors' liability for losses resulting from the misapplication of company property are to be found in the case-law. Examples are:

(1) the application of funds in breach of what is now section 151 of the Companies Act 1985;[5]

(2) the payment of compensation to a director in breach of section 312;[6]

(3) the making of a loan to a director in breach of what is now section 330;[7]

(4) the payment or recommendation to pay dividends out of capital;[8]

(5) the unlawful issue of bonus shares or shares at a discount;[9]

(6) the payment of unauthorised commission to a broker for placing shares;[10]

(7) the allotment of shares by directors to themselves or their friends at par when they would be able to find purchasers willing to take them at a premium;[11]

(8) any ultra vires disposition of a company's assets,[12] unauthorised payment of remuneration to a director,[13] or bribe paid to a third party;[14]

(9) the execution of a guarantee and debenture in breach of the articles and not *bona fide* in the interests of the company;[15]

---

1   Ibid, at 564. As to the ratification issue, see **16.23.1**.

2   *Industrial Development Consultants Ltd v Cooley* [1972] 2 All ER 162 (discussed further at **16.9**).

3   *Re Derek Randall Enterprises Ltd* [1990] BCC 749 (CA). No doubt this assumes no further loss by the company.

4   *Zerco Ltd v Jerrom-Pugh* [1993] BCC 275 (CA).

5   *Steen v Law* [1964] AC 287 (PC); *Selangar United Rubber Estates Ltd v Cradock (No 3)* [1968] 1 WLR 1555; *Wallersteiner v Moir (No 1)* [1974] 1 WLR 991 (CA). *Belmont Finance Corp Ltd v Williams Furniture Ltd* [1980] 1 All ER 393 (CA).

6   *Re Duomatic Ltd* [1969] 2 Ch 365.

7   *Wallersteiner v Moir (No 1)*, above.

8   *Flitcroft's Case* (1882) 21 Ch D 536 (CA); *Allied Carpets Group plc v Nethercott* [2001] BCC 81, *Bairstow v Queens Moat Houses plc* [2001] EWCA Civ 712, [2001] 2 BCLC 531.

9   *Hirsche v Sims* [1894] AC 654 (PC).

10   *Re Faure Electric Accumulator Co* (1889) 40 Ch D 141.

11   *Parker v McKenna* (1875) 10 Ch App 96.

12   *Russell v Wakefield Waterworks Co* (1875) LR 20 Eq 474. This is expressly preserved by section 35(3) of the Companies Act 1985.

13   *Re George Newman & Co* [1895] 1 Ch 674 (CA). See also *Guinness plc v Saunders* [1990] 2 AC 663 (HL), discussed in **16.9**, although the House of Lords did not use the language of misapplication.

14   *E Hannibal & Co Ltd v Frost* (1988) 4 BCC 3 (CA).

15   *Rolled Steel Products v British Steel Corporation* [1985] 2 WLR 908 (CA); see further as to this case, **6.7–6.8**.

(10) the signing of blank transfer forms in respect of securities owned by the company which were transferred without consideration and without the authority of the full board of directors;[1]

(11) the payment of a debt owed by a third party.[2]

Where directors are liable for misapplication of a company's funds, they may be charged compound interest.[3]

16.9 Avoidance of conflict of interest and duty

Directors are in general bound by the broad principle, affecting all persons who are subject to fiduciary duties, that 'no-one, having such duties to discharge, shall be allowed to enter into engagements in which he has, or can have, a personal interest conflicting, or which possibly may conflict, with the interests of those whom he is bound to protect'.[4] This principle equally applies if the director has an 'outside' duty which clashes or may clash with his fiduciary duties to the company.[5] It is a principle that may be invoked by the company only, and not by the director by way of a defence to proceedings instigated to compel performance of the conflicting duty.[6] It has at times been suggested that it is too broad a principle to be strictly applicable in all situations,[7] but it is none the less the underlying basis of the more specific fiduciary duties discussed in the following sections, as well as being a distinct principle in its own right.[8]

This last point is illustrated by *Industrial Development Consultants v Cooley*.[9] Here the managing director of a design and construction company, being himself a successful architect, failed in an attempt to obtain for the company a valuable contract to do work for a local gas board. He was subsequently approached by the board with an offer to take up the contract in his private capacity, the board still indicating that it was not interested in letting the company have the contract. He concealed this offer from the company and, by misrepresenting that he was in

1   *Bishopsgate Investment Management Ltd v Maxwell* [1993] BCC 120 (CA).
2   *DEG-Deutsche Investitutions-und Entwicklungsgesellschaft mbH v Kosky* [2002] 1 BCLC 479.
3   *Wallersteiner v Moir (No 2)* [1975] QB 373 (CA), applying principles established in relation to defaulting trustees. See further, *Gore-Browne on Companies* 44th edn (Jordans, loose-leaf) at 27.6.2.
4   *Aberdeen Rly Co v Blaikie* (1854) 1 Macq 461 at 471–472 (HL (Sc)), *per* Lord Cranworth LC; see also *North-West Transportation Co Ltd v Beatty* (1887) 12 App Cas 589 at 593 (PC); *Bray v Ford* [1896] AC 44 at 51–52 (HL); *Regal (Hastings) Ltd v Gulliver* [1942] 1 All ER 378 at 381; [1967] 2 AC 134n at 137 (HL); *Boulting v ACTAT* [1963] 2 QB 606 at 635 (CA); *New Zealand Netherlands Society 'Oranje' Inc v Kuys* [1973] 1 WLR 1126 at 1129 (PC); *Queensland Mines Ltd v Hudson* (1978) 52 ALJR 399 (PC); *Guinness plc v Saunders* [1990] 2 AC 663 (HL); *CMS Dolphin Ltd v Simonet* [2001] 2 BCLC 704 at 728–734; *Bhullar v Bhullar* [2003] EWCA Civ 424, [2003] 2 BCLC 241.
5   *Transvaal Lands Co v New Belgium (Transvaal) Land and Development Co* [1914] 2 Ch 488 (CA); and see further, **16.22**.
6   *Boulting v ACTAT*, above.
7   See eg ibid; *Phipps v Boardman* [1967] 2 AC 46 at 124, *per* Lord Upjohn, dissenting. *New Zealand Netherlands Society 'Oranje' Inc v Kuys*, above, at p 1130. For a brief comment as to the fairness of the principle as it applies to 'secret profits', see **16.18.3** and the sources cited there.
8   See *Phipps v Boardman*, above, at 103, 111. This principle is clearly more aptly described as a 'principle' rather than as a 'duty', although its application may lead to duties imposed on directors, eg duties of disclosure. See Vinelott J in *Motivex Ltd v Bulfield* (1986) 2 BCC 99, 403 (following *Tito v Waddell (No 2)* [1977] 3 All ER 129); this case is discussed further in **16.23.3**.
9   [1972] 2 All ER 162.

poor health, procured the company to release him from his service contract, in order that he could take up the contract for himself. It was held by Roskill J that he was liable to account to the company for the profit which he obtained from performing the contract, on the footing that he should have informed the company of the board's offer to him and that, after the offer was made, he 'embarked on a deliberate policy and course of conduct which put his personal interests as a potential contracting party with the [gas board] in direct conflict with his pre-existing and continuing duty as managing director of the [company]'.[1]

A further example is provided by the House of Lords' decision in *Guinness plc v Saunders*.[2] Here, a director of Guinness, which was engaged in making a takeover bid for the shares of another company, agreed to provide services to Guinness in connection with the bid for a substantial fee, the size of which was dependent on the value of the bid. In the absence of a properly authorised contract,[3] it was held by the House of Lords that the director had put himself into a position where there was an irreconcilable conflict between his personal interests and his duty, in consequence of which he had no claim to an equitable allowance for his services. See also the recent Court of Appeal decision in *Bhullar v Bhullar*,[4] where, on similar facts to those in *Industrial Development Consultants Ltd v Cooley*, the court stressed the universality and inflexibility of the principle in any situation where a reasonable person looking at the facts would think that there was a reasonably sensible possibility of conflict.

16.10 Disclosure of interests in contracts at general law

Subject to modification by the articles, the requirement to avoid a conflict of duty and interest means that a director is under a duty to disclose to the shareholders in general meeting the nature of any interest which he has in a contract to which the company is or is to be a party.[5] In the event of the director failing to disclose his interest to the meeting, or of the meeting refusing to sanction his interest, two consequences follow.[6] In the first place, the contract is voidable at the option of the company against any party thereto who has notice of the breach of duty,[7] though its right of avoidance will lapse if it affirms the contract,[8] or it delays

---

1   [1972] 2 All ER 162, at 173–174.
2   [1990] 2 AC 663.
3   The articles of Guinness would have permitted such a contract provided that it had been approved by the full board of directors (along the lines of standard articles referred to in the following sections). Instead, it was only the sub-committee of the board charged with facilitating the takeover which had purported to enter into a contract. This 'contract' was void.
4   [2003] EWCA Civ 424, [2003] 2 BCLC 241.
5   *Aberdeen Rly Co v Blaikie* (1854) 1 Macq 461 (HL (Sc)); *Gwembe Valley Development Co Ltd v Koshy* [2003] EWCA Civ 1048, [2004] 1 BCLC 131
6   Under some articles, the director may in addition be liable to disqualification.
7   *Hely-Hutchinson & Co Ltd v Brayhead* [1968] 1 QB 549 (CA); *Cowan de Groot Properties Ltd v Eagle Trust plc* [1991] BCLC 1045 at 1116–1117.
8   See *MacPherson v European Strategic Bureau Ltd* [1999] 2 BCLC 203.

unduly before rescinding, or the rights of *bona fide* third parties intervene.[1] Secondly, any profit which the director derives from the contract is recoverable from him by the company,[2] even if he can show that it is unfair for the company to have the profit and/or that the transaction was fair and reasonable and/or that he could have made the same amount of profit after disclosure.[3] It should be noted, however, that when all that he has done is to fail to disclose his interest in a sale to the company of property which he acquired in his own right free from any duty to hold it on trust for the company, his profit on the resale is not accountable and the company's only remedy is to rescind (which makes it particularly important that the company should rescind quickly before anything happens to bar this right).[4] If the general meeting sanctions the director's interests in the contract, the contract ceases to be voidable and the director may retain any profit arising out of it. On the resolution for approval, the director may vote in his own interests on any shares of which he is the holder, except where to do so constitutes fraud or 'oppression'.[5]

16.11 Statutory duty to disclose interests in contracts

These duties imposed by general law are supplemented by a number of provisions in Part X of the Companies Act 1985.[6] In general, section 317 makes it the duty of every director interested directly or indirectly in any way in any contract, proposed contract, transaction or arrangement with a company of which he is a director to declare the nature of his interest at a meeting of directors,[7] and an unlimited fine on conviction on indictment may be imposed for default. The section does not prejudice any rule of law restricting directors of a company from having any interest in a contract with the company;[8] in other words, the general law described in **16.10** must be complied with.[9]

In the case of a proposed contract the declaration must be made at the meeting of the directors at which the question of entering into the contract is first taken into consideration, or if the director was not at the date of that meeting interested in the proposed contract, then at the next meeting of the directors held after he became so interested. Whether the director becomes interested in a contract after it is made, the declaration must be made at the first meeting of the directors held

---

1 Ibid; *Victors Ltd v Lingard* [1927] 1 Ch 323. It is submitted that only the general meeting, and not the board, should have the right to affirm the contract: see *Re Cardiff Preserved Coke and Coal Co* (1862) 23 LJ Ch 154; *North-West Transportation Co Ltd v Beatty* (1887) 12 App Cas 589 at 600 (PC).

2 *Aberdeen Rly Co v Blaikie* (1854) 1 Macq 461 (HL (Sc)); *Imperial Mercantile Credit Association v Coleman* (1873) LR 6 HL 189.

3 *Costa Rica Rly Co v Forwood* [1901] 1 Ch 746 at 761 (CA); *Gray v New Augarita Porcupine Mines Ltd* [1952] 3 DLR 1 at 15 (PC).

4 *Cavendish-Bentinck v Fenn* (1887) 12 App Cas 652; *Re Lady Forrest (Murchison) Gold Mines Ltd* [1901] 1 Ch 582; *Burland v Earle* [1902] AC 83; *Jacobus Marler Estates Ltd v Marler* (1913) 114 LT 640n (PC).

5 *North-Western Transportation Co Ltd v Beatty*, above; *Burland v Earle*, above, at 94; *Harris v A Harris Ltd* 1936 SC 183; *Baird v Baird & Co (Falkirk) Ltd* 1949 SLT 368; see **16.23** and **17.4**.

6 In addition to that described here, see those discussed in **16.14** *et seq.*

7 Section 317(1).

8 Section 317(9).

9 Save insofar as it is modified by the articles as described in **16.12**. For a valuable analysis, see Griffiths, 'Declaring an Interest: the Companies Act 1985, s 317 and the Regulation of Self-dealing' [1997] CfiLR 95. For the recommendations of the Law Commission, see **16.13**.

after the director becomes so interested.[1] A general notice given to the directors of a company by a director to the effect that: (a) he is a member of a specified company or firm and is to be regarded as interested in any contract which may, after the date of the notice, be made with that company or firm; or (b) he is to be regarded as interested in any contract which may after the date of the notice be made with a specified person who is connected with him,[2] is a sufficient declaration of interest in relation to any contract so made, provided that it is given at a meeting of the directors, or the director takes reasonable steps to ensure that it is brought up and read at the next meeting of the directors after it is given.[3]

Section 317 requires disclosure to a duly convened meeting of the full board of directors,[4] and where the director is already interested, the contract must be presented for consideration and approval, not as a *fait accompli*.[5] A failure formally to declare an interest common to all members of the board and, *ex hypothesi*, known to all, is unlikely to be regarded as a breach of the section.[6] Similarly, it has been held that a company could not rely upon the section where the failure to declare an interest, a variation of a director's service contract, was a purely technical breach since all the directors were aware of the variation.[7] It is important to bear in mind that this amounts to a dispensation on equitable grounds, where any other result would have been unjust.[8] It does not support any general dispensing with the requirements of section 317,[9] since there appear to be sound policy reasons for, in general, requiring formal declarations of interest, in particular that they draw the attention of the directors specifically to the duties that the law imposes on them and that they will be minuted and permanently recorded.[10]

Section 317 also applies to a 'shadow director'.[11] Such a person obviously cannot declare his interest at a meeting of the directors. He is required to inform the directors by notice in writing, which must be either a specific notice before the date of the meeting if the matter relates to an existing or proposed contract and section 317(2) would have required disclosure at that meeting had the person been a director, or a general notice under section 317(3).

---

1   Section 317(2).
2   The relevance of 'connected person' is with regard to the provisions regarding substantial property transactions and loans. It is defined in section 346 and discussed in **16.16**.
3   Section 317(3) and (4).
4   *Guinness plc v Saunders* [1988] BCLC 607 (CA), affirmed on other grounds [1990] 2 AC 663. See also *Gwembe Valley Development Co Ltd v Koshy* [2003] EWCA Civ 1048, [2004] 1 BCLC 131, at paragraphs 51 and 59, where the point was emphasised in the context of the relevant articles of association rather than section 317 as such.
5   *Re Nuneaton Borough AFC Ltd (No 2)* [1991] BCLC 44 at 59–60.
6   *Lee Panavision Ltd v Lee Lighting* [1992] BCLC 22 at 33 (CA).
7   *Runciman v Walter Runciman plc* [1992] BCLC 1084. See also, *MacPherson v European Strategic Bureau Ltd* [1999] 2 BCLC 203.
8   Ibid at 1093 and 1097. See also, *Re Dominion International Group plc* [1996] 1 BCLC 572 at 598–600.
9   And article 85 of Table A, with which, in practice, it will often have to be read. See **16.12**.
10   [1992] BCLC at 1095. See also *Neptune (Vehicle Washing Equipment) Ltd v Fitzgerald* [1995] 1 BCLC 352 where it was held that a sole director was obliged to make a section 317 declaration of interest.
11   Section 317(8). See **16.2**.

16.12 The effect of releasing provisions in the articles

The outcome of these rules is that no less than three distinct duties of disclosure exist: direct disclosure to the general meeting (at general law) and disclosure to the board (under section 317 of the Companies Act 1985); there is also a requirement of disclosure to the general meeting and the public through the accounts (under sections 232 and 233 and Schedule 6).[1] In practice, however, the articles almost invariably contain provisions which release directors from the first of these duties,[2] provided that section 317, which is mandatory in operation, is complied with and (in most cases) that, with some specified exceptions, the interested director does not vote upon any board resolution by which the contract or his having an interest therein is approved, and is not counted in the quorum for such resolution.[3] Such provisions are valid and, provided they are strictly complied with, neither of the two remedies prescribed at general law for breach of the general law duty of disclosure – ie rescission of the contract and an account of profits – can be invoked by the company.[4] On the other hand, any failure to comply with the relevant provisions of the articles renders both remedies available to the company,[5] subject to the limitations thereon which have already been mentioned. A breach of section 317 does not of itself render the contract voidable, although that result may follow from the general law principles described above,[6] nor does it give the company a separate right to damages.[7]

Article 85 of Table A is the current standard provision. It provides that: 'Subject to the provisions of the Act, and provided that he has disclosed to the directors the nature and extent of any material interest of his, a director notwithstanding his office . . . may be a party to, or otherwise interested in, any transaction . . . with the company . . .'. The drafting of this article has been judicially criticised, but it has been held that its effect is that the whole thrust of the Act, and in particular the specific requirements for disclosure under section 317, must be read into it.[8] On that basis, disclosure under article 85 had to be 'to the board at a meeting and at the meeting when the relevant contract first comes to be considered'.[9]

---

1   See **14.12**.
2   See eg Table A, articles 85 and 86 described below and see further, **16.23.3**.
3   See articles 94 and 95 of Table A.
4   *Imperial Mercantile Credit Association v Coleman* (1871) 6 Ch App 558 (revd on other grounds (1873) LR 6 HL 189).
5   *Imperial Mercantile Credit Association v Coleman* (1873) LR 6 HL 189; *Hely-Hutchinson & Co Ltd v Brayhead* [1968] 1 QB 549 (CA).
6   *Hely-Hutchinson & Co Ltd v Brayhead*, above; *Guinness plc v Saunders* [1990] 1 All ER 653 at 664–665 *per* Lord Goff of Chievely. Lord Templeman (ibid at 662) seemed to think that the *Hely-Hutchinson* decision decided the contrary, but it is thought that the view of Lord Goff is to be preferred. See also, *Lee Panavision Ltd v Lee Lighting Ltd* [1991] BCLC 575 at 583 and *Cowan de Groot Properties Ltd v Eagle Trust plc* [1991] BCLC 1045 at 1113.
7   *Coleman Taymar Ltd v Oakes* [2001] 2 BCLC 749. However the company will have a right to claim equitable compensation or an account of profits; see **16.10** and *Gwembe Valley Development Co Ltd v Koshy* [2003] EWCA Civ 1048, [2004] 1 BCLC 131.
8   *Lee Panavision Ltd v Lee Lighting* [1991] BCLC 575. This decision was upheld by the Court of Appeal ([1992] BCLC 22) on other grounds (see **16.7**) and the CA expressly declined to express a view on this point.
9   Ibid at 583–584, *per* Harman J. As to the construction of a slightly different article, see *Cowan de Groot Properties Ltd v Eagle Trust plc*, above, at 1113–1114.

16.13 Interpretation of the rules as to disclosure

Various decisions have been given as to the meeting of 'interest' in this context, though in considering them it should be remembered that most of them are decisions on particular provisions in company articles and are thus not necessarily applicable directly to other such provisions or to section 317 of the Companies Act 1985.[1] A director has been held to be interested in a contract with another company in which he was a shareholder[2] or a firm of which he was a member,[3] in a contract to allot shares or debentures to him,[4] and in a debenture granted to release him from a personal guarantee of a debt.[5] It goes without saying that a director is 'interested' in an arrangement whereby he provides services to the company (whether as chairman of directors, managing director, executive director or otherwise) for a remuneration; on the other hand, an agreement whereby he is appointed chairman or managing director without any (or any additional) remuneration is merely a delegation of power and not a contract in which he is 'interested'.[6] It is expressly provided by section 317(6) that a transaction or arrangement within section 330, ie loans and related dealings,[7] made by a company for a director or for a person connected with a director[8] is to be treated as a contract in which that director is interested for the purposes of section 317, if it would not otherwise be so treated, and whether or not the transaction or arrangement is prohibited by section 330.

Under section 317, 'the nature' of the director's interest must be disclosed by him, and the articles cannot reduce this obligation. It has been said in addition that disclosure must be 'full and frank'.[9] The result is that, generally speaking, it will not be enough for the director merely to say 'I am interested' in the relevant contract; however, there is no hard and fast rule as to how far disclosure must go. 'The amount of detail must depend in each case upon the nature of the contract or arrangement proposed and the context in which it arises.'[10] It has been held[11] that directors negotiating an agreement whereby their contracts of service are terminated in return for compensation for loss of office are not bound to disclose past breaches of duty which would entitle the company to dismiss them without

---

1   Note, in particular, that the modern Table A (**16.12**) refers to 'material interest', which is clearly narrower than the reference to 'interest' in the 1948 Table A, and might well not comprehend the situations in the case in the next two footnotes.

2   Even as a trustee (*Transvaal Lands Co v New Belgium (Transvaal) Land and Development Co* [1914] 2 Ch 488), though not if he is a bare trustee without duties to perform (*Cowan de Groot Properties Ltd v Eagle Trust plc* [1991] BCLC 1045 at 1115).

3   *Imperial Mercantile Credit Association v Coleman* (1873) LR 6 HL 189.

4   *Neal v Quin* [1916] WN 223; *Cox v Dublin City Distillery (No 2)* [1915] 1 Ir R 145.

5   *Rolled Steel Products Ltd v British Steel Corporation* [1984] BCLC 466 (CA). See also *Lee Panavision Ltd v Lee Lighting Ltd* [1991] BCLC 575 (contract including indemnity for director).

6   *Foster v Foster* [1916] 1 Ch 532; *Runciman v Walter Runciman plc* [1992] BCLC 735.

7   See **16.17.1**.

8   'Connected person' is defined in section 346 and discussed in **16.14**.

9   *Fine Industrial Commodities Ltd v Powling* (1954) 71 RPC 253 at 262, *per* Danckwerts J. Standard articles following article 85 of Table A require disclosure of the nature *and extent* of any material interest.

10   *Gray v New Augarita Porcupine Mines Ltd* [1952] 3 DLR 1 at 14, *per* Lord Radcliffe. See also *Movitex Ltd v Bulfield* [1988] BCLC 104 at 121, *DEG-Deutsche Investitions-und Entwicklungsgesellschaft mbH v Koshy* [2002] 1 BCLC 478 at 555–556.

11   *Healey v SA Française Rubastic* [1971] 1 KB 946, approved in *Bell v Lever Bros Ltd* [1932] AC 161 at 228, 231 (HL).

compensation, but this is somewhat difficult to accept, and the opposite view has more recently been taken.[1]

The Law Commissions subjected section 317 to an extremely thorough analysis. A number of possibilities for amendment were considered and their Report[2] makes the following recommendations.

(1) The disclosure of immaterial interests would be excluded by provisions that the section would not apply where a director satisfied the court that the interest did not give rise to a real risk of an actual conflict of duty and interest or that the other directors were aware of the nature and extent of his interest before the transaction was approved.[3]

(2) There would be exemptions relating to:
   (a) a director's interest in his own service contract where that had been considered by the board or a duly authorised committee thereof;[4]
   (b) interests of which a director had no knowledge;[5] and
   (c) the interest of a sole director.[6]

(3) A director would be obliged to declare the nature and extent of his interest,[7] and the section 317 requirements would be extended to cover the interests of 'connected persons'.[8]

(4) There should be a Register of Directors' Interests, but this would be open to inspection only by directors.[9]

(5) Failure to disclose an interest should render a contract voidable and there should be other civil remedies along the lines of those which are provided in section 322.[10]

These suggestions seem very sensible and balanced and were in general supported by the Company Law Review Steering Group. Further the Government in *Modernising Company Law* indicated its intention to reform all the provisions in Part X. Exactly how will be done alongside the proposed statutory code of general duties remains to be seen.

---

1   *Horcal Ltd v Gatland* [1983] BCLC 60, especially at 65–67. Cf, however, the view of Robert Goff LJ on appeal, *obiter*: [1984] BCLC 549 at p 554. See also *Item Software (UK) Ltd v Fassihi* [2003] EWHC 3116 (Ch) at paragraph 51, [2003] 2 BCLC 1 at 18.

2   *Company Directors: Regulating Conflicts of Interest and Formulating a Statement of Duties*, Law Com No 261, Scot Law Com No 173, Part 8. See generally, **16.24**.

3   Paragraphs 8.9 to 8.33.

4   Paragraphs 8.41 to 8.45.

5   Paragraphs 8.55 to 8.57.

6   Paragraphs 8.76 to 8.88, thus reversing part of the decision in *Neptune (Vehicle Washing Equipment) Ltd v Fitzgerald* [1995] 1 BCLC 352, footnote 10 at p 504. However, the interest would have to be recorded in the proposed new register of interests (see below).

7   Paragraphs 8.93 to 8.96, although this may be required already; see the discussion in the previous paragraph.

8   Paragraphs 8.58 to 8.62. As to the meaning of connected person, which is relevant for many of the other existing statutory provisions, see **16.14**.

9   Paragraphs 8.63 to 8.75.

10 Paragraphs 8.97 to 8.120. The Commissions also think that the criminal penalty should be removed, but the question of decriminalisation of parts of the Companies Act is something that the Review of Company Law is examining generally, and so they make no final recommendation.

16.14   Specific rules regarding directors' interests in contracts

Even if the general rules as to disclosure are complied with, a contract in which a director is 'interested' will be voidable if it is not made *bona fide* in the company's interests, and for the proper purposes, in accordance with the first two fiduciary principles discussed above. If the director is actually a party, he will most likely not have a defence to an action for rescission because he will be aware of the relevant breach of duty. Furthermore, certain types of contract in which a director is 'interested' are subject to special rules and restrictions in the Companies Act 1985 over and above those just mentioned. These rules and restrictions relate particularly to directors' service contracts, substantial property transactions involving directors, and loans to and related deals with directors. These are examined in the following sections.[1]

It should be noted that most of these rules and restrictions apply to shadow directors as much as to directors.[2] Further, many of them also apply to 'persons connected' with directors, so that avoidance of them is not easily effected. It is appropriate to describe such persons at this stage.

By section 346, a connected person is someone who is not a director of the company who falls within one of the following categories.[3]

(1) A director's spouse or infant child or step-child.[4]
(2) An associated body corporate; this is basically a body corporate[5] in which a director and any person connected with him has a 20% interest. The interest may be either an interest in equity share capital[6] or the control of one-fifth or more of the voting power at general meetings.[7]
(3) The trustee (other than under an employees' share scheme or a pension scheme) acting in that capacity of any trust under which a director, his spouse or infant children or an associated body corporate are or may be a beneficiary.
(4) A partner of a director or connected person, acting as such.
(5) A Scottish firm in which a director or connected person is a partner.

16.15   Directors' service contracts

It should be noted first that these have their own special rules in Table A, article 84 of the Companies Act 1985, and in the articles commonly adopted by public companies in imitation of Table A. Further, the articles are usually more liberal in respect of voting and quorum requirements[8] than the articles governing

---

1   Note also the controls where directors exceed their powers: section 322A, discussed in **6.23**.
2   As to shadow directors, see **16.2**.
3   For a fuller explanation, see *Gore-Browne on Companies* 44th edn (Jordans, loose-leaf) at 27.11. The Law Commissions (*Company Directors: Regulating Conflicts of Interest and Formulating a Statement of Duties,* Law Com No 261, Scot Law Com No 173, Part 14; see generally, **16.24**) have recommended extending the definition to include cohabitants (including of the same sex), adult children, parents and siblings, and that the Review of Company Law considers simplifying the definition of an associated company.
4   Including an illegitimate child.
5   This expression, defined in section 740, is used to catch foreign as well as British companies.
6   'Interest' is defined widely by reference to Schedule 13, as to which see **15.22.2**.
7   Note the qualifications in section 346(6) regarding this category of connected person.
8   See article 97 of Table A.

directors' contracts in general. Where, as in article 84, the articles vest in the directors as a whole the authority to enter into a service contract with one of their number, such a contract is not binding unless it has been approved by the whole board of directors.[1]

Secondly, section 319 contains important restrictions on the length of service contracts.[2] The section applies to the employment[3] of a director by a company and, where the company is a holding company, to the employment of any of its directors within the group,[4] provided that the company is a company within the meaning of the Act or registered under section 680, and except where the company is the wholly owned subsidiary[5] of any body corporate, wherever incorporated.[6] It is prohibited for any company thus falling within section 319 to incorporate in any agreement providing for such a director's employment[7] a term whereby that employment may continue, other than at the instance of the company, for more than five years, if during that time it cannot be terminated by the company by notice or can be terminated by notice only in specified circumstances, unless that term is first approved by a resolution of the company in general meeting or, in the case of a director of a holding company, by a resolution of that company in general meeting. However, as the only purpose of section 319 is the benefit and protection of shareholders, the specific requirements of the section can be waived if there is fully informed and unanimous informal agreement of the shareholders to a director's employment contract lasting more than five years.[8]

Where a director is, or is to be, employed under an agreement with similar restrictions on its being terminated, and, more than six months before the end of this agreement, a further agreement is entered into under which he is to be employed with the company, or with the group where he is a director of a holding company, the unexpired part of the old agreement must be added to the period of the new agreement. If the result is a term of more than five years, general meeting sanction as above must be obtained. However, this does not apply where the new agreement was entered into in pursuance of a right conferred on the party to the agreement other than the company.[9]

Before a resolution approving a term longer than five years can be passed, a written memorandum setting out the proposed agreement containing the term must be available for inspection by members of the company at the company's registered office for at least 15 days before the relevant meeting, and at the meeting itself.[10]

---

1   *UK Safety Group Ltd v Heane* [1998] 2 BCLC 208.

2   For other provision controlling service contracts, see **15.21**.

3   Whether under a contract of service or a contract for services; section 319(7)(a).

4   Ie that company and its subsidiaries; section 319(7)(b).

5   See section 736(2), by which a company is deemed to be the wholly owned subsidiary of another if it has no members except that other and the latter's wholly owned subsidiaries or persons acting on behalf of that other or its wholly owned subsidiaries.

6   Section 319(4).

7   Section 319 does not therefore apply just to a contract directly between a director and his company, and cannot be evaded by, eg, the use of a contract between the company and another company which the director controls.

8   *Atlas Europe Ltd v Wright* [1999] BCC 163 (CA), applying the principle described in **13.2**.

9   Section 319(2).

10   Section 319(5).

A term which contravenes section 319 is void to the extent that it contravenes the section, and the agreement is deemed to contain a term entitling the company to determine it at any time by reasonable notice.[1] In other words, the agreement is deemed to be made for five years subject to its being determinable at any time within that period by reasonable notice.

For some years, concern has been expressed regarding the length of directors' service contracts, particularly in the case of listed companies (see also Chapter 11 and **15.3**), and the Combined Code now requires contract or notice periods of no more than one year, so that directors are not entitled to excessive compensation in the event of their contract being terminated. Reflecting these developments, the Law Commissions[2] recommended that the time-limit in section 319 be reduced to three years and applied, to prevent evasion of the section, to rolling contracts. The Steering Group, and the Government in *Modernising Company Law* generally supported these recommendations, although it is possible that longer service contracts might be permitted with special resolution approval.

16.16   Substantial property transactions

Any contract by which a company sells to or buys from a director property of any sort, and any other property dealings between directors and their companies, are subject to the general rules already described. The provisions of sections 320 to 322 of the Companies Act 1985 reinforce these general rules, in particular by imposing a requirement of general meeting approval similar to that required by the general law[3] which had in practice been modified by articles of association[4] until the introduction (in 1980) of what are now sections 320 to 322.[5] Further, the sections do not catch only contracts between directors and their companies, since they apply to 'arrangements', a deliberately broad word, and to deals with shadow directors[6] and connected persons.[7]

The statute applies to an arrangement for the acquisition[8] from a company[9] of one or more non-cash assets[10] of the requisite value by a director of the company

---

1   Section 319(6).

2   *Company Directors: Regulating Conflicts of Interest and Formulating a Statement of Duties*, Law Com No 261, Scot Law Com No 173, Part 9. See generally, **16.24**.

3   See **16.10**.

4   See **16.12**.

5   It has been held that a solicitors' firm was negligent for failing to advise its client company that a particular transaction fell within section 320: *British Racing Drivers' Club Ltd v Hextall Erskine & Co* [1997] 1 BCLC 182.

6   See **16.2**.

7   See **16.14**.

8   This clearly indicates any dealing, whether by way of sale, gift, exchange or whatever. By section 739(2), the acquisition of a non-cash asset includes the creation of an estate or interest in, or a right over, any property and the discharge of any person's liability, other than a liability for a liquidated sum.

9   Within the meaning of the Act (see section 735) or registered under section 680. This includes a sale by a receiver acting as agent for the company: *Demite Ltd v Protec Health Ltd* [1998] BCC 638.

10   'Non-cash asset' is defined in section 739(1) as 'any property or interest in property other than cash (including foreign currency)'. This clearly includes a lease (*Niltan Carson Ltd v Hawthorne* [1988] BCLC 298) and the benefit of a deposit paid on a contract to purchase property (*Duckwari Ltd v Offerventure Ltd* [1995] BCC 89 (CA)), but not a right to a sum of money such as compensation for termination of a service contract (*Lander v Premier Pict Petroleum Ltd* [1998] BCC 248).

or its holding company or a person connected with such a director, and conversely, to an arrangement for the acquisition by a company of one or more non-cash assets of the requisite value from such a director or connected person. To fall within the section, the value of the asset or assets must be more than £10,000 or 10% of the company's asset value, subject in the latter case to a minimum of £2,000.[1] The value of the asset acquired is to be determined in the context of the particular circumstances of the transaction or arrangement, and is not necessarily limited to market value when its worth to a director or connected person is greater.[2] The amount of a company's asset value is the value of its net assets as determined by reference to its last annual accounts prepared and laid under Part VII,[3] or its called-up share capital if no such accounts have been prepared and laid at the relevant time.[4]

However, section 320 does not apply in the following circumstances:

(1) where the company is the wholly owned subsidiary of any body corporate, wherever incorporated;[5]

(2) to an arrangement for the acquisition of a non-cash asset, if the asset in question is to be acquired by a holding company from any of its wholly owned subsidiaries or from a holding company by any of its wholly owned subsidiaries or by one wholly owned subsidiary of a holding company from another wholly owned subsidiary of that same holding company;[6]

(3) to an arrangement for the acquisition of a non-cash asset entered into by a company which is being wound up, unless the winding-up is a members' voluntary winding-up;

(4) to an arrangement whereby a person is to acquire an asset from a company of which he is a member if the arrangement is made with him in his character as such member;[7]

(5) to a transaction on a recognised investment exchange which is effected by a director or connected person through the agency of an independent broker.[8]

An arrangement to acquire an asset in the circumstances described is forbidden unless it is first approved by a resolution of the company in general meeting[9] and, if the director or connected person is a director of its holding company or a person connected with such a director, by a resolution of the holding company in general meeting. Whereas not every last detail of the arrangement must be

---

1   Reading section 320(2) as if it included the words 'whichever is the lesser': *Niltan Carson Ltd v Hawthorne*, above. The onus is on the party alleging breach of the section to prove that the value exceeded the requisite value.

2   *Micro Leisure Ltd v County Properties Developments Ltd (No 2)* [2000] BCC 872.

3   See **14.2**.

4   Section 320(2).

5   Section 321. A body corporate is deemed to be the wholly owned subsidiary of another if it has no members except that other and the latter's wholly owned subsidiaries or persons acting on behalf of that other or its wholly owned subsidiaries: section 736(2).

6   Section 321(2).

7   Section 321(3).

8   Section 320(4).

9   It has been doubted whether the informal assent of all members (see **13.2**) would satisfy this particular statutory requirement (*Demite Ltd v Protec Health Ltd*, above at p 648), but *quaere* in the light of the subsequent Court of Appeal decision in *Atlas Europe Ltd v Wright* [1999] BCC 163 and the later decision in *Re Conegrade Ltd*, [2002] EWHC 2411, [2003] BPIR 358, ChD.

approved, the central aspects of it, such as the price to be paid in return for a sale of assets, must be covered.[1] By section 322, a breach of this requirement renders the arrangement and any transaction entered into in pursuance of it[2] voidable at the instance of the company,[3] except in the following circumstances:

(1) if restitution of any money or other asset which is the subject-matter of the arrangement or transaction is no longer possible, or the company has been indemnified in respect of loss or damage suffered by it under section 322;

(2) if avoidance would affect rights acquired for value by a third person not a party to the transaction or arrangement who acted in good faith and without actual notice of the contravention; or

(3) if the arrangement is within a reasonable time affirmed by the company in general meeting, and by a resolution in general meeting of its holding company if it involves a director of the holding company or a person connected with such a director.

These exceptions are the only circumstances in which the right to avoid is lost and a lapse of time is not by itself a bar to avoidance.[4]

In addition, the party to an arrangement not so approved and any director of the company not a party to it who authorised it or a transaction entered into in pursuance of it are liable, whether or not the arrangement has been avoided, to account to the company for any gain made directly or indirectly by the arrangement or transaction, and are jointly and severally liable to indemnify the company for any loss or damage resulting from it. The liability to indemnify the company against loss extends to any subsequent decline in the market value of an asset after its acquisition,[5] but it is limited to loss arising from the acquisition and does not include losses arising from associated transactions, for example in respect of a borrowing effected to make the acquisition.[6] However, a connected person and a director not a party are excused from liability if they can show that at the time the arrangement was entered into, they did not know the relevant circumstances constituting the contravention, and where the arrangement is with a person connected with a director, that director is not liable if he shows that he took all reasonable steps to secure the company's compliance with the section. These statutory liabilities are expressly stated to be without prejudice to any liability imposed otherwise, ie under the common-law rules already discussed in **16.10**.

---

1   *Demite Ltd v Protec Health Ltd* [1998] BCC 638. The consideration to be paid may not be crucial, but the shareholders must have sufficient information to make their approval an informed one; *Clydebank Football Club Ltd v Steedman* 2002 SLT 109.

2   Such a transaction does not have to be one which the company is compelled to enter into as a result of the arrangement: *Re Duckwari plc* [1997] BCC 45 at 49.

3   But not illegal: *Niltan Carson Ltd v Hawthorne*, above.

4   *Demite Ltd v Protec Health Ltd*, above. In this respect, the statutory remedy differs from the general law remedy of rescission: see **16.10**.

5   *Duckwari plc v Offerventure Ltd* [1998] 2 BCLC 315.

6   *Re Duckwari plc (No 3)* [1999] 1 BCLC 168 (CA), the sequel to the decisions referred to above. It is submitted, though, that the directors might be liable for such losses by reason of a breach of their duty to act in good faith and for the proper purposes as described earlier. It appears that the claim in the litigation involving Duckwari plc was founded solely on a breach of section 320.

The Law Commissions[1] recommended amendments to the provisions discussed here. First, they consider that section 320 should permit a company to enter into a contract that is conditional on subsequent shareholder approval.[2] Secondly, they think that, for clarity, covenanted payments under service contracts and payments under section 316(2) should be exempted,[3] as should sales by administrators; administrative receivers should have the option of seeking court approval as an alternative to shareholder approval.[4]

16.17   Loans to directors and others

The Companies Act 1985 contains comprehensive prohibitions on companies making loans to and entering into equivalent transactions on behalf of directors and persons connected with directors. These replaced a prohibition in the Companies Act 1948 which was both easily avoided and, it seems, often evaded. As loans and similar transactions must be disclosed in the accounts,[5] the task of ensuring compliance with the provisions falls to some extent on the auditors. Subject to the general exceptions described below, the prohibitions fall into two categories: first those applying to all companies, and secondly those applying only to 'relevant companies'. The sections concerned are some of the most complex to be found in the companies legislation.[6]

16.17.1   Prohibitions on all companies

By section 330(2), no company may lend money[7] to any of its directors or to a director of its holding company, nor may it guarantee[8] or provide security in connection with a loan made by a third person to such a director. In addition, a company must not assume or have assigned to it any rights, obligations or liabilities under a transaction which, if it had been entered into by the company, would have contravened section 330(2),[9] nor must it take part in any arrangement whereby another person enters into a transaction which, if it had been entered into by the company, would have contravened section 330(2), and under the arrangement that person has obtained or is to obtain any benefit from the company or its holding company or a subsidiary of the company or its holding company.[10]

---

1   *Company Directors: Regulating Conflicts of Interest and Formulating a Statement of Duties*, Law Com No 261, Scot Law Com No 173, Part 10. See generally, **16.24**.
2   Paragraphs 10.8 to 10.10.
3   Paragraphs 10.11 to 10.13. As to section 316, see **16.20**.
4   Paragraphs 10.14 to 10.19.
5   See **14.12**.
6   In their Consultation/Discussion Paper (LCCP No 153, SLCDP No 105), the Law Commissions proposed a rewriting of the provisions governing loans, but the question of simplification of the companies legislation became a matter for the Review of Company Law, so their final Report did not take this any further.
7   'Loan' must be construed in its ordinary sense as a straightforward lending of money to be returned in money or money's worth – see *Champagne Perrier SA v HH Finch Ltd* [1982] 3 All ER 713, a case concerned with the predecessor to section 330 (section 190 of the 1948 Act). The arrangement in this case was what under the Act is a 'quasi-loan' (see **16.17.2**).
8   Or indemnify: section 331(2).
9   Section 330(6). If a company does arrange for this in contravention of the prohibition, the transaction is treated has having been entered into on the date that the company enters into the arrangement.
10   Section 330(7).

16.17.2 Prohibitions on relevant companies

A 'relevant company' is basically a public company or a company within a group which contains a public company.[1]

The prohibitions on relevant companies extend in particular to dealings with 'connected persons',[2] to what are termed 'quasi-loans', and to 'credit transactions'. The last two terms are dealt with below.

By section 331(4), a 'quasi-loan' is a transaction under which a creditor pays, whether by agreement or otherwise, a sum for a borrower, or reimburses expenditure incurred by a third party for the borrower, on the terms that the borrower or someone on his behalf will reimburse the creditor, or in circumstances giving rise to a liability on the borrower to reimburse the creditor. For the purpose of the prohibitions, the company will be the creditor who pays money or reimburses expenditure to a third party for the director or connected person, the latter being the 'borrower' in the statutory definition liable to repay the sum to the company.[3]

A 'credit transaction' is defined as a transaction under which one party (the creditor)

(1) supplies any goods or sells any land under a hire-purchase or conditional sale agreement;[4]
(2) leases or hires any land or goods in return for periodical payment; or
(3) otherwise disposes of land or supplies goods or services[5] on the understanding that payment (whether in a lump sum or instalments or by way of periodical payments or otherwise) is to be deferred.[6]

The prohibitions on relevant companies fall under five heads. Such a company must not:

(1) make a loan or quasi-loan to a director of it or of its holding company;
(2) make a loan or quasi-loan to a person connected with such a director; or
(3) enter into a guarantee or provide any security in connection with a loan or quasi-loan made by any other person for such a director or a person so connected.[7]

There are two qualifications to these first three prohibitions. First, where a relevant company is a member of a group of companies (meaning a holding company and its subsidiaries), heads (2) and (3) do not apply to prohibit the relevant company from making a loan or quasi-loan to another member of that

---

1   The full definition in section 331(6) refers to a company which: (a) is a public company; (b) is a subsidiary of a public company; (c) is a subsidiary of a company of which another subsidiary is a public company; or (d) has a subsidiary which is a public company.
2   See **16.14**.
3   Any reference to the person to whom a quasi-loan is made is a reference to the borrower, and a borrower's liabilities under a quasi-loan include the liability of any person who has agreed to reimburse the creditor on behalf of the borrower: section 331(4). A good example of a quasi-loan is to be found in *Champagne Perrier SA v HH Finch Ltd*, above, where a company paid bills for a director, on the basis that he would repay at a future date. Another example would be the provision of a credit card on similar terms.
4   These bear the same meaning as in the Consumer Credit Act 1974 (see section 189 thereof): section 331(10).
5   Services means anything other than goods or land: section 331(8).
6   Section 331(7).
7   Section 330(3).

group or entering into a guarantee or providing any security in connection with a loan or quasi-loan made by any person to another member of the group by reason only that a director of one member of the group is associated[1] with another member.[2] Secondly, a relevant company may make a quasi-loan to one of its own directors provided that it contains a term requiring the director or a person on his behalf to reimburse the company incurring the expenditure and provided that the amount of the quasi-loan and of any existing outstanding relevant[3] quasi-loans does not exceed £5,000.[4]

The fourth and fifth prohibitions rule that a relevant company must not:

(4) enter into a credit transaction as creditor for a director of it or of its holding company or a person connected with such a director; or

(5) enter into any guarantee or provide any security in connection with a credit transaction made by any other person for such a director or connected person.[5]

By section 335, there are two exceptions to heads (4) and (5). The first allows a relevant company to enter into, or guarantee, a credit transaction of the sort described so long as the aggregate of the value of that transaction and existing ones outstanding does not exceed £10,000.[6] Secondly, a relevant company whose ordinary course of business includes such transactions can enter into one with a director or connected person if it does so on its usual terms, ie the director, etc, is treated no differently from the way in which the company would treat an unconnected person of the same financial standing.[7]

16.17.3 *General exceptions*

In addition to the limited exceptions already discussed, sections 334, 336, 337 and 338 provide for a number of general exceptions to the prohibitions on loans and related dealings in section 330. These are as follows:

(1) *Loans of small amounts.* Section 334 exempts entirely loans made to a director of the company or of its holding company if the aggregate of such loans outstanding does not exceed £5,000.

(2) *Transactions in favour of a holding company.* By section 336, none of the prohibitions against loans, quasi-loans and credit transactions applies where the deal is with or in favour of a company's holding company; in the absence of this exception, a holding company might well be caught as a director or connected person.

(3) *Directors' expenditure.* Under section 337, a company can provide its directors with funds (but only up to £20,000 in respect of relevant companies) to enable them to perform their duties or to meet expenditure incurred or to be

---

1   Association is defined in section 346(4), discussed in **16.14**.
2   Section 333.
3   A quasi-loan is relevant if it was made to the director by virtue of this exception by the company or by its subsidiaries or, where the director is a director of the company's holding company, any other subsidiary of that company.
4   Section 332.
5   Section 330(4).
6   Section 335(1). The full definitions, which are quite complex, of 'value' etc are contained in sections 339 and 340. For a full description, see *Gore-Browne on Companies* 44th edn (Jordans, loose-leaf) at 27.14.3.
7   Section 335(2).

incurred for the purpose of their duties. This is subject to a requirement of disclosure to and approval by the general meeting, or, failing such approval, to repayment within six months of the conclusion of the meeting.[1]

(4) *Moneylending companies.* These companies[2] can, by section 338, make loans, etc, to directors, etc (but only up to £100,000 in the case of relevant companies which are not banking companies), if they are made on the ordinary terms, ie the director, etc, is treated no differently from the way in which the company would treat a person of the same financial standing without a connection with the company.[3]

16.17.4 Remedies and criminal penalties

The Companies Act 1985 makes express provision for civil remedies and criminal penalties[4] in respect of contraventions of section 330. By section 341, a transaction or arrangement in breach is voidable at the instance of the company[5] unless:

(1) restitution of any money or other asset which is the subject-matter of the transaction or arrangement is no longer possible;

(2) the company has been indemnified under section 341(2)(b)[6] for the loss or damage suffered by it; or

(3) any rights acquired *bona fide* for value and without actual notice of the contravention by a person other than the person for whom the transaction or arrangement was made would be affected by its avoidance.

In addition, or alternatively, and without prejudice to any other liability,[7] where a prohibited transaction or arrangement has been made by a company with a director of it or of its holding company or with a person connected with such a director, any of these persons and any other director who authorised the transaction or arrangement is liable to account to the company for any gain made directly or indirectly by the transaction or arrangement, and jointly and severally liable to indemnify the company for any loss or damage resulting from it. However, a connected person or an authorising director is excused from civil liability if he shows that, at the time the arrangement or transaction was entered into, he did not know of the relevant circumstances constituting the contravention, and where an arrangement or transaction is with a person connected with a director, that director is not liable if he shows that he took all reasonable steps to secure the company's compliance with section 330. As prohibited loans etc are

---

1 Section 337(3) and (4).

2 Defined in section 338(1).

3 More generous provision may be made for loans for house purchase and improvement if such loans are ordinarily made on similar terms to employees and do not exceed £100,000.

4 The criminal penalties under section 342 are restricted to relevant companies, their directors, etc.

5 See *Tait Consibee (Oxford) Ltd v Tait* [1997] 2 BCLC 349 (CA).

6 Presumably, if the company relies on general law to recover any loss or damage (see footnote 7, below), this bar to avoidance will not apply.

7 Ie under the general law. In *Wallersteiner v Moir (No 1)* [1974] 1 WLR 991, it was held that a director receiving a loan in breach of section 190 of the 1948 Act (the predecessor to the provision consolidated in section 330) was liable for misfeasance and to compensate the company for any loss. It is submitted that the same result would follow a breach of section 330. In addition, profit recoverable under section 341(2) (see below) would be recoverable as a matter of general law.

merely voidable at the option of the company, the company can sue to enforce a prohibited loan, in addition to using the statutory remedies.[1] However, it cannot recover money paid thereunder on the basis of a constructive trust, as a loan is merely voidable and property in the money passes to the borrower.[2]

Despite canvassing a range of possible amendments in their Consultation Paper, the Law Commissions finally recommended[3] only one change to the provisions on loans and related dealings,[4] namely that the distinction between relevant and other companies should be abolished and the basic prohibitions should apply to all companies. The Company Law Review Steering Group supported this, but took a strict view in general, thinking that the number of exceptions should be reduced.[5]

16.18   Secret profits

These is a broad principle, developed from the law as to trustees and agents that any profit acquired by a director through holding the office of director must as a matter of law be accounted for to the company, unless the director has disclosed the profit and the circumstances in which he acquired it to the company in general meeting and his retention of it has been sanctioned by an ordinary resolution or by the acquiescence of all the individual members entitled to vote thereon, or unless he is protected by an appropriately worded provision of the articles.[6] This principle overlaps considerably with, but does not fully embrace, the rule that directors must not misapply the assets of the company[7] and also the rule that directors must disclose any interest in a contract involving the company as a party.[8]

16.18.1   *Various types of secret profit*

In the leading case of *Regal (Hastings) Ltd v Gulliver,*[9] the plaintiff company had formed a subsidiary company which was to take up a lease of two cinemas, but the owner of the cinemas insisted that the subsidiary should have a paid-up capital

---

1   *Currencies Direct Ltd v Ellis* [2002] 1 BCLC 193, decision upheld on other grounds: [2002] EWCA Civ 779, [2002] 2 BCLC 482.

2   *Re Ciro Citterio Menswear plc* [2002] EWHC 293 (Ch), [2002] 1 BCLC 672, distinguishing what was said in *Wallersteiner v Moir (No 1)* [1974] 1 WLR 991; see footnote 7 at p 516. This follows from the difference in wording between the current provision and that which it replaced, although the judge did not explicitly make this point.

3   *Company Directors: Regulating Conflicts of Interest and Formulating a Statement of Duties*, Law Com No 261, Scot Law Com No 173, Part 12. See generally, **16.24**.

4   See also the comment on the drafting of these provisions in footnote 6 at p 513.

5   See *Modern Company Law for a Competitive Economy: Developing the Framework*, March 2000, Annex C, paragraphs 28–30, paragraph 4.21 of *Completing the Structure*, and paragraph 6.15 of their *Final Report*.

6   See further as to these matters, **16.23.3**. The principle is equally applicable to former directors, provided that they have acquired the profit from an opportunity which the company is still actively pursuing: *Island Export Finance Ltd v Umunna* [1986] BCLC 460; *CMS Dolphin Ltd v Simonet* [2001] 2 BCLC 704.

7   Misapplications do not necessarily involve profit to the director, but may do so; conversely, the making of a secret profit does not necessarily involve loss to the company (which is of the essence of a misapplication), but may do so.

8   An interest in a contract of the company does not necessarily produce a profit for the director, but may do so; conversely, the making of a secret profit does not necessarily involve having an interest in a contract of the company, but may do so.

9   [1942] 1 All ER 378, [1967] 2 AC 134n (HL).

which, in the honest opinon of the plaintiff's board, was greater than the plaintiff could afford to subscribe. The ordinary directors accordingly subscribed at par for part of the balance themselves, the remainder being taken up by 'outsiders' in the name of the chairman of directors and by the plaintiff's solicitor. The whole transaction had been carried out with a view to a sale of the two cinemas, together with another cinema which the plaintiff itself owned, as a going concern, but ultimately the shares of the plaintiff and of the subsidiary were purchased instead at a price substantially above par. The plaintiff company sued the ordinary directors, the chairman and the solicitor for an account of their profits on the resale. It was found that they had all acted honestly throughout, but nonetheless the ordinary directors, who had taken their shares as beneficial owners, were held liable to account to the plaintiff, it being said that only disclosure to and approval by the general meeting would have saved them. On the other hand, the chairman escaped liability because the 'outsiders' who beneficially owned the shares for which he had subscribed owed no fiduciary duties to the company. The solicitor escaped also, on the ground that, although owing fiduciary duties to the company as its solicitor, his breach thereof could be and was effectively sanctioned by the board.

The effect of this decision is sometimes reversed, or substantially modified, by a provision in the articles,[1] but it submitted that its scope is wide enough to render a director liable to account when, through being aware of confidential information which comes to him because he is a director – an example is information as to an impending takeover – he makes a profit through buying and selling the company's own shares. The party entitled to claim the account would, of course, be the company; the decision in *Percival v Wright*[2] substantially curtails, if not totally bars, any claim by an individual shareholder in such a case unless he can establish some material misrepresentation by the director.

This general prohibition against the acquisition of secret profits is applicable to, *inter alia*, any secret commission or 'bribe' received by a director in the course of negotiating business transactions on the company's behalf,[3] any secret benefit coming to him in the course of any takeover bid for the company's shares or any reconstruction or amalgamation involving the company,[4] and profit derived through the use of confidential information which comes to the director's knowledge through his position on the board.[5] On the other hand, a director who will be leaving his company pursuant to an agreement between the company and his new employer to transfer part of the business of the company, and who is not involved in the negotiations, is not obliged to account in respect of undisclosed

---

1   As to this, see **16.23.3**. In Table A to the 1948 Act, the decision was reversed (article 78). In the modern Table A it is instead modified by article 85.

2   [1902] 2 Ch 421. See **16.3**.

3   *Boston Deep Sea Fishing and Ice Co Ltd v Ansell* (1888) 39 Ch D 339 (CA). For a discussion of the law relating to bribes in a company law context, see Birds, Chapter 6 in Birks (ed), *The Frontiers of Liability*, vol 1 (Oxford University Press, 1994).

4   *General Exchange Bank v Horner* (1870) LR 9 Eq 480. The Companies Act 1985 reinforces this position: see sections 313 to 316, described in **16.20**.

5   This case may also, if the information is property and is misused to the company's detriment, amount to a misapplication of company property as described in **16.8**. For recent examples of the application of the principle, see *Gencor ACP Ltd v Dalby* [2000] 2 BCLC 734, *CMS Dolphin Ltd v Simonet* [2001] 2 BCLC 704.

benefits he will receive from his new employer.[1] Where a director resigns and then exploits a maturing business opportunity of the company, he is accountable for the profits properly attributable to the breach of duty, as is also a company that he has formed in order to exploit the opportunity.[2]

16.18.2 Remedies available to the company

The *Regal (Hastings)* decision[3] establishes that, in an action for account of profits based upon his principle, it is no answer for the director to allege by way of defence that the company could not itself have acquired the relevant profit, or had *bona fide* decided not to try to acquire it, or in any event had not suffered any loss by virtue of the director having acquired it. However, evidence that an opportunity to enter into the transaction out of which the profit arose had been offered to and rejected by the company, then subsequently offered to the individual directors after a reasonable period of time had elapsed, may be enough to persuade the court that the profit was not derived by virtue of the director's position as such. It will be a question of fact in each case.[4] But it would seem that no defence is furnished by establishing any of the following matters:

(1) that the director acted honestly and in good faith throughout;[5]
(2) that the profit was acquired through the use of the director's own property and/or skill as well as through his directorship;[6]
(3) that disclosure to the general meeting would have been a mere formality because at a general meeting the director had or could have summoned sufficient votes to pass a resolution approving his retention of the profit;[7]
(4) that none of the shareholders at the time of the proceedings for an account was a shareholder at the time when the profit was made.

If a director employed under an express contract of service makes a secret profit without due authorisation, the company can not only recover the profit, but also dismiss him without compensation, even though this breach of duty does not occur more than once. It does not matter that the company in fact effects the dismissal on some other insufficient ground and only finds out about the secret

---

1 *Framlington Group plc v Anderson* [1995] 1 BCLC 475, distinguishing the Australian High Court decision in *Furs Ltd v Tomkies* (1936) 54 CLR 583, where the departing director was closely involved in the negotiations and held accountable for the secret profit he made.

2 *CMS Dolphin Ltd v Simonet* [2001] 2 BCLC 704. Lawrence Collins J characterised the breach as a breach of trust, relying in particular on *Cook v Deeks* [1916] AC 554 (PC) and *Canadian Aero Service Ltd v O'Malley* (1973) 40 DLR (3d) 371 (SC (Can)), as well as the general principle exemplified in *Regal (Hastings) Ltd v Gulliver* [1942] 1 All ER 378, [1967] 2 AC 134n (HL). His judgment was referred to in *In Plus Group Ltd v Pyke* [2002] EWCA Civ 370, [2002] 2 BCLC 201 at 220 as a valuable recent analysis of the law governing the no conflict and no profits rules.

3 [1942] 1 All ER 378, [1967] 2AC 134n (HL). See also, eg, *Industrial Development Consultants Ltd v Cooley* [1972] 2 All ER 162, discussed in **16.9**.

4 See the Canadian case of *Peso Silver Mines Ltd v Cropper* (1966) 58 DLR (2d) 1 (Canadian SC); and the decision in *Queensland Mines Ltd v Hudson* (1978) 52 ALJR 399 (PC), where it was clear that the company had given up all interest in the transaction and was fully informed, albeit informally, of the director's intention to take up the opportunity himself. It was held therefore that the director was not accountable for the profit he made.

5 *Regal (Hastings) Ltd v Gulliver*, above; and see *Phipps v Boardman* [1967] 2 AC 46.

6 See ibid; *Industrial Development Consultants v Cooley*, above.

7 *Regal (Hastings) Ltd v Gulliver*, above.

profit after the dismissal.[1] However, a director entering into an agreement to terminate his contract of service is not bound to disclose an intention to commit a breach of fiduciary duty. So non-disclosure does not make the agreement void for mistake, nor is any compensation paid recoverable.[2]

It is submitted that where a director receives a secret profit which has not been derived from the use of the company's property or which does not amount to a bribe, the profit does not become the property of the company to such an extent that it can follow investments or other property into which the money is put. Until the decision of the Privy Council in *Attorney-General of Hong Kong v Reid*,[3] this proposition seemed unarguable, being based upon the decision in *Lister & Co v Stubbs*,[4] where the Court of Appeal held that the relation between a bribed agent and his principal was that of debtor and creditor, not of trustee and beneficiary. In *Attorney-General of Hong Kong v Reid*, the Privy Council held that a bribe taken by a fiduciary belonged in equity to his principal.[5] However, it is thought that there is no mandate for regarding the holding in *Attorney-General of Hong Kong v Reid* as extending to a situation such as that exemplified by *Regal (Hastings) Ltd v Gulliver*.[6] On the other hand, it does seem clearly to support the view that, where the profit has been derived directly from the use of the company's property (which, as has been pointed out in **16.8.1**, may in this context include confidential information of a special and valuable nature), the profit is impressed with a trust in favour of the company, and for this reason is traceable.[7]

16.18.3   *Comment on the secret profits rule*

It is clear that the English courts may apply the secret profits rule strictly and it has been argued that it is applied too strictly. It has been said that it penalises the

---

1   *Boston Deep Sea Fishing Co v Ansell* (1888) 39 Ch D 339 (CA).
2   *Horcal Ltd v Gatland* [1984] BCLC 549 (CA). Neither is any salary paid while the director is working out his contract recoverable, though he would, as admitted in that case, be accountable for any secret profit made. *Quaere* whether a director is under a duty to disclose a breach of duty already committed; see footnote 1 at p 507. But a director's fiduciary duty does not necessarily come to an end when he ceases to be a director: *Island Export Finance Ltd v Umunna* [1986] BCLC 460.
3   [1994] 1 AC 324.
4   (1890) 45 Ch D 1.
5   In effect, overruling *Lister & Co v Stubbs*, although technically the Privy Council cannot overrule an English Court of Appeal decision.
6   See Boyle (1995) 16 Co Law 131. However, see *United Pan-Europe Communications NV v Deutsche Bank AG* [2000] 2 BCLC 461 (CA) at 482 to 484, which suggests that a proprietary remedy may be imputed in respect of a secret profit if the circumstances warrant it.
7   See the form of the order, for instance, made in *Phipps v Boardman* [1967] 2 AC 46 (HL) referred to in the speech of Lord Cohen at 99. The correctness and applicability of the decision in *Reid* has been much discussed in books and articles on the law of restitution. For a useful summary of the arguments and appropriate references, see Ferran *Company Law and Corporate Finance* (Oxford University Press, 1999), pp 199–203. There is considerable Commonwealth authority supporting the view that equitable compensation may be awarded for breach of this and other fiduciary duties, but this has not yet really been explored in English cases; see *Gore-Browne on Companies*, 44th edn (Jordans, loose-leaf) at 27.15.2.

honest and leads to absurd results, especially in that the company may receive a windfall.[1]

While such criticisms appear at first sight to be well founded, and it has been further argued that the courts should move away from the strict accountability of the director who benefits secretly from his position towards the notion of whether he took advantage of a genuine corporate opportunity,[2] it is thought that there is merit in the strict rule at least as respects directors of large companies and of companies with widely dispersed shareholders.[3] After all,[4] such directors are generally well-paid fiduciaries;[5] a strict rule can have the positive effect of encouraging them to do all they can for their companies in terms of pursuing opportunities and, last but by no means least, the prohibition is only against *secret* profits, so that if disclosure is made to and approval obtained of the company in general meeting, the director is relieved of any possibility of a breach of duty.[6]

---

1   For the most persuasive criticism, based at least partly on the courts' failure to require a genuine conflict of duty and interest, see Jones (1968) 84 LQR 472, attacking particularly the *Regal (Hastings)* case, above and the subsequent decision in *Phipps v Boardman* [1967] 2 AC 46 (HL) concerning a solicitor in a fiduciary position. The same cannot easily be said of a case like *Industrial Development Consultants Ltd v Cooley* [1972] 2 All ER 162, where the director certainly did not act honestly and where, it is thought, there was a real conflict of duty and interest; see **16.9**. The same certainly cannot be said where the profit has resulted from a misapplication of company property, ie a breach of trust of the sort involved in *Cook v Deeks* [1916] 1 AC 554 (PC); see **16.8**. For consideration of the economic aspects, see Bishop and Prentice (1983) 46 MLR 289.

2   For suggestions along these lines, see the Canadian Supreme Court decision in *Canadian Aero-Service Ltd v O'Malley* (1973) 40 DLR (3d) 371. For an application of the reasoning in this case in an English case, see Hutchinson J in *Island Export v Umunna* [1986] BCLC 460 at 478–479. See the discussion in *Farrar's Company Law*, 4th edn (Butterworths, 1997) Chapter 27, where it is pointed out that the recent decisions of the highest courts (the House of Lords in *Guinness plc v Saunders* [1990] 2 AC 663 (see **16.9**) and the Privy Council in *Attorney-General of Hong Kong v Reid* [1994] 1 AC 324) have adopted an uncompromisingly strict approach to the application of the equitable principles governing fiduciaries. See also, eg, *Paragon Finance plc v DB Thakerar & Co* [1999] 1 All ER 400 (CA) and *JJ Harrison (Properties) Ltd v Harrison* [2001] EWCA Civ 1467, [2002] 1 BCLC 162. The recent periodical literature includes Lowry and Edmunds, 'The Corporate Opportunity Doctrine: The Shifting Boundaries of the Duty and its Remedies' (1998) 61 MLR 515.

3   As far as small companies are concerned, breaches of the duty must often in practice be waived either by the articles or by the consent of the members (who, of course, will often be the same people as the directors). The Company Law Review Steering Group favoured a strict rule: see *Modern Company Law for a Competitive Economy: Developing the Framework*, March 2000, paragraph 3.63.

4   For this sort of argument in full, see Prentice (1967) 30 MLR 450 and (1974) 50 Can Bar Rev 623, and Beck, 'Corporate Opportunity Revisited', *Studies in Canadian Company Law*, vol 2, p 224.

5   As opposed to, eg, the solicitor in *Phipps v Boardman*, above. Even if they are not, the court can allow them such remuneration, in effect allowing them to retain part of their profits, as in *Phipps v Boardman*, above, and *O'Sullivan v Management Agency and Music Ltd* [1985] 3 WLR 448 (CA).

6   Further, the articles may lessen or even possibly exclude the obligation of disclosure (see **16.23.3**) and the director can also seek relief if he has acted honestly and reasonably under section 727 of the Companies Act 1985 (see **16.23.4** especially the comment in footnote 3 at p 534).

16.19   Prohibition on option dealings

The 'secret profits' rule has been reinforced by a number of statutory provisions.[1] Section 323 of the Companies Act 1985 makes it a criminal offence for a director to buy either:

(1) a right to call for delivery at a specified price and within a specified time of a specified number of 'relevant shares' or a specified amount of 'relevant debentures'; or

(2) a right to make delivery of 'relevant shares' or 'relevant debentures' on such terms; or

(3) a right at his election to call for or make delivery of 'relevant shares' or 'relevant debentures' on such terms.[2]

'Relevant shares' and 'relevant debentures' are shares and debentures respectively in the company of which the director is a director, or in any body corporate which is the company's subsidiary or holding company or a fellow subsidiary of the company's holding company, provided that they are listed on a stock exchange, whether in Great Britain or abroad. The section applies to shadow directors,[3] and 'price' includes any consideration other than money.[4] The section does not, however, prohibit a director from buying convertible debentures or options to subscribe for shares or debentures.[5]

Section 327 applies section 323 to the wife or husband or infant child (including a stepchild and adopted child) of a director who is not himself or herself a director, but it is a defence for such a person charged to show that he or she had no reason to believe that his or her spouse or parent (as the case may be) was a director of the company.

The Law Commissions[6] recommended the repeal of sections 323 and 327 on the ground that they are obsolete, their subject matter now being adequately covered by the provisions on insider dealing examined in Chapter 20, and by The Stock Exchange's Model Code.

16.20   Payments in connection with loss of office

Sections 312 to 315 of the Companies Act 1985 require the disclosure to and approval by the general meeting of certain types of payment made to directors connected with the loss of their office.

Section 312 prohibits the making of any payment by a company to a director of the company by way of compensation for loss of office or as consideration for or in connection with his retirement from office, unless particulars of the proposed

---

1   In addition to those described in this section, note also the statutory obligation of directors and members of their families to disclose any interests they have in shares or debentures (see **15.22** *et seq*) and the general controls on insider dealing and market abuse (not confined to company directors) described in Chapter 20.

2   No civil consequences are indicated, but presumably the law as to illegal contracts applies to any prohibited option.

3   Section 323(4); see **16.2**.

4   Section 323(3)(c).

5   Section 323(5).

6   *Company Directors: Regulating Conflicts of Interest and Formulating a Statement of Duties*, Law Com No 261, Scot Law Com No 173, Part 11. See generally, **16.24**. The Company Law Review Steering Group agreed.

payment, including the amount thereof, have been disclosed to the members[1] of the company and the proposal has been approved by the company. A director receiving such a payment in breach of the requirements is liable to repay it, and the directors responsible for its being made are also liable. However, the section covers only payments made to compensate for the loss of the office of director. It does not cover payments made to compensate for the loss of a position as employee or payments which the company is contractually obliged to make, for example compensation payable under the terms of a managing director's service contract.[2]

Section 313 imposes the same requirements in respect of payments made to a director by the company or any other person in connection with the transfer of the whole or any part of the undertaking or property of the company. A payment in breach of section 313 is unlawful and the director is deemed to have received it in trust for the company.

Section 314 deals with similar payments when made in connection with the transfer to any persons of all or any of the shares in the company resulting from any of the following types of takeover bid:

(1) an offer made to the general body of shareholders;
(2) an offer made by or on behalf of some other body corporate with a view to the company becoming its subsidiary or a subsidiary of its holding company;
(3) an offer made by or on behalf of an individual with a view to his obtaining the right to exercise or control the exercise of not less than one-third of the voting power at any general meeting of the company;
(4) any other offer which is conditional on acceptance to a given extent.

When such a payment is to be made to a director, the director is under a duty to take all reasonable steps to secure that particulars of it, including its amount, are included in or sent with any notice of the offer made for their shares which is given to any shareholders.[3] If this duty is not discharged or the making of the proposed payment is not approved as described below, any sum received by the director on account of the payment is deemed to have been received by him in trust for any persons who have sold their shares as a result of the offer, and the expenses incurred by him in distributing that sum among those persons must be borne by him and not retained out of that sum. The approval must be given, before the transfer of any shares in pursuance of the offer, by a meeting, summoned for the purpose, of the holders of the shares to which the offer relates and of other holders of shares of the same class as any of those shares.[4]

Section 316 supplements the above sections in important ways. First, in relation to all the sections, the payments referred to do not include any *bona fide* payment

---

1   Including members with no or restricted voting rights: *Re Duomatic Ltd* [1969] 2 Ch 365.
2   *Taupo Totara Timber Co v Rowe* [1978] AC 537, a Privy Council decision on the identically worded section 191 of the New Zealand Companies Act 1955, followed in Scotland in *Lander v Premier Pict Petroleum Ltd* [1998] BCC 248.
3   A fine may be imposed on a defaulting director and on any person who fails to include or send the particulars, having been properly required to do so by the director: section 314(3).
4   Section 315(1). If these are not all the members of the company and the articles make no provision for such a meeting, the provisions of the Act and of the articles relating to general meetings apply to this meeting, with, if appropriate, such modifications as the Secretary of State may direct: section 315(2). If the meeting is not quorate, and the adjourned meeting is similarly not quorate, the payment is deemed to have been approved for the purposes of the section: section 315(3).

by way of damages for breach of contract or by way of pension in respect of past services.[1] Secondly, avoidance of sections 313 to 315 is prohibited by the following provisions. Where, in proceedings for the recovery of any payment received by any person on trust by virtue of the sections, it is shown that: (a) the payment was made in pursuance of any arrangement entered into as part of the agreement for the transfer in question, or within one year before or two years after that agreement or the offer leading thereto; and (b) the company or any person to whom the transfer was made was privy to the arrangement, the payment is deemed, except in so far as the contrary is shown, to fall within the relevant section.[2] In addition, if, in connection with a transfer within either section: (a) the price to be paid to a director whose office is to be abolished or who is to retire from office for any shares held by him in the company is in excess of the price which could at the time have been obtained by other holders of the like shares; or (b) any valuable consideration is given to any such director, the excess or the money value of the consideration is deemed to be a payment made to him by way of compensation for loss of office or as consideration for or in connection with his retirement from office.[3] Finally, section 316(4) provides that nothing in sections 313 to 315 prejudices the operation of any rule of law requiring disclosure to be made of any payments within the sections or any other like payments.[4]

Even if a payment falling within these sections is duly approved, it can still be invalid if made gratuitously and not for the benefit of the company as a whole, in the absence of an express power in the memorandum.[5]

The Law Commissions[6] recommended a number of changes to sections 312 to 316. These include:

(1) greater disclosure of covenanted payments;[7]
(2) extending section 312 to cover uncovenanted payments for the loss of any office in the company or its group;[8]
(3) amending section 314 to cover unconditional takeover offers;[9]
(4) prohibiting the offeror from voting at meetings held under section 315;[10] and
(5) that all the sections should cover directors of the company's parent company.[11]

---

1   Section 316(3).
2   Section 316(1).
3   Section 316(2).
4   Eg disclosure in the accounts of compensation payments (see **14.10**).
5   *Gibson's Executor v Gibson* 1980 SLT 2. This is merely a particular application of the law as to corporate gifts (see **6.13**).
6   *Company Directors: Regulating Conflicts of Interest and Formulating a Statement of Duties*, Law Com No 261, Scot Law Com No 173. See generally, **16.24**. The Company Law Review Steering Group generally agreed with these recommendations.
7   Paragraphs 7.6 to 7.26. They do not recommend subjecting covenanted payments to the regime of approval under the sections (approving this aspect of the decision in *Taupo Totora Timber Co v Rowe*, footnote 2 at p 523).
8   Paragraphs 7.38 to 7.48, reversing one aspect of the decision in *Taupo Totara Timber Co v Rowe* above.
9   Paragraphs 7.57 to 7.59, but they do not recommend that section 314 covers schemes of arrangement under section 425 (see **19.17**) as there is adequate disclosure in such a case.
10 Paragraphs 7.60 to 7.65.
11 Paragraphs 7.68 to 7.72.

16.21 Duty with regard to competing

Despite the general strict rule that a director must avoid positions of conflict between his duty to the company and his own interest, there is no general prohibition against a director competing with his company, whether on his own account or by virtue of his being director of another company in the same field of business.[1] Further, in the absence of some special circumstance, a director commits no breach of duty merely because he takes steps so that, on ceasing to be a director, he can immediately set up in business in competition with the company or join a competitor of it.[2] This, however, is subject to any express agreement to the contrary between the director and the company, and, if the director is also an employee of the company, the court may in appropriate circumstances be prepared to imply into his contract of employment a term that he should not perform services for a competitor, even in his spare time.[3] In addition, of course, freedom to compete does not comprehend licence to disclose confidential information belonging to his company.[4]

It is not uncommon for a director to undertake, formally or informally, to act in accordance with the instructions of an 'outsider' or as representative of such an 'outsider'. This can arise when a holding company has nominee directors on the board of its subsidiary, or when the right to appoint a director is given to a class of shareholders or a debenture-holder or class of debenture-holders. It is not necessarily unlawful for a director to be in such a position, provided that he does not conceal his position, has the consent of the company,[5] preserves a substantial degree of independent discretion as to how he shall exercise his powers,[6] and, if a divergence occurs between the interests of the company and those of the 'outsider', does not subordinate the former to the latter as a means of resolving the conflict.[7] Directors cannot validly contract with an outsider as to how they will vote at future board meetings, but this does not preclude them from agreeing, in a contract entered into bona fide in the interests of the company, that they will take such further action as is necessary to carry out that contract.[8]

The potential responsibility of the 'outsider' for the acts of the directors was in issue in *Kuwait Asia Bank EC v National Mutual Life Nominees Ltd*,[9] where a bank held a beneficial interest in 40% of the issued shares of a company and had

---

1   *London v Mashonaland Exploration Co Ltd v New Mashonaland Exploration Co Ltd* [1891] WN 165, approved in *Bell v Lever Bros Ltd* [1932] AC 161 at 195–196 and followed by the majority of the Court of Appeal in *In Plus Group Ltd v Pyke* [2002] EWCA Civ 370, [2002] 2 BCLC 201. However, Sedley LJ (ibid at 222–227) expressed some doubts and compare *Scottish Co-operative Wholesale Society Ltd v Meyer* [1959] AC 324 at p 368 and, for a detailed analysis and trenchant criticism, see Christie, 'The Director's Fiduciary Duty Not to Compete' (1992) 55 MLR 506.

2   *Balston Ltd v Headline Filters Ltd* [1990] FSR 385; *Framlington Group plc v Anderson* [1995] 1 BCLC 475.

3   See, in particular, *Hivac Ltd v Park Royal Scientific Instruments Ltd* [1949] Ch 169. Such a term will not always be implied; ibid.

4   As to confidential information, see **16.8.1**.

5   See *Kregor v Hollins* [1913] 109 LT 225 at 231.

6   *Boulting v ACTAT* [1963] 2 QB 606 at 626–627; *Clark v Workman* [1920] Ir R 107.

7   See, in particular, *Scottish Co-operative v Meyer*, above. For useful comments on the position of nominee directors, see Boros (1989) 10 Co Law 211 and (1990) 11 Co Law 6, and Crutchfield (1991) 12 Co Law 136.

8   *Fulham Football Club Ltd v Cabra Estates plc* [1992] BCC 863 (CA), following the decision of the High Court of Australia in *Thorby v Goldberg* (1964) 112 CLR 597.

9   [1990] BCLC 868 (PC).

nominated two of its employees to be directors of the company. It was held that in the performance of their duties, the directors were bound to ignore the interests and wishes of the bank and could not plead any instruction from the bank as an excuse for any breach of their duties. In the absence of evidence that the bank had exploited its position and interfered with the affairs of the company, it was neither vicariously nor personally liable for any negligence of the directors.

16.22   Directors' duties of skill and care

The second major aspect of directors' duties concerns the standard of skill and care expected of a company director. Many of the reported cases on this question were decided around the end of the nineteenth century or in the early years of the twentieth century and hence really before the existence of 'professional' company directors. For this reason, perhaps, the standards imposed thereby are surprisingly low.[1] While a legal account of the duties of care and skill must still pay some attention to these decisions, there are a number of reasons why they may not in fact represent the present law. This matter is considered further in **16.22.1**.

With this qualification in mind, the starting-point is the judgment of Romer J in *Re City Equitable Fire Insurance Co Ltd*,[2] which contains a useful review of the early authorities and which reduced the principles found therein to three general propositions.

First, 'a director need not exhibit in the performance of his duties a greater degree of skill than may reasonably be expected from a person of his knowledge and experience'.[3] Thus there is no objective standard of the reasonable director. In one case,[4] a 'country gentleman' director failed to study a set of accounts and subsequently proposed a dividend which in fact was paid out of capital. He was absolved from liability for negligence because he could not be expected to realise the significance of the accounts. Such an extreme result seems unlikely nowadays, and if a director is also employed under a contract of service, it will in any event contain an implied term requiring him to show objectively reasonable skill in the performance of the duties.[5]

Secondly, 'A director is not bound to give continuous attention to the affairs of his company. His duties are of an intermittent nature to be performed at periodical board meetings... He is not, however, bound to attend all such meetings, though he ought to attend whenever, in the circumstances, he is reasonably able to do so.'[6] Clearly this proposition, like the first, will often be expressly or impliedly displaced. In accordance with it, in one early case,[7] a 'figurehead' director, who never attended board meetings and who therefore

1   For general critiques, see Finch, 'Company Directors: Who Cares about Skill and Care?' (1992) 55 MLR 179 and Riley, 'The Company Director's Duty of Care and Skill: the Case for an Onerous but Subjective Standard' (1999) 62 MLR 697. See also the recommendations of the Law Commissions discussed at **16.24**.
2   [1925] Ch 407 (affirmed ibid on other grounds by CA).
3   Ibid at p 428. It was often said that a director was liable only for 'gross negligence'.
4   *Re Denham & Co* (1883) 25 Ch D 752.
5   Cf *Lister v Romford Ice & Cold Storage Co Ltd* [1957] AC 555, where a term of this nature was read into the service contract of an ordinary employee. See also *Jackson v Invicta Plastics Ltd* [1987] BCLC 329 at 347, comparing the duty of care owed by a director with that owed by an employee.
6   [1925] Ch 407 at 429.
7   *Re Cardiff Savings Bank, The Marquis of Bute's Case* [1892] 2 Ch 100.

failed to prevent the active director conducting the company's affairs improperly, was held not to have been negligent. Such a result is perhaps unlikely these days.[1]

Thirdly, 'In respect of all duties that, having regard to the exigencies of business, and the articles of association, may properly be left to some other official, a director is, in the absence of grounds for suspicion, justified in trusting that official to perform such duties honestly.'[2] Thus directors have escaped liability where subordinates to whom they properly delegated functions relating to the company's finances misrepresented the company's financial position, with the result that the directors paid or recommended the payment of dividends out of capital.[3] It must be stressed, however, that there must be no grounds for suspicion, and the director who, having delegated a function, keeps an eye on its performance, cannot maintain that he did not know what was going on.[4]

It should be noted that a director is not the agent of his co-directors,[5] and the other officers of the company are not the agents of the directors.[6] Thus the mere fact that a director or officer is liable for breach of duty does not of itself render the remaining directors liable. Their liability can be established only if it can be shown that they were negligent in accordance with the standards of skill and care expected of them, or if they participated, however slightly,[7] in the breach, or sanctioned the conduct constituting the breach.

16.22.1 *Modern developments in respect of the duties of care and skill*

There are echoes of the propositions found in *Re City Equitable Fire Insurance Co Ltd*[8] in more recent authorities, but it seems that the law is fast moving towards a more objective and thus demanding standard of care and skill for company directors. As already mentioned, an objective standard of care and skill will be required in any event of a director employed under a contract of service, that is an executive director, so that the discussion here is concerned solely with the position of non-executive directors.

In *Dorchester Finance Co Ltd v Stebbing*,[9] Foster J applied the propositions laid down in *Re City Equitable Fire Insurance Co Ltd*, but held that non-executive directors

---

1   See *Dorchester Finance Co Ltd v Stebbing* [1989] BCLC 498, where failure to participate in the company's activities and the resulting failure to discover the defaults of the managing director on the part of the directors in question were regarded as negligent, and *Re Simmon Box (Diamonds) Ltd* [2000] BCC 275; see **16.22.1**.

2   [1925] Ch 407 at p 429. See also the discussion in two recent cases which concerned the permissibility of delegation in the context of applications for the disqualification of directors for unfitness under section 6 of the Company Directors Disqualification Act 1986 (see **15.16.4**): *Re Westmid Packing Services Ltd* [1998] 2 BCLC 646 at 653 (CA) and *Re Barings plc* [1999] 1 BCLC 433 at 486–489.

3   See, in particular, *Dovey v Cory* [1901] AC 477.

4   Cf *Department of Health and Social Security v Wayte* [1972] 1 WLR 19.

5   *Cargill v Bower* (1878) 10 Ch D 502; *Re Denham & Co* (1883) 25 Ch D 752.

6   *Weir v Barnett* (1877) 3 Ex D 32; *Weir v Bell* (1878) 3 Ex D 238 (CA).

7   See, especially, *Re Lands Allotment Co* [1894] 1 Ch 617 (CA), where a chairman of directors, who signed the minutes relating to an ultra vires investment of company funds and announced the investment to the company in general meeting in terms indicating his assent thereto, was held liable as a participant in this misapplication of company funds. See also *Ramskill v Edwards* (1885) 31 Ch D 100 and *Bishopsgate Invesment Management Ltd v Maxwell* [1993] BCC 120 (CA).

8   [1925] Ch 407.

9   [1989] BCLC 498 (decided in 1977, although unreported until 1989).

who were either qualified accountants or who had considerable accountancy and business experience had been negligent in signing blank cheques which allowed the managing director to misappropriate the company's money. This indicates recognition of the concept of the professional director, although, in contrast, the legislature declined the opportunity to impose an objective standard on some company directors,[1] and more recently the Privy Council[2] cited *Re City Equitable Fire Insurance Co Ltd* with approval.[3]

On the other hand, section 214 of the Insolvency Act 1986[4] requires a director to display a higher standard of skill and care lest he be found liable for wrongful trading. The section refers to the conduct of 'a reasonably diligent person having both – (a) the general knowledge, skill and experience that may reasonably be expected of a person carrying out the same functions as are carried out by that director in relation to the company, and (b) the general knowledge, skill and experience that that director has'. Although of course liability for wrongful trading can be imposed only when the company is in insolvent liquidation, this provision has been cited in two recent decisions[5] as an accurate statement of the director's common-law duty of care and skill. This does not mean, though, that, for example, a director will not be able to rely upon others. In the first of these cases,[6] it was held that, provided he observed the standard laid down in section 214, a director was entitled to trust people in positions of responsibility until there was reason to distrust them. So a director was not liable for the theft of company money by someone who was a senior partner in an eminent firm of solicitors when he had no reason to doubt the other's honesty. In contrast, in *Re D'Jan of London Ltd*,[7] a director who signed an insurance proposal form without checking its contents was regarded as negligent. In *Re Simmon Box (Diamonds) Ltd*,[8] the only director of the company, who abjectly surrendered to the person who acted as de facto director, was held to have been negligent, as was the director in *Re Westlowe Storage and Distribution Ltd*,[9] who failed to ensure that the company benefited properly from the transactions it was engaged in when it was his responsibility to ensure that a proper accounting system was in place.

Further support for the view that the courts are likely to impose a higher standard of care and skill on directors than a simple reading of the old authorities would suggest is found in some of the case-law on the question of whether or not a

---

1   The Supply of Goods (Exclusion of Implied Terms) Order 1982, SI 1982/1771 excludes from section 13 of the Supply of Goods and Services Act 1982, which lays down a generally objective standard of skill and care in contracts for the supply of a service, the services rendered to a company by a director of the company in his capacity as such. Section 13 would have applied anyway only to directors appointed under a contract. The exclusion cannot affect the duties owed by a director in some other capacity, eg as employee (see above).

2   *Kuwait Asia Bank EC v National Mutual Life Nominees Ltd* [1990] BCLC 868 at 892.

3   Even repeating the proposition that directors were only liable for gross negligence.

4   Especially subsection (4)(a); see **15.17.2**.

5   *Norman v Theodore Goddard* [1991] BCLC 1028 at 1030–1031, *per* Hoffmann J; *Re D'Jan of London Ltd* [1993] BCC 646 at 648 *per* Hoffmann LJ. A similar analogy with the statutory provisions dealing with insolvency has been drawn in Australia, in consequence bringing an objective standard to the duties of care and skill (including the duties of non-executive directors): see *Daniels v Anderson* (1995) 16 ACSR 607 (NSWCA).

6   *Norman v Theodore Goddard*, above. See also *Equitable Life Assurance Society v Bowley* [2003] EWHC 2263 (Comm), [2004] 1 BCLC 180.

7   Above.

8   [2000] BCC 275.

9   [2000] BCC 851.

director should be disqualified for unfitness under section 6 of the Company Directors Disqualification Act 1986.[1]

16.23 Factors relieving a director from liability for breach of duty

There are a number of ways in which a director who is prima facie liable for a breach of directors' duties may be relieved from such liability. These are examined in the following sections.

16.23.1 Ratification by the general meeting

As already indicated at various stages of this chapter, a breach of duty by a director may often, but not always, be 'cured' through his conduct being disclosed to the general meeting and ratified thereat by the passing of an ordinary resolution.[2] The notice summoning a meeting for this purpose should make it clear that the purpose or one of the purposes of the meeting is to sanction the relevant conduct of the director; if it does not, the notice may be held insufficient and the resolution ineffective.[3] However, the director may vote upon any shares that he holds in favour of his conduct being sanctioned, provided that this does not constitute 'fraud' or 'oppression'.[4]

The dividing line between those breaches of duty which are capable of ratification and those which are not is not at all easy to draw. Some types of breach have been expressly established as ratifiable,[5] namely failing to disclose an interest in a contract to which the company is a party,[6] obtaining a secret profit not involving a misapplication of company property,[7] negligence,[8] and using a

---

1   See especially *Re Landhurst Leasing plc* [1999] 1 BCLC 286 at 344, *Re Barings plc* [1999] 1 BCLC 433 at 486 to 489. See Walters, 'Directors duties: the impact of the Company Directors Disqualification Act 1986' (2000) 21 Co Law 110.

2   Ratification should be distinguished from an exercise of power by the general meeting where the meeting validly performs the relevant act itself, as opposed to approving its prior performance by the board. The distinction is brought out in a comparison between the first instance judgment of Plowman J and the judgments of the Court of Appeal in *Bamford v Bamford* [1970] Ch 242. The *locus standi* of a minority shareholder to challenge the validity of the resolution may well turn upon the distinction; see **17.6**. For an interesting article challenging the conventional view of ratification and arguing that, as opposed to a prospective release from liability, it can bind only the minority and not the company unless the director provides consideration or it is given under seal, see Partridge (1987) 46 CLJ 122.

3   *Kaye v Croydon Tramways Co* [1898] 1 Ch 358 (CA).

4   See in particular *North-West Transportation Co v Beatty* (1887) 12 App Cas 589 (PC); *Burland v Earle* [1902] AC 83 at 94 (PC); *Northern Counties Securities Ltd v Jackson & Steeple Ltd* [1974] 1 WLR 1133 at 1146. Cf, however, the views of Vinelott J in *Prudential Assurance Co Ltd v Newman Industries Ltd (No 2)* [1980] 2 All ER 841 at 862–863. The question of 'fraud on the minority' is discussed in more detail at **17.4**.

5   In addition, acting in excess of power, though intra vires the company, is ratifiable, whether a breach of duty or not: *Irvine v Union Bank of Australia* (1877) 2 App Cas 366 (PC); *Grant v United Kingdom Switchback Railways* (1880) 40 Ch D 135 (CA).

6   *North-West Transportation Co v Beatty*, above.

7   *Regal (Hastings) Ltd v Gulliver* [1967] 2 AC 134n (HL).

8   *Pavlides v Jensen* [1956] Ch 565.

power for an improper purpose.[1] In all cases, there is an overriding qualification that the director must have acted *bona fide* in the interest of the company.[2]

The following breaches of duty are not capable of ratification by the general meeting:[3]

(1) one involving a lack of *bona fides* on the part of the director;[4]
(2) one resulting in the company performing an illegal or *ultra vires* act;[5]
(3) one resulting in the company performing an act which, although lawful and *intra vires*, cannot be done under the articles without some special procedure such as a special resolution;
(4) one bearing directly upon the 'personal rights' of individual shareholders, as defined in the articles;[6]
(5) one involving a 'fraud on the minority', that is whereby a majority of the shareholders or the directors succeed in expropriating at the expense of the minority the 'money, property, or advantages' of the company.[7]

16.23.2 Ratification by the consent of all members

It is clear that any breach of duty by directors which is ratifiable by ordinary resolution, as described above, is equally ratifiable by the informal approval of every member who would have the right to vote on such a resolution.[8] However, there are *dicta* in recent cases indicating that the principle of unanimous approval goes further than this and that, whether given before or following the breach, it is effective to relieve a director from liability for *any* breach of duty, provided only that the breach is not *ultra vires* the company and does not involve a fraud on its creditors.[9] Such a fraud[10] seems likely to arise only when a company is in danger of going out of business in an insolvent state.

---

1 *Alexander v Automatic Telephone Co* [1990] 2 Ch 56 at 67 (CA); *Hogg v Cramphorn Ltd* [1967] Ch 254; *Bamford v Bamford*, above. If the impropriety was an improper allotment of shares, as in the latter two cases, the votes on the improperly allotted shares should not be used on the resolution.

2 This is expressed in most of the cases cited above and is supported by *Daniels v Daniels* [1978] Ch 406 in respect of liability for negligence.

3 For a fuller discussion in the context of minority shareholders' actions where the question is of paramount importance, see **17.2–17.4**.

4 *Attwool v Merryweather* (1867) LR 5 Dq 46n; *Mason v Harris* (1879) 11 Ch D 97 (CA).

5 *Re Exchange Banking Co Flitcroft's Case* (1882) 21 Ch D 519 (CA).

6 Eg, refusal to register a transfer of shares for an improper purpose.

7 *Burland v Earle* [1902] AC 83 at 93 (PC). See also especially, *Cook v Deeks* [1916] 1 AC 554 (PC), the facts of which were given at **16.8.1** and *Shaker v Al-Bedrawi* [2002] EWCA Civ 1452, [2003] 1 BCLC 157 at 198. Cf *Regal (Hastings) Ltd v Gulliver*, above, discussed in **16.18.1** where the opportunity to make the profit was not 'expropriated' from the company and the breach was ratifiable. There are, however, difficulties with this analysis: see *Gore-Browne on Companies* 44th edn (Jordans, loose-leaf) at 27.21.1; Davies, *Gower's Principles of Modern Company Law* 6th edn (Sweet & Maxwell, 1997), pp 644–648; Wedderburn [1957] CLJ 194 and [1958] CLJ 93; Sealy [1967] CLJ 83 at 102 *et seq*; Beck, in Ziegel (ed), *Canadian Company Law*, vol II, pp 232–238.

8 *Re Duomatic Ltd* [1969] 2 Ch 365; *Re Gee & Co (Woolwich) Ltd* [1975] Ch 52, see **13.2**.

9 *Re Horsley and Weight Ltd* [1982] Ch 442 (CA) at 454; *Multinational Gas and Petrochemical Co v Multinational Gas and Petrochemical Services Ltd* [1983] Ch 258 (CA) at 269 and 289–290; *Rolled Steel Products Ltd v British Steel Corporation* [1984] BCLC 466 (CA) at 508–509.

10 Eg, the taking of excessive remuneration by directors as in *Re Halt Garage (1964) Ltd* [1982] 3 All ER 1016.

This principle seems acceptable in theory, given that ratification in this context means simply the company's waiving of its right to sue a director. It is obviously perfectly proper for a fully informed company to take such a decision in respect of any breach of duty, subject to the qualifications mentioned.

As regards breaches of duty which are beyond the capacity of the company, account must also be taken of section 35.[1] Although section 35(1) abolishes the effect of *ultra vires* as far as third parties are concerned, section 35(3) expressly preserves the duty of directors 'to observe any limitations on their powers flowing from the company's memorandum'. Further, action which but for subsection (1) would be beyond the capacity of the company may be ratified by special resolution, but such ratification does not affect any liability incurred by the directors; relief from such liability must be agreed to separately by special resolution. It is clear therefore that a breach of duty which consists only of directors exceeding their powers under the memorandum is ratifiable (or can be relieved, to use the statutory language) by special resolution. It seems arguable that another effect of the statute is to make such breaches ratifiable by the consent of all members.[2] It would be odd for the law to require the formality of a special resolution in the face of the fully informed consent of all members and the subsection does not expressly contain the requirement of a general meeting. On the other hand, the first part of section 35(3), referring to ratification in the sense of approval of an act rather than relief from liability, does state that such ratification can be given only by special resolution, and the second part uses the word 'must'.

It is submitted, however, that if the directors' breach of duty involves more than merely an excess of their powers under the memorandum, it is not necessarily ratifiable by special resolution. If the breach is otherwise ratifiable by ordinary resolution,[3] then clearly the *ultra vires* nature of it can be cured under section 35(3). However, if it is not so ratifiable, it is thought that only the unanimous consent of the members will suffice.

16.23.3 Provisions in the articles

Section 310 makes void any provision, whether contained in the articles of the company or any contract with the company or otherwise, for exempting any officer of the company or any person (whether an officer or not) employed by the company as auditor from, or indemnifying him against, any liability which by virtue of any rule of law would otherwise attach to him in respect of any negligence, default or breach of duty or breach of trust of which he may be guilty in relation to the company.[4] Until an amendment made by the Companies Act 1989,[5] it was arguable that section 310 rendered void policies of professional indemnity insurance effected by companies on behalf of their directors and officers.[6] To cure the uncertainty in the face of a growing demand and market for

---

1 See **6.11**.
2 A statutory written resolution (see **13.4.1**) could be used by private companies.
3 As described in **16.23.1**.
4 Only an exemption or indemnity provided by the company, not one provided by a third party, is caught by the section: *Burgoine v London Borough of Waltham Forest* [1997] BCC 347.
5 Section 137.
6 There has never been any concern about liability insurance effected and paid for by directors themselves.

this type of insurance,[1] section 310(3)(a) now provides that the section does not prevent a company from purchasing and maintaining for any officer or auditor insurance against the liabilities in subsection (1).[2] Further, a company is permitted to indemnify any officer who is a successful defendant in civil or criminal proceedings or who successfully applies for relief under section 144[3] or section 727.[4]

Exactly what provisions in articles section 310 covers has been the subject of much academic debate,[5] but for many years there was no relevant case-law. The problem arose because Table A, the model form of articles of association, contains provisions, in both its 1948 and 1985 versions, which do appear to modify and even in part exclude the duties of directors; in the 1985 Table A, these are articles 85 and 94; in the 1948 Table A, which will continue to apply to many registered companies, they are articles 78 and 84. Clearly, these articles must be valid as they have statutory authority.[6] The problem is whether, and if so to what extent, articles adopted by companies which do not follow them exactly are valid.

The problem arose for the first time judicially in *Movitex Ltd v Bulfield*.[7] Here the company in question had articles similar to but slightly more extensive than article 84 of the 1948 Table A. These allowed a director to have interests in and profit from transactions in which the company was interested, provided that he disclosed his interest to his fellow director and, in most instances, did not vote on the matter or, if he did vote, that his presence was not to be counted in the quorum.[8] However, in certain circumstances, a director could vote and be so counted.[9]

Vinelott J held that the articles were valid and did not infringe section 205 of the 1984 Act (now section 310). In doing so, he recognised that there was a difficult point of construction to be resolved in reconciling the articles with the section. He rejected the argument that articles could rewrite the content of directors' duties so long as they did not purport to exempt directors from liability for breaches of duty not ratifiable by the general meeting or from breaches of duties stemming from a mandatory rule of statute. He reasoned, applying *dicta* of Megarry V-C in *Tito v Waddell*[10] that the general principle forbidding directors (and others in fiduciary positions) from putting themselves in a position where their duty to the company might conflict with their own interest was not a *duty* in the strict sense of

---

1   For a very useful review, see Finch, 'Personal Accountability and Corporate Control: the Role of Directors' and Officers' Liability Insurance' (1994) 57 MLR 880.
2   This does not automatically validate all such insurance so that, eg, indemnity against the deliberate commission of a breach of duty could be unenforceable on public policy grounds; see Birds *Modern Insurance Law* 4th edn (Sweet & Maxwell, 1997), Chapter 12. The existence of any insurance of this sort must be disclosed in the directors' report: Schedule 7, Part 1, para 5A.
3   See **7.16**.
4   See **16.23.4**.
5   See Baker [1975] JBL 181; Birds (1976) 39 MLR 394; Parkinson [1981] JBL 335; Gregory (1982) 98 LQR 413.
6   This point was not, however, made in *Movitex Ltd v Bulfield*, discussed below, where Vincent J was at pains to reconcile what is now section 310 and the relevant articles in Table A, implying that if he could not do so, the articles in Table A would be invalid: *sed quaere*.
7   (1986) 2 BCC 99, 403; for a fuller discussion, see Birds (1987) 8 Co Law 31.
8   See **16.12**.
9   Cf article 84(2) of the 1948 Table A and article 94 of the 1985 Table A. The difference from these provisions was that the number of circumstances where voting was allowed was greater.
10 [1977] 3 All ER 129 at 247.

the word, but simply a disability. It thus did not fall within the wording of section 310. The company could exclude the general principle in its articles, providing in effect that specified situations did not give rise to a conflict of duty and interest, provided that it did not exclude the duties of directors properly so-called.

On this analysis, it would seem that the non-excludable *duties* of directors are those obligations which seek to prevent a director from damaging the interests of the company. These probably comprehend the primary duties of good faith and proper purpose,[1] the duty to show proper care and skill, the duty not to misappropriate company property, and any statutory duty imposed on directors. However, the general rule imposing accountability for secret profits, as well as that avoiding a transaction involving a conflict of duty and interest, would, on Vinelott J's analysis, be excludable, so long as the director acts in good faith.[2] It is submitted that this result is acceptable as a matter of policy,[3] although it must be recognised that the distinction between duties and disabilities drawn in *Tito v Waddell* and relied on in *Movitex Ltd v Bulfield* has increasingly been questioned in recent case-law in the Court of Appeal.[4] On this basis, perhaps, Vinelott J's analysis could be challenged. On the other hand, there are recent authorities[5] where the validity of articles similar to those in issue in *Movitex Ltd v Bulfield*, which have not followed exactly those in Table A, has not been challenged on the basis that they infringe section 310.

---

1   Although as the proper purposes doctrine (see **16.7**) is derived from the articles, it must in principle be excludable in the sense that the articles can define the range of purposes in respect of which a power is properly exercisable; see Birds (1976) 39 MLR 394 at p 400.

2   Indeed, Vinelott J expressly held that article 78 of the 1948 Table A, which excludes accountability for secret profits in a particular situation, was consistent with what is now section 310. He seems to have assumed that liability for secret profits (as to which see **16.18** *et seq*) is imposed only when there is a conflict of duty and interest, but this is not the case as the speeches in *Regal (Hastings) Ltd v Gulliver* [1942] 1 All ER 378 make clear; simply, a director is under a duty to account for a secret profit obtained by use of his position. It could be argued that this is a duty which is subject to section 310 and thus non-excludable. Article 78 was perhaps a statutory aberration; it was not replaced in exactly the same form in the 1985 Table A – instead of excluding a duty to account totally, part of article 85 of the 1985 Table A excludes it only if the director has disclosed his profit to his fellow directors, thus making the subject-matter of the former article 78 subject to the same requirement as directors' interests in contracts, etc (see **16.12**).

3   It may also accord with the intentions of the Greene Committee (Cmnd 2627, 1925, paragraphs 46 and 47), who recommended the introduction of what is now section 310, although it is somewhat difficult to discern their intention other than that clauses excusing directors' liability for negligence should be outlawed. Vinelott J's conclusion, though not his reasoning, is similar to that reached by Parkinson, op cit, footnote 5 at p 532.

4   *Gwembe Valley Development Co Ltd v Koshy* [2003] EWCA Civ 1048, [2004] 1 BCLC 131 at paragraphs 104 to 108, referring to the earlier Court of Appeal analyses of the fiduciary's duty of loyalty in *Paragon Finance plc v DB Thakerar & Co* [1999] 1 All ER 400, and *JJ Harrison (Properties) Ltd v Harrison* [2001] EWCA Civ 1467, [2002] 1 BCLC 162. The Law Commission commented that the decision in *Movitex Ltd v Bulfield* 'does draw very difficult distinctions' (*Shareholder Remedies*, Law Com No 246, 1997, paragraph 6.26). The effect of the Review of Company Law is likely to be the replacement of section 310 by more specific provisions: see *Modern Company Law for a Competitive Economy: Developing the Framework*, March 2000, paragraph 3.74.

5   Including *Gwembe Valley Development Co Ltd v Koshy*.

16.23.4 *Discretionary relief from liability by the court*

Section 727(1) of the Companies Act 1985[1] allows the court which has found a director or other officer[2] liable for negligence, default, breach of duty or breach of trust to relieve him from liability, wholly or partly, on such terms as it thinks fit, provided and only provided that the director establishes the three distinct matters specified in the section, namely:

(1) that he acted honestly;
(2) that he acted reasonably; and
(3) that, having regard to all the circumstances, he 'ought fairly to be excused'.

It is possible for a director to succeed on the first two points, yet fail on the third, which is a matter for the court's discretion in each case.[3]

16.24 Enforcement of civil liabilities against directors

It is all very well for the law to impose what are generally strict duties on company directors, as described in the previous pages of this chapter. What may well be much more important in practice is that the law provides effective ways in which breach of those duties can be remedied. While the company can always take action, that is, for obvious reasons, not likely in many cases in practice. For that reason, and despite the fact that, as we have seen,[4] a director's duties are generally owed only to the company itself, in certain circumstances a minority shareholder may be able to institute proceedings. These circumstances are fully explored in the next chapter.

When a company is in liquidation, a breach of duty will be much easier to litigate since the liquidator will in general have the conduct of the action in the company's name. Further, if the breach falls within section 212 of the Insolvency Act 1986,[5] he, or the Official Receiver, or any creditor or contributory, may instead be able to invoke the simpler procedure of a summons in the liquidation.

If a director dies, his estate remains liable for any breach of duty he may have committed, including any wrongful dealing with the company's property such as a payment of dividend out of capital or sale of its assets at an undervalue.[6] A discharge in bankruptcy does not release a director from liability for a fraudulent breach of duty[7] or a claim for a refund of secret profits, for the retention of them is a breach of trust.[8] The company can prove in the bankrupt estate for the secret profit.

If two or more directors are implicated in the same breach of duty, their liability is joint and several: accordingly, if in the same transaction they have each

---

1 Cf the equivalent section 61 of the Trustee Act 1925, from which this provision was adapted.
2 Or an auditor.
3 *Re J Franklin & Son Ltd* [1937] 2 All ER 32. See further as to section 727, *Gore-Browne on Companies* 44th edn (Jordans, loose-leaf) at 27.21.5 and for a very useful review of recent case law, Edmunds and Lowry, 'The continuing value of relief for directors' breach of duty', (2003) 66 MLR 195. It is curious that the section was not at least pleaded in *Regal (Hastings) Ltd v Gulliver* [1967] 2 AC 134n (HL) (see **16.18.1**), the facts of which look like the sort of case where relief should be considered: see Birds (1976) 39 MLR 394 at 397.
4 See **16.3**.
5 See **15.17.4**.
6 *Ramskill v Edwards* (1885) 31 Ch D 100; *Re Sharpe* [1892] 1 Ch 154 (CA).
7 Insolvency Act 1986, section 281(3).
8 See *Emma Silver Mining Co v Grant* (1881) 17 Ch D 122.

misappropriated company assets, each of them is liable for the total amount so misappropriated by himself and his co-directors.[1] If one of them has been rendered liable, he can usually recover contributions from any of the other directors who were responsible also.[2]

16.25 Reform of the law on directors' duties

As will be clear by now, various proposals have been made or are under consideration to reform the law governing directors' duties in a number of respects. It could be said that there are three major problems with the law in this area. The first, namely, the complexity and overlap of the many and varied rules governing directors' fiduciary duties, will be evident from the account given in this chapter. This makes the law difficult to comprehend for the lawyer, never mind the often-untrained company director. Few would probably argue that it is unnecessary to have strict fiduciary duties, but it is not at all clear that they require such a mass of legal rules. The second major problem could be said to relate to the relatively low standard of care and skill required of a company director by the law, although as we have seen (**16.23.1**), the courts are by themselves in effect reforming the law in this area. The third relates to the fundamental duty to act honestly 'in the interests of the company'. Many argue that a test which gives particular primacy to the interests of shareholders needs reformulating in modern times, although whether the reformulation proposed by the Company Law Review Steering Group and accepted by the Government will effect any real change must be open to doubt, as discussed in **11.6**.

It is certain that the result of the Review of Company Law[3] will result in changes, building on the work of the Law Commissions' Report of 1999 – *Company Directors: Regulating Conflicts of Interests and Formulating a Statement of Duties.*[4] Although most of the Law Commissions' detailed recommendations have already been mentioned at the appropriate points in this chapter, there are some general considerations arising out of their Report and the subsequent work of the Company Law Review that this section seeks briefly to address.

The Law Commissions' Report was a valuable review of many aspects of the law governing directors' duties.[5] It built on the earlier English Law Commission Report on *Shareholder Remedies,*[6] which is considered in Chapter 17, in particular by identifying the 'guiding principles' for law reform in this area, referring also to the principles identified in the Review. In the context of directors' duties, the headline principles are identified as:

(1) accessibility of the law;
(2) certainty;
(3) graduated regulation of conflicts of interests; and
(4) efficient disclosure.[7]

---

1   See, eg, *Re Carriage Co-operative Supply Association* (1884) 27 Ch D 322.
2   See generally, *Ramskill v Edwards*, above.
3   See generally, **1.7** and Chapter 22.
4   Law Com No 261, Scot Law Com No 173.
5   As to their use of economic analysis, see **1.9**. See further for varied comments on the Report, *Directors' Conflicts of Interests*, Andenas and Sugarman (eds) (Kluwer, 2000).
6   LC No 246, 1998.
7   See Part 3 of the Report. 'Efficiency' has much to do with the economic analysis relied upon in the Report; see the comments in **1.8**.

The meaning of principles 1 and 2 is fairly self-evident. Principle 3 implies that the law should range from:

(a) prohibiting certain transactions where there is a real risk of prejudice to persons other than directors or shareholders; to

(b) requiring shareholder approval of matters where there is a risk of prejudice to shareholders; to

(c) disclosure after the event to shareholders; and to

(d) disclosure to the board before the event, provided that this is efficient.

Principle 4 should exclude disclosure of what is immaterial, but also ensure that directors and shareholders receive the information they need to exercise their respective functions.

In line with these principles, the Commissions' first recommendation[1] was for a partial codification of directors' duties. They favoured a non-exhaustive codification drafted in clear language to make the law more accessible and coherent. The statement would also be set out on the statutory forms that must be completed when a director is appointed[2] with an acknowledgement by a director that he has read the statement and it was thought that the DTI should also consider the production of pamphlets explaining directors' duties. It is thought that the arguments in favour of these changes were persuasive and, perhaps, that the Law Commissions were right to reject arguments in favour of full codification of directors' duties, primarily on the ground that it would affect the dynamic development of the law. However, the Company Law Review Steering Group took a rather different view. They favoured an exhaustive code, stating:[3]

> We have not been able to think of any new principles, nor areas where it is desirable to leave scope for the judges to develop completely new ones. There would also be an objection of principle to the judges inventing wholly new bases of liability for company directors, with retrospective effect, rather than new obligations being imposed prospectively and after democratic debate by Parliament. We are therefore inclined to favour the proposed restatement being treated as exhaustive. Our view at this stage is that the restatement should set out all the general duties which apply to directors in the exercise of their functions as such. The only other duties which apply to them will be those which are imposed by other provisions of the legislation.

They maintained this view through to their Final Report and it was accepted by the Government in the White Paper, *Modernising Company Law*.[4] Although some will continue to have doubts about the sense and feasibility of having an exhaustive code,[5] it now seems inevitable that such a code will appear in the next Companies Bill.[6] This will include the second major recommendation made by the Law Commissions,[7] namely codification of the duty of care and skill along the same lines as section 214 of the Insolvency Act 1986.[8] As noted earlier,[9] the modern law

---

1   Part 4 of the Report.

2   Forms 10 and 288a; see **4.5** and **15.19**.

3   See *Developing the Framework*, at paragraph 3.82.

4   Cm 5335, July 2002, paragraph 3.5.

5   See for example Worthington, 'Reforming Directors' Duties', (2001) 64 MLR 439; Birds, 'The Reform of Directors' Duties' in De Lacy (ed) *The Reform of UK Company Law* (Cavendish, 2002).

6   A draft was included in the draft Bill appended to the White Paper.

7   Part 5 of the Report.

8   As to section 214, see **15.17.2**.

9   See **16.23.1**.

has probably now adopted this mixed subjective/objective standard, but it seems obviously sensible to make the position absolutely clear in statutory form.[1]

The bulk of the Law Commissions' Report was concerned with the detailed statutory duties in Part X. On consultation, they raised the question whether some sections in this Part could be repealed on the ground that in effect they duplicated what the general law would provide anyway.[2] The responses supported their view that there was no case for such a general repeal, primarily because the provisions in Part X provide protection that is superior to the general law. None the less, they considered that some provisions could be safely repealed.[3] Further, they proposed a fairly large number of amendments to improve the law and these have been noted at the appropriate places earlier in this chapter. Most of them are to satisfy the principle of efficient disclosure and were supported by the Company Law Review Steering Group and the Government. A further important point, which was referred to the general review for further consideration, was that there should be a single code of remedies and effects to replace what they describe as the 'bewildering variety of civil sanctions' applying to the provisions of Part X.[4] It is expected that an attempt to provide this as part of a general codification of remedies will be made in the promised Companies Bill, although this is a far from easy task.

---

1   The introduction of a 'business judgment' rule was rejected. This is a rule, developed in the United States (and a form of which has just been introduced in Australia), which absolves a director from liability for negligence if he is not interested in the subject of the business judgment, he is informed about it to the extent that he reasonably believes is appropriate and he reasonably believes that it is in the best interests of the corporation.
2   And in the case of listed companies by the *Listing Rules*.
3   Namely sections 311 (see **15.3**), 381(5) and (11) (see **15.21**) and 323 (see **16.19**).
4   See Part 15 of the Report.

Chapter 17

Shareholders' Remedies

17.1 Introduction

This chapter is concerned with various remedies available to minority shareholders. Such remedies are in practical terms the only effective way of enforcing directors' and controlling shareholders' duties (outside the context of the company's liquidation). It will be seen that these remedies are also very much concerned with actions or conduct by the company or its officers which infringe the rights, or prejudice the interests, of individual shareholders or groups of shareholders. The first part of this chapter is concerned with the rule in *Foss v Harbottle*[1] and the minority shareholders' actions which are allowed by exception to it.

The second part of this chapter deals with two interrelated statutory remedies. A member of a company may petition on the ground of unfair prejudice under Part XVII of the Companies Act 1985 or petition to have the company wound up on the 'just and equitable' ground now contained in section 122(1)(g) of the Insolvency Act 1986.

It will be seen that well-justified minority shareholders' complaints are still thwarted by the undue technicality and doctrinal obscurity of the *Foss v Harbottle* rule. It is true that the statutory minority remedies now rest upon a broader and more liberal judicial discretion, the use of which has much improved the lot of minority shareholders in small or medium-sized private companies. However, their beneficial effect is largely confined to such companies, as these remedies are not an appropriate way of coping with corporate abuse or gross incompetence in public listed companies. In response to many criticisms over the years, the Department of Trade and Industry referred the issue of the enforcement of shareholders' rights and remedies to the Law Commission in December 1994. Their Report[2] proposes replacing the common law derivative action with a statutory derivative action, essentially giving the court power to grant leave for such an action subject to specified guidelines.[3] The Department of Trade and Industry has broadly supported the recommendations,[4] and it may be expected that changes will emanate from the current Review of Company Law.[5]

The last part of this chapter is concerned with the Department of Trade and Industry's range of powers to investigate companies. This may be done informally by civil servants or by the formal appointment of inspectors. The Department is

---

1   (1843) 2 Hare 461.
2   *Shareholder Remedies*, Report No 246, 1997, Cm 3769.
3   These are outlined in **17.10.1**. The Report also proposes changes to the statutory unfair prejudice remedy; see footnote 8 at p 557.
4   *Shareholder Remedies, A Consultative Document*, November 1998, URN 98/994. See further *Modern Company Law for a Competitive Economy: Developing the Framework*, paragraph 4.65, *Completing the Structure*, paragraph 6.5.87, *Final Report*, paragraph 7.48 and *Modernising Company Law*, Cm 5553–1 (July 2002), 3.18.
5   See generally, **1.7** and Chapter 22.

also given the power to follow up its investigation by bringing various types of civil proceedings. While these powers are more than ample in terms of the letter of the law, their use has been much restrained by the customary bureaucratic caution and inertia. These habits tend only to be set aside where a clear *prima facie* case of serious corporate abuse, already publicised in the press, affects the affairs of a public listed company. Even then it is the powers to investigate the affairs of the company (or the ownership of or dealings in its shares) that are likely to be employed. The powers to bring civil proceedings are almost never used. The power to wind up already failed or defunct public companies is occasionally resorted to.

PART 1: MINORITY SHAREHOLDERS' ACTIONS

17.2 The rule in *Foss v Harbottle*

There is a general principle of company law[1] that minority shareholders cannot sue for wrongs done to their company or complain of irregularities in the conduct of its internal affairs. This principle has come to be known as the rule in *Foss v Harbottle*,[2] from the decision in which it was first clearly established. The cases[3] show that this rule rests upon two related propositions: (a) the right of the majority to bar a minority action whenever they might lawfully ratify alleged misconduct; and (b) the normally exclusive right of the company to sue upon a corporate cause of action. In *Edwards v Halliwell*,[4] Jenkins LJ elucidated the relationship between these two propositions by contending that the will of the majority, *vis-à-vis* the minority, is to be identified with that of the company. Consequently, to say that the company is *prima facie* the proper plaintiff (claimant) in actions concerning its affairs is only another way of saying that the majority, within the limits of their power to ratify, have the sole rights to determine whether or not a dispute shall be brought before the courts.

The courts have justified the policy expressed by the rule by certain practical arguments of convenience. In *Gray v Lewis*,[5] James LJ justified the principle, that any body corporate is the proper plaintiff in proceedings to recover its property, by pointing to the obvious danger of a multiplicity of shareholders' suits in the absence of a rule such as *Foss v Hartbottle*. 'There might be as many bills as there are

---

1   In *Hodgson v NALGO* [1972] 1 WLR 130, Goulding J held that the rule in *Foss v Harbottle* did not apply to the case of an *unregistered* trade union since it was incapable of suing in its own name. *Dicta* in *MacDougall v Gardiner* (1875) 1 Ch D 13 at 25, *Cotter v NU Seamen* [1929] 2 Ch 58 at 71 and *Edwards v Halliwell* [1950] 2 All ER 1064 at 1066 were applied. The two latter cases established that the *Foss v Harbottle* rule *does* apply to unions that have been given the statutory right to sue in their own name. See further, *Taylor v NUM* [1985] BCLC 237.

2   (1843) 2 Hare 461. As to the historical development of the rule, see Wedderburn (1957) Camb LJ 194 and (1958) Camb LJ 93; Boyle (1965) 28 MLR 317; Baxter (1987) 38 NILQ 6; see also Drury (1986) 45 CLJ 219. See generally Boyle, *Minority Shareholders' Remedies*, Cambridge Studies in Corporate Law, CUP 2002.

3   *Foss v Harbottle* (1843) 2 Hare 461 at 492–493 and 494–495; *Mozley v Alston* (1847) 1 Ph 790 at 800; *Burland v Earle* [1902] AC 83 at 93 (PC); *Pavlides v Jensen* [1956] 1 Ch 565 at 575.

4   [1950] 2 All ER 1064 at 1066. However, this does not provide an explanation for 'wrongdoer control' in actions based on the 'fraud on a minority' exception to the rule.

5   (1873) 8 Ch App 1035 at 1051. This problem of abuse of procedure could of course be handled by the courts in other ways (eg the power to stay or consolidate actions). See Boyle (1965) 28 MLR 317.

shareholders multiplied into the number of defendants.' This situation would be aggravated where suits were discontinued at will, or dismissed with costs against plaintiff shareholders unable to meet these costs.[1] In *MacDougall v Gardiner*,[2] Mellish LJ observed the futility of ignoring the majority's power to ratify. If 'something has been done irregularly which the majority are entitled to do regularly, or if something illegally which the majority of the company are entitled to do legally, there can be no use having litigation about it if the ultimate end of which is that a meeting is called and then ultimately the majority gets its wishes'. In this case, the Court of Appeal refused to allow a minority shareholder to complain of the refusal by the chairman of a shareholders' meeting to call a poll.[3] It is well established that a mere breach of the fiduciary duties that directors owe to their company is ratifiable and hence cannot be the subject of a minority shareholder's action.[4] The same is true of an act by directors beyond the authority conferred upon them by the articles, or an irregularity in the appointment of directors.[5] The rule has also been applied to allegations by a minority shareholder that the directors have been engaged in practices in breach of the competition rules in Articles 85 and 86 of the Treaty of Rome, with the intention of damaging the company.[6]

17.3 The exceptions to the rule

The rule does not extend to a case where the act complained of is either illegal[7] or *ultra vires*, or is a fraud upon the minority,[8] and there is also an exception in cases where the act done, although regular in form, is unfair and oppressive as against the minority.[9] This will include acts by directors which are an abuse of powers contained in the memorandum and while not beyond the capacity of the company

---

1   See *La Compagnie de Mayville v Whiteley* [1896] 1 Ch 788 at 807; *Mozley v Alston* (1847) 1 Ph 790 at 799; *Lord v Cooper Miners* (1848) 2 Ph 740.
2   (1875) 1 Ch D 13 at 25. See also James LJ at 22.
3   This decision is not easy to reconcile with *Pender v Lushington* (1877) 6 Ch D 70, which established that the right to vote at shareholders' meetings is a personal right for which a shareholder may sue. It would be idle to pretend that all the cases on shareholders' 'individual' rights (as an exception to the rule) can be reconciled. For an exploration of the difficulties and a suggested solution, see Baxter, 'The Role of the Judge in Enforcing Shareholder Rights' [1983] Camb LJ 96.
4   *Burland v Earle* [1902] AC 83 (PC); *Dominion Cotton Mills v Amyott* [1912] AC 546 (PC); *Pavlides v Jensen* [1956] Ch 565; *Heyting v Dupont* [1961] 1 WLR 843 (CA); *Bentley-Stevens v Jones* [1974] 1 WLR 638; *Lee v Chou Wen Hsien* [1984] 1 WLR 1202 (PC). As to directors' fiduciary duties, see Chapter 16.
5   *Grant v UK Switchback Railways* (1888) 40 Ch D 135 (CA); *Mozley v Alston* (1847) 1 Ph 790.
6   *O'Neil v Ryan* [1990] 2 IR 200.
7   'Illegal' in this context should be understood as meaning either 'contrary to company law' or 'so plainly illegal that the directors have acted in abuse of their powers'. Where all that is alleged is that the company has engaged in conduct that is contrary to the general law in the sense that it may result, or has resulted, in a criminal prosecution of the company, a shareholder will not have a remedy: *Australian Agricultural Co v Oatmont Pty Ltd* (1992) 8 ACSR 225 (CA) NT.
8   *Alexander v Automatic Telephone Co* [1900] 2 Ch (CA); *Hope v International Financial Society* (1877) 4 Ch D 327; *Simpson v Westminster Palace Hotel* (1860) 8 HLC 712; *Clinch v Financial Corp* (1868) 4 Ch App 117. See the cases on 'fraud on a minority' discussed at **17.4**. As to the *ultra vires* doctrine, see Chapter 6.
9   See the cases establishing the principle that the majority in general meeting must act *bona fide* in the interests of the company as a whole (eg in altering the articles to the prejudice of a shareholder or class of shareholders). These cases are examined in **5.27**.

(and therefore void at common law) may only be approved by the unanimous consent of the shareholders.[1] It does not apply to a case where the matter in question requires, by virtue of a provision either in the Companies Act 1985 or in a company's memorandum or articles, a special or extraordinary resolution,[2] for to allow a company to ratify an act requiring the sanction of a special or extraordinary resolution by refusing to be party to proceedings would be to enable a bare majority to do that which can only be done by a three-quarters majority. A unanimous though informal agreement by the shareholders will effectively amend the articles without a special resolution.[3]

A single shareholder may sue in his own name to restrain an act which is an infringement of his individual rights,[4] for example a wrongful refusal to accept his vote at a general meeting of the company[5] or a wrongful exclusion of him from the board of directors.[6] The rule of *Foss v Harbottle* has, of course, no application to any statutory right conferred by the Companies Act 1985 on individual shareholders or a minimum number of them.[7] There is also judicial authority for the view that the rule has no application to any individual right conferred by the articles or memorandum.[8] However, whether such rights are an exception to the rule or are beyond its scope is largely a matter of language.

It is sometimes said that a minority shareholder has the right to have any provision in the articles enforced as part of his contract of membership. This proposition has received some support in judicial *dicta*,[9] but it appears contrary to two principles of company law. The first of these is that a member of a company is entitled only to enforce rights conferred upon him by the contract of membership, as defined by section 14(1) of the Companies Act 1985, in his capacity as a

---

1   *Rolled Steel Products Ltd v British Steel Corporation* [1985] 2 WLR 908 (CA).
2   *Baillie v Oriental Telephone Co* [1915] 1 Ch 503 at 515 (CA); *Cotter v NU Seamen* [1929] 2 Ch 58
     at 69–70; *Edwards v Halliwell* [1950] 2 All ER 1064 at 1067 (CA). Further, the notice of such a
     resolution must give a fair and reasonably full statement of the facts if the resolution is to
     bind the minority: *Kaye v Croydon Tramways* [1898] 1 Ch 538 (CA); *Tiessen v Henderson* [1899]
     1 Ch 861; *MacConnell v E Prill & Co* [1916] 2 Ch 57. Cf *Normandy v Ind Coope & Co Ltd* [1908]
     3 Ch 84.
3   *Cane v Jones* [1980] 1 WLR 1451. However, such an agreement requires registration under
     section 380; see **13.18**.
4   *Johnson v Little's Iron Agency* (1877) 5 Ch 687 (CA); *Wood v Odessa Waterworks Co* (1881) 42 Ch
     D 636; *Clark v Workman* [1920] 1 Ir R 107 at 112; *Davies v Commercial Publishing Co of Sydney*
     [1901] NSW (Eq) 37 at 47–48; *Edwards v Halliwell* [1950] 2 All ER 1064 (CA). As to
     difficulties about this 'exception', see footnote 3 at p 541, above.
5   *Pender v Lushington* (1877) 6 Ch D 70 at 81.
6   *Pullbrook v Richmond Consolidated Co* (1878) 9 Ch D 610; *Harben v Phillips* (1883) 23 Ch D 14
     (CA).
7   As to the rights of members (in respect of meetings) as to notice of resolutions, the
     requisitioning of meetings, circulating resolutions, etc, see Chapter 13. As to the right of
     shareholders to petition under Part XVII of the 1985 Act, see **17.14**.
8   *Edwards v Halliwell* [1950] 2 All ER 1064 at 1067 *per* Jenkins LJ (CA).
9   *Wood v Odessa Waterworks* (1889) 42 Ch D 636; *In Re Harmer* [1959] 1 WLR 62 at 87 *per*
     Harmer LJ (CA) (but this was a case of a petition under section 210 of the 1948 Act); and
     Bamford v Bamford [1968] 3 WLR 317 *per* Plowman J. In the Court of Appeal, Plowman J's
     decision was affirmed on other grounds and his remarks as to the right to enforce the articles
     as a contract received no support: *Bamford v Bamford* [1969] 2 WLR 1107.

member *qua* member.[1] The second principle, which such a general right to enforce articles would appear to offend, is the *Foss v Harbottle* rule itself. This rule prevents actions by minority shareholders for internal irregularities, such as breaches of the articles. Where such a breach does not involve the infringement of the individual rights conferred upon a shareholder, it has been held that a breach of the articles may be ratified by the majority.[2]

17.4 The 'fraud on a minority' exception to the rule

The 'fraud on a minority' exception to the rule demands more extensive consideration than do the other exceptions to the rule, as it has occasioned considerable litigation. The scope of this exception to the rule is important in determining the extent to which minority shareholders may enforce the duties owed by directors to their company,[3] by way of a 'derivative action'.[4]

The relationship between the *Foss v Harbottle* rule and the fraud on a minority exception to it was considered by Lord Davey in 1902[5] in a passage which has frequently been quoted, and was adopted by the Privy Council in 1912.[6] Lord Davey notes that an exception would be made to the principle of the company as proper plaintiff where 'the persons against whom relief is sought themselves hold and control the majority of shares in the company and will not permit an action to be brought in the name of the company'. This has come to be known as the element of 'wrongdoer control' and is discussed at **17.5**. As regards the kind of wrongful conduct for which the minority may maintain an action,[7] these are 'confined to those in which the acts complained of are of a fraudulent character or are beyond the powers of the company. A familiar example is where the majority are endeavouring directly or indirectly to appropriate to themselves money or property, or advantages which belong to the company, or in which the other shareholders are entitled to participate . . .'.[8]

---

1   See *Hickman v Kent or Romney Marsh Sheepbreeders' Association* [1915] 1 Ch 881. The decision in *Hickman* has been the subject of some criticism by academic writers on the ground that its reasoning is not consistent with all the other authorities on the shareholders' contract. This much-debated issue is examined at **5.18**. These arguments, however, do not dispose of the problem posed by the *Foss v Harbottle* rule itself.

2   *Grant v UK Switchback Railways* (1888) 40 Ch D 135 (CA).

3   Where the *Foss v Harbottle* issue is raised by motion at the outset of the proceedings, the court may not, on the one hand, 'assume as fact every allegation in the statement of claim as in a true demurrer'. On the other hand, the plaintiff is not required to prove 'fraud' and 'control' before he can establish his title to prosecute the action: *Prudential Assurance Co Ltd v Newman Industries (No 2)* [1982] Ch 204.

4   A shareholder does not necessarily have to be strictly a minority shareholder; a 50% shareholder has been held entitled to bring a derivative action: *Barrett v Duckett* [1993] BCC 778.

5   *Burland v Earle* [1902] AC 83 at 93 (PC).

6   *Dominion Cotton Mills v Amyot* [1912] AC 546 (PC); see also *Cook v Deeks* [1916] AC 554 (PC); *Foster v Foster* [1916] 1 Ch 532 at 547.

7   Ie an action in their own names, as a 'mere matter of procedure in order to give a remedy for a wrong which would otherwise escape redress, and it is obvious that in such an action the plaintiffs cannot have a larger right to relief than the company itself would have if it were plaintiff . . .'.

8   Earlier case-law clearly establishing the distinction between the right to bring an action in the company's name and the right to bring a minority shareholders' action on its behalf can be found especially in *East Pant Du United Lead Mining Co v Merryweather* (1864) 2 H & M 234 and *Atwool v Merryweather* (1868) 5 Eq 464n.

An instructive illustration is to be found in cases where an act is authorised by the votes of interested directors given at a general meeting. In the absence of fraud or oppression such votes in general meeting are valid, and a minority suing to set aside the transaction will fail;[1] but if the directors are seeking to appropriate to themselves property which belongs to the company as a whole, a resolution of the company in general meeting carried by their votes cannot validate the transaction, and a single shareholder or a minority of shareholders can obtain relief.[2] Misappropriation of corporate property extends to property (or contracts) which 'belong in equity' to the company.[3] Here the directors are accountable for a non-ratifiable breach of trust and not merely for a breach of their fiduciary duty.

In *Daniels v Daniels*,[4] Templeman J reviewed the authorities referred to above in an application to strike out the plaintiff's statement of claim (in a minority shareholder's action) on the ground that no cause of action was shown because no fraud was alleged. For the plaintiffs it was argued that any breach of fiduciary duty by directors could be a ground of action. The defendants contended that no cause of action was shown because the statement of claim did not allege fraud, and in the absence of fraud minority shareholders are unable to maintain a claim on behalf of the company against the majority.[5] Templeman J rejected this proposition as not consistent with the authorities, including *Pavlides v Jensen*.[6] The principle that he 'gleaned' from these authorities is 'that a minority shareholder who has no other remedy may sue where directors use their powers, intentionally or unintentionally, fraudulently or negligently in a manner which benefits themselves at the expense of the company'.[7] The cases which Templeman J particularly relied upon (as demonstrating that the word 'fraud' in this context does not mean literal or 'common-law fraud') are *Cook v Deeks*[8] and *Alexander v Automatic Telephone Co.*[9] His decision is valuable in clarifying the meaning of 'fraud on a minority' and restricting the scope of *Pavlides v Jensen*. The court's reasoning was clearly intended to be within the principles earlier laid down by higher courts. The facts alleged in the pleadings could well have led to the conclusion at a full hearing that the defendants had either appropriated property belonging in equity to the company (*Cook v Deeks*) or had acted in bad faith in exercising their power to sell

---

1   *North-West Transportation Co v Beatty* (1877) 12 App Cas 589 (PC); *Burland v Earle* [1902] AC 82 (PC); *Baird v Baird & Co (Falkirk)* 1949 SLT 368. As to the distinction between the duty of directors in respect of circulating notices of meetings (and accompanying circulars), and their right to vote at the meeting which results, see *Northern Securities v Jackson and Steeple* [1974] 1 WLR 1133. See also *Clemens v Clemens Bros Ltd* [1976] 2 All ER 268 applying *dicta* of Sir Richard Baggallay in *North-West Transportation v Beatty*, above, at 593.

2   *Cook v Deeks* [1916] 1 AC 554 (PC); *Menier v Hooper's Telegraph Works* (1874) 9 Ch App 350.

3   *Cook v Deeks*, above. See **16.8.1–16.8.2** as to the distinction between a mere breach of fiduciary duty and the misappropriation of property which 'belongs to equity' to the company. See further *Bracken Partners Ltd v Gutteridge* [2003] EWCA Civ 1875, [2004] 1 BCLC 377 (CA).

4   [1978] Ch 406.

5   Ibid at 408.

6   [1956] Ch 565.

7   [1978] Ch 408 at p 414.

8   [1916] 1 AC 554 (PC).

9   [1900] 2 Ch 56.

the company's property (*Automatic Telephone*). As Templeman J was at pains to demonstrate, neither of these propositions amounts to an allegation of fraud.[1]

17.5 'Wrongdoer control'

In *Pavlides v Jensen*,[2] the directors of a company did not, in the strict legal sense, control the company they were alleged to have harmed by their negligence. They were, however, a majority of the directors on the board of its holding company. Danckwerts J held that the action failed on two grounds. First, because the sale of the company's mine at a gross undervalue was not alleged to be fraudulent or an *ultra vires* act, but merely negligent and therefore open to ratification. Secondly, he held that there was not sufficient control exercised by the alleged wrongdoers to enable them to stifle any attempt to institute proceedings in the name of the company. The 'shareholders of the shareholding company could in general meeting decide differently and disagree with the directors of that company'.[3] Such a rigorous approach to this second aspect of 'fraud on a minority' does not appear to be entirely consistent with the cases discussed above.[4]

Vinelott J, in *Prudential Assurance Co Ltd v Newman Industries (No 2)*,[5] was prepared to extend the concept of 'wrongdoer control' so that it would apply not only where the wrongdoers were a majority, but also where it could be shown that unless the minority could be allowed to sue on the company's behalf, the interests of justice would be defeated in that an action which ought to be pursued on behalf of the company could not be pursued. Thus, in Vinelott J's view, 'wrongdoer control' comprehends '*de facto* control' as well as *de jure* control (of the kind insisted upon by Danckwerts J in *Pavlides v Jensen*). It would, on this view, also comprehend a situation where a majority of the board of directors are deceived by the wrongdoers so that the question of bringing civil proceedings will never be put to the shareholders.

Unfortunately, the Court of Appeal[6] (on appeal from Vinelott J) would have none of this. First of all, the court repudiated the whole 'justice of the case' principle as ground for departing from the rule in *Foss v Harbottle* and therefore as the theoretical basis employed by Vinelott J. The court was fully aware of the policy

---

1   For further discussion of this case in the periodical literature, see Wedderburn (1978) 41
     MLR 569 at p 571 [1978], Rider [1978] Camb LJ 270, Prentice 41 Conveyancer 47 (1979);
     Boyle (1980) 1 Co Law 3. In *Prudential Assurance v Newman Industries (No 2)*, Vinelott J's
     attempt at a radical restatement of the principle behind the 'fraud on minority cases'
     received no support in the Court of Appeal: [1982] Ch 204. See Boyle (1981) 2 Co Law 264.
     A similar approach was taken by Megarry V-C in *Estmanco (Kilner House) Ltd v Greater London
     Council* [1982] 1 WLR 2. See Birds (1982) 2 Co Law 31 and 77; see also, more recently, *Barrett
     v Duckett* [1995] 1 BCLC 73.
2   [1956] Ch 565.
3   Ibid at 577.
4   See especially, *Heyting v Dupont* [1964] 2 WLR 843 (CA) which accepted the following
     observation of Jessel MR in *Russell v Wakefield Waterworks* (1875) 20 Eq 474 at 480, which had
     been rejected by Danckwerts J in *Pavlides v Jensen*, above, '... that is not a universal rule; that
     is, it is a rule subject to exceptions, and the exceptions depend very much on the necessity of
     the case; that is the necessity of the court doing justice'. See also *Hodgson v NALGO* [1972] 1
     WLR 130 at 140.
5   [1980] 2 All ER 841 at 871–877.
6   [1982] Ch 204. See Boyle (1981) 2 Co Law 264.

problem caused by *de facto* control of public companies,[1] but remained unconvinced that Vinelott J's test of '*de facto* control' was a practical test, particularly as it involves a full dress trial before the test is applied. Instead, the court suggested that 'it may well be right' for the judge trying the preliminary issue[2] to grant a sufficient adjournment to enable a meeting of shareholders to be convened by the board. This is to enable the judge to reach a conclusion (ie as to wrongdoer control) in the light of the conduct of, and proceedings at, the meeting. Where the company has an independent board with adequate information, then the board is entitled to make a commercial assessment of the advantage to the company in taking civil proceedings (whether that assessment be sound or unsound). Where a shareholders' meeting is held, it seems that its function is not (as in *Hogg v Cramphorn*[3]) to ratify or approve an exercise of power by directors. Instead their function, in the event that they do not adopt the proceedings initiated by the minority, is to help clarify the judge's mind as to whether or not wrongdoer control exists. This ignores the difficulty of determining the motivation and conflicting interests of various shareholders at a company meeting.[4]

In *Smith v Croft (No 2)*,[5] Knox J stressed the need for an appropriate independent organ of the company to decide that it was not in the commercial interest of the company to pursue the action. In that case, a majority within the minority was allowed so to decide. Such an independent majority within the minority must reach its conclusions on grounds genuinely thought to advance the company's interests. Its decision is then treated as that of a 'corporate independent organ' which can properly prevent the plaintiff minority shareholders from suing. It is for the judge to determine whether the 'majority within the minority' has fairly reached its decision. It is not his function to say whether its decision is right or wrong. This approach is certainly a judicial innovation which will make a derivative action extremely difficult to bring except in the smallest private companies.[6]

17.5.1 The Civil Procedure Rules

What are now[7] the Civil Procedure (Amendment) Rules[8] set out the procedures governing derivative actions. This applies where a company is alleged to be entitled to claim a remedy and a claim is made by one or more members of the

---

1   The court observed that the term 'control' embraces a broad spectrum extending from an overall absolute majority of votes at one end to a majority of votes at the other end made up of those likely to be cast by the delinquent himself plus those voting with him as a result of influence and apathy.

2   As to the procedural basis on which this issue may be raised by the defendants, see *Smith v Croft (No 2)* [1988] Ch 114, see below.

3   [1967] Ch 254. See **17.6**.

4   The incomplete and unsatisfactory character of the Court of Appeal's observations stems from the fact that, on appeal, the *Foss v Harbottle* rule became irrelevant because the defendant company, Newman Industries, had 'adopted' the action against the real defendants. Thus the court's observations were entirely obiter and indeed the court refused to hear argument from counsel on the question.

5   [1988] Ch 114.

6   For a general comment, see Sealy, in Pettet (ed), *Company Law in Change* (Stevens, 1987), Chapter 1.

7   This replaces RSC Order 15, rule 12a, which was preserved in an appendix to the Civil Procedure Rules 1998.

8   SI 2000/221; see Schedule 2, Part 19, rule 19.9.

company for it to be given that remedy.[1] The company for whose benefit the remedy is sought must be a defendant to the claim.[2] After the claim form has been issued, the claimant must apply to the court for permission to continue the claim, and may not take any other step in the proceedings except to serve the claim form and supporting documents on the defendants, which must be done 14 days before the court is to hear the application.[3] Any other step requires the permission of the court.[4] If the court on hearing the application gives the claimant permission to pursue the claim, the defence must be filed within 14 days after the date on which permission is given or such period as the court may specify.[5] The court may order the company to indemnify the claimant against any liability in respect of costs incurred in the claim.[6]

17.6 The exercise of directors' powers for improper purposes

It is well established that if directors exercise their powers *mala fide* or for an improper purpose this is not only a breach of duty to the company, but is a matter of which the minority are entitled to complain.[7] Thus, where the directors use their power to issue shares to retain control by giving themselves a majority voting power at the expense of those rightly entitled to a majority of votes, a shareholder may seek an injunction to protect the rights of the majority.[8]

In *Hogg v Cramphorn*,[9] Buckley J held that, where shares were issued to trustees for the benefit of the company's employees as part of an elaborate scheme to defeat a takeover bid, this was an improper use of the power to issue shares even if it was done in good faith for the benefit of the company. Although a minority shareholder was entitled to sue despite the *Foss v Harbottle* rule, the court directed a meeting to be held at which defendants undertook that the wrongly issued votes would not be used.[10] Thus the success of the minority's action depended upon whether or not the director's misconduct would in fact be ratified in general meeting.[11] In *Bamford v Bamford*,[12] the Court of Appeal adopted a similar approach where the majority had ratified an improper issue of shares shortly after

---

1   Rule 19.9(1).

2   Rule 19.9(2).

3   These are the application notice and written evidence in support of the application; rule 19.9(5).

4   Rule 19.9(6).

5   Rule 19.9(6).

6   See **17.10** as to applications for indemnity, which are now heard with the application for leave.

7   *Alexander v Automatic Telephone Co* [1900] 2 Ch 56 (CA); *Re Smith & Fawcett Ltd* [1942] Ch 304 (CA). See **16.7**, as to the duty of directors to act in good faith in the interests of their company. Where bad faith takes the form of a bribe, a constructive trust may be imposed on the proceeds of the bribe: *Att-Gen for Hong Kong v Reid* [1994] 1 AC 324 (PC). See **16.18.2**.

8   *Punt v Symons* [1903] 2 Ch 506; *Piercy v Mills* [1920] 1 Ch 77. In both these cases the 'majority and minority were already arrayed for battle on a specific issue when the latter attempted to create reinforcements by issuing additional shares': Buckley J in *Hogg v Cramphorn* [1967] 2 Ch 254 at 269 (decided in 1963).

9   [1967] Ch 254. For a fuller discussion of this case in the context of directors' duties, see **16.7**.

10   It is not clear whether Buckley J would have allowed a general meeting to ratify if the directors had acted *mala fide*.

11   It should be noted that the majority and minority were not already 'arrayed for battle on a specific issue'. See Buckley J in [1967] Ch 254 at 269.

12   [1969] 2 WLR 1107.

proceedings commenced. The natural inference to be drawn from these decisions is that the use of directors' powers for an improper or collateral purpose may be the subject of a minority shareholder's suit even though such conduct is open to ratification. Further, a minority action will be defeated if such ratification takes place. Both these propositions appear at first sight to be contrary to the well-established principles on which the *Foss v Harbottle* rule and the exceptions to it rest.[1] It is possible to regard the reasoning in Buckley J's judgment in *Hogg v Cramphorn* as primarily directed to the issue before the court, namely the improper issue of shares. The minority shareholder complained of a wrong neither to himself nor primarily to the company. It was, as Buckley J pointed out,[2] an attempt 'to deprive the majority of their constitutional rights', which attempt would 'cease to have any force' if (leaving aside the wrongly issued shares) the majority in fact approved of what had been done. If a minority are allowed to vindicate the rights of the majority, it is obvious that if the majority agree to what has been done, then *cadit quaestio*. Alternatively, it may be that the duty to exercise powers for a proper purpose, especially the power to allot shares, is owed directly to shareholders.[3]

17.7   The enforcement of statutory 'fiduciary' duties

Certain provisions in Part X of the Companies Act 1985 impose statutory duties upon directors and 'connected persons'.[4] These duties are intended to avoid a conflict of duty and interest arising. In the case of section 320 (substantial property transactions involving directors) and section 330 (prohibition of loans, etc, to directors) there are statutory civil remedies following the pattern of those already available under the rules of equity which apply in the case of a breach of fiduciary duty on the part of directors. Any transactions or arrangements which infringe section 320 or 330 are voidable (on certain conditions) at the instance of the company.[5] In addition, there is both liability to account for gains (profits) made in breach of those sections and liability to indemnify the company for any loss or damage resulting.[6]

It was seen that these provisions in principle overlay the long-established rules laid down by the courts of equity and the remedies already afforded. However, it is clear that Parliament was seeking to do more than duplicate the existing law and thus intended to provide more effective civil remedies against the more flagrant forms of abuse of their fiduciary duty by directors. These remedies will be more effective in that they may not be modified in any way by provisions in the articles[7] nor by ratification by the general meeting (except insofar as section 322(2)(c) expressly provides for this by making affirmation within a reasonable period a bar

---

1   See, eg, *MacDougall v Gardiner* (1875) 1 Ch D 13 (CA); *Burland v Earle* [1902] AC 83 (PC); *Edwards v Halliwell* [1950] 2 All ER 1064 (CA).

2   [1967] Ch 254 at 269. In *Bamford v Bamford* [1969] 2 WLR 1107 (CA) this passage from Buckley J's judgment was cited with approval. However, the judgment of Harman LJ appears to assume a minority shareholder's action could not have been brought in any event.

3   See *Re A Company* [1987] BCLC 82; *John Crowther Group v Carpets International plc* [1990] BCLC 460 at 464, and **16.3**, above.

4   See **16.16** and **16.17**.

5   See sections 322(1) (as to substantial property transactions) and 341(1) (loans).

6   See sections 322(3) and 341(2) (in respect of section 330).

7   See **16.24.3**. Thus disclosure to and approval by an independent board of directors is not a ground of relief.

to the statutory form of rescission at the instance of the company provided by section 322(1)). It should be noted that the company's right to an accounting for gains and to an indemnity for losses (section 322(3)(b)) is not barred by loss of the statutory right to rescission by reason of affirmation by the shareholders in general meeting or otherwise.[1] In the case of the prohibition on loans, quasi-loans, etc, to directors and connected persons in section 330, the right to avoid transactions and arrangements in breach of the section cannot be barred by affirmation by the shareholders.[2] Again, the right to an accounting for gains and to an indemnity for losses may be pursued by the company 'whether or not' the company is still able to, or chooses to, seek to avoid transactions or arrangements in contravention of section 330.[3]

It is clearly open to argument that these new statutory remedies might be the basis of a derivative action by a minority shareholder even though he cannot bring his case within the fraud on a minority exception to the *Foss v Harbottle* rule. Obviously there would have to be a contravention of either section 320 or 330 which was not within any of the exceptions provided[4] or for which any particular defendant had no defence under the relevant statutory provision. It is true that various civil remedies are expressed to be available to the company ('voidable at the instance of the company', 'to account to the company', 'to indemnify the company'), but it is of the nature of derivative proceedings that corporate rights are enforced for the company's benefit.[5] There is nothing in these sections which expressly excludes a minority action. This might well be brought under the '*ultra vires* and illegality' exception to the *Foss v Harbottle* rule[6] which has always been understood to include not only acts *ultra vires* the objects clause but acts which are prohibited by provisions of the Companies Acts or otherwise illegal.[7] Furthermore, it is possible, where recovery is sought for the company's benefit, to bring a derivative action under this exception to the rule.[8] No doubt, in this event 'wrongdoer control' of the company must be shown as one of the conditions for allowing a derivative action to proceed (ie even though it is not founded upon fraud on the minority).[9]

Where a minority shareholder seeks only a declaration or injunction for a breach of a statutory duty,[10] it is questionable whether the proceedings should be properly classified as derivative and that, therefore, the issue of 'wrongdoer

---

1   See section 322(4): 'whether or not it has been avoided in pursuance of subsection (3) above'.
2   See section 341(1).
3   See section 341(2).
4   Sections 331 and 333–338.
5   See **17.8**.
6   See **17.3**.
7   Thus the infringement of what was then section 54 of the 1948 Act can be regarded as one ground for allowing a minority action in *Wallersteiner v Moir (No 1)* [1974] 1 WLR 991, and see *Smith v Croft (No 3)* [1987] BCLC 355. See *Anderson v Hogg* 2000 SLT 64. This Scottish decision was in part reversed on appeal (2002 SLT 354), but without disturbing the Lord Ordinary's comments on this point.
8   See **17.8** and *Russell v Wakefield Waterworks* (1875) 20 Eq 474. See *Taylor v NUM* [1987] BCLC 237.
9   See **17.5**.
10   This form of relief would be more appropriate to an alleged contravention of section 309 (directors to have regard to the interests of employees) and section 319 (contracts of employment of directors – see section 319(5)). See *Devlin v Slough Estates* [1983] BCLC 497.

control' has any relevance. A minority shareholder may therefore have more difficulty in establishing *locus standi*.

Where a member of a company successfully petitions under Part XVII of the 1985 Act (**17.13**), the court may make an order authorising civil proceedings to be brought 'in the name and on behalf of the company' (see **17.16**). Where such an order is obtained, then it is clear that any remedy available to the company in respect of sections 320 and 330 might be pursued.[1]

17.8 Procedure in minority shareholders' actions in England

In American law, a representative action by shareholders to enforce corporate rights, by seeking the recovery of damages for or property belonging to their corporation, is termed a 'derivative' action (ie one derived from the corporation's right of action). Lord Denning first adopted this usage,[2] and the courts have long recognised that certain special rules apply to a minority shareholder's action brought for this purpose. The rules now to be discussed apply[3] where, under the 'fraud on a minority' or *ultra vires* exceptions to the rule in *Foss v Harbottle*, the claimant shareholder seeks to recover damages for breach of duty from directors (or third parties) or the restitution of property for the company. Such an action must be brought in the 'derivative' form by the claimants 'on behalf of themselves and all the other shareholders of the company other than the defendant'.[4] 'The reason the action takes this form is that the minority shareholder is not in a position to see that the action is brought in the name of the company itself to enforce the company's rights.[5] Although this type of shareholder's action is brought for the benefit of the company, the company must be joined as a nominal defendant as well as the real defendants against whom relief is sought. The reasons for this are succinctly explained in the judgment of Chitty LJ in *Spokes v Grosvenor Hotel Company*.[6]

---

1   However, in *Re Carrington Viyella plc* (1983) 1 BCC 98, 751, a breach of what was then section 47 of the Companies Act 1980 was held not to amount to unfair prejudice in a petition under section 75 of that Act.

2   See *Wallersteiner v Moir (No 2)* [1975] QB 373 at 391, citing Gower, *Modern Company Law* 3rd edn (Stevens, 1969), at p 587. Such an action is not available to a shareholder seeking declaratory relief in respect of a statutory right; *Devlin v Slough Estates* [1983] BCLC 497. See (1982) 3 Co Law 261.

3   The procedural points discussed in **17.8–17.10** do not apply in Scotland. See Paterson (1981) 2 Co Law 155.

4   *Spokes v Grosvenor Hotel Co* [1897] 2 QB 124 at 128–129 (CA). See also *Mosely v Koffyfontein Mines Ltd* [1911] 1 Ch 73 (CA) at 81, where the distinction between shareholders' actions to enforce the rights of the company and other shareholders' actions is clearly expressed in the judgment of Fletcher Moulton LJ. See also *Prudential Assurance v Newman Industries (No 2)* [1982] Ch 204; *Heron International v Lord Grade* [1983] BCLC 244 (CA).

5   *Beattie v Beattie Ltd and Beattie* [1938] Ch 708 at 718 *per* Greene MR. See also *Burland v Earle* [1902] AC 83 at p 93 *per* Lord Davey (PC). See, however, the judgment of Denning MR in *Wallersteiner v Moir (No 2)* [1975] 2 QB 373 at 391 where the representative form is treated as a 'formula' that may be 'discarded'. See also *Taylor v NUM* [1985] BCLC 237. However, this does not appear to be consistent with earlier authority. Moreover, such a practice might harm the right of other minority shareholders to intervene where the proceedings are not being properly prosecuted.

6   [1897] 2 QB 124 at 128 (CA).

To such an action as this the company are necessary defendants. The reason is obvious: the wrong alleged is done to the company, and the company must be a party to the suit in order to be bound by the result of the action and to receive the money recovered in the action. If the company were not bound they could bring a fresh action for the same cause if the action failed, and there were subsequently a change in the board of directors and in the voting power. Obviously, in such an action as this, no specific relief is asked against the company; and obviously, too, what is recovered cannot be paid to the plaintiff representing the minority, but must go into the coffers of the company.

This type of action can be brought by a shareholder even in respect of wrongs committed against the company before he became a shareholder,[1] but such an action if commenced by a member may not be continued by him when he ceases to be a member, although the court may allow the action to be continued by another member.[2] The conduct of a shareholder may debar him from bringing this type of shareholder's action. If he has participated in the wrongful act of which he complains, the application of the 'clean hands' doctrine will result in his suit being dismissed.[3] Further, such an action must be brought genuinely in the interests of the company and not for the benefit of a rival company which has fostered the litigation and indemnified the plaintiff against costs.[4] The distinctive characteristic of a shareholder's 'derivative' action is that 'what is recovered cannot be paid to the plaintiff representing the minority, but must go into the coffers of the company'.[5] Hence, such an action should not be combined with a claim for a wrong done to the claimant shareholder personally.[6] As in other representative suits, the claimant, as *dominus litis* until judgment, can discontinue or settle an action at his pleasure.[7] However, unless the settlement is embodied in a formal judgment, a second action may be brought by another shareholder.[8] The Court of Appeal has held that a director does not owe a shareholder a personal duty of good faith where the company's assets have been misappropriated, even if this causes a loss in the value of the claimant's shares. Such a claim must be brought in the form of a derivative action.[9]

A minority shareholder's derivative action cannot be pursued (even if otherwise well grounded) once the company is in liquidation. This is because the corporate cause of action is then vested in the liquidator. The shareholder should seek

---

1   *Seaton v Grant* (1867) LR 2 Ch App 459; *Bloxham v Metropolitan Rly* (1868) LR 4 Ch App 337.
2   *Birch v Sullivan* [1957] 1 WLR 1247. Such an action may not be brought if the company has been dissolved; *Coxon v Gorst* [1891] 2 Ch 73; *Clarkson v Davies* [1923] AC 100 (PC).
3   *Towers v African Tug Co* [1904] 1 Ch 558 (CA); *Nurcombe v Nurcombe* [1984] BCLC 557.
4   *Forrest v Manchester, Sheffield & Lincolnshire Rly* (1861) 4 De GF & J 126.
5   *Spokes v Grosvenor Hotel Co* [1897] 2 QB 124 at 128 (CA).
6   *Stroud v Lawson* [1898] 2 QB 44 (CA). Another view was expressed by Vinelott J in *Prudential Assurance v Newman Industries (No 2)* [1980] 2 All ER 841. However, the Court of Appeal (in the same case; [1982] Ch 204) took a very different view of the possibility of combining representative actions in tort with derivative actions for breach of fiduciary duty. Such a possibility was rejected by the Court of Appeal. See Boyle (1981) 2 Co Law 264 at 266.
7   *Re Alpha Co* [1903] 1 Ch 203.
8   See *Gray v Lewis* (1873) 8 Ch App 1035 at 1051. At an earlier stage in the proceedings the court has power to remove a plaintiff from control of a representative action where another of the class represented intervenes on the ground that the action is not being adequately prosecuted; *Re Services Club Estates Syndicate* [1930] 1 Ch 78 (a debenture-holder's action).
9   *Stein v Blake (No 2)* [1998] 1 BCLC 573, applying *Prudential Assurance v Newman Industries* [1982] Ch 704. See further, *Johnson v Gorewood* [1999] BCC 474 (CA).

redress from the liquidator. If the liquidator refuses unreasonably, the shareholder can then apply to the court.[1]

17.9 Overlapping personal and corporate claims

The overlap between personal claims and corporate claims (derivative or otherwise) was fully explored by the House of Lords in *Johnson v Gore Wood & Co*,[2] where there were parallel claims against a firm of solicitors by a dominant shareholder and the company which for all practical purposes was his 'corporate embodiment'. The House of Lords refused to strike out the appellant's claim in so far as it sought to enforce not only duties owed personally as shareholder but related to personal losses distinct from those suffered by the company. Lord Bingham indicated the principles involved:[3]

> On the one hand the court must respect the principle of company autonomy, ensure that the company's creditors are not prejudiced by the action of individual shareholders and ensure that a party does not recover compensation for a loss which another party has suffered. On the other hand the court must be astute to ensure that the party who has in fact suffered a loss is not arbitrarily denied fair compensation.

Lord Millett addressed the key issue that arises where the company suffers a loss caused by the breach of a duty owed both to the company and the shareholder:[4]

> In such a case the shareholder's loss, in so far as this is measured by the diminution in the value of his shareholding or the loss of dividends, merely reflects that suffered by the company in respect of which the company has its own cause of action. If the shareholder is allowed to recover in respect of such loss, then either there will be double recovery at the expense of the defendant or the shareholder will recover at the expense of the company and its creditors and other shareholders. Neither course can be permitted. This is a matter of principle; there is no discretion involved. Justice to the defendant requires the exclusion of one claim or the other; protection of the interests of the company's creditors requires that it is the company which is allowed to recover to the exclusion of the shareholder.

These principles, which are based on a well-known passage in *Prudential Assurance Co Ltd v Newman Industries*,[5] Lord Millett conceded, have not always been faithfully observed.[6] He criticised a passage in the judgment of Thomas J (in the New Zealand Court of Appeal) in *Christenson v Scott*.[7] This accepted that a diminution in the value of the plaintiff's (claimant's) shares can be considered a personal loss and not a corporate loss. Lord Millett was 'unable to accept this reasoning as representing the position in English law'.[8]

Lord Millett made it clear that the reflective loss which a shareholder may not recover extends beyond the diminution in the value of the shares. It extends to the loss of dividends and all other payments which the shareholder might have

---

1   *Fargro Ltd v Godfroy* [1986] 1 WLR 1134, applying *Ferguson v Wallbridge* [1935] 3 DLR 66.
2   [2002] 2 AC 1. The decision of the House of Lords was applied in *Day v Cook* [2002] EWCA Civ 592, [2002] 1 BCLC 1 (CA).
3   Ibid at 36. As to these recoverable losses, see Lord Bingham's judgment at 36–37.
4   [2002] 2 AC at 62.
5   [1982] Ch 204 at 222 to 223.
6   He made clear his disapproval of *Fisher (George) (GB) Ltd v Multiconstruction Ltd* [1995] 1 BCLC 260 at 266 and *Barings plc (In administration) v Coopers & Lybrand* [1997] 1 BCLC 427 (CA).
7   [1996] 1 NZLR 273.
8   [2002] 2 AC at 66.

obtained from the company if it had not been deprived of its funds. All transactions or putative transactions between the company and its shareholders must be disregarded.

Later cases establish qualifications to the principle established in *Johnson v Gore Wood & Co*. It will not apply where a company has not settled its claim, but has been forced to abandon it by reason of impecuniosity attributable to the wrong done to it by the wrongdoer sued by the claimant shareholder.[1] It also did not preclude a beneficiary under a trust, where the assets of the trust consisted of 70% of the company's shares, bringing an action against a trustee for the profit made by the latter in breach of trust. To prevent such an action, the defendants had to show that the whole of the claimed profit reflected what the company had lost and which the company had a cause of action to recover.[2]

17.10 Minority shareholders' right to an indemnity in a derivative action

In *Wallersteiner v Moir (No 2)*,[3] the Court of Appeal recognised that a minority shareholder who brings a derivative suit[4] may have a right to an indemnity against the company in respect of his costs. This right was held to be closely analogous to the indemnity which a trustee is entitled to in respect of proceedings on behalf of the trust property or in the execution of the trust.[5] Fundamentally, the right will depend on whether the minority shareholder acted in good faith and reasonably in bringing proceedings. The Court of Appeal modelled the procedure for applying to the court to claim the indemnity on that already well established in the case of a trustee.[6]

An indemnity order application is heard as part of the application for permission to continue the claim in derivative proceedings.[7] The Master in the exercise of his discretion can give approval for the continuance of the action to various stages: 'until close of pleadings, or until after discovery or until trial (rather like a legal aid committee does)'.[8] Indeed, this might extend to the claimant's costs down to judgment. Assuming that on the hearing the claimant was authorised to proceed, he would 'be secure in the knowledge that, when the costs of the action should come to be dealt with, this would be on the basis, as between himself and the company, that he had acted reasonably and ought *prima facie* to be treated by the trial judge as entitled to an order that the company should pay his costs'.[9] Moreover, the Court of Appeal adds the extremely important rider that these costs would normally be taxed on a basis not less favourable than the

1   *Giles v Rhind* [2002] EWHC Civ 1248, [2003] 1 BCLC 1. See further *Giles v Rhind* (No 2)
     [2003] EWHC 2830, [2004] 1 BCLC 385.
2   *Shaker v Al-Bedrawi* [2002] EWCA Civ 1452, [2003] 1 BCLC 157.
3   [1975] QB 373.
4   A *Wallersteiner* order will not be made in a shareholders' action which is not a derivative one,
     but at the end of the proceedings an order for costs may be made on a common fund basis if
     the result of the case is beneficial to members generally; *Marx v Estates and General Ltd* [1976]
     1 WLR 380 at 392. See also *Re A Company* [1987] BCLC 82.
5   See *Hardoon v Belilios* [1901] AC 118 (HL).
6   See *Beddoe, Re Downes v Cottam* [1893] 1 Ch 557.
7   The Civil Procedure (Amendment) Rules 2000, Schedule 2, Part 19, rule 19.9(7).
8   [1975] QB 273 at 392 *per* Denning MR.
9   [1975] 1 QB 373 at 405 *per* Buckley LJ.

common fund basis, and should indemnify him against any costs he may be ordered to pay to the defendants.[1]

In a later decision,[2] Walton J gave a somewhat cautious and restrictive interpretation of the Court of Appeal's decision in *Wallersteiner*. He indicated that, in order to hold the balance fairly between plaintiffs (claimants) and defendants, it is incumbent on the claimant, in applying for a *Wallersteiner* order for costs, to show that it is genuinely needed. Even when an order is granted, it is appropriate to leave some proportion of the costs to be borne by the claimants, since otherwise there would be no incentive for the claimant to prosecute the action effectively. This might ultimately result in the action being dismissed for want of prosecution. It has been held that an indemnity order does not confer a lien over the company's assets or any damages recovered in a successful derivative action. Thus where the company is later put into administration, as being unable or likely to be unable to ay its debts, no equitable lien exists to give priority in respect of the indemnity order.[3]

In *Wallersteiner v Moir (No 2)*,[4] the Court of Appeal held that legal aid was not available to a shareholder bringing a derivative action.[5] The majority, against the views of Lord Denning MR, also refused to countenance the adoption of the American contingency fee system. [6] Now that civil legal aid is no longer generally available, the possibility of using the modern system of a conditional fee agreement might be considered.[7] The regulations permit a maximum 'success fee' and the use of such agreements in derivative actions might be open to challenge in so far as they detract from the right of the company in such proceedings to receive all the proceeds of a successful action. Even if the success fee were not restricted to damages etc recovered in a successful action, its recovery might have a serious impact on the ability of the defendant directors to discharge their liabilities.

17.10.1   The Law Commission's recommendations for a statutory derivative action

As indicated earlier, the Law Commission[8] has recommended the replacement of the common law by a new statutory derivative action in cases where there has been

---

1   Ibid at 405 *per* Buckley LJ and 392 *per* Denning MR.

2   *Smith v Croft* [1986] 1 WLR 580. Applied in *Re Charge Card Services Ltd* [1986] 3 WLR 697 in a creditor's application for costs in a winding-up. Cf *Jaybird Group Ltd v Green* [1986] BCLC 319 (decided in 1981). Here a less restrictive approach was taken. The criterion applied was that of an honest, independent and impartial board of directors.

3   *Qayoumi v Oakhouse Property Holdings plc* [2002] EWHC 2547 (Ch), [2003] 1 BCLC 352.

4   Above.

5   [1975] 1 QB 373 at 400–401.

6   Ibid at 373.

7   See sections 58 and 58A of the Courts and Legal Services Act 1990. Conditional fee agreements are regulated by the Conditional Fee Agreements Order 2000, SI 2000/823 and the Conditional Fee Agreements Regulations 2000, SI 2000/692.

8   *Shareholder Remedies*, Report No 246, 1997, Cm 3769. See Boyle, 'The New Derivative Action', (1997) 18 Co Law 256. The recommendations are based on Commonwealth models, especially those in Canada; as to the relevance of such models, see Part 16 of the preceding Consultative Paper No 142 (July 1996).

an alleged breach of directors' duties.[1] Notice would have to be given to the company at least 28 days before the commencement of the action, specifying the grounds for it, and the leave of the court to maintain the action would have to be sought at an early stage. In deciding whether or not to grant leave, the court would consider all relevant circumstances including the following:

(1) whether the applicant is acting in good faith (although this would not be a pre-requisite to the grant of leave);
(2) whether the action would be in the interests of the company, with leave being refused if this were not the case;
(3) whether the alleged wrong has been, or may be, approved by the company in general meeting; effective ratification would be a bar to continuing;
(4) whether the general meeting has resolved not to pursue the action;
(5) the views of an independent organ; and
(6) the availability of alternative remedies.

It can be seen that much of this reflects the way that the common law has developed, as described in the previous sections. Although the benefit of having the basis for the derivative action laid out in modern statutory form cannot be denied, many commentators have felt that the approach is somewhat restrictive, especially in allowing ratifiability of a wrong to continue to play an important role.[2]

17.11 Shareholders' actions to enforce rights against the company

Where a minority shareholder seeks a remedy *against* the company under any of the exceptions to the rule in *Foss v Harbottle*, then the special rules which apply to the 'derivative' type of representative action, described at **17.8**, do not apply. Whenever he seeks to enforce a right which he enjoys together with other shareholders, or some class of them, he may sue in the representative form.[3] However, a representative action is not obligatory in such cases. He may instead sue simply in his own name.[4] In either event, the normal remedy against the company will be to seek an injunction[5] or bring an action for a declaration.[6] Where the representative form of proceedings is employed, the 'clean hands'

---

1   Although in *Modernising Company Law*, Cm 5553–1, 2002, at 3.18, the DTI left it open to question as to whether the Law Commission's work would be implemented, their more recent view, as expressed on the Company Law Review website (http://www.dti.gov.uk/cld/review.htm) is more positive.
2   For generally critical comments on the earlier Consultation Paper No 142, the provisional views in which were largely followed in the Report, see Sugarman (1997) 18 Co Law 226 and 274, Lowry (1997) 18 Co Law 247, Riley (1997) 18 Co Law 260, Moran (1997) 18 Co Law 264. The difficulties in deciding what breaches of directors' duties are ratifiable are discussed in **16.23.1**.
3   See now rule 19.6 in the Civil Procedure (Amendment) Rules 2000. See, eg *Pender v Lushington* (1877) 6 Ch D 70; *Mosely v Koffyfontein Mines Ltd* [1911] 1 Ch 73, affirmed *sub nom Koffyfontein Mines v Mosley* [1911] AC 409 (HL).
4   *Simpson v Westminster Palace Hotel Co* [1860] 8 HLC 712; *Sidebottom v Kershaw, Leese & Co Ltd* [1920] 1 Ch 154 (CA).
5   *Wood v Odessa Waterworks* (1889) 42 Ch D 636; *Pender v Lushington* (1877) 6 Ch D 70.
6   *Edwards v Halliwell* [1950] 2 All ER 1064 (CA); *Sidebottom v Kershaw, Leese & Co Ltd* [1920] 1 Ch 154 (CA); *Greenhalgh v Arderne Cinemas Ltd* [1951] Ch 286 (CA). A shareholder may now seek a judgment in an action against his company: section 111A of the Companies Act 1985.

doctrine may apply to the conduct of the claimant.[1] The claimant in such an action has the right to control the conduct of proceedings, as *dominus litis* until judgment.[2]

In shareholders' actions *against* the company it is not necessary to join the directors as parties, unless some form of relief is sought against them in addition to the remedy against the company. However, in such an action, it is possible to seek relief by way of injunction against the company while joining the directors as co-defendants in order that relief may be claimed against them for the company's benefit.[3] In such an action, the two forms of relief sought should arise out of a series of related transactions. The court will not allow what is in substance a derivative suit to be brought in the guise of a representative action in tort (eg the tort of conspiracy).[4]

17.12   Proceedings in the company's name

The proper persons to give instructions for the commencement of an action to enforce any right of the company, or to obtain redress for a wrong done to the company, or to recover its property, are the directors; and the company itself is the only proper claimant in such an action,[5] though it cannot appear in person, either as claimant or defendant, and, except in the county court,[6] can only be represented by counsel.[7] Whether before or in a liquidation, the company's name alone should appear as claimant, it being improper to add the directors or liquidators as plaintiffs unless some relief is claimed by them in their individual capacity.

Although the directors are the proper persons to give the instructions for commencing such an action, it was long ago held that effect should be given to the wishes of a majority of the shareholders when they desire that proceedings should be taken to protect the company's rights, and that an action may be commenced in the company's name as claimant by such a majority, or even in case of urgency by one or more shareholders who believe that they have the support of a majority, and subsequently obtain the sanction of a resolution of the company.[8] An interim injunction may be obtained in such an action before their sanction has been

---

1   *Burt v The British Nation Life Insurance Association* (1859) 4 De G & J 158. But cf *Mosely v Koffyfontein Mines* [1911] 1 Ch 73 (CA), an action to restrain future illegal acts.
2   See above as to the 'derivative' type of action. This principle applies to any representative action.
3   See *Russell v Wakefield Waterworks Co* (1875) LR 20 Eq 474 at 481–482; *Bagshaw v Eastern Union Rly* (1849) 7 Hare 114, affirmed 2 Mac & G 389; *Hogg v Cramphorn* [1967] 2 Ch 254.
4   *Gray v Lewis* (1873) 8 Ch App 1035 at 1050; *Russell v Wakefield Waterworks Co* (1875) 20 Eq 474 at 479; *Duckett v Gover* (1877) 6 Ch D 82; *Burland v Earle* [1902] AC 83 at 93 (AC); *Prudential Assurance v Newman Industries (No 2)* [1982] Ch 204; *Heron International v Lord Grade* [1983] BCLC 244 at 281–283.
5   *Prudential Assurance v Newman Industries (No 2)* [1982] Ch 204.
6   *Charles P Kinnell & Co v Harding Wace & Co* [1918] 1 KB 405 (CA).
7   *Frinton & Walton UDC v Walton & District Sand Co* [1938] 1 All ER 649; *Tritonia v Equity & Law Life Assurance Society* [1943] AC 584 (HL (Sc)). But see further Chapter 3, footnote 2 at p 44.
8   *Pender v Lushington* (1877) 6 Ch D 70; *Imperial Hydropathic Hotel Co v Hampson* (1883) 23 Ch D 1 (CA); *La Compagnie de Mayville v Whitley* [1896] 1 Ch 788 (CA); it seems difficult to reconcile these cases with *Salmon v Quin & Axtens* [1909] AC 422 (HL), and *Automatic Self-Cleansing Filter Co v Cunninghame* [1906] 2 Ch 34; but they have been often followed. See also *Marshall's Valve Gear Co v Manning* [1909] 1 Ch 627.

procured. But if it ultimately appears that the majority is not in favour of the proceedings,[1] the name of the company as claimant will be struck out.[2]

In *Breckland Group Holdings Ltd v London & Suffolk Properties*,[3] a shareholder was restrained from continuing a legal action in the company's name where the articles provided that actions in the company's name could be commenced only with the consent of two particular directors. The shareholder who brought the action argued unsuccessfully that the directors would have to agree to take proceedings as this was obviously in the company's best interests.[4]

PART 2: A STATUTORY REMEDY FOR MINORITIES

17.13 Power of the court to grant relief on a petition alleging unfair prejudice

The Cohen Committee[5] designed what used to be section 210 of the Companies Act 1948 as a procedure to meet the specific problems of minority oppression. It was realised that a 'just and equitable' winding-up under what is now section 122(1)(g) of the Insolvency Act 1986,[6] though it might be kept in reserve, was usually inappropriate, and a derivative action was frequently unavailable owing to the restrictive nature of the *Foss v Harbottle* rule. The Jenkins Committee,[7] when it came to review section 210, found its provisions restrictive in various respects. It made a number of proposals which were originally enacted in section 75 of the Companies Act 1980. The most important of these changes is that the basis on which a court may grant a petition is no longer that of oppression but that of 'unfair prejudice'. These provisions are now contained in Part XVII (sections 459 to 461) of the Companies Act 1985, as amended by the Companies Act 1989.[8]

---

1 If such approval is obtained, the action may proceed in the company's name; *Danish Mercantile Co Ltd v Beaumont* [1951] Ch 680 (CA). This decision of the court of Appeal was followed in *Alexander Ward & Co Ltd v Samyang Navigation Co Ltd* [1975] 1 WLR 673 (HL (Sc)).

2 *Silber Light Co v Silber* (1878) 12 Ch D 717; *East Pant Du Lead Mining Co v Merryweather* (1864) 2 H & M 254; *Duckett v Gover* (1877) 6 Ch D 82. Where it is intended to bring a genuine minority action (ie under one of the exceptions to *Foss v Harbottle*) and action should not be commenced in the company's name; *Alexander v Automatic Telephone Co* [1900] 2 Ch 56 at 69 *per* Lindley MR (CA).

3 (1988) 4 BCC 542. See also **15.11**.

4 For further details on procedure, especially motions to strike out the company's name and security for costs under section 726 of the Companies Act 1985, see *Gore-Browne on Companies* 44th edn (Jordans, loose-leaf) at 28.11.1 and 28.11.2 and Boyle, *Minority Shareholders' Remedies*, (Cambridge Studies in Corporate Law, CUP 2002), chapters 4 and 5.

5 Cmnd 6659 (1945), paragraph 60.

6 As to which, see **17.17**.

7 Cmnd 1749 (1962).

8 See the Law Commission's Report on 'Shareholder Remedies' (Cm 3769 (1997)). One of the Commission's proposals is to create a 'New Additional Unfair Prejudice Remedy for Small Companies' (Part 3). This will provide a cheaper simplified procedure in the case of the exclusion from management in small 'partnership type' private companies. The Report also proposes the adoption of an additional provision in Table A to assist the internal resolution of shareholder disputes in private companies. The new regulation proposed will provide a shareholder exit article for smaller private companies (see Part 5).

Section 459(1) allows a member[1] to apply to the court by petition for an order under the section. The ground on which he may petition (and on which the court must be satisfied that the petition is well founded)[2] is as follows: that the company's affairs are being or have been conducted in a manner which is unfairly prejudicial to the interests of its members generally or of some part of the members (including at least himself) or that any actual or proposed act or omission[3] on its behalf is or would be so prejudicial.[4]

17.13.1 The concept of unfair prejudice

It is readily apparent that the abandonment of the term 'oppressive' (in the old section 210 of the 1948 Act) and the judicial gloss put upon it[5] has been given its intended effect by the judiciary. 'Bad faith' and 'lack of probity' (and their associated burden of proof) are now irrelevant. Similarly, the use or threatened use of majority shareholders' voting power is not a requirement. The term 'unfair prejudice', whether analysed as a 'standard' or a 'concept', is a relatively more objective one which is concerned with running the company in a way that is clearly unfair in its consequences to the complaining shareholder, even if the respondents can claim to have acted in the best of good faith.

It is, however, clear that the petitioner does not have to establish the infringement of a shareholder's right given by some other aspect of company law. The concept of unfairness cuts across the distinction between acts which do or do not infringe rights attaching to shares.[6] It has also been judicially observed[7] that unfairness is a familiar concept employed in ordinary speech – often by way of contrast to infringement of legal rights. The court may pay regard to wider equitable considerations. For example, in a 'quasi-partnership' type company, the court may take account of legitimate expectations of members.[8] On the other hand, the plain infringement of a shareholder's right (eg to be given accurate

---

1   This may theoretically include a passive majority – it is not necessarily restricted to a minority member (see *Re Baltic Real Estate Ltd (No 1)* [1993] BCLC 499, cf *Re Baltic Real Estate Ltd (No 2)* [1993] BCLC 503).

2   See section 461(1). See *Re A Company* (No 004175 of 1986) [1987] 1 WLR 585.

3   See *Re Kenyon Swansea Ltd* [1987] BCLC 514.

4   The procedural rules to be followed are now set forth in a statutory instrument, the Companies (Unfair Prejudice Application) Proceedings Rules 1986, SI 1986/2000.

5   See *Gore-Browne on Companies* 44th edn (Jordans, loose-leaf) at 28.12 for a summary of the old case-law on section 210.

6   In *Re A Company (No 008699 of 1985)* [1986] 2 BCC 99, 024; see also *McGuinness v Bremner plc* [1988] BCLC 673 (Ct of Sess). The conduct complained of in a section 459 petition must relate to the manner in which the affairs of the company are conducted. In *Nicholas v Soundcraft Electronics* [1993] BCLC 360 (CA), the non-payment of debts owed by a holding company to its subsidiary (where this was an attempt to keep the group afloat in financial difficulties) was held not to constitute unfair prejudice in the conduct of the subsidiary's affairs. It does not include acts of a shareholder carried out in a personal capacity outside the course of the company's business: *Re A Company (No 001761 of 1986)* [1987] BCLC 141. Where a shareholder's refusal to sell his shares is a private matter, it is no part of 'the conduct of the company's affairs': *Re Legal Costs Negotiators Ltd* [1999] 2 BCLC 171 (CA).

7   Ibid, *per* Hoffmann J.

8   *Re Kenyon Swansea Ltd* [1987] BCLC 514. Cf *Re Postgate and Denby (Agencies) Ltd* [1987] BCLC 8; see also, *Re A Company, ex parte Schwartz (No 2)* [1989] BCLC 427 and *Re Elgindata Ltd* [1991] BCLC 959.

accounting information as prescribed in the Companies Act 1985) could also be the basis of an allegation of unfair prejudice.[1]

17.13.2 O'Neill v Phillips

In *O'Neill v Phillips*,[2] for the first time the House of Lords had an opportunity to consider the scope of the unfair prejudice remedy. Lord Hoffmann gave the only reasoned judgment. The case concerned a building construction company whose original 'proprietors' first allowed the petitioner, an employee, a minority holding and a directorship. Later he was left alone on the board as in effect *de facto* managing director. Subsequent changes included a profit sharing agreement. Some of these profits were later capitalised by the issue of non-voting shares. Discussions took place with a view to the petitioner obtaining a 50% shareholding but no agreement was, in the event, concluded. In a later building recession, the company's position worsened. The petitioner was excluded from managing the company. The profit sharing arrangement was later terminated and the petitioner left the company and brought a petition under section 459. The trial judge dismissed his petition but it succeeded in the Court of Appeal[3] from whence the respondent appealed to the House of Lords.

Lord Hoffmann's exegis of 'unfair prejudice' in section 459(1), as in his earlier Court of Appeal judgment in *Re Saul D Harrison & Sons plc*,[4] relies on two essential points. These are the fundamentally promissory nature of the basis on which relief may be granted, and secondly, that the same principles underlie both the just and equitable winding up remedy and the unfair prejudice remedy.

As regards the first point, he observes[5] that a member of a company will not ordinarily be entitled to complain of unfairness unless there has been some breach of the terms on which he agreed that the affairs of the company be conducted. These terms are contained in the articles of association and sometimes in the collateral agreements made between shareholders.

> In a quasi-partnership company, there will usually be understandings between the members at the time they entered into the association. But there may be later promises, by words or conduct, which it would be unfair to allow a member to ignore. Nor is it necessary that such promises should be independently enforceable as a matter of contract. A promise may be binding as a matter of justice and equity, although for one reason or another ... it would not be enforceable in law.[6]

Lord Hoffmann relies strongly on Lord Wilberforce's *locus classicus* in *Ebrahimi v Westbourne Galleries*[7] to underpin the second point: there will be cases in which equitable considerations make it unfair for those conducting the affairs of the company to rely upon their strict legal powers. 'This unfairness may consist in a

---

1   See, eg *Re A Company, ex parte Shorter* [1990] BCLC 384. Cf *Re A Company, ex parte Schwartz* [1989] BCLC 427. See further *Re A Company, ex parte Harries* [1989] BCLC 383, where an old allotment in breach of statutory pre-emptive rights was found to be evidence of unfair prejudice.

2   [1999] 2 BCLC 1. For a discussion of the theoretical implications of this decision, see Thomas and Ryan, 'Section 459, public policy and freedom of contract' (2001) 22 Co Law 177 and 198.

3   [1997] 2 BCLC 739.

4   [1995] 1 BCLC 14 at 19–20.

5   [1999] 2 BCLC 1 at 8.

6   Ibid at 10–11.

7   [1973] AC 360 at 379. See **17.17**.

breach of the rules or in using rules in a manner which equity would regard as contrary to good faith.'[1] Lord Hoffmann traces the principles upon which the court decides the alleged conduct is unjust, inequitable or unfair back to nineteenth-century cases such as *Bisset v Daniel*[2] and the distinction between the legal and equitable approach to the use of powers.

Lord Hoffmann is clearly aware of drawing too close an analogy between a 'just and equitable' winding up and the notion of unfairness in section 459. He observes that 'the parallel I have drawn ... does not mean that conduct will not be unfair unless it would have justified an order to an order to wind up the company'.[3] He later adds: 'The parallel is not the conduct which court will treat as justifying a particular remedy but the principles upon which it decides that the conduct is unjust, inequitable or unfair.'[4] The difficulty with this approach is that it does not make it sufficiently clear that a just and equitable winding up order may be made in circumstances of a breakdown in mutual confidence where it is impossible to hold that the respondent has acted unfairly. The most obvious example (well established before *Westbourne* but not changed by it) is where there is deadlock between corporate partners which they are incapable of resolving.

Lord Hoffmann's use of the term 'good faith' (to cover, it seems, both 'just and equitable' and 'unfairness') is perhaps unfortunate. In *Westbourne*, the House of Lords[5] specifically rejected the test of 'bad faith' as the basis for a just and equitable winding up and overruled the Court of Appeal on the issue. The petitioners need not show bad faith in the sense that the respondents had not acted in good faith in the company's interests. In the case of section 459 petitions, it is well established[6] that a breach of directors' duties may enable the court to find unfair prejudice. It is clear that a breach of fiduciary duties, even if the breach does not involve bad faith, may in appropriate circumstances justify relief under section 459. It is thus difficult to grasp in what more generic sense the term 'good faith' is employed.[7]

Certainly, Lord Hoffmann's judgment also makes clear that 'exercising rights in breach of some promise or undertaking' is not the only form of conduct which will be regarded as 'unfair' for the purposes of section 459. For example, there may be some event which puts an end to the basis upon which the parties entered into association with each other, making it unfair that one shareholder should insist upon the continuance of the association. Thus Lord Hoffmann's observations on the term 'unfair prejudice' are valuable as a conceptual analysis. It is debatable

---

1   [1999] 2 BCLC at 8.

2   (1853) 10 Hare 493, 68 ER 1022.

3   [1999] 2 BCLC at 9.

4   Ibid. See further the judgment of Neill LJ in *Re Saul D Harrison & Sons plc* [1995] 1 BCLC 14 at 30–32 as to the differences between the two remedies. See, however, *Re Guidezone Ltd* [2000] 2 BCLC 321 at 356–357, where Jonathan Parker J interprets Lord Hoffmann's judgment to mean that the jurisdiction of the court on hearing an unfair prejudice petition is co-extensive with the jurisdiction in a winding up; *sed quaere*; see also *Re Phoneer Ltd* [2000] 2 BCLC 241. See Acton, 'Just and equitable winding up; the strange case of the disappearing jurisdiction' (2001) 22 Co Law 134.

5   [1973] AC 360 at 379. It has also been rejected as the test of unfair prejudice. See *Gore-Browne on Companies* 44th edn (Jordans, loose-leaf) at 28.13.2.

6   See *Gore-Browne on Companies* 44th edn (Jordans, loose-leaf) at 28.13.7. Lord Hoffman's earlier judgments have been important on this point. Lord Hoffmann draws an analogy to 'continental systems' which introduce a general requirement of good faith in contractual performance.

7   [1999] 2 BCLC at 11.

whether they have the full weight of the *ratio decidendi* of a House of Lords' decision. His observations do not amount to a re-statement of the pre-existing body of case-law. Earlier decisions are not overruled. It neither extends nor restricts the range of circumstances which may amount to unfair prejudice.

17.13.3 Breach of directors' duties

A question that was raised by most commentators[1] on section 459 is how far a breach (or breaches) of directors' fiduciary duties may be of assistance in establishing unfair prejudice. Or, to put it another way, to what extent is section 459 of use in circumventing the limitations of the 'fraud on a minority' exception to the rule in *Foss v Harbottle*?[2] In three cases which took the form of applications to strike out petitions under section 459 (on the basis that there was no case in law for the respondents to answer), the allegations in the petition referred to various breaches of duty by directors. Hoffmann J (who heard all three applications),[3] in rejecting these applications to strike out, clearly regarded allegations of breach of fiduciary duty as capable of establishing unfair prejudice to minority shareholders in a private company or a small unlisted public company.

The contention that the facts (eg a crude misappropriation of assets by a majority shareholder) would have readily warranted the bringing of a derivative action will not bar a petition under section 459.[4] Moreover, a breach of directors' fiduciary duties not to mislead shareholders when making statements supporting one of two rival takeover bids is capable (at a later full hearing of a section 459 petition) of establishing unfair prejudice.[5] Where the petitioners were fraudulently induced to sell their shares in a private company to a small public company (as part of a manifestly dishonest scheme), Hoffmann J refused to strike out a petition merely on the ground that the matters complained of constituted wrongs to the petitioner as defrauded vendors of their former private company's shares and as a wrongfully dismissed managing director (as regards one petitioner) of that company. Once again, it was held that the interests of a member are not limited to his strict legal rights since the use of the word 'unfairly' in section 459 enabled the court to have regard to wider equitable considerations.[6]

The developments described above are encouraging for shareholders in private companies, but there is less encouraging news in respect of public listed companies with widely dispersed shareholders. It is in this type of company, of course, that the restricting aspects of 'fraud on a minority', and especially wrongdoer control,[7] prevent shareholders' derivative suits having much impact on the still serious problem of corporate abuse. In *Re Carrington Viyella plc*,[8] in a petition in respect of a publicly listed company, it was held by Vinelott J that failure to obtain shareholders' approval for the chairman's long-term contract of

---

1   Eg *Gore-Browne on Companies* 44th edn (Jordans, loose-leaf) at 28.13.7.
2   As to 'striking out' and 'case management' in a section 459 petition, see *Gore-Browne on Companies*, 44th edn (Jordans, loose-leaf) at 28.12A.
3   *Re A Company* [1986] 1 WLR 281; *Re A Company* [1986] BCLC 382; *Re A Company* [1986] BCLC 376. See also, *Re A Company, ex parte Burr* [1992] BCLC 724 and *Re Ghyll Beck Driving Range Ltd* [1993] BCLC 1126.
4   See [1986] 1 WLR 281 at p 284.
5   *Re A Company* [1986] BCLC 382.
6   *Re A Company* [1986] BCLC 376; *McGuinness v Bremner plc* (1988) SLT 891.
7   See **17.5**.
8   (1983) 1 BCC 98, 951; see (1983) 4 Co Law 164.

employment, as required by section 319 of the Companies Act 1985,[1] did not amount to unfairly prejudicial conduct within section 459(1).[2] Other section 459 cases involving public companies[3] have rejected petitions principally on the ground that there is no room in this context for allegations of failure to meet legitimate expectations outside what is contained in the company's public documents, ie its memorandum and articles, prospectus or listing agreement, etc. It was arguable that the previous wording of section 459, which referred to 'the interests of some part of the members (including at least himself)', made relief under the section more difficult in the case of public listed companies, on the grounds that the alleged unfair prejudice had to differentiate or discriminate between the interests of classes or groups of shareholders. Whatever the force of this argument,[4] the current wording of section 459(1), as revised by the Companies Act 1989[5] – 'unfairly prejudicial to the interests of its members generally or some part of its members' – has removed this particular difficulty, and it can no longer be an answer to a section 459 petition concerning a public company where the majority remains passively indifferent, that the unfair prejudice has been suffered by all shareholders alike (or all but a handful who are also the wrongdoers). There is no evidence that the Jenkins Committee, in reforming the old section 210, intended to exclude such companies from the wide discretion it proposed should be conferred upon the court by what is now Part XVII of the 1985 Act.

Another aspect of the enforcement of directors' duties by means of a petition under section 459 which remains unclear is the director's duty of care. It would seem that the Jenkins Committee[6] intended that the reformed statutory remedy might be used in this regard, although the courts decided otherwise[7] in the case of the old section 210. Where serious mismanagement causes real economic harm to the company's business (and therefore to the value of the members' interest) the general conceptual developments examined earlier should enable the courts to hold that unfair prejudice has been established. The terminology in section 459(1) (referring to 'any actual or proposed act or omission of the company including an act or omission on its behalf ' where this 'is or would be so prejudicial') should be of assistance here. Once again, however, a petition in the case of a public listed company may present greater difficulty. In *Re Elgindata Ltd*,[8] Warner J was of the view that the court would ordinarily be very reluctant to treat managerial decisions as unfairly prejudicial conduct but that it would be open to the court in an appropriate case to find that serious mismanagement of a company's business could constitute unfair prejudice. Disagreement between the

---

1   See **16.15**.

2   It was also held that the failure of a controlling shareholder to comply with an undertaking given to the Secretary of State for Trade and Industry in order to avoid a reference to the Monopolies Commission did not affect the rights of the petitioning shareholders; this finding is wholly understandable.

3   *Re Blue Arrow plc* [1987] BCLC 585, *Re Ringtower Holdings plc* (1989) 5 BCC 82.

4   It was accepted in *Re A Company* [1988] 1 WLR 1068 but rejected in *Re Sam Weller and Sons Ltd* [1990] Ch 682.

5   See Schedule 19, paragraph 11. The wording now mirrors that in section 27 of the Insolvency Act 1986, which gives a remedy to members and creditors unfairly prejudiced when a company is in administration; see **21.29**.

6   Cmnd 1749 (1962), paragraphs 207–8.

7   *Re Five Minute Car Wash Service* [1966] 1 WLR 745.

8   [1991] BCLC 959.

parties as to whether a particular managerial decision was commercially sound is clearly not enough. Shareholders realise that the value of their shares will depend upon the measure of competence in management. A breach by a director of his duty of care and skill must, however, be distinguished from the quality of management turning out to be poor. An example of unfair prejudice might be 'where the majority shareholders, for reasons of their own, persisted in retaining in charge of the management of the company's business a member of their family who was demonstrably incompetent'.[1]

17.13.4 'Legitimate expectations'

In a number of cases, it has been held that in the case of a small private 'quasi-partnership' type company, the court may take account of the 'legitimate expectations' of members.[2] However, in a more substantial company such a 'concept' has no place.[3] More recently, the Court of Appeal[4] has emphasised that in general members have no legitimate expectations beyond the legal rights conferred on them by the constitution of the company. This applies unless it can be shown that a 'legitimate expectation' arises out of a fundamental understanding between shareholders, which formed the basis of their association. This may confer a right to participate in management.[5]

In *O'Neill v Phillips*,[6] Lord Hoffmann has cast some doubt on the significance of the concept of 'legitimate expectation'. Lord Hoffmann, as he readily concedes, was the 'author' of this term in respect of exclusion from participation in management in a 'partnership type' private company. In *O'Neill*, Lord Hoffmann insists that this term, taken from public law, is only a 'label' to be attached to a conclusion that unfair prejudice has been established. 'The concept of a legitimate expectation should not be allowed to lead a life of its own, capable of giving rise to equitable restraints in circumstances to which the traditional principles have no application.'[7]

It was largely on this basis that the petitioner's claim failed in the House of Lords. Overruling the Court of Appeal, Lord Hoffmann upheld the trial judge's finding that there were no 'legitimate expectations' to participate in management or share in profits, even if it could be said that the petitioner had suffered in his capacity as 'stakeholder' in the company rather than employee.[8] Lord Hoffmann was rightly concerned to repudiate the erroneous notion that a section 459 petition can be used to obtain what he calls 'no fault divorce'.[9] Counsel had argued that where confidence and trust had broken down, in a quasi-partnership, one 'partner' ought to be entitled at will to require the other partner (or partners)

---

1   *Per* Warner J in *Re Elgindata Ltd* [1991] BCLC 959 at 993, applied in *Re Macro (Ipswich) Ltd* [1994] 2 BCLC 354.

2   See *Re Kenyon Swansea Ltd* [1987] BCLC 514.

3   *Re Postgate & Denby (Agencies) Ltd* [1987] BCLC 8. *Re Blue Arrow plc* [1987] BCLC 585. It clearly has no application in the case of a listed plc: *Re Astec (BSR) plc* [1998] 2 BCLC 556 at 589. See further, *Gore-Browne on Companies* 44th edn (Jordans, loose-leaf) at 28.13.4–28.13.5.

4   *Re Saul D Harrison & Sons plc* [1995] BCLC 14 at 19–20.

5   *R&A Electrical Ltd v Haden Bill Electrical Ltd* [1995] 2 BCLC 280. *Re Regional Airports Ltd* [1999] 2 BCLC 30.

6   [1999] 2 BCLC 1.

7   [1999] 2 BCLC 1 at 11.

8   Ibid at 12–13 and 15.

9   Ibid at 13.

to buy out his shares without having to show unfairness. This 'stark right of unilateral withdrawal' is rejected as quite unsupported on authorities. Lord Hoffmann noted that indirect support came from the Law Commission Report on *Shareholder Remedies*.[1]

The Court of Appeal has held[2] that, even in a quasi-partnership type company, the remedy provided by section 459 does not extend to a member/director who wishes entirely for his own reasons to sever his connections with the company and *de facto* has done so. In this situation, the member cannot use allegations of unfair prejudice to justify obtaining a full discounted value for his shares, where he has been offered a purchase based on a minority discounted valuation.

17.14 'Member *qua* member'

It was a clear distinction between the old remedy under section 210 of the Companies Act 1948 and the remedy of just and equitable winding up (as reinterpreted by the House of Lords in *Ebrahimi v Westbourne Galleries Ltd*)[3] that a petitioner had to complain in his capacity as 'member *qua* member' under section 210[4] but not, at any rate in the case of a 'quasi-partnership', under what is now section 122(1)(g) of the Insolvency Act 1986. 'It is obvious that in a small private company it is legalistic to segregate the separate capacities of the same individual as shareholder, director or employee. His dismissal from the board or from employment by the company will inevitably affect the real value of his interest in the company expressed by his shareholding.' However, in the first fully reported case (on what was then section 75 of the Companies Act 1980), Lord Grantchester QC appeared to apply the 'member *qua* member' test to an unfair prejudice petition.[5]

In later decisions, the phrase 'interests of some part of the members' has been more flexibly interpreted so as to free it from this particular shackle on the old section 210. In one case, in which the company was 'a classic example of a quasi-partnership', Vinelott J strongly expressed the view *obiter* (and has amplified it extrajudicially[6]) that the introduction of the term 'interests' allows the court to avoid the 'member *qua* member' approach and take account of the same 'interests' (granted the need to prove unfair prejudice) as in a just and equitable winding-up. Hoffmann J[7] observed that 'the interests of a member who had ventured his capital in a small private company might include the legitimate expectation that he would continue to be employed as a director – so that his dismissal would be unfairly prejudicial to his interests as a member'. This was related to other allegations of unfairly prejudicial behaviour and linked to the wider principle that 'the interests of a member are not necessarily limited to his strict legal rights'.[8]

Even in the case of a 'quasi-partnership' type of company, dismissal from employment and a position on the board will not necessarily establish unfair

---

1 　*Shareholder Remedies* Law Com No 246 (1997), Cm 3769, at paragraph 3.66.
2 　*Re Phoenix Office Supplies Ltd* [2002] EWCA Civ 1740, [2003] BCLC 76 at 89 (Auld LJ) and 91 (Jonathan Parker LJ). As to valuation of shares. See **17.16**.
3 　[1972] AC 360. See **17.17**.
4 　See, eg *Re Five Minute Car Wash Service* [1966] 1 WLR 745.
5 　[1983] Ch 178.
6 　*Re A Company* [1983] BCLC 151 and (1985) 6 Co Law 21 at 30.
7 　*Re A Company* [1986] BCLC 382.
8 　For a discussion on this aspect of 'unfair prejudice' see **17.13.2**.

prejudice. This is made clear by Nourse J in *Re London School of Electronics.*[1] This case concerned a company which provided courses of study in electronics in conjunction with City Tutorial College Ltd (CTC), the majority shareholder. The petitioning minority shareholder's complaint was that the two individuals who owned the shares in CTC had resolved at a board meeting of the London School of Electronics (LSE) to transfer substantially all of the LSE students to CTC (and to register all new students for the electronics course with CTC) on the grounds that that was necessary to qualify for recognition by an American university as a degree course. The petitioner was subsequently removed from his office as director. The petitioner had then set up a rival establishment and taken away a number of pupils enrolled at the LSE. The following passage in the judgment of Nourse J indicates when dismissal may provide evidence of unfair prejudice.

> In my judgment it was CTC's decision to appropriate the B.Sc. students to itself which was the effective cause of the breakdown in the relationship of mutual confidence between quasi-partners. Furthermore, that was clearly conduct on the part of CTC which was both unfair and prejudicial to the interests of the petitioner as a member of the company. It is possible, although I do not so decide, that CTC would have been entitled to relieve the petitioner of his teaching duties before June 1983. It is even possible, although it is much less likely, that CTC, had it gone through the appropriate formalities, could have properly removed the petitioner as a director of the company. But none of that is to say that CTC was entitled to take the extreme step of determining to deprive the petitioner of his 25 per cent interest in the profits attributable to the B.Sc. students.

In another sense, the unfair prejudice remedy is not confined to members. Section 459(2) allows those to whom shares have been transferred[2] or transmitted by operation of law to petition. Section 460 also gives such a right to the Secretary of State (after powers of investigation have been used), but this has been almost totally ignored by the Department of Trade and Industry.[3]

As will be seen below, in regard to members a section 459 petition is often combined with a petition for a just and equitable winding-up. It has long been established that a contributory's winding-up petition may not be brought if he has no tangible interest. This prevents such petitions where the company is insolvent. It has been held[4] that this also bars a petition under section 459. It is not entirely clear why this should always be so. Thus the victim of unfair prejudice might still wish his shares bought by a wealthy respondent protected from the company's creditors by limited liability.

Although a petitioner for relief under section 459 must be a shareholder before he can petition, he is entitled after he becomes a shareholder to support his petition by relying on conduct that took place before he became a shareholder.

---

1   [1986] Ch 211. See *Re A Company (No 004377 of 1986)* [1987] BCLC 94. See also, *Re Alchemea Ltd* [1998] BCC 964 where the company was formed as a co-operative and the members were paid wages and re-imbursed for their expenses. In consequence, they complained that the conduct affected their position as employees not as members.

2   The use of the term 'transferred' in section 459(2) does not permit those with an equitable interest in shares (who are not registered as shareholders) to petition; *Re A Company (No 007838 of 1985)* (1986) 2 BCC 98, 952. Those who are in no sense members cannot petition: *Re A Company* [1986] BCLC 391.

3   See *Gore-Browne on Companies* 44th edn (Jordans, loose-leaf) at 28.15.

4   *Re Commercial and Industrial Insulations Ltd* [1986] BCLC 191; as to a winding-up order, see *Re Chesterfield Catering Ltd* [1977] Ch 623.

Section 459(1) applies not just to continuing conduct but to conduct that occurred in the past.[1]

17.15 The 'alternative remedy'

What is now section 125(2) of the Insolvency Act 1986 requires the court, on hearing a winding-up petition presented by members of the company as contributories on the ground that it is just and equitable, to grant a winding-up order 'if it is of the opinion (a) that the petitioners are entitled to relief either by winding up the company or by some other means and (b) that in the absence of any other remedy it would be just and equitable that the company should be wound up'. The section then emphasises this second point with the addition of this rider: '... but this does not apply if the court is also of the opinion both that some other remedy is available to the petitioners and that they are acting unreasonably in seeking to have the company wound up instead of pursuing the other remedy'.

This 'alternative remedy' provision, as it is usually called, has now become even more important since section 459 of the Companies Act 1985 has become a remedy of a more inclusive nature than the old section 210, and since it obviously furnishes a more satisfactory range of remedies which contrast favourably with the stark and 'sledgehammer' outcome of a successful petition under what is now section 122(1)(g) of the Insolvency Act 1986.[2] There will still of course be cases where it is not possible to petition successfully under both of these statutory minority remedies. Thus in *London School of Electronics*,[3] it was held that there was no overriding requirement (in a petition under what is now section 459 of the Companies Act 1985) that it should be just and equitable to grant relief or that the petitioner should come to court with clean hands. However, the misconduct of a petitioner might still be relevant in a number of ways. The two most obvious are that it might render the conduct of which the petitioner complained, even if prejudicial, not unfair. Secondly, even if the treatment (by the respondents) of the petitioner was still found to be unfair and prejudicial, it might affect the relief granted by the courts. The 'clean hands' doctrine clearly applies to a just and equitable winding-up petition. However, the Privy Council has held that even if the petitioning minority shareholder has been partly responsible for the breakdown in the relationship between the parties, if his conduct was not the cause of the breakdown he will not be prevented from obtaining a winding-up order on the just and equitable grounds.[4]

In a petition for a just and equitable winding-up,[5] unfair prejudice does not have to be shown. Moreover, it is not necessarily part of the petitioner's case that the respondents have acted unjustly or inequitably. Thus where petitions under both section 459 of the Companies Act 1985 and section 122(1)(g) of the

---

1 See *Lloyd v Casey* [2002] 1 BCLC 455 at 466–467, applying *Re Quickdrome Ltd* [1988] BCLC 370 and *Bermuda Cable Vision Ltd v Calica Trust Co Ltd* [1998] AC 198 (PC).

2 See *Practice Direction (Companies Court; Contributories Petition)* [1990] 1 WLR 490. This draws practitioners' attention to the undesirability of including as a matter of course a petition for winding up as an alternative to an order under section 459. This should be done only if a winding-up is the relief that the petitioner prefers or if it is considered that it is the only relief to which he is entitled.

3 [1986] Ch 211, 233. See **17.14**.

4 *Vujnovich v Vujnovich* [1990] BCLC 227 (PC).

5 See **17.17**.

Insolvency Act 1986 are presented, the court may, as Nourse J did in *Re R A Noble (Clothing) Ltd*,[1] dismiss the former petition and grant the latter.

Where, however, the petitioner (whether or not he has petitioned under both sections) could succeed under either remedy, the importance of section 125(2) of the Insolvency Act 1986 and the 'alternative' remedy principle will come into play. Thus section 125(2) will point the court firmly in the direction of section 459 (and its ampler and more appropriate remedial solutions) whenever the petitioner can establish 'unfair prejudice' to the satisfaction of the court. The 'alternative remedy' need not be section 459 as such.

17.15.1 The offer to buy as a bar to a winding-up

A reasonable offer to buy out the petitioner's shares at a fair price (with appropriate expert valuation) may suffice. In *Re A Company*,[2] Vinelott J observed that the jurisdiction under what is now section 125(2) is discretionary. The court would be at least entitled to refuse to make a winding-up order if satisfied that the petitioner was persisting in asking for such an order, and that it would be unfair to the other shareholders to make that order having regard to any offer they made to the petitioner to meet his grievance in another way. The petitioner was also held to have acted unreasonably in refusing to accept the respondent's offer to purchase his shares at a valuation. The date when the adequacy of the respondent's offer has to be determined is the date of the hearing and not that of the presentation of the petition. 'It is as much an abuse of the process of the court to persist in a petition which, because of a subsequent offer, is bound to fail as it would be to present a petition which on the facts existing at the time of presentation is bound to fail.'[3] This gives the respondents, faced with a petition under section 122(1)(g) every incentive to negotiate an adequate offer to buy out the petitioner by means of a fair and independent valuation, ie where no price can be agreed. To make sure the respondent continued to show sincerity until the completion of the 'buy-out', Vinelott J decided not to dismiss the petition outright. It was merely 'stood over' to enable the parties to agree the terms of submission to an arbitration or valuation by an expert. When agreement was reached 'the matter could be mentioned to the court and the petition stayed'. If there was any disagreement, Vinelott J continued, he would 'then hear further argument'.

Whenever possible, it would seem, a winding-up order with all its potential for the destruction of an otherwise viable business and with harsh consequences for the innocent employees will be denied whenever a viable alternative remedy is available. In the case before Vinelott J (referred to above), the court rejected the argument that in a small quasi-partnership type company the petitioner is entitled to reject an alternative 'buy-out' remedy on the ground that (as in partnership law) he is entitled to a share of 'partnership' assets on their realisation. The only qualification to this proposition admitted by Vinelott J was that where the petitioner (excluded from a quasi-partnership despite the underlying assumption of a right to participate) has always insisted on a winding-up as the only remedy, then the argument that he was entitled to that remedy might have succeeded. On

---

1   [1983] BCLC 273.
2   *Re A Company* [1983] 1 WLR 927. See also, *Re Copeland & Craddock Ltd* [1997] BCC 294 (CA): a petitioner allowed to proceed in the hope of bidding for the business when it was sold by the liquidator.
3   Applying *Bryanston Finance Co v De Vries (No 2)* [1976] 2 WLR 41.

the facts of this case that was not so. From the time of exclusion from participation, the petitioner had indicated a willingness to sell to his co-shareholders at a fair price to be negotiated.

The principle so firmly stated in these first-instance decisions on the 'alternative remedy' has been reviewed by the Court of Appeal in *Virdi v Abbey Leisure.*[1] Where a petitioner is entitled in principle to a just and equitable winding-up, an offer by the respondent majority shareholders to buy his shares, under a provision in the articles, at a fair value to be agreed by an accountant, could reasonably be refused by the petitioner. The trial judge was held to be wrong in the exercise of his discretion under section 125(2), in deciding to strike out the petition. The Court of Appeal accepted that an accountant acting under the procedure in the articles would value them on a discounted basis as a minority holding. The petitioner was entitled to insist on his normal right to a *pro rata* valuation, which would result from an order for a just and equitable winding-up. Balcombe LJ[2] observed that the courts have shown a general inclination (under both sections 459 and 122(1)(g)) towards a valuation on a *pro rata* basis. Balcombe LJ also stressed that in a just and equitable winding-up based on the principles laid down by the House of Lords in *Ebrahimi v Westbourne Galleries,*[3] 'legal rights and obligations conferred or imposed on shareholders by the constitution of the company may be subject to equitable considerations'. This freed the petitioner from his obligation under the articles.[4]

17.15.2 The offer to buy as a bar to an unfair prejudice petition

In a number of cases[5] the courts have stressed that, where there is an irretrievable breakdown which is the fault of neither petitioner nor respondent, pre-emptive rights provisions in the articles should be sought rather than a petition under section 459 on the ground of unfair prejudice. Where the court concludes that unfair prejudice to the petitioner could not be established at a full hearing, this is obviously right. However, some decisions go further than this on motions to strike out unfair prejudice petitions. These would bar a petitioning minority shareholder from complaining about unfair prejudice if no attempt has been made to use the machinery provided by the articles for determining the fair value of the party's shares.[6] In view of the Court of Appeal's observations in *Virdi v Abbey Leisure,*[7] these decisions would appear to be open to question where the provision in the articles allows only for a discounted minority holding basis of valuation if,

---

1   [1990] BCLC 342. The Court of Appeal also held that the discretion of the trial judge exercised under section 125(2) could be reviewed by the Court of Appeal not only on the ground of principle but on the ground of whether the petitioner had acted reasonably.

2   [1990] BCLC 342 at 350. Balcombe LJ referred in particular to *Re Bird Precision Bellows Ltd* [1984] BCLC 395.

3   [1973] AC 360. See **17.17**.

4   [1990] BCLC 342 at 350.

5   *Re R A Noble (Clothing) Ltd* [1983] BCLC 273; *Re A Company* [1986] BCLC 362; *Re A Company* [1987] BCLC 94. See further, *Re A Company, ex parte Kremer* [1989] BCLC 365, where such a petition was struck out on this basis. See likewise, *Re Castleburn Ltd* [1991] BCLC 89. But cf *Re A Company, ex parte Harries* [1987] BCLC 383 at 398.

6   See Hoffmann J in *Re A Company* [1987] BCLC 94 at 102, cited by the same judge in *Re A Company, ex parte Kremer* [1989] BCLC 365 at 368. Admittedly, this is qualified in respect of cases of 'bad faith or plain impropriety or where the articles provide for some arbitrary or artificial method of valuation'.

7   [1990] BCLC 342 see **17.15.1**.

under a successful section 459 petition, a *pro rata* basis would be appropriate. The observations of the Court of Appeal are applicable to unfair prejudice petitions even though the case itself concerned a just and equitable winding-up.[1]

This process has been taken a stage further by Lord Hoffmann in *O'Neill v Phillips*.[2] He took the opportunity to clarify the law and practice on the 'offer to buy' as a bar to an unfair prejudice petition. This is perhaps the most useful as well as innovatory aspect of the House of Lords' judgment in *O'Neill*. Lord Hoffmann noted that this issue was *obiter* in that it did not arise for decision on the facts of the case. 'Nonetheless, the effect of an offer to buy the shares as an answer to a petition under section 459 is a matter of such great practical importance that I invite your Lordships to consider it.'[3]

The point of the list of criteria, set out under five headings, is to establish that a reasonable offer has been made so that the exclusion of the petitioner from the business of the company will not be treated as unfairly prejudicial. The petition will be struck out. First, the offer must price the shares at a fair value. As in the existing case-law, this will normally be on a *pro rata* basis, though there may be cases in which it will be fair to take a discounted value. Secondly, if not agreed, the value must be determined by a competent expert (eg an accountant agreed by the parties). Thirdly, the offer should be to have the value determined by the expert as an expert (not full arbitration nor the half way house of an expert who gives reasons). The objective is economy and expedition. Fourthly, both parties should have the same access to information about the company relating to the value of the shares, and should have the right to make submissions to the expert. Fifthly, normally the offer should cover the costs of the petitioner, but the respondent should be allowed a reasonable opportunity to make an offer before being obliged to pay costs.

Lord Hoffmann, like other members of the judiciary involved in section 459 petitions, has long been aware of the dangers of the destructive effect of costs where such petitions are unnecessarily pursued. 'It is therefore very important that participants in such companies should be allowed to know what counts as a reasonable offer', he rightly observes.[4] This has done much to settle and clarity an area of law and practice. It may well prove to be the aspect of *O'Neill* of most lasting importance to the practitioner. Where a petitioner and a respondent were both making offers for each other's shares, the court allowed the respondent to succeed as having made the more reasonable offer. The latter had adequate funds

---

1   See *Re A Company, ex parte Harries* [1989] BCLC 383 at 398 *per* Peter Gibson J, who anticipated the Court of Appeal in *Virdi v Abbey Leisure* [1990] BCLC 342. See also, *Re A Company, ex parte Holden* [1991] BCLC 597. See *Re Vocam Europe Ltd* [1998] BCC 396 where the court stayed a section 459 petition on the basis of an arbitration clause in an agreement between the parties.

2   [1999] 2 BCLC 1.

3   [1999] 2 BCLC 1 at 15. A failure to make a reasonable offer may exacerbate the unfairness alleged: *Richards v Lundy* [2000] 1 BCLC 376.

4   [1999] 2 BCLC at 16. See *Re A Company, North Holdings Ltd v South Tropics Ltd* [1999] BCC 746 (CA) where Morritt LJ emphasised the need for active case management at an early stage in order to reduce the time and expense involved in ascertaining a fair price for the petitioner's shares. This was the first appeal concerning section 459 proceedings under the Civil Procedure Rules 1998. See further, *Re Rotadata Ltd* [2000] 1 BCLC 123.

available whereas the petitioner lacked funds and made a vague offer lacking in detail and insufficiently specific in vital details.[1]

17.16   The remedies available to the court: section 461

To the original remedies[2] available to the court under section 210 of the Companies Act 1948, new specifically procedural remedies were added in 1980 on the basis of the Jenkins Committee's proposals. These were that the court may 'require the company to refrain from doing or continuing an act complained of by the petitioner or to do an act which the petitioner has complained it omitted to do' and it may 'authorise civil proceedings to be brought in the name of or on behalf of the company by such person or persons and in such terms as the court may direct'.[3]

It is not surprising that in the case of most successful petitions (and there were few of them under the old section 210) the remedy sought by the petitioners, and granted by the court, is that of purchase of the minority's shares by the majority. As a solution to intra-corporate disputes in small private companies this is still the most attractive choice among the remedial solutions offered by section 461.[4] It is likewise not surprising that there have been a number of decisions in the reports (and others unreported) on the related questions of the method of valuing the minority's shares and the date on which that valuation should be made.

In *Re Bird Precision Bellows*,[5] Nourse J considered the legal basis for valuing the minority's shares where a 'buy-out' order is made. He emphasised that there was no rule that the price of a minority holding in a small private company be fixed on a *pro rata* basis (according to the value of the shares as a whole), or, alternatively, that the price should be discounted to reflect the fact that the shares were a minority holding. He indicated, however, that the court would employ the *pro rata* basis where the shares had been acquired on the incorporation of a quasi-partnership company, and it was thus expected that the shareholders would participate in the conduct of the affairs of the company.[6] The valuation would be

---

1   *West v Blanchet* [2000] 1 BCLC 795 at 803. As to the proper role of mediation in shareholder disputes, see Corbett and Nicholson, 'Mediation and section 459 petitions' (2002) 23 Co Law 274.

2   These are a wide power to 'make such order as it thinks fit for giving relief in respect of the matters complained of and further powers to order the complainants' shares be bought by the company (with a consequent reduction of capital) or by the majority from the minority (or vice versa)'. The court has power to give this relief against an ex-shareholder: *Re A Company* [1986] BCLC 68. There is also a power to 'regulate the conduct of the company's affairs in the future' and to alter the articles and memorandum. See *Gore-Browne on Companies* 44th edn (Jordans, loose-leaf) at 28.17.

3   See section 461(2).

4   In exceptional circumstances, the court may order the majority to sell their shares to the minority (eg where a pre-emption agreement between majority and minority has been made): *Re Brenfield Squash Racquets Club* [1996] 2 BCLC 184.

5   [1984] Ch 419. As to the proper method of valuing a private company's share capital, see *Re a Company* [1986] BCLC 362 at 368, *Re Regional Airports* [1999] 2 BCLC 30 at 84–100 and *Profinance Trust SA v Gladstone* [2000] 2 BCLC 516.

6   This would also apply, in such a company, where the minority were ordered to purchase the majority's shares. If a company's articles provide machinery for a sale of the minority shareholder's shares, and a fair means of assessing the value of the shares, a member seeking to sell his shares on a breakdown of relations with other shareholders should not ordinarily be entitled to complain of unfair conduct if he has made no attempt to use the machinery provided: *Re A Company* [1987] 1 WLR 102.

on a discounted basis where, in an exceptional case, the minority had acted so as to deserve exclusion. This would also apply where the shares were allotted or later acquired as an investment in a private company. The Court of Appeal confirmed Nourse J's exercise of his discretionary power while emphasising the wide nature of the first instance court's power once unfair prejudice was shown.[1] The Court of Appeal emphasised that the overriding consideration[2] is that the valuation must be fair and equitable between the partners. The specific power (in what is now section 461(2)(d)) 'to provide for the purchase of the shares of any member of the company by other members' is subject to the wide discretion in section 461(1): 'make such order as it thinks fit for giving relief in respect of the matters complained of '. The Court of Appeal affirmed, but did not reopen, Nourse J's exercise of this discretion since it was a matter for the court of first instance rather than an appellate court. However, the court accepted that in a quasi-partnership case the '*pro rata*' solution was a proper exercise of the judge's discretion.[3] By implication they also accepted Nourse J's observation that in other cases the discounted minority interest method would be more appropriate.[4]

The same overriding requirement in valuing shares (that the price should be fair) will govern the choice of date for this purpose. Various dates have been chosen (eg the date of the unfair prejudice, the date of the petition,[5] the date when the valuation is made,[6] or the date of a consent order that shares should be purchased 'at such a price as the court should therefore determine'). The petitioner's own conduct, though not precluding a finding of unfair prejudice in his favour, may affect the date chosen by the court in exercising its discretion.[7] In the appropriate case, however, fairness may sometimes require that the shares be valued at a date earlier than the petition.[8] A petitioner may be unfairly prejudiced by the company's action in appointing the auditors as valuers when they are not independent, in the sense that the auditors could not reasonably approach the

---

1   [1986] 2 WLR 158 (CA). An allegation that the petitioner's shareholding is worthless was held not to be a ground for striking out a petition. The expert evidence conflicted, and the petition was allowed to go to trial. *Guinness Peat Group plc v British Land Co plc* [1999] 2 BCLC 243 (CA).

2   Ie after the court is satisfied that unfair prejudice has been established.

3   This was the basis applied by the same judge in another 'quasi-partnership' case, *Re London School of Electronics* [1986] Ch 211.

4   The same principles apply where the court has to exercise its powers on the basis of a consent order made after an earlier hearing with a provision for the matter of valuation to be settled by a judge. This was what had happened in *Re Bird Precision Bellows*, above. The court also held that the consent order did not constitute an agreement that interest should be awarded. There was no other basis on which interest could be awarded before the principal sum (the valuation) was determined.

5   *Re London School of Electronics* [1986] Ch 211. In *Virdi v Abbey Leisure Ltd* [1990] BCLC 342, the Court of Appeal noted the general inclination of the courts towards a *pro rata* basis of valuation. Cf *Howie and Others v Crawford* [1990] BCC 330. As to the valuation of shares in a private company as a going concern being sold on the open market, see *Re Planet Organic Ltd* [2000] 1 BCLC 366.

6   Ie the date of the Master's certificate.

7   See *Re London School of Electronics* [1986] Ch 211 where Nourse J considered a choice between the date of presentation of the petition and the date of valuation. He chose the former because of the petitioner's behaviour. See also *Re Cumana Ltd* [1986] BCLC 430 (CA).

8   *Re OC Transport Services Ltd* [1984] BCLC 251. Here by any later date the value of the petitioner's shares had been influenced by the reorganisation of its capital to allow another company to take the benefit of its unused capital allowances. See also *Re A Company* [1983] 1 WLR 927.

task of valuation without following the advice they had already given in different circumstances.[1]

The additional powers conferred by section 461(2)(b) and (c), (referred to earlier), allowing civil proceedings to be brought, have not yet been much invoked. However, in one case, which went to the Court of Appeal, the court hearing the petition appointed a receiver and manager,[2] permitted civil proceedings in the name of the company against certain of its creditors and ordered the cancellation of an issue of shares. The Court of Appeal[3] made certain further orders as to how the litigation should be controlled and conducted, while rejecting the argument that the original petitioner was not a suitable person to leave in charge of such litigation. The court also decreed that the debts of various creditors connected with the company (including the appellants and the respondents) 'be made subordinate to the outside creditors'. Where a derivative action is brought for misappropriation of the company's assets and the claimant later commences unfair prejudice proceedings, the derivative action can in due course be merged with those proceedings. The court can still grant a tracing order as it has power to give such a proprietary remedy under section 461.[4]

The power of the court under section 461(2)(c) to 'authorise civil proceedings to be brought in the company's name' has not yet shown its full potential. If the concept of 'unfair prejudice' in section 459 is to encompass grave corporate abuse (including serious negligent mismanagement) in public listed companies, it may become a more commonly sought remedy. Such proceedings would essentially amount to a thinly disguised derivative action[5] with the statutory concept of 'unfair prejudice' rather than the *Foss v Harbottle* concept of 'fraud on a minority' determining the issue of access to an action in the company's name or for its benefit. The simple wording of section 461(2)(c) leaves unanswered a number of questions as to the conduct and control of civil proceedings permitted under section 461.[6] For example, could the court exercise its discretion, in an appropriate case, to allow '*pro rata* recovery' where to require the proceeds of an action to be restored to the company would only benefit the wrongdoers left in control of the company? Another important question is whether the company would be responsible for the costs of an unsuccessful litigation permitted by the

---

1   *Re Benfield Greig Group plc* [2001] EWCA Civ 397, [2002] 1 BCLC 65.

2   See also *Re A Company (No 00596 of 1986)* [1987] BCLC 133.

3   In *Cyplon Developments Ltd* (CA) 3 March 1982 (*Lexis* transcript). See also *Re Whyte* (petitioner) 1984 SLT 330, where the court interdicted the holding of a meeting because the resolution to be passed would have removed a managing director from a committee responsible for company litigation. The effect of the resolution would have been to put the litigation under control of the defendants. As to the appointment of a receiver to protect the petitioner's interests, see *Wilton Davies v Kirk* [1998] 1 BCLC 274.

4   *Clark v Cutland* [2003] EWCA Civ 810, [2003] 2 BCLC 393 at 401–404, per Arden LJ. The court's powers under sections 459 and 461 are not limited by the restrictions, whether of policy or principle, of the rule in *Foss v Harbottle*. For a contrary view, see Hirst, 'In what circumstances should breaches of directors' duties give rise to a remedy under ss 459–461?', (2003) 24 Co Law 100.

5   See *Re A Company* [1986] 1 WLR 281 at 284. Such relief (ie court proceedings in the name of the company to recover sums improperly paid out by the company) was refused where an administrative receiver had already been appointed: *Re a Company* [1992] BCC 542. In *Lowe v Fahey* [1996] 1 BCLC 262, where the only substantive relief sought was a claim on behalf of the company against a third party, the petitioner was not allowed to proceed under section 459. A derivative action was the appropriate remedy.

6   See *Gore-Browne on Companies* 44th edn (Jordans, loose-leaf) at 28.17.9.

court (or the costs awarded in an action which succeeded but the defendant could not pay). In other words would the petitioner, put in charge of such proceedings, be at least as well protected as if he had the benefit of a *Wallersteiner* order[1] in a derivative action? Even if that is a fairly safe assumption, this would still not meet the point that the petitioner under section 459 must hazard the risk of costs at least until the stage when the issue of unfair prejudice is determined.[2] To that extent a derivative action, even in the case of a small private company, will be more attractive assuming that the difficulties of establishing 'fraud in a minority' can be overcome. The issue of costs can be resolved (at least to a particular stage in the litigation) at an early stage in an application before the Master.[3]

It may be fairly observed that a justifiable assertion by a minority shareholder of a serious breach of directors' duties (especially the duty of care) may fall between the alternative remedies of a derivative action on the one hand and a section 459 petition on the other. This is much more likely to be the case where a public listed company is concerned. Thus, it is to be hoped that the recommendations of the Law Commission, outlined in **17.10.1**, will eventually become law.

17.17 Just and equitable winding up as a minority shareholder's remedy

The preceding treatment of Part XVII of the Companies Act 1985 (petitions on the ground of unfair prejudice) sought to relate that type of relief to the alternative (but much older) remedy of a contributory's (ie a member's) petition for a just and equitable winding-up under what is now section 122(1)(g) of the Insolvency Act 1986. It was seen that the concept of a 'quasi-partnership' type of company (which was first developed by the House of Lords[4] in restating the principles applicable to just and equitable winding up), has in recent years been applied in the context of petitions under section 459.[5] Another important link between the two statutory remedies is the 'alternative remedy' requirement now contained in section 125(2) of the Insolvency Act 1986. This is an important factor in the exercise of judicial discretion, whether or not the petitioner combines a petition under section 459 of the Companies Act 1985 with one under section

---

1   See, however, *Smith v Croft* [1986] 1 WLR 580 where Walton J gave a rather restricted interpretation to *Wallersteiner v Moir (No 2)* [1975] QB 373 (CA); see further, **17.10**.

2   As to the award of costs where unfair prejudice is established and the petitioner's shares are ordered to be purchased, see *Re Elgindata Ltd (No 2)* [1993] BCLC 119 (CA).

3   *Smith v Croft* [1986] 1 WLR 580 implies that an interim order for costs will be given only where it is genuinely needed (eg the claimant cannot afford to sue) and even then some proportion of the costs must be borne by the claimant.

4   *Ebrahimi v Westbourne Galleries Ltd* [1973] AC 360, discussed below.

5   See earlier sections of this chapter for the relationship between these two statutory minority remedies. See **17.13.2** and **17.15**.

122(1)(g) of the Insolvency Act 1986. In *Ebrahimi v Westbourne Galleries*,[1] the House of Lords reviewed the nature and scope of the 'just and equitable' ground. It was emphasised that this ground should not be confined to special categories of situation.

It is clear that the effect of the House of Lords' decision is to extend the range of circumstances in which an order may be made on the just and equitable ground. The extent of the extension is still not entirely clear. Lord Wilberforce and Lord Cross of Chelsea delivered the only reasoned speeches. Although the case on its facts involved exclusion from participation in management, the observations made are of general significance in relation to the just and equitable ground. Lord Wilberforce also emphasised that references to 'quasi-partnerships' are confusing in the context of section 122(1)(g) except insofar as they recognise that concepts of probity, good faith and mutual confidence produced by the law of partnership are relevant to the exercise of the power to wind up on the just and equitable ground.

Lord Wilberforce emphasised that the mere fact that the exclusion of a director from participation in a company accords with the powers conferred by section 303 of the Companies Act 1985 and the articles of a company is not conclusive. The effect of section 122(1)(g) of the Insolvency Act 1986 is to enable the court 'to subject the exercise of legal rights to equitable considerations; considerations, that is, of a personal character arising between one individual and another, which may make it unjust, or inequitable, to insist on legal rights, or to exercise them in a particular way'.[2] Lord Wilberforce declined to define in an exhaustive manner the circumstances where the court would effect such a 'subjection'. He confined himself to a description of the type of situation which would typically give rise to the subjection of the legal rights or powers to the equitable considerations. He stated that such a situation:

> ... may include one or probably more of the following elements: (i) an association formed or continued on the basis of a personal relationship, involving mutual confidence – this element will often be found where a pre-existing partnership has been converted into a limited company; (ii) an agreement, or understanding, that all, or some (for there may be 'sleeping' members), of the shareholders shall participate in the conduct of the business; (iii) restrictions upon the transfer of the members' interest in the company – so that if confidence is lost, or one member is removed from management, he cannot take out his stake and go elsewhere.[3]

The primary importance of the decision of the House of Lords is to reject the view that the petitioner must prove that his exclusion was not *bona fide* in the

1   [1973] AC 360 (HL (E)). The House of Lords was influenced by a number of Commonwealth decisions where the principles governing just and equitable winding up had been developed on similar lines. See, in particular, *Re Straw Products Pty Ltd* [1942] VLR 222 at 223 and *Re Wondoflex Textiles Pty Ltd* [1951] VLR 467 at 458 cited in the speech of Lord Wilberforce. See also, *Tench v Tench Bros Ltd* [1930] NZLR 403; *Re Sydney and Whitney Pier Bus Service Ltd* [1944] 3 DLR 468; and *Re Concrete Column Clamps Ltd* [1953] 4 DLR 60, which were also referred to by Lord Wilberforce. See also, *Re Tivoli Freeholds* [1972] VR 445. For further examination of the implications of the House of Lords' decision, see Chesterman (1973) 36 MLR 129 and Prentice (1973) 89 Law Quarterly Review 107. See Prentice, ibid, pp 123–4, on the application of the principle to directors' refusal to transfer shares and on this see Lord Cross of Chelsea's speech.
2   [1973] AC at 379. See *Clemens v Clemens Bros* [1976] 2 All ER 268 at 282 for an application of this passage outside a just and equitable winding-up. *Sed quaere.*
3   [1973] AC at 398.

interests of the company or such that no reasonable man could consider it to be in the interests of the company. The decision established, on a positive note, that the court possesses jurisdiction under section 122(1)(g) to order winding up where the circumstances disclose some underlying obligation in good faith and confidence that the petitioner should participate in management so long as the business continues. Expulsion justifies the assertion of that jurisdiction at least where the expulsion results in the loss of participation in profits and leaves the party expelled as a locked-in shareholder.[1]

The application of the above principles to situations *not* involving expulsion remains to some degree uncertain.[2] The position also remains uncertain where a (private) company has adopted the increasingly uncommon practice of distributing profits by way of dividend. However, it does not appear that an exclusion either from participation in management or from participation in profits is essential. Any course of dealing which produces a breakdown in mutual confidence may well suffice to justify the making of a winding-up order under section 122(1)(g),[3] unless that breakdown in mutual confidence is referable to the conduct of the complainant shareholders.[4] It is also possible that retention of profits which excludes members from participation by way of dividend will justify a winding-up order where this defeats the members' expectations and leaves the petitioner unable to realise the full value of his shares.[5]

An important issue is the relationship between the just and equitable winding-up and the unfair prejudice remedies. As seen earlier in this chapter, there are some circumstances where one of these remedies may be available and the other will not be, but there are other circumstances, of which the situation exemplified in the *Westbourne Galleries* case is probably a classic example, where both remedies may be available. The issue of which remedy might prevail has been examined in **17.16**.

17.18 Earlier cases consistent with *Westbourne*

There are other English and Scottish cases decided before *Westbourne* which can still be regarded as consistent with it. A company was wound up where there were only three shareholders, each holding one-third of the capital, and an article directed that if one shareholder offered his shares to the others and they refused to purchase, the company should be wound up. In this case the winding-up was on the ground that it was just and equitable, and that though the article was not binding on the court it formed a reason for holding that the company ought to be wound up.[6] In another case there were only two shareholders, each of whom was a director, one holding a single share, and the other the remainder of the issued

---

1   See *Lewis v Haas* 1971 SLT 57 (Ct of Sess) and *Re Davis & Collett* [1935] Ch 593.
2   An example of the application of the principles in *Westbourne Galleries*, above, in the context of a joint venture company is *Re A & BC Chewing Gum* [1975] 1 WLR 579.
3   See eg *Jesner v Jarrad Properties Ltd* [1993] BCLC 1032 (Ct of Sess). See also *Re Pauls Federated Merchants Ltd* (30 July 1976, unreported), where Brightman J applied the *Westbourne* decision to a company which was not a quasi-partnership.
4   Cases such as *Re Yenidje Tobacco Co* [1916] 2 Ch 246 (CA); *Re Sailing Ship Kentmere Co* [1897] WN 58, and *American Pioneer Leather Co* [1918] 1 Ch 556 must now be interpreted not merely as cases establishing that deadlock in management justifies a winding-up order, but as illustration of the wide concept of section 122(1)(g) established in *Westbourne Galleries*, above.
5   *Re A Company, ex parte Glossop* [1988] 1 WLR 1068.
6   *Re American Pioneer Leather Co* [1918] 1 Ch 556.

capital: namely 1,501 shares. The latter having usurped the whole powers of the company, the former, though holding one share only, successfully petitioned for a winding-up order.[1]

17.19   Loss of 'substratum'

The court will wind up a company even within one year of its formation, although it may be solvent, if it appears that it has become impossible to carry on the business for which it was formed.[2] Thus where the mine which a company was formed to work could not be found,[3] or the patent it was to work was not granted,[4] or the bulk of its property had been sold and its capital exhausted,[5] or there was no reasonable probability of obtaining the benefit of the contract it was formed to carry out,[6] a winding-up order was made. The *substratum* of the company was also held to have vanished where a bank had ceased to carry on banking business[7] or the mine which the company was working proved worthless,[8] or a company formed to amalgamate three syndicates for speculating in seats for the Diamond Jubilee proposed, after losing money over that speculation, to do other financial business,[9] or a single steamship company had lost its only ship and proposed with a small sum of cash to carry on business as a charterer of ships.[10] The sale by the company of the only business it has ever carried on, even if the carrying on of that particular business was stated in its memorandum as the first object, will not justify an order being made under this paragraph if, under its memorandum, it has power to resume that or any other kind of business.[11]

Compulsory acquisition of the property of a company for the purposes of nationalisation will not apparently render it in any case immediately liable to be wound up under section 122(1)(g).[12] In some of the earlier cases, the court has paid attention to what appears to be the most important object of the company

---

1   *Thomson v Drysdale* 1925 SC 311.
2   This principle was first suggested in the case of *Suburban Hotel Co* (1867) 2 Ch App 737.
3   *Re Haven Gold Mining Co* (1882) 20 Ch D 151.
4   *Re German Date Coffee Co* (1882) 20 Ch D 169.
5   *Re Diamond Fuel Co (No 2)* (1879) 13 Ch D 400 (CA).
6   *Re Blériot Manufacturing Aircraft Co* (1916) 32 TLR 253.
7   *Re Crown Bank* (1890) 44 Ch D 634.
8   *Re Red Rock Gold Mining Co* (1886) 61 LT 785.
9   *Re Amalgamated Syndicate* [1897] 2 Ch 600.
10 *Pirie v Stewart* (1905), 6 F 847 (Ct of Sess).
11 *Re Kitson & Co* [1946] 1 All ER 435; *Re Taldua Rubber Co* [1946] 2 All ER 763; *Galbraith v Merito Shipping Co* 1947 SC 446. In the first of these cases, Lord Greene MR suggested that if after selling its business a company was obviously unable, eg for lack of capital, to carry on any business which under its memorandum it had power to carry on, this might afford a ground for a winding-up order: [1946] 1 All ER at 440. He also suggested that different considerations might arise if the main business which the company was originally intended to carry on was never acquired on incorporation, so that it did not start its career in the way the original shareholders bargained for (ibid at p 438). See also *Re Eastern Telegraph Co* [1947] 2 All ER at 111, where Jenkins J stated that this case was not one of the contemplated objects failing *ab initio*.
12 *Re Eastern Telegraph Co* [1947] 2 All ER 104.

appearing in its memorandum.[1] In others, this has not been decisive.[2] It is, however, clear that the memorandum must be construed on a question of this kind in the same way as it would be construed for any other purpose.[3]

17.20 Fraudulent and illegal companies

A company may also be wound up on the just and equitable ground where the company was in its inception fraudulent and hopelessly embarrassed by actions for rescission, and where a winding-up is the best means of recovering money from the promoters,[4] or where the company never had a real foundation and was a mere 'bubble',[5] or is formed to carry on an illegal business, such as dealing in lottery bonds.[6]

The court will not, however, wind up a company because it is not prosperous,[7] or its chance of success small,[8] unless the company passes a special resolution for liquidation; thus except where the company is insolvent the mere fact that it has passed an ordinary resolution that it be wound up, and that the directors be directed to present a petition therefore, will not justify the making of an order.[9] A contributory whose shares are fully paid up must establish that he has a tangible interest in the winding-up. To do this the petition must show a *prima facie* probability that the company is solvent and consequently there will be substantial assets for distribution.[10]

1   *Re Red Rock Gold Mining Co* (1889) 61 LT 785; *Re Coolgardie Consolidated Gold Mines* (1897) 76 LT 269; *Stephens v Mysore Reefs (Kangundy) Mining Co* [1902] 1 Ch 745.

2   With the words only slightly differing from those in the cases cited in the previous note, Warrington J held that other mines were within the original contemplation of the company; *Pedlar and Road Block Gold Mines* [1905] 2 Ch 427; and see *Campbell v Australian Mutual Provident Society* (1908) 77 LJPC 117.

3   *Re Kitson & Co* [1946] 1 All ER 435. See *Butler v Northern Territories Mines of Australia* (1907) 96 LT 41; see also *Cotman v Brougham* [1918] AC 514 (HL).

4   *Re Thomas Edward Brinsmead & Sons* [1897] 1 Ch D 406 (CA); cf *Re Diamond Fuel Co* (1879) 13 Ch D 400 (CA); and *Re General Phosphate Corp* [1893] WN 142.

5   *Anglo-Greek Steam Co* (1866) LR 2 Eq 1; *Re West Surrey Tanning Co* (1886) LR 2 Eq 737; *Re London and County Coal Co* (1867) LR 3 Eq 355.

6   *Re International Securities Corp* (1908) 99 LT 581, where Swinfen-Eady J also held that the company was conducted in a fraudulent manner.

7   *Re Langham Skating Rink Co* (1877) 5 Ch D 669 (CA); *Re Suburban Hotel Co* (1867) 2 Ch App 737.

8   *Re Kronand Metal Co* [1899] WN 15. See, however, *Davis v Brunswick (Australia) Ltd* [1936] 1 All ER 299.

9   *Re Anglo-Continental Produce Co* [1939] 1 All ER 99.

10 *Re Expanded Plugs Ltd* [1960] 1 WLR 514; *Re Othery Construction Co* [1966] 1 WLR 69.

PART 3: THE DEPARTMENT OF TRADE AND INDUSTRY'S POWERS TO INVESTIGATE COMPANIES AND THEIR SECURITIES

17.21 Introduction

Under the Companies Act 1985,[1] the Department of Trade and Industry is given powers to appoint inspectors to investigate the affairs of a company.[2] The DTI may also conduct its own investigations into a company's affairs by more informal enquiries. As the result of its own investigations, or as the result of the publication of a report by inspectors, the DTI has the power to bring proceedings on behalf of the company or to petition for a winding-up order. The Department of Trade and Industry has the power to appoint inspectors to investigate the ownership of a company. It may also appoint inspectors to investigate share dealings which are in contravention of certain provisions of the Companies Act 1985.[3]

17.22 Investigation of the affairs of the company

As regards the investigation of the affairs of a company,[4] the Department of Trade and Industry is obliged to appoint an inspector if the court orders it to do so.[5] Section 431(2)(c) provides that the DTI may appoint inspectors 'in any case, on the application of the company'. The DTI may at its discretion appoint an inspector on the application of a specified number of minority shareholders.[6] This application must be supported by evidence showing that the applicant or applicants have good reason for requiring the investigation. In addition, security for the costs of the enquiry, not exceeding £5,000, must be provided. The maximum amount of the security may be further increased by statutory instrument. These powers have been very little used.[7]

The DTI may also appoint an inspector under section 432(2)[8] if there are circumstances suggesting any of the following:

---

1 These provisions of the Act were amended by Part III of the Companies Act 1989. The references in this part of this chapter to the 1985 Act are to it as so amended.
2 The powers conferred by Part XIV of the Companies Act 1985 apply to registered companies. As to unregistered companies, see Schedule 22 to the Companies Act 1985, as amended by section 71 of the 1989 Act.
3 Ie sections 323, 324 and 328 (restrictions on share dealings by directors and their families, etc). See also section 446.
4 An inspector, appointed under either section 431 or 432 to investigate the affairs of a company, has the power, if he thinks it necessary, to investigate the company's holding or subsidiary company 'or a subsidiary of its holding company or a holding company of its subsidiary'. This applies to any body which *is* a subsidiary, etc, or which 'has at any relevant time *been*', etc: Companies Act 1985, section 433. For the statutory definition of the relationship of holding and subsidiary company, see section 736. See further **3.8.1**.
5 Section 432(1).
6 Section 431(2)(a) and (b). The applicants must consist of not less than 200 members of the company or of members holding not less than one-tenth of the shares issued in the case of a company having share capital. In the case of a company not having share capital, the applicants must consist of not less than one-fifth in number of the persons on the company's register of members.
7 It will be seen that this is linked with the DTI's power to obtain repayment of the expenses of an inspection.
8 Section 423(3) allows the DTI to appoint an inspector where the company is in course of a voluntary liquidation.

(1) that the company's business is being conducted with intent to defraud its creditors or the creditors of any other person, or otherwise for a fraudulent or unlawful purpose or in a manner which is unfairly prejudicial to some part of its members, or that any actual or proposed act or omission of the company (including any act or omission on its behalf) is or would be so prejudicial, or that it was formed for any fraudulent or unlawful purpose; or

(2) that persons concerned with its formation or the management of its affairs have in connection therewith been guilty of fraud, misfeasance or other misconduct towards it or towards its members; or

(3) that its members have not been given all the information with respect to its affairs which they might reasonably expect.

A provision inserted in section 432 by the Companies Act 1989 allows the Secretary of State to appoint inspectors under section 432(2) on terms that 'any report that may be made is not for publication'.[1]

Although more use has been made of what is now section 432, prior to the 1967 Act the DTI had been inclined only to exercise its discretion in cases where notoriety in the press had already caused serious public concern. This cautious policy had been defensible to the extent that the mere announcement of a DTI inspection can do a company's business reputation irreparable harm on The Stock Exchange and elsewhere before any abuse is proven. On the other hand, this reaction of the business community may in part reflect the limited use of this power in the past.

To overcome this difficulty, the DTI was given new powers in the Companies Act 1967 to obtain the information it needs more quickly and informally. These additional powers[2] enable the DTI to compel the production of any books and papers it may specify.[3] The DTI may lay any information before a justice of the peace to obtain a warrant giving power to enter and search premises for the books and papers they require.[4] Penalties are also provided for the destruction of documents and for furnishing false information.[5]

The rules of natural justice have been held not to apply to the discretion exercised by the DTI in appointing inspectors to investigate the affairs of a company.[6] So long as the Secretary of State is acting within his powers[7] and is in good faith, his decision cannot be challenged. His decision does not imply there is any case against the company or its management and he cannot be made to reveal the evidence which has led him to act. The Secretary of State may appoint

---

1   See section 432(2A).

2   Companies Act 1985, section 447.

3   This power is wide enough to include the provision of an explanation not only of the text of a document but also, *inter alia*, its creation, authorship, accuracy, completeness etc: *Attorney-General's Reference (No 2 of 1998)* [1999] BCC 590 (CA).

4   Section 448. See section 449, which provides for security of information obtained under section 447 and for the permitted disclosure of this information in certain cases (eg examination of persons by inspectors appointed to conduct an investigation, or with a view to bringing criminal proceedings).

5   Ibid, sections 450 and 451. The 1985 Act also confers powers on inspectors, approved by the DTI to conduct a formal investigation, to enable them to compel the attendance of witnesses: sections 434 and 436.

6   *Norwest Holst v Secretary of State for Trade* [1978] 3 WLR 73 (CA).

7   In the *Norwest* case, the inspector had been appointed under what is now section 432(2)(c), but this decision would apply to any other statutory discretion to appoint inspectors or to take proceedings.

inspectors to investigate matters which may also be the subject of criminal proceedings.[1]

17.22.1 *Informal investigations under section 447*

The vast majority of investigations by the DTI are carried out under section 447. Members of the Company Investigation Branch or other competent individuals can be authorised, among other things, to seek the production of documents or to require explanations of any document from the person who produces it.[2] These are confidential fact finding inquiries, but there is a disclosure regime that allows, for example, information to be passed on to other regulators. Investigations under section 447 are carried out, for example, where there are grounds for suspicion of fraud, misfeasance or misconduct unfairly prejudicial to shareholders or where there has been a failure to supply shareholders with information they may reasonably expect. It has been held that an inspector appointed to make an informal investigation under section 447 cannot be cross-examined (in subsequent winding-up proceedings) either as to his reasons for investigating under section 447 or as to why he thought it in the public interest that the company be wound up under section 440.[3]

It has been held that the court will not exercise powers of review (on the basis of orders of prohibition and certiorari under RSC Order 53[4]) in the case of officers of the Department of Trade and Industry exercising powers under section 447. The principle of bias did not apply to an investigation under section 447, since under this section the officers are exercising a police function and not a judicial or quasi-judicial function. However, a complainant may be entitled, on the ground of unfairness, to an order quashing a notice under section 447(2) (requiring the production of documents relating to the company's finances) on the basis that the notice is unreasonably and excessively wide.[5]

The Companies (Audit, Investigations and Community Enterprise) Bill 2003[6] will amend the powers to investigate under section 447. While not changing the basis of an inspection or making any changes of substance to the grounds for an investigation, the Bill seeks to strengthen the regime. It will give investigators a general power to require relevant information and strengthen their power to require documents. For example, it will enable them to require a person to explain his or her conduct or to give his or her opinion about something. It will also exclude liability for breach of confidence so that individuals and business can feel able to volunteer information in response to an informal DTI enquiry. The Bill will also give inspectors and investigators a power to require entry on to a company's business premises and to remain there for the purposes of the investigation.

---

1   *Re London United Investments plc* [1992] BCLC 285 (CA).
2   Or from any past or present officer or employee of the company.
3   *Re Golden Chemical Products Ltd* (1979) *The Times*, 8 December, *per* Deputy Judge Michael Wheeler QC.
4   See now the Civil Procedure Rules 1998, Schedule 1 at 1.90.
5   *R v Secretary of State for Trade, ex parte Perestrello* [1980] 3 WLR 1.
6   See Part I, chapter 3. The Bill was introduced in to the House of Lords, December 2, 2003.

17.23   The conduct of proceedings by inspectors

The Court of Appeal has held[1] that although the proceedings before inspectors are not judicial or quasi-judicial,[2] but are of an administrative nature, yet the characteristics of the proceedings require the inspectors to act fairly. In this sense, the rules of natural justice apply. Thus, if they were disposed to condemn or criticise anyone in a report, the inspectors must first give him a fair opportunity to correct or contradict the allegation against him. For this purpose, an outline of the charge will usually suffice. So long as the inspectors acted fairly they were not subject to any set rules procedure. The Court of Appeal held that directors were not entitled to refuse to answer questions put to them by the inspectors until they were shown the transcripts of evidence and the documents used against them, and had been allowed to cross-examine witnesses. The inspectors were held to have acted fairly, and in accordance with rules of natural justice,[3] by undertaking that no one would be criticised in the report without first being told in general terms of the allegation against him and being afforded an opportunity to give an explanation. The inspectors were prepared to make known the purport of the relevant evidence and documents. The directors' refusal to give evidence on these terms was unjustified.

Where an officer or agent of the company or other body corporate refuses to answer questions which are put to him by inspectors, the latter may 'certify the refusal under their hand to the court'.[4] The House of Lords has held that an officer or agent of the company examined by the inspectors is entitled to refuse to answer questions on the ground that the answers would incriminate him. But if such a witness does so, the matter may be referred to the court under section 436(2).[5] The issue of self-incrimination is one which the court not the inspectors should decide.[6]

It has been seen that an investigation is not a judicial enquiry, and the proceedings should be conducted in private. However, it has been held that the inspector is entitled to the assistance of anyone whose presence is reasonably necessary, and that a person examined could not object to the presence of a

---

1   *Re Pergamon Press Ltd* [1970] 3 WLR 792 (CA), affirming the decision of Plowman J [1970] 1 WLR 1075. See also *Maxwell v Department of Trade and Industry* [1974] 1 QB 523 (CA).

2   See *Re Grosvenor and West End Railway Terminus Hotel Co Ltd* (1897) 76 LT 732; *Hearts of Oak Assurance Co Ltd v Attorney-General* [1932] AC 322 (HL).

3   The Court of Appeal referred, as to the rules of natural justice, to *Russell v Duke of Norfolk* [1949] 1 All ER 109; *Ridge v Baldwin* [1964] AC 40 (HL); *Wiseman v Borneman* [1969] 3 WLR 706 (HL); *R v Gaming Board for Great Britain, ex parte Benaim* [1970] 2 QB 417 (CA).

4   Companies Act 1985, section 436(2). The same procedure applies to a refusal to produce to the inspectors any book or document which it is the duty of such an officer to produce under section 434 or 435, or to a refusal 'to attend before inspectors when required so to do'.

5   The power conferred by section 436 now extends to 'any person'. See **17.25**.

6   See further, *Gore-Browne on Companies* 44th edn (Jordans, loose-leaf) at 28.23 as to the right to refuse to disclose information given to the company's bankers and those entitled to 'professional legal privilege'. See also, *Re London United Investments* [1992] BCLC 285, in which the Court of Appeal held that the privilege against self-incrimination is not a basis for refusing to answer questions.

shorthand writer.[1] Parties involved in the investigation may be represented by counsel.[2]

17.24 The inspectors' report and subsequent proceedings

A copy of any report of inspectors appointed to investigate into the affairs of a company is admissible in any legal proceedings as evidence of the opinion of the inspectors in relation to any matters contained in the report.[3] Moreover, section 434(5) of the Companies Act 1985 provides that an answer given by a person to a question put to him under the powers conferred by section 434 (as to the conduct of investigations by inspectors) may be used in evidence against him.[4]

17.25 The power to examine on oath and obtain documents

Section 434(3) of the Companies Act 1985 gives an inspector power to examine any person on oath and to administer an oath accordingly. Section 434(1) imposes a duty on all officers and agents of the company to produce documents, attend before the inspectors and give assistance in connection with the investigation. Section 434(2) amplifies this duty. It provides that if the inspectors consider that a person other than an officer or agent of the company (or other body corporate) is, or may be, in possession of any information concerning its affairs, they may require that person to produce to them any books or documents[5] in his custody or power. They may also require such a person to attend before them and otherwise to give them all the assistance, in connection with the investigation, which he is reasonably able to give (and it is the duty of such a person to comply).[6] In certain circumstances, section 435(1) gives inspectors power to request disclosure of documents relating to the bank accounts of directors (or past directors) of the company or other body corporate whose affairs are being investigated. This may apply where the director maintains (or has maintained) a bank account of any description, whether alone or jointly with another person, and whether in Great Britain or elsewhere. However, this can be done only if the inspectors have reasonable grounds to believe that the following types of payment have been paid into, or out of, the account. These are of three types.

---

1   *Re Gaumont-British Picture Corp* [1940] 1 Ch 506.
2   See *McClelland, Pope and Langley Ltd v Howard* [1968] 1 All ER 569n. As to the Department of Trade and Industry's decision to publish a report and furnish it to various interested parties, see the Companies Act 1985, sections 437 and 441. See *Gore-Browne on Companies* at 28.24.
3   Companies Act 1985, section 441(1). The report is certified by the Secretary to be a true copy of such report (and it must be received in evidence etc).
4   See, eg, *R v Seelig* [1991] BCLC 869; *Re London United Investments plc* [1992] BCLC 285. See further as to the use of evidence so obtained in subsequent proceedings, *Gore-Browne on Companies* at 28.25.2. The power to obtain evidence under section 434 applies also to investigations into the ownership of the company under section 442, and to an investigation into share dealings under section 446.
5   Ie in relating to the company or other body corporate.
6   See *Re an Enquiry into Mirror Group Newspapers plc* [1999] 1 BCLC 690 as to when a refusal to respond to the inspector's questions will be held reasonable.

(1) Emoluments or part of the emoluments of his office as such director, particulars of which have not been disclosed in the accounts of the company or other body corporate for any financial year contrary to paragraphs 24 to 26 of Schedule 5.

(2) Any money which has resulted from, or been used in, the financing of various types of transaction, arrangement or agreement which are in breach of various provisions listed by section 435(2).

(3) Any money which has been in any way connected with any act or omission, or series of acts or omissions, which constituted misconduct (whether fraudulent or not) on the part of that director towards the company or body corporate or its members.

17.26 Civil proceedings by the Department of Trade and Industry

The DTI may now act on the basis of its powers to obtain documents and other information from the company without a formal investigation by the Department's inspectors. It still retains the power to take proceedings after receiving an adverse report by an inspector.

The DTI can bring any action the company itself might bring if it appears that such proceedings ought to be brought in the public interest.[1] The DTI's power to petition for a winding-up likewise depends on its opinion of what is in the public interest.[2] Again, the DTI may act not only on the basis of an inspector's report, but under its new power to obtain information without a formal public enquiry. Where it was sought in ordinary civil proceedings (as opposed to a winding-up petition, as to which see below) to use an inspector's report, it was held inadmissible since it contained only opinions. If the inspector's opinions (contained in their report) were referred to in an affidavit to be used in interlocutory proceedings, they may be struck out as containing inadmissible evidence.[3]

In a winding-up petition by the DTI, where the accuracy of an inspector's report is not disputed, the court may act on the basis of the report although it is supported only by the affidavit of a DTI official.[4] Where allegations against a company and its officers are contested, the DTI must support the petition 'by evidence of true evidential value'.[5] A challenge to a report (on which a petition by the Secretary of State is based) means 'a challenge by someone with knowledge of the facts coming along and saying the inspectors' report is wrong, and being willing to put forward an affidavit and be cross-examined, and to be judged in the witness box on the evidence which he puts forward in contradiction of the inspectors' report'.[6] Even if the report is challenged in the above sense, it ought

---

1   Section 438(1).

2   See now section 124(4)(b) of the Insolvency Act 1986. See section 124A as to the reports and statutory sources of information on the basis of which the Secretary of State may conclude that it is expedient in the public interest that a company should be wound up. A voluntary liquidation will no longer inhibit the exercise of this power: *Re Lubin Rosen and Associates Ltd* [1975] 1 WLR 122.

3   *Savings and Investment Bank Ltd v Gasco Investments (Netherlands) BV* [1984] 1 WLR 271.

4   *Re Allied Produce Co* [1967] 1 WLR 1964; *Re Travel & Holiday Club* [1967] 1 WLR 71.

5   *Re ABC Coupler Engineering Co* [1962] 1 WLR 1236. As to the evidence admissible in a compulsory winding-up brought by the Department of Trade, see *Re Koscott Interplanetary (UK) Ltd* [1972] 3 All ER 82.

6   *Re Armvent Ltd* [1975] 3 All ER 441 at 446 *per* Templeman J.

to be treated as *prima facie* evidence and it ought to be left to the judge in any case, having read the report and having seen the witnesses, to make up his own mind whether it is just and equitable to wind up the company.

> The whole machinery of the inspector's report was evolved in order to enable the Secretary of State to present a winding up petition where he considers the public interest so demands. It would be unfortunate if, once the Secretary of State has reached that conclusion on proper grounds based on the inspector's detailed report, the court should go right back to square one and start again as though the inspector had never come on the scene at all.[1]

The DTI also possesses the power to seek relief under section 460 of the Companies Act 1985, if it appears to it that the affairs of a company are being conducted in a manner unfairly prejudicial to some part of the members. Here the DTI is not required to have regard to the public interest, and it may seek to enforce this minority shareholders' remedy either in addition to or instead of a winding-up petition.[2]

17.27 Expenses in investigations and proceedings by the DTI

One of the attractions for shareholders in seeking the intervention of the Department of Trade and Industry, under section 432 of the Companies Act 1985, is that the expenses of the investigation and any consequent proceedings brought by the DTI must be defrayed in the first instance by the Department.[3] The Department is entitled to repayment of these expenses if the report of the inspector results in a successful prosecution in a criminal court, or a judgment in a civil court, to the extent specified in an order made in those proceedings.[4] In addition, a company for whose benefit civil proceedings have been brought by the DTI is liable to repay the expenses 'to the amount or value of any sums of property recovered by it as a result of those proceedings'.[5]

Where the DTI appoints an inspector 'otherwise than of the Department's own motion' the company can also be made to contribute from its own resources to the costs of inspection and subsequent proceedings. Thus where, under section 432(1), the court orders an inspection, the DTI has no choice in the matter, and it is only fair that the company should be liable 'except so far as this Department otherwise direct'. But shareholders who apply under section 431 are also liable to repay the DTI 'to such extent (if any) as the Department may direct', even though

---

1   Ibid.
2   See **17.14**.
3   Section 439(3); but see section 439(5).
4   Section 439(2).
5   Section 439(3). Any amount for which the company is liable under section 439(3) is a first charge on the sums or property recovered. But in the case of a civil action brought on behalf of the company, the DTI is required to indemnify the company against costs or expenses incurred by the company in connection with the proceedings: section 438(2). Thus the company may have to contribute from the proceeds accruing to it from a successful action, but it cannot be prejudiced by an unsuccessful action. It has been held that 'the amount or value of any sums recovered by the company' (as limiting what it may be liable to pay to the DTI under section 439(3)(b)) includes the costs recovered by the company: *Selangor Rubber Estates Ltd v Cradock (No 4)* [1969] 2 WLR 1773. However, the DTI's duty to indemnify the company for the expenses of litigation includes costs ordered to be paid by the company to other parties: *Selangor United Estates v Cradock (No 1)* [1967] 1 WLR 1168 at 1173.

here it is not compelled to appoint an inspector.[1] Where minority shareholders do not make a formal request under section 431, but confine themselves to persuading the DTI to act 'of its own motion' under section 432(2), the Department has no power to make the minority or the company contribute to the expenses of an inspection. Thus if the DTI chooses to act under section 432(2), it will recover its expenses only in the event of successful proceedings resulting from the inspector's report. There is provision for rights of contribution as between any of the parties who may become liable to repay the Department's expenses.[2] What the DTI cannot recover must of course be paid by public funds.[3]

17.28 The DTI's power to investigate the ownership of shares

Under section 442 of the Companies Act 1985, the Department of Trade and Industry has power to investigate the ownership of shares of a company. Where it appears to the DTI that there is good reason so to do, it may appoint one or more competent inspectors to investigate and report on the membership of any company and otherwise with respect to the company for the purpose of determining the true persons who are or have been financially interested in the success or failure (real or apparent) of the company, or are able to control or materially influence its policy.[4]

Where an application for an investigation under the section is made to the Department of Trade and Industry with respect to particular shares or debentures of a company, in the case of a company having a share capital, either by not less than 200 members or by members holding not less than one-tenth of the shares issued, or in the case of a company not having a share capital, by not less than one-fifth in number of the persons on the register of members, then the DTI is to appoint an inspector to conduct the investigation unless it is satisfied that the application is vexatious. Where inspectors are appointed, their terms of appointment must include any matter insofar as the Secretary of State is satisfied that it is reasonable to be investigated.[5] Section 442(3C) permits the Secretary of State to proceed instead under section 444 where he deems it more appropriate. The Secretary of State may, before appointing inspectors, require the applicants to give security up to an amount not exceeding £5,000 for the payment of the costs of the investigation.[6]

Subject to the terms of an inspector's appointment, his powers are to extend to the investigation of any circumstances suggesting the existence of an arrangement or understanding which, though not legally binding, is or was observed or likely to be observed in practice and which is relevant to the purposes of his investigation.[7]

---

1 Section 439(5).
2 Section 439(9); and see section 439(8).
3 Section 439(10).
4 Section 442(1).
5 Section 442(3), (3A).
6 This amount may be increased by the Secretary of State by order: see section 442(3B).
7 Section 442(4). With the necessary modifications, certain of the provisions governing an investigation of the company's affairs by inspectors are applied to investigations under section 442 of ownership of shares. These provisions are section 433(1) (power to investigate related companies), section 434 (production of documents, etc), section 436 (obstruction of inspectors) and section 437 (inspector's report).

Where it appears to the DTI that there is good reason to investigate the ownership of any shares in or debentures of a company but that it is unnecessary to appoint an inspector for the purpose, under section 442 they may require any person whom they have reasonable cause to believe to have or to be able to obtain any information as to the present and past interests in those shares or debentures and the names and addresses of the persons interested and of any persons who act or have acted on their behalf in relation to the shares or debentures to give any such information to the Secretary of State.[1]

17.29   Power to impose restrictions on shares or debentures

Part XV of the Companies Act 1985 gives the Department of Trade and Industry power to impose restrictions on shares[2] 'in connection with an investigation' under section 442 or 444 (investigation of the ownership of a company).[3] The DTI may invoke these powers where it appears to it that there is difficulty in finding out the relevant facts about any shares (whether issued or to be issued). In that event, the DTI may by order direct that the shares shall be subject, until further order, to the restrictions imposed by section 454.

So long as any shares are directed to be subject to the restrictions imposed by Part XV of the Act, the following provisions of section 454(1) apply:

(1) any transfer of those shares, or in the case of unissued shares any transfer of the right to be issued with them and any issue of them, is void;
(2) no voting rights are exercisable in respect of those shares;
(3) no further shares are to be issued in right of those shares or in pursuance of any offer made to their holder;
(4) except in a liquidation, no payment shall be made of any sums due from the company on those shares whether in respect of capital or otherwise.

Section 454(2) and (3) contain provisions which amplify the effect of these restrictions. Where shares are subject to the restrictions imposed in (1) above, any agreement to transfer the shares, or in the case of unissued shares the right to be issued with the shares, is void.[4] Where shares are subject to the restrictions imposed in (3) and (4), any agreement to transfer any right to be issued with *other* shares in right of those shares or to receive any payment on those shares (otherwise than in a liquidation) is void.[5]

Where the Department of Trade and Industry makes an order directing that shares shall be subject to such restrictions, or refuses to make an order directing that shares cease to be subject thereto, any person aggrieved may apply to the

---

1   Section 444(1). See further, *Gore-Browne on Companies* 44th edn (Jordans, loose-leaf) at 28.28.1.
2   Part XV applies to debentures as well as to shares: section 445(2).
3   This power can also be invoked under Part VI of the Companies Act 1985. See section 216. See *Re Geers Gross plc* [1987] BCLC 253, and *Re FH Lloyd Holdings plc* (1985) 1 BCC 99, 407 as to the application of these provisions to foreign shareholders; see also *Re Ricardo Group (No 1)* [1989] BCLC 566, *(No 2)* [1989] BCLC 766 and *(No 3)* [1989] BCLC 771.
4   'Except an agreement to sell shares on the making of an order under section 456(3)(b).' 'Sale' means a sale for cash, not an exchange of shares: *Re Westminster Property Group plc* [1985] BCLC 188 (CA).
5   Except on an agreement to transfer any such right on the sale of the shares on the making of an order under section 456(3)(b).

court for an order directing that the shares be no longer subject to the restrictions.[1] If the order was made by the court under section 216(1) (non-disclosure of shareholding), the application may be made by the person aggrieved or by the company.[2]

Section 456(3) states the conditions on which the court, or the Secretary of State, may make an order that shares shall cease to be subject to the restrictions imposed by section 454. These are that the court or, as the case may be, the Secretary of State, is satisfied that the relevant facts about the shares have been disclosed to the company, and no unfair advantage has accrued to any person as a result of the earlier failure to make disclosure. Alternatively an order under section 456(3) may be made if the shares are to be transferred and the court (in any case) or the Secretary of State (if the order is made under section 210 or 445) approves the sale. Section 456(4) gives the court a power to order the sale of shares on the application of the Secretary of State (unless the restrictions were imposed by the court under section 216) or the company. On such an application the court may also order that the shares shall cease to be subject to the restrictions imposed. Where shares are sold by an order made under section 456(4), the proceeds of sale, less the costs of sale, shall be paid into court for the benefit of the persons who are beneficially interested in the shares. Such persons may apply to the court for payment of the whole[3] or part of the proceeds. On an application under section 457(1), the court must order the payment to the applicant of the whole of the proceeds of sale (together with any interest) or, if any other person had a beneficial interest in the shares at the time of their sale, such proportion of those proceeds (and interest thereon) as is equal to the proportion which the value of the applicant's interest in the shares bears to the total value of the shares.[4]

17.30 Powers to investigate share dealings

Under section 446 of the Companies Act 1985, the Department of Trade and Industry is given power to appoint 'one or more competent inspectors' if it appears to the DTI that circumstances suggest a contravention of section 323 (dealing by directors in options for quoted securities of their company) or of section 324 and Schedule 13 (obligation of directors to notify their company of interests in the securities of their company).[5] Such inspectors are to carry out such investigations as are requisite to establish whether or not contraventions have occurred, and to report the results of their investigation to the DTI. In making such an appointment, the DTI may limit the period of the inspector's investigation or confine it to shares or debentures of a particular class (or both).[6]

The powers given to inspectors to obtain documents relating to a company, and to examine its officers and agents on oath, by sections 434 to 436, with some modifications, apply to investigations into share dealings under section 446.[7] As it applies to an investigation under section 446, the reference to 'any other body

---

1 Section 456(1) and (2).
2 *Re Lonrho plc* [1988] BCLC 53.
3 This is subject to any order as to costs for the benefit of the applicant made under section 457(3).
4 Section 457(2).
5 This includes the extension (under section 325) of section 324 to spouses and children of directors. As to section 323, see **16.19** and as to section 324, **15.22**.
6 Section 446(2).
7 Section 446(3).

corporate whose affairs are being investigated under section 433(1)'(in sections 434 to 436) is to have substituted for it a reference to 'any other body corporate which is, or has at any relevant time been, the company's subsidiary or holding company'. The powers given by sections 434 to 436 also apply (for the purposes of an investigation under section 446) to persons authorised under the Financial Services and Markets Act 2000.[1] In the specific context of insider dealing and market abuse,[2] that Act confers powers of information gathering and investigation in respect of dealings in securities on the Financial Services Authority.[3]

Section 446 provides that inspectors appointed under it may (and must if so directed by the DTI) make interim reports to the Department, and on the conclusion of their investigation they must make a formal report.[4] The DTI may cause such a report to be published.[5] The expenses of an inspection under section 446 must be defrayed by the DTI out of moneys provided by Parliament.[6]

---

1 Section 446(4) as amended by the 2000 Act.
2 See Chapter 20.
3 Financial Services and Markets Act 2000, sections 165–177.
4 Section 446(5).
5 Section 446(5). A report may be written or printed as the DTI may direct.
6 Section 446(7).

Chapter 18

The Public Issue of Securities

18.1 Legislative background

This chapter is concerned with listing and public offers of securities. Listing is a regulatory process by which securities become eligible to be traded on an organised market.[1] It does not necessarily involve the sale of any securities, although in practice it is often combined with a sale of securities. The main concern of the law and regulatory rules relating to listing is to ensure that, following listing of a company's securities, there will be a proper market, meaning one in which investors are able, at any point in time, to make fully-informed investment decisions (eg to buy or sell). A public offer of securities is an invitation to the general public to buy securities.[2] A public offer can be made in respect of listed or unlisted securities and in practice it is common for a public offer to be made of securities that are to be listed. The focus of the law relating to public offers runs parallel to that relating to listing in that it aims to ensure that adequate disclosure is made in respect of the securities offered for sale. However, as a public offer will not always involve securities that are to be traded on an organised market, the law relating to public offers is more directly concerned with the fairness of the particular sale transaction involved in the public offer, whereas the law relating to listing has a broader focus on the fairness of the operation of the market as a whole.

Historically, public issues of securities were regulated by the companies legislation. The first move away from the companies legislation as the source of regulation resulted from the need to implement three EC directives on listed securities.[3] Listed securities are securities admitted to official listing in a Member State which, in the United Kingdom, means admitted to the Official List of the UK Listing Authority.[4] These directives were first implemented into the law in the United Kingdom in 1984 by means of regulations.[5] The effect of these regulations was, broadly, to disapply the relevant provisions of the companies legislation in relation to listed securities. The companies legislation continued to apply to unlisted securities and, on consolidation of that legislation, the relevant provisions governing unlisted securities were contained in Part III and certain sections of Part IV of the Companies Act 1985.

While these events were occurring, a fundamental review of the whole body of securities law was undertaken on behalf of the Department of Trade and Industry by their adviser, Professor LCB Gower.[6] On the basis of this report, but in a form inevitably altered by the usual consultation processes and the pressures of various

---

1   This is an explanatory definition. There is no legal definition of the term.
2   This is an explanatory definition. The legal definition (see **18.22**) is more complex.
3   The Admissions Directive (No 79/279); The Listing Particulars Directive (No 80/390); and The Interim Reports Directive (No 82/121).
4   See further **18.4**.
5   The Stock Exchange (Listing) Regulations 1984, SI 1984/716.
6   *Review of Investor Protection*, Part I (Cmnd 9125) 1984. See also Part II (1985), Chapter 6.

interest groups affected, the Financial Services Act 1986 introduced a new 'securities law' to regulate most aspects of the financial markets in the United Kingdom. Part IV of the Financial Services Act 1986 regulated listed securities. Changes to Part IV[1] that were made in 1995 were intended to implement the EC Public Offers Directive[2] in so far as it affects listed securities. Largely because Part IV was already based on Community law, the impact of this Directive on the regime governing listed securities was not especially great. Part VI of the Financial Services and Markets Act 2000 contains the new provisions on official listing that replace Part IV of the Financial Services Act 1986. It recasts the requirements for official listing in simpler, more modern language but makes few substantive changes. A significant change that took place in advance of the enactment of the new regime was that the London Stock Exchange ceased to be the United Kingdom's listing authority following the transfer of responsibility to the Financial Services Authority, the United Kingdom's financial regulator. It is a requirement of the European directives on listing that Member States should have a competent authority to perform certain functions in connection with listing. The transfer of this role from the London Stock Exchange to the Financial Services Authority was prompted by an internal re-organisation of the Stock Exchange and its decision to operate as a more commercial and internationally orientated organisation.[3] Given that decision, it was deemed to be inappropriate for the Stock Exchange to continue to carry the regulatory responsibilities that are imposed on national listing authorities.[4]

The three EC directives on listed securities mentioned above have now been consolidated in the Consolidated Admissions and Reporting Directive ('CARD').[5] This Directive pursues the policy of minimum harmonisation and mutual recognition, which was developed in the 1980s as a mechanism to give effect to the objective of a single capital market within the EC.[6] Minimum harmonisation is intended to remove significant differences between the regulatory systems of Member States and thereby create the conditions under which mutual recognition can be implemented. The essence of mutual recognition is that compliance with the legal and regulatory processes in one Member State is recognised as being compliance with those in other Member States. In respect of listed securities, the objective is that listing particulars approved in one Member State should be accepted in other Member States in which an issuer seeks a listing (the host State). The extent to which the CARD gives effect to that objective is, however, quite limited. There are two main reasons for this. One is the policy of minimum harmonisation, which, in principle, leaves Member States free to impose additional requirements.[7] The other is that the mechanisms that give effect to the Directive's objective contain limitations and exceptions which, in

---

1   Made by the Public Offers of Securities Regulations 1995, SI 1995/1537.
2   No 89/298.
3   The London Stock Exchange is now a listed company on the London Stock Exchange.
4   The transfer was effected by the Official Listing of Securities (Change of Competent Authority) Regulations 2000, SI 2000/968.
5   Directive 2001/34/EC [2001] OJ L184/1. The Major Holdings Directive (88/627/EEC, [1988] OJ L348 62) is also included in the consolidation. The CARD is implemented in the UK by the provisions of Part VI of the Financial Services and Markets Act 2000 and the UKLA *Listing Rules*.
6   See **18.27** and Moloney *EC Securities Regulation* (OUP 2002) pp 66–76.
7   In the UK, such requirements are referred to as 'super-equivalents'. Article 8(1) of the CARD expressly provides for such provisions.

effect, provide considerable leeway for a member state in which a listing is being sought on the basis of listing particulars approved in another member state to impose additional requirements.[1] The new Prospectus Directive (discussed below) attempts to resolve these problems both in relation to listing and public offers.

The Public Offers Directive ('POD') was much more significant in relation to the regulation of unlisted securities.[2] The Directive applies where securities are offered to the public for the first time in a Member State irrespective of whether a listing is sought for the securities which are the subject of the offer. The core obligation contained in the Directive is that the person making the offer publishes a prospectus. Where the offer relates to securities that are to be listed, the content of the prospectus is determined by the relevant provisions of the CARD.[3] Where the offer relates to securities that are not to be listed, the information required to be contained in the prospectus is less demanding.[4] There are a number of important exceptions to the requirement to produce a prospectus including so-called 'Euro-securities',[5] offers made to persons in the context of their trade, profession or occupation, offers to a restricted circle of persons, and offers where the selling price of the securities exceeds a threshold.[6] The Government decided to implement the POD so far as it relates to unlisted securities by means of regulations made under section 2 of the European Communities Act 1972.[7] So far as it relates to listed securities, it is implemented by sections 84–87 of the Financial Services and Markets Act 2000.

The new Prospectus Directive[8] aims to resolve some of the problems associated with the operation of mutual recognition under the POD and the directives consolidated in the CARD. When it takes effect[9], it will bring to an end the distinction between 'official' and other forms of listing, replacing it with the concept of admission to trading on a regulated market. The obligation to publish a prospectus will apply either when a public offer[10] is made or when relevant

---

1   See eg article 38(1) of the CARD, which permits a host Member State to require that listing particulars include information specific to the market of the host Member State.

2   The reason being that listed securities were already subject to the three directives mentioned above (see footnote 3 on p 589), which are now consolidated in the CARD.

3   Article 7 of the POD refers to the Listing Particulars Directive, now consolidated in the CARD.

4   Recital 8 of the POD explains that this is justified 'so as not to burden small and medium sized issuers unduly'.

5   See article 3(f) of the POD for a definition. Eurobonds are a form of Euro-security.

6   See Moloney, footnote 6 at p 590, pp 181–185 for more detail.

7   The Public Offers of Securities Regulations 1995, SI 1995/1537. The provisions of Part V of the Financial Services Act 1986 relating to unlisted securities were intended to replace Part III and certain sections of Part IV of the Companies Act 1985 but were never brought into force. The scope of Part III and the relevant sections of Part IV of the Companies Act 1985 was wider than that of the Prospectus Directive and, to the extent that the two regimes did not overlap, the limited nature of the power to make regulations under section 2 of the European Communities Act 1972 meant that the Government could not make amendments to the Companies Act 1985. Accordingly, there remains a rather untidy category of circumstances in which it is necessary still to have regard to the provisions of the Companies Act 1985.

8   Directive 2003/71/EC, [2003] OJ L345/64.

9   Member States are required to implement the Directive in national law by 1 July 2005. For a discussion of the implications for the UK see FSA Discussion Paper 14 *Review of the listing regime* (July 2002).

10   Unlike the POD, the new Prospectus Directive defines a public offer (see article 2(1)(d)).

securities are admitted to trading on a regulated market. Provision is made for a prospectus to be split into a registration document, a securities note and a summary, thereby enabling subsequent issues to be made simply by the publication of new versions of the latter two documents. As regards disclosure standards, the objective is to enhance the current level of disclosure by implementing the International Disclosure Standards adopted by IOSCO.[1] The possibility of different disclosure standards for different markets and types of investors is preserved by the directive notwithstanding the ending of the distinction between 'official' and other forms of listing. The Directive also enhances the 'passport' characteristic of a prospectus[2] approved by a home Member State by removing in almost all instances[3] the ability of a host State to impose additional requirements.

The central principle underlying the regulation of public issues of securities in both the EC and United Kingdom is that of mandatory disclosure to investors of information relating to an issuer.[4] Three justifications are generally offered in support of this approach. [5] The first is that mandatory disclosure promotes investor confidence and investor protection. This claim is based on the role of mandatory disclosure in making information relating to an issuer available to investors so as to allow them to make informed decisions on the valuation of investments. The second is that mandatory disclosure prevents fraud by requiring information to be made public which might otherwise be withheld. The third is that mandatory disclosure promotes efficient capital markets and efficient capital allocation. This claim is based on the role of mandatory disclosure in making capital markets informationally efficient, meaning that they correctly reflect relevant information regarding an issuer in prices: when this occurs, the process of allocating capital to competing uses is more efficient than if such decisions are made on the basis of partial information or speculation.

In respect of the EC legislative measures, an additional policy (and the cause of much of the complexity evident in the legislation) is that of creating a single market in capital and financial services. While the legal competence of the EC is respect of the wide-ranging programme of harmonisation in this area may not always be clear[6], it now seems to be accepted that a harmonised form of mandatory disclosure is a pre-requisite for the emergence of a single capital market. The notable change represented by the new Prospectus directive is the rejection of the previous approach through 'minimum standards' directives, which left consider- able   power   to   host   Member   States   and   effectively   prevented   the

---

1   IOSCO is the International Organisation of Securities Commissioners. A related development
     is the requirement that all companies whose securities are admitted to trading on a regulated
     market in the EU must implement International Accounting Standards from 1 January 2005
     (see Reg 1606/2002 [2002] OJ L243/1). Detailed disclosure standards will be set by the
     European Securities Committee, whose function is to advise the Commission on the detailed
     implementation of the securities directives.
2   See also **18.27**.
3   Article 23 permits the host State, in exceptional circumstances following the failure of
     remedial action taken by the home Member State, to take appropriate measures to protect
     investors.
4   The term is often associated with US securities regulation, but it has a long history in the
     United Kingdom. As noted by Moloney, op cit, p 177 the UK introduced mandatory
     disclosure and registration requirements for prospectuses in the Companies Act 1900.
5   See generally Moloney, op cit, pp 118–128.
6   See, for a discussion of this issue Moloney, op cit, pp 136–140.

operation of mutual recognition. The obstacles which have in the past frustrated the operation of mutual recognition have now been largely removed[1], opening up the possibility of it becoming a practical reality for issuers rather than an option which has largely been ignored (mainly for reasons of cost and complexity) under the POD regime. It remains to be seen whether the trend towards greater integration of capital markets will eventually lead to the emergence of a single EC authority with responsibility for regulating listing, public offers and financial markets.[2]

18.2 The regulatory framework

The broad framework of the regulatory control of listed and unlisted securities is as follows.

(1) Securities which are to be admitted to official listing are governed by Part VI of the Financial Services and Markets Act 2000. The detailed requirements vary slightly depending on whether the securities to be listed are 'transferable securities' subject to the Prospectus Directive and on whether the listing is sought in connection with a public offer of the securities.[3]

(2) First-time public offers of unlisted securities which are within the scope of the Prospectus Directive are regulated by the Public Offers of Securities ('POS') Regulations 1995.[4]

(3) Offers of securities falling outside both Part VI and the Public Offers of Securities Regulations are subject to the provisions of section 21 of the Financial Services and Markets Act 2000, which regulates the activity described as 'financial promotion'.

(4) Certain matters relating to the allotment of shares and debentures remain subject to the Companies Act 1985.

(5) Special rules apply where a company wants to make a simultaneous offer of its securities in two or more Member States.[5]

Offers of securities are brought within the regulatory framework irrespective of whether those securities are offered for cash or for a non-cash consideration. This point is notable because the relevant provisions of the Companies Act 1985 (and earlier companies legislation) only applied to securities offered to the public 'for subscription or purchase'. This phrase was interpreted by the courts to mean

---

1   It is not possible to say that they have been completely removed as the 'maximum harmonisation' principle adopted by the new Prospectus directive applies only to issuer disclosure and not the conditions for admission to listing.

2   See Hertig and Lee 'Four predictions about the future of EU securities regulation' [2003] 3(2) JCLS 359.

3   The meaning of 'public offer' is considered at **18.22**. Part IV also applies where securities are simply admitted to official listing without an accompanying offer of any sort. Introductions of this kind are not especially common for UK incorporated companies but can occur where, for example, shares are already admitted to and traded upon a foreign market and are introduced to UK listing in order to enhance their international marketability and liquidity. This process is referred to as 'secondary listing': see generally I MacNeil and A Lau 'International Corporate Regulation: Listing Rules and Overseas Companies' 50(4) ICLQ 787 (2001).

4   SI 1995/1537.

5   These are contained in regulation 20 of and Schedule 4 to the POS Regulations.

subscription or purchase for cash[1] which meant that, for example, an offer made by a bidder to acquire the shares of the target by means of a share-for-share exchange was not caught. The change of policy embodied in the current law was based on a recommendation by Professor Gower in *The Review of Investor Protection*.[2]

18.3   Private and public companies

A private company may not offer its securities to the public[3] nor may its securities be admitted to official listing.[4] The Companies Act 1985 does not contain a complete definition of what is meant by an 'offer to the public' for this purpose.[5] Uncertainty as to the precise scope of the phrase 'an offer to the public' was one of the criticisms levelled at the regulatory regime contained in the Companies Act 1985 and it is unfortunate that the phrase has had to be retained even for the limited purpose of a prohibition imposed only on private companies.[6]

A business conducted through the corporate form is usually established as a private company. At a later stage, its proprietors may choose to convert it into a public company[7] precisely in order to be able to sell their shareholding or raise additional capital by offering its securities to the public. Starting life as a private company allows the proprietors to operate the business under more relaxed rules governing the maintenance, increase and reduction of share capital than those applicable to public companies.[8] For most types of business at the early stages of their development, their operations are unlikely to be hampered by the prohibition on offering securities to the public because, in any event, few external investors are likely to be interested in investing in such untested operations. If and when a business has established itself as a successful and profitable trading venture, the proprietors may consider it to be worthwhile subjecting the company to the more rigorous regulations imposed on public companies and their capital in return for acquiring the freedom to exploit the company's reputation by offering its securities to the public.

However, this familiar picture of the business that is established in private company form and built up over a number of years until it is of a size and has a reputation that would make the raising of capital through issues of securities to the public a viable option, was challenged in the late 1990s by the emergence of fast-growing internet and other technology companies. A notable phenomenon during this period was the willingness of investors (assisted by modifications made to the *Listing Rules*) to invest in such companies despite the absence of a trading

---

1   *Government Stock and Other Securities Investment Co Ltd v Christopher* [1956] 1 All ER 40, [1956] 1 WLR 237. See also section 744 of the Companies Act 1985.

2   (1984) Cmnd 9125.

3   Section 81 of the Companies Act 1985.

4   Section 75(3) FSMA 2000 and regulation 3(a) of The FSMA 2000 (Official Listing of Securities) Regulations 2001, SI 2001/2956.

5   Some guidance is provided by sections 58 and 742A of the Companies Act 1985.

6   The matter could be resolved if, following implementation of the new Prospectus directive, the definition of an offer to the public contained in article 2 (1)(d) of that directive were applied also to the prohibition contained in section 81(1). That, however, is unlikely to occur if the directive is implemented by regulations made under section 2 of the European Communities Act 1972.

7   The procedure for conversion is contained in sections 43–48 of the Companies Act 1985. See **4.11**.

8   See Chapter 7.

record or of profitability. Such companies had to be in public company form in order to exploit this investor interest.

18.4   The UK Listing Authority and the London Stock Exchange

With effect from 1 May 2000, the Financial Services Authority (FSA) assumed the role of UK Listing Authority. [1] Before that, responsibility for matters relating to listing lay with the London Stock Exchange. The FSA's approach to the transfer was to maintain business as usual and, accordingly, it adopted requirements for listing that were for most purposes the same as those previously imposed by the London Stock Exchange.

A distinction must now be drawn between the listing of securities and their admission to trading on a securities market. Securities are admitted to listing by the FSA in its role as Listing Authority and, separately, are admitted to trading on a recognised investment exchange's market for listed securities. Securities that have completed both processes are said to be admitted to official listing on a stock exchange.

An applicant for official listing must comply with the requirements of Part VI of the Financial Services and Markets Act 2000 . It must also comply with the UK Listing Authority's requirements for listing which are set out in a publication entitled the *Listing Rules*. The *Listing Rules* have statutory backing under Part VI of the Financial Services and Markets Act 2000.

To qualify for official listing, an applicant must ordinarily satisfy certain criteria relating to the length of time it has been trading, the value of the securities for which listing is sought and the proportion of securities that will be held by the public once listing has taken place. These criteria mean that official listing can normally be sought only by established businesses of a certain size which have a substantial trading record. These requirements are modified, however, for innovative growth companies in technology sectors, such as computer hardware and services and the internet. Such companies can seek a listing without satisfying the three-year trading record requirement provided they meet certain size requirements. In most cases, the persons who have built up a business must accept some dilution of their formal[2] control of the company in order to satisfy the requirement for the appropriate percentage of the company's securities for which listing is sought to be in the hands of the public. The costs and expenses involved in seeking and maintaining an official listing are significant and this is an additional consideration which can dissuade smaller companies from taking this step.[3]

---

1   The change was given effect by the Official Listing of Securities (Change of Competent Authority) Regulations 2000, SI 2000/968.

2   There is much discussion about the extent to which practical, as opposed to formal, control is lost when the ownership of a company's securities becomes dispersed via a flotation. The persons who built up the business will, more likely than not, remain in managerial control after the securities are listed. Outside shareholders, individually, are unlikely to own enough of the company's securities to be able to exercise much control over the managers and may be too widely dispersed to be able to act effectively as a collective group. Also, they may be disinclined to take collective action, preferring instead the simple option of selling their shares if the managers of the company underperform. These issues of corporate governance are discussed further in Chapter 11.

3   'New Equity Issues', Bank of England Quarterly Bulletin, May 1990, p 243.

The London Stock Exchange presently has two markets: its main market for listed securities, which has a separate sub-division, techMARK for innovative high growth technology companies; and the 'Alternative Investment Market' (AIM) for smaller and growing companies. This market began operating in June 1995. The background to the establishment of the AIM was that research conducted by the Exchange indicated that, notwithstanding a decline in the use of the Unlisted Securities Market, a predecessor lower-tier market, there was still a demand for a new source of funding and trading for smaller companies as an alternative to the main market for listed securities. AIM may appeal to companies which cannot satisfy the requirements for official listing, and also to companies which are eligible for official listing but which are attracted to the lower admission criteria and less onerous continuing obligations imposed on companies trading on AIM. Also, the costs of obtaining and maintaining admission to AIM are considerably lower than those of the main market.[1] Some companies may view admission to the AIM as the first step in the process leading to full listing.

18.5   Criteria for admission to listing

The conditions to be fulfilled by an applicant for official listing and the listing procedure are set out in the *Listing Rules*. For an applicant seeking a listing for its shares, the usual important admission requirements are as follows.

(1)   The market value of the shares to be listed must be at least £700,000[2] (but, in practice, an applicant may have difficulty in finding a broker or issuing house to sponsor the issue[3] and may find the costs involved make an official listing prohibitively expensive unless the value of the securities involved is substantially greater than this).

(2)   The company must normally have a trading record of at least three years and must have audited accounts for those three years.

(3)   The company must have carried on an independent business which is supported by its historic revenue earning record for at least the period covered by the accounts required in (2).

(4)   The company's directors must collectively have appropriate expertise and experience for the management of its business and must in general be free of conflicts between their duties to the company and their personal interests, or other duties.

(5)   If the company has a controlling shareholder (ie one who can exercise, or control the exercise of, 30% or more of the rights to vote at general meetings or who can control the appointment of directors who are able to exercise the

---

1   A particular area of saving is in relation to sponsors. Unlike applicants for official listing, applicants for admission to the Alternative Investment Market do not require a sponsor. Having a sponsor is an expensive requirement because, under the *Listing Rules*, sponsors must give a confirmation that, having made due and careful inquiries, they have satisfied themselves that the rules have been complied with. Sponsors must perform extensive (and expensive) due diligence exercises in order to be in a position to provide such confirmation. AIM companies must have nominated advisers, but nominated advisers are not required to give this confirmation.
2   In an application for the admission of debentures the equivalent figure is £200,000.
3   *Listing Rules*, Chapter 2 sets out the requirement to have a sponsor.

majority of votes at board meetings), the company must be capable of at all times operating and making decisions independently of the controlling shareholder.

(6) At least 25% of the shares must be in the hands of the public after the flotation.

(7) The company must be able to state that it is satisfied, after due and careful inquiry, that it has sufficient working capital for at least the next twelve months.

For technology companies these requirements are modified to allow for admission without a three-year trading record. In such cases, applicants must have a minimum market capitalisation of £50 million and must be selling a minimum volume of new or existing shares on flotation of £20 million. They must undertake to provide quarterly financial reports (as opposed to the six-monthly reports generally required).

18.6 Criteria for admission to trading on the London Stock Exchange

Companies that seek to have their securities admitted to the London Stock Exchange's market for listed securities must comply with the *Listing Rules* but they are not subject to significant additional admission criteria imposed by the Exchange. Applicants to the Alternative Investment Market do not need to comply with the *Listing Rules* but they must satisfy AIM's own criteria for admission. There is no requirement for a minimum (or maximum) market value of the securities for which admission is sought, there is no minimum trading record and no requirement for a minimum proportion of the securities to be in public hands. A company joining AIM must satisfy the following requirements.

(1) The company must be duly incorporated or otherwise validly established according to the laws of its place of incorporation or establishment.

(2) The company must be permitted by its national law to offer its securities to the public. In the UK this means that it must be a public limited company.

(3) The securities to be traded on the market must be freely transferable.

(4) The company must appoint and retain a nominated adviser and a nominated broker.

(5) The company must state that it has sufficient working capital for its present requirements.

(6) The company must accept continuing obligations with regard to such matters as preparation of accounts, completion of transfers of securities and dealings in securities by directors and employees.

18.7 Offers of securities otherwise than through the London Stock Exchange

A company is not obliged to seek admission to one of the markets of the London Stock Exchange in connection with an offer of its securities. Securities can be offered and traded without having been first admitted to a formal market. This form of trading in securities is sometimes described as 'over the counter' trading (although in modern trading conditions, such transactions are more likely to be concluded via telephone and computer links than face to face). An advantage of having securities admitted to a formal market is that this can facilitate trading in them by the widest possible range of investors and thus enhance the liquidity of the securities. Admission of its securities to a formal market can also increase a company's status and make it easier for it to raise capital from other sources. In return for these advantages, however, the company is likely to have to agree to abide by certain continuing obligations imposed by the market and will certainly have to incur the expense of admission and membership fees.

A company which has had its securities admitted to an overseas market can offer those securities to investors in the United Kingdom without also seeking to have the securities admitted to trading on the London Stock Exchange. For example, specialised debt securities which are targeted mainly at expert investors (eg Eurobonds) are commonly listed on the Luxembourg Stock Exchange but offered to investors in the City of London and elsewhere throughout the world without being formally admitted to any other market.

One effect of the programme of harmonisation of requirements for the public offering and listing of securities in the laws of the Member States of the European Union is that it is becoming increasingly easier for a company to offer securities that are listed on an Exchange in one State to investors in other States.[1] This provides opportunities for competition between Exchanges in different countries for listing business.

18.8 'Offers for subscription' and 'offers for sale'

A large-scale issue to the general investing public can take one of two forms. A direct offer to the public (known as an 'offer for subscription' or a 'prospectus offer') was the traditional method of making a large-scale public issue. Where it is used, investors subscribe for shares to be allotted directly by the company. The issuing house advises and helps to arrange the issue, including underwriting and sub-underwriting arrangements. Today, however, this method is rarely used when a company offers its securities to the public for the first time, although subsequent capital-raising exercises through rights issues commonly adopt this form. The more usual method of large-scale initial public issue takes the form of an 'offer for sale'. Here the whole of the shares in issue are normally taken up by an issuing house which then itself offers them to the public for purchase. The issuing house, not the company, takes prime responsibility for the success of the issue. Since the shares are allotted to it, the issuing house acts as a principal rather than agent (of the issuer) and will need to arrange for its own risk to be underwritten. The issuing house does not become a registered holder of the shares it agrees to purchase. Indeed, it is common for the company to issue the renounceable allotment letters[2] not to the issuing house but directly to those who purchase the shares from the issuing house.

---

1   See further **18.1**.
2   See **7.8**.

18.9 Placings, intermediaries offers, rights issues and open offers

The incidental costs of making an offer for sale or for subscription (including underwriting fees, advertising expenses and publicity costs, and legal and financial advisers' fees) can be very large. For a company that wants to raise a relatively small amount of capital by way of an offer of shares, these costs may be prohibitive. An appropriate method of marketing for smaller offers may be a placing. A placing is a marketing of securities to a limited class of persons (eg clients of the issuing house which is sponsoring the issue).[1] It does not involve an offer to the public at large, with the result that publicity expenses and advertising costs can be kept relatively low in comparison to an offer for sale or for subscription. An intermediaries offer is essentially a variant form of placing involving the marketing of the securities to the clients of a number of financial intermediaries.[2] Placings are now commonly carried out through the process of 'bookbuilding'. This involves investors providing indications to an issuer's financial adviser as to their take up of the offer at different (theoretical) price levels. This information is then used to set the actual price for the offer.

A rights issue is an issue to the existing members of the company which gives them the right to subscribe in proportion to their existing holding of shares in the company (or of the class of shares involved). This is now the most common method for companies already listed to raise new capital, although the amounts raised by such issues individually are much less than in the case of initial public offers.[3] The costs of rights issues, in the sense of the expenses of the issue, are proportionally less than in the case of a general public offer, but, because it is customary to offer the new shares on more favourable terms than would be available under a public offer the company may raise less capital in proportion to the shares issued than would have been raised by an offer to the public generally.[4]

The shares are usually offered to the existing shareholders by means of renounceable letters or other negotiable instruments (this is a requirement of the *Listing Rules* for rights issues of shares which are to be listed[5]). Existing shareholders may take up their rights or renounce them in whole or in part. A shareholder can choose to renounce the offer but still take advantage of the discount element normally included in the rights issue price. In effect, the renouncing shareholder sells the value of the right which was offered to him.[6] Provided the rights issue is at a discount to the market price of the company's existing shares, a purchaser may be prepared to pay the existing shareholder for this right. Inexperienced investors may not appreciate that they can, by selling their rights, secure the financial equivalent of the discount that is offered to investors who take up the rights issue.[7] To guard against this, the *Listing Rules* contain a protective provision requiring rights which are not taken up to be sold

---

1   *Listing Rules*, Chapter 4, paragraph 4.7.
2   *Listing Rules*, Chapter 4, paragraph 4.10.
3   As to the Stock Exchange requirements, see the *Listing Rules*, Chapter 4, paragraphs 4.16–4.21.
4   See further Ferran, *Company Law and Corporate Finance* (Oxford University Press, 1999) Chapter 18.
5   *Listing Rules*, Chapter 4, paragraph 4.16.
6   The market is said to be in 'nil paid rights'.
7   See Ferran, op cit, p 610 for a worked example.

on the market for the benefit of the existing shareholders who were entitled to them.[1]

Where a listed company wants to raise new capital through an issue of its ordinary shares, it is *prima facie* obliged by section 89 of the Companies Act 1985[2] to do so by means of a rights issue in favour of its existing shareholders. This obligation can be disapplied. A public company is permitted to disapply the statutory pre-emption requirement by special resolution for a period of up to five years.[3] Under Pre-emption Guidelines agreed between representatives of companies, institutional investors and the London Stock Exchange, there are limits on the amount of securities that may be included in a special resolution disapplying section 89. The Pre-emption Guidelines are not formal regulatory rules but companies have the assurance that a disapplication resolution which complies with those guidelines will be supported by their institutional shareholders.

An open offer is similar to a rights issue in that it is an offer of new securities to existing investors in those securities in proportion to their existing holdings but is not made by means of a renounceable letter of allotment. Also it operates on the basis of a shorter timetable than a rights issue, which can help to minimise costs associated with the issue, such as underwriting costs.[4]

18.10   Convertible issues

A 'convertible issue' is a term which relates not to the method of issue but to the hybrid type of security involved. In the usual form, convertible debentures are offered with the right to convert at a future date into ordinary shares. The attraction of this type of investment is that it gives the investor the security of a fixed interest security, which may be particularly important where the funding is sought to capitalise a new, and perhaps somewhat risky, venture, combined with the opportunity to convert into 'equity' shares when the success and profitability of the company is established.

18.11   The function of the sponsor

In major public issues,[5] a crucial role is performed by the company's sponsor, who will normally be its corporate broker or investment bank.[6] The sponsor not only acts as financial adviser to the company but will have the task of directing the strategy of the issue and co-ordinating the activities of the other professional advisers concerned (stockbrokers, auditors, reporting accountants and solicitors). Where the securities are to be listed in London, the sponsor also has specific obligations which it owes to the FSA as the Listing Authority to ensure that the

---

1   *Listing Rules*, Chapter 4, paragraph 4.19. But if the premium obtained over the subscription price (net of expenses) does not exceed £3, the proceeds may be retained for the company's benefit.
2   See **7.5**.
3   Section 95.
4   *Listing Rules*, Chapter 4, paragraph 4.22. The matter of underwriting charges in the United Kingdom capital markets has been a controversial area and the subject of a reference to the Competition Commission. On this, and the response of the markets, see Ferran, *Company Law and Corporate Finance* (Oxford University Press, 1999) Chapter 18 and *Guide to Share Issuing Good Practice for Listed Companies* (Bank of England, October 1999).
5   An applicant for admission to the Alternative Investment Market does not require a sponsor.
6   *Listing Rules*, Chapter 2 sets out the requirements relating to sponsors.

company satisfies the listing criteria and is guided through the listing process.[1] The name and good reputation of the sponsor has a considerable influence on the reception that will be given by the financial press and the stock market to the issue. This is linked with the understanding that the broker or issuing house, before it agrees to sponsor an issue, will be aware of the need to protect its reputation with the investing public, especially the institutional investors who may be involved both as underwriters and sub-underwriters and as straightforward investors.[2]

18.12 Underwriting

A contract of underwriting is an agreement that, if the whole or a certain proportion of the issue is not applied for by the public, the underwriters will themselves apply or find persons to apply for the balance or a certain proportion of the balance of the issue. Where the underwriters undertake merely to find persons to apply for shares the remedy of the company in case of breach is in damages only.[3] Where the underwriters undertake to apply for the shares themselves, the company can hold the underwriters to their promise by placing them on the register of members.

The underwriters receive a commission whether they are called upon to take up any securities or not.[4] The maximum amount of commission that can be paid to underwriters from the proceeds of an issue of shares is regulated by sections 97 and 98 of the Companies Act 1985.[5]

18.13 Official listing: the function of the 'competent authority'

Part VI of the Financial Services and Markets Act 2000 contains the regulatory framework applicable to the listing of securities. The FSA (as competent authority) may admit to the official list such securities and other things as it considers appropriate.[6] A financial instrument is considered a 'security' for this purpose if it can be admitted to the official list.[7] The Listing Rules provide some examples of financial instruments that can be admitted to listing but ultimately the issue turns on whether the conditions in the Listing Rules relating to the relevant securities are satisfied.[8] Section 74 stipulates that no security to which the section applies may be admitted to listing except in accordance with the provisions of Part VI.

---

1   See further, *Listing Rules*, Chapter 2.
2   See *Gore-Browne on Companies* 44th edn (Jordans, loose-leaf) at 10.15 as to the initial searching enquiry that will be given by the issuing house to a company 'coming to market'.
3   See *Gorrissen's Case* (1873) 8 Ch App 507.
4   The meaning of 'underwriting' was declared by the Court of Appeal after hearing evidence in *Re Licensed Victuallers' Mutual Trading Association* (1889) 42 Ch D 1. A modern judicial analysis of underwriting structures is provided by Hobhouse LJ in *County Ltd v Girozentrale Securities* [1996] 1 BCLC 653 at 670–673. See also *Eagle Trust plc v SBC Securities Ltd* [1995] BCC 231 (role and duties of underwriter).
5   See **4.21**.
6   Section 74(2).
7   Section 74(5).
8   See Chapter 3, paragraphs 3.14-3.27 of the *Listing Rules*. The Treasury has a residual power to exclude certain types or categories of securities from official listing: section 74(3)(b) FSMA 2000.

Section 74(4) gives the FSA the power to make 'listing rules' and it is this power which provides the statutory backing for the *Listing Rules*. The FSA has a delegated power to make law by regulating applications for listing and specifying the detailed criteria for admission to listing within widely drawn enabling provisions of the Act. In performing this rule-making function, the FSA must as a matter of EC law comply with the EC directives relating to listing.[1] The Act, however, does not say that the FSA must comply with the directives. This appears to have been done so that a question of *ultra vires* may not arise by reason of any failure to comply with the directives. It is intended that companies which comply with the *Listing Rules* should not be imperilled.

18.14   Application for listing

Section 75 deals with applications for listing. These must be made to the FSA as the UK Listing Authority 'in such manner as may be required by listing rules'. Section 75 also prohibits an application for listing of any securities except 'by or with the consent of the issuer of the securities concerned'. 'Issuer' is defined as the person by whom the securities have been or are to be issued.[2] Where, for example, an investment institution which owns a substantial holding of shares or other securities in a public company seeks a listing for these securities, this requires the consent of the company.

Section 75 also defines the responsibilities of the FSA for 'vetting' applications for listing. It provides for admission to official listing only if the *Listing Rules* and other requirements are complied with and specifies the circumstances in which an application for listing may or must be refused. The FSA may refuse an application if it considers that the admission of the securities would be detrimental to the interests of investors because of any matters relating to the issuer.[3] An application may also be refused where the issuer has failed to comply with listing obligations imposed by another Member State when the securities are already listed there.[4]

A decision must be notified to the applicant within six months of the date of its receipt. Where the applicant has been required to give further information, the six-month period will run from the time when the information is supplied. Where the FSA fails to notify within this period, it is 'taken to have refused the application'.[5]

A refusal by the FSA to admit securities to listing may be referred by the applicant[6] to the Financial Services and Markets Tribunal,[7] which is empowered to direct the FSA as to the action to be taken.[8] A party to a reference to the

---

1   The Secretary of State, however, has preserved a power to enable him to ensure that international obligations are complied with. See section 410.
2   Reg 4 of the FSMA 2000 (Official Listing of Securities) Regulations 2001, SI 2001/2956.
3   Section 75(5) FSMA 2000.
4   Section 75(6) FSMA 2000.
5   Section 76 and the *Listing Rules*, Chapter 1.
6   Reference to the applicant removes any doubt over the category of person to whom the CARD gives the right of appeal. The FSA 1986 did not contain a provision similar to section 76(6) FSMA 2000 but it was decided in *R v International Stock Exchange ex parte Else (1982) Ltd* [1993] BCC 11 that the right (previously contained in Article 15 of the Admissions Directive) was conferred on the company alone and not shareholders.
7   Section 76(6). Part IX sets out the powers and procedure of the tribunal.
8   Section 133(4). The tribunal is able to consider any evidence, whether or not it was available to the FSA at the material time: s133(3).

Tribunal may with permission appeal to the Court of Appeal (in Scotland, the Court of Session) on a point of law arising from a decision of the Tribunal.[1]

The FSA has the power to discontinue and suspend listing.[2] This is obviously an important weapon in enforcing compliance with its rules relating to original admission to listing as well as to continuous reporting and dealing requirements. One of the grounds on which listing will be cancelled is where the securities in question are no longer admitted to trading on a recognised investment exchange's market for listed securities.[3]

18.15 Part VI prospectuses and listing particulars

Section 79 of the Financial Services and Markets Act 2000 empowers the FSA as the UK Listing Authority to require as a condition of admission of securities to listing the production and publication of a prospectus or a set of listing particulars. A prospectus is mandatory where the securities for which the listing is sought are to be offered to the public in the United Kingdom for the first time prior to their admission to the Official List, unless the offer is within one of the exemptions provided by Schedule 11 to the Act.[4] The exemptions provided by Schedule 11 mirror those relating to unlisted securities provided by the Public Offers of Securities Regulations 1995 and they are considered further in that context.[5] For the moment, it suffices to note that an offer of shares for sale or subscription would be unlikely to fall within an exemption. With regard to placings, although there is an exemption where securities are offered to no more than 50 persons, there will often be more than that number of placees involved in a placing. A typical rights issue made by a listed company will also usually be too large to benefit from any of the exemptions.

For the purposes of Part VI, it is expressly provided that a person is to be regarded as offering securities if he makes an offer relating to the securities which, if accepted, would give rise to a contract to issue or sell the securities or if he invites a person to make such an offer.[6] Thus, an offer for this purpose means not only an offer in its strict contractual sense but also an invitation to treat. A person is to be regarded as offering securities to the public if he offers them to any section of the public, whether selected as members or debenture-holders of a company, or as clients of the person issuing the prospectus, or in any other manner.[7] This

---

1   Section 137, implementing article 19 of the CARD (previously article 15 of the Admissions Directive). However, no actions for damages will lie against the FSA or its members, officers or employees for any thing done or omitted in good faith in discharge of their functions: section 102.

2   Section 77. Securities whose listing is suspended under this section are to be treated for the purposes of sections 96 (obligations of issuers) and 99 (fees payable to the competent authority) as still being listed.

3   See Chapter 1, paragraph 1.19 of the *Listing Rules*.

4   See **18.22**.

5   The *Listing Rules* already contain an exemption from the obligation to produce listing particulars or a prospectus in respect of new shares of a class which is already listed where the new shares would increase the class by less than 10%: *Listing Rules*, Chapter 5, paragraph 5.1(f) and paragraph 5.27(e).

6   Section 103(4) FSMA 2000.

7   Section 103(6) of and Schedule 11 (para 1) to the FSMA 2000 in respect of listed securities and regulation 6 of the POS Regulations in respect of unlisted securities. Note that section 742A of the Companies Act 1985 adopts a similar approach, which applies for the purposes of the section 81 prohibition against a private company making a public offer.

precludes any argument that it is not necessary to produce a prospectus in respect of a placing of securities or a rights issue: it cannot be said that the offer, in either case, is not an offer to the public simply because it is made to a section of the public rather than to the public at large.

The detailed requirements concerning the contents of listing particulars and prospectuses are set out in Chapters 5 and 6 of the *Listing Rules*. Listing particulars relating to an application for admission of shares must include a mass of information about the applicant and its share capital, and financial information about the applicant as well as its recent development and prospects. Information is also required about the applicant's group structure and its management. These detailed requirements are to a large extent derived from the Listing Particulars Directive.[1] Article 7 of the Public Offers Directive provides that the contents of a prospectus relating to a public offer of securities for which listing is being sought must be determined in accordance with the Listing Particulars Directive subject to adaptations appropriate to the circumstances of a public offer. Such relevant adaptation includes the terms (eg as to price) on which the securities are being offered. Once the new Prospectus Directive is implemented in detail, it will be the instrument which regulates the content of listing particulars.[2]

Since listing particulars and prospectuses are subject to virtually the same rules governing their form and content, it can appear that little of substance turns on the fact that in some cases where Part VI applies the applicant for listing must produce a prospectus whilst in others it must produce listing particulars. The consequences of failing to provide all of the required information, or of providing false or misleading information, are the same in either case.[3] Where the distinction matters is in relation to the persons who can be held liable for inaccurate or incomplete information in the document. If the document is a set of listing particulars the following are potentially liable: the issuer; directors of the issuer; any person who accepts and is stated in the particulars as accepting responsibility; and any person who has authorised the contents of the particulars.[4] If the document is a prospectus, the offeror is, in addition to the persons just mentioned, also potentially liable.[5] It is possible that some offerors of securities may play little part in preparing the prospectus, for example where they are employees of a company who are offering their shares in the company for sale in conjunction with an offer of new shares by the company itself. The potential unfairness of holding people responsible for information over which they had no control is dealt with by a provision to the effect that an offeror will not be responsible where he makes an offer in association with the issuer and where the documentation is drawn up primarily by the issuer or by a person acting on the issuer's behalf.[6]

1　Now consolidated in the CARD. See paragraph 6.1.
2　See articles 5(1) and 7. It contains a general duty of disclosure similar to that contained in article 11(1) of the POD.
3　Section 90 FSMA 2000 (taken together with section 86).
4　Regulation 6 of The FSMA 2000 (Official Listing of Securities) Regulations 2001, SI 2001/2956. The regulation does not expressly refer to the 'shelf registration' system operated by the UKLA, which permits issuers to replace listing particulars with a 'shelf document' and 'issue note'. It would seem correct in principle to assume that regulation 6 does extend to this system as it is the functional equivalent of listing particulars.
5　Regulation 10 SI 2001/2956. In many instances, but not all, the issuer and the offeror will be the same entity.
6　Regulation 10(2) of SI 2001/2956.

18.16 The issuer's general duty to disclose

In addition to the information specified by the *Listing Rules* or otherwise required by the FSA, section 80 imposes an overriding duty of disclosure in respect of what must be contained in any listing particulars submitted under section 79. The overriding duty of disclosure also applies in relation to a prospectus required by section 84 and the *Listing Rules*. The duty is imposed on those responsible for the listing particulars or prospectus.[1] The prospectus or, as the case may be, the listing particulars must contain 'all such information' as investors and their professional advisers would reasonably require, and reasonably expect to find there, for the purpose of making an informed assessment of: (a) the assets and liabilities, financial position, profits and losses, and prospects of the issuer of the securities; and (b) the rights attached to the securities involved in the issue.[2] A qualification to this general obligation is that what is required is information 'which is within the knowledge of any person responsible for the prospectus or, as the case may be, listing particulars or which it would be reasonable for him to obtain by making enquiries'.[3] As a further guide, it is provided[4] that in determining what information is required to be included in a prospectus or in listing particulars by virtue of section 80, regard is to be had to the following factors. These are, first, the nature of the securities and of the issuer; secondly, the nature of the persons likely to consider their acquisition (eg professional investment managers). The third factor is the fact that certain matters may reasonably be expected to be within the knowledge of professional advisers of any kind which those persons may reasonably be expected to consult.[5] It would seem that this provision is intended to indicate that if professional investment advisers receive more detailed documentation appropriate to their skills and level of understanding, the ordinary investors for whom they act may receive simpler documentation which they will be more likely to comprehend. This is reflected in the current practice of issuing investors at large with 'mini-prospectuses'.[6] The full documentation is made available to professional investors and advisers and to those members of the public who ask for it.

Provision is made for the FSA to exempt from the obligation to disclose in the prospectus, listing particulars or supplementary documents on the ground that the disclosure of certain information would either be contrary to the public interest or would be seriously detrimental to the issuer of the securities.[7] In the latter case, the FSA may not exempt essential information from the obligation of disclosure.[8]

---

1   Section 80(1) does not state expressly on whom the duty is imposed, but this is the implication of section 80(3).
2   Section 80(1). This implements Article 21(1) of the CARD and Article 11(1) of the Public Offers Directive.
3   Section 80(3).
4   Section 80(4). Regard must also be had to information which the FSA has required to be made available (or itself made available) under section 96.
5   Regard must also be had to information which the FSA has required to be made available (or itself made available) under section 96.
6   The contents of a mini-prospectus are regulated by the *Listing Rules*, Chapter 8, paragraphs 8.12–8.13. The authorisation for the issue of a mini-prospectus is contained in Chapter 8, paragraph 8.24 where the FSA exercises the statutory power conferred by section 98. See further **18.19**.
7   Section 82(1).
8   Section 82(2).

18.17   Supplementary Part VI prospectuses and listing particulars

In the United States federal securities law administered by the SEC, there is a policy of 'continuous disclosure'[1] in respect of publicly issued prospectuses, on the ground that securities issued thereunder will continue to be sold and resold in a market influenced by the publicly issued prospectus. For reason of costs and administrative burden, the Financial Services and Markets Act 2000 does not go that far, but it does in certain circumstances require a document called, as the case may be, a supplementary prospectus or supplementary listing particulars to be issued before the commencement of dealings in the securities (ie after their admission to the Official List).[2] The circumstances are a significant change in any matter required to be in the prospectus or listing particulars or the emergence of a significant[3] new matter which would have been disclosed had it arisen at the time of preparation of the prospectus or listing particulars. The supplementary prospectus or listing particulars must be submitted in advance to the FSA for its approval in accordance with the *Listing Rules*.[4]

18.18   Pre-publication vetting of Part VI prospectuses and listing particulars

Independent pre-publication vetting of the information contained in a prospectus or set of listing particulars can be an important safeguard for investors.[5] It can help to ensure that all of the required information has been included and that the information has not been stated in a way which is likely to create a false impression. Knowing that the information will be subject to vetting may also serve to deter those who would otherwise have been tempted deliberately to mislead or to conceal information. Professor Gower described the vetting role played, at that time, by the London Stock Exchange as being 'in practice, a more effective protection to investors than the legal sanctions'.[6] Under section 75 of the Financial Services and Markets Act 2000, as supplemented by the *Listing Rules*, the documents must be submitted in draft to the FSA as the UK Listing Authority and must be formally approved by the FSA prior to publication.[7]

18.19   Power to control information

The FSA acting as the UK Listing Authority is given a general power to specify in the *Listing Rules* the requirements to be complied with by the issuers of listed securities. It may also specify the sanctions or measures it will take in the event of non-compliance. This may include publishing the fact that the issuer has broken

---

1   In the case of listed securities in Britain there is of course the Interim Reports Directive (now consolidated in the CARD) and the relevant listing requirements. See the *Listing Rules*, Chapters 9–11.
2   Section 81.
3   'Significant' means significant for the purpose of making an informed assessment of the matters required to be disclosed under section 80(1): see section 81(2).
4   Section 81(3) provides a defence where the issuer or the person responsible for the listing particulars is unaware of the change or the new matter.
5   Gower, *Review of Investor Protection* (Cmnd 9123, 1984), Part I, paragraphs 9.16–9.23 and Part II, paragraphs 6.10–6.12.
6   *Review of Investor Protection*, Part I, paragraph 9.12.
7   *Listing Rules*, Chapter 5.

the rules. The issuer may be required to publish any information and the FSA itself may be authorised to do so if the issuer fails to do so.[1]

Section 98 gives the FSA the power to control advertisements[2] where there is the publication of a prospectus or listing particulars in connection with an application for listing. There may be no publication of an advertisement[3] in the United Kingdom unless the contents of the advertisement (or other information) have been submitted to the FSA. The latter may either approve the contents or authorise publication without such approval.[4]

Those who contravene section 98, if they are authorised persons, will be treated as having 'contravened a requirement imposed by or under' the Financial Services and Markets Act 2000 and will be subject to the disciplinary measures made available to the FSA by Part XIV of the Act. Authorised persons are persons who are authorised to carry on regulated activity[5] in the United Kingdom. Issuing houses (nowadays often part of an integrated investment bank) and corporate brokers would be among the category of persons who are required to seek authorisation. It is a criminal offence for any person to infringe section 98.[6] The regulatory authorities are empowered to seek injunctions to restrain contraventions of requirements[7] imposed by or under the Act and to apply for restitution orders in respect of breaches which have occurred.[8] Private persons may also seek damages for losses resulting from contravention of relevant FSA rules.[9]

Where advertisements to which section 98 applies have been approved or authorised by the FSA, no civil liability will be incurred by those responsible for publishing the information if 'that information and the listing particulars (or prospectus), taken together, would not be likely to mislead persons of the kind likely to consider the acquisition of the securities in question'.[10] This excludes the possibility of a civil remedy (under section 90 or at common law), where the information, publication of which has been officially sanctioned, is not misleading when read in conjunction with other information publicly available. However, this will not preclude a claim where the information is still misleading, even when taken together with the information in the prospectus or listing particulars and, where relevant, supplementary documents.

Where, under the *Listing Rules*, the publication of a prospectus is required, the securities must not be offered to the public in advance of publication of the prospectus.[11] Contravention of this prohibition is an offence and is also actionable

---

1 Section 96.
2 This extends to other information of a kind specified in the *Listing Rules*.
3 *Listing Rules*, Chapter 8, paragraphs 8.23–8.27 specify various documents for the purposes of section 98 and indicate whether the Stock Exchange's approval is required before publication or whether publication without prior approval is permitted.
4 See section 98(1).
5 See sections 19, 22 and the Financial Services and Markets Act 2000 (Regulated Activities) Order 2001, SI 2001/544.
6 Section 98(2). A defence is made available by section 98(3) when a person issues an advertisement to the order of another person in circumstances in which he believed on reasonable grounds that it had been approved by the FSA.
7 Including rules refered to in the FSA Handbook as 'Conduct of Business Rules'.
8 See sections 380 and 382.
9 Section 150. The relevant rules are conduct of business rules. 'Private person' is defined in the FSMA 2000 (Right of Action) Regulations 2001, SI 2001/2256.
10 Section 98(4).
11 Section 85(1).

at the suit of any person who suffers loss as a consequence, subject to the defences and other incidents applying to actions for breach of statutory duty.[1]

18.20 Registration of Part IV prospectuses and listing particulars

On or before the date on which a prospectus or a set of listing particulars is published as required by the *Listing Rules*, section 83 requires that it must be delivered for registration to the Registrar of Companies. A statement to this effect must be included in the prospectus or particulars.

18.21 Public offers of unlisted securities

Public offers of unlisted securities are regulated by the Public Offers of Securities Regulations 1995[2] which implement the Public Offers Directive into UK law. Much of the Directive is drafted in precise language, and to a considerable extent the Regulations simply adopt the wording of the Directive. The Directive and the Regulations do not draw a significant distinction[3] between public offers made through a formal market (such as the Alternative Investment Market of the London Stock Exchange) and other public offers.

The core requirement of the Regulations is contained in regulation 4(1)[4] which provides that:

> When securities are offered to the public in the United Kingdom for the first time the offeror shall publish a prospectus by making it available to the public, free of charge, at an address in the United Kingdom, from the time he first offers the securities until the end of the period during which the offer remains open.

Any person who makes a public offer of securities may be subject to this requirement since it is not limited in its application to offers made by the company which is the issuer of the securities. Thus a traditional offer for sale on behalf of a company is within the scope of the Regulations. An offer by a large investor of its shareholding in a particular company may also be covered by the Regulations, provided that the offer is of sufficient magnitude to constitute an offer to the public and those securities have not been the subject of an earlier public offer in the UK.

The prospectus must be delivered to the Registrar of Companies for registration prior to publication.[5] There is, however, no requirement for mandatory pre-publication vetting of prospectuses relating to unlisted securities, which, given the widely acknowledged benefits of the vetting process, may be regarded as an unfortunate lacuna in the regulatory framework. The structure of the Alternative Investment Market makes no provision for vetting of prospectuses.[6]

Contravention of Regulation 4 by an authorised person is treated as a breach of the relevant Conduct of Business Rules, whilst contravention by any other person

---

1   Section 85(5). Section 86 extends this requirement to prospectuses.
2   SI 1995/1537.
3   Note regulations 8(4), 8(5) and 15(1)(d) where the fact of securities being admitted to dealings on an approved exchange has some relevance.
4   See articles 4, 9, 15 and 16 of the Directive.
5   Regulation 4(2), implementing article 14.
6   The absence of vetting creates a particular problem with regard to mutual recognition of prospectuses throughout the European Community. See **18.27**.

is an offence.[1] Contravention by an authorised or an unauthorised person is also actionable at the suit of any person who suffers loss as a result, subject to the defences and other incidents applying to actions for breach of statutory duty.[2]

18.22   An 'offer to the public' of 'securities'

The requirement to publish a prospectus is triggered by the making of an offer to the public in the United Kingdom of securities. The expression 'offer to the public' is not defined by the Public Offers Directive, which, in its preamble, explains that 'so far it has proved impossible to furnish a common definition of the term public offer and all of its constituent parts'. Regulations 5 and 6 attempt to define the expression in the same terms as are used in Part VI of the Financial Services and Markets Act 2000. An 'offer' includes an invitation to treat as well as a strict contractual offer;[3] and under regulation 6 an offer to a section of the public, whether selected as members or debenture holders of a company, or as clients of the person issuing the prospectus, or in any other manner, constitutes an offer to the public. A person offers securities to the public in the United Kingdom if, to the extent that the offer is made to persons in the United Kingdom, it is made to the public.[4]

The Prospectus Directive exempts various types of offer from its scope.[5] These exemptions are reflected in regulation 7,[6] which deems certain offers of securities not to be offers to the public. The exempted offers in regulation 7 include the following.

(1) Offers to persons in the contexts of their trades, professions or occupations.[7]
(2) Offers to no more than 50 persons.[8] Previously, the law in the United Kingdom did not specify a threshold number of offerees below which an offer was not to be regarded as an offer to the public. This important exemption enables small-scale offers to be made without excessive regulation.[9]
(3) Offers made to a restricted circle of persons whom the offeror reasonably believes to be sufficiently knowledgeable to understand the risks involved.[10]
(4) Offers in connection with underwriting.[11]

---

1   Regulation 16. A person is not to be regarded as having contravened regulation 4 by reason only of a prospectus not having fully complied with the requirements of the regulations as to form and content of prospectuses.
2   Regulation 16(4).
3   Regulation 5.
4   Regulation 6. An offer to any section of the public, however selected, is a public offer.
5   Article 2.1.
6   These exemptions also apply to the requirement under Part VI to publish a prospectus instead of listing particulars. For the purposes of Part VI, the exemptions are contained in section 84(1) of and Schedule 11 to the FSMA 2000 but, in substance, they are the same as those that apply to public offers of unlisted securities which are discussed in the text.
7   Regulation 7(2)(a) and (in respect of listed securities) Schedule 11, paragraph 3.
8   Regulation 7(2)(b); and see also Schedule 11, paragraph 4.
9   They are regulated by section 21 of the FSMA 2000; see **18.26**.
10   Regulation 7(2)(d) and (7); and see also Schedule 11, paragraph 6.
11   Regulation 7(2)(e); and see also Schedule 11, paragraph 7.

(5) Offers of securities by a private company to its existing members, employees or debenture holders, or to members of the families of existing members and employees.[1]

The Public Offers Directive applies only to 'transferable securities', which are defined as including shares in companies and debt securities having a maturity of at least one year.[2] Accordingly, the Public Offers of Securities Regulations 1995 do not require the publication of a prospectus in respect of an offer of short-term debentures which will mature within one year.[3] Also reflecting the scope of the underlying Directive,[4] there are exemptions from the requirement to publish a prospectus in respect of bonus shares, that is shares issued on a fully paid basis to existing shareholders,[5] shares or debentures offered in connection with a takeover bid or merger,[6] and shares or debentures offered by employers to employees or former employees or members of their families.[7]

18.23   Form and content of prospectuses

Where a prospectus is required, its form and content must comply with the requirements set out in Schedule 1 to the Regulations. The information required to be included relates to the issuer and its capital, financial position, activities and organisation, the offeror (if different from the issuer), the persons responsible for the prospectus, the securities and the offer.[8] The information in a prospectus must be presented in as easily an analysable and comprehensible a form as possible.[9]

There is an overriding duty of disclosure which is very similar to, but not precisely the same as, the duty of disclosure imposed by section 80 of the Financial Services and Markets Act 2000 in respect of listed securities. Under regulation 9, a prospectus relating to unlisted securities must contain all such information as investors would reasonably require, and reasonably expect to find there, for the purpose of making an informed assessment of the assets and liabilities, financial position, profits and losses and prospects of the issuer and of the rights attaching to the securities. In determining the information required to satisfy the overriding duty of disclosure, regard is to be had to the nature of the securities and of the issuer;[10] and the duty is qualified to the extent that it is only information which is within the knowledge of the persons responsible for the prospectus, or which it would be reasonable for them to obtain by making enquiries, that must be

---

1   Regulation 7(2)(f) and (8); this exemption does not have an equivalent in Schedule 11 because the securities of a private company may not be admitted to listing. Other 'restricted circle' exemptions are in respect of offers to members of a club or association (regulation 7(2)(c); Schedule 11, paragraph 5 and of offers to governments or local or public authorities (regulation 7(2)(g); Schedule 11, paragraph 8.
2   Article 3(e). For 'securities' subject to the regulations see regulation 3, and for 'securities' subject to Part VI see section 74(5).
3   Regulation 3(2)(a); see also Schedule 11, paragraph 22.
4   See Article 2.2.
5   Regulation 7(2)(m); see also Schedule 11, paragraph 14.
6   Regulation 7(2)(k) and (l) and (10); see also Schedule 11, paragraphs 5,12 and 13. .
7   Regulation 7(2)(o) and (12); see also Schedule 11, paragraphs 16.
8   These detailed requirements are derived from Article 11 of the POD.
9   Regulation 8(3), implementing Article 11.2.
10   Regulation 9(3).

disclosed.[1] Once the new Prospectus Directive is implemented, it will be the instrument which regulates the content of prospectuses.[2]

As permitted by the Directive, the regulations make provision for the modification of the information required to be included in a prospectus in particular circumstances.[3] For example, where a company makes a number of public offers in the United Kingdom of its securities within one year, it may be relieved of the obligation to publish a full prospectus each time. In respect of second and subsequent offers, the company may instead publish a prospectus which contains only the differences which have arisen since the publication of the full prospectus and which are likely to influence the value of the securities. This prospectus must be accompanied by the earlier full prospectus or must refer to it.[4] Where the person offering the securities is not the company issuing them, and is not acting in pursuance of an agreement with that company, he can omit information from the prospectus that would otherwise be required if that information is not available to him because he is not the issuer and he has been unable, despite making such efforts (if any) as are reasonable, to obtain it.[5] Provision is also made for applications to be made to the FSA in its role as UK Listing Authority for permission to omit information that would otherwise be required to be included: this extends one of the advantages of the regime governing listed securities to unlisted securities.[6]

18.24 Supplementary prospectuses

Where a prospectus has been registered in respect of an offer of securities and an agreement in respect of those securities can still be entered into in pursuance of the offer, there may be a need to publish one or more supplementary prospectuses. This need arises if, during the relevant period, there is a significant[7] change affecting any matter contained in the prospectus which was required to be included, a significant[8] new matter arises which would have been so required if it had arisen when the prospectus was prepared, or there is a significant inaccuracy in the prospectus.[9] However, where the person who delivered the prospectus for registration is unaware of the matter which gives rise to the need for a

---

1   Regulation 9(2). However, unlike section 80, in determining the information required to be included, there is no express provision permitting account to be taken of the nature of the persons likely to consider the acquisition of the securities, or the fact that certain matters may reasonably be expected to be already within the knowledge of professional advisers of any kind which likely investors could be reasonably expected to consult. This may have the effect of imposing a heavier onus of disclosure under the regulations than that under the Act. See further **18.1**.

2   See articles 5(1) and 7. The former contains a general duty of disclosure similar to that contained in article 11(1) of the POD. See further **18.1.**

3   Regulation 8(2), (4), (6) and regulation 11. Regulation 8(5) paves the way for an approved exchange to dispense altogether with the requirement to publish a prospectus, where the offer is of a class of securities which is already admitted to dealings on that exchange and will increase the class by less than 10%.

4   Regulation 8(6).

5   Regulation 11(2).

6   Regulation 11(3).

7   Defined by regulation 10(2).

8   Ibid.

9   The last of these does not have an equivalent in section 81 of the Financial Services and Markets Act 2000.

supplementary prospectus, he is under no duty to comply unless he is informed of it by a person who is responsible for the prospectus; any person who is responsible for the prospectus is under a duty to provide the relevant notification.[1] A supplementary prospectus must be delivered to the Registrar of Companies for registration.[2]

18.25 Control of information

Any advertisement, notice, poster or document (other than a prospectus) announcing a public offer of unlisted securities for which a prospectus is required must not be issued or caused to be issued to the public in the United Kingdom by the person making the offer, unless it states that a prospectus is or will be published and gives an address in the United Kingdom from which it can be obtained.[3] Contravention of this requirement by an authorised person amounts to a breach of the relevant Conduct of Business Rules made by the FSA under the Financial Services and Markets Act 2000. An unauthorised person who breaches this requirement is guilty of an offence. Contravention by an authorised or unauthorised person is also actionable at the suit of any person who suffers loss, subject to the defences and other incidents applying to actions for breach of statutory duty.[4]

18.26 Regulation of invitations to engage in investment activity under the Financial Services and Markets Act 2000

Apart from the regulation of prospectuses and listing particulars, another way in which the regulatory structure seeks to filter out unsuitable investment information is through section 21 of the Financial Services and Markets Act 2000, which establishes the so-called 'financial promotion' regime. Under this section, invitations (including advertisements) or inducements to engage in investment business which are issued in the United Kingdom must be issued by, or with the approval of, authorised persons. Authorised persons must comply with the FSA's Conduct of Business Rules when issuing, or approving for issue, investment advertisements. The responsibility so imposed on authorised persons acts as a safeguard against invitations or inducements containing false or misleading information or failing to provide adequate information. The expression 'engage in investment activity' is defined by reference to 'controlled activities' which are defined in subordinate legislation[5] and it would certainly include an advertisement containing an offer of securities. Thus, an offer of unlisted securities which, for some reason relating either to the nature of the securities or the type of offer, is not subject to the Public Offers of Securities Regulations 1995 does not necessarily escape from the regulatory net, since it may be caught in any event by section 21. Contravention of section 21 is an offence and an agreement entered into in

---

1 Regulation 10(4).
2 Regulation 10(1).
3 Regulation 12.
4 Regulation 16.
5 Section 21(8) and the FSMA (Financial Promotion) Order 2001, SI 2001/1335 (as amended). Note that, while there is considerable overlap, 'controlled activities' are not the same as 'regulated activities'. See Blair (ed) *Butterworths Annotated Guide to the Financial Services and Markets Act 2000* (Reed Elsevier, 2003) pp 29–34.

breach of the section may be unenforceable, with the innocent party being entitled to recover any money or property he has parted with as well as compensation.[1]

Section 21 is subject to a number of exemptions. Particularly important exemptions in the context of public offers of securities are those which relate to prospectuses, listing particulars and associated documents. As well as catching invitations and inducements that would not otherwise be regulated, section 21 also *prima facie* brings within its scope prospectuses and listing particulars which are subject to the requirements of Part VI of the Financial Services and Markets Act 2000 or, as the case may be, of the Public Offers of Securities Regulations 1995. A requirement to comply with section 21 as well as Part VI or the Public Offers Regulations could be regarded as amounting to excessive regulation and this result is prevented by appropriate exemptions: listing particulars, supplementary listing particulars, Part VI prospectuses, supplementary prospectuses and other advertisements relating to listed securities published with the approval of the FSA or in accordance with the *Listing Rules* are exempt from section 21;[2] prospectuses, supplementary prospectuses and other advertisements relating to unlisted securities which are the subject of a public offer that is regulated by the Public Offers of Securities Regulations are also exempted from the scope of section 21.[3]

18.27 Mutual recognition of prospectuses and listing particulars in Member States of the European Community

With a view to encouraging the development of a pan-Community capital market, the Member States of the Community have adopted mutual recognition provisions. These allow securities to be offered, or admitted to listing, in a number of Member States on the basis of a prospectus or set of listing particulars which has satisfied the requirements imposed by one of those States. Satisfying the requirements of one State can thus be said to act as a passport for the offering or listing of the relevant securities in other Member States. Under European law, mutual recognition is governed by article 21 of the Public Offers Directive and articles 38–40 of the Consolidated Admissions and Reporting Directive ('CARD'). Schedule 4 to the Public Offers of Securities Regulations makes provision for the recognition in the United Kingdom of prospectuses and listing particulars approved in other Member States. Implementation of the new Prospectus Directive will result in changes to the provisions of Schedule 4 as the Directive will, in most circumstances, require the FSA to recognise prospectuses (or listing particulars) approved in other Member States and remove the power to require additional information to be included in the document.[4]

To qualify for use as a passport throughout the Community, a prospectus or set of listing particulars must first be approved in one Member State. This poses a difficulty in the United Kingdom in relation to prospectuses relating to unlisted securities, because they are not required to be vetted or approved by an independent authority prior to publication. To ensure that companies do not

---

1 Section 30. Note that there is nothing to stop a customer holding the other party to the contract.
2 Reg 71 of the Financial Promotion Order, SI 2001/1335.
3 Reg 72 of the Financial Promotion Order, SI 2001/1335.
4 See **18.1** regarding the background to the Directive.

have to seek a listing solely in order to benefit from the mutual recognition provisions, section 87 FSMA 2000 makes provision for the submission to, and the approval of, the FSA as the UK Listing Authority of prospectuses relating to offers of unlisted securities. The section 87 procedure can be used only where the United Kingdom is one of the Member States in which the securities are to be offered, but it is not restricted to companies having their registered office in the United Kingdom or another Member State. An application under section 87 does not amount to an application for listing and the costs involved should be much smaller than those incurred in seeking a full listing.

18.28 Remedies for false, misleading or incomplete statements in connection with offers of securities

Part VI of the Financial Services and Markets Act 2000 provides a single type of statutory remedy in respect of three distinct situations, namely:

(1) the inclusion of false or misleading information in a prospectus or set of listing particulars (including supplementary prospectuses and listing particulars);
(2) failure to disclose the information required to be included in a prospectus or set of listing particulars (including supplementary prospectuses and listing particulars); and
(3) failure to publish, when required, a supplementary prospectus or set of listing particulars.

A virtually identical statutory remedy in respect of unlisted securities is provided by regulation 14 of the Public Offers of Securities Regulations 1995. The Part VI remedy is considered below, with reference to the equivalent provisions in respect of unlisted securities.

Various other remedies for deceit, misrepresentation and negligence must also be considered since they are applicable to offers which fall outside Part VI and the Public Offers of Securities Regulations 1995 and to statements made otherwise than in prospectuses, listing particulars and related documents. These remedies are also potentially applicable in respect of false statements in prospectuses and listing particulars, but considerations such as the burden of proof or range of possible defendants are likely to lead investors to favour the statutory claims. It would seem undeniable that the range of overlapping remedies can create unnecessary confusion in this area of the law.

18.29 The statutory remedy for false, misleading or incomplete statements

Section 90 of the Financial Services and Markets Act 2000 creates liability for loss as a result of any untrue or misleading statement in listing particulars or the omission from them of any matter required to be included by section 80 (general duty of disclosure) or section 81 (supplementary listing particulars). The section applies, *mutatis mutandis,* to non-listing prospectuses.[1] Failure to publish sup-

---

1   Section 87(5) and Schedule 9 FSMA 2000.

plementary listing particulars or prospectuses when required is similarly actionable.[1]

The 'person or persons responsible'[2] for any prospectus or set of listing particulars[3] are made 'liable to pay compensation to any person who has acquired[4] any of the securities in question and suffered a loss in respect of them as a result of any untrue or misleading statement', etc. As is appropriate to a misrepresentation and non-disclosure remedy[5] intended to protect investors in the context of a public issue, the elements of 'reliance' and 'inducement' (required by the common law of misrepresentation) have been abolished. The element of causation ('as a result of') remains. Further, it is specifically provided that actual knowledge by the claimant when he acquired the securities that the statement was false or misleading, etc, may be raised and proved as a defence against an action based on section 90.[6] It is obviously important that in a public issue investor remedy of this type, those who acquire securities without reading the prospectus or listing particulars but nevertheless suffer a loss because of false or misleading statements (or the omission of information that is required to be disclosed[7]) should have a remedy. This is because the market price is affected by the responses of other investors when the truth becomes known. The original price those investors were in general prepared to pay can be properly said to relate to the accuracy of the information made available to the investing public.[8]

A less satisfactory feature of section 90 is the nature of the 'compensation' payable to a person who has acquired securities and 'suffered a loss'. Similar terminology employed in section 2(1) of the Misrepresentation Act 1967 has generally been understood to give a tort measure of damages (ie based on 'out of pocket' losses) rather than losses based on 'loss of expectation of bargain' (the traditional[9] contractual measure). Although it is possible that the draftsman may have intended otherwise (or perhaps hoped to leave the matter to the courts), it is regrettable, especially in an investor protection Act, that the answer cannot be given with any certainty. It seems that, whatever the basis of awarding compensation, section 90 does not impose contractual liability. Like other remedies for false or misleading statements (where these cannot be regarded as incorporated

---

1   Section 90(3). See regulation 14(1) for the equivalent provision in respect of unlisted securities.

2   This expression is defined at length by regulation 6 of the FSMA 2000 (Official Listing of Securities) Regulations 2001 SI 2001/2956, examined below. Primarily it is the 'issuer' and its directors.

3   Or, where appropriate, supplementary prospectuses or listing particulars. See section 90(10).

4   See the definition of 'acquisition' in section 90(7). The question of who may seek relief on this basis is considered below.

5   This is a common feature of such remedies in American and Commonwealth securities regulation legislation. See Rider and Leigh French, *The Regulation of Insider Trading* (Macmillan, 1979).

6   Section 90(5) and Schedule 10, paragraph 6, FSMA 2000. Regulation 15(5) is the equivalent provision for unlisted securities.

7   Where the prospectus or listing particulars require that a statement be made that no information can or need be given on a certain matter, failure to do so also comes within this remedy: section 90(3) and, in respect of unlisted securities, regulation 14(2).

8   Welch, 'Breach of Prospectus Requirements' (1985) 6 Co Law 246. See further Ferran, *Company Law and Corporate Finance* (Oxford University Press, 1999) Chapter 17.

9   It is true that in some respects the rules governing damages in contract and in tort have, in recent years, 'grown together'. This, however, does not affect the point made in the text.

in the terms of a contract), failure to carry out promises will not ground relief.[1] Undertakings of various kinds are commonly given in both public issue and takeover documents.

18.30   Who may be sued and who may sue under the statutory remedy?

To the first of these questions an ample answer is given by section 90 of the Financial Services and Markets Act 2000 and the relevant subordinate legislation.[2] Primarily it is the 'issuer of the securities' and (where the issuer is a body corporate) the directors of the issuer at the time the listing particulars were submitted to the FSA as Listing Authority.[3] The offeror of securities is also a responsible person save where the offeror is making an offer in association with the issuer and the issuer is primarily responsible for the documentation.[4] Responsibility also extends to those who accept, and are stated in the prospectus or particulars as accepting, responsibility for the document. That will include those who accept responsibility for 'any part' of the document. It also covers those who authorise the contents of all or part of the document. These provisions cast a wide net. They will clearly cover an issuing house performing its usual functions (whether or not the relevant prospectus relates to an offer for sale). They will also catch an 'expert'[5] (eg a valuer or reporting accountant) who is responsible for that part of the contents of the prospectus or listing particulars for which he has taken responsibility.[6] The liability imposed by section 90 does not extend to those giving advice on the contents of the prospectus or particulars in a professional capability (eg solicitors).[7]

Liability to pay compensation under section 90 is ignored in determining the amount to be paid on subscription for the shares in question or as to the amount paid up or deemed to be paid up.[8] This preserves the formal requirements on the raising of share capital.

The provisions relating to those who may seek a remedy under section 90 are less clearly spelt out than is the case in regard to those made responsible for the prospectus or listing particulars. Section 90 (1) itself refers to 'a person who has acquired securities to which the particulars apply '. Section 90(7) then states that references in section 90 'to the acquisition by any person of securities include references to his contracting to acquire them or any interest in them'.[9] This phraseology is not wholly free from ambiguity. It obviously means that not only those who have become registered owners of the securities in question but also

---

1   In Scotland, promises are legally enforceable but the obligation arsing from a promise is not, strictly speaking, contractual.
2   Part 3 of SI 2001/2956. Regulation 13 is the equivalent provision in respect of unlisted securities.
3   Regulation 6, SI 2001/2956. It also includes those named in the prospectus or listing particulars who have authorised their naming as present or future directors: regulation 6(1) (c). As to issues of securities concerned with a take-over by share exchange, see regulation 7.
4   Regulation 10(2), SI 2001/2956.
5   See the definition of 'expert' in paragraph 8 of Schedule 10 to FSMA 2000.
6   Regulation 6(1)(d), SI 2001/2956.
7   Regulation 6(4), SI 2001/2956.
8   Regulation 6(5), SI 2001/2956. See regulation 13(5) of the POS Regulations in respect of unlisted securities.
9   See regulation 14(5) of the POS Regulations in respect of unlisted securities.

who have agreed to purchase or subscribe for them (or options in them) may resort to the relief provided by section 90. It seems that claimants under section 90 may include market purchasers provided, and to the extent that, they can show that their loss results from the inaccuracies in, or omissions from, the prospectus or listing particulars.[1] Regulation 14 of the Public Offers of Securities Regulations 1995 does not track the wording of section 90 exactly, and it has been judicially suggested that claims under that provision may be limited to initial subscribers or purchasers,[2] but that would seem to be an unduly restrictive interpretation.

18.31 Defences available to persons responsible

Section 90(2) sets out a series of defences by reference to Schedule 10.[3] The principal defence is that the person responsible can satisfy the court that he 'reasonably believed',[4] having made such enquiries (if any) as were reasonable, that the statement was true and not misleading.[5] It must also be shown he continued in that belief until the securities were acquired. Alternatively, he may show that the securities were acquired before it was reasonably practical for steps to be taken to bring a correction to the attention of persons likely to acquire the securities, or that before the securities were acquired he had taken all such steps as it was reasonable for him to have taken to secure that a correction was brought to the attention of those persons. Another alternative defence is that he continued to believe (that the statement was true, etc) until after the commencement of dealings in the securities following their admission to the listing. Here he must satisfy the court that the securities were acquired after such a lapse of time that he ought in the circumstances to be reasonably excused.[6]

Reasonable reliance on statements made on the authority of an expert is a further defence,[7] and there is a defence against liability for loss resulting from a statement made by an official or contained in an official document.[8] A defence to the failure to publish required supplementary prospectuses or listing particulars is available to a person who can establish that he reasonably believed that no such supplementary document was required.[9]

---

1   This interpretation is borne out by the wording of paragraph 1(3)(d) of Schedule 10 to FSMA 2000 which implies that liability may occur after the commencement of dealings.

2   *Possfund Custodian Trustee Ltd v Diamond* [1996] 2 All ER 774.

3   See regulation 15 in respect of unlisted securities.

4   That is, at the time when he submitted the prospectus or listing particulars to the FSA. For prospectuses relating to unlisted securities, the relevant time is when the prospectus is delivered to the Registrar of Companies for registration: regulation 15(1).

5   Or that the matter that was omitted (where the omission of required information caused the loss) was properly omitted.

6   Schedule 10, paragraph 1(3)(d). The equivalent defence in respect of unlisted securities is contained in regulation 15(1)(d). This defence bears out the inclusion of 'market purchasers' in the initial period of dealing as among those who may sue. Note Schedule 9, paragraph 5(1) which modifies the defence as it applies to prospectuses which do not relate to securities that are to be listed and which are brought within Part VI for mutual recognition purposes.

7   Schedule 10, paragraph 2(2).

8   Schedule 10, paragraph 5, ie where these statements, etc, are included in the prospectus or listing particulars. See regulation 15(2) and (4) for the equivalent provisions in respect of unlisted securities.

9   Schedule 10, paragraph 7. The equivalent provision in respect of unlisted securities is regulation 15(6).

18.32 The relationship of the statutory remedy to the common-law remedies

Section 90(6)[1] is careful to preserve 'any liability which any person may incur apart from this section'. An investor in securities is thus free to pursue claims based on misrepresentation or negligence.[2] There are good grounds for the retention of the remedy of rescission for misrepresentation because, whereas he can only seek compensation under section 90, rescission allows the investor to set aside the contract for the acquisition of the securities and thus to unwind completely the original bargain. Also rescission can be sought on the basis of a purely innocent (ie non-negligent) misrepresentation. However, otherwise (and in particular with regard to the right to damages in English law under section 2(1) of the Misrepresentation Act 1967) there appears still to be an unnecessary and confusing overlap in remedies. It is a matter of regret that the question of overlap remains unresolved. Section 2(1) of the 1967 Act is available only against the other party to the investment contract (eg the issuing house in the case of an offer of sale) and is thus more restricted in its 'target' than section 90 of the 2000 Act. Moreover, it would appear to require the proof of 'reliance' and 'inducement'. On the other hand, since the only defence is reasonable ground for belief (and not the other defences in Schedule 10 to the 2000 Act), it may sometimes be worth pleading in addition to section 90. However, none of these distinctions was worth preserving, and it would have been a simple matter to disapply section 2(1) in the context of investment contracts within the scope of section 90.[3]

18.33 The common-law remedies: the right to rescind a contract of allotment for material misrepresentation

An allottee's right to rescind the contract of allotment may arise in the case of any allotment of shares by a company whether public or private. An action for rescission must be brought by the subscriber against the company as the other party to the contract of allotment. Where the shares are not allotted directly to subscribers by the company, a right of rescission may not be exercised against the company. In the case of an offer for sale, the issuing house is the 'subscriber' and the investors who obtain securities from the issuing house do so by 'purchase'. Clearly, any remedy by way of rescission will be against the issuing house.

A contract to take shares, like other contracts, is voidable if induced by misrepresentation, whether such misrepresentation is fraudulent or innocent: that is to say the contract is valid until repudiation, but upon repudiation is terminated as from the date when the shareholder gives notice that he requires to be relieved of his shares. This is subject, however, to the rule discussed later that he must actually take proceedings to enforce his right (if it is not admitted) before the company goes into liquidation, and that he must come promptly for relief. Accordingly, if there is a material misrepresentation in the listing particulars or, as the case may be, the prospectus upon which a shareholder relied when applying

---

1   See regulation 14(4) for the equivalent provision in respect of unlisted securities.
2   Or in contract in a suitable case.
3   Something similar to this has been done in regard to a promoter's duties of disclosure to his company in section 90(8). This equitable duty is disregarded as regards the duty to disclose information in the prospectus or listing particulars.

for shares offered by way of subscription, he is entitled, if he seeks relief within a reasonable time after learning the truth, and before the company is in liquidation, to have his name removed from the register, and the amount he has paid upon the shares returned to him,[1] with interest from the time of payment.[2] But it must be noted that only the shareholder who applied for the shares on the faith of the prospectus is entitled to relief; the remedy does not extend to a purchaser from another shareholder who is not a party to the misrepresentation.

18.34 Responsibility for statements

Questions can arise concerning the responsibility of the company, its directors and its professional advisers for statements made in connection with a public offering of securities. In the case of the statutory remedy under the Financial Services and Markets Act 2000, subordinate legislation identifies those responsible.[3] In the case of the common-law remedies such as rescission, a company is responsible for the statements of its directors, general agents and special agents who are acting within the scope of their authority[4] which includes persons whose acts are subsequently ratified;[5] a company is also responsible for statements which, to the knowledge of its directors, were made before the contract and which induced it or which formed the basis of it.[6] In each case, the company's responsibility does not depend on whether the representations were known to be false or not.[7]

Representations made even before the company was in existence, or made by persons who are strangers to the company, may become, by the subsequent knowledge of the directors, the responsibility of the company, as where an application for shares was made before the company was incorporated upon the faith of a prospectus prepared by a promoter, and the company later adopted the prospectus and allotted the shares.[8]

If a statement is actually included in listing particulars or in a prospectus, the company may find it difficult to deny that the statement formed the basis of the contract to take the shares. The cases establish that the statement will be so treated unless the company expressly dissociates itself from the report and warns investors that they must take the report for what it is worth:[9] the distinction is between showing that it is repeating on hearsay what it has been told, and affirming the matter as a fact.[10] However, such disclaimers of responsibility must be read in the

---

1   The best statement of the effect of the cases will be found in *Re Scottish Petroleum Co* (1883) 23 Ch D 413 (CA).

2   *Karberg's Case* [1892] 3 Ch 1 (CA) (where the rate of interest was fixed by the court at 4 per cent).

3   See **18.30**. Regulation 13 of the Public Offers of Securities Regulations 1995 provides an equivalent code in respect of unlisted securities

4   Thus where the directors know that one of their body is obtaining subscriptions for shares, the company is responsible for representations made by him: *Hilo Manufacturing Co v Williamson* (1911) 28 TLR 164.

5   *Lynde v Anglo-Indian Hemp Co* [1896] 1 Ch 178.

6   Ibid.

7   This last proposition is not accurately stated in the headnote to *Collins v Associated Greyhound Racecourses* [1930] 1 Ch 1, but is correctly stated in the judgment.

8   *Karberg's Case* [1892] 3 Ch 1; *Tamplin's Case* [1892] WN 146.

9   *Mair v Rio Grande Rubber Estates* [1913] AC 853; *Karberg's Case*, above; *Lynde v Anglo-Italian Hemp Co*, above; *Re Pacaya Rubber Co* [1914] 1 Ch 542.

10 *Re Reese River Silver Mining Co* (1867) 2 Ch App 604 at 615.

light of section 3 of the Misrepresentation Act 1967, which invalidates any unreasonable[1] contractual term that would exclude or restrict liability for misrepresentation. Also, such a disclaimer cannot be included in a prospectus or a set of listing particulars relating to securities which are to be listed, because the *Listing Rules* specifically require the directors of the issuer (or, in some cases, the issuer itself) to state expressly that they take responsibility for the information contained in the listing particulars.[2] Also, under the Public Offers of Securities Regulations 1995, a prospectus relating to an offer of unlisted securities which is made or authorised by the issuer of the securities must contain a declaration by the directors that, to the best of their knowledge, the information accords with the facts and that there is no omission likely to affect the import of the information.[3]

18.35　Loss of the right to rescind

It is a general principle of law that where a party having a right to rescind his contract, after having knowledge of such right, performs any act affirming his contract, he cannot afterwards set up his right to avoid the contract.[4] Therefore, any act by a shareholder recognising his position as a member of the company after knowledge of the misrepresentation, such as by selling or trying to sell the shares,[5] attending meetings,[6] signing proxies, paying calls, or accepting dividends,[7] will prevent the member from obtaining rescission, even though performed under a mistake as to rights,[8] unless he has meanwhile definitely elected to rescind the contract, as by commencing proceedings.[9]

The shareholder must, moreover, come within a reasonable time after learning the truth; for the rights and interests of other persons intervene, and the aggrieved shareholder will not be allowed to wait and see whether the speculation turns out to be a favourable one, and then, according to the result, retain the benefit or repudiate the loss.[10] As the intervention of the rights of others prevents the right of the applicant to rescind, it may well be that even a charge on the uncalled capital in favour of debenture-holders will prevent relief, but this has not been definitely decided.[11] The occurrence of a winding-up, whether the assets are sufficient to pay the creditors or not, brings in other rights (ie those of the

---

1　Reasonableness is judged in accordance with section 11(1) of the Unfair Contract Terms Act 1977. The burden of establishing that a term is reasonable is on the person who wishes to rely on it: section 11(5). There is no equivalent in Scotland to section 3.

2　*Listing Rules*, Chapter 5, paragraphs 5.2–5.5. Special provision is made for listing particulars relating to an issue of securities in connection with a takeover, where the directors of the target alone can take responsibility for information in the listing particulars relating to their company (paragraph 5.3(b)). Only the company, and not its directors, is required to take responsibility for information in listing particulars relating to international securities such as eurobonds: *Listing Rules*, Chapter 23, paragraph 23.11.

3　Schedule 1, part III, paragraph 10(1).

4　*Clough v London and North-Western Railway* (1872) LR 7 Ex 26 (Ex Ch).

5　*Ex parte Briggs* (1866) LR 1 Eq 483. Cf *Crawley's Case* (1869) LR 4 Ch App 322.

6　*Sharpley v Louth and East Coast Railway* (1876) 2 Ch D 663.

7　*Scholey v Central Railway of Venezuela* (1869) LR 9 Eq 266, note.

8　*Re Dunlop-Truffault Cycle Co* (1896) 66 LJ Ch 25.

9　*Tomlin's Case* (1898) 1 Ch 104.

10　*Downes v Ship* (1868) LR 3 HL 343; *Houldsworth v City of Glasgow Bank* (1880) 5 AC 317 (HL).

11　For the principle see: *Re Scottish Petroleum Co* (1883), 23 Ch D 413 (CA); *Tennant v City of Glasgow Bank* (1879) 4 App Cas 615 (HL).

creditors or contributories) so as to render rescission impossible;[1] for upon the commencement of a liquidation the creditors or other shareholders are the persons interested in retaining the name of the shareholder upon the register, and against them he has no claim to set aside his bargain.[2]

It is not enough merely to serve the company with notice of repudiation. The complainant must either procure the company to remove his name from the register of members, or commence proceedings to compel it to do so,[3] subject to the exception, however, that if he has *agreed to be bound* by a test case brought by another shareholder, he may await the decision of such case,[4] or if in an action for calls he has set up a counterclaim for rescission, he is in time.[5] In an action for calls, it is not a sufficient defence to set up misrepresentation and repudiation of the shares. The defence must be coupled with a counterclaim for rescission of the contract and rectification of the register, or, if the action is brought in a court where such counterclaim cannot be entertained, a statement must be made that relief is being claimed in the proper court. If the delay has been so long that rescission will not be granted, the defence will fail.[6]

'Where a person has contracted to take shares in a company and his name has been placed on the register, it has always been held that he must exercise his right of repudiation with extreme promptness after the discovery of the fraud or misrepresentation.'[7] What is a reasonable time is a question of fact, and will vary with the circumstances of each case, but in practice a shareholder should not delay at all after he knows the facts which entitle him to relief. 'The delay of a fortnight in repudiating the shares', said Baggallay LJ,[8] 'makes it to my mind doubtful whether the repudiation in the case of a going concern would have been in time. No doubt where investigation is necessary some time must be allowed, as in *Central Railway Co of Venezuela v Kisch*.[9] But where, as in the present case, the shareholder is at once informed of the circumstances he ought to lose no time in repudiating.' There are conflicting authorities on whether it is possible to rescind if some of the shares originally acquired have since been sold.[10] As shares are fungible securities, it is doubtful in principle whether disposal of part of the original holding should bar rescission, since the investor can always go into the market to buy substitute

---

1   *Tennent v City of Glasgow Bank* (1879) 4 App Cas 615 (HL); *Burgess's Case* (1880) 15 Ch D 507, this being the case of a solvent company.

2   *Tennent v City of Glasgow Bank* (1879) 4 App Cas 615; *Stone v City and County Bank* (1877) 3 CP 282 (CA); *Oakes v Turquand* (1867), LR 2 HL 325; *Burgess's Case* (1880) 15 Ch D 507; *Re Scottish Petroleum Co* (1883) 23 Ch D 413.

3   *Re Scottish Petroleum Co* (1993) 23 Ch D 413 (CA); *First National Reinsurance Co v Greenfield* [1921] 2 KB 260; but see **12.9**.

4   *Re Scottish Petroleum Co* (1883) 23 Ch D 413; *Pawle's Case* (1869) 4 Ch App 497; *Hare's Case* (1869) 4 Ch App 503. The pendency of other cases will not save him if there is no agreement to be bound by their result (see cases cited in this note).

5   *Whiteley's Case* [1900] 1 Ch 365.

6   *First National Reinsurance Co v Greenfield* [1921] 2 KB 260.

7   *Per* Lord Davey in *Aaron's Reefs v Twiss* [1896] AC 273 at 294. See also *Sharpley v Louth and East Coast Railway* (1876) 2 Ch D 663 at 685.

8   *Re Scottish Petroleum Co* (1883) 23 Ch D at 434. See also *Re Christineville Rubber Esttes* [1911] WN 216 (four months); *Taite's Case* (1867) LR 3 Eq 795 (a month sufficed).

9   (1867) LR 2 HL 99. In this case two months was allowed, but it was stated that it was necessary that the complainant should come 'with the utmost diligence' (*per* Lord Romilly at 125).

10   *Re Metropolitan Coal Consumers' Assn Ltd* (1890) 6 TLR 416 (no rescission if part sold); *Re Mount Morgan (West) Gold Mines Ltd* (1887) 3 TLR 556 (rescission still possible despite sale of part).

shares and in that way put himself into a position to give back the full portion of what he acquired in return for his money back.[1]

18.36 An action for deceit

Besides the right to rescission of his contract to take shares, the shareholder may also claim damages against the persons who fraudulently induced him to become a shareholder, and this right does not cease when the company goes into liquidation. The company itself may be sued for fraudulent statements made by those for whom it is vicariously responsible.[2] Those responsible for the prospectus, so long as they have knowledge of the falsity of the statements made, are liable in deceit whether or not rescission of the allotment is obtained. 'Those responsible' will clearly embrace promoters, directors and issuing houses (as well as experts in respect of reports made by them).

There is a clear distinction between an action for deceit and an action for rescission of contract. In the latter case, it is only necessary to show that the contract was induced by an untrue statement of a material fact, whether made innocently or not,[3] while to sustain an action for deceit it is necessary to show that the defendant acted fraudulently – ie made the untrue statement either knowing it to be false or without belief in its truth, or recklessly, not caring whether it were true or false.[4] Thus liability would attach if the defendant 'shut his eyes to the facts or purposely abstained from inquiring into them'. It would not be enough to show that the statement was made through want of care.[5]

The House of Lords has held that if the misrepresentation complained of was contained in the prospectus, only original subscribers, and not purchasers of shares, can obtain damages for deceit; for the function of the prospectus is exhausted once the allotment is made,[6] unless the prospectus was in fact issued with a view of inducing persons to become purchasers of shares. The latter inference will be the natural one to draw today in the context of normal public issues accompanied by the publication of the prospectus or at least a 'mini-prospectus' in national newspapers. If this is the case, the directors and other persons issuing it with this object will become liable for losses suffered by those who bought shares, even from strangers. It is not necessary that the representation should be direct to the person injured; it is sufficient if it be made to another (eg to a newspaper) with the intent that it shall be repeated to and acted upon by the person who is subsequently injured.[7] 'But to bring it within the principle, the injury must be the immediate and not the remote consequence of the representation thus made ... It must appear that such false representation was

---

1   *Smith New Court Securities Ltd v Scrimgeour Vickers (Asset Management) Ltd* [1997] AC 254 (HL), at 262 *per* Lord Browne-Wilkinson.
2   Section 111A of the Companies Act 1985, as inserted by the Companies Act 1989, which reverses the effect of the decision in *Houldsworth v City of Glasgow Bank* (1880) 5 App Cas 317 (HL, Sc).
3   *Karberg's Case* [1892] 3 Ch 1 at 13 (CA); *Lagunas Nitrate Co v Lagunas Nitrate Syndicate* [1899] 2 Ch 392 at p 423 (CA).
4   *Derry v Peek* (1889) 15 App Cas 337 at 374 (HL).
5   *Derry v Peek* (1889) 14 App Cas at 375 and 376; *Angus v Clifford* [1891] 2 Ch 449 (CA).
6   *Peek v Gurney* (1873) LR 6 HL 277 at 400 and 411. A subscriber who has sold his shares and subsequently repurchased them cannot obtain relief: *In re Bank of Hindustan, China and Japan* (1873) LR 16 Eq 417.
7   *Andrews v Mockford* [1896] 1 QB 372 (CA); *Barry v Crosskey* (1861) 2 J & H 1.

made with the direct intent that it should be acted upon by such third person in the manner which occasions the injury or loss.'[1]

The misstatement must be of an existing fact, and not merely an unduly sanguine expression of hope or an exaggerated view of the advantages the company offers. A general commendation of his wares by a trader is not a false statement, even if too highly coloured. 'Anticipation of future results is not a statement of fact.'[2] 'If you are looking to the language as only the language of hope, expectation, and confident belief, that is one thing: but you may use language in such a way as, although in the form of hope and expectation, it may become a representation of existing facts';[3] and to say that something is expected when in reality it is not expected, or that directors have an intention to do something when they have not, is a misstatement of fact.[4] For example, a statement that property has been acquired which has not in fact then been acquired will be ground for an action against directors, even if the property be acquired a few days after the allotment of the shares.[5] A misrepresentation of law is not a misstatement of fact which will give any remedy against directors.[6]

If a false or misleading statement is made, it is no protection to the defendants to say that the claimant had means of ascertaining the truth and was negligent in failing to inspect documents referred to in the prospectus or to make other enquiries, for he is entitled to rely on the statements made to him.[7] If before allotment the directors discover a mistake in the prospectus, it is fraud to allow applicants to remain under the mistaken belief and accept an allotment.[8] It is the duty of the directors to point out the mistake in unambiguous terms, and not merely to send a new prospectus correctly stating the facts. 'Assuming a fraud to have been committed, it obviously lies on those who rely upon a subsequent explanation to show that such explanation was quite clear.'[9]

In an action for deceit, the motive with which the statement was made is immaterial, for a person is liable for a false statement knowingly made, even if he has no intent to defraud.[10] It is not necessary to show that the false statement was the sole inducing cause if it forms a substantial ground for taking the shares,[11] and the courts pay little attention to a cross-examination as to the weight attached to each statement by the applicant, holding that a material misrepresentation likely to induce the application is enough, unless the claimant admits that he did not act

---

1   Cited from *Barry v Crosskey* with approval by Lord Cairns in *Peek v Gurney* (1873) LR 6 HL 377 at 413.
2   *Per* Lord Esher MR, in *Bentley v Black* (1893) 9 TLR 580 (CA).
3   *Per* Lord Halsbury LC in *Aaron's Reefs v Twiss* [1896] AC 273 at 284 (HL).
4   *Edgington v Fitzmaurice* (1885) 29 Ch D 459 (CA); *Karberg's Case* [1892] 3 Ch 1 at 11 (CA).
5   *McConnel v Wright* [1903] 1 Ch 546 (CA).
6   *Beattie v Lord Ebury* (1872) 7 Ch App 777, (1874) LR 7 HL 102; *Rashdall v Ford* (1865) LR 2 Eq 750; *Bentley v Black* (1893) 9 TLR 580.
7   *Reynell v Sprye* (1851) 1 De GM & G 660; *Arkwright v Newbold* (1881) 17 Ch D 301; *Aaron's Reefs v Twiss* [1896] App Cas 273; *Gluckstein v Barnes* [1900] AC 240 at p 251; *Redgrave v Hurd* (1881) 20 Ch D 1; *Alliance & Leicester Building Society v Edgestop* [1994] 2 All ER 38 [1993] 1 WLR 1462.
8   *Brownlie v Campbell* (1880) 5 App Cas 925 at 950; *Davies v London and Provincial Co* (1878) 8 Ch D 459 at 475.
9   *Arnison v Smith* (1889) 41 Ch D 348, *per* Lord Halsbury at 370.
10 *Derry v Peek* (1889) 14 App Cas 337 at 374; *Smith v Chadwick* (1884) 9 App Cas 187; *Arnison v Smith* (1889) 41 Ch D 348 (CA).
11 *Edgington v Fitzmaurice* (1885) 29 Ch D 459.

upon it.[1] If, however, the court comes to the conclusion that the particular misrepresentation did not affect the claimant's mind, and that he would still have taken the shares if he had known the truth, he will have suffered no damage, and cannot recover. The court may come to this conclusion either from the claimant's answers in cross-examination or from his conduct, or from the nature of the misrepresentation relied upon.[2]

If a statement is true at the time it is made, but becomes untrue before the allotment of the shares (eg if a director named in the prospectus has meanwhile resigned), it will be good ground for rescinding the contract,[3] and there is authority for the view that it may give a cause of action for deceit.[4]

18.37   Misleading omissions

Either in an action for deceit or in an action for rescission the omission of material facts may amount to a misrepresentation.[5] Thus, in a prospectus describing land purchased by the company as 'eminently suitable' for its operations, the *innocent* omission to state that the land had been scheduled to a town planning resolution and that the company would not be entitled to compensation for the removal of buildings unless they had been erected with the previous consent of the local authority was held sufficient to entitle an allottee of shares to rescission against the company.[6] Again, the omission of the names of the real vendors and the interpolation of a nominal vendor to conceal the true facts may be sufficient to entitle subscribers to relief,[7] but this rule applies only if the omission renders the prospectus as it stands misleading,[8] or the omissions are (in the words of James LJ) 'omissions amounting in effect to false statements',[9] or if the omission is of something which there was a duty to disclose. Lord Cairns said: 'There must, in my opinion, be some active misstatement of fact, or, at all events, such a partial and fragmentary statement of fact, as that the withholding of that which is not stated makes that which is stated absolutely false.'[10] 'There must be something more than mere non-disclosure proved before misrepresentation is established: it must, I

---

1   *Per* Lord Halsbury in *Arnison v Smith* (1889) 41 Ch D 348 at 369 (CA). And see *Smith v Chadwick* (1884) 20 Ch D 27 (CA), 9 App Cas 187 (HL).
2   *Smith v Chadwick* (1884) 9 App Cas 187; *Macleay v Tait* [1906] AC 24 (HL); *Nash v Calthorpe* [1905] 2 Ch 237.
3   *Anderson's Case* (1881) 17 Ch D 373; *Re Scottish Petroleum Co* (1883) 23 Ch D 413 (CA). This will also be the case if the other directors know that one of the directors is on the point of resigning when they go to allotment: *Re Kent County Gas Co* (1906) 95 LT 756.
4   *Brownlie v Campbell* (1880) 5 App Cas 924 at 950 (HL Sc); *Briess v Woolley* [1954] AC 333 at 353–354 (HL). Cf *Arkwright v Newbold* (1881) 17 Ch D 301 at 325 and 329, and *Bradford Building Society v Borders* [1941] 2 All ER 205 at 228 (HL).
5   *Central Railway Co of Venezuela v Kisch* (1867) LR 2 HL 99; *Oakes v Turquand* (1867) LR 2 HL 325, 342; *Cackett v Kewsick* [1902] 2 Ch 456. It has been suggested that a concealment may be a ground for rescission of the contract to take shares, which would not be sufficient to ground an action of deceit against directors (see *per* Lord Cairns in *Peek v Gurney* (1873) LR 6 HL 377 at 403), but later cases do not draw the distinction.
6   *Coles v White City (Manchester) Greyhound Association* (1928) 45 TLR 230. See also *Ross v Estates Investment Co* (1868) LR 3 CH 682.
7   *Components Tube Co v Naylor* [1900] 2 Ir R 1.
8   *McKeown v Boudard Peveril Gear Co* [1896] WN 36 (CA); *New Brunswick and Canada Rail and Land Co v Conybeare* (1862) 9 HL C711; *Peek v Gurney* (1873) LR 6 HL 377 at 403.
9   *Gover's Case* (1875) 1 Ch D 182 at 189 (CA).
10   *Peek v Gurney* (1873) LR 6 HL 377 at 403.

think, be shown that the non-disclosure is the non-disclosure of something the disclosure of which would falsify some statement in the prospectus.'[1]

Furthermore, 'if by a number of statements you intentionally give a false impression and induce a person to act upon it, it is none the less false although if one takes each statement by itself there may be a difficulty in showing that any specific statement is untrue'.[2] Thus the prospectus must be taken as a whole, 'and everybody knows that half a truth is no better than a downright falsehood'.[3]

As regards statements that are misleading in the sense that they can bear more than one meaning, the law used to be stated that it is not material in what sense the directors intended the words to be understood if they are in fact untrue or misleading.[4] However, this formulation was rejected by the Privy Council in *Akerheilm v De Mare*[5] in favour of a more subjective test of the defendant's honesty. The following passage from the opinion of the Privy Council shows that in an action for deceit the subjective state of mind cannot be ignored:

> The question is not whether the defendant in any given case honestly believed the representation to be true in the sense assigned to it by the court on an objective consideration of its truth or falsity, but whether he honestly believed the representation to be true in the sense in which he understood it albeit erroneously when it was made. This general proposition is no doubt subject to limitations. For instance, the meaning placed by the defendant on the representation made may be so far removed from the sense in which it would be understood by the reasonable person as to make it impossible to hold that the defendant honestly understood the representation to bear the meaning claimed by him and honestly believed it in the sense to be true.[6]

The qualification in the latter part of this passage accords with the view of Lord Blackburn in *Smith v Chadwick*[7] that 'if with intent to lead the plaintiff to act upon it they put forth a statement which they know may bear two meanings, one of which is false to their knowledge, and thereby the plaintiff, putting that meaning upon it, is misled, I do not think they can escape by saying he ought to have put the other'. It is essential, of course, that the claimant proves that he understood the statement in the sense in which it is false.[8] Further, in considering whether a statement is misleading, the prospectus must be considered as a whole and if the tendency is to deceive there is no need to point out some one or more statements which are absolutely untrue.[9]

18.38   The Misrepresentation Act 1967

The changes introduced into the English law of innocent misrepresentation by the Misrepresentation Act 1967 would allow a claim for damages against the company for a misrepresentation made by or on behalf of the company. As part of the general law, this Act will apply to any misrepresentation made by or on behalf

---

1   *Per* Eve J, in *Re Christineville Rubber Estates* [1911] WN 216, and see *R v Bishirgian* (1936) 154 LT 499 (CCA).
2   *Per* Halsbury LC, in *Aaron's Reefs v Twiss* [1896] AC 273 at 281.
3   *Per* Lord Macnaghten in *Gluckstein v Barnes* [1900] AC 240 at 250 and 251 (HL).
4   See *Greenwood v Leathershod Wheel Co* [1900] Ch 421; *Arnison v Smith* (1889) 41 Ch D 348 at 372, *per* Lindley LJ (CA); *Arkwright v Newbold* (1881) 17 Ch D 301 at 322 and 323 (CA).
5   [1959] AC 789 (PC), where the Privy Council refused to follow *Arnison v Smith*, above.
6   [1959] AC 789 at 805.
7   (1884) 9 App Cas 187 at 201.
8   *Smith v Chadwick* (1882) 20 Ch D 45 at 73 (CA); (1884) 9 App Cas 187 (HL).
9   *Aaron's Reefs v Twiss* [1896] AC 273; *R v Kylsant* [1932] 1 KB 442 (CCA).

of the company which has induced subscribers to enter into a contract of allotment on the faith of it. It is not confined, as are the civil remedies now provided by the Financial Services and Markets Act 2000, to public issues of securities nor to written statements in a formal prospectus or set of listing particulars. This Act does not apply to Scotland.

Under section 2(1) of the Misrepresentation Act 1967:

> where a person has entered into a contract after a misrepresentation has been made to him by another party thereto, and as a result thereof he has suffered a loss, then, if the person making the misrepresentation would have been liable to damages in respect thereof had the misrepresentation been made fraudulently, that person shall be so liable notwithstanding that the misrepresentation was not made fraudulently, unless he proves that he had reasonable ground to believe and did believe up to the time that the contract was made that the facts represented were true.

It is clear that an action based on section 2(1) of the Act must be brought against the other party to the contract. It has been seen that in an offer for sale this will be the issuing house.

Section 2(2) of the Misrepresentation Act 1967 confers a discretion upon the court, in the case of an innocent misrepresentation, to award damages in lieu of a decree of rescission where in the circumstances of the case it is in the interest of justice to do so. It should be noted that there is no *right* to damages in lieu of rescission on the part of either party to the contract. Section 2(2) allows for damages to be awarded in lieu of rescission from which it appears that the court may only award damages if the claimant has not lost his normal right to rescission.[1]

18.39   The measure of damages

The overriding principle in an action at common law for deceit or under section 2(1) of the Misrepresentation Act 1967[2] is that the victim of the tort is entitled to be compensated for all actual loss flowing directly from the transaction induced by the wrongdoer.[3] In some circumstances, the difference between the price paid for property and the market price that it would have had on the date of the transaction but for the tort may be the appropriate measure of this loss but in others a different measure, such as the difference between the price paid for the property and the price at which it was later disposed of, may be required in order to give the claimant full compensation in accordance with the general principle.

---

1   This analysis of section 2(2) is supported by *Zanzibar v British Aerospace (Lancaster House) Ltd* QBD, [2000] 1 WLR 2333. Section 2(3) is intended to prevent any possibility of 'double recovery' where claims under subsection (1) and subsection (2) are combined. On the measure of compensation under section 2(2), see *William Sindall plc v Cambridgeshire County Council* [1994] 1 WLR 1026.
2   *Royscot Trust Ltd v Rogerson* [1991] 2 QB 297; *East v Maurer* [1991] 1 WLR 461.
3   *Smith New Court Securities Ltd v Scrimgeour Vickers (Asset Management) Ltd* [1997] AC 254 (HL). But note that the House of Lords expressed some criticism of the *Royscot* decision, where this deceit measure of damages was applied to claims under section 2(1) of the Misrepresentation Act 1967.

18.40   An action for negligent misstatement

Since the leading decision of the House of Lords in *Hedley Byrne & Co Ltd v Heller & Partners Ltd*,[1] it is possible to argue that the directors and others responsible for a prospectus may owe a duty of care to those intended to rely on the prospectus in respect of negligent misstatements it contains. So long as the 'special relationship' giving rise to such a duty of care can be established, an action for the tort of negligence might lie. The special relationship may arise in pre-contractual negotiations, and those who may be held liable for negligent statements need not be persons who carried on, or held themselves out as carrying on, the business of advising: *Esso Petroleum Co Ltd v Mardon*.[2] In many instances, the remedies afforded by section 2(1) of the Misrepresentation Act 1967[3] and section 90 of the Financial Services and Markets Act 2000 will provide better protection to investors in company securities than an action for common-law negligence. Both these statutory provisions place the burden of disproving negligence upon the defendant. In an action for negligent misstatement, as in any other action for negligence, the burden of establishing negligence rests upon the claimant. However, in contrast with the remedies in the Financial Services and Markets Act 2000, an action in tort will apply to the private as well as to the public issue of company securities.

It has been seen that an action for damages under section 2(1) of the Misrepresentation Act 1967 will only lie as between the contracting parties. An action for the tort of negligent misstatement would allow a wider range of possible claimants and defendants. However, the courts will not lightly extend the duty of care under *Hedley Byrne*.[4] *Al Nakib Investments (Jersey) Ltd v Longcroft*[5] concerned a prospectus issued in connection with a rights issue. The court held that, because the purpose of the prospectus was to invite subscriptions for shares, there was insufficient proximity for a duty of care to arise between the directors and those persons (including existing shareholders of the company) who used the prospectus for the different purpose of purchasing further shares in the market. This case was distinguished in *Possfund Custodian Trustee Ltd v Diamond*,[6] where, in relation to a prospectus relating to a general public offer of securities, as opposed to a rights issue, it was held that there was an arguable case for the existence of a duty of care to market purchasers and that the issues merited full consideration at trial.

18.41   Criminal liability for false or misleading statements in prospectuses

The Financial Services and Markets Act 2000 contains, in section 397, a general 'all purpose' criminal sanction to deal with false and misleading statements. This section clearly applies to public issues but also 'underpins' many other provisions in the Act concerning transactions in securities.

---

1   [1964] AC 465. See also *WB Anderson Ltd v Rhodes* [1967] 2 All ER 850; *Mutual Life & Citizens Assurance Co Ltd v Evatt* [1971] 2 WLR 23 (PC).
2   [1976] 2 WLR 583 (CA).
3   This Act does not apply in Scotland.
4   *Caparo Industries plc v Dickman* [1990] 2 AC 605, [1990] 1 All ER 568, [1990] 2 WLR 358, [1990] BCLC 273, [1990] BCC 164.
5   [1990] 3 All ER 321, [1991] BCLC 7, [1990] BCC 517.
6   [1996] 2 All ER 774.

Section 397(1) makes it an offence for anyone to make a statement, promise or forecast which he knows to be misleading, false or deceptive. It also comprises dishonestly concealing any material facts and covers recklessly making (dishonestly or otherwise) a statement, promise or forecast which is misleading, false or deceptive. [1] The offence is 'investment related' in that the accused must make the statement (or conceal the facts dishonestly) for the purpose of inducing, or being reckless as to whether it may induce, another person to enter into, or offer to enter into, or to refrain from entering into, a relevant agreement. [2] The 'other person' need not be the person to whom the statement is made or from whom the facts are concealed. [3]

It has been held that a statement which is superficially true but actually untrue because of the omission of relevant information can be a false statement. [4] Such a statement could also be described as misleading or deceptive. [5] The terms 'misleading, false or deceptive' are not mutually exclusive in scope but they do differ slightly in degree. For instance, it would not be possible to describe an over-optimistic profit forecast as 'false' until the actual profit figures are known, [6] but, even without the actual figures, it might be possible to establish that the forecast was a misleading interpretation of the information on which it is based.

The offence of dishonest concealment of any material facts requires more than merely the omission of information, and in order to establish an offence under this section it must be shown that what has been said is incorrect or inaccurate because of what has been omitted. [7] This means that there is a very considerable overlap between the *actus reus* of the 'concealment' offence and the 'making' offence. A person is dishonest if he realises that he would be so judged on the standards of ordinary honest people, even though he does not consider himself to be dishonest by his own standards. [8]

Another provision in section 397 [9] goes beyond statements or concealments and is concerned with conduct which has the effect of market manipulation or market rigging. An offence is committed by someone 'who does any act or engages in any conduct which creates a false or misleading impression as to the market in, or the price or value of any relevant investments'. This must be done for creating that false impression and thus inducing others to acquire, dispose of, subscribe for, or underwrite investments. [10] A defence of reasonable belief that the act or conduct in question will not create a false or misleading impression is available to the accused. [11]

---

1   These criteria are derived from section 13 of the Prevention of Fraud (Investment) Act 1958 (now repealed).

2   A relevant agreement is, in essence, one falling within the scope of FSMA 2000: see section 397(9) and (10). Section 397(1) also applies to inducing another to exercise or refrain from exercising, any rights (eg options) conferred by those investments.

3   Eg the section covers statements made to an adviser which are intended to induce the adviser's client to enter an investment agreement.

4   *R v Kuylsant* [1932] 1 KB 442; *R v Bishirgian, etc* [1936] 1 All ER 568.

5   *Oakes v Turquand and Harding* (1867) LR 2 HL 325 at 342–343.

6   *R v Bates* [1952] 2 All ER 842 at 845.

7   *R v MacKinnon* [1959] 1 QB 150 at 154.

8   *R v Ghosh* [1982] QB 1053.

9   Section 397(3).

10   Inducing others to refrain from investing in these ways is also within section 397(3) .

11   Section 397(5)(a). As to the jurisdictional limits to section 397, see section 397(6) and (7). As to the penalties for conviction on indictment or summarily, see section 397(8).

The provisions of Part VIII of the Financial Services and Markets Act 2000 relating to market abuse overlap to some extent with section 397. In particular, section 118(2)(c) identifies, as a form of market abuse, behaviour which would be regarded by a regular user of the market as likely to distort the market in investments of the kind in question. The availability of the regulatory procedure and sanctions established by Part VIII for dealing with this form of market abuse is likely to limit resort to prosecutions under the market manipulation provisions of section 397.[1]

18.42 Section 19 of the Theft Act 1968

The Theft Act 1968, which does not apply in Scotland, contains, in section 19, a special provision to deal with dishonest statements in writing by officers of corporate bodies or unincorporated associations. It provides that 'an officer or person purporting to act as an officer of a body corporate or unincorporated association who, with intent to deceive its members or creditors about its affairs, publishes or concurs in publishing a written statement or account which to his knowledge is or may be misleading, false or deceptive in a material particular' is liable to a maximum sentence of seven years' imprisonment. Even under the more narrowly worded section 84 of the Larceny Act 1861 (the predecessor of section 19), which referred simply to 'false' statements, the courts gave it a liberal interpretation so as to include misleading or deceptive statements or omissions. Thus, in *R v Kylsant*[2] a prospectus relating to the issue of debenture stock said that the company paid a dividend in every year between 1921 and 1927. This was literally true, but it gave the misleading impression that the company during this period had made trading profits, whereas in fact substantial trading losses had been made. It was only able to pay dividends from reserves earned in earlier years. The fact that the dividends were paid from these 'hidden reserves' was not disclosed in the prospectus. Lord Kylsant, who knew the true state of affairs and was responsible for the prospectus, was convicted.

Section 19 of the Theft Act 1968 must certainly be given at least as wide an interpretation by the courts so long as an intention to deceive can be established. However, it does not extend to false promises or forecasts nor to oral statements.

---

1 The FSA is empowered to bring prosecutions under section 397 (section 401) but its policy in respect of prosecutions appears to exclude the imposition of a financial penalty under section 123 (power to impose penalties in cases of market abuse) once a decision has been taken to prosecute. See FSA Handbook, Regulatory Processes, Enforcement, paragraph 15.4.3G.

2 [1932] KB 442 (CCA). See further *R v Bishirgian* (1936) 154 LT 499 (CCA).

Chapter 19

Takeovers and Mergers

19.1 Introduction

This chapter is concerned with the legal machinery for merging and reconstructing companies. Some of this machinery is contained in legislation,[1] but the bulk of it is to be found in the City Code on Takeovers and Mergers and the Rules Governing the Substantial Acquisitions of Shares.[2] This self-regulatory body of rules, under the auspices of the Panel on Takeovers and Mergers, does not have the full force of law in the sense of being established by legislation, but has nonetheless proved to be a fairly effective mechanism for policing takeovers and mergers. In addition to the City Code, the *Listing Rules* require detailed information to be disclosed in the document making a takeover bid about the character of the offeror and the precise terms of the offer, and listed companies must notify the Company Announcements Office of a number of matters relating to a takeover or merger or consequent upon it.[3]

Takeovers and mergers have other important dimensions which are beyond the scope of this book. For example, they may lead to a reference by the Office of Fair Trading to the Competition Commission under the Enterprise Act 2002, or to the European Commission for offers with a Community dimension under the EC Merger Control Regulation.[4] The purpose of the investigations which follow such references is to establish if the proposed mergers are likely to have anticompetitive effects.[5] If they do, they will either be blocked or have conditions attached to them so as to remove the anti-competitive effects. There are also taxation implications for the offeror and the shareholders of the offeree,[6] and there are employment law consequences under the Acquired Rights Directive, as implemented by the Transfer of Undertakings (Protection of Employment) Regulations 1981.[7]

19.2 The Takeover Panel and its administration of the Code

When the machinery of the Panel was reconstituted in March 1969, it became a purely supervisory body and the day-to-day administration of the Panel business was taken over on a full-time basis by the Panel Executive – consisting of the Director-General, the Deputy Director-General(s), the Secretary and their staff

---

1   Principally the Companies Act 1985 and the Insolvency Act 1986.
2   The Code is available at www.thetakeoverpanel.org.uk.
3   For details, see *Gore-Browne on Companies* 44th edn (Jordans, loose-leaf) at 29.26.
4   EC Regulation 139/2004 [2004] OJ L24/1, replacing the previous EC Merger Regulation (No 4064/89) as from 1 May 2004.
5   See Furse, *Competition and the Enterprise Act 2002* (Jordans, 2003), Chapter 3. The UK and EC systems adopt different approaches to the determination of whether mergers are likely to have anti-competitive experts.
6   See *Gore-Browne on Companies* 44th edn (Jordans, loose-leaf) at 30.12 to 30.14.
7   See, eg McMullen, *Business Transfers and Employee Rights* (Butterworths, loose-leaf, 1998).

reporting directly to the Chairman.[1] The day-to-day business of the Panel, which the Panel Executive administers, consists chiefly of monitoring all takeover and merger transactions to ensure as far as possible that the proposals and the manner of their execution conform to the spirit and to the detailed provisions of the Code, on the basis that such rulings are subject to reference to the full Panel. The Director-General or his Deputies are available at all times to give rulings on points of interpretation of the Code. They will endeavour to give these rulings as promptly as is necessary to ensure the free functioning of the takeover and merger business. Companies and their advisers are encouraged to consult the Panel Executive on points needing clarification either by telephone or by meetings at short notice.

The main functions of the full Panel in its supervisory role are to consider progress reports of the Director-General and matters of policy, which it does at regular quarterly meetings, and to hear:

(1) appeals against rulings of the Director-General;
(2) references by the Panel Executive;
(3) disciplinary cases; and
(4) cases of exceptional importance where the Chairman is of the opinion that the Panel should be fully informed.

The Code incorporates a section describing the procedure that will be followed when the full Panel's decision is required. In general, proceedings are informal and private, consistent with ensuring that all parties are given a fair hearing. Principals (whether companies, individuals or their advisers) present their case in person, without representation by lawyers. All parties are usually present at the hearing and see the papers submitted to the Panel by each other party unless, exceptionally, evidence is of a commercially confidential nature, when the full Panel may be prepared to hear evidence in the absence of some or all of the other parties concerned.

If there appears to have been a breach of the Code, the Panel Executive invites the person concerned to appear before the full Panel for a hearing. He is informed by letter of the nature of the alleged breach and of the matters which the Director-General will present. If any other matters are raised at the hearing, he is allowed to ask for an adjournment. If the Panel finds that there has been a breach, it may have recourse to private reprimand or public censure or, in a more flagrant case, to further action designed to deprive the offender temporarily or permanently of his ability to enjoy the facilities of the securities markets. The Panel may refer certain aspects of a case to the Department of Trade and Industry, the Financial Services Authority or another appropriate body. No reprimand, censure or further action will take place without the person concerned having 48 hours to serve notice of appeal to the Appeal Committee of the Panel. However, it is the Panel's policy, in the case of important or controversial matters, to publish its

---

1   The Chairman, two Deputy Chairmen and three independent members (who are industrialists) are nominated by the Governor of the Bank of England and the bodies represented on the Panel are: the Association of Investment Trust Companies, the Association of British Insurers, the Confederation of British Industry, the National Association of Pension Funds, the Institute of Chartered Accountants in England and Wales, the Association of Private Client Investment Managers and Stockbrokers, the British Bankers' Association, the London Investment Banking Association and the Investment Management Association.

conclusions and the reasons for them. In this manner, its own activities are subject to public scrutiny.

There is a right of appeal[1] to the Appeal Committee where the Panel both finds a breach of the Code and proposes to take disciplinary action, and in a case where it is alleged that the Panel has acted outside its jurisdiction or where the Panel refuses to recognise or ceases to recognise a market-maker or fund-manager as an exempt market-maker or fund manager. An appeal may also lie with leave of the Panel against decisions which, although not strictly of a disciplinary nature, inflict in the view of the Panel serious hardship on an individual or company. No appeal, however, lies against a finding of fact or against a decision of the Panel on the interpretation of the Code.

The Appeal Committee does not normally hear new evidence. If the Appeal Committee considers that there may be material new evidence which could not have been presented to the Panel, then it would normally remit the matter to the Panel for further consideration. Proceedings before the Appeal Committee are conducted in a similar way to those before the Panel.

If an appeal is upheld, the appellant is consulted on the form of statement (if any) which should be published. If an appeal is dismissed, the findings of the Panel are published and any steps decided upon by way of penalty implemented.

19.3 The sanctions available to the Panel

The Panel is not a statutory body and its decisions do not have the force of law. Furthermore, it is no answer on a failure to consult the Panel Executive that a legal opinion has been obtained on the interpretation of a rule.[2] It has to be recognised that the City Code is a voluntary one; this has advantages in that the General Principles and Rules contained in it may go beyond, or be at least in advance of, anything which could be laid down in legislation and may be more readily adapted to changing circumstances as well as more quickly and flexibly administered. But voluntary rules inevitably suffer from the disadvantage that they depend in the main upon voluntary observance and often lack explicit sanctions which can be enforced. It is for this reason that the Panel – and, indeed, all the Institutions associated with it – attach the highest importance to a loyal observance of the Code and to support for the Panel's rulings by all concerned. This duty to observe the Code rests particularly, of course, upon directors of companies affected. But shareholders as well should recognise that if they wish their investment generally to be protected by orderly markets and integrity on the part of those whose conduct may affect them, there may be occasions when in spite of some short-term disadvantage they should accept and support the operations of the Code.

Although the Panel is not a statutory body and its decisions do not have legal force, its decisions remain fully effective unless and until they are set aside by a

---

1   The Court of Appeal has held that decisions of the Panel and its Appeal Committee are in principle open to judicial review but in the particular case an application for judicial review was rejected: *R v Panel on Take-overs, ex parte Datafin plc* [1987] QB 815. Sir John Donaldson MR indicated that the relationship between the Panel and the court should be historic rather than contemporaneous. The court should allow contemporary decisions to take their course, considering the complaint and intervening, if at all, later and in retrospect by declaratory orders. See also *R v Panel on Take-overs and Mergers, ex parte Guinness plc* [1990] 1 QB 146.

2   See the Panel's statement in Mooloya Investments Ltd and Customagic Manufacturing Company Ltd (20 July 1978).

court of competent jurisdiction. It is acknowledged by government and other regulatory bodies that those who seek to take advantage of the facilities of the securities market in the United Kingdom should conduct themselves in matters relating to takeovers in accordance with the best business standards and so according to the Code. Therefore, for those who do not do so, by way of sanction, the facilities of those markets may be withheld. The Financial Services and Markets Act 2000 gives effect to this principle by permitting the FSA to 'endorse' the Takeover Code and the Substantial Acquisition Rules (SARs). The FSA has done so[1] and the result is that breaches of the Code or SARs can lead to enforcement action being taken by the FSA, such as the imposition of fines or the withdrawal of authorisation to engage in regulated activity.

In 1987, the Department of Trade and Industry (DTI) arranged a formal review of the framework for the working and authority of takeovers. It was decided that the Panel would continue in its current form to administer, as a self-regulatory body, takeover activity in the United Kingdom. Nevertheless, it does operate within a legal framework. The Panel is designated as an authority to receive restricted[2] information from the FSA, the UKLA and information acquired by the DTI under 'books and papers' inspections pursuant to section 447 of the Companies Act 1985.[3] The FSA requires practitioners to co-operate with Panel enquiries and investigations. The DTI have their own far-reaching investigative powers[4] and the Panel can request that they should be invoked.

19.4 The scope and form of the Code

The Introduction to the Code states that those who wish to take advantage of the facilities of the securities markets in the United Kingdom should conduct themselves in matters relating to takeovers according to the Code and that such persons are required to observe the spirit of the Code. Types of transaction which are explicitly stated in the Code as being subject to its regulations, in addition to self-evident takeover transactions, include partial offers and offers by a parent company for shares in its subsidiary. Certain other transactions where control[5] of a company is to be obtained or consolidated also fall within the area to which the Code applies, including transactions effected by way of schemes of arrangement[6] and reverse takeovers. The Code does not apply to offers for non-voting non-equity capital unless they are offers required by the Code applying to convertible securities, options or other subscription rights outstanding.[7]

Whether or not the Code applies to a particular company is determined by the characteristics of the company which is the offeree or potential offeree, or in which control may change or be consolidated. The Code applies to offeree public

---

1   See FSA Handbook MAR 4.2.1R. Endorsement applies equally to altered provisions of the Code: see section 143(6) FSMA 2000, in respect of which the FSA has issued the relevant notification (see FSA Handbook MAR 4.2.2G).
2   This refers to the restriction on disclosure of confidential information contained in s348 of the FSMA 2000.
3   See section 349 of FSMA 2000 and the FSMA 2000 (Disclosure of Confidential Information) Regulations 2001, SI 2001/2188. See Chapter 17 regarding DTI investigations under the Companies Act 1985.
4   Ibid.
5   See Introduction to the Code, paragraphs 3 and 4.
6   Ie under sections 425 and 427 of the Companies Act 1985. See **19.18**.
7   See Rule 15 of the Code as to when an offer will be required for convertible securities.

companies, listed or unlisted, which are resident in the United Kingdom, the Channel Islands or the Isle of Man.[1] In addition to applying to all public companies, it governs private companies which have (a) filed a prospectus for the issue of equity share capital during the preceding ten years or (b) whose shares have been listed within that period, or in whose equity share capital dealings have been advertised in a newspaper or electronic price quotation system regularly for a continuous six-month period within those years or (c) whose equity share capital has been subject to a marketing arrangement as described in section 163(2)(b) of the Companies Act 1985 at any time during the previous ten years (eg dealings on the Unlisted Securities Market).

The provisions of the Code fall into two distinct categories. First, there are the General Principles, of which there are ten. These are intended to be 'general principles of conduct to be observed in takeover and merger transactions'. They are a 'codification of good standards of commercial behaviour and should have an obvious and universal application'. The second and larger part of the Code consists of Rules (of which there are now 38).[2] Some of these 'are no more than examples of the application of the general principles whilst others are rules of procedure designed to govern specific forms of takeover and merger transactions practised in the United Kingdom'.

The Code emphasises that a legalistic and literal interpretation should not be given to any part of the Code. It is framed 'in non-technical language and is, as a measure of self-discipline, administered and enforced by the Panel, a body representative of those using the securities markets and concerned with the observance of good business standards and not the enforcement of the law'.

19.5   The Principles of the Code

The Code first of all states its guiding philosophy. This is that the 'spirit as well as the precise wording' of the General Principles and the Rules be observed. Furthermore, 'the General Principles and the spirit of the Code will apply in areas or circumstances not explicitly covered by any Rule.' It is conceded that (in accordance with the principles of company law) boards of directors and their advisers have a duty to act in the best interests of their shareholders. But the General Principles and the Rules inevitably impinge on the freedom of action of boards and persons involved in takeover and merger transactions. This applies to the board and advisers of both the offeror and offeree companies. However, 'there are limitations in connection with such transactions on the manner in which pursuit of these interests can be carried out'. The Principles indicate those areas where the Code impinges on the traditional freedom of action of boards in takeover battles or agreed mergers.[3]

A number of the Principles are concerned with fair treatment of shareholders, including equal treatment of different classes of shares, as well as among members of each class. Thus, 'rights of control must be exercised in good faith and the

---

1   The Code also applies to Irish companies listed in the United Kingdom. It does not apply to open-ended investment companies.

2   There are also Notes to the Rules which are intended to furnish a more detailed guidance as to how the Rules are to operate.

3   See *Gore-Browne on Companies* 44th edn (Jordans loose-leaf), for text of the Principles at 29.7.

oppression of a minority is wholly unacceptable', and 'all shareholders of the same class of an offeree company shall be treated similarly by an offeror'.[1]

General Principle 10 indicates where the acquisition of a degree of control by a person (or persons acting in concert)[2] will necessitate a general offer to all other shareholders. A similar obligation may arise where control is consolidated.[3]

The Code[4] imposes a general duty on the directors of both offeror and offeree companies, when advising their shareholders not to have regard to their personal or family shareholdings or to their personal relationships with their companies. It is shareholders' interests as a whole, together with those of employees and creditors, which should be considered.[5]

A number of the Principles of the Code are concerned with the adequacy of information (and opinions) given to the shareholders of an offeree company. General Principle 4 requires that shareholders must be given sufficient information and advice to enable them to reach a properly informed decision and must have sufficient time to do so. No relevant information may be withheld. General Principle 2 is concerned that there should be equality of information available to all shareholders. Neither the offeror, the offeree company nor their advisers may furnish information to some shareholders which is not available to all. As to the standard of accuracy required, any document or advertisement addressed to shareholders containing information or advice from the board of an offeror or an offeree company (or their advisers) must, as in the case of a prospectus, be prepared with the highest standard of care and accuracy.[6]

The Code also requires 'every endeavour to prevent the creation of a false market in the share of an offeror or offeree company'.[7] There are also Principles dealing with the frustration of a bona fide offer by the board of an offeree company[8] and requiring that an offeror be able to implement an offer once it has been announced.[9]

19.6 The Rules

The scope of a book of this nature does not permit a full account of the 38 Rules of the Code (and their attendant Notes). These make up the bulk of the Code. The Rules are intended to regulate the whole process by which a takeover bid (or agreed merger) is conducted, from its initial launch to its (hopefully) successful completion. There are detailed provisions regulating the preliminary stages. These include the approach to the board of the offeree[10] company and the announcement of the offer or approach.[11] The General Principles of the Code will

---

1   General Principles 8 and 1 respectively. This of course expresses the gist of a similar principle
     of company law. In other respects, however, the Principles and Rules go further than existing
     company law.
2   As to 'persons acting in concert', see the 'Definition' section to the Code..
3   This Principle is elaborated by Rule 9. See **19.9**. There is an obligation on the person
     acquiring such control to ensure that it will be possible to implement such a general offer.
4   General Principle 9.
5   This, broadly speaking, also reflects the requirements of company law: see Chapter 16.
6   General Principle 5.
7   General Principle 6.
8   General Principle 7.
9   General Principle 3.
10   Rule 1.
11   Rule 2.

govern the offeree board's consideration of the offer. It should be observed that the Code requires the offeror to give evidence of financial (and other) ability to implement the offer.[1] Furthermore, where the offer comes within the statutory provisions for possible reference to the Competition Commission, it must contain a term stating that it will lapse if there is a reference to the Commission by the Secretary of State for Trade and Industry before the closing date for the offer, or the date (whichever is later) when it is declared unconditional.[2]

Besides the Rule governing the timing and contents of offer announcements,[3] the Code makes elaborate provision as to the information that must be given to the shareholders of the offeree company.[4] This includes the shareholding by the offeror company in the offeree company.[5] It also includes (in the case of a securities exchange offer) shareholding in the offeror and (in any event) shares in the offeree in which the directors of the offeror are interested. A similar disclosure must be made as to shareholdings owned or controlled by persons 'acting in concert'[6] with the offeror. It likewise applies to holdings owned or controlled by any persons who, prior to the posting of the offer document, have irrevocably committed themselves to accept the offer.[7] There is also provision for disclosure of directors' service contracts in respect of the offeree company. This applies in the case of documents sent to shareholders of the offeree company (by the board of the offeree) which recommend either acceptance or rejection of an offer.[8]

The Code makes provision for profit forecasts and for asset valuations.[9] The policy expressed by the Code is that information concerning profit forecasts may be vital to the shareholders' assessment of the merits of a takeover proposal. General Principle 5 requires that takeover documents must be prepared with the same standard of care as if the document were a prospectus. However, whereas in a prospectus it is the proper practice to make a conservative estimate of profits (so as not to inflate the price of securities offered for sale), in a takeover document it may mislead shareholders to err on the conservative side in estimating profits. In any event, since there are obvious hazards in such forecasting, Rule 28 lays down precise and stringent requirements as to the preparation of forecasts. Directors are required to state the assumptions, including commercial assumptions, upon which they base their profit forecasts. Although such forecasts are the sole responsibility of the directors making them, the accounting bases and assumptions must be reported on by the offeror's auditors (or reporting accountants) as well as by its merchant bank or other financial adviser mentioned in the offer document. This is not required where the forecast is made by an offeror offering solely cash.[10]

---

1   Rule 2.5.
2   See Rule 9.4 and Rule 12.
3   Rule 2. Rule 2 stresses the importance of secrecy prior to an announcement.
4   See Rules 23–27.
5   Rule 24.3.
6   The term 'persons acting in concert' is widely used throughout the Code and is thus defined in the Definitions which preface the Code.
7   Rule 25.3 imposes a parallel duty on the offeree company in respect of a document advising its shareholders on an offer.
8   Rule 25.4. In the offer document itself it should be stated (except in the case of an offeror offering solely cash) whether the offeror's directors' emoluments will be affected by a successful acquisition of the offeree: Rule 24.4.
9   See Rules 28 and 29.
10   Rule 28.3.

It may be noted that, although the common law as to misrepresentation is ill adapted to provide a remedy for predictions (eg profit forecasts) or opinions (eg asset valuations), the law of contract, being concerned with the enforcement of promises, is more apt for such purposes. Since an offer document will, as its name indicates, produce a contract between the offeror company and the shareholders in the offeree who accept its terms, legal redress will be available in the case of a misleading forecast (or unsound valuation) which events show to be widely inaccurate. The Panel has recognised that legal responsibility may arise from statements made in takeover documents. If legal proceedings are initiated or threatened in such circumstances the Panel will normally suspend its own enquiries.[1]

Rule 29 also stipulates that where a valuation of assets is given in connection with a takeover offer, the board of the offeror should be supported by the opinion of a named independent valuer and the basis of the valuation clearly stated.[2]

A number of Rules in the Code relate to what has been termed the 'mechanics of the formal offer'.[3] These concern such matters as what is permissible in respect of the revision and extension of offers, and as to the withdrawal of acceptances. Provision is made as to how and when an offer may be declared unconditional. It should be noted that copies of all offer documents (and other announcements or documents bearing on a takeover) must be lodged with the Panel at the same time as they are dispatched to their intended recipients.[4]

19.7   Partial offers

In Rule 36 the Code tries to curtail any unfairness to shareholders that may arise from 'partial offers'. Although such offers for less than 100% of a company's shares (or a class thereof) may sometimes be justified, Rule 36 states that the Panel's consent is required for *any* partial offer and it then lays down guidelines as to how and when that consent may be given. The rationale for limiting the use of partial offers is not made clear by the Code. It can be argued, however, that they deviate from the general principle[5] adopted by the Code that a person who acquires control of a company should be required to make an offer to all the shareholders (the mandatory bid rule). A policy of limiting the use of partial offers supports the mandatory bid rule as partial offers are in effect exceptions to the mandatory bid rule.

In the case of an offer which would result in the offeror holding shares carrying less than 30% of the voting rights[6] of a company, consent will not normally be given. Where the result will be control of between 30% and 100%, such consent will not normally be given if the offeror (and 'persons acting in concert') have acquired shares in the offeree company during the previous twelve months. Where an offer is made which would result in the offeror holding shares carrying

---

1   See the Panel's Report for the year ending 31 March 1978, p 13.
2   Rule 29.2.
3   Ie Rules 30–34.
4   Rule 19.7.
5   General Principle 10.
6   These are defined by the Code as 'all the voting rights attributable to the share capital of a company which are currently exercisable at a general meeting'. However, the Panel should be consulted where rights exercisable only in restricted circumstances have in fact been exercisable for a long time, or it may be considered that the shares in question have voting rights for the purpose of the Code.

30% or more of the voting rights, a comparable offer must be made to each class. Acquisition of 30% of the voting rights is also critical in 'triggering' an obligation under Rule 9 to make an extended offer to other voting shareholders. In the case of a partial offer which could result in the offeror holding over 30% (but less than 50%) of the voting rights of the offeree, the precise number of shares offered for must be stated. The offer may not be declared unconditional as to acceptance unless acceptances are received for not less than that number. Any offer which would result in the offeror holding shares carrying 30% or more of the voting rights must be conditional, not only on the specified number of acceptances being received, but also on approval by 50% of the voting rights not held by the offeror and persons not acting in concert with it.[1]

Today partial offers are rarely made *ab initio.* Instead, a tender offer under the Substantial Acquisition Rules (discussed later)[2] is made. Rule 36 also provides for partial offers which are intended to increase a holding to a higher level. Here it will have more relevance.

19.8 Restrictions on dealings

The wider context of the regulation of insider dealing is considered in the next chapter. The City Code was early in this field in so far as insider dealing in the context of a takeover bid or merger is concerned. The main restriction is found in Rule 4. This forbids persons who are privy to the intention to make an offer (or to the preliminary negotiations) from dealing in the securities of the offeree company from the time when there is reason to suppose that an approach is contemplated until the issue of a press announcement (or the termination of the previous discussions). Furthermore, no such dealings shall take place in the securities of the offeror except where the proposed offer is not deemed price-sensitive. Rule 4 also imposes a general injunction of confidentiality upon anyone privy to such information making recommendations to any other person as to dealing in the relevant securities.

Rule 5 restricts the speed with which, just before and during an offer, voting shares and rights over voting shares of a company may be acquired by a person, or those acting in concert with him, whose aggregate holding of shares and rights over shares would thereby rise to or through 30% of the voting rights in that company. It also restricts acquisitions of voting shares and rights over shares by a person whose holding is between 30 and 50%. Acquisitions falling within either category are not permitted before the announcement of a firm intention to make an offer, unless the acquisition immediately precedes and is conditional upon such an announcement being made with the public recommendation of the board of the offeree company.

However, once a takeover proposal is announced, all parties may (subject to certain other provisions of the Code) deal subject to daily disclosure to the Stock

---

1   See *Gore-Browne on Companies* 44th edn (Jordans, loose-leaf) at 29.20 as to the possibilities of waiver by the Panel, and as to how Rule 36 applies to different classes of shares.
2   See **19.11**.

Exchange, the Panel and the press.[1] This disclosure must be made on a daily basis (whether on or off the market and at whatever price) in respect of purchases of shares in the offeror or offeree. The basic freedom to purchase is posited on the basis that it is 'undesirable to fetter the market'. However, the Code implicitly recognises that this philosophy of the unfettered market may well give an unfair advantage to the offeror and those acting in concert with it.[2] Thus Rule 6.2 requires that if the offeror (or any person acting in concert) purchases securities during the offer period at above the offer price (being the then current value of the offer), the offer must be increased to not less than the highest price paid for the security so acquired.[3]

In certain cases, Rule 11 requires that offers in respect of a class of shares shall either be in cash or be accompanied by a cash alternative.[4] This obligation applies when shares of any class (under offer in the offeree company) are purchased[5] for cash by the offeror (and any person acting in concert) during the offer period and within 12 months prior to its commencement and the shares purchased carry 10% or more of the voting rights exercisable at a class meeting of that class.[6] It also applies to mandatory offers made under Rule 9.[7] The Panel may give its consent to dispense with this obligation. Additionally, the panel may also excuse the offeror from paying the highest price (under Rule 11) in a particular case.[8]

19.9 The mandatory offer to the remaining shareholders

Rule 9 exists to prevent the problem of the 'locked in' minority shareholder arising. It is also designed to discourage acquisition of de facto control by stealth and through payment of a control premium to a select group of shareholders. In certain circumstances, this Rule requires an existing offer to be extended to the remaining shareholders hitherto excluded from it. Rule 9 applies where any person *acquires*, whether by a series of transactions over a period of time or not, shares which (taken together with shares held or acquired by persons acting in concert with him) carry 30% or more of the voting rights of a company. Rule 9 also

---

1 See Rule 8.1. This obligation applies not only to the 'parties to a takeover or merger transaction' but to their 'associates' – not only where they deal for their own account but also where 'associates' deal for the account of investment clients (see Rule 8.2). Disclosure of dealing by major shareholders (meaning those owning or controlling 1% or more of any class of relevant securities of an offeror or the offeree company) is also required. 'Associates' is elaborately defined in the definition section of the Code; see *Gore-Browne on Companies*, 44th edn (Jordans, loose-leaf) at 29.10.
2 Rule 8.3 and Rule 16 (special deals with favourable conditions).
3 Immediately after the purchase it must be announced that a revised offer will be made in accordance with Rule 6. Where practical, disclosure must be made of the number of securities purchased and the price paid. Rule 7.1 also requires an immediate announcement to be made if the offer has to be amended where purchases give rise to obligations under Rules 6, 9 and 11.
4 This must be valued at not less than the highest price paid (excluding stamp duty and commission) for the shares of that class purchased during the offer period and within 12 months prior to its commencement.
5 Eg through the market or by private purchase.
6 See Rule 11(1)(b) re obligations arising when shares are purchased for cash during the offer period only.
7 Rule 9.5. See **19.9** re mandatory offers.
8 Rule 11.3. See the note thereto as to the 'relevant factors' that the Panel will take into account.

applies where any person, together with persons acting in concert, *holds* not less than 30% but not more than 50% of the voting rights, and such a person or any person acting in concert, acquires in any period of twelve months additional shares carrying more than 1% of the voting rights. In either of these situations, those concerned must extend an offer[1] to the holders of any class of equity share capital whether voting or non-voting. This offer must also be made to the holders of any class of voting non-equity share capital in which such person or persons acting in concert with him hold shares.[2]

The Code contains other provisions to curb rapidly repeated takeover bids or improper defensive tactics by the offeree company. Thus it prevents those who have made an offer, which has lapsed or been withdrawn, from making another offer within the next 12 months for the same company, except with the permission of the Panel.[3]

Rule 21 is designed to amplify further General Principle 7. The latter condemns any action by the board of an offeree company which is designed to frustrate a *bona fide* takeover bid unless such action has the approval of the shareholders in general meeting. Rule 21 is concerned with the issue of any authorised (but unissued) shares or the issue or grant of options in respect of such shares, or convertible debentures. The board of the offeree company may not issue such securities during the course of the offer, or even before the date of the offer if the board has reason to believe that a *bona fide* offer is imminent, unless the approval of the shareholders in general meeting is obtained. There is a similar prohibition on the sale, disposal or acquisition of 'assets of material amount' and on 'entering into contracts otherwise than in the ordinary course of business'.[4]

19.10   Assessing the Code's effectiveness

Whatever the criticism levied at an earlier stage in their development,[5] the Code on Takeovers and Mergers, and the Panel which administers it, are now generally regarded as a successful example of self-regulation. The Code is sometimes held up as a model that might be followed in other areas of City activity which are in need of more effective self-regulation.[6] It is certainly so regarded by the senior

---

1   The offer so extended must comply with the condition set out in Rule 9.5; eg it must be in cash or be accompanied by a cash alternative. Such offers must be conditional upon the offeror having received acceptance in respect of shares which, together with the shares acquired or agreed to be acquired before or during the offer, will result in the offeror, etc holding shares carrying more than 50% of the voting rights. See Rule 9.3.

2   Offers for different classes of equity capital must be comparable. Here the panel must be consulted in advance. This rule is complex in its varied applications. It has an extensive Note giving detailed interpretation, in particular as to 'persons acting in concert'.

3   Rule 35. This also applies on an acquisition of shares of the offeree company which may result in an obligation to make an offer as required by Rule 9. See also Rule 35.2 partial offers and 35.3 (delay of six months before acquisition above the offer price).

4   Rule 21 does not apply to contracts to issue shares, etc already entered into. In special circumstances the Panel may give its consent to dispense with this rule.

5   See Davies, *The Regulation of Takeovers and Mergers* (Sweet & Maxwell, 1976), pp 39–46 for criticism of the 1974 version of the Code. Much of this is still true as regards enforcement and sanctions. See also McCrae and Cairncross, *Capital City* 2nd edn (Eyre & Methuen, 1985), pp 150–157.

6   See L C B Gower, *Review of Investor Protection* Cmnd 9125 (1984) at paragraphs 9.09–9.11.

staff of the Panel[1] and by the City institutions who have to live with the Code and the Panel's rulings. It can be argued that the Code admits of regular and rapid amendments in response to the lessons of experience. It is not staffed by civil servants with a bureaucratic mentality, but by those knowledgeable of the problems of effective regulation of takeover bids. Further, the Panel has built up wide support from all the City and governmental bodies concerned.

In 1987, the Secretary of State for Trade and Industry instigated a full review of the powers and personnel and rules of the Panel. Although it was considered that some measures could be provided which would strengthen the regulation of takeovers, it was decided that the Panel would continue as a self-regulatory body. It was felt overall that the Panel had, in general, worked effectively in ensuring fair treatment for all shareholders, regardless of whether takeovers succeed or fail. A self-regulatory system was preferred to a statutory underpinning, which would be slower and would encourage more formal litigation through appeals against the Panel's decisions.

Nevertheless the unofficial status of the Panel's Executive has drawbacks when it has to investigate abuses. This encouraged the Panel to withdraw from the field of policing 'insider dealing' and to welcome sanctions imposed by the criminal law. A lack of the power to subpoena witnesses, and the inhibiting effect of the laws of defamation, are said to curb the effectiveness of the Panel as an investigatory body. However, this has not in general hindered it in seeking compliance with the administration of the Code and in resolving disputed interpretations. Further, it appears that the Panel enjoys qualified privilege in the conduct of investigations into alleged breaches of the Code.[2] However, the publication of critical reports may still be inhibited by the law of defamation and contempt.

Endorsement of the Takeover Code by the FSA[3] has led to the sanctions for breach of the Code becoming largely aligned with those available to the FSA in respect of regulatory contraventions under the FSMA 2000. Thus, the FSA may withdraw authorisation, initiate disciplinary measures, undertake investigations, impose financial penalties, issue a public censure, apply for an injunction to restrain a breach, require restitution to be made or seek a court order requiring restitution. There is also the possibility of public censure of individuals or institutions being undertaken by the Panel. Such a sanction, where very substantial financial advantages are at issue, may seem feeble, especially in the case of those who will not need to maintain the goodwill of the Panel in the future. Yet the Panel still resorts to such censure even where it has found culpable (if not deliberate) breaches of important rules of the Code.[4]

19.11 The Substantial Acquisition Rules

Certain much-discussed abuses which have occurred in the last few years have shown both the strengths and the limitations of the Panel and the other

---

1   For a review of the 5th edition of the Code by Peter Lee, Deputy Director of the Panel, see (1981) 2 Co Law 99. See also Morse, 'Controlling Takeovers – The Self-Regulation Option in the United Kingdom' [1998] JBL 58.

2   See *Graff v Shawcross, Macdonald and Frazer*, 10 October 1980. See (1981) 2 Co Law 33. Caulfield J's observations were obiter, but they would apply to investigations by other self-regulatory bodies.

3   See **19.3**.

4   See the 'statements' section of the Panel website (www.thetakeoverpanel.org.uk) for recent examples.

self-regulatory bodies. The problem of what are known as 'dawn raids' seems in the end to have produced a reasonably effective response. The practice of making a 'dawn raid', by rapid and organised early trading to acquire a substantial interest in a target company, first attracted widespread comment in the case of the acquisition of Consolidated Gold Fields by Anglo-American Trust.[1] Frequently, such raids were carried out through a complex web of subsidiaries and associates acting, often, through foreign nominees. The principal objection to this practice is that it favoured the interests of large institutional investors (eg pension funds), who were able to make a rapid response to a purchasing raid and so gain (at a favourable price) an advantage from which the small individual investor was excluded. The Department of Trade and Industry refused the opportunity to legislate for new disclosure provisions,[2] and encouraged the self-regulatory bodies to cope with the problem. At the prompting of the Panel and the Stock Exchange, the Council for the Securities Industry (which has since ceased to exist) produced a set of rules to curb the more blatant forms of market raid.[3]

The Substantial Acquisition Rules are rules which restrict the speed with which a person (and any person acting with him) may increase to between 15 and 30% his holding of voting rights in a company resident in the United Kingdom, the shares of which are listed or otherwise traded on the Stock Exchange or AIM. They are issued on the authority of the Panel and are administered by the Panel Executive. They do not apply to a person whose acquisitive action or intention is such as to make him subject to the Code.

The Rules provide that a person who proposes to acquire shares which would result in his holding 15% or more, but less than 30%, of the then exercisable voting rights in a relevant company may do so only:

(1) by acquiring less than 10% of the voting rights within a period of seven days, unless the only acquisition within the seven-day period is from a single shareholder;

(2) by means of a tender offer whereby he advertises a firm offer to make such an acquisition if shares are tendered to him by a date at least eight days after it is advertised; or

(3) by acquiring shares immediately prior to and conditional upon the announcement by the person making the acquisition of a firm intention to make an offer for the company (whether or not the posting of the offer is subject to the fulfilment of any condition) which is publicly recommended by the board of the offeree company.

In a tender offer, the buyer makes a firm offer to purchase a specified number of shares at a fixed price or up to a maximum price. In a maximum price tender, he indicates the maximum price which he is prepared to pay and invites shareholders to tender at that price or at any lower price. He then accepts all shares tendered at the price (the striking price) at which his needs are met which may be at or below

---

1   See (1980) 1 Co Law 66 at 218 and 303.
2   It contended that the problems of appropriate drafting and effective administration of legislation once drafted were too great to overcome the problems of defining and locating 'concert parties' acting through foreign nominees. However, what is now the Companies Act 1985 has improved the disclosure provisions in respect of 'concert parties' and increased the power to 'freeze' dealings in suspect shares under the 1985 Act. See **12.9.7** and **17.28**.
3   'Rules Governing Substantial Acquisitions of Shares', 11 December 1980. See (1981) 2 Co Law 2.

the maximum price. The striking price is paid for all tenders which are accepted (subject, if necessary, to *pro rata* scaling down or balloting of shares tendered at the striking price). If the tender is not fully satisfied, the maximum price applies provided the minimum percentage specified in the tender offer is subscribed. In a fixed price tender, if the tenders exceed the number of shares sought, they will be scaled down *pro rata*. Both maximum price tender offers, and fixed price tender offers may be made on the London Stock Exchange or elsewhere.[1]

The Rules set out the information which must be included in the advertisement announcing a tender offer. They also provide that a person who, as a result of an acquisition, comes to hold 15% or more of the voting rights in a company must publicly disclose his total holding (distinguishing between acquisitions and holdings of shares and rights over shares and specifying the nature of any rights concerned) by 12 noon on the business day following the acquisition. He must thereafter similarly disclose any further acquisitions which increase his holding to and beyond any whole percentage figure above 15% of the voting rights.

Rule 37 of the Code concerns the impact upon corporate control where the powers to redeem and purchase a company's shares under powers in the Companies Act[2] are exercised. It may require the directors of the company and those acting in concert with them to make a general offer. Rule 37 provides that when a company redeems or purchases its own voting shares, a resulting increase in the percentage voting rights (carried by the shareholders or the directors and persons acting in concert with them) will be treated in principle as an acquisition for the purposes of Rule 9 (ie will require a mandatory offer). However, subject to prior consultation, the Panel will normally waive this obligation to make a general offer if there is an independent vote of the shareholders and certain other procedures are followed.[3]

19.12 The proposed thirteenth directive on takeovers

Following 14 years of negotiations, it appears that an EC Directive on takeovers will soon be approved.[4] Contrary to fears that were expressed in respect of earlier drafts[5], the Directive is unlikely to have a major impact on the role of the Takeover Panel and the operation of the Takeover Code in the UK. Political disagreements over the role and regulation of takeovers within the EU resulted in the Directive being framed more at the level of broad principle than detail, thus allowing considerable freedom to Member States as regards implementation. For example, although the Directive follows the approach of the Takeover Code in adopting a mandatory bid rule, definition of the control threshold which triggers a mandatory bid is left to Member States.

---

1   SARs rule 4(1)(a) and (c).
2   Under Part III, Chapter VII of the 1985 Act. See **7.17** *et seq.*
3   See Appendix I. 'Whitewash Guidance Note'. See also Rule 37.3 (Redemptions or Purchases of Offeree Company Shares) and Rule 37.4 (Redemptions or Purchases of Offeror Shares). Rule 38 is concerned with dealings by connected exempt market-makers.
4   See COM/2002/0534 final – COD 2002/0240. For the history of the proposal see *Gore-Browne on Companies* 44th edn (Jordans, loose-leaf) at 40.5–40.16.
5   The United Kingdom reacted strongly to early drafts fearing that the Takeover Panel might have to be established on a statutory footing and thus would lose the benefits of its non-statutory status. In particular, the DTI expressed concern that the proposal would have the result that litigation could be used as a tactic for delaying or preventing takeovers.

The Directive is a minimum standards directive and does not attempt to introduce extensive harmonisation of takeover rules throughout the EU. In principle, Member States can therefore adopt more stringent national provisions provided they comply with the minimum requirements. Provision is also made for Member States to opt out of/into two of the most significant and controversial provisions of the Directive: article 9, which relates to defensive measures taken by an offeree company and article 11 (the so-called 'breakthrough' provision), which allows restrictions of transfer and voting rights to be disapplied for certain purposes. That provision clearly opens up the possibility of very different systems of takeover regulation being preserved in the different Member States and the objective of establishing a single market in capital and financial services being frustrated.

19.13 Reconstruction and amalgamation under section 110 of the Insolvency Act 1986

It is possible for a company to carry out a sale of its undertaking in two distinct ways: the sale of the undertaking may be effected: (a) before liquidation, under powers contained in the memorandum, but this is only possible when a liquidation is not in immediate contemplation; or (b) in contemplation of, or after the commencement of, a voluntary liquidation, under the powers now contained in sections 110 and 111 of the Insolvency Act 1986.[1]

However, a power in the memorandum to sell its undertaking (ie (a)) may not be used to enable the company to avoid compliance with the provisions of section 111 (examined below). In reversing earlier decisions[2] which upheld such a course, the Court of Appeal[3] held that the proper function of the memorandum was to deal with the objects of the company during its corporate life and not after that life has come to an end. Thus it is not part of the corporate objects to define the distribution of assets in a winding-up (including a section 110 reconstruction).

19.14 Procedure under sections 110 and 111

The procedure under section 110 of the Insolvency Act 1986 is as follows: the company[4] will usually go into a members' voluntary winding-up,[5] and pass a special resolution authorising the liquidator to sell the undertaking under section 110. These powers may also be given to a liquidator in the case of a *creditors'* voluntary winding-up. Here the sanction of the court or the liquidation

---

1   These provisions now apply to both a members' and a creditors' voluntary winding-up. See section 110(3). See Chapter 21, below as to voluntary winding up.
2   See *Gore-Browne on Companies* 44th edn (Jordans, loose-leaf) at 30.3. If such a power is appropriately drafted, it may allow the sale of the company's undertaking not only for cash but for shares, ibid.
3   *Bisgood v Henderson's Transvaal Estates* [1908] 1 Ch 743.
4   For the purposes of section 110, the 'transferor company' (ie the one put into voluntary liquidation) must be a registered company. But the transferee company may be a 'company within the meaning of this Act or not': section 110(1). However, the transferee must be a company and not an individual. See *Gore-Browne on Companies* 44th edn (Jordans, loose-leaf) at 30.6.1.
5   The resolution sanctioning the sale may be either before, concurrent with, or after the resolution for voluntary winding up: section 110(6).

committee must be sought.[1] However, the sale can take place before winding up and authority can then be given to distribute shares. The authority may be general, or may be confined to a specified sale, to be made in accordance with a scheme of reconstruction or a draft agreement submitted to the meeting. To avoid unpleasant mistakes, it is advisable that the resolution authorising the sale of the property should be submitted simultaneously with the winding-up resolution, so that if the former is not carried the latter may also be dropped: otherwise the company will find itself in liquidation without any scheme for selling its business.[2] Both the voluntary winding-up and the authority for a sale require a special resolution; but they may be passed together at the same meeting.[3] Express notice of each resolution must, however, be given to the shareholders, specifying that a sale is intended under section 110,[4] and if the directors derive any special advantage a notice which does not disclose this fact is insufficient.[5] But it is no objection to a scheme of reconstruction that it openly gives a bonus to directors.[6]

Where a draft agreement for sale is prepared, the special resolution may refer to and approve it, and no other scheme of reconstruction is necessary. But power should be taken for the agreement to be carried out with or without modifications.[7]

19.15 Rights of dissenting shareholders

If any member of the company[8] being wound up who has not voted for the special resolution expresses his dissent from the resolution in writing, addressed to the liquidator and left at the registered office of the company[9] not later than seven days after the passing of the resolution, he may require the liquidator either to abstain from carrying the resolution into effect or to purchase his interest[10] at a price which, if not settled by agreement, shall be determined by arbitration.[11] In such an arbitration, the dissentient has to prove the value of his interest. If a person who ought to be, but is not, on the register of members gives notice of

---

1   See Insolvency Act 1986, section 110(3)(b).
2   *Cleve Financial Corp* (1874) 16 Eq 363; *Clinch v Financial Corp* (1869) 4 Ch App 117; *Thomson v Henderson's Transvaal Estates* [1908] 1 Ch 765 (CA).
3   See section 110(6).
4   *Imperial Bank of China v Bank of Hindustan* (1868) 6 Eq 91; *Re Irrigation Company of France, ex parte Fox* (1871) 6 Ch App 176 at 193.
5   *Kaye v Croydon Tramways* [1898] 1 Ch 358 (CA); *Tiessen v Henderson* [1899] 1 Ch 861; *Clarkson v Davies* [1923] AC 100 (PC).
6   *Southall v British Mutual Life Association* (1871) 6 Ch App 614. As to payments made to directors for loss of office (or retirement), see the provisions of section 313 of the Companies Act 1985, discussed at **16.20**.
7   As to the forms of consideration, the liquidator may give to the transferee company's shareholders, see the wide terms of section 110(2) and (4).
8   This includes the executors of a deceased member, even if the articles declare that they shall not have the rights of a member until they are registered; *Llewellyn v Kasintoe Rubber Estates* [1914] 2 Ch 670 at 679 (CA).
9   In the case of a Rhodesian company, under similar words in the Colonial Ordinance, Warrington J held that a notice actually served on the liquidator in England and not left at the registered office was sufficient, and that the liquidator could waive service at the office: *Brailey v Rhodesia Consolidated* [1910] 2 Ch 95.
10   The notice must in terms state both alternatives for the liquidator to choose from, or it will be inoperative: *Re Demerara Rubber Co* [1913] 1 Ch 331; *Re Union Bank of Kingston-upon-Hull* (1880) 13 Ch D 808.
11   Section 111(2), (3) and (4).

dissent, the court may, on making an order for rectifying the register, declare that it shall relate back, so as to render the notice of dissent effective.[1] If the liquidator elects to purchase a dissenting member's interest, the purchase money must be paid before the company is dissolved, and be raised by the liquidator in such manner as may be determined by special resolution. Articles used often to provide that shareholders dissenting shall not have the rights given them by this section, or that the value of their interests shall be determined in some way other than by arbitration under the Act. But such provisions are invalid, for the articles cannot negate a provision in the statute for the benefit of the whole body,[2] and they are not an agreement settling the price within the meaning of section 111(4).[3] If the company being wound up is in difficulties, the value of the interest of such members is, of course, very small. These safeguards for dissenting shareholders in section 111 of the Insolvency Act 1986 apply to the case of section 110 in a members' voluntary liquidation. Where section 110 is used in a creditors' voluntary winding-up, section 111 has no application.[4]

Schemes of reconstruction under section 110 may be upset by a dissentient minority on the ground that some of the provisions are an infringement of the rights of the minority, which the majority cannot impose upon them.[5] If proceedings are taken to set aside a sale to another company after the agreement for sale has been executed, the purchasing company must be made a defendant to the action,[6] and if the method of distributing the purchase consideration can be severed from the provisions for sale, the sale may stand good, leaving the proper distribution of the shares to be made according to the rights of the members of the vendor company.[7] The resolution for winding up is not invalidated by reason of its being coupled with an invalid resolution dealing with the distribution of the purchase consideration.[8]

The arrangement for a sale under section 110 can provide for the manner in which the consideration is to be paid, but cannot determine how it is to be distributed among the members of the vendor company, as this must be done in strict accordance with their rights.[9] It will be seen that this introduces a serious difficulty where there are either preference or other shares having special rights in the distribution of surplus assets. If one million shares of £1 each are to be distributed, and the rights of the holders of preference shares to the extent of £200,000 are that they shall be paid in full the amount of such shares before any repayment is made to the holders of ordinary shares, who shall say how many shares in the new company would be equivalent to a payment in full of the amount of the preference shares?

---

1   *Re Sussex Brick Co* [1904] 1 Ch 598 (CA).
2   *Payne v Cork Co* [1990] 1 Ch 308; *Bisgood v Henderson's Transvaal Estates* [1908] 1 Ch 743 at 758 (CA).
3   *Baring-Gould v Sharpington Combined Pick and Shovel Syndicate* [1899] 2 Ch 80 (CA).
4   See section 111(1).
5   As to the provisions which may lawfully be inserted in a scheme of reconstruction under section 110 (eg as to time-limits for members to apply for shares and as to the disposal of shares unapplied for), see *Gore-Browne on Companies* 44th edn (Jordans, loose-leaf) at 30.5.
6   *Doughty v Lomagunda Reefs* [1903] 1 Ch 673 (CA).
7   *Wall v London and Northern Assets Corporation* [1898] 2 Ch 469 (CA).
8   *Thomson v Henderson's Transvaal Estates* [1908] 1 Ch 765 (CA); *Cleve v Financial Corp* (1873) 16 Eq 363.
9   *Griffith v Paget* (1877) 5 Ch D 894 and 6 Ch 514; *Simpson v Palace Theatre* [1893] WN 91; affirmed by Court of Appeal (1893) 9 TLR 470.

It is often attempted to meet the difficulty by giving holders of preference shares in the old company preference shares in the new; but this will not prevail over the rights of any of the old company's preference shareholders who insist on getting the full value of their shares before the old company's ordinary shareholders get anything.

The result is that in companies where there are preference shares, a reconstruction under section 110 alone is not possible unless either there is power in the articles of association to meet the circumstances of the case, or the preference shareholders consent unanimously,[1] or those who do not consent to the proposed distribution also dissent from the whole scheme, so as to be paid out under section 111.[2]

19.16   The protection of creditors

If after a voluntary winding-up of a company has been commenced an order is made within one year for winding it up, the special resolution is not valid unless sanctioned by the court: section 110(6). This sanction cannot be given in the voluntary winding-up. It will be effective only if given when the company is in compulsory liquidation.[3] When a scheme is unfair or improper this may be a ground for the court making a compulsory order on the application of dissatisfied shareholders;[4] but, 'generally speaking, the only persons who could raise this question or ask for an order . . . would be the creditors'.

If creditors of the company, instead of proving in the liquidation and having their claims met in the ordinary way, accept securities in the transferee company, then they have the power, under section 110(6), to impeach any arrangement which proves unsatisfactory to them within this 12-month period.[5] This means that a scheme under section 110 may remain liable to be impeached for this period.[6]

19.17   Duties of the liquidator under sections 110 to 111

The liquidator must apply the funds which he receives from the new company in paying the costs of the liquidation and any debts which the old company is bound to pay, and in buying out dissentient members. If anything remains, it must be distributed among the members of the old company according to their rights.[7] If

---

1   Note that the court does not draw the inference that shareholders not represented at the meeting have consented; *Re North-West Argentine Rly* [1900] 2 Ch 882.

2   Such a scheme has, however, been brought before the Court of Appeal under what is now section 425 of the Companies Act 1985, so as to bind the preference shareholders: *Sorsbie v Tea Corp* [1904] 1 Ch 12 (CA). However, this case conflicts with other decisions on the relationship between sections 110 and 425.

3   *Re Callao Bis Co* (1889) 42 Ch D 169 (CA).

4   *Re Consolidated South Rand Mines* [1909] 1 Ch 491.

5   *Re City & County Investment Co* (1879) 13 Ch D 475 (CA).

6   In *Re New Flagstaff Mining Co* [1889] WN 123, the company itself applied to the court for a supervision order.

7   If the real value of the assets received by the transferee company exceeds the nominal amount of the shares issued by it, then the transferee company must transfer a sum equal to the amount in value to the share premium account: *Henry Head & Co v Ropner Holdings* [1952] Ch 124. See sections 131 to 132 of the Companies Act 1985 for relief from section 130. See **7.15**.

the cash which the liquidator receives is not sufficient for the above purposes, he must raise cash by selling or mortgaging the shares or other property which he receives from the new company. The shares remaining over he will distribute among the members of the old company who have not been bought out.

The contract for sale usually provides that the purchasing company shall take over all the assets and pay all the liabilities of the old company, so that the business of the old company can be wound up at once; but such an arrangement does not relieve the liquidator of the old company from the obligation of seeing that the debts are duly paid before the old company is dissolved: to leave everything to the new company is 'a gross dereliction of duty by the liquidator',[1] and if he fails to pay income tax due from the company he will be personally liable to the Crown for the amount.[2]

If a liquidator makes a mistake in distributing the purchase shares, and has none left to correct his mistake, the court cannot upon a summons give damages against him.[3] Whether in an action damages could be recovered is doubtful.

As regards the new company, the same considerations will apply as in the case of a purchase from ordinary vendors, and the usual provisions will apply concerning the filing of contracts with the Registrar of Companies.[4]

Upon a reconstruction being carried into effect, the liquidator should wind up the old company with all possible speed, and, after making up his accounts, should call and advertise the meeting or meetings for receiving those accounts as provided in what is now section 94 of the Insolvency Act 1986. He should then make a return to the Registrar of the meeting or meetings having been held, and at the end of three months from the registration of the return the company is dissolved,[5] subject, however, to the power of the court to reopen the dissolution.[6] The importance of this is that sometimes claims arise for damages, or on other grounds, which, if the company were still in existence, might give rise to great difficulties. The liquidator will have to pay all the debts of which he knows;[7] but claims for damages may arise unexpectedly, and if the shares of the new company have been distributed there is nothing to meet such claims. A contract between the old and the new companies that the new will satisfy the liabilities of the old company cannot be enforced against the new company by creditors of the old for their own benefit, unless it has been made part of a scheme sanctioned under section 425 of the Companies Act 1985.[8]

The decisions[9] by the courts on the relationship between section 425, which provides for an alternative procedure for a reconstruction, as described in **19.18**, and section 110 of the Insolvency Act 1986 are difficult to reconcile. However, they

---

1   *Pulsford v Devenish* [1903] 2 Ch 625; *Argill's v Coxeter* (1913) 29 TLR 355; *Re Aidall* [1933] 1 Ch 323 at 327 (CA).
2   *Re New Zealand Joint Stock Corp* (1907) 23 TLR 238.
3   *Re Hill's Waterfall Co* [1896] 1 Ch 947.
4   See also **7.10**.
5   Section 201 of the Insolvency Act 1986.
6   See section 110(6) and **19.16**. Sections 106 and 201 will govern the final meeting and dissolution, where it is a *creditors'* voluntary liquidation.
7   The liquidator will be personally liable, however, if he does not secure the payment of claims of which he has notice: *Pulsford v Devenish* [1903] 2 Ch 625; *Re New Zealand Joint Stock Corp* (1907) 23 TLR 238; *Re Aidall* [1933] 1 Ch 323 at p 327 (CA).
8   *Craig's Claim* [1895] 1 Ch 267 (CA).
9   See *Sorsbie v Tea Corp* [1904] 1 Ch 12 (CA); *Re General Motor Cab Co* [1913] 1 Ch 377 (CA); *Re Sandwell Park Colliery* [1914] 1 Ch 589; *Re Guardian Assurance Co* [1917] 1 Ch 431 (CA).

appear to require that when a 'so-called' scheme is really a sale and transfer of assets under section 110, then that section must be complied with and cannot be evaded by petitioning for a scheme of arrangement under section 425.[1] However, this proposition is open to question as an unwarranted restriction on the powers conferred on the court by sections 425 to 427 of the Companies Act 1985.[2]

19.18 Procedure under section 425 of the Companies Act 1985

A reconstruction can be carried out in pursuance of a compromise or arrangement under section 425, which applies not only as between the company and the creditors or any class of them, but as between the company and the members or any class of them. This section provides that where any compromise or arrangement[3] is proposed between a company[4] and its creditors or any class of them, or between the company and its members or any class of them the court may, on the application[5] of the company, or any creditor or member of the company, or the liquidator, order a meeting of the creditors or class of creditors, or of the members or class of members, as the case may be, to be called. If at the meeting so ordered a majority, in number representing three-quarters in value of the creditors or class of creditors, or members[6] or class of members, present either in person or by proxy, agree to the compromise or arrangement, and it is also sanctioned by the court, it will be binding on all the creditors or the class of creditors, or on the members or class of members, as the case may be, and on the liquidator and the contributories of the company.

An order under the section is of no effect until an office copy has been delivered to the Registrar for registration, and a copy of every order must be annexed to every copy of the memorandum issued after the order has been made, or in the case of a company not having a memorandum, of every copy so issued of the instrument constituting or defining the constitution of the company.[7]

---

1 See the judgment of Astbury J in *Re Anglo-Continental Supply Company* [1922] 2 Ch 723. Where there are preference shares and this creates difficulties in making a distribution under section 110 of the Insolvency Act 1986, then a scheme under section 425 of the Companies Act 1985 has been upheld. See the *Tea Corp* and *Sandwell Park* cases cited in the footnote above.

2 For a further discussion of this question, see *Gore-Browne on Companies* 44th edn (Jordans, loose-leaf) at 30.7.

3 This includes a reorganisation of the share capital by the consolidation of shares of different classes or by the division of shares into shares of different classes or by both those methods: section 425(6).

4 'Any company liable to be wound up under the Act': section 425(6).

5 *Ex parte* by originating summons under RSC Order 102, rule 5 (England). See now *Practice Direction (Companies Court: Schemes of Arrangement and Capital Reductions)* [1997] 1 WLR 1 (Sir Richard Scott V-C).

6 As to the approval of members in the case of a company limited by guarantee, see *Re NFU Development Trust Ltd* [1972] 1 WLR 1548. Brightman J held that in such a company each member had in law the identical financial stake in the company. Thus a three-quarters majority of those present and voting satisfied the requirements of section 425(2).

7 Section 425(3).

19.19 The information required by section 426

The Companies Act 1985 imposes certain requirements, by section 426, as to giving information in relation to schemes under section 425. Section 426 provides that where a meeting is convened under section 425 there shall:

(1) with every notice summoning the meeting which is sent to a creditor or member, be sent also a statement explaining the effect of the scheme and in particular stating any material interests of the directors of the company, whether as directors or as members or as creditors of the company or otherwise, and the effect thereon of the scheme, in so far as it is different from the effect on the like interests of other persons;[1] and

(2) in every notice summoning the meeting which is given by advertisement, be included either such a statement or a notification of the place at which and the manner in which creditors or members entitled to attend the meeting may obtain copies of the statement.[2]

Where the scheme affects the rights of debenture-holders, the statement must give the like explanation as respects the trustees[3] of any deed for securing the issue of the debentures as it is required to give as respects the company's directors.[4]

Where there has been a failure to include an explanatory statement in an advertisement or to indicate where copies might be obtained, the fact that no prejudice is suffered as a result of the omission does not enable the court to dispense with the requirements of section 426. Fresh meetings with proper notice are necessary.[5]

Where the material interests of directors change, after the notices required by section 426 have been sent out, there is, strictly speaking, no requirement under that section for information about this later change to be sent to those who have already received notice under this section. Nevertheless, the court will take any change in directors' material interests into account in deciding whether to confirm a scheme under section 425. The court will have to be satisfied that no reasonable shareholder would change his decision on how to act on the scheme if the changes had been disclosed.[6]

The practice is to apply by originating summons for an order to convene the requisite meetings,[7] and if the appropriate majorities are obtained to apply by petition to the court for its sanction to the scheme.

The responsibility for determining what creditors or members are to be summoned to any meeting, as constituting a class, rests upon the applicant. If the meeting is incorrectly convened or constituted, or an objection is taken to the

---

1   As to what is sufficient disclosure of the interests of the directors see: *Rankin & Blackmore* 1950 SC 218; *Peter Scott* 1950 SC 507; *Coltness Iron Co* 1951 SLT 344; *Property Investment Trust Corp Ltd* 1951 SLT 371.
2   They are entitled to have a copy free of charge: section 426(5).
3   See *Second Scottish Investment Trust Corp Petitioners* 1962 SLT 392.
4   As to the sanctions imposed upon the company and officers in default for failure to comply with section 426, see section 426(6). There is also an obligation on directors and trustees for debenture holders to give the necessary particulars as to their interests: section 426(7).
5   *Scottish Eastern Investment Trust* 1966 SLT 285.
6   *Re Minster Assets plc* [1985] BCLC 200; *Re Jessel Trust Ltd* [1985] BCLC 119.
7   A copy of the proposed statement under section 426 should form part of the evidence in support of the summons. This, of course, applies to proceedings in England.

presence of any particular creditors as having interests competing with the others, the objection must be taken on the hearing of the petition for sanction, and the applicant must take the risk of the petition being dismissed.[1]

The classic test of what is a class for the purposes of what is now section 425 was laid down by Bowen LJ in *Sovereign Life Assurance Co v Dodd:*[2] 'it must be confined to those persons whose rights are not so dissimilar as to make it impossible for them to consult together with a view to their common interest'. In *Re Hellenic & General Trust Ltd,*[3] a majority of the ordinary shares of a company were owned by a wholly owned subsidiary whose holding company sought to acquire all the sub-subsidiary's shares under a section 425 scheme. Templeman J held that there was a sufficient community of interest between the holding and the subsidiary companies so that the latter was to be regarded as being in the purchasers' camp rather than in the vendors. Consequently, there was a sufficient difference of interest from that of the dissenting minority shareholders for two separate class meetings to be required. As in fact only one class meeting had been held for all the ordinary shareholders the scheme under section 425 could not be confirmed. It must be observed that this seems a rather strained interpretation of Bowen LJ's *dictum,* of which it has been said that the 'emphasis here is on rights, which are not dissimilar, and the rights in question must surely be against the company in respect to the shares or debts in question. Extraneous interests should surely be disregarded'.[4] Moreover, Templeman J's decision does not accord with previous English and Commonwealth decisions that the members of a single class of shares (or debenture-holders or unsecured creditors, as the case might be) should, for the purpose of organising meetings, be treated as one class even though there are clear conflicts of interest between them.[5] However, if different amounts are paid on shares, or certain shareholders have paid amounts in advance of calls, this makes various classes of shareholders, and separate meeting must be called.[6]

In sanctioning a scheme, the court may ignore the fact that a class has not consented if it be proved that upon an immediate distribution of the assets none would be available for that class.[7] The power of the court to sanction a scheme is a discretionary one, as to which see **19.23**.

At meetings held in pursuance of section 425 proxies are allowed, and foreign creditors must be taken into account.[8] The treatment of foreign creditors must depend on the terms of the scheme, and the conduct of meetings in this as in other respects is governed entirely by the court's directions. The court may allow

---

1   *Practice Note* [1934] WN 142 (England).
2   [1892] 2 QB 573 at 583.
3   [1976] 1 WLR 123 at 125–126.
4   This quotation is from a note by J A Hornby in (1976) 39 MLR 207 at 208.
5   See *Re Alabama New Orleans, Texas and Pacific Junction Rly* [1891] 1 Ch 213; *Re Holders Investment Trust Ltd* [1971] 2 All ER 289. See also the Australian and South African cases discussed by Hornby in (1976) 39 MLR 207; *Re AW Allen Ltd* [1930] VR 251; *Re Chevron (Sydney) Ltd* [1963] VR 249; *Re Jax Marine Pty Ltd* [1967] 1 NSWR 145; *Re Landmark Corp Ltd* [1968] 1 NSWR 759; *Rosen v Bruyns* 1973 (1) SA 815(T). This simply means that a scheme under section 426 or other statutory provisions will not fail simply for not having separate meetings. The court may still refuse to sanction it on other grounds. See also *Re RMCA Reinsurance Ltd* [1994] BCC 378.
6   *Re United Provident Assurance Co* [1930] 2 Ch 477.
7   *Sorsbie v Tea Corp* [1904] 1 Ch 12 (CA); *Re Oceanic Steam Navigation Co* [1939] Ch 41.
8   *Re Queensland National Bank* [1893] WN 128.

the result of proxies to be communicated by telex or cable from distant places.[1] A form of proxy is settled in chambers for use at such meetings; the shareholder signing it cannot, when the company is in liquidation, leave the decision to his proxy,[2] but when the company is not in liquidation he may use any proper form of proxy, whether lodged before the meeting or not.[3] Directors who, pursuant to the order of the court, get proxies for or against a scheme are bound to use them. A proxy appointing a person to act for a shareholder at a class meeting and to vote either for or against a scheme of arrangement empowers the holder to vote against a resolution to defer the consideration of the scheme.[4] Meetings of shareholders not convened exactly in accordance with the directions of the court may be held good, if in the result a sufficient number of the shares are accounted for,[5] but it is most advisable to comply strictly with the directions.

If there are debentures to bearer or share warrants, the holders must produce them at the meeting, or otherwise prove their title to be treated as debenture-holders before the vote is taken.[6]

19.20   The court's powers under section 427

Section 427 of the Companies Act 1985 confers upon the court certain additional powers which it may exercise on an application under section 427 for the court's sanction for a compromise or arrangement. A common use of these powers enables what is broadly the equivalent of an amalgamation under section 110 of the Insolvency Act 1986 to be carried out under sections 425 to 427.[7] Indeed, for the powers given by section 427 to be employed, it must be shown to the court that the compromise or arrangement has been proposed for the purposes of, or in connection with, a scheme 'for the reconstruction of any company or companies or the amalgamation of any two or more companies'. It must further be shown that under the scheme the whole or any part of the undertaking or the property of any company concerned in the scheme is to be transferred to another company. Section 427(2) terms the first-named company the 'transferor company' and the second the 'transferee company'. Where these conditions are met, the court may either by the order sanctioning the compromise or arrangement or by any subsequent order make provision in respect of any of the matters which are set out below.

In contrast with an amalgamation under section 110 of the Insolvency Act 1986, a scheme carried out under sections 425 to 427 has the advantage of effectively overriding[8] the objections of dissenting shareholders and creditors. The problem of preference shareholders' entitlement and the difficulties of the arbitration procedure to settle the claims of dissenting shareholders do not arise. Furthermore, dissenting creditors may not threaten the validity of a scheme by seeking to

---

1   *Re English, Scottish and Australian Bank* [1893] 3 Ch 385 (CA).
2   *Re Magadi Soda Co* [1925] WN 50.
3   *Re Dorman, Long & Co* [1934] Ch 635. The judgment in this case contains an exhaustive exposition of the law relating to proxies and will repay careful study.
4   *Re Waxed Papers* (1937) 156 LT 452 (CA).
5   *Re Anglo-Spanish Tartar Refineries* [1942] WN 222.
6   *Re Wedgwood Coal Co* (1877) 6 Ch D 627.
7   As to the relationship between section 110 of the Insolvency Act 1986 and sections 425 to 427 of the Companies Act 1985, see **19.17**.
8   The appropriate consents required by section 425, as well as the sanction of the court, having been obtained.

put the company into compulsory liquidation within one year, as may occur in a transfer of assets under section 110(6). On the other hand, the procedure under section 425 will inevitably entail court proceedings (in respect of the meeting ordered by the court and its subsequent sanction of the scheme). Under section 110, no application to court may be made unless shareholders or creditors have some ground to challenge the transfer of assets by the liquidator.

The matters as to which the court can make provision under section 427 of the Companies Act 1980 are as follows:

(1) the transfer to the transferee company of the whole or any part of the undertaking and of the property or liabilities of any transferor company;
(2) the allotting or appropriation by the transferee company of any shares, debentures, policies, or other like interests in that company which, under the compromise or arrangement, are to be allotted or appropriated by that company to or for any person;
(3) the continuation by or against any transferee company of any legal proceedings pending by or against any transferor company;
(4) the dissolution, without winding up, of any transferor company;
(5) the provision to be made for any persons who, within such time and in such manner as the court directs, dissent from the compromise or arrangement;
(6) such incidental, consequential, and supplemental matters as are necessary to secure that the reconstruction or amalgamation shall be fully and effectively carried out.

Section 427(4) states that where an order under the section provides for the transfer of property or liabilities, that property is, by virtue of the order, transferred to and vests in the transferee company, and those liabilities are by virtue of the order, transferred to and become the liabilities of, the transferee company. Any property, if the order so directs, vests freed from any charge which is by virtue of the compromise or arrangement to cease to have effect. The expression 'property' includes property, rights and powers of every description,[1] and the expression 'liabilities' includes duties, but not a duty to serve under a contract of personal service.[2]

The normal procedure under the section is first to obtain an order under section 425 sanctioning the scheme.[3] Then application will be made in chambers under section 427 in accordance with RSC Order 102, rule 7(2)(b), to which the transferee company should be a party.[4]

---

1   Such property and rights do not include the rights of the transferor company under contracts of service with its employees: *Nokes v Doncaster Amalgamated Collieries* [1940] AC 1014 (HL); and do not include rights to carry forward losses and wear and tear allowances for income tax purposes: *United Steel Companies v Cullington* [1940] AC 812 (HL). Nor does section 427(2) extend to the rights, duties or powers of an executor: *Re Skinner (deceased)* [1985] 1 WLR 1043.
2   Section 427(6): *Nokes v Doncaster Amalgamated Collieries*, above. Section 427(5) requires a copy of the court order to be delivered to the Registrar for registration within seven days of the court making the order.
3   Where the scheme provides for one company assuming the liabilities of another, a meeting of the creditors of the latter is not necessary: *Clydesdale Bank* 1950 SC 30.
4   *Practice Note* [1939] WN 121 (England).

19.21 The Companies (Mergers and Divisions) Regulations 1987

The Companies (Mergers and Divisions) Regulations 1987[1] implement Council Directive No 78/855/EEC, which concerns mergers of public limited liability companies, and Council Directive No 82/891/EEC, which concerns the division of public limited liability companies. Both the mergers and the divisions in question involve the transfer of the undertaking, property and liabilities of public companies ('transferor companies') to other public companies or, in some cases, companies, whether or not public, formed for the purpose of the merger or division ('transferee companies').

The transfer of the undertaking, etc of the transferor company must be in exchange for shares in the transferee company with or without additional cash payment. In British company law, these mergers or divisions take place under sections 425 to 427 of the Companies Act 1985. To comply with the directives, the regulations amend the Act by inserting a new section 427A and a new Schedule 15B. Section 427A provides that, in the case of mergers or divisions within the scope of the regulations, sections 425 to 427 shall have effect subject to the provisions of that section and Schedule 15B. A court may sanction a compromise or agreement under section 425 only if it complies with Schedule 15B.

The main requirements of Schedule 15B[2] are that three-quarters (measured by value) of each class of the shareholders of the transferee companies involved at a meeting agree, and that the draft terms of the merger or division are drawn up by the directors of the companies involved and published by the Registrar of Companies. There is also provision for directors' reports containing special information and the reports of independent experts containing specified information. All these documents and the relevant company accounts must be made available to shareholders.[3]

19.22 Composition with debenture-holders and other creditors

Under the powers given by section 425 of the Companies Act 1985, if the requisite majority of debenture holders agree to forgo their security, and accept preference shares in the new company in exchange for their debentures in the old company, their decision, if confirmed by the court, will be binding upon the minority who oppose the exchange,[4] and an agreement whereby a new company agrees to purchase all the assets and pay a composition to the creditors will be enforced, even though a large sum may be subsequently offered by another person.[5] Since the Insolvency Act 1986 came into force, it is very likely that a scheme of reconstruction affecting the rights of creditors (secured or otherwise) will have been preceded by the appointment of an administrator under Part II of the 1986

---

1   SI 1987/1991.
2   See *Gore-Browne on Companies* 44th edn (Jordans, loose-leaf) at appendix to Chapter 30 at pp 30.041–30.050.
3   Section 427A and Schedule 15B do not apply where the company in respect of which the compromise or arrangement is made is being wound up. See further, *Gore-Browne on Companies* at 30.11.B and 30.11.C.
4   *Re Empire Mining Co* (1890) 44 Ch D 402; *Re Alabama New Orleans etc, Rly Co* [1891] 1 Ch 213 (CA); *Follit v Eddystone Granite Quarries* [1892] 3 Ch 75 at 85.
5   *Re Oriental Bank* [1887] WN 109 at 112.

Act. One of the purposes for which an administration order can be made is the sanctioning of a scheme of arrangement under section 425 of the Companies Act 1985.[1]

A company can effect compromises or arrangements with its creditors without going into liquidation, for section 425 applies to companies not in the course of being wound up, as well as to companies which are being wound up.[2] The result is that with the sanction of the court any compromise or arrangement between the company and its creditors, or any class of such creditors, may be made binding on all such creditors or class of creditors and the company, provided that it has been submitted to a meeting of the creditors or class of creditors summoned under the direction of the court and approved by a majority in number representing three-quarters in value of such creditors or class of creditors present either in person or by proxy. If the company is in liquidation, the compromise or arrangement may be made binding on the liquidator and contributories, and any compromise or arrangement between the company and its members, or any class of its members, may equally be made binding.

In the case of the reconstruction of a company, if the creditors of the old company are to be paid in full at once, their consent need not be asked to a reconstruction; but if they are to accept a composition, or to take shares or debentures in the new company in satisfaction of their claims, or to accept deferred payment, their consent must be obtained to a scheme of composition.

19.23 The rights of dissenting shareholders and creditors

The sanction of the court to the scheme is essential,[3] and in determining whether such sanction should be given, the duties of the court are twofold: first, to see that the resolutions are passed by the statutory majority, and secondly, to see whether the proposal is such that an intelligent and honest man, a member of the class

---

1   Section 8(3)(c) of the Insolvency Act 1986 previously referred to a section 425 scheme of arrangement as being one of the purposes for which an administration order could be made. That is no longer the case, but a section 425 scheme of arrangment falls within the more broadly defined purposes of an administration order found in Schedule 16 (paragraph 3) to the Insolvency Act 1986 (as amended by the Enterprise Act 2002). As to administration, see Part 3 of Chapter 19. Where there is an estimated deficiency for creditors affected by section 425, subordinated creditors can be excluded from the scheme: *Re British Commonwealth Holdings plc* [1992] BCC 58. *Re Maxwell Communications Corporation plc* (No 3) [1993] BCC 369 considers the position of contractually subordinated unsecured creditors in relation to a scheme of arrangement under section 425. Vinelott J held that a contract which has been freely made between a debtor and a creditor to the effect that, in the event of the insolvency of the debtor the creditor should be subordinated to other unsecured creditors, is valid. In such circumstances, the joint administrators of Maxwell Communications Corporation plc were entitled to exclude the subordinated creditors from a scheme of arrangement. See also *Re British and Commonwealth Holdings plc (No 3)* [1992] 1 WLR 672.

2   But the court may decline to approve a scheme of arrangement if it is an object of the scheme to avoid a winding up and the consequent investigation of the company's affairs by a liquidator: *Re Halley's Department Store Pte Ltd* [1996] 1 SLR 70, HC (Spore).

3   After the resolutions approving the scheme have been passed, in meetings summoned by the court under section 425, the company presents a petition to the court for its sanction under RSC Order 102, rule 5(1)(h). The petition need not state that the company is carrying on business: *Re Great Universal Stores Ltd* [1960] 1 WLR 78. The procedure differs in detail in Scotland.

concerned and acting in respect of his interest, might reasonably approve.[1] But although shareholders acting honestly are usually much better judges of what is to their commercial advantage than the court can be, this proposition is of little value when it is proved that the majority of a class have voted or may have voted in the way they did because of their interests as shareholders of another class.[2]

In a recent unreported case,[3] the objectors to a scheme for demerger under section 425 represented a number of American health care providers. They contended that a payment of dividend *in specie* to be made after the scheme was completed would render the company unable to meet potential damages awards that could be made against it in pending tobacco litigation in the United States. It was held that the authorities showed that the objectors had a right to be heard, even though they were not members of the company, but that the court's primary concern under section 425 was the effect of the scheme between the company and its members. The terms of the scheme were such that there would be no net reduction of the company's capital value. Nothing in the scheme's terms suggested that its purpose was to deprive objectors of any assets they might recover in US litigation. The scheme was sanctioned.

A scheme will not be sanctioned if the terms of the scheme are such that it does not qualify as a 'compromise or arrangement' between the company and its members within section 425. These words 'compromise' and 'arrangement' imply some element of accommodation on each side and are not apt to describe a total surrender of the rights of one side. Where in a scheme concerning a guarantee company the rights of members were being expropriated without any compensating advantage, such a scheme was held by Brightman J not to be capable of being sanctioned under section 425: 'The word "compromise" implies some element of accommodation on each side. It is not apt to describe total surrender. A claimant who abandons his claim is not compromising it. Similarly, I think the word "arrangement" in this section implies some element of give and take. Confiscation is not my idea of arrangement.'[4] Brightman J also found that the scheme was unreasonable, that is one which 'properly examined, no member voting in the interests of members as a whole could reasonably approve'.[5]

It has nevertheless been held, in *Re Savoy Hotel Ltd*,[6] that a scheme is an 'arrangement' between the company and its members (for the purposes of section 425) even though the applicant (which was not the company) sought to acquire all the company's A and B shares[7] (other than those already held) in exchange for shares in the applicant or cash sums. As a matter of jurisdiction, this 'arrangement'

1   *Re Alabama, New Orleans, etc, Rly Co* [1891] 1 Ch 213 (CA); *Re English, Scottish 7 Australian Chartered Bank* [1893] 3 Ch 385 (CA); *Re Dorman, Long & Co* [1934] Ch 635; *Re National Bank* [1966] 1 WLR 819.
2   *Carruth v Imperial Chemical Industries* [1937] AC 707 at 769 *per* Lord Maugham (HL); *Re National Bank*, above. See *Re Holders Investment Trust Ltd* [1971] 1 WLR 583.
3   *Re BAT Industries plc v BAT Reconstructions Ltd*, unreported, 3 September 1998, Neuberger J (Transcript 0001165 of 1998).
4   *Re NFU Development Trust Ltd* [1972] 1 WLR 1548 at p 1555. The *dictum* of Bowen LJ in *Re Alabama, etc, Rly Co* [1891] 1 Ch 213 at 243 was applied.
5   Ibid.
6   [1981] 3 All ER 646.
7   The holders of the A shares owned approximately 97% of the company's total equity, but only 51% of the votes. The holders of the B shares owned only 2.3% of the equity but were entitled to 48% of the votes. Moreover, 65% of the B shares carrying 31% of the votes were owned, either beneficially or as trustee, by the company's board.

was within section 425 since the scheme would affect the contractual relationship between the company and its members by requiring the company to register the applicant in the place of the existing shareholders as the holders of the company's shares. Nevertheless, Nourse J held[1] that the court had no power to sanction the scheme since the company itself had not given its consent to the scheme through a decision either of its board or of the company in general meeting. The judge's reasoning turns largely on the legislative history of section 425 and a slender line of judicial *dicta*. The application before Nourse J was for the summoning of separate meetings of the A and the B shareholders.[2] He refused to exercise his discretion to order such meetings where the much greater number of A shareholders could override the advantage that weighted voting would normally give to the B shareholders. The reason given was that this would circumvent the essential requirement of the company's consent. A sounder basis for the decision might have been that the court had no power to circumvent the special voting rights attached to the B shares. It should still have been possible, following earlier authority,[3] to hold separate meetings for the two different classes of shares. The scheme, however, could only effect a transfer of that class of shares which at its own meeting gave the degree of consent required by section 425. Admittedly, this would still have had the effect of defeating the object of the scheme proposed by the applicant.

It has been held[4] that it is not a valid objection to a scheme under section 425 that its aim in essence was a purchase by an outsider of all the issued shares of the company, and that this was attempting to do under sections 425 to 427 what should have required approval by 90% of the shareholders under Part XIIIA of the Companies Act 1985 (as to which see **19.24**). The latter gives dissenting shareholders the right to be bought out. Plowman J refused to accept that what was then section 209 of the 1948 Act thus limited the court's jurisdiction under what is now section 425: 'In the first place, it seems to me to involve imposing a limitation or qualification either on the generality of the word "arrangement" under section 206 [section 425 of the 1985 Act] or else on the discretion of the court under that section. The legislation has not seen fit to impose such a limitation on terms and I see no reason for implying any.'[5] Plowman J maintained that these two statutory methods of amalgamation involved different considerations and approaches to reconstructions. Under Part XIIIA, the scheme need never come to court unless the minority bring it. If they do, they have the burden of demonstrating unfairness. In this respect there is good reason for requiring a small majority.

If the resolution has been passed by the statutory majority, but members of the class sufficient to have prevented the obtaining of the statutory majority appear on

---

1   [1981] 3 All ER 646.
2   Note that his decision as to the sanction of the court was not as to the merits of the scheme since these had not yet been submitted to the meetings of shareholders affected or voted upon. Instead, in refusing to order any meetings, he held that as a matter of law the scheme was incapable of sanction by the court.
3   As to the practice in holding meetings where different classes of shares are concerned, see **19.18**.
4   *Re National Bank* [1966] 1 WLR 819.
5   Ibid at p 829. In *Re Hellenic and General Trust* [1976] 1 WLR 123 at 127–129. Templeman J reached a different conclusion while attempting to distinguish *National Bank* on its facts. For a critique of the decision in *Hellenic*, see *Gore-Browne on Companies* 44th edn (Jordans, loose-leaf) at 30.10.3.

the hearing of the petition and oppose it, such opposition will be ignored if the change of mind was induced by a misleading circular: *quaere* whether a change of mind not so induced would be regarded.[1]

19.24 Compulsory acquisition of shares under Part XIIIA of the Companies Act 1985

Part XIIIA[2] amended the law on compulsory acquisition of shares. It substituted nine new sections for three sections (428 to 430) in the Companies Act 1985. The reform of these provisions had been long delayed, having originally been proposed by the Jenkins Committee[3] in 1962. The new restatement on Part XIIIA is almost entirely based on a memorandum by The Law Society's Standing Committee on Company Law.[4]

One of the more obvious flaws in the old legislation was that, on a literal interpretation, it allowed class rights to be overridden where an offeror obtained a nine-tenths level of acceptances from the shareholders of a company as a whole, even though the terms of the offer might be much more attractive to one class than to another. Such behaviour would of course have been a breach of the Code on Takeovers and Mergers. It will be seen that section 429 prevents this happening. Even now, however, there is no definition of a 'class of shares' for the purposes of Part XIIIA. Its meaning is simply assumed. What is meant by a 'class of shares' or a 'class right' has never been entirely clear since it is not defined in the Companies Act 1985 and, until fairly recently, this has been true of the case-law. The decision in *Cumbrian Newspaper Group Ltd v Cumberland and Westmorland Herald, Newspaper and Printing* Co[5] makes the matter more complex than earlier commentators had thought.[6] Scott J held that rights given to certain individual shareholders (eg to nominate a director to the board or a right of pre-emption over the company's shares) are to be regarded as class rights and are therefore protected by the class rights protection provisions of the Companies Act 1985,[7] even if the rights are given to individuals and do not attach to any particular shares. Nevertheless, a distinction may have to be drawn, so far as Part XIIIA is concerned, since it refers to 'a class of shares' and not to 'class rights' or 'rights attached to any class of shares'. The term 'a class of shares' accords better with the more traditional concepts of class rights. This requires a distinct class, or classes, of shares to be differentiated from each other by distinctive rights attaching to a particular type of share. These rights usually relate to voting, dividend or capital rights but, so long as they are attached to identifiable shares, could include particular rights of another kind. This concept of 'class of shares' would seem much more appropriate to the purpose and scope of Part XIIIA of the Companies Act 1985.

---

1   *Re Waxed Papers* (1937) 156 LT 452. Cf *Re National Bank* [1966] 1 WLR 819, where the non-disclosure of the bank's accounts was held entirely proper under the law applicable to banks at that time.

2   Inserted by Schedule 12 to the Financial Services Act 1986.

3   Cmnd 1762, paragraph 294.

4   November 1984. This was given the approval of the Law Reform Committee of the Senate of the Inns of Courts and the Bar. See Milman (1985) 6 Co Law 129.

5   [1986] 3 WLR 26.

6   See Polack [1986] CLJ 399, and the criticisms in **8.7.1**.

7   Ie sections 125 and 127.

It will be seen that a number of features in Part XIIIA are better adapted than the old law to contemporary takeover practice (eg in giving a choice of consideration to the offeree). The solutions adopted tend to imitate those of the Code on Takeovers and Mergers.

19.25   The power of compulsory acquisition

Section 428 of the Companies Act 1985 provides the defined meaning for the purposes of Part XIIIA of a number of terms used in sections 429 to 430E. The most important of these terms is that of 'takeover offer' in section 428(1). It is only takeover offers coming within this definition which will confer on the offeror the power of compulsory acquisition of a dissenter's shareholdings conferred by sections 429 and 430.[1] For the purposes of these provisions, then, a 'takeover offer' means an offer to acquire all the shares, or all the shares of any class or classes in a company, *other than* those which at the date of the offer are already held by the offeror. It is further required that it is an offer on terms which are the same in relation to all the shares to which the offer relates or, where those shares include shares of different classes, in relation to all the shares[2] of each class. Where the 'bidder' invites offers with the intention of accepting them, this does not amount to a 'takeover offer' as defined by section 428(1).[3]

The powers conferred by section 429 distinguish between two types of takeover offer. This is indicated by the definition in section 428(1), which refers to an offer to acquire all the shares, *or* all the shares of a particular class or classes. Section 429(1) deals with 'a case in which a takeover offer does not relate to shares of different classes'. In that case, if the offeror has, by virtue of acceptances of the offer, acquired or contracted to acquire not less than nine-tenths in value of the shares to which the offer relates, he may give a section 430 notice leading to compulsory acquisition of those shares that he had not acquired. In the case of a takeover offer which relates to shares of different classes, he must obtain (by virtue of acceptance of the offer, etc) nine-tenths in value of the shares of any class of shares to which the offer relates.[4] Thus, if the offeror wishes to acquire all the shares in a company with several classes of shares, it must achieve the appropriate level of acceptance *vis-à-vis* each class. It can, of course, use the powers conferred by sections 429 and 430 in the case of any class of shares where it does achieve that level of acceptances.

---

1   This is equally true of a minority shareholder's right to be bought out by the offeror under sections 430A and 430B. These provisions are discussed at **19.27**. This definition excludes the possibility of 'partial bids' that a loose interpretation of the earlier section arguably allowed.

2   'Shares' primarily means shares which have been allotted on the day of the offer. However, a takeover offer may include among the shares to which it relates all or any of the shares that are subsequently allotted before a date specified in, or determined in accordance with, the terms of the offer: section 428(2). The terms offered in relation to shares must be the same in relation to all the shares, or, as the case may be, all the shares to which the class relates: section 428(3). A limited variation is allowed to meet the requirements of foreign law: section 428(4).

3   *Re Chez Nico (Restaurants) Ltd* [1992] BCLC 192 at 203–204.

4   Section 429(2).

Section 429(3) imposes a four-month 'deadline' as the maximum period following the date of the offer[1] during which notices starting the process of compulsory acquisition can be given.[2] It is also provided that no such notice may be given after the end of the period of two months beginning with the date on which the offeror has acquired, or contracted to acquire, shares that satisfy the nine-tenths minimum. Practice in making takeover offers, and the need to comply with the Code on Takeovers and Mergers, are likely to keep the exercise of these powers well within the relevant statutory periods.

Subject to certain safeguards, section 429 allows an offeror to acquire shares during the offer period *otherwise* than under the offer. Clearly, there is a need to protect those who have sold their shares under the offer. Section 429(8) makes sure that the 'side purchases' permitted do not give those who have sold to the offeror (other than by acceptance of the terms of the offer) a better bargain. It, first of all, permits such purchases where the 'acquisition consideration'[3] does not exceed the value of the consideration specified in the terms of the offer. Alternatively, such purchases are permitted if the terms of the offer are subsequently revised so that, when the revision is announced, the value of the 'acquisition consideration' at the time of acquisition (or a contract to acquire) no longer exceeds the value of the consideration specified in those terms. If either of these conditions is met, the shares so purchased 'count' towards the nine-tenths level of acceptances required by section 429(1) and (2). If not, they are of course excluded from this calculation.

Section 430D allows joint offers to be made 'by two or more persons'.[4] So far as they acquire, or contract to acquire, the necessary shares under the takeover offer, the offerors do so jointly. However, so far as they acquire shares apart from the offer (ie within the limits allowed by section 429(8)), they may do so jointly or separately.[5] Section 430E makes special provision for the acquisition of shares by the 'associates' of the offeror. (This elaborately defined term is discussed later.) It was seen that for the purposes of sections 429 and 430, a takeover offer must extend to all the shares, or all the shares of any class or classes in a company. For this purpose, however, shares held or contracted for by associates of the offeror

---

1   It is possible for the terms of a takeover offer to make provision for its revision and for acceptances on the previous terms to be treated as acceptances on the revised terms. Section 428(7) provides that for the purposes of Part XIIIA the revision of such terms is not to be regarded as the making of a fresh offer. The date of the offer remains the date on which the original offer was made.

2   As to the formal requirements for the offeror giving a section 429 notice, see section 429(4) to (5). Criminal sanctions are provided for failing to send a copy to the company: section 429(6) and (7). Section 429(4) requires the statutory declaration at or about the same time as the first section 429 notice is served. In *Re Chez Nico (Restaurants) Ltd* [1992] BCLC 192 at 205, this provision was held to be directory and not mandatory and was not intended to nullify the whole procedure. On the facts, the failure to comply with the procedure for fourteen days would not affect the right to acquire the shares. Section 429(5) does not require that the section 429 notice be signed personally. It may be signed by an authorised agent such as a solicitor: ibid.

3   This is defined as the valuable consideration for which they were acquired or contracted to be acquired. See section 429(8)(a).

4   Although the definition of the 'offeror' in section 428(8) refers to the 'person making a takeover offer', it is clear from section 430E(8) that an offeror may be an individual. In practice, offerors, whether single or joint, are likely to be registered companies.

5   Section 430D(2). See sections 430D(3) and (7) for the consequential changes made to the other provisions in Part XIIIA in the case of joint offerors.

are not to be counted. Thus the offeror must obtain nine-tenths acceptances from the remainder of the shares (or class of shares as the case may be) without counting on shares acquired (or contracted for) by the offeror's associates to make up the required level of acceptances.[1] This applies to acquisitions at the time when the offer is made as well as shares obtained subsequently. An exception is made for shares acquired during the offer period by associates of the offeror which satisfy the same conditions[2] that must be satisfied by an offeror acquiring shares otherwise than by acceptance of the takeover offer.

The term 'associates'[3] is widely defined[4] to include nominees of the offeror, companies in the same group as the offeror,[5] and bodies corporate in which the offeror is substantially interested.[6] It also includes any person[7] who is a party to an agreement with the offeror for the acquisition of shares, or in an interest in shares. This must amount to an 'acquisition agreement' within section 204 of the Companies Act 1985.[8] Where an offeror is an individual, his 'associates' include his or her spouse and any minor child or stepchild.[9]

The powers of compulsory acquisition conferred by Part XIIIA apply to shares of any kind, but obviously not to debentures. However, convertible securities are to be treated as shares in the company if they are convertible into shares or rights to subscribe for shares.[10]

19.26 The 'price' payable to those whose shares are compulsorily acquired

Once a valid notice under section 429 of the Companies Act 1985 is given to those whose shares the offeror is entitled to acquire, the offeror then becomes both entitled and bound to acquire those shares on the terms of the offer. One of the improvements in the new Part XIIIA is that it deals with the situation where the terms of the original offer gave those who accepted its terms a *choice* of consideration. Here any notice under section 429 must give particulars of the choice. The holder of the shares to be acquired must be given six weeks to make his choice in a formal written communication. The notice must also provide for the eventuality of the holder failing to make a choice. It must specify which consideration will apply in that event.[11] The fact that the terms of the original offer set a time-limit or other conditions as to the choice of consideration to be made by shareholders accepting the offer will not prevent those whose shares are to be compulsorily acquired under section 429 from still retaining that choice.[12] Special

---

1   Section 430E(1).
2   Ie in section 429(8)(a) and (b). See section 430E(2). See above.
3   This is a term used in the Code on Takeovers and Mergers where it is likewise widely defined.
4   See section 430E(4)–(8).
5   See section 430E(5).
6   Section 430E(6). Two criteria are used: the company or its directors are accustomed to act in accordance with the offeror's directions or the offeror has one-third or more of the voting power at general meetings.
7   Or a nominee of such a person.
8   See **12.9.6**. See Section 430E(7) as modifying section 204(5) and (6).
9   Section 430E(8).
10   See section 430F. As to how such securities should be treated in respect of the class share to which they belong, see section 430F(2).
11   Section 430(3).
12   Section 430(4).

provision is made for the situation where a non-cash consideration is chosen by the holder of the shares and the offeror is no longer able to provide it. Here the consideration shall be taken to consist of an amount of cash payable by the offeror which at the date of the notice is equivalent to the chosen consideration.[1]

Six weeks from the end of the section 429 notice the offeror must begin to complete the process of compulsory acquisition by sending a copy notice to the company, and must pay or transfer to the company the consideration for the shares to which the offer relates. This must (in the case of registered shares) be accompanied by an instrument of transfer executed on behalf of the shareholder by someone appointed by the offeror. On the receipt of this, the company must register the offeror as holder.[2] Any sums received by the company in this process are to be held in trust for those whose shares have been acquired.[3]

19.27 The right of minority shareholders to be bought out

Where an offeror, whether in a bid for all the shares of a company or in a bid for a class or classes, has obtained acceptance of the offer (whether by acquisition or contract to acquire) by nine-tenths of the shareholders (or those of the class or classes concerned), then those who have not been acquired may demand to be bought out.[4] The shares already held (ie acquired or contracted to be acquired) by the offeror 'count' towards the nine-tenths level of acceptance required to 'trigger' the dissenting shareholder's right to be bought out. It was seen that these shares do not 'count' in order to 'trigger' the offeror's right compulsorily to acquire the shares.[5]

Once a dissenting shareholder has exercised his rights, the offeror is entitled and bound to acquire the dissenter's shares 'on the terms of the offer or on such terms as may be agreed'.[6] Where the takeover offer gave a choice of consideration to those who accepted its terms, this choice is preserved for dissenting shareholders who exercise their rights to be bought out.[7] If the parties cannot agree on the terms of the offer, then either side may apply to the court. The terms may then be 'such as the court thinks fit'.[8] Unlike the equivalent jurisdiction where the offeror compulsorily acquires shares, there is no guidance from reported judicial decisions. It may be noted, however, that the court here has no

---

1   Section 430(4). This solution also applies where the consideration was to be provided by a third party who is no longer bound or able to provide it (eg a put option from a merchant bank). This in effect legislates the decision in *Re Carlton Holdings* [1971] 1 WLR 918.

2   Section 430(5) and (6). As to bearer shares and shares to be allotted, see section 430(7) and (8).

3   Section 430(9). Provision is made as to appropriate banking of such sums, and as to what enquiries and other steps must be taken where those entitled cannot be traced. See section 430(10)–(15).

4   Section 430A(1) and (2). As to the notice of the rights to buy which an offeror must give the dissenters, the time allowed for the exercise of their rights and the sanctions for failure by the offeror to comply, see section 430A(3), (4), (6) and (7).

5   Where the offeror can and does exercise his rights to acquire the shares of those who have not accepted the offer, they cannot exercise the right to be bought out: section 430A(5).

6   Section 430B(2).

7   Section 430B(3). Similar provision is made as in the case of an offeror compulsorily acquiring shares where the consideration is not in cash and the offeror is no longer able to provide it, etc. See section 430B(4).

8   Section 430C(3).

power to prevent the shareholder having his shares bought. It can only change the terms. It would appear that there has been very little need for this form of relief, but together with the right to be bought it forms a useful protection when minority shareholders are 'locked into' a company under the overwhelming control of the offeror.

19.28 Applications to the court by dissenting shareholders

As was the case under the previous legislation , there is a provision in Part XIIIA of the Companies Act for dissenting shareholders to apply to court. This application must be made within six weeks of when the notice to acquire the shares (under section 429) is given.[1]

The court may be asked to do two things. It may order that the offeror shall not be entitled and bound to acquire the shares. This is the same power as existed under the earlier legislation.[2] Thus the case-law in respect of application under this earlier legislation may still be relied upon.[3] It is thus explored in the pages that follow. Section 430C(1) also allows the court to 'specify terms of acquisition different from those of the offer'. This allows the court more flexibility in meeting the claims of the applicant. It may encourage more judicial intervention than is evidenced by the reported cases. However, the same factors that have made Chancery Division an awkward forum in which to examine the true merits of a takeover bid will still apply. These include judicial reliance on the nine-tenths level of acceptance as indicating that sound commercial judgment must be behind the decision of such a large majority. There is also the difficulty for dissenting shareholders in matching the means, access to expert advice, and internal corporate information that the offeror will have at its command. Nevertheless, the necessity for a public hearing where dissenters apply to the court will place some restraint upon those who frame the terms on which a successful takeover offer is made. Where this has not been contested by the offeree company (or another bidder), this may be all the more necessary.

There are two other new provisions in section 430C which may prove useful. The court has always tended to encourage applicants by the award of costs even when their application fails. Section 430C(4) now enjoins this as a general rule, unless the application has been unnecessary or vexatious, or there is unreasonable delay or other misconduct in the prosecution of the application. The Court of Appeal has considered the meaning of 'vexatious' in section 430C(4). In allowing an appeal against the judge's decision that an application under section 430C(1) was vexatious, the court[4] found that there were sufficient grounds[5] for it to consider the fairness of the offer. This meant that the application was not so obviously unsustainable or impossible of success as to amount to an abuse of the process of the court. There is also a new power for the court to deal with the

---

1 Section 430C(1). If an application to court is pending, the power to acquire is suspended: section 430C(2).
2 See section 428(4) in the original provisions of the Companies Act 1985.
3 That will not of course be true of decisions upon the 'procedural' aspects of Part XIIIA, insofar as changes have been made.
4 *Re Britoil plc* [1990] BCC 70.
5 The offeree board's original defence document put a value on the shares 40% above the offer. The later recommendation of the offer by the board did not come to the applicant's attention.

problems of 'untraceable shareholders'.[1] Where the offer needs additional acceptance to make up the nine-tenths level required, the court may make an order authorising that such untraced shareholdings be treated as acceptances. The section contains obvious safeguards to prevent abuse. Thus reasonable enquiry must have been made to trace the shareholders, and the consideration must be shown to be fair and reasonable. This imposes a tougher and more objective standard than the courts usually apply in applications under this section. There is, finally, an overriding requirement that the court must conclude that such an order is just and equitable, having regard in particular to the number of shareholders who have been traced but who have not accepted the offer.

It is well established that there rests upon dissenting shareholders a heavy onus of proof if they are to show that a scheme which holders of 90 per cent of the shares have accepted, is unfair. In *Re Sussex Brick Co*,[2] Vaisey J observed that it was not sufficient for the applicant to set out in his affidavit certain criticisms which undoubtedly show that a good case could be made 'for the formulation of a better scheme, of a fairer scheme, of a scheme which would have been more attractive to the shareholder, if they could have understood the implications of the criticisms'. The courts are clearly influenced by the high proportion of shareholders who must assent to a scheme under what is now section 430C. Vaisey J, in *Re Sussex Brick Co*, said that it was difficult to 'predicate unfairness' where the good faith of the transferee company is not challenged and there is no case of any intentional misleading of the offeree shareholders. A dissenter under section 430C is faced with the very difficult task of showing that 'he, being the only man out of step in the regiment, is the only man whose views should prevail'. These principles were followed by Plowman J in *Re Grierson, Oldham & Adams Ltd*,[3] where the fact that holders of 99% of the shares had approved the scheme, and that the price offered was slightly above the market price,[4] was held to indicate that there was no unfairness. In estimating whether a 'fair value' is being paid for the shares, the market price is a good indication of such value. The real value of the transferor company and its assets to the transferee company is not as a rule to be taken into account.[5] The new power in section 430C(1) enabling the court to specify different terms of acquisition may now encourage more judicial scrutiny.

Where the Part XIIIA procedure was misused to expropriate a minority shareholder in a small private company, the Court of Appeal allowed his application.[6] There two shareholders who already held 90% of the shares set up a company as a vehicle through which to compulsorily acquire the shares of the remaining shareholder. However, it does not follow that the approving shareholders must always be wholly independent of the transferee company. This is merely a factor to be taken into account by the court in exercising its discretion, the weight to be given to it depending on the circumstances of the case.[7]

---

1   Section 430C(5).
2   [1961] Ch 289n following *Re Hoare & Company* [1933] 150 LT 374; *Re Evertite Locknuts* [1945] Ch 220; *Re Press Caps Ltd* [1949] Ch 434 (CA).
3   [1968] Ch 17.
4   See also *Re Sussex Brick Co* [1961] Ch 289n.
5   *Re Press Caps Ltd* [1949] Ch 434 (CA); *Re Grierson, Oldham & Adams Ltd* [1968] Ch 17.
6   *Re Bugle Press Ltd* [1961] Ch 270 (CA).
7   See *Sammel v President Brand G M Co* (1969) (3) SA 629, at 677–691.

It has recently been held that the court will be much more inclined to exercise its jurisdiction under section 430C where the bidder is *not* an outsider, but a director and shareholder in the target company and it is shown that the information made available to dissenting shareholders falls far short of what should have been provided. In *Re Chez Nico (Restaurants) Ltd*,[1] Browne-Wilkinson V-C supported this statement of principle by adverting to various disclosure provisions in the City Code on Takeovers and Mergers which had not been complied with.[2] There had also been a failure to comply with the restrictions on advertising contained in section 57 of the Financial Services Act 1986.[3]

Under the Part XIIIA procedure, there is no provision (equivalent to section 426 in a scheme under sections 425 to 427) requiring information to be given to the shareholders to whom the offer is made. It would appear that the lack of full disclosure will not necessarily amount to unfairness.[4] In *Gething v Kilner*,[5] however, Brightman J accepted that the directors of an offeree company owe a duty towards their own shareholders which 'clearly includes a duty to be honest and a duty not to mislead'. Any minority shareholder in an offeree company could properly complain if they were being wrongfully subjected to the power of compulsory purchase, conferred by section 429 on the offeror company, as a result of a breach of the above-mentioned duty by the board of the offeree company in recommending the offer. The minority shareholders would have to show bad faith or conduct so unreasonable as to amount to bad faith.

---

1 [1992] BCLC 192 at 206–212.
2 Ibid at p 209. The court indicated that the liability considered in *Coleman v Myers* [1977] 2 NZLR 225 might also have applied; as to this, see **16.3**.
3 Ibid at 210–211.
4 *Re Evertite Locknuts* [1945] Ch 220; Roxburgh J in *Re Press Caps* [1948] 2 All ER 638 held that an order for discovery will not be made on an application by originating summons under what is now section 430C in the absence of special circumstances. But see *Coni v Robertson* [1969] 1 WLR 1007. This latter decision was followed in *Re Lifecare International plc* (1990) BCLC 227 on the basis that the position applicable at the time of *Re Press Caps* has been changed by what is now RSC Order 24, rules 3 and 8. In *Lifecare*, the discovery sought related to the professional advice given to the board of the offeree company. It did not call for 'an extensive investigation of the company's affairs'. Cross-examination was also allowed on the expert evidence submitted by affidavit.
5 [1972] 1 WLR 337.

Chapter 20

Insider Dealing and Market Abuse

20.1 Introduction

The purpose of this chapter is to give an account of some of the provisions that exist to attempt to ensure that markets in company shares and other securities operate fairly. In one sense they are part of the law of securities regulation or investor protection or certainly at least at the 'margins of company law'.[1] But as Davies points out,[2] every quoted company has an interest in activities which, if unregulated, could distort the true value of the company. Indeed, company law has for a long time contained measures that can penalise directors and other insiders who make a profit or avoid a loss by trading in the shares of their companies. See in particular the rule against 'secret profits'[3], the prohibitions on option dealings,[4] and the requirement for directors to disclose their interests in company securities.[5] Other controls include provisions of the City Code on Takeovers and Mergers[6] and the Model Code for Securities Transactions for Directors.[7] In this context, readers are reminded that, although a company may penalise directors who have profited from insider dealing, the general law does not provide an effective remedy for the other party who has lost out,[8] but provisions in the Financial Services and Markets Act 2000 (FSMA 2000) may go some way to remedying this.[9]

20.2 Insider dealing

Essentially, insider dealing involves the deliberate exploitation of unpublished price-sensitive information, obtained through or from a privileged relationship, to make a profit or avoid a loss by dealing in the securities of a company, when the price of the securities would be materially altered if the information were

---

1   Davies and Gower, *Principles of Modern Company Law* 7th edn (Sweet & Maxwell, 2003), p 749.
2   Ibid.
3   See **16.18**.
4   See **16.19**.
5   See **15.22**.
6   See **19.8**.
7   Now part of the *Listing Rules*.
8   See **16.3**. In the case of a transaction on the Stock Exchange or other investment exchange, it may in fact be impossible to discover who the other party is.
9   See the excellent survey by Davies, op cit, chapter 29. See also for an exhaustive account, *Gore-Browne on Companies* 44th edn (Jordans, loose-leaf) at chapter 12.

disclosed. For some years the balance of opinion has supported the view that such dealing is wrong and should be the subject of legal sanctions.[1]

The specific criminal law provisions concerning insider dealing are now contained in Part V of the Criminal Justice Act 1993, implementing the EC Directive on Insider Dealing.[2] This Directive had a tortuous history, but has a philosophy firmly based on the importance of maintaining and fostering confidence in the integrity of the EC's securities markets by promoting 'smooth markets' where there is equality of information.[3] The United Kingdom had first made insider dealing a specific criminal offence in 1980,[4] and re-enacted the provisions with minor amendments in the Company Securities (Insider Dealing) Act 1985. The 1993 Act, completely replacing the 1985 Act, retains many of the central elements of the former law, but has refashioned and modified them in important respects.[5] Essentially there is one offence of insider dealing, although it can be committed in three ways:

(1) by dealing in securities the price of which will be affected by the inside information which is in that person's possession;[6]
(2) by encouraging another person so to deal;[7] and
(3) by disclosing the inside information to another person.[8]

The scope of this offence is examined in the following sections.

There have been relatively few prosecutions for insider dealing since 1980. This partly reflects the difficulties in detecting the crime but also the prevailing view that prosecutions should be brought only when there can be little doubt as to the individual's lack of integrity. The somewhat special nature of this crime is also reflected in the requirement that prosecutions can be brought only by or with the consent of the Secretary of State or the Director of Public Prosecutions.[9] On conviction on indictment, a person can be imprisoned for up to seven years and/or receive an unlimited fine,[10] indicating that the legislature regards the

---

1   There has, none the less, been much debate over the morality or immorality of insider dealing, particularly in the United States where controls have existed since the 1930s, and the subject has spawned a voluminous literature. A dated although comprehensive guide to the position in many countries is Rider and Leigh Ffrench's *Regulation of Insider Trading* (Macmillan, 1979). For a detailed account of the new law, see Rider and Ashe, *Insider Crime* (Jordans, 1993). See also Lomnicka [1994] JBL 173 and, for an interesting critique, Alcock (1994) 15 Co Law 67.

2   89/592/EEC. The statutory references in this section are to the 1993 Act. As to the new Directive on Market Abuse (including insider dealing), which replaces this Directive, see **20.10** (and cf **2.4**), although it is likely that the UK will keep the provisions described here.

3   In contrast, the North American controls are based more on notions of abuse or misappropriation of information obtained in a relationship founded on trust or confidence.

4   Part V of the Companies Act 1980.

5   Note that not all the provisions concerning insider dealing are in the 1993 Act: eg, the provisions regarding investigations remain in the Financial Services Act 1986; for a detailed consideration of these, see *Gore-Browne on Companies* 44th edn (Jordans, loose-leaf) at 12.31. The Government has been criticised for the way in which it implemented the Directive; see *Gore-Browne on Companies* at 12.18.

6   Section 52(1).

7   Section 52(2)(a).

8   Section 52(1)(b).

9   Section 61(2).

10 On summary conviction, the punishment is restricted to the usual limits of magistrates' courts.

offence as a very serious one,[1] but the courts have not imposed punishments which might operate as a substantial deterrent. In practice criminal prosecutions for insider dealing are much less likely anyway, as almost any case falling within the provisions of the 1993 Act will also amount to market abuse, which, as will be seen, is punishable by civil penalties.

The Criminal Justice Act 1993 expressly provides, by section 62(2), that 'no contract shall be void or unenforceable by reason only' that it is entered into in contravention of the Act. However, the courts may well use well-established principles of public policy to deny specific performance of an executory contract entered into in breach of the Act.[2]

20.3 Securities covered

A wide range of securities is covered by the insider dealing law. The provisions first define the securities, then define the circumstances and conditions which will bring those securities within the parameters of the insider dealing law, and then set out the circumstances of dealing in those securities with which the law is concerned.

The list of securities includes shares and debentures in companies, and rights and options under contracts in relation to such shares and debentures.[3] Dealing in these securities is within the Act if: (a) the transaction occurs on a regulated market; or (b) the person dealing either relies on, or is himself acting as, a professional intermediary. Regulated markets are prescribed by Order[4] and include the Stock Exchange, other recognised investment markets in the United Kingdom and some major investment exchanges in the European Economic Area (EEA).[5] In addition, the security must satisfy one of a number of conditions, in particular that it is officially listed in a State within the EEA or that it is admitted to dealing on, or has its price quoted on or under the rules of a regulated market.[6] A professional intermediary is defined[7] as a person who carries on a business of acquiring or disposing of securities, whether as an agent or principal, or a business of acting as an intermediary between persons taking part in any dealing in securities. The purpose of these provisions is to exclude from the scope of criminal liability a truly private deal executed off the market without the involvement of a market professional.

---

1 It is also an extraditable offence and one to which the provisions for the seizure and forfeiture of profits in the Criminal Justice Acts of 1988 and 1993 apply.

2 See *Chase Manhattan Equities v Goodman* [1991] BCLC 897. This decision was concerned with the previous legislation where the equivalent to section 62(2) used 'voidable' rather than 'unenforceable'. As to whether this might make a difference, see *Gore-Browne on Companies* 44th edn (Jordans, loose-leaf) at 12.20, where other potential civil consequences are also discussed.

3 See Schedule 2 to the 1993 Act. Public sector debt securities and various other financial instruments are also covered; see *Gore-Browne* on Companies 44th edn (Jordans, loose-leaf) at 12.21.

4 The Insider Dealing (Securities and Regulated Markets) Order 1994, SI 1994/187.

5 Note that the criminal offence is territorially limited by section 62 so that dealing must either take place on United Kingdom markets or with or through professional intermediaries based in the United Kingdom. The encouragement and disclosure offences can be committed if either the insider or the recipient was in the United Kingdom at the time. Of course, offences of similar scope should now exist in most European countries in any case.

6 Section 54(1) and the 1994 Order.

7 Section 59(1).

Inside information

By section 56, information must satisfy four characteristics in order to be inside information for the purposes of the Act. First, it must relate to particular securities or to a particular issuer, or particular issuers, of securities and not to either securities or issuers in general. Thus information is inside information even if it does not relate to a particular issuer but does relate to the industry within which that issuer operates, so it may come from within or without the issuer. A classic example of information relating to a particular issuer is a decision to make a takeover bid for that issuer. Further, 'information shall be treated as relating to an issuer not only where it is about the company itself, but also where it may affect the company's business prospects' (such as the gain or loss of a major contract, or possible government or EU intervention).[1] The exclusion of 'general information' would appear to exclude information, like unpublished information regarding government economic policy or the bank rate, which might be expected to impact on the market in a general way, although it is difficult to identify where the line should be drawn.[2]

Secondly, the information must be either specific or precise. The Directive requires only that information be precise, so it seems that UK law is wider in this respect. An example of specific information is that a takeover bid is to be made; an example of precise information is the price at which the bid is to be made: either is within the definition. The essential point is that rumours or casual remarks will not satisfy the requirement.

Thirdly, the information must not have been made public. Section 58 provides four specified situations where information is deemed to have been made public, but these are not exhaustive. The specified situations are:

(1) when information is published in accordance with the rules of a regulated market for the purpose of informing investors and their advisers;

(2) when information is placed in records which, by virtue of any enactment, are open to inspection by members of the public;

(3) if information can be readily acquired by those who are likely to deal in any of the securities to which it relates or of an issuer to which the information relates; or

(4) if the information is derived from information which has been made public (such as conclusions drawn by market analysts from information made public).

Further, information may[3] be treated as having been made public even though it can be acquired only by persons exercising diligence or expertise, or where it is communicated to a section of the public rather than the public at large, or where it can be acquired only by observation, or it is communicated only on payment of a fee, or it is published outside the United Kingdom. It is notable that the law does not require a period for information to be digested. It is public as soon as, among other things, any of the four events listed above occurs.

---

1   Section 59(4).
2   As to whether or not this is consistent with article 1 of the Directive, see *Gore-Browne on Companies* 44th edn (Jordans, loose-leaf) at 12.22.
3   It does not have to be so treated.

Fourthly, the information must be such that if it were made public, it would be likely to have a significant effect on the price[1] of any securities. The purpose of this requirement seems self-evident and sensible, and its application should not cause many difficulties.[2]

20.5 Who is an insider?

It is in respect of the definition of who is an insider that the structure of the 1993 Act is significantly different from that of the previous UK law.[3] Under the way the previous law defined the term, an insider had to be a director, officer or employee of, or professional adviser to, the company in question, in other words someone who almost inevitably stood in a fiduciary position or under a duty of confidentiality. The 1993 Act does not require a nexus of the same sort. Under section 57, a person has information as an insider if, and only if, it is, and he subjectively knows that it is, inside information, and he has it, and subjectively knows that he has it, from an inside source. This latter phrase is further qualified so that a person has inside information from an inside source if, and only if: (a) he has it through being a director, employee or shareholder of an issuer of securities or through having access to the information by virtue of his employment, office or profession; or (b) the direct or indirect source of his information is a director, employee or shareholder. So anyone can be an insider, even if they have had no previous connection with the issuer, provided that they get inside information from an inside source; the latter though has to be a director, officer, employee, shareholder or professional adviser.[4] However, it may be difficult to prove that the person in question knew that the information was inside information from an inside source and therefore make prosecutions more difficult.

It is conventional in this area to distinguish by description between the types of insider in paragraphs (a) and (b) above. The first, who must have the connection with the company, is the primary insider. The second is the secondary insider or tippee.[5]

20.6 The offences in detail

As indicted earlier, there are three separate offences under Part V of the 1993 Act. The first is the dealing offence (section 52(1)) and its two essential elements are: (a) an individual has information as an insider; and (b) he must then deal in securities that are price-affected securities in relation to the information. 'Dealing' is comprehensively defined in section 55 as the acquisition or disposal of securities, whether as principal or agent, or the direct or indirect procurement of an acquisition or disposal by any other person. A person is considered as dealing if he procures an acquisition or disposal of a security if the security is acquired or disposed of by a person who is his agent or nominee or is acting at his direction in

---

1 'Price' includes value. Section 56(3).

2 Provided that complex disputes of the sort discussed in *Gore-Browne on Companies* 44th edn (Jordans, loose-leaf) at 12.22.3 do not occur.

3 The effect may not be significantly different.

4 The inclusion of shareholders, as required by the directive, is quite a new departure for UK law. For a detailed discussion of who is an insider, see *Gore-Browne on Companies* 44th edn (Jordans, loose-leaf) at 12.23.

5 There was an unsuccessful attempt in Parliament to have the description 'tippee' enshrined in the legislation.

relation to the acquisition or disposal. Contracts to acquire or dispose of securities which are never executed are nonetheless caught, because of the wide definition of the terms 'acquire' and 'dispose'.[1] Crucially, however, a decision not to acquire or dispose securities, which may well be based on inside information, is not covered by the Act, presumably because it would be almost impossible to provide relevant evidence.

The second offence is the encouragement offence (section 52(2)(a)), involving an individual who has information as an insider encouraging another (who may be a company) to deal in securities that are (whether or not that other knows it) price-affected securities in relation to the information, knowing or having reasonable cause to believe that the dealing would take place.[2] It should be noted that the offence fastens solely on the conduct and state of mind of the insider who encourages another; it matters not whether the other person knows what is going on nor whether in fact that other person deals. Whether 'encouragement' for this purpose covers only an explicit recommendation or goes further and covers mere 'hints' such as by a nod or a wink is not clear.[3]

The third offence is that of unauthorised disclosure of inside information by an individual (section 52(2)(b)), that is disclosure otherwise than in the proper performance of the functions of his employment, office or profession. It is irrelevant whether or not the insider intends or suspects that the other will deal on the basis of the information.[4]

20.7 Defences

Section 53 contains a number of defences to the section 52 offences.[5] The first three apply to both the dealing and the encouragement offences.[6] It is a defence to these if the defendant shows:[7]

(1) that he did not, at the relevant time, expect the dealing to result in a profit which was attributable to the fact that the information was price-sensitive information in relation to the securities; for this purpose, 'profit' includes the avoidance of a loss;[8]

---

1   Section 55(2) and (3).

2   This replaced the former, very similar, counselling and procuring offence

3   For more detailed consideration, see *Gore-Browne on Companies* 44th edn (Jordans, loose-leaf) at 12.26.

4   In this respect, the offence is wider than the old law. What is not clear is the position of what are called multiple-function fiduciaries, who may in one capacity hold information which it is improper to disclose but who have another capacity in respect of which it would be appropriate to disclose, eg someone acting as a trustee of a fund including certain shares who is also a director of the company in question. As an insider he cannot disclose information which may cause the value of the shares to drop, but as a trustee it may be his duty to act on the information. This problem is not confined to the context of insider dealing laws: eg many of the regulatory rules effected under the auspices of the Financial Services Act 1986 may clash with traditional fiduciary duties. It raises the issue of the effectiveness of so-called 'Chinese walls' and was considered by the Law Commission (*Fiduciary Duties and Regulatory Rules*, Law Com No 236 (1995)). For further consideration, see *Gore-Browne on Companies* 44th edn (Jordans, loose-leaf) at 12.30 and the sources there cited.

5   There are also a number of specific defences in Schedule 1 relating to market making, stabilisation and market information; for more detail, see *Gore-Browne on Companies* at 12.29.

6   With minor differences in wording for the second defence.

7   This clearly imposes the burden of proof on the defendant.

8   Section 53(6).

(2) that at the time he believed on reasonable grounds that the information had been disclosed widely enough to ensure that none of those taking part in the dealing would be prejudiced by not having the information;

(3) that he would have done what he did even if he had not had the information.

There are two defences to the offence of disclosing information. The first is if the defendant shows that he did not, at the time he disclosed the information, expect any person, because of the disclosure, to deal in the securities on a regulated market, or through or with a professional intermediary. The second is if he shows that although he had such an expectation at the time, he did not expect the dealing to result in a profit (or avoid a loss) attributable to the fact that the information was price-sensitive information in relation to the securities. Note that in both these instances, it is not necessary to show, in contrast to the second defence (above) to the dealing and encouragement offences, that the expectations were reasonable.

20.8 Market Abuse

Under Part VIII of the FSMA 2000, the Financial Services Authority (FSA) has the power to reprimand publicly, or impose an unlimited fine on, persons who engage in market abuse. It is also indirect market abuse if a person requires or encourages (by action or even inaction) another to engage in behaviour that if done by the defendant would have amounted to direct market abuse. Market abuse is basically defined as behaviour in relation to any qualifying investments, which is likely to be regarded by regular users of the market as falling below the standard reasonably expected of a person in that position; and which falls within at least one of the three categories described below.[1] The behaviour can be that of one person or more than one acting together.[2] The FSA gives further guidance on what investments count as 'traded on a market' and on the type of behaviour that counts in its Code of Market Conduct ('the COMC').[3]

Behaviour 'likely to be regarded by regular users of the market as falling below the standard reasonably expected of a person in that position' is quite a complicated concept. The standard is set by the hypothetical regular users of the market because it is their confidence that would be damaged.[4] The FSA seems to take the view that 'likely to' generally means little more than a bare possibility.[5] This test could, in theory, be used by 'market insiders' to impose cosy protective standards against 'market outsiders' or to excuse low but common standards of behaviour amongst such insiders. Much therefore depends on the evidential rules and guidance in the COMC.

The three categories of behaviour are the following:

---

1   Financial Services and Markets Act 2000 (hereafter FSMA), section 118.
2   FSMA 2000, section 118(1), (5), (6), (9) and (10).
3   FSA Handbook, MAR 1.3 and 1.11. See below.
4   The official definition is 'a reasonable person who regularly deals on the market in investments of the kind in question', FSMA 2000, section 118(10) and has been described as 'a cousin of the courts' reasonable man'.
5   Policy Statement: Code of Market Conduct (FSA, April 2001) paragraphs 4.10 and 5.3 to 5.5.

(1) behaviour based on information not generally available to those using the market but which if available to a regular user would be likely to be regarded by him as relevant in deciding the terms on which to deal in such investments (ie insider dealing);

(2) behaviour likely to give a regular user a false or misleading impression as to the market or value of such investments (ie misleading statements and practices); or

(3) behaviour that would be regarded by a regular user as likely to distort the market in such investments (ie rigging the market).[1]

20.8.1 The three categories of market abuse

These three categories mirror specific criminal offences, although their scope is not identical. We have already examined the crime of insider dealing; the other offences are now contained in section 397 of FSMA 2000. The definitions in the context of market abuse are objective. Neither intent nor actual knowledge needs to be proved. This wide drafting is deliberate and does give rise to serious definitional problems.

Where the market abuse is of the first type (based on 'insider dealing'), no status as an 'insider' has to be shown. However, information which 'can be obtained by research or analysis by or on behalf of users of a market' is deemed to be 'generally available'.[2] That does stop all 'inequality of information' being sufficient to prove market abuse, but information still does not have to be 'known' to be inside information. It just has to amount to an informational advantage that a regular user of the market would consider relevant and reasonable not to expect the person to exploit. In theory, the FSA could accept that regular users of markets really should expect informational advantages to be exploited unless obtained through a breach of confidence. Then this type of market abuse would be little wider in scope (albeit still easier to prove) than the crime of insider dealing. The FSA's approach to this issue can be seen in the COMC, as explained below.

Examples of the second type of market abuse include the case of an internet user (perhaps a disgruntled employee) publishing a false announcement about a company that, for example, it is going to face a massive compensation suit, just so as to destroy the company's share price, whether or not he stood to gain financially,[3] and a company's failure to inform the markets of a major new development as required by the market or listing rules.[4] Squeezing or cornering a market is probably the clearest example of the third type of market abuse, which otherwise tends to overlap with the second type.

20.8.2 Safe harbours

There are three 'safe harbours', by showing any of which a defendant will be absolved from responsibility for market abuse. These apply if the defendant can show that:

---

1   FSMA 2000, section 118(2).
2   FSMA 2000, section 118(7).
3   See the statement in Standing Committee A, 2 November 1999, cols 683 and 684.
4   Ibid, col 676.

(1) his behaviour conformed to the FSA's rules that exclude market abuse;[1]

(2) his behaviour conformed to certain rules in the City Code on Takeovers and Mergers, accepted by the FSA (with the Treasury's approval) as excluding market abuse;[2] or

(3) his behaviour conformed to FSA guidance in the COMC that the FSA considers excludes market abuse.[3]

There are also two partial defences that exclude potential liability for fines but not public reprimands, namely that the defendant believed, on reasonable grounds, that the behaviour did not amount to direct or indirect market abuse; and that he took all reasonable precautions and exercised all due diligence to avoid engaging in direct or indirect market abuse.[4] The onus is on the defendant in representations to show to the FSA that 'there are reasonable grounds for it to be satisfied' that the defences are met, but the FSA is required to issue a policy indicating the circumstances that would satisfy it. It must also publish the general policy that it will follow on when and how much it will fine.[5] It should be noted that, subject to these points, there is no requirement of *mens rea* in the offence of market abuse.[6] In this respect, the provisions of the Code of Market Conduct are crucial.

20.9 The Code of Market Conduct

The 2000 Act only defines the outer limits of what can constitute market abuse. The FSA is required to draw up a COMC, in effect evidential rules but also offering valuable guidance on the scope of the standard, to help determine whether or not behaviour does amount to market abuse.[7] The purpose of the Code is to allow the FSA the sort of flexibility that the non-statutory Takeover Panel has to adapt and amend its rules in the face of rapidly changing market practices.[8] The COMC may specify behaviour that does and does not amount to market abuse. It may also specify factors that will be taken into account by the FSA when deciding other cases, particularly as it may make different provisions for different persons and circumstances.[9]

The exact status of the Code was much discussed by the Joint Committee that looked at the Bill that became the 2000 Act.[10] It has to 'give appropriate guidance to those determining whether or not behaviour amounts to market abuse'.[11] The FSA has used its power to specify circumstances giving rise to further safe harbours to list nine such circumstances.[12] Otherwise the Code 'may be relied upon so far as it indicates whether or not that behaviour should be taken to amount to market

---

1   FSMA 2000, section 118(8). These are rules relating in particular to stabilisation, Chinese Walls and the provisions of the *Listing Rules* relating to disclosures, their timing, content, method of release and standard of care to be applied.

2   FSMA 2000, section 120.

3   FSMA 2000, section 122(1).

4   FSMA 2000, section 123(2).

5   FSMA 2000, section 124.

6   As to the controversy this caused, see *Gore-Browne on Companies* 44th edn (Jordans, loose-leaf) at 12.40.3.

7   FSMA 2000, section 119(1).

8   See Chapter 19.

9   FSMA 2000, sections 119(2) and (3).

10 Joint Committee, First Report, Part VII.

11 FSMA 2000, section 119(1).

12 MAR 1.1.10, marked 'C' in the COMC.

abuse.'[1] It is not entirely clear who is doing the relying. If it is the FSA, this might make behaviour that it has specified as being market abuse almost unarguably market abuse. However, the Economic Secretary said:

> Where someone breaches the code it will not, however, be conclusive that he has committed market abuse. The FSA will have to prove that his behaviour comes within the definition as set out in [FSMA]. In that case the code will carry evidential weight.[2]

If the relying is by one of the persons whose behaviour is being challenged, this appears to widen the safe harbours but only if the person can show he consciously relied upon factors in the COMC that suggested that his behaviour was not market abuse.

A first draft Code was produced in a Consultation Paper, but proved so controversial that the FSA set up groups to consider the matter further. A second Consultation Paper taking these into account was produced and has formed the basis of the current COMC.[3] All this redrafting produced a COMC that is considerably longer and more complex than the first draft. This is partly because it incorporates the underlying provisions of the 2000 Act, but also because more guidance and examples have been given to try and cut down the number of enquiries with which the FSA will have to deal. The COMC concentrates on elucidating what is 'behaviour', the 'regular user test' and the three categories of market abuse, which it refers to as 'misuse of information', 'false and misleading impressions' and 'distortion'. There is also guidance on what amounts to 'encouraging or requiring' for indirect market abuse.

20.9.1 Behaviour

The COMC does not give a comprehensive definition of behaviour, but does give a list of what might be included, namely dealing in, arranging dealing in, causing, procuring, advising others to deal in, disseminating information on, providing corporate advice on, or managing, qualifying investments (ie those dealt in on a UK market) or dealing in underlying commodities or investments. The Code reiterates that inaction can be market abuse, in particular, failure to make prompt and adequate disclosure when under a legal or regulatory obligation to do so.[4]

20.9.2 Regular user test

The COMC confirms the statutory test as being based on 'hypothetical' not 'actual' regular users. In other words, the fact that a particular market and its regular users accept behaviour that falls within one of the three categories, does not necessarily excuse the behaviour.[5] However, the FSA accepts that this will be a quite exceptional situation and is more likely to lead to new guidance for the future than enforcement against past actions. The rules and normal practices of the markets (including overseas markets) will always be taken into account and will usually be taken as indicating what legitimate behaviour is. However, the FSA is reluctant to let a UK firm channel business through a less regulated overseas market to evade UK rules. Nevertheless, it has stressed:

---

1 FSMA 2000, section 122.
2 Standing Committee A, 2 November 1999, col 685.
3 Consultation Paper 10, FSA, June 1998; Feedback Statement on Responses to CP 10, FSA, June 1999; Consultation Paper 59, FSA, July 2000.
4 Handbook MAR 1.3.
5 MAR 1.2.4 and 1.2.8–1.2.11.

In particular, the new market abuse regime is not intended to affect activities which form part of the normal transaction of business on prescribed markets. Such activities will include, amongst others, position-taking, market making, the execution of customer orders and hedging.[1]

The COMC reiterates that market abuse does not generally require 'any intention or purpose to be present in order for behaviour to fall below the objective standards'.[2] Behaviour can only be abusive if it falls below the reasonable user test, but that test does not impose a uniform standard. It varies according to the person's experience, skill and level of knowledge and the markets and investments concerned.[3]

20.9.3 Misuse of information

To be misuse of information, a person must deal or arrange deals where four conditions have to be met:

(1) The behaviour must be based on the information, that is the information must be a, but not necessarily the, reason for the behaviour.[4]

(2) The information must not be generally available. The FSA does not have to show actual or even constructive knowledge of this status on the part of the user, but a list of factors similar to those in the Criminal Justice Act 1993, section 58(2) and (3)[5] is given to determine whether information is objectively available. Information available by diligent research or observation of a public event, even if through lack of resources or opportunity not available to others, is still deemed to be generally available.[6]

(3) The information must be relevant. The COMC does not require information to be specific or precise or indeed price-sensitive,[7] but they are factors that the FSA will consider along with how current and reliable (near to the source) it is and what other information is available. Where 'soft information' about the future is concerned, the significance of the information and its apparent level of certainty will be important. The information does not have to emanate from a source connected to the investments affected, eg it can be official information or information about the supplies of a commodity.[8]

---

1   Consultation Paper 59, paragraph 6.13. The FSA has confirmed that current Takeover Code rules do not permit or require market abuse, MAR 1.2.12, and reiterated its concern not to prevent innovation, MAR 1.2.13.

2   MAR 1.2.5.

3   MAR, paragraph 1.2.3.

4   MAR, paragraph 1.4.4(1), a similar test to misrepresentation at common law.

5   See **20.4**.

6   MAR, paragraphs 1.4.4(2), 1.4.5–1.4.8.

7   Compare the requirements for insider dealing.

8   MAR, paragraphs 1.4.4(3), 1.4.9–1.4.11. 'Relevant' here seems to be close to the US concept of general materiality: *TSC Industries Ltd v Northway Inc* 426 US 438 (1976). The US Supreme Court has also said when considering the US equivalent of market abuse, Rule 10b–5, that determining the materiality of soft information requires 'balancing of both the indicated probability that the event will occur and the anticipated magnitude of the event', *Basic v Levinson* 485 US 224 (1988) at 238. Exactly how they are balanced off is not so clear, see SEC Financial Reporting Release No 36 7 Fed Sec L Rep (CCH) 501 (1989).

(4) The information must be of the type where disclosure would reasonably be expected either because there is a legal or regulatory requirement, eg listing or transparency rules (disclosable information); or it is publicly announced routinely, eg changes in interest rates or in published credit ratings (announceable information). Information is disclosable or announceable if it is reasonably clear that it will have to be disclosed or announced at some point in the future, but information based merely on research or surveys is never disclosable or announceable.[1]

This fourth condition does narrow the scope of the statutory definition.

The FSA has specified five safe harbours[2] in respect of misuse of information:

(1) The deal was required by a legal or regulatory or contractual obligation.

(2) The deal was not based on or influenced by the information, which will be presumed if Chinese wall requirements have in effect been met, or in fact the individuals in possession of the information were not involved in the deal and they had no contact with those who were.

(3) The information is trading information (ie that someone intends to deal), unless it is about a possible takeover bid or primary market activity. Unlike the market information defence under the Criminal Justice Act 1993, the behaviour does not have to be reasonable.

(4) The information is information about acquiring or disposing of an equity stake (including a takeover), but the dealing is for or on behalf of the potential offeror and for the sole purpose of pursuing the principal transaction. This does not allow dealing aimed at providing financial protection, eg selling a put option that will not lead to delivery of the stock to the potential offeror.

(5) Agreeing to underwrite.

Finally, it should be noted that under misuse of information, it is not a defence that the person did not expect a profit to be made (or loss avoided) from the information. As the FSA has pointed out, 'the mischief being prevented is abuse of the market rather than personal gain.'[3]

20.9.4 False or misleading impression

Rather than give a single definition, the COMC lays down a general requirement that a false or misleading impression is one that is likely (a real, not fanciful, albeit not necessarily 50% plus chance) to give a regular user a materially false or misleading impression (although it may not be the only effect) of, or give thereto a price, value or volume of trading.[4] The COMC then lists four categories of such behaviour:

---

1   MAR, paragraphs 1.4.4(4), 1.4.12–1.4.18. Thus mere consideration of, and certainly negotiations over, a merger, takeover or major contract can be 'disclosable' for this purpose, even though under The Listing Rules, paragraphs 9.1–9.5 there is no immediate obligation to disclose.
2   MAR, paragraphs 1.4.19–1.4.30.
3   Consultation Paper 59, paragraph 6.55.
4   MAR, paragraph 1.5.4.

(1) *Artificial transactions.* In an attempt to distinguish legitimate hedging or customer order transactions from wash trades and other fictitious transactions, the COMC has had to introduce an amazingly complex definition interestingly involving a 'principal rationale' defence. An artificial transaction is where:

(a) a person enters into a transaction or series of transactions in a qualifying investment or relevant product;

(b) the principal effect of the transaction or transactions will be, or will be likely to be, to inflate or depress the apparent supply of, or apparent demand for, or the price or value of a qualifying investment or relevant product such that a false or misleading impression is likely to be given to a regular user; and

(c) the person knows, or could reasonably be expected to know, that the principal effect of the transaction or transactions on the market will be, or will be likely to be, to inflate or depress the apparent supply of, or apparent demand for, or the price or value of a qualifying investment or relevant product such that a false or misleading impression is likely to be given to a regular user. The defence is that the regular user would regard the principal rationale for the transaction in question as a legitimate commercial rationale and the way in which the transaction is to be executed as proper.[1]

The FSA lists a number of factors that it will take into account, like whether the transaction causes a brief price fluctuation and what interest the person might have in that fluctuation.[2]

(2) *Disseminating information.* Here the abusive behaviour is where a person disseminates information which is, or if true would be, relevant information, they know, or could reasonably be expected to know, that the information disseminated is false or misleading; and they disseminate the information in order to create a false or misleading impression (this need not be the sole purpose for disseminating the information but will be an actuating purpose).[3]

This is an odd definition since it is difficult to see how dissemination can be 'in order to create' the impression if the person does not actually know that the information is false or misleading. The problem the FSA is struggling with is to distinguish between the inevitable passing on of market rumours and promulgating them to mislead.[4] In the first draft of the COMC, the behaviour could only be abusive if the person had an interest in the investment. That is still a factor to be considered but since disinformation may be disseminated deliberately before an interest is acquired, it has been dropped as a pre-condition.

(3) *Dissemination of information through an accepted channel.* Where information is to be disseminated, for example, through the Stock Exchange's Regulatory News Service, the person responsible for its submission remains under a positive obligation to take reasonable care to ensure that it is not false or misleading. Accidental misreporting of transactions or figures could be

---

1   MAR, paragraph 1.5.8.
2   MAR, paragraph 1.5.11.
3   MAR, paragraph 1.5.15.
4   Internet bulletin boards and chat rooms have made this form of abuse particularly easy.

market abuse unless the person has taken sufficient care to try and prevent such mistakes.[1]

(4) *Course of conduct*: The test here is similar to that in (1) above, but covers a course of conduct other than transactions causing or likely to cause the impression. Again there is a purpose defence.[2]

The FSA has also specified three safe harbours in respect of false or misleading impressions, namely certain regular market transactions like arbitrage between different markets and stock-lending, reporting legitimate transactions as required by law or regulation and dissemination of false or misleading information by a firm through innocent employees (eg because of Chinese walls).[3]

20.9.5 Distortion

As the FSA admitted:

> it is difficult to define when a market is distorted . . . It is fair to say that regular users of a particular market will be familiar with the normal range or price movements that can be expected in certain market conditions, given the market's structure and the products traded on it. The FSA considers that a price is likely to be distorted when price movements deviate from such expected norms. Such a distortion may not be due to any particular course of behaviour by a market participant, but may be caused instead by extreme market conditions beyond the control of market users.'[4]

There are two circumstances which the COMC defines as abusive distortion:

(1) *Abusive squeezes*: where, with a, although not necessarily the, purpose of distorting prices, a person has a significant influence over supply, demand or delivery mechanisms of an investment or the underlying product, and directly or indirectly holds positions under which he expects delivery of them. It is the combination that can be abusive. Having a significant influence over supply, indeed extracting 'super-normal' profits thereby, is not of itself abusive. The abuse is cornering the market and then using the position to distort.[5]

(2) *Price-positioning*: where a person enters into transactions or a series of transactions where a, although not necessarily the, purpose of which is to move the price materially higher or lower, ie ramping prices of an investment or a relevant index.[6]

20.9.6 Encouraging and requiring

Strictly the COMC only applies to section 118 and not section 123 of the 2000 Act, and so the FSA has only issued guidance on what amounts to 'requiring or encouraging'.[7] However, as the whole point of section 123 is to aggregate the encouraged or required 'actus reus' of another party with the 'mens rea' of the

---

1   MAR, paragraphs 1.5.18–1.5.20. This appears to be the issuer rather than any corporate broker as *The Listing Rules* impose their obligations on the former.
2   This heading is particularly relevant to commodity derivatives markets and the movements of stocks and transport of the underlying commodity.
3   MAR, paragraphs 1.5.23–1.5.29.
4   Consultation Paper 59, paragraphs 6.72.
5   MAR, paragraphs 1.6.13–1.6.18.
6   MAR, paragraphs 1.6.9–1.6.12.
7   MAR, paragraphs 1.8.

instigator, any COMC provisions on both elements must still apply. Otherwise the total package would not amount to market abuse if it had all been done by the instigator.

In such indirect market abuse, the instigator does not have to benefit from the behaviour and the other party does not himself have to be 'guilty'. Most of the guidance is about to whom inside information can be released, but except in the most obvious cases (regulators, advisers, negotiating parties, employees where necessary for their functions), it seems that it can be released only within the terms of the *Listing Rules*, Takeover Code, etc and even then with a warning that it is inside information.[1] Thus, although the market abuse provisions do not mention disclosure, the COMC appears to deem disclosure outside the strict terms of the *Listing Rules*, Takeover Code, etc as being encouragement at least if there is no clear warning as to the information's confidentiality.

Little guidance is given to intermediaries whose clients engage in market abuse. They will not themselves be found to have encouraged or required 'unless the intermediary knew or ought to have known that the originator was engaging in market abuse' in which case they may be committing direct market abuse.[2]

20.9.7 *Conclusions on the COMC*

In summary, market abuse through misuse of information, or disseminating false or misleading information through accepted channels, can be committed negligently. In other cases, defendants have either to show that their principal motive was a proper one or, which is probably harder, to rebut any suggestion of an improper motive. In addition to these slight reductions to the original scope of market abuse, the FSA has created safe harbours and other exceptions, as well as giving helpful examples in the COMC. Given the complexity of all of these definitions of market abuse and the many factors that will be taken into account, the FSA will give informal oral advice as situations arise. It also recognises that there is a need for practitioner training in this area, although the changes created by the market abuse regime are going to be greater for non-practitioners who, until now, have only had to be concerned with the rather ineffective criminal sanctions for insider dealing.

20.10 The EC Directive on Insider Dealing and Market Manipulation

The Directive on insider dealing has been replaced by Directive 2003/6/EC on Insider Dealing and Market Manipulation.[3] By October 2004, a market abuse regime should be adopted across Europe. Although the European obligation to have separate insider dealing provisions has disappeared, it is expected that the UK will retain its criminal regime for insider dealing. Although the European provisions are based on the UK regime, there are significant differences, most notably no regular user test and few safe harbours. As with the UK regime, companies can be found 'guilty' but the Directive does not clarify the position of Chinese Walls and attribution. It is not yet clear what changes the FSA will consider necessary to make the COMC comply with the Directive.[4]

---

1 MAR, paragraphs 1.8.5–1.8.7.
2 MAR, paragraphs 1.8.8.
3 Directive 2003/6/EC (2003) OJ L 96/16.
4 As to implementation, see **2.4**.

20.11   Enforcement

The enforcement of the market misconduct regime was a whole new responsibility for the FSA where its reach extends far beyond those engaged in the business of financial services. It has a choice of sanctions, namely whether to prosecute through the courts for insider dealing, making false or misleading statements or creating a false or misleading impression to the market, to publicly reprimand or impose its own fines for market abuse, or if the defendant is a member of an Recognised Investment Exchange (RIE) or Recognised Clearing House(RCH), leave the matter to their disciplinary procedures. The Treasury does have the power (with the consent of the Attorney General and the Secretary of State) to give written guidance on which course to take. This is a reserve power but may be necessary as the right to prosecute is shared by a number of authorities in England, Wales and Northern Ireland, whereas the power to reprimand or fine is solely the FSA's.[1]

The position is complicated further by the supplementary powers given to the FSA. The FSA and the Secretary of State have the power to apply to the High Court for injunctions to prevent breaches of the criminal provisions; and restitution on behalf of those affected by any such breaches.[2] The FSA alone may apply to the High Court for injunctions, restitution or penalties in respect of market abuse, but it also has the power to order restitution for market abuse itself, subject to following its disciplinary procedures.[3]

20.11.1   Injunctions

The seeking of an injunction does not require there to have been a criminal offence or market abuse, but the court must be satisfied that there is a 'reasonable likelihood' of one, or of one continuing. The injunction may extend to anyone 'knowingly concerned' in a crime (the wide definition of market abuse does not need such an extension). It can also order an asset freeze of those who may have already been involved.[4] However, the FSA will only consider seeking an injunction if it appears serious misconduct has been involved, continuing damage may be done to market confidence or investors' interests and private undertakings (or other intervention in the case of authorised firms) are not considered sufficient.[5]

If the FSA does seek an injunction, it can also ask the court to order restitution and fine the defendant if market abuse has already been committed.[6]

20.11.2   Market abuse proceedings

As seen earlier, one of the distinctive features of the market abuse regime is the power of the FSA to impose a civil penalty, although breaches of the COMC or failure to follow guidance issued by the FSA will not automatically lead to market

---

1   FSMA 2000, section 130. As to prosecutions, see *Gore-Browne on Companies* 44th edn (Jordans, loose-leaf) at 12.42.2. To avoid confusion, the FSA can, when it proposes to investigate or act on market abuse, order any RIE or RCH not to conduct or continue conducting an inquiry under their rules: section 128.
2   FSMA 2000, sections 380 and 382.
3   FSMA 2000, sections 381 and 383 to 386 and 392.
4   FSMA 2000, sections 380 and 381.
5   Enforcement, Chapter 6; Consultation Paper 17, paragraphs 131 to 134.
6   FSMA 2000, sections 129 and 383.

abuse proceedings. The FSA has laid out the criteria that it will consider[1] as it is required to publish a statement of policy on fining for market abuse.[2] The statutory list of criteria require it to consider, when proposing a fine, the seriousness of the behaviour's effect on the market, whether the behaviour was deliberate or reckless and whether the penalty is being imposed on an individual.

The FSA's own provisions on sanctions for market abuse[3] list the following factors:

(1) the adverse effect on the market;
(2) the extent to which the behaviour was deliberate or reckless;
(3) whether the individual is an individual;
(4) the amount of profits accrued or loss avoided;
(5) conduct following the contravention;
(6) disciplinary record and compliance history;
(7) previous action taken by the FSA; and
(8) action taken by other regulatory authorities.

A particular issue that arises with market abuse is the relationship between the FSA and the Takeover Panel. If issues of market abuse arise during a takeover bid, the FSA will consult closely with the Panel,[4] which can itself ask the FSA for assistance. Although some concern has been raised by the Panel that allegations could be used as a tactical weapon in a takeover bid, there is no evidence of that at least as yet and the fact that compliance with the Takeover Code is a safe harbour against an allegation of market abuse is clearly important in this respect.

20.11.3 Restitutionary orders

To maintain orderly settlement in the market, the imposition of a fine does not make a transaction void or unenforceable.[5] However, for any form of market misconduct, the FSA may apply to the High Court for a restitutionary order against anyone; or make a restitutionary award itself against any authorised firm and, in the case of market abuse against anyone, subject to its disciplinary procedures. It may only pursue such restitutionary claims for accrued profits or losses suffered 'as a result' of the contravention or market abuse on behalf of anyone 'to whom the profits ... are attributable; or who has suffered the loss or adverse effect'. There are also reasonable belief and due diligence defences.[6] It is not likely that these orders will be sought or made very often,[7] if only because, as we have seen earlier, there will often be no specific victim of market abuse. In the words of the FSA,[8]

> The rationale for the ... market abuse regime in the UK is ... directed at protecting the integrity of market mechanisms, rather than protecting the interests of any particular group of market users ... We do not anticipate that the exercise of the FSA's restitution powers would normally be appropriate for the purposes of disgorging profits for the benefit of, for example: "[c]ontemporaneous traders" – ie persons

---

1   ENF, paragraphs 14.4.1 and 2.
2   FSMA 2000, sections 124 and 125.
3   ENF, paragraphs 14.6.2 and 14.7.4.
4   ENF, paragraphs 14.9.
5   FSMA 2000, section 131.
6   FSMA 2000, sections 382(1) and (8), 383(1), (3) and (10) and 384(1) and (6).
7   See ENF, Chapter 9.
8   Consultation Paper 17, paragraphs 155 and 158.

trading in the market at the same time as persons found to have been insider dealing or misusing information in a manner which constitutes market abuse [or] [c]ompanies or issuers whose investments have been the subject of manipulation, insider dealing or information misuse.

Chapter 21

Corporate Reconstruction an[...]

PART 1: GENERAL

PART 1: GENERAL

21.1 Introduction

There are a number of options for a company which is experiencing serious financial difficulties. The first is to continue to trade despite the underlying difficulties, in the hope that the crisis will prove to be temporary and capable of being quickly resolved. This may only be possible for so long as the company is able to pay its debts as they fall due or, to the extent that it is not, its creditors are prepared to tolerate late payment. If the financial difficulties are more serious, the company may try to come to some formal arrangement with its creditors regarding the repayment of its debts but, for a company with a large number of creditors, reaching agreement with all of them may not be practicable.[1] There are now a number of statutory procedures which a company can invoke to bind all of its creditors to a voluntary arrangement which has been agreed with some of them. Schemes of arrangement under section 425 of the Companies Act 1985, which require the approval of the court, are considered in **19.18** to **19.23**. Another procedure is the voluntary arrangement scheme contained in Part 1 of the Insolvency Act 1986. The options were widened even further in respect of small companies by the introduction of a new voluntary arrangement procedure in the Insolvency Act 2000 which inserted a new Schedule A1 into the Insolvency Act 1986. The latter procedure is coupled with a moratorium on the enforcement of creditor rights during the currency of the procedure.

Administration and liquidation are governed by the Insolvency Act 1986 as amended by the Enterprise Act 2002, the relevant provisions of which came into force on 15 September 2003. Administration and liquidation are similar procedures, to the extent that they both involve the appointment of a qualified insolvency practitioner to a company and the displacement of the company's existing board of directors from their management function. A company can resolve to go into liquidation (or to be wound up, liquidation and winding-up being synonymous terms) or can be forced compulsorily into liquidation by order of the court. Commonly, although not necessarily, it would be creditors of the company who would seek a winding-up order. Under the Insolvency Act 1986 an administrator could only be appointed by order of the court. The persons who can apply for an administration order include the company itself, and also its creditors. The facility of court appointment is still available but the Enterprise Act 2002 now allows out-of-court appointment either by the company itself or by

---

1 Many large company rescues are accomplished outside formal insolvency procedures by means of consensual 'workouts'. This is the so-called 'London Approach'; on which see the Bank of England website – www.bankofengland.co.uk and also J Flood 'Corporate Recovery: The London Approach' (1995) 11 Insolvency, Law and Practice 82; J Armour and S Deakin 'Norms in Private Insolvency Procedures: The London Approach to the Resolution of Financial Distress' [2001] *Journal of Corporate Law Studies* 21.

...tor who holds a 'qualifying' floating charge. It is likely that court ...s will now be made only in a small minority of cases perhaps in ...where there is some doubt about the validity of the security or where it is ...that the out-of-court appointment of an administrator would not be ...gnised overseas.

...Where liquidation and administration differ most significantly is in their ...intended purpose. Liquidation of a company involves the cessation of its business, the realisation of its assets, the payment of its debts and liabilities, and the distribution of any remaining assets to the members of the company. At the end of a liquidation, a company is wound up and ceases to exist. Administration, in contrast, is designed primarily as a rescue procedure aimed at facilitating the survival of the company's business either in whole or in part. The legislation states that an administrator must perform his functions with the objective of (a) rescuing the company as a going concern, or (b) achieving a better result for the company's creditors as a whole than would be likely if the company were wound up (without first being in administration), or (c) realising property in order to make a distribution to one or more secured or preferential creditors. The statute sets out this hierarchy of objectives and an administrator can only descend the list of objectives if he thinks that it is not reasonably practicable to achieve any of the preceding objectives.

The administration procedure was first introduced into English law by the 1980s insolvency legislation[1] and its enactment resulted largely from recommendations made by a committee under the chairmanship of Sir Kenneth Cork. The Cork Committee was appointed by the Department of Trade and Industry in 1977 to review insolvency law and practice and, in its report,[2] the Committee identified the absence of a statutory procedure to assist ailing but basically sound companies as one of the key deficiencies of insolvency law at that time.

The Insolvency Act 1986 also regulates some aspects of the receivership process. Receivers are persons appointed by secured creditors in order to realise their security. Under the Act, a distinction is drawn between 'administrative receivers' and other receivers. Administrative receivers are, broadly, receivers appointed under floating charges on the whole or substantially the whole of the chargor company's property. The role of administrative receivers is considerably more important than that of other types of receiver. Since it is a remedy for secured creditors, receivership is considered in Chapter 10 but certain aspects of the procedure which are regulated by the Insolvency Act 1986 are mentioned in this chapter. The Enterprise Act 2002 has abolished the right to appoint administrative receivers in the generality of cases insofar as 'new' floating charges are concerned, ie floating charges created after the coming into force of the legislation on 15 September 2003.[3] Holders of floating charges in existence

---

1   The reforms were first enacted in the Insolvency Act 1985. This was replaced by the Insolvency Act 1986, which consolidated the earlier Insolvency Act and also certain other provisions (including some in the Companies Act 1985) relevant to insolvency. The principal factors underlying the legislative reforms and consolidation of insolvency law in 1985 and 1986 are discussed in Fletcher, 'The Genesis of Modern Insolvency Law – An Odyssey of Law Reform' [1989] JBL 365.

2   *Insolvency Law and Practice*, Cmnd 8558 (1982).

3   See section 72A of the Insolvency Act 1986 as inserted by section 250 of the Enterprise Act 2002.

before that date retain the right to appoint an administrative receiver. Moreover, there are still some exceptional cases set out in the legislation where the holders of floating charges may still appoint administrative receivers even after the coming into force of the Enterprise Act 2002 regime.[1]

Insolvency law is a subject in its own right and it is not appropriate in a company law textbook to attempt to provide much more than an overview of the various insolvency procedures and the ways in which they are regulated by the insolvency legislation. Specific aspects of insolvency law, in particular, the manner in which transactions entered into in the twilight period of the company's solvency are liable to be held void or set aside, merit closer examination.

21.2 The definition of insolvency[2]

There are two principal, although not exclusive or exhaustive, tests of insolvency: a company is insolvent if it is unable to pay its debts as they fall due ('cash flow' insolvency); it is also insolvent if its liabilities exceed its assets ('balance sheet' insolvency). Under the Insolvency Act 1986,[3] a company may be compulsorily wound up where the court is satisfied that it is insolvent in either of these senses; where it is demonstrated that a company is or is likely to become insolvent in either of these senses, this may also lead to the appointment of an administrator.[4]

Failure to pay a debt which is due and not disputed amounts to evidence of cash flow insolvency.[5] Thus a company which has a policy of late payment of bills could find itself the subject of a petition for a winding-up or administration order. Such a petition will not be struck out at an early stage as a form of improper pressure and an abuse of the process of the court, because, as Staughton LJ explained in *Taylor's Industrial Flooring*,[6] creditors, not late payers, are more worthy of insolvency law's protection:

> Many people today seem to think that they are lawfully entitled to delay paying their debts when they fall due or beyond the agreed period of credit, if there is one ... This can cause great hardship to honest traders, particularly those engaged in small businesses recently started. Anything which the law can do to discourage such behaviour in my view should be done.

The position is different if there is a bona fide dispute about a debt. A petition based on a disputed debt will usually be dismissed because the procedure is

---

1   Section 72B of the Insolvency Act 1986 and subsequent sections as inserted by section 250 of the Enterprise Act 2002.

2   See, generally, RM Goode, *Principles of Corporate Insolvency Law*, 2nd edn (Sweet & Maxwell, 1997) Chapter 4. The extensive Australian case-law on the various tests of insolvency is reviewed in Keay, 'The Insolvency Factor in the Avoidance of Antecedent Transactions in Corporate Liquidations' (1995) *Monash University Law Review* 305.

3   Sections 122 and 123.

4   See now Schedule B1 to the Insolvency Act 1986, paragraph 11. For a disputed administration application and the consideration of these tests see *Re Colt Telecom Group plc (No. 2)* [2003] B.P.I.R. 324.

5   *Taylor's Industrial Flooring Ltd v M & H Plant Hire Ltd* [1990] BCLC 216, [1990] BCC 44 (where the Court of Appeal held that an order could be granted even though the petitioner had not previously served a statutory demand): *Cornhill Insurance plc v Improvement Services Ltd* [1986] 1 WLR 114, (1986) 2 BCC 98, 942; *Re A Company (No 006273 of 1992)* [1992] BCC 794 (presentation of winding-up petition not restrained despite company's cross-claim for a larger amount).

6   [1990] BCC at 51.

ill-equipped to resolve factual disputes.[1] However, it will not be dismissed where the petitioning creditor has a good arguable case and the dismissal would deprive the petitioner of a remedy, injustice would otherwise result, or there is some other sufficient reason for the petition to proceed.[2]

Balance sheet insolvency for the purpose of winding-up or administration applications is defined as an excess of liabilities over assets, and contingent and prospective liabilities must be taken into account in the assessment. Prospective liabilities include an obligation to repay a loan in one year's time[3] and an undisputed claim for unliquidated damages for more than a nominal amount.[4] Contingent liabilities are distinguishable from prospective liabilities in that a prospective liability is a binding liability which has not yet matured, whilst a contingent liability is a liability which may never mature because it is dependent on an event which may or may not occur.[5] An example of a contingent liability is the liability of a guarantor under a guarantee.

Prospective and contingent liabilities must be 'taken into account' in determining whether there is balance sheet insolvency. In *Re A Company (No 006794 of 1983)*,[6] it was held that taking into account contingent liabilities does not mean simply adding up the principal amount of those liabilities and deducting the total from the assets, but rather involves considering whether, and if so when, they are likely to becoming present liabilities. An examination of the likelihood of contingent liabilities become present liabilities also takes place when liabilities are admitted for proof in a winding-up and, at that stage, contingent liabilities may be discounted to reflect the fact that they are uncertain. The Insolvency Act 1986 does not specify how contingent liabilities (and indeed prospective liabilities which are not yet certain in amount) are to be valued for the purpose of the balance sheet insolvency test but, presumably, some guidance would be had from the practice of admission of such liabilities for proof on winding-up.

The balance sheet insolvency test also requires valuation of assets. Valuation, however, is not an exact science and different valuers might well disagree about the value of an asset. A particular difficulty is that the Act does not indicate whether the assets are to be valued on the basis of the company's business being sold as a going concern or on the basis of the assets being broken up and sold separately; the former basis would usually be expected to produce a higher figure.

The company's assets include any unpaid capital unless this has been declared reserve capital under section 120 or 124 of the Companies Act 1985;[7] but the prospect of acquiring future assets from continued trading or from other sources is ignored.[8]

---

1   *Re Claybridge Shipping Co SA* [1981] Com LR 107, [1997] 1 BCLC 572 (CA); *Alipour v Ary* [1997] 1 BCLC 557 (CA); *Re A Company (No 006685 of 1996)* [1997] 1 BCLC 639.

2   *Re Claybridge Shipping Co SA* [1981] Com LR 107, [1997] 1 BCLC 572 (CA).

3   *Byblos Bank SAL v Al Khudhairy* (1986) 2 BCC 99, 550 at 99, 562.

4   *Re Dollar Land Holdings plc* [1994] 1 BCLC 404.

5   *Re British Equitable Bond and Mortgage Corp Ltd* [1910] 1 Ch 574; *Winter v IRC* [1961] 3 All ER 855; *Stonegate Securities v Gregory* [1980] Ch 576, in particular at 579 *per* Buckley LJ.

6   [1986] BCLC 261. Although this case concerned an earlier statutory provision, the reasoning would still seem to be applicable.

7   *Re Bristol Joint Stock Bank* (1890) 44 Ch D 703; *Re European Life Assurance Society* (1870) LR 9 Eq 122; *Re Suburban Hotel Co* (1867) 2 Ch App 737.

8   *Re European Life Assurance Society,* above; but the prospect of acquiring further assets before future liabilities are due will be relevant where the court is exercising a discretion; *Byblos Bank SAL v Al-Khudhairy,* above at 99, 562.

21.3   The regulation of insolvency practitioners

Until the reforming legislation of the 1980s, it was possible to act as a liquidator or receiver without holding any relevant professional qualifications or having any previous experience. This could be exploited by unscrupulous persons to their own advantage, because the controllers of a company could elect to put the company into liquidation and appoint a sympathetic liquidator who, through ignorance, inexperience or complicity, would agree to the sale of the company's business at a low price to another company controlled by the same persons. This stratagem allowed the controllers to continue the business free from the burden of existing debts; meanwhile the creditors of the old company were left with claims which, in all probability, would never be paid.

Under the Insolvency Act 1986, it is an offence for an unqualified person to act as an insolvency practitioner in relation to a company.[1] Apart from the Official Receiver, who is regulated as an officer of the court, all liquidators, provisional liquidators, administrators, administrative receivers and supervisors of voluntary arrangements act as insolvency practitioners.[2] The principal way[3] of obtaining the appropriate qualification is through membership of one of the recognised professional accountancy bodies[4] or of The Law Society.[5] Specific restrictions prevent undischarged bankrupts, persons disqualified under the Company Directors Disqualification Act 1986 and persons subject to the mental health legislation from acting as insolvency practitioners,[6] and there are also bonding requirements.[7] Only individuals may act as insolvency practitioners.[8]

PART 2: VOLUNTARY ARRANGEMENTS

21.4   The use of voluntary arrangements

The Insolvency Act 1986 provides a procedure for voluntary arrangements between a company and its creditors and members (CVAs). A voluntary arrangement approved by the majority of creditors and members of a company in accordance with the Act can be made binding on all of them. Under the Insolvency Act 1986 as originally enacted, the procedure governing voluntary arrangements was less formal than that governing administration, though administration procedures have now been steamlined by the Enterprise Act 2002 in particular by the introduction of the facility for out-of-court appointments of

---

1   Section 389. But see now section 389A which permits the Secretary of State to authorise 'company doctors' to act as nominees and supervisors of voluntary arrangements.
2   See also section 388.
3   The Secretary of State can also grant direct authorisations: section 392. This function can be (but, as yet, has not been) delegated to a 'competent authority'.
4   Guidance notes issued by the accountancy bodies (and also by the Secretary of State) indicate that 'independence' is a further requirement. If, eg, one of the partners of an individual who is otherwise qualified to act as an insolvency practitioner has in the previous three years been the auditor of a company, that individual is not qualified to act as an insolvency practitioner in relation to that particular company.
5   Section 390(2). See generally Part XIII and the Insolvency Practitioners Regulations 1990, SI 1990/439.
6   Section 390(4).
7   Section 390(3) and the Insolvency Practitioners Regulations 1990.
8   Section 390(1).

administrators. In practice, however, 'stand alone' voluntary arrangements were relatively uncommon when compared to the overall number of insolvencies. Voluntary arrangements combined with administrations are more common.[1] One important factor which may explain why the 'stand alone' voluntary arrangement procedure has not been more widely used wass the absence of a moratorium on creditors' rights. The company is not given a breathing space in which to try to come to an arrangement with its creditors. Whilst negotiations are ongoing, individual creditors can continue to press for payment and can commence or continue proceedings for that purpose; secured creditors can enforce their security; landlords, suppliers of goods on hire purchase and others who have supplied goods to the company on credit terms can continue to exercise their contractual rights. The administration procedure does provide a moratorium and it is for this reason that a voluntary arrangement is often combined with that procedure.

Under the Insolvency Act 2000 provision is now made for reform of the company voluntary arrangement procedure by the introduction of a moratorium. The legislation, as drafted, is limited in its effect because the moratorium is limited to small companies, defined by reference to section 247 of the Companies Act 1985 which uses turnover, balance sheet totals and number of employees as the qualifying conditions.[2] The reform had been preceded by extensive consultation exercises.[3] A statutory moratorium in company voluntary arrangements is viewed as a measure that will help to facilitate the creation of a more failure-tolerant environment and a rescue culture that will promote business enterprise and entrepreneurship.

The Insolvency Act 2000 also made some changes to the voluntary arrangement without a moratorium procedure. The effect of the legislation is that there are now two types of voluntary arrangement procedure:

(1) CVAs without a moratorium which are governed by Part 1 Insolvency Act 1986 as amended by Insolvency Act 2000.
(2) CVAs with a moratorium as governed by Insolvency Act 2000 which inserted a new Schedule A1 into the Insolvency Act 1986. The substantive provisions are contained in this schedule.

Even if a company satisfies the eligibility criteria for obtaining a CVA with a moratorium the directors may prefer to go down the non-moratorium route as this procedure is more informal and affords greater privacy. If it is desired to obtain the benefit of a moratorium the old-style CVA can still be coupled with the appointment of an administrator. The latter appointment brings about a moratorium.

---

1   Section 8(3)(b) to the Insolvency Act 1986 as originally drafted specifies the approval of a voluntary arrangement as one of the purposes for which an administration order may be made.
2   Schedule A1 to the Insolvency Act 1986.
3   *The Insolvency Act 1986. Company Voluntary Arrangements and Administration Orders. A Consultative Document* (DTI, 1993) and comments by Rajak (1993) IL&P 111; Penn [1994] JIBL 3; Wood (1993) 4 PLC 4. *The Insolvency Act 1986. Revised Proposals for a New Company Voluntary Arrangement* (DTI, 1995). *Our Competitive Future: Building the Knowledge Driven Economy* (DTI, 1998) paragraph 2.13, noted by TS Braithwaite (1999) 3 Comm LJ 19. *A Review of Company Rescue and Business Reconstruction Mechanisms* (Insolvency Service, 1999).

21.5 CVA without a moratorium – Part 1 Insolvency Act 1986 as amended

A voluntary arrangement is based upon a proposal to the company and its creditors for a composition in satisfaction of its debts or a scheme of arrangement of its affairs. The proposal must provide for some person to act as trustee or otherwise to supervise its implementation. That person is referred to as the 'nominee' and must be a licensed insolvency practitioner.[1] An administrator or liquidator may designate himself as the nominee of a proposed voluntary arrangement, although he is not required to do so.

The proposal may be made:

(1) by the directors of the company (where the company is not in administration or being wound up);
(2) by the administrator, where an administration order is in force; and
(3) by the liquidator, where the company is being wound up.[2]

21.6 Outline of the procedure

In broad outline, the procedure governing a voluntary arrangement is as follows. Where the designated nominee is someone other than the existing administrator or liquidator of a company, he must make a report to the court stating whether he considers that the proposal should be considered at meetings of creditors and of the company.[3] The nominee will usually work closely with the proposers of the arrangement in making this report but, in any event, there are statutory obligations on the proposers to provide him with information.[4] The role of the court at this stage is largely administrative. It does not vet the proposal nor approve the nominee's report. A report to the court is not required where an administrator or liquidator designates himself as the nominee.

The nominee must then summon meetings of the creditors and of the company[5] to decide whether to approve the proposed voluntary arrangement.[6] The meetings may modify the proposal in certain respects, but the modifications must not be so extensive as to change the character of the proposal so that it is no longer a composition in satisfaction of the company's debts or a scheme of arrangement in respect of its affairs.[7] Also, the meetings are specifically prohibited from approving any proposal that would interfere with the rights of a

---

1   Section 1(2). But see however section 389A Insolvency Act 1986 as introduced by section 4 of the Insolvency Act 2000 which allows the Secretary of State to authorise persons who are not qualified insolvency practitioners to act as nominees and supervisors of CVAs. This measure is designed to promote the rescue culture by opening up CVA work to so-called 'company doctors', ie specialists in corporate turnaround who are not necessarily insolvency practititoners.
2   Section 1.
3   Section 2. The period for submitting this report is 28 days or such longer period as the court may allow.
4   Section 2(3) and rules 1.3 (directors' proposal) and 1.10 (administrator's or liquidator's proposal).
5   Section 3. Where the nominee is not the liquidator or administrator, the summoning of meetings is subject to directions from the court: section 3(1). The procedural aspects of the meetings are governed by the Insolvency Rules 1986, Part 1, chapter 5.
6   Section 4.
7   Section 4(2).

secured creditor to enforce his security or with the priority of a debt which is afforded preferential status by the Insolvency Act 1986, unless the secured creditor or, as the case may be, preferential creditor concurs.[1]

Under the unreformed CVA procedure both meetings of member and creditors had to approve an proposed voluntary arrangement but this is no longer the case. The effect of section 4A is that where different decisions are taken at each of the two meetings the decision taken at the creditors' meeting shall prevail subject to the right of a member to go to court to challenge this conclusion within 28 days of the date of the creditors' meeting. On such an application the court has wide discretionary powers including the power to make such order as it thinks fit.[2]

21.7 The effect of the approval of the voluntary arrangement

If the voluntary arrangement is approved by the requisite majorities at the creditors' and company meetings,[3] it:

(1) takes effect as if made by the company at the creditors' meeting; and
(2) binds every person who in accordance with the Rules had notice of, and was entitled to vote at, the meeting (whether or not he was present or represented at the meeting) or would have been so entitled if he had had notice of it

as if he were a party to the voluntary arrangement.[4]

Creditors who are entitled to vote at the meeting include those whose debts are unliquidated or unascertained provided the chairman agrees to put an estimated minimum value on them,[5] as well as those who debts are liquidated and presently due.

The court may, if the company is being wound up or an administration order is in force, stay the winding-up or discharge the administration order and give such directions with respect to the conduct of the winding-up or the administration as it thinks appropriate for facilitating the implementation of the approved voluntary arrangement.[6]

21.8 Implementation of the proposal

Once a voluntary arrangement has been approved, the nominee becomes its supervisor.[7] The supervisor's role is to carry out the functions conferred on him

---

1   Section 4(3) and (4). The interpretation of the term 'security' can be problematic: cf *March Estates plc v Gunmark Ltd* [1996] BPIR 439 and *Razzaq v Pala* [1998] BCC 66.

2   Section 4A(6) of the Insolvency Act 1986.

3   The detailed procedural aspects are governed by the Insolvency Rules 1986 (rules 1.13–1.21). Broadly, more than three-quarters in value of the creditors present in person or by proxy and voting on the resolution must support the arrangement for it to become effective (rule 1.19); at the meeting of members the equivalent requirement is that more than one half in value (determined by reference to voting rights) of the members present in person or proxy and voting on the resolution must support the arrangement (rule 1.20).

4   Section 5. *Inland Revenue Commissioners v Adam and Partners Ltd* [1999] 2 BCLC 730, applying *Johnson v Davies* [1999] Ch 117. The facility to bind unknown creditors is very valuable and was introduced by section 2 and Schedule 2 of the Insolvency Act 2000.

5   *Doorbar v Alltime Securities Ltd* [1995] BCC 1149 (CA).

6   Section 5(3), subject to the qualification in section 5(4).

7   Section 7(2).

by the arrangement.[1] The supervisor must notify all creditors and members of the company who are bound by the arrangement when it is complete and must provide them with an account of receipts and payments.[2] A copy of the notice and account sent to the creditors and members must also be filed with the Registrar of Companies and the court.[3]

21.9 Challenging the approval of a voluntary arrangement or the supervisor's decisions

A specific right to challenge the decision to approve a voluntary arrangement is conferred on certain persons by section 6. The challenge may be based on the substantive ground that the arrangement unfairly prejudices the interests of a creditor, member or contributory of the company, or may relate to material irregularities at or in relation to either of the meetings. The persons with standing to bring a claim under section 6 are those who were entitled to vote at either of the meetings, the nominee or a replacement nominee, and the company's liquidator or administrator.[4] The challenger must move swiftly, because an application under section 6 may not be made after the period of 28 days beginning with the first day on which the results of the creditors' and company meetings were reported to the court.[5] Any irregularity at or in relation to a meeting does not invalidate the approval given by that meeting unless it is challenged successfully under section 6.[6]

Where the court is satisfied that one or other of the grounds is made out, it may revoke or suspend approvals given by the meetings and may give directions for the summoning of further meetings, either to consider a new proposal from the person who made the original proposal or to reconsider the original proposal.[7] The court itself has no power to devise a new proposal for consideration at creditors' and company meetings.

Any of the company's creditors or any other person who is dissatisfied by any act, omission or decision of the supervisor can apply to court. The court can confirm, reverse or modify the supervisor's act or decision, give him directions or make such other order as it thinks fit.[8]

The court may also appoint substitute supervisors.[9]

---

1   Ibid.
2   Rule 1.29(1) and (2).
3   Rule 1.29(3).
4   Section 6(2).
5   Section 6(3). An application under the equivalent provision in the personal insolvency regime (section 262) failed in *Doorbar v Alltime Securities Ltd* [1995] BCC 1149 (CA). See also *Re Sweatfield Ltd* [1997] BCC 744 (application under section 6; held no material irregularity established).
6   Section 6(7).
7   Section 6(4). If the original proposer fails to put forward a new proposal in accordance with the court's direction, the court must revoke the direction and revoke or suspend the earlier approvals: section 6(5). The court may also give supplemental directions: section 6(6).
8   Section 7(3).
9   Section 7(5) and (6).

21.10   Terminating a voluntary arrangement

The supervisor himself has a general right to apply to the court for directions in relation to any particular matter arising under the voluntary arrangement, and may also apply to the court for a winding-up order or an administration order to be made.[1] Such an application may become necessary if the company fails to fulfil the terms of a CVA whether by failing to meet a payment due to creditors or otherwise. There has been substantial litigation on the effect of subsequent liquidation on the CVA and on the status of funds collected by the CVA supervisor prior to liquidation.[2] Fortunately, a lot of the difficulties in this area have been clarified by the decision of the Court of Appeal in *Re NT Gallagher & Son Ltd*.[3] The court said that so long as the terms of the arrangement were clear, funds collected by a supervisor were held on trust exclusively for the benefit of the CVA participants. Moreover, the fact that the CVA proposal did not use the terminology of 'trust' was not material. The fate of the CVA trust and its survival on liquidation depended on the terms of the arrangement. The court said that to treat a trust created by a CVA as continuing notwithstanding the liquidation of the company did not produce such unfairness to post-CVA creditors so as to warrant a termination default rule. Peter Gibson LJ observed:

> Further, as a matter of policy, in the absence of any provision in the CVA as to what should happen to trust assets on liquidation of the company, the court should prefer a default rule which furthers rather than hinders what might be taken to be the statutory purpose of Part 1 of the Act. Parliament plainly intended to encourage companies and creditors to enter into CVAs so as to provide creditors with a means of recovering what they are owed without recourse to the more expensive means provided by winding up or administration, thereby giving many companies the opportunity to continue to trade.

It should be noted that creditors whose debts have not been fully discharged by CVA trust moneys may prove for the balance in the liquidation.

21.11   Reinforcing the integrity of the law

Parts of the reforms of the CVA procedure introduced by the Insolvency Act 2000 were designed to reinforce the integrity of the law. The new section 6A makes it an offence for a company officer to seek to obtain the approval of a CVA by making false representations. Section 7A imposes a 'whistle blowing' obligation on a nominee/supervisor.[4] If it appears to the nominee/supervisor that a past or present officer of the company has been guilty of an offence in connection with the moratorium or voluntary arrangement he is obliged to report the matter to the appropriate authority, ie the Secretary of State, forthwith. He is also obliged to provide the Secretary of State with information and documents in his possession that relate to the matter in question.

---

1   Section 7(4). An example of such an application is *Re FMS Financial Management Services Ltd* (1989) 5 BCC 191.
2   See eg *Re Excalibur Airways Ltd* [1998] 1 BCLC 436; Re *Maple Environmental Services Ltd* [2000] BCC 93; *Welsby v Brelec Installations* [2000] 2 BCLC 576; *Re Kudos Glass Ltd* [2000] 1 BCLC 390.
3   [2002] 1 WLR 2380.
4   Inserted by section 2 and Schedule 2 to the Insolvency Act 2000.

21.12 CVAs with a moratorium – Insolvency Act 1986, Schedule A1

It is for the directors of the ailing company to apply for the moratorium. They must produce sufficient evidence that the proposed voluntary arrangement has a reasonable prospect of success and that the company is likely to have sufficient funds during the moratorium to enable it to carry on business. It is provided by section 1A of the Insolvency Act 1986 that where the directors of an eligible company intend to make a proposal for a voluntary arrangement, they may take steps as laid down in Schedule A1 of the Insolvency Act 1986 to obtain a moratorium.

Under paragraph 4(1) of Schedule A1 a company may not apply for a moratorium if it is subject to a subsisting insolvency procedure. There are also anti-abuse provisions to prevent the company from having the benefit of a number of unsuccessful moratoria in rapid succession. A moratorium, for example, is precluded if a previous moratorium has been in force during the previous 12 months unless the moratorium ended with the coming into effect of a voluntary arrangement which has not ended prematurely. Certain companies including insurance and banking companies and companies connected with the financial markets are excluded from the possibility of obtaining a moratorium.

Directors proposing a moratorium are obliged to submit to the nominee the terms of the proposed voluntary arrangement together with a statement of affairs and any additional information requested by the nominee which the latter needs to form a statement of opinion.[1] Before a moratorium can be obtained the nominee is required to form a favourable opinion as to the prospects for obtaining approval of the proposal and as to whether the company will have sufficient funds to carry on business during the moratorium. The nominee should also indicate whether meetings of the company and its creditors should be called.[2] The directors must then file with the court the terms of the proposed arrangement, a statement of the company's affairs, a statement that the company meets the moratorium eligibility criteria, a statement of the nominee's agreement to act and also the statement of the nominee's opinion.[3]

In general the effect of the moratorium in relation to a company voluntary arrangement (CVA) is the same as that which applies to a company in administration. The major difference lies in the fact that the directors maintain the management reins during a CVA. Under the moratorium:[4]

(1)   no winding up petition may be presented except on public interest grounds or under the Financial Services and Markets Act 2000 or Banking Act 1987.
(2)   An administration application cannot be made.
(3)   No meeting of the company can be called or requisitioned except with the consent of the nominee or by leave of the court.
(4)   A voluntary winding up resolution cannot be passed.
(5)   An administrative receiver cannot be appointed.

---

1   Schedule A1 to the Insolvency Act 1986, paragraph 6(1).
2   Schedule A1, paragraph 6(2).
3   Schedule A1, paragraph 7.
4   See generally Schedule A1, paragraph 12.

(6)   Steps cannot be taken to enforce any security over the company's property or to repossess goods in the company's possession under any hire-purchase agreement except by leave of the court.

(7)   Where the company has rented premises a landlord cannot forfeit the lease by peaceable re-entry for non-payment of rent or breach of any other condition of the lease except with the leave of the court and subject to such requirements as the court may impose.

(8)   Legal proceedings may not be commenced or continued or executions levied against the company or its property except with the leave of the court.

(9)   Any pending winding up petitions will be stayed and section 127 of the Insolvency Act 1986, which invalidates dispositions of the company's property after the presentation of a winding up petition, will be disallowed.

(10)   A floating charge is precluded from crystallising during the moratorium.[1]

(11)   Security granted by the company during the moratorium may only be enforced if there were reasonable grounds for believing that it would benefit the company.[2]

(12)   Public utility suppliers may not require the discharge of outstanding debts as a condition of making further supplies during the period of the moratorium but a personal guarantee of payment may be obtained from the nominee.[3]

There are other prohibitions which attract criminal liability on the part of the company and any company officer who permitted the contravention without reasonable excuse. The company may not obtain credit greater than £250 without informing the creditor that a moratorium is in force[4] nor may a company dispose of its property otherwise than in the ordinary course of business unless there are reasonable grounds for believing that the disposal will benefit the company and the disposal has been approved by committee or the nominee.[5] In addition the company may not pay a pre-existing debt or liability unless there are reasonable grounds for believing that it will benefit the company and the payment has been approved by the nominee or committee.

A company may dispose of property in its possession that is subject to a hire purchase agreement or to a security interest provided that the holder of the proprietary interest consents or the court grants leave.[6] Where the security was, as created, a fixed charge the proprietary rights of the charge holder are transferred to the proceeds of sale. Where the property was subject to a hire purchase agreement or a fixed charge it is a condition of any consent or leave that:

(1)   the net proceeds of the disposal; and

---

1   Schedule A1, paragraph 13.
2   Schedule A1, paragraph 14.
3   Section 233 of the Insolvency Act 1986 as amended.
4   Ibid, paragraph 17
5   Ibid, paragraph 18.
6   Ibid, paragraph 20. The terms of this provision are somewhat curiously drafted and are to be contrasted with, paragraphs 70–72 Schedule B1 to the Insolvency Act 1986 which applies to a company administration.

(2) a sum equalling the deficit between the net proceeds of disposal and the net amount which would be realised by a sale of the assets at market value as determined by the court

must be applied towards discharging the sums secured by the fixed charge or payable under the hire-purchase agreement.[1]

The moratorium comes into force on various filings being made.[2] It lasts initially for a maximum period of 28 days and during this time meetings of the company and creditors must be held to consider the proposal. There is provision for the moratorium to be extended by a majority of creditors to a date not later than two months from the date on which the meetings are first held.[3] The nominee must inform a meeting that is considering an extension of various matters; of the nominee's work to date; the expenditure to date and the projected spend during the period of the extension.[4] An extended moratorium may always be cut short by the decision of a creditors' meeting.[5]

The relevant meetings must decide whether or not to approve the proposals with or without modifications and it is specifically provided that secured creditors and preferential creditors must consent to any proposals that adversely affect their rights.[6] Directors are obliged to give the nominee at least seven days notice before the meetings of modifications that they intend to propose.[7] The procedures relating to the approval of proposals, effectiveness of decisions taken at meetings, challenges to decisions and implementation of CVAs are basically the same as for CVAs without a moratorium under Part 1 of the Insolvency Act 1986.[8]

During the currency of a moratorium a nominee is required to maintain an ongoing surveillance of the company's affairs pertaining to the prospects of the arrangement being approved and the sufficiency of funds and nominees who form a negative opinion on either of these matters are required to withdraw their consent to act.[9] The same requirement to withdraw consent obtains if the nominee becomes aware that the company was not eligible for a moratorium or where the directors fail to provide sufficient information to enable the monitoring obligations to be fulfilled.[10] Withdrawal of consent brings the moratorium to a premature conclusion. A nominee who fails to act or acts precipitately may find his conduct subject to challenge under Schedule A1, paragraph 26, which empowers any person affected by the moratorium who is dissatisfied with the conduct of the nominee to apply to the court. The court may make a wide variety of orders to redress the situation complained of.

---

1   Schedule A1, paragraph 26.
2   Ibid, paragraph 8.
3   Ibid, paragraph 32 and Rule 1.19(2) Insolvency Rules 1986.
4   Ibid, paragraphs 32(3) and 32(4).
5   Ibid, paragraph 32(6).
6   Ibid, paragraph 31(5).
7   Ibid, paragraph 31(7).
8   Ibid, paragraphs 36–38.
9   Ibid, paragraph 24.
10   Ibid, paragraph 25.

PART 3: ADMINISTRATION

21.13   The role of administration

The statutory framework of the administration procedure is contained in Part II of the Insolvency Act 1986. The Enterprise Act 2002 revamped completely the administration procedure and substituted a whole new Part II.[1] The relevant law is now essentially contained in Schedule B1 to the Insolvency Act 1986 as supplemented by the Insolvency Rules 1986 (as amended).

The administration regime was brought into being by the Insolvency Act 1986 following the recommendations of the 1982 Cork Committee on Insolvency Law and Practice report.[2] Cork suggested the introduction of a wholly new corporate insolvency mechanism designed primarily to facilitate the rescue and rehabilitation of the viable parts of the company in financial difficulties. Cork tended to view receivership through somewhat rose-tinted business rescue spectacles stating that the power of the floating charge holder to appoint a receiver and manager of the whole property and undertaking of a company has been of 'outstanding benefit to the general public and to society as a whole . . .'[3] adding:

> Such receivers and managers are normally given extensive powers to manage and carry on the business of the company. In some cases, they have been able to restore an ailing enterprise to profitability, and return it to its former owners. In others, they have been able to dispose of the whole or part of the business as a going concern. In either case, the preservation of the profitable parts of the enterprise has been of advantage to the employees, the commercial community, and the general public.

The Cork Committee envisaged that the new administration procedure would be used primarily in cases where the company had not granted a debenture secured by a floating charge. It did not wish however that the procedure should be confined to such cases.[4]

As enacted in Part II of the Insolvency Act 1986, the administration order procedure contained a number of features which curtailed its effectiveness.[5] First, the procedure was too heavily court-centred. Only the court was empowered to appoint an administrator on application to it by the company or its directors or by a creditor of the company. There was no facility whereby out-of-court appointments could be made – whether by the company or by its creditors. Secondly, a floating charge holder had an effective veto on the appointment of an administrator. In one sense this was because administration was viewed as an alternative to receivership but also because during the period of administration the company, under the control of the administrator, could continue to trade and incur debts and these debts were payable in priority to claims secured by the floating charge but not in priority to those secured by a fixed charge. A floating

---

1   The 'old' administration regime contained in the former Part 11 remains in force as far as building societies and certain public utility companies are concerned – see section 249 of the Enterprise Act 2002.

2   *Insolvency Law and Practice*, Cmnd 8558 (1982). Prentice, Oditah and Segal, 'Administration: The Insolvency Act 1986, Part II' [1994] LMCLQ 487 considers further the reasons for the introduction of the administration procedure, its evolution and effect.

3   Cmnd 8558, at para 495.

4   Cmnd 8558, at para 497.

5   See generally Insolvency Service *A Review of Company Rescue and Business Reconstruction Mechanism, Report by the Review Group* (May 2000) and also Hunter 'The nature and functions of a rescue culture' [1999] JBL 491.

charge holder could find his security devalued by post-administration debts and liabilities and giving the floating charge holder power to prevent this state of affairs from developing was seen as a necessary balancing measure. Thirdly, there was no statement of overarching statutory objectives or hierarchy of purposes. Section 8(3) of the Insolvency Act 1986 specified various purposes for whose achievement an administration order might be made namely:

(a) the survival of the company, and the whole or any part of its undertaking, as going concern;
(b) the approval of a voluntary arrangement;
(c) the sanctioning of a compromise or arrangement between the company and its creditors; and
(d) a more advantageous realisation of the company's assets than would be effected on a winding up.

An administration order could also specify more than one purpose but there was no explanation in the legislation as to whether one purpose could take precedence over another.

A fourth feature of the administration order procedure that may have detracted from its usefulness was the presence of gaps in the statutory moratorium. After the presentation of a petition for the appointment of an administrator and during the currency of an administration order there was a embargo laid down by statute on the enforcement of security rights and other claims against the company. While the embargo was pretty extensive in its ambit it did not cover situations where a landlord of business premises occupied by a company in administration forfeited the lease for breach of covenant and peacefully retook possession.[1]

Fifthly, the administration procedure was somewhat open-ended. There were no time-limits apart from a requirement to hold a meeting of creditors within three months of appointment and to lay a statement of the administrator's proposals before such a meeting. This period could be extended by the court. The administration procedure did not to an end automatically on the expiry of a particular time frame or the occurrence of another event. There was the possibility that administration might drag on indefinitely. Basically an administrator was required to apply to the court for the administration order to be discharged if it appeared to him that the purpose or each of the purposes specified in the administration order had been achieved or was no longer capable of achievement.[2]

Sixthly, the exit routes from administration into liquidation were procedurally difficult and cumbersome to negotiate. For example creditors' voluntary liquidation is a more cost effective alternative than compulsory liquidation under the control of the court but there were considerable difficulties in going down the creditors' voluntary liquidation route.[3]

---

1   See generally *Re Lomax Leisure Ltd* [2000] BCC 352 where the various authorities were analysed by Neuberger J.
2   Section 18(2) of the Insolvency Act 1986 as originally drafted.
3   For a discussion of some of the problems see *Re Mark One (Oxford Street) plc* [1998] BCC 984.

21.14 The Enterprise Act 2002 and the Rescue Culture

The Enterprise Act 2002 must be seen against the backdrop of the stakeholder rhetoric of the 'New Labour' government elected in 1997.[1] The statute aims to make the UK a better place in which to do business. Even the title of the legislation suggests a new social order. Whereas before we had insolvency legislation, now we have enterprise law.[2] The legislation was designed to strengthen the foundations of an enterprise economy by establishing an insolvency regime that encouraged honest but unsuccessful entrepreneurs to persevere despite initial failure. In other words, the aim was to promote a culture in which companies that could be rescued were, in fact, rescued.[3]

The Enterprise Act 2002 can also be viewed in the context of the late 1990s technology and internet driven boom but at the same time, with a government fearful of the economic downturn and recession of the early 1990s.[4] There was a feeling that suitable mechanisms should be in place to prevent or at least to mitigate the consequences of banks 'cutting rough' in any future recession.[5] To this end the receivership model was seen as too heavily creditor oriented.[6] Essentially the concern was that the power to appoint a receiver has been too readily used by banks to protect their investment and that the effect of this was to drive too many companies unnecessarily into insolvency.

The new legislation borrows from overseas models but it is not a direct transplant. There has been a lot of refashioning and reshaping. One distinguished US commentator has observed:[7]

> ... if an American banker is very, very good, when he dies he will go to the United Kingdom. British banks have far more control than an American secured lender could ever hope to have. Receiverships on the British model are unknown and almost unthinkable in the US. A US banker could barely imagine a banker's Valhalla in which

---

1   For a full theoretical discussion of these issues, see V Finch, *Corporate Insolvency Law: Perspectives and Principles* (Cambridge University Press, 2002) and in particular chapters 8 and 9 and see also V Finch 'Re-Invigorating Corporate Rescue' [2003] JBL 527; S Frisby 'In Search of a Rescue Regime: the Enterprise Act 2002' (2004) 67 MLR 247; A Belcher *Corporate Rescue* (Sweet & Maxwell, 1997) The specialist insolvency journals *Insolvency Lawyer*, *Insolvency Intelligence* and *Insolvency Law and Practice* also contain a wealth of literature on the new administration procedure and practical problems thrown up by the same.

2   The legislation was preceded by a 2001 White Paper *Productivity and Enterprise: Insolvency – A Second Chance* Cmnd 5234 (2001).

3   In the *Productivity and Enterprise* White Paper it was suggested that the result would be a procedure that would be as flexible and cost-effective as administrative receivership, but one in which the administrator will owe a duty of care to all creditors, unsecured creditors will have the opportunity for input and participation and the process will be subject to the oversight and direction of the court in a public and transparent way.

4   See the discussion in S Davies (ed.) *Insolvency and the Enterprise Act 2002* (Jordans, 2003) at pp 13–14.

5   See the statement by the government minister in *Hansard*, Standing Committee B, Enterprise Bill, 15th Sitting, 9 May 2002 at col 602.

6   The White Paper *Productivity and Enterprise: Insolvency a Second Chance* (2001) at para 2.5 talked about 'making changes which will tip the balance in favour of collective insolvency proceedings – proceedings in which all creditors participate, under which a duty is owed to all creditors and in which all creditors may look at o an office holder for an account of his dealings with company's assets'.

7   See Westbrook 'A Comparison of Bankruptcy Reorganisation in the US with the Administration Procedure in the UK' (1990) 6 Insolvency Law and Practice 86 at 87.

a bank could veto a reorganisation as a UK bank may effectively veto an administration by appointing an administrative receiver.

The US Bankruptcy Code has traditionally been seen as very 'pro-debtor' compared with the UK position which, by contrast, is seen as 'pro-creditor'.[1] In the US, corporate reorganisation proceedings are governed by Chapter 11 of the Bankruptcy Code 1978 and are almost always begun by a voluntary petition filed by the corporate debtor.[2] The filing brings about a moratorium on enforcement proceedings against the debtor or its property and the incumbent management normally remain in place during the early stages at least of the reorganisation proceedings. As the Department of Trade and Industry review of company rescue and business reconstruction mechanisms points out, on the three standard tests, the United States corporate reorganisation law should be classed as pro-debtor rather than pro-creditor – it provides for an automatic stay on creditor enforcement proceedings; secondly, it allows unimpeded petitions for reorganisation and thirdly, it allows the company's board to remain in control during reorganisation.[3] The Enterprise Act 2002 moves English law in the direction of Chapter 11 but it still falls considerably short of the US regime. The administration procedure still involves handing control of the company over to an outsider and moreover there is no method by which secured creditors can be 'crammed' down, ie forced to accept a reorganisation plan against their wishes. The possibility for 'cramdown' is a feature of the US system. Nevertheless, in many ways the Enterprise Act 2002 has repaired the perceived defects in the old administration order procedure. One commentator has remarked that:[4]

> The government deserves much praise for seeking out this middle ground between, on the one hand, the ancient regime in the UK, dominated by the banks through the instrumentality of receivership and, on the other, Chapter 11 with its increasingly criticised partisanship favouring the debtor. If, as is to be hoped, all interests – secured and unsecured creditors, management, investors, insolvency practitioners – give this reforming Act a fair wind, we may yet see the most dynamic insolvency regime in the world.

21.15 Purposes of administration

Under the Insolvency Act 1986 the floating charge holder had an effective veto on the appointment of an administrator.[5] With the new regime this veto disappears and is replaced by an effective veto on the identity of the proposed administrator. Perhaps a more significant change effected by the Enterprise Act 2002 has been in relation to the purposes of the administration order. We have a new hierarchy of purposes specified which administration is supposed to serve.[6] An administrator must perform his functions with the objective (a) of rescuing the company as a

---

1   See generally D Milman 'Reforming Corporate Rescue Mechanisms' in J De Lacy (ed.) *The Reform of United Kingdom Company Law* (Cavendish, 2002) at p 415.

2   For a synopsis of Chapter 11 see R Broude 'How the Rescue Culture came to the United States and the myths that surround Chapter 11' (2000) 16 Insolvency Law and Practice 194.

3   May 2000 at pp 38–41. The Review Group however concluded at p 33 of its report that 'it would be wholly inappropriate to attempt to replicate Chapter 11 in the UK, where the business culture and economic environment are quite different'.

4   See H Rajak 'The Enterprise Act and Insolvency Law Reform' (2003) 24 Company Lawyer 3.

5   Section 9 of the Insolvency Act 1986 as originally drafted.

6   Schedule B1, paragraph 3(1).

going concern unless he thinks that it is not reasonably practicable to achieve that objective or objective (b) would achieve a better result for the company's creditors as a whole. Objective (b) means achieving a better result for the company's creditors as whole than would be likely if the company were wound up without first being in administration. The third objective of administration specified in the legislation is realisation of property in order to make a distribution to one or more secured or preferential creditors. An administrator may only pursue this third objective if he thinks that it is not reasonably practicable to achieve of the first two objectives and he does not unnecessarily harm the interests of the creditors of the company as a whole.[1]

The first objective is preservation of the business of the company rather than preservation of the company as an empty corporate shell. The point was made during the parliamentary debates that rescuing the company on its own is a pointless objective in that a company that has nothing, does nothing and has no purpose is of no use.[2] On the other hand, the objective of preserving all or part of the company's business would be beneficial to employees, to creditors who may be paid out of the proceeds of the sale of the business or from future profits and additionally beneficial to the overall economy. Great emphasis was placed on the importance of preserving a business activity in the company and not just rescuing empty corporate shells. The government stressed that the first priority was to rescue the company as a going concern with much of its business intact. 'We would not want the administrator to rescue the company if it is to the detriment of creditor value'.[3]

Another question arising from the hierarchy of purposes specified in the legislation is the administrator's decision to move from one to the other. Choices within the hierarchy are governed by the test of what is reasonably practicable but the arbiter of choice appears to be the administrator. The legislation refers to what he 'thinks' rather than to what on reasonable grounds he might believe. If an administrator has been appointed by a qualified floating charge holder out of court and then moves rapidly to the conclusion that the only practicable option is to make distributions to secured and preferential creditors then administration seems suspiciously like administrative receivership in another guise. The question arises whether the administrator's beliefs on the feasibility of alternatives are challengeable in court either by the company or by unsecured creditors. Paragraph 74 provides that a creditor or member of a company in administration may apply to the court claiming that the administrator is acting or has acted so as unfairly to harm the interests of the applicant whether alone or in common with some or al other members or creditors or is proposing to act in such a manner. The court if it adjudges the complaint to be well-founded may make such order as it thinks appropriate including regulating the administrator's exercise of his functions or requiring the administrator to do or not to do a specified thing. Some ammunition for a court challenge may come from the administrator's duty under paragraph 49 in the statement setting out proposals for achieving the purpose of administration to explain why objectives (a) or (b) cannot be achieved.[4]

---

1   Ibid, paragraph 3(4).
2   See the comments by Lord Hunt of Wirral in the House of Lords – *Hansard,* HL Debs, col 765, 29 July 2002.
3   See the comments by the relevant Minister, Lord McIntosh of Haringey, in *Hansard,* HL Debs, col 766, 29 July 2002.
4   Schedule B1, paragraph 49(2)(b).

It should be noted however that the relevant test is what the administrator 'thinks' and not what he 'reasonably believes'. While the state of a man's mind may be as much a fact as the state of his indigestion, the 'thinks' test leaves little scope for judicial review. It is not generally the practice of the courts to second-guess the commercial judgments of administrators and other discretionary decision makers. During the parliamentary debates on the Enterprise legislation the relevant Minister explained that:[1]

> The administrator is the person on the ground who is best placed to judge whether or not a particular objective is reasonably practicable, in the light of his experience and professional judgment . . . [I]t will be for the administrator to reach a conclusion as to whether or not the objectives are reasonably practicable, taking into account all the circumstances of the particular case of which he or she is aware at the time.

Dr Vanessa Finch has suggested that the legislative reliance placed on the administrator's opinion makes it virtually impossible for a court to interfere with the administrators' judgments provided that these are made in good faith.[2] Another commentator offers an even more pessimistic prognosis stating that:[3]

> the likely practical effect of the paramount regard to what is in the best interest of the company's creditors as a whole is that there will be a few instances where the administrator performs his functions with the objective of rescuing the company as a going concern. After all, the interests of creditors are more often than not to be paid as much as possible and as quickly as possible. Those primarily interested in a rescue are likely to be employees, guarantors of any debts of the company and shareholders, interests to which the administrator is not expressly required to have regard.

When paragraph 74 is however read in conjunction with paragraph 3(4)(b), which requires the administrator not unnecessarily to harm the interests of the creditors of the company as a whole, it seems clear that there is scope for judicial second-guessing of administrators' decisions in contexts other than the purposes of administration. Take the situation where a company has two assets, one of which is essential to the carrying on of a company's business and the other of which is not. The administrator then decides to sell the key asset, perhaps because it is a bit more easily saleable, so as to make distributions to secured and preferential creditors even though the sale has a crippling effect on the further viability of the company. In these circumstances, it would seem that the administrator has acted in a way that has unfairly and unnecessarily harmed the interests of members (and perhaps creditors) of the company. Therefore his conduct is amenable to redress under paragraph 74 whereas it seems that if an administrative receiver had behaved in a similar fashion his conduct could not be impeached. An administrative can choose to exercise or not to exercise the power of sale over a particular sale. According to the Privy Council decision in *Downsview Nominees v First City Corp*[4] the only constraint on the administrative receiver's choices is the criterion of good faith. In Professor Goode's words, *Downsview* suggests that:[4]

> The receiver . . . is entitled, if he so chooses, to decide not to continue the company's business, and to sell a part of the business which would be better kept. It would also

---

1   *Hansard*, HL Deb, col 768, 29 July 2002.
2   See V Finch 'Re-Invigorating Corporate Rescue' [2003] JBL 527 at 546.
3   See L Linklater 'The Enterprise Act: Fulfilling Great Expectations' (2003) 24 Company Lawyer 225.
4   [1993] AC 295.
5   Goode, *Principles of Corporate Insolvency Law*, 2nd edn (Sweet & Maxwell, 1997) at p 242.

seem that he can select a particular asset to realise for the benefit of his debenture holder even though the removal of that asset would damage the company's business and there are other assets to which he could resort and on which the business is less dependent.

21.16   Entry routes into administration

There are now a variety of routes into administration. An administrator can now be appointed by the court; by a qualified floating charge holder out of court or by the company itself upon giving prior notice to a qualified floating charge holder.

The court route into administration most closely resembles the old procedure but even here there are still some differences. An application to the court for the making of an administration order may be made by the company itself or its directors or by one or more of its creditors.[1] Notice of the application has to be served on any person who has appointed or may be entitled to appoint an administrator or on any qualified floating charge holder who is or may be entitled to appoint an administrator. The latter is then afforded the opportunity to appoint an administrator out of court.[2] The former power which a qualified floating charge holder had to appoint an administrative receiver has now effectively been abrogated.[3] Before an administration order may be made there is a threshold insolvency condition – the court must be satisfied that the company is or is likely to become unable to pay its debts. Moreover, it must also the satisfied that the 'administration order is reasonably likely to achieve the purpose of administration.'[4] Superficially at least this marks a substantial change from the old wording under which the court was required to consider that the making of an order 'would be likely to achieve' one or more of the statutory purposes. The predominant judicial interpretation was that all that was required was a 'real prospect' of these statutory purposes being accomplished.[5] A higher standard requiring the evidence to show that the purpose or purposes will more probably than not be achieved was favoured in a few early cases[6] but that standard was generally rejected in favour of the less rigorous test.

The new legislation does not entail a full-blown balance of probabilities test but it does appear to raise the evidentiary hurdle. It may be however that it is not a productive exercise to compare the old and the new legislation in this respect. Under the old there were four disjunctive statutory purposes[7] whereas under the new there is a clear hierarchical list of objectives. It should also be remembered that court-appointed administrators are likely to be in a distinct minority under the new regime. Qualified floating charge holders and the company itself may not

---

1   Schedule B1, paragraph 12(1).
2   Pursuant to Schedule B1, paragraph 14.
3   Enterprise Act 2002, section 250 though there are a number of exceptional cases where such a power of appointment still exists and moreover holders of qualifying floating charges created before the coming into force of the Enterprise Act on 15 September 2003 have their old entitlements still intact.
4   Schedule B1, paragraph 11.
5   *Re Harris Simons Construction Ltd* [1989] 1 WLR 368, [1989] BCLC 202, (1989) 5 BCC 11; *Re SCL Building Services Ltd* (1989) 5 BCC 746, [1990] BCLC 98; *Re Primlaks (UK) Ltd* [1989] BCLC 734; *Re Rowbotham Baxter Ltd* [1990] BCLC 397, [1990] BCC 113; *Re Chelmsford City Football Club (1980) Ltd* [1991] BCC 133; *Re Arrows Ltd (No 3)* [1992] BCLC 555.
6   *Re Consumer and Industrial Press Ltd* [1988] BCLC 177, (1988) 4 BCC 68; *Re Manlon Trading Ltd* (1988) 4 BCC 455.
7   Section 8(3) Insolvency Act 1986 as originally drafted.

appoint out of court and one wonders what the merits are in going to court considering the inevitable additional expense. Court appointments may be confined to a residual category of case where a company has no substantial secured borrowings but where unsecured creditors are disenchanted with the management of the company and wish to see company reconstruction under the steering hand of an outsider notwithstanding the objections of existing management.

The overall effect of the Enterprise Act 2002 is to pay great deference to the wishes of secured creditors and this is seen in two provisions relating to court appointment of administrators. First, under paragraph 36 Schedule B1 where an administration application is made by somebody other than a qualified floating charge holder, the latter may intervene in the proceedings and suggest to the court the appointment of a specified person as administrator. The court is obliged to respond positively to this intervention unless it thinks it right to refuse the application 'because of the particular circumstances of the case'. Furthermore, under paragraph 35 the court is required automatically to accede to administration applications made by qualified floating charge holders and there is no threshold insolvency test in the case of such applications. Floating charge holders may invoke this facility rather than utilise their out-of-court appointment powers in cases where an administrator may be called upon to take control of company property or perform other functions in a foreign jurisdiction. Schedule B1, paragraph 5 provides that an administrator is an officer of the court (whether or not he is appointed by the court).[1] Nevertheless, a foreign tribunal may not accord recognition to an administrator appointed by a qualified floating charge holder out of court.

21.17 Out of court appointments by qualified floating charge holders

The main route into administration is likely to be out of court appointments by floating charge holders pursuant to Schedule B1, paragraph 14. The new administrator has a different set of functions to perform than the old style administrative receiver. Nevertheless, one of the functions is making distributions to secured and preferential creditor. Where this function is performed and where the appointor is a floating charge holder the similarities between new guise administration and administrative receivership seem quite strong. It has been suggested that the reforms introduced by the Enterprise Act 2002 will be better understood if approached with the concept of transmutation in mind.[2] In other words, it may be better be describe the reforms as a 'transmutation' or 'merger' of the administrative receivership and administration procedures rather than as being the end of administrative receivership.

It should be noted however, that the holder of a pre-Act floating charge who is entitled still to appoint an administrative receiver may instead appoint an administrator. The early success of the legislation will be determined partly by the extent to which such appointments are made but the omens are not very optimistic. There seems to be little incentive for lenders to give up the advantages

---

1   As an officer of the court an administrator probably becomes subject to the somewhat ill-defined obligation enunciated in *Ex parte James* (1874) LR 9 Ch App 609 to act honourably and fairly.

2   See S Davies (ed.) *Insolvency and the Enterprise Act 2002* (Jordans, 2003) at pp 40–41.

and control that they have under administrative receivership. Being seen to embrace the new administration regime as part of the rescue culture may bring some publicity benefits but the solid tug of money may exert a contrary pull.[1]

The right to appoint an administrator out of court is conferred on the holder of a qualifying floating charge as defined in paragraph 14. This definition is not free from controversy and may engender considerable controversy in the years to come. Under paragraph 14(2) a floating charge qualifies if it is created by an instrument which:

(a) states that this paragraph applies to the floating charge;
(b) purports to empower the holder of the floating charge to appoint an administrator of the company; and
(c) purports to empower the holder of the floating charge to appoint an administrative receiver.

It is not altogether clear whether these are disjunctive or conjunctive conditions. In other words, it is not clear whether the relevant debenture must provide both that the relevant paragraph applies and also empower the floating charge holder to appoint an administrator or whether it suffices if the debenture does either one of these things. There is also some ambiguity about the 'property' condition in paragraph 14(3). The simpler scenarios is where the floating charge or a number of floating charges collectively together relate to the whole or substantially the whole of the company's property. Paragraph 14(3) also refers however to a situation where 'charges and other forms of security' together relate to the whole or substantially the whole of the company's property and at least one of which is a qualifying floating charge. What is meant by other forms of security is not entirely clear and whether it embraces 'quasi-security', ie functionally equivalent legal devices.

Before appointing an administrator a qualifying floating charge holder must give two days' written notice to the holder of a prior qualifying floating charge.[2] A floating charge is treated as prior if it was first in point of time or if it is entitled to priority by virtue of a priority agreement between the two charge holders.

The floating charge holder is not obliged to give any notice to the company of the intention to appoint an administrator. A company may have administration foisted upon it against its wishes. An administrator must perform his functions with the overarching objective of rescuing the company as going concern but a company may wished to be saved from this fate particularly where the existing management are of the view that any temporary trading difficulties can be alleviated without recourse to formal insolvency processes. Again in this respect administration via the floating charge holder can be likened to administrative receivership. A floating charge holder was not required to give prior notice to the

---

1   See the comments in S Davies (ed.) *Insolvency and the Enterprise Act 2002* (Jordans, 2003) at p 97. Rule 2.67 of the Insolvency Rules 1986 now provides that one of the expenses of the administration will be 'the amount of any corporation tax on chargeable gains accruing on the realization of any asset of the company …'. It appears that such expenses are payable in priority to floating charge realizations pursuant to Schedule B1, paragraph 99(3) whereas in an administrative receivership they would not come out of the realizations – see *Re Buchler v Talbot* [2004] UKHL 9, [2004] 2 WLR 582. Thus 'administrative receiverships look more attractive where capital gains are likely to be an issue' – see Sims and Briggs, 'Enterprise Act 2002 – Corporate Wrinkles' [2004] Insolvency Intelligence 49 at 53.

2   Schedule B1, paragraph 15. There is an exception if the holder of any prior floating charge has consented in writing to the making of the appointment.

corporate debtor of his intention to appoint a receiver[1] and the absence of a prior notice requirement still obtains in those cases where the appointment of an administrative receiver is still permissible. English law contrasts in this respect with some other jurisdictions including Canada which introduced a statutory notice requirement in 1992. Section 244 of the Canadian Bankruptcy and Insolvency Act requires that a secured creditor who intends to enforce a security over all or substantially the whole of the debtor's property should send a prescribed notice to the debtor. The security interest cannot be enforced until ten days after service of the notice. The grace period is designed to allow the debtor time to put in place alternative funding arrangements or else to invoke one of the debtor reorganisation mechanisms. In defence of the English position one could say that administration is intended to serve as a debtor reorganisation mechanism.[2]

A charge holder who is contractually entitled to appoint a receiver is under no duty to refrain from doing so on the grounds that it might cause loss to the company or its creditors. It has been held that, in exercising the right to appoint, no duty of care is owed to either the debtor or to guarantors of the secured debt. A chargee is given the power to appoint a receiver to protect his interests, and the decision to exercise that power cannot be challenged, except possibly on the ground of bad faith.[3] Likewise the decision of a qualified floating charge holder to appoint an administrator cannot be impeached by a company that is concerned about the destruction of economic value that such an appointment might entail. As one commentator remarks:[4]

> Banks will be able to use the streamlined appointment procedure in all cases, not merely situations of urgency, and they will be able to determine who should be appointed to the post of administrator. This gives the banks the power to insert their chosen administrator with speed and without regard to the other creditors or the courts.

21.18 Out of court appointments by the company or its directors

The company or its directors are also enabled to appoint an administrator out of court on giving five days notice which identifies the proposed administrator to floating charge holders.[5] The notice of intention to appoint must be accompanied by a statutory declaration stating inter alia that the company is or is likely to become unable to pay its debts; that the company is in liquidation and that none of the other factors precluding an appointment are present.[6] An appointment must be made not later than ten days after notice of intention to make an appointment is filed with the court.

There are certain anti-abuse provisions.[7] A company cannot invoke this out-of-court administration procedure if the company has come out of administration under such procedure within the previous 12 months or if the company has been the subject of a moratorium under a 'small company' company voluntary

---

1   See eg *Gomba Holdings UK Ltd v Homan* [1986] 1 WLR 1301.
2   See generally McCormack, 'Receiverships and the Rescue Culture' [2000] CfiLR 229.
3   *Downsview Nominees v First City Corp* [1993] AC 295.
4   V Finch, 'Re-invigorating Corporate Rescue' [2003] JBL 527 at 535.
5   Schedule B1, paragraphs 22 and 26.
6   Ibid, paragraph 27.
7   Ibid, paras 23–25.

arrangement in the previous 12 months or a winding up petition has been presented and has not yet been disposed of. The limitations built into the legislation may be seen as a necessary measure to prevent certain unscrupulous companies and directors from making continuous use of moratorium procedures to the disadvantage of their creditors. The company can always go into administration during this period but this must be done through the courts and not by means of the out-of-court route.

21.19   Effect of the appointment of an administrator

The appointment of an administrator displaces the board of directors from their existing management functions. Under paragraph 67 an administrator is required on his appointment to take custody or control of all the property to which he thinks the company is entitled. The administrator is obliged to manage the affairs, business and property of a company. It is provided in paragraph 64 that a company in administration or an officer of a company in administration may not exercise a management power without the consent of the administrator and 'management power' is interpreted to mean any power which could be exercised so as to interfere with the exercise of the administrator's powers. The Enterprise Act 2002 does not change anything in this regard from the position under the Insolvency Act 1986. The directors of a company remain in office but they lose their management powers during administration. It may be that one way of cutting down in expense would be for the administrator to delegate certain day-to-day tasks to the 'old' management team but retaining overall strategic control himself.

Apart from such 'grace and favour' actions by the administrator however there is no scope in the process for existing management. The legislation places decisive faith in the established skills of the UK insolvency profession.[1] The US Chapter 11 is almost at the other end of the spectrum for in that system the corporate debtor remains in control of the business during the reorganisation process though the bankruptcy court may appoint a trustee to oversee operations if the management are suspected of fraud.[2] While the board of directors remain in overall charge of the business it may be that the composition of the board will change quite significantly during the rescue and renewal period. Be that as it may, there is quite a difference in the formal approach of the law between the US and England. This has been accounted for by reason of the difference in business philosophy on either side of the Atlantic. In the US there is less of a stigma attached to business failure. It is seen as part and parcel of entrepreneurial endeavour and if one business fails there should be scope for picking up the pieces and starting afresh. Management are not seen as blameworthy whereas in Britain there may be a view that since the existing management are the very people who got the company into financial difficulties they are least qualified to take it out of such difficulties.[3] The British approach has its critics. As one commentator remarks:[4]

> The English approach is founded upon the outdated philosophy that those who have managed the company so that it requires protection should not be allowed to

---

1   See V Finch, 'Re-invigorating Corporate Rescue' [2003] JBL 527 at 549.
2   See generally, V Finch, *Corporate Insolvency Law: Perspectives and Principles* (Cambridge University Press, 2002) pp 195–204.
3   See G Moss QC 'Chapter 11: An English Lawyer's critique' (1998) 11 Insolvency Intelligence 17.
4   See Phillips, *The Administration Procedure and Creditors' Voluntary Arrangements* (Centre for Commercial Law Studies, QMW, 1996) at p 16.

continue to manage it. As a proposition it is fundamentally flawed. Not all directors of insolvent companies are unfit to manage them ...

The administrator has very wide powers to manage the company's business and to deal with its assets in order to achieve the purposes of administration. Thus the administrator may allow the company to continue to trade, to dispose of its assets and to commence or continue legal proceedings. The administrator has the power to remove directors and to appoint any person to be a director, whether to fill a vacancy or otherwise.[1] He can also call meetings of members and of creditors,[2] and has a general power to apply to the court for directions in carrying out his functions.[3]

A person dealing with an administrator in good faith and for value is not concerned to inquire whether the administrator is acting within his powers.[4] There are, nevertheless, various disclosure obligations which are designed to ensure that persons who have an interest in the company or who have dealings with it are aware of its new status.[5] In particular, every invoice, order for goods or business letter which is issued by or on behalf of the company or the administrator after the commencement of administration must also contain the administrator's name and a statement that the affairs, business and property of the company are being managed by the administrator.[6]

21.20   The statutory moratorium

One of the most important features of the administration procedure is the moratorium. The commencement of the administration procedure imposes a freeze on proceedings or executions against the company and its assets. This provides a breathing space during which the company has an opportunity to make arrangements with its creditors and members for the rescheduling of its debts and the reorganisation and restructuring of its affairs.[7]

By virtue of the moratorium:

(1) No resolution may be passed or order made for the winding-up of the company though this does not apply to winding up petitions on public interest grounds under section 124A of the Insolvency Act nor to winding up petitions presented by the Financial Services Authority under section 367 of the Financial Services and Markets Act 2000.[8]

---

1   Schedule B1, paragraph 61.
2   Ibid, paragraph 62.
3   Ibid, paragraph 63.
4   Ibid, paragraph 59(3).
5   See rule 2.10 of the Insolvency Rules.
6   Schedule B1, paragraph 45.
7   The operation of the moratorium throughout the administration is modified in respect of market charges, that is charges arising out of dealings in securities. The modifications of the law of insolvency in respect of market charges are made by Part VII of the Companies Act 1989. See also the Financial Collateral Regulations 2003 for enforcement rights in respect of financial collateral. These regulations were enacted to give effect to the EC Financial Collateral Directive, Directive 2002/47/EC.
8   Schedule B1, paragraph 42.

(2) No steps may be taken to enforce any security over the company's property[1] or to repossess goods in the company's possession under any hire-purchase agreement[2] except with the leave of the court and subject to such terms as the court may impose; and or else with the consent of the administrator.

(3) No legal process[3] including distress[4] may be instituted or continued against the company or its property except with the leave of the court and subject to such terms as the court may impose or else with the consent of the administrator.

(4) Under section 11(3) of the Insolvency Act no steps could be taken to enforce any security over the company's property with security being defined as 'any mortgage, charge, lien or other security.' After some uncertainty and vacillation the courts held that a landlord's right to forfeit a lease for breach of covenant by peaceful re-entry did not fall within the definition of security. A right of re-entry was not security over a lease but simply a right to terminate the lease and restore the lessor to possession of his own property.[5] The Insolvency Act 2000 extended the moratorium so as to catch a landlord's right of forfeiture by peaceable re-entry. This position is now reflected in paragraph 43(4).

When an administration order takes effect in respect of a company any administrative receiver of the company shall vacate office and moreover, any receiver of part of the company's property shall vacate office if the administrator requires him to.[6] According to paragraph 42 the moratorium applies to a company in administration and there is also provision in broadly similar terms in paragraph 44 for an interim moratorium and this begins to bite from the time that an administration application is presented. The interim moratorium is intended to ensure that the status quo is maintained and the company's business and assets are protected pending the outcome of the hearing. The interim moratorium is also brought into being by the filing of a notice of intention to appoint an administrator out of court either by a qualified floating charge holder or by the company or its directors. The interim moratorium continues pending the hearing of the administration application or where a notice has been served, for five days from filing unless an administrator has been appointed beforehand.

---

1   Ibid, paragraph 43(2).

2   Ibid, paragraph 43(3) and defined by paragraph 111 as including conditional sale agreements, chattel leasing agreements and retention of title agreements.

3   The proceedings in question are legal proceedings or quasi-legal proceedings such as arbitration: *Bristol Airport v Powdrill* [1990] Ch 744, [1990] 2 All ER 493, [1990] 2 WLR 1362, [1990] BCLC 585, [1990] BCC 130. This can include applications to industrial tribunals: *Carr v British International Helicopters Ltd* [1993] BCC 855. A 'legal process' requires the assistance of the court and therefore the service of a notice making time of the essence is not within this category: *Re Olympia and York Canary Wharf Ltd* [1993] BCC 154; *McMullen & Sons Ltd v Cerrone* [1994] BCC 25. See now on 'legal process' for the purpose of the moratorium *Re Railtrack plc* [2002] 2 BCLC 755 and see also *Environment Agency v Clark* [2001] Ch 57.

4   The essential feature of distress is that the assets distrained are seized and detained by the distrainor: *Bristol Airport v Powdrill* [1990] Ch 744.

5   Although it was held in one case that 'security' for the purposes of relevant provisions of the Insolvency Act 1986 included a landlord's right to forfeit a lease (*Exchange Travel Agency v Triton Property Trust* [1991] BCLC 396), this has not been followed in later decisions: *Razzaq v Pala* [1998] BCC 66; *Re Lomax Leisure Ltd* [1999] 2 BCLC 126. See also *Re Park Air Services plc* [1999] 1 BCLC 155 (HL).

6   Schedule B1, paragraph 41.

21.21 Relaxation of the moratorium

With the leave of the court or with the administrator's consent, security may be enforced, goods may be repossessed and other legal processes may be instituted or continued notwithstanding the fact that the company is in administration. Under the old substantially re-enacted provisions of the Insolvency Act 1986 there have been a number of test cases in which the courts have had an opportunity to spell out their approach to the granting of leave.

The leading authorities are the decisions of the Court of Appeal in *Bristol Airport plc v Powdrill*[1] and *Re Atlantic Computer Systems plc (No 1)*.[2] In the former case it was held that the exercise by an airport authority of its rights under the Civil Aviation Act 1982 to detain an aircraft for non-payment of landing charges constituted a 'step taken to enforce security' and thus came within the statutory moratorium. The Court of Appeal held that the first-instance judge had properly taken into account the relevant factors and properly exercised his discretion in refusing leave to enforce the security. Particularly telling factors against the airports were that none of the company's aircraft were on their runways at the commencement of the administration and had only arrived there subsequently because of the administrator's decision to continue the business; the airports had acquiesced in the administrator's proposal to sell the business as a going concern, which detention of the aircraft would prevent; and the airports had benefited financially from the continuation of the business by the administrator because they had received payment of substantial fees. In other words, having supported the administration when it suited them, the airports could not later seek to enforce a right which was inconsistent with the achievement of the purpose of the administration.[3]

The Court of Appeal in *Powdrill* accepted that its reasoning would extend to a case where the holder of ordinary possessory lien[4] or similar right was requested by an administrator to give up the chattels subject to the right. Refusal to comply with the request would amount to a step taken to enforce security and would fall within the statutory moratorium. The Court of Appeal accepted that it would be practically inconvenient and costly for the holder of every lien to have to apply to court for leave but[5] thought that these potential difficulties would be mitigated in practice by the fact that the administrator and the holder of the lien could simply agree the matter between themselves without the intervention of the courts.

Re Atlantic Computer Systems plc (No 1) decided the narrow point that where a company in administration has leased goods and then sub-leased the goods to customers, those goods nevertheless remain in the possession of the company for the purposes of the moratorium. The Court of Appeal, nevertheless, granted leave to lessors and security holders to recover their property and to enforce their security. The court also took the opportunity to set out in general terms the

---

1   [1990] Ch 744, [1990] 2 All ER 493, [1990] 2 WLR 1362, [1990] BCLC 585, [1990] BCC 130.
2   [1992] Ch 505, [1992] 1 All ER 476, [1992] 2 WLR 367, [1991] BCLC 606, [1990] BCC 859.
3   [1990] Ch at p 767 *per* BrowneWilkinson V-C.
4   Under section 246, liens and similar rights on the company's books, papers or other records are unenforceable against 'office-holders', a category which includes administrators. On lien-holders, see also *Re Sabre International Products Ltd* [1991] BCLC 470.
5   Staughton LJ at 772 considered that the effect of the statutory moratorium should be kept carefully under review.

approach of the court to leave applications[1] as this could assist administrators in deciding whether to grant consent themselves and thus help to make applications to court for leave the exception rather than the rule.

The underlying principle is that an administration for the benefit of unsecured creditors should not be conducted at the expense of those who have proprietary rights except to the extent that this may be unavoidable.

(1)   The onus is on the applicant to establish a case for leave to be granted.

(2)   The moratorium is intended to assist in the achievement of the purpose for which the administration order was made. If granting leave to the applicant is unlikely to impede that purpose, leave should normally be given.

(3)   In other cases, the court should balance the legitimate interests of the applicant and the legitimate interests of the other creditors of the company.[2]

(4)   In carrying out the balancing exercise great importance is normally to be given to the proprietary interest of the applicant. In general, so far as possible the administration procedure should not be used to prejudice those who were secured creditors or lessors at the commencement of the administration.

(5)   It will normally be sufficient ground for the grant of leave if significant loss would be caused to the applicant by the refusal. But if substantially greater loss would be caused to others by the grant of leave, or loss which is out of all proportion to the benefit which leave would confer on the applicant, that may outweigh the loss to the applicant caused by a refusal.

(6)   In assessing the respective losses, the court will have regard to matters such as:
      (a)   the financial position of the company;
      (b)   its ability to pay rental arrears and continuing rentals (or, in the case of security, to meet its obligations under its loans);
      (c)   the administrator's proposals;
      (d)   the period for which the administration order has been in force and is expected to remain in force;
      (e)   the effect on the administration if leave is given and on the applicant if it is refused;
      (f)   the end result sought to be achieved by the administration;
      (g)   the prospects of that result being achieved; and
      (h)   the history of the administration so far.

(7)   In considering these suggested consequences it will often be necessary to assess how probable they are.

(8)   Other factors, such as the conduct of the applicant, may also be relevant.

(9)   The above conditions will also apply to a decision to impose terms if leave is granted. They will also apply to a decision whether to impose terms as a condition for refusing leave. An example of refusal to grant leave on terms is provided by *Re Meesan Investments*,[3] where leave to enforce security was

---

1   Nicholls LJ, delivering the judgment of the court, also reflected that the range of circumstances in which leave could be sought would vary almost infinitely thus making guidelines inadequate, and noted that first-instance judges in the Commercial Court had more practical experience of the procedure than the members of the Court of Appeal.

2   For an example of the operation of this balancing process, see *Re Meesan Investments Ltd (Royal Trust Bank v Buchler)* (1988) 4 BCC 788, [1989] BCLC 130.

3   [1989] BCLC 130.

refused but the administrator was ordered to return to court in two months' time if the secured property had not been sold by then. The guidelines envisage refusal on terms becoming a common phenomenon.

(10) On applications to enforce security, an important consideration will often be whether the applicant is fully secured. If he is, delay in enforcement is likely to be less prejudicial than in cases where his security is insufficient.

(11) Unless the issue can be easily resolved, it is not appropriate on a leave application for the court to resolve a dispute about the existence, validity or nature of a security which the applicant seeks leave to enforce. The court needs to be satisfied only that the applicant has a seriously arguable case.

Wrongful refusal by an administrator to allow an owner of goods to repossess them could render the administrator liable to pay compensation.[1]

It appears that the Enterprise Act 2002 was not intended to change existing law on leave to exercise proprietary rights and that the courts should be free to continue to carry out this balancing exercise on a case-by-case basis. On the other hand, while the Enterprise Act 2002 is respectful of proprietary rights an argument could be made that having regard to the overall thrust of the legislation a slightly different emphasis could be placed on the various factors that make up the *Atlantic Computers* equation. Administrations should be shorter under the new procedure – carried out quickly and efficiently to paraphrase Schedule B1, paragraph 4. In these circumstances it seems less of an injustice that an owner of goods should be shut out from exercising his proprietary rights during the entirety of the administration period.

The *Atlantic Computers* case makes it clear that there is no 'expenses of administration' principle similar to an 'expenses of liquidation' principle. In other words, an owner of equipment leased to a company in administration and who is precluded from recovering possession of the equipment by virtue of the statutory moratorium cannot insist on payment of the rental amounts during the currency of the administration as an expense of the administration. The new power of an administrator to make distributions under paragraph 66 may possibly provide partial relief to an owner of equipment in this situation. The provision empowers an administrator to make a payment otherwise than in accordance with the normal rules of priority if he thinks it likely to assist achievement of the purpose of administration. The more common scenario though for the application of this provision is where an essential supplier insists on the discharge of earlier debts as a condition of making further essential supplies.

21.22 Power to deal with charged property

In many cases, in order to achieve the purposes of administration, the administrator will need to be able to use or dispose of all the company's property, including that part of it which is charged to a third party, eg the company's bankers. Schedule B1, paragraph 70 gives the administrator certain powers to deal with property charged to third parties and chattels owned by third parties but in

---

1   *Barclay Mercantile Business Finance Ltd v Sibec Development Ltd* [1992] 2 All ER 195, [1992] 1 WLR 1253, [1993] BCLC 1077, [1993] BCC 148. The basis of this jurisdiction is the administrator's position as an officer of the court. Whether an administrator could be liable for conversion was left open.

the company's possession, irrespective of the wishes of the chargees or owners. There is a distinction between, on the one hand, assets subject to a fixed charge (or to hire-purchase agreements),[1] and, on the other, assets subject to a floating charge.

In the case of assets subject to a floating charge, the administrator is given power to dispose of such assets or otherwise exercise his powers in relation to them as if the assets were not subject to the floating charge. Accordingly, the administrator can deal with such assets and dispose of them as he sees fit without reference to the floating charge holder and without being fettered by any contractual restrictions contained within the floating charge, for example a negative pledge clause.

The reference in paragraph 70 to a floating charge means a charge which, as created, was a floating charge.[2] Accordingly, the crystallisation of the floating charge prior to the administration order would not prevent the administrator from exercising these wide powers.

Where the administrator disposes of floating charge assets, the holder of the floating charge is given the same priority in respect of any of the company's property directly or indirectly representing the assets disposed of as he would have had in respect of the assets subject to the floating charge. If, for example, the administrator sells plant and machinery subject to the floating charge, the proceeds of the sale will fall within the floating charge and the holder of the charge will be entitled to the same priority as against third parties (eg holders of subsequent floating charges) in respect of the proceeds as he had in respect of the plant and machinery disposed of.

As regards assets subject to a fixed charge (as created) or goods which are in the possession of the company under a hire-purchase agreement, the administrator may apply to court in accordance with Schedule B1, paragraphs 71 and 72, for an order authorising him to dispose of the property. The court may make such an order if it is satisfied that the disposal (with or without other assets) of the fixed charge assets or goods acquired on hire purchase would be likely to promote the purpose, or one or more of the purposes, specified in the administration order. The court order will authorise the administrator to dispose of the assets or goods as if they were not subject to the fixed charge or, as the case may be, as if the owner's rights under the hire-purchase agreement were vested in the company. Schedule B1 paragraphs 71(3) and 72(3) provide that the court must make it a condition of any such order that.

(1) the net proceeds of the disposal; and
(2) a sum equalling the deficit between the net proceeds of disposal and the net amount which would be realised by a sale of the assets at market value as determined by the court

must be applied towards discharging the sums secured by the fixed charge or payable under the hire-purchase agreement.

Section 15 of the Insolvency Act 1986 is the predecessor provision to paragraphs 71 and 72 and its operation was considered in *Re ARV Aviation Ltd*.[3] Knox J held that the task of the court in leave applications was to balance the prejudice that would be felt by the secured creditor by the making of an order against the

---

1   This term includes conditional sale agreements, chattel leasing agreements and retention of title agreements: Schedule B1, paragraph 111.
2   Ibid, paragraph 111.
3   (1988) 4 BCC 708, [1989] BCLC 664.

prejudice that would be felt by those interested in the promotion of the administration purpose, in this case the unsecured creditors, if it were not made. The view that the court takes of the open-market value of the assets which the administrator seeks leave to sell is extremely important because it is this amount which the administrator is required to discharge as a condition of obtaining leave. In *ARV Aviation*, Knox J proceeded on the assumption that the purpose of this condition was to protect to the maximum practicable extent the secured creditor.[1] With a view to achieving this purpose, Knox J held that the granting of leave could be a two-stage process, with the open-market valuation being assessed some time after the making of the order granting the administrator leave to dispose of the assets.

Leave may be sought in circumstances where the administrator and the secured creditor[2] are unable themselves to agree on a valuation; but such a dispute is not an essential prerequisite of the jurisdiction.[3] Where a secured creditor consents to the sale of the charged assets,[4] the administrator may not use the statutory mechanism to retain the proceeds of the sale but must deal with these proceeds in accordance with the terms on which the secured creditor has agreed to release its security.[5]

Where assets are subject to more than one fixed charge and the court makes an order authorising the disposal of such assets, the proceeds of sale must be applied towards discharging the sums secured by the securities in their order of priority.[6]

21.23   Status of the administrator

The administrator wears a couple of hats. Paragraph 5 provides that an administrator is an officer of the court whether or not he is appointed by the court. Paragraph 69 however states that in exercising his functions the administrator acts as the company's agent. Under general principles, an agent is not liable under a contract which he makes on behalf of his principal. Accordingly, an administrator would not be personally liable on any contract entered into by him in the course of acting as administrator, except in so far as the contract otherwise provides. However, in a suitable case, the court may oblige the administrator to comply with a contractual obligation of the company by granting an injunction.[7]

In acting as the company's agent in contractual matters, the administrator will commit a breach of duty if he fails to observe the limits imposed by the company's objects clause.[8] If the administrator has acted honestly and reasonably, under section 727 of the Companies Act 1985 the court may relieve him from liability for this breach of duty.[9]

Although the normal rule is that an agent is not personally liable on his principal's contracts, the Insolvency Act makes special provision for the payment of debts and liabilities incurred during the administration under contracts

---

1   *Mutatis mutandis*, the same underlying purpose would exist where the administrator seeks leave to dispose of goods in the possession of the company under a hire-purchase agreement.
2   Or supplier of goods on hire purchase, as the case may be.
3   *Re ARV Aviation Ltd*, above.
4   Or a supplier of goods on hire purchase consents to the sale of those goods.
5   *Re Newman Shopfitters (Cleveland) Ltd* [1991] BCLC 407.
6   Schedule B1, paragraph 71(4).
7   *Astor Chemicals Ltd v Synthetic Technology Ltd* [1990] BCLC 1, [1990] BCC 97.
8   *Re Home Treat Ltd* [1991] BCLC 705, [1991] BCC 165.
9   Ibid.

entered into by the administrator.[1] The special provision also applies to debts and liabilities incurred during the administration under contracts of employment adopted by the administrator after the first fourteen days from his appointment.[2] The nature of the provision is that a statutory charge, ranking in priority to the administrator's statutory charge for his own remuneration and expenses[3] and to any floating charge, is imposed on the company's property in respect of the said debts and liabilities. Strictly, these statutory charges arise only when the administrator vacates office but the ordinary practice is for administrators to meet obligations, including salaries and other payments due to employees, as they arise during the continuance of the administration.

It is central to a procedure intended to facilitate the recuperation of the financial health of a struggling business that, if at all possible, business continuity should be maintained. Until the matter was litigated in the course of the administration of Paramount Airways Ltd (litigation which reached the House of Lords and which is reported as *Powdrill v Watson*),[4] the standard practice of administrators who chose to continue businesses was to inform employees that, despite the continuation of the business, their contracts would not be adopted and that no personal liability would be assumed by the administrators in respect of them. The underlying aim of this practice was to take the employees' contracts outside the scope of the statutory charge and hence ensure that payments arising from them did not rank in priority to the administrators' own remuneration and expenses.

In *Powdrill*, the House of Lords held that this practice was ineffective. The mere assertion of non-adoption was judged to be without legal effect because adopting was a matter not merely of words but of fact. If administrators continued after the fourteen-day grace period to employ staff and to pay them in accordance with the terms of their previous contracts, they would be held to have adopted those contracts. Accordingly, as well as payments due in respect of services actually rendered by employees during the course of, and for the benefit of, the administration, sums in respect of wages accruing during contractual notice periods or in respect of damages payable for failure to give such notices, as well as pension contributions in respect of these periods, would be entitled to the statutory 'super priority'.

The outcome of the Paramount Airways litigation caused considerable consternation amongst insolvency practitioners. They argued that it undermined the 'rescue culture' because administrators would be reluctant to retain employees with a view to continuing the business if this meant that they might not be able to recover their own remuneration and expenses, the company's resources having been exhausted by payments to employees. A new Insolvency Act was hurriedly enacted to clarify the position and these provisions are now reflected in paragraphs 99(5) and 99(6).

---

1   Schedule B1, paragraph 99(4).

2   Schedule B1, paragraph 99(5). Note that the statutory charge is limited to debts and liabilities incurred while he was administrator.

3   This statutory charge is conferred by Schedule B1, paragraph 99(3). On what falls within the category of administration expenses, see *Re Atlantic Computers*, above and *Re A Company (No 005174 of 1999)* [2000] 1 WLR 502.

4   [1995] 2 AC 394, the decision of the Court of Appeal ([1994] 2 All ER 513), which was varied by the House of Lords with respect to holiday pay entitlements, is noted Fletcher (1994) 15 Co Law 145; Davies (1994) 23 ILJ 141.

Under this regime liabilities to pay sums by way of wages or salary[1] or by way of contribution to an occupational pension scheme which are in respect of services rendered after the adoption of the contract are 'qualifying liabilities' and, as such, they are entitled to the priority afforded by the statutory charge. Payments in respect of services rendered before the adoption of the contract are to be disregarded. Payment in lieu of contractual notice periods and damages for breach of contract are not payments in respect of services rendered after adoption and thus would not be qualifying liabilities.[2]

An administrator may incur liability in tort as an agent and, as an officer of the court, is subject to the rule in *ex parte James*[3] which requires him to do the fullest equity.[4]

21.24   Duties of the administrator

The first duty of the administrator is to take into his custody or under his control all the property to which the company is or appears to be entitled.[5] Where the administrator seizes or disposes of property which does not belong to the company, then, provided that at the time of such seizure or disposal he believed and had reasonable grounds for believing that his actions were justified, he is not liable to any third party in respect of resulting loss or damage except to the extent that it was caused by his own negligence.[6]

Secondly, the administrator must manage the affairs, business and property of the company.[7] In the initial period of the administration, the administrator must discharge this management obligation subject to any directions from the court. Once the creditors have approved the administrator's proposals, the administrator must manage in accordance with those proposals or with any revision of the proposals approved by a creditors' meeting.[8] Some latitude is given to an administrator however in that he is allowed to manage in accordance with insubstantial revisions of the proposals approved by him.

21.25   The administrator's proposals

The formulation of proposals is an important stage in the administration procedure. As soon as is reasonably practicable and in any event within 8 weeks after the company enters administration[9] (or such longer period as the court or creditors may allow pursuant to paragraphs 107 or 108), the administrator must produce proposals for achieving the purpose of administration. A statement of the proposals must be sent to all creditors (so far as their addresses are known)

---

1   See *Re A Company (No 005174 of 1999)* [2000] 1 WLR 502.
2   It is clear that under the general law, damages for breach of contract are not 'wages or salary': *Delaney v Staples* [1992] 1 AC 687 at pp 692–93, [1992] 1 All ER 944, [1992] 2 WLR 451, [1992] ICR 483.
3   (1874) LR 9 Ch App 609.
4   In *Powdrill*, above, the rule in *ex parte James* was applied by the Court of Appeal to require the administrator to pay interest on the sums payable to employees.
5   Schedule B1, paragraph 67.
6   Section 234(3) and (4).
7   Schedule B1, paragraph 68(1).
8   Ibid.
9   Ibid, paragraph 49.

and also to the Registrar of Companies.[1] Members must also be informed of the proposals, either by being sent a copy of the statement or by publication of a notice informing them of their right to apply for a copy free of charge.[2] A copy of the statement of proposals must also be laid before a meeting of the company's creditors if such a meeting is held.[3]

Forthwith on appointment, the administrator must[4] require certain persons, in particular the officers of the company, to submit a statement of affairs giving details of *inter alia* the company's assets, debts and liabilities and of creditors and of securities held by them.[5] The information produced is likely to be of considerable assistance to the administrator in the drawing-up of his proposals.

An administrator's proposals may not result in non-preferential entitlements being paid ahead of preferential entitlements or one preferential creditor of the company being paid a smaller proportion of his debt than another.[6] More generally, respect for proprietary rights is clearly demonstrated by paragraph 73(1)(a) which provides that an administrator's statement of proposals may include any action which affects the right of a secured creditor of the company to enforce his security. Secured creditors' rights are inviolate in this respect and this respect there is a clear contrast between the English legislation and chapter 11 of the US Bankruptcy code. Generally speaking however, creditors need to approve a chapter 11 corporate reorganisation plan and approval signifies a majority in number and two-thirds in amount, valued by the extent of the outstanding debt, of each class of creditors. As a general rule, it is imperative that every impaired class of creditors approve the plan though 'cramdown' is possible. 'Cramdown' refers to the process whereby a plan may be confirmed despite a class of creditors voting down the plan. A secured class of creditors may be crammed down if it receives the value of its collateral plus interest over time, while an unsecured class may insist that equity owners receive nothing if a plan is to be approved over its objection. Objecting creditors are protected by both a 'best interests' test and also a 'feasibility' test. Under the 'best interests' test, each objecting creditor must receive at least as much under the plan as it would in liquidation. The 'feasibility' test' requires that debtor must be reasonably likely to be able to perform the promises it made in the plan.[7]

21.26 The meeting of creditors

Under paragraph 51 an initial creditors' meeting must be held as soon as reasonably after the company enters administration and in any event within ten weeks though this time limit can be extended by the court or by the creditors. The meeting is preceded by the creditors and members being sent a copy of the

---

1 Ibid, paragraph 49(4).
2 Ibid, paragraph 49(6).
3 Ibid, paragraph 51(3).
4 This is a mandatory obligation on the administrator: Schedule B1, paragraph 47(1). But he can release individual persons from their obligation to comply: Schedule B1, paragraph 48(2).
5 They must comply within 11 days of being given notice of the requirement by the administrator unless the administrator extends the period: Schedule B1, paras 48(1) and 48(2).
6 Schedule B1, paragraphs 73(1)(a) and (b).
7 For a general discussion see V Finch, *Corporate Insolvency Law: Perspectives and Principles* (Cambridge University Press, 2002) at pp 195–204.

administrator's proposals which must be done at the latest within 8 weeks of the company entering into administration. The relevant periods are shorter than the three months required under section 23 of the Insolvency Act 1986 but the periods were lengthened during the course of the parliamentary passage of the Enterprise Act 2002. In initial drafts the relevant periods were four weeks and six weeks but these tight time limits were criticised for being unrealistic. It must be remembered that the administrator's statement of his proposals will have to be a detailed document setting out the history of the company, its present financial position and future plans during the administration as well as providing sufficient financial information to enable the creditors to decide whether or not they should approve the proposals.

There was a view that unrealistically short time-scales would lead to significant number of applications being made to the court for extensions. This would give rise to more costs and take up more time for insolvency practitioners and creditors. Consequently, the time-scales were amended so as more closely to reflect the day-to-day practicalities of administration. It should be noted however that under paragraph 4 the administrator must perform his functions as quickly and efficiently as is reasonably practicable.

An administrator has power to dispense with the requirement to hold an initial creditors' meeting if the company, in his belief, is at either of two extremes. The first scenario is where he thinks the company is fully solvent, ie the company has sufficient property to enable each creditor to be paid in full.[1] The second situation is where the company has insufficient property to make a distribution to unsecured creditors other than by virtue of the ring-fencing provision.[2] The decision about not holding a meeting is based upon the administrator's subjective assessment and in the opinion of certain commentators is 'ripe for abuse'.[3] On the other hand, an administrator can be forced to hold an initial creditors' meeting if so requested by creditors of the company whose debts amount to at least 10% of the total debts of the company.[4]

The initial creditors' meeting may perform an important function in ensuring the accountability of administrators especially where an administrator has been appointed out of court by a floating charge holder. An administrator is required to perform his functions in the interests of creditors of the company in the whole. The creditors' meetings may help to ensure that more than lip-service is paid to this obligation. During the parliamentary debates an amendment was suggested but rejected which would make an initial creditors' meeting mandatory in all instances. In favour of this proposition it was pointed out that the administrator is given extensive powers to manage the company's affairs, business and property without interference from anyone and that, at the very least, he should report to the creditors at one meeting what he proposes to do. It was said:

> Creditors must be given a chance to voice their concern and they should not be denied that right, particularly where the administrator thinks the company has insufficient property to enable a distribution to be made to unsecured creditors.

---

1   See generally Schedule B1, paragraph 52(1).
2   What is now section 176A Insolvency Act 1986 which sets aside a proportion of floating charge recoveries for the benefit of unsecured creditors.
3   See S Davies (ed.), *Insolvency and the Enterprise Act 2002* (Jordans, 2003) at p 152.
4   Schedule B1, paragraph 52(2).

> These creditors will recover nothing and they . . . must be satisfied that nothing can be done for them and to be able to test that at the meeting.[1]

The Government did not demur at the suggestion that creditors had the right to be involved in the process of administration. The amendment was resisted however on the basis that it would:

> add unnecessarily to costs, burden the courts and reduce the returns for those creditors who did have a financial interest. . . . [T]he virtues of creditors' meetings are grossly exaggerated. It costs a lost of money for the boss of a small company to attend a creditors' meeting, possibly more than he is owed.

This point however lacks total conviction especially when the suggested alternative – recourse to the courts – is likely to be even more costly and productive of delay.

The meeting of the creditors convened to consider the administrator's proposals has limited powers. It can accept the administrator's proposals in toto but any modification favoured by the meeting can be incorporated into the proposals only with the administrator's consent.[2] If the administrator and the creditors cannot reach agreement, the matter must be referred back to the court. The court may provide that the appointment of the administrator shall cease to have effect from a specified time and make such consequential order as it thinks fit, or adjourn the hearing conditionally or unconditionally or make an interim order or any other order that it thinks fit.[3] This can include allowing the administration to proceed despite the creditors' opposition.[4] It may also make a winding up order on a winding up petition that has been suspended while the company is in administration.

Where agreement is reached, the administrator must again report the outcome to the court and must also inform creditors and the Registrar of Companies.[5] There is provision under paragraph 56 for the administrator to summon further creditors' meetings if directed to do so by the court or so requested by creditors whose debts amount to at least 10% of the total debts of the company. The administrator's role after the proposals have been approved is to manage the company in accordance with the proposals. Ordinarily, any proposed substantial revisions to the proposals must be put to the creditors at a creditors' meeting[6] but it has been held that the court has jurisdiction itself to authorise deviation from the original proposals in an exceptional case, eg where the delay involved in convening a meeting could be fatal to the chances of success of the revised proposal.[7] If revised proposals are not approved, the administrator can continue to follow the old proposals, or, if his experience leads him to conclude that the purpose of the administration is incapable of achievement, he may apply to court under paragraph 79 for his appointment to cease to have effect.

---

1   *Hansard*, HL Debs, col 783, 29 July 2002.
2   Schedule B1, paragraph 53(1).
3   Ibid, paragraph 59(2).
4   *Re Maxwell Communications Corp* [1992] BCLC 465 at p 467; *Re Structures & Computers Ltd* [1998] BCC 348 at p 353.
5   Schedule B1, paragraph 54(6).
6   Ibid, paragraph 55(2).
7   *Re Smallman Construction Ltd* (1988) 4 BCC 784, [1989] BCLC 420.

21.27 The committee of creditors

A creditors' meeting may also decide to establish a creditors' committee. The creditors' committee may require the administrator to attend on the committee at any reasonable time and may also require the administrator to provide the committee with information about the exercise of his functions.[1]

21.28 Cases where urgent action is required

The legislative scheme envisages the administrator managing the day-to-day conduct of the company's affairs for the period during which he is making investigations and inquiries with a view to formulating the proposals for the achievement of the administration purposes; but, before any radical steps are taken to achieve those purposes, the creditors are to be given an opportunity to consider and review what the administrator proposes to do. Underlying this structure is the assumption that, in return for the moratorium imposed by the administration procedure, creditors are to have an important say in the conduct of the administration.

What this standard scheme ignores, however, is the possibility of circumstances arising in which the company's interests dictate that the administrator should act very quickly, perhaps even before there is an opportunity to convene a meeting of the creditors. If, for example, the administrator is offered a generous price for the business conditional upon the sale being concluded in accordance with a tight timetable which does not allow for the holding of a creditors' meeting, what can and should the administrator do? Under the legislation the administrator has wide powers even before his proposals are approved by the creditors, but do they extend to selling off the company's business prior to the holding of the creditors' meeting?

Lawrence Collins J answered this question in the affirmative in *Re Transbus International Ltd.*[2] He said:[3]

> I am satisfied that a better view would be that administrators are permitted to sell the assets of the company in advance of their proposals being approved by creditors.... Paragraph 68(2) of the Schedule requires the administrators to act in accordance with directions of the court 'if the court gives[them]'. This appears to be a deliberate choice to adopt wording that mirrors the interpretation which Neuberger J had put upon the previous provisions [in *Re T & D Industries plc*[4]] the same policy arguments apply.

Lawrence Collins J said in many cases the administrators will be justified in not laying any proposals before a meeting of creditors. This is so where the requirements of paragraph 52 are satisfied, eg where unsecured creditors are going to receive no payment. He said that if in such cases the administrators were prevented from acting without the direction of the court it would mean that they would have to seek the directions of the court before carrying out any function throughout the whole of the administration. This ran counter to the goal of the Enterprise Act 2002 which reflected a conscious policy to reduce the involvement of the court in administrations, where possible.

---

1   Schedule B1, paragraph 57.
2   [2004] 2 All ER 911.
3   At paragraphs 12–13 of the judgment.
4   [2000] 1 WLR 646.

21.29 Protection of the interests of creditors and members

Any creditor or member of a company in administration may apply to the court under paragraph 74(1) claiming that either the administrator is acting or has acted so as unfairly to harm the interests of the applicant (whether alone or in common with some or all other members or creditors) or that the administrator proposes to act in such a way. This provision substantially re-enacts section 27 of the Insolvency Act 1986 with some modifications of language.[1] Paragraph 74 (2), on the other hand, is wholly new. It enable a creditor or member of a company in administration to apply to the court claiming that the administrator is not performing his functions as quickly or as efficiently as is reasonably practicable.

On such an application, the court may make such order as it thinks fit for giving relief in respect of the matters complained of, or adjourn the hearing conditionally or unconditionally, or make an interim order or any other order that it thinks fit.[2] An order under paragraph 74 may, in particular:[3]

(1) regulate the administrator's exercise of his functions;
(2) require the administrator to do or not to do a specified thing;
(3) require a meeting of creditors to be held for a specified purpose;
(4) provide for the appointment of the administrator to cease to have effect nd make such consequential provisions as the court thinks fit.

However, an order under paragraph 74 must not impede or prevent the implementation of a voluntary arrangement approved by the creditors or any compromise or arrangement sanctioned under section 425 of the Companies Act 1985 or, where the application for the paragraph 74 order has been made more than twenty-eight days after the approval of any proposal or revised proposals put forward by the administrator, the implementation of those proposals or revised proposals.[4]

In *Re Charnley Davies Ltd*,[5] it was held that the administrator had not acted negligently in the timing or the manner of the sale of the business of various companies in the Charnley Davies group. Millett J commented that an allegation of negligence only does not constitute an allegation of management in a manner which is unfairly prejudicial to the creditors and that, accordingly, it does not fall within the scope of section 27 of the Insolvency Act 1986. The language of paragraph 74 is different referring to 'unfairness' rather than 'unfair prejudice' but whether this warrants a difference in outcome as regards negligence allegations remains to be seen.

21.30 Replacing an administrator and vacation of office

Schedule B1, paragraphs 87–89, deal with the replacement of an administrator and paragraphs 90–95 are concerned with filling vacancies in the office of

---

1 In particular the legislature has departed from the expression 'unfairly prejudicial to the interests' to 'unfairly to harm the interests'. Whether this heralds substantive change awaits judicial interpretation.
2 Schedule B1, paragraph 74(3).
3 Ibid, paragraph 74(4).
4 Ibid, paragraph 74(6).
5 [1990] BCLC 760, [1990] BCC 605.

administrator. Under paragraph 87 an administrator may resign only in pre-scribed circumstances. An administrator may also be removed from office by order of the court and he is required to vacate office if he ceases to be qualified to act as an insolvency practitioner in relation to the company.

Generally, a person who has ceased to be the administrator of a company obtains a discharge from liability in respect of any action of his as administrator. Generally, the discharge takes effect from such time as the court may determine or, in the case of an administrator appointed out of court, at a time appointed by resolution of the creditors or the creditors' committee. The release discharges the administrator from liability in respect of any action of his as administrator.[1] The release however, does not prevent the court from exercising its powers under Schedule B1, paragraph 75, which allows the court to examine the conduct of an administrator for possible misfeasance on the application of the Official Receiver, the liquidator or any creditor or contributory of the company. On an examination of an administrator's conduct under paragraph 75 the court may order him (a) to repay, restore or account for money or property; (b) to pay interest or (c) to contribute a sum to the company's property by way of compensation for breach of duty or misfeasance.

The question of entitlement to fill a vacancy in the office of administrator depends on who made the initial appointment. Where the original appointment was made by the court, the court may replace the administrator.[2] Where an administrator was appointed out of court either by a qualified floating charge holder, the company itself or by its directors, the original appointor may replace the administrator.[3] The court however, under paragraph 95 has a general power to effect a replacement if satisfied that reasonable steps have not been taken to make a replacement or that for another reason it is right for the court to make the replacement.

21.31 Exit routes from administration

Under the Insolvency Act 1986 the exit routes from administration were somewhat inconvenient. In particular it was cumbersome to move from an administration to a creditors' voluntary liquidation (CVL). The latter was more cost effective than a compulsory liquidation but section 11(3) of the Act precluded the passing of a voluntary winding up resolution while the company was still in administration. Moreover, the relevant date for the calculation of preferential debts was the date of the passing of the winding up resolution whereas in cases where administration was followed immediately by a winding up order it was the date of entry into administration.[4] Certain preferential creditors could be disadvantaged by the different dates and for this reason might oppose a voluntary winding up. It took a great deal of judicial dexterity to resolve these difficulties.

---

1   Schedule B1, paragraph 98(1).
2   Ibid, paragraph 91.
3   Ibid, paras 92–94.
4   Section 387 Insolvency Act 1986. The relevant provisions were amended by the Enterprise Act 2002 and section 387(3A) stipulates that in relation to a company which is in administration the relevant date is the date on which the company enters administration.

Jacob J came up with a practical solution in *Re Mark One (Oxford Street) plc*,[1] holding that the court was empowered to order that the administrator make payments to preferential creditors as if the voluntary liquidation were a compulsory liquidation or that payments made by the administrator to the future liquidator should be on trust for the benefit of the previously preferential creditors.

The Enterprise Act 2002 streamlines the exit routes from administration and enables the company to move directly from administration to a CVL on the filing by the administrator of a requisite notice with the registrar of companies. The new procedure can be operated in cases where the administrator thinks that there are funds to make distributions to unsecured creditors (paragraph 83).[2] An administrator has an unfettered power to make distributions to secured and preferential creditors during the currency of an administration but payments to unsecured creditors require the permission of the court (paragraph 65). It seems clear from the overall thrust of the legislation that administration should not be the main vehicle for payment of unsecured creditors given the fact that an administrator must perform his functions as quickly and efficiently as is reasonably practicable.[3] Where there are effectively no funds left for payment of unsecured creditors paragraph 84 provides a fast track route from administration into dissolution of the company. Again this requires the filing of a requisite notice by the administrator with the registrar of companies. Dissolution is deemed to occur automatically three months after the filing of the notice though there is a mechanism whereby this period may be extended.

The effect of the legislative changes is that now there are nine possible exit routes from administration:

(1) Under paragraph 76 administration comes to an end automatically one year after a company goes into administration though this period may be extended either by the court or with the consent of creditors. Under the Insolvency Act 1986 there was no automatic time-limit in this respect and administrations were potentially open-ended. There was an unlimited period for the completion of an administration. Administrations were seen as too long drawn-out and cumbersome and the costs of an open-ended and potentially lengthy administration constituted a significant barrier to entering administration. The new legislative drafting reflects desire to speed up the administration process especially when viewed in combination with an administrator's duties under paragraph 4 to perform his functions as quickly and efficiently as is reasonably practicable. In the early drafts of the legislation however the relevant period was three months rather than twelve months. This was seen as too restrictive and unrealistic in many instances with applications to the court for extensions of time becoming the norm. After strenuous lobbying by professional bodies the time scales were lengthened.

(2) By court order on an application made by the administrator pursuant to paragraph 79. This paragraph requires the administrator to apply to the court if he thinks that the purpose of administration cannot be achieved in relation to the company or that the company should not have entered into

---

1   [1998] BCC 984.
2   The administrator becomes liquidator unless the creditor nominates somebody else.
3   Schedule B1, paragraph 4.

administration or a creditors' meeting has required him to make the application.

(3) Under paragraph 80 where an administrator appointed out of court files a notice that the purpose of the administration has been sufficiently achieved.

(4) By court order under paragraph 81 on an application made to it by a creditor who claims that there was an improper motive on the part of an administration applicant or an out of court appointor.

(5) Pursuant to paragraph 82 where the court makes a winding up order on public interest grounds.

(6) Where the administrator files a notice to put the company into a creditors' voluntary liquidation.

(7) Where the administration files a notice to dissolve the company.

(8) Where creditors fail to agree to the administrator's proposals or revised proposals and the court makes a termination order pursuant to paragraph 55(2).

(9) Also by court order where the administrator's actions have unfairly harmed either creditors or members – paragraph 74(4).

21.32 Expenses of administration and post-administration financing

Paragraph 99(3) provides that where a person ceases to be an administrator, his remuneration and expenses shall be charged on and payable out of property of which he had custody or control immediately before cessation and will be payable in priority to any floating charge.

The new legislative framework has been criticised for the absence of any specific provision for the financing of corporate rescues.[1] As one commentator observes[2], the legislation:

> fails to address the difficulty that an administrator may face in obtaining funding, especially in a situation where it would be desirable for him to be able to offer security but, at the time of his appointment, the assets of the company were already subject to fixed security or were subject to a negative pledge preventing the company from granting security over the assets. There is no provision which would allow the administrator to proceed in a manner which may be contrary to or affect the rights of such a person and, being an officer of the court, he must act honourably towards such a person.

New finance is often critical to the survival of the business of the company. Unless such finance is available from some source the assets of the company may have to be sold on a piecemeal basis and the company will be forced into liquidation. As the Department of Trade and Industry pointed out in 'Review of Company Rescue

---

1   See however Rule 2.67 of the Insolvency Rules 1986 as amended. There was no equivalent to this under the original regime and it might be argued that it is sufficiently broadly worded so as to permit post-administration financing to be recognized as one of the expenses of the administration.

2   See McKnight, 'The Reform of Corporate Insolvency Law in Great Britain' [2002] JIBL 324 at 327.

and Business Reconstruction Mechanisms', new secured finance is only available to support a rescue procedure in the UK where the existing secured creditors agree or where there are unsecured assets or sufficient equity in unsecured assets.[1] In the parliamentary passage of the Enterprise Act the government resisted an amendment that would have created a statutory framework for super-priority financing after the administration process has commenced.[2] It was wary of creating a situation that would essentially guarantee a return to lenders advancing funds on the basis of such priority irrespective of the commercial viability of the rescue proposals. In its view, the issue of whether to lend to a company in administration was a commercial one that was best left to the commercial judgment of the lending market. A lender might take into account the viability of the rescue proposals and the availability of free assets to serve as collateral, amongst other things.

Reference was made during the parliamentary debates to the experience in the US but the official line was that it would be inappropriate to attempt to replicate the chapter 11 provisions in the UK where the business culture and economic environment are quite different. In the US, post petition financing, as it is called, is dealt with in paragraph 364 of the Bankruptcy Code. Under this provision, any credit extended to the corporate debtor during the reorganisation process has priority over pre-petition unsecured claims. If the extension of credit is in the ordinary course of business, then the priority gained is automatic. If, on the other hand, the extension of credit is outside the ordinary course of business, then the priority must be authorised by the court prior to the granting of credit. In the absence of any agreement by the lender to the contrary, a corporate debtor can obtain confirmation of a reorganisation plan only by ensuring payment of the post-petition lender in full at the confirmation stage. Moreover, even if the reorganisation plan fails, post-petition debts will have priority over unsecured pre-petition debts in the ensuring liquidation.

There may be a significant number of cases where the a company's assets are secured to such an extent that the granting of priority over simply pre-petition unsecured creditors offers new lenders little chance of recovery in any subsequent liquidation. In these circumstances, meaningful priority means priority over pre-filing secured creditors. Article 364(d) of the US Bankruptcy Code expressly allows the court to authorise debtors in possession to grant new lenders priority over pre-filing secured creditors in narrowly defined circumstances. The relevant provision however incorporates protection for affected secured creditors by requiring the debtor to prove that it cannot obtain the loan without granting such a security interest and that the pre-filing secured creditor is adequately protected against loss. The US courts appear to apply these requirements strictly. In consequence, the 'priming' of prior secured lending is permitted only relatively infrequently. In effect, a priming loan may not be granted unless the court concludes there is sufficient value in the collateral to protect fully both old and new lenders.[3]

---

1   See pp 33–35 of the Review Group report and see also V Finch, *Corporate Insolvency Law: Perspectives and Principles* (Cambridge University Press, 2002) at pp 301–305.

2   See the House of Lords parliamentary debates for 29 July 2002, and see also the extensive discussion in S Davies (ed.) *Insolvency and the Enterprise Act 2002* (Jordans, 2003) at pp 19–26.

3   See generally R Broude, 'How the Rescue Culture came to the United States and the Myths that surround Chapter 11' (2000) 16 Insolvency Law and Practice 194.

There are other incentives built into the system to encourage post-petition financing. Firstly, while Article 9–202 of the US Commercial Code validates the functional equivalent of the floating charge – a blanket security interest on shifting collateral, a general security interest over all a company's property appears to be much less common in the US context.[1] Moreover, Article 552 of the US Bankruptcy Code terminates the effect of a blanket security interest in its application to property acquired after the bankruptcy petition has been filed though there are exceptions. The curtailment of the blanket security interest may be one of the factors that encourages a pre-petition lender to continue funding the company.

In Ireland under the 'court examinership' procedure that is designed as a corporate rescue procedure like administration there are also special statutory provisions in place to facilitate the financing of companies in financial difficulties.[2] During the period of examinership, a company enjoys protection from its creditors like a company in administration. The relevant legislation allows the examiner – a court-appointed official, normally an accountant – to certify liabilities incurred during the protection period where such liabilities are essential to ensure the survival of the company as a going concern.[3] The liabilities so certified then rank with the examiner's own expenses ahead of all other liabilities including pre-examinership secured liabilities. The 'certification of liabilities' procedure can be used to cover borrowings made by the company during the period of examinership. In the leading case – *Re Atlantic Magnetics Ltd*[4] – the Irish Supreme Court interpreted the original legislation to mean that assets already secured by fixed charges may be used for the purposes of fresh borrowings. The end result of this and other decisions is that virtually any expenditure, including additional company borrowings, can be deemed 'expenses' if so certified by the examiner.

The Irish legislation has however been amended to provide that liabilities certified by the examiner should rank after the claims of fixed charge holders although still ahead of floating charges.

21.33 The administrator as an 'office-holder'

The Insolvency Act 1986 gives certain rights and privileges to categories of insolvency practitioners defined as 'office-holders'. An administrator is within the definition of an office-holder for certain purposes.

As an office-holder, an administrator can attack transactions which took place prior to his appointment on the grounds that they amount to transactions at an undervalue, preferences, extortionate credit transactions, vulnerable floating charges or transactions defrauding creditors. These special powers are also enjoyed by liquidators and are considered further below. Unlike a liquidator, an administrator does not have standing to bring proceedings for fraudulent or wrongful trading.

---

1   See generally for a comparative treatment G McCormack, *Secured Credit under English and American Law* (Cambridge University Press, 2004).
2   See generally on this procedure T Courtney, *The Law of Private Companies* (Butterworths, 2002) Chapter 23.
3   Irish Companies (Amendment) Act 1990, section 10.
4   [1993] 2 IR 561.

Suppliers of gas, electricity, water and telecommunications services cannot make it a condition of continuing the supply that the administrator pays outstanding charges. This protection is given to the administrator as an office-holder. However, the supplier can require the administrator to give a personal guarantee in respect of any new supplies.[1]

The powers which an administrator, as an office-holder, enjoys in relation to investigating the conduct of the company's affairs prior to his appointment are the same as those enjoyed by a liquidator.

21.34 An overview of the new administration procedure

In analysing the features of the revamped administration order procedure and the steps leading up to its enactment a number of conclusions can be reached. Firstly, the lobbying power of banks and related groups is evident in the whole process. Commentators have spoken of banks winning the battle for the Enterprise Bill.[2] It is possible to see and read this at various levels. On one level one could say that the government are rightly sympathetic and sensitive to the concerns expressed by City practitioners and are motivated by a desire to make the legislation workable on the ground. A more critical and cynical view would see the outcome of the lobbying process as an abject surrender on the government's side to naked self-interest on the part of banks. Banks in this perspective are solely concerned with boosting their own short-term profit levels and are not motivated by any wider societal concerns or issues of long-term economic performance.

Viewed in the round, banks did not come too badly out of the Enterprise Act 2002 reforms. As far as existing lending agreements are concerned, the right to appoint an administrative receiver is preserved and even in the case of new lending agreements, there are still a substantial number of exceptional instances which continue to permit the appointment of an administrative receiver. Moreover, in one guise the 'new' administration procedure is simply administrative receivership under another name, with a few bells and whistles attached. The administrator has wider duties than an administrative receiver to consider the interests of creditors as a whole but an administrator can be appointed out of court by a floating charge holder and can made distributions to secured and preferential creditors. Banks also derive a short-term benefit under the Enterprise Act 2002 from the abolition of Crown preference. It is intended that this should be offset by the requirement that a proportion of floating charge recoveries should be set aside or ring fenced for the benefit of unsecured creditors. Crown Preference however disappears for all insolvencies with immediate effect whereas the ring fencing provisions only kick in for new lending agreements ie those entered into after the coming into force of the Enterprise Act 2002 on 15 September 2003.

The administration procedure in the UK was born out of receivership. The Cork Committee saw the new procedure as being particularly appropriate in cases where a company had not created a floating charge over substantially the whole of its property and consequently there was no secured lender in a position to appoint a receiver over the entirety of the company's business operations. The Insolvency

---

1   Section 233.
2   See J Willcock 'How the Banks Won the Battle for the Enterprise Bill' [2002] Recovery 24 at 26. The quote is attributed to David Mond of Hodgsons.

Act 1986 rebranded the receiver of substantially the whole of a company's business as an administrative receiver. This rebranding exercise has been carried a stage further by the Enterprise Act 2002 with the administrative receiver appointed by a floating charge holder being transmuted into an administrator whose first objective is to try to rescue the company as a going concern unless he thinks that this is not reasonably practicable. Nevertheless, one of the essential features of receivership remains, ie the board of directors lose control of the corporate decision-making machinery. It could be argued that if one is designing a corporate rescue framework from scratch one would not start with receivership. In the US there was a different starting point and a different end result though it must be remembered that the notion of privately-appointed receiverships is almost unknown in the United States. In the US the existing management keep the apparatus of power while the company is undergoing the reorganisation process.

Finally, one might conclude that, while the Enterprise Act 2002 and the revamping of the administration procedure are not wholly devoid of substance, the Act also contains a whole lot of 'spin'. Some persons may find it unsurprising, and indeed reassuring, out that beneath New Labour clothes lurk 'old' Conservative concepts. For others, it is somewhat disappointing that the rhetoric of fundamental and far-reaching reform is not necessarily matched by the reality.

PART 4: THE COMPULSORY LIQUIDATION OF COMPANIES

21.35 Compulsory winding-up

We now turn to consider the liquidation or, as it is also called, the winding-up of companies. The first type of winding-up procedure is the compulsory liquidation, which entails the presentation of a petition requesting that the court make a winding-up order and appoint a liquidator. All companies incorporated under the Companies Act 1985 and the statutes which it replaced are subject to the winding-up jurisdiction of the court under the Insolvency Act 1986.[1] Overseas companies registered under the branch registration regime[2] or the place of business regime[3] may also be compulsorily wound up, as may unregistered companies[4] including foreign companies which carry on business in Great Britain but which are not registered.[5] The winding up jurisdiction of the courts has now been extended by the EC Regulation on Insolvency Proceedings (Council Regulation No 1346/2000). The Regulation gives an English court jurisdiction to wind up any company whose centre of main interests is in England even though

---

1 Section 117 of the Insolvency Act 1986 deals with the respective jurisdictions of the High Court and county court.

2 Oversea Companies and Credit and Financial institutions (Branch Disclosure) Regulations 1992, SI 1992/3179.

3 Companies Act 1985, Part XXIII.

4 Defined for this purpose by section 220 of the Insolvency Act 1986. See *Re Witney Town Football and Social Club* [1993] BCC 874; *Re Normandy Marketing Ltd* [1993] BCC 879.

5 The court must be satisfied that there is a sufficient connection with the jurisdiction. It has been held that this does not necessarily have to be the presence of assets in the jurisdiction: *Re Real Estate Development Co* [1991] BCLC 210; *Re A Company (No 00359 of 1987)* (also reported as *International Westminster Bank plc v Okeanos Maritime Corp*) [1988] Ch 210, [1987] 3

the company may be incorporated elsewhere. The Regulation is discussed in detail at paragraph **21.59** below.

Under Schedule B1, paragraph 42, while a company is in administration no resolution may be passed nor order made for the winding up of the company. The same prohibition also applies under the interim moratorium, which obtains whenever an administration application is pending or where notice to appoint an administrator out of court has been filed.

21.35.1   Grounds for a compulsory winding-up order

Section 122 of the Insolvency Act 1986 sets out the grounds upon which a company may be wound up by the court.

The most common ground upon which petitions are presented is that the company is unable to pay its debts. Section 123 of the Insolvency Act 1986 contains the definition of inability to pay debts. The cash flow and balance sheet tests of insolvency discussed in **21.2** are tests of inability to pay debts for this purpose. In addition, a company is deemed unable to pay its debts:

(1) if a creditor (by assignment or otherwise) to whom the company is indebted in a sum exceeding £750 then due has served on the company, by leaving it at the company's registered office, a written demand (in the prescribed form) requiring the company to pay the sum so due and the company has for three weeks thereafter neglected to pay the sum or to secure or compound for it to the reasonable satisfaction of the creditor; or

(2) if, in England and Wales, execution or other process issued on a judgment, decree or order of any court in favour of a creditor of the company is returned unsatisfied in whole or in part; or

(3) if, in Scotland, the induciae of a charge for payment on an extract decree, or an extract registered bond, or an extract registered protest, have expired without payment being made; or

(4) if, in Northern Ireland, a certificate of unenforceability has been granted in respect of a judgment against the company.

Unpaid creditors of a company may consider commencing winding-up proceedings against the company as an alternative to suing it for payment. As a debt collection mechanism, winding-up proceedings may be swifter and, for the individual creditor, less expensive than a claim that may not come to trial for some time; on the other hand, winding-up is a collective procedure for the benefit of creditors generally and it does not benefit specific creditors individually.[1] However, if the company disputes the debt and the court accepts that the dispute

---

All ER 137, [1987] 3 WLR 339, [1987] BCLC 450; *Re Eloc Electro-Optieck and Communicatie BV* [1982] Ch 43, [1981] 2 All ER 1111, [1981] 3 WLR 176; *New Hampshire Insurance Co v Rush & Tompkins Group plc* [1998] 2 BCLC 471; *Re Latreefers Inc* [1999] 1 BCLC 271. See also *Banque des Marchands de Moscou v Kinderley* [1951] 1 Ch 112 (CA); *Re Compania Merabello San Nicholas SA* [1973] Ch 75; *Re Allobrogia Steamship Corp* [1978] 3 All ER 423. There must be a reasonable possibility that the winding-up order would benefit those applying for it and the court must be able to exercise jurisdiction over one or more persons interested in the distribution of the company's assets.

1   See generally, F Oditah, 'Winding Up Recalcitrant Debtors' [1995] LMCLQ 107.

is genuine,[1] the petition will usually be dismissed because the procedure is ill-equipped to deal with the resolution of factual disputes. It may be held to be an abuse of process to have proceeded by way of statutory demand instead of by claim,[2] in which case the creditor may be held liable to indemnify the company for its costs.[3] Also, the company may be able to resist the making of a winding-up order by establishing that its failure to pay resulted otherwise than from neglect, for example where it can show that the demand was never received.[4]

If a debt is disputed in part but the part of the debt which is undisputed is above the statutory minimum a petition can still validly be presented.[5] If a creditor makes a statutory demand for more than was actually due, provided the amount that was due was more than £750, any winding-up order made by the court on the basis of the demand remains valid.[6]

Where the petitioner succeeds in establishing a ground on which a winding-up order may be made, it has been said that he has a prima facie right to a winding-up order.[7] However, in all cases, the court has discretion whether or not to order winding-up. Since winding-up is a collective procedure for the benefit of creditors generally, one situation where the court may exercise its discretion against winding-up is where other creditors in the same class[8] oppose the making of the order. In this case, the court will usually have regard to the majority of the creditors and will refuse the petition if it is opposed by the majority.[9]

A specific case where there can be a difference of opinion between groups of creditors is where some creditors favour a compulsory winding-up whilst others

---

1   *R Claybridge Shipping Co SA* [1981] Com LR 107, [1997] 1 BCLC 572 (CA); *Alipour v Ary* [1997] 1 BCLC 557 (CA); *Re A Company (No 006685 of 1996)* [1997] 1 BCLC 639. But dismissal in these circumstances is a rule of practice only and it must give way in circumstances that make it desirable for the petition to proceed, such as where the petitioner would otherwise be without a remedy: *Claybridge*. See also *Re Janeash Ltd* [1990] BCC 250 (no genuine claim).

2   *London Wharfing Co* (1866) 35 Beav 37; *Re Brighton Club and Norfolk Hotel Co* (1865) 35 Beav 204; *Re London and Paris Banking Corp* (1875) 19 Eq 444; *Re Gold Hill Mines* (1883) 23 Ch D 210; *Mann v Goldstein* [1968] 1 WLR 1091; *Stonegate Securities Ltd v Gregory* [1980] Ch 576; *Re Wallace Smith Group Ltd* [1992] BCLC 989.

3   *Re A Company (No 0012209 of 1991)* [1992] 2 All ER 797, [1992] 1 WLR 351, [1992] BCLC 865 followed in *Re A Company (No 00751 of 1992)* [1992] BCLC 869.

4   *Re London and Paris Banking Corp* (1875) 19 Eq 444; *Re A Company* [1985] BCLC 37; and see *Re Cannon Screen Entertainment Ltd* [1989] BCLC 661.

5   *Re Tweeds Garage Ltd* [1962] 1 Ch 406; *Re Trinity Insurance Co Ltd* [1990] BCC 235; *Taylor's Industrial Flooring Ltd v M&H Plant Hire (Manchester) Ltd* [1990] BCC 44, [1990] BCLC 216; *Re Pendigo Ltd* [1996] BCC 608; *Re Bydand Ltd* [1997] BCC 915.

6   *Cardiff Preserved Coal and Coke Co v Norton* (1867) 2 Ch App 405. On costs in these circumstances, see *Re A Company (No 008122 of 1989), ex parte Transcontinental Insurance Services Ltd* [1990] BCLC 697.

7   See *Re Demaglass Holdings Ltd* [2001] 2 BCLC 633; *Re Lummus Agricultural Services Ltd* [2001] 1 BCLC 137.

8   *Re Crigglestone Coal Co Ltd* [1906] 2 Ch 327 (unsecured creditors in different class from secured creditor for this purpose); *Re Leigh Estates (UK) Ltd* [1994] BCC 292. See section 195 which provides for the holding of meetings to ascertain the wishes of creditors (or contributories) on matters relating to the winding up of the company.

9   *Re Chapel House Colliery Co*, above; *Re Uruguay Central and Hygueritas Rly Co of Monte Video* (1873) 11 Ch D 372; *Re St Thomas's Dock Co* (1876) 2 Ch D 116.

are content for the company to be wound up voluntarily. This situation is discussed at **21.39–21.46**.

21.35.2 *Persons who may present a petition*

Section 124 of the Insolvency Act 1986 provides that a petition for the winding-up of a company may be presented to the court by all or any of the following whether acting together or separately:

(1) the company;
(2) the directors of the company;
(3) any creditor or creditors of the company (including any contingent or prospective creditor or creditors);
(4) any contributory or contributories.[1]

A petition presented by the directors does not require the approval of the shareholders. In *Re Instrumentation Electrical Services Ltd*,[2] Mervyn Davies J held that all the directors had to join in the petition. The position may be different where the decision to seek a winding-up is embodied in a formal board resolution, because it is the duty of all directors to implement such resolutions.[3]

An administrative receiver is expressly empowered by the Act[4] to present or defend a petition for the winding-up of the company over which he has been appointed.[5] An administrator[6] or the supervisor of a CVA[7] can also present a winding up petition.

A contributory, which means, broadly, any present or past member of the company, is not entitled to present a winding-up petition unless either: (a) the number of members is reduced below two; or (b) the shares in respect of which he is a contributory, or some of them, were originally allotted to him, or have been held by him and registered in his name, for at least six months during the eighteen months before the commencement of the winding-up or have devolved on him through the death of a former holder. The term 'contributory' is considered further at **21.52**.

---

1 Other statutory provisions empower specific bodies to seek winding-up orders on other grounds; eg, under section 124A of the Insolvency Act 1986, the Secretary of State can seek the winding-up of a company on public interest grounds (see *Re Titan International Inc* [1998] 1 BCLC 102).
2 (1988) 4 BCC 301.
3 See *Re Equiticorp International plc* (1989) 1 WLR 1010 (directors' petition for an administration order).
4 Section 42 and Schedule 1, paragraph 21. Whether a receiver who is not an administrative receiver has this power depends upon the construction of the debenture under which he was appointed: *Re Emmadart Ltd* [1979] 1 Ch 540. For an example of an administrative receiver's petition, see *Re Television Parlour plc* (1988) 4 BCC 95.
5 Section 14 and Schedule 1, paragraph 21. The clerk of the magistrates' court, the Secretary of State and the Financial Services Authority are other persons who can petition for winding-up on various grounds. Note also the power of the Official Receiver to petition for the winding-up of a company which is being wound up voluntarily: section 124(5).
6 Insolvency Act 1986 Schedule 1, paragraph 21 and Schedule B1, paragraph 60.
7 Section 7(4)(b) and Schedule A1, paragraph 39(5)(b) Insolvency Act 1986.

A contributory who has not paid calls upon his shares will be permitted to petition only in very special circumstances[1] and will usually be required to pay the amount of his unpaid calls into court.[2] A contributory must also prove that he has an economic interest in the winding-up: this requirement can be satisfied by showing that he is liable for calls on partly paid shares or, if the shares are fully paid, by establishing that there is some prospect of assets being available to him in the winding-up.[3] The company's articles of association cannot take away the right of a member to petition for the company's winding-up.[4]

In practice most petitioners will be creditors of the company. A creditor may petition whether he is secured or unsecured.[5] The creditor may be the original creditor of the company or an assignee of the debt.[6]

A contingent or prospective creditor of the company is also entitled to petition.[7]

21.35.3   The hearing of the petition

Section 125 of the Insolvency Act 1986 states that the court, on hearing the petition, may:

(1) dismiss it;
(2) adjourn the hearing conditionally or unconditionally;
(3) make an interim order;
(4) make any order that it thinks fit;
(5) make a winding-up order.

The court cannot refuse to make a winding-up order on the basis only that the company's assets have been mortgaged to an amount equal to or in excess of those assets or that the company has no assets.[8]

If a petition has been presented by the members of a company as contributories on the ground that it is just and equitable that the company should be wound up, the court, if it is of the opinion: (a) that the petitioners are entitled to relief either by winding up the company or by some other means; and (b) that in the absence of any other remedy it would be just and equitable that the company should be wound up, may make the order. However, if the court is of the opinion that some other remedy is available to the petitioners and that they are acting unreasonably

1   The holder of share warrants to bearer, who is not the original allottee, cannot present a petition: *Re Wala Wynaad India Gold Mining Co* (1882) 21 Ch D 849; see also *Re Patent Steam Engine Co* (1878) 8 Ch D 464 (company neglected to register persons who established their title to shares for more than six months: held they were entitled to petition); *Re Gattopardo Ltd* [1969] 1 WLR 61; *Re A Company* [1894] 2 Ch 349.

2   *Re Crystal Reef Gold Mining Co* [1892] 1 Ch 408.

3   *Re Rica Gold Washing Co* (1879) 11 Ch D 36; *Re Greenhaven Motors Ltd* [1997] BCC 547. See generally on disputed petitions by contributories, *Alipour v Ary* [1997] 1 BCLC 557 (CA).

4   *Re Peveril Gold Mines* [1898] 1 Ch 122 (CA).

5   The secured creditor does not invalidate his security: *Moor v Anglo-Italian Bank* (1879) 10 Ch D 681; *Re Borough of Portsmouth etc Tramways Co* [1892] 2 Ch 362; *Re Great Western (Forest of Dean) Coal Consumers' Co* (1882) 21 Ch D 769; *Re Cambrian Mining Co* [1881] WN 125.

6   *Re Paris Skating Rink Co* (1877) 5 Ch D 959 (CA); *Re Montgomery Moore Ship Collision Doors Syndicate* [1903] WN 121.

7   *Re Dollar Land Holdings plc* [1993] BCC 823; *Tottenham Hotspur plc v Edennote plc* [1995] 1 BCLC 65.

8   Section 125(1). *Bell Group Finance (Pty) Ltd v Bell Group (UK) Holdings Ltd* [1996] BCC 505.

in seeking to have the company wound up instead of pursuing that other remedy, it may refuse to make the order.[1]

Once made, a winding-up order operates in favour of all creditors and contributories of the company as if made on the joint petition of a creditor and a contributory.[2]

21.35.4 Commencement of the winding-up

On the making of a winding-up order the commencement of the liquidation relates back to the time at which the petition was presented. However, if before the presentation of the petition the company had passed a resolution for voluntary winding-up, the winding-up of the company is deemed to have commenced at the time that resolution was passed (whether it was for a members' or creditors' voluntary liquidation).[3] The relation back is important because of some of the results which follow upon the commencement of the winding-up, such as its effect upon dispositions of the company's assets.

21.36 The effect of a winding-up order on dispositions of assets

Section 127 of the Insolvency Act 1986 states:

> In a winding-up by the court, any disposition of the company's property, and any transfer of shares, or alteration in the status of the company's members, made after the commencement of the winding-up is, unless the court otherwise orders, void.[4]

In *Re French's (Wine Bar) Ltd,*[5] the company had contracted to sell its assets prior to the commencement of its winding-up. Vinelott J held[6] that the completion of the contract did not constitute a disposition of the company's property within what is now section 127, because that section relates only to property in which the company is beneficially interested. The company had entered into an unconditional contract to sell the property and the contract was specifically enforceable. Accordingly, the beneficial interest in the property had passed to the purchaser before the commencement of the winding-up.

Vinelott J cautioned that it did not follow that the completion of any contract would in all circumstances fall outside the section. If, for example, the contract was conditional or voidable by the company, the waiver of the condition or the confirmation of the contract might amount to a disposition, as might the variation of contractual terms. Vinelott J stated that, in practice, unless a contract was

---

1   Section 125(2). See **17.15**.
2   Insolvency Act 1986, section 130(4).
3   Section 129 of the Insolvency Act 1986. The time will be noted on the petition itself by the court when it is presented. The section also states that 'unless the court, on proof of fraud or mistake, directs otherwise, all proceedings taken in the voluntary winding up are deemed to have been validly taken'.
4   This section does not apply to dispositions giving rise to market charges: section 175(4) of the Companies Act 1989. Note also the disapplication of section 127 in the circumstances provided for in regulations 16 and 119 of the Financial Markets and Insolvency (Settlement Finality) Regulations 1999, SI 1999/2979.
5   [1987] BCLC 499, (1987) 3 BCC 173.
6   Citing *Re Gray's Inn Construction Co Ltd* [1980] 1 All ER 814, [1980] 1 WLR 711 and *Re Margart Pty Ltd, Hamilton v Westpac Banking Corp* (1984) 9 ACLR 269, [1985] BCLC 314 (realisation of floating charge security). See also *Wiley v Commonwealth of Australia* (1995) 13 ACLC 1, at 556.

plainly specifically enforceable and there was no possible dispute, it would be prudent to seek the court's approval for completion.

The operation of section 127 in relation to payments into and out of a company's bank account has generated some case-law. The simplest view is that all such payments are dispositions of property[1] but the cases do not fully support this view. It is established that payments into an overdrawn account are dispositions of the company's property for the purposes of section 127.[2] The argument that a payment into an account which is in credit is also a disposition within section 127[3] was considered and rejected in *Re Barn Crown Ltd*,[4] where such a payment, made by cheque, was characterised as amounting simply to an adjustment of entries in the statement recording the account between the bank and the company.

In respect of payments out of an account, the leading authority is now the decision of the Court of Appeal in *Hollicourt (Contracts) Ltd v Bank of Ireland*.[5] In this case it was held that a payment by a company to a creditor, made by a cheque drawn on a bank account in credit, after the presentation of the winding up petition, was a disposition of the company's property in favour of the creditor but did not constitute such a disposition in favour of the bank. The court said that in honouring the cheque the bank was merely acting on the company's mandate as its agent. There was, in its view, a restitutionary liability on the payee of the cheque to reimburse the company but no liability on the part of the bank. Mummery LJ said:[6]

> the policy promoted by section 127 is not aimed at imposing on a bank restitutionary liability to a company in respect of the payments made by cheques in favour of the creditors, in addition to the unquestioned liability of the payees of the cheques... The section impinges on the end result of the process of payment initiated by the company ie. the point of ultimate receipt of the company's property in consequence of a disposition by the company. The statutory purpose ... is accomplished without any need for the section to impinge on the legal validity of intermediate steps, such as banking transactions, which are merely part of the process by which dispositions of the company's property are made. This is not a restitutionary situation where the bank has been unjustly enriched as against the company and where the general law requires the restitution of the benefit.

In *Hollicourt* the relevant account was in credit at all material times but the Court of Appeal suggested that even if the company's bank account were in overdraft, the result would be the same in respect of a claim for recovery as against the bank. According to the court the need for a complex analysis of whether payments were made out of an account that was in debit or in credit could not be justified on any sensible view of the purpose of section 127. The court strongly disapproved of observations in *Re Gray's Inn Construction Co Ltd*[7] which appeared to suggest that (i) all post-presentation cheques drawn in favour of third parties on a company's bank account, whether that account is in credit or in debit, involve a disposition of

---

1   *Re McGuinness Bros (UK) Ltd* (1987) 3 BCC 571 at 574.
2   *Re Gray's Inn Construction Ltd*, above; *Re McGuinness Bros (UK) Ltd*, above.
3   This argument, which derives some support from dicta in *Re Gray's Inn Construction Co Ltd*, and *Re McGuinness Bros (UK) Ltd*, above, is examined in more depth in Goode, *Principles of Corporate Insolvency Law*, 2nd edn (Sweet & Maxwell, 1997) at pp 427–429.
4   [1994] 4 All ER 42, [1994] BCC 381.
5   [2001] Ch 555 endorsing the ruling of Lightman J in *Coutt & Co v Stock* [2000] BCC 247.
6   [2001] Ch 555 at p 563.
7   Above.

the amount of the cheque in favour of the bank and are invalidated by the statutory provision, unless validated by the court and (ii) in consequence of statutory avoidance of such dispositions, the bank may be liable in proceedings by the liquidator for the amount of the dispositions of property, albeit only to the extent that the amounts prove to be irrecoverable from the creditors who were paid.

The safest course for anybody dealing with a company that has a petition on file is for an application to be made to the court for a validating order. The court can make such an order even before the hearing of the winding-up petition.[1] The court can authorise particular dispositions or the general continuance of trading (including, for that purpose, the continued operation of the company's bank accounts). The court can validate prospective dispositions or grant retrospective validations. In *Re Gray's Inn Construction*,[2] it was held[3] that the bank was entitled to have validated retrospectively payments in and out of the account before it became aware of the petition. Buckley LJ stated that 'a disposition carried out in good faith in the ordinary course of business[4] at a time when the parties are unaware that a petition has been presented may, it seems, normally be validated by the court unless there is any ground for thinking that the transaction may involve an attempt to prefer the disponee in which case the transaction would probably not be validated'. It was also accepted that dispositions which did not reduce the value of assets (such as sales of assets at full value or for more than they were worth) would normally be validated. In general, the court, in considering whether to grant the validating order, will consider whether the disposition would be for the benefit of the company's creditors.[5] A disposition that allows one pre-liquidation creditor to receive payment in full whilst other creditors are limited to the dividends that they will receive in the liquidation will be sanctioned only where this will benefit the creditors as a whole.[6]

Section 127 does not in itself afford a statutory remedy towards the recovery of property disposed of after the commencement of the liquidation. Recourse must be had to the rules for the tracing of property and, accordingly, no claim will be upheld against a *bona fide* purchaser for value without notice.[7]

Section 127 states that every transfer of shares or alteration in the status of the company's members made after the commencement of the winding-up is void unless the court orders otherwise. No transfer can be effected without registration

---

1   *Re AI Levy (Holdings) Ltd* [1964] Ch 19.
2   [1980] 1 All ER 814, [1980] 1 WLR 711.
3   Citing *Re Wiltshire Iron Co* (1868) LR 3 Ch App 443; *Re Neath Harbour Smelting and Rolling Works* (1887) 56 LT 727 at p 729; *Re Liverpool Civil Service Association* (1874) LR 9 Ch App 511; see also *Re Clifton Place Garage Ltd* [1970] Ch 477, approving *Re Steane's (Bournemouth)* [1950] 1 All ER 21; *Re TW Construction* [1954] 1 WLR 840.
4   See also *Denney v John Hudson & Co Ltd* [1992] BCLC 901. Expenditure incurred in defending an unfair prejudice petition is not incurred in the ordinary course of business where the essence of the claim is a dispute between shareholders: *Re Crossmore Electrical and Civil Engineering Ltd* (1989) 5 BCC 37.
5   *Re AI Levy (Holdings) Ltd*, above. See also *Re A Company (No 007523 of 1986)* (1987) 3 BCC 57; *Re Sugar Properties (Derisley Wood) Ltd* (1978) 3 BCC 88; *Re Tramway Building & Construction Co Ltd* [1988] Ch 293, [1988] 2 WLR 640, (1987) 3 BCC 443; *Re Webb Electrical Ltd* (1988) 4 BCC 230; *Re Rafidain Bank* [1992] BCC 376.
6   *Re Gray's Inn Construction*, above. See also more generally for a statement of the relevant principles governing validation orders under section 127, *Rose v AIB Group (UK) plc* [2003] EWHC 1737 (Ch), [2003] 1 WLR 2791.
7   *Re J Leslie Engineering Co Ltd* [1976] 1 WLR 292. See also *Rose v AIB Group plc* [2003] 1 WLR 2791.

of that transfer in the register of members of the company. The register cannot be rectified without leave of the court. Nevertheless, as between the vendor and purchaser of shares under a contract equitable rights arise which are not affected by this section, and the purchaser can claim through his vendor any payments made in the liquidation in respect of the shares, and the vendor may, when calls are made (but not before), enforce his right to indemnity.[1]

21.37 Appointment of the liquidator

On a winding-up order being made by the court, the Official Receiver becomes the liquidator of the company and continues in office until another person is appointed as liquidator by the creditors or contributories of the company.[2] The liquidator who is appointed will usually be the person nominated by the creditors.

If there is any vacancy in the office of liquidator this is filled by the Official Receiver until a further appointment is made.[3]

21.37.1 The liquidator's status

As in the case of directors, it is not easy to state succinctly yet accurately the position occupied by a liquidator. In several cases there will be found statements to the effect that he is a trustee for the creditors, or, in the case of a solvent company, for the contributories. Thus, Lord Selborne says, 'The hand which receives the calls necessarily receives them as a statutory trustee for the equal and rateable payment of all the creditors',[4] and James LJ speaks of the assets as being 'fixed by the Act of Parliament with a trust for equal distribution among the creditors'.[5] The House of Lords has confirmed that a liquidator is not a trustee in the strict sense, while also holding, in the context of a taxing statute, that when a company enters liquidation it ceases to be 'the beneficial' owner of its assets.[6] But it must not be inferred that all the results follow which would ensue if the liquidator were a trustee in the full sense of the word; and in particular it is to be noted that the property in the assets remains vested in the company and does not pass to the liquidator. But the court may on the application of the liquidator by order direct that all or any part of the property belonging to the company or held by trustees on its behalf shall vest in the liquidator by his official name: section 145 of the Insolvency Act 1986. When a liquidator makes a contract he does so in the name of the company; thus if he employs a solicitor in the company's business he is not personally liable for the costs.[7] A liquidator:

---

1   See sections 550 and 567 of the Companies Act 1985 and section 160(2) of the Insolvency Act 1986; *Re Onward Building Society* [1891] 2 QB 463 (CA); *Hughes-Hallet v Indian Mammoth Gold Mines* (1883) 22 Ch D 561.

2   Section 136(2). The appointment arises 'by virtue of his office'. The Official Receiver is a civil servant and should not be confused with an administrative receiver.

3   Section 136(3).

4   *Re Black & Co's Case* (1872) 8 Ch App 254 at p 262 (CA).

5   *Re Oriental Inland Steam Co* (1874) 9 Ch App 557 at p 551 (CA). See also *Re Flack's Case* [1894] 1 Ch 369; *CIR v Olive Mill* [1963] 1 WLR 712; *Re Movitex Ltd* [1992] 2 All ER 264, [1992] 1 WLR 303, [1992] BCLC 419, [1992] BCC 101 (position of trustees and beneficiaries considered by way of analogy in determining whether creditors were entitled to an order for the inspection of books and records).

6   *Ayerst v C & K (Construction) Ltd* [1975] 3 WLR 16 (HL).

7   *Re Anglo-Moravian Hungarian Junction Rly Co* (1875) 1 Ch D 130 (CA).

... is a person having a prima facie right to costs [out of the estate], but he is not in the ordinary sense a trustee. He is a person appointed by the court to do a certain class of things; he has some of the rights and some of the liabilities of a trustee, but is not in the position of an ordinary trustee. Being an agent employed to do business for a remuneration, he is bound to bring reasonable skill to its performance.[1]

Similarly, Romer J has said 'In my judgment the liquidator is not a trustee in the strict sense'.[2]

It is clear that the liquidator occupies a fiduciary position.[3] As such, he must avoid conflicts between his interests and his duties[4] and must not make a secret profit out of his position. It may be safely asserted that the liquidator has all the duties an agent would have; but it is suggested that he is liable only to the company and not directly, prior to its dissolution, to third parties, even though they be creditors or contributories, for negligence apart from misfeasance or personal misconduct.[5] If, however, the liquidator 'has misapplied or retained or become liable or accountable for any moneys or property of the company, or been guilty of any misfeasance or breach of trust in relation to the company', he can be brought to account by any creditor or contributory on a summons under section 212 of the 1986 Act.

The liquidator represents creditors and contributories alike, and should bear an even hand between them.[6] He should afford reasonable assistance and facilities to persons seeking information to enforce their rights,[7] but in cases of litigation he usually requires parties desiring access to the books and documents of the company to obtain an order for inspection under section 155(1) of the 1986 Act. This provides that the court may make an order for inspection of the books and papers of the company by creditors and contributories, and any books or papers of the company may be inspected accordingly but not further or otherwise. Orders under section 155(1) are rarely granted.[8] The section does not restrict any statutory right of a government department or person acting under its authority: section 155(2).

The liquidator, being an officer of the court, will be directed to deal fairly:[9] for example, he may be ordered to repay moneys paid to him under a mistake of law. Instances of this rule may also be found in cases under the Bankruptcy Acts.[10]

Where a liquidator has properly carried on the business of the company after his appointment, the post-liquidation creditors are entitled to be paid out of the

---

1   *Per* Cotton LJ in *Re Silver Valley Mines* (1882) 21 Ch D 381 at p 392 (CA).

2   *Knowles v Scott* [1891] 1 Ch 717 at 721 and 723. As to the possibility of recovering damages against a liquidator for neglect of statutory duty (even though there is no evidence of wilful default), see *Gore-Browne on Companies* 44th edn (Jordans, loose-leaf) at 32.5.

3   *Silkstone and Haigh Moor Coal Co v Edey* [1900] 1 Ch 167.

4   *Re Corbenstoke Ltd (No 2)* [1990] BCLC 60, (1989) 5 BCC 767.

5   *Knowles v Scott* [1891] 1 Ch 717 at 723. See also *Stewart v Engel* [2000] BCC 741 (exclusion clause precluded claim that liquidator had acted negligently).

6   *Re Palmer Marine Surveys Ltd* [1986] 1 WLR 573; *Re P Turner (Wilsden) Ltd* [1987] BCLC 149.

7   *Re Sir John Moore Gold Mining Co* (1879) 12 Ch D 325 at p 328 (CA).

8   *Re Brazilian Sugar Factories* (1887) 37 Ch D 83; *Re DPR Futures Ltd* [1989] 1 WLR 778, [1989] BCLC 634, (1989) 5 BCC 603.

9   *Re Regent Finance and Guarantee Corp* [1930] WN 84.

10 See, eg, *ex parte James* (1874) LR 9 Ch App 609 (CA); *ex parte Simmonds* (1885) 16 QBD 308 (CA); *Scranton's Trustee v Pearse* [1922] 2 Ch 87 (CA).

assets of the company, in priority to its creditors at the commencement of the winding-up.[1]

21.37.2 Duties and powers of a liquidator

Once made, a winding-up order operates in favour of all creditors and contributories of the company.[2]

The liquidator's primary duty is to collect in and realise the assets of the company and then to distribute the proceeds amongst the creditors of the company and, if any surplus remains, to the members in accordance with their rights. The fundamental tenet governing the making of distributions in a liquidation is that the free assets of the company must be distributed rateably among the company's unsecured creditors. If the assets of the company are insufficient to meet all of the unsecured debts, such debts abate equally. This method of distribution is known as the *pari passu* rule. The *pari passu* rule, which also applies to voluntary liquidations, is subject to a number of qualifications or exceptions.[3]

As soon as a winding-up order is made, the powers of the directors to manage the business of the company are terminated. To allow these to continue would be inconsistent with the liquidator's duty and power to collect in the assets of the company for the collective benefit of all of the creditors.

The liquidator has a range of specific duties and powers. He must take into his custody or bring within his control all the property to which the company is or appears to be entitled.[4] He can require any person who has in his possession or control any property, books or papers or records to which the company appears to be entitled to deliver up the same to him.[5] In exercising the powers conferred on him by the Insolvency Act 1986 to collect in the assets of the company, the liquidator is an officer of the court and is subject to its control.[6] If the liquidator mistakenly seizes property owned by a third party, he will not incur any liability for having seized or subsequently disposed of the property, provided he had reasonable grounds for believing that he was entitled to make the seizure. This protection, which is afforded by section 234(3) and (4), does not extend to any loss or damage resulting from the seizure or disposal which is caused by the liquidator's negligence. In the event of the liquidator's entitlement to make a seizure being disputed, the court can resolve the dispute.[7]

Section 167 of and Schedule 4 to the Act set out the powers of a liquidator in a compulsory winding-up. These are divided into powers which may be exercised with the sanction of the court or the liquidation committee[8] and powers which are exercisable by the liquidator without such sanction. The powers which can only be exercised with the appropriate sanction include conducting litigation and carrying on the business of the company so far as is necessary for the beneficial winding-up of the company. Amongst the things that a liquidator can do without

---

1   *Re National Arms and Ammunition Co* (1885) 28 Ch D 474 at p 481 (CA); *Re Great Eastern Electric Co* [1941] Ch 241.
2   Section 130(4).
3   See Part 6, below.
4   Section 144.
5   Section 234 and rule 4.185.
6   Rule 4.181.
7   *Re London Iron & Steel Co Ltd* [1990] BCLC 372, [1990] BCC 159.
8   See **21.37.3**, for a brief description of the status and function of the liquidation committee.

sanction are selling the company's property and raising money and giving security on the company's assets. A person who deals for value and in good faith with a liquidator need not be concerned whether any requisite consent from the liquidation committee or the court has been obtained by the liquidator.[1]

Certain specific powers relating to the holding of meetings, settling of lists, making of calls, proving of debts and other matters in the administration of a compulsory liquidation are formally vested in the court by the Act but are delegated to the liquidator by the Insolvency Rules 1986.[2]

Where the liquidator intends to carry on the business of the company he may do so only where this is necessary for the beneficial winding-up of the company. This limitation on his power reflects the fact that the primary objective of liquidation is the orderly winding-up of a company and the distribution of its assets to its creditors rather than rescue and rehabilitation. Necessity in this context has been described as mercantile necessity as opposed to absolutely compelling force.[3] On this basis, something which is highly expedient for the beneficial winding-up of the company would be permitted; where a liquidator has a reasonable expectation of selling the business as a going concern (which usually results in a much higher price being paid by a purchaser than on a sale on a break-up basis),[4] the liquidator may thus be allowed to carry on the business with this objective in mind. In cases of doubt the liquidator can always apply to the court for guidance; he is allowed to apply to the court for directions in relation to any matter arising during the course of the liquidation.[5]

The prudent liquidator will always have regard to the wishes of the majority of those with the most substantial interest in the assets of the company.[6] The liquidator has power to summon general meetings of creditors and contributories to ascertain their wishes in respect of any particular aspect of the conduct of the liquidation. If the holders of more than one-tenth in value of the creditors or contributories request a liquidator to summon such meeting he is duty-bound to do so.[7] If any person is aggrieved by an act or discretion of the liquidator, he may apply to the court for an order reversing or modifying that act or decision. The court has power to make any order it thinks fit on such an application.[8]

It should be noted that under what is now Schedule B1 paragraph 38 of the Insolvency Act 1986, an administrator can apply to the court to convert the liquidation into an administration. This would be the appropriate course of action if the liquidator thinks that corporate rescue is a realistic possibility.

21.37.3   *The liquidation committee*

A liquidation committee may be established under section 141 of the Insolvency Act 1986. Either the liquidator or one-tenth in value of the creditors may summon

---

1   Rule 4.184.
2   Section 160 makes provision for delegation.
3   *Re Wreck Recovery and Salvage Co* (1880) 15 Ch D 353.
4   Tax losses may be available to the purchaser of a business sold on a going-concern basis.
5   Section 168(3).
6   The liquidator should not deny those solely concerned in the outcome of the liquidation the opportunity even of throwing good money after bad: *Re Agricultural Industries* [1952] 1 All ER 1188.
7   Section 168(2); see also section 195, which states that the court may have regard to the wishes of creditors and contributories in all matters relating to a winding-up and may direct that such meetings shall be held if it thinks fit.
8   Section 168(5).

general meetings of the company's creditors and contributories for the purpose of determining whether a liquidation committee should be established.[1]

The liquidation committee will consist of at least three and not more than five creditors of the company elected at the creditors' meeting which decides to establish the liquidation committee.[2] In the case of a solvent winding-up, up to three contributories may become members of the liquidation committee.[3] Once the liquidation committee has been duly constituted, the liquidator has a duty to keep it informed in respect of matters arising out of the conduct of the winding-up and to supply it with information.[4] The purpose of the liquidation committee is not only to sanction the exercise by the liquidator of the powers conferred upon him but also to perform the function of a watchdog to ensure that the liquidator carries out his function in a proper manner.

In two circumstances the functions of the liquidation committee are vested in the Secretary of State.[5] The first is where the Official Receiver is the liquidator of the company. The second is where there is no liquidation committee (eg where the creditors and contributories decide not to have one) but the liquidator is a person other than the Official Receiver.

21.38 Ceasing to act as liquidator

Section 172 of the Insolvency Act 1986 deals with the removal and resignation of a liquidator from office.

A liquidator may be removed from office only by one of the following methods:

(1) an order of the court;[6]
(2) a resolution of a general meeting of the company's creditors summoned specifically for that purpose;
(3) where the liquidator was appointed by the Secretary of State, by a direction of the Secretary of State.

There are restrictions on the power of the creditors to remove a liquidator who was appointed by the Secretary of State or by the court.[7]

A liquidator may resign only in certain circumstances prescribed in rule 4.108 of the Insolvency Rules 1986. The liquidator may only resign following the procedure laid down in the rule on the grounds of ill health or if he intends to cease to practise as an insolvency practitioner or if there is some conflict of interest or change in personal circumstances which precludes or makes it impracticable for him to discharge his functions as liquidator of the company.

---

1   Section 141.
2   Rule 4.152.
3   Ibid. A person may not be a member of the liquidation committee in his capacity as both a creditor and a contributory rule 4.152(4). For the procedure followed where the creditors decide not to form a liquidation committee, see rule 4.154.
4   Rule 4.155.
5   Section 141(4), (5). The Secretary of State has the functions vested in him 'except to the extent that the rules otherwise provide'.
6   *Re Corbenstoke Ltd (No 2)* [1990] BCLC 60, (1989) 5 BCC 767 (removal from office on grounds of conflict of interest and duties); *Re Edennote Ltd* [1996] BCC 718 (CA) (creditors could remove the liquidator if they had lost confidence in him on reasonable grounds); *Deloitte and Touche AG v Johnson* [1999] 1 WLR 1605 (PC).
7   Section 172(3).

In certain circumstances, a liquidator must vacate his office. If a liquidator ceases to be qualified to act as an insolvency practitioner in relation to the company in question, for example if the specific bond required by the Act becomes invalid, he automatically vacates office.[1] Where a final meeting is held and the liquidator's report on the completion of the winding-up is received, the liquidator vacates office as from the date he gives notice to the court and the Registrar of Companies that the final meeting has been held.[2]

The time when a liquidator will obtain his release depends upon the manner in which he vacates office.[3] Where the liquidator has obtained his release he is discharged from all liability both in respect of acts and omissions during the course of the winding-up and otherwise in relation to his conduct as liquidator. However, the Insolvency Act 1986 specifically provides that nothing contained in any release will prevent a misfeasance summons being issued under section 212 of the Act.

PART 5: THE VOLUNTARY LIQUIDATION OF COMPANIES

21.39   Introduction

The most common type of winding-up procedure is the voluntary, winding-up. It is voluntary in the sense that the procedure has to be initiated by the company itself (although, of course, a company does have power to present a petition).[4] A creditor cannot compel a company to wind itself up voluntarily.

There are two types of voluntary liquidation both of which are considered below. If the company's directors are able to swear a declaration of solvency the liquidation will be a members' voluntary liquidation. In this type of liquidation, all creditors will be paid in full. If there is no declaration of solvency, the liquidation will be a creditors' voluntary liquidation in which the creditors may not be paid in full.

21.40   Resolutions for voluntary winding-up

Section 84 of the Insolvency Act 1986 sets out the circumstances in which a company may be wound up voluntarily:

(1) when the period (if any) fixed for the duration of the company by the articles expires, or the event (if any) occurs, on the occurrence of which the articles provide that the company is to be dissolved, and the company in general meeting has passed a resolution requiring it to be wound up voluntarily;

(2) if the company resolves by special resolution that it be wound up voluntarily;

(3) if the company resolves by extraordinary resolution to the effect that it cannot by reason of its liabilities continue its business, and that it is advisable to wind up.

---

1   Section 172(5).
2   Section 172(8).
3   Section 174 and rules 4.121 and 4.123–4.125.
4   See **21.35.2**.

Once a resolution has been passed under (1), (2) or (3) above, a copy of it must be filed with the Registrar of Companies within fifteen days.[1]

It is unusual nowadays for the articles of association of a company to provide for the company's duration to be limited or for it to be wound up on the occurrence of any specified event. If there are such provisions in the articles, it is the directors' duty to call a general meeting for the purposes of considering a resolution that the company be wound up.

A resolution under paragraph (3) will be passed only when it is intended that the liquidation is to be a creditors' voluntary winding-up.

21.40.1   Commencement of a voluntary liquidation

A voluntary winding-up (whether members' or creditors') is deemed to commence at the time the resolution under section 84 is passed by the members in general meeting.[2]

21.40.2   Consequences of resolution to wind up

Once a resolution has been passed, a company must cease to carry on its business except in so far as continuance may be deemed necessary for its beneficial winding-up.[3] Any transfer of shares in the company not made to or with the sanction of the liquidator or any change in the status of the company's members will be void.[4]

Notice of the resolution must be given by advertisement in the *London Gazette* within fourteen days.[5]

The Act provides that the corporate existence and the powers contained in the memorandum of association continue, notwithstanding anything in its constitution, until such time as the company is finally dissolved.[6] This provision is, obviously, necessary to ensure that the liquidator has the ability to wind up the company in an orderly manner.

21.41   The declaration of solvency

If the directors of a company propose to recommend to the members that the company be wound up voluntarily in a members' voluntary liquidation, they will also have to consider whether or not they can swear a statutory declaration of the company's solvency. Only if a majority of directors consider the swearing of a statutory declaration to be possible will they be able to recommend such course of action to the members.

The statutory declaration of solvency must state[7] that the directors have made a full inquiry into the company's affairs and that they have formed the opinion that

---

1   Sections 84(3) and 194.
2   Section 86. Where a resolution is passed at an adjourned meeting, it is treated as having been passed at the time it was actually passed, not at any earlier date: section 194. It has been held that it is not possible to pass resolutions for winding-up that are conditional upon the happening of specified events: *Re Norditrack (UK) Ltd* [2000] 1 WLR 343, not following *Re Powerstore (Trading) Ltd* [1997] 1 WLR 1280 and *Re Mark One (Oxford Street) plc* [1999] 1 WLR 1445 on this point.
3   Section 87(1).
4   Section 88.
5   Section 85.
6   Section 87(2).
7   Section 89(1).

the company will be able to pay its debts in full, together with interest at the official rate[1] within such period not exceeding twelve months from the commencement of the liquidation as may be specified in the declaration. In addition, the declaration must contain a statement of the company's assets and liabilities as at the latest practicable date before the making of the declaration.[2]

A director must not decide to join in the swearing of a declaration of solvency lightly. The Insolvency Act 1986 provides that any director making a declaration of solvency, without having reasonable grounds for the opinion that the company will be able to pay its debts in full together with interest at the official rate within the period specified in the declaration, will be liable to imprisonment or a fine or both.[3] There is a presumption that a director did not have reasonable grounds for his belief that the company would be able to so pay its debts if in fact the debts are not paid within the period specified in the declaration.[4] The Act imposes criminal liability in this respect to ensure that directors do not swear declarations of solvency and proceed by way of members' voluntary liquidation in which control rests substantially with the members and not with the creditors, who may be more interested in making a thorough investigation into the directors' conduct of the business. This is particularly important in the case of a private company where the directors have majority shareholdings and therefore would have the power to appoint a friendly liquidator (although the liquidator must be a qualified insolvency practitioner even in a members' voluntary winding-up).

If a declaration of solvency is not sworn, the liquidation must proceed as a creditors' voluntary winding-up.

There is a procedure for converting a members' voluntary liquidation to a creditors' voluntary liquidation where the liquidator forms the opinion that the company will be unable to pay its debts in full (together with interest at the official rate) within the period specified in the directors' declaration of solvency.[5]

21.42 Appointment of a liquidator

In a members' voluntary winding-up, the company in general meeting has the power to appoint one or more liquidators. On the appointment of a liquidator all of the powers of the directors cease, except in so far as the members or the liquidator sanction their continuance.[6] If a vacancy occurs, the company in general meeting may fill it [7]

In a creditors' voluntary winding-up, the procedure for appointing a liquidator is more complex. Under section 98 of the Insolvency Act 1986 the company, having decided to wind itself up because of its inability to pay its debts, has a duty to summon a meeting of its creditors in accordance with the procedure specified in the Act. Both the members and the creditors at their respective meetings may nominate a person to be liquidator. If there are different nominees the creditors' choice normally prevails,[8] although any director, member or creditor may apply

---

1   For the 'official rate' see section 189(4).
2   Section 89(2)(b); see also *De Courcy v Clement* [1971] Ch 693.
3   Section 89(4).
4   Section 89(5).
5   Section 95, 96.
6   Section 91.
7   Section 92. The members' ability in this respect is expressly made subject to any arrangement with the company's creditors.
8   Section 100(2).

to court for an order appointing the members' nominee or some other person as the liquidator.[1] The creditors have power to fill any vacancy in the office of liquidator that may arise during the course of the winding-up.[2]

Under section 108(1) of the 1986 Act, the court has a power to appoint a liquidator in any voluntary winding-up if 'from any cause' there is no liquidator acting.

On the appointment of a liquidator in a creditors' voluntary winding-up, the directors' powers cease except in so far as the liquidation committee (or if there is no liquidation committee the creditors) sanction their continuance.[3]

A liquidator in a voluntary winding-up must be a qualified insolvency practitioner. A liquidator in a voluntary winding-up is not an officer of the court but, otherwise, the status of the liquidator is as discussed at **21.37.1** in relation to compulsory windings-ups.[4]

21.43   The liquidation committee

In a creditors' voluntary winding-up, the creditors may resolve to form a liquidation committee to exercise the functions conferred on it by the Insolvency Act 1986.[5] The committee may consist of up to five creditors and, if the creditors do not object, five members of the company. If the creditors object to the members' nominees having the right to sit on the committee, such nominees cannot act as members of the committee unless the court so directs.[6]

21.44   Powers and duties of a voluntary liquidator

The fundamental duty of a voluntary liquidator is the same as that of a liquidator in a compulsory winding-up. He must collect in and realise the assets of the company, apply the proceeds in satisfaction of the company's debts and liabilities and distribute any remaining proceeds to the members of the company in accordance with their rights under the memorandum and articles.[7] The *pari passu* rule applies with respect to distributions.

In a voluntary winding-up, the liquidator has the same specific powers as are conferred on a liquidator in a compulsory winding-up by section 167 of and Schedule 4 to the Insolvency Act 1986. Where sanction is required to exercise a particular power, it can be given by an extraordinary resolution of the company in a members' voluntary winding-up; in a creditors' voluntary winding-up the liquidator may obtain the requisite sanction from the court, the liquidation committee or (if there is no liquidation committee) from the creditors.[8] Although the matters requiring sanction in the case of a compulsory winding-up include conducting   litigation   and   carrying   on   the   company's   business,   a

---

1   Section 100(3).
2   Section 104.
3   Section 103; see also **21.44**, for certain limitations on the powers of liquidators; see **21.43** for a discussion of the liquidation committee.
4   *Re TH Knitwear (Wholesale) Ltd* [1985] Ch 275.
5   For the role of a liquidation committee in a compulsory winding-up see **21.37.3**.
6   The court may direct other persons to act as members of the liquidation committee: section 101(3).
7   Sections 107 and 165(5).
8   Section 165.

liquidator in a voluntary winding-up can exercise both of these powers without formal sanction.[1]

A voluntary liquidator also has the power to settle lists of contributories, make calls, pay debts, adjust the rights of contributories and to deal with other matters connected with the administration of the liquidation.[2]

In a creditors' voluntary winding-up, the timing is such that it is possible for the members to nominate a liquidator before a meeting of the creditors has been held, thus giving them an opportunity to decide who should fill that office. However, section 166 of the Insolvency Act 1986 now provides that in a creditors' voluntary liquidation the liquidator nominated by the members may not exercise his powers prior to the first meeting of creditors without the sanction of the court except where the exercise of his powers is:

(1) to take into custody or under his control all the property to which the company is or appears to be entitled;
(2) to dispose of perishable goods and other goods the value of which is likely to diminish if they are not immediately disposed of; and
(3) to do all such other things as may be necessary for the protection of the company's assets.

Under section 112, the liquidator or any contributory or creditor may make an application to the court to determine any question arising in the winding-up of the company including the exercise of certain powers of the liquidator. The court may make such order as it thinks just in the circumstances.[3]

Finally, where in the case of a voluntary winding-up no liquidator has been appointed or nominated by the company, the director must not exercise any powers except with the sanction of the court or (in the case of a creditors' voluntary winding-up) so far as may be necessary to call a meeting of creditors or prepare a statement of affairs in accordance with the Act. The directors may, however, exercise their powers in the circumstances described in (2) and (3) above. Failure to have regard to these limitations on the exercise of powers will result in a fine.[4]

21.45   Ceasing to act as a voluntary liquidator

Section 171 of the Insolvency Act 1986 states that a liquidator in a voluntary winding-up may be removed only:

(1) by an order of the court; or
(2) in the case of a members' voluntary winding-up by a resolution of the company in general meeting passed at a meeting summoned for that purpose; or
(3) in the case of a creditors' voluntary winding-up by a resolution of the company's creditors passed at a meeting summoned for that purpose.

---

1   Section 165(3).
2   Section 165(4).
3   *Re Movitex Ltd* [1992] 1 WLR 303 is an example of an application made by creditors under section 602 of the Companies Act 1985 (which was replaced by section 112 of the Insolvency Act 1986). Scott LJ, with whom the other members of the Court of Appeal agreed, assumed, without deciding, that a post-liquidation debt would not provide the desired *locus standi* for such an application.
4   Section 114.

Additional procedural requirements apply where the liquidator has been appointed by the court under section 108.[1]

A voluntary liquidator vacates office automatically if he ceases to be a person qualified to act as an insolvency practitioner in relation to the company or when the final meetings of members and creditors (in the case of a creditors' voluntary liquidation) have been held and notice of the same has been given to the Registrar of Companies.[2]

Under section 108 of the 1986 Act, the court retains power on cause being shown to remove a voluntary liquidator' and appoint another in his place. A court may use this power to appoint an additional liquidator or replace a retiring liquidator.[3] An applicant must show cause why the liquidator should be removed.[4] The cause may lie in some unfitness or unsuitability of the liquidator, whether this be personal or arising from the particular circumstances of the case, for example some conflict of interest.[5] In *Re Keypak Homecare*, a liquidator was removed because of his relaxed and complacent conduct of the liquidation, although there was no evidence of misconduct or conflicts of interest.

In a voluntary liquidation, the liquidator may resign in the prescribed circumstances, which are the same as in a compulsory winding-up.[6]

The time at which a voluntary liquidator obtains his release depends on the manner in which he vacates office.[7] The release operates to discharge the liquidator from all liability in respect of acts and omissions in the course of his winding-up and otherwise in relation to his conduct as liquidator. It does not give him immunity from misfeasance proceedings under section 212 of the 1986 Act.[8]

21.46 The relationship between voluntary liquidation and other insolvency-related procedures

The fact that a company is being wound up voluntarily does not prevent any creditor or contributory from presenting a petition to the court requesting a winding-up order.[9] Where, however, the petition is presented by a contributory, the court must be satisfied that the rights of the contributories will be prejudiced by the continuation of the voluntary winding-up and that some benefit would accrue from making a winding-up order.[10]

Where a creditor presents a petition, he is not required to show that he would be prejudiced by the continuance of the voluntary liquidation.[11] However, although a creditor is entitled *ex debito justitiae* between himself and the company to a

---

1   Section 171(3). On section 108 appointments see **21.42**.
2   Section 171(4) and (5).
3   *Re Sunlight Incandescent Gas Lamps Co* [1900] 2 Ch 728; *Re Sheppey Portland Cement Co* [1892] WN 184.
4   *Re Keypak Homecare Ltd* [1987] BCLC 409, (1987) 3 BCC 558.
5   *Re Sir John Moore Gold Mining Co* (1879) 12 Ch D 325 (CA); *Re Adam Eyton* (1887) 36 Ch D 299 (CA); *Re London Flats* [1969] 1 WLR 711; *Re Charterland Goldfields* (1909) 26 TLR 132.
6   See **21.38**.
7   Section 173.
8   Section 173(4).
9   Section 116.
10   *Re National Company for the Distribution of Electricity* [1902] 2 Ch 34.
11   Older cases (eg *Re New York Exchange* (1888) 39 Ch D 415 (CA); *Re Russell Cordner & Co* [1891] 2 Ch 171; *Re Medical Battery Co* [1894] 1 Ch 444 emphasised that point, but the need to show prejudice was removed by the Companies Act 1929.

winding-up order,[1] as between himself and the other creditors the court will normally give effect to the wishes of the majority.[2] The majority, both in number and value, is considered but the majority in value is more significant than the numerical majority.[3] As Diplock LJ stated in *Re JD Swain Ltd*:[4]

> For the wishes of the petitioner to overrule those of the majority of the creditors there must be some reason why the wishes of the majority should be overridden ... [the petitioner must] show some reason why the remedy under the voluntary winding-up is not an adequate remedy for him.

In *Re Lowestoft Traffic Services Ltd*,[5] Hoffmann J noted that the decision whether to grant the winding-up order lay in the court's discretion and that, in exercising this discretion, the court would consider a range of matters including: the number, value and quality of the creditors for and against the petition; the possible or probable motives of these creditors; and general principles of fairness and commercial morality. Because it is a matter of discretion, it may not be strictly correct to speak of an onus of proof on the petitioner to demonstrate to the court reasons why the order should be made[6], but if no such reasons are put before the court this may result in the discretion being exercised against the making of a winding-up order.

If a company has already been dissolved under the voluntary liquidation, the creditor or contributory will be unable to present a petition because the court will have no jurisdiction to make a winding-up order.

While a company is in administration, no resolution may be passed or order made for the winding up of a company and the same prohibition applies while an administration application is pending or where notice has been filed with the court for the out-of-court appointment of an administrator. There are now straightforward procedures for exiting from an administration to a creditors' voluntary liquidation. The administrator is empowered to activate this procedure where he thinks that (a) the total amount which each secured creditor of the company is likely to receive has been paid to him or set aside for him and (b) that a distribution will be made to unsecured creditors of the company if there are any. The administrator can send a notice to the registrar of companies and on registration of the notice the company shall be wound up as if a resolution for voluntary winding up were passed on the day on which the notice is registered. The creditors have the power to nominate a liquidator but in the absence of any such nomination the administrator shall automatically be appointed liquidator.[7]

The fact that there is a voluntary arrangement in force under Part I of the Insolvency Act 1986 does not prevent a company from being wound up voluntarily. However, where a company is in the course of being wound up, the power to make a proposal under section 1 of the Insolvency Act 1986 rests with the liquidator and not the directors of the company. In the case of small companies

---

1   *Re James Millward & Co* [1940] Ch 333.
2   Section 195.
3   *Re HJ Tomkins & Sons Ltd* [1990] BCLC 76. See also *Re William Thorpe & Son Ltd* (1989) 5 BCC 156.
4   [1965] 1 WLR 909 (CA) at p 915B adopted by Harman J in *Re Medisco Equipment Ltd* [1983] BCLC 305.
5   [1986] BCLC 81, (1986) 2 BCC 945.
6   *Re Lowestoft Traffic Services Ltd*, above; *Re Palmer Marine Surveys Ltd* [1986] 1 WLR 573; *Re Falcon RJ Developments Ltd* [1989] BCLC 437, (1987) 3 BCC 146.
7   Schedule B1, paragraph 83 Insolvency Act 1986.

that satisfy the eligibility criteria specified in what is now Schedule A1 to the Insolvency Act 1986 and hence enjoy the benefit of a moratorium when directors are proposing a voluntary arrangement, no resolution may be passed or order made for the winding up of the company during the currency of this moratorium.[1]

The fact that an administrative receiver has been appointed over the assets of the company does not prevent the company from being wound up voluntarily.

PART 6: THE CONDUCT OF LIQUIDATIONS

21.47 Introduction

In this part we explore some of the most important aspects of both compulsory and voluntary liquidations. In general terms, the liquidator's fundamental duty is to collect in and realise the assets of the company and to apply the proceeds in discharging the debts and liabilities of the company in accordance with the *pari passu* rule. Any remaining surplus belongs to the members of the company and must be distributed to them in accordance with their rights under the company's memorandum and articles. Closer examination of the detailed aspects of liquidations can be left to specialist texts but this part indicates the main areas of complexity.

21.48 Creditors' claims

A liquidator need only apply the company's assets in payment of creditors' debts and liabilities which have been admitted to proof in the liquidation. If a creditor in a compulsory liquidation fails to submit a proof, or for some reason his claim is not admissible to proof, the liquidator cannot, in normal circumstances,[2] take it into account in making distributions.[3] In a voluntary winding-up (whether members' or creditors'), the liquidator may require creditors to submit proofs.[4]

Admissibility to proof in both compulsory and voluntary liquidations is governed by Part 4, Chapter 9 of the Insolvency Rules 1986. All debts and liabilities, including contingent debts and debts due in the future, can be proved, provided the company is subject to them at the date when it goes into liquidation or becomes subject to them after the date of the liquidation by reason of obligations previously incurred.[5] A debt or liability need not be fixed or liquidated in amount.[6]

The position with regard to secured creditors and the submission of proofs is as follows. Generally speaking, the liquidation of a company does not affect a secured creditor's rights (subject to what is said below about the priority of preferential claims over the claims of the holder of a floating charge and the invalidation of certain security interests). The secured creditor is free to realise his security without reference to the liquidator. Thus, where the value of the security

---

1   Schedule A1, paragraph 12(1)(c) Insolvency Act 1986.
2   Note rule 4.67(2) which provides for an exceptional case where, by order of the court, a debt which has not been the subject of a proof may be treated as if it had been proved for the purpose of paying a dividend.
3   Rule 4.73(1) and (3).
4   Rule 4.73(2) and (3).
5   Rule 13.12 defines 'debt' and 'liability'.
6   Ibid.

is more than sufficient to discharge the debt or the security is a floating charge on all of the company's assets, the secured creditor may simply choose to enforce his security outside the liquidation. It is possible for a secured creditor voluntarily to surrender his security and prove for his debt as if he were unsecured[1] but there can be few circumstances in which it would be advantageous for a creditor to give up his security in this way.

If a secured creditor realises his security but the amount so realised is insufficient to discharge the debt, he may prove for the balance in the liquidation.[2] A secured creditor also has the option of valuing his security and submitting a proof for the balance. In that case, the liquidator can offer to redeem the security at the value stated in the proof,[3] which he may well choose to do where he considers that the value stated in the proof is less than the value which the assets subject to the security could fetch on a disposal, although, because there is some scope for the secured creditor to revise the value stated in his proof,[4] the matter may then become one for negotiation between the liquidator and the creditor.

A secured creditor, part of whose secured claim is preferential, may, if he realises his security, appropriate the proceeds of the realisation to the non-preferential element of his claim in a liquidation.[5]

21.49   Proof of debts and rights of set-off

Where, before a company goes into liquidation, there have been mutual credits, mutual debits or other mutual dealings between the company and any creditor of the company proving in the liquidation, an account must be taken of what is due from each party to the other in respect of the mutual dealings, and the sums due from one party must be set off against the sums due from the other. If, after the operation of the set-off, there is still a balance owing from the company to the creditor, that balance is the amount provable by the creditor in the liquidation. Alternatively, if the result of the operation of the set-off is that an amount remains owing to the company from the creditor, the creditor must pay that amount to the liquidator and it is part of the company's assets available for distribution.[6]

Thus, the result of the operation of a right of set-off is that, to the extent of the amount set off, the creditor in effect obtains repayment of the amount owing to him from the company in priority to the company's general creditors. From the company's viewpoint, the amount of assets available to repay its general creditors is reduced by the amount of the debt which the creditor is allowed to set off but, in turn, the company is spared the trouble and potential expense involved in suing the creditor for the amount owing to it to the extent that this is diminished by the set-off. The operation of set-off is said to facilitate proper and orderly adminis-tration of insolvent estates.[7] It has also been described as a method of doing

---

1   Rule 4.88(2). Note rule 4.96 which deems a secured creditor to have voluntarily surrendered (unless the court grants relief) if he omits to disclose his security in his proof.
2   Rule 4.88(1).
3   Rule 4.97.
4   Rules 4.84 and 4.95.
5   *Re William Hall (Contractors) Ltd* [1967] 2 All ER 1150, [1967] 1 WLR 948.
6   Rule 4.90.
7   *National Westminster Bank Ltd v Halesowen Presswork & Assemblies Ltd* [1972] AC 785, [1972] 1 All ER 641, [1972] 2 WLR 455; *Re Maxwell Communications Corp plc (No 3)* [1993] 1 All ER 737, [1993] 1 WLR 1402, [1993] BCC 369.

justice between the parties;[1] it is considered that it would be unjust for a creditor to have to pay the whole of the debt which he owes to the company while, in respect of the amount which the company owes to him, he is allowed only to prove for a dividend in the company's liquidation.[2] In practice, it is creditors who most obviously benefit from the operation of set-off but, because its purpose is wider than simply the benefiting of one particular party and extends to ensuring the proper administration of insolvent estates, set-off is regarded as mandatory and it is not possible to contract out of the relevant provisions of the Insolvency Rules 1986.[3]

The conditions governing the availability of set-off in liquidation are, first, that there must be debts, credits or dealings between the company and the person seeking to assert a right of set-off and, secondly, that these debts, credits or dealings must be mutual. The interpretation of these conditions has spawned a considerable amount of case-law.[4] In brief, mutual debts are liquidated amounts owing from each of the parties to the other. 'Mutual credits' is a wider term than 'mutual debts',[5] and means credits which will eventually result in money claims such as where one party, who is indebted to the other, supplies the other party with property on the basis that the property is to be resold and the proceeds handed over.[6] Mutual dealings are arrangements in which the parties extend credit to each other in respect of individual sums, with the intention, express or implied, that at some point the individual sums will be brought into account and set off against each other.[7] Each claim must result in a liability to pay money; for example, a claim to the return of goods cannot be set off against a money debt.[8] 'Mutual dealings' is the widest term and could encompass both mutual debts and mutual credits.

The requirement for mutuality means that a joint debt cannot be set off against a several debt. For the same reason, money held by the company for a specific purpose or on trust cannot be set off against a debt owed to the company.[9] In *MS Fashions Ltd v BCCI SA*,[10] mutuality was found to exist in a tri-partite situation. BCCI, a bank, went into liquidation and was owed money by various companies. These debts had been guaranteed by the companies' directors, the directors being described as 'principal debtors' in the documentation, and, as security, the directors had deposited sums with the bank. The Court of Appeal held that the liability of the directors as principal debtors and the liability of the bank for the deposits[11] could be set off against each other so that the effect of the set-off was

---

1　*Forster v Wilson* (1843) 12 M&W 191 at 203–204.

2　*Stein v Blake* [1996] AC 243, [1995] 2 All ER 961 (HL) (a bankruptcy case, but the principle is the same).

3　*National Westminster Bank Ltd v Halesowen*, above.

4　See generally, Wood, *English and International Set-off* (Sweet & Maxwell, 1989); Derham, *Set-off* 2nd edn (Clarendon Press, 1996); and Derham, 'Some Aspects of Mutual Credit and Mutual Dealings' (1992) 108 LQR 99.

5　*Palmer v Day & Sons* [1895] 2 QB 618.

6　*Rolls Razor Ltd v Cox* [1967] 1 QB 552, [1967] 1 All ER 397, [1967] 2 WLR 241.

7　*Ross Razor v Cox*, above.

8　*Eberle's Hotels & Restaurant Co v Jones* (1887) 18 QBD 459.

9　*Exparte Caldicott* (1884) 25 Ch D 716; *Re City Equitable Fire Insurance Co Ltd (No 2)* [1930] 2 Ch 293; *Young v Bank of Bengal* (1836) 1 Moore Ind App 87; *National Westminster Bank v Halesowen*, above.

10　[1993] Ch 425, [1993] 3 All ER 769, [1993] 3 WLR 220, [1993] BCLC 1200, [1993] BCC 360.

11　This was held not to be money held for a special purpose such as to destroy mutuality.

automatically to reduce or extinguish the indebtedness of the companies to the bank. However, in a later case also arising out of the collapse of BCCI, the House of Lords held that sums deposited with the bank by third parties as security for borrowing could not be set off against sums owing to the bank by the borrowers. The distinction between the cases was that, in the latter case, the depositors had not undertaken personal liability to the bank; accordingly, the element of mutuality was missing.[1]

There has, historically, been some uncertainty regarding the operation of set-off in relation to contingent debts.[2] The recent decision of the House of Lords in *Secretary of State for Trade and Industry v Frid*[3] raised this issue in an acute form. In that case a company went into voluntary liquidation and its liabilities included notice pay and redundancy payments due to some ex-employees. Upon the company failing to meet these payments to employees, the Secretary of State became liable to make the same out of the National Insurance Fund. The Secretary of State was then entitled by statute to be subrogated to the rights and remedies of the employees against the company. A proof was submitted in respect of this claim less the amount of a VAT refund to which the company was entitled and which the Crown claimed should be set off against the amount of the proof.

The liquidator rejected the set-off claim pointing out that the relevant insolvency date was the date of the winding up resolution. At that time there was an undoubted liability on the part of the Crown to refund the overpaid VAT but the liability from the company to the Crown by virtue of statutory subrogation was purely contingent. There was only a possibility that such a debt would come into existence afterwards. There was a significant obstacle to allowing set-off in these circumstances in the shape of the decision of the Court of Appeal in *Re A Debtor (No 66 of 1955)*,[4] where it appears to have been decided that a surety under a pre-insolvency guarantee was not entitled to set-off unless he had actually paid the debt before the insolvency date. On the other hand it was decided by Brightman J in *Re DH Curtis (Builders) Ltd*[5] that the set-off provisions applied to debts arising under statute. In other words, the mutuality required by the statute did not mean that the claims sought to be set off were contractual claims.

Lord Hoffmann in *Frid* observed:

> If a statutory origin does not prevent set-off in the case of debts due and payable at the insolvency date, I do not see why it should make any difference that the statute creates a contingent liability which exists before the insolvency date but falls due for payment and is paid afterwards. The term 'mutual debts' does not in itself require anything more than commensurable cross-obligations between the same people in the same

---

1 *Re Bank of Credit and Commerce International SA (No 8)* [1998] AC 214 (HL). The BCCI cases are extensively noted. Articles and notes include R Mokal, 'Resolving the MS Fashions "Paradox"' [1999] CfiLR 106; G McCormack, 'Charge Backs and Commercial Certainty in the House of Lords' [1998] CfiLR 111; C Rotherham, 'Charges Over Customers' Deposit Accounts' [1998] CLJ 260; Rm Goode, 'Charge Backs and Legal Fictions' (1998) 114 LQR 178; R Calnan, 'Fashioning the Law to Suit the Practicalities of Life' (1998) 114 LQR 174.

2 An additional complication to that discussed in the text is that arising from the rule against double proof (a rule which is illustrated by *Barclays Bank Ltd v TOSG Trust Fund Ltd* [1984] AC 626, [1984] 1 All ER 1060, [1984] 2 WLR 650); a contingent claim, such as one arising under a guarantee, may not be admissible to proof for that reason and, if it is not provable, it will also not be capable of being the subject of set-off.

3 [2004] UKHL 24, [2004] 2 WLR 1279.

4 [1956] 1 WLR 1226.

5 [1978] Ch 162.

capacity. How those debts arose – whether by contract, statute or tort, voluntarily or by compulsion – is not material.

The House of Lords suggested that all that was necessary was that there should have been 'dealings' (in an extended sense which included the commission of a tort or the imposition of a statutory obligation) which gave rise to commensurable cross-claims.[1] There were no additional requirements that had to be satisfied before set-off could be recognised.

A secured debt may be set off against an unsecured debt; the existence of a security does not destroy mutuality.[2] However, a creditor who relies on his security to enforce his debt does not prove in the liquidation and is not subject to set-off.[3]

21.50   The company's assets

The liquidator must get in and realise the company's assets.[4] Assets which are not beneficially owned by a company fall outside the scope of its liquidation and are not available to meet the claims of its general body of creditors. Instead, the persons who are beneficially entitled to the property are entitled to invoke equitable claims to recover their property.

The decision of the House of Lords in *Barclays Bank Ltd v Quistclose Investments Ltd*,[5] demonstrates the operation of the principle that trust assets fall outside the normal rules governing distribution of assets in liquidation. Rolls Razor Ltd was a company in serious financial difficulties but it had managed to declare a dividend. Lacking available funds to pay the dividend, and being unable to raise them from its bank, the company entered into an arrangement with Quistclose, whereby Quistclose agreed to lend the money on condition that the company would use it only to pay the dividend and, if that could not be done, that it would return the money to Quistclose. The House of Lords held that this arrangement amounted to a relationship of a fiduciary character or trust in the form of a primary trust to pay the dividend and, if that failed, a secondary trust in favour of Quistclose. It was

---

1   See, paragraph 24 of the judgment.
2   *Ex parte Barnett* (1874) LR 9 Ch App 293; *Hiley v People's Prudential Assurance Co* (1938) 60 CLR 468.
3   *Re Norman Holding Co Ltd* [1990] 3 All ER 757, [1991] 1 WLR 10, [1990] BCLC 1, [1991] BCC 11.
4   Sections 144 and 148 (compulsory liquidation). The duty is not spelt out in relation to a voluntary liquidator in a voluntary winding-up but a liquidator must necessarily collect in the assets of the company in order to be able to fulfil his duty (section 107) to distribute the proceeds amongst those who are entitled.
5   [1970] AC 567, [1968] 3 All ER 651, [1968] 3 WLR 1097. On the 'Quistclose Trust' see Worthington, *Proprietary Interests in Commercial Transactions* (Oxford University Press, 1996) Chapter 3; Goodhart & Jones, 'The Infiltration of Equitable Doctrine into English Commercial Law' (1980) 43 MLR 489; Millett, 'The Quistclose Trust: Who Can Enforce It?' (1985) 101 LQR 269; Rickett, 'Different Views on the Scope of the *Quistclose* Analysis: English and Antipodean Insights' (1991) 107 LQR 608; Bridge, 'The Quistclose Trust in a World of Secured Transactions' (1992) 12 OJLS 333; ; L Ho and P St J Smart 'Reinterpreting the Quistclose Trust: A Critique of Chambers' (2001) 21 OJLS 267.

further held that the primary trust had failed[1] and that Quistclose was entitled to recover the money.

The Quistclose trust is a device which has been upheld in a number of later cases[2] but the jurisprudential basis of the trust identified in the *Quistclose* case itself has been questioned. Lord Millett in *Twinsectra Ltd v Yardley*[3] said that the Quistclose trust was an entirely orthodox example of the kind of default trust known as a resulting trust. He went on to say:[4]

> The lender pays the money to the borrower by way of loan, but he does not part with the entire beneficial interest in the money, and in so far as he does not, it is held on a resulting trust for the lender from the outset ... When the purpose fails, the money is returnable to the lender, not under some new trust in his favour which only comes into being on the failure of the purpose, but because the resulting trust in his favour is no longer subject to any power on the part of the borrower to make use of the money. Whether the borrower is obliged to apply the money for the stated purpose or merely at liberty to do so, and whether the lender can countermand the borrower's mandate while it is still capable of being carried out, must depend on the circumstances of the particular case.

A policy question raised by the Quistclose trust is whether the law should recognise and give effect to this interest, given that it occurs in transactions which, in economic terms, are often indistinguishable from secured loans; unlike a secured loan, a Quistclose trust does not require registration, and hence disclosure, at Companies House. The same policy question can arise where assets are sold to a company on credit terms which provide that title to the assets will not pass until debts owing from the company to the supplier have been paid for in full.[5] Like a charge, a retention of title clause also achieves the effect of giving credit to the company whilst at the same time allowing the creditor to protect its position with a proprietary interest; but because the creditor's interest is retained in its own property rather than taken on property of the company, legally it is not a charge and does not require registration; in the event of liquidation leading to a breach of the terms on which the assets were supplied, the creditor can simply assert its proprietary claim to the assets supplied.

---

1   Although, as Goodhart & Jones, op cit, point out at p 494, n 28, it is arguable whether this was in fact the case unless it is accepted that there were also other conditions attached to the loan. Millett, op cit, suggests that the primary purpose for which the loan was made available was to ensure the survival of the company, a purpose which certainly failed.

2   These include *Re Northern Developments Holdings Ltd* (unreported); *Carreras Rothmans Ltd v Freeman Mathews Treasure Ltd* [1985] Ch 207; *Re EVTR Ltd* [1987] BCLC 464, (1987) 3 BCC 389; *Re Kayford Ltd* [1975] 1 All ER 604, [1975] 1 WLR 279; *Re Lewis of Leicester Ltd* [1995] BCC 514; *Hurst-Bannister v New Cap Reinsurance Corp Ltd* [2000] Lloyd's Rep IR 166 (principles of *Barclays Bank Ltd v Quistclose Investments Ltd* were to be applied widely); cf *Re Multi-Guarantee Co Ltd* [1987] BCLC 257; *Re Holiday Promotions (Europe) Ltd* [1996] BCC 671.

3   [2002] UKHL 12, [2002] 2 All ER 377.

4   At paragraph 100 of the judgment.

5   This is the simplest type of retention of title clause. Suppliers sometimes insert more elaborate clauses into their supply contracts, whereby title is also claimed to the proceeds of resales or to goods manufactured from those supplied. More elaborate clauses have tended not to be regarded favourably by the courts.

Various law review bodies have criticised the law in this area on the grounds that it appears to be concerned more with form rather than substance.[1] Retention of title provisions have attracted more attention than Quistclose trusts, with the most widely supported suggestion being that such provisions should be brought within the scope of revised law relating to security interests. Despite calls for reform stretching back over a number of decades, however, successive governments have shown little enthusiasm for extensive reform in this area.[2] The recent Law Commission consultation paper on Registration of Security Interests[3] has once again whetted the appetite for reform but whether the government rises to the bait remains to be seen.

21.51 The order of payment of debts and liabilities and the *pari passu* rule

Although the *pari passu* rule is a fundamental tenet of insolvency, there are a number of ways in which the principle of *pari passu* distribution is qualified.[4] We have already seen how the operation of insolvency set-off can in effect allow one creditor to be paid in advance of other creditors, which cuts across the *pari passu* rule, and how trust assets fall entirely outside the ambit of the *pari passu* rule. Other important illustrations of the qualified nature of the *pari passu* principle include the position of secured creditors (who may, subject to the special rules discussed below governing debts secured by a floating charge, enforce their security outside the liquidation) and the ranking of liquidation costs and expenses and of preferential debts.

The precise order of application of funds in a liquidation is:[5]

(1) costs and expenses of the liquidation including the liquidator's remuneration;
(2) preferential debts;
(3) ordinary debts;
(4) deferred and subordinated debts; and
(5) any balance remaining is distributed to members in accordance with their entitlements under the company's memorandum and articles.

---

1   *Report of the Committee on Consumer Credit* Cmnd 4596 (1972); *Report of the Review Committee on Insolvency Law and Practice* Cmnd 8558 (1982); Diamond, *Review of Security Interests in Property*, (1989). See also, Bridge 'Form, Substance and Innovation in Personal Property Security Law' [1992] JBL 1.
2   See Chapter 10.
3   July 2002. On the consultation paper see McCormack 'Quasi-Security and the Law Commission Consultation Paper on Registration of Security Interests' [2003] LMCLQ 80.
4   Oditah, 'Assets and the Treatment of Claims in Insolvency' (1992) 108 LQR 459; Belcher and Beglan, 'Jumping the Queue' [1997] JBL 1. For trenchant criticism of the pari passu principle see R Mokal, 'Priority as Pathology: The Pari Passu myth' [2001] CLJ 581; R Mokal, 'The Search for Someone to Save: A Defensive Case for the Priority of Secured Credit' (2002) 22 OJLS 687 and for other perspectives see G McCormack, *Secured Credit under English and American Law* (Cambridge University Press, 2004) chapter 1 and V Finch, 'Security, Insolvency and Risk: Who Pays the Price?' (1999) 62 MLR 633.
5   Sections 107 and 115 (voluntary liquidations) and 143 and 156 (compulsory liquidations) and section 175 and rule 4.218 (both types of liquidation).

21.51.1 Preferential debts

Preferential debts rank equally among themselves after the expenses of the winding-up and must be paid in full, unless the assets are insufficient to meet them, in which case they abate in equal proportions.[1] Also, whilst preferential debts rank behind debts secured by fixed charges, so far as the assets of the company available for payment of general creditors are insufficient to meet them, they have priority over the claims of debentures secured by, or the holders of, any floating charge created by the company and must be paid accordingly out of any property comprised in or subject to that charge.[2] The fact that the floating charge may have crystallised prior to the commencement of the winding-up does not deprive the preferential debts of this special priority, because it is expressly provided by section 251 that a floating charge for this purpose means a charge created as such.

Schedule 6 to the Insolvency Act 1986 sets out the categories of preferential debts. As amended by the Enterprise Act 2002,[3] this now covers only up to four months' back-pay to employees and former employees (up to a prescribed maximum limit per employee) as well as unpaid holiday pay and contributions to state and occupational pension schemes. Giving these preferential status in winding-up is a way of protecting the interests of creditors who are not in a position to negotiate an enhanced position, through charge or trust mechanisms, for themselves.[4]

21.51.2 Liquidation expenses

Liquidation expenses rank before preferential debts but behind debts secured by fixed charges. Since preferential debts enjoy a priority over debts secured by a floating charge, the logical position might appear to be that be that liquidation expenses also rank before debts secured by floating charges. In 1970 in *Re Barleycorn Ltd*,[5] the Court of Appeal accepted this proposition. Essentially their reasoning proceeded along the following lines. The expenses of winding up are payable out of an insolvent company's funds in priority to the claims of unsecured creditors, whether preferential or otherwise. The claims of preferential creditors, so far as unpaid out of the company's funds, are payable out of the debenture-holder's funds. It therefore follows that the expenses of winding up are payable out of the debenture-holder's funds. *Barleycorn*, however, has recently been overruled by *Buchler v Talbot*[6] where the House of Lords made it clear that the general costs and expenses of liquidation could not be paid out of floating charge realisations. Lord Hoffmann suggested that the reasoning in *Barleycorn* was based on false logic. He said:[7]

> If A has priority over B in respect of payment out of the proceeds of Blackacre and B has priority over C in respect of payment out of the proceeds of Whiteacre, why does it follow that A has any right to payment out of Whiteacre?

---

1   Section 175(2)(a).
2   Section 175(2)(b).
3   Which abolished preferences that the Crown used to have in respect of unpaid taxes of various sorts.
4   See generally, LA Bebchuk and JM Fried, 'The Uneasy Case for the Priority of Secured Claims in Bankruptcy' [1996] 105 Yale LJ 857.
5   [1970] Ch 465.
6   [2004] UKHL 9 [2004] 1 All ER 1289.
7   At paragraph 27.

With respect, however, Lord Hoffmann's criticism seems premised on the assumption that Whiteacre and Blackacre are completely distinct assets. The criticism falls away if Whiteacre is seen as merely part of Blackacre. The House of Lords, however, was strongly attracted to the idea that there were two separate funds. Lord Millett said:[1]

> In considering the incidence of the costs and expenses of the winding up it must be borne in mind that there are two distinct funds: (i) the proceeds of the free assets which belong to the company and are administered by the liquidator in a winding up and (ii) the proceeds of the assets comprised in a floating charge which belong to the charge holder to the extent of the security and are administered by the receiver. In principle ... the costs of administering each fund are borne by the fund in question.

In his view, each fund bore its own costs of administration and neither was required to bear the costs of administering the other. The expenses of a winding up were borne by the assets comprised in the winding up ie the company's free assets, and the receivership expenses were borne by the assets comprised in the floating charge. The floating charge brought into existence a second fund with its own set of priorities. Lord Millett went on to say however that the costs of realising a particular property must be distinguished from the general expenses of the winding up or receivership. The costs of realisation were deductible from the proceeds of the property realised, whether it was realised by the liquidator or by the receiver.

Buchler v Talbot was decided on the basis that floating charge assets constitute a separate fund distinct from the company's own assets and that the charge holder 'owns' these assets. The decision could possibly be criticised on the basis that it ignores the fundamental nature of a 'charge'. As traditionally understood, a charge does not involve the transfer of ownership as such to the charge holder but merely gives the latter a right of recourse to the property for payment of the debt or performance of the obligation secured. Indeed in *Re BCCI (No 8)*,[2] Lord Hoffmann appeared to accept that a charge does not confer 'ownership' per se on the charge-holder. He described a charge as a security interest created without any transfer of title or possession to the beneficiary.

Some would see the decision in *Buchler v Talbot* as being undesirable on more general policy grounds. The suggestion in the case is that, since winding up is little more than an orderly mechanism for the recovery and distribution of the company's free assets for the benefits of general creditors, it brings no benefits to floating charge holders, who therefore should not be expected to pay for it. On the other hand, some months previously in *Re Pantmaneog Timber Co Ltd*,[3] the House of Lords confirmed the long established proposition that liquidation proceedings serve the public interest more generally and result in benefits to a far broader range of interested parties,

Since liquidation expenses enjoy 'super priority', the range of expenses encompassed within this category is especially important. Rule 4.218 of the Insolvency Rules 1986 defines the various expenses payable out of the assets and the order in which they are payable. The liquidator's own remuneration is included in the list of liquidation expenses. The courts have also expanded the concept of 'liquidation expenses' to include liabilities incurred before the

---

1   At paragraph 62.
2   [1998] AC 214.
3   [2004] 1 AC 158.

liquidation in respect of property afterwards retained by the liquidator for the benefit of the insolvent estate. Consequently, more or less automatically included (although in theory the matter is in the discretion of the court) are continuing rent or hire purchase charges in respect of land or goods in the possession of the company which the liquidator continues to use for the purposes of the liquidation.[1]

Among the items listed in Rule 4.218 are 'any necessary disbursements by the liquidator in the course of his administration . . .'. In *Re Toshoku Finance (UK) plc,*[2] it was held by the House of Lords that the liability to corporation tax is a sum which, by statute, is payable by a company in respect of profits or gains arising during a winding up. Therefore it is a 'necessary disbursement' which the liquidator has to make in the course of his administration. It was a liquidation expense and that was the end of the matter. According to Lord Hoffmann, who spoke for the House of Lords, rule 4.218(1) was intended to be a definitive statement of what counted as an expense of the liquidation. The courts will interpret rule 4.218 to include debts that, under the *Lundy Granite Co*[3] principle, are deemed to be expenses of the liquidation but the heads of expense listed in rule 4.218(1) are not subject to any implied qualification. In particular, Lord Hoffmann rejected the proposition that rule 4.218(1) created only an outer envelope within which expenses were contained ie it was necessary to come within rule 4.218(1) to count as a liquidation expense but that was not sufficient.

Costs incurred by a liquidator in an unsuccessful attempt to recover assets were not originally included in the concept of liquidation expenses.[4] Millett J's analysis to this effect, in *Re MC Bacon Ltd (No 2),* was confirmed by the Court of Appeal in *Lewis v IRC,*[5] but the Enterprise Act 2002 alters the position somewhat. Under section 253 of this Act, it is only possible for a liquidator to pursue such proceedings with the sanction of creditors and the costs of such proceedings are now deemed to be a liquidation expense.[6] It is up to the unsecured creditors therefore whether they choose to take their 'pot' or whether they authorise the liquidator to try to augment this pot by challenging allegedly improper transactions.

21.51.3 *Deferred debts and subordinated debts*

As among ordinary unsecured debts, the pari passu rule generally prevails. However, section 74(2)(f) creates a category of deferred debt: any sum due to a member of a company (in his character of a member) by way of dividends, profits or otherwise is not deemed to be a debt of the company, payable to that member in a case of competition between himself and any other creditor not a member of the company; but such sum may be taken into account for the purpose of the final

---

1   *Re International Marine Hydropathic Co* (1884) 28 Ch D 470; *Re Lundy Granite Co* (1871) LR 6
     Ch App 462; *Re Oak Pits Colliery Co* (1882) 21 Ch D 322; *Re Atlantic Computer Systems plc* [1992]
     Ch 505, where the earlier authorities and the general principle are reviewed.
2   [2002] UKHL 6, [2002] 1 WLR 671.
3   (1871) LR 6 Ch App 462.
4   *Mond v Hammond Suddards* [1999] 3 WLR 697; *Re MC Bacon Ltd (No 2)* [1991] Ch 127.
5   *Re Floor Fourteen Ltd, Lewis v IRC* [2001] 3 All ER 499.
6   Rule 4.218(1)(a) Insolvency Rules now refers to expenses or costs which are properly
     chargeable or incurred by the official receiver or the liquidator 'in preserving, realising or
     getting in any of the assets of the company or otherwise relating to the conduct of any legal
     proceedings which he has power to bring or defend whether in his own name or the name of
     the company . . .'.

adjustment of the rights of the contributories among themselves. The House of Lords has said that sums due to a member in his character as such are sums arising from claims based on the statutory contract in section 14 of the Companies Act 1985[1] and other rights and liabilities conferred and imposed by that legislation.[2] On this basis, a claim for compensation for misrepresentation whereby an investor is induced to acquire shares in a company is not a deferred debt for the purposes of section 74(2)(f).

Whether a creditor can by contract choose to opt out of the *pari passu* rule and defer his debt to other debts of the company was, until recently, unclear.[3]

However, in *Re Maxwell Communications Corp plc (No 3)*[4] Vinelott J, following Australian and South African authority,[5] held that it was legally possible for a creditor to opt out of the *pari passu* rule and to contract to defer his debts to other debts of the company. Earlier House of Lords' authorities that, in the view of some commentators,[6] cast doubt upon the validity of subordination agreements were distinguished. Although there was clear authority that the *pari passu* principle was mandatory to the extent that a creditor could not, by contract, obtain a better position than that which the *pari passu* principle afforded him,[7] this did not prevent a creditor from agreeing to a worse position. Similarly, the ruling that insolvency set-off was a mandatory procedure[8] did not preclude the court from upholding a subordination agreement since, unlike set-off, which was a procedure from which the company as well as its creditors could potentially benefit, the *pari passu* principle operated only in favour of creditors and, therefore, they were free to waive the benefit. Vinelott J considered that it was important, particularly at a time when insolvency increasingly had international ramifications, for English law to give effect to contractual subordination arrangements in the same way as other jurisdictions.

21.52 Contributories

Under section 74 of the Insolvency Act 1986, every present and past member is liable to contribute to the assets of the company on winding-up and is therefore a contributory.[9] Section 74 then limits the amount of the contribution that can be

---

1   See **5.17**.

2   *Soden v British & Commonwealth Holdings plc* [1997] BCC 952 (HL).

3   The question produced much literature, a sample of which includes Wood, *English and International Set-Off* (Sweet & Maxwell, 1989), Chapter 17; Johnson, 'Debt Subordination: The Australian Perspective' (1987) 15 ABLJ 80; Johnson, 'Contractual Debt Subordination and Legislative Reform' [1991] JBL 225.

4   [1993] 1 All ER 737, [1993] 1 WLR 1402, [1993] BCC 369.

5   *Horne v Chester & Fein Property Developments Pty Ltd* (1986) 11 ACLR 485; *Re Carbon Developments (Pty) Ltd* [1993] 1 SA 493.

6   More detailed post-*Maxwell* assessments of debt subordination include R Nolan, 'Less Equal Than Others – *Maxwell* and Subordinated Unsecured Obligations' [1995] JBL 485; Ferran, *Company Law and Corporate Finance* (Oxford University Press, 1999), Chapter 16.

7   *British Eagle International Air Lines v Compagnie Nationale Air France* [1975] 2 All ER 390, [1975] 1 WLR 758 (HL).

8   *National Westminster Bank Ltd v Halesowen Presswork & Assemblies* [1972] AC 785, [1972] 1 All ER 641, [1972] 2 WLR 455 (HL).

9   Contributory being defined by section 79 as meaning any person who is liable to contribute. This category does not include persons who are ordered to make a contribution as a result of liability for fraudulent or wrongful trading: section 79(2).

required of a contributory. Consistent with the principle of limited liability, no contribution can be required from any present or past member of a limited company in excess of the amount unpaid in respect of the shares held, or previously held. No contribution can be required from a past member who ceased to be a member one year or more before the commencement of the winding-up.[1] Past members are, in addition, liable to contribute only where present members appear to be unable to make the contributions required of them and, furthermore, are not liable to contribute in respect of debts or liabilities contracted by the company after they ceased to be members.[2]

21.53 Distribution of remaining assets

The liquidation process may result in a surplus remaining after the expenses, costs and debts have been paid in full, although it would be comparatively rare for this to happen. Where there is a surplus, the question arises as to its distribution. Section 107 of the Insolvency Act 1986 provides that in the case of a voluntary liquidation, remaining assets are to be distributed among the members according to their rights and interests in the company. The equivalent provisions governing compulsory liquidations are sections 143 and 154, which provide for the distribution of remaining assets among the persons entitled to them.

The distribution of any surplus must take into account the rights conferred on the members by the terms of the company's memorandum and articles of association but, leaving aside any special provisions made by these documents, the position is as follows. Where there are shares having a preference as to capital, the amount paid on those shares must be repaid before any amount is paid to those whose rights are deferred, such as the holders of ordinary or deferred shares in the company. It now seems to be generally accepted that the annexation to preference shares of the right to receive back their capital on a winding-up in priority to ordinary shares is an exhaustive delimitation of the capital rights attaching to the preference shares, so that their holders are excluded from any participation in any surplus after all capital has been returned.[3]

Where, however, all the shares rank equally among themselves and the same amount has been paid up on each of them, the surplus is distributed in repayment of the capital paid up on those shares rateably, according to the number of shares. If more has been paid up on some shares than on others, equalisation must first be achieved, usually by paying back the amount which exceeds that which has been paid in respect of all of the shares.[4]

If all capital has been repaid but there still remains a surplus then, unless the articles otherwise provide, it is divisible amongst the shareholders in proportion to the nominal amount of the share capital held by them respectively, and not in proportion to the amount paid up on their shares.[5] Where there has previously been a reduction of capital, the shares rank only at the reduced amount.[6]

---

1   Section 74(2)(a).
2   Section 74(2)(b)–(c).
3   See **8.4.1**; *Scottish Insurance Co v Wilsons & Clyde Coal Co* [1949] AC 462.
4   *Re Exchange Drapery Co* (1888) 38 Ch D 171.
5   *Birch v Cropper* (1889) 14 App Case 525.
6   *Re Espuela Land and Cattle Co (No 2)* [1909] 2 Ch 187.

PART 7: SPECIAL POWERS OF LIQUIDATORS AND OTHER OFFICE HOLDERS IN INSOLVENCY PROCEEDINGS

21.54 A liquidator's ability to disclaim property

Section 178 of the Insolvency Act 1986 gives a liquidator the power by giving notice to disclaim any onerous property notwithstanding that he has taken possession of it, endeavoured to sell it or otherwise exercised rights of ownership in relation to it. This is a potentially very important power to rid a company in liquidation of assets which are subject to liabilities, thus rendering retention undesirable from the point of view of a beneficial realisation of the assets of the company for the benefit of the creditors generally. For the purposes of the section, 'onerous property' means any unprofitable contract and any other property of the company which is unsaleable or not readily saleable or is such that it may give rise to a liability to pay money or perform any other onerous acts. It can include statutory exemptions or licences, such as a waste management licence.[1]

Once effectively made, the disclaimer operates to determine as from its date the rights, interests and liabilities of the company in respect of the property disclaimed. It does not, however, except insofar as is necessary for the purpose of releasing the company from any liability, affect the rights or liabilities of any other person interested in that property.[2]

Under section 178(6) of the 1986 Act, any person sustaining loss or damage in consequence of a disclaimer is deemed a creditor of a company to the extent of the loss or damage sustained and may prove for that loss or damage in the winding-up of the company.[3]

Under section 179, a disclaimer in respect of any leasehold property does not take effect until such time as a copy of the disclaimer has been served on every person claiming under the company as underlessee or mortgagee and either:

(1) no application is made under section 181 (see below) in respect to that property within fourteen days; or
(2) where such an application under section 181 has been made the court directs that the disclaimer shall take effect.

Under section 181 of the Act, which applies not only to disclaimers of leasehold property but also to disclaimers of any other onerous property, any person who has an interest in the disclaimed property or who is under any liability in respect of it (not being a liability which would be discharged by the disclaimer[4]) may apply to the court for an order to have the disclaimed property vested in it. Where the application is made by a person who is under a liability in respect of the disclaimed

---

1   *Re Celtic Extraction Ltd* [2001] Ch 475.
2   Section 178(4).
3   *Re Park Air Services plc* [1999] 1 All ER 673 (HL) (landlord entitled to prove for statutory compensation for loss of his right to future rent and compensation assessed in the same way as damages for breach of contract).
4   An original lessee of a lease which has been assigned remains liable for the rent notwithstanding disclaimer by the assignee's liquidator: *Warnford Investments Ltd v Duckworth* [1979] Ch 127; *WH Smith Ltd v Wyndham Investments Ltd* [1994] BCC 699; *Hindcastle Ltd v Barbara Attenborough Associates Ltd* [1996] BCC 636, [1997] AC 70 (HL). However, for new leases this is now subject to the Landlord and Tenant (Covenants) Act 1995, which provides for an assignor to be released of its obligations upon assignment.

property, the court will not make the order unless it considers that it would be just to do so for the purposes of compensating that person.

The court cannot make an order under section 181 vesting leasehold property in any person claiming under the company as underlessee or mortgagee except on terms making that person:

(1) subject to the same liabilities and obligations which the company was subject to under the lease at the commencement of the winding-up; or

(2) if the court thinks fit, making the person who has the property vested in it subject to the same liabilities and obligations as that person would be subject to if the lease had been assigned to him at the commencement of the winding-up.

Where either an underlessee or mortgage is unwilling to accept a vesting order on the above terms the court can order that the property be vested in any person who is liable as guarantor or surety (whether alone or jointly with the company) to perform the lessee's covenants under the lease.[1]

Section 168(5) allows persons who are aggrieved by an act or decision of a liquidator to apply to court; the court may confirm, reverse or modify the act or decision complained of, and make such order in the case as it thinks just. *Re Hans Place Ltd*[2] was an attempt to use this provision to challenge a liquidator's decision to disclaim a lease. The court held that it did have jurisdiction to consider the complaint but that it could interfere only where the liquidator had acted in bad faith or had made a perverse decision.

21.55 Office-holders

Office-holders are given certain special powers under the insolvency legislation. Who an office-holder is depends on the power in question, but the category can include administrators, administrative receivers (but not other receivers), supervisors of voluntary arrangements, liquidators and provisional liquidators.

21.55.1 *Utilities*

Suppliers of gas, electricity, water and telecommunications services cannot make it a condition of continuing the giving of the supply that the office-holder pay outstanding charges, but the supplier can require the office-holder to give a personal guarantee in respect of any new supplies.[3] For this purpose administrators, administrative receivers, supervisors of voluntary arrangements, liquidators and provisional liquidators all count as office-holders.

21.55.2 *Transactions at an undervalue*

An administrator or a liquidator, as an office-holder, has the power to make an application to court in respect of transactions at an undervalue.[4] If the application is successful, the court must make such order as it thinks fit for restoring the position to what it would have been if the company had not entered into the transaction.[5]

---

1   Section 182(3). For the procedural requirements as to disclaimer see rule 4.187 *et seq.*
2   [1993] BCLC 768.
3   Section 233.
4   Section 238.
5   Section 238(3).

The Insolvency Act 1986 defines a transaction[1] at an undervalue as one where:

(1) the company makes a gift to a person or otherwise enters into a transaction with a person on terms that provide for the company to receive no consideration; or

(2) the company enters into a transaction with a person for a consideration the value of which, in money or money's worth, is significantly less than the value, in money or money's worth, of the consideration provided by the company.

The first limb of the definition envisages a total absence of any consideration passing to the company, while the second limb covers the case where there is some mutual consideration but significantly differing in amounts. The second limb was considered in *Re MC Bacon Ltd*[2] where Millett J made the following observations:

(1) a comparison must be made between the value obtained by the company for the transaction and the value of the consideration provided by the company;

(2) both values must be measurable in money or money's worth;

(3) both values must be considered from the company's point of view.

Millett J held that the granting of a debenture by a company in return for its bank forbearing from calling in its overdraft and continuing to make advances was not within the scope of the second limb of the definition of a transaction at an undervalue. In granting the debenture, the company had parted with nothing of value: the granting of the debenture meant that assets of the company were appropriated for the payment of a debt, but those assets were not depleted or diminished in value. Further, the consideration which it received in return was not something which was capable of being valued in monetary terms.

This reasoning would seem to be equally applicable to the giving of a guarantee, other than a guarantee which is caught by the first limb as being granted as a gift or for no consideration. A guarantee creates a contingent obligation but does not normally deplete or diminish the company's assets (although conceivably it could be treated as having that effect where, at the time when the guarantee is given, it is certain or virtually certain that it will be called upon). Whether a transaction is within the section is tested at the time when it is entered into,[3] so that if a guarantee, when given, is not within its scope later payment under that guarantee should not amount to a transaction at an undervalue.

Re MC Bacon thus limits the scope of office-holder's power in respect of transactions at an undervalue quite considerably. Where it may prove to be most useful is in relation, first, to gifts made by a company prior to its administration or liquidation and, secondly, to cases where the company has sold assets for

---

1   The term 'transaction' is defined in section 436 of the Act to include 'a gift, agreement or arrangement'.

2   [1990] BCLC 324, [1990] BCC 78, Millett J's analysis of the provision was adopted by Balcombe LJ in *Menzies v National Bank of Kuwait SAK* [1994] BCC 119, and by Sir Christopher Slade in *Agricultural Mortgage Corpn plc v Woodward* [1995] 1 BCLC 1 (both cases on section 423 of the Insolvency Act 1986). See also *Phillips v Brewin Dolphin Bell Lawrie Ltd* [2001] 1 WLR 143.

3   Sections 238(2) and 240.

considerably less or, as the case may be, bought assets for considerably more than their true worth.[1]

There is one way in which a transaction which would otherwise amount to a transaction at an undervalue can be saved. The court may not make an order in respect of a transaction at an undervalue if it is satisfied that: (a) the company entered into the transaction in good faith and for the purpose of carrying on its business; and (b) at the time when it did so, there were reasonable grounds for believing the transaction would benefit the company.[2] Good faith, propriety of purpose and reasonableness must all be established to the satisfaction of the court; if any of these elements is missing, the transaction remains vulnerable.

There is a time-limit on the power of an administrator or liquidator to attack a transaction at an undervalue. The transaction must have taken place at a 'relevant time'.[3] There are two elements to the definition of 'relevant time'. First, the transaction must be entered into within a specified period before the onset of the administration or liquidation. The transaction at an undervalue must have taken place either at a time within the period of two years ending with the onset of the administration or liquidation, or at a time between the making of an administration application in respect of the company and the making of an administration order on that application.[4]

Secondly, it is only a relevant time for the purposes of the provisions relating to transactions at an undervalue if, at the time, the company is unable to pay its debts within the meaning of section 123 of the Act or if it becomes unable to pay them within the meaning of that section in consequence of the transaction. This requirement, however, is deemed to be satisfied, unless the contrary is shown, where the transaction in question is entered into by the company with a person who is connected with the company.[5]

The court is given a very wide power to make such order as it thinks fit for the purpose of restoring the position to what it would have been if the company had not entered into the transaction. The court also has power to set aside transactions at an undervalue in applications brought under section 423.[6] There is no time-limit on applications under this section and, as well as liquidators and administrators, supervisors of voluntary arrangements and victims of transactions[7] have standing to seek an order under this section although, if the company is in administration or liquidation, a victim must obtain the leave of the court[8] Whoever brings the claim, it is treated as made on behalf of every victim of

---

1   *Re Barton Manufacturing Co Ltd* [1998] BCC 827 (gratuitous payments ordered to be repaid to liquidator in application under section 238); *Phillips v Brewin Dolphin Bell Lawrie Ltd* [2001] 1 WLR 143 where the House of Lords held that there was no reason why the consideration for a transaction should not be provided by a third party.
2   Section 238(5).
3   Section 240.
4   See also section 240(3).
5   Section 240(2). For the definition of a person connected with the company, see sections 249 and 435.
6   A transaction at an undervalue for this purpose is defined by section 423(1). So far as companies are concerned, the definition is the same as that under section 238.
7   A litigant in proceedings against a company who has a chance of success in those proceedings can be a 'victim' for this purpose: *Pinewood Joinery v Starelm Properties Ltd* [1994] BCC 569. See also, *Re Ayala Holdings Ltd* [1993] BCLC 256 and *Agricultural Mortgage Corp plc v Woodward*, above (application by mortgagee).
8   Section 424(1)(a).

the transaction.[1] The court can make an order under this section only where it is satisfied that the transaction was entered into by the company for the purpose of putting assets beyond the reach of any person who is making, or may at some time make, a claim against the company or of otherwise prejudicing the interests of such a person in relation to the claim which he is making or may make.[2] The need to establish this purpose inhibits the use of the power contained in this section.[3]

21.55.3 *Voidable preferences*

An administrator or liquidator may apply to the court for an order on such terms as the court thinks fit, for restoring the position to what it would have been if the company had not given a preference.[4] A company gives a preference to a person if:

(1) that person is one of the company's creditors or a surety or guarantor for any of the company's debts or other liabilities; and
(2) the company does anything or suffers anything to be done which (in either case) has the effect of putting that person into a position which, in the event of the company going into insolvent liquidation, will be better than the position he would have been in if that thing had not been done.

These elements of the definition of preference must be determined objectively: a preference arises in the event that the objective effect referred to occurs. However, the court may not make an order to reverse the preference unless the company which gave the preference was influenced in deciding to give it by a desire to put the recipient in a better position in an insolvent liquidation than he would have been in if the preference had not been given.

A desire to prefer is narrower than intention in that a person may be held to have 'intended' the necessary consequences of his acts even though he does not desire them to happen: to be held to have desired it, the company must be shown positively to have wished to improve the creditor's position in its insolvent liquidation. A company is 'influenced' by a desire to prefer where it is a motivating factor, but it need not be the only or the predominant one.[5] The desire must be present at the time when the preference is given.[6]

Where the preference is given to a person connected with the company (otherwise than by reason only of being its employee) at the time that the preference was given then the company is presumed, unless the contrary is shown,

---

1   Section 424(2).
2   Statutory predecessors of this section, which also applies to individual insolvents, can be traced back to 1571. See *Arbuthnot Leasing International Ltd v Havelot Leasing & Ors (No 2)* [1990] BCC 636; *Menzies v National Bank of Kuwait SAK*, above; *Chohan v Saggar* [1994] BCC 134; *Agricultural Mortgage Corp plc v Woodward*, above.
3   Section 425 specifies orders which can be made in respect of a transaction defrauding creditors (such specific provision to be without prejudice to the general power of the court).
4   Section 239.
5   *Re MC Bacon*, above; *Re DKG Contractors Ltd* [1990] BCC 903; *Re Beacon Leisure Ltd* [1991] BCC 213, [1992] BCLC 565; *Re Fairway Magazines Ltd* [1992] BCC 924, [1993] BCLC 643; *Re Agriplant Services Ltd* [1997] BCC 842.
6   *Wills v Corfe Joinery Ltd* [1997] BCC 511.

to have been influenced in deciding to give the preference by the requisite desire.[1]

A company may be held to have given a preference by giving an unsecured creditor a security over the company's assets. However, in a case such as *Re MC Bacon*, where the debenture was granted to avert the calling-in of the company's overdraft and the immediate liquidation which would have followed if the bank had withdrawn its support, the requisite desire to prefer may not be established. Another example of a possible preference is the decision to pay some debts but not others: the creditors whose debts are paid are obviously placed in a much better position than those who remain unpaid and who become subject to the moratorium in administration or, as the case may be, become obliged to prove for their debts in the company's liquidation.[2]

The fact that something has been done in pursuance of an order of the court does not prevent that thing from constituting the giving of a preference. This provision is intended to prevent, for example, the company submitting to a judgment against itself by the person to be preferred and then arguing that it had no choice in giving the preference because of the judgment.

The preference is vulnerable only if it was given at a relevant time. This means, in the case of a preference given to a person who is connected with the company (otherwise and by reason only of being its employee), a period of two years ending with the onset of the administration or liquidation. In the case of a preference which is not given to a person connected with the company then the relevant period is six months ending with the onset of the administration or liquidation. In addition, the time between the presentation of a petition for the making of an administration order and the making of such order is a relevant time. A time will be a relevant time, however, only if the company is unable to pay its debts within the meaning of section 123 of the Act when the preference is given or becomes unable to pay its debts within the meaning of that section in consequence of the preference (but there is no presumption as to such inability even in relation to connected persons).

The same definition of the onset of the administration or liquidation applies as in the case of transactions at an undervalue.

21.55.4 Court orders in respect of transactions at an undervalue and preferences

The court is given a very wide discretion to make orders for the purpose of restoring the position to what it would have been if the company had not entered into the transaction or preference. Without prejudice to the generality of this discretion, the court is also given the power to make the following orders:[3]

(1) to require any property transferred as part of the transaction, or in connection with the giving of a preference, to be vested in the company;

---

1   Section 239(6). See, eg, *Katz v McNally* [1999] BCC 291 (CA). See also *Re Brian D Pierson (Contractors) Ltd* [2000] 1 BCLC 275. See also, *Re Thirty-Eight Building Ltd* [1999] BCC 260 (trustees of employees' pension scheme were not within the connected person category).

2   As in *Katz v McNally*, above, where debts owing to members of the family that controlled the company were repaid. See also, *Re Brian D Pierson (Contractors) Ltd*, above, where bank loans were repaid in order to reduce the exposure of directors under personal guarantees that they had given to the bank.

3   Section 241.

(2) to require any property to be so vested if it represents in any person's hands the application either of the proceeds of sale of property so transferred or of money so transferred;

(3) to release or discharge (in whole or in part) any security given by the company;

(4) to require any person to pay, in respect of benefits received by him from the company, such sums to the administrator or liquidator as the court may direct;

(5) to provide for any surety or guarantor whose obligations to any person were released or discharged (in whole or in part) under the transaction, or by the giving of the preference, to be under such new or revived obligations to that person as the court thinks appropriate;

(6) to provide for security to be provided for the discharge of any obligation imposed by or arising under the court order, for such an obligation to be charged on any property and for the security or charge to have the same priority as a security or charge released or discharged (in whole or in part) under the transaction or by the giving of the preference; and

(7) to provide for the extent to which any person whose property is vested by the order in the company, or on whom obligations are imposed by the order, is to be able to prove in the winding-up of the company for debts or other liabilities which arose from, or were released or discharged (in whole or in part) under or by the transaction or the giving of the preference.

An order relating to a transaction at an undervalue or a preference may affect the property of, or impose any obligation on, any person, whether or not he is the person with whom the company in question entered into the transaction or, as the case may be, the person to whom the preference was given. However, such an order:

(1) must not prejudice any interest in property which was acquired from a person other than the company and was acquired in good faith and for value, or prejudice any interest deriving from such an interest; and

(2) must not require a person who received a benefit from the transaction or preference in good faith and for value to make a payment to the administrator or liquidator, except where that person was a party to the transaction or the payment is to be in respect of a preference given to that person at a time when he was a creditor of the company.[1]

Section 241(2A), inserted by the Insolvency (No 2) Act 1994, amplifies the concept of good faith in this context. A person who has notice of the relevant surrounding circumstances and of the relevant proceedings, or who was connected with, or an associate of, either the company in question or the person with whom the company entered into the transaction or to whom the company gave the preference, is presumed, unless the contrary is shown, not to be in good faith. The relevant surrounding circumstances are the fact that the company entered into the transaction at an undervalue or, as the case may be, the circumstances which amounted to the giving of a preference by the company in question.[2] A person has notice of administration proceedings if he has notice of

---

1   Section 241(2), as amended by the Insolvency (No 2) Act 1994.

2   Section 241(3) as amended by the Insolvency (No 2) Act 1994.

the fact that a petition has been presented or an order has been made; and a person has notice of liquidation if he has notice of the fact that a petition has been presented or of the fact that the company has gone into liquidation.[1]

The proceeds of an action to set aside a preference are held by the office-holder for the benefit of its general creditors and do not fall within the scope of a floating charge on its assets.[2] The reasoning underlying this is that the power to attack a preference is granted only to the liquidator and administrator and is not available to the company itself; therefore the proceeds of an action in respect of a preference cannot be the subject of a charge granted by the company on its assets and they are held separately by the administrator or liquidator for the benefit of unsecured creditors.[3]

The Act[4] specifically states that the provisions relating to transactions at an undervalue and preferences apply without prejudice to the availability of any other remedy, even in relation to a transaction or preference which the company had no power to enter into or to give.

21.55.5 *Extortionate credit transactions*

A liquidator or administrator may apply to the court in respect of an extortionate credit transaction which was entered into within three years of the date of the administration order or, as the case may be, when the company went into liquidation.[5]

A transaction is extortionate if, having regard to the risk accepted by the person providing the credit:

(1) the terms of it are or were such as to require a grossly exorbitant payment to be made (whether unconditionally or in certain contingencies) in respect of the provision of the credit; or

(2) it otherwise grossly contravened ordinary principles of fair dealing.

It is to be presumed, unless the contrary is proved, that a transaction is extortionate.

An order in respect of an extortionate credit transaction may contain one or more of the following, as the court thinks fit:

(1) provision setting aside the whole or part of any obligation created by the transaction;

---

1   Section 241(3A) and (3C), as inserted by the Insolvency (No 2) Act 1994. See also section 241(3B), which deals with the situation where liquidation follows immediately upon administration.

2   *Re Yagerphone* [1935] 1 Ch 392. This ratio in the case was that payment of a debt due to an unsecured creditor prior to crystallisation bound the debenture holder but Bennett J's obiter statement as to the application of the proceeds recovered on a preference claim is widely regarded as correct: see *Re MC Bacon Ltd (No 2)* [1991] Ch 127 at p 137. See also *Re Floor Fourteen Ltd, Lewis v IRC* [2001] 3 All ER 499; *Re Oasis Merchandising Services Ltd, Ward v Aitken* [1997] 1 All ER 1009.

3   Wheeler, 'Swelling the Assets for Distribution in Corporate Insolvency' [1993] JBL 256 but see now R Parry, 'The Destination of Proceeds of Insolvency Litigation' (2002) 23 Company lawyer 49; A Keay, 'Another way of skinning a cat: Enforcing directors' duties for the benefit of creditors' [2004] Insolvency Intelligence 1.

4   Section 241(4).

5   Section 244. These provisions follow closely the terms of sections 137–139 (inclusive) of the Consumer Credit Act 1974.

(2) provision otherwise varying the terms of the transaction or varying the terms on which any security for the purposes of the transaction is held;

(3) provision requiring any person who is or was a party to the transaction to pay to the office-holder any sums paid to that person, by virtue of the transaction, by the company;

(4) provision requiring any person to surrender to the administrator or liquidator any property held by him as security for the purposes of the transaction; and

(5) provision directing accounts to be taken between any persons.

The power to attack any transaction as being extortionate may be exercised concurrently with any other powers exercisable in relation to that transaction.

21.55.6 Avoidance of floating charges

Floating charges created by the company within a specified period prior to the commencement of the administration or the liquidation (a 'relevant time') will be invalid[1] except to the extent of the aggregate of:

(1) the value of so much of the consideration for the creation of the charge as consists of money paid or goods or services supplied to the company at the same time as, or after, the creation of the charge. The value of any goods or services supplied by way of consideration for a floating charge is deemed to be the amount in money which at the time that they were supplied could reasonably have been expected to be obtained for supplying the goods or services in the ordinary course of business and on the same terms (apart from the consideration) as those on which they were supplied to the company;[2]

(2) the value of so much of that consideration as consists of the discharge or reduction, at the same time as, or after, the creation of the charge of any debt of the company;[3]

(3) the amount of such interest (if any) as is payable on the amount falling within para (1) or (2) in pursuance of any agreement under which the money was so paid, the goods or services were so supplied or the debt was so discharged or reduced.

The phrase 'at the same time as' which is used in section 245 was considered by the Court of Appeal in *Re Shoe Lace Ltd.*[4] Not following authorities on a statutory predecessor to section 245,[5] the Court of Appeal held that whether the

---

1   Section 245.

2   Section 245(6).

3   This would appear to reverse the decision in *Re Destone Fabrics Ltd* [1941] Ch 319. Section 245 preserves (contrary to the recommendations of the Review Committee on Insolvency Law and Practice Cmnd 8558 (1982), paras 1561–1562) the decision in *Re Yeovil Glove Co Ltd* [1965] Ch 148, whereby in respect of a floating charge created in favour of a bank to secure an overdrawn account, if payments are made into the account after the creation of the charge, these will, under the rule in *Clayton's Case* (1816) 1 Mer 572, go to reduce the pre-charge indebtedness, so that cheques drawn on the account after the creation of the charge will be money paid to the company thereafter and the charge will therefore be valid to this extent.

4   [1993] BCC 609 (also reported as *Power v Sharp Investments Ltd*).

5   *Re Columbian Fireproofing Co Ltd* [1910] 2 Ch 120 and *Re F & E Stanton Ltd* [1929] 1 Ch 180, which had held that a delay between the creation of the charge and the giving of consideration would not bring a charge within the scope of the section if the person seeking to uphold the charge could establish a good reason for the delay.

consideration for the charge was given at the same time as the creation of the charge is a mechanical issue determined solely by the clock, subject only to *de minimis* delays.

In *Re Fairway Magazines Ltd*,[1] the company was indebted to its bank and this debt was personally guaranteed by one of its directors. As part of a series of measures designed to keep the company alive, the director lent sums of money to the company which, at his request, were paid directly into the company's overdrawn bank account. A debenture was granted to the director as security for these advances. The effect of paying the borrowed money into the company's bank account was to reduce the director's personal liability under the guarantee. This led to a corresponding reduction in the amount for which the director would be required to lodge a proof in the liquidation of the company in respect of his payments under the guarantee. Instead, to the extent of the reduction of his exposure as an unsecured creditor, the director became a secured creditor.

Mummery J held that payments made by the director which were paid into the company's bank account were not in substance paid to the company for its benefit, since the effect of the payments was merely to substitute a secured debt for an unsecured debt. Therefore, the arrangement was avoided by section 245 because the payments were not 'paid . . . to the company' as required by section 245(1)(a).[2]

A floating charge is created at a relevant time if:

(1) in the case of a floating charge created in favour of a person who is connected with the company it is created at a time in the period of two years ending with the onset of insolvency;

(2) where the floating charge is not created in favour of a person connected with the company, it is created at a time in the period of twelve months ending with the onset of insolvency; or

(3) in any case it is created at a time between the presentation of a petition for the making of an administration order in relation to the company and the making of such an order on that petition.

In addition, in a case where the floating charge is created in favour of a person who is not connected with the company then the company must at that time be unable to pay its debts within the meaning of section 123 of the Act or become unable to pay its debts within the meaning of that section in consequence of the transaction under which the charge is created.

The definition of the onset of the insolvency for the purpose of section 245 is the same as for transactions at an undervalue.

21.56　Other powers

The Insolvency Act 1986 contains various powers which office-holders and other insolvency practitioners[3] can call upon to assist them in their task of collecting in the assets of the company for the benefit of the creditors. The powers are

---

1　[1992] BCC 924, [1993] BCLC 643.

2　*Re Orleans Motor Co Ltd* [1911] 2 Ch 41; *Re Matthew Ellis Ltd* [1933] Ch 458; *Re GT Whyte & Co Ltd* [1983] BCLC 311.

3　Nominees under voluntary arrangements and the Official Receiver are not generally regarded as office-holders, but the Official Receiver is an office-holder for the purposes of sections 235 and 236. See now *Re Pantmaenog Timber Co Ltd* [2004] 1 AC 158.

extensive: in *Re British & Commonwealth Holdings plc (No 2)*,[1] Woolf LJ described the powers contained in Part IV of the Act as 'a remarkable armoury of summary weapons with which to assist "office holders" ... to perform their functions'.

In outline the relevant powers include the following.

(1) A power to get in the company's property. Under section 234 of the Act, where a person has in his possession or control any property, books, papers or records to which the company appears to be entitled, the court may require that person to pay, deliver, convey, surrender or transfer the same to the office-holder. An office-holder for this purpose means an administrator, an administrative receiver, a liquidator or a provisional liquidator.

(2) Under section 235, specified persons can be compelled to give to the office-holder any information concerning the company and its promotion, formation, business dealings or affairs generally and may be required to attend on the liquidator at such times as he may reasonably require. The persons who have this duty to co-operate with the office-holder include the existing and former officers of the company and also those who have been its employees in the past year.

If a person fails in his duty to co-operate under section 235 he is liable to a fine. In addition to those who are office-holders under section 234, the Official Receiver is also an office-holder in this case.

(3) Power to apply to court for an examination of certain persons.[2] The office-holders who have this power are administrators, administrative receivers, liquidators and provisional liquidators, and also the Official Receiver. Examinations under this power, which is conferred by section 236, are private. In compulsory liquidations, the Official Receiver also has power to apply to the court for public examinations.[3]

The court may on the application of an office-holder under section 236 summon to appear before it any officer of the company, any person known or suspected to have in his possession any property of the company or supposed to be indebted to the company, or any person whom the court thinks capable of giving information concerning the promotion, formation, business dealings, affairs or property of the company.[4]

---

1   [1992] Ch 342, [1992] 2 All ER 801, [1992] 2 WLR 931, [1992] BCLC 641, [1992] BCC 165 and 172; affirmed *sub nom British and Commonwealth Holdings (Joint Administrators) v Spicer and Oppenheim* [1993] AC 426, [1992] 4 All ER 876, [1992] 3 WLR 853, [1993] BCLC 168, [1992] BCC 977.

2   Section 236.

3   Section 133. See *Re Wallace Smith Trust Co Ltd* [1992] BCC 707. This power has extra-territorial effect; *Re Seagull Manufacturing Co Ltd* [1993] Ch 345, [1993] 2 All ER 980, [1993] 2 WLR 872, [1993] BCLC 1139, [1993] BCC 241. Note *Re Campbell Coverings Ltd (No 2)* [1954] Ch 225 where it was held that the power to apply for a public examination applies to voluntary liquidations. In *Bishopsgate Investment Management Ltd v Maxwell* [1993] Ch 1, [1992] 2 All ER 856, [1992] 2 WLR 991, [1992] BCC 222, the point was not decided but the Court of Appeal accepted that a public examination might be available in a voluntary liquidation by virtue of section 112.

4   Section 236(2).

21.57 Dissolution of companies

Section 201 of the Insolvency Act 1986 deals with the dissolution of a company which has been wound up voluntarily. Where the liquidator has filed his final accounts and returns,[1] the Registrar of Companies will put these on the company's file. On the expiration of three months from the registration of those returns the company is deemed to be dissolved. The court has power, on the application of the liquidator or any other interested party, to make an order that the dissolution of the company takes place at some later date if the court thinks fit.[2]

In a compulsory winding-up, the Official Receiver, if he is the liquidator of the company and believes that the realisable assets are insufficient to cover the expenses of the winding-up and that no further investigation of the company's affairs is required, may apply to the Registrar of Companies for the early dissolution of the company.[3] If the Official Receiver gives such a notice this is registered by the Registrar of Companies. At the expiry of three months from the date of registration of the notice the company is dissolved. Where a notice has been given by the Official Receiver in this respect, any creditor or contributory of the company or any administrative receiver may apply to the Secretary of State for a direction if he considers that:

(1) the realisable assets of the company are sufficient to cover the expenses of the winding-up;
(2) the affairs of the company do require further investigation; or
(3) for any other reason the early dissolution of the company is inappropriate.[4]

The Secretary of State may give directions enabling the winding-up of the company to proceed as if the Official Receiver had not given a notice requiring the early dissolution of the company to the Registrar of Companies. His powers in this respect include the power to make a direction deferring the date at which the dissolution of the company is to take effect.[5]

Where in a compulsory winding-up no application is made by the Official Receiver for an early dissolution, the provisions of section 205 of the Insolvency Act 1986 apply. When the liquidator has filed his final returns or the Official Receiver has filed a notice stating that he considers the winding-up to be complete, the Registrar of Companies will register those returns or the notice as the case may be. At the end of a three-month period beginning with the date of that registration the company is dissolved.[6]

Again, the Official Receiver or any other person interested in the company's dissolution may apply to the Secretary of State for a direction deferring the date of the dissolution.[7]

When a company is dissolved, its corporate existence ceases. It no longer has any officers or agents who can be served with notices or other proceedings on behalf of the company. It is not infrequently the case, however, that there are

---

1 Section 94 (members' voluntary); section 106 (creditors' voluntary).
2 Section 201(3).
3 Section 202(2).
4 Section 203(2).
5 Section 203(3).
6 Section 205(2).
7 Section 205(3), with a right of appeal to the court if the Secretary of State refuses to grant a deferral.

persons who have grievances or claims involving the company which they still wish to enforce.

Under section 651 of the Companies Act 1985, on the application of the liquidator of the company or any other person appearing to be interested the court may make an order declaring the dissolution to be void.[1] This power will be exercised where, upon a reconstruction, the new company, after agreeing to satisfy the liability of the old company,[2] has failed to perform its obligations and the old company has been dissolved. Note, however, that the order, if made, will not validate any purported corporate activity of the company carried out prior to the making of the order.[3] It has been stated that, ordinarily, the purposes of restoring a company to the register are to enable the liquidator to distribute an overlooked asset or a creditor to make a claim which he has not previously made.[4] The jurisdiction can be used to put a creditor in a better position than he would otherwise have been in.[5]

Generally, such applications must not be made after the end of the period of two years from the date of dissolution of the company, but applications for the purpose of bringing proceedings against the company for damages for personal injuries or under the Fatal Accidents Act 1976 may be brought at any time subject to any applicable limitation periods.[6]

Once a company is dissolved, all property and rights whatsoever which may still be vested in or held on trust for the company immediately before its dissolution (including leasehold property, but not including property held by the company on trust for any other person) are deemed to be *bona vacantia*[7] and vest in the Crown, subject to its right to disclaim. Section 656 of the Companies Act 1985 lays down the conditions upon which such disclaimer may be made by the Crown.

21.58 Defunct companies

Aside from winding-up, a company may also cease to exist if it is struck off the register in accordance with the procedures contained in sections 652 and 652A–F of the Companies Act 1985. The Registrar of Companies can activate the striking off procedure[8] or a private company, acting through its directors, can apply to the Registrar for striking off.[9] Provision is made for the possible restoration to the register of any company struck off under these procedures by order of the court on the application of specified persons including members and creditors of that

1   *Re Townreach Ltd* [1995] Ch 28. On the effect of restoration to the register see: *Allied Dunbar Assurance plc v Fowler* [1994] BCC 422.

2   *Re Spottiswoode, Dixon and Hunting* [1912] 1 Ch 410.

3   *Morris v Harris* [1927] AC 242 (HL).

4   *Re Forte's Manufacturing Ltd* [1994] BCC 84 at p 87 *per* Hoffmann LJ.

5   Ibid.

6   Section 651(4) and (5). The court has power to direct that the period between the dissolution of the company and the making of the order under the section shall not count for limitation purposes: section 651(6).

7   Section 654 of the Companies Act 1985.

8   Section 652.

9   Section 652A.

company.[1] If a company is dissolved by being struck off the register, its property becomes *bona vacantia* vesting in the Crown.[2]

21.59   EC insolvency regulation

The winding up jurisdiction of the courts has now been supplemented by the EC Regulation on Insolvency Proceedings (Council Regulation No 1346/2000). The Regulation is in force from 31 May 2002 and applies in all the EU Member States, except Denmark which exercised an 'opt-out'. It applies to collective insolvency proceedings involving the partial or total disinvestment of the debtor and the appointment of a liquidator (Art 1). The expression 'liquidator' in the context of the Regulation has a far broader meaning than it does under domestic English law. In the Regulation setting 'liquidator' means any person or body whose function it is to administer or liquidate assets of which the debtor has been divested or to supervise the administration of his affairs. In particular the expression includes administrators and supervisors of company voluntary arrangements.

There are many oddities and incongruities of language throughout the Regulation. It is specifically stated to apply to the collective proceedings listed in Annex A even though company voluntary arrangements, for example, do not necessarily entail the partial or total divestment of a debtor. For the UK the procedures listed in Annex A are:

(a) winding-up by or subject to the supervision of the court;
(b) creditors' voluntary winding up (with confirmation by the court);
(c) administration;
(d) voluntary arrangements under insolvency legislation;
(e) bankruptcy or sequestration

A creditors' voluntary winding-up, which is the most convenient form of winding-up in practice, does not invariably involve confirmation by the court, but there is a facility under the widely drafted section 112 of the Insolvency Act 1986 whereby court confirmation may be sought and it is likely that this will become a matter of routine where the liquidation potentially involves foreign assets

The aim of the Regulation is that the opening of main insolvency proceedings in a Member State should have immediate and universal effect throughout the European Union (Art 3(1)). Would the commencement of administration in England through the appointment by a floating charge holder of an administrator out of court produce such an effect throughout the EU? In other words, would the courts in other EU Member States construe the Regulation as having this effect? There are certain factors pointing them in the direction of this construction. First, under the Enterprise Act 2002 an administrator is deemed to be an officer of the court, whether or not he is actually appointed by the court.[3] Secondly, the Virgos-Schmit Report on the draft EU Convention on Insolvency Proceedings

---

1   Section 653. Only members or creditors may seek such an order if the company was struck off under section 652. A wider category of persons has standing to apply if the striking off was under section 652A. See *Re Blenheim Leisure (Restaurants) Ltd (No 2)* [1999] All ER (D) 1070. For possible reforms in this general area see Company Law Review, Final Report, vol 1 (2001), paragraphs 11.17–11.20.
2   Section 655.
3   Enterprise Act 2002, Schedule B1, paragraph 5.

(which preceded and foreshadowed the provisions of the Regulation)[1] referred to the definition of 'court' in the Convention/Regulation and suggested that the expression was to be construed in a very broad sense as covering 'not only the judiciary or an authority which plays a similar role to that of a court or public authority ... but a person or body empowered by national law to open proceedings or make decisions in the course of those proceedings'. While the Virgos-Schmit Report has no official status and was not agreed to by all the EU Member States, nevertheless it is of persuasive authority. Thirdly, while Blackburne J in. In *Re Salvage Association*[2] accepted that the Regulation, and in particular Art 3(1) thereof, appear to be premised on the assumption of court activation of insolvency proceedings he suggested that a broader, purposive interpretation is possible.

21.59.2 Jurisdiction to open main insolvency proceedings

Jurisdiction to open insolvency proceedings is given to the Contracting State in whose territory the centre of the debtor's main interests is situated (Art 3). These proceedings are intended to have universal effect and application, although subject to a whole host of enumerated exceptions. There is a presumption that the centre of main interests of a company or other legal person is at the place of the registered office. The Regulation seems to make the assumption that the area of greatest economic activity of a bankrupt will be in the state where the bulk of assets and liabilities exist, but this may not be the case. The 'centre of main interests' (COMI) expression is one that is capable of varying judicial interpretation. It is questionable whether any greater certainty is introduced by the statement in Recital 13 of the preamble to the Regulation that the centre of main interest 'should correspond to the place where the debtor conducts the administration of his interests on a regular basis and is therefore ascertainable by third parties'. On a purely pragmatic level, however, the courts in a Member State that are first seised of an insolvency matter may well be inclined to assert jurisdiction. In cases of doubt, therefore, it behoves a party whose personal interests would be best served by the opening of proceedings in a particular Member State to initiate insolvency proceedings in that state even though it is debatable where the debtor's centre of main interests are situated.

The English courts have adopted an expansive approach to jurisdiction under the Regulation. In *Re Daisytek-ISA Ltd*,[3] Daisytek-ISA Ltd was the holding company of a group of trading companies – including French and German-incorporated subsidiaries – and the question arose whether an English court had jurisdiction to make an administration order in respect of each of the companies on the basis that their centre of main interests was in England, notwithstanding the foreign incorporation. It was held that the court was required to consider the scale of the interests administered at a particular place and their importance and then to consider the scale and importance of its interests administered at any other place that might be regarded as its centre of main interests. On the evidence he took the view that the majority of the group's administration was conducted from its head office in Bradford and, therefore, England was the centre of main interests for

---

1   The Report can be found in an Appendix to Moss, Fletcher and Isaacs *The EC Regulation On Insolvency Proceedings* (Oxford University Press, 2002).
2   [2003] 3 All ER 246.
3   [2003] BCC 562.

each subsidiary within the group. In determining the centre of main interests of each subsidiary, he held that the most important 'third parties' referred to in Recital 13 are the potential creditors.[1]

Potentially the most significant decision thus far on the Regulation is that in *Re BRAC Rent-A-Car International Inc*,[2] where it was held that an English court had jurisdiction under the Regulation to grant an administration order in respect of a non-EU company where its centre of main interests was in England. In this case the company was incorporated in Delaware in the US but it had no employees in the US. All of its employees worked in England with contracts of employment governed by English law apart from a small number in a branch office in Switzerland. All the company's trading activities were carried out by way of contracts with subsidiaries and franchisees that were governed by English law. Lloyd J decided that in the circumstances an English court had jurisdiction. In his view, by dint of both a literal reading and also a purposive interpretation of the Regulation, the only test for the application of the Regulation in relation to a given debtor is whether the centre of the debtor's main interests is in a relevant Member State and where a debtor that is a legal person is incorporated.

21.59.3 *Jurisdiction to open secondary insolvency proceedings*

Article 3(2) of the Regulation assigns jurisdiction to open secondary insolvency proceedings. The basis of jurisdiction in this situation is that there is an 'establishment' within the jurisdiction. In those circumstances insolvency proceedings may be commenced, but the scope must be confined to the assets situated within the Member State. In other words, secondary insolvency proceedings have an exclusively territorial, as distinct from universal, effect. The opening of secondary proceedings may have the effect of safeguarding local preferential creditors whose claims would be regarded as non-preferential by the law of the main proceedings, and indeed this may be a prime motive for the institution of such proceedings. The jurisdictional crutch is a debtor's establishment and the latter is defined as meaning 'any place of operations where the debtor carries out a non-transitory economic activity with human means and goods'. It seems clear from this that the mere presence of assets within a particular jurisdiction is not sufficient for the assumption of jurisdiction. Nevertheless, the basis of jurisdiction is not cast iron and leaves ample leeway for local courts favourably disposed to local creditors. Park J, however, resisted the temptation to exercise jurisdiction in *Telia v Hillcourt*[3] and appeared to reject the proposition that the mere presence of business premises within the jurisdiction would constitute an 'establishment'.

21.59.4 *Applicable law*

The applicable law is the law governing insolvency in the state where the proceedings are opened (Article 4). The possibility of proceedings being started in two or more jurisdictions with differing laws applying means that the principle of universality has been abandoned, and conflicts between different priority rules will inevitably arise. An attempt to minimise these problems is made by restricting

---

1   See also *Re Enron Direct* [2003] EWHC 1437, [2003] BPIR 1132 and *Geveran Trading Co Ltd v Skjevesland* [2003] BCC 209.
2   [2003] 2 All ER 201.
3   [2002] EWHC 2377 (Ch).

the 'effects' of secondary proceedings to the 'assets of the debtor situated in the territory' of the Member State where secondary bankruptcy is opened (Article 27). There are often conflicts, however, concerning the *situs* of assets between the laws of different Member States and consequently this provision will not eliminate all difficulties. Article 4 sets out a number of matters which are specifically referred to the law governing the opening of the proceedings and which are both substantive and procedural in nature. These include:

(a) the debtors against whom insolvency proceedings may be brought;
(b) the assets which form part of the estate;
(c) the powers of the liquidator;
(d) the effects of insolvency on current contracts to which the debtor is a party;
(e) rules governing the lodging, verification and admission of claims; and
(f) priority ranking of creditors.

21.59.5 Referrals to legal orders other than the law of the insolvency forum

Notwithstanding the terms of Article 4, the law of the insolvency forum does not regulate all substantive and procedural matters pertaining to the insolvency proceedings. There are a number of specific referrals to other legal systems, which are set out in Articles 5–15. Article 5, for example, recognises the rights of secured creditors with a valid claim to assets under the law of the place where the assets claimed are situated. This means that creditors can acquire security by complying with the conditions necessary in the law of the place where the prospectively secured assets are located, safe in the knowledge that their secured status will not be disturbed by the commencement of insolvency proceedings in another Member State.[1] The effect of Article 6 is to preserve certain set-off rights. Article 4(2)(d) states that the law of the insolvency forum shall govern the conditions under which set-offs may be invoked, but set-off rights can still be claimed if they are permitted by the law applicable to the insolvent debtor's claim. It is clear from the *BCCI*[2] litigation that set-off rights differ significantly as between Member States, and Article 6 is a valuable safeguard for creditors who have entered into certain transactions on the basis that set-off rights would be available. It should be noted that it is not the law of the creditor's claim (the 'active' claim) that governs the availability of set-off, but rather the law of the insolvent debtor's claim (the 'passive' claim) and the latter law may be the law of a non-EC Member State.

Article 7 preserves seller's rights under reservation of title clauses where the assets in question are situated in a Member State other than that of the insolvency forum. Article 8 reaffirms the generally accepted principle of private international law that questions of title to immovable property are governed exclusively by the *lex situs*. The effects of insolvency proceedings on contracts conferring the right to acquire or make use of immovable property are governed solely by the law of the Member State within whose territory the immovable property is situated. Article 9 is aimed at protecting the integrity of payment systems and financial markets. It provides that the effects of insolvency proceedings on the rights and obligations of the parties to a payment or settlement system or to a financial market shall be governed solely by the law of the Member State applicable to that system or market. This preserves the full enforcement of Part VII of the Companies Act 1989

---

1 The wording of Article 5 would appear to accord recognition to the English floating charge.
2 *Re Bank of Credit and Commerce International SA (No 10)* [1997] Ch 213.

under which the provisions of market contracts or the rules of the exchange or clearing house with respect to default and settlement will prevail over the general law of insolvency.

It is provided in Article 10 that the effect of insolvency on employment contracts and relations shall be governed by the law applicable to the contract of employment. The preamble to the Regulation states that the purpose of this provision is to protect both employees and jobs. The intention is that the law applicable to the employment contract would determine, for example, whether liquidation operates to terminate or to continue employment contracts. Other important employment law related matters are left to the law of the insolvency forum including the preferential status of employee claims in a liquidation. It may be that the precise interrelationship between the two sets of provisions on the employment aspects of insolvency will require detailed working out.

21.59.6 *Recognition of insolvency proceedings*

Article 16 provides that insolvency proceedings, once validly commenced, shall be recognised in all other member States, with the proceedings having the effect they have in the State where the proceedings were commenced. If unqualified, this statement would import true universality. However, as already noted, it is subject to the right to open secondary insolvency proceedings. Implementation of the Regulation should promote the rescue culture since an administrator's powers will be recognised throughout the Community, and the stay on creditor enforcement actions will be equally recognised. On the other hand, the fact that secondary proceedings cannot include the debtor rehabilitation provisions of a particular jurisdiction may act as a significant impediment to the rescue culture. For example, an administrator who is trying to formulate and implement a rescue plan could find the plans frustrated by the actions of a group of creditors in a particular jurisdiction who take the view that a secondary liquidation in that jurisdiction would better serve their interests.

There is also the practical point of obtaining recognition in a foreign jurisdiction for an administration order granted by an English court. While the effect of an administration order is theoretically immediate and universal throughout the Community, the practical implications of legal and cultural differences remain. One commentator has suggested that a European database of companies going into either administration or liquidation ought to be contemplated. One can hardly disagree with the proposition that the 'Regulation has clearly set a high onus on lawyers practising cross-border insolvency law: that of being able to reach out to their foreign counterparts, even those with little experience of cross-border matters, and convince them, in simple terms, that the order which they obtained carries with it a body of law which they might not know about but which will nevertheless have a necessary impact upon them'.[1]

21.59.7 *Liquidators' powers*

Under Article 17, a judgment opening insolvency proceedings has the same effect in all Member States as it has in the State where proceedings were opened. Moreover, the liquidator in the main liquidation has the same powers in all Member States as the powers that are conferred on him by the State where the

---

1   See M Haravon 'English Administration Order Binding ... in France' [2003] *Insolvency Intelligence* 38.

proceedings are opened.[1] In particular, it is emphasised that the liquidator will have the power to remove assets from any jurisdiction except where rights in rem or reservation of title are an issue.[2] In exercising his powers, however, a liquidator must comply with the provisions of local law especially with regard to procedures for the realisation of assets. It has been suggested that some attempts to exploit the full potential of Articles 17 and 18 might provoke recourse to Article 26 – the public policy exception to the Community-wide enforceability of insolvency proceedings.[3]

21.59.8 Relationship between main and secondary liquidations

Having strayed from the principle of universality, the Regulation has the difficult task of determining the relationship between two sets of proceedings. There is a duty laid on the primary and secondary liquidators to communicate with one another promptly.[4] Moreover, a secondary liquidation can be stayed for up to 3 months at the request of the liquidator in the main proceedings, although the court in the secondary proceedings granting the stay may require the liquidator in the main insolvency proceedings to take any suitable measure to guarantee the interests of the creditors in the secondary proceedings and of individual classes of creditors.[5] A request by the liquidator for a stay may be rejected only if it is manifestly of no interest to the creditors in the main proceedings. The stay may be extended for further 3-month periods at a time, but the stay may be lifted by the court where it no longer appears justified having regard to the interests of creditors. A composition in the secondary proceedings may not become final without the consent of the liquidator in the main proceeding. Such consent cannot be withheld if the financial interests of the creditors in the main proceeding are not affected by the composition.

Any surplus remaining in a secondary bankruptcy after payment of all claims must be passed to the main liquidator, but this may be a case of 'shutting the stable door after the horse has bolted'. There may be little or nothing left in the secondary pot after the claims of local preferential creditors have been satisfied. Article 32 attempts to preserve unity between the main and secondary insolvency proceedings by declaring that any creditor may lodge his claim in the main proceedings and in any secondary proceedings. Moreover, subject to creditor objections, the liquidators in the respective proceedings are obliged to engage in consolidated cross-filing of claims that have already been lodged in the proceedings for which they were appointed. The principle of mutual recognition and equality of treatment of creditors is reinforced by Article 39, which states:

> Any creditor who has his habitual residence, domicile or registered office in a member state other than the state of the opening of proceedings, including the tax authorities and social security authorities of member states, shall have the right to lodge claims in the insolvency proceedings …

As far as other EC Member States are concerned, this eliminates the rule in *Government of India v Taylor*[6] that foreign revenue authorities are not competent to

---

1   Article 18.
2   Articles 5 and 7.
3   See Rajak [2000] *CfiLR* 180 at 193.
4   Article 31.
5   Article 33.
6   [1955] AC 491.

submit proofs in English insolvency proceedings, although the rule remains in force for non-EC states. One important proviso is that while foreign revenue claims may be treated as preferential under the relevant foreign law, as far as English law is concerned they are strictly non-preferential, with the foreign revenue authorities swelling the army of unsecured creditors.

21.59.9 An Assessment of the Regulation

The Regulation is to be welcomed for introducing a measure of harmonisation of bankruptcy and insolvency law throughout the European Community. There are significant gaps, though, which may increase uncertainty. It is silent on the central issue of the priority of creditors, leaving the claims to be settled according to the law governing the particular insolvency. In view of different priority rules in different countries, it may often be crucial to establish which is the 'main' and which is the 'secondary' liquidation. The creditors proving in the main liquidation may call on assets from all Member States, whereas the secondary liquidator may collect only assets within the jurisdiction in which he has been appointed. This difference, when coupled with the power of the liquidator of the main liquidation to remove assets from any Member State and effectively to suspend the secondary liquidation, with court sanction, makes the test to determine which constitutes the 'main' liquidation of great significance. The test however, lacks complete clarity.

Overall the effect may be that small creditors who claim in a local secondary liquidation may lose out to more powerful creditors with the ability to hedge their bets by proving in more than one set of proceedings. Moreover, if the system encourages duplicate claims, much money may be wasted in trying to prevent duplicate recovery. A better system might have been to give all power to the liquidator in the main proceedings and provide that a secondary liquidator was a mere minion for the collection of assets to be transferred to the main proceedings for distribution according to the law governing those proceedings.

Ambiguities in the text may ultimately be ironed out by a process of judicial interpretation, but clarification and uniform interpretation across the Community is likely to take some time. The jurisdiction of the European Court of Justice (ECJ) to hand down interpretative rulings is more restricted than its standard competence under what is now Art 234 of the EC Treaty. The Regulation was adopted under Title IV of the EC Treaty, and Art 68 applies on preliminary rulings. The jurisdiction to refer is limited to courts or tribunals of a Member State against whose decisions there is no judicial remedy under national law. Such a reference can and must be made where the court or tribunal considers that a decision on a question of interpretation of the Regulation is necessary to enable it to give judgment in a case pending before it. The crucial question is whether, in respect of the particular case pending before the court, there are any rights of appeal. It may be many years before a significant body of jurisprudence builds up on the interpretation of the Regulation.

Chapter 22

The Company Law Review and the Future of Company Law in the UK

22.1 Introduction

> Company law can help business or it can hinder it. Company law can encourage entrepreneurship, promote growth, enhance international competitiveness and create the conditions for investment and commitment of resources, whether of savings or employment. Or it can frustrate entrepreneurs, inhibit growth, restrict competitiveness and undermine the conditions for investment.
>
> Too much of British company law frustrates, inhibits, restricts and undermines. It is over-cautious, placing too high a premium on regulation and avoidance of risk. The company remains the choice of corporate vehicle for over a million businesses, and the core principles established by company law have served our economy well for over 150 years. But significant parts are outmoded or have become redundant and they are enshrined in law that is often unnecessarily complicated and inaccessible.[1]

This brief description of the current state of company law provides the background to, and the justification for, the present process of reform. As has been noted at a number of places throughout this book, company law has been the subject of a fundamental review since 1998 leading to the publication of a White Paper in July 2002.[2] A new Companies Bill to be introduced before the end of the current British Government's term was to be the outcome of the review process with the aim that it will 'be the most radical revision of the law since the mid nineteenth century and is intended to last for at least a generation'.[3] Quite when in fact the promised wide-ranging Bill will materialise is not at the time of writing clear. However it seems unlikely that there will be legislation within the stated timetable.

The first chapter of this book (at **1.7**) gave a brief overview of the review process. This chapter attempts to identify the core themes of the review in a slightly more reflective and fuller manner. As already noted, individual chapters have highlighted, in our view, the most significant detailed proposals that are likely to be implemented eventually.[4]

When the company law review began, the then President of the Board of Trade, Margaret Beckett, said that the framework of company law:

---

1 The Company Law Review Steering Group, *Modern Company Law for a Competitive Economy: Final Report*, (DTI, 2001), Volume I, Foreword, paragraphs 1 and 2, at p ix.
2 *Modernising Company Law*, Cm 5553.
3 White Paper, paragraph 5.1.
4 The literature on company law reform in general since the Company Law Review Steering Group published its Final Report (see below) includes De Lacy (ed), *The Reform of United Kingdom Company Law* (Cavendish, 2002), Wheeler, *Corporations and the Third Way* (Hart, 2002), Meeks, 'Reporting to shareholders: the proposals in the company law review', (2003) 3 JCLS 191, Freedman, 'One size fits all; small business and competitive legal forms', (2003) JCLS 123.

is essentially constructed on foundations which were put in place by the Victorians in the middle of the last century. There have been numerous additions, amendments and consolidations since then, but they have created a patchwork of regulation that is immensely complex and seriously out of date.[1]

The purpose of the review was, according to Mrs Beckett, 'to play an important part in modernising the nation and ensuring that our economy is well placed for the challenges which lie ahead'.[2] Thus she made it clear that company law is integral to a competitive economy. The principal objective of the review was therefore to be the development of a company law that would contribute in a positive way to building a competitive economy.

At the outset, the review identified a number of key problems with the law. These included an outdated structure; complexity arising from over-formal language, excessive detail, over-regulation and opaque structure whereby it is difficult to identify those rules which apply only to private companies.[3] As was observed in the first consultation paper, such complexity causes substantial costs in terms of management time and professional fees.[4] Certain provisions were considered to be obsolete or ineffective. In addition, the DTI adopted the view that the backward looking nature of company law impedes efficiency.[5] The review also identified directors' duties, the conduct of corporate meetings and share-holder control over directors' pay as areas of company law requiring legal reform. The aim of the consultation process and the review was to bring about an up-to-date company law framework, based on principles of consistency, pre-dictability and transparency. The extent to which the process will achieve this aim depends upon the nature of the field legislation. It remains to be seen whether the proposed and planned reforms will result in a coherent, clear and transparent company law that will benefit the UK's economy.

22.2   The company law review process

Although established by the Secretary of State for Trade and Industry, the review was an independent process led by a Steering Group of company law experts, academics, business people and others. In addition, a Consultative Committee gave the Steering Group an opportunity to discuss its ideas and proposals. A number of Working Groups and Working Parties contributed to the review by considering specific aspects of company law in detail. During the course of the

---

1   DTI, *Modern Company Law for a Competitive Economy*, March 1998. DTI/Pub 3162/6.3k/3/98/NP, Foreword, p.i.
2   Ibid.
3   DTI, *Modern Company Law for a Competitive Economy*, March 1998. DTI/Pub 3162/6.3k/3/98/NP, paragraph 3.2. See also our critique in Chapter 1.
4   Ibid, paragraph 3.3.
5   Ibid, paragraph 3.4.

review the DTI published 11 consultation documents, culminating with the Final Report in July 2001.[1]

The Government's response in July 2002 in the two-volume White Paper, *Modernising Company Law*,[2] outlined its policies on most of the major issues with a request for comments on specific questions where the Government had not yet formed a final view. The White Paper also contained draft clauses for a Companies Bill and stated that there were plans for further draft clauses and draft statutory instruments to follow in later months. A response to the Government's White Paper was published by the Trade and Industry Committee in its Sixth Report of Session 2002–03[3] and the Government responded to that in the Select Committee on Trade and Industry's Thirteenth Report.[4]

22.3 The main features of company law identified by the Steering Group

The main objectives laid out by the Company Law Review Steering Group in its Final Report provide a backdrop against which to consider the substantive recommendations. The foreword to the Final Report states:

> A key principle has been that company law should be primarily enabling or facilitative – it should provide an effective vehicle for business leadership and enterprise to flourish freely in a climate of discipline and accountability. We need an accessible framework for channelling the resources of the community to wealth generation. Small companies should be liberated from many of the constraints that were originally designed for large businesses. The framework should provide the necessary safeguards to allow people to deal with and invest in companies with confidence. It should enable our companies to be competitive in a global market where business can choose which jurisdiction to adopt for their regulation. Our law should provide the maximum possible freedom combined with the transparency necessary to ensure the responsible and accountable use of that freedom. We should strip out regulation that is no longer necessary. We should make more effective and accessible those rules which enable markets to work efficiently and which prevent patterns of abuse that disrupt and add cost to economic activity. Finally, company law should reflect the reality of the modern corporate economy, where those who run successful companies recognise the need to develop positive relationships with a wide range of interests beyond shareholders – such as employees, suppliers and customers.
>
> The potential rewards are great:
>
> A framework for business that puts small companies first, not last.
>
> A reduction in costs and burdens for all businesses.

---

1   The full list of papers issued is *Modern Company Law for a Competitive Economy*, March 1998; *The Strategic Framework*, February 1999, URN 99/654; *Company General Meetings and Shareholder Communication*, October 1999, URN 99/1144; *Company Formation and Capital Maintenance*, October 1999, URN 99/1145; *Reforming the Law Concerning Oversea Companies*, October 1999, URN 99/1146; *Developing the Framework*, March 2000, URN 00/656; *Capital Maintenance: Other Issues*, June 2000, URN 00/880; *Registration of Company Charges*, October 2000, URN 00/1213; *Completing the Structure*, November 2000, URN 00/1335; *Trading Disclosures*, January 2001, URN 01/542; *Final Report*, July 2001, URN 01/942 and 00/943.

2   *Modernising Company Law*, Cm 5553-I and Cm 55553-II.

3   House of Commons Trade and Industry Committee, *The White Paper on Modernising Company Law*, Sixth Report of Session 2002–03, HC 439 (hereinafter, 'Sixth Report').

4   House of Commons Trade and Industry Committee, Thirteenth Report of Session 2002–03, *Government Reply to the Commons' Sixth Report of Session 2002–03 on White Paper on Modernising Company Law*, HC 1022, 18 July 2003 (hereinafter, 'Thirteenth Report').

> A climate which encourages people to set up businesses and make them grow.
> A framework which promotes international competitiveness, encourages inward investment, and provides flexibility and responsiveness to changing business needs.
> Clear rules which enable people to deal with and invest in companies with confidence.
> Renewed public confidence in the legitimacy of an approach to wealth-creation that is based on clear and widely accepted principles.
> In short, the prize is a modern company law for a competitive economy.[1]

This demonstrates an emphasis towards a liberal approach to regulation encouraging trade relations with safeguards based on transparency. We now consider the main proposals in the White Paper and the responses to them.

22.4   The White Paper

The White Paper identifies the following aspects of company law that are in need of reform:

(1) approach to small companies;
(2) improving governance: shareholders and decision making, directors, and reporting and audit;
(3) institutional arrangements; and
(4) other ways of simplifying and streamlining company law.

22.4.1   Small companies

The White Paper states that the starting point for company law should be the needs of the small company with additional provisions specific to larger companies where necessary. In the words of the White Paper: '[C]ompany law should make it easy to start and run businesses'.[2] Thus the aim is to simplify the law in order to ease the start up and running of businesses. The main objective for small companies is to avoid unjustified burdens and to provide flexibility so that the law can adapt easily to developments and changing technology. From this point of view the proposals include removing the requirement for private companies to hold annual general meetings unless members want them[3] and to simplify the rules on written resolutions to make it easier for private companies to take decisions.[4] In general the intention is that new legislation will distinguish between public and private companies but will put private companies first. Additional safeguards are to be added where public companies are involved.[5]

The Trade and Industry Select Committee in its Sixth Report welcomed the decision to draft new legislation with the small company primarily in mind and with additional requirements for larger companies where necessary.[6] Indeed, the Select Committee did not add anything substantial to these particular proposals.

---

1   *Final Report*, Foreword, paragraphs 9 and 10 at pp xi–xii.
2   *Modernising Company Law*, paragraph 1.3, p 15.
3   Ibid, paragraphs 2, 11–12, pp 18–19.
4   Ibid, paragraphs 2.26–30, pp 21–22.
5   Ibid, paragraph 1.6, pp 15–16.
6   Sixth Report, HC 439, paragraph 6, p 5.

22.4.2 *Improving Governance*

Improving governance was examined in three main areas: shareholders and decision making, directors; and the third examining corporate reporting and audit.

(1) Shareholders and decision making

A number of proposals have been made relating to shareholders and decision-making in companies. First, alterations are likely to be made to the two main constitutional documents; the separation between the memorandum and the articles of association[1] will be removed. The requirement to have an objects clause will be abolished, since the view expressed in the White Paper, in line with that of the Company Law Review, is that today, it no longer serves any useful purpose except internally.[2] The new form of constitution will be alterable by special resolution.[3] The Government has proposed, in accordance with recommendations in the Review, that separate model constitutions be prepared in simpler, clearer language for public and private companies.[4] These are likely to be drafted after the Bill has been fully prepared.[5] With regard to the decision-making procedures, one of the main deregulatory proposals is to reverse the current default rule requiring companies to hold annual general meetings unless, in private companies, all members agree to dispense with them.[6] The proposal is that private companies will no longer be required to hold annual general meetings[7] nor to lay the accounts or re-appoint the auditors annually at a general meeting,[8] unless they decide by ordinary resolution to meet. The draft Bill replicates the current position that an individual member may require an annual general meeting, the laying of accounts and the reappointment of auditors in any year.[9] The Government points to some disadvantages with this approach, namely that it would enable a single dissenting shareholder effectively to undermine the deregulatory purpose of the private company reforms, that it does not sit comfortably with the opt-in approach to the default rules, and that it would add further complexity.[10]

Whilst public companies will be required to hold annual general meetings, they will also have the option to decide unanimously to dispense with them.[11] The Bill is also likely to contain provisions to enable companies to take further advantage of communications technology as an alternative means of fulfilling the functions of a meeting.[12] The notice periods for company meetings are likely to be aligned to a

---

1   See Chapter 5.
2   *Modernising Company Law*, paragraph 2.2, p 17.
3   Ibid, paragraph 2.3, p 17, and draft clauses 20–23.
4   Ibid, paragraph 2.4, p 17.
5   What remains unclear is the extent to which, if at all, these changes will be retrospective, that
     is apply to companies registered before the new Act is implemented. One assumes that
     existing companies will be able to adopt the new form of constitution but, if they do not (and
     many may not do so through inertia or ignorance), it is not yet clear, for example, whether
     the existing section 14 of the 1985 Act (see **5.17**) will continue to apply to them.
6   See **13.4.6**.
7   *Modernisng Company Law*, paragraphs 2.10–12, pp 18–19, and draft clauses 128–131.
8   Ibid, paragraph 2.11, p 18.
9   Ibid, draft clauses 136–139.
10   Ibid, paragraph 2.12, pp 18–19.
11   Ibid, paragraph 2.13, p 19, and draft clauses 130–131.
12   Ibid, paragraph 2.15, p 19.

minimum of 14 days and shorter notice if a sufficient majority of shareholders agree.[1]

Additionally the Government intends that the voting powers of proxies will be enhanced so that proxies will be able to speak and to vote on a show of hands as well as on a poll and join with others in demanding a poll.[2] The Government also proposes a new right for a sufficient body of members to require a scrutiny of any poll that would be conducted by a registered auditor.[3]

In order to link the annual general meeting more closely to the annual reporting cycle, the draft Bill requires the annual general meeting of private companies to be held within ten months of the end of the previous financial year and the annual general meeting of public companies to take place within six months of the financial year-end.[4]

The White Paper states that the Bill will effectively abolish the extraordinary resolution[5] as a separate category of resolution and any current extra-ordinary resolutions will be replaced by a requirement for a special resolution. Special resolutions will be valid with only 14 days' notice in line with the intended revised minimum notice period for general meetings.[6] Members' resolutions and statements received in time to be circulated with the notice of the meeting should be circulated to all members at the company's expense.[7]

In order to enable small companies to make decisions quickly and efficiently they will be allowed, under the proposed reforms, to pass a written ordinary resolution with a simple majority and a written special resolution with 75% of the eligible votes.[8] Additionally, as long as a resolution can be received or converted by the recipient into legible form, electronic communication of any such resolution will be possible.[9]

A reform proposal worthy of consideration pertains to the rights of beneficial owners. The White Paper indicates that the Government recognises the concerns of beneficial owners who may not be the registered members.[10] Thus the Government is keen to amend the law to make it possible for companies to be able to recognise the rights of the holders of beneficial interests in shares at the request of the registered member.[11] The Government is also considering the Company Law Review's recommendation that companies should be compelled to recognise the rights of another person as being entitled to exercise specific rights if the registered member so requests.[12]

The Government's stance in the White Paper on the role of institutional investors is cautious. The White Paper identifies three specific concerns: shareholder activism, lack of transparency in the voting system and conflicts of interest. The Treasury took up the issue of shareholder activism as part of its

---

1   Ibid, paragraph 2.17, pp 19–20, and draft clauses 148–149.
2   Ibid, paragraphs 2.18–19, p 20, and draft clause 153.
3   Ibid, paragraph 2.19, p 20, and draft clauses 164–165.
4   Ibid, paragraph 2.16, p 19 and draft clause 141.
5   See **13.16**.
6   *Modernising Company Law*, paragraphs 2.21–22, p 20 and draft clause 157.
7   Ibid, paragraph 2.24, p 21, and draft clauses 150, 158 and 160.
8   Ibid, paragraphs 2.26–2.27 and draft clauses 170–175.
9   Ibid, paragraphs 2.29–2.30 and eg draft clause 149.
10 This occurs more widely now since the introduction of CREST; see **9.3.3**.
11 *Modernising Company Law*, paragraphs 2.37–2.41, p 23.
12 Ibid, paragraph 2.41, p 23.

response to the Myners Report on Institutional Investment in the UK.[1] In the White Paper, the Government endorses the proposals of the Company Law Review for improving the effectiveness of the voting process and voting transparency in quoted companies, in particular by a requirement for companies to disclose the results of polls at general meetings on their websites and in annual reports as well as by a new right for members to require a scrutiny of any poll.[2] The Government appears to be more reluctant to tackle the issue of conflicts of interests through company law, saying that it would set out its position fully at a later date.[3] The response to the Government's comments by the Trade and Industry Select Committee in the Sixth Report indicate a lack of optimism for the role of institutional investors as corporate governance actors:

> Ultimately, the primary concern of institutional investors is to maximise the returns on their investments. Whilst this may bring with it some pressure on companies hoping to attract funds from institutional investors to ensure that they have adequate corporate governance systems in place, there is a limit to the extent to which the institutional investors are willing or able to police the probity of the UK's companies.[4]

However, the Government believes that institutional investors have a key role to play in ensuring the good governance of the companies in which they invest and considers best practice guidelines to be the most efficient way of achieving higher levels of corporate behaviour.[5] The Government has suggested that it will monitor the situation and take action if necessary.

(2) Improving governance: directors

The role of directors and the regulation of their activities has been a major component of debate about the future of company law. The Law Commissions set out the broad parameters of the discussion on directors in their report which was published in 1999 which focussed on directors' duties and conflicts of interests.[6] The Company Law Review built upon the recommendations made by the Law Commissions of England and Wales, and Scotland and also considered the broad question of to whom directors should owe their duties and be responsible. The Government endorsed the Company Law Review's controversial conclusion that:

> the basic goal for directors should be the success of the company in the collective best interests of shareholders, but that directors should also recognise, as the circumstances require, the company's need to foster relationships with its employees, customers and suppliers, its need to maintain its business reputation, and its need to consider the company's impact on the community and the working environment.[7]

This is otherwise known as the 'enlightened shareholder' view.[8] Under this theoretical framework the Government has also supported the recommendation by the Law Commissions and the Company Law Review to codify the directors'

---

1   Published on 6 March 2001.
2   *Modernising Company Law*, para 2.45, p 24.
3   Ibid, paragraph 2.47, p 25.
4   Sixth Report, HC 439, paragraph 120, at p 38.
5   Thirteenth Report, paragraph 24.
6   Law Commission and Scottish Law Commission *Report on Company Directors: Regulating Conflicts of Interests and Formulating a Statement of Duties* (July 1999, ISBN 010 144 362 5). See further Chapter 16.
7   Ibid, paragraph 3.3, p 26.
8   See the discussion in Chapter 11, especially at **11.6**.

common-law duties.[1] The draft put forward by the Government in the White Paper[2] emphasises the need for directors to consider both the short and long-term consequences of their actions and take into account, where practicable, relevant matters such as their relationships with employees and the impact of the business on the community and on the environment. Additionally the draft requires a director to exercise the care, skill and diligence of a reasonably diligent person with both: the knowledge, skill and experience which may reasonably be expected of a director in his or her position; and any additional knowledge, skill and experience which the particular director has.[3] The Government suggests specifically that if the draft is adopted, the existing section 309 of the Companies Act 1985[4] would disappear.[5] The conclusion expressed by the Trade and Industry Select Committee in its Sixth Report is that the law should aim to provide a framework to promote the long-term health of the company taking into account the interests of the shareholders and broader corporate social and environmental responsibilities and that specific duties of care should be set out in other legislation covering areas such as health and safety, environmental and employment law and insolvency law *vis-à-vis* creditors. The Select Committee concluded that the draft statement represented a step forward because, 'for the first time, it explicitly recognises that good managers will have regard to a broader range of considerations than value to shareholders, which on its own may lead to short-termism'.[6] The draft code is currently being revised to minimise the possibility of different interpretations on the provisions.

The White Paper's identification of the role of non-executive directors as a key aspect of corporate governance with respect to both accountability and business prosperity gives support to the work of Derek Higgs. The Higgs *Review of the role and effectiveness of non-executive directors* (hereinafter 'Higgs Review') was published by the DTI in January 2003.[7] This was welcomed by the Trade and Industry Select Committee in its Sixth Report stating that the proposals set out in the Higgs Review were modest but can contribute to good corporate governance standards without being overly prescriptive.[8] Following these endorsements, the proposals set out in the Higgs Review have been incorporated into the latest Combined Code on Corporate Governance revised by the Financial Reporting Council.[9] Significantly, the Higgs Review advocates a 'comply or explain' approach and this has been followed in the revised Code.

The issue of directors' training was considered by both the Higgs Review and the Tyson Report on recruitment of non-executive directors.[10] One advance has been to require the provision of training. The Government noted in its response to the Sixth Report that the Tyson Report recommended that a body such as the Financial Reporting Council or the London Stock Exchange bring together

---

1   See also **16.25**.
2   Schedule 2 in Volume II.
3   See **16.22**.
4   Scc **16.6**.
5   *Modernising Company Law*, paragraph 3.5, p 26.
6   Sixth Report, paragraph 22, at p 10.
7   See also **11.5.6**.
8   Sixth Report, HC 439, paragraph 49.
9   Financial reporting Council, *The Combined Code on Corporate Governance*, July 2003, available at http://www.frc.org.uk. See also Chapter 11.
10   *Tyson Report on the Recruitment and Development of Non-Executive Directors* (2003) (hereinafter 'Tsyon Report').

training providers and companies to establish guidelines to ensure that practical training programmes for directors provide what is needed and that useful information about such programmes is easily accessible on a timely basis.[1]

The Government also plans to prohibit the appointment of corporate directors.[2]

(3) Improving governance: company reporting and audit

In the White Paper, the Government states the objectives in relation to company reporting as follows:

> Good company reporting is essential. It provides information to shareholders, as well as creditors, employees and others who may have an interest in companies and their activities. Equally the need for information has to be balanced against the cost to the company of collecting and publishing that information, as well as the cost to readers in finding the information they are seeking. More information is not necessarily better information; and the Government is firmly committed to improving the quality rather than the mere quantity of company reporting.[3]

From this starting point a broad range of proposals are made. First, the Government confirms that the detailed rules on the form and content of annual financial statements and other reports such as the new operating and financial review and the summary statement will be the responsibility of a new Standards Board.[4] This will, according to the Government, remove existing overlaps between primary legislation and non-statutory rules and will enable technical and detailed rules to be made by a specialist rule-making body and to be updated and amended quickly and easily. The Standards Board will involve companies and users of reports in the development of rules.[5] The Government's expectation is that the Financial Reporting Council will act as an umbrella body for the Standards Board.[6]

A very important change to the reporting framework is the proposed removal of the directors' report[7] and its replacement by a short supplementary statement and, for 'the most economically significant companies', an operating and financial review (OFR).[8] Thus in future companies will be required to prepare (a) financial statements, (b) a supplementary statement, (c) for the most economically significant companies, an OFR, and (d) for quoted companies a directors' remuneration report. All companies may publish an optional summary statement. The supplementary statement will replace the directors' report for companies that do not have to provide an OFR with the aim of such statement offering a fair review.

A further proposal is for a reduction in the time allowed for private companies to deliver their accounts and statements from ten months to seven months[9] and also to require a private company that lays its annual accounts and statements at a

---

1   Thirteenth Report, paragraph 7.
2   *Modernising Company Law*, paragraphs 3.32–3.34, pp 31–32.
3   Ibid, paragraph 4.1, p 33.
4   Ibid, paragraphs 4.5–4.7, p 34.
5   Ibid, paragraph 5.16, p 47.
6   Ibid, paragraph 5.27, p 49.
7   See Chapter 14, Part 3.
8   *Modernising Company Law*, paragraphs 4.9, 4.15 and 4.28ff, pp 34–40.
9   Ibid, paragraph 4.24, p 37.

meeting to do so within ten months.[1] Additionally, small and medium-sized companies will no longer be given the opportunity of filing abbreviated accounts at Companies House.[2] Quoted companies will also be required to publish their accounts on their website within four months of their year-end.[3] Part of the simplification of accounts proposals for small companies will include an increase in the thresholds for defining a small company to the EU maximum of £4.8 million turnover, £2.4 million balance sheet total or 50 employees.[4] Any changes made at the European level would also have to be considered.

Arguably the most controversial proposal under this heading is the introduction of the OFR. Many quoted companies already produce such a report in accordance with the 1993 Statement on the OFR published by the Accounting Standards Board. The main objective of the proposed OFR is to provide more qualitative and forward looking reporting, in addition to information that is quantitative, historical or about internal company affairs. The detailed rules for the compilation of the OFR will be devolved to the Standards Board. However, the Government gives an indication of the basic contents of the OFR in the White Paper. Thus draft clause 73 sets out the objective of the review as 'providing such information as will permit the members of the company, as of the approval date, to make an informed assessment of the company's operations; its financial position; and its future business strategies and prospects.' The Government proposes a compulsory content with core elements as well as a duty on directors to consider other matters that would be relevant to achieving the review objective. The compulsory matters, or core elements listed in draft clause 74, include (a) a statement of the company's business in the financial year to which the operating and financial review relates; (b) a fair review of performance during the financial year and of the position of the company at the end of that year; and (c) a fair projection of the prospects for the company's business and of events which will, or are likely to, substantially affect that business. Those non-mandatory matters listed in draft clause 75, which must at least be considered for inclusion if the directors feel they are materially relevant, include:

(a) the management structure of the company;
(b) receipts from, and returns to, members of the company in the financial year to which the operating and financial review relates in relation to shares held by them;
(c) the company's policies in relation to employment by the company;
(d) the company's policies on environmental issues relevant to the company's business;
(e) the company's policies on social and community issues relevant to the company's business;
(f) the company's performance in the financial year to which the operating and financial review relates, in carrying out the policies mentioned in paragraphs (c) to (e);
(g) matters not falling within the preceding paragraphs which affect, or may affect, the company's reputation.

The response of the Trade and Industry Select Committee was to say that the proposed OFR would be a marked improvement on current minimum reporting

---

1   Ibid, paragraph 4.25, p 37.
2   Ibid, paragraph 4.26, p 37.
3   Ibid, paragraph 4.50, p 42.
4   Ibid, paragraph 4.19, p 36.

standards because it would help to give a more rounded, clearer view of both past operations and future prospects of companies. The Committee is less pessimistic than others about the division into 'core' and 'other' matters and argues that there will be pressure from investors and others for companies to raise their standards of reporting.[1]

The spirit and reasoning behind the reporting and accounting rules have for a long time been emphasised in preference to a prescriptive 'cook book' of rules that would encourage a narrow interpretation of the standards. From this point of view, the Government proposes the adoption of administrative enforcement rather than criminal sanctions for failure to comply with reporting standards. Thus criminal penalties should be reserved only for an intent to deceive or mislead by making a false statement to an auditor or for deliberate false accounting or failure to deliver accounts to the registrar or members.[2] This approach was endorsed by the Trade and Industry Select Committee, which stated that the effect of the law should be to encourage proper disclosure rather than merely punish directors for failing to do this.[3]

The role of auditors is also clearly relevant to the reporting regime. The Government gives support to the Company Law Review's recommendations to extend the statutory role of auditors in relation to the OFR and the cash flow statement, as well as an extension of auditors' rights to information from the company.[4]

Following the ENRON disaster the Government also commissioned a review of the liability of auditors. A number of questions arose after ENRON in particular that of auditor independence and the Government has stated its intention to put in place a package of measures dealing with auditor independence set out in detail in the report by the Coordinating Group on Audit and Accounting Issues. These are contained in the Companies (Audit, Investigations and Community Enterprise) Bill, which at the time of writing is before Parliament.[5] The Auditing Practices Board is also to develop necessary standards on auditor independence. As regards audit committees Sir Robert Smith led a Review, the conclusions of which have been incorporated into the revised Combined Code by the Financial Reporting Council.

22.4.3   *Rule-making and keeping company law up to date*

The Government intends to develop a new company law that is sufficiently flexible to be kept up to date and respond to changes in the environment in which companies operate. Thus to enable it to develop with modern business practices, the Government has endorsed the recommendations of the Review that the Bill should allow much of the technical detail to be amended by secondary legislation and that there should be a greater role for non-governmental institutions in keeping company law up to date and effective.[6] From this perspective the Government makes the following proposals in the White Paper. The new Standards Board should be given power to make detailed rules on the form and

---

1   Sixth Report, paragraphs 68–70.
2   *Modernising Company Law*, paragraphs 4.44–4.46, pp 40–41.
3   Sixth Report, paragraph 79.
4   *Modernising Company Law*, paragraph 4.47, p 41.
5   See **22.6**.
6   *Modernising Company Law*, paragraph 5.3, p 44.

content of financial statements and reports as well as responsibility for keeping the Combined Code under review, together with the power to make rules requiring companies to disclose whether they have complied with the Combined Code.[1]

22.5 Reforms outside the White Paper

Alongside the proposals in the White Paper, which will constitute the main body of the company law reform programme, there have been other developments towards further specific reforms. Notably, these include an initiative for community interest companies which will be purpose-designed to operate in the community interest within the existing framework of company law. They are intended to demonstrate that a business operates in the community interest and re-invests its profits for the community. This proposal arises out of a recommendation by the Strategy Unit Report on the voluntary sector.[2]

Other proposals have been brought forward in response to the ENRON debacle and other corporate scandals. In particular, the Government commissioned reports into the role and effectiveness of non-executive directors[3] and also on auditor liability and independence.[4] Many of the recommendations arising from these reviews have been incorporated into the revised Combined Code and the Companies (Audit, Investigations and Community Enterprise) Bill. This Bill sets out possible measures to implement independent auditing standards, and introduces monitoring and disciplinary procedures on the professional accountancy bodies. The Bill also seeks to enable the Secretary of State to delegate to the Financial Reporting Council (FRC) powers to recognise the professional bodies. The Bill extends the remit of the Financial Reporting Review Panel so that it can look at interim as well as annual accounts and reports; it gives to the Financial Reporting Review Panel (FRRP) a power to require information from companies it is investigating; and provides an opening for the Inland Revenue to pass information on defective accounts to the FRRP. The Bill extends the Secretary of State's power to require more detailed disclosure of non-audit services provided by auditors to companies. It gives additional powers to auditors to obtain information from companies and requires directors to state that they have not withheld relevant information from their auditors. The Bill also contains measures to strengthen the company investigations regime.[5]

The Law Commissions have also been active on company law reform initiatives. The Reports noted above on the duties of directors have played an important role in the government's policy developments and its proposals in the White Paper. It now seems that the earlier Report of the Law Commission on shareholders' remedies[6] will be implemented at least in part. In addition, at the request of the Government, the Law Commissions have been investigating the issue of company charges. This came about after the Company Law Review's Final Report highlighted the technical complexity of the area of registration of company

---

1   Ibid, paragraphs 5.7–5.14, pp 45–46.
2   See the Companies (Audit Investigations and Community Enterprise) Bill.
3   The Higgs Review, noted above.
4   The Co-ordinating Group on Audit and Accounting Issues, *Final Report to the Secretary of State and Chancellor of the Exchequor*, URN 03/567, noted above. The issue of auditor independence was also explored in a report published by the Treasury Committee in July 2002, entitled *The Financial Regulation of Public Limited Companies*, Sixth Report of Session 2001–2002 (HC 756).
5   See **17.22.1**.
6   At least to introduce a statutory derivative action; see **17.10.1**.

charges and made recommendations of its own, including replacing the current scheme with a system for notice filing that would encompass functionally equivalent legal devices. The Law Commissions of England and Wales and Scotland have thus simultaneously, but separately, looked at the issue of charges. The Law Commission published its consultation paper in July 2002[1] recommending the introduction of an electronic notice-filing system which would cover a seller who takes purchase money security over an asset purchased with the finance provided and that notice-filing should also cover certain quasi-security interests such as hire-purchase agreements and retention of title clauses. Final reports are due in 2004.[2]

22.7   Conclusion

Company law in the UK has been subject to a phenomenal amount of 'official' scrutiny over the last decade. There have been promises of a radical modernisation of the company law regime, mostly regarded as a necessity if Britain's economy is to compete effectively in a global market. Perhaps as a result of the amount of time spent examining the problems, the end result is likely to be disappointing when viewed against the strong promises. In fact it has been possible to observe a watering down of the approach. For example, the opening consultation paper hinted at the possibility of broadening significantly the scope of company law but, by the time the Final Report was published, the enlightened shareholder value approach had established itself as the guiding principle. The enlightened shareholder value philosophy has clearly shaped the character of the specific reforms, in particular those proposed in relation to directors' duties and also for designing the rules for the OFR. This approach to company law is likely to continue to be a bone of contention. Some of the witnesses to the Sixth Report have evidently not fully resigned themselves to such a philosophy.[3]

The process of the development of company law reform has in part aimed to combat the fragmented structure of company law in the UK. Yet the reforms which appear separately from those proposed in the White Paper, although arguably justifiably separate, may well open the door to criticisms of the reform programme. Inevitably, by separating the reforms there will be risks of fragmentation, one of the problems that the Company Law Review set out to dispel from its beginning.[4] Although this chapter has concentrated on the UK position, the reader must not forget the continuing importance of the European Union to the development of UK company law, as explained in Chapter 2. We have already at **1.7.1** criticised the narrowness of the Company Law Review in this respect. Even though the European Commission has recognised the need to modernise its approach,[5] developments in the UK must be viewed alongside developments at a European level.

---

1   Law Commission, Consultation Paper on the *Registration of Security Interests: Company Charges and Property other than Land* (June 2002, ISBN 011 730249x).
2   See further **10.38**.
3   See for example, the evidence supplied by the TUC and the Corporate Social Responsibility Coalition.
4   Note the trenchant criticisms expressed by the Select Committee in the Thirteenth Report!
5   See **2.1**.

At this point it is not possible to judge if the proposed reforms will create the modern, competitive company law regime that the Company Law Review set out to achieve. In the absence of a Bill, let alone any completed reforms, such a judgment will have to wait.

Index

References are to paragraph numbers